FOREST
AND CRAG

Mountains of the Northeast

FOREST
AND CRAG

A HISTORY OF HIKING, TRAIL BLAZING, AND ADVENTURE IN THE NORTHEAST MOUNTAINS

By
Laura and Guy Waterman

APPALACHIAN MOUNTAIN CLUB
Boston

Maps by Judy Jacobs
Text design by Dede Cummings/IPA
Cover design by Carol Stephens/IPA
Cover photograph by Ned Therrien

Published by the Appalachian Mountain Club
5 Joy Street, Boston, Massachusetts 02108

Distributed by The Talman Company, Inc.
150 Fifth Avenue, New York, New York 10011

FIRST EDITION

Library of Congress Cataloging-in-Publication Data
Waterman, Laura.
    Forest and crag : a history of hiking, trail blazing, and adventure in the
Northeast mountains / by Laura and Guy Waterman.
        p.   cm.
    Bibliography: p.
    Includes index.
    ISBN 0-910146-75-6.   ISBN 0-910146-73-X (pbk.)
    1. Hiking—New England—History.   2. Mountains—New England—
Recreational use—History.   I. Waterman, Guy.   II. Title.
GV199.42.N38W38 1989
917.4—dc19   88-18875

The paper used in this publication meets the minimum requirements of the
American National Standard for Information Sciences—Permanence of Paper
for Printed Library Materials, ANSI Z39.48-1984.∞™

Printed in the United States of America

10 9 8 7 6 5 4 3 2   90 91 92 93

FOR FREE AS AN EAGLE,
  THESE ROCKS WERE HIS EYRIE;
AND FREE AS AN EAGLE
  HIS SPIRIT SHALL SOAR.

  —From a Scottish lament

Contents

Figures
and
tables

Figures

Tables

Illustrations

Preface

In 1979 the Appalachian Mountain Club asked us to write a history of
Northeastern hiking and climbing. We thought it would be a long job,
that it might take as long as three years. Ten years later, here it is.

During the early part of those ten years, we found out how little we
knew about the history of the mountains which we thought we knew so
well. We also found out how little we knew about the methods of historical research. Fortunately we also quickly learned how extraordinarily
friendly and helpful are the librarians and knowledgeable mountain historians of this region when they see that you are really in love with your
subject—and really do need professional guidance.

The idea behind this book was that someone should bring together the
mountain recreation history of the entire region: the White Mountains,
the Green Mountains, and the Adirondacks, of course, but also the
friendly Catskills, aloof Katahdin, the multifarious mountains of western Maine, Mount Desert, splendid individual mountains like Monadnock, Greylock, and Ascutney, New York's Hudson Highlands,
Connecticut's Litchfield Hills, Massachusetts's Holyoke Range, Boston's
Blue Hills, the Berkshires and the Taconics, the Shawangunks, the Sleeping Giant. The history of each of these ranges and mountains could be
found. But the sources were scattered, were generally anecdotal, and
lacked historical perspective. The idea of integrating the histories of all
the mountains of the Northeast in one book offered opportunities for
comparing and contrasting the pace of change, and for placing all the
delightful anecdotes in some sort of relation to social history and Americans' evolving attitudes toward mountains and wilderness.

We are told that what distinguishes history from mere chronology is
generalization. As we read the sources, we came to feel that, for all the
rich storehouse of anecdotes on Northeastern hill walking, no one had
really attempted to grope toward generalizations about this history, to

synthesize the wealth of information or analyze the major shifts in people's perspective on the hills. We have tried to draw some of these generalizations. We hope our first efforts may stimulate others to study the material with improved insight, to challenge our ideas, and gradually to shape a truer history of these hills and their interesting relationship to the people who have come to see them, to climb them, to build trails on them, to find adventure and fun and inspiration and consolation among them.

Writing this history required three big tasks. Tasks may be the wrong word, because it often implies drudgery, and each of our tasks was pure pleasure.

First, we spent uncounted hours at libraries, historical societies, and the archives of hiking and trail clubs from Bangor, Maine, to Brooklyn, New York. We visited exactly two dozen college libraries to learn how their outing clubs began or what rambles their students took during, say, the 1860s. We chased down rumors of scrapbooks and journals in the attics of sons and daughters of great trail-builders of the 1920s. To find a sketchbook of summer life at a New Hampshire mountain resort about 1900 we went to a senior citizen condominium outside Washington, D.C. To find records of the building of the Appalachian Trail in Massachusetts, we prowled the basement storage rooms of the county courthouse in Pittsfield and were invited into the homes of the descendants of the original trail-builders. To find the field notes of early surveyors crossing the mountains of Maine, we immersed ourselves in the remarkable files of the James W. Sewell Company in Old Town, kept in wooden cabinets in a locked basement storeroom. Most of this phase, however, involved long hours at libraries and historical societies, where we formed friendships with some of those helpful librarians, friendships that may outlast this book.

Second, we went to see people. We wrote to every trail-builder or hiking club leader or early winter climber who seemed to have made major contributions to twentieth-century hiking history, more than one thousand individuals. We met so many interesting outdoorspeople, each with much to tell us. Many were in their eighties or nineties. The outdoor life must be health giving, because these folk were still bustling with energy. Our senior interviewee was the skier Jackrabbit Johannsen, 106 years old when we talked with him and still skiing, still swift in repartee as he once had been on the long boards; when we left after five hours of talk, he gave Laura what Guy thought was a dangerously affectionate hug. The people we met were probably the greatest reward we had from writing this book.

Third, we went to the mountains. We thought we should get to know the ranges and important peaks that we might have missed in our two lifetimes of hiking in this region. We discovered some wonderful hiking country and hidden treasures we'll return to. We bushwhacked along the

Monument Line over Katahdin's rugged slopes. We traced as best we could the original ascent route on Mount Marcy on its 150th anniversary and the historic Belknap-Cutler expedition to Mount Washington on its 200th. With the help of then seventy-five-year-old Ray Evans, who grew up in Crawford Notch, we searched for the remains of an elaborate trail network on the Rosebrook Range, now completely trailless. With George Libby, one of Connecticut's master trail maintainers, we stood at Grand Junction, once the confluence of three great trails, now swallowed up in a welter of small-lot housing on all sides. With local expert Richard Scaramelli, we rambled the old worn paths of the long-gone Half Way House hotel on Monadnock and stood on the spot where (probably) Thoreau camped in 1860. For the rest of our lives, wherever we hike, we will hear the echoes of the footsteps of the first explorers, the grunts and puffs of those who labored to build the first trails, the laughter of those who hiked these trails twenty or fifty or one hundred years ago.

So much could be written about Northeastern mountains. In the end we were forced to be selective, or this book would have been too heavy to lift. Therefore, for example, we have largely omitted the interesting and vital history of conservation of mountain country—not because it's un-important but because it's too important to tuck into a hiking history. In general we have concentrated on the beginnings of things. You'll learn relatively more about how the Appalachian Mountain Club or the Ap-palachian Trail or the pursuit of peakbagging got started, relatively less about the subsequent institutional history of the AMC or the AT or the Forty-Sixers. When it comes to events after about 1950, we grow skepti-cal of the ability of historians to form objective judgments. Until more time has elapsed to put recent events into perspective, we're all guessing as to what's important, what's really happening out there. So Part Five (since 1950) is deliberately more sketchy than the first four parts. Throughout the book, space limitations forced difficult choices. Origi-nally we'd planned to integrate technical rock and ice climbing into the story of hiking and trail building. This didn't work. After eight years of researching and writing both subjects in one history, we had to concede that the worlds of technical climbers and of hikers and trail-builders are, for most people, separate and unrelated worlds. So the former will be another book some other time. For that matter, throughout our research, we kept finding other histories that someone should write, before much of the evidence submerges into oblivion: the Appalachian Trail, the Ap-palachian Mountain Club, the summer camp movement, the social phe-nomenon of New York City hiking clubs, search and rescue activity in Northeastern mountains, and much more. Other authors, other books.

For what we have covered, we have made every effort to find all availa-ble sources and to report accurately what people did, without passing judgment on whether the modern hiker would approve or not. Many ex-perts on specific regions or time periods kindly read our drafts and pointed out errors or omissions. We are extremely grateful for this help, but acknowledge that any errors that yet remain are solely the responsibility of the authors. Indeed, if any readers notice errors or substantial omissions, it would be most helpful if they would point them out for future printings. Please send any comments to the authors care of AMC Books, 5 Joy St., Boston, MA 02108.

A few observations on selected points may help, before you start reading this book. About reference notes: we have tried to devise a system whereby the general reader will not be distracted by a lot of obtrusive footnotes, but the interested follow-up reader or researcher may nevertheless find the source of each piece of information or quotation, as well as references for more detailed data on each major subject. All the notes are at the back, in the Notes section. To find the source of any quotation or idea, note the page number and the first three words in the quotation; then find the appropriate reference note in the back. If you don't care about sources, you can skip the notes entirely and not miss anything of substance.

On spelling of names, we follow authoritative local texts. For example, the building on Monadnock was called Half Way House, according to Allen Chamberlain, author of *Annals of the Grand Monadnock;* but Robert L. Hagerman tells us, in his book *Mansfield: The Story of Vermont's Loftiest Mountain,* that Mansfield's corresponding emporium was Halfway House. We adopt local usage, at the expense of consistency. Adirondak Loj is a special case. When the lodge was first built its name was spelled conventionally: *Adirondack Lodge.* After the Deweys took it over, they invoked their ideas of spelling reform and changed it to its present *Adirondak Loj.* Readers will find we spell it conventionally when describing events before the Dewey era and switch to the reformed spelling after the Deweys came in.

On elevations of peaks, we use figures given in the most recent editions of leading guidebooks.

One point of difficulty for us: some women these days find it insulting to read about Mrs. John Doe, when she should be called by her own name, Jane Doe. Unfortunately nineteenth-century sources do not always tell us what women's first names were. Thus you will read about Mrs. Henry Buermeyer (chapter 18) and Mrs. George Witherle (chapter 30), simply because that's how the contemporary accounts identify them, and we were unable to track down their first names. Particularly frustrating is the case of Miss M. F. Whitman, who was a very admirable and interesting person, frequently alluded to in early records of the Appalachian Mountain Club—but always as Miss Whitman or M. F. Whitman. We were able to uncover the first names for many of the women you will read about in these pages, but alas, not all.

In fact, the whole question of how to treat the role of early women climbers was a troubling one for us. Our first idea was that it would be

wrong or patronizing to have separate chapters dealing with women hikers in the nineteenth century. As we studied the history of those times,
however, we realized that women first came to the mountains with enormous burdens that their male contemporaries simply didn't have to cope
with, both in terms of entrenched social mores that frowned upon displays of outdoor vigor by women, and in terms of dress codes that required women to bushwhack through dense forests and to snowshoe
through deep snow while wearing long, heavy skirts. The accomplishments of path-breaking women hikers of the nineteenth century, therefore, in our opinion, were extraordinary, and could be adequately
acknowledged only by separate chapters (chapters 12 and 26). Where,
however, it seemed appropriate to write about women's part in the history of hiking along with the men's, we have done our best to integrate
them.

Enough preamble. Let's go to the mountains. We immensely enjoyed
writing this book, and we hope you enjoy reading about these wonderful
forests and crags, the "sun-flecked narrow paths" that wander through
them, and the energetic and colorful, sometimes eccentric, often marvelous men and women who shaped the modern hiker's mountain world.

Laura and Guy Waterman
East Corinth, Vermont

Acknowledgments

Never, to paraphrase Churchill, was so much owed by just two people to so many, many others. We think of almost numberless instances where people we didn't know went out of their way to help our research, and there is no way we can possibly acknowledge our debt. To give just two examples: When we visited the Berkshire School library and found their records of early trail work incomplete, librarian Jane Carver, with no prodding from us, wrote to a large number of Berkshire alumni from the late 1920s to find out if they could fill in the missing information. When we visited aging Carl O. Chauncey, former chairman of the New England Trail Conference and one of the truest gentlemen we've ever met, he produced all his old notebooks and other records and simply gave them to us. Time and again individuals we'd never met before went to considerable trouble to assist our research. Our gratitude and good feeling toward these people know no bounds.

Some whose help was crucial on particular subjects are mentioned in the Reference Notes. Otherwise, with far too many individuals to mention, we place an arbitrary limit at forty names. Originally we planned to hold the list to twenty-five, but we couldn't cut it that short. Even now we are excruciatingly conscious of how grateful we are to the forty-first, forty-second, and forty-third, or even the eighty-third, all of whom go unacknowledged, but not unappreciated.

Forty? Okay. When we entered our first library for our first day of research, nervous and intimidated by the size of our job and our inadequacy for it, almost the first person we met was Walter Woodman Wright, the distinguished chief of Dartmouth College Library's Special Collections (now retired): the patience, support, and guidance he gave that first day was the beginning of constant support and guidance since then from this mild, generous, and most knowledgeable of White Mountain authorities. In the Adirondacks, James A. Goodwin occupies a special niche, for over fifty years the master trail-builder, guide, winter climber, rock climber, and historian; the magnanimity of his help, whenever we called on him, was unbelievable and literally indispensable. It's hard to say who's next, but it's an understatement to say we feel especially grateful for the expertise and friendly counsel of, for the White Mountains, Fran Belcher, Peter Crane, Charles Fobes, Guy Gosselin, Ned Therrien, and especially Douglas Philbrook; for Vermont, Bill Gove, Jack Harrington, Gary Thomas Lord, John Paulson, and especially Reidun Nuquist; for the Adirondacks, Pete Fish, Tony Goodwin, Grace Hudowalski, Herbert McAneny, David Newhouse, Peggy O'Brien, Bill White, and especially Mary MacKenzie; for the Catskills, Fr. Ray Donahue, Michael Kudish, and Ed West; for the Hudson Highlands, Elizabeth Levers, Julian Salomon, and Robert Schulz; for the Berkshires, Dick Bailey, George Wislocki, and Kay Wood; for Connecticut, Ned Greist, George Libby, and especially Kornel Bailey; for Monadnock (and more), Richard Scaramelli; for the change in perception of mountain landscape, Louis Cornell and Sara Cornell; for friendship and support throughout, Molly Burns Snyder; and for reading nearly the entire manuscript and providing professional advice with candor but tact, Annie Barry, Tom Bassett, and Jonathan Waterman.

Does that come to thirty-seven, if we count the Cornells as one? Well, not really, but we'll deliberately miscount. That leaves us three whom we wish especially and eternally to acknowledge.

David M. Sherman, a high official in the National Park Service, has an energy and accomplishment level that we've never seen excelled. For the past seven years he has deluged us with ideas and printed source material, opened doors and solved problems for our research, tirelessly and promptly reviewed drafts and answered questions, and most of all sent us unfailing encouragement and enthusiasm. In dark days when we wondered if we really could finish this job, we knew there was no way we could fail to honor his confidence in what we were attempting. We have the feeling that we are just two of dozens for whom this indefatigable counselor is an inspiration and constant helper.

An inimitable, indestructible scholar-in-disguise-as-a-hobbit, now approaching his tenth decade on this earth, is the former reference librarian at Amherst College, private collector of mountain books, and lifelong hiker, trail worker, and bushwhacker, E. Porter Dickinson. Shortly after we had just been introduced, he dispatched to us a box full of a score of rare books from his private collection which he knew would be valuable to our research. From then on, Uncle Porter constantly raised questions, suggested obscure sources, reviewed manuscript, recalled anecdotes, debated interpretations, and prodded us to action, rarely interrupting the flow of sparkling conversation even when seated at the piano to call up an Austrian mountain song or a Norwegian lament. What a privilege to know him.

Most of all we wish to salute Bradley J. Snyder for his complete and thorough editing of the entire manuscript. Of many good writers and editors we've had the benefit of working with, none brings more skill, imagination, intelligence, and wit to the task of improving someone else's book. It is a little appreciated art, but we appreciate it. *Forest and Crag* is much the better for his sustaining help.

That's forty who were our strongest support on the substantive side of producing this history. On the mechanical side, no less vital to the result, we wish to thank Arlyn Powell, who signed us up to do the job; Nancy Rich, who helped a lot on finding and selecting illustrations and in countless other ways; Linda Buchanan Allen and Margo Shearman, who edited the final manuscript; Susan Cummings, who shepherded us through the production process; David Goodnow, who kept our two typewriters in good repair for ten years; the young woman at the copy center, whose name we don't even know but who always made sure our copying jobs were done speedily and flawlessly; Nancy Frost and Beth Thompson of the East Corinth post office, who handled our voluminous mailings, both incoming and outgoing, with efficiency and good cheer; and Bev Longo and the others at the Blake Memorial Library in East Corinth, who ably responded to all our requests for library support.

Abbreviations

ADK	Adirondack Mountain Club
AMA	Ascutney Mountain Association
AMC	Appalachian Mountain Club
AMR	Adirondack Mountain Reserve
AT	Appalachian Trail
ATC	Appalachian Trail Conference
ATIS	Adirondack Trail Improvement Society
BOC	Bates Outing Club
CAHC	College Alumni Hiking Club
CCC	Civilian Conservation Corps
CCHC	City College Hiking Club
CFPA	Connecticut Forest and Park Association
CHC	Camel's Hump Club
CMC	Chocorua Mountain Club
DEC	Department of Environmental Conservation
DOC	Dartmouth Outing Club
ESMC	Eastern States Mountain Club
GE	General Electric Company
GMC	Green Mountain Club
GMNF	Green Mountain National Forest
GNP	Great Northern Paper Company
IOCA	Intercollegiate Outing Clubs of America
JBL	Johns Brook Lodge
LPC	Lake Placid Club
LT	Long Trail
LTP	Long Trail Patrol
MATC	Maine Appalachian Trail Club
MIT	Massachusetts Institute of Technology
MITOC	MIT Outing Club
MPC	Metropolitan Park Commission (Boston area)
MTT	Maine Trail Trotters
MVHC	Mohawk Valley Hiking Club
NETC	New England Trail Conference
NHHH	New Hampshire Hundred Highest
NPS	National Park Service

NYHC	New York Hiking Club
NY-NJTC	New York-New Jersey Trail Conference
OH	Old Hutmen
PATC	Potomac Appalachian Trail Club
PIPTC	Palisades Interstate Park Trail Conference
R & D	research and development
REI	Recreational Equipment, Inc.
RPI	Rensselaer Polytechnic Institute
RUA	Restricted Use Area
SMC	Stratton Mountain Club
SOA	Shore Owners' Association (Lake Placid)
UMO	University of Maine, Orono
USDA	U.S. Department of Agriculture
USGS	U.S. Geological Survey
UVM	University of Vermont
VIA	Village Improvement Association (Bar Harbor)
WAIA	Waterville Athletic and Improvement Association
WMNF	White Mountain National Forest
WMS	Winter Mountaineering School
WOC	Wilton Outing Club
WODC	Wonalancet Out Door Club
YMCA	Young Men's Christian Association

Introduction: The mountains

T HIS book is about people climbing the mountains of the northeastern United States. We shall tell about how people first saw these hills; the first tentative explorations onto the heights; the obstacles and adventures met in those early days; the gradual evolution of mountain recreation and how people began to come to the hills for pleasure and pastime; how enjoyment of the mountains changed from the first truly recreational hill walking of the 1830s to the post-Civil War vacations of the 1870s, to the turn of the century tramping and camping, to that of the 1920s and 1930s, to the postwar boom of hiking and backpacking; the special craft of trail building and its successor art, trail maintenance; and the exceptional hardships and rewards of going up into these hills in winter.

Our book will focus on people. A kaleidoscope of colorful characters have cascaded across the stage of Northeastern hiking history. But before we summon up the heterogeneous human cast, let us start by introducing the one constant backdrop throughout: the mountains themselves. They too have distinct personalities.

The three chief ranges

The mountains of the Northeast are variously clustered. Three distinct ranges lie across the northern part of the region: the Adirondacks of New York, the Green Mountains of Vermont, and the White Mountains of New Hampshire. (Readers may wish to consult the map on the frontispiece which shows where the mountains lie.) These three ranges are clearly spaced apart from each other, with broad valleys between: Lake Champlain separates the Adirondacks from the westernmost Green Mountains, while the pastoral Connecticut River valley separates the easternmost Green Mountains from the Benton Range and Moosilauke, western outposts of the White Mountains.

All three ranges have summits that rise above treeline, which is reached somewhere between 4,000 and 5,000 feet. The Green Mountains are the lowest, with but five peaks that reach 4,000 feet in elevation. The Adirondacks and White Mountains contain between forty and fifty 4,000-footers. For years the locals counted exactly forty-six 4,000-footers in each of these ranges, but more recent surveys have ended that symmetry. The White Mountains now claim forty-eight. The Adirondack faithful still like to climb their original list of forty-six, but concede that several on that list fall a bit short of 4,000 feet.

A striking feature of the taller mountains is the land above treeline, sometimes called the alpine zone. The largest such area is in the Presidential Range of the White Mountains, where a chain of a half-dozen peaks is well above timberline and a substantial rolling upland between them exhibits many of the characteristics of the Arctic tundra. Lesser but still impressive alpine zones are found on the Franconia Ridge, on the western side of the Whites; on Mount Mansfield and, in miniature, on Camel's Hump in Vermont; and on the highest half-dozen peaks of the Adirondacks. Among Maine's mountains, which we'll get to presently, additional alpine zones are found, notably the broad "tableland" of Katahdin. Ferocious weather attacks these alpine zones, especially in winter. Winds elsewhere regarded as hurricane force are routine in these alpine zones. The fastest observed land-surface wind speed in the world was clocked at 231 mph at the summit observatory on Mount Washington. Taken with cold temperatures, frequent low visibility due to clouds and blowing snow, plus erratic changeability, Northeastern winter weather more than makes up for the region's lack of high elevation or consistent dramatic relief.

THE ADIRONDACKS. The name Adirondacks applies to an extensive area—larger than the entire state of New Hampshire—that includes a wealth of lakes and streams, deep forests, villages and towns, as well as mountains. This book deals with that relatively small section within the Adirondacks where its tallest mountains are concentrated: the "high peaks" region. The high peaks form a roughly circular cluster within which the mountains run in north-south ridges: the Dix Range farthest east, the Colvin and Nippletop groups next, the Great Range, the MacIntyres, and so on out to the remote Sewards in the west. Between these ridges lie deep passes, some with lakes whose settings amid the steep mountainsides are uncommonly picturesque. The Ausable Lakes that lie east of the Great Range, and Avalanche Lake and Lake Colden just east of the MacIntyres, are two examples of some of the most striking mountain scenery to be found anywhere.

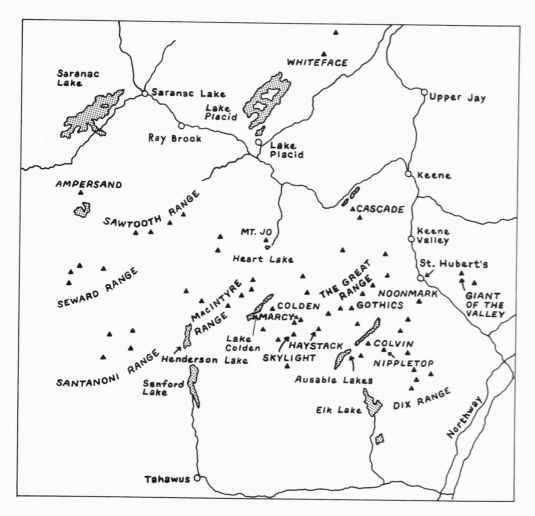

Figure 0.1. The High Peaks region of the Adirondacks

Mount Marcy (5,344 ft.) is the Adirondacks' best-known peak, for the unsubtle reason that it is highest. With its nearby neighbors, Haystack (4,960 ft.) and Skylight (4,926 ft.), it forms a triumvirate of lofty summits, all far from roads and surrounded by a wilderness of lesser mountains that form the heart of the high peak region. An eloquent nineteenth-century essayist, Charles Dudley Warner, described the prospect from the top of Marcy thus:

> From horizon to horizon there is a tumultuous sea of billows turned to stone. You stand upon the highest billow; you command the situation; you have surprised Nature in a high creative act; the mighty primal energy has only just become repose.

Among the lower billows in this sea, Gothics (4,736 ft.) is especially admired as a sharply defined personality, its steep sides swept bare by landslides and its summit balanced high on a narrow ridge. To the east, the slender silhouette of Mount Dix (4,857 ft.) is only a shade less impressive. Other peaks that compel notice are Colden (4,714 ft.) and Algonquin (5,114 ft.), towering over Avalanche Lake facing each other, and two more independent figures that stand apart from the rest: the massive, sprawling Giant of the Valley (4,627 ft.) and the graceful, aloof Whiteface (4,867 ft.). Two small but exquisite jewels in the Adirondack tiara are Noonmark (3,556 ft.), at the northern outposts of the Colvin-Nippletop Range, and Ampersand (3,352 ft.), far off in the west.

Less noted for beauty, but infamous for its wildness and inaccessibility, the Seward Range lies to the west of the rest of the high peaks, save only Ampersand. Roads and trails have been slower to reach the Sewards, and we shall find that this has given them a special position in the history of mountain exploration of the Adirondacks.

THE GREEN MOUNTAINS. If you took the half-dozen parallel ridges of the Adirondacks, peeled them off the map, and stuck them back on as a single long chain, you would approximate the Green Mountains of Vermont (which actually extend into Massachusetts and Canada).

The Green Mountains are the lowest of the three chief ranges. The tops of these ridges are sometimes not much more than gentle swells of forest above cultivated valleys. They are truly green mountains, heavily vegetated, rich in evergreens, ferns, and lush understory. Their "lack of Wagnerian grandeur" has been identified by one reporter as their chief virtue:

> They are friendly, gentle mountains. . . . [They] inspire affection, not awe or terror. They are close, familiar places, appropriate to the small and human landscape of Vermont.

But all up and down the state, the ridge from time to time swoops skyward into mountain crests of noble stature.

The high point of Vermont, Mount Mansfield (4,393 ft.) expresses the general tendency of the Green Mountains: it is an elongated north-south ridge, whose profile has been compared by imaginative viewers to a human head lying face up. Thereby its prominent features gain such undignified appellations as Forehead, Nose, Lips, Chin, and Adam's Apple. Mansfield's long silhouette is a readily identifiable feature of the Vermont skyline from many points east and west.

Even more recognizable, less than 20 miles due south where the Green Mountain ridge breaks into the sky again, is the Camel's Hump (4,083 ft.). One of the most graceful outlines of any mountain in the Northeast, the Hump got its name from someone who fancied that its profile resembled a one-humped camel (with its head down). Competing viewers

Figure 0.2. The Green Mountains

called it Camel's Rump, or the Couching Lion. That's *couching*, not *crouching*; it's a term from medieval heraldry, and that name commands fierce loyalty from the mountain's most devoted admirers.

South of Camel's Hump, a chain of peaks forms a continuous rugged skyline for 50 miles, subsiding somewhat south of Killington Peak (4,241 ft.). Here is the largest concentration of truly *mountainous* mountains in the state. But both to the south and north recur individual peaks with distinct personalities, the most memorable lying far to the north: the sharp-pointed Jay Peak (3,861 ft.).

While the bulk of Vermont's mountains lie in these great north-south ripples from Jay Peak, less than 10 miles from Canada, to Glastenbury (3,748 ft.) and its neighbors around Bennington in the south, a handful of individual mountains or small clusters of peaks are scattered elsewhere throughout the state. One especially picturesque group orients around Lake Willoughby, way up in the northeast corner. Nearby is an independent mountain of merit, Burke (3,267 ft.). Much farther south, on the banks of the Connecticut, lies a completely isolated little peak of classically graceful proportions, Ascutney (3,150 ft.).

THE WHITE MOUNTAINS. The largest and highest range, with the longest history of climbing, is New Hampshire's White Mountains.

The White Mountains are bunched in a big, pear-shaped area in the northern half of New Hampshire. Like the Adirondacks, these mountains tend to form a series of parallel north-south ridges, from the Kinsman Ridge of the west, past the Franconia Ridge, Twin Range, Willey Range, the Presidentials, the Carters, to the Baldface-Royce group that lies right on the Maine border. Three of the deep "notches" (New Hampshire parlance for mountain pass) that cut through these ranges from north to south have played important roles in the history of the White Mountains, and all three now have paved highways through them— Pinkham, Crawford, and Franconia notches.

The most famous mountain is predictably the highest, Mount Washington (6,288 ft.). In fact, the top three peaks in the Presidentials— Washington, Adams (5,774 ft.), and Jefferson (5,712 ft.)—are the three highest summits in the Northeast, and the Presidential Range, which they dominate, is far and away the most extensive above-treeline area in the region.

In addition to this renowned alpine zone, the Presidentials have another characteristic feature: large, semicircular valleys rimmed by steep walls, called glacial cirques. These souvenirs of the Ice Age appear elsewhere too, as on Maine's Katahdin, but nowhere are they as numerous and spacious as in the Presidentials. Much of the White Mountains' climbing history centers on the Presidential Range, and some of its more exciting moments take place in the great cirques: Tuckerman, Huntington, and Ammonoosuc ravines on Mount Washington; King, Castle, and

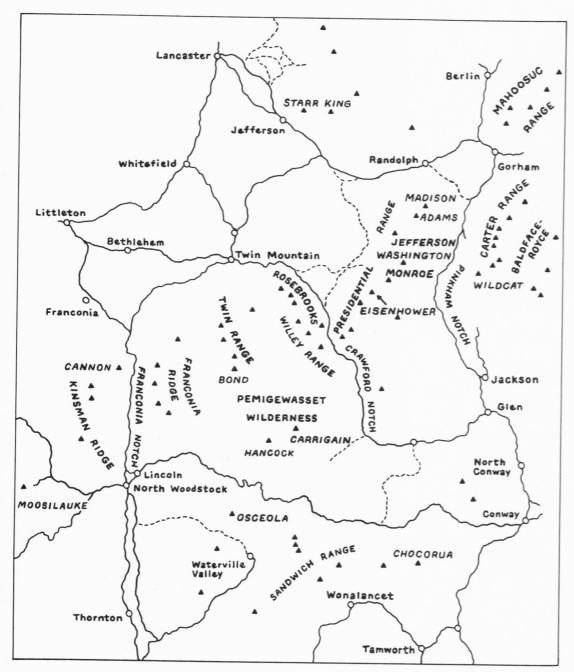

Figure 0.3. The White Mountains

Jefferson ravines and Madison Gulf in the Northern Presidentials, and the Great Gulf, nestled right in the middle of all the highest peaks.

Next in height to the Presidentials, but scarcely less in inspirational scenery and climbing enjoyment, is the Franconia Ridge near the western edge of the mountains. In between lies a vast area of mountains and forested valley known as the Pemigewasset Wilderness. Of many striking peaks in this area, irreverently nicknamed "the Pemi," two of exceptional beauty and personality are Mount Bond (4,698 ft.), with its wild cirque formed by the slender, spiny West Bond on the north and rock-bound Bondcliff on the south; and Mount Carrigain (4,680 ft.), the quintessential eastern mountain, in lordly isolation at the south end of the Pemi, with its deep-cut sides, majestic ridges, and hidden secrets.

Around the perimeter of the Whites are other mountains with personalities of their own: glamorous little Chocorua (3,475 ft.), whose rocky spire must adorn more calendars and postcards than any other peak in New England; big, friendly Moosilauke (4,802 ft.), the gentle giant at the southwest extremity of the range, where it enjoys a sociable relationship with the towns whose horizons it dominates; and the twisty, thorny, prickly Mahoosuc Range, at the wild northeast end of the White Mountains.

The mountains of Maine

These three big ranges—Adirondacks, Green Mountains, White Mountains—are neatly set off one from another. The picture becomes a bit more jumbled as it continues into Maine. Across the New Hampshire line, the border between Canada and the United States swings sharply northward. Hugging that border, a wide swath of land runs northeast from the White Mountains, roughly 60 miles wide (measuring southeast from the Canadian line) and 100 miles long (northeast from New Hampshire). This 60-by-100-mile belt swarms with more or less discontinuous mountains and small ranges, in isolation or in clusters, spilling out northeast from the White Mountains like schoolchildren dashing out at recess. Several of these mountain groups are as impressive as almost anything else in the Northeast, but overall they lack the continuity and cohesiveness of the three great ranges of the other states.

The previously mentioned Mahoosucs, which begin in New Hampshire, carry on into Maine as its westernmost range, culminating in Old Speck (4,180 ft.). South of the Mahoosucs lie Mounts Caribou, Speckled, and a charming family of lower peaks, across Evans Notch from the Baldface-Royce group. Moving north and east one encounters a succession of bold, independent Maine mountains, all with highly individual personalities: Elephant (3,774 ft.), Saddleback (4,116 ft.), Abraham (4,049 ft.), the Crockers (4,168 ft.), the great-horned ridge of the

Figure 0.4. The mountains of Maine

Bigelows (4,150 ft.), and off to the east the bristling Barren-Chairback range. Around the huge irregular coastline of Moosehead Lake are arranged the pleasing forms of Big Squaw (3,196 ft.), Boundary Bald (3,640 ft.), and the Spencers (3,240 ft.), plus a mountain-in-miniature that demonstrates that great elevation is not essential to vivid distinctiveness: Kineo (1,860 ft.), perched on a slender peninsula, square in the middle of the immense lake.

Beyond Moosehead, the last of these mountain heights fall off. Northward from the north shore of Moosehead extend the vast, rolling north woods of Maine, with no significant peaks rising above the endless forest —a canoeist's and sportsman's paradise, but without much interest for the hill walker. Due east from Moosehead, after the final bulwarks of Jo-Mary (2,904 ft.) and the Spencers, the land also drops into low woods.

But 25 miles farther east, Maine erupts in one final display of mountaincraft: Katahdin (5,267 ft.). This is the East's most remarkable single peak, a true mountain of steep, rugged ridges and enormous glacial cirques, a vast alpine tableland above, thick coniferous forests below, and far enough north to give its weather the quality of a much higher peak. Seen from the south, Katahdin appears as a solitary monolith, a huge, rammed-earth fortification jutting imperiously above the forests and waters of eastern Maine. From east or west, one discovers that it is merely the mightiest of a considerable range of many other fine peaks, most of which today lie within the boundaries of Baxter State Park.

Beyond this mountain group, to north and east there are no further mountains within the United States. Therefore, although political boundaries often fail to match geographical features elsewhere, in this case each of the four northeasternmost states has a unique and distinctive range neatly set apart (except between New Hampshire and Maine) from the others.

The lower hills

Throughout New England and New York, the smaller mountain ranges have considerable historical importance, scenic interest, and grand opportunities for hiking (see the frontispiece).

Rugged hills line the coast of Maine. Notable among these are the sea cliffs of Mount Desert Island and the more rounded contours of the Camden Hills. Down along the coast is a landmark familiar to ocean mariners: Mount Agamenticus (691 ft.).

The pride of southern New Hampshire is the Grand Monadnock (3,165 ft.), whose solitary eminence has given the name to a whole class of similar *monadnocks*, a term that the dictionary defines as "an isolated rocky hill or mountain rising above a peneplain." Its twin-summited kid brother, Pack Monadnock (2,300 ft.), lies just east, while similar low monadnocks sit across the Connecticut River in Vermont.

Western Massachusetts is a virtually unrelieved conglomeration of modest-sized hills: the Berkshires. Here forest lies side by side with farm in a pleasing mixture of the pastoral and the wild. The poet laureate of the Berkshires during the 1920s, Walter Prichard Eaton called them

> long horizontals . . . covered with second-growth forest, and criss-crossed with old roads which invite exploration. . . . They are true wilderness gardens. . . . The wild and the cultivated are close companions in our country.

Greylock (3,491 ft.), in the far northwest corner of the state, is the highest, a gentle, Moosilauke-like mass. One of the most striking mountains in western Massachusetts is that diminutive gothic, Monument Mountain (1,700 ft.). Along the Massachusetts—New York line, the Taconic Range spreads its highlands, topped by the near-perfect "Dome of the Taconics," Mount Everett (2,602 ft.). Though linked topographically more with the Taconic Range, Greylock is commonly regarded as part of the Berkshires scenically. Hills continue to dot the landscape as one moves eastward. Even in the Connecticut River valley, lovely illustrations of the union of the wild and the cultivated can be found in the Holyoke Range (878 ft.) and its neighbor, Mount Tom (1,202 ft.). Still farther east lie Toby (1,269 ft.), Wachusett (2,006 ft.), and Watatic (1,832 ft.), and, overlooking Boston itself, the Blue Hills (635 ft.).

The Litchfield Hills are the nearest thing to mountains in northwestern Connecticut. They are charming, furry little hills, and splendid hiking country. Central Connecticut abounds in red-hued trap-rock crags, such as the Hanging Hills of Meriden (1,024 ft.) and the rock climbers' Ragged Mountain (754 ft.). Down near Long Island Sound snoozes the graceful silhouette of the Sleeping Giant (700 ft.).

Separated from New England by the broad Hudson valley, the Catskills loom not far beneath the four northern ranges in geographic extent and height. Because of their more southerly latitude and significant geological differences, the Catskills afford the flavor of an experience all their own. Not a true mountain range but, properly speaking, an eroded peneplain, they seem less jagged and dramatic on top. But the deep-cut cloves (Catskillian for stream valley) and steep mountainsides abound in beauty, legend, and hiking pleasure.

Southeast of the Catskills lies an altogether different ridge of "mountains," the Shawangunk escarpment, famed for its abundance of cliffs of white conglomerate, known as the best rock-climbing playground in the eastern United States. Still farther southeast, the Hudson Highlands have been compared with the European Rhineland for scenic beauty. It may be that the most elegant single "mountain" of the entire northeast is

1,352-foot Storm King, as seen from across the Hudson at Breakneck Ridge. Spilling out to the West lie the broken hills of Bear Mountain and Harriman Parks. Moving on into New Jersey, one meets the Ramapos and the Wyanokies, all marvelous hiking country, of which an earlier admirer wrote:

> . . . the woods, the heavens, the hills
>   Are not a world today
> But just a place God made for us
>   In which to play.

PART ONE

Mountains as "daunting terrible": Before 1830

Mountain climbing in the northeastern United States, pursued for pleasure, is relatively young. Prior to the 1830s, few people tried to reach the summits of the region's highest hills. Those who did were there primarily for business reasons; they were adventurers after rumored precious stones; military men seeking a lookout; land surveyors obliged to run town or property lines across high terrain; or hunters or lumbermen whose work led them up ridges. Not until after the American Revolution (1776–83) is there record of anyone climbing a significant peak for anything like recreational reasons. For the first fifty years of the nation's existence, these instances remain rare.

The nearly complete absence of a mountain recreation impulse was not unique to Americans of that era. Although some cultures have appreciated and even revered mountain scenery for many centuries, most did not.[a] Europeans avoided mountains or regarded them with fear and superstition until modern times. Appreciation of mountain landscape, as well as purely recreational climbing, whether of the Alps or of lesser hills like those of England's Lake District, were rarely heard of until the eighteenth century. The first ascent of Mont Blanc, often cited as the starting point of modern mountaineering, came in 1786, but European climbs remained isolated, almost eccentric events until the next century.

People didn't climb because they didn't perceive mountains in the same way we do today. Mountains were, at best, difficult and unpleasant places to get to; at worst, ugly or terrifying or the rumored abode of evil spirits or horrid creatures. One knew little about mountains, and the unfamiliar is always a little scary. "Here bee dragons," the old maps

---

[a]The Chinese and some other Asian civilizations took a positive view of mountains as early as 200 B.C. The Incas in the years 1400–1800 A.D. lived among the Andes with acceptance and reverence. Considerable discussion of early non-European attitudes may be found in Michael Charles Tobias and Harold Drasdo, eds., *The Mountain Spirit* (Woodstock, N.Y.: The Overlook Press, 1979).

say. Seventeenth-century geographers disputed whether the Caucasus were 115 or only 59 miles high—that's not in the dim Dark Ages of Beowulf but in the 1600s of Galileo and Milton. A minor British poet writing in 1679 referred to the Lake District hills, later so romanticized by Wordsworth's generation, as "Hillocks, Mole Hills, Warts, and Pibbles."

This European attitude was the cultural heritage of the American colonists. When they first came to the New World, the earliest European explorers saw mountains in the nearby interior, but there was no campaign to go climb them. The Italian navigator Giovanni da Verrazano mentions in 1524 "high mountains back inland," which were probably the White Mountains. French explorer Samuel de Champlain saw and named the Isle de Monts Desert in 1604. Englishman John Smith drew a map in 1614 depicting Mount Agamenticus on the coast of Maine as "Snadoun Hill," and recorded sightings of Maine's Camden Hills and Boston's Blue Hills. Even those ranges farther inland, out of sight of the sea, were sighted relatively early: the Adirondacks in 1535 by a French missionary near Montreal; the Green Mountains in 1609 by Champlain on a voyage down the long lake that now bears his name; the Catskills by the Dutchman Henry Hudson, also in 1609.

When the Pilgrims landed near Plymouth in 1620, and other settlements began to dot the New England coast thereafter, the mountains did not immediately assume a significant role in the settlers' lives. Sheer survival was their preoccupation. As one historian described the first days in the New World:

> At the start, all the colonizing enterprises were tentative. The little troops landed at the edge of the dark forest, the ships withdrew beyond the eastern horizon. Now was the time for survival. . . . The people of Charlestown, on Massachusetts Bay, in 1630 took shelter in empty casks before the first rude huts went up. In Jamestown the palisade and magazine for stores took precedence over individual convenience.

For these first settlers, clinging to life in a new harsh and hostile environment, occasional glimpses of high peaks to the north and west must have seemed uninviting in the extreme. Mountains aside, the unyielding wilderness of thick forest alone was daunting:

> A waste and howling wilderness,
> Where none inhabited
> But hellish fiends, and brutish men
> That devils worshipped.

When the earliest pioneers pushed westward to the Berkshires, they called them "horrid hills." Even as late as 1760, soldiers approaching the

Vermont hills south of Lake Memphremagog saw "even higher mountains, crammed together helter skelter, so that the land was overcrowded with them," and their fictional narrator (in Kenneth Roberts's *Northwest Passage*) can only despair: "We were coming to a terrible country: no doubt of that."

The Native Americans who were in this region before the European settlers reportedly had little to do with the higher mountains. No trace of trails to summits, no cairns, or any other evidence of climbing the bigger peaks was found. For the Indians these mountains had no practical uses. They could not be farmed. The upper elevations were rarely frequented by game. Routes of travel naturally avoided ups and downs where possible and clearly kept away from the thick, stunted, coniferous forests of the higher reaches. In the lower, less intimidating hills—the Catskills, Hudson Highlands, Shawangunks, the miniature mountains of southern New England— Indians hunted and even made seasonal use of natural rock shelters. On these more accessible heights, Indians may even have built trails; the Indian origins of the Housatonic Range Trail seem uniquely suggested by an item in the trail description in the *Connecticut Walk Book*—that is, the crossing of a small stream by the name of Naromiyochknowhusunkotankshunk Brook. But the Indians shunned the higher peaks of the northern ranges because of religious beliefs: they felt those heights were the abode of great spirits who resented intrusion. Katahdin, for example, was said to be the stronghold of a terrifying storm god, Pamola, part man and part eagle and several times larger than life. The sole report of an Indian attempt on a major peak concerns Katahdin, and that imprudent brave turned back before reaching the top.[b]

Under these circumstances, one could expect that no mountain climbing took place in the New World for several generations after the Pilgrims landed in 1620. In fact, both Katahdin and the Adirondacks went unexplored for well over a century, nor can any record of anyone's visiting the higher Green Mountains be found.

This background makes Darby Field's ascent of Mount Washington in 1642 an astonishing achievement. Just twenty-two years after the first tenuous foothold at Plymouth, the highest peak in the entire region was climbed. Field's ascent indeed touched off a minor flurry of expeditions to Mount Washington, all in the same summer.

Then, that spasm spent, colonial America reverted to ignoring mountains, while turning full attention to taming the wilderness at hand. Relatively few ascents of any mountains were recorded during the remaining colonial years. Some of these reports concern rangers

---

[b]There is interesting evidence that Indians in the Rockies and Sierra did climb many of the high mountains, hunted sheep and eagles on their upper slopes, and even built cairns on summits. White men making "first ascents" on 14,345-foot Blanca Peak in Colorado and 13,165-foot Cloud Peak in Wyoming reported finding Indian structures on the tops. See Chris Jones, *Climbing in North America* (Berkeley, Calif: University of California Press, 1976), pp. 22–23. No such evidence on 5,000-foot elevations of the White Mountains or Adirondacks has come to light.

hunting for hostile Indians, such as the party led by Capt. Samuel Willard to the top of Monadnock in 1725 for its first recorded ascent. Other reports involved land speculators such as Ira Allen, who ran a town line up Mount Mansfield in 1772. A hunter named Chase Whitcher is credited with the first ascent of Moosilauke sometime during the 1770s, allegedly in pursuit of a moose. Any knowledge of the extent of such pre-Revolution climbing is, of course, limited by the scant evidence. We can never know how many adventurous individuals scrambled to mountaintops. We do know that no one who wrote of those years hints of much interest in climbing; and since those ascents of 1642 *were* described by early chronicles in some detail, other ascents might have received attention as well.

Besides, the northern sections of New England were sparsely populated until fewer than fifteen years before the American Revolution, so few people were physically near the mountains for most of that period. For a couple of generations prior to 1760, the northeastern United States was the scene of a struggle between English and French imperial aspirations. The French government encouraged its Indian allies to harass any English pioneers who attempted to settle northern New England. It became hazardous to be the first settler anywhere much beyond the coasts of New Hampshire and Maine. As a result, northern New Hampshire, inland Maine, and virtually all of Vermont remained without permanent settlement until the threat of French-inspired Indian raids was reduced by British victory over the French at Quebec in 1761. This is why so many northern New England towns were settled in the 1760s—and none before.

If New England's higher mountains remained largely unexplored until after the Revolution, the Adirondacks were even less known and visited. The leading historian of that range, Alfred L. Donaldson, writes:

> Stanley had found Dr. Livingstone and familiarized the world with the depths of Africa before the average New Yorker knew anything definite about the wonderful wilderness lying almost at his back door.

As late as 1756, the standard map of New York showed no details of the whole northern mountainous region, simply labeling it "Cauchsachrage an Indian Beaver Hunting Country." "This country, by reason of mountains, swamps, and drowned lands, is impassable and uninhabited." *Cauchsachrage*, a name essentially retained in one of the region's peaks today, was variously translated "dismal wilderness" and "beaver-hunting grounds."

Far off in the north woods of Maine, lonely Katahdin also stood remote from European settlement. In 1763 the General Court of Massachusetts (which then controlled Maine) directed a thorough investigation of the Penobscot River watershed. Capt. Joseph Chadwick, a leading surveyor of the time, was appointed to explore and describe the country and to determine the feasibility of a road from Fort Pownal (now Fort Point) to Quebec. He came back with a detailed journal, a rough map, and a negative conclusion about the Pownal-Quebec road scheme. Chadwick also turned in the first description of Katahdin, which he called Satinhungemoss Hill, in these terms:

> Being a remarkable Hill for highteth & figr the Indines say that this Hill is the hightest in the Country. That thay can ascend so high as any Greens Grow & no higher. That one Indine attempted to go higher but he never returned.
>
> The hight of Vegetation is as a Horizontal Line about halfe the perpendiciler hight of the Hill a & intersects the tops of Sundrey other mountines. The hight of this Hill was very apperent to ous as we had a Sight of it at Sundre places Easterly
>
> Westerly at 60 or 70 Miles Distance—It is Curious to See—Elevated above a rude mass of Rocke large Mountins—So Lofty a Pyramid.

Chadwick's map gives the first pictorial representation we have of Katahdin, along with various other peaks. But like many government reports and maps before and since, Chadwick's papers were filed away and do not seem to have touched off any great rush to climb the mountains of Maine. It was forty years before the next recorded effort to reach lordly Katahdin. Like the Adirondacks, it remained unseen and unexplored, far off in the "dismal wilderness"—"impassable and uninhabited."

After the Revolution, American life became more settled, and opportunities for exploration and mountain climbing opened up. Beginning with a widely reported expedition to Mount Washington in 1784, scattered instances of climbing appeared. Soon after the turn of the nineteenth century, even remote Katahdin was climbed. Sometime after 1820 —later than in Europe—new perceptions of mountain landscape began to catch hold, leading to considerable interest in mountain recreation and even mountaintop buildings.

But until then mountains were seen, in the words of a seventeenth-century British traveler writing about New Hampshire's Northern Presidentials, as "daunting terrible, being full of rocky Hills, as thick as Molehills in a Meadow, and cloathed with infinite thick Woods." No place for a sensible person, obviously.

Chapter 1

Darby Field on Mount Washington

Considering the time and circumstances, Darby Field's ascent of what we now call Mount Washington is as noteworthy a mountaineering achievement as any other in this history.

Imagine how the first settlers perceived "the White Hills" (as the White Mountains were first known). The earliest maps of New England offer a primitive representation of the coastline and the location of settlements along it. Beyond the coast, though, are large blank areas marked as wilderness, with the general course of major rivers drawn in, sometimes by guesswork, and at their sources a vague indication of high mountains. One is reminded of the map in *The Hobbit,* where J. R. R. Tolkein shows the friendly settled regions of hobbits, elves, and men—and then an arrow pointing up beyond the northern wastes with the notation "Far to the North are the Grey Mountains & the Withered Heath whence came the Great Worms." To the New Englander of the 1640s, the White Mountains must have been equally shrouded in mystery, dread, and inaccessibility. Here bee dragons indeed.

Yet, with but a toehold of colonial settlement scarcely established, Field set off on his great adventure.

Darby Field was born in Boston, England, around 1610, and came to what is now the United States apparently to escape religious persecution, probably in 1636. He moved to New Hampshire in 1638, settling first in Exeter. Early records of Exeter's settlement include Field among those who "could not write." By 1642 he had moved again to the area around what is now Durham, New Hampshire.

In that year, accompanied by several Indians, he set out along the coast to the mouth of the Saco and thence up the river until he reached a settlement of Indians where the river forked, in the foothills south of Mount Washington (see figure 1.1). From there he picked up local guides to take his party farther north toward the big peak. When the locals refused to go up the mountain itself, Field and his original companions made the ascent alone. The whole journey took eighteen days, probably during the month of June.

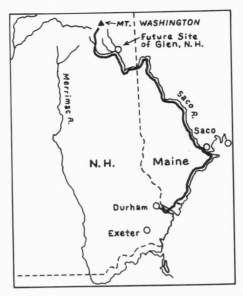

Figure 1.1. Darby Field's itinerary, 1642 Darby Field lived in Durham, New Hampshire, in 1642. In an eighteen-day trip, he journeyed along the coast to the Maine seaport of Saco, and up the Saco River to an Indian settlement, possibly in the vicinity of today's town of Glen, New Hampshire. From there, with directions from local Indians, he climbed Mount Washington.

Mount Washington was in a moderately testy mood for its first visitors. Field encountered "terrible freesing weather"; clouds hung around the lower flanks of the mountain. When the summit party returned to the local Indians they had left below, they "found them drying themselves by the fire, for they had a great tempest of wind and rain." However, as sometimes happens, the summit plateau was clear and relatively windless, and Field thought he saw the Atlantic Ocean, as well as many other mountains and lakes.

In view of the historical importance of this ascent, we would like to be able to state with precision what his route was. The uncertainties of the evidence preclude sweeping conclusions on this point, and the changes in historians' guesses as to the route make an interesting story on their own.

Until remarkably recently, only one account of Darby Field's climb was known. This appeared in a journal kept by Gov. John Winthrop of Massachusetts:

> His relation at his return was, that it was about one hundred miles from Saco, that after 40 miles travel he did, for the most part, ascend, and within 12 miles of the top was neither tree nor grass, but low savins, which they went upon the top of sometimes, but a continual ascent upon rocks, on a ridge between two valleys filled with snow, out of which came two branches of Saco river, which met at the foot of

the hill where was an Indian town of some 200 people. Some of them accompanied him within 8 miles of the top, but durst go no further, telling him that no Indian ever dared to go higher, and that he would die if he went. So they staid there till his return, and his two Indians took courage by his example and went with him. They went divers times through the thick clouds for a good space, and within 4 miles of the top they had no clouds, but very cold. By the way, among the rocks, there were two ponds, one a blackish water and the other reddish. The top of all was plain about 60 feet square. On the north side there was such a precipice, as they could scarce discern to the bottom.

Considering the antiquity of the event, this paragraph offers a surprising number of clues to Field's route. The Indian village that he reached, at the fork of "two branches of Saco River," may have been near the present village of Glen on Route 16. The description of ascending a rocky ridge between two valleys filled with snow seems vivid. But which of the many ridges separating glacial cirques on that side of Mount Washington?

For years historians favored the theory that Field went up the Ellis River into Pinkham Notch, turned due west up to Boott Spur, and then circled around the headwall of Tuckerman Ravine to ascend the final summit cone. This certainly follows "a ridge between two valleys filled with snow," Tuckerman Ravine and the Gulf of Slides. A troublesome point, however, is that Winthrop's account says that the rivers draining the two valleys "met at the foot of the hill where was an Indian town of some 200 people." If Boott Spur's east ridge was climbed, that would place the Indian town way up in Pinkham Notch, on the steep slopes just south of the present Appalachian Mountain Club camp, an inhospitable place for a settlement. Furthermore, if local Indians came with Field for a considerable distance before refusing to climb the peak itself, the village is more likely to have been several miles to the south; two rivers meeting there would drain valleys more to the west. Field describes the ridge as lengthy, another point against the Boott Spur–east ridge theory. These points invited the conjecture that Field and his companions might have gained Boott Spur via the Rocky Branch and the Montalban Ridge (see figure 1.2).

At any rate, the earliest guesses put the route definitely up Boott Spur, either by way of the Ellis or the Rocky Branch:

In Lucy Crawford's *History of the White Mountains*, originally published in 1846, the author gives Field's route as "near 'Tuckerman's Ravine.' "

The first careful examination of the question by someone with a scholar's credentials was by Edward Tuckerman, in his chapter "Exploration of the White Hills" in Starr King's *The White Hills*, published in 1859; Tuckerman was certain Field went up Boott Spur and thought it "likely" he went up the Ellis.

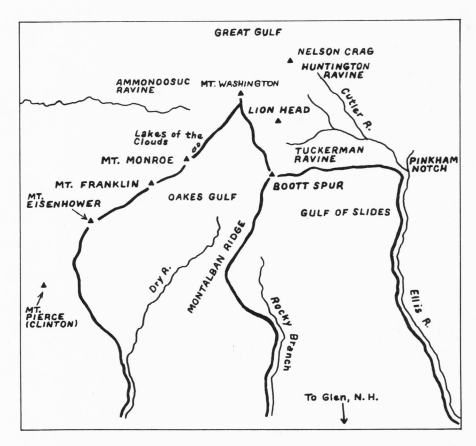

Figure 1.2. Darby Field's route for ascending Mount Washington, 1642 Until 1984 most White Mountain historians believed that Darby Field ascended Mount Washington via Boott Spur, first going up either the Ellis River (the route of today's New Hampshire Route 16) or Rocky Branch and the Montalban Ridge. A dramatic discovery of new evidence in 1984 produced a new theory: that he might have ascended via the southern peaks, going over Mount Eisenhower, Mount Franklin, and Mount Monroe en route.

The next writer to publish an independent analysis of the Winthrop source seems to have been Frederick Tuckerman, in a 1921 article in *Appalachia*; this second Tuckerman was less confident of which approach to Boott Spur was used, saying only that the route went "up the valley either of Rocky Branch or of Ellis River."

In 1930 John Anderson and Stearns Morse published *The Book of the White Mountains*, in which they opted for the Montalban Ridge.

In 1942 Warren Hart came out for the Ellis River and the east ridge theory.

Frederick W. Kilbourne, a most respected general source on the White Mountains, hedged on this question: he placed the route on "the ridge (Boott Spur) between Tuckerman's and the valley of the Dry, or Mount Washington, River"; there are three or four ridges between those two ravines, and Kilbourne didn't say which was Field's route.

Whichever ridge it was, Winthrop's references to ponds and to the precipices are generally taken as evidence that Field visited Lakes of the Clouds and that he went to the edge of the Great Gulf, a stupendous gorge with precipitous sides north of the summit.

Through the centuries during which the lone Winthrop source was puzzled over, a letter written by a Maine magistrate named Thomas Gorges sat silently in the wings unnoticed. Gorges served as deputy governor of the province of Maine, on behalf of his cousin in England who had received a charter for Maine in 1639. Gorges was thus on the scene near the mouth of the Saco River when Darby Field passed through in 1642. On June 29, 1642, Gorges wrote a letter to his cousin relating what he knew of Field's ascent.

The original of that letter was apparently lost. But Thomas Gorges made a practice of rough drafting his letters in copybooks that contained miscellaneous notes and entries. Ten such copybooks were not destroyed. One included the draft of that June 29, 1642, letter describing Field's climb.

For three centuries, totally unknown to White Mountain scholars or aficionados, these copybooks from the years 1640–43 were held by the Mallock family (into which Gorges had married) in their manor in an obscure English village 3,000 miles from the windswept summit of Mount Washington. In 1948 the Mallock family papers were turned over to the City Library of Exeter, Devon. By this time the Gorges letters were "in a sorry state, having lain neglected, exposed to water and rats. . . . water-stained, blotted, frayed at the edges, matted together, disarranged." Yet there, in that ancient, musty, and nearly unreadable copybook, was that slender thread leading back into the oblivion of early colonial times, providing long-forgotten information about the first ascent of Mount Washington.

Still another generation was to pass before the White Mountain community became aware of the find. Finally the Exeter Library called the material to the attention of American colonial history scholars, and in 1978 the Maine Historical Society published an unobtrusive volume under the title *The Letters of Thomas Gorges*. For another six years this volume sat on library shelves before a Vermont history professor (and White Mountain hiker), Gary Thomas Lord of Norwich University, pointed out to White Mountain historians the significant paragraph about Darby Field's climb. Significant indeed: Gorges's account preceded Winthrop's in time, having been written within a month of the ascent, based apparently on direct evidence provided by Field himself. Since Gorges and Winthrop are known to have been in communication, it is possible that Winthrop had his information secondhand from Gorges or others. In short, 342 years after the event, a second source—and probably an even more direct one—on Darby Field's pioneering climb had come to light.

The key paragraph is in a letter dated June 29, 1642:

> This much I certify of accordinge as it was sent to me by him that discovered them [the white hills] whose name was Darby Feild [sic] of pascataqua who about a month since with some 3 or 4 Indians undertook the voyage, went first to Pigwackett, a place on the Saco river accordinge to my draught now 23 leagues from Mr Vines his house, hence he travailled some 80 miles as he sayeth & came to a mountain, went over it, & a 2d & a 3d, at length came to a ledge of rocks which he conceaved to be 12 miles high, very steep, uppon which he travailed going to a rocke that was at the end of that which he judged 2 miles high, very steep, yet he adventured up, but one Indian accompaynge him, the most being fearfull. At the top it was not above 20 foot square, wher he sate with much fear some 5 hours time the clouds passing under him makinge a terrible noyse against the mountains. Thence he discovered some 80 miles farther a very (*glorious*) white mountain & between 2 other great mountains as he judged some 100 miles [. . .] a mighty river bearing North & by East from him of which like or sea he could see noe end. On this mountain, he mett with terrible freesing weather and, as I took it, on the top of the ledge or rocke & at the foot of them were 2 litle ponds, 1 of a curious red colour, the other black. The [latter] dyed his handkerchief very blacke, the former did not alter the collours. Ther wer many rattle snakes but he receaved noe harm.

Gorges's letter included at least one striking new hint of Field's route. He speaks of going over three preliminary summits before ascending the final summit cone. This "new" evidence, not mentioned in Winthrop's account, gives strong reason to suspect that Field did not first ascend Boott Spur but rather came up over the ridge where the Crawford Path now ascends, and over Mounts Eisenhower, Franklin, and Monroe, past the Lakes of the Clouds, and up the summit cone via the southwest. The Gorges letter also emphasizes Field's passing by two ponds—presumably the Lakes of the Clouds. This has prompted historians to look more closely at Winthrop's allusion to his passing these ponds "by the way." Furthermore, if Field came over Boott Spur and went around the rim of Tuckerman Ravine, why did not such close and prolonged views of that spectacular cirque receive more attention than the Great Gulf (which he does mention)? The evidence is so vague that the earlier Boott Spur theory cannot be dismissed, but the Crawford Path ridge is certainly now a distinct possibility.

When news of the Gorges letter broke on the White Mountain history community in 1984, bemused historians were reminded of the truth in that seeming paradox pronounced sixty-six years earlier by eminent Victorian biographer Lytton Strachey, when predicting that nineteenth-century history could never be written. "We know too much about it," observed Strachey. "Ignorance is the first requisite of the historian—ignorance, which simplifies and clarifies, which selects and omits." As our ignorance of Field's climb was reduced by access to a second source, our former assurance about where he went was all suddenly confused. Having more information, we "know" less.

We know even less about *why* Field climbed. What inspired this obscure illiterate immigrant to a hostile wilderness to make such a perilous journey so early?

It is not clear whether Field set out from home with the explicit idea of climbing the highest mountain, or whether that goal overtook him once he was up in the wild country. No one could have known that the apex of the White Hills was in fact the highest mountain of the entire Northeast. It is possible that his journey had other original motives but that as he got closer to the mountain his purpose centered on an ascent, which on its accomplishment became the most important event of the trip. However, the general assumption of posterity, that he deliberately set forth to climb the big mountain that had been seen from the coast and spoken of by the natives, could also be correct.

One theory is that Field was an adventurer, a man of imagination and courage. Warren W. Hart writes; "It seems probable that he went because he felt the call of the wilderness, a call ever irresistible to him in whose veins flows the restless blood of the explorer." Another possible motive is that Field was looking for a route to the fur country that was then enriching Quebec traders—a kind of first-generation northwest passage quest. A more worldly purpose is more often cited: "It is far more probable that the reports brought by Indians of the fabulous treasures of the mountains led to Field's long, arduous and really perilous journey."

It seems likely that Field's motivation was "fabulous treasures." Adventuring for wealth had been in the New World air for more than a century, whereas mountaineering for whatever reason certainly had not. The Spaniards in South America, Mexico, and even in the American Southwest sometimes literally struck pay dirt. Whether or not Field had heard of Pizarro and Cortés, the explorations by the Spanish in the ringing name of gold and silver must have been known to him. Indeed Field thought he had found diamonds among Washington's summit rocks, but like many "fabulous treasures" adorned with an overdose of imagination and wishful thinking, they performed on closer inspection a reverse alchemy and became baser stuff: quartz crystals and "Muscovy glass" (mica).

Whatever Field's motives, his adventurous spirit was advanced for its time. His climb took place more than a century *before* the Revolution.

More time elapsed between Field's ascent and the construction of the first well-maintained path up Mount Washington than has elapsed since. A nineteenth-century author points out that Field's ascent was 125 years before even the ascent of Mont Blanc, an event often cited as the first modern mountain climb, and comments:

> The exploit of [Field] is far more remarkable in its way than that of the brave Swiss, since he had to make his way for eighty miles through a wilderness inhabited only by beasts of prey, or by human beings scarcely less savage, before he reached the foot of the great range; while Balmat lived under the very shadow of the monarch of the Alps.

Furthermore, this author goes on to point out, guides and chamois hunters knew the lower slopes of the Alps well, while Field's eighteen-day journey was through terra incognita, where, for all he knew, lay only "the Grey Mountains & the Withered Heath whence came the Great Worms."

For a time Field had rival claimants for the first ascent honors on Washington. Jeremy Belknap, in his history of New Hampshire, originally credited Walter Neal and Henry Josselyn with accompanying Field. Neal was an agent for a group sent "to discover lakes, and to settle a trade with the Indians." Belknap also set the date as 1631. He corrected these errors in later editions of his history, but the 1631 date (or sometimes 1632) and Neal's name were picked up in other accounts. Today historians find no evidence of Neal's having climbed the mountain, though he is known to have been exploring the general area during the 1630s.

After the first ascent, Field returned about a month later to climb the mountain again, this time with other settlers. These men brought back samples of the summit crystals. Interest ran high that summer; after Field's two trips, still other ascents were made, including one by Thomas Gorges and Richard Vines, both magistrates of the province of Maine. New Englanders, however, were not destined to become wealthy from mountaintop riches. After these three ascents in a single summer, it is acknowledged that the treasures were false, and interest in the White Hills waned. Further ascents may have occurred, but they went unreported and are unlikely to have been frequent. Not until 1725 did a few widely scattered reports of people climbing Mount Washington and other New England peaks begin to trickle in. With the absence of treasure, no further incentive for such a frivolous and hazardous pursuit presented itself to the sober colonial mind. The mountains loomed once more as "daunting terrible."

Chapter 2

Ira Allen on Mount Mansfield

Whoever set up mountains in New Hampshire had nothing whatever to do with arranging those of Vermont. The two states have an entirely different relationship with their hills.

In New Hampshire, the mountains are virtually all in one place (except Monadnock), a wide belt in the northern part of the state, so thickly clustered that settlers knew there was no point in trying to farm anywhere near them. New Hampshire mountains are distinct scenery, separate and apart from the rest of the state. Aside from a brief (albeit colorful) period of logging, the sole and obvious economic use of the hill region by the locals has been tourism. As tourist bait, they're first rate: full of craggy cliffs, high alpine zones, deep notches flanked by picturesque mountainsides.

In Vermont, the mountains are at once less important and more important. They are less mountains. They are less of a tourist attraction because they are neither so high nor so dramatic. What's more, they are not all in one convenient place but stretch from one end of the state to the other in continuous longitudinal sinews. This very continuity makes them *more* important in the everyday lives of Vermonters all over the state. They are a persistent presence, visible from just about every town, a topographical fact of life to anyone trying to move even a short way across the state. Vermont is indeed the Green Mountain State, in a sense that one would not normally speak of New Hampshire as the White Mountain State. The resident of Portsmouth, Nashua, Manchester, Keene, or even Concord or Laconia, is far more conscious of the seacoast, or Lake Winnipesaukee, or maybe Monadnock, or even of Boston, than he is of Mount Washington. But any Vermonter has the Green Mountains in his soul.

The Vermont hills really are vividly *green* too. With only a few acres of alpine zone scattered over a handful of peaks, the dominant impression they leave is of endless ridges and folds of emerald. The verdure is unrelieved. From a distance you see the trees; walking beneath the trees you see the understory, the wood sorrel and the mayflower, the ferns, and the mosses; everywhere green.

To the settlers, the state-long backbone of hills was one state-long problem, a divider:

> It was an obstruction to commerce, a hindrance to communication, a formidable obstacle to the gregarious. The mountains had to be crossed and climbed. The wily rivers flushing the steep flanks had to be tamed; forests skidded out of the hills; intractable snows navigated in winter; barns and homesteads had to be fixed on the rocky slopes. The barrier was an eternal dare; it gave year-round battle.

Because of French and Indian hostility, little of Vermont was settled prior to 1760. Then the floodgates opened. By the end of the decade, in the years just before the American Revolution, the tide of settlement was lapping against the flanks of even the highest peaks, so that in 1772 a surveyor was running property lines *over* Mansfield itself, the highest summit—but then, this was no ordinary surveyor . . .

As every Vermont schoolchild knows, Ethan and Ira Allen are renowned among the influential figures in the state's early history. To contemporaries in colonial America, *notorious* might have been a better word than *renowned*. When northern and western Vermont first became habitable after 1761, a hot dispute arose about whether or not the new territory should be under the control of New York. In the early 1770s a band of independent-minded and action-loving Vermont settlers took arms to drive out the New York influence. These desperadoes became known as the Green Mountain Boys. The Allens were among them.

Twentieth-century schoolchildren know the Green Mountain Boys as patriotic heroes who routed the British from Fort Ticonderoga for one of the earliest American victories in the Revolution. In fact, this band of frontier rowdies probably fought more against the New Yorkers than the British. Their leader, Ethan Allen, known today as a great patriot, was ill-famed then as a land speculator, radical pamphleteer, and outlaw. New York placed a price on his head.

The Allen family, which had many male children and few scruples, came to Vermont from northwestern Connecticut. New England's premier historian, James Truslow Adams, says of the Allens, "The family seems to have been a hot-tempered, boastful, swash-buckling sort, carving fortunes for themselves out of the frontier." Before their diverse careers were concluded, one or another of the brothers had seen the insides of prisons in three countries. Ethan was a hell-raiser at the time of the Revolution and before. During the Revolution, he alternated between fighting on our side and scheming with the British to pull Vermont out of the new United States. Three other brothers were moving around northwestern Vermont back in the early 1770s, bent on making a killing in land speculation. One of these was Ira, who was born on May 1, 1751, in Cornwall, Connecticut, and moved to Vermont in 1770.

Ira Allen was just nineteen years old when he got to Vermont. He was "a short, well-built young man, brown-haired, with fine brown eyes glancing alertly out of a handsome face." He was one of his brother Ethan's original Green Mountain Boys and played no small role in the subsequent military and diplomatic history of Vermont's entry into the Union in 1791. His biographer refers to him unequivocally as "Founder of Vermont." His personality contrasted sharply with his more flamboyant brother's, as another Vermont historian has noted:

> Ira, the brilliant, the imperturbable, and, alas, the sometimes devious. Unlike the extroverted Ethan, he preferred to move in the shadows, making quiet and, if necessary, questionable deals, and in the end getting what he wanted without much fuss or fanfare. Few men were so influential in the affairs of early Vermont.

To political and diplomatic historians, Ira Allen is either schemer or statesman, but he enters the history of mountain climbing because of his dealings as a land speculator and surveyor during the early 1770s. Ira had been one step ahead of Ethan in recognizing the future economic value of the Burlington area, with its fertile farmland and strategic location on Lake Champlain. At age twenty-one he was determined to get in on the ground floor. By agreeing to conduct the initial land survey, he was able to secure rights to about one-third of a remote and uninhabited town by the name of Mansfield. In 1772, with a company of fellow adventurers, he set out to find and survey this new town, dreaming of rich farms and flourishing commerce.

What he found was "a tremendous range of mountains": Mount Mansfield jutting 4,393 feet into the sky, capped by a barren alpine zone, with long tumbling ridges of spruce-fir forest and jagged boulders on all sides. So much for rich farms and flourishing commerce. Undeterred by injuries to himself or by discouragement among his partners or by long rainy spells ("for three of the last days I believe that not one of us had a dry thread on us"), Ira Allen ran his survey line right through the very crest of the ridge. The line he ran crosses the mountain feature known today as the Adam's Apple, at an elevation of 4,060 feet, less than one-half mile from the highest point of the mountain. Since he was there to see his land, it is possible that he walked on up to the top to view what lay to the south.

For 1772 this was a formidable mountain to climb, way up in the wilds of uninhabited Vermont. Though we now see his climb as a mountaineering accomplishment, Ira Allen viewed it through the eyes of a land speculator:

> I was the owner of very near one-third of the town, and could not discover lands that would [make] one good farm. This gave Baker [a companion on the survey] an opportunity to pass many hard jokes on me respecting my purchase, &c.

The future founder of Vermont was not about to tie up his fortunes in a precipitous mountainside. On his return to the principal landowners of the town of Mansfield, he reported the land as covered, not with spruce and fir, but with "gum-wood," which he described as "tall Straight trees that had a gum, much like the gum on cherry trees, &c." His descriptions did not dwell on the steepness or elevation of the land. When the chief owners were looking over his map, he took aside another minority owner ("an ignorant fellow") and hinted at purchasing his land. When this dupe reported Allen's interest in further purchases, the principal owners became convinced that Allen considered Mansfield a bargain, came back to him, and bought him out at a good price. "Having closed this business satisfactory to myself," recalled young Allen smugly, "I returned to my brothers' and had a hearty laugh with my brothers Heman and Zimri, on informing them respecting the gum-wood, &c."

Ira Allen's climbing exploits did not end with the probable first ascent of Mansfield. Before returning to civilization to hoodwink his partners, he and four other backwoodsmen journeyed farther inland on the Winooski River (then known as Onion River), and up the Mad River to the main ridge of the Green Mountains around Breadloaf. Then for 16 miles they apparently followed close to the ridge crest all the way to Brandon Gap—"Taking the range of the Green Mountains lengthwise," complained the other men—before dropping off on the west side. If this is a correct reading of their itinerary, it means they bushwhacked 40 miles in three days, the last 16 along the crest of the mountains, roughly along the future Long Trail, and over or near perhaps half a dozen 3,000-foot peaks (see figure 2.1). Battell (3,482 ft.), Boyce (3,323 ft.), Kirby (3,140 ft.), Burnt Hill (3,030 ft.), Worth (3,234 ft.), Romance (3,145 ft.), Gillespie Peak (3,366 ft.), Cape Lookoff (3,320 ft.), and Mount Horrid (3,216 ft.) —all lay along their path.[a]

Ira Allen had something of the climber's spirit. Once during his mountain survey work, he scaled a tall spruce that stood at the edge of "a ledge I judged to be at least 300 feet perpendicular." With his hatchet he climbed until he was near the top, which he lopped off, so as to set his compass on the stump and take various bearings from that airy perch.

> While thus amusing myself, the day being some windy, a sudden gust of wind caused the top of the tree to wave over the ledge aforesaid. At this unlucky moment for the first time, I chanced to cast my eyes down the tree, waved by the wind over, it had the appearance that I was going to the bottom. This gave me sensations not easily expressed.

[a]Allen's account of this march is not explicit as to how much of the time was spent on the ridgetop and how many peaks were climbed. Our account accepts the interpretation given by Llew Evans in "Mount Mansfield: Capstone of Vermont," *Appalachia* (June 1944), p. 42. Others who have examined Allen's account question whether he spent that much time on the crest—for example, letter from Thomas D. S. Bassett to L&GW, July 16, 1985.

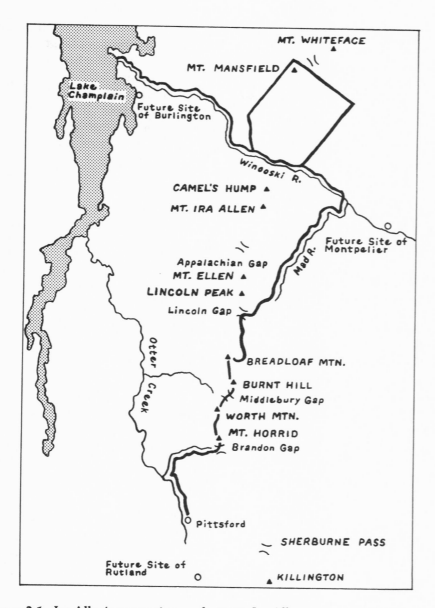

Figure 2.1. Ira Allen's mountain travels, 1772 Ira Allen ran survey lines for the town of Mansfield, Vermont, in 1772, during the course of which he crossed very nearly over the summit of Mount Mansfield, possibly making its first ascent. Later on the same trip, he traveled south over mountain country traversed by the Long Trail today.

On another occasion, Allen found himself at the top of the cliff, which angled steeply down for 60 feet, then dropped perpendicular for nearly 100 feet. For the pleasure of trundling a large boulder off the upper part of this cliff, he took off his shoes and worked his way down to it, using the narrow cracks in that part of the cliff. This may have been Vermont's first rock climbing. When he was dislodging the boulder, a projecting corner of it brushed against him, very nearly dislodging him as well—after which "I moved carefully to the top of the hill."

After these early days, Ira Allen became more interested in economic and political developments than in boulder trundling or climbing around precipices. He disappears from the pages of this history to carry on a checkered career closely tied to the fortunes of his adopted state. At moments when fate deposited him in prisons in England and France, he must have recalled with longing his footloose days of roaming the Green Mountains.

Chapter 3

The Belknap-Cutler expedition to Mount Washington

The Belknap-Cutler expedition to Mount Washington in 1784 was a landmark event in several respects. It is the first well-documented mountain climb in North America, the first for which we have more than a few cryptic sentences of description; indeed, it is richly recorded by no fewer than three of the participants. It is thought to have been the occasion on which the mountain was named, in honor of General (not yet President) Washington. The climb also marks the first time in America when serious scientists visited and observed that strange new world above treeline. It also brings to us some engaging personalities of men who were prominent in their day and vivid in ours, thanks to their very human expressions of the difficulties of their trip.

The impact of these scientists' accounts on people of their own day and on subsequent mountain-climbing history was important. Popular reports of this trip, mostly by Jeremy Belknap, were immediately circulated and created more interest in the White Mountains than had existed during colonial times. The scientific reports, mostly by Manasseh Cutler, were less noticed at first but kindled sparks of interest that ultimately flared into the first major burst of mountain-climbing enthusiasm in the New World: the invasion of the botanists during the 1820s, 1830s and 1840s. Close on the heels of the botanists came other scientists, artists, writers, and soon the entire first generation of White Mountain recreationists.

The Belknap-Cutler party was the progenitor of those large, leisurely groups that meandered northward from Massachusetts during the following century, taking several weeks to make a slow circuit up through Pinkham Notch and down through Crawford or perhaps Franconia Notch. This itinerary was to become a "standard tour" for vigorous pedestrians (see chapter 15). In fact, as we retell the story of this pioneering expedition, the reader may note several points in which the problems encountered in 1784 bear striking resemblance to hiking trips up Mount

Washington not just fifty or seventy-five years later but even in our own day. It all began with Belknap and Cutler in 1784.

Of the dozen or so individuals who assembled for this expedition, the figures of principal interest are:

The Reverend Jeremy Belknap of Dover, New Hampshire, a Harvard graduate, minister, and historian, who wrote the first history of the state of New Hampshire, and who published several accounts of the climb. Belknap, however, was apparently too overweight to make it up the mountain himself: "Being the heaviest person in the company, you may depend on it that I was not the nimblest," he wrote to a friend.

The Reverend Manasseh Cutler of Ipswich, Massachusetts, a lawyer, minister and early scientist, member of the American Academy of Arts and Sciences, with a reputation as New England's first important botanist. Cutler seems to have been the driving force behind the scientific activities of the group. (Belknap and Cutler corresponded extensively after the expedition, and the picture of the two scientific gentlemen that emerges from that correspondence is most sympathetic. Belknap was an endlessly curious inquisitor, good humored and modest about his own scientific knowledge and a rambling raconteur in his letters. Though Cutler moved among the political and intellectual leaders of the new nation, he too was gentle and self-effacing in the letters, with a quiet sense of humor.)

Col. Joseph Whipple, who operated a large farm in the next valley north of the Presidentials, then a remote and inaccessible settlement of Dartmouth, now called Jefferson, New Hampshire (no relation to Dartmouth College, which lies much farther south and west on the Connecticut River). Colonel Whipple was the largest landowner and leading public figure in the backwoods mountain towns north of the White Mountains. As a young man he had "left family, friends, social life, civilization and a good business behind, and penetrated the trackless forest, founded a town in a wilderness, and set in motion numberless wheels of varied industries." The brother of a signer of the Declaration of Independence and himself a collector of customs in Portsmouth, he seemed to enjoy the dual role of aristocrat in Portsmouth (then a prominent city) and pioneer in the north country (then a frontier). He must have been a man of energy and enterprise, a curious blend of pioneer and patrician. When he joined the party at Conway, the last settlement south of the mountains, he was accompanied by his black manservant.

Capt. John Evans, a local "ax-man," who also joined the group at Conway. Captain Evans had built the road through Pinkham Notch ten years earlier, at which time he had twice climbed the big peak. Evans was employed as "guide" for the mountain and was accounted the most knowledgeable person about Mount Washington.

Others in the party included a leading scientist, Joshua Fisher of Beverly, Massachusetts, president of the Massachusetts Medical Society; the Reverend Daniel Little of Kennebunk, Maine, celebrated for his missionary work among Indians of the north woods; Enoch Whipple of Rochester, New Hampshire; other amateur scientists from the Boston area; and other locals to serve as guides through lower New Hampshire, carry equipment, and otherwise help out. Altogether the party numbered at least a dozen people. The precise number is difficult to state with certainty, since the various accounts sometimes count and sometimes don't count the "ax-men," guides, and other attendants.

This impressive contingent traveled northward from Ipswich through New Hampshire, observing the changing picture of what was then a frontier of sorts, until they passed the last human habitation, the cabin of Benjamin Copp in the intervale of what is now the town of Jackson. From there it took nine hours to ride the last eight miles up the forest road to the height-of-land, very near where the Appalachian Mountain Club's north country headquarters now stands in Pinkham Notch.

Here they camped in a meadow near beaver ponds, perhaps those that are still there today. Turning their horses out in the meadow, they set about doing what the AMC was to do more than a century later: they "built a hut"—but while the AMC's famed huts were to be solid and spacious, the Belknap-Cutler party's consisted of "poles and bark, with an hemlock bed." Not that everyone pitched in; the portly Belknap reports that "while the hut was building" he and Little strolled out on the meadow to have a look at the mountain. From this vantage point, they saw it as "two very high peaks and several ridges"; probably they took Boott Spur to be an independent summit, since it appears so from where they stood that day. Later that same afternoon, Belknap and Enoch Whipple went out in the meadow again so that Whipple could take a compass bearing on their objective. This time the Reverend Mr. Belknap succeeded in falling into "a deep hole full of water up to my hips," which rendered him "ill all night; feverish and weak."

The next morning—July 24, 1784—dawned fair, and the party, like so many Washington climbers since, failed to allow for the changeability and severity of this mountain's now notorious weather. They started up, all but Colonel Whipple's servant, who was left in charge of the camp. At first they kept the Cutler River (which they named) on their left, which means that the start of their route was probably not far from the present Tuckerman Ravine Trail.

Not all the party got very far. At the first steep section, Fisher developed a "pain in his side" and went back to camp. For the next two hours, the group's pace was slowed by having to wait for its slowest member—a plight not infrequently encountered by subsequent parties. The Reverend Mr. Belknap was proving a bit too stout and "found my breath fail." Declining the offer of others in the party to descend with him, he returned to camp alone, a reasonably adventurous undertaking for an inexperienced and overweight man on a trackless mountainside in 1784. After a nap, the two campbound gentlemen explored the beaver ponds. There and in camp they reported "insects very troublesome." Late July is not normally the height of the ill-famed black fly season in New England's mountains, but many twentieth-century hikers will attest the persistence of "troublesome insects" at almost any time of the summer. They were there in 1784.

The route of the ascent is not at all clear. The various accounts mention the group keeping the Cutler River on their left but eventually crossing it before starting the steepest part of their climb (see figure 1.2). Whether this crossing was in fact the main Cutler River or one of its tributaries cannot be ascertained. Either way, they did some steep scrambling: they report this part of the climb "exceedingly steep . . . loose rocks covered with very long and thick green moss," and "like steep stairs," requiring "utmost exertions."

As with Darby Field, historians have taken various stabs at interpreting the accounts and come up with different theories on the 1784 itinerary. For years most students of the sources placed the route through Tuckerman Ravine, or over Boott Spur, or both. Some support was also marshaled for the view that the party went more directly, over Lion Head. However, on the bicentennial of the event, July 24, 1984, a party of eight White Mountain history buffs reenacted the ascent, carefully reexamining the evidence on the ground, and concluded that a route over Nelson Crag seemed to fit best the descriptions in the originals.

The most complete account is Cutler's. He spoke of reaching a "first summit" from which the main peak appeared as a "Sugar-loaf" rising above a "plain"—a description that could put them on Boott Spur, Lion Head, or Nelson Crag. The first summit is described as possibly 100 or 150 feet higher than the plain; and the plain as extending to the west and northwest "with an easy declivity to the north-west." These two points keep Boott Spur and Nelson Crag in the running but greatly reduce the prospects of Lion Head. The sugarloaf is described as lying to the southwest; and views were obtained to the "N. E., N., and N. W.," where "several mountains towered their heads, and seemed to vie with those we were ascending, but still far below them." These points fit perfectly the prospect from Nelson Crag, the other mountains being the Northern Presidentials, not visible from either Boott Spur or Lion Head. Cutler's description of the ascent to the first summit also better fits Nelson Crag than either of the other two, if one assumes that by following the north bank of the Cutler River they actually were diverted up its northernmost tributary without realizing it, a common occurrence when bushwhacking up a stream.

Little's account is briefer, but it is noteworthy that he describes the final ascent as proceeding "by regular steppings on the Northerly side." It would be awkward to go around to the northerly side from either Boott Spur or Lion Head, nor are there intervening steps between those two eminences and the summit; whereas from Nelson Crag, the ascent is on the northerly side of the summit cone, and there are at least two intervening steps, Ball Crag and an unnamed bump.

Belknap's various accounts are far more general and seem consistent with any of the three approaches. The readier availability of Belknap's descriptions may have led most readers to rely on them and thus not to examine the route question as closely as a reading of the Cutler account makes possible.

As they climbed the final summit cone, the party "had the mortification to be involved in a dense cloud" that swirled about them and soon became so dense that it precluded views during the rest of their time above treeline. They would not be the last visitors disappointed by having no views from the top.

As careful scientists, they recorded with precision their times: left camp at 6:15 A.M.; reached the first summit at 11:32 A.M.; the true summit at 1:06 P.M. Deducting one hour and thirty-eight minutes for rests, they took five hours and thirteen minutes for the ascent. This meticulous accounting of times shows up periodically in subsequent Northeastern climbing and has also encountered criticism as an overly mechanical, competitive, or unpoetic approach to the mountains. To Cutler and his early associates, it was all part of their scientific method.

Once upon the summit, the conclave huddled in the chilly mist, measuring the temperature at 44 degrees Farenheit. They estimated the height of the mountain as close to 10,000 feet, off by about 4,000 feet; but to many a subsequent novice hiker Washington has seemed to be much more than 6,288 feet. In their time they found the height impressive. The learned Cutler could list only four higher peaks in the world: "Andes" (20,280 ft.), Mont Blanc (14,432 ft.), the Peak of Teneriffe (13,178 ft.), and Gammi (10,110 ft.).

Other scientific observations were impeded by damage to their instruments and by the temperature—"as cold as November"—which "nearly deprived [Cutler] of the use of his fingers." The Reverend Mr. Little and Colonel Whipple inaugurated a two-hundred-year tradition of graffiti by carving "N.H." on the summit rock, and a lead plate with their names engraved was deposited under a loose stone. They enjoyed a lunch of "partridges and neats tongue," but because of the cloud and cold they made no further scientific investigations and began the descent (at 3:57 P.M.).

On the way down they got lost, befuddled by the dense cloud. Once off the summit cone, they started down the headwall of one of the steep ravines, either Tuckerman or Huntington. The going became exceedingly steep and rough, until at one point Captain Evans, who as guide was going first, "slipped, and was gone out of sight." At first the shouts of his companions went unanswered, and they became alarmed, fearing that he "was either killed, stunned, or had received some kind of disaster which rendered him unable to answer us." At length the enterprising Colonel Whipple worked his way down to where he could shout to Evans, who turned out to be "happily, without any other damage, than tearing his clothing." Considerably shaken, the group reascended to the plateau and started down again when they could find a less steep course (they were coolheaded enough to note the time of this second descent as 5:50 P.M.). If the Nelson Crag theory is true as to the route of ascent, Huntington Ravine seems more likely to have been the scene of this excitement on the descent than Tuckerman. Cutler's Journal describes the gully down which they started as growing "wider, more steep, and slippery" near the bottom, where the guide fell; that after his slip, the guide found himself almost to the bottom; and we read in Belknap's History that the rest of the party reascended by means of "a winding gully of a more gradual ascent." The description of the descent route fits the gully known to modern ice climbers as Yale Gully, with the reascent going up either Diagonal or Damnation gullies, as they are now called. However, it would be rash to state with any assurance that this is where the party was in 1784. The description is so vague as to preclude anything more than conjecture.

Darkness overcame the party on the way down. They spent a rainy, chilly night huddled around a fire, "par-boiled and smoke-dried"—not the last unplanned bivouac on Mount Washington. In the morning they soon rejoined the base camp vigilants, and continued their journey north through Pinkham Notch to Colonel Whipple's farm in Jefferson, no doubt to unwind for a spell. Then the expedition moved south through the western (later Crawford) notch.

This ascent was not without minor controversy. In an altercation in Conway afterward, a Captain Heath infuriated Captain Evans by claiming that in the clouds they had missed the true summit. These doubts were shared by Colonel Whipple himself, who began to think that a higher summit lay considerably west of their high point. So did a local figure of consequence, Paine Wingate, a leading minister and future congressman and senator. When queried on the point, the mild Cutler remained "pretty firm in the belief that we were on the highest summit," but would not be "obstinate" on the point and agreed the cloud cover left their observations "so imperfect and confused, that I am almost ashamed to say anything about them." All hoped a later ascent would clarify the question, and for the next two years plans to go up again were repeatedly formed and postponed. Heavy involvement with the settlement of the Ohio frontier and other duties prevented Cutler from getting back to the mountains for twenty years. No later ascent by Colonel Whipple is recorded. Belknap from the start was less enthusiastic about trying again himself, cheerfully pointing out,

Two hundred-weight of mortality, and a pair of lungs by no means related to the *adamantine ones*, which Pope was laughed at so much about, are very inconvenient in the ascending line, unless an aerostatic machine could be contrived, and even then I suspect my brain would be giddy with the sudden elevation. It is a discouraging circumstance to my making a second attempt.

Since none of the original journals questions whether the party reached the summit, it seems likely that they did. It is worth noting that, save Colonel Whipple, none of the doubters mentioned in Belknap's letter were present during the climb. Possibly local jealousies were aroused when the event attracted so much notice. Colonel Whipple's skepticism is more difficult to explain, though from Jefferson (his home) Washington does not always appear to be the highest peak. It is true that an ascent via Nelson Crag would take them over two or three subsidiary bumps, and Ball Crag could certainly be mistaken for a summit in extremely low visibility. From either Boott Spur or Lion Head, no lesser eminence would confuse them. There is no way to confirm or deny the account with certainty after two hundred years, but history has chosen to ignore the doubts raised by Colonel Whipple and the others.

The 1784 expedition was significant because of the attention it received. The story was initially circulated through the writings of the ever expansive Belknap, who kept a journal of the trip, immediately wrote to various friends and relations about the ascent, prepared an account for publication in 1786 by the American Philosophical Society of Philadelphia, had the same piece published by the *American Museum or Repository* in 1788, and still later included an account in volume III of his full-dress *History of New Hampshire,* published in 1792. These accounts were read and quoted extensively in early nineteenth-century writings about the mountains. At least two other members of the party, Cutler and Little, kept journals of the climb. Twenty years later (1804) Cutler returned to climb Washington again, this time accompanied by two other eminent scientists of the day, botanist William D. Peck and astronomer-mathematician Nathaniel Bowditch. This second scientific team took many observations on the alpine vegetation, publication of which attracted the attention of the next generation of American botanists and led to the first wave of extensive upper-elevation mountain exploration on the North American continent.

The Belknap-Cutler party thus is as much the starting point of modern mountain climbing in the United States as any single event.

Chapter 4

Alden Partridge: The first regionwide hiker

IN the length and breadth of Vermont, one of the few places where you get little sense of the state's mountains is about halfway up on its eastern edge, just above where the White River flows into the Connecticut. Here it's as hilly as ever, but Mount Ascutney is too far south, Burke and Pisgah too far north, and the main spine of the Green Mountains too far west to be of much influence on the daily life of the local Vermonters. Ironic, then, that in this little low pocket, in the town of Norwich, just across the river from Dartmouth College, was born possibly the greatest pre–Civil War mountain walker of the entire northeastern United States.

Alden Partridge was born in 1785, just one generation after the Connecticut Valley was settled. He started his college education at Dartmouth in 1802 but transferred to the U.S. Military Academy at West Point in 1805 to begin a military career. After graduation in 1806, he stayed on at West Point to teach mathematics. He rapidly developed some advanced ideas about practical education—progressive for that age but downright radical for a military school. He believed in teaching modern languages, for example, not just Latin and Greek. His broad abilities resulted in his appointment as superintendent of West Point in 1815, at the age of thirty. In his brief but eventful tenure, he was innovative in curriculum and administration, enormously popular with the student corps, but an object of suspicion for his faculty and senior officers. When he insisted on assuming command of West Point for the academic year 1817–1818, despite not having been reappointed, he was court-martialed and dismissed.

Captain Partridge's ideas about military education for the citizen-soldier next found expression in founding the American Literary, Scientific and Military Academy at Norwich, Vermont, in 1819. He made the institution the focus of his energies and his educational theories for the next quarter-century. He has been called the father of the private military school movement. The academy moved to Middletown, Connecticut, in 1825, then back to Norwich, changing its name to Norwich University in 1834. Partridge was president till 1844; he died suddenly in 1854. The university moved to Northfield, Vermont, in 1866, where it continues today and still provides a broad military education, with fitting emphasis on vigorous outdoor exercise.

All his life Captain Partridge was a walker. He was intensely interested in climbing the mountains of the Northeast. In fact, considering the primitive transportation of the early nineteenth century, Partridge probably ranged more widely throughout the region than anyone until Arnold Guyot came along in midcentury (see chapter 13). Mount Washington several times felt his stride, as did the Southern Presidentials, Lafayette and Moosilauke; many remote peaks in Maine; Ascutney, Camel's Hump, Killington, and Mansfield; the Grand Monadnock; Greylock; a variety of lesser peaks in Vermont, Massachusetts, and Connecticut; as well as the Catskills and Hudson Highlands (see the frontispiece). He never visited the Adirondacks, but hardly anyone else had either in his day.

Our first record of Partridge on a mountain is climbing Round Top and High Peak in the Catskills in October 1810. By that time, though, he is known already to have climbed and measured heights in the Hudson Highlands. Since he was at West Point beginning in 1805, he may have been out around those hills any time after that. He later referred to having taken mountaintop scientific observations "since the year 1809." Among the summits he climbed in that area were Bear Mountain, Anthony's Nose, Mount Beacon (two summits), Breakneck Ridge, Bull Hill (or Mount Taurus), Crow's Nest, and Storm King.

In the summer of 1811 Partridge made his first trip to the White Mountains. While the usual procedure was to ride or take the stage to Rosebrook's inn in the great notch later called Crawford's, Partridge walked the 76 miles from Norwich, Vermont. At Rosebrook's, with the host's son for a guide, he went up a route that approximated the later Crawford Path, then a trackless forest. On the ridge they went over all the intermediate summits of Clinton, Eisenhower, Franklin, and Monroe (none of them yet named), ate dinner at the high mountain ponds (today's Lakes of the Clouds), and reached the top of Mount Washington at 1:00 P.M. When clouds settled in, together with rain ("mixed with hail, and a few flakes of snow"), they got turned around descending the summit cone and found themselves back on top again after two hours' wandering. A more careful descent this time took them down to treeline by dark, where they spent a supperless and mostly sleepless night, unable to build a fire in the damp. The next day they returned to Rosebrook's and breakfasted, after which the tireless Partridge began his walk back to Norwich, reaching it in three days.

Later that year Partridge joined some Dartmouth students for a climb of Killington. In 1817, the summer before his dismissal from West Point, he climbed Moosilauke and Ascutney.

In 1818, Partridge took a weeklong excursion in which he walked 200 miles and climbed both Camel's Hump and Mansfield, despite the fact that it rained on five of the seven days, "during the whole of which my clothes were not once dry." His climb of Camel's Hump on September 16 was a bushwhack from the north, during a furious rainstorm, taking all day, ending with "not a dry thread in my clothes, and somewhat fatigued, having ate nothing, nor drunk anything but water during the day." The very next morning he went on to Stowe to meet a friend with whom he went up Mansfield the following day. With the benefit of a faint trail for part of this ascent, they bushwhacked down the north end of the peak and wound around to the steep east flank, getting down at 5:00 P.M. "as usual, drenched with the water which fell from the bushes in passing through the woods." Thereupon the Captain continued on to Waterbury alone, arriving at 10:00 P.M., having covered 34 miles (including the traverse of Mansfield) that day.

On all his climbs, Partridge carried measuring instruments and calculated summit altitudes, a lifelong preoccupation. In the period between leaving West Point and founding Norwich Academy, he exercised this passion professionally as one of three commissioners representing the United States in determining the Maine-Canada border following the War of 1812. This responsibility took Partridge to the north woods of Maine, where he clambered along the steep, heavily forested ridges on the national boundary. However, exactly which mountains he climbed is not clear from the documents of this period.

The scope of Partridge's interest in mountains of the Northeast is well demonstrated in two letters he wrote to the *National Intelligencer* in 1816 and 1820. In these he recited observations he had made all over the region since 1809, and described his ambitions to cover the entire northeastern United States, plus portions of Canada, in a projected series of long walks.

Having personally inspected such a broad cross section of Northeastern hill country, Alden Partridge was in a better position than most of his contemporaries to form opinions about its overall structure. One theory, which he shared with Benjamin Silliman, then the leading scientific mind in the United States, was that New England's mountains formed two great chains, in the outline of a V, meeting in New Haven, Connecticut. The Green Mountains chain stretched through Vermont, the Berkshires, and the Litchfield Hills to its origin at West Rock near New Haven. To the east, the Moose Hillock range ran all the way from northern Maine down through the White Mountains, Monadnock, and the Blue Hills, to its origin at East Rock. (Professor John Ritchie of Yale, an enthusiastic hiker of the early twentieth century, as well as a loyal son of Eli, irreverently summed up this theory: "The Green Mountains end in West Rock in New Haven, the White Mountains in East Rock. All trails lead to Yale!")

The founding of Norwich Academy gave Captain Partridge a chance to develop his beliefs in the value of "physical education," a modern term that he used in 1820. In a "Lecture on Education" delivered that year, he charged that American education suffered from "the entire neglect, in all our principal seminaries, of physical education, or the due cultivation and improvement of the physical powers of the students." Along with vigorous military exercises and agricultural pursuits, Norwich students under Partridge were encouraged to take "pedestrian excursions" to provide "practical education opportunities which would correspond with classroom studies," including measuring the elevations of mountaintops. An academy catalog expressed the underlying educational philosophy:

> It was seen that our systems of education tended to weaken, and in too many cases to destroy the animal man; that systematic *exercise* was necessary even to the full development of the mental powers.

And again:

> The physical power gained in the rigid exercise we demand, makes it easy to sustain the additional amount of study, and leaves still a large balance of health and strength in our favor.

To Partridge physical exercise should take place in the great outdoors, not inside a gymnasium. The student excursions were more than afternoon strolls, for Partridge believed that "on these excursions youth became accustomed to endure fatigue and privation, and also to take care of themselves." The marches went long distances, rain or shine, up hill and over dale. One cadet wrote of an all-day storm: "We continued our course as if too proud of the appelation of soldiers to be conquered by adverse winds and rain."

One of the first excursions set the tone. In late August 1821 Partridge led a group of eight thirteen- and fourteen-year-old cadets, along with sundry professors and Dartmouth students, on a three-day march of 76 miles from the academy to Crawford Notch. After sitting out one rainy day, they climbed Washington via Ethan Allen Crawford's new trail, the lead hikers accomplishing the 8 miles and 4,500-foot elevation gain in five hours. Partridge's notes proudly credit fourteen-year-old Master Lewis Davis as "the first who gained the summit." Some of the adults straggled in three hours later. They spent a cold night on the summit plateau and the next morning descended by the original Crawford Path to Ethan's inn by 11:00 A.M. That same day Partridge and some others walked 28 miles to Littleton. The next day it was 30 more miles in an all-day rain, then back to Norwich the following day. One of the professors on this trip was twenty-year-old George P. Marsh, later to serve in Congress and in a variety of diplomatic posts. He was an early writer on what we would today call environmental themes. It may be that Marsh acquired some of his appreciation of the natural world from early exposure to Captain Partridge and his ideas about the value of outdoor life.

During October 8–10, 1821, the entire cadet corps walked from Norwich Academy to Woodstock, Vermont, and back. The following spring came a 145-mile march roundtrip to Concord, Massachusetts. In October 1822 the youths marched to Montpelier where Vermont's governor reviewed their exhibition drills.

In September 1823 Partridge led twenty-seven cadets to Manchester, Vermont, to climb Mount Equinox and measure its elevation. They covered 150 miles in four days, Partridge noting that on the final day "a youth of 16 years of age walked by my side 45 miles." Their route of ascent was recalled by one of the cadets as "very steep indeed so much so that we had to hold on trees, or whatever came in our way to prevent our falling backward." This student appreciated the trip, however: "The view alone I consider as a full compensation for the trouble it was to get here. None but those who have been witnesses of such a scene can have any idea of its grandeur."

The year 1824 saw walks to Burlington, Vermont, and elsewhere, including Killington, in the spring and the White Mountains in the fall. The latter excursion was noteworthy in that it included two cadets destined for future achievements: Thomas G. Clemson, founder of Clemson University, and Gideon Welles, secretary of the Navy in President Lincoln's cabinet. In this year one of the leading mountain botanists, Joseph Barrett, was on the Norwich faculty and took four cadets to the Presidentials for a combined excursion and scientific investigation.

In 1825, when the academy moved temporarily to Middletown, Connecticut, Partridge and his students were removed from direct access to the northern ranges. Nevertheless, the long excursions continued, to places like Washington, D.C. (1826) and Niagara Falls (1827—1,300 miles in four weeks), with shorter marches into the hills of northwestern Connecticut, where "we scaled their lofty summits." Connecticut was duly impressed; the Middletown *Sentinel* observed:

> These young men, owing to the mode of instruction and exercise adopted by their teachers, present a fine, hardy appearance. They travel mostly on foot, carrying their clothing in their knapsacks.

When the Academy moved back to Vermont, excursions continued to the previously named objectives, as well as to Lafayette (1837).

As superintendent, Partridge was along on most of these excursions, setting the pace on the more arduous ones. Cadet accounts are studded with awestruck mentions of "the Captain" who "seemed to progress as fast up the mountain as a common man would on a level road." One journal concluded a 29-mile day with this comment: "All (except the Captain) were very much fatigued." Another records:

> Captain Partridge is about forty years old, of a spare but robust temperament; he is extremely active and indefatigable in all bodily exercises,

and especially in walking. He has been known to travel forty-five miles a day, for several days in succession, without any special necessity, and often when there were two feet of snow upon the ground. His limbs are pliable and nervous: he traverses the steepest hills, with as much agility, as if he were walking on a plain.

At the age of forty-five Partridge made the following walking trips:

152 miles in three days for the purpose of climbing Monadnock

220 miles in four days to climb on the Holyoke Range, again averaging over 50 miles per day

300 miles on another Massachusetts round-trip, covering 64 miles on the last day of the return

There is a tale of his starting out from Concord, New Hampshire, for Hanover, to which a stagecoach was just departing. The driver of the stage, seeing Partridge start walking, said, "Get aboard, Captain, we start immediately," to which Partridge remarked, "No, you will overtake me." About 6 miles up the road, the stage finally overtook the pedestrian and the driver reined up. But Partridge said, "No, you have to change horses three or four miles ahead, and I will be there." By the time fresh horses were harnessed, the Captain had been and gone. This process was repeated all day, the stage passing the man, then stopping at the next town, where the man would pass the stage. According to the tale, "when the horses galloped up to the hotel in Hanover, there sat Captain Partridge on the porch reading."

When Alden Partridge first began climbing Northeastern mountains there were essentially no trails, and the peaks were still regarded by most people as "daunting terrible." Except in the best of weather, Partridge had to assume that an hour or two of travel through timberline scrub would leave him and his clothing not only scarred and torn but often soaking wet as well. He writes of "not having had my clothes dry in some instances for six days in succession." At his death mountains were more fashionable, and summit houses adorned many of the peaks the Captain had seen as wild places, but there were still few trails and no hiking clubs.

In this context, Partridge ranks as the first great regionwide mountain climber of the Northeast. Indeed, few people since have covered so much of the region for such difficult climbing by the standard of the day. From West Rock to Mansfield, from Anthony's Nose and Round Top to the wild ridges of the far-off Maine border, and virtually all the major peaks between, Partridge climbed everywhere.

As a man proud of his prowess, he is also the first in what became an elite fraternity of superhikers who saw the mountains as a supreme testing ground for human effort and achievement. Partridge believed in covering a lot of ground. This philosophy has not dominated Northeastern climbing; the friendly contours of the region's hills have invited a more relaxed and easygoing pace for the majority of recreationists. But there is a parallel tradition of responding to the more rugged challenge that can also be found in these low hills. With the possible exception of Darby Field, about whom we know so little, the first to respond to this challenge was Alden Partridge.

Chapter 5

The Crawfords of Crawford Notch

ACCORDING to the old story, it was in 1771 that a hunter named Timothy Nash, in hot pursuit of a moose, climbed a tree on the southern flanks of Cherry Mountain hoping to get a better view of his quarry. What he saw was of considerably more historical importance than the north end of the southbound moose. Among the towering ridges of the main chain of the White Mountains, there opened a deep defile that appeared to cut directly through the otherwise impassable heights. This was the great Notch of the Mountains, later called Crawford Notch, a place destined to play a major role in Northeastern hiking history.

Nash followed this narrow vale, threading among some of the region's tallest peaks and more imposing cliffs, until he emerged into settled regions below—the towns of Conway and Tamworth. Then he went straight to Gov. John Wentworth to inform him about this notch and the use that could be made of it. The colonial governor was delighted and offered Nash a tract of land if he could get a horse and a barrel of rum through from Lancaster. Somehow Nash succeeded, with the help of a hunting buddy, though the rum, it was said, "was taxed heavily, in its own substance, however, to ensure its passage, and reached [the other end of the notch] in a very reduced condition." We know nothing of how the horse came through the day, but the two hunters ended up with the land known today as Nash and Sawyer's Location, which extends from the notch northward to just beyond the site of the Fabyan House, near what is now the Bretton Woods ski touring center.

This was the widely told fiction of the nineteenth century—that Nash was the first person to see or pass through the White Mountain Notch. The truth is that the Indians knew of it, and it is most unlikely that earlier settlers were unaware of the passage. One source suggests that Nash "had noted the existence of an old Indian trail" through the notch. According to a local newspaper of the 1880s, this path was used by settlers at least as early as 1764.

It was also the quality of legend that portrayed Nash as a rustic hunter chasing a moose. In fact, Timothy Nash was a leading citizen of the town of Lancaster, New Hampshire, appointed to a committee of five charged with the responsibility "to look out and mark" roads that might improve that new town's contact with other areas. This committee was appointed in 1767, so Nash might have been looking for feasible routes at least four years earlier than 1771.[a]

Discovery or rediscovery, 1771 or earlier, this event was important to the history of the mountains. Today we think of Crawford Notch as one of a triumvirate of coequal notches of the White Mountains, the others being Pinkham and Franconia. In the late eighteenth century, however, the route through Crawford Notch was peculiarly important as a vital throughway between the settlements of the upper Connecticut River valley and the seacoast trading centers, principally Portland, Maine, then a port of considerable commerce.

At first the lonely wilderness path was not much of a road. Nathaniel Hawthorne heard a fellow traveler tell how it took him eighteen days to get from the Connecticut River to Conway around 1785, a trip Hawthorne could do in a single day in 1835, and we in less than two hours today. (In truth, eighteen days seems like an exaggeration even for the original road, when one considers that Darby Field got to the top of Washington from the coast in that time with no road at all.) The road was somewhat improved around 1785, but in 1791 the state legislature still balked at seating a representative from Coos County "on account of lack of evidence of his election, due to the difficulties of communication." The road was upgraded again in 1803, if still reportedly "not much better than a bridle path, although passable for the chaise, ox-cart and team wagon." As commercial traffic through the notch gradually increased, scattered houses along its lonelier stretches began to do a modest business as inns. This inn business, still small for the first two decades of the nineteenth century and oriented toward transporting goods to and from markets, began to generate a trickle of sightseers who came to view the scenic wonders of the notch. As mentioned in chapter 3, in the wake of Manasseh Cutler's scientific expeditions, botanists began to take a growing interest in the vegetation of the alpine zone. They were soon followed by other scientists, artists, writers, and the just plain curious. This trickle grew to a respectable flow of visitors

---

[a]One historian has uncovered two pieces of evidence that tend to place Nash's discovery earlier than the traditionally ascribed 1771 date. One is a letter signed by the surveyor general of lands ordering the reward of land to Nash and Sawyer, dated February 20, 1771. Assuming normal administrative lag in processing such an order, and assuming the horse was not taken through in winter, this letter would place Nash's "discovery" at least as early as 1770. The other is a crude map, carved in scrimshaw on a powderhorn by Daniel Beede in 1771, which shows the notch as "Grate Pass," suggesting that its existence was known of and accepted by the locals. Beede was a settler in Sandwich, to the south of the notch. These two items were discovered by Douglas A. Philbrook, president of the Mount Washington Summit Road Company, an amateur historian whose private collection of White Mountain material rivals any institutional collection. The letter concerning the award of land has never been published, but the powderhorn map was described by Philbrook in "The Grate Pass Powderhorn," *Appalachia* (June 1966), pp. 25–37.

during the 1820s, to a steady stream of tourists during the 1830s and 1840s, and to a flood of mountain vacationers by midcentury.

Before the botanists or anyone else could climb Mount Washington in great numbers, however, a more feasible ascent route was needed. Cutler's two climbs, like those of Field, had been bushwhack ordeals, through dense thickets, up the steep eastern or southeastern sides of the range.

The first path up Mount Washington was cut at the instigation of Col. George Gibbs, a mineralogist and one of the first scientists encouraged by Cutler to visit the White Mountains. Gibbs made more than one trip to Mount Washington, apparently around the year 1809. During one of these trips he arranged to have a path cut through the scrub growth, the belt of stunted fir and spruce just below treeline that is the most difficult obstacle to the higher Northeastern summits. A close reading of the sole direct reference to this path, by an 1816 party, places it most probably through Tuckerman Ravine. Local climbers used a path up from the east for the next generation or so; this could have been Gibbs's path, although it may have ascended Boott Spur from a point farther south.

Most visitors might have continued to approach Mount Washington from the east, had it not been for a series of developments: the improvement of the road through Crawford Notch in 1803; the deterioration of the Pinkham Notch road; the subsequent increase in traffic through Crawford Notch; and finally the arrival there of the Crawford-Rosebrook family which saw an opportunity on the mountain and seized it.

The coming of the Crawfords

Around 1791, when the notch road was open but still rough, a young woodsman named Abel Crawford took over a settler's cabin just north of the gateway of the notch. In the winter of 1792, his wife's father, Capt. Eleazar Rosebrook, moved from Vermont to join him in that homestead, soon after which Abel moved on through the notch to new land 12 miles south. Now there were two branches of the Rosebrook-Crawford family, one on either end of the notch: the elder Rosebrook on the original site about 6 miles north of the notch's narrowest point (the "Gateway"), and Abel and Hannah Crawford down in Hart's Location about 6 miles south of the Gateway.

Initially both branches of the family worked farms, but the land was not meant to afford agricultural prosperity. They soon realized that providing room and board to travelers coming through the notch was a more promising livelihood. They worked on improving the notch road, aided by state funds in 1803, and gradually built up their inn-keeping business as traffic between Portland and parts west came to use this key thoroughfare more and more.

By 1816 Rosebrook was dying of cancer, and he persuaded his grandson (Abel's son) Ethan Allen Crawford to come take care of him. The following spring, Ethan obtained further help from another Rosebrook grandchild, his cousin Lucy. When the old man passed away that fall, Ethan and Lucy were entrenched in the original Crawford homestead. On November 1, 1817, they were married and began their long, sometimes stormy, always colorful career as stewards of the notch and the western approaches to Mount Washington.

For the next twenty years Ethan and Lucy operated the mountain inn that Rosebrook had established, rebuilding after a fire in 1818, and expanding in 1832 to make it "the largest house in Coos County." Old Abel and Hannah also continued to take in travelers at Hart's Location until Abel's death at the age of eighty-five in 1851; toward the end, this inn was run by Abel's son-in-law, Nathaniel P. Davis. In 1828 the Crawfords built a third family house for the accommodation of the notch trade, this one halfway between the other two, right at the Gateway of the Notch. Here they installed Ethan's younger brother, Thomas J. Crawford, sixth of Abel's eight sons. This house prospered because of its strategic location at the Gateway; eventually its nearby successor grew into a major resort, known as the Crawford House, operating there in opulent splendor until its close during the 1970s.

Most of the lodgers at the Crawfords' gave little thought to the mountain heights. From 1803 when the road became passable for wagons, the notch was an important avenue of commerce. All year long cargoes of commodities streamed back and forth between Portland and the other coastal cities, and northern Vermont and the upper Connecticut Valley. Smuggling was said to be part of the trade. Winter brought no interruption to traffic; during the early days, winter was almost an easier time to move goods through the mountain passes, with as many as 150 sleds passing through the notch in a single day. Thus much of the inn business came from teamsters and farmers transporting their goods to market and bringing back their supplies.

Little by little, however, a tourist trade based on the magnificent mountain scenery began to emerge. The Rosebrook-Crawford innkeepers detected the start of this new business and became the first to capitalize on it.

As mountaineers and guides, the Crawfords have suffered the fate of many a legend: that of uncritical adulation in the eyes of posterity. Nearly every writer of White Mountain lore for the past century and a half has painted two-dimensional images in sunny pastels of Ethan as the genial mountain giant, performing Herculean feats of strength; Abel as the noble old patriarch of the hills; and their patient, hardy, pioneer-stock wives, Lucy and Hannah. Someday perhaps the more intriguing, more complex story of this interesting family will be written, shedding light in some of the darker corners, the internal stresses and strange personality characteristics of the principals. But that lies beyond the scope of this history.

Legend is nonetheless fundamentally correct in assigning to the Crawfords a major place in the history of Northeastern climbing. The first substantial wave of White Mountain tourists were guided up Mount Washington by this unique family: first by Captain Rosebrook, then Abel and Ethan, later Thomas, and still later Abel's son-in-law Nathaniel Davis, as well as by various others employed by the family at their several inns. The first mountain trails to receive regular and frequent use were the two cut by the Crawfords. The first personalities to receive major attention as figures associated with Northeastern mountains were Abel and Ethan. Both of these men, but especially Ethan, recognized the value of their colorful reputations as mountain "characters" and overlooked no opportunity to add to their own legends.

The Crawford Paths

Soon after the road was made passable for wagons and stages in 1803, Captain Rosebrook began occasionally guiding curiosity-seekers through the woods and along the scrub of the long southwesterly ridge to the summit of Washington. As early as 1808 he contemplated clearing a trail. By 1819 the tourist trade was sufficiently brisk to induce Abel and Ethan to cut the 8¼-mile trail that has survived to this day, though considerably relocated in places, as the oldest continuously used hiking trail in the Northeast.[b] (See figure 5.1.)

The Crawford Path has always been a fine mountain trail. Its lower stretches cross a slope of lovely large spruce—much still virgin today—that gradually diminish in height and give way to birch and fir before the path suddenly curves into an open col between the peaks we now call Clinton and Eisenhower. The views from then on are such as to delight any lover of New England hill country. As the trail winds along and up the long ridge, it climbs over the graceful dome of Eisenhower, the open plateau of Franklin, and the fortresslike double-peaked Monroe, from which it drops down to the two little mountain tarns known originally as Blue Ponds (now Lakes of the Clouds). All the while, sweeping views to the distant horizons, with the endless waves of mountain ridges, compete with the dominant view ahead: the massive pyramid of the Northeast's largest mountain, Washington. From the lakes on, the trail winds slowly back and forth up the huge cone, as if reluctant to approach too directly into such an august presence.

---

[b]The phrase *oldest continuously used hiking trail* needs the qualification that for a period of a few years during the early 1870s the Crawford Path was so little used as to become overgrown and, in Paul Doherty's phrase, "all but forgotten" (Doherty, "Pathway of the Giant," *Appalachia* [Dec. 1969], p. 608). In the description that follows, it should also be noted that the Crawford Path itself is not regarded as going directly over the summits of the lower peaks, though short side trails or loops lead to them.

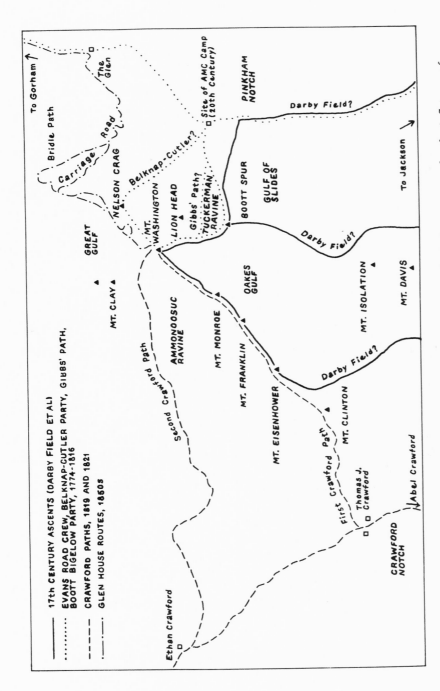

Figure 5.1. Changing approaches to Mount Washington, 1642–1862 Over the years, under the influence of changing conditions of transportation, the dominant direction for climbers approaching Mount Washington shifted several times: from the southeast for the earliest ascents; the east for those around 1800; the southwest and west during the heyday of the Crawfords; and finally, about the middle of the nineteenth century, to the northeast.

The Crawford Path was at first but a slight improvement over the old bushwhack routes. One of the first parties to hike it described it as "obscure, often determined only by marked trees, some of which 'old Crawford' alone could discover." In the scrub above treeline, in dense fog, even Abel was "perplexed" at one point for almost an hour before picking up his trail. By 1820, however, when Alden Partridge walked up, he found that "the logs and underbrush are all cut out of the way and it is good walking."

In 1829 the opening of the inn at the Gateway brought more pedestrian traffic, and the path started to become worn enough to be followed readily. In 1840 the Crawfords widened and leveled the path so as to make it suitable for horses. This was the first of many mountain bridle paths built before the Civil War (see chapter 8). Old Abel, then seventy-four, was the first man to ride horseback all the way to the top of Mount Washington.

Like the family, the Crawford Path has acquired some misinformation as part of its legend. It was not, for example, the first trail built up Washington; that was Gibbs's path. Nor was it the route used by Ethan Crawford for most of his widely celebrated guided ascents.

Two years after building the Crawford Path with his father, Ethan cut a different trail, this time with Charles Jesse Stuart of Lancaster, New Hampshire. Ethan's second "Crawford Path" ran along the valley parallel to the southwest ridge until it reached the base of Ammonoosuc Ravine, then climbed the due west spur to the summit. This trail received more use than the Crawford Path during the 1820s, as Ethan used it almost exclusively and left the original path to his father. Like its predecessor, the new path was rough: an 1824 climber described it as "a narrow footpath . . . impeded by rocks, stumps, fallen trees, bogs, morasses, and frequently by streams of water across which had fallen some neighboring tree that served as a bridge." Ethan had plans to make it passable for horses as early as 1827 but never finished the upper parts. In 1837 it still was full of "deep mud holes, the tangled roots, and the projecting stones and timber." After Horace Fabyan took over the business at the north end of the notch in the early 1840s, he improved the trail, making it a bridle path competitive with the newly improved Crawford Path. During the 1860s this route was taken by the Cog Railway and thereafter it ceased to be much used for foot or horse traffic.

The Lancastrians on the Northern Presidentials

Mount Washington was always the chief attraction, but the other magnificent peaks of the Presidentials finally achieved due notice, primarily through the expeditions in the summer of 1820 by a festive group of local citizens from nearby Lancaster. Their objective on the first trip was simply to reach the summit of Washington, there to bestow official names on the other peaks of the range. For this purpose they planned a trip of three days. As guide, Ethan Crawford was "loaded equal to a pack-horse, with cloaks and necessary articles for two nights, with a plenty of what some call 'Black Betts' or 'O-be-joyful.' " When the party reached the summit, an orgy of mountain-naming christened Mounts Adams, Jefferson, Madison, and Monroe, and (finding the 1820 roster of presidents outnumbered by the available peaks, even including the incumbent) Franklin and Pleasant (today called Eisenhower). Prolonged toasts were pronounced, probably with diminishing precision, to each statesman and his alpine namesake, followed by cheers and a good time. The toasts and cheers were sufficiently convivial to cause Ethan some concern about whether the party could negotiate the descent safely: when called on to provide another toast himself, the guide "could only express my feelings by saying I hoped all of us might have success and return to our respective families in safety, and find them in health: which was answered by a cheer from all, as they had cheered at other times before, when anyone had drunk a toast."

The Lancastrians proved themselves more than merrymakers, however. A month later (August 1820), three of the original party, this time accompanied by other neighbors, returned for a six-day expedition with the serious objective of measuring the heights of the newly named peaks. They also took compass bearings from the summit of Washington to its northern satellites and to such points as Haystack (now Lafayette), Moose Hillock (now Moosilauke), and Corway Peak (now Chocorua; measured from Mount Pleasant). On the last night (August 31) they camped on the very top of Washington, the first people to spend a night on the summit. The Lancastrians were the first hikers known to explore that "daunting terrible" terrain of the Northern Presidentials and to climb Jefferson, Adams, and Madison: 178 years had passed between the first recorded ascent of Washington and the first recorded ascents of the northern peaks (see figure 5.2).

With regard to the Lancastrians' 1820 ascents, a curious question may be raised as to whether there was agreement on the original names of the Northern Presidentials. A detailed account written in 1823 by one of the Lancastrians, Adino Nye Brackett, clearly identifies Adams and Jefferson as we now know them. Adams, says Brackett, is "known by its sharp terminating peak, and by being the second north of Mount Washington" and Jefferson is "situated between the two first." However, Brackett told a Pinkham landowner for whom he subsequently did survey work that Jefferson was the more northerly peak, and Adams the one closer to Washington, "to correspond with the order of the succession of the four Presidents." Furthermore, the field notes of their survey have survived and record the following points proceeding north from Washington in this order: "Bald Rocks, North" (perhaps what we call Mount Clay); "grass large field" (the

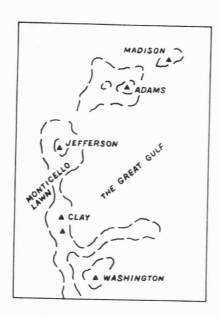

Figure 5.2. The Northern Presidentials The peaks of the Northern Presidentials were named by the Lancastrians' expedition of 1820. Their field notes and other historical evidence raise a question about whether some of the Lancastrians intended to apply the name Adams to what we call Jefferson today, and vice versa.

acreage now called Monticello Lawn); "Top of Mount Adams"; "Best spring in the world" (an opinion since expressed of the spring at Edmands Col, lying north of our Jefferson and south of our Adams); "top of Mount Jefferson"; "top of Mount Madison." Quite possibly in the exuberant christening and toasting a month earlier, some of the celebrants had understood that the peaks were named in order south to north, while others went by elevation. Brackett was inconsistent, as the above quotations indicate. Brackett's written version has prevailed for posterity, but it took at least a generation to clear up the confusion. One party in 1824 referred to Jefferson as "second to Washington alone—while to the south [sic], Adams, Madison and Monroe 'in quick succession rise' "—an apparent reference to what we would call Monroe, Franklin, and Eisenhower! An 1839 gazetteer attaches the name of Lafayette to Eisenhower. As late as 1853 the knowledgeable G. P. Bond, in drawing the first detailed map of the White Mountains, reversed Adams and Jefferson vis-à-vis our present names, as did the well-known Eastman guidebook of 1858.

Meanwhile, back on Mount Washington and its new hiking paths, the Crawfords' tourist trade was growing as early as the 1820s. By the summer of 1828 Ethan was spending "most of this summer in ascending the mountain" with his guests. The Crawfords' inns and their paths set the style for mountain recreation in the White Mountains before the Civil War. People would take long trips to the scenic areas, sticking to the valleys and roads, but would plan on staying possibly two nights at one of the Crawfords' establishments. On the day between, they would climb the mountain. Sometimes they would take two days or even more for the hike, spending an exciting night or two out. The Crawfords built a variety of rude shelters on the mountain to make two-day ascents more comfortable. Visitors went up under the guidance of Abel or Ethan or, after 1830, one of their hired hands. Thomas Crawford had a man named Garland who is mentioned as guiding Crawford House guests in 1834, for example. Visitors might ride part of the way on horseback but until the 1840s had to switch to walking for most of the difficult stretches.

The tourists were people who had leisure and could afford to take these long pleasure trips. Leading public figures of New England were among those who made the climb. Daniel Webster was taken up by Ethan on a cold, foggy day, with no view, in the summer of 1831. It became almost an obligatory mark of a vigorous public man of New England in those years that he had made the ascent of Mount Washington.

In the historical development of how people climbed New England's highest peak, at least five swings of the compass needle may be observed. Transportation greatly influenced these changes.

1. The first ascents, by Darby Field and his contemporaries, seem to have been from the south, since the jump-off point was the Indian settlement on the Saco.
2. With construction of the road through Pinkham Notch in 1774, ascents came from due east: Evans in 1774, the Belknap-Cutler party in 1784, and the earliest nineteenth-century botanists.
3. As the Crawford Notch road became a widely used thoroughfare after 1803, the southwest approach over the long ridge of the southern peaks became the preferred route. With construction of the Crawford Path on this ridge in 1819, climbs from the east virtually ceased.
4. With the opening of the second Crawford Path and its improvement during the 1820s, a due west approach took more of the traffic.
5. Finally, as we shall note in chapter 8, when the railroad from Portland reached Gorham, New Hampshire, in 1851, creating the first rail link to the mountains, traffic reverted to Pinkham Notch and the Glen. With development first of the bridle path and then of the carriage road, the ascent was again most often made from the east, or slightly northeast.

The invasion of the botanists

If most of the Crawfords' guests stuck to the trails, one class of visitors began to wander off trail and, indeed, into every nook and cranny of the range. These were the botanists who took up the torch from Manasseh Cutler. The opportunity to study the succession of vegetative zones, culminating in the arctic environment of the tundra, became an irresistible attraction as a living laboratory for the next generation of botanists. Two of the best-known names arrived in 1816: Jacob Bigelow, for whom the flatlands south of the summit cone are named (Bigelow Lawn); and Francis Boott, after whom Boott Spur is named. Bigelow was one of the young nation's top scientists, just appointed a professor at Harvard, and a leader in the Linnaean Society, a botanical professional society formed in 1814. Boott was destined to spend most of his career in England and was less celebrated on this side of the Atlantic. During the 1820s and 1830s a succession of important botanists arrived, each contributing new botanical findings as the unique world of the Presidentials' "alpine gardens" unfolded to a fascinated scientific community. Perhaps the most important was William Oakes, who first came in 1825 and was back regularly thereafter. Oakes inspired a battalion of talented followers, the more illustrious of whom were James W. Robbins, who thoroughly explored the Northern Peaks and the Great Gulf beginning in 1829, and for whom one of the rarest alpine plants is named; and Edward Tuckerman, who first visited in 1837 and kept returning for many years to come, and whose name is immortalized in the best-known single locale of the entire Presidentials, Tuckerman Ravine. As early as 1829, Oakes was writing to Robbins, "There is now no corner of any extent or promise that has not been visited"—yet Oakes himself found and investigated two new areas when in 1843 he penetrated the upper reaches of the cirque from which the Dry River originates (now called Oakes Gulf). In 1846 he walked into the previously neglected "dark ravine" (as he called it) that lies north of the well-known Tuckerman, forbidding Huntington Ravine, steepest of the entire range. Tuckerman is credited with a possible "first ascent" of Mount Willey, on the western wall of Crawford Notch. It is conceivable that between 1825 and 1848—the years when Oakes was inspiring others—the Presidential Range was hiked more intensively, albeit by a tiny band of dedicated men, than it has been in any generation since, when almost everyone sticks to established trails.

But for the generality of Mount Washington tourists before 1850, it was the Crawford family's mountain. The Crawfords basked in the limelight. Abel served several terms in the state legislature. At the age of eighty he still drove a four-horse team through the notch regularly and was described as "erect and vigorous as one of those pines on yonder mountain," with long white hair and a "fresh, ruddy face . . . always expressive of good humor." Ethan's enormous size and physical strength fueled countless tales. Accounts differ, but apparently he stood well over six feet and was said to be capable of lifting 500 pounds, wrestling bears, and carrying tourists up (or down) the last part of the trail. He roamed the hills tirelessly and knew them well. In addition to his climbs on Washington, Ethan is credited with discovering the beautiful little pond that now bears his name, tucked behind the range west of the notch, and he guided tourists there as well. Though he clearly had physical and possibly psychological problems by the mid-1830s, he was widely admired during his prime. One youthful visitor recalled years later,

> Honest, simple minded, kind hearted, tall, erect as the lordly pine, with the strength of a giant and the gentleness of a woman, he truly deserved to be called one of nature's noblemen.

Not all the Crawfords' contemporaries were so impressed. One visitor remembers of venerable old Abel only that he was "very deaf," that Tom Crawford was "intemperate" with his wife, and that supper at Ethan's was "poor" and the cider "very bad." The lack of pretty girls and music was a subject of complaint. Another visitor referred to Ethan as "that coarse, long-legged fellow," while the noted traveler N. P. Willis was "disappointed" and thought the real Ethan fell short of the carefully cultivated legend:

> He is a large man, and strong in muscle, but I have seen fifty larger and stronger in my own town. There is nothing remarkable in his manners or conversation. His voice is stentorian, and his style is marked by a rude bluntness and an apparent consciousness that something original is expected of him.

Whatever their human frailties, family dissensions, and the murkier corners of their psyches, the Crawfords surely merit the rank accorded them by their admirers as great mountain men of their day. They played an extremely important role in the Northeast's awakening interest in its mountain scenery. The trails they cut blazed the way for mountain recreation for countless thousands to come.

Chapter 6

The Monument Line surveyors
on Katahdin

Howeveʀ intimidating the prospect of ascending mountains such as Mansfield or the Northern Presidentials in their trailless days, no Northeastern mountain then or now compared with that "prince of eastern mountains . . . wild, grand, and solitary," Katahdin.

The vast, unbroken, mysterious north woods of Maine constituted a barrier, both physical and psychological, far more effective than any obstacles on the way to the other mountains in New England. Katahdin was not even definitely seen until Joseph Chadwick's exploration in the 1760s. One of the early climbers, William Larrabee, described it thus: "It stood alone, rising from a vast forest plain, like an island from an illimitable ocean." As a schoolteacher, Larrabee undoubtedly chose his references with care: "illimitable ocean" is the phrase with which Milton describes the realm of Chaos and ancient Night:

> . . . a dark
> Illimitable ocean, without bound,
> Without dimension, where length, breadth, and height,
> And time, and place, are lost . . .

That is how the vast Maine woods appeared to those early travelers—"unbroken, silent, and desolate." This was the stronghold of Pamola, the storm god.

Katahdin was both difficult to reach and, once reached, difficult to ascend. It is a steep, high mountain, especially on its south and west sides, where it was first approached. More than any other Eastern peak, it bears comparison to the much higher mountains of the western United States.

Thus, long after the Belknap-Cutler party had made Mount Washington reasonably famous and Ira Allen had run his survey over Mansfield, Katahdin remained little more than a rumor that lay somewhere up in the great north woods. In 1785, the year after the Belknap-Cutler climb, Belknap heard reports from north woods travelers of:

> a mountain, which the Indians call Tadden, i.e., the highest, and say it is bald-pated like our Saconian Mountains, and exceeds them in altitude.[a]

Belknap discounted these tales on the grounds that Indians didn't climb mountains and were "very poor judges" of altitude. So, for nearly two more decades, Katahdin remained a rumor.

Maine was part of Massachusetts until 1820. Shortly after 1800 the Commonwealth decided to find out more about its extensive "Eastern Lands." Charles Turner, Jr., of Scituate, Massachusetts, was hired to conduct a survey of the area. Over a period of several summers Turner explored with wandering feet the dark unbottomed infinite north woods of interior Maine. In 1804 this assignment took him to "Catardin."

The party that moved up the waters of the West Branch of the Penobscot River beneath the southern flanks of the mighty mountain saw one long, steep, broody bank 2,000 feet high.[b] This gargantuan fortress bristles with dense coniferous growth and jutting rock slabs. It was obvious that they would find no easy line of approach here. Twelve years after the Turner party's expedition, a great landslide tore off a wide swath of mountainside, leaving bare earth and rock from top to bottom of this giant slope, and opening a breach for subsequent parties. This was the Abol slide. But in 1804 there was no breach—just one seemingly impregnable wall (see figure 6.1).

Turner's group of eleven men left their canoes at 8:00 A.M. on Monday, August 13, 1804. Seeking an opening, they worked around toward the west to the ridge now followed by the Hunt Trail. The woods that lay between them and the mountain had recently burned, and the going was difficult over twisted and charred trunks seasoned with raspberry brambles. After following Katahdin Stream for awhile, they bore right onto the steep ridge that took them steadily upward. The fire had not burned the ridge, so at first they found the climbing easier. Toward treeline, however, they were forced to clamber over boulders and through the denser scrub growth, the footing obscured by "a deep green moss."

At length the ridge emerged suddenly on "a plane [sic] of rocks with coarse gravel in the interstices, and the whole covered with a dead bluish moss." This remarkable plain is what we call today Katahdin's "Tableland" (though Turner's account applies that term to the forest plain below). Here the going was much easier. The day was uncharacteristically

---

[a]By Saconian Belknap evidently meant those mountains in which the Saco River rose—that is, the White Mountains.
[b]Actually the total rise from river to summit is more than 4,600 feet (ca. 600 ft.–5,267 ft.), but the ground slopes gradually up for three miles to about the 2,500-foot level, then rises very steeply to 4,500 feet, then more gradually again to the top.

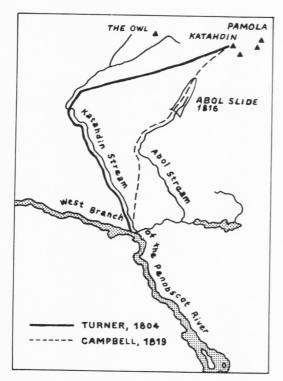

Figure 6.1. Earliest ascents of Katahdin, 1804–1819 In 1804 surveyor Charles Turner, Jr., did not have the advantage of direct access from the south via the Abol Slide, which did not fall until 1816. Therefore, Turner approached Katahdin from the west, following a route not unlike that of today's Hunt Trail or Appalachian Trail. In 1819 Colin Campbell's survey team went up the freshly fallen Abol Slide, a route often used ever since.

"very calm and sultry." A mile and a half of easy walking brought them to the top at 5:00 P.M., having climbed for nine hours.

The stronghold of Pamola had fallen. A long 162 years after Darby Field stood on Washington, Charles Turner stood on Katahdin.

Another fifteen years passed before this remote wilderness admitted another party to the heights of the great mountain. Again the climb was part of a survey, this time assigned to determine the boundary between British Canada and the United States following the War of 1812. From 1817 to 1820, teams were stalking the north woods of Maine making their surveys and turning in their reports. In October 1819 a British team under the leadership of Colin Campbell was in the field near Katahdin, and Campbell himself led a small party up the mountain. Campbell had one clear advantage over the 1804 party: in 1816 the great Abol slide had occurred. Campbell's party became the first of a host of Katahdin climbers to use this slide as a route of ascent. In the long history of diverse approaches to Katahdin over the next century and a half, the Abol Slide has remained the one route in more or less continuous use ever since Campbell first went up it in 1819. In August 1820 another team of surveyors returned, this time with representatives of both British and U.S. boundary observers, and again used Campbell's approach via the West Branch and Abol Slide.

The initial ascents of the distant eyrie of the storm god Pamola were remarkable enough achievements, but the real epics took place in the second wave of explorers, again there as surveyors, but for a new reason and with a far more difficult assignment from a mountaineering standpoint. These were the Monument Line surveyors of 1825–33.

Scarcely had the national boundary between Maine and Canada been tentatively established, when the state of Maine was created as a unit independent of Massachusetts. To provide for orderly development of the interior, it was decided that a single baseline would be run clear across the new state from east to west, as a reference from which all subsequent town and property lines could be measured. As the starting point for this baseline, the authorities chose a "monument" on the eastern boundary with Canada. This monument was the point at which the boundary ceases to follow a water course and runs due north. Specifically, the "monument", as a physical entity, was a yellow birch tree around which iron hoops were affixed in 1817.

The line running due west from this yellow birch was known as the Monument Line and is an extremely important reference point in Maine's political geography. No doubt the state politicians who decreed the establishment of the Monument Line were aware that those who actually ran the line with transit and chain were in for a tough time crossing the north woods. They little knew how tough it would be.

In 1825 Joseph C. Norris, Sr., and his son were hired to run the Monument Line, and they started surveying due west from the monument. Since the project was not agreed upon until July 20 of that year, the Norrises and their small party of assistants got underway late in the year. It was November before they made the unhappy discovery of what kind of terrain lay due west of that yellow birch (see figure 6.2).

The first 40 miles found them running their chain across low and frequently marshy land, crossing one sizable lake (Caribou), till they reached the Sebois River, a tributary of the East Branch of the Penobscot, and in another mile the East Branch itself—so far, no problems. The next seven and a half miles took them over a low swell of less than 2,000 feet, but if the skies to the west were clear, father and son must have been growing increasingly apprehensive. Immediately before them lay the wild valley of the Wassataquoik Stream, of which no record existed of any previous human visits. Beyond that, great lumps of mountain ridge loomed. Bad luck had aimed the Monument Line directly at the heart of the Katahdin group of mountains.

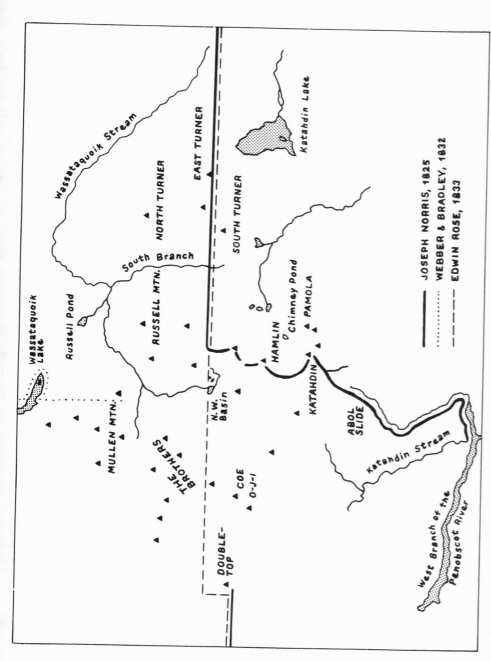

Figure 6.2. Monument Line surveyors on Katahdin, 1825–1833 In 1825 Joseph Norris conducted the first attempt to run the Monument Line over the rugged country north of Katahdin. Stopped by the precipitous drop into the Northwest Basin, his party escaped by a bold maneuver that included making the fourth ascent of Katahdin and the first ascent of Hamlin. In 1832 surveyors Webber and Bradley attempted to run a line south toward Katahdin but stopped when they saw the view south from Mullen Mountain. In 1833 Edwin Rose finally completed the Monument Line through this difficult country.

On the night of November 7, 1825, the Norris party camped at the foot of the Turner range, the first of the outlying ridges. The next day they ran their chain over the top of 2,441-foot East Turner and on over the shoulder of 3,123-foot South Turner, so close to its top (within 160 vertical feet) that they might have walked over to the open summit. This was arguably a first ascent of that now popular peak with its striking view of the Katahdin range from Pamola to the North Peaks in all its mountain glory. The way over the Turners had given them a taste of what lay ahead; the field notes describe it as "steep and broken, composed of ledges and large rocks . . . a mass of huge rocks, among which grows a dense thicket of shrubbery . . . scrubby, and mostly bent or broken down by the snow."

The view from South Turner was not encouraging. One can almost hear the compressed sigh of 160 years ago as the surveyors tersely recorded, "Our line will pass over the N. part of Katahdin."

After dropping 1,400 feet of rugged terrain in about one mile, "the steepest land we have seen," they camped in the valley of the South Branch, having covered just three miles that day. On November 9 they laboriously chained their way up to the 4,000-foot level on the northern edge of the Tableland of Katahdin itself—to gain only two miles and about 2,300 feet of elevation in one day. The upper mountainside was a tangle of gigantic rocks covered with moss, "which conceals the apertures and renders the traveling highly dangerous." A thick stand of young spruce grew up through the dead and twisted remains of a former stand of spruce and fir, "so interwoven from one tree to another that it requires uncommon exertion to crawl through them." Here they camped at 4,000 feet on a November night, without water or sleep, as they stayed up all night trying to keep a fire going with scrub growth, none of it thick enough to burn long or dry enough to burn hot.

On November 10 they soon crested out on the ridge, only to discover that before them lay "perpendicular ledges and precipices" plunging to a jumble of boulders and thickets 1,200 feet below. Joseph Norris and his son had discovered the Northwest Basin of Katahdin. On the far side, where their survey line was supposed to run, they beheld a dense mass of low vegetation, the edge of that bushwhacker's nightmare known now as the Klondike (and scarcely ever visited even today); beyond it rose yet another mountain, "a ledge almost perpendicular of about 2000 ft."—the Brothers. In fact the Brothers are no steeper on the east side than the land over which the Norrisses had run, so the "almost perpendicular" characterization was an exaggeration—surely a pardonable one in view of what they had been through and their anxiety about getting out of this terrain. At this point, Norris's field notes simply state, " . . . so we cannot continue our line."

The party now faced the problem of extricating itself from a remote perch, surrounded by wilderness, at a time of year when a sudden snowstorm could quite effectively trap the party. The isolation of the location can be judged from the observation that, after the Monument Line survey was completed eight years later, more than half a century passed before the next pair of eyes saw the Northwest Basin. To get back out, after spending another night camped high in "cold intense," the Norris group did a bold thing: they headed straight across the Tableland for the summit of Katahdin, to pick up the known route of descent down the Abol Slide. In the course of this retreat, therefore, these remarkable climbers pulled off the fourth recorded ascent of the main peak and almost certainly the first ascent of the neighboring peak, Hamlin.

The descent added to the epic. At first enveloped in cloud, the group started down too far to the east. When they struck steep terrain here, two of the party slipped and suffered minor injuries. Deciding that this was a "dangerous way to travel," they camped yet another night in the scrub—their third in a row at probably 3,500 feet or more in November on Katahdin. In the morning they were able to locate the Slide and get down safely. Once in the lowlands they retreated to civilization over lakes and streams that were rapidly freezing over, providing still more excitement but no mountains.

The next year, the elder Norris resumed work on the Monument Line but quite sensibly decided to omit, for the time being, the 16 miles between where he had stopped on that chilly November 10 and Lake Chesuncook, well to the west of the Katahdin mountains. After completing the line to the west, he tried to chain east from Chesuncook later in 1826 and in 1827 but was stopped by the imposing side of 3,488-foot Doubletop, and his awareness that if he did get over Doubletop, things would only get worse from there on. This left a gap of about 8 miles of rugged Katahdin terrain over which the Monument Line remained unsurveyed.

Five years after Norris quit the field, John Webber was appointed by the land agents of Maine and Massachusetts to clear up the uncompleted survey lines around the Katahdin massif. With Zebulon Bradley, Webber spent a considerable part of 1832 in the rough mountain wilderness north of the Monument Line. One town line took them over the east flank of the Traveler, northernmost of the Katahdin group. Another ran south over Pogy Mountain, crossed the beautiful Wassataquoik Lake, rimmed with wilderness mountains, and struck straight over Mullen Mountain, aiming to link up with the Monument Line (see figure 6.2). They also made a halfhearted stab at extending the Monument Line itself but got no farther than Norris had when confronted with the steep drop into the Northwest Basin.

The challenge was finally accepted the following year by yet a third Monument Line party, headed by Edwin Rose. With four co-workers, Rose returned to the north peaks and found Norris's 1825 cairn perched on the rim of the precipitous east wall of the Northwest Basin. Rose took a compass bearing on the basin floor, where the Monument Line chanced to go right along the outlet of one of the two little ponds in the basin (now called Lake Cowles). Three of his companions thrashed their way down around the edge of the cliff to the outlet of the pond and erected a cairn there. Having confirmed the accuracy of the line, he and his other helper then made the descent, "which is extremely dangerous traveling owing to the perpendicular pitches, many of them are from 50 to 100 feet."

More obstacles remained. The surveyors worked their way through the edge of the Klondike, finding it "rough and bad running a line." After that came the ascent of South Brother from the east, a formidable course entered in the field notes simply as "rough ascent to a little north of the peak of this mountain." Having descended from the Brothers, Rose faced the final barrier of "Double Capped Mountain," the peak that had stopped Norris in 1827 coming from the west ("very difficult to run a line owing to the steepness of its ascent"). When they came off Doubletop, the line did not neatly dovetail with Norris's 1827 line, so the Monument Line has ever since exhibited a slight offset at that point.

Thus after eight years was completed the Monument Line. The surveys of Norris, Webber and Bradley, and Edwin Rose form a significant chapter in the early days of Northeastern climbing. Their work led them to known or probable first ascents of Doubletop, South Brother, East Mullen, South Turner, East Turner, with an outside possibility of Hamlin and Fort as well; had given them the fourth ascent and first from that side of Katahdin itself; and had taken them into the Northwest Basin and the Klondike, two of the loneliest and most interesting pieces of landscape in New England, apparently never seen before and fated to remain among the least-known until well into the twentieth century. As professionals doing their work, these men are not known for other mountain-climbing exploits. What they achieved in that wild pocket north of Katahdin, however, gives them front rank among Northeastern mountain explorers.

When the surveyors left, climbers were not long in following. By the 1830s attitudes toward the mountains were changing from dread of the "daunting terrible" to starry-eyed pursuit of the "sublime." Katahdin became an objective for those seeking adventure of a special kind. But for nearly half a century, they confined their attentions to Katahdin itself and the southernmost end of the massif. The "rough and rocky" land of the Northwest Basin, the Klondike, and the northern outreaches of the storm god Pamola, over which Norris and Rose, Webber and Bradley had struggled, fell back into wilderness again—"unbroken, silent, and desolate."

Chapter 7

Janus on the heights during the 1820s

THE ROMAN deity Janus had two faces, one to look forward, the other back. Northeastern Americans had such contrasting perceptions of their mountains during the 1820s.

On the more prominent and accessible peaks of the southern part of the region—in the Catskills and the Holyoke Range, on Massachusetts's Greylock, New Hampshire's Monadnock, possibly Vermont's Ascutney —the first mountaintop structures were built during the 1820s. These constructions, including two genuine hotels, looked forward toward a time of acceptance and enjoyment of the scenic hills. Yet during the same decade, society's continuing ignorance of the magnificent Adirondacks looked backward toward the old colonists' view of mountains as "waste and howling wilderness."

Both perceptions were very much alive in the 1820s. Before 1820 the negative view definitely prevailed. A few curious travelers inspected the closer peaks. For example, during a long tenure as president of Yale, Timothy Dwight made many vacation tours throughout the Northeast, on which he took special note of the mountains he saw. He is known to have climbed Greylock in 1799, Everett in 1781, and Catskill peaks in 1815. But except for Dwight, Partridge, and a handful of similarly inquisitive academics, those with any desire to climb were few and far between. By the 1830s the balance tipped decisively the other way. With the discovery and ascent of New York's Mount Marcy, the first recreational sorties to Katahdin, and the transition from the rustic inns of the Crawfords to first-class hotels in the White Mountains, not to mention considerably more activity among the lower peaks, the people of the Northeast fully embraced the mountain scenery. The 1820s were a time of transition.

The Blue Hills, which lie to the south of Boston, had the only known "mountaintop" structure built before 1820. In May of 1798 the owner and patrons of nearby Billings Tavern erected an observatory on the top of Great Blue Hill, intended to enhance the enjoyment of sightseers and picnickers on that modest elevation (635 ft.). No doubt it was primitive; reportedly it "blew down" in 1802. However, it was also said to be "three stories high," so it deserves notice as the first mountain "house" of the Northeast. A permanent observatory atop Great Blue Hill dates from 1830, when Harvard University put up a 20-foot tower and began using it for serious weather observations (see table 7.1).

Meanwhile, however, the prototype of mountain tourist development took form on the Holyoke Range in the Massachusetts section of the Connecticut River valley. There in 1821 was erected the Prospect House. It was built because the view from Mount Holyoke was already a magnet for picnickers and sightseers. In a geography textbook published in 1813, the only U.S. "mountain" from which a view is described—"a most beautiful prospect"—is Mount Holyoke. Some sort of facility was probably there even before 1821; Partridge referred to Mount Holyoke in 1818 as "a place of fashionable resort, on account of the fine prospect from its summit." However, tradition gives the structure of 1821 the honor of being the first genuine "hotel." The prime mover in this historic enterprise was Samuel F. Lyman, a young law student who raised $120 in subscriptions and materials and organized a crew of scores of Northampton and Hadley townspeople (one report says three hundred!) to help carry up materials and erect the hotel. It was a festive house raising, with good spirits nurtured by "a little water with a good deal of brandy in it." The result was a 15-by-22-foot structure that was enlarged in 1822, with a second footpath up the west side of the mountain in 1824. Under later proprietor James W. French, this summit house was enlarged again (1851), a road built (1850), and finally an inclined railway (1854), which in its heyday carried as many as 125,000 tourists a year. Even during that first summer of 1821, no fewer than 6,000 visitors thronged the Northeast's first summit house. In 1825 it rated a mention in *The Fashionable Tour*, one of the first travelers' guides.

Travel accounts by Timothy Dwight and others indicate that a number of Massachusetts hills had become popular picnic spots by the 1820s, from the Blue Hills through Mounts Wachusett and Toby, to the Holyoke

Table 7.1

MOUNTAINTOP STRUCTURES, 1820–1830

Date	Structure	Range/mountain
1821	Prospect House	Mount Holyoke
1823	Catskill Mountain House	Catskills
1824	Fife's "sufficient building"	Monadnock
1825	Crawfords' "camps"	Washington
1825	Possible building	Ascutney
1826	Dinsmore's "shantee"	Monadnock
1830	Permanent observatory	Great Blue Hill
1830	Williams students' observatory	Greylock

Range and its neighbor, Mount Tom, and on to such Berkshire eminences as Monument Mountain and East Mountain, and Mount Everett, then the "Dome of the Taconics" (see frontispiece).

The state's highest peak, Greylock, had a "road" to its top, built from the north and apparently maintained by a local farmer, Jeremiah Wilbur, in the late eighteenth century. Another road led to the Hopper valley on the west side of the mountain (see figure 7.1). On May 12, 1830, a noisy horde of Williams College students cut a path from the end of this road to the top in a one-day blitz, armed with axes, bush hooks, crow bars, hoes and tin horns. Though denounced as "a visionary scheme" by critics not yet prepared to acknowledge the sublimity of mountain scenery, the Hopper Trail has lasted ever since. It ranks not far behind the Crawford paths in antiquity. A rough observation tower was also built on top that day in 1830, and improved in 1841. In those years the slopes of Greylock were more cleared than now, a stage road crossed the southern shoulder near Jones Nose, and various informal routes of ascent may have been in use by locals.

The prime mountaintop resort, however, was launched just two years after the Prospect House, in New York's Catskills. The Hudson Valley had been thickly settled well before the Revolution. Regular stage service between New York and Albany passed within sight of Catskill peaks as early as 1784, and daily after 1798. On the Hudson River, passengers plying to and fro on leisurely sloops contemplated the land of Rip Van Winkle for hours. Picnickers and curiosity seekers had been climbing the ridge west of the Hudson that forms the eastern rampart of the northern Catskills. Two lakes lay nestled there, between two modest mountains, with a prominent flat rock on the edge of the escarpment that commanded a sweeping view of the river valley. In the early years of the nineteenth century, this picturesque spot was called Pine Orchard; the name is delightfully symbolic of the contrast between wildness and human associations, so appealing to the evolving new attitudes towards mountains. In 1819 the first shanty was thrown up on that level rock outlook. In 1822 a 60-foot addition was erected and a "Rural Ball" held on September 18. This event was a smashing success, to which a large and enthusiastic crowd flocked, spent the night, visited nearby Kaaterskill Falls, and wound up the next day with a huge dinner at a tavern in the valley. The business opportunities at Pine Orchard were now too obvious to ignore. On July 4, 1823, the Catskill Mountain House opened its doors (see figure 7.2). Livery service was provided from the town of Catskill, where boats, stages, and later trains arrived from New York and other points. In 1824 the building was substantially rebuilt and enlarged, and a further expansion in 1825 brought it to a frontal length of 140 feet, four stories high in one section, three in another, with accommodations for sixty visitors. In subsequent remodeling, it acquired an imposing front piazza supported by thirteen massive Corinthian columns, and

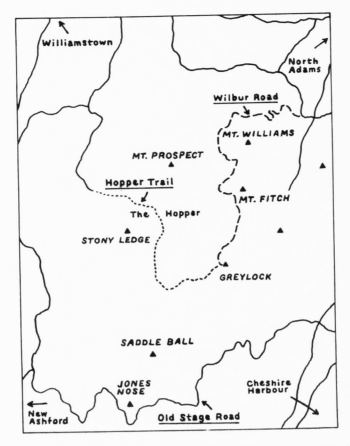

Figure 7.1. Greylock in 1830 The earliest roads and the Hopper Trail, built in 1830, are shown. This map accepts the view that Wilbur's "road" closely approximated the modern Notch Road to the top of Greylock. A competing view is that Wilbur's road more nearly followed the later Bellows Pipe Trail, well to the east. (For the route of this trail, see figure 23.2.)

eventually came to have three hundred rooms and to entertain more than five hundred guests at a time. This was the right building in the right place at the right time. The Catskill Mountain House instantly achieved economic success and social prestige. As attitudes toward mountain scenery changed, the well-to-do flocked to this well-known resort. Artists and writers discovering the Catskills initially centered their attentions on Pine Orchard, many of them as guests at the Mountain House. The view from the piazza was extolled with extravagance. The proprietors judged their clientele correctly, quickly moving past the rustic homeliness of the Crawfords to provide elegance for America's rising elite, as well as distinguished European visitors. Within a few years of opening, the Catskill Mountain House had become

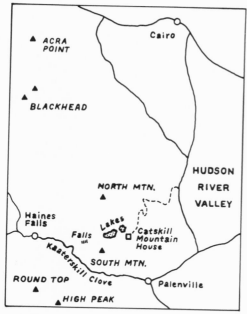

Figure 7.2. The Catskill Mountain House in the 1820s The Catskill Mountain House was built in 1823 on a ledge overlooking a sweeping view of the Hudson River valley to the east. Nearby were picturesque attractions, such as two lakes (today modified so as to form one large lake), Kaaterskill Falls, Kaaterskill Clove, and North and South mountains, not to mention a variety of viewpoints, sequestered nooks, and natural features linked by paths for the pleasure of Mountain House guests.

an early symbol of the economic and social flowering of the new Republic . . . a refuge for our well-to-do merchants . . . a showcase for foreign visitors.

The remarkable thing about the Catskill Mountain House was its extraordinary dominance of the Catskill scene for so long. During the post–Civil War years, things changed, larger and more elegant hotels arose, and people discovered that there were many mountains in the Catskills besides those overlooking North and South lakes. But for more than a generation, Pine Orchard *was* the Catskills. Mountain trails were largely limited to those built by and for the Mountain House. Guests were richly accommodated with an extensive network of paths, ornamented with rustic ladders, designated vistas, and places to rest. The guests climbed North and South mountains, with occasional longer expeditions to High Peak and Round Top.

The flowering of mountain tourism at the Catskill Mountain House beginning in 1823 occupies an extremely important niche in the history of Northeastern mountain climbing. At this point the mountains of northern New England were still beyond the pale of popular interest, still "daunting terrible." The first signs of change were there, in the Crawfords' rudimentary guiding business, but the gulf between the centers of civilized life and the rugged mountain heights was still too great. On that rock ledge within sight of the sloops on the Hudson, the first major breach of the mountain wilderness was made. The early and spectacular success of the Catskill Mountain House was a harbinger of a new era in the Northeastern mountains.

Meanwhile in southern New Hampshire, the Grand Monadnock was launched on its career of popularity that has earned it the title of second-most-climbed mountain in the world, deferring only to Japan's holy Fuji-yama. It is indeed a mountain made for people (see figure 7.3). A craggy rockbound summit is supported by long ridges of matchless views, below which charming dells and nooks invite exploration—all boiled down to manageable size, allowing the whole to be sampled comfortably in an easy day, yet varied enough to satisfy many days' tramping. At least as far back as the 1820s its attractions as an eminently *enjoyable* mountain were overcoming the old colonial antipathy for wilderness. By 1825 a local newspaper called it "a fashionable place of resort for people of pleasure." By that time several routes of ascent seem to have been in use, possibly as many as six. Certain evidence of its popularity by the 1820s is the scramble of at least three different entrepreneurs to set up business on the high land south of the summit rocks. In the summer of 1823 Josiah Amadon published an advertisement in the local paper claiming to have "erected a convenient building" at which "good refreshment" would be furnished, "near the pinnacle of said Mountain."[a]

In 1824 John Fife announced the opening of "a sufficient building" on the bank of a brook southeast of the summit rocks, where he offered all kinds of "meats and drinks," even including "spirituous liquors." By the following summer he was advertising his building as a "shantee" and inviting one and all to celebrate the Fourth of July there. Even more substantial was the "shantee" built by Thomas Dinsmore and his partners in July 1826. The foundations of this building may still be seen on the mountain, along with a nearby rock on which the initials of Dinsmore and his associates, plus the year 1826, are inscribed. Dinsmore found enough business to justify regularly staffing the shantee on Thursdays through Sundays. This kind of entrepreneurial hustling is ample evidence that the Grand Monadnock was already aswarm with trampers by the 1820s, as it has been ever since.

---

[a]Whether Amadon ever really had more than ambitions of putting up a building is not clear, as the next summer he advertised that he "proposes to erect something like a HOTEL on the summit of GRAND MONADNOCK, by the 17th of August Inst" (*New Hampshire Sentinel*, Aug. 6, 1824, p. 3); and two years after that a further advertisement finally announced that Amadon and a partner (one Levi Bigelow) "have opened a HOTEL" (*New Hampshire Sentinel*, Aug. 4, 1826, p. 3). By that time Fife and Dinsmore were in business before him. Amadon's claims are therefore omitted from table 7.1.

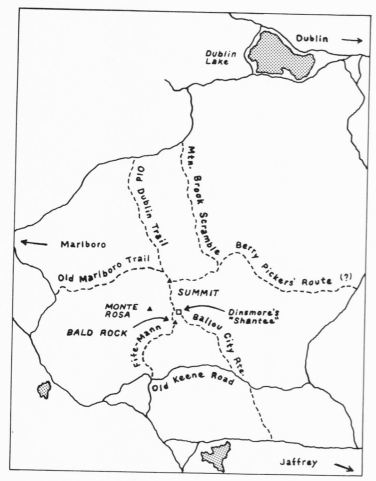

Figure 7.3. The Grand Monadnock in the 1820s At least six routes for climbing Monadnock were in use by the 1820s. Four of these were reasonably formal hiking trails. During the 1820s, three buildings were built on the southern shoulder, the most substantial being Thomas Dinsmore's "shantee," erected in July 1826. Already this popular mountain was aswarm with hikers, as it has been ever since.

Neighboring "monadnocks" in southern New Hampshire, such as Pack Monadnock, Uncanoonuc, and Kearsarge South, probably had a smaller volume of hiking traffic. Definite evidence that at least Kearsarge South was so honored exists in the form of initials carved into the summit rock that can be traced (with some difficulty) today: dates of 1820 (possible), 1821 (definite), and 1830 (signed by A. M. Sawyer and S. Gale) can be found.

Separate and apart from the Green Mountains (much as Monadnock is from the Whites), Vermont's Ascutney has bestowed much pleasure on the people who live beneath its graceful contours at least as far back as 1820. A reasonably respectable trail—developed enough to be called a "road" in the terminology of the preautomobile era—was put up the mountain by 1822. In September 1823 some Norwich Academy cadets climbed Ascutney, one of them noting in his journal,

> During the last year the enterprising citizens of Windsor have cut a road nearly to the top and the mountain is now visited by a great number for the purpose of enjoying a view of its beautiful scenery.

The aforementioned *The Fashionable Tour in 1825*, which ignores the greater ranges as beyond the pale of fashion at that date, praises Ascutney for "the rich and diversified prospect afforded from its summit," clearly implying that a trail suitable for the fashionable tour existed. In 1825 Revolutionary War hero General Lafayette made a triumphal tour on which the New Hampshire mountain was named in his honor. A corresponding tribute was hatched in Vermont to build a "road" to the top of Ascutney and erect thereon a building, with the idea of giving the distinguished visitor a ride up "so that the Kingdoms of the Earth from this point might be shown him." Aside from whether the gallant champion of republicanism would have wished to see "kingdoms" of any stripe in the New World, his triumphal tour proved to be on too tight a schedule to permit a mountain excursion. The general's coach clattered into Windsor, Vermont, in the early hours of the morning, stopped long enough for the hero to munch a fast breakfast at John Pettes's Coffee House, grace the assembled citizenry with a short oration from the balcony of that emporium, and charge off again to the next lucky town by 9:30 A.M. Meanwhile, it is unclear whether the new "road" up Ascutney was completed in 1825, and also whether it represented a widening of the 1822 or earlier path or a brand new road. It is not even known whether a building was built on the summit at that time, though this was part of the plan. Nonetheless, Mount Ascutney is the first Vermont mountain of consequence known to have a definite summit trail, one of the earliest in the Northeast.

While these more southerly summits blossomed as tourist attractions, the Adirondacks remained almost literally unknown to the general public. A few small towns dotted the fringes of the high peaks, but their settlers were the only humans who seemed aware of the scope of the mountain wilderness of upstate New York. Whiteface was thought to be the highest peak of the range at perhaps 2,500 feet—surely not as tall as High Peak in the Catskills. (Actual altitudes: High Peak, 3,655 ft.; Whiteface, 4,867 ft.; Marcy, 5,344 ft.) Most people knew more about Katahdin than about any of the mountains of the wild Cauchsachrage. Longer than any other Northeastern mountain group, the Adirondacks retained the stigma (or badge of honor, depending on the viewpoint) of howling wilderness. Its highest peak (Marcy) was not climbed for 195 years after Mount Washington. Its first trail had to wait for half a century after the Gibbs's Path cut through the scrub of Tuckerman Ravine (see table 7.2).

The first records of direct confrontation with the Adirondack High Peaks are those of a handful of enterprising surveyors who drew the assignment of running boundary lines for the earliest divisions of this vast, wild land. One Charles Brodhead ran the earliest survey line through the highest country, June 1797, along the south bounds of the Old Military Tract and McComb's Purchase (see figure 7.4). It is an extraordinary line, crossing the Adirondacks from Giant to Wallface. The terrain was tough; one modern land surveyor who is also an accomplished mountaineer has commented with due respect,

> Even today, I'm not sure I would willingly set out to repeat his line, and it must have been quite the undertaking in those days.

The southeast corner of the Old Military Tract, where Brodhead started, is around 1,800 feet on a small eminence (Bald Peak today) southwest of the village of Elizabethtown. For 2½ miles Brodhead slabbed westward along the flanks of minor peaks before dropping down to Roaring Brook. Here he stood at the base of cliffs on the northeast ridge of Giant, "a Mountain which is impossible to to [sic] climb over which the line goes." For the next three-fourths of a mile he fought his way up 1,400 feet of terrain similar to what Norris faced on the north slope of Katahdin (Norris was twenty-eight years later, be it noted). At

Table 7.2

A COMPARISON OF THE ADIRONDACKS WITH OTHER
NORTHEASTERN RANGES

First known ascents of highest peaks	*First definite trails*
1642: Mount Washington (White Mountains)	1809: Gibbs' Path on Mt. Washington (White Mountains)
1725: Monadnock (southern New Hampshire)	1820: worn track to and up Abol Slide, Katahdin (Maine)
1742: South Mountain[a] (Catskills)	1822: "road" up Ascutney (Vermont)
1772: Mansfield (Green Mountains)	1823: paths for guests of the Catskill Mountain House (Catskills)
1804: Katahdin (Maine)	1824: Fife-Mann Trail on Monadnock (southern New Hampshire)
1837: Mount Marcy (Adirondacks)	1859: Wilmington trail up Whiteface (Adirondacks)

[a]*No good estimates of first ascents in the Catskills, of which Slide Mountain is the highest.*

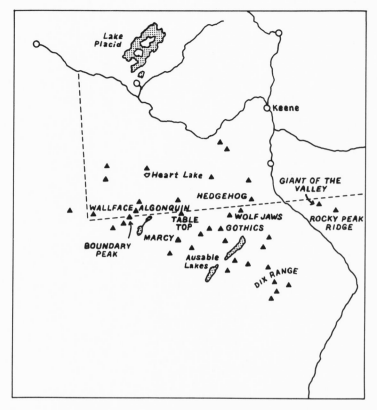

Figure 7.4. Brodhead's Adirondack survey, 1797 Long before the Adirondack high peaks were explored by others, surveyor Charles Brodhead ran a line that crossed extremely rugged mountain country. En route he was forced to climb close to the tops of half a dozen 4,000-footers, fighting blowdowns, late spring snow, and precipitous ledges. Even by modern bushwhackers' standards, it was an amazing feat.

several points the surveyor was forced to offset his line to avoid cliffs, then to fight his way back up. Two feet of snow at the 4,000-foot level complicated the job. Finally he crossed the summit of Giant, the line passing within 300 lateral yards of the 4,627-foot summit. As with other surveyors, it is not unlikely, though impossible to substantiate, that the advantages of a good viewpoint might have induced him to take the time to walk over to the true summit. In the case of Giant the topography is such that the summit would provide a uniquely profitable prospect. Adirondack historians therefore credit Brodhead with the first ascent of the first Adirondack 4,000-footer—the Giant of the Valley on June 2, 1797. The line next dropped, "descending steep rocks, no Timber . . . Land rough," until it crossed the comparatively "Leavel Land" of the Ausable River valley about where St. Hubert's now stands. On the other side of the valley the line climbed over the choppy terrain of Hedgehog and the north slopes of the Wolf Jaws before dropping into the Johns Brook valley not far from the present site of Johns Brook Lodge. Next came the jumble of hummocks north of Marcy. It is often overlooked, in the credits paid to the Redfield-Emmons pioneers on Marcy in 1837 (see chapter 10), that Brodhead passed scarcely more than 2 miles north of the great peak a full forty years earlier. His line ran aslant the sharp east ridge of Table Top, across the northern end of its sprawling uplands at elevations of up to 4,100 feet, then on over the sharp bluff just northwest from Indian Falls and down into the dip just below Avalanche Pass. Modern peakbaggers who know Table Top principally for its ferocious blowdown will not be surprised at Brodhead's description of almost two centuries ago: "Top the mountain—very rough chief of the timber fallen down by the wind." Beneath the tangled blowdown, a foot of snow hid good footing. From the dip on the far side of Table Top, Brodhead's line climbed the 4,700-foot level on the MacIntyre Range, passing over Boundary Peak and within a half-mile of the second-highest peak in the Adirondacks, Algonquin. He then plunged over 50-foot cliffs and down a long, wooded, rocky slope to Indian Pass and around the edges of Wallface, where his notes are disappointingly uncommunicative.

Brodhead's 1797 trip is the Adirondacks' first documented record of people up in these high peaks. He and his party climbed high on a half-dozen of the "Adirondack forty-six," the list of 4,000-footers: Rocky Peak Ridge, Giant, Lower Wolf Jaws, Table Top, Algonquin, Iroquois. He cannot be said with certainty to have stood on the true summit of any of these, but it is probable that he was on the very top of Giant, and not beyond possibility that he stepped over to Algonquin as well. Whatever the number of summits trod, Brodhead's trip was an amazing achievement. The terrain was as formidable as almost any comparable distance in the Northeast. Nor could he dodge obstacles except by strict offset procedures but had to stay right on his straight line, wherever it took him. Add to the normal difficulties of Adirondack bushwhacking the further rigors of snow at the upper elevations—2 feet on Giant!—and the black flies that must have been out at lower elevations in early June. Recall that this was not a one-day outing but a protracted march through totally unknown country, Brodhead carrying surveying equipment, day after day. Brodhead's accomplishment must rank high in any evaluation of early Northeastern mountain climbing.

The surveyors' ascents are the only documented records of Adirondack climbs prior to the 1830s. Besides Brodhead, a man named Rykert ran a line over Dix in 1807, and John Richards's surveys took him up Big Slide in 1812 and Whiteface in 1814. But the chief historical fact about the Adirondacks at this time is not what was climbed but what was *not* climbed; in an era when the Catskill Mountain House clientele were ambling up half a dozen Catskill peaks; when the Crawfords had three inns and two well-used paths up Mount Washington; when Alden Partridge was leading his cadets up every mountain they could walk to; when even Katahdin had been climbed several times by at least three different routes—still the central core of the Adirondack high peaks remained virtually untrodden, untouched, and unknown.

Part Two

Mountains as sublime: 1830–1870

THE CATSKILL Mountain House and the more primitive mountain structures of the 1820s were straws in a gathering wind. By midcentury, Americans' neglect or fear of their mountains had been transformed into a grand passion for them. Tourists swarmed to mountain vacation centers, writers and poets extolled the majesty of the peaks, artists painted them, philosophers contemplated them—and increasingly some hardy souls went and climbed them.

The fashionableness of mountains after 1830 reflected a profoundly important change of attitude toward the mountains. To the pioneers in New England, as we've seen, mountains had been difficult, useless, hostile, obstacles to farming and travel, sanctuaries for French and Indian enemies, foreboding shrines of frightening superstitions. With the conquest of the wilderness on the eastern seaboard, especially after the flush of optimism that followed national independence, fear of the mountains waned. Wilderness began to attract, not repel.

European perceptions of mountains had already changed during the eighteenth century; American ideas were just a little behind. In her landmark book with the indicative title *Mountain Gloom and Mountain Glory*, Marjorie Hope Nicolson points out the shift that occurred in Europe:

> During the first seventeen centuries of the Christian era, "Mountain Gloom" so clouded human eyes that never for a moment did poets see mountains in the full radiance to which our eyes have become accustomed. Within a century—indeed, within fifty years—all this was changed. The "Mountain Glory" dawned, then shone full splendor.

The new attitudes were delayed in reaching America, probably because colonial Americans were too close to the genuine difficulties and dangers of wilderness. Mountains were too much of a real threat. Roderick Nash observes:

> Enthusiasm for wilderness . . . developed among sophisticated Europeans surrounded by cities and books. So too in America the beginnings of appreciation are found among writers, artists, scientists, vacationers, gentlemen—people, in short, who did not face wilderness from the pioneer's perspective.

Mountain history was at this point profoundly influenced by ideas of the "sublime," an important concept to Europeans of the late eighteenth century and one that caught on with invigorating fervor in America of the early nineteenth. The concept of the sublime was articulated by such influential English writers as Edmund Burke (*Essay on the Sublime and the Beautiful*, 1756) and infused the widely read aesthetic judgments of John Ruskin during the nineteenth century. The term *sublime* was applied to rough, uncontrolled nature, in which the viewer was awed by tremendous size and power in the landscape. The sublime was tinged on the one hand with dread and on the other with spellbound rapture. It was slightly terrifying but still elevating in that it reminded the viewer of the awesome majesty of nature—and, for many, of God—in comparison with which mere man was humbled.

Mountains, of course, were quintessentially sublime. A check of the list of some nine attributes assigned to the sublime in Burke's original essay, shows they are all to be found in mountains: vastness, power, obscurity, privation (darkness, solitude, silence), difficulty, magnificence, light, sound, and loudness (as during mountain storms); and most of all "ideas of pain and danger . . . whatever is in any sort terrible." Viewing the Alps, Lord Byron exulted:

> All that expands the spirit, yet appals,
> Gather around these summits, as to show
> How Earth may pierce to Heaven, yet leave vain
>   man below.

Formal European aesthetic theory may seem remote from climbing American mountains, and it is. But it was when these ideas or something like them permeated society that people began to look at mountain terrain differently and the active history of New England mountain climbing began. In the ideas of Burke and Wordsworth lay the seeds of the Catskill Mountain House and Mount Washington's Cog Railway—and eventually the Appalachian Trail and the Appalachian Mountain Club hut system, the Adirondack Forty-Sixers, and every backpacker ranging the high country today.

All the qualities of mountains that had most appalled the early Americans coping with the wilderness—rugged precipice, vast impenetrable forest, foaming cataract, mountain storms with all their awesome retinue of rolling clouds, flashing lightning, violent winds, and tormented landscape—now began to inspire their descendants with feelings of the sublime. The very term became a kind of code word in descriptions of American mountains. Not everyone used it with the precision of Burke or Ruskin, but they were beginning to get the idea.

Jeremy Belknap gave an unusually early American expression to these sentiments in his account of the 1784 ascent of Mount Washington, in which he waxed eloquent on the view from Pinkham Notch:

> Almost everything in nature, which can be supposed capable of inspiring ideas of the sublime and beautiful is here realized. Aged mountains, stupendous elevations, rolling clouds, impending rocks, verdant woods, chrystal streams, the gentle rill, and the roaring torrent, all conspire to amaze, to soothe and to enrapture.

Timothy Dwight, traveling throughout New England in the decade before and after 1800, also was among the first to be amazed, soothed, and enraptured by mountain scenery rather than repelled. Dwight specifically uses the term *sublime* in describing Mount Everett, but the more important point is that the whole of his mountain description is suffused with the ideas referred to here, to a greater extent than the writings of any other American this early.

Even the "goal-oriented" Captain Partridge caught the new attitudes. On Camel's Hump in 1818, he called the view

> grand and sublime. It truly exhibited the works of the Creator on a magnificent scale . . . [The foul weather] diminished nothing, but, on the contrary, rather added to the grandeur of the scene. . . . The whole appeared to me as strangely illustrative of the original state of chaos.

But such observations were episodic and pallid compared with what was to come. By 1825 a traveler through the Hudson Valley was extolling the Hudson Highlands as uniting "all the charms of novelty, with the highest emotions of the sublime." Moving on to the Catskills, the same writer found them "truly majestic and sublime," as did many more who stood transfixed on the ledge at Pine Orchard.

A White Mountain traveler in Crawford Notch found that

> the sublime and awful grandeur of this passage baffles all description. . . . No words can tell the emotions of the soul, as it looks upward, and views the almost perpendicular precipices which line the narrow space between them; while the senses ache with terror and astonishment, as one sees himself hedged in from all the world besides.

A visiting minister wrote of the same hills "whose beauty, and grandeur, and sublimity my poor pen possesses no power to describe." The poor pen was willing to try, however; the prospect from the summit of Washington was soon

> sublime in the highest degree, but it is the sublimity of nature, unaided and alone, or rather, of nature's God. Art has had no hand in the manufacture of the objects exhibited, or in their presentation.

Needless to say, Katahdin evoked feelings of the sublime as powerfully as any single peak in the East. Thomas Wentworth Higginson, after his first view of the mountain, called it "more absolutely isolated, more precipitous, more sublime" than any other mountain of the Northeast.

The pursuit of the sublime was part of many important roots in early nineteenth-century thought which began to come to full flower in America about 1830: romanticism, the passion for landscape painting embodied by the Hudson River school, the transcendentalism of the Concord writers and philosophers. For all this mosaic of American thought, mountains held a powerful attraction.

In art these impulses gave birth to the so-called Hudson River school, which had more to do with mountains than rivers, and as much to do with the White Mountains as those that overlooked (Catskills) or sourced (Adirondacks) the Hudson River. Some critics prefer to call it the White Mountain school. Whatever its name, it was a movement of realistic nature painting that took shape during the 1820s, led by Thomas Cole and his celebrated pupil, Frederic Church. Artists flocked to the mountain regions. One painter depicted the Saco River with its banks lined by the white umbrellas of . . . other painters! Many of them were active hikers, not just valley-bound appreciators. Cole was on many a Catskill summit, often lingering on top to catch the last light of the fading day and its special effect on the landscape; on one occasion, descending in the dark, he lost his way and spent a harrowing night in the woods, falling into deep streams (he couldn't swim!), groping through caves, loving every terrifying but romantic moment. The first ascent party on Mount Marcy included an artist, Charles Cromwell Ingham.[a] Another, Alexander Wyant, is credited with the first ascent of Mount Macomb in 1872. Church was well acquainted with the Katahdin massif. Today's technical climbers on the cliffs of Frankenstein in Crawford Notch normally assume these intimidating crags must be appropriately named for the mad monster; not so—for the painter, Godfrey Frankenstein. The effusive attentions paid to mountains by the leading artists of this pre–Civil War generation had a lot to do with attracting tourists there. According to one authority, describing the impact of Cole's visit to the crags of Mount Desert on the Maine coast:

---

[a]Ingham's presence on such a venture reflects a standard practice in exploration during the early nineteenth century. Lacking photography, the explorers employed artists to illustrate what they discovered. The juxtaposition of this practical need with the artists' growing fascination with mountain scenery proved a fruitful common interest.

[September 3, 1844] will go down in the records as the day on which Bar Harbor summer colony was founded. . . . On that day, Thomas Cole . . . drove across Mount Desert Island to stay at Lynam's at Schooner Head.

Artists in residence at major resorts were common. One astute inn-keeper in North Conway, New Hampshire, even made special arrangements to attract leading artists, giving them a sizable discount on their bills and sending their noontime meals out to wherever they might choose to paint that day—on condition that they sign all their pictures as painted in North Conway. This was a practical entrepreneur's recognition of the influence of art on public opinion.

As the Hudson River school painted mountains in the middle of its canvas, so the transcendentalist movement in literature found few locales so conducive to its spiritual instincts as the uplifted hill country. Ralph Waldo Emerson was an inveterate hill walker:

> I think 'tis the best of humanity that goes out to walk. In happy hours, I think all affairs may be wisely postponed for this walking. Can you hear what the morning says to you, and believe *that*? Can you bring home the summits of Wachusett, Greylock and the New Hampshire hills? . . . Can you bottle the efflux of a June moon, and bring home the top of Uncanoonuc? The landscape is vast, complete, alive.

Besides these local hills, Emerson climbed Monadnock, Mansfield, and Washington. William Cullen Bryant ("Go forth, under the open sky, and list / To Nature's teachings") often accompanied Cole in Catskill ramblings. James Russell Lowell climbed distant Mount Kineo in Maine. John Greenleaf Whittier summered in New Hampshire's Sandwich Range. Nathaniel Hawthorne sojourned in the Berkshires and occasionally traveled through the White Mountains, where he found material for short stories from such places and events as Mount Washington ("The Great Carbuncle"), the Cannon Mountain profile ("The Great Stone Face"), and the landslide that came down around the Willey House in Crawford Notch ("The Ambitious Guest"). James Fenimore Cooper climbed no mountains but was personally acquainted with the Eastern hardwood forest, and his novels displayed a deep respect for the same wilderness that had so repelled the Puritans.

But the writer most prominently identified with wilderness and the mountains was Henry David Thoreau. Beginning with a climb of Washington at age twenty-two in 1839, Thoreau was often among the hills, both nearby eminences such as Wachusett (1842), Monadnock (1844, 1852, 1858, 1860), Greylock (1844), and the hills of southern Vermont (1856), and more remote peaks such as Katahdin (an unsuccessful attempt in 1846) and Washington (a second climb in 1858). Thoreau's climbs and journeys through the mountains of the Northeast were on the whole no more than standard for their day, although he seems to have camped out more than most of his contemporaries. He achieved no "first ascents" or remarkable discoveries. More important, he accepted in a positive way those wilderness qualities that had dismayed the previous generation. People heard his clarion call about these qualities. Perhaps no one before or since has placed wilderness values so much at the core of existence. Fannie Hardy Eckstorm, the Maine historian who emphatically did not admire Thoreau's scientific pretensions or his woodsmanship, focused on his wilderness values: "Thoreau stood at the gateway of the woods and opened them to all future comers with the key of poetic insight."

An incident that symbolizes the central place of mountains for American writers is the picnic atop Monument Mountain in the Berkshires on August 5, 1850, at which Nathaniel Hawthorne was introduced to Herman Melville, accompanied by Oliver Wendell Holmes. This was the American equivalent of those prestigious gatherings at the Turk's Head presided over by Dr. Johnson almost a century earlier—but, appropriately, taking place on a wild mountaintop instead of in an elegant London coffeehouse. Though none of the three literary giants present wrote up the occasion, two of the publishers who arranged it reported delightedly on the party scrambling over the rocks at the summit pinnacles, "puns flying off in every direction like sparks among the bushes":

> We scattered over the cliffs, Herman Melville to seat himself, the boldest of all astride a projecting low stick of rock while Dr. Holmes peeped about the cliffs and protested it affected him like ipecac. Hawthorne looked wildly about for the great carbuncle. Mathews read Bryant's poem. The exercise was glorious.

But though all the more celebrated names of American transcendentalism touched on Northeastern mountains, it remained for a lesser figure of the time to write the book that truly captured the spirit of the pre-Civil War vision of the hills. *The White Hills* appeared in 1859—that is, not at the start, but at the full flood both of antebellum mountain tourism and romantic preoccupation with the sublime. It was an overnight bestseller, striking a responsive chord in that generation of awestruck mountain tourists.

Thomas Starr King was born in New York City on December 17, 1824, and moved to Charlestown, Massachusetts, at age ten. When he was fifteen his father died, and the boy was forced to go to work, becoming first a schoolteacher, then a bookkeeper in the Charlestown Navy Yard, with no time or money for mountain sojourns.

However, this slender youth with the rich and powerful voice seized every opportunity for self-improvement, read avidly, attended evening lectures, and at age twenty began to preach. An eloquent, passionate speaker, he was soon accounted one of the finest preachers in Boston.

Within a year he was appointed minister of the Universalist Church in Charlestown. Three years later, not quite twenty-four years old, he was installed as pastor at the Hollis Street Unitarian Church in Boston. His circle of acquaintances rapidly expanded to include Emerson, Whittier, Longfellow, and fellow preachers Henry Ward Beecher and Edward Everett Hale.

The following summer he made his first trip to the White Mountains and in 1850 began a ten-year practice of summering there, usually at the Alpine House in Gorham. (A rumor that he visited the White Mountains as a boy of twelve or thirteen, which occasionally appears in print, has been pretty well discredited by White Mountain historians.) Beginning in 1853 he began sending articles about the mountains to the *Boston Transcript*. In 1859 these articles formed the basis of a book called *The White Hills: Their Legends, Landscape, and Poetry*.

The very next year, the Reverend Mr. King accepted a call to a church in San Francisco. In short, he was in the White Mountains for fewer than a dozen summers. In California he preached the antislavery crusade and roamed the mountains sufficiently to have a California peak (along with one in New Hampshire) named after him. At age thirty-nine, Thomas Starr King was dead of pneumonia.

Meanwhile *The White Hills* had become an immediate and continuing success. It is a book hard to classify, one that would probably not be written and certainly not published today. It is in part a guidebook to the mountain region, part an anthology of poetry about mountains in general, part a retelling of all the old legends and famous incidents (the Willey slide disaster gets eleven pages of prose, followed by a forty-stanza poem), part a series of reflective essays on how to appreciate mountain scenery and comprehend its religious meaning. The book is 403 pages long, its chapters organized mostly by regions ("The Pemigewasset Valley and Franconia," "The Notch and its Vicinity," "The Glen," and so forth), with two special chapters contributed by Edward Tuckerman on the history of exploration and on the vegetation. Interspersed are short and long excerpts from the mountain poetry of a broad range of bards. Also of contemporary charm are more than sixty line drawings. An opening quotation is appropriately from Ruskin, assuring us that the Garden of Eden must have been in a mountain setting.

The sublime never had a more enthusiastic advocate in the White Mountains. Riding up Mount Washington's carriage road, looking across the Great Gulf at the Northern Presidentials, Starr King wrote:

> There is no such view to be had east of the Mississippi of mountain architecture and sublimity. . . . We call them barren, but there is a richer display of the creative power and art on Mount Adams yonder than on any number of square miles in the lowlands of New England equal to the whole surface of that mountain.

In the midst of a ten-page Ruskinian peroration, he intones:

> The great mountains rise in the landscape as heroes and prophets in history, enobled by what they have given, sublime in the expressions of struggle and pain, invested with the richest draperies of light, because their brows have been torn, and their cheeks been furrowed by toils and cares in behalf of districts below. Upon the mountains is written the law, and in their grandeur is displayed the fulfillment of it, that perfection comes through suffering.

The sublime, yes—but also the pastoral. New Hampshire at midcentury was more completely cleared of forest than ever before or since. In the eyes of the Unitarian minister, agricultural pursuits juxtaposed nicely with mountain crags. He wrote approvingly of the Pliny Ridge "on which, far up towards the summit, the wilderness has been displaced by smiling farms." A 50-acre field of rye high on the slopes of Mount Moriah, a desecration that would offend lovers of wilderness today, was to Starr King an asset that

> made a visit to the Village of Gorham a greater delight. . . . Nature had plainly been longing for the necessity of the agriculture that would bind a new sheaf for her harvest of hues.

For all this, however, King strongly valued wilderness as well. As the bridle paths were built during the 1850s, he could recall with nostalgia the days when rougher paths were the only means of ascent. He linked up with the Gorham guide James Gordon to explore previously uncharted routes on the wilder sides of the Northern Presidentials. He and Gordon were said to have led the first party to ascend King Ravine (named for him) on Mount Adams in 1857.

No one lingered more lovingly on the splendors of New Hampshire's humble hills. Madison and Adams appeared to him as

> a lioness and lion crouched side by side, half resting, half watching, with muscles ready in a moment for vigorous use. . . . those of Madison a little more feminine than those of Adams, but both majestic.

From the Glen, the five chief Presidentials seemed at one time "petals . . . of a mighty flower" and at another, in an extended analogy, a vocal quintet (Madison as soprano, Clay alto, Adams tenor, Jefferson baritone, Washington bass).

Mountains had to be appreciated in precisely the right way, "at the fitting hour of the afternoon and through a favoring air." One particular view of Madison (from a hill 4 miles west of Gorham) was best "after tea, and before sunset, when the light is most propitious." The slightest change of place or time of day altered the perfection of the vision.

What a great difference is made in the effect of a landscape by a very slight change of position on the road. . . . Sometimes the beauty of scenes depends on the hour when you visit them, sometimes on the nicely calculated distance. . . . Some hills need rain, or a thick air, to tone down the raggedness of their foreground, and reveal the beauty of their lines. Others show best under the noon-light; others demand the sunset glow.

Starr King's purple rhapsodies were usually effective, but sometimes his metaphors misfired, as in this description of the view from the top of Willard: "A man stands there as an ant might stand on the edge of a huge tureen." The grand style was vulnerable to parody; no matter—Shakespeare and Beethoven and even the Bible can be delightfully parodied. Starr King's anthem of celebration of New Hampshire's mountains won the praise of White Mountain chronicler Frederick Kilbourne, that it "will never be equaled or superseded in its field." Even with today's altogether different social climate and tastes, a modern reader who approaches the book with leisure to linger and an appreciation of its context will find it an inspiration without equal. In its day it guided a generation of tourists to come to and appreciate the White Hills, in the era of bridle paths and summit houses.

Chapter 8

The first mountain tourists

THE ARTISTS, writers, and philosophers set the tone for the age, or at least for those with leisure. Mountain sojourns became an increasingly popular pastime—not just two-day stops at the quaint, rustic Crawfords', but two-week, monthlong, or even summerlong sojourns in mountain vacation centers. The first full generation of mountain tourists had arrived.

Nor was this leisure class a tiny elite of millionaires. A detailed study of 1850s hotel registers in the White Mountains by Peter B. Bulkley demonstrated that a remarkably broad social spectrum participated in mountain vacations, including "a very significant degree of patronage from those of more modest economic means and lower occupational rank." Americans from all walks of life viewed the mountains as sublime.

During the middle years of the nineteenth century, at least three categories of mountain climbers were present.

Summer tourists and the guides who escorted them accounted for the greatest number of hikers on the big peaks such as Washington and Lafayette, Mansfield and Camel's Hump, as well as on mountaintops associated with summer vacation centers such as Pine Orchard or Maine's Mount Desert. These people are what this chapter's mostly about.

Local residents also climbed neighboring mountains more than before, it seems likely, but the evidence is insufficient to judge how many locals climbed or how often. Typically the majority of the resident population seems to have ignored or even resented the mountains. A traveler coming through Franconia Notch encountered a small sawmill set up right in the notch itself, and when he asked the operator about the famous Old Man's profile, he received the answer "Dunno—never see it." A man who had farmed on the flanks of Camel's Hump for twenty years told another traveler that he had never hiked that graceful peak: "The furthest up I've be'n is that spur yonder. The cows got loose once and I had t'er go up there and get 'em." Another, whose farm was near the Northern Presidentials, responded to an inquiry about them, "Oh, drat the mountains! I never look at 'em. Ask the old woman." Starr King asked a farmer in

Gorham what he thought of the scenic Presidentials overlooking his fields; said the farmer, "It's nice, but we often have 'em here." Another farmer in Randolph told King irritably that he "wish[ed] they was flat." Nevertheless several accounts show that local people climbed Moosilauke as a frequent pastime, and Burlington Vermonters climbed Mansfield and occasionally Camel's Hump. Early chroniclers of Mount Washington, Moses Sweetser and Edward Tuckerman, allude to "Jackson people" using an old path (Gibbs's?) up the eastern side of Mount Washington. Lower elevations such as Vermont's Ascutney, New Hampshire's Monadnock, the Camden Hills of Maine, the Holyoke Range in Massachusetts, Meriden's Hanging Hills (Connecticut), and the Hudson Highlands doubtless were often climbed by the locals.

The professionals, the third category of climbers, were this generation's successors to the Monument Line surveyors of Katahdin (chapter 6). A lot of boundary lines were run in the middle years of the century, many of them in hill country. Now mapmakers were out there too: the first respectable map of the White Mountains was produced in 1853 by Prof. G. P. Bond of Harvard. Timber cruisers roamed the hills of northern New England in large numbers. In the early days one could set a sawmill anywhere and start cutting, but by midcentury each lumber king had to be looking for the best stands left, to get there before his competitors. So they sent cruisers ranging all over the hills, doubtless going over many a summit on their way. Equally anonymous to history were the hunters roaming the mountain regions. Nameless in dark oblivion let them dwell.

But the tone of the age was set by the mountain tourists. All the Northeastern mountain areas were inundated by this first wave of recreationists. The Catskills, the Berkshires, and the White Mountains were engulfed. The Green Mountains began to see more visitors. Even lonely Katahdin became a shrine for hardy adventurers. And, trailing all the rest, even the wild Adirondacks finally drew attention.

This first period of recreational climbing had a clearly discernible beginning and end, with characteristics that were quite different from those of later periods. From its beginnings in the 1830s, the wave of mountain tourism rose sharply in the 1840s and reached flood tide in the 1850s. During the Civil War the wave subsided, continuing to ebb for another ten years. Not until the late 1870s did mountain tourism again reach the heights of the 1850s. Furthermore, there are unique qualities to those years, 1830–70, so that in one sense we shall not look upon their like again.

Travel to and fro consumed a major share of any mountain trip. Stagecoach and boat were the original modes of access. It took all day to get from New York City to the Catskills, two or even three days from Boston to the White Mountains. These early methods of travel had a flavor all their own.

Prerailroad modes of transportation generated their own self-contained social life. Hour after hour passed aboard the spacious decks of steamers—before that, on the even more leisurely and elegant sailing sloops—or jouncing along in four- or six-horse coaches. Early journals revel in the repartee among travelers, mild flirtations among the younger set, maneuvering as to who would ride inside and who on top of the coach, speculations about one's fellow travelers, their backgrounds and intentions, and the colorful personalities of the stage drivers and sailors to whom the long, slow journeys were a way of life. Minor mishaps could escalate to major trauma due to muddy roads, rough waters, or equipment breakdowns. It was all a richly varied and unpredictable part of the mountain vacation experience.

On October 8, 1851, an event of portent for Hudson valley hiking history occurred: the first train of the Hudson River Railroad made the run from New York City to Albany. In the same year the Atlantic and St. Lawrence opened connections from Portland, Maine, to Gorham, New Hampshire. Already during the 1840s rail lines had been constructed between the Massachusetts towns of Springfield and Pittsfield, and from the Hudson River to Pittsfield, providing access by train to the Berkshires from both east and west. In 1842 the Housatonic Railroad wound through northwest Connecticut from Bridgeport to West Stockbridge. In 1848 rail service reached Keene, New Hampshire, at the base of Monadnock. The Vermont Central pushed through to Burlington in 1849, passing close to many of the Green Mountains en route.

The railroad's cataclysmic change in speed was more than arithmetic: it altered, immediately and forever, the flavor of the trip to the mountains. The contrast was even sharper than that between sloop and steamboat. Railroad trips were faster, thus occupying less of the traveler's time. Train trips were more hectic, certainly noisier, and involved less social interplay among travelers or between travelers and drivers. On the other hand, railroad travel had a new kind of excitement and bustle. For many travelers, trains seemed to have a personality of their own in ways that perhaps steamboats and coaches did not, and that surely today's airplanes and buses do not.

The railroads not only changed the trip there, they also changed the mountain vacation centers themselves. Consider the alterations in life at Gorham, New Hampshire, after 1851, for example. At last it was possible for Bostonians to be in the playground of New England in one day; they could now entrain at Boston in the morning, change at Portland, Maine, and step off in the shadow of the Northern Presidentials by 5:00 P.M. From an inconsequential cluster of houses, Gorham rapidly became an important tourist center. Two high-class hotels sprang into being. Population increased fourfold between 1850 and 1860. Climbing patterns completely changed too. Mount Washington, almost invariably climbed from the west and southwest for the preceding twenty years, suddenly turned its face eastward: in the following twenty years, the regular climbing route began at the Glen, and the old Crawford Path was so little used that it became almost extinct. Mountains such as Moriah, Hayes, and Baldcap, scarcely heard of before, became popular climbing objectives. Corresponding impacts were felt in the Catskills and the Berkshires as the railroads lapped the miles and licked the valleys up.

If antebellum transportation had its own style, so did the hotel accommodations of the era. These were the years when the Catskill Mountain House reached the height of its prestige as undisputed monarch of mountain resorts. After the Civil War other grand hotels might eclipse it in size but none in style. Its estate of 3,000 acres included North and South lakes, much of North and South mountains and, above all, that classic view from the columned piazza. On an American tour from 1834 to 1836, the British traveler and writer Harriet Martineau gazed on that view and glowed that she would rather have missed the prairies, the Mississippi, and even Niagara than this view. In 1847, a step farther into the mountain country, the Laurel House opened a kind of middle-class sister establishment, but no other major competitor appeared in the Catskills until the 1870s.

In the White Mountains, Crawford Notch, where it all started, remained a center for hotel activity, but the Crawfords themselves became anachronisms as the day of the grand hotel inexorably approached the notch. Their rough buildings, no matter how expanded to fit in the extra guests now coming to the mountains, could never pretend to elegance. Old Abel, Ethan, and Thomas were simple innkeepers, mountain guides, and raconteurs around the common room fire of a cool summer's evening, but they could satisfy neither the numbers nor the expectations of the new generation of mountain tourists. During the 1830s and 1840s came a new breed of city-bred professional hotel managers. Horace Fabyan, who arrived in 1837, symbolized the change; he was a businessman from Portland, not born in a frontier cabin in the notch. Fabyan's accommodations could pretend to the epithet *grand*, boasting as many as one hundred rooms, as well as such displays as a 60-foot carpeted living room. Equally grand hotels opened in the other White Mountain notches, notably the Glen House in Pinkham Notch in 1852 and the Profile House in Franconia Notch in 1853.

In Vermont mountain tourism did not catch hold as widely as in New Hampshire, but the 1850s saw some moves in this direction. In 1850 a Stowe innkeeper enlarged his dwelling, named it the Mansfield House, and played up its proximity to Mount Mansfield in his advertising. Mountain-ringed Manchester became a major resort, the Equinox House opening there in 1853. Lake Willoughby—until 1850 "hardly accessible, on either side"—bloomed with the opening of the Lake House in 1852.

The Berkshires saw a slightly different kind of development, more like what happened later elsewhere. Instead of patronizing grand hotels, the gentry who vacationed in Lenox and Stockbridge chose to build their own magnificent estates and mansions. This movement is often dated from Samuel Ward's estate in Lenox, built in 1846, but the 1850s was when the first generation of the Berkshires' stately mansions rose among the hills. Perhaps because of this trend, relatively few public accommodations of grand style appeared in the hill country of western Massachusetts. Stockbridge's Red Lion Inn (enlarged in 1848) was one notable exception; others included the Stockbridge House and the Curtis House in Lenox.

For most people who came to these mountain centers, enjoyment of the surroundings largely took the form of armchair mountaineering—gazing at the sublime and picturesque views from rockers on the verandas of the hotels and boardinghouses in the valleys beneath the heights. A few hiking trails were built, attesting the fact that actually walking up high places was no longer the exclusive province of the adventurous or eccentric. Still, pre-1870 hiking centered on a few prestigious peaks, and most of the rich profusion of ridges and summits was visited little or not at all.

The decade of the 1850s witnessed a phenomenon in Northeastern mountain history that rose quickly and faded almost as fast: the era not of hiking trails but of bridle paths and summit houses. There were buildings on mountains before 1850, and a few would remain into the twentieth century. But during the 1850s bridle paths and summit houses were seen as the norm, the principal mode of operation on a mountain. Even hotels were built on the very tops. More New England peaks offered overnight summit accommodations, albeit often quite primitive, before the Civil War than at any time later in history.

This fashion is as remarkable for its quick demise as for its rapid growth. During the 1860s and first half of the 1870s, mountain tourism went into a downward phase of its cycle. Many of the bridle paths and summit buildings lost patronage, were not maintained, and were essentially lost. Only the big-name attractions survived continuously: Washington, Mansfield, Moosilauke. There was a brief renewal of interest during the 1880s, with sporadic instances later. But never again did so many mountains have both summit buildings and bridle paths or even maintained roads to the very top as during the ten years before the Civil War.

As described in chapter 7, buildings atop Massachusetts's modest eminences were a fashion of the 1820s. The 1850s boom was largely a phenomenon of Starr King's White Hills and the Green Mountains of Vermont.

The White Mountains

During the 1850s there were five routes up Mount Washington: all five were passable by horses. These were the two original Crawford Paths: the Davis Path, built up the Montalban Ridge in 1845; the new Glen

House bridle path, completed by 1852; and the Stillings Path, built the same year primarily to haul building material from the north side (Randolph) for the summit hotels. There were no purely pedestrian paths to the top of the mountain. By contrast, a generation earlier there had been two paths (maybe three, counting the Gibbs or Jackson Path), all designed for foot travel. A generation later there were half a dozen ways to go up, but no horse could comfortably use any route but the carriage road (see figure 8.1).

The first hotel on the summit of Washington opened in 1852, and the following year a second opened as well. By 1854 the two hotels were under one management. Various other buildings have crowded onto the summit over the years since. The top of Mount Washington became one of the major tourist attractions of the Northeast and hummed with a busy commercial life from the 1850s on. Its preeminence as a tourist attraction was assured when a carriage road to the top was completed in 1861 and a cog railroad in 1869.

Almost every other peak in the White Mountains that had any trail at all had a bridle path, and most of these also had a summit building, whether a full-service hotel or a simple structure for protection from bad weather (see figure 8.2).

Lafayette's original path, built in 1826 (today's Greenleaf Trail), was widened for horseback use in 1853. A second trail, built around 1850, had already been converted (today's "Old Bridle Path") in 1852. Toward the end of the decade a summit building was erected; this was not a hotel, just a primitive refuge, the foundations of which are still evident.

Moosilauke had its first bridle path (today's Glencliff Trail) in 1840. A second was built in 1858 and widened to become the carriage road a few years later. In 1859 a third bridle path was built from Benton (now the Benton Trail). In 1860 the Prospect House was built on the very top and operated as a hotel for more than eighty years. Unlike Washington and Lafayette, Moosilauke also had two purely foot paths, probably a reflection of this gentle giant's perennial popularity as a friendly neighborhood mountain for Sunday excursions by the locals.

Mount Moriah enjoyed a brief moment of unwonted prominence when the railroad first arrived in Gorham. In 1854 a bridle path was built to the top and a building roughly comparable to Lafayette's was erected just below the summit, though this was of log while Lafayette's was of stone. Moriah was a fashionable objective as long as its domineering neighbor, Washington, had only bridle paths. In 1861, as soon as the carriage road to the top of Washington opened, Moriah's path and building fell into disuse. Eventually the former partially and the latter completely disappeared.

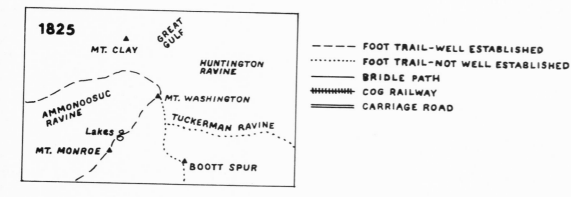

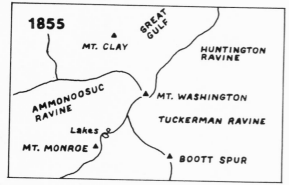

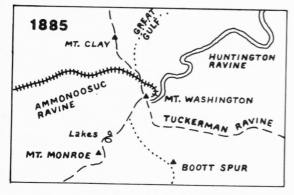

Figure 8.1. Paths on Mount Washington, thirty-year intervals: 1825–1885 Big changes took place on Mount Washington during the middle of the nineteenth century, reflecting powerful shifts in people's attitudes toward mountain climbing and in their expectations about how to ascend the big peak. In the 1820s there were just two well-established foot trails. The 1850s saw the ascendancy of bridle paths: of five routes to the summit, all five were passable on horseback. After the Civil War, however, tastes changed again: a carriage road displaced one bridle path, a cog railway displaced another, and purely foot travel resumed on other approaches.

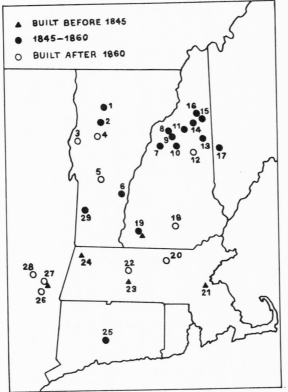

Key to numbers

1. Mansfield
2. Camel's Hump
3. Snake Mountain
4. Lincoln Peak
5. Killington
6. Ascutney
7. Moosilauke
8. Bald Peak
9. Lafayette
10. Osceola
11. Willard
12. Chocorua
13. Kearsarge
14. Washington
15. Moriah
16. Hayes
17. Pleasant
18. Uncanoonuc
19. Monadnock
20. Wachusett
21. Great Blue Hill
22. Sugar Loaf
23. Holyoke Range
24. Greylock
25. West Peak
26. Overlook Mountain
27. Pine Orchard
28. Tower Mountain
29. Equinox

Figure 8.2. Mountaintop buildings in the Northeast Mountaintop buildings, ranging from primitive shelters to comfortable hotels, were largely a phenomenon of the middle of the nineteenth century. Of almost thirty such structures, a majority were built during the years 1845-60. Many of these had fallen into ruins by the twentieth century. This map does not include fire towers and ski facilities, both of which were twentieth-century phenomena.

Mount Willard was an early entry, with a bridle path in 1846 and a modest hut on top. For many years full carriages carried Crawford House guests up Willard.

Mount Pleasant (known today as Eisenhower) had a bridle path during the late 1840s, starting from the hotels north of the notch.

Mount Kearsarge in the town of Bartlett enjoyed a reputation as a splendid point from which to view the higher peaks. Perhaps as early as 1845 a building appeared on its top. A succession of fires and cycles of disuse led to many later versions, one still in ruins by the 1980s. During the 1850s there was at least a bridle path to the top, with intermittent efforts to improve it for use by carriages.

At the north end of Franconia Notch, little Bald Mountain had a very popular bridle path to its top during the 1850s, and an observatory building of sorts.

Mount Osceola, the dominant peak in Waterville Valley, had a bridle path during the 1850s. There was also a structure on top but apparently very primitive.

When a hotel opened in Waterville Valley in the 1860s, a path for horses was opened north past Greeley Ponds all the way through to Crawford Notch. It was claimed that some accomplished equestrians thereby rode all the way to the top of Washington from Waterville in a single day.

These bridle paths were not, as one might suppose, the apex of a graduated pyramid or system of paths of all kinds; they were virtually all there were on the White Mountains. The tip of the iceberg was bigger than the rest. From all that can be gleaned from old maps, guidebooks, and contemporary accounts, very few other mountains had paths of any kind to their summits. Berry pickers had worn tracks on some other peaks known to be habitat for the savory whortleberry—the Moats, Welch, Baldface, and others. There were no trails on the Carter Range or Wildcats, and none on the many mountains in the broad Pemigewasset Wilderness, except for the valley-level fishermen's trails (which were probably well tramped).

South of the White Mountains, Monadnock had already had a foretaste of the mountain house fashion, with the "shantees" of Fife and Dinsmore during the 1820s. During the 1850s the bridle path–summit house fever spread to Monadnock and produced a considerable upgrading of facilities there. In 1855 or 1856 a nearby farmer named Joseph Fassett built a frame cabin halfway up the south side of the mountain and improved the trail for use by wagons. Fassett's did a booming business as a refreshment stand for a couple of years, but the sudden death of the proprietor ended this enterprise. It was soon succeeded by a far more important one. In 1860 Moses Cudworth purchased a tract of land that included a small flat area within a few hundred feet of Fassett's. During that year and the following, Cudworth began to erect buildings to accommodate guests and their horses overnight. Cudworth operated there on a modest basis for two or three years, but when he sold out his successors, George D. and Abbie J. Rice, put up a comfortable three-and-a-half-story hotel with the capacity for one hundred guests. Though fire razed this first Half Way House in 1866, the profitability of the site on so popular a mountain quickly brought about its replacement, and Monadnock's Half Way House flourished well into the twentieth century. Such a handsome hotel required a first-class carriage road to its door. Nevertheless, the rugged upper contours of the mountain resisted the bridle path craze, and it remained accessible only by foot paths.

A similar picture may be seen in Vermont: wherever mountains were regularly visited, bridle paths or carriage roads soon appeared. Buildings providing overnight accommodations sprouted on three peaks where there had been none before the 1850s.

Mount Mansfield received attention from both the west (Underhill) and east (Stowe) side. The former was convenient to the city of Burlington and accordingly invited the attentions of local residents. The latter proved an ideal site for a mountain vacation center and soon attracted the summer tourist set.

As early as 1830 a survey was begun for a road partway up the west side. When that was built is uncertain, but in 1850 the first Halfway House on the Underhill side was put up at the end of that road, about one mile short of the summit ridge. In 1856 Underhill entrepreneurs erected a small summit building on the Nose. In 1859 or 1860 the Halfway House Trail was made passable for horses (see figure 8.3).

Until the late 1850s contemporary accounts indicate that the west side of the mountain was the more common approach. Mansfield may have enjoyed local popularity from the city of Burlington, less than 20 miles away, comparable to that of Moosilauke. The local newspaper admonished its readers in 1859,

> An occasional trip to the top of Mansfield Mountain is becoming one of the necessaries of life to all who dwell in sight of that noble elevation.

However, it was the east side and the town of Stowe where mountain tourism ultimately became more firmly established, beginning with the arrival of William Henry Harrison Bingham. A lawyer who acquired title to considerable land on the east side of the mountain, Bingham progressively developed the tourist business out of Stowe. In 1856 he opened his own "Halfway House" on the east side; in 1857 he established a small hotel at the 3,600-foot level; in 1858 he moved this building on up to just under the Nose; by 1860 he was enlarging this hotel and doing a thriving business. In 1864 he built an enormous hotel in Stowe. Along with these developments went the inevitable bridle path up the east ridge to the Nose. This evolved by stages into a carriage road, completed to the hotel by the 1870s.

The Mansfield "summit" hotel enjoyed a reputation as "a far more complete hotel than any other summit house in New England." "Cozy" bedrooms took in fifty people, with a comfortable sitting room, dining room, and bar also provided. Before long there was even a high-altitude croquet court outside on the tundra. As early as 1860, an enthusiastic press hailed Bingham's lofty emporium as "the Astor House of those altitudes."

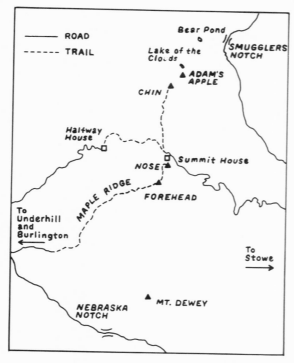

Figure 8.3. Mount Mansfield in 1860 Vermont's highest peak had two hotels by 1860: a Halfway House built on the Underhill-Burlington side in 1850, and a series of overnight accommodations at different locations on the Stowe side, culminating in a very fashionable hotel—"the Astor House of these altitudes" —near the summit ridgeline by 1858. By 1870 a carriage road ascended the latter side to bring guests in comfort to this hotel, while both a bridle path and a foot trail (on the Maple Ridge) afforded access from the west.

At about the same time tourist activity began to grow on Camel's Hump. In 1859 Samuel Ridley and sons of North Duxbury erected a hotel in a clearing 3/10 miles below the summit. A carriage road provided direct access from the railroad station to within 3 miles of the summit, a bridle path proceeding from there. By the early 1870s, however, both hotel and carriage road had fallen into disuse and disrepair. The hotel reportedly burned in 1875.

During the 1850s efforts to put a road up Ascutney finally bore fruit, when a carriage road was built in 1858, predecessor of today's auto road, though in a different location. When D.C. Linsley's new 14-foot-by-20-foot stone house opened on the top on September 4, 1858, a crowd of three hundred was on hand for a full dinner, "interesting speeches," and a musical salute by the Windsor Cornet Band.

Joseph Seavey Hall, shortly to become proprietor of the buildings atop Mount Washington, was living in East Burke, Vermont, in 1853 and cut a trail to the top of Burke Mountain. This was later enlarged to be a bridle path.

The 1850s is also when the Lake Willoughby circle of mountains became popular. The Willoughby Lake House opened in 1852 and soon fostered bridle paths to the tops of Pisgah (then called Ananance) and possibly Hor. No summit buildings were constructed.

Both Equinox in the south and Jay in the north end of the state had roads to the top by 1860.

In the modest resurgence of interest in summit building during the 1880s, some other Vermont mountains added to the ranks of mountain houses and roads, Killington, Lincoln, and Snake among them. But these peaks were not part of the 1850s summit development boom.

Maine

In Maine, Mount Pleasant had a summit building as early as 1845, together with a bridle path that eventually matured into carriage road status. Mount Desert's network of bridle paths and carriage roads began to grow during the 1850s, though its first true summit building, the lodge on Green (now called Cadillac) Mountain, was not built until 1866 and the major tourist boom there was definitely a post-Civil War occurrence.

One of the more bizarre manifestations of the bridle path–summit house craze of the 1850s was a proposal that might have profoundly altered the future character of Katahdin had the project not died a merciful death. Influential voices in Maine politics doubtless envied the commercial successes that brought tourists and their dollars to Mounts Washington, Lafayette, and Mansfield, and to Pine Orchard. In 1856 the state legislature chartered a road to be built from the Aroostook Road at Stacyville (see figure 9.1) all the way to the very summit of Katahdin. Two years later these authorities employed David Haynes to survey the centerline, and Haynes in turn took on Marcus Keep (of whom much more in chapter 9) and Charles Lyon as chainmen, with Thomas H. Haynes as axman. These four men journeyed to remote Chimney Pond, where they camped on November 3, a very late date to be out in the mountains and that far north. (An early December climb of Washington in the same year was regarded with nearly superstitious dread as perilous in the extreme.) Nevertheless, on November 4, the survey party climbed to the top "and commenced our survey of the road at a corner of a rock marked K, it being the highest part of the mountain." These optimistic roadmakers marked a centerline down a slide not far from today's Saddle Trail, a rugged hiking trail by any standards and nothing but absurd for carriages. Indeed, Haynes's field notes show that the route from "the brink of the precipice" to the inlet of Chimney Pond was surveyed by means other than point-to-point chaining, "as the face of the mountain is such that I was doubtful of obtaining correct measure with the chain." Over the next few days, the men methodically surveyed the proposed route to the Aroostook Road, despite storms and a 12-inch snowfall on November 7. Whether or not even a bridle path could ever have been built up Katahdin was never put to the test, as no further steps seem to have been taken and the project disappeared from history.

There is no record of a building on the top of little Mount Kineo in the nineteenth century, perhaps because it was such a short distance from the hotel on Moosehead Lake. Meanwhile, the big, wild mountains of western Maine—Bigelow, Saddleback, Abraham, the Crockers, and their neighbors—remained untamed.

The fascination with bridle paths and summit houses during the 1850s set the dominant tone for the first wave of mountain recreation. The tourists of that generation did not perceive mountains as the pedestrian preserves that their children did, beginning in the late 1870s, or as we do today.

Remember, the generation of the 1850s had newly discovered the sublimity of mountain scenery, and it was this visual and inspirational experience that they sought, not exercise. It was the age of Starr King, not of Partridge, nor yet of Cook and Peek (who during the 1880s thundered along mountain tops and cut steep hiking trails). Placing hotels on summits was a symptom of an urge to tame wild mountains that not many years before had been seen as frightening and inhospitable. Veneration and awe had replaced fear and distrust of the alpine heights. So the mountain lovers of the 1850s wanted to look at mountain scenery either from the vantage points in the valleys below or by riding up to see the summit prospects. This objective could perfectly well be satisfied from the comfort of a coach, or at least on horseback. (The horses bagged a lot of peaks in those days, or rather bagged one peak a lot of times—one guide claimed his horse had climbed Mount Washington sixty-eight times.) It did not yet occur to the riders that it could be fun to get off and walk. As one writer said of Monadnock,

> Though it is very tiresome to walk to the top of it, people often do so, for the sake of the wide prospect which they can there behold.

Mountains were to be seen. They were not yet primarily—as they became after the Civil War—places to walk.

Chapter 9

Katahdin: A test for the adventurous

To the average citizen of Boston or New York in the 1850s, anyone who climbed any mountain must have seemed irrationally fond of exertion and discomfort. But those who did go to the hills knew they could often attain their goal with bridle paths and summit houses, and as many as five thousand people did reach the top of Mount Washington each year.

The spirit of mountaineering, the pursuit of the difficult, required some greater challenge. To walk up a carriage road or bridle path or well-marked trail afforded ample opportunity to behold the sublime, but it lacked the ambiance of genuine adventure.

Katahdin filled this need for challenge. During the late 1840s and 1850s, the region's "greatest mountain,"[a] still no easy peak to reach, much less climb, and still without a trail, became a test for the adventurous, a "lodestone of great power," challenging those for whom the White and Green mountains were already too accessible. A small but distinctive parade of interesting personalities made expeditions to Pamola's stronghold, which often met them with stern rebuffs. Recall that the peak had been climbed no more than half a dozen times as late as 1836—which was just one year before Horace Fabyan introduced modern hotel management to the tourist-thronged Mount Washington area.

Even for this remote citadel, however, time and distance were eroding, though the north woods put up a stubborn defense against change. By the 1830s large-scale logging operations were moving up the East Branch of the Penobscot (see figure 9.1). In 1832 the Aroostook Road sliced through the wilderness, passing the town of Sherman, roughly 25 miles due east of Katahdin. In 1835 William Hunt established his homestead on the Wassataquoik Stream and the East Branch, with a road connecting it to the Aroostook Road at the little settlement of Stacyville. When logging began on the Wassataquoik in 1841, tote roads pushed in still closer to the peak, rough and temporary but nonetheless useful to would-be Katahdin climbers while they lasted. By 1845 logging roads reached

---

[a]The original Indian words from which we derive the name Katahdin are said to have meant "greatest mountain." See, for example, Hakola, *Legacy of a Lifetime*, p. xiii.

almost to Russell and Pogy ponds, not 10 miles northeast of the Tableland. This proved as close as civilized transportation could get to Katahdin until well into the 1880s, however.

In 1836 the first serious botanical investigations, in the spirit of Cutler, Boott, and Bigelow from a generation before, were finally introduced on Katahdin. Three professors—George Washington Keely and Phineas Barnes from Colby College in Waterville, Maine, and Jacob Whitman Bailey of West Point, New York—attempted the Abol Slide. It proved a challenging trip just to get to the mountain and back. Several days' journey on horseback were followed by several days' slogging on foot up "a

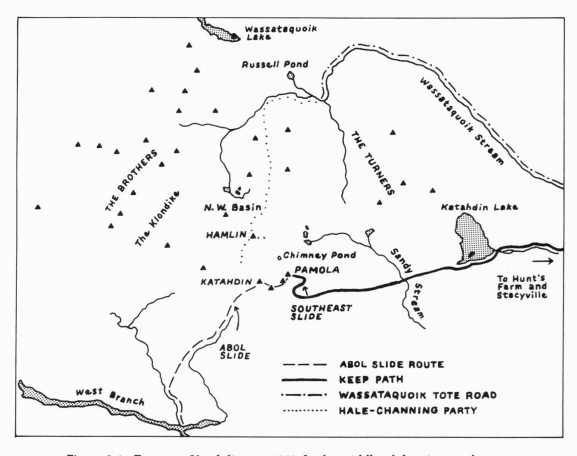

Figure 9.1. Routes to Katahdin, ca. 1850 In the middle of the nineteenth century, Katahdin became a test piece for the adventurous hiker. Several parties climbed the Abol Slide. In 1845 two young Cambridge (Massachusetts) intellectuals, Edward Everett Hale and William Francis Channing, took advantage of the newly built Wassataquoik tote road to make an attempt from the north. A few years later the remarkable backwoods minister Marcus Keep built the first true hiking trail into the Katahdin massif and began escorting parties there regularly.

blind path (if path it might be called) which was scarcely passable, although we were on foot. It was so obstructed by fallen trees, tangled roots, bushes and mud holes." At length they reached a pair of primitive log huts crowded with lumbermen, smoke, and, incongruously, a copy of a Sir Walter Scott novel (*The Heart of Midlothian*). Here they hired two "athletic" loggers named McAstlin as guides (though neither had ever been on the mountain), wrapped pork, tea, bread, and salt in blankets, and, slinging these loads over their shoulders, proceeded to bushwhack through the woods toward the foot of the Abol Slide. Plagued by deteriorating weather and an especially difficult stretch of burnt-over woods, they at last reached the "wild confusion" of fractured talus at the base of the slide. After rolling in their blankets for a damp bivouac low on the slide, they started up in a "drizzling mist." Keely and Bailey turned back when they saw the weather worsening; Barnes and the McAstlins went to the top but soon returned "thoroughly drenched, and much fatigued." Even the return journey through the woods was harrowing:

> The heavy rain in the morning had completely drenched the trees and bushes, so that every one we touched sent down upon us a shower, which soon wet us to the skin. Climbing over fallen trees, stumbling at tangled roots, now by main force making a passage through the bushes, and anon falling prostrate, as some rotten branch gave way, to which we had trusted for support, we at last reached the "burnt wood," with much less clothing upon us than when we began our journey. . . . In the endeavor to avoid one swamp, we got into a dozen, besides adding several miles to the length of our route.

With all this effort, success was by no means assured. Two of these three professors failed to reach the top. Another 1836 party, a few days before, missed the prize altogether. Thoreau failed to make the summit in 1846.

In 1836 the state of Maine authorized a geological survey, comparable to the one in New York during which Mount Marcy was first climbed. For state geologist Maine turned to an interesting individual named Charles Thomas Jackson, a brilliant but never quite successful scientific mind, brother-in-law of Ralph Waldo Emerson, and the man for whom Mount Jackson in the Presidential Range was named. This complex man seemed always on the verge of greatness, never there. In scientific pursuits, he is alleged to have worked out the principles of the telegraph, even a working model, but failed to follow up on it, allowing a colleague named Samuel F. B. Morse to see it through. He is also said to have suggested the use of ether as an anesthetic for extracting teeth but turned that idea over to W. T. G. Morton, who thereby became the father of modern dentistry. Similarly in the history of Northeastern mountains: in his travels through western Maine in 1838, Jackson had plans to explore both Saddleback and Bigelow, two major peaks of rugged contours, which might have given him place as a significant explorer of Northeastern mountains, but in both cases bad weather and early snowfalls (October 10 on Saddleback!) disrupted his plans. In the Presidentials, during a subsequent geological survey of New Hampshire, Jackson's reputation was sufficient to win him the honor of having a major peak named after him, yet most hikers now assume that Mount Jackson was named for President Andrew Jackson. One student of early American science says of Jackson:

> His was a wonderful scientific fertility and originality, greater perhaps than any American had ever possessed before. He was the first scientist in New England who lived up fully to European standards. . . . [He was] constantly overflowing with ideas, both concrete and vague, simply had no time in which to carry them out to see where they would lead.

In quest of Maine's geological survey, Jackson devoted considerable attention to the state's mountains during the years 1836–38. After some lesser climbs in the Camden Hills and Mount Desert in the first year, Jackson took a party to Katahdin in 1837, making what was then still an uncommon ascent on September 23. The Abol Slide was their route. Once again Maine's great mountain put up stiff defenses. The party hit wild weather, including cold, snow, wind, and low visibility, and almost started down the wrong way from the summit. Disaster was averted through the foresight of a Penobscot Indian in the party, who had hastily constructed a series of small cairns during the ascent, which they followed back to the top of the slide. In 1838 Jackson and his surveyors spent much time in the western mountains of Maine. Their principal climb of note was Mount Abraham. Although they did not reach the highest point, the south summit, which they did reach, was no easy ascent; even today's peakbaggers rate it a tough objective.

These are the only records of attempts on Katahdin before 1845. When expeditions resumed in that year, it was with an unmistakable sense of deliberately seeking out mountaineering challenge. In 1845 two bright young men of the Massachusetts intellectual elite made a pioneering attempt on Katahdin from the north. Edward Everett Hale was a grandnephew of Revolutionary War Hero Nathan Hale; son of a crusading editor who founded the *North American Review*; brother of Lucretia, who wrote children's books, notably *The Peterkin Papers*; and he was destined for a long career himself as Unitarian clergyman, chaplain of the U.S. Senate, and author, whose best-known work was the popular short story "The Man without a Country." His partner was William Francis Channing, son of William Ellery Channing, a leading Unitarian minister and confidant of Emerson and Thoreau. William Francis Channing was an inventor of some accomplishment with several patents, including the first electric fire alarm telegraph. Hale and Channing had climbed many mountains together: both had worked on Jackson's New Hampshire geological survey in the early 1840s. In the summer of 1845 they determined to test their mettle on an ascent of Katahdin. While they did some botanizing on this trip on behalf of the botanist Asa Gray, basically it was a recreational jaunt. A stagecoach took them to the last regular stop, a backwoods town called Mattawamkeag, where they hired a lumberman named Jackins as a guide. On up the road to Stacyville and in to Hunt's farm they went. From this point they took advantage of the lumbering then just starting to invade the Wassataquoik watershed, walking from lumber camp to lumber camp until they were somewhere in the vicinity of Russell Pond, due north of Katahdin (see figure 9.1). The ascent to the tableland was "steep and hard," characterized by the usual "impassable" scrub evergreens. When they emerged above treeline, they became the first people to tread the north peaks of the massif since the Monument Line surveyors and assuredly the first to be there for recreational reasons. Apparently the little party got as far as Hamlin Peak when darkness fell. To spend the night, they dropped down to shelter on the east side (possibly on the Hamlin Ridge), built a fire, and huddled in blankets. A beautiful night and glorious sunrise ill prepared them for a sudden clouding-up and downpour of rain the next day. Clutching their blankets about them, they went on in the storm, building small cairns to guide their return. When they reached the Saddle and started up the main peak, the precipitation turned from rain to hail. They made a prudent retreat. The walk back across the tableland was a trying experience:

> If you can imagine three men, tightly wrapped in blanket cloaks, with caps bound closely down, strolling along over a bald mountain ridge with a wind like a mill stream knocking them backwards as it chose, and tumbling them and theirs among the rocks, I hope you will do it. There was something ghastly in the sight, for a very slight distance in the fog gave a hazy, indistinct outline to the gracefully flowing drapery,—though the horizontal lines of hail gave evidence enough of the nature of the enemy which we were pressing against so desperately. One was reminded at once of Tiffany's fine drawing of the involuntary race of the *violenti* in Dante's Inferno.

Entering the trees, they lost their way and "went down by a longer and more unpleasant route than we went up." The bushwhacking ordeal was somewhat relieved by the storm's letup, and they were able to reach one of the lumber camps by nightfall. Thus ended the first intentional effort to open a regular climbing route on Katahdin other than the Abol Slide. "Pamola," concluded Hale, "knows how to defend himself from intrusion."

In 1846 two other young men attempted a third approach, walking overland from Hunt's, a long trek through rolling woods, until they reached the base of a slide on the long ridge that descends from the Pamola Peak, at the east end of the celebrated Knife Edge ridge, for which Katahdin is justly famous. On the first try the two youths went partway up this slide and then turned back. For one of them, however, the lure of Pamola's stronghold became irresistible. The Reverend Marcus Keep became the first in a distinguished line of mountaineers who have made Katahdin their special bailiwick: Keep during the forties and fifties, Hamlin during the sixties and seventies, Witherle during the eighties and nineties, and finally Leroy Dudley, the greatest of twentieth-century guides, beginning in 1895, the year after Keep's death.

Those who wrote about Keep described him as "a little odd" and "peculiar in more respects than one." He was a huge man with enormous feet, one leg a bit shorter than the other, "somewhat uncultivated in appearance." Strong-willed, iracund, a prodigious hiker and load-carrier, he always led the way for his parties, "not only because he knew it best, but because it was a right belonging to him as the strongest." He interrupted his ground-eating hiking pace only to let others rest. Sometimes, entering the woods alone, "he would start off and be gone for a week without letting anyone know where he was going." His politics were conservative; one client called him

> so conservative that I was about to say that he leaned backwards. . . .
> He was like the Scotchman who prayed that the Lord would keep him
> right because when he once took a wrong way it was so terribly hard to
> change him.

Born in Vermont and educated at Middlebury College and various theological seminaries, the Reverend Mr. Keep adopted the life of a home missionary in distant Fort Kent, one of the northernmost villages in Maine, on the Canadian border, beginning in 1846. His ecclesiastical career thereafter took him to a variety of tiny settlements in Maine's northeastern reaches, ending in the town of Ashland, where he died in 1894 at the age of seventy-eight.

From the very beginning of his years as a missionary, a major side-interest of his life was the great mountain. That first unsuccessful attempt in 1846 merely whetted his appetite. In 1847 Keep led a party of seven, primarily Maine ministers, back to that slide on the east ridge, well to the east of the Abol Slide, and thereby reached the easternmost outpost of the massif, Pamola Peak. Then they set out across the exposed Knife Edge Ridge to the main summit, the first party known to have made this traverse, one of the glories of Northeastern hill walking. This tightrope crossing took them between sharp drops on both sides, especially dramatic being those into the "great basin" enclosed by Pamola on the southeast, the main summit's ramparts on the southwest, and the rugged Cathedral Ridge on the west. From jewel-like Chimney Pond, the great east walls of this amphitheater rise well over 2,000 feet to form a most exceptional mountain spectacle. Most of the party was appalled by the difficulties and dangers of the Knife Edge, but not Keep. The scene electrified the young cleric, who resolved to return to explore this rugged massif further. The party descended by returning along the Knife Edge and down the east ridge, which later became known as the Keep Ridge. The trip involved two nights spent in the woods, a rare instance of camping out among sporting parties of that era, but Keep seems not to have been daunted by the hardships.

Within a month the Herculean minister was back, this time finding his way onto the floor of the Great Basin, becoming the first person known to have reached Chimney Pond. What thoughts occupied the backwoods preacher as he enjoyed the privilege of gazing on that magnificent amphitheater, one of the East's most compelling mountain images, went unrecorded. Keep was a doer, not a contemplator.

The next summer he returned and, with John Stacy, marked out the first real trail on Katahdin, which became known as the Keep Path. It ran through the woods from Hunt's farm, up the east ridge and across the Knife Edge. When, later that year, the lumber companies cut a tote road through to Katahdin Lake, the Keep Path became the most logical route up the mountain, and Keep's services as a guide naturally became much in demand. From 1849 to 1861, Keep led parties at least once a year, sometimes more often.

In 1849 the Reverend Mr. Keep married Hannah Taylor. In the same year he guided her and others on the first women's ascent of Katahdin (see chapter 12). On this 1849 trip Keep and his party indulged in what proved a futile attempt to name the prominent peaks along the Knife Edge. The true summit was dubbed Moriah; the next eminence south of that (which Keep and his contemporaries thought looked higher) was to be Cario; across the Knife Edge what we now call Chimney Peak was called Etna; Pamola was called Alma. This nomenclature does not appear to have been adopted by anyone else.

In 1861 a state geological team employed Keep's guiding services. This brought together two of the great characters of this era of Northeastern climbing history: the backwoods pastor Keep, and the nationally known geology professor Charles H. Hitchcock, whose subsequent New Hampshire geological survey did so much to open up climbing in the White Mountains.

After 1861 Keep seems to have stopped going to Katahdin. Not until 1881 is there reference to his guiding there again; then it was to escort Charles E. Hamlin up the peak. This was Keep's last guiding venture.

Meanwhile a few other hardy spirits continued to find Katahdin a fit challenge during the bridle path–summit house years when the vast majority of mountain recreationists basked in the less intimidating White Hills of Starr King.

In 1847 a small squad of scientists led by Aaron Young, appointed to conduct a botanical survey of the state of Maine, went in via the northern approaches pioneered by Hale and Channing. This, however, did not become a regular route at this time.

During the 1850s several parties made use of Keep's Path, even without the great man's guiding services: another minister named John Todd in 1852; William L. Jones and his brother, also in 1852; a large party that included the well-known reformer Thomas Wentworth Higginson in 1855; the Rev. Joseph Blake (who had been in the unsuccessful 1836 party mentioned earlier) in 1856, this time successful; a Bowditch party (Henry I. Bowditch, his teenage son, and three teenage nephews) also in 1856; and Col. Luther B. Rogers with a party of twenty-two a year or two later. In 1856 Frederic Church, the artist, and Theodore Winthrop, who wrote up their climb in *Life in the Open Air*, made their ascent, using the old Abol Slide route; Church was often about Katahdin in those years, but this is the first record of his having climbed to the summit.

These tales of bushwhacking through blowdown, burnt-over brush, and bogs with pork and bread slung over the shoulder in blankets, cold and damp bivouacs on the open slides, clambering over the Knife Edge, lengthy approach marches, and smoky lumber camps—all speak of a world different from the fashionable tour of other Northeastern mountain regions. Katahdin remained, right up to the Civil War, a test for the adventurous—a long, long way from the elegance of the Glen House ballrooms, the Catskill Mountain House's columned piazza, or Mr. Bingham's "Astor House of those altitudes" on Mansfield.

But as wild as Katahdin was, there remained yet one entire region of the Northeast that in some ways was wilder still. It is finally time that this history draw the curtain hiding the last holdout of unexplored mountain wilderness in the Northeast: the Adirondacks.

Chapter 10

The Adirondacks at last

T HE ADIRONDACK high peaks yielded grudgingly to civilization. A few settlements took root shortly after 1800 around the fringe of the main mountains, with a total population of about five hundred in the hamlets of Keene, Keene Flats (today's Keene Valley), and North Elba (today's Lake Placid). There is no evidence that these settlers climbed the high peaks, except for the isolated surveyors noted in chapter 7, but they doubtless knew the mountain horizon well as a backdrop to their daily lives. The rest of the world, however, knew little about either these pioneers or the mountains among which they dwelt. To many Americans, the Adirondacks remained desolate wilderness, the wild Cauchsachrage of the early maps. Most people assumed that the Catskills were the highest and most scenic mountains in New York State.

Whereas rumors of precious stones had attracted Mount Washington's first visitors during the seventeenth century, and dreams of riches from land speculation prompted Mount Mansfield's exploration during the eighteenth century, a sober scientific program brought the first party to Mount Marcy during the nineteenth century. New York was, with Massachusetts and Maine, one of the first states to be smitten with zeal to know more about its own geology. In 1819, a ten-thousand-dollar appropriation from the legislature funded a geological survey of Albany and Rensselaer counties (near Albany). The surveyor's job fell to Amos Eaton, a brilliant and colorful personality who had mastered scientific studies while serving a jail term for land fraud. Though he was never to go to the Adirondacks himself, Eaton played a key role in putting together the expeditions that did.

In 1824 Eaton founded the Rensselaer School (now Rensselaer Polytechnic Institute), and in 1830 he hired a Williams College graduate, Ebenezer Emmons, as junior professor of chemistry. About the same time, one of the new students who enrolled was from Hingham, Massachusetts; his name was James Hall.

In 1835 Eaton took the lead among scientists urging the state legislature to fund a survey of New York State's natural resources, with emphasis on geology, and to include the unexplored northern wilds of the Adirondacks. In 1836 the legislature authorized the survey. Eaton also had the ear of Gov. William Learned Marcy, and at his recommendation, the second district, which included the vast wilderness tract, was placed under the direction of his former protégé, Emmons, now a full professor of natural history at Williams College. His former pupil, Hall, now a promising young geologist, was named assistant director. Emmons was just thirty-seven years old; Hall was twenty-five.

Immediately upon receiving the appointment, Emmons embarked on a general tour of the second district, assigning Hall to investigate the iron ores of the McIntyre Iron Works, a mining venture on the southern edge of the high peaks wilderness, in 1836.

It should not be assumed that their previous association as teacher and student at Rensselaer had resulted in a close friendship between Emmons and Hall. On the contrary, the two were distinctly unlike in personality —Emmons sensitive, emotional, and adventurous, Hall physically strong, tough, ambitious. As an undergraduate Hall had borrowed four hundred dollars from Emmons, a sum that was never repaid and remained a source of friction between the two. A letter from Emmons to Hall dated February 18, 1837, shows that the two were at odds over the loan in the very year in which they embarked together on the Marcy exploration. On scientific matters they disagreed, and Hall publicly criticized Emmons's final report. Following the survey they vied for the permanent post of state geologist. Hall won the job and went on to have a long, eventful, and prestigious career as director of the state museum. Emmons settled for the post of state agriculturalist and later moved to North Carolina to become state geologist there, never returning to his native Northeast.

Meanwhile, however, independent of the official survey, another scientist of authority, ability, and vigor was headed their way. William C. Redfield was the first of a minor Adirondack tradition of self-trained, physically robust, indefatigably inquisitive scientists who have taken a keen interest in New York's high peaks over the years. Apprenticed to a harness- and saddle-maker at the age of thirteen and never formally trained in the sciences, Redfield had a lifelong consuming curiosity about natural phenomena, combined with extraordinary energy and physical hardiness, qualities that carried him far among the scientists of that day. Having already made a reputation in meteorology, Redfield was branching out into other fields by the 1830s. In 1843 he helped found the American Association for the Advancement of Science and became its first president. He demonstrated his pedestrian prowess at age twenty-two when he walked 700 miles to visit his mother in Ohio, completing the trip in just 27 days, an average of close to 30 miles per day. Though in his late fifties on his two trips to the Adirondacks in 1836 and 1837, he seemed often to be the prime mover of the party, not put off by vicissitudes, always anxious to be on the move. His journal for one day records:

> I got the party out of bed & breakfast at 7 A.M. instead of 6 as agreed. Party afraid of rain!!! With much demuring got embarked at 9 A.M.

Redfield's curiosity about the north woods led him to contacts with the McIntyre Iron Works, since its properties extended into an unknown mountainous region that was part of the district assigned to Emmons and Hall for geological investigation. Redfield wanted to be a part of so intriguing a venture.

In August 1836 Redfield and Hall met at McIntyre village to join three of the Iron Works partners, Archibald McIntyre, Duncan McMartin, and David Henderson, along with three "woodsmen" of their employ, and David C. Colden, a socially prominent New Yorker and friend of Henderson's. The woodsmen certainly included John Cheney, destined to become Mount Marcy's first and most famous guide, and possibly Harvey Holt. Though primarily an exploratory venture, this 1836 party made some important discoveries of places and pleasures that were to become well-known to Adirondack walkers of later generations.

On a four-day trip, from August 17 to 20, these men traveled up what was then known as the eastern branch of the Hudson River, today called the Opalescent River (see figure 10.1). Redfield remarked that they "found the woods very difficult to penetrate." Fighting brush all that first day—as have Adirondack bushwhackers throughout the high peaks since—they camped at 4:00 P.M. on the banks of the river.

The next day, August 18, the party continued up the Opalescent to "the outlet of a beautiful lake situated between two high mountains estimated by us to be 2 to 3000 feet above the surface of the lake." This lake they named after the wealthy Colden. Its outlet was the site of their second camp.

On August 19 the party awoke to a steady drizzle, dampening their exploratory ambitions. Despite the rain, Henderson and Cheney walked completely around the lake. When the skies cleared, McMartin, McIntyre, and Hall walked up the lakeside to the gap at the northern end. Here, not far through the woods,

> they found a narrow deep Lake bounded abruptly by the precipices of the 2 mountains and discharging its waters into Lake Colden by a descent of 100 or more feet. Into this narrow Lake the avalanches from the upper parts of the mountain had slidden and rendered the Gorge impassable.

This was wild, cliffbound Avalanche Lake. To many Adirondack aficionados this happy discovery must rank scarcely lower in importance than

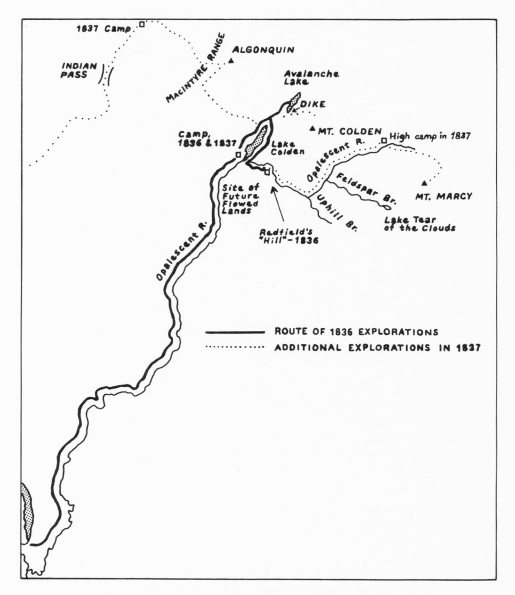

Figure 10.1. Explorations around Mount Marcy, 1836–1837 The first explorers to penetrate the heart of the Adirondack high peaks region placed a camp on the shore of Lake Colden in 1836. Returning there in 1837, they mounted successful ascents of both Marcy and Algonquin, the two highest peaks in New York State. Thus was opened up the last of the Northeast's major ranges.

the first ascents of the high peaks. The precipices are indeed vertical rock walls that reach a height of 200 feet in places, above which the mountainous terrain continues steeply up for 1,800 feet on the east to Mount

Colden, and only a bit less abruptly for more than 2,000 feet on the west to the summits of the MacIntyre Range. Even for today's mountain walkers, Avalanche Lake is an awe-inspiring and almost painfully beautiful place. These earliest explorers must have been doubly struck by the dramatic setting and the unrelenting verticality of the nearly encircling rock walls.

But to Redfield, accompanied by Henderson and (probably) Cheney, fell what was to become the most important discovery of that day for the future of the Adirondacks. They continued up the Opalescent as it flows down into Lake Colden from the mountain heights for what Redfield estimated as 2 miles. Here the curious scientist climbed a "hill" on the south bank and took note of three major peaks within view: one on the west side of Lake Colden, which we now call Algonquin; one on the east side, which he described as "surmounted by a beautiful dome of rock the whole apparently of difficult ascent"—Mount Colden; and, most important, "a third high peak" slightly north of east, which he judged to be (and which in fact was) the highest of all. This seems to have been the first close-up look at Marcy.

Redfield realized that all these summits were lofty indeed and that here, not in the Catskills, lay New York State's highest mountains. The pursuit of that "third high peak," or what he elsewhere dubbed the "High Peak of Essex," became the prime object of the expedition of the following summer.

On their return from Lake Colden, Redfield and most of the others went back to civilization. Hall, McIntyre, and two of the woodsmen went north through spectacular Indian Pass to North Elba, where they were joined by Emmons. On September 20, 1836, Emmons and Hall climbed Whiteface. While that peak had been climbed before, this ascent was noteworthy for two discoveries. First, they measured its altitude as 4,855 feet (compare with today's 4,867 ft.), documenting for the first time that the Adirondacks were indeed considerably higher than the Catskills. Second, they spotted the "High Peak of Essex"—the same "third high peak" noted by Redfield a month earlier—and speculated that it might be the highest in the region. The explorers were finally closing in on Marcy.

In his own journey through Indian Pass during the summer of 1836, Emmons not only saw but climbed Wallface. From the top, he looked over and measured the stupendous cliff that forms the west side of the pass. By peering over the edge, Emmons revealed the adventurous streak that being in the mountains brought out in him. He was thrilled by the giant precipice: "Probably the greatest natural curiosity in the State, except the falls of Niagara," he said.

The summer of 1837 found Emmons, Hall, and Redfield back in the Adirondacks to pursue their geological survey. On August 1, the three scientists assembled at the Iron Works with a large party, including their McIntyre village hosts, McIntyre and Henderson (McMartin had died during the intervening year); the woodsmen who acted as guides, including Cheney and Holt; botanist John Torrey and a young assistant of his, just graduated from Princeton, John Miller; Emmons's son, Ebenezer, Jr.; the artist, Charles Cromwell Ingham; and sundry others. The party that moved north into the high country around Lake Colden was drawn from this large assortment of men. Those who went to the summit of the High Peak of Essex have been reduced, by careful examination of the evidence, to Emmons, Hall, Redfield, Henderson, Torrey, Ingham, and at least two of the guides, probably Cheney and Holt.

On August 3, the summit party left McIntyre, traveled up the Opalescent, and occupied the camp built on the shores of Lake Colden the previous year. The next day they began the ascent. The route retraced Redfield's of the year before, up the Opalescent, but continued higher over unexplored ground. They turned north with the stream at "the South elbow," where Uphill Brook joins the Opalescent. They continued, following the river (now little more than a stream), up the high valley between Marcy and Colden, to establish what they called "Holt's Camp" at the "extraordinary elevation of 3700 feet." They were right below a point where the river steepens perceptibly to form a deep gorge. That afternoon Emmons and Redfield explored farther up the gorge for about half a mile (see figure 10.1).

August 5, 1837, dawned cold; their field notes comment on ice on the vegetation. The party was up and away by 7:30, and by 8:40 Redfield recorded them as having climbed out of the steep river bed 1,000 feet above their camp. They stood at the base of Marcy's summit cone. But their final labors were not easily accomplished. Redfield wrote,

> We immediately found ourselves entangled in the zone of dwarfish pines and spruces, which with their numerous horizontal branches interwoven with each other, surround the mountain at this elevation. These gradually decreased in height, till we reached the open surface of the mountain, covered only with mosses and small alpine plants, and at 10 A.M. the summit of the High Peak of Essex was beneath our feet.

Thus 195 years after the first ascent of Mount Washington, 65 years after Mount Mansfield's, and 33 years after Katahdin's, the Adirondacks' highest peak was finally climbed. With the Catskill Mountain House in its fifteenth year of opulent entertainment and hotels of similar pretensions arising in the heart of the White Mountains, a small band of men looked out from the ice-encrusted top of Marcy over a wealth of tumultuous mountain country unbroken by civilization and nearly all unclimbed. Emmons measured the altitude at 5,467 feet (today measured at 5,344 feet), which Redfield observed was 1,650 feet higher than the Catskill peak previously recorded as the state's highest. Hall estimated that there were twenty peaks higher than any in the Catskills (a conservative guess, it turns out; the number is more like thirty). Emmons offered the opinion that "there are probably few places in North America where Nature is invested with more magnificence and solitude than on these mountain peaks."

On the descent they headed more directly down to their high camp, then returned to the shores of Lake Colden. But their mountain explorations were by no means over. On August 7 the party traveled north to Avalanche Pass. The feature that most struck them on this, the second visit to that lonely seclusion, was a great gully rent in the side of Mount Colden at the south end of Avalanche Lake. The Colden Dike rises steeply enough to daunt most modern hikers, its surface composed of irregular, water-smoothed rock steps, its sides being vertical or overhanging rock walls up to 80 feet in height—a scene of "sublime grandeur" to Redfield but charged with challenge to the climbing instincts of Emmons. The latter ascended an estimated 1,200 to 1,500 feet up the narrow chasm, no little accomplishment for its day. Emmons described the climb as "steep and difficult of ascent." Redfield's account specifies that Emmons made the climb, not mentioning any other names. Perhaps the rest of the party remained below and watched the adventurous survey director with apprehension.

On August 8 the party ascended the steep, forested mountainside west of Lake Colden, reaching the top of the MacIntyre Range, thereby achieving the first recorded ascent of Algonquin, second only to Marcy among Adirondack elevations. Though covering little more than a mile of horizontal distance, by Redfield's reckoning, they took a long time for the ascent, bogging down again in the timberline scrub. They did not reach the summit until 1:00 or 1:20 P.M. Seeing bad weather on its way, they hurried down the west side of the peak, following a steep ravine, and camped north of Indian Pass. The following morning, in an all-day rainstorm, they trooped soggily out through the pass and back to the Iron Works.[a]

Later that summer, apparently—Emmons's reports do not give the date—Emmons made an ascent of Nippletop (4,620 ft.), the highest summit in the group that lies between the Great Range and the Dixes. His route appears to have begun from a settler's house to the south, going up to the notch between Dix and Nippletop, and then to the top from the east. At some point during these survey years, Emmons also studied the geological formation in the steep streambed that courses down the side of Cascade Mountain (plainly visible from today's highway through

---

[a]Emmons and Redfield were certainly among the group that visited the Colden Dike and traversed Algonquin. It is uncertain whether Hall remained with the party after the Marcy climb. Already he had received the appointment to direct the survey in the fourth district, the western part of the state. His own published description of the Marcy climb mentions no other ascents, and alludes to his leaving for the west "in a few days" (Hall, *Albany Daily Advertiser*, Aug. 15, 1837, p. 2). The accounts by others do not mention his presence.

Cascade Pass), possibly also making the first ascent of this peak.[b] He also made an attempt to reach the remote Seward but was unsuccessful, since that peak was so far from settlements. It is in this flanking range of 4,000-footers that the mountain named for the chief surveyor of the second district lies: 4,139-foot Mount Emmons.

The Emmons-Hall-Redfield explorations and ascents of 1836 and 1837 loom large in the opening up of the Adirondack high peak region. These two trips accomplished as much for the Adirondacks as several landmark events had done for the White Mountains years earlier. Like Darby Field, they made the first recorded ascent of the range's highest summit. Like Belknap and Cutler, they called attention to the range for a generation of subsequent climbers. Like Oakes and the other botanists, they made important scientific observations. There was even a little of the éclat of the Monument Line surveyors in Emmons's daring dash up the Colden Dike. Whereas these various landmark events in New England climbing unfolded over almost two centuries, the three scientists and their Iron Work hosts and woodsmen compressed all their achievements into two summers.

The credit for what they did deserves to be widely shared. Among the scientists, Redfield seems to have been a driving force on both sides, his enthusiasm and energy belying his age. Emmons clearly had a climber's instincts; where others might look from below, Emmons had to go bounding up to peer over the top of Wallface, scramble up the Colden Dike, respond to the challenge of any rugged climb he saw. Aside from the scientists, the Iron Works partners played an important role in the explorations. David Henderson in particular seems to have been up for whatever beckoned, being the one to circumambulate Lake Colden on that rainy morning when the scientists stayed in camp; joining Redfield in the exploratory probe up the upper Opalescent; being on the summit party. The artist, Ingham, is not credited with a lead role in the explorations, but his sketches were published in Emmons's report and added significantly to popular interest in the mountains. Lastly, the "woodsmen" employed as guides and campmakers deserve as much credit as the rest. Foremost among these seems to have been John Cheney.

The same year that Emmons's final geological survey report appeared, a writer named William Hogan identified Marcy, Seward, and Whiteface as the three highest peaks and said that none reached 3,000 feet, that all were "susceptible of cultivation to their summits." As late as 1854, the

---

[b]While Emmons does not explicitly report how high he climbed in this gully, his cryptic notes have been interpreted by at least one source as possibly indicating he climbed to or near the summit of Cascade (4,098 ft.). The evidence is in Emmons, *Geology*, p. 229, where he describes the geological formation in the streambed as continuing "above the slide, where it is concealed by soil, moss, and the underbrush of the forest." Mary MacKenzie, town historian of Lake Placid and North Elba, points out that this wording is reasonably solid evidence that Emmons was up there to look, and being that high, may well have gone on to the summit (letter to L&GW from Mary MacKenzie, Oct. 7, 1980, and conversation, March 1, 1981).

first editor of the *New York Times,* Henry J. Raymond, spent a week on the back roads of the region and found it hopelessly uncivilized, "less known than the newest state on the western borders of the American Union." To Hogan and Raymond, and many of their readers, the Catskills still reigned supreme as the foremost mountains of New York.

By the 1840s and 1850s, however, Whiteface Mountain was starting to attract something like the regular tourist attention being given to the White and Green mountains. It was the only Adirondack peak of consequence that had a summer vacation center nearby. Though still small when compared with contemporary New England meccas, or with Adirondack vacation spots of the 1870s and later, Lake Placid at midcentury had "quite a tourist infestation." Ascents of Whiteface were reported with some frequency in early travel books and old letters, and a trail existed at least as early as 1859.

For the true mountaineering spirits, however, Marcy was destined to become the lodestone of the range. Less than six weeks after the first ascent, a New York journalist named Charles Fenno Hoffman got in touch with Cheney to hire him for a trip up the great peak; though failing to reach the top, Hoffman was treated to a stormy bivouac in Indian Pass, providing lots of excitement and good copy for newspaper accounts and a book called *Wild Scenes in the Forest.* In 1839 a Vermont scientist named Farrand Northrop Benedict made what may have been the second ascent of Marcy. The more regular sequence of documented ascents does not get underway until 1846, when Cheney guided up the Reverend Joel T. Headley, who produced another glowing tribute to the Adirondack wilderness, entitled (in various editions over the years) *The Adirondack; Or, Life in the Woods* or *Letters from the Backwoods and the Adirondac.* In 1847 Cheney guided up Charles Lanman, a prolific nature writer and artist of the American landscape, who further spread the word of Marcy and the high peak wilderness in his *Adventures in the Wilds of the United States.* It is indicative of the difference between the tourist-thronged White Mountains and the still-remote Adirondacks in the 1850s that two of the decade's most widely read books about the former were entitled *The White Hills: Their Legends, Landscape, and Poetry* and *Historical Relics of the White Mountains* (implying so much human history as to produce "legends," "relics," and "poetry"); while for the latter, Headley's and Lanman's titles conjure up "backwoods," "wilds" and "adventures."

These well-publicized ascents brought to public attention the first great Adirondack mountain guide, John Cheney. Cheney was originally hired by the Iron Works as a hunter who could provide game and fish for the hungry miners' table, but his growing knowledge of the forests and crags to the north led to his being assigned the job of guiding visiting parties that wished to explore the high peaks. Both the explorers of 1836–37 and the writers who followed extolled his woodsmanship, hunting prowess, and quiet but forceful personality. Thus was launched the first legend of the great Adirondack guides. Cheney was not impressive physically; those who met him were always surprised, having heard of his fabulous reputation as a backwoodsman. "I expected," wrote Lanman, "to see a huge, powerful, hairy Nimrod; but, instead of such, I found him small in stature, bearing more the appearance of a modest and thoughtful student, gentle in his manners, and as devoted a lover of nature and solitude as ever lived." Others refer to him as "an amicable, kind-hearted man," "quiet and gentle . . . amiable," "loved and esteemed by all." As a mountain man, Cheney probably contributed as much to the ascent of Marcy as either Redfield or Emmons, being the senior guide and expected to know the terrain of the area. He was probably on the climb of Algonquin three days later. For the occasional ascents of Marcy that took place before 1850, Cheney was the most frequently employed guide. That the Adirondack guides were not primarily *mountain* guides is attested by the fact that, for all Cheney's woodsmanship and knowledge of the country south of Marcy, there is no record of his exploring summits other than Marcy and Algonquin—no jaunts over Haystack or Skylight, no bushwhacks to Santononi or Allen. (Surely any such feats would have been eagerly cited by one of the admiring writers who lauded "this formidable Nimrod.") He once claimed an ascent of Seward in 1850, having wandered up in pursuit of the obligatory moose, but the tale is not given much credence. For all his celebrity status as the conqueror of Marcy, Cheney remained fundamentally a hunter.

The other guide known to have been on the 1837 party, Harvey Holt, did some other mountain guiding as well. One rumor survives that Holt had cut a trail up Marcy in 1836, but the meager quality of the evidence and Holt's lack of interest in pressing that historic claim later (in a lifetime that extended to 1893) makes the story questionable.

By the late 1850s, ascents of both Marcy and Whiteface were more frequent. John Brown's daughter Annie wrote of an overnight excursion to Whiteface in 1857 as if it were commonplace.[c] Keene Valley joined Lake Placid as an increasingly acceptable summer tourist destination.

Nevertheless, when compared with the highly developed state of mountain tourism in New Hampshire and even Vermont during this decade of Starr King and William Henry Harrison Bingham, the Adirondacks of John Cheney and the other mountain guides remained a rough country, little-populated, with unsophisticated tourist accommodations, and with most of the high peaks still unclimbed. According to the chronicler of their first ascents, only ten of the forty-six 4,000-footers had been climbed before the Civil War. The bridle paths and summit houses that adorned so many mountaintops in New England were completely missing in the land of the Cauchsachrage. The entire era had simply passed them by.

---

[c]The fiery abolitionist who ended at Harpers Ferry kept a farm in the Adirondacks, which is now a tourist attraction on the outskirts of Lake Placid.

Chapter 11

The mountain guides

SOMETIME around 1850, Adirondack mountain climbing underwent a change. Until then, climbers had approached the high peaks (except for the isolated Whiteface) from the McIntyre Iron Works and the southwest. Around 1850 a transition began to Keene Valley, or Keene Flats as it was first known, and the easterly routes (see figure 11.1). This shift in the center of gravity of Marcy climbing is somewhat analogous to changes in the approaches to Mount Washington, as noted in chapter 5 (see figure 5.1).

The movement from the Iron Works to Keene Valley reflected irresistible economic and social changes. The Iron Works was in a state of decline and ceased operating after 1857. On the other hand, Keene Valley was beginning to attract its first mountain tourists.

Associated with these underlying forces was a change in the principal Marcy guide, from John Cheney to Old Mountain Phelps. Orson Schofield Phelps had worked at the Iron Works and thus undoubtedly had been aware of Cheney's climbs. It is not recorded whether he ever climbed Marcy by Cheney's route during these years. In 1845 Phelps moved to Keene Valley, and from this side he cut the first true trail up the peak—that is, partially cleared, not merely blazed. The trail began between the Ausable Lakes, crossed the Bartlett Ridge, dropped into Panther Gorge, and climbed an old slide to treeline and the final walk to the summit. This was probably the second formal trail up an Adirondack peak (following the one around 1859 on Whiteface). Phelps cut it in 1861—the same year that a carriage road was completed on Mount Washington, which already had five bridle paths. Over this trail Phelps guided many a mountain walker, becoming the premier mountain guide of his generation.

Speaking of guides immediately raises a problem of definition. The northeastern United States never developed a full-fledged profession of *mountain* guides. In at least two north woods centers—Maine and the Adirondacks—a clearly distinguishable body of professional guides emerged, but in both cases their chief jurisdiction was the woods and waters of the flatlands. They were primarily hunting and fishing guides, and

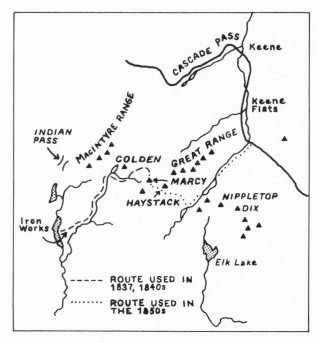

Figure 11.1. Changing approaches to Mount Marcy, 1837–1860 About 1850
Adirondack climbing underwent a significant change, comparable to shifts in
approaches to Mount Washington as shown earlier (figure 5.1). Before 1850
Mount Marcy climbers approached from the Iron Works, which lay to the
southwest. During the 1850s, as tourism began to take root in Keene Flats
(later Keene Valley) and in other towns to the north, more parties began to
approach Marcy from the northeast, using the Ausable Lakes as a starting
point. The chief proponent of the latter approach was the colorful guide Old
Mountain Phelps.

their itineraries almost invariably took their parties to lakes and wooded
camping places along the waterways that penetrated the seemingly endless forests of Maine and northern New York. Within this domain, the
guides built an expertise and mystique that gave them Bunyanesque stature in the north woods vacation areas and fringe settlements.

Even for the nineteenth-century woodsman, guiding seems rarely to
have been a full-time profession. These men made their living from the
backcountry in a multitude of activities, no one of which was richly re-
munerative, but all of which could be strung together over the seasons to
produce an adequate subsistence. They guided, hunted, and fished in the
summer months; ran trap lines, worked for lumber companies, or cut ice
in the winter; perhaps made maple syrup in the spring. Some of them
owned or worked small farms. But during the season when vacationing
sportsmen invaded the north woods, the guides happily shouldered their
axes and guns, pocketed their fees, and took to the woods.

Guides may have been rough and unlettered, but the occupation was considerably more demanding than many trades of the day. There were both objective and subjective requirements. The objective requirements were for the guide to know his terrain well enough to get parties to and from a reasonable selection of destinations; to be a sound all-around outdoorsman, skilled with gun, rod, paddle, and especially ax; to cook; to erect primitive shelters at every new location (normally consisting of a few hewn logs, roofed over with bark strips or boughs); to build a fire in wet weather and maintain it all night in cold weather. Among the early backcountry vacationers, the tradition of each climber carrying a pack had not firmly taken root, so the guide often carried the lunch, everyone's extra clothing, and all other necessary freight.

The subjective requirements were equally demanding if a guide wished to acquire standing that would guarantee a demand for his services. A guide worth rehiring ought to have a fund of good stories and a raconteur's ability to tell them well around a campfire. A certain image of quaintness or local color became a desirable attribute. Clients began to look for a mix of woodsiness, humor, saltiness, deft mastery of the understated monosyllabic repartee, the well-worn, never washed article of clothing, a certain intransigence and independence.

An idealized picture of the north woods guide took shape not only in the novels of James Fenimore Cooper but in many a travel book description. Nature writers etched unforgettable word portraits of these sons of the forest that may or may not have borne much resemblance to the originals—though, in some cases, the originals then sought to live up to the myths. "Adirondack" Murray called them a "noble class of men," "models of skill, energy, and faithfulness":

> Bronzed and hardy, fearless of danger, eager to please, uncontaminated with the vicious habits of civilized life. . . . Among them an oath is never heard, unless in moments of intense excitement. Vulgarity of speech is absolutely unknown. . . .
> . . . The wilderness has unfolded to them its mysteries, and made them wise with a wisdom nowhere written in books. The wilderness is their home.

Another Adirondack admirer purred:

> If he is the right kind of a guide, he will be at the same time your "philosopher and friend." He will initiate you into the mysteries of woodcraft. . . . He will cook for you when you are hungry, and find a cold stream for you when you are thirsty. He will tell you endless stories . . . when you are in the talking mood, and keep a discreet silence when you are meditative. And when you are sleepy he will make for you a bed of fragrant balsam boughs.

"The Maine guide," gushed a later writer, " . . . is the best fellow in the world; it is both pleasant and profitable to share a canoe or tent with him."

The relationship between guide and client in the north woods had many subtleties. To be sure, the guide's role was often pure and simple that of manservant—that is, cook, porter, fire tender. Yet he was also in some ways a teacher and almost a leader, as when finding and stalking the hunter's quarry, or showing a client how to run a rapids or prepare a camp. Maine vacationers were told, as late as 1912, "It is the guide of course who personally conducts the trip, furnishing the canoe and securing the provisions." The Adirondack guide "should resemble a general," according to one awed sportsman. The better clients strove to become good woodsmen themselves and valued the example and counsel of their untutored mentors. There is no doubt that, in many cases, guide and client found a mutual respect and a rich companionship in their days spent together in remote settings. This is not to say that in every case, or even in a majority, the relationship approached the ideal; doubtless many clients saw their guides only as manservants and treated them as such, while many guides saw clients only as rich city folk to be separated from their money. Even Lyman Eppes, one of the great Adirondack guides, was praised as "respectful, which . . . quality he evinced by always sitting apart from our party." The ambivalence of the relationship is evident in a description of Adirondack guides as those men "who for years used to lead, serve and entertain us." Note the effortless juxtaposition of "lead, serve." Here is a 1910 description of Maine guides:

> The guides of the north woods are in almost all cases as much companions as servants. They keep their places and are respectful, but they are, with few exceptions, men of a certain independence of character and know their own worth; they value their self-respect to the point of sensitiveness.

In both Maine and the Adirondacks, the guides eventually created professional organizations, but it is noteworthy how late this step was taken: 1891 in the Adirondacks, and not until 1933 in Maine. In other words, this formality took place in both instances *after* the most celebrated guides had passed from the scene and the work had degenerated— with honorable exceptions—into a far less romantic job of escorting well-heeled novices over well-known rivers and trails to well-trampled campgrounds for as fat a fee as the goose could be fleeced for. The guides' associations, in some ways resembling trade unions in their antiromantic pursuit of better wages and working conditions, belonged to an era in which the role of the guide in true backcountry adventure had faded.

Ironically the guides' own successes as trail cutters led to less need for their services. Blazed trails in the high peaks meant that summer vacationers could make their own way. As the years went by and transportation improved, more and more mountain vacationers came who could not afford to hire guides. Equipment improved. Camping became easier. More self-motivated hikers entered the woods. The last full generation of guides, it is said, hastened their own demise by becoming more expert in the art of padding a bill than of paddling a canoe or finding a mountain. As Adirondack historian Paul Jamieson observed, "Leatherstocking was losing his innocence."

But back in the nineteenth century, professional guides played a significant role in the history of mountain climbing. Ethan Allen Crawford and others of his family or their employees were paid guides on Mount Washington, perhaps the Northeast's first to play that role more or less regularly. Others stand out in White Mountain lore: James Gordon of Gorham, Benjamin F. Osgood of the Glen House, the Lowe family of Randolph, James Clement of Moosilauke. But guiding in the White Mountains was never able to take firm root because the hills were too soon filled with well-marked trails. Tourists, based in accommodations close to the mountains, had no need of services that were deemed essential to penetrate the remote fastnesses of the Adirondacks and Maine. By 1876 the leading guidebook writer, M. F. Sweetser, observed:

> There are but few guides left among the White Mountains, since most of the popular routes are now so plain and easy as to render that profession unprofitable.

The pattern was the same in other regions where mountains were climbed by summer folk. Certain local woodsmen became well known as dependable guides for climbing and camping excursions—James Dutcher of Slide Mountain in the Catskills is a good example—but as trails were built, the need for such services soon declined.

In Maine the profession of guiding developed into a regular occupation more successfully than anywhere else in the Northeast. Indeed, by the 1890s nonresidents of the state were legally prohibited from camping or building fires in the Maine woods without "being in charge of a registered guide." To climb Katahdin in 1912, a traveler first went to Moosehead Lake's Mount Kineo resort or to the Northeast Carry, "for at Kineo and the Carry may be obtained *the first requirement* of such a journey, a guide." Nevertheless, the Maine guides were, on the whole, even less involved with climbing mountains than those elsewhere. Hunting and fishing trips, or just plain quiet canoe trips, were their chief pursuit. Outside of Katahdin, records of Maine guides climbing peaks are scarce to nonexistent.

It is in the Adirondacks, where trails and mountainside hotels were as yet undeveloped, that the image of the old mountain guides of the nineteenth century comes through strongest of all. Here were the largest living legends and the guides most associated with major feats of exploration and mountain adventure, from Cheney and Holt on Marcy; to the highly respected Indian, Mitchell Sabattis, and the black, Lyman Eppes, Sr.; the grim antisocial hermit, Alvah Dunning, and the much employed and ever popular Bill Nye, both of whom recorded significant "first ascents" with surveyor Verplanck Colvin during the 1870s.

Still, all these were hunting and fishing guides who occasionally climbed peaks. The first to focus primarily on the mountains was Orson Schofield Phelps. Born in Vermont (as were several of the great guides: Ethan Crawford, Marcus Keep, Bill Nye) on May 6, 1817, Phelps moved with his father to Schroon Lake in 1830. When the Iron Works began hiring in 1832, the fifteen-year-old Orson signed on and worked there until 1845. Then, at age twenty-eight, he married, moved over to Keene Flats (Keene Valley), and "settled down to a sixty-year existence of little work and increasing celebrity."

Phelps is not known to have participated in any of the Adirondack climbs of the early days, but after moving to Keene Valley, he began to take an interest in the high places. He was in the party that first climbed Marcy from the east in 1849. He cut the first two trails on the peak: the standard route from the Ausable Lakes over the Bartlett Ridge to the head of Panther Gorge; and the long Johns Brook route from the northeast. He guided parties up Marcy frequently from the 1850s on. He it was who escorted the first two women up. He is reported to have climbed it more than one hundred times.

Phelps paid attention to other peaks beside the big Cloud-splitter. In his 1849 climb, he and two partners made the first ascent of Haystack, the third-highest peak in the Adirondacks and considered by many Adirondack partisans as a more rugged and impressive climb than Marcy. In 1854 he climbed the Giant of the Valley with George and Levi Lamb. Later he cut a trail over Hopkins to the Giant. He is known to have made some of the earliest ascents of difficult peaks such as Nippletop and Gothics. In 1873, at age fifty-six, he was with Colvin on the first recorded ascents of Mount Colvin and of Skylight, fourth highest peak and another remote and rugged climb.

Phelps's importance owed partially to his guiding career's coinciding with the tentative beginnings of summer tourism in Keene Valley. With his strong love for the high places and his distaste for other work, he was probably the most active guide from 1850 through the early 1870s. He was certainly the most widely known. Among his regular and more famous clients were artist Frederick Perkins, writer Charles Dudley Warner, and several leading clergyman of the time, Horace Bushnell, James B. Shaw, and Joseph H. Twichell.

Adirondack historians differ in their appraisals of Phelps as a guide. Alfred Donaldson judged him harshly: "He was not a great guide. Indeed, many did not consider him even a good one." Herbert McAneny reports that his colleagues among the Keene Valley guides regarded him as "lazy, shiftless, and lacking in the sturdier qualities that made a competent guide." A nineteenth-century writer alludes to "the vulgar estimate of his contemporaries, that reckoned Old Phelps 'lazy.' "

On the other hand, Russell Carson excused other shortcomings because of qualities that his critics generally conceded:

> He was a great guide because, in addition to a guide's equipment of woodcraft and knowledge of topography, he had the soul of a philosopher and poet, and a fine appreciation of the beauties and sublimities of nature. With the skill of an artist, he displayed all the wonders of his mountains to the appreciative tourist. . . . Probably no guide in all Adirondack history loved the peaks and his profession as he did.

Phelps also was a true backwoods "character" and worked hard at being one, especially as he got older. Guidebook writer Seneca Ray Stoddard described him as

> a little man, about five feet six in height, muffled up in an immense crop of long hair and a beard that seemed to boil up out of his collar band. Grizzly as the granite ledges he climbs, shaggy as the rough-barked cedar, but with a pleasant twinkle in his eye and an elasticity to his step equaled by few younger men. He likes to talk and delivers his sage conclusions and whimsical oddities in a cheery, chirrupy, squeaky sort of tone—away up on the mountain as it were—an octave above the ordinary voice, somewhat suggestive of the warblings of an ancient chickadee.

In 1878 Charles Dudley Warner devoted a full-length essay in the Atlantic entitled "A Character Study" to this "true citizen of the wilderness," this "primitive man." Warner's literary skill may have done more for Phelps's reputation than almost thirty years of guiding had done. He drew a vivid picture of the archetypal old mountain guide:

> One does not think of Old Phelps so much as a lover of nature—to use the sentimental slang of the period—as a part of nature itself. . . . A sturdy figure, with long body and short legs, clad in a woollen shirt and butternut-colored trousers repaired to the point of picturesqueness, his head surmounted by a limp, light-brown felt hat, frayed away at the top, so that his yellowish hair grew out of it like some nameless fern out of a pot. . . . His features were small and delicate, and set in the frame of a reddish beard, the razor having mowed away a clearing about the sensitive mouth, which was not seldom wreathed with a child-like and charming smile. . . . small gray eyes, set near together; eyes keen to observe and quick to express change of thought; eyes that made you believe instinct can grow into philosophic judgement.

Warner conceded that other guides might be better trappers or hunters or even better guides—"but Old Phelps was the discoverer of the beauties and sublimities of the mountains."

Fascinated readers of the *Atlantic* were introduced to all the beloved eccentricities: the "shambling, loose-jointed gait, not unlike that of the bear," the picturesque apparel ("His clothes seemed to have been put on him once for all, like the bark of a tree, a long time ago"), the quaint nicknames for Marcy ("Mercy") and Dix ("Dixie"), the distaste for soap ("thing that I hain't no kinder use for"), and the colorful terminology (a bushwhack was "a reg'lar random scoot of a rigmarole").

The *Atlantic* article was widely read and secured its subject's lasting fame. Probably the most enthralled reader of all was Old Mountain Phelps. It is reported that after 1878 the old guide "devoted himself, too obviously at times, to living up to the literary halo in which he had been unexpectedly lassoed." He "took to posturing a little and lost some of his naturalness."

His critics are probably harsher on Old Mountain Phelps than they need to be. They may have been correct that he was not a great guide in the terms by which most guides were evaluated—axmanship; shooting; fishing; willingness and ability to carry huge loads, erect overnight lean-tos, paddle all day, tend fire all night. But in a quite different meaning of the term, he apparently was in a class by himself—through his ability to project his appreciation of the high, wild mountains to others, to "guide" them into a deeper appreciation of the craggy summits and dark ravines. No doubt there was a touch of the charlatan about the wizardry of his images, which probably sat poorly with the other, more earthy guides. But few visionaries are untainted by at least a faint aroma of quackery. He clearly seems to have had a hold on many of the intellectuals of the day who visited the Adirondacks. The learned divine Horace Bushnell would spend hours in conversation with Phelps, around a campfire or on the heights. Many tales credit him with being genuinely affected by mountain scenery. The Reverend Frederick Baylies Allen wrote to Carson:

> Phelps was a man of a good deal of sentiment, and delicacy of feeling. The first year we camped on the upper Ausable, it was on the bank at the right, toward Mount Marcy. We objected, saying the Gothics Mountains were not in sight from there. He answered very seriously, "That's the reason I put the camp here. Some kinds of scenery you don't want staring you in the face all the while. You want to row out on purpose to see it. You don't want to hog the Gothics Mountains."

Ultimately, Old Mountain Phelps's contribution was his inspirational devotion to mountain climbing and to "Mercy" above all. When he first climbed it, Marcy probably had seen fewer than ten ascents. In the next decade it became a regular tourist run, to the extent that the Adirondacks yet had tourists. The guide who took them up there more often than anyone else was "that wily scamp."

Chapter 12

The Austin sisters and their legacy

OBSERVANT readers—or at least half of them—may have noticed that so far Northeastern mountaineering history has been a man's world. During colonial times, when mountains were "daunting terrible," there is indeed no record whatever of women on mountaintops—absolutely none. After the establishment of the Crawfords' primitive tourist trade on Mount Washington, however, women were not long excluded.

These women who pioneered on the heights in the period between 1820 and 1870 contended with attitudinal obstacles far more severe than the mountains' objective defenses. It was, to put it mildly, not an age when women either expected or were expected to show athletic vigor or an adventurous bent. The overcoming of psychological barriers is often more difficult than surmounting physical obstacles. But the physical obstacles were drastically augmented for women by the fact that social mores required them to wear ankle-length dresses when climbing mountains. When all of these factors are taken into account, the achievements of pioneering women on the heights are as impressive as any accomplishments of their male counterparts before them.

In 1821 three young sisters, Eliza, Harriet, and Abigail Austin, had recently moved from Portsmouth to Jefferson, New Hampshire. On August 31 of that year, the trio showed up at Ethan Crawford's. "They were ambitious," records Lucy Crawford in her *History*, "and wanted to have the honor of being the first females who placed their feet on this high and now celebrated place, Mount Washington." Three men accompanied them: one of the 1820 Lancastrians' merry Northern Presidentials troop (see chapter 5), Charles Jesse Stuart; a brother, Daniel Austin; and an Austin farm tenant, Mr. Faulkner, to carry baggage. Stuart was engaged to Eliza, and they were married the following summer.

Stuart was a veteran of one year's climbing experience, so they set out without a guide. This party took several days to accomplish a climb that Crawford took his guests up in just one, or with one overnight. For two days they meandered uphill along Ethan's new trail, staying at the rough camps that he had built. The third day dawned stormy, so they stayed in camp. As the rain persisted, they sent the hapless Faulkner down to summon Ethan's aid. Crawford, then lame from an ax wound to his heel, hobbled up on a cane, while Faulkner fled back to Jefferson, pleading he had grain to look after. On the fourth day, braced by Crawford's reassuring presence and a more favorable turn in the weather, they completed the ascent by noon. Ethan was impressed by the "heroism" of the Austin sisters, as well as by their propriety: "Everything was done with so much prudence and modesty by them; there was not a trace or even a chance for reproach or slander." These assurances probably reflect the uneasiness men felt at that time about how women could possibly manage on the inhospitable terrain of mountains, especially if nights were to be spent out in necessarily cramped shelters.

The Austin sisters were pathbreakers in their modest way, perhaps as much as Darby Field two centuries earlier. From their hesitant, faltering, but nonetheless successful ascent of Washington flowed a gradually strengthening tradition of female mountaineering that will unfold in these pages in the achievements of M. F. Whitman and the Pychowska women in the 1880s, Laura Banfield on Marcy in the winter of 1908, Laura Cowles and some other women on the Long Trail in the 1920s, a small army of New York–area hikers on the trails of Harriman Park and the Hudson Highlands in the 1930s, and innumerable other women trampers and snowshoers, trail-builders, and hiking club presidents of the twentieth century. It all began with Eliza, Harriet, and Abigail Austin on Mount Washington in the first week of September 1821.

The Crawfords were at first ambivalent about the idea of women climbing. For the next three years, no women climbed Mount Washington. In 1825 a tourist from Boston brought his sister along (unnamed in the accounts), and they prevailed upon Lucy to accompany them for the second women's ascent. After again waiting out an extra day of bad weather at high camp, they had an uneventful if strenuous ascent. After Lucy's experience on this climb, however, the Crawfords discouraged ladies from trying Mount Washington, "as we thought it too much of an undertaking."

When another Boston party, consisting of an older couple and their two daughters and one son, showed up, Ethan did not accompany them, sending along William Howe as guide in his place. The mother and one of the daughters turned back in "a dismal hurricane" on the summit cone, but Louisa Jane Park and her father struggled on to reach the top. "It was a desperate business," recalled Dr. Park grimly. "I have experienced gales in the Gulf Stream, tempests off Cape Hattaras, tornadoes in the West Indies, and been surrounded by water spouts in the Gulf of Mexico, but I never saw anything more furious or more dreadful than this." As they descended, they met a concerned Ethan Crawford who was hastening to the rescue in the storm.

Men who "escorted" these early women climbers expressed their disapproval in journal entries at the Crawfords' following the ascents. Dr. Park wrote:

> Gentlemen, there is nothing in the ascent of Mount Washington that you need dread. Ladies, give up all thoughts of it; but if you are resolved, let the season be mild, consult Mr. Crawford as to the prospects of the weather, and with every precaution, you will still find it, *for you*, a tremendous undertaking.

The male companion of three women who made an 1825 ascent of Washington advised future lady visitors to the Crawfords' mountain: "Do not attempt it, at least, *never but in fair weather."*

In the next year or two, however, Ethan Crawford was converted, perhaps pressured by Lucy and probably shrewdly sensing an untapped segment of the tourist business. He refurbished one of his camps with separate quarters for men and women. As he improved his path to accommodate horses for a much greater share of the distance, the number of women who climbed Washington picked up, and by the 1830s they were no longer a rarity. During this decade Abel Crawford also began guiding women up the mountain via the older Crawford Path. So did guides from Thomas's Crawford House.

Women climbers are unreported elsewhere in the White Mountains until Mrs. Daniel Patch made the ascent of Moosilauke in 1840 or shortly thereafter. She is said to have brought her teapot along and had a brew on top. Like the Austins, Mrs. Patch was a local woman, not a tourist.

In 1839, in the Adirondacks, a notable female made an accidental ascent which has found its way into the lasting lore of the land of the Caughsachrage. Along with Marcy, Whiteface was the peak that attracted most attention before the Civil War. From the south, as usually seen, it stands out as a clear, graceful pyramid, the closest thing to Mount Fuji–like symmetry found in the Northeast. But the northern slopes of Whiteface are less regularly shaped, meandering off in a formless array of ridges and humps. On these northern flanks, before they descend to the lower hills that stretch to Canada, there arises one last swell of forested upland that forms a subsidiary sister peak to the great Whiteface. This 4,270-foot mountain is designated Esther. How it got its name is an odd story.

North of these sprawling outreaches of Whiteface, a road cut through the wilderness connecting the settlements of Wilmington and Franklin Falls. On this road was the farm of the McComb family. Among the children of this family a girl named Esther was born about 1824. According to a tradition recounted by an old-timer nearly a century later, the McCombs prohibited their children from climbing the mountains. Esther, it is said, had a burning ambition to climb Whiteface. At the age of fifteen, in the year 1839, mountaineering spirit overcame filial duty, and she took off for the summit of Whiteface.

There were of course no trails, and the farm girl is not likely to have carried a compass. She worked her way uphill in the general direction of her objective, finally heading for what looked like the highest summit. When she got there she was indeed on the highest land in her immediate vicinity—but could clearly see the majestic top of Whiteface still a couple of miles away and 600 vertical feet above. According to tradition, Esther McComb had reached the top of that subsidiary peak now known by her first name.

The tale seems inconsequential, but recall the way mountains had been perceived only a few years before—as dangerous and inaccessible places, the abode of wild beasts, if not of evil spirits—and consider that the backwaters of the road between Wilmington and Franklin Falls in 1839 cannot have been at the forefront of the new perceptions of the sublime. The Redfield-Emmons ascents had only just occurred. Virtually no recreational mountaineering can have come to the attention of a fifteen-year-old farm girl. In the annals of the forty-six Adirondack high peaks, fewer than ten others had been climbed in 1839. Add to these constraints the nature of the terrain: Esther today is one of the tougher bushwhacks of the forty-six, the imbosked top reached only after battling tangled scrub growing chaotically on a rocky slope. Many is the party of peakbaggers that has easily bagged Whiteface but turned back short of Esther's true summit.

For a girl, alone, with no experience on mountains of that elevation, in a year like 1839, the accomplishment of Esther McComb merits recognition as a mountaineering feat, although not a major one.

On top of Esther she was still short of her original goal, so she plunged back into the puckerbrush and continued on. She never made it to Whiteface, spending a chilly night somewhere in the scrub. A search party found her in the morning, alive and well. Tradition credits her mother with naming the peak as a casual joke. The name and the legend have lasted.

In the late 1850s two local women, Mary Cook and Fannie Newton, made the first known ascent of Marcy by women. They came up from Keene Valley, escorted by Old Mountain Phelps, Harvey Holt, and five locals. Mary Cook was said to have been "of generous proportions" and slow, but she climbed the peak again in 1861 with two more women, Orpha and Teresa Bruce, this time employing Phelps's trail and his guidance. In the meantime, in 1859 Mitchell Sabattis, the great Indian guide, escorted Mr. and Mrs. B. J. Lossing up from the old Iron Works side. Otherwise, ascents of Adirondack peaks by women seem to have been rare. As late as 1873 a Keene Valley woman claimed the first woman's ascent of Haystack.

In 1849 Marcus Keep sought to arrange the first woman's ascent of Katahdin by a party of five women, including his future wife, Hannah Taylor, of Lincoln, Maine. A forceful and prickly personality like Keep tended to arouse local antagonisms. Another party soon formed, with the express objective of beating Keep's party to the prize. Mrs. E. Oakes Smith, with the first woman's ascent of Kineo already on her record, and a Bangor, Maine, woman named M. C. Mosman, made the long trip up the Keep Path, accompanied by James H. Haines and David Mosman. (Haines had accompanied Keep on his first and unsuccessful go at Katahdin in 1846, and some kind of bad feeling had evidently grown between them.) On August 11 Smith and her party reached Pamola. They declared that this goal qualified as the "Top of Mount Katahdin," as they contended in a note smugly left for the Keep party to discover a week later.

Undaunted, Keep brought the five women in his party up that far and on August 20, 1849, crossed the Knife Edge, "where *no foot* of better halves had been," to reach South Peak, which at that time was thought to be the highest point of the mountain. All five women made it that far, with no great difficulties on the infamous Knife Edge—"like children walking upon a crooked rail or stone fence," Keep observed. Hannah Taylor, who was by then Hannah Taylor Keep, and Esther Jones of Enfield, Maine, then continued to the last summit on the ridge, which is now known to be the true summit of Katahdin. The cairn they built that day may have been the first on that spot. It is possible that this cairn has existed in some state of repair ever since. It is one of the most important cairns in the Northeastern mountains, as it marks not just the top of Katahdin, but also the northern terminus of the 2,100-mile Appalachian Trail. Thus Hannah Taylor Keep and Esther Jones made a distinctive contribution to Northeastern mountain-climbing history.

In 1855 one Katahdin party led by the prominent intellectual Thomas Wentworth Higginson was notable for including no fewer than six women, whose first names only were preserved: Rachel, Fanny, Mary, Theo, Kate, and Alice. The group made the long trip via Hunt's farm and the Keep path. On the way in they gradually shed the refinements of civilization, the men changing from suits to brightly colored shirts, the women from skirts to bloomers, though they seem to have been nattily enough attired withal. (Rachel, for example, wore a white sunbonnet, lined with blue, all the way.) One of the women was the first to reach the top of the slide. "Sometimes we were tugged along by gentlemen, and sometimes offered to help gentlemen along." The party reached Pamola; like Mrs. Oakes Smith, they did not cross the Knife Edge to the true summit. Still they concluded,

> Our moral is that there is more real peril to bodily health in a week of ball-room than in a month of bivouacs.

Since Higginson's female companions did not cross the Knife Edge, Hannah Keep and Esther Jones deserve the high honors as the only women to stand on the true summit of Katahdin until perhaps as recently as one hundred years ago.

The next generation saw a far more vigorous participation by women in mountain walking, unleashing such untrammeled spirits as Lucia and Marian Pychowska, Isabella Stone, M. F. Whitman, and Laura Banfield. Until then, the constraints of the antebellum world restricted what women could do in the mountains, though it could not entirely stop the Austin sisters, Mrs. Patch, Hannah Taylor Keep, Mrs. Oakes Smith, or little Esther McComb.

Chapter 13

The elder Hitchcock and Arnold Guyot

In the relaxed and diffident age of Starr King, bridle paths and summit houses, two individuals stand out from the carriage set, two who exemplify something of the more robust spirit of mountaineering to come.

Edward Hitchcock, noted geologist and educator, was a devoted champion of mountain climbing during its early years. Born in Deerfield, Massachusetts, on May 24, 1793, Hitchcock became a student of the geology of the Connecticut River valley, including the Holyoke Range and other local hills. By 1817, at age twenty-four, he was writing papers and corresponding with the renowned Professor Benjamin Silliman at Yale and working on a geological map of the entire region. In 1825 he was appointed to the faculty of Amherst College. Over the years his professional stature as one of New England's most knowledgeable geologists brought him fame and involvement in the early state geological surveys in Massachusetts, New York, and Vermont. In 1845 he was elevated to the presidency of Amherst College, turning his talents to broader educational and social questions.

Throughout this luminous career as scientist and educator, Hitchcock followed Alden Partridge in emphasizing the value of physical education. In an 1830 address entitled "The Physical Culture Adapted to the Times," Hitchcock pleaded for equal emphasis on physical as well as mental training, deploring "the neglect of early physical education" and advocating that students devote three to six hours per day to "mechanical or agricultural pursuits." As president of Amherst from 1845 to 1854, he counseled students and faculty alike to spend vacations "among the mountains, the valleys, the gorges, the beetling cliffs, the caverns, the mines, the wild cataracts, and the deep solitudes."

Hitchcock himself explored and led his students up most of the principal eminences of the state. He climbed Greylock, Everett, Monument Mountain, many other summits in the Berkshires, Mount Toby (which he tried unsuccessfully to rechristen "Mount Metawampe"), Wachusett, Dorset in southern Vermont (which he called "Aeolus"), Tom, and numerous other mountains, always reserving a special fondness for the

Holyoke Range, which he called "the gem of Massachusetts mountains." Recalled one admirer: "Down to the last years of his life few could climb mountains or break rocks with him—few could endure so much fatigue as he on a geological excursion."

The Amherst president probably did more to popularize hill walking in Massachusetts than anyone else (if we exempt the indirect influence of the transcendentalist writers) until Albert Hopkins got rolling in Williamstown. For thirty years Hitchcock roamed the hills, led parties of young people, prodded his colleagues to get out and walk, wrote about mountains for periodicals of the day, conducted serious geological surveys in both Massachusetts and Vermont (while serving as an adviser for New York State), and generally both preached and practiced the minimountaineering of Massachusetts at midcentury. Besides all these attainments, Edward Hitchcock fathered a man who made even more important contributions to Northeastern climbing history in the next generation: Charles H. Hitchcock, director of New Hampshire's seminal geological survey in the years around 1870.

While Edward Hitchcock was president of Amherst and prowling the Holyoke Range, an even more strenuous mountaineer arrived in the United States from the Alps. In 1848 the Swiss scientist Arnold Henri Guyot, at age forty already well known for his studies of glaciers, came to the United States. He immediately settled upon the exploration, measurement, and mapping of the entire Appalachian chain from upper New England to Georgia as his life's work. After six years of varied employment, mostly in Massachusetts, he was appointed to a Princeton professorship in 1854, an association that lasted until his death in 1884. In those thirty years, he was a popular teacher, prolific producer of research papers, coauthor of a series of geography textbooks for public school use, and, in the words of his newspaper obituary, "remarkable not only for his wisdom and scientific attainments, but also for his great gentleness and humility." At the time of his death, a scientific colleague described his personality as "singularly pure and sweet" and guessed that "he probably had not an enemy in the world." One of his associates once called him (be it noted that the professor was fifty years old when this assessment of his impact on the opposite sex was offered)

one of the loveliest of men for any one to have for a companion, and one of the few I could understand a lady falling in love with.

Every summer Guyot took to the hills. Probably no individual covered a wider variety of mountains throughout the region than Arnold Guyot between 1849 and the late 1870s. Only Alden Partridge bears comparison to him in the scope of his travels throughout the Northeast. Guyot made extensive explorations—not just a climb or two—in the White Mountains, the Adirondacks, the Catskills, with more modest amounts of time spent among the upper elevations of Vermont, the Shawangunks, Massachusetts, and Connecticut. For all this, he was even more active in the southern Appalachians, but that side of his career lies not within the scope of this book. With pardonable hyperbole, one Appalachian Trail authority notes,

> Indeed, he seems to have climbed up almost every major peak that the A. T. passes over from New Hampshire to Georgia in a time when most of these mountains had no trails or roads to the top! A most interesting individual.

The name of this Swiss immigrant has been much memorialized in the hills of his adopted country. There is a Mount Guyot in the Twin Range of the White Mountains, another of the same name in the southern Appalachians, and a Guyot Hill in the Shawangunks of New York, not to mention other peaks named for him in California, Colorado, Utah, and Alaska, and even a crater on the moon—this geographical spread reflecting the breadth of his investigations.

Guyot's relentless researches left the landscape littered with exposed fallacies. Before he went to work, Mount Washington was still thought by many to be the highest peak east of the Mississippi; he demonstrated that the southern Appalachians had many higher peaks. Ante Guyot, the Catskills were perceived as the area adjacent to the Catskill Mountain House, period; he proved that Slide Mountain was the highest in the range, and identified and mapped squads of other mountains to the south and west. Previous measurements of summit altitudes he corrected in wholesale lots; Guyot's figures compare quite closely to currently accepted data.

When Guyot began his excursions in 1849, mountain climbing was beginning to grow in popularity but on a highly selective basis. In the Catskills, climbing was concentrated around the Catskill Mountain House. No one bothered with peaks south of Overlook or west of Hunter. In the White Mountains, people climbed Washington and its neighbors, or Lafayette, Moosilauke, or some of the southern tier of peaks. In the Adirondacks, they stuck with Marcy or Whiteface.

But Guyot had his own agenda. In each of these ranges, he was powerfully attracted to those summits that rose off the beaten track, the unclimbed mysteries of each area, the hidden jewels. From a mountaineering history viewpoint, Guyot's most interesting achievements were the exploration of some of these more challenging but hitherto overlooked ranges: Carrigain in the White Mountains, the Seward Range in the Adirondacks, and just about everything west of Hunter and south of Overlook in the Catskills.

In late August 1857 Guyot was in the White Mountains, traveling with a large party that included Herbert Torrey (another in that prolific dynasty of outdoors-lovers), S. Hastings Grant (Torrey's foster brother), and the mapmaker Harvey Boardman. After two ascents of Mount Washington in four days, Guyot and Grant arose at 5:30 A.M. on August 26, climbed Mount Willard before breakfast at the Crawford House, boarded the stage to Bartlett, and with a local guide named Bill Hatch were off into the unknown wilderness of the Sawyer River before 11:00 A.M. (see figure 18.1). There ensued what Grant called "six hours of about the hardest tramping in the woods that I was ever connected with." By 5:00 that afternoon they were camped at the base of the massive mountain form of Carrigain, then "untraversed and unexplored." That evening our intrepid explorers were just a bit nervous for having seen enormous bear tracks (9 inches by 5 inches) in a swampy place en route. On August 27, they rose early and at 6:00 A.M. began the ascent, "over fallen trees, through thick undergrowth we pass, and all the time climbing, climbing," until they arrived on top at 10:00 A.M., elated in spite of "scratched face and hands, bruised feet, and well-torn clothes." Their route is not specified in Grant's account. Wherever it was, Carrigain, for men with neither trail experience nor knowledge of the terrain, was a tough antagonist. Fourteen years later, J. H. Huntington called it "a noble mountain with precipitous cliffs and deep gorges on either side." A later writer explained the exceptional steepness of its hiking trails by saying, "But that is a climber's mountain, really." After more than an hour on top, they descended and were back out to the Crawford Notch road by about 6:00 P.M. "I never went through more, in two days, of toil and exertion," concluded Grant. This ascent of Carrigain was not unlike many an adventure of the 1880s when the Randolph crew and Prof. Charles Fay were at the peak of their zestful exuberance. But before the Civil War it was an isolated and exceptional event in White Mountain climbing. So out of the mainstream was it in those days of bridle paths and summit houses, that Professor Fay himself was unaware of its existence, crediting George Vose in 1869 with Carrigain's first ascent.[a]

Soon after his arrival in the United States, Guyot was engaged by the Smithsonian Institution to set up a series of thirty-eight weather stations throughout New York State. For one of the sites he selected the McIntyre Iron Works, and while there (in 1849 or 1850) he climbed Marcy. Returning in 1863 with his nephew Ernest Sandoz, Guyot set out for the remote Seward Range. Unfortunately the record is unclear as to where Guyot and Sandoz were. They climbed one of the higher summits, Sandoz ascending a second peak as well. Authorities on Adirondack climbing history are divided in speculating which two peaks they reached. Verplanck Colvin and

---

[a]Guyot's route on Carrigain is subject to a good guess. In his article "On the Appalachian Mountain System" (*American Journal of Science and Arts*, 31, 2d series [May 1861], p. 183), he gives a barometric reading for the "Eastern Spur" of Carrigain. This most likely means Vose Spur. This could signify (though there is no way to say with certainty) that they first went toward what we now call Carrigain Notch and ascended the extremely steep flank of Vose Spur and then on over another intermediate hump before reaching the top of Carrigain (see figure 18.1). If so, it was a sensational climb for 1857.

others credit them with reaching Mount Seymour but not Seward. Others, including George Marshall, who examined the question closely, think Sandoz may have been on Seward itself. After weighing all the evidence, Russell Carson threw up his hands and declared it "impossible to tell from the meagre data whether they came out on Seward or Seymour." In either case, they were way off in mountainous wilderness of a character unattempted by anyone else in the Adirondacks before the Civil War.

Through much of the 1860s and 1870s, Guyot devoted extensive time to the Catskills. He and his aides carefully determined and mapped the location of all the peaks of consequence; named them, sometimes revising traditional nomenclature when it was confusing (thus reducing the number of "Round Tops" and "North" and "South" mountains); and painstakingly measured elevations. Like almost everyone else, Guyot started out assuming that Kaaterskill High Peak was the highest in the range. It did not take him long to discover that Black Head was higher; he called it 3,945 feet to High Peak's 3,664 feet. Then his assistant, Henry Kimball, who had been climbing Catskill peaks since 1847 and was convinced that the Pine Orchard peaks were not the highest, escorted him up Hunter, which they measured at 4,038 feet. Finally in 1872, at age sixty-five, Guyot climbed and measured Slide Mountain and determined that it was in fact the apex of the Catskills, 4,205 feet by his measurement. Before he was through, Guyot and his assistants had climbed at least twenty-seven and possibly closer to thirty of the thirty-four peaks listed by today's Catskill 3,500 Club as being more than 3,500 feet. The impact of Guyot's studies on how people perceived the Catskills was revolutionary. No longer were they a tame little collection of picturesque peaks and vales within strolling distance of the Mountain House's columned piazza. As Guyot proved,

> The wilderness of the Adirondacks is more extensive but hardly more complete than that of the pathless forests of the Southern Catskills, the habitual haunts of numerous bears, wild cats and occasional panthers.

Perceptions had come full circle. Until the 1830s people believed that the Adirondacks had little to offer and that the Catskills were New York's highest mountains. Now in the 1870s, as people began to flock to the Adirondacks, it took this inquiring Swiss scientist to point out that there was more wilderness in the Catskills than lay within the compass of Pine Orchard.[b]

---

[b]Guyot's measured elevations are noted in almost all cases as made by mercury or aneroid barometer. To measure in this way requires being physically on the summit—reasonable proof that he or one of his assistants climbed each peak thus measured. In the June 1880 *American Journal of Science* (pp. 449–51), Guyot gives elevations of seventy-three summits, including subsidiary peaks in several instances, of which all but four were by barometer. Of the 3,500-foot peaks, unquestionably he or his aides were on twenty-seven of the thirty-four. There is doubt as to whether he crossed Cornell and Big Indian en route to others, and possibly Rocky and Balsam Cap as well. He apparently did not climb Sherrill, and probably not Balsam Lake, nor North Dome.

Nonetheless, if Carrigain, the Sewards, and the entire field of the Catskills were Guyot's most important and interesting tours de force, they by no means exhaust the list of his Northeastern mountain travels. In the White Mountains, besides the Presidentials and Carrigain, he is thought to have climbed Moosilauke, Lafayette, Lincoln ("South Peak" of Lafayette), Cannon, Kinsman, Cherry, Moriah, Carter Dome, Wildcat, Willey, the Tripyramids, Whiteface, Passaconaway, Chocorua, Sandwich Dome, and Deception. In the Adirondacks, besides the Sewards and Marcy, there is evidence he climbed Whiteface, Algonquin, Colden, Dix, Nippletop, Santanoni, Wallface, and Boreas. In Vermont he measured Mansfield, Camel's Hump, Killington, Pico, Shrewsbury, Equinox, and Herrick (near Rutland). Farther south, he was on the Grand Monadnock, Greylock, Everett, Wachusett, the Hanging Hills around Meriden, Connecticut, New York's Shawangunks, and, as mentioned, virtually all the Catskill peaks of consequence.

The list would be a considerable accomplishment for a twentieth-century peakbagger with high-speed roads and motorcars, lightweight camping equipment, and groomed hiking trails. In the mid-nineteenth century, with the state of Northeastern mountain climbing described in the preceding chapters, Guyot's accomplishment is in a class by itself.

Myron Avery, himself a tramper extraordinaire in a later era, recognized in Guyot a peerless predecessor. He called him

> beyond question, the most thorough explorer who ever penetrated the Appalachian Mountain system. . . . Guyot acquired an extensive knowledge of the Appalachian Mountains, such as has never been possessed by any other person and under conditions which can never again be duplicated.

Chapter 14

Wintering over on Moosilauke and Washington

UNTIL just before the Civil War there is virtually no evidence that anyone seriously considered climbing the higher mountains of the Northeast
in winter. The summit houses of the 1850s were boarded up and abandoned in the fall. Starr King made one journey through the White Hills
one winter but kept himself bundled up snugly in a sleigh that glided over
the snows of the valley roads. Thomas Cole and others went up to look
at the icy spectacle of Kaaterskill Falls in February but not to the Catskill
summits.

Early nineteenth-century, Northeasterners considered mountains dangerous in winter. J. H. Spaulding wrote of Crawford Notch in 1855:

> For two-thirds of the year a more desolate place can hardly be imag-
> ined than this Notch. Dismal winds moan through the leafless trees,
> and through the fissures of the rocks; . . . Woe, then, to poor mortal-
> ity, when the snow falls fast, and the king of tempests rides on the
> wings of the hurricane through the clouds, armed with winter's cold,
> blinding sleet, and avalanches of ice!

Going above treeline in winter was particularly dreaded. As late as the
1850s, people feared what they called "frost clouds." Whatever this phenomenon was, "to be caught in its folds would probably be fatal."

The first known successful ascent of Mount Washington under wintry
conditions (though not in the calendar's winter, strictly speaking) arose
from a legal proceeding.[a] The case involved one of the many wrangles
over ownership and rights to the summit businesses. One of the dispu-
tants required a legal process to be served on the summit buildings. It

---

[a]There are rumors of a party on Moosilauke in 1800 when snow was on the mountain, but that lofty
eminence often has snow in October and April so there is no certain grounds for assuming that this
was a winter ascent (Little, *History of Warren*, p. 460). An entry in the register of the Crawford
House for December 4, 1836, by two Bangor, Maine, men reports: "Visited Mt. Washington today—
found the snow three foot deep—the day has been uncommon mild and pleasant." (New Hampshire
Historical Society collections; reprinted with permission). There is no indication of how high this
party went on the mountain.

happened to be December of the year 1858. The dread of winter climbing notwithstanding, the law must be served. One of the Glen House guides, B. F. Osgood, was prevailed upon to lead a deputy sheriff, Lucius Hartshorne, up the carriage road. On the morning of their historic climb, December 7, 1858, the lucky party happened on good weather. They reached the summit without trouble, where they found the view "sublime beyond the power of description." Nevertheless they feared to stay long, "as delay was dangerous in the extreme." Having nabbed his mountain, Sheriff Hartshorne noted with no little alarm a buildup of clouds in the southwest. "They knew it was a frost cloud," reported the local newspaper, " . . . and they hastened to avoid it." Not a moment too soon did our intrepid travelers make it below treeline, where "it came upon them. So icy and penetrating was its breath, that to have encountered its blinding, freezing power on the unprotected height, would have been to have perished with it as a pall to cover them." Quickly they descended to the Glen House where their friends anxiously awaited them, "well knowing the danger attending this never before accomplished feat."

The second winter ascent of Washington—and for the purist, the first true calendar-winter ascent—is credited to J. H. Spaulding, F. White, and C. C. Brooks. On February 10, 1862, the three men snowshoed to the Halfway House and bivouacked there "upon an old straw bed, laid on a snowdrift." Starting at sunrise the next morning, leaving their snowshoes behind, and apparently without crampons of any kind, they began their ascent on one of those rare mornings of perfect stillness that befall winter climbers so seldom on the Presidential Range. Almost immediately as they began the turn above their camp, the mountain steepened and steps had to be cut in the icy slopes. Their apprehension was great:

> One false step or careless motion, in such a place, would have sent us down, down, and given us a name with other victims of rashness. . . .
> As the pieces of ice went whirling down like a heavy shower of hail, at least eight hundred feet below, a shudder, such as teaches poor mortality its weakness, came over us.

As they approached the summit, storm clouds began to build up in the east, the wind picked up, and mist scudded past them, frosting their faces and clothing. Before conditions became too difficult, however, they reached the summit where the rime covering the buildings and summit boulders greatly impressed these three men, the first to see that famous summit under midwinter conditions. Clambering up a large drift, they removed an attic window and entered. They brought a stove up from below, found wood, and made a circle of mattresses around the stove. They seem to have managed rather well, considering that they were trapped there by the storm's fury for thirty-six hours. They sat out the entire next day (the then president's birthday), and spent a second night satisfactorily despite a temperature drop to -5 degrees. The morning of February 13 broke to "the most magnificent sunrise scenes that imagination can picture." Descent was accomplished without incident. The first full-scale winter ascent and overnight stay on Mount Washington was history.

Winter's special challenges

Early fears of "frost clouds" seem irrational in this era of regular winter climbing, but in point of fact the objective obstacles to climbing Northeastern mountains in winter are considerable. It is cold, of course. Zero is a common daytime temperature on all major mountains of the Northeast; -20 is not so common, -40 most unusual. Compared with other mountains, these are not especially troublesome temperatures. What is extraordinary is the wind. The Presidentials are famous for their high winds, and the fastest surface wind speed ever recorded was on Mount Washington: 231 mph, on April 12, 1934. Winter climbers above treeline can normally expect to be staggered by winds of 30–60 mph. Gales of 75–100 mph or more—elsewhere regarded as a hurricane—occur regularly each winter. Such winds often are associated with blowing snow and ice, adding reduced visibility to the problems. Full-scale winter storms can be as ferocious on those little hills as anywhere else outside the polar regions.

Men with such diverse backgrounds as Adm. Robert Peary, the Arctic explorer who first reached the North Pole; Noel Odell, veteran of attempts in the 1920s to climb Mount Everest; and Bradford Washburn, who knows Mount McKinley as well as anyone—all agree that winter storms can be as bad on Mount Washington as anything in the Arctic, the Himalayas, or Alaska. One world-class climber who has made significant first ascents in the notorious Patagonian ice cap, has said, "Mount Washington is the coldest place I've ever been," though he conjectures that the highest peaks like Everest might be colder in winter. "Patagonian winds are about comparable," he said, "but it's much warmer down there." Another big-mountain climber told the authors:

> When I went to the Harvard Cabin [on Mount Washington] this winter I brought one extra layer of clothes with me than I carried up on Annapurna South. The clothes I figured I needed in severe conditions in Huntington Ravine and on the Alpine Gardens are approximately what I'll take with me on Nanga Parbat, 26,700 ft., except I'll try to carry some additional coverage in my pack.

The severity of Northeastern winter weather should not be exaggerated. On many days each winter, when the wind is calm and skies clear, above-treeline travel is easy and pleasurable. During occasional winters, snowfall is delayed past January 1; on good days one can stroll up in running shoes. On December 27, 1982, one climber walked up Mount Washington in shorts. (One year and one day later, the same climber was blown off his feet in an unsuccessful attempt to move above treeline on the Franconia Ridge.)

Objective conditions of cold and wind are probably as bad or worse in some other mountain ranges. But because of the limited scale of Mount Washington and the consequent limited commitment required, climbers actually *climb* in much worse weather than they would elsewhere. On Washington, the area in which the most severe conditions are found is limited to the relatively small above-treeline zone; once one is down among the trees, that dreaded wind is suddenly manageable again. Not so on McKinley or Everest: there, there is no place to hide. Climbers do not even think of trying to climb those mountains during storms. The result is that northeastern U.S. climbers gain real experience in dealing with incredibly bad conditions, in which climbers elsewhere simply stay holed up inside a tent or snow cave, or down low at base.

Another peculiarity of Northeastern winter climbing is the perverse changeability of the weather. Mountain storms elsewhere may be just as bad but apparently are a bit more predictable. The prudent climber can usually manage to avoid having to move in the worst conditions. In the northeastern United States, the weather's fickleness is notorious, and with the relative safety of the trees nearby, climbers may find themselves trying to move in driving winds, low visibility, and extreme cold, where elsewhere no one would move.

Some of these considerations have been summed up by one climber who knows both New England and Alaskan mountains well, reflecting on several years as climbing ranger for Denali National Park (Denali is the traditional local name for McKinley) followed by a brief return visit to some Northeastern mountains in winter:

> One of the great psychological boons to the Whites is that treeline usually represents safety from the wind. . . . Then too is New Hampshire's psychological benefit of easy access. You can usually find it in your bones to stumble back to a roadhead. . . . Climbers on Denali simply don't venture out into winds like we experienced on top of Moosilauke because there is nothing safe to retreat to. So [in Alaska] I have never climbed in conditions as stormy as the ones I went out of my way to experience in the White Mountains. In winter of '75–'76, Brad Washburn told a naive group of Explorers that the White Mountains in winter were the best place possible to train for an ascent of Denali. He was right. However, years later, I have discovered that 6 trips up Denali still did not leave me adequately prepared for . . . the wind in Huntington's and a "stroll" up the gentle giant, Moosilauke.

Thus, paradoxically, it is the small scale and limited commitment of the winter climbing in the Northeast that makes these mountains an arena in which some of the most difficult adverse-weather climbing is actually practiced.

One of the most experienced Western climbers, a veteran of many years of winter climbing in the Cascades of Washington State, has offered these comments on Northeastern winter climbing and climbers:

> [Western climbers] don't really have it so tough, however. In New England, . . . in spite of the extremely severe climate, snowshoers swarm up these peaks all winter. Difficulty of travel that would limit western snowshoers to a trickle seems to incite the locals. . . . The people who climb these mountains in winter in "normal" conditions of subzero temperatures and 30-mph wind are just plain tough. There's no place else where people get out of the car when weather conditions are that hostile.

It is not entirely coincidental that the second winter ascent of 20,320-foot McKinley, though attempted by climbers from all over the world, was finally pulled off, in February 1982, via the technically demanding Cassin Ridge, by a three-person party, two of whom were from New England.[b] The New Englanders were accustomed to continuing climbing in wind and cold on days when others might have holed up. As one wilderness training leader has put it, "If you've camped in the White Mountains in the winter time, then you're prepared, as far as conditions, for a climb anywhere."

Again, the hardships of Northeastern winters should not be overstated. The difficulties are confined to above-treeline zones, the Presidentials most of all. Below treeline the wind and visibility problems are virtually eliminated. Here the major obstacle is the depth of the snow, which obscures summertime trails effectively and makes travel without skis or snowshoes literally impossible for any significant distance except under conditions of a strong crust, a well-beaten path, or an atypically snow-free winter. Still, in their benign moods, these little mountains become almost as easy to climb in winter as in summer. When the wind is manageable, temperatures moderate, and visibility good, even the formidable alpine zone is a pleasant place. At such times all that need be feared is the changeability of the weather. In special cases, winter climbing can actually be easier than summer. Bushwhacking through blowdown or uneven terrain is decidedly easier on deep, well-consolidated snow (though decidedly tougher on deep,

---

[b]Jonathan Waterman and Michael Young. Both had trained extensively in the Presidentials and Katahdin. During one winter, Waterman was the Appalachian Mountain Club caretaker in Tuckerman Ravine, with Young ensconced in neighboring Huntington Ravine as Harvard Mountaineering Club caretaker, and that winter they constantly roamed above treeline and in the steep gullies in all kinds of weather. (Jonathan Waterman is not related to the authors, as far as he or we know.) The third climber on the McKinley winter climb trained in Scotland, another land of little mountains, ferocious weather, and tough climbers. See Roger Mears, "Cassin Ridge in Winter," *Mountain* (July–Aug. 1983), pp. 24–29. The first winter ascent, done in 1967, did not include New Englanders or Scots; it was via the nontechnical West Buttress.

unconsolidated snow). Descending a packed snow path can be less taxing than descending rocky trails in summer. But such circumstances are the exception, not the rule.

Had nineteenth-century climbers encountered good days in the mountains they would have had no trouble climbing in winter. But most of the active summer climbers lived a long way off in Boston, or Portland, or New York, so they simply were not nearby to take advantage of the good days. The dominant tone in nineteenth century accounts of Northeastern mountains in winter is their dreariness. The romantics who were thrilled by the sublimity of rugged mountain heights in August found even their warm ardor chilled by the sight of the same crags in winter. Wrote Thomas Cole:

> There is beauty, there is sublimity in the wintry aspect of the mountains; but their beauty is touched with melancholy, and their sublimity takes a dreary tone.

The cheery summer resort of Sugar Hill lost its charm in the winter months to the nineteenth-century viewer:

> It must be a tedious place in winter: the cold is extreme: the winds are severe: there are few or no entertainments. . . . The principal occupations of the inhabitants are eating and sleeping.

Thus an important part of the explanation of the dearth of pre-1880 winter climbs was simply that no one cared to come up to the mountains at all during that season.

North country locals could get around expertly in the woods in winter. The early settlers had learned snowshoeing from the Indians. Some of the Indian-hunting rangers of the eighteenth century conducted their grisly business on snowshoes in mountainous country, though neither their quarry nor they would have reason to be at upper elevations at that season. Ethan Crawford and Charles Stuart scouted the second Crawford Path on snowshoes, but nothing indicates they were on the higher slopes on those trips. Hunters, trappers, loggers, and maple syrup producers were abroad in the forests during the winter months. Some of these early woodsmen must have been tough and resourceful on their snowshoes, and who will ever know if some of them occasionally went to tops of mountains for whatever impulses may have stirred them. But in general mountaintops simply were not a necessary or even a sensible object of their travels. Categorical assertions that *no* high mountains were *ever* climbed in winter would be hazardous. All the prudent historian can venture is that no *recorded* ascents took place before 1840, very few until 1880, and that regular recreational winter climbing of higher mountains in the Northeast did not begin until after 1890.

The earliest known record of a winter ascent is preserved in a letter from one of Capt. Alden Partridge's schoolboys, writing to his parents in Perth Amboy, New Jersey, on January 20, 1840. Young Edward Crowell tells of fifteen cadets from Norwich University tramping 23 miles to the base of Mount Ascutney, where they spent the first night at an inn at the foot of the mountain; climbing the peak the next day through deep snow without snowshoes, taking seven exhausting hours to do it; and spending the night on top, sleeping in blankets on a bough bed in a crude snow cave. The weather seems to have provided what a modern climber would call "full conditions"—that is, Master Crowell reports that "it was snowing rapidly and the wind was blowing a hurricane." The locals knew of no previous winter ascent and predicted they would neither make the summit nor remain out all night. "However," Crowell writes with Partridgian pride, "we toughed it out."

In 1853, when Thomas Wentworth Higginson visited Carter Notch, he was impressed with a rugged local woodsman named Bill Perkins. His narrative mentions that Perkins had climbed Wildcat Mountain in winter:

> Over the brow of that mountain our guide had passed in snow shoes;
> . . . "It was considerable of a clear day (he said, briefly), and he
> thought there might be something to see up there—and there was."

If this passing mention can in truth be taken to mean a midwinter ascent to the summit of 4,397-foot Wildcat, it is the first recorded winter ascent of a 4,000-foot mountain in the Northeast. Within the next ten years, there followed one unsuccessful attempt (at least) on Mount Washington in 1856, and the two successful climbs described at the start of this chapter.

These few tentative advances were all the precedent there was for the first major winter mountaineering program, which began in 1869: the winterlong occupation first of the summit of Moosilauke, and then of Mount Washington itself.

Moosilauke in 1869–70

It is a measure of the vision of Joshua Henry Huntington that the idea of wintering over on the top of Mount Washington came to him even before the mountain—or almost any other Northeastern mountains either— had ever been climbed in winter. In the summer of 1858, Huntington first broached the idea to Charles H. Hitchcock, the son of the Amherst College president, during a geological research trip to Lake Champlain. In the next ten years efforts to obtain financing never quite succeeded. Finally in 1868 Hitchcock was appointed to direct a geological survey for the state of New Hampshire. He selected Huntington as his top assistant. However, the Tip Top House declined the men's request to use the building for their project. Unexpectedly, the owner of the summit house on Moosilauke volunteered the use of his facility. Hitchcock quickly agreed and wrote excitedly to Huntington—so excitedly that his handwriting was illegible and Huntington thought the mountain in question was Monadnock. Whatever the peak, Huntington eagerly accepted the opportunity.

The two scientists were anxious to learn more about what winter was really like up there amid the "frost clouds" and the dreaded weather. Mount Washington had all along been their primary objective and still was. But, as the tenth highest peak in the White Mountains, with the 4,802-foot summit sufficiently above the treeline to be exposed to full-scale alpine conditions, Moosilauke seemed a fit trial run for the great Washington venture.

Initially Hitchcock lined up a Dartmouth student, Arthur C. Page, to accompany Huntington on the first winter occupation of an above-tree-line zone. Either because of second thoughts about the prudence of spending the winter up there or for some other good reason, Page soon landed a job in Georgia for the winter and withdrew from the project. This new setback, however, proved a blessing in disguise, because it opened the way for a young photographer from Warren, New Hampshire, named A. F. Clough. As events were to show, not even Huntington could surpass the redoubtable Mr. Clough in his passion for winter-above-treeline hardships.

It was well into November 1869 before they began the work of hauling wood and provisions up the bridle path, using horsepower as long as conditions permitted. On November 23, Huntington and Clough started up, assisted by some local men and a team to haul a heavy-laden wagon. Huntington described the scene:

> As we came where the trees were small, we perceived that it was growing cold. When a mile from the summit, we were met by such a blast of wind, with driving snow, that we were compelled to halt. The men who had gone forward soon returned, driven back by the fierceness of the blast. They reported that the snow was in such immense drifts that it would be impossible for the horses to pass. Our only resource was to return to the foot of the mountain.

It was a discouraged crew who gathered for the evening meal. Some were frostbitten, and none but the optimistic James Clement, Moosilauke's most experienced guide, believed the mountain would be climbed with horses and loaded wagons that winter. But, of course, mountain weather is ever known for its changeableness, and the next two days were "charming"—clear and cold—and the work went on at a feverish pace until on November 26, with Moosilauke's rounded summit dome once again enveloped in cloud, the last loads were taken up, hoarfrost adhering to all. At last all was ready, and on December 31 Clough and Huntington ascended the mountain for the final time to take possession of their summit home. They were to remain there for two months.

Scarcely were they ensconced in their winter quarters than on January 2, 1870, they were greeted with a raging storm. This time it was not the cold that was their enemy, but unseasonal warmth and rain—enough to flood the floor of their room, the wind driving the rain through the cracks and chinks in the summit building. Clough, a man who seemed to revel in nature's holocausts, determined to measure the speed of this furious wind. He succeeded in doing so by literally crawling out on the rocks and holding the anemometer up to the force of the gale, where he clocked a strong 97.5 mph—the greatest wind velocity ever recorded to that date. "When he reached the house," Huntington wrote, "he was thoroughly saturated, the wind having driven the rain through every garment, although they were of the heaviest material, as though they were made of the lightest fabric."

Now their real battle with the storm began. Toward evening the wind increased, blowing the glass out of the windows, creating such a draft that it extinguished the fire, broke the lights, even snuffed out the hurricane lamp. "Darkness and terror reigned," wrote Huntington, "but calmness, with energy, were requisites for such an occasion." Not without a struggle, the two men got the situation back in hand by nailing boards across the windows and using blankets to stuff the cracks. Clough's entry in his diary for this storm reads:

> If it blows much harder it may sweep us, house and all off the crest. They would have a first class inn then down at North Benton. If we go it will be by wind. We can go swift and well but how the devil shall we light. Blow and hang if you will. I have my boots, coat and hat on all right for a start. H. looks as though he was all right, all but his eyes; some fright there, for they stick out. I am not quite calm.

The winter of 1870 passed well for the two observers who were now both in their element. For the first time a scientist and a photographer could study, from a winter mountaintop, the ever-changing clouds, the buildup of winter snows, the constant renewal and erosion of ice crystals on rocks and trees, the patterns of drift created by wind. It proved a valuable opportunity for meteorological study. Hitchcock later commented on what was learned on Moosilauke: "In some respects, the Mount Washington phenomena have not equalled those upon Moosilauke." On the clear days they could see the glistening Washington, and both knew that this training on Moosilauke was preparation for larger things. Clough wrote:

We often asked ourselves the question, "Shall we next winter occupy the top of that mountain?" And I think that it was as fully settled in our minds then as at any time after, if the necessary funds could be raised.

On the last day of February they descended the mountain. The day was violent, with temperatures between 0 and -17 and wind up around 70 mph. They loaded a sled and started down the southeast side. When they hit the exposed ridge they could not stand against that wind and the sled was soon splintered on the rocks. Huntington wrote of their precarious situation:

> Here we were, the wind blowing seventy miles per hour, and the thermometer at zero or below. What was to be done? A decision must be made at once. To remain here only for a moment, without putting forth severe physical efforts, we should become statues only too lifelike. We pulled the broken sled with its load over the side of the ridge where the wind was not quite so furious, and Clough went back to get a sled, which had been left two days before, where we first came on the ridge.

With difficulty they managed to reload and finally made it to the shelter of the trees. The Moosilauke winter adventure was over.

Ten years after Huntington and Clough's winter sojourn their feat was duplicated by two local boys, Jim Clement and his brother, D.Q. Jim Clement, as has been mentioned, was the foremost local guide for Moosilauke, a tough winter woodsman who thoroughly enjoyed the challenge of cold and storms. D.Q. kept a journal that is an utterly disarming account of two brothers having a marvelous time in the face of some atrocious storms, mingled with patches of beautiful weather. Unlike their scientific predecessors, Jim and D.Q. Clement had no support team, no specialized equipment, and hardly any visitors. They improvised crampons ("I have to put spikes on my boots") and ice axes (" a cane with a steel point on it"), and tugged their provisions up on a hand-drawn sled ("Jim has got a good sled"). When they went down for more supplies, if conditions were right, they'd ride the sled down the carriage road ("When the snow is glare how fast I go, more than a mile a minute"). During the good weather they roamed the top of the mountain, observing animal tracks, occasional birds, frost feathers, and other wind sculpture. But blizzards, high winds, and bitter cold plagued them as much as they had Huntington and Clough, though the locals enjoyed every minute of it.

> In February we have hard storms. We go out to see them form and burst . . .
> The flakes come down so thick you can not see six feet through them. It is as though some one sifts meal from the sky. All the time flash and crash rip out of it. . . .

While this storm rages Jim smokes, makes the fire roar and seems full of bliss. He is fond of the strange and wild. Since I was born, says he, there has been no such storm as this.

Washington in 1870–71

Meanwhile, as the winter of 1870–71 approached, Huntington and Clough, with the full support of Hitchcock, were bursting to take on Mount Washington. But though spirits were willing, lack of funding remained an apparently insuperable problem, until at the last moment a curious figure stepped forward. In July of that summer, one S. A. Nelson of Georgetown, Massachusetts, approached Hitchcock, asking to join the summit party for the winter. Hitchcock was understandably cool toward this inexperienced volunteer. As the autumn dragged on, with no money in sight for the project, Nelson added to his persistent requests that he might be able to raise five hundred dollars. Upon hearing this, Hitchcock promptly sent him a formal invitation. When Nelson joined the mountain team, an unassuming, slightly built man, he came to stay; he remained on the mountain through May and proved a dependable and resourceful team member.

In the course of the fund-raising efforts, Hitchcock had pricked the interest of the War Department's newly created "Bureau of Telegrams and Reports for the Benefit of Commerce," an Army unit concerned with weather observation and forecasting. (That phrase "for the benefit of commerce," a bureaucratic rationale for the Army's involvement in weather observation, was to become an ironic slogan for the Mount Washington team.) The Army sent no money, but it did agree to supply an observer and 3 miles of telegraphic wire, all of which proved to be of great value. In early December Sgt. Theodore Smith arrived, becoming the fourth member of the summit team.

One other individual became involved. Howard A. Kimball, a Concord, New Hampshire, photographer, signed on as an alternate to Clough. The two worked together smoothly, one or the other being on the summit most of the winter.

The mountain did not fail to show them its best—or worst. Even before they moved in, as the group prepared the interior of the small building erected for their use, an October storm of wind and driving rain brought excitement. As the battering increased, Huntington saw the door start to give and began to think fast about what they would need to do should it blow in. In the next moment

   . . . in it came. The boards and planks lying about in the building, were thrown in every direction. I never saw boards move about so lively, they seemed to have lost their weight. I knew they were heavy enough the other day, when I put them in the building. We tried to put the door in place, but with all our efforts we could not get it near the doorway; . . . We put the door against the side of the building and tried to push it along, but when about six inches of it became exposed, in it came again.

They finally nailed a board to the floor inside the door, bracing a plank against that to hold the door in place while they nailed it fast—nailing themselves in until the storm passed.

Finally on November 12, 1870, Huntington moved in, his thirteen-year ambition realized. After eighteen days alone, he was joined by Clough and Kimball on November 30, by Smith and Nelson shortly thereafter.

Of their first thirty days on the mountain, the photographers enjoyed but three on which conditions permitted work outside. On December 15, the temperature was -15 degrees, with winds clocked at 92 mph, though they did not dare to try measuring at the peak of the gale: "It was not safe to venture out with the anemometer, unless we wanted to take an airline passage to Tuckerman's Ravine." This was the first test of the new building, and the men realistically were not certain it would stand the pounding of the Presidential wind. They took the precaution of putting hardtack in their pockets and "had axe and saw handy to cut their way out if needed." It should be more than casually noted what this action implied: had their shelter been destroyed in those conditions and at night, they could not fail to be sensible of the consequences. They were in a true life-threatening situation, not playing games up there like a recreational climber out for the day above treeline. Yet Sergeant Smith shouted to the others above the roar of the storm that "if we were blown down into Tuckerman's Ravine, it would be for the 'benefit of commerce,' and so, of course, all right."

Except for the hints provided on Moosilauke during the winter before, this was the first time that people had experienced firsthand the full fury of Mount Washington's winter storms. On December 29 Kimball wrote:

This morning I went out to see if we could make some negatives during the day. I had barely got out, when the wind swept me, with resistless force, away from our entrance or door, and I only saved myself from the rude handling and probable bruising, by catching the chain which passed over the building. It hurled me with such power as to swing me in toward the depot into a snow drift, which was much better than to have been swept upon the rocks covered with the frost feathers. How was I to face such a wind and get back? I tried several times, each time carried back by the force of the wind, the velocity of which, at times, must have been as high as seventy miles an hour, but not steadily thus. There were lulls when it did not reach more than forty miles an hour, and in one of these I crawled back on "all fours," and got into the Observatory, determined to stay there as long as the wind blew so furiously; and we have decided, without much question, that it will be impossible to make a photograph today.

During a storm on February 4 and 5, winds of more than 100 mph rattled the building. Wrote Nelson in his journal: "We shout across the room to be heard. . . . Everything movable is on the move. Books drop from the shelves, we pick them up, replace them only to do it again and again." After two days of this, the men gathered at breakfast to talk over the experience, "recalling many laughable incidents, and agreeing that we rather enjoyed the night's experience than otherwise, that it was a sublime affair . . . but all things considered, were unanimous in the opinion that once a fortnight was quite enough for such grand displays of the storm-king's power."

A cheerful sangfroid was their style that winter. On January 23, Nelson's journal reads: "Temperature tonight ten P.M.—minus 40 degrees; a changeable climate this." At midnight of the February storm, the wind exceeding 100 mph, he wrote, "Really there is quite a breeze just now." Huntington observed, "It is sometimes difficult to be perfectly cool, particularly when the thermometer gets below -40, as the chances of escape are very small should the house be crushed. But in general it only furnishes excitement enough to keep off the *ennui* incident to an isolated life."

Life wasn't all hard work and storms. For good weather spells, Huntington and Smith worked out a sled ride on the northeast shoulder of the mountain; about a mile long, it was appraised as "slightly hazardous, but full of fun and exciting." Once when Huntington raised a flag on the summit at the request of a party from Littleton, Smith and Nelson got together and formed the "Republic of Washington. . . . We only lack three things to make our new government a success: a national debt, internal revenue, and two custom-houses, one on the carriage road and the other on the railway."

Huntington loved the mountains in their fury. "Mountains without clouds are spiritless and tame," he wrote. "Whether we watch the storm as it approaches, or feel its force as it breaks in all its fury on the summit, there is a grandeur and sublimity in these manifestations that fills the mind with awe and wonder." Yet for all his love of wildness, he was equally touched by the tender beauties to be seen. Frequently he called the others out of bed for a beautiful sunrise. Wrote Nelson on one occasion: "Professor found today some beautiful frost-wings; just as perfect in form and feathering as a real wing; they were beautiful indeed."

The first long winter on Mount Washington wound down reluctantly. As late as May 7 and 8, a furious snowstorm, with winds of 90 mph, dumped almost 3 feet of new snow at treeline and kept the summit crew trapped for two days. But that was winter's last blast. On Sunday, May 14, with Sergeant Smith and the photographers already departed, Huntington walked out of the observatory at 9:00 A.M. to descend the mountain for the last time of that long winter. The mountain gods paid their final tribute to this kindred spirit, escorting him down with winds of 48 mph and temperatures of 14 degrees. Nelson worried about the bad conditions but knew Professor well enough not to stop him. Nelson then lingered on to savor the summit solitude for a few days.

From a mountaineering standpoint, the occupation of Washington during winter and repeated ascents by the observers under diverse conditions was a tour de force. By comparison, polar exploration was in its infancy. This was almost twenty years before Fridtjof Nansen crossed the Greenland ice cap, an event sometimes taken as the kickoff of serious Arctic-Antarctic work. The race for the poles was not to come until the 1890s and later. The winter weather experienced by Huntington and his friends on Moosilauke and Washington was something that only the native peoples of the far north and a handful of Arctic pioneers had ever seen.[c]

For raw guts and determination, the exploits of Huntington and his mates deserve to be ranked not far below the polar expeditions of the next generation—of Peary, Amundsen, Scott, and Shackleton. If that assessment is fair, it is interesting to note how little known is the name of Huntington, much less those of Clough, Nelson, and Smith; probably not one in fifty of today's ice climbers in the ravine that bears his name could identify Joshua Henry Huntington.

---

[c] A few remarkable polar journeys predated the winter occupation of Mount Washington, such as Samuel Hearne's explorations in North America's "barren lands" in 1769–72, Capt. John Franklin's travels over much of the same ground in 1819–22, and Capt. John Ross's discovery of the magnetic pole in 1829–33. All of these expeditions included more than one winter spent in the extreme north. Most of the better-known Arctic and Antarctic epics, however, came after the 1870s.

Part Three

Mountains as places to walk: 1870–1910

THE FIRST wave of recreational climbing in the Northeastern mountains receded as fast as it had risen. The era of bridle paths and summit houses in the 1850s faded away with the start of the Civil War. The war interrupted mountain vacations for five years, but the hiatus in public taste for mountain scenery lasted more like fifteen years. When people's interest in mountain climbing resumed during the 1870s, it took a very different form. Instead of the transcendentalist vision of the sublime, the postwar recreationists were walkers and climbers, full of practical-minded energy.

We should recall that the generation of the 1850s was not so much interested in *climbing* mountains as in simply being among them—or on their tops, if they could ride up. A fair proportion of Starr King's generation was far more concerned with gazing at panoramas and experiencing the sublime than in actually walking uphill, which could be fatiguing. While the top of Mount Washington was often crowded, a summit register placed on Mount Adams in 1854 had fewer than twenty names in it two decades later. Beyond their familiar summits the vacationing gentry of the 1850s seldom strayed, and the isolated forays off the beaten track by an occasional Guyot were uncommon and considered moderately eccentric. When Thoreau or Hale or Channing sought a sporting climb, it was usually (as with the novice adventurer in the region today) on the few well-known peaks. Monadnock, Greylock, Wachusett, Katahdin, Washington and Lafayette were among Thoreau's objectives, for example—not, one notices, Carrigain or Gothics or the Traveler. So the late 1870s generation of mountain walkers were the first real hikers in the modern sense of the term.

Why did the tourists who flocked to the Tip-Top houses and Sunset Rocks during the 1850s lose interest during the 1860s and the first half of the 1870s, only to come back with even greater enthusiasm during the late 1870s and 1880s? Diminished interest in mountains after 1860 is explained initially by the outbreak of a major war. That it lasted ten years after the war ended is harder to explain. A tentative hypothesis may be drawn from observing a similar pause in mountaineering activity immediately following World War II. It may be that, when a nation's young men have been thrown into a shooting war on a large scale, they get all the experience with adventure that they want for a while. The synthetic or self-imposed adventure of mountain climbing may seem a waste of time to veterans of for-real dangers such as so many young American faced in the Civil War and World War II.[a]

Besides, a change in national mood was working itself out during the 1860s. The old romantic order was fading. The mystic vision of the mountains from afar gave way to a more practical and energetic realism. In 1860 Starr King left the East and took his romantic vision to the greater heights of the Sierra. Thoreau died in 1862. Professor Emmons died in 1863, outliving his old Marcy colleague, Redfield, by six years. Their stalwart guide, John Cheney, was in his seventieth year before the decade was over, his pioneering explorations reduced to memories. In 1869, brooding bitterly in her decaying Vermont farm, seventy-six-year-old Lucy Crawford passed away, far from her beloved notch, where she and the mountain giant Ethan had once symbolized the White Hills to a generation of travelers, a generation now long gone. Within six years Lucy's wild notch had a railroad track running through it.

After the Civil War, a surge of lusty economic expansion and preoccupation with material gains washed away what was left of transcendentalist fervor. Spiritual renewal on quiet mountaintops was not all that attractive to a nation on the march toward industrial progress. A Dartmouth student group touring the White Mountains in 1871 showed little reverence for the sublime:

> We failed to observe . . . the majesty and sublimity of that region. We not only failed to be impressed, but spoke with such comical levity of everything, that I fear we should have shocked those who profess to feel a reverence for the White Hills.

Nevertheless, rather suddenly after about 1875, new waves of mountain-lovers came forward but with different goals and different attitudes. This new generation loved walking. It was an age of doers, not dreamers. It was a time for action, full of energy and purpose. So when they returned to the mountains, they came now to climb and hike, to form

---

[a]World War I involved European youth fully as much as World War II, but not so many Americans. That earlier conflict was almost over before many U.S. troops saw action. Similarly, though the Korean conflict presented every bit as much war as any other to those who were directly involved, the country as a whole was not as pervasively affected. The Vietnam fighting had a profound effect on American society, but it did not have the same *kinds* of effects, stemming from direct personal involvement with danger, which the Civil War and World War II had for so large a part of the young generation of Americans.

hiking clubs, to build foot trails (not bridle paths), and to go up all the ranges they could find (not just the standard handful of traditional peaks). Mountains became outstanding places to walk.

For the wealthy and the middle class alike, a new kind of summer vacation evolved during the post–Civil War years. The pattern was altogether different from today's weekends, long weekends, and two-week vacations. In the early stages of the great industrial boom, the average working person faced a sixty-hour work week—ten hours a day for six days each week. Thus, the phenomenon of the hiking weekend was a later development, awaiting not only the arrival of the automobile (after 1900) but also the availability of at least Saturday afternoons free from job commitments (after 1920). On the other hand, college teachers and others had the entire summer off, where many now take on summer school or consulting duties. So back then it was not uncommon for families to spend all summer in the mountains. Wives and children would pack huge trunks and remove to a mountain vacation center for weeks at a time, husbands and fathers commuting by the railroad to join them when they could. Through the leisurely summer, social patterns evolved around a variety of diversions, from fancy dress balls to croquet matches and long carriage rides.

In the bustling prosperity of the post–Civil War era, mountain vacations began to show divergent strains. On the one hand, these years constituted America's Gilded Age—years of industrial expansion, huge fortunes, lavish entertainments and amusements, garish displays of wealth, and a lot of bad taste. On the other hand, impecunious students and others of modest means were looking for the least expensive way of seeing the mountains. The wealthy gave the mountains the Grand Hotel. The needs of the latter group spawned the lowly boardinghouse.

The Grand Hotels were truly grand. If the Catskill Mountain House never lost its top rank, not one but two Catskill resorts that opened in 1880 actually exceeded the Pine Orchard relic in capacity and luxury, if not in taste. These were the Grand Hotel at Pine Hill (450 guests), with a marble fountain gushing spring water in the very rotunda through which the guests strolled, and the stupendous Hotel Kaaterskill (1,000 guests!). The latter had the effrontery to rise like an exhalation on South Mountain, within two miles of the Mountain House itself, and to parody its gilt-age grandeur in a vulgar display of even more wealth and luxury. By the end of the nineteenth century, the fashionable vacationer in the Catskills could choose among no fewer than twenty-nine hotels capable of taking in more than 100 guests. In the nearby Shawangunks, the identical twins Albert and Alfred Smiley opened establishments that reached grand hotel proportions, though with a quiet dignity befitting both the Quaker traditions of the owners and the subtler charms of the Shawangunk landscape. In the White Mountains, grand hotels flourished in all three of the great notches: the Glen House in Pinkham Notch, the Profile House in Franconia, and several in the notch where Abel Crawford had pioneered. (Here, as everywhere, the railroads played an active role in providing ready access to the notches and the resort centers.) If the longitudinal Green Mountains afforded a poor arrangement for resort centers, even in Vermont the Mansfield House now hosted 300 guests, and a brief tourist prosperity blossomed around Killington in the 1880s and 1890s, continuing to do so at Manchester, Lake Willoughby, and Lake Memphremagog. While Katahdin and the Maine woods rebuffed all grand hotel pretensions, Maine's seacoast hills put in a more successful claim to participation in the Gilded Age: by the end of the 1860s Bar Harbor on Mount Desert had some ten hotels, by 1875 fifteen, and by 1888 eighteen, the largest of which could accommodate 600 guests; the Rangeley Lakes area began to attract vacationers; and on Moosehead Lake, under the flinty cliff of Mount Kineo, a substantial resort developed.[b] In Massachusetts, no major resort business ever took hold, because the spirit of the Berkshires lay in the grand private estates that moneyed summer folk built, especially in Lenox—they called these cottages, but their owners followed the hounds, formed cricket teams, and employed more than one hundred servants for a single "cottage."

It should not be supposed that mountain vacation accommodations were limited to palaces. In the shadow of the giants in almost all the mountain areas, a large number of smaller inns and simple boarding-houses prospered. They could not offer chandeliers or fountains in the lobby, but their rates were within the means of a much broader segment of vacationers. In the Catskills, for example, the Ulster & Delaware Railroad's opening in 1870 converted all the towns along the way into "summer-boarding centers." The guidebooks of the time had page after page of advertisements for these more mundane accommodations, some with photos that betray that many were little more than large Victorian houses with rooms rearranged and cut up to take in boarders. "Can Accommodate 20 Boarders," or "Accommodates 20" are typical of the advertisements of such places. By the 1890s, noted one guide, "nearly every Catskill man's home is a little paradise and filled with summer boarders." Many of them were moderately priced. At a time (1893) when it cost $4.00 or $5.00 for an opulent night at the Catskill Mountain House, or $3.00 at the Overlook, most boardinghouses in the towns along the U & D cost $1.50 or $2.00 per night.

---

[b]Dreams of a grand resort, if not the reality, even approached Katahdin. In 1861 Charles Hitchcock, the geologist, had sat at Chimney Pond and speculated that a hotel would be just the thing on the quiet shoreline of this pristine tarn, "the most romantic spot for a dwelling-house in the whole state." Hitchcock's dreams also envisioned "a good carriage road" to Chimney Pond and a "bridle path from there to the summit" (*Sixth Annual Report of the Secretary of the Maine Board of Agriculture* (1861), p. 399). As a hotel man, Hitchcock was a great geologist. This dream never got any farther than Marcus Keep's scheme for a road to the top. Pamola's stronghold remained inviolate.

Between these extremes one could find an intermediate kind of mountain center, frequented by moderately well-off vacationers with summertime leisure, especially teachers, ministers, and a few businessmen who arranged for extended time off. These were places such as the Ravine House in Randolph, New Hampshire, or Adirondack Lodge. Monadnock always remained more of a middle-class haven; although no large-scale hotel grew up, beginning in the 1870s regular summer visitors found hospitable lodging at the Half Way House, the Ark, and the Shattuck Inn, the latter two lying at the southeastern foot of the mountain. After 1875 it was these places—smaller, intimate, moderately comfortable but not ostentatiously luxurious—from which the second wave of recreational climbing largely emanated.

Hill walking became popular close to the big cities too, wherever wild uplands were available close by. It is hard to know how much recreational hiking was done by city folk in the early part of the nineteenth century, but it is clear that by the 1880s, and especially the 1890s, picnic and sightseeing outings to nearby woodsy hills were a popular pastime. Around Boston, the Blue Hills and the Middlesex Fells were favorite retreats; escaping up from New York, the Fresh Air Club and other earnest pedestrians roamed the Hudson Highlands; and from Connecticut's cities, strollers headed for the Sleeping Giant, the Hanging Hills of Meriden, New Haven's "Four Rocks," or other trap-rock outcrops in which the state abounds. Springfield's urban trampers had the Holyoke Range, those of Portland had Blackstrap Hill.

Most hiking was done by small groups of families or friends, but at least one organized club fielded much larger parties. The Appalachian Mountain Club's excursions tended to be crowded, sociable events, both for day-trips to the nearby Blue Hills, Middlesex Fells, or Wachusett, or for multiday "field meetings" at spots in the White Mountains (usually) or elsewhere (occasionally). On one hike in the Middlesex Fells on May 19, 1883, no fewer than 210 exuberant Appalachians turned out, but parties of more than 100 were the exception. A note on the May 15, 1886, Middlesex Fells trip apologizes that "owing to the uncertainty of the weather, there were only about seventy-five members and friends who participated." For the AMC field meetings, total trip attendance typically ranged from 100 to 150, though for any particular day's climb, parties were normally more like 20 to 40.

Overnight camping trips—the word *backpacking* is a twentieth-century invention—made a tentative beginning in the late nineteenth century. However, this practice was not a major focus of mountain recreationists until later.

The characteristics of Northeastern mountain climbing in the years 1870–1910 came together gradually, shaped by a number of forces that combined to form the modern Northeastern hiking milieu:

The art of walking—pleasure in pure pedestrian perambulation—swept the country. It had to be only a matter of time before the joys of walking on level ground extended to walking up mountains.

The two principal ranges—the White Mountains and Adirondacks—were explored thoroughly by scientific survey teams, revealing for everyone that not just a few big-name peaks but an abundance of varied mountains might make excellent places to walk.

Railroads completed the work, begun before the Civil War, of providing speedy access to vacation centers throughout the mountain region.

Guidebooks appeared, offering instruction to the new generation of mountain walkers, not only on where to find trails but on how to go hiking, what clothing and equipment to take, how to pack a knapsack or blanket roll, even how to walk uphill.

Hiking clubs formed.

Women, embarking on the stormy road to suffrage in 1920, took to the hills in great numbers and with growing independence, although they still labored under the frightful burden of dress codes that seem ludicrous today.

Maps of the mountains made hiking easier and safer. Guyot's 1880 map of the Catskills was matched by skillfully executed maps of the White Mountains and Adirondacks.

The first fatalities for recreationists on mountains occurred during the 1850s. By the end of the century, enough incidents had accumulated to provide a stark reminder to all future hikers that these little hills could be places of peril as well as pleasure.

Concerned conservationists roused campaigns to set aside large tracts of mountain land, both public and private, to preserve the hiking and climbing environment for their own generation and later.

All these forces, coming together largely in the years between 1870 and 1910, did much to shape the Northeastern mountain world we know today.

Chapter 15

The pleasures of pedestrianism

UNABASHED joy in the pleasures of pure pedestrianism exploded all over the national scene right after the Civil War. City dwellers strolled the avenues. Vacationers paced the country lanes. Well-known national figures extolled the virtues of the vigorous constitutional. The editor of the *New York Times*, John Huston Finley, annually walked the perimeter of Manhattan Island on his birthday, a distance of 32 miles and presumably a far less hazardous undertaking then than now. A few zealots took off on long-distance walks rarely matched in this century.

Perhaps America's greatest pure walker ever was Edward Payson Weston (1839–1929). Every day except Sunday (when he never exercised), Weston walked 12–15 miles as a matter of course. In 1863 he claimed the record time for walking from Philadelphia to New York, which he did in twenty-three hours and twenty-nine minutes. On October 29, 1867, Weston started walking west from Portland, Maine. One month and 1,235 miles later, he pulled into Chicago (having rested every Sunday en route). In 1870 he walked 100 miles in fewer than twenty-four hours. Weston kept up his walking feats through a long and cheerful life, bettering both his Philadelphia–New York and Portland–Chicago times when more than sixty years old, getting all the way from New York to San Francisco on foot at age seventy, and still vigorously pacing along till shortly before his death at age ninety.

This growing interest in walking during the 1860s, 1870s, and 1880s may be compared to the national interest in running almost exactly one hundred years later. A vigorous afternoon's walk was a regular ritual for many men. Doubtless the carriage rider of that day smiled at the sight of earnest walkers along suburban roadways much as the auto driver of our day is amused at the equally earnest joggers along the sidewalks of main thoroughfares.

Victorian scruples notwithstanding, women joined the foot-bound traffic. Newspapers proclaimed, "It is a common sight on pleasant mornings to see couples and trios of young ladies taking their constitutional on the avenues." One article assured its readers that such women were not English actually but genuine American females: "Perhaps their ruby complexions, the result of their regular outdoor exercise, induces the conclusion that they are English maidens."

For vacationers with more than a few days to spare, "the pedestrian tour" began to be as fashionable as the former carriage-driving tour. Walking country roads was easier and more pleasant before the coming of the automobile and hard-surface roadways, though dustier in some seasons and muddier in others. Besides, unlike the carriage rider, the pedestrian could leave the road at a whim, cut across the open fields or through woods, or "linger among sweet-scented wild flowers." From modest beginnings during the 1840s, the extended pedestrian tour's popularity blossomed during the 1860s and 1870s for those with large blocs of leisure in summertime: students, professors and schoolteachers, ministers, aspiring artists or writers, visiting foreign travelers. Solitary or paired ramblers were usually men, but larger parties were often mixed or even all-women groups, and a few families.

When applied to the New England mountain region, the extended pedestrian tour at first meant mostly walking around the roads of the region, without actually climbing many mountains themselves. Careful examination of the evidence suggest that, while pedestrian tours of mountain regions flourished chiefly during the 1860s and the first half of the 1870s, actual mountain *climbing* was very limited until the late 1870s. Nevertheless, these pedestrian tours were an important preliminary in the history of mountain walking.

Two or three rambling companions might travel very light, putting up at inns in larger towns and at farmhouses in the country, paying for their meals wherever they could find them. Gatherings of half a dozen or more voluble strollers might arrange for a baggage wagon to be towed by a horse; the horse and wagon carried all their camping equipment and extra clothing, and gave them at least the option of bringing their own food and roughing it by camping out. Economy was the word: a Portland student group did a sixteen-day walking tour of the White Mountains at an average cost of $11.86 per person. Lightweight equipment, so prized a part of today's backpacking scene, had not yet arrived and was not necessary from any viewpoint save that of the hard-working horse: a recommended tent "weighs but fifty pounds," and the "compact" cook-stove could roast a turkey and support "an eight-quart kettle, six-quart tea-kettle, two-quart coffee pot, fry-pan, two square and one round pans, a dipper, gridiron, tent-collar, and eight feet of telescope funnel," the whole nesting neatly into a 27-pound bundle at a cost of $15.00.

The pedestrian tour was a relaxed and casual affair, as this description of a Williams College outing in 1860 attests:

> We seldom walked together along the road. We were scattered along a
> distance of two or three miles, usually in different squads. The first

was composed of the more ambitious—those who walked "on time." The next were the more conservative ones, who pursued the even tenor of their way, never hastening, and seldom halting. They were always the least fatigued. The last were the footsore and the weary, who kept near the wagon, which was generally behind.

As mentioned, climbing mountains was a distinctly secondary objective of these long walks. The by now traditional peaks might be climbed but more in the spirit of taking in popular sightseeing attractions than as the principal focus of the journey. The British novelist Anthony Trollope, doing the pedestrian tour when he was over in 1861, advised readers, "Ascend Mount Washington on pony. That is *de rigeur.*" Trollope also recommended the ascent of Mount Willard: "It is but a walk of two hours, up and down, if so much." Other White Mountain peaks climbed by 1860s pedestrians were limited chiefly to Lafayette, Kearsarge, Red Hill (near Lake Winnipesaukee), and, less often, Moosilauke. While one was ambling through Vermont, climbs of Mount Mansfield, the Camel's Hump, or Equinox might be diverting. Walks along the Connecticut River valley would certainly take in Ascutney, if one was that far north; farther south, it would be the Holyoke Range and possibly Mounts Tom and Toby. But more challenging mountaineering ventures were discouraged. A widely read how-to-do-it manual of the day cautioned,

> Avoid all nonsensical waste of strength, and gymnastic feats before and during the march; play no jokes upon your comrades, that will make their day's work more burdensome. Young people are very apt to forget these things.

The pedestrian tour of mountain regions in the 1860s and 1870s thus *preceded* the second wave of true climbing. These walkers were not climbers, save for obligatory strolls up the standard three or four peaks. The passion for pedestrianism should be viewed as one of the forces that *contributed to* the burst of mountain climbing that began in the 1870s, rather than as a part of climbing history per se.

From most of the leading colleges of the Northeast, students sallied forth on these pedestrian tours of the mountains. Moses F. Sweetser, the White Mountain guidebook writer of 1876, took satisfaction in observing,

> It is pleasing to see so many of the undergraduates of the New England colleges taking up this form of exercise and visiting the mountains in small squads of active service.

Another tour guide purred: "There is a certain age when young men glory in pedestrianism, and see in it a source of great pleasure."

The origins of college pedestrianism can be traced to Mount Holyoke College and the vigorous principles of its founder, Mary Lyon. A strong believer in physical exercise, Lyon wrote into the "Book of Duties" for young women at her seminary:

> The young ladies are to be required to walk one mile per day till the snow renders it desirable to specify time instead of distance, then three quarters of an hour is the time required.

In 1839 Mount Holyoke inaugurated an annual "Mountain Day," on which classes were canceled and "all young ladies were expected to walk and climb in the surrounding country." On the first Mountain Day in 1839, fifty students rode in farmers' wagons to the foot of Mount Holyoke (the hill, not the college) and climbed on foot to its summit. The Mountain Day tradition later caught on at other colleges.

Harvard walking traditions also blossomed early. References to pedestrian tours of the White Mountains may be found during the 1850s. Energetic sons of Harvard discovered Georgianna Falls back in the woods of lower Franconia Notch and made one of the earliest recorded crossings of the Pemigewasset Wilderness in 1859.

But it was Dartmouth that established its claim to being the college most associated with the White Mountains. Back on July 18, 1836, a Dartmouth student signed in to the Crawfords' register as "Erastus Everett, on a pedestrian tour from Dart. College." Like the examples of Mount Holyoke and Harvard, that was unusually early. In the years between 1866 and 1876 it was an "established custom" for a handful of Dartmouth's incoming senior class to "do" the mountains. Parties of seven to fifteen students would roam the roads through the notches, visiting the standard scenic attractions, followed by a wagon and team drawing their tents, extra clothing, and cooking supplies. Mountains were climbed—but not many. Washington and Lafayette were on the list almost every year. One recurring theme in these tours is the repeatedly expressed preference for Lafayette over Washington; the latter was too crowded, barren, and hackneyed, said the college travelers.[a] Willard was another standard ascent, sometimes also Cannon or Chocorua or more outlying peaks such as Ascutney. Oddly enough, Moosilauke, which later became Dartmouth's favorite mountain, does not seem to have figured

---

[a]We see here the beginnings of a long rivalry between the claims of the world-famous tourist-thronged Mount Washington and its associated resorts versus those of the lesser-known Franconia Ridge and its fiercely loyal partisans. Besides the Dartmouth students, a visiting minister in 1874 found Lafayette "much more awe-inspiring" than Washington (the Reverend F. W. Sanborn, "How Frank and I Spent Two Weeks in the White Mountains of New Hampshire," 1874, manuscript in the collections of the New Hampshire Historical Society, p. 45). This strongly held minority view reappears down through history, persisting today in partisans who steadfastly prefer the AMC's Green-leaf Hut to those in the Presidentials, and in rock climbers who extol the climbing on Cannon cliff as a richer mountaineering experience than the far more popular and accessible crags in the Mount Washington valley.

prominently in these nineteenth-century tours. But the students generally avoided any taxing mountaineering exploits. On the 1871 holiday lark, three of the party of thirteen started out to attempt the crossing of the Pemigewasset Wilderness but turned back when they saw more signs of bear than they found conducive to relaxed sleeping in the open.

The innocent wonder of antebellum mountain tours was replaced on these Dartmouth outings by a more laconic and conscious sophistication. The students refused to be impressed by the sublimity of the peaks. They ridiculed the size of Profile "Lake" ("Why not call it Profile Ocean?"), scoffed at stories about the violent weather ("those northwesters in former days when it required two men to hold one's hair on"), held that Hanover's own trout brooks were prettier than the Flume, and devoted considerably less attention to the view from Mount Washington than to the glimpses of young women in the towns through which they sauntered. The outdoor life was seen with a new realism:

> In *poetry* the "mossy couch" charms us, and the sleeper as he reposes on the broad bosom of Mother Earth appears sublimely independent; but in *practice* it is an entirely different affair. Instead of fragrant flowers breathing delicious perfume in the summer air, you get a bug in your ear, and the unevenness of the ground sends rheumatic twinges through your agonized frame.

By 1874 they were mildly joshing the whole idea of these pedestrian tours:

> But here, some one says, why did you go to the Mountains? Why did you go, foot sore and weary, many a mile to see what you could see at home just as well? We answer, because every one else does it.

Indeed everyone else did. College pedestrians came from all over New England during the 1860s and 1870s.

Brown University in Providence, Rhode Island, had an active student group interested in pedestrian tours of the mountain region. Twice during the Civil War, in 1862 and again in 1864, a troupe of about a dozen students from Brown spent their summers walking through the White Mountains and climbing the more accessible peaks. The instigator and leader of these 600-mile rambles was Warren R. Perce, but the scribe who wrote up their experiences sported the unforgettable monicker of Xenophon Demosthenes Tingley. Their rambles were archetypes of the 1860s and 1870s student pedestrian tours. Their route went from Manchester north past New Hampshire's big lakes to Chocorua, on up into Pinkham Notch, over Washington to Crawford's, around to the north and down through Franconia Notch, then out to the Connecticut Valley—very much the standard itinerary. The youths walked the whole way, carrying light packs and trailed by a faithful horse drawing a wagon for their tents, food, cooking gear, and guns—in those days dinner might be enriched by a partridge or other small game procured by an able marksman or lucky shot along the way. Most days they walked the unpaved roads through the mountain notches, passed by an occasional carriage or horseman, pausing for lunch in a field or by a woodland stream, gazing at the mountain vistas on every hand, and talking about whatever college men talk about, then as now. They took turns guiding the horse. They never walked on Sundays, attending services either in local churches or of their own devising in a pastoral or sylvan setting. The mountains they climbed included Chocorua, Kearsarge, Washington, and the Southern Presidential chain of Monroe, Pleasant, and Clinton. For the Southern Presidentials, they dispatched the long-suffering horse from Glen House around to Crawford's by the valley roads, while they walked up the carriage road to Washington's summit and down the Crawford Path over the southern peaks. During the succeeding decade, Brown students continued this tradition: a Dartmouth party in 1871 mentions encountering two sophomores and a freshman from Brown in the vicinity of Franconia Notch.

Yale students roamed the White Mountain notches, climbing Washington, Lafayette, and Willard, as well as the Berkshires and the Green Mountains.

Wesleyan students were afoot on Connecticut's hills and often as far north as Mount Holyoke—the mountain, not just the women's college—and over to the Catskills and north to the White Mountains.

Williams College owed its strong mountain tradition to the proximity of Greylock. Williams groups also "did" the White Mountain tour on occasion. During the 1870s students enjoyed a respite from classes on "Mountain Day" in June and "Scenery Day" in October. Theoretically everyone turned out to climb Greylock on such occasions but actual practice was spotty.

Students of Middlebury College, set on the flanks of the Green Mountains, did considerable mountain rambling, at least up to about 1880. Like their counterparts at Mount Holyoke, Dartmouth, and Harvard, Middlebury students started early; during the 1840s, they often strolled to nearby points like Chipman's Hill, Belden Falls, and Otter Creek. By the 1870s, the student newspaper complained that widespread interest in long walks was retarding the development of sports at Middlebury.

Colby College students walked among the hills of Maine on a regular basis during the 1870s. A student newspaper column of that decade took the form of discursive essays written as if the writer were rambling over the hills with his readers, talking on diverse subjects.

Nonstudent groups also roamed the mountains, some with colorful names.

The Pemigewasset Perambulators were an 1866 party of a dozen men from the Boston area who did *not* venture into the Pemigewasset

Wilderness, their name notwithstanding, but did the standard tour, with climbs of Mounts Washington, Lafayette, and Willard.

The Oatmeal Crusaders did the tour in 1875 in a group of twenty-three, a young British bard memorializing their exploits in deft classical iambic pentameter:

> "O Friend! beneath the beechen shade apart
> On oatmeal porridge how intent thou art;"
> So Virgil sang, when Tityrus went camping
> With Meliboeus, out from Mantua tramping.
> I too will pipe my rustic oaten song;
> In measures rough, and with untutored tongue
> I'll sing of you, New Hampshire's last invaders, . . . "

This went on for thirty-nine pages, the last set of verses saluting their completion of the walk in Fryeberg, Maine, a town surely unaccustomed to hearing itself addressed thus: "Sweet Fryeberg! here accept the faltering verse / In which a stranger would thy praise rehearse, . . . "

The Bummers was a slang name evidently common to that era. Two young scamps from Salem, Massachusetts, called themselves "Two Bummers" on an 1867 tour recorded in 222 pages of daily journal, much of it more concerned with their elaborate flirtations along the way and at the Glen House and other grand hotels than with the few mountains they climbed (or rode up). A quartet of travelers from Woburn and Amesbury, Massachusetts, walking 224 miles during a leisurely month among the hills, recalled their school days together by calling themselves the "Woburn High School Bummers."

Sometime toward the end of the 1870s the popularity of the pedestrian tour began to wane. The decline can be followed in this sample of reports of Williams's Mountain Days during the 1870s:

[In 1870] The freshman expedition up Greylock on Mountain Day forgot to take an ax, and suffered much with the cold. By the rest of the college the mountains were comparatively neglected.

[In 1872] Our semi-annual Mountain Day is a great institution; long may she wave! . . . Although comparatively few of the students now visit the mountains on these holidays, the name by which they were formerly known remains.

[In 1878] The students delicately hinted to the faculty that they would love to have Mountain Day at the time of the baseball game with Harvard, for the laudable purpose of having a large cheering section at Cambridge for the game.

[In 1879] A number of students went to Pittsfield, Mountain Day, thinking that they could find the most delightful scenery. They say the Pittsfield hills are full of nymphs and fairies. . . .

After 1880, New England college publications mention few accounts similar to those described thus far—at Dartmouth, for example, none. An 1883 student article at Colby alludes to "old-time pedestrians" as if long walks were rarely undertaken anymore. As the students' elders turned to more energetic mountain hiking after 1875, fewer accounts of the long road walks appear in other publications as well. Whether pure pedestrianism had simply run its course or succumbed to new conditions and changing times is hard to say.

Moses Sweetser claimed that the popularity of the country walk suffered because of "the alarming development of the 'tramp' scourge during the last few years, and the ferocious brutality of many of the tramps." According to Sweetser, the local population that had once opened hospitable doors to pedestrian ramblers grew more suspicious as the "tramp" became more common.

Another reason for the decline in walking tours might have to do with the rising prices of hotels and boardinghouses. Not only were hotels growing grander, but it is possible that farmers' wives, who at first took in college boys out of kindness, began to charge a fair price.

In the colleges, the decline of walking is associated with the rise of organized athletics. A Middlebury student, class of 1845, had given as the reason for long walks, "In our college days we had no gymnastics or regular athletic games, but there was an ample variety of pleasant walks for those so inclined." Now during the 1870s came baseball to Dartmouth College, and in 1878 a football match between two "tens" aroused interest: though "few of the spectators understood the game, yet it had the charm of novelty." Baseball became very popular during the 1880s, while football emerged during the 1890s. Concomitantly, pedestrian tours disappeared from Dartmouth, and neither walking nor hiking was in vogue for an entire generation of Hanover students—until the formation of the Dartmouth Outing Club in 1909 brought it all back in style. In other colleges as well, the rise of organized athletic programs seemed to dry up student interest in long walks.[b] In 1883, Colby's student newspaper observed with pleasure the advent of baseball and of a new gymnasium, noting that "irrepressible energies" had formerly lacked these outlets and thus were directed into pedestrian excursions:

> If our "far away" predecessors practiced the giant swing less, they took longer walks into the adjoining country; if they know not of the excitement and glory of the base-ball field, they contrived to invest their rural

---

[b]It should be mentioned that student walking tours did not entirely cease after 1880, though they certainly seemed to disappear almost completely at Dartmouth and other colleges where they had been so popular during the 1860s and 1870s. At MIT, oddly enough, where no evidence is found of involvement before 1880, accounts of such tours show up in the student journal, *The Tech*, during the later decade—see issues of May 21, 1884, pp. 201–2; May 20, 1885, pp. 201–3; Feb. 17, 1887, pp. 134–35; Feb. 16, 1888, pp. 131–34; Feb. 20, 1890, pp. 129–32; and March 6, 1890, pp. 145–48.

rambles with enough perilous and romantic adventures, to satisfy that external craving of student hearts for excitement.

There is some evidence that this connection between the rise of organized athletics and the decline of walking extended beyond college campuses. At least one writer credits the growth of athletic clubs in New York City during the early 1880s with delaying the start of hiking clubs in the New York area for a full generation.

In one sense the pedestrian tour has but trifling significance for the history of mountain *climbing*, since these walkers reached few summits. But in another sense, these perambulations may be viewed as the prelude to a continuing strain in Northeastern hiking. There have always been people who love a mild walk, who are truly devoted outdoorspeople, but who avoid strenuous uphills and who sometimes actually disdain summits. Theirs is a legitimate tradition, going all the way back to the Oatmeal Crusaders and the perambulations of the Pemigewasset Perambulators and Xenophon Demosthenes Tingley.

Chapter 16

Adirondack Murray's Fools

THE RISE of mountain resorts in New England was a steady development that had begun with the Crawfords and merely accelerated after 1870. The White Mountains, Mount Mansfield, Mount Desert, Kineo— each had well-established traditions of tourism. Even Katahdin was a test for the adventurous as early as the 1840s. Certainly the Catskills had been mining tourist gold since the 1820s. For all these places, then, increased popularity after 1870 was merely a continuing evolution.

But in the Adirondacks—still largely that "realm of mystery" to the vacationing set—the change came more abruptly. To a remarkable degree, that change pivoted on the publication of a single mythopoetic book in the year 1869, written by one of the most colorful and controversial figures to put his stamp on the history of the Northeastern mountains.

The man who wrought this change, William Henry Harrison Murray, came into the world on April 26, 1840, at a farm in Guilford, Connecticut. "A big, husky, brawny lad," he worked his way through Yale. Despite the physique of a wrestler, the verbal virtuosity of an Athenian orator, the shrewdness of a poolroom gambler, and the moral philosophy of a patent medicine salesman, young Murray incongruously entered— the ministry! After working his way through three smaller Connecticut churches in less than six years, he landed in the pulpit of the prestigious Park Street Congregational Church in Boston, at age twenty-eight. Elmer Gantry would have been envious.

"Handsome and good-natured and powerfully built, full of life and enthusiasm," Murray and his lovely wife "fairly took Boston by storm." His spell-binding oratory established his reputation rapidly. His admiring biographer tells us:

> There has perhaps never been an American clergyman who held, continuously, such vast audiences under the spell of his high rhetoric and persuasive delivery as did Mr. Murray during the years that he occupied Boston pulpits.

This period of heady success was short-lived. Murray's Rabelaisian appetites led him to involvements that may be best described as outside the scope of this book and that cost him the Park Street pulpit. He left the ministry at age forty, and the lovely wife shortly thereafter, embarking on a checkered career in which he failed at several business, tried his hand at popular fiction writing, and traveled to Texas, Canada, Europe, Africa, Vermont, and ultimately home to Guilford, Connecticut, where he retreated into the seclusion of his ancestral home. He died on March 3, 1904, in the room where he had been born sixty-four eventful years before.

This intriguing figure bulks large in our story because he changed the history of Adirondacks climbing. The not-so-very-reverend Murray visited the Adirondacks first when just two years out of Yale (1864) and soon became a regular summer tourist. Not that *he* climbed mountains:

> Now, tramping is something I never admired. I can get along very well tramping down hill, but when the path begins to run upward, I always get in and ride.[a]

But a certain level of outdoor exercise in that wilderness setting was just to his liking. In the fall and winter of 1866 he began writing up his experiences for the *Meriden Literary Recorder*. (He was then, if briefly, minister at Meriden, Connecticut.) Murray brought the articles out in book form in April 1869—"some say on the first," according to the oblique observation of Adirondack historian Alfred L. Donaldson, for reasons that speedily will become clear.

The book that "kindled a thousand campfires and taught a thousand pens how to write of nature" was a modest-sized (236 pages) volume entitled *Adventures in the Wilderness, or Camp-Life in the Adirondacks*. It was a combination of travelogue, nature worship, how-to guide for the aspiring camper, and compendium of backwoods yarns. To the modern reader it does not appear more informative or entertaining than the books of Hoffman, Headley, or a dozen others who previously had written of the Adirondack wilderness. To many critics of his day and later, the book was wildly inaccurate or fanciful. Some chapters, Donaldson comments, are so exaggerated that "a literal construction of them reflects more on the reader than the author." The feats of courage and skill performed by Murray's guides made Natty Bumppo seem overcautious and bumbling. The curative powers of the clean air and pure water could conquer any disease. The plenitude of deer for the hunter and trout for the angler portrayed a Nimrod's Eden. The unspoiled woods described by Murray blithely ignored an already bustling lumber industry ravaging many sections of the rich Adirondack forests.

---

[a]Murray made this comment when confronting the regular trail up Whiteface, which struck him as altogether too steep.

Yet the book was an instant sensation. Immediately it sold out, as did repeated reprintings. "It displaced the popular novel of the day," reports one historian. "Everybody seemed to be reading it, and a great many people were simultaneously seized with the desire to visit the region it described." Henceforth the lion of Boston's Park Street Church was christened "Adirondack Murray." According to one bemused historian:

> Either the timing of the book's appearance matched a growing desire to get out-of-doors or Murray caught some note others had missed; the effect of the book was phenomenal. By June 1869, the book had created a stampede to the woods.

That was the summer of what were dubbed "Murray's Fools" (hence Donaldson's oblique comment). The tourists who jammed the roads and railroads to the Adirondacks completely overwhelmed the existing supply of boardinghouses, hotels, food, carriages, boats, and guides. A contemporary satirical account described a crowded train heading north on which "up and down the double range of seats, . . . behold! all the passengers were studying 'Murray.' " When the train disgorged its passengers at Whitehall, the throng was

> a moving phantasm of sea-side hats, water-proofs, blanket-shawls, fish-poles, old felts, mackintoshes, reticules, trout-rods, fish-baskets, carpet-bags, guns, valises, rubber-boots, umbrellas, lap-rugs, hunting-dogs, guide-books, and maps. There were old women, misses, youngsters, spinsters, invalids, students, sports, artists, and jolly good fellows. Behind followed innumerable vans, crates, and barrows of miscellaneous baggage. Two packages of "Murray" and one case of "Hamlin's Magic Oil" brought up the rear.

Murray's Fools went to seek lovely woods untouched by ax, peaceful waters teeming with trout, and an instant cure for tuberculosis and a score of other ailments. What they found was an uncommonly wet summer that year, black flies, inadequate lodging and transportation, guides who jacked up prices in a perfectly natural working of supply-demand economics, and a tremendous traffic of other tourists all looking for the same things and all having read the same book. For many, disillusionment quickly ensued: "the stampede into the woods in June was a stampede out in August." But the Adirondacks as a whole were never the same unspoiled wilderness again. The word was out.

Adirondack tourism, so long delayed, now ran rampant. Between 1869 and 1875, the number of hotels and boardinghouses reportedly rose from about fifty to more than two hundred. By the 1880s the region was almost as much a center for tourists as the White Mountains or the Catskills.

By some estimates, more tourists could be accommodated in the Adirondacks during the late nineteenth century than during the midtwentieth. Almost 1,000 visitors could be entertained at seven hotels in Keene Valley alone. Another 1,200 could put up at Upper Saranac, almost 1,500 at Lake Placid, while down at Lake George seventeen hotels could take in more than 3,000 tourists in season. Prospect House at Blue Mountain Lake was said to be the first hotel in the world to have electric lights in every bedroom, and its magnificent masquerade balls were attended by the Tiffanys, the Astors, and the Stuyvesants.

But the grand hotel was never as characteristic a feature of the Adirondacks as it was of the White Mountains or Catskills. The more typical accommodations deliberately sought to convey a taste of the wilderness that the public had associated with the Adirondacks from of old. Enterprising men acquired sites at remote and picturesque places, built substantial lodges for a wealthy clientele, hired a fleet of guides to take them hunting, fishing, and camping, and sought to establish a unique aura that appealed to vacationing sportsmen. "Riches and rusticity were combined" and "symbolized both harmony with nature and triumph over it."

The archetype of such enterprises was Paul Smith's on Lower St. Regis Lake, able to handle one hundred guests by 1875 and five hundred before Smith's death in 1912, with an associated colony of well-appointed cabins and an entourage of highly regarded guides. In 1887 a travel brochure marveled,

> Paul Smith's is a surprise to everybody; an astonishing mixture of fish and fashion, pianos and puppies, Brussels carpeting and cowhide boots. . . . feathers and fishing rods, point lace and pint bottles.

The backwoods host and raconteur who concocted this "astonishing mixture" was himself

> a man of contradictions, a hunter and guide on first-name terms with millionaires and presidents, a man who made his fortune exploiting the wilderness but drew both ire and admiration by speaking out in favor of protecting the forest.

At Lower St. Regis Lake, Paul Smith presided genially over a dependable flow of prominent businessmen who delighted in being treated familiarly by this homespun north woods Mark Twain. His was the model of success toward which many another Adirondack "camp" aspired.

Even more vintage Adirondack were the large private summer camps. To the old guides a "camp" might have been a rude hut slapped together with hewn logs and bark. The Adirondack "camp" of the Gilded Age belonged to an altogether different classification of architecture: opulent palaces of rustic log, massive stone fireplaces, cathedral ceilings buttressed by rough-hewn beams, stuffed trophy heads adorning the pine walls. "Morgans,

Whitneys, Vanderbilts, and Rockefellers presided over vast woodland retreats," according to one account. Said to be the most extravagant of all was Pine Knot, the "camp" of William West Durant on Raquette Lake, where the fusion of wilderness with ostentation was symbolized in the bent twigs over the veranda forming the wealthy owner's initials.

Several associations of the well-to-do formed self-contained communities of summer affluence. Among these, the Adirondack League Club near Old Forge was especially extensive, with holdings of 100,000 acres. An indirect consequence of such large holdings was that private ownership often impeded the less responsible operations of lumbermen. Those who paid for large tracts of wilderness did not care to look at a wasteland of stumps and slash.

Adirondack visitors after the Civil War included the country's social and cultural elite. Theodore Roosevelt spent three summers at Paul Smith's in the 1870s, indulging his outdoor interest by compiling a catalogue of the birds of the Adirondacks: he identified ninety-seven species. Robert Louis Stevenson was a tubercular patient at Saranac Lake during the 1880s. President Benjamin Harrison, J. P. Morgan, and Alfred Vanderbilt were vacationers in what had been the desolate wilderness of the Cauchsachrage. The poet Henry Van Dyke became a devotee of Ampersand Mountain and its nearby lake. Composer Victor Herbert was a summer resident of Lake Placid for twenty-five years. Francis Parkman, Mark Twain, William James, Felix Adler, and Yale's President Noah Porter were among the distinguished figures that frequented the woods and waters of upstate New York. Philosopher William James spent a night camped in Panther Gorge in 1898, "one of the happiest lonesome nights of my existence and I understand now what a poet is."

As elsewhere, the centers from which Adirondack hiking, climbing, and trail-building history was written were neither the grand hotels and great "camps," nor the lowly boardinghouses, but a handful of moderately sized inns. In the Adirondacks, an especially large role was played by three establishments that occupied strategic spots relative to the high peaks (see figure 16.1):

1. The Beede House, later to evolve into the Ausable Club, at the northern end of the valley of the Ausable Lakes, the eastern base for climbs of Marcy and Haystack

2. Adirondack Lodge, at the base of the northern approaches to Marcy and the MacIntyre range

3. The Lake Placid Club, at the base of Whiteface and a future starting point for much winter climbing

The story of these three centers of Adirondack climbing is best told in connection with the specific events that they spawned. As in the White

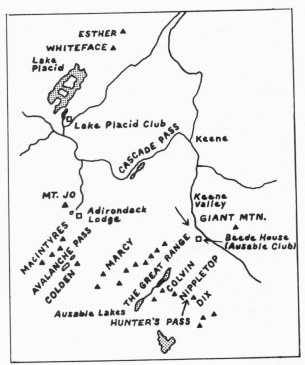

Figure 16.1. Three centers of Adirondack hiking, late nineteenth century
When recreational hiking grew more popular in the last quarter of the
nineteenth century, three establishments became the dominant centers from
which Adirondack hikers set forth: the Beede House (which later became the
Ausable Club), Adirondack Lodge on Heart Lake, and the world-famous Lake
Placid Club. Each was associated with colorful personalities who helped
shape the unique character of each hiking center.

Mountains, these events did not occur until the last quarter of the nineteenth century (see especially chapter 21). Before they could, one more
ingredient was needed. The catalyst required to set these events in motion was the coming, in rapid succession, of the two great scientific surveys of the principal mountain regions, conducted just before the curtain
rose on the second wave of recreational climbing.

Chapter 17

The younger Hitchcock and Verplanck Colvin

Few events changed Northeastern climbing history as rapidly and radically as two post–Civil War scientific surveys. In 1868 the state of New Hampshire authorized a geological survey and appointed Charles H. Hitchcock as state geologist. Four years later New York State authorized a topographical survey, with Verplanck Colvin as superintendent.[a]

Before Hitchcock and Colvin, the two principal Northeastern ranges were known and used but superficially. A few leading peaks were climbed (considerably more in the White Mountains than in the Adirondacks), but in both ranges the majority of interesting mountains were essentially untouched and untraveled.

After the surveys were completed, nearly every corner of the two ranges was known, explored, and publicized. Within a very few years, large numbers of trampers came to climb them, trails were built, guidebooks published, accurate maps distributed, and the second wave of recreational climbers washed over the whole of both ranges. It has never receded.

---

[a]The jobs that Hitchcock and Colvin were asked to do were not unprecedented; only their zeal and thoroughness were. The concept of a scientific survey of American lands traces back to Thomas Jefferson and his sponsorship of the Lewis and Clark exploration of 1803–6, the travels of Zebulon Pike (for whom Colorado's Pikes Peak is named) in 1805–7, and the formation of the U.S. Coast Survey in 1807. At the state level, the first systematic geological survey was one in North Carolina in 1823–25. In the Northeast, in 1830, Massachusetts authorized both a topographical survey by Simeon Borden and a geological survey by Edward Hitchcock, the Amherst scientist-educator and mountain enthusiast. Connecticut followed suit in 1835. In New York State, Amos Eaton had conducted county surveys as early as 1820, and the statewide survey, involving Emmons and Hall, was launched in 1836. In other Northeastern states, the dominant figure in pre–Civil War surveys was Charles Thomas Jackson, who directed surveys in Maine (1836–38), Rhode Island (1839), and New Hampshire (1839–41). A second Maine survey was held by C. H. Hitchcock (1861). Vermont stumbled through several false starts and turnover among directors before completing its geological survey in the late 1850s. A convenient summary of the history of state scientific surveys may be found in Dirk J. Struik, *Yankee Science in the Making*, pp. 239–45. For more detail see Anne Marie Millbrooke, "State Geological Surveys of the Nineteenth Century" (Ph.D. diss., University of Pennsylvania, 1981); and Mary C. Rabbitt, *Minerals, Lands, and Geology for the Common Defence and General Welfare—Before 1879*, pp. 314–15. The complex convolutions of Vermont's efforts to inventory its own geology are traced in T. D. Seymour Bassett, *A History of the Vermont Geological Surveys and State Geologists* (Essex Junction, Vt.: Essex Publishing, 1976) see especially pp. 1–11; see also Henry M. Seely, "Twentieth Century History of Vermont: Part II: The Geology of Vermont," *The Vermonter* (Feb. 1901), pp. 53–67.

Hitchcock and Colvin played similar roles in opening up the two principal mountain regions of the Northeast—yet two more dissimilar personalities can scarcely be imagined.

Charles Henry Hitchcock was born on August 23, 1836, son of the distinguished Edward Hitchcock of Amherst College. Birth, training, and his own talent and temperament all combined to assign him a leading place in American science. He graduated Phi Beta Kappa from Amherst in 1856 and spent the next five years partly as assistant to his father in the Vermont geological survey and partly in teaching at Amherst, Yale, and Andover Theological Seminary. In 1861 the younger Hitchcock struck out on his own as state geologist for Maine. In the mid-1860s he spent a year of study in London and was appointed professor at Lafayette College. In 1868 the New Hampshire survey was authorized, and on September 8, 1868, the governor appointed the thirty-two-year-old Hitchcock state geologist of New Hampshire. Simultaneously it was arranged with Dartmouth College to name him professor of geology and mineralogy, a post he held for forty years. Upon retirement, he went to Honolulu and undertook extensive geological investigations of the volcanic islands and mountains of Hawaii, publishing his findings in 1909. This closed his distinguished career as one of the country's leading scientists of the late nineteenth century. He returned to New Hampshire and lived on in comfortable retirement until his death in 1919 at age eighty-three.

Verplanck Colvin was born on January 4, 1847, of Albany parents well enough endowed that young Verplanck did not need to seek gainful employment. After starting and stopping the study of, in turn, law, geology, and topography, he had apparently equipped himself for no definite career. He was a strange young man, tall, dark, but not handsome. His social relations ranged from awkward and strained to overtly hostile. He never married—like Dickens's Mr. Lorry, he was a bachelor in his cradle. As a youth he vacationed in the Adirondacks, there forming his one and only lifelong interest: the exploration, ascent, and mapping of the high peaks. At age eighteen he was making sketch maps of the region. When landslides rent the appropriately named Avalanche Pass in 1869, the twenty-two-year-old Colvin was there within a week to view the scene, take notes, and write up a detailed account for the Albany newspapers. That winter he mastered the art of snowshoeing and accompanied a hunter into the wild Indian River country, where he shot a bear. (His predilection for telling the world each of his adventures was the butt of some gentle ridicule; after frequent narrations of a mountain lion kill, he acquired the nickname "Panther.") At the age of twenty-three, Colvin made his first major exploration, picking out with characteristic daring, the most remote of all the high peaks, the Seward Range. The next year he joined State Botanist Charles H. Peck to climb Mount Dix, the highest in the eastern Adirondacks; under their direction, guides blazed and cleared the first complete trail up Dix. On the strength of all this show of interest, he won appointment in 1872 to a newly formed State Park Commission.[b] Though but twenty-five years old, Colvin wrote its final report. Although the state legislature did not immediately accept the park proposal, it did authorize a topographical survey of the Adirondack region. Colvin promptly landed the job as superintendent. The topographical survey and the state land survey that the legislature authorized ten years later and assigned to the same staff became Colvin's life work for the next twenty-eight years. When he finally resigned in 1900, Colvin lived on in Albany for twenty years. It was not a dignified end. Nursing vengeance for what he felt was failure to appreciate his role in saving the Adirondack wilderness, he came up first with a scheme for a railroad through the heart of the Forest Preserve, and later a project for mining lands in the wilderness that he had fought so long to preserve. He lived for years with the only man who ever seemed to find him possible to get along with, his former assistant and boyhood friend, Mills Blake, but he took to wandering the streets muttering to himself and was eventually consigned to a mental institution. There, still at war with the world, he died in 1920.

The contrast in these two men is obviously striking.

Hitchcock, even at thirty-two years old, was an eminent geologist, well traveled, had studied abroad, and had participated in geological surveys in Vermont and Maine as well as New Hampshire. Colvin is not known for anything outside the work of the New York topographical survey and the subsequently authorized state land survey.

Hitchcock participated in professional societies and was the fledgling Appalachian Mountain Club's first councillor of topography. Colvin seems to have had no outside interests, except one professional society, the Albany Institute.

Hitchcock was an erudite man with a gentle sense of humor, an able and popular manager of the many men who worked harmoniously together on the New Hampshire survey. Colvin was a narrow zealot, controversial, almost completely humorless: he feuded with the U.S. Geological Survey, the state engineer's office, and the state legislature, which rarely appropriated the funds he requested; the guides he hired for the survey work regularly quit on him; and he seems to have managed a long-standing personal relationship with only one other person, Mills Blake.

One can imagine Hitchcock enjoying an occasional sociable cocktail with his colleagues, always in moderation. Colvin, who did nothing in moderation, not only never drank but demanded the strictest temperance of and enforced it on all the rough-hewn backwoodsmen who worked under him.

---

[b]In addition to his Adirondack experience, Colvin had partially prepared himself by a smaller-scale survey of the Helderbergh Hills near Albany. He also traveled in the Southern states and in the Rocky Mountains.

Hitchcock presided over a buoyant staff and, while not absent from the field himself, left many of the more adventurous explorations to his younger colleagues and college students. Colvin personally led all the most difficult work, with energy bordering on the demoniac, often reserving the greatest hardships for himself alone or with the accompaniment of a single guide.

The story of the New Hampshire survey is studded with illustrious names of resourceful young men: Huntington, Vose, Clough, Upham, Morse, and many more. The story of the New York survey comes down to us mostly as that of one man, Colvin, though Blake and some of the guides were thoroughly capable of contributing when they were given a chance.

If these contrasting accounts portray Hitchcock in a positive and Colvin in a negative light, we should delve a little deeper. For all his competence and his impact on White Mountain history, Hitchcock is not a striking figure, not nearly as interesting a personality as his father (see chapter 13). Assuredly Colvin *was* interesting. Though a difficult and ultimately demented personality, he was also incredibly and admirably creative as well as energetic. For his wilderness explorations, he invented a portable boat, a brass lantern (which permitted no compass interference), and a stout leather haversack for the all-weather protection of maps and field notes. His driven compulsiveness made him a significant force in the movement for preserving the Adirondack wilds. He was a passable artist and one of the most compelling writers on wilderness who has ever come through the Northeast. A novelist would be bored by Hitchcock but would hugely enjoy Colvin for a protagonist.

The top assistants on those two surveys were almost as strikingly different in character as their superiors. Joshua H. Huntington was flamboyant, imaginative, always proposing—and executing brilliantly—the daring stroke; he it was who conceived the spectacular plan for wintering over on the summit of Mount Washington, and of course was among those who did it. Mills Blake was faithful, plodding, wholly reliable under the worst of conditions into which Colvin placed him, but is not known to have originated a single idea of consequence. It is perhaps fitting that their names should be immortalized in the region's topography by such disparate features, Huntington's in the most dramatic and rugged of all the great rock-crested ravines on Mount Washington, Blake's in an obscure wooded summit not even 4,000 feet in height—located, naturally, just down the ridge from and distinctly lower than Mount Colvin.

While Hitchcock and Colvin, Huntington and Blake exhibited four radically different personalities, they shared one common trait: a burning desire to climb mountains, ill-concealed under motives of science. They were all intensely interested in scientific observation, to be sure, but strongly intermingled with that quest for knowledge was a sheer love of adventure and getting to the top. This common drive for climbing worked to make both surveys into landmarks in the climbing history of the Northeast.

The geological survey of New Hampshire

Although the White Mountains had become a popular vacation center by 1868, it will be recalled that relatively few peaks were climbed regularly. Thirteen years earlier a White Mountain writer had observed,

> As yet, there are many deep glens and wild crags in all this mighty pile of mountains, where the explorer had never left the print of his feet upon the moss.

It was to these deep glens and wild crags that the New Hampshire geological survey turned.

In the fall of 1869 Hitchcock drew up his plans and selected his two principal assistants: George L. Vose of Paris, Maine, and Joshua H. Huntington of Norwich, Connecticut. To round out the staff he relied chiefly on Dartmouth students during the summers; Hitchcock seems to have employed the survey work as a teaching device, with almost one-fourth of the class of 1871, for example, working on the survey.

For the summer of 1869 Vose was assigned to concentrate on the White Mountains and thereby "to furnish the most accurate map of the mountains ever drawn." Vose knew his subject well from childhood hiking trips going back to 1838 and from extensive summer excursions during the 1860s. In 1869 Vose was mostly in the Sandwich Range, where he climbed Chocorua, Passaconaway, and Whiteface, making detailed observations from their summits. In September Vose determined to ascend Carrigain, figuring that its location "almost exactly in the centre of the vast group of White and Franconia mountains" would offer a matchless panorama for topographical observations. With George F. Morse of Portland, Maine, an accomplished artist who specialized in accurate sketches of summit panoramas, and a Bartlett, New Hampshire, man named John C. Cobb for guide, Vose approached the mountain from the Sawyer River valley (see figures 17.1 and 18.1). The key to Carrigain's southeastern approach is Signal Ridge, a striking knife-edge (by New England standards) that leads off from the principal summit a few hundred feet below the top and runs nearly level toward the southeast at about 4,000 feet, with impressive sweeping slopes that drop sharply off both sides for more than 1,000 feet. The eastern and steeper side of this knife-edge is supported by steep buttresses into which are etched exceptionally steep watercourses. The present trail starts up the first of these brooks and then slabs gently over to the ridge; Vose's party took a higher and steeper brookbed. This in turn forks again, and here they took the more southerly fork, naming its precipitous ledgy course Cobb's Stairs in honor of their local guide. On the first day they climbed for two hours partway up the "magnificent slope," at first in the stream, then beside it,

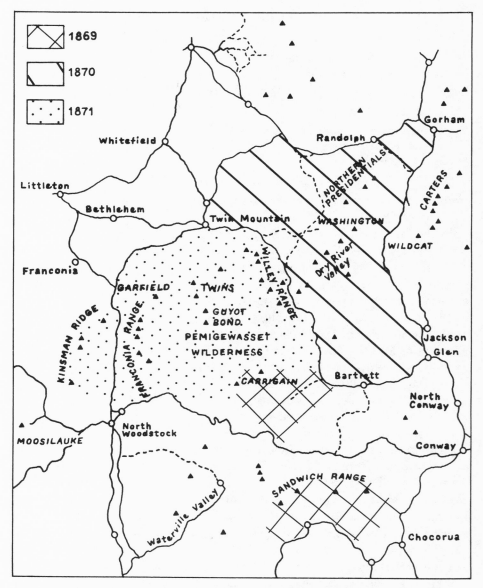

Figure 17.1. Areas covered by the Hitchcock survey, 1869–1871 The interior of the White Mountains was systematically explored for the first time by Charles H. Hitchcock and his associates, who conducted the geological survey of New Hampshire during the years 1869–71. In the process, these men made the first recorded ascents of several major peaks and discovered many interesting features well known to modern hikers.

stumbling now into some hidden chamber beneath the moss, now lifting ourselves up by the friendly branches of spruce and pine [*sic*], now

sinking exhausted into the soft green bed beneath our feet, now winding around some fallen tree, still up, up, up we go, panting and strain-
ing, with every muscle called into play and every drop of blood in
vigorous motion.

After spending the night at an improvised camp on this steep mountainside, they pushed on in the morning, taking only compass and notebooks, battling the scrub conifers, until

one more lusty pull, and a rough scramble through the bushes and over
the rocks, and we stand upon a narrow ridge, from which the great
green carpet of forest spread out like a map beneath.

To their disappointment, clouds had closed in and their views were at
first limited, so that they sat down and made a fire and for several hours
waited out the bad weather. They did not realize until they had begun to
descend that they had not been on the summit, since clouds hung in tight
around the summit cone (a not uncommon occurrence).

For reasons that are not recorded, Vose's tenure with the Hitchcock
survey was brief. No account of his activities in 1870 survives, the map
he was to furnish was apparently never made, and he soon resigned.
Huntington remained then as the principal assistant.

The focus of the Hitchcock survey in the summer of 1870 was a thorough investigation of the Presidential Range in the widest possible sense
of the term—the entire 30-by-15-mile area bounded by the Israel's,
Moose, Peabody, Ellis, and Saco rivers (figure 17.1). Hitchcock and
Huntington headed the field trips, with Dr. Nathan Barrows and Edward
Hitchcock, Jr., Charles's brother, and six Dartmouth seniors as assistants. The party stocked up on supplies and then took to the woods to live
in "extempore camps" for long periods. While no new ascents were recorded, the survey team combed all the subsidiary ridges and valleys,
"one after another, till all had been explored." It is a great loss that no
detailed field notes remain telling of their explorations from day to day,
but they are known to have repeated King's ascent of his ravine on Mount
Adams and to have spent considerable time in the large Dry River basin
and its various offshoots. The numerous steeper slopes of the range were
not avoided; as an illustration, Hitchcock and his assistants scrambled
around on the Webster cliffs that form the east wall of Crawford Notch.
Hikers keeping to the well-groomed trails today but gazing out over the
huge slopes of tangled forest can appreciate the kind of travel that Hitchcock and his assistants undertook throughout the range day after day.

The following summer the survey turned attention to the area west of
Crawford Notch (see figure 17.1). If the major peaks of the Presidentials
had been well known, those of the Pemigewasset were scarcely even
named. This immense north country mirkwood had been traversed at

least twice, and fishermen were conversant with the East Branch and its main tributaries, but knowledge of the mountains was limited to the ranges that form its western (Franconia) and eastern (Willey Range) borders, plus Carrigain to the south. That left an area of 10 miles square that was virtually unknown. You could have taken Manhattan Island from the Battery to George Washington Bridge and laid it east-west between Mounts Liberty and Nancy and its tallest buildings of today would have sunk out of sight of any road of that era, behind the encompassing mountain ridges. The high range of peaks in the interior—later given the names of North and South Twin, Guyot, and the Bonds—may never have been climbed at all. Though the immense forests of the Pemigewasset were later thoroughly logged over and lumber camps and railroads sprang up all over, that period was still twenty years in the future. When Hitchcock's men entered the "Pemi," it was the largest area of major mountains yet unexplored in the White Mountains.

Hitchcock and Huntington, along with eleven Dartmouth students, formed the 1871 party. An important member of the group was Warren Upham, then an undergraduate but a keen participant on some of the more arduous undertakings and one who retained his enthusiasm for the hills after graduation, becoming active in the Appalachian Mountain Club upon its formation later that decade. This group began a one-month sojourn in those woods on June 17, 1871.

> Our houses were hastily extemporized sheds; our beds a few boughs of ferns placed upon boards; our food consisted of stale crackers and preserved meats, save a rare taste of trout and berries gathered in climbing mountains, and the luxury of an occasional basket of provisions sent by kind friends at the Profile House; and we were our own servants.

During that month and subsequent, more limited expeditions that summer, the Pemigewasset explorations included traverses of the Twins-Bonds range, Garfield Ridge, and Willey Range. Carrigain was reached by Upham from the north, probably a second ascent (after Guyot's of 1857). Among the other peaks climbed, which may represent first ascents, were South Twin and possibly North, by Hitchcock and one Dartmouth student; Guyot and Bond, by Upham and another student; and Garfield (then Haystack), by C. H. Conant, C. W. Hoitt, and Jonathan Smith. Hitchcock's forces also discovered two remarkable flumes cut deeply into the side of Mount Willard and did a roped descent to the Devil's Den, that dark cave just below the top of Willard's precipitous south face. In 1871, working west of Franconia Notch, they discovered Kinsman Pond and made possible first ascents of the twin peaks of the Kinsmans.

Hitchcock began submitting annual reports in 1869 and 1870, the major results appearing as *The Geology of New Hampshire* in 1874. Most of the survey's mountain exploration was done in 1870 and 1871. Coming during the period of transition between the bridle path era of the 1850s and the explosion of pedestrian hiking and trail building after 1875, it could not have been better timed to play a key role in pointing the way for that second generation of recreational climbers.[c]

The topographical survey of New York

The Adirondack survey entered upon a region far wilder than even the Pemigewasset segment of the White Mountains.

Verplanck Colvin had already displayed a flair for mountain exploration, most notably in his exploration of the Seward Range in 1870 with guide Alvah Dunning. The pair made a long approach via canoe and afoot, climbing not just Seward but also Donaldson and possibly (though not definitely) Emmons as well. Depending on whether Guyot and Sandoz had reached Seward earlier, an uncertain question, Colvin and Dunning accomplished between one and three first ascents of Adirondack 4,000-foot peaks in this one trip.

The early years of the topographical survey were the most significant for mountain exploration and discovery. In 1872, 1873, and 1875 (1874 was mainly spent on office work), Colvin personally led field trips in climbing a score of the high peaks, including first ascents recorded of such difficult objectives as Skylight, Gray Peak, Colvin, and Upper Wolf Jaw (see figure 17.2). He also discovered two tiny tarns nestled way up amongst the highest of the hills, Moss Pond and Lake Tear-of-the-Clouds. In the process, he opened up a new and shorter route to Marcy from the southwest. Many of his forays probed land previously untrodden and unmapped: the high, turbulent plateau southwest of Marcy, the long approach to the Seward Range from the east, the high traverse from Dix to Nippletop to Mount Colvin.

These pioneering explorations are shown in figure 17.2, but two highlights should be stressed here.

One was the discovery of Lake Tear-of-the-Clouds and the shorter route to Marcy. On September 16, 1872, Colvin and one guide, Bill Nye, had just made the first recorded ascent of Gray Peak when they dropped down to this lonely, hidden pool. They guessed, and subsequently demonstrated, that this was the highest source of the Hudson River. Descending along its outlet, Feldspar Brook, they discovered that this itinerary opened a shortcut to Marcy from the southwest, more direct than the old Emmons-Redfield circuitous route that Cheney had used to guide parties during the 1840s and 1850s. Subsequently a trail was cut along the direct

[c]An important phase of the Hitchcock survey, already mentioned (chap. 14), was the winter ascent and occupation of first Moosilauke (1869–70) and then Washington itself (1870–71). This was the arena in which J. H. Huntington most shone.

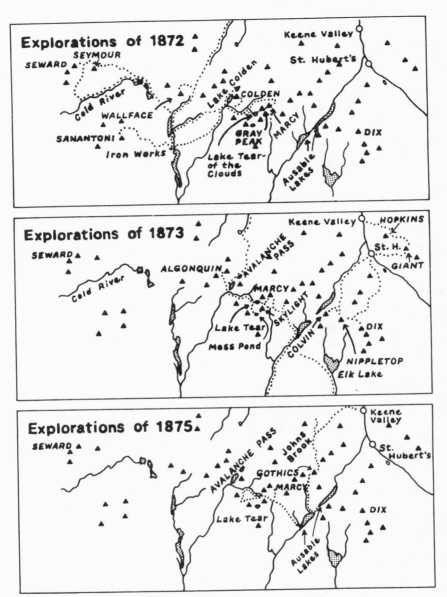

Figure 17.2. Explorations of the Colvin survey, 1872–1875 The interior of the Adirondacks was systematically explored for the first time by Verplanck Colvin and his associates, who conducted the topographical survey of New York. Their most important explorations from the standpoint of climbing history were in the years 1872, 1873, and 1875. Among their accomplishments were first ascents of Gray Peak (1872), Skylight and Colvin (1873), the opening of a new route to Marcy via Lake Tear-of-the-Clouds, and the thorough exploration of the complex mountain country south and southwest of Marcy.

route, after which the old original route fell into disuse, and the ancient track disappeared. Colvin regarded the discovery of Lake Tear and the shorter route to Marcy as among his most significant achievements.

The second landmark event is the ascent of Skylight (4,926 ft.) on August 28, 1873, by Colvin, Old Mountain Phelps, and two others. At this time Skylight was probably the highest unclimbed peak in the Northeast and the region's last really major virgin summit. This climb thus marks the final passing of an era that had begun with Darby Field on Washington 231 years earlier. Note well. It is fitting that this epochal ascent should fall to such major figures in this history as Verplanck Colvin and Old Mountain Phelps. It is also noteworthy that it was done with some style: the party traversed the peak, descended into unknown terrain on the far side, discovered Moss Pond, another tiny tarn high amongst the high peaks, and traced a circuit through that dense woods back to Lake Tear and on back to their camp in Panther Gorge. It was an important day in Northeastern climbing.

The process by which Colvin accomplished his work was the direct opposite of the orderly, relaxed, and enjoyable ways of Hitchcock's team in the more cultivated mountains of New Hampshire. On repeated occasions Colvin and his guides would fight their way to a mountain summit, arriving finally by late afternoon; the superintendent would become completely absorbed in taking every possible measurement until at length he realized that he could no longer see the instrument readings in the twilight gloom. Only then would he permit the party to begin the descent, whereupon they were often benighted in the midst of precipitous mossy and damp ledges, where they would shiver and hop around till dawn. Like as not it might rain, or perhaps snow or sleet, and in the morning they would limp into camp. Not surprisingly, the guides on such outings might refuse to work for him again. For various reasons, field work was often delayed until late fall, so that summit observations had to be made during intermittent snowstorms and long periods of sub-freezing temperatures; or lakes that they had boated across on the way in would be found half frozen on their return.

Colvin's talent for crepuscular descents through trackless wilderness was repeatedly documented. For example:

On 3,859-foot Snowy Mountain on August 4, 1872: "Bread, without water, made our lunch, and at dusk we hurried as best we could down from the lonely crag, to be soon overtaken by darkness, compelled to wrap our blankets around us, and, making the tree roots pillows, there pass the night."

On 2,278-foot Bald Mountain on August 28, 1872: They worked till sunset, then groped down "a long and toilsome descent among the rocks and ledges, where it was almost impossible to see the way," until making camp by a small stream where, wrapped in blankets, they slept "with no other roof between us and the stars than the slight swaying foliage of the trees."

On Giant on August 13, 1873: They didn't start up until 3:30 P.M., quickly completed measurements as the sun set, then felt their way down "off the trail . . . feeling, not seeing" till a moonrise at 1:00 A.M. enabled them to continue down and back to the valley.

On Dix on August 17, 1873: "Absorbed in our work we were startled by the sunset to the conspicuousness that night had already settled in the chasm valleys below. It would be impossible to descend in the dark, amid the cliffs and ledges."

On Algonquin on September 6, 1873: Benighted on the summit, they made a perilous descent during which Colvin took a bad fall off a ledge, sustaining painful bruises.

The guides who suffered through these escapades and much worse, had heavy demands placed upon them. Aside from the standard tasks of guides—building bark huts, keeping all-night fires, carrying 50–60 pounds through trackless mountain country—they had to furnish their own blankets and tarps, cups, plates, and cutlery, as well as to carry tents, cooking gear, lamps, axes, and brush hooks, plus a wide variety of heavy and sometimes delicate survey equipment. The workday was deemed to start at 7:00 A.M. and to conclude at sunset (not counting the maintenance of all-night fires in colder weather). No work was allowed on Sundays—but no pay either, except for the cook. Declared Colvin: "Not a particle of alcoholic or fermented liquor of any kind—even for medicinal purposes—was used, carried, or permitted to be used or carried by any member of the party."[d]

If this seemed a harsh and cheerless regimen, some observers have noted that the tougher guides of those years—men such as Nye and the two Phelpses (Orson and his son, Ed), for example—repeatedly returned to work for Colvin. They may have shared his desire to climb the peaks, but they also may have respected him, as he endured every hardship fully as much as they. Indeed he reserved the most difficult climbs and forced marches for small parties, always including himself. Russell Carson was able to find in 1927 a number of Colvin's guides still living. "On the whole these men speak well of him," he reported. "It was the shirkers whom he antagonized."

The superintendent in turn respected good woodsmen. Almost every annual report includes a comment or two like this one from the 1874

[d]Colvin was a lifelong teetotaler. When lobbying for appointment to the Adirondack survey job, he invited some fifty influential Albany politicians to a grand reception, at which he served no food and no drink but ice water. Though the guests were outraged and left early, Colvin thought the party a grand success.

report: "Almost all of them [the guides] were faithful, intelligent, and skillful men."

What stands out most in Colvin's accounts is his burning desire to *climb* the mountains. His is perhaps the first true *climber's* spirit in the northeastern United States—in the sense of a relentless desire to get to the top of whatever he saw, especially if it had not been reached before. A peak in the Ausable Lakes region attracted him as "unascended, unmeasured and—prominent as it was—unknown to any map." Finding the ascent difficult, he was delighted to discover the final few feet ending in a "cliff almost impregnable"; the top was to him "a seat upon a throne that seemed the central seat of the mountain amphitheatre." With uncharacteristic understatement he commented, "The knowledge that it was a mountain hitherto unascended . . . made the ascent more interesting." Fittingly, this peak was thereafter called Mount Colvin.

After 1875 the incredible pace and hardships of the first four years were not sustained. Furthermore, from a mountaineering standpoint, of course, the major unexplored summits and passes of the high peaks had been reached in the trips between 1872 and 1875. During the winter of 1877, for two weeks in February, Colvin snowshoed around the woods and lakes southwest of the high peaks. This was an adventurous winter camping trip at that time, but the only mountain he ascended was "Seventh Lake Mountain" and its "broad but elevated summit" on February 15. In late 1883, as the topographical survey continued to work extensively in the Marcy area, Mills Blake put in some trying days on Marcy under extremely wintry conditions. During the later 1880s and 1890s, field work tended more and more toward tedious town boundary measurements. In 1891 the U.S. Geological Survey began its own work on Adirondack mapping. The first man in charge was Maj. John Wesley Powell, a towering figure in the exploration of western lands. Interestingly, Colvin and Powell cooperated reasonably well, but when the latter left the scene, Colvin was soon at odds with his successors. His arguments with the state legislature became increasingly frequent and bitter. At last in 1900 Colvin exploded and resigned.

Any evaluation of Colvin's contributions must be checkered. It seems hard to believe that after all those decades of work on the survey, Verplanck Colvin was still but fifty-three years old when he resigned. It is even harder to believe that after all that work he had still failed to produce the promised map of the Adirondacks. Many of Colvin's contemporaries judged him harshly. The state engineer who was sent to take over Colvin's papers when the survey was officially terminated in 1900 was dismayed to find the offices

> filled with a mass of camp equipage, snow shoes, tents, canoes, guns, traps, etc. It looked as though there was sufficient equipment for a trip to the North Pole. There was also an enormous mass of notebooks. I

should say there must have been many hundreds—possible thousands
—piled in the rooms without any method or system, but simply
thrown on the floor and piled up.

Colvin's status as a conservationist is assured by his unrelenting and
ultimately successful labors to make the Adirondacks a protected park.
(More evidence of his contributions in this field appears in chapter 31.)
But today's environmentalists would be horrified by his regular practice,
upon reaching summits, of ordering the guides to clear trees to facilitate
surveying. Not just a few trees: on flatter summits, he literally required
that acres be felled in order to allow his instruments to peer in all directions. While burning brush on the summit of Mount St. Regis, his party
started a fair-sized forest fire and was forced to beat a hasty retreat with
the camp and instruments. Today many people would also be offended to
note that although he was enchanted at the sight of two eagles soaring
above Marcy on October 22, 1875, Colvin expressed his relationship to
these wild creatures by reporting that they "soared past us majestically,
unmindful of revolver shots." His late-years schemes for railroads and
mining in the Adirondack wilderness have been mentioned.

However, history has not been so shortsighted as to judge Verplanck
Colvin in terms only of the accuracy of his mathematics or the constancy
of his conservationism. His impact on the Adirondack Mountains went
beyond that of any other man. In those first years of high-pitched energy, the Colvin surveys fundamentally altered the wilderness character
of the region. This change was of course also a function of the influx of
vacationing tourists and others, whose arrival owed more to Adirondack
Murray and the march of economic and social events than it did to the
surveyors. But the exploration and charting of the heart of the mountain
wilderness was the work of Colvin and his men. They climbed every major range and all the highest summits, fixed their locations and altitudes
with accuracy remarkable for the day, and took much of the mystery
from the forested fastness. If this work was not accomplished by the most
careful scientist, that is not surprising. But, as one recent evaluation expressed it, "If it had not been for a man like Colvin with his touches of
compulsive madness who would have done the job?"

Other considerations aside, his writings evoked an authentic image of
true wilderness that inspired not only his own generation but others to
come, down to our own day. One of today's closest students of
Adirondack history, Philip Terrie, regards Colvin as personally a
"crank" and "as looney as they come" but has high words for his writings
and their impact:

> The Colvin reports are collectively one of the great, largely undiscov-
> ered treasures of American nature writing and contain significant ele-
> ments of a genuine wilderness aesthetic, a new way of perceiving the

wilderness. . . . The chief importance of Colvin lies not in how he influenced current policy but in his descriptions of what life in the wilderness was actually like. His narratives are a living testament to the spiritual satisfaction of intimacy with the wilderness.

Colvin's measurements on the previously little-known Haystack and Skylight established them as the third and fourth highest in the Adirondacks, eclipsing the claims of such better-known giants as Whiteface and Dix. There lies another indication of the difference in degree of wilderness between the Adirondacks and other parts of the Northeast: imagine "discovering" Jefferson and Monroe's status as third and fourth highest in the White Mountains in 1873—that was four years after the Cog Railway was opened in *their* crowded neighborhood.

Chapter 18

The first hiking clubs

NEW ENGLAND is often regarded as the wellspring of individualism; yet it was here that the first organized associations of hikers were born. In fact, for half a century, hiking clubs were a peculiarly Northeastern institution—so much so that during the 1920s those who sought to build the 2,100-mile Maine-to-Georgia Appalachian Trail found with dismay that the only existing hiking or trail-building groups were in the Northeast.

The Alpine Club of Williamstown, Massachusetts

It all began in the quiet college village of Williamstown, Massachusetts. During the 1860s Williams College gave the little community an enterprising turn of mind. This was the presidency of the great Mark Hopkins, one of the most inspiring and influential educators of his day; President James Garfield was to define his idea of education as "a simple bench, Mark Hopkins on one end and I on the other." Williamstown was awash in Hopkins family members at that time, and one of them, Prof. Albert Hopkins, was a vigorous pedestrian in his late fifties who, as a youth in 1836, had accompanied Ebenezer Emmons during some of his geological investigations in the Adirondacks. Albert Hopkins loved the Berkshire hills around Williamstown. His biographer reports:

> Not a glen or cascade, not a ledge of rock or isolated boulder or majestic tree on all these hills and among these mountains had escaped his closest attention.

In April 1863 Professor Hopkins came up with the idea of forming a hiking club.[a]

---

[a]Professor Hopkins seems to have been a congenital organizer of outdoor clubs. During the 1830s, then a new young faculty member, he organized both the Natural History Society of Williams College (Grace Greylock Niles, *The Hoosac Valley: Its Legends and History* [New York: G. P. Putnam's Sons, 1912], p. 403) and the Horticultural and Landscape Gardening Association (Rudolph, *Mark Hopkins and the Log*, p. 142). In 1864, the year after he founded the Alpine Club, he also fathered the Sunrise Club (*Williams Alumni Review* [Feb. 1935], p. 160).

The original membership of the Alpine Club of Williamstown drew not so much from the students of all-male Williams College, but from energetic and enthusiastic young women of the college community. The twelve founding members included nine women—two from the Hopkins family (Carrie and Louisa)—plus three Williams professors, two of whom were also Hopkinses (Albert and Harry). Over the next two years the membership doubled but retained a female majority. The offices, also dominated by women, were not your standard president, vice president, and so forth, but consisted of leader (Fanny Dewey), chronicler (Professor Hopkins), secretary-treasurer (Carrie Hopkins), bugler (Fanny Whitman), and surgeon (Bessie Sabin). One active participant worth noting for future reference was a young scientist, Williams graduate, and hiking enthusiast named Samuel Hubbard Scudder; he was to play a lead role in the Appalachian Mountain Club more than a decade later.

The objectives of this path-breaking group were:

> To explore the interesting places in the vicinity, to become acquainted, to some extent at least, with the natural history of the localities, and also to improve the pedestrian powers of the members.

The pedestrian powers were soon being worked on. On May 2, 1863, the first hike by an organized club in America took place, a modest 6-mile jaunt from Williamstown to Birch and Prospect glens, "over fields and rough wagon roads." By the end of 1863, the Alpine Club had launched nineteen excursions, meriting its name by ascending such local alps as Greylock, Arbutus, Audubon, Anthony, Bald, and, on a two-day camping expedition, Vermont's Mount Equinox. In 1864 the club enjoyed eighteen more excursions, including a three-day camping trip in the relatively isolated and wild Hopper valley, tucked behind enfolding ridges of Greylock. During this trip the party climbed "the steepest face of Greylock," got lost on the descent, and embarked on a long bushwhack "tearing through the underbrush, sinking in the decayed vegetation, tumbling over precipices, panting, tired," until at length they just made it out to a road in the last daylight. The club organized nineteen excursions in 1865, including its first and last trip to the White Mountains.

This last was a twelve-day expedition during late August. The tour stuck to the standard White Mountain fare until the last day, with visits to Franconia Notch, the Silver Cascade, Glen Ellis Falls, and Diana's Baths, and ascents of Willard and Washington. After spending the night on the summit of Mount Washington, the party exited with a flourish, first climbing over Clay, Jefferson, Adams, and Madison, then at 3:30 P.M. dropping a little way down the "easterly ridge" (now the Osgood Ridge) and then straight down through the woods by compass, heading for Dolly Copp's Imp Cottage. They seem to have followed roughly the course of the present Daniel Webster (Scout) Trail, but for them it was first a "tangle of scrub," then a "steep acclivity" and finally a long bush-whack through thick woods, over fallen trees and rocks, sinking into soft moss and leaves. Night overtook them long before they reached the bottom. They proceeded by lighting matches to check the compass and trying to keep the sound of Madison (now Culhane) Brook on their left. Finally they invoked Fanny Whitman's function as bugler:

> Refreshed by a pull at the Chaplain's brandy-flask, the Bugler at-
> tempted to blow a blast, but failed to make it very effective. But now
> and then we tried again, and woke the echoes of the mountain-side, in
> the hope of reassuring an anxious friend below. We had been nearly
> four hours in the woods when we heard, or seemed to hear, the sound
> of a distant horn.

Eventually they heard the barking of dogs at the Copps' farm and made it safely down to Imp Cottage, only to arise at an early hour to catch the Gorham train and Portland boat back home.

Curiously enough, this was one of the last excursions of the Alpine Club of Williamstown. Professor Hopkins was losing interest, devoting himself increasingly to religious missionary work instead. Scudder moved to Harvard. The core of twenty-four members began to disperse from the little college town. Scheduled trips ceased in 1866, and though the club remained formally organized and had occasional reunions, it lived "rather in the pleasant memories of the past than in the exploits of the present."

New York City's earliest walking clubs

Another energetic college teacher was Columbia University's Professor of Botany John Torrey—the first of several Torreys to leave his imprint on Northeastern walking circles. Torrey was on the first ascent party of Mount Marcy (see chapter 10). A distinguished teaching career followed, winding up at Columbia. There, sometime in the 1860s—the exact year is hidden amongst conflicting evidence—he organized the Torrey Botanical Club. Though formally devoted to botanical pursuits, the club inherited the physically robust interpretation of that science from the legacy of Oakes and Tuckerman. From the beginning the club had an active program of field trips throughout the New York area on daylong excursions, and farther afield in New England, New Jersey, and Pennsylvania on trips of two or three days, or sometimes longer. If not truly a mountain-climbing club, the Torrey Botanical Club has always been a vigorous bunch, still going strong today.

New York's oldest club that officially devoted itself to mountain walking for its own sake was the Fresh Air Club. This pioneering group of city pedestrians was organized in 1877 by Henry E. Buermeyer, Mrs. Buermeyer, and their friend William B. ("Father Bill") Curtis. The Fresh Air Club lasted a century, finally disbanding in 1979. According to one version of a hoary club legend, the name came from one bitter cold day when Curtis and Buermeyer were striding about the streets of New York, coatless, when a well-wrapped taxi rider muttered audibly, "Huh! Just some of those fresh air cranks!" Curtis was delighted and instantly adopted the sobriquet as the official name for their nascent walking club.

"What the Appalachian Mountain Club did for New Hampshire," says one account, written in 1916, "the Fresh Air Club did for the country within a fifty-mile radius of New York." Hikes were scheduled every Sunday, with Curtis going out on Friday to scout the route. The usual locale was the Hudson Highlands, including Storm King, Bear Mountain, and Anthony's Nose. Formal hiking trails had yet to be built in this area, but the hills abounded in old wood roads. Rail connections were used to get to and from hikes. By the twentieth century the club had a well-entrenched tradition, which may have started in Curtis's day, of an afternoon tea break. Club members stashed tea pots around their favorite hiking haunts, would start up a small fire, and brew a pot of tea on the spot. "If a tree leaf or so found its way into the pot, it was left there. Such was their forest ritual."

The Fresh Air Club at first drew its membership primarily from New York City's men's athletic clubs of the 1870s and 1880s. "Father Bill" Curtis was known as one of the outstanding all-around athletes of his day. Mrs. Buermeyer was said to have been "one of the first women to ride a bicycle in this country." With that background, it is perhaps not surprising that, from its earliest days right up until World War II, the Fresh Air Club enjoyed an awesome reputation for the vigor of its hikes. Its members went out in all kinds of weather, disdaining overcoats on the coldest days. The walking was fast-paced, the itineraries ambitious. Recalls one New York area hiker who saw Fresh Air Club trampers whizzing by on the Harriman Park trails in the 1920s and 1930s,

> The story was if someone stopped to fasten his shoestring, he wouldn't catch up with the rest until they met at the railroad station.

Despite Mrs. Buermeyer's early role the group soon became strictly "men only," not just in membership but even on hikes, except for four specified Sundays when "women friends of members are invited." In fact, the Fresh Air Club was generally restrictive in membership. Far from promoting growth, the club discouraged publicity and sought to retain an aura of exclusivity and elitism based on the physical prowess of its walkers.

A New York club that flourished briefly was the Westchester Hare and Hounds, another athletics-oriented group, growing out of the Harlem Athletic Club. Its brief career terminated with absorption into the Fresh Air Club.

White Mountain Club of Portland, Maine

Portland, Maine, was a center of interest in the White Mountains during these early years. The second important "mountain club" of the Northeast was born there in 1873. Called the White Mountain Club of Portland, Maine, its principal organizers and leaders included George L. Vose, pioneer on Carrigain and elsewhere for the New Hampshire Geological Survey; John F. Anderson, a close friend of Vose, chief engineer of the Portland & Ogdensberg Railroad and designer of the rail route through Crawford Notch; Abner Lowell, an early promoter and director of the Mount Washington carriage road; George Frederick Morse, a professional craftsman and sketcher of the White Mountains, who had been with Vose on Carrigain; and Maj. John M. Gould, an especially energetic hiker and author of a manual called *How to Camp Out.*[b]

Organized in 1873, with Lowell as president, the club launched a period of vigorous and imaginative hiking exploration, fading only as the still more active Appalachian Mountain Club came to dominate the hiking scene and to absorb the energies of leading White Mountain climbers. During its brief ascendancy, the Portland Club devoted much attention to exploring little-visited regions.

Carrigain was a special favorite of club members. "It is," wrote an anonymous chronicler of one early outing, "none of your civilized mountains, the resort of tourists, made easy of ascent by footpaths, carriage ways and railroads, like your tame Mt. Washington. It is a savage peak, rising remote in the wilderness." The club was organized at a camp during an 1873 ascent of that "savage" peak, via the Cobb's Stairs route of Vose's 1869 attempt (see chapter 17; figure 18.1). In August of 1874 they returned, this time with Vose carrying a barometer to measure the elevation; "a bottle with records" was left on top. In June 1875 the club repeated the ascent up the South Fork and Cobb's Stairs. In August four men led by a Mr. Fox went up the next fork north from Cobb's Stairs, coming out farther along Signal Ridge, proceeding over the summit and down the north slope of the mountain, and walking out the East Branch through the still virgin Pemigewasset Wilderness to North Woodstock—a three-day trip, and a rather committing one for the time.

---

[b]The Portland group's special affection for the Carrigain area is attested by the naming of the three principal summits that directly overlook Carrigain Notch: Vose Spur, Mount Anderson, and Mount Lowell.

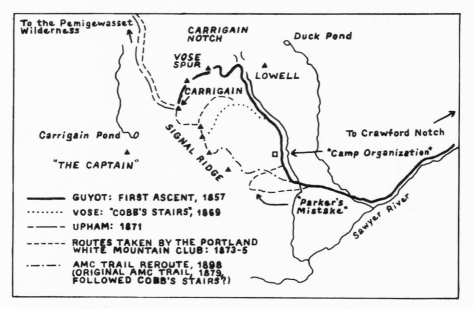

Figure 18.1. Early routes up Mount Carrigain, 1857–1898 Relatively remote from roads, Carrigain remained unclimbed until Arnold Guyot's ascent in 1857, evidently via Carrigain Notch and Vose Spur. The Portland White Mountain Club, however, made several ascents during the mid-1870s. Indeed the club was organized during a camping trip in the Carrigain area. Club members ascended and descended by several routes and named numerous features in the area, including "The Captain," a then little-visited, smaller, sharp-pointed summit southwest of Carrigain. On one occasion a Portland party lost its way and involuntarily explored some new country—cheerfully identifying their itinerary thereafter as "Parker's Mistake."

Another area of wildness explored by the Portland White Mountain Club was the Mahoosuc Range, a rambling and rugged spine of middling-sized peaks that runs for 30 miles from just north of the Presidentials in a northeasterly direction into Maine, culminating in 4,180-foot Old Speck. The club was in this range to climb Goose Eye Mountain as early as September 1875. They passed through the dark, boulder-strewn defile of Mahoosuc Notch in a trip in June 1880 and climbed Old Speck on July 4, 1881. Like the Carrigain area, the Mahoosucs were wild and little-visited terrain before the Portland White Mountain Club set foot there.

The Portlanders were also active closer to home, climbing such Maine mountains as Tumbledown Dick, Speckled Mountain, the Bethel Hills, and Blackstrap Hill, a local favorite just 7 miles from downtown Portland, with a 65-foot wooden observation tower on top, which collapsed in a 1914 storm.

It was the rise of the broader-based Appalachian Mountain Club that spelled the decline and demise of the smaller club. For awhile Portlanders resisted being absorbed by the AMC, voting unanimously against amalgamation in 1878. But five years later, club meetings were attended by but five to nine forlorn souls. Field meetings were canceled if Major Gould was not there to run them. By February 20, 1884, the minutes sadly noted:

> The weather prevented an audience and the speaker of the evening from attending. Time spent in desultory conversation. (Dr. Wm. Atwood buried today.)

That was the last entry in the annals of the once proud and adventurous White Mountain Club of Portland, Maine.

The Appalachian Mountain Club

These modest and tentative beginnings in Williamstown, New York, and Portland suggested that the concept of a club devoted to Northeastern hiking, mountain exploration, and related pursuits was an idea whose time had come. It remained for a twenty-nine-year-old MIT physics professor and a small circle of his Boston hiking friends to conceive the basic structure and program of what became and remained the largest and most influential club in Northeastern hiking and climbing: the Appalachian Mountain Club.

In 1873, the same summer in which the Portland men were organizing on Carrigain, Prof. Edward C. Pickering made his first visit to the New Hampshire hill country. Over the next two summers, Pickering met others equally enthusiastic about rambling over the peaks and passes. In the summer of 1875, during conversations with John B. Henck, Jr., and J. Rayner Edmands, Pickering began to develop the idea of an organized club for the purposes of exploring hitherto unascended peaks, measuring elevations, recording data, building trails, and mapping the vast playground of forested mountains.

They profited from the examples of the Portland White Mountain Club and the Alpine Club of Williamstown, not only in a general sense but by recruiting veterans from those organizations. The Harvard faculty had fortunately made two recent acquisitions whose club experience Pickering solicited. One was Edward F. Morse, formerly active in the Portland group, who transferred from Bowdoin to Harvard during the 1870s. The other was Samuel H. Scudder, the dynamo of the Williamstown Alpine Club, now in Cambridge and affiliated with Harvard variously as university lecturer, assistant librarian, and assistant in the Museum of Comparative Zoology.

But the Williamstown club was defunct and the Portland group too narrowly devoted to "amusement rather than scientific study or exploration," so Pickering decided to form a new club. The idea germinated on hiking trips in the summer of 1875. Early that winter, Pickering and Henck issued invitations to twenty or thirty like-minded White Mountain vacationers to meet in room 11 of MIT's Rogers Building on January 8, 1876. Among the group of thirty or so present, were Pickering, Henck, Morse, Scudder, and Charles E. Fay. There and then was born the Appalachian Mountain Club, which today stands as the oldest continuously operating mountain-climbing organization in the United States.

A remarkable group of mountain lovers accepted the new club as the right kind of organization in the right place at the right time, and made it the outlet for their enormous talents and energies:

Edward C. Pickering. In addition to his initiating role, Pickering served as the club's first president.

Samuel H. Scudder. The ex-Williamstown tyro succeeded Pickering as president in 1877. He also conceived the idea of a regular publication, *Appalachia.*

Charles E. Fay. From the founding meeting, this unquenchable little man threw his dynamic exuberance into the club's exploratory work. He succeeded Scudder as the third club president in 1878, serving three other terms (1881, 1893, 1905), became councillor of explorations in 1879, and edited *Appalachia* for forty years. His primary contribution was sparking the adventurous side of club activities, both in bold explorations of the remaining unvisited corners of the White Mountains and in excursions to the western United States and the Canadian Rockies.

William G. Nowell (rhymes with *Howell*). Like Pickering, Nowell had come to the mountains first in 1873 but had settled on Randolph, New Hampshire, as his summer base. He was the first person in Northeastern mountain history to take a serious and sustained interest in trail building. From his base in Randolph, Nowell spearheaded the development of the system of trails in the Northern Presidentials. Nowell served as councillor of improvements of the club for the first three years, from 1876 to 1878, and gave that post both its emphasis on trail construction and its tremendous importance in club activities from the very beginning.

J. Rayner Edmands. Edmands first went to the White Mountains in 1868 and for the next forty years pursued a wide range of interests among them. His first club office was councillor of explorations, but during those early years he was primarily a leader in scientific activities. Around 1890 he transferred his energies and prodigious capacity for work to trail construction and improvement. In both roles he imparted depth and force to the AMC's early programs. Like Nowell, he assured club emphasis on trail building. He served as president in 1886.

William H. Pickering. Younger brother of Edward the first (president), William was an even more active hiker than his brother. By 1879 he was said to have explored more than one hundred peaks in the White Mountains. He became councillor of explorations for three years, from 1880 to 1882, succeeding Fay, and much later served two terms as president. Like Fay, he assured club emphasis on adventurous exploration.

Of great significance for the AMC's early prestige was the association of the Hitchcock survey leaders with the club. Hitchcock himself agreed to be the original councillor of topography; in the club's second year he assumed the post of councillor of explorations. In 1878 Huntington succeeded him in that post; then Huntington became councillor of natural history from 1879 to 1881. Warren Upham, the Dartmouth student who did so much useful work for the survey, was an active member and served in both improvements and natural history posts.

These talented founders were succeeded by a second generation of competence and energy: Louis Cutter, Rosewell Lawrence, Ralph Larrabee, and Parker B. Field (direct descendant of Darby), to name a few of the more prominent. The extraordinary efficiency of the early AMC led Thomas Wentworth Higginson to observe,

> It seems to me that if anywhere there is a universe in need of administration, it might well be turned over to the Appalachian Mountain Club.

A key factor in the success of the club was its early recognition that times were changing for women. At its second meeting the club voted to admit women to membership. Although club offices remained dominated by men, the activities certainly were not. A number of AMC women were among the more adventurous explorers, while Mrs. Nowell and other women joined in trail work. Early club excursions seem to have involved women more than men. The 1887 "August Camp" at Katahdin—about as ambitious an expedition as you could find in New England in those days—consisted of nine men, ten women. The earliest winter trips to the White Mountains often had more women than men (see chapter 32). The decision not to remain an all-men preserve was a vital one for the AMC's success in becoming the dominant outdoor club of the Northeast.

From a charter membership of 34, the club grew rapidly. By the end of 1876 membership had reached 92. By 1880 it was up to 320, and by 1886 it reached an early plateau of 715. For a while thereafter growth occurred at a more sedate pace. By 1898 membership had passed 1,000.[c]

As the new organization took shape in its first decade, a variety of pursuits engaged the attentions of its members: placing registers on mountaintops, drawing panoramas and maps of the region's ranges, recording scientific observations in the mountains, producing a journal that has become one of the club's signal contributions (*Appalachia*), and engaging in what became the club's three prime functions, which we shall hear much more about in these pages—excursions, explorations, and improvements (by which was meant principally the building of trails and shelters).

Late nineteenth-century outdoors clubs

Other groups besides the outdoor clubs mentioned thus far were organized during the late nineteenth century.

The Catskill Club, 1875, was a short-lived organization of Catskill Mountain House guests. They do not seem to have done much walking, preferring to be conveyed to choice picnic spots in a grand wagon, trimmed with evergreens and club flags, the club name imprinted in gold letters on the side. The leader of the group, George Harding, later broke with the Mountain House to establish the Hotel Kaaterskill.

The Agassiz Association, 1875, originated as a Lenox (Massachusetts) High School group formed to investigate natural history in the Berkshire countryside, within a radius of 5–10 miles. Under the encouraging influence of Harlan H. Ballard, librarian and curator of the Berkshire Athenaeum in Pittsfield, additional chapters were formed elsewhere, the association's membership reaching ten thousand by the early twentieth century. Though emphasizing scientific pursuits, the association's focus was outdoors and must have involved many walking excursions.

The Wlwascackbwgmsaesfssjhe Pedestrian Association, 1881, is the magnificent appellation of a group whose origins, accomplishments, and demise were alike shrouded in obscurity. The name surfaces once: in a summit register sign-in sheet atop Carter Dome on July 17, 1881, with the names of Adrian and Augustus Scharff, William L. Worcester, George M. Sinclair, and Charles E. Ioraven as officers. Their time for ascending the then new trail from Carter Notch was a thoroughly respectable fifty minutes (compare with the 1980s AMC Guidebook time of ninety minutes) so

[c]Appalachian Mountain Club members have been known by a variety of nicknames. In general, club members were referred to during the nineteenth century as "Appalachians." Gradually during the first half of the twentieth, this term was supplanted by "Appies." Sometimes "AMCers" has been used. In the early days at least one circle of hikers called them "Apes" (see letter from Marian Pychowska to Isabella Stone, Apr. 4, 1880, jointly owned by George N. Kent and Douglas A. Philbrook). A bit later we find them called "Apps" (by James P. Taylor, in unidentified page proofs in the James P. Taylor Papers, collections of the Vermont Historical Society).

there were clearly some formidable hikers among the long-forgotten and unsung Wlwascackbwgmsaesfssjhe.[d]

The Waterville Athletic and Improvement Association, 1888, was a product of a resurgence in hiking and trail building in the Waterville Valley during the 1880s and 1890s. Like its neighbors to the east—the Wonalancet Out Door Club, 1898, and the Chocorua Mountain Club, 1908—its story appears in chapter 22.

A climbing club on the Sleeping Giant, 1889, was formed by ten New Haven trampers, led by J. Walter Bassett of Yale. This group built a clubhouse on one of the ridges of the Giant, but does not seem to have been active elsewhere.

The Intermediates, around 1890, was a walking club formed in the Haines Falls section of the Catskills, out of which grew a fun-loving aggregation calling themselves the Lingernot Society (around 1905). The Lingernots awarded a variety of degrees to members, based on distances hiked and mountains climbed. A "Doctor of Pedestry," for example, required walking 300 miles in one season, including at least one walk of 35 miles; twenty mountains, including the five highest in the Catskills; and the exploration of "one peak never before conquered by a member of the society." At one time 30 miles of trails were maintained by the Lingernots on High Peak and Round Top.

The Sierra Club, 1892, was originally modeled on the AMC. Not primarily a Northeastern club, it is mentioned here only to indicate the timing of its origin relative to other outdoor clubs, and because ultimately it sprouted regional chapters in the Northeast that have adopted regular hiking and climbing programs.

The Field and Forest Club, about 1900, seems to have been the only major outdoor club in the Boston area besides the AMC. The date of its origin is hard to establish, but by 1904 it was going strong and soon thereafter had a regular schedule of Saturday outings to such places as the Blue Hills, Middlesex Fells, Neponset Meadows, and Lynn Woods. With a membership of two hundred, it was certainly an active walking group around the city's open spaces during those years, but its interest in hiking seems to have subsided and eventually expired sometime after the mid-1920s, although as late as 1936 the *AMC White Mountain Guide* referred readers to a map and trail description "issued by" the Field and Forest Club (for the trail between Watatic and Wachusett).

These examples attest the diversity of the late nineteenth-century organizations with a strong interest and participation in walking, whose destinies ranged from those of the Northeast's largest, the AMC, and the influential nationwide Sierra Club, to that of the less prestigious Wlwascackbwgmsaesfssjhe Pedestrian Association.

---

[d]One can only regret that no evidence has survived of hikes by this club in Connecticut. Therefore it is not known whether the Wlwascackbwgmsaesfssjhe ever crossed the Naromiyochknowhusunkotankshunk (see the introduction to Part One).

Chapter 19

The first mountain guidebooks

THE PUBLICATION of guidebooks was an important influence in the growth of mountain recreation during the latter part of the nineteenth century. Understandably, guidebook history paralleled trail-building history. As with trails, some guidebooks had come to life during the earlier years of the century, but these were not mountain climbers' guides. Not until the 1870s did guidebooks, in the modern sense, make their appearance.

General travel guides were commonplace in the young nation during the early nineteenth century. G. M. Davison's *The Fashionable Tour in 1825* is an early illustration of this genre. Theodore Dwight, traveling nephew of his famous traveling uncle Timothy, produced a guide called *The Northern Traveller*, which went through several editions beginning in 1825 and described interesting routes through New England and parts of New York, as far as Saratoga Springs and even Niagara Falls—though not yet the Adirondacks. Nathaniel Willis penned one of the best-known and most literate guides, *American Scenery*, in 1840. A considerable library of guidebooks to the Northeast emanated from the prolific publishing house of John Disturnell of New York, beginning in 1842.

By the 1850s guidebooks specific to the White Mountain region began appearing with instructions for routes up the popular peaks. Samuel C. Eastman was the most noteworthy producer of White Mountain guidebooks in this and the following decade. He is credited with authorship of the "Guide to the Lakes and Mountains of New Hampshire," a forty-five page brochure put out by the Boston, Concord & Montreal Railroad in 1852. In 1858 *The White Mountain Guide*, a full-length book, appeared under his own name. Subsequent editions appeared in 1859 and almost annually from 1863 on. Other early guidebooks, less specific to the White Mountains but covering the major peaks such as Washington, Lafayette and Willard, included H. M. Burt's *Illustrated Guide of the Connecticut Valley*, *Appleton's Handbook of American Travel*, Osgood's *New England: A Handbook for Travellers*, and various guides by John Disturnell and Charles Newhall Taintor.

The first modern guidebook to White Mountain hiking trails, how-ever, dates from 1876. This was a crucial year in many ways for the open-ing of the modern era of mountain recreation. In 1876 no fewer than three distinct mountain centers had their first real guidebooks: the White Mountains, Maine, and the Catskills. This was also the year in which the Appalachian Mountain Club was formed; the first full year of operation of the strategically vital railroad through Crawford Notch; the year the Beede House opened on the approaches to the Ausable Lakes; the year the Putnam Camp took root; and the year when William Nowell and Charles Lowe inaugurated the modern trail era on Mount Adams.

In 1876—two years after Hitchcock's *Geology of New Hampshire* ap-peared—Moses Foster Sweetser had ready for publication the first guide-book to contain route descriptions for the ascents of virtually all the peaks, together with accounts of sights along the way and the prospect to be seen from each major summit. Sweetser's *The White Mountains: A Handbook for Travellers* was a stout, handsome, red-jacketed book des-tined to go through many editions, the regular companion of the serious White Mountain hiker until it was displaced by the AMC's guidebooks, which began to appear in 1907 and replaced most others after 1916. To write this guide, Sweetser himself walked many of the paths and pathless routes; he told Frederick Tuckerman that he had climbed more than eighty peaks in the White Mountains to prepare his guide. For expert assistance in climbing all these peaks, so many of them previously unknown or little-visited, Sweetser made arrangements with Hitchcock's chief assistant, the rugged and tireless Joshua Henry Huntington. Thus there is a direct lineal descent from the Hitchcock survey in 1868–74 to the Sweetser guidebook series that commenced in 1876, not simply in generally calling attention to the various peaks, but in the key role played by Huntington in both en-deavors. Sweetser's guidebook in effect transmitted to a new generation of mountain recreationists the detailed knowledge of routes of ascent that the Hitchcock survey team had discovered.

A new generation of guidebooks for the Adirondacks began to appear about the same time. Of course, Verplanck Colvin's *Reports* had been more widely read than Hitchcock's, being written with more verve. One admirer comments that Colvin "could make a routine survey report sound like a story of a dash to the North Pole, yet stick to literal truth"; Adirondack historian Paul Jamieson insists that Colvin "imparts to the ascent of four-thousand footers a zest worthy of the Alps and the Himalayas." Soon guidebook writers followed along to spread the word about routes to the summits and trails Colvin eulogized. Seneca Ray Stoddard began issuing his series in 1874. Edwin Wallace brought out his version almost annually beginning in 1875. An earlier version of Wal-lace's appeared as a kind of appendix to H. P. Smith's *Modern Babes in the Woods* in 1872. Wallace's guides were not as significant for the moun-tains as those of Stoddard. While neither of these blanketed the

Adirondack high peaks as thoroughly as Sweetser's had the White Mountains, that fact simply reflects the greater degree of wildness still left in the land of the Cauchsachrage, even after Colvin had passed through.

In Maine, north woods guidebooks primarily concerned with waterways and camping areas appeared during the period. The very first to mention any mountain was a small booklet prepared by John M. Way in 1874, which contained primarily hiking and canoeing information but included advice on how to climb both Kineo and Katahdin. However, the first thorough series covering Maine's mountains began with Capt. Charles A. J. Farrar's *Illustrated Guide-book for Rangeley, Richardson, Kennabago*, etc., which came out in 1876, with new editions appearing often throughout the 1880s. These were soon followed by Lucius L. Hubbard's *Summer Vacations at Moosehead Lake and Vicinity: A Practical Guide-book for Tourists*, beginning in 1879; Thomas Sedgewick Steele's *Canoe and Camera: A Two Hundred Mile Tour through the Maine Forests*, beginning in 1880; George Henry Haynes's *Seaside, Mountain and Lake Summer Resorts . . .* , beginning in 1886; and Leroy Thomas Carleton's *Carleton's Pathfinder and Gazetteer of the Hunting and Fishing Resorts of the State of Maine* in 1899.

In the Catskills, Walton Van Loan's series of guidebooks began coming out in 1876, and included a modest amount of information on what peaks made pleasant strolls, though far more on what valley accommodations were available. Van Loan soon had competitors. Samuel E. Rusk brought out a Catskills guide in 1879. Later the Ulster & Delaware Railroad issued more detailed guidebooks to the region.

Toward the end of the nineteenth century, the Berkshires and even the low hills of Connecticut had guidebooks for "walks and rides." Examples included Clark W. Bryan's *The Book of Berkshire* (1887), Rollin H. Cooke's *Drives and Walks in the Berkshire Hills* (1895), and James D. Dana's *The Four Rocks of the New Haven Region, with Walks and Drives about New Haven* (1891). Many hills of southern New England had been covered in the earlier generation of more general or regional guides, such as *Appleton's General Guide to the United States and Canada* (issued almost annually during the 1860s and 1870s) and Burt's *Illustrated Guide of the Connecticut Valley* (beginning in 1866).

There is an interesting point of contrast between the first generation of guidebooks and their modern counterparts. The early guidebooks devoted little time to describing the trail, evidently assuming that the hikers of that day could find their way once they knew where the trail started— or that they would hire a guide. The view from the summit, on the other hand, received lavish attention, reflecting the continuing influence of the Starr King era's absorption with sublime scenery. In contrast, modern guidebooks give detailed descriptions of every bend in the trail—and almost nothing on the view from the top. For example, contrast the

Sweetser guidebook's account of the Moat range with that given in the modern AMC guidebook. As late as the 1918 edition, the Sweetser guide devoted six and a half pages to North and South Moat. The trail description consists of one sentence for North Moat, two sentences for South Moat, with no details given. The views from the top consume the rest of the entry: over six pages' worth! In the 1987 edition of the *AMC White Mountain Guide*, the trail description takes almost two full pages, while summit views rate portions of two sentences, with no details given. This difference in guidebook emphasis is suggestive of differences in the purpose and spirit of climbing between the early climbers and their descendants of the late twentieth century.

The guidebooks completed the setting of the stage. The railroads had opened easy access to the mountains. The grand hotels provided opulent accommodations for the wealthy, the cheaper boardinghouses more modest facilities for the middle class. The passion for the pleasures of pedestrianism had brought the country out on foot, extolling the virtues of wholesome exercise. The scientific surveys had identified all the wealth of mountains that awaited the adventurous excursionist. The trail-builders were preparing pathways to the ridges and summits. The guidebooks pointed out exactly where to go and what to see.

Chapter 20

The first trail systems

W HILE growing numbers of hill walkers were tramping around established trails and well-known summits during the late nineteenth century, two other smaller groups were doing deeds that merit closer attention. These two elites were numerically small, but their accomplishments bulk large on the horizon of Northeastern mountain history.

Let us recall how, back in 1876, the newborn Appalachian Mountain Club's three most significant functions came under the headings of excursions, improvements, and explorations. Of these, excursions were pursued by the vast majority of the membership. But though improvements and explorations involved few individuals, their significance as divergent strains in Northeastern mountaineering for the next century and beyond, cannot be overstressed. Not only within the AMC and the White Mountains but throughout the region we shall find these two impulses vibrant throughout the twentieth century. Since these terms sound quaintly archaic today, we start by asking what the early Appalachians meant by *improvements* and *explorations*.

Improvements and explorations

Very simply, *improvements* referred to building trails and shelters; *explorations* meant investigating peaks, ridges, and valleys hitherto unexplored.

Back in 1876 the forces of improvements and explorations saw themselves as mutually supporting, or at least not conflicting. Yet within these two concepts lay the seeds of two profoundly different perceptions of the mountains and people's relationship to mountains, two divergent paths along the wild and scenic vistas, reflecting two fundamentally separate sets of values.

The improvers build trails to enable club members and the public to get up into the mountains, shelters to accommodate them there, maps and guidebooks to help them find their way around the hills in safety.

The explorers set off for hitherto unvisited valleys and sally forth up steep ridges to apparently inaccessible crags, thereby physically and spiritually turning their backs to the public that the improvers seek to serve.

Both sides deeply love the mountains. But one strives to share them with others and to provide trails and facilities to make their time in the mountains more comfortable, while the other cherishes the wildness of the hills, their very uncomfortableness, the spice of which depends on the rugged demands it exacts from those hardy enough to pursue it.

The improvements camp looks at the splendor of mountain scenery and sees a natural wealth to be shared; the explorations camp seeks adventure of a more personal kind.

The word *improvement* signals the thought behind trails, shelters, maps, and guidebooks: that these *improve* the experience that people can enjoy in the mountains. To the explorer, the idea that people could improve on the experience that nature provides is sacrilege.

This divergence persists down through the years in the recurring debate within the venerable halls of the AMC over how many huts to build in the mountains, how civilized a service to provide at them, how much trails should be "hardened." The explorations wing goes into such challenging pursuits as winter climbing, rock climbing, ice climbing, and bushwhacking—efforts to preserve the zest and risk of exploration. Meanwhile the improvements wing branches off into increasingly commodious camps, accommodations for family vacations in the mountains, and eventually a variety of educational programs intended to broaden and deepen public enjoyment of the hills. In this divergence, apparent in the very earliest organizational structure of the AMC, lie the taproots of the debate between preservation and use which divides the conservation movement of the late twentieth century.

But it should not be construed that this division was explicitly recognized in the early years of AMC. Certainly it did not appear to the founders as a problem. Referring to four individuals who will be met in the chapters that follow, Charles Fay and Herschel Parker were explorers to the core; J. Rayner Edmands and Louis Cutter were ardent improvers— but all four found a comfortable home in the new club. Indeed one reason why the AMC became and remained the dominant mountain club of the Northeast may well be traced to its combining under one organizational roof both the improvers and the explorers.

The same divergent paths were being trod in the Adirondacks, on Katahdin, along the Green Mountains—the difference between those seeking the last great adventures to be wrung from the Northeastern hills and those promoting the greatest trail-building era these same beloved hills have ever seen.

The earliest hiking trails

Trail building in the Northeastern mountains, as an isolated, discontinuous pursuit, can be traced back to the path through the scrub up Tuckerman Ravine, cut by order of Colonel Gibbs in 1809. Close on the heels of that pioneering track came the two Crawford paths, the trail built up Lafayette in 1826, and the paths to peaks farther south during the period from 1820 to 1830: North and South mountains in the Catskills, Ascutney, Monadnock, Greylock. During the 1850s and 1860s, mixed up with all the bridle paths and carriage roads of the Starr King era, came more trails on Mount Washington in New Hampshire, Mansfield and Camel's Hump in Vermont, Whiteface and Marcy in the Adirondacks, Greylock in Massachusetts. But with one exception, these were isolated from one another, not linked into any system of trails.

Waterville Valley

The single exception—one place where a true system of hiking trails was built before the Civil War—was in Waterville Valley. The cluster of paths that grew up here, the Northeast's first trail system, is associated with the special character of the resort that developed at that quiet little "town at the end of the road," and with one remarkable figure who stood at its center.

Nathaniel Greeley moved into the isolated, peaceful, mountain-rimmed valley of Waterville, New Hampshire, around 1830, built his log cabin, and cleared his land. As early as 1835, according to the accepted account, a man with lung trouble spent a restful convalescence at the Greeleys' and asked to return as a boarder the following summer. Fishermen then and tourists later followed suit. When the railroad reached Plymouth in 1853, 20 miles to the south, Greeley's inn became a major tourist target. But the railroad never got closer than that, never entered the mountain sanctuary where Greeley held sway. This fact enabled the innkeeper to dominate the scene and create a uniquely pedestrian-oriented resort in Waterville Valley.

Greeley was evidently a commanding personality. In 1862 one visitor described the sixty-year-old former pioneer as "proprietor of the Valley and everything in it." As a host he left an indelible visual impression:

> His spare form was somewhat bent and gnarled. His features were full of odd lines and produced an effect of good-natured grotesqueness that was quite taking. He was very bright and quick at retort and had an immense amount of executive energy that he carried into everything.

Few mountain hotel men recognized and capitalized on the appeal of the peaks as early or as aggressively as Greeley. His was truly one of the more entrepreneurial minds of early mountain recreation. During the 1850s he cut or arranged for the cutting of not merely the usual assortment of gentle paths to nearby waterfalls and outsized boulders but also a considerable variety of substantial hiking trails even by modern standards (see figure 20.1). He built one bridle path, leading to the summit of Osceola, the highest of the mountains that ring Waterville Valley. To its neighbor Tecumseh, he gave a footpath. An old berry pickers' track up Mount Welch was soon opened for use by the summer folk as well, and a path was worked out to connect Welch to Tecumseh. On the sprawling minimassif southeast of the valley, Sandwich Dome, Greeley's men cut a new trail starting at a point across the road from the one up Welch. Shorter paths led to a variety of natural beauty spots north of the inn, including the ponds that bear the host's name. Thus, in the era of bridle paths and summit houses, Waterville Valley became uniquely more a hiker's haven than a rider's.

For the vigorous equestrian, Greeley established three bridle paths over formidable mountain terrain, connecting with neighboring valleys and other resorts. The first of these paths ran northeast across the southern edge of the Pemigewasset Wilderness to Crawford Notch, about 30 miles of rough country; some claimed that a good horseman could ride all the way from Greeley's inn to the top of Mount Washington in one day. A second path twisted east and south through the heavily forested gap between Sandwich Dome and the Tripyramids, past Flat Mountain's low summits, to the settlements of Whiteface, Sandwich, and Tamworth. Both these transwilderness trails, built around 1860, proved difficult to keep open, and the latter soon was obliterated, that gap becoming known as "Lost Pass." The third trail ran west over a height-of-land to North Woodstock, not clearly finished until the 1870s.

Little of Greeley's original trail system survives today. The trails on Osceola, Tecumseh, and Sandwich Dome were in different places from today's trails. Those connecting Welch and Tecumseh and through Lost Pass were lost. Only one of the three long bridle paths survived, today's Tripoli Road. No trails existed on the Tripyramids in Greeley's day, for the very good reason that the landslides that later opened the routes for today's trails had not yet slid.

Greeley's trail system was ahead of its time. As late as 1875, nowhere else in the mountains of the Northeast was there anything approaching a modern trail system.

Beginning in the 1870s, however, throughout the region, a variety of true trail systems or clusters of footpaths began to take form. These reflected the newly emerging enthusiasm for mountain walking. The trails were usually built by people from the mountain vacation centers, either by the hired hands of the hotels or inns, or by the summer folk who stayed at such places. Figure 20.2 shows the approximate periods of peak trail-building activity and how this phenomenon surfaced all over the region at about the same time.

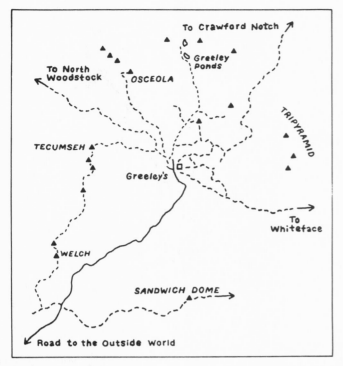

Figure 20.1. Waterville Valley trails, 1850s The first true system of hiking trails took root in Waterville Valley in the White Mountains during the 1850s. In addition to the medley of short walks to scenic attractions, note that trails extended to several major summits that rimmed the secluded valley. Other hotels provided short walks, but Nathaniel Greeley was the first to open pedestrian paths to a number of sizable nearby mountains.

Nowell, Lowe, and the AMC trail-builders

In the White Mountains 1876 was a pivotal year. The AMC was organized, Sweetser produced the first serious White Mountain guidebook. And in the same year the first mountain trail of the new era was cut. In light of subsequent events, it is fitting that this first trail originated in Randolph, New Hampshire, was conceived by a Randolph summer resident, and cut by a year-round Randolph man.

William G. Nowell was cast from the mold of earlier Renaissance men such as Cutler and Belknap—a minister, physician, and schoolteacher who found time for much outdoor recreation. Educated at Bowdoin, he was teaching high school in Malden, Massachusetts, when he began summering at Randolph in 1873. Then thirty-six, he was known for "great physical strength and hardihood," breaking late autumn ice in Snyder Brook for a swim. Yet he was also a warm family man and sensitive nature-lover who adorned trail reports with such passages as this:

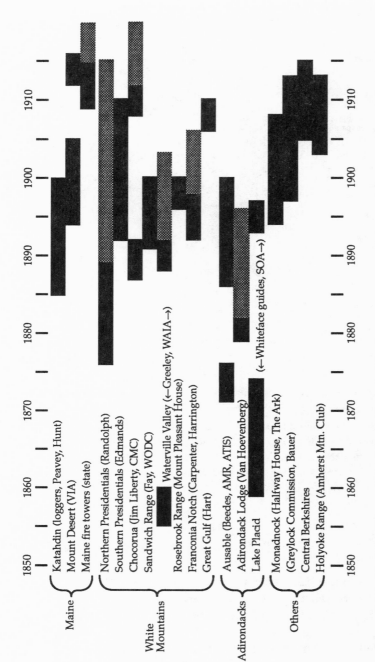

Figure 20.2. Trail building activity throughout the Northeast, 1870–1910 Modern hiking trails were first built during the period 1870-1910 throughout the Northeast. In just two locales, activity began earlier: Waterville Valley in the White Mountains, and Whiteface Mountain in the Adirondacks. Otherwise, the pattern was similar all over the region, beginning with the Ausable area (Adirondacks) and the Northern Presidentials (White Mountains) during the 1870s. The decades just before and just after 1900 were particularly active.

When the setting sun is flooding the green valley below with misty gold, bathing the shoulders and penetrating the uttermost recesses of the ravines of the Great Range with warm hues of rose and purple, and transmuting the stony gray peaks aloft into amethyst, those who linger on this little mountain [Boy Mountain, where he had just built a trail] till near the coming of the night shadows, will not fail to perceive why the Club should prize what has been done here in its name during the past season.

Even before the AMC was formed, Nowell had been instrumental in arranging for a trail to be cut from Randolph into the Northern Presidentials. The man whom Nowell paid to cut it was another of the great figures of early Randolph—Charles E. Lowe. A year younger than Nowell, Lowe had moved to Randolph from Maine. When Nowell and other summer visitors began to ask local residents to help build trails and guide mountain parties, Lowe seized the opportunity. He was a trained surveyor and blessed with a "companionable" nature, both qualities valuable in a guide. Of his seven children, three followed him in that role. The Lowes should not be perceived as primitive backwoodsmen, however; Charles Lowe and several of his descendants down to the present day have been community leaders in Randolph, serving as selectmen, delegates to the state legislature, and postmasters.

Nowell and Lowe were but the first two actors to appear on the crowded Randolph stage (see chapter 22), but they were superstars. The modern era of trail building can be dated from the construction of the Lowe's Path up Mount Adams from Randolph. Lowe began work in 1875 and completed it the following year. Over half a century after the first trail up the Southern Presidentials to Washington was completed, a fully cleared trail now reached the Northern Presidentials for the first time.

With the formation of the Appalachian Mountain Club in 1876, Nowell was invited to be its first councillor of improvements. He was a fortunate choice. Like later great Northeastern trail-builders who followed the path he first dreamed of, Nowell combined the gleam-in-the-eye of the visionary with the ax-in-the-hand of the doer. He planned trails all over the White Mountains, and with his own two feet and hands he went to work to build them.

Thinking big, Nowell's very first report as councillor of improvements, read to a club gathering on May 10, 1876, boldly listed twenty "Paths to be Made." Like many a grand vision, Nowell's schemes foundered on the hard rock of reality, in this case New Hampshire granite. One of his successors, A. E. Scott recalled four years later:

We remember with what . . . enthusiasm we looked forward to the November meeting, picturing in our minds a report of twenty smooth paths, eight feet wide, free from trip roots, the trees along their sides spotted with the Club hatchet, and the rocks on the mountain-tops blazing with "A. M. C." And, while we look back with pride on the work that has been accomplished from year to year, our experience forces us to admit, that wielding an axe on a mountain-side, or lugging stones on the ledges with which to build cairns, in midsummer, has a cooling effect on one's ardor in path-building, if not on the temperature of one's body; and that the many so-called improvements must be accomplished slowly, and by hard labor.

Nevertheless, what Nowell and others achieved in the first five years of the AMC's existence was to lay the cornerstone of the first great trail-building era (see figure 20.3).

Lowe's Path, completed in 1876, was followed up with a spur leading into King Ravine, from which a rougher track led up the headwall to Mount Adams. Some lesser trails in the Presidentials and around Randolph were also cut.

Also, in 1877, under Nowell's guidance, Lowe cut a good trail from near the Glen House into scenic Carter Notch, following Nineteen-Mile Brook. With improvements to an old fisherman's trail from Jackson, this made a through route from the Glen to Jackson. In 1879 a Jackson resident, Jock Davis, cut a trail from the Notch up Carter Dome.

The Glen House guide, Benjamin F. Osgood, began cutting major trails about this time. In 1878 he opened a way up Madison from the Glen House, following the long sweeping ridge that ever since has borne his name. Three years later he completed a trail that branched low into the Great Gulf to Spaulding Lake, then very wild and little-visited terrain.

In 1879 the AMC arranged for Jock Davis and his father to cut a good trail directly to Tuckerman's from the road through Pinkham Notch. Until that year the trail reached only as far as the Crystal Cascade, a popular tourist destination then as now.[a]

In the same year Maj. Curtis Raymond of Boston, a summer guest at the Glen House, undertook to reopen an old path from the carriage road into Tuckerman Ravine, ever since known as the Raymond Path.

---

[a]Nowell had envisioned the trail into Tuckerman's "for the more hardy and adventurous" (Nowell "Report of the Councillor of Improvements," *Appalachia* [June 1887], p. 197)—little foreseeing the army of trampers of every size and description that would one day swarm up the Tuckerman Ravine Trail. According to guidebooks of the early 1880s, the Raymond Path was far better built than Jock Davis's direct trail from the notch road, though it is the latter that has become the trade route. Herbert Allen, who climbed Mount Washington sixty times between 1900 and 1942, recalled that until the 1920s the Raymond Path was more heavily used than the Tuckerman Ravine Trail (conversation with Dan H. Allen, his grandson, March 6, 1988).

Figure 20.3. **Trail building in the White Mountains, 1876–1880** Following formation of the Appalachian Mountain Club in 1876, the first sustained period of trail building began in the White Mountains. Beginning with Lowe's Path from Randolph to the summit of Mount Adams, trail-builders went to work within the next four years, from Randolph and the Glen House in the north, to Albany and Waterville Valley in the south, as well as in Crawford Notch and the Moat Range. The modern age of trail building was underway at last.

During this time several trails were cut on the Moat Range, a highly accessible and attractive chain of summits overlooking Conway and North Conway.

At Hincks's instigation, Lowe cut a trail up Mount Willey from its southern flank in 1878. Another, apparently older, trail branched off this to Ethan Pond.

Mount Carrigain, so oft explored by the Portlanders, finally had a definite trail cut in 1879, following roughly the Cobb's Stairs bushwhack route of 1869.

Over in Waterville Valley, the AMC joined forces with an active group of hikers who summered there to enhance their network of trails. Greeley's old bridle path connecting Waterville with the Swift River valley above Albany Intervale was improved and extended northward by Sawyer Pond and River to end at Livermore Mills near the foot of Carrigain. A trail from Waterville over Noon and Jennings Peaks to Sandwich Dome (then often called Black Mountain) was constructed for the AMC by Greeley and his men. During this period also, the trail between Waterville and North Woodstock (today's Tripoli Road) was definitely established and maintained for the first time. The Watervillians also cut a new trail up Tecumseh, probably the direct ancestor of today's trail.

At the end of a little road west of Conway (where the Kancamagus Highway now streams across the wilderness), a farmer by the name of James M. Shackford discovered, as had Randolph's Lowe and Jackson's Davis, that he could earn money both by contracting to cut trails for the AMC and by taking in tourists who liked to hike on those trails. In 1880 Shackford cut trails from the end of the road up Oliverian Brook to Mount Passaconaway and on up the Swift River to picturesque Sabba Day Falls. From the falls, AMC trail-builders made halfhearted efforts to cut a trail up Tripyramid, but it was years before this was established.

In these first five years, besides trails, the AMC's Improvements Department built a number of shelters, or "camps" as they were then called. Two of the most widely used were on Lowe's Path at the site of today's "Log Cabin" shelter, and in Carter Notch, a rude, three-sided shelter that antedated the present hut by thirty-five years. In 1879 W. B. Parker directed the construction of a shelter in Tuckerman Ravine, probably the first in that region where now so many shelters are available to backpackers. For many years these and other backwoods buildings were so casually constructed that it was not uncommon for a severe storm to destroy a shelter or two each year. Only after repeated rebuildings and some major changes in design did the AMC begin to put up buildings in the mountains that lasted.

Chapter 21

Three Adirondack trail centers

I$_F$ White Mountain trails were sparse before 1870, Adirondack trails were even less developed. Indeed the first definite mountain trail on the high peaks of upper New York State was not cut until the 1850s—so Adirondack trail history is scarcely 130 years old, as this is written; some hikers can personally recall more than half of that history.

Prior to the 1870s, Whiteface Mountain was the only scene of more than token trail building. Surprisingly, no fewer than four separate paths were cut up Whiteface before anything much happened elsewhere. Whiteface had long been the best-known Adirondack peak and had been thought to be the highest until Emmons proved otherwise in 1837. It was frequently ascended during the middle of the century, and by 1859 guide Andrew Hickok cut the Adirondacks' first formal mountain trail, from his home near the present Flume bridge on the Ausable River, a few miles east of Wilmington village. In 1865 Bill Nye turned his talented hand to constructing the first cleared route from Lake Placid to the peak, following a prominent slide on the southwest side; the upper portions of Nye's original route ran north and west of the present Lake Placid approach. As we saw, the early bridle path–summit house era had passed the Adirondacks by, but in 1870 the Adirondacks' first and only bridle path to a summit was built on the east side of Whiteface by the proprietor of the Whiteface Mountain House in Wilmington. Running north of the subsidiary Marble Mountain, instead of south as the 1950 relocation and present trail does, this route was 6.5 miles long. In 1872 two innkeepers from Franklin Falls, Russ and Sam French, built a fourth route up Whiteface from the north.[a] By this time newspaper accounts refer to Whiteface as frequented by tourists fully as much as Marcy, the accessibility of the former balancing the prestige of the latter's elevation (see figure 21.3).

In 1861 Old Mountain Phelps cut Marcy's first trail; it led from Wells Camp on the Upper Ausable Lake, along Shanty Brook, over Bartlett

---

[a] One of the Beedes told Russell Carson that he recalled a trail up Esther, also built by Russ French, possibly earlier than this one up Esther's more celebrated big brother (Carson, *Peaks and People*, p. 97). Such a trail is otherwise undocumented, however, Esther remaining trailless until a ski trail was built during the 1950s.

Ridge just south of Haystack, into Panther Gorge, and from there up an old slide to the summit. Phelps also put in a trail of sorts through Johns Brook valley to Marcy, work later enhanced by his son, Ed Phelps, and another guide, Seth Dibble; however, it was little used and probably never thoroughly bushed out.

During the 1860s, the Phelpses (father and son) cut a trail out of Keene Valley to Hopkins Mountain, and later extended it along the ridge to Giant, though that part may not have been well articulated. (When Colvin's surveyors traveled this route in 1873, no mention was made of a trail, even though Ed Phelps may have been in the party. One who passed that way in 1874 said there was "no regular trail all the way.")

Still, none of this activity produced a true trail system in the Waterville sense—that is, a variety of footpaths emanating from the same mountain center. The creation of true trail systems in the Adirondacks finally began during the 1870s. Four distinct forces generated virtually all of the Adirondacks' trails between 1870 and 1910:

1. The Colvin survey

2. The opening of the Beede House on the approaches to the Ausable Lakes in 1876 and its eventual takeover by the Adirondack Mountain Reserve around 1890

3. The opening of Adirondack Lodge on Heart Lake by Henry Van Hoevenberg in 1880

4. The formation of the Shore Owners' Association of Lake Placid in 1893 and of the Lake Placid Club in 1895

The Colvin survey

The Colvin survey's contribution to permanent trails was small in mileage but strategically important in pointing the way into what had previously seemed impenetrable wilderness. In 1871 Colvin's guides cut a trail up Mount Dix from Elk Lake. In 1873, working for Colvin, Old Mountain Phelps and others cut the first trail up Haystack, third highest in the range. Colvin's men next cut a trail from Lake Colden up Algonquin, second highest, and in 1875 (Phelps again) up Skylight, fourth highest. In addition, Colvin worked out better approaches to Marcy from both west (by Lake Tear) and east (avoiding Bartlett Ridge). Thus Colvin left new trails up each of the four highest peaks in the Adirondacks. The effect of all this in producing a sense of the whole range opening up to mountain recreation was incalculable. The scene was now set for the three great centers of Adirondack trail work.

The Ausable region

Summer visitors flocked to Keene Valley during the 1870s. The attraction of the mountains, well known to but a select few before, started to be more widely recognized. Much of the original development of facilities for the mountain pedestrian was the work of the Beede family, who owned key acreage for approaches to the Ausable Lakes and their rich retinue of surrounding peaks. Beedes ultimately filled Keene Valley much as Crawfords had dominated their notch fifty years before. Orlando Beede knew the peaks in that area as well as anyone, even Old Mountain Phelps. In 1871 he cut a long trail through the pass between Noonmark and Round Mountain and up the valley of the Bouquet River to the summit of Dix, easternmost giant of the high peaks, eighth highest, and one of the most striking summits in the Northeast, with deep valleys plunging to both east and west. In 1873 and 1874 he opened a direct way up Giant. In 1875 he supervised cutting of a trail up the peerless Noonmark via its northeast depression (see figure 21.1).

In 1876 Orlando's father, Smith Beede, built "Beede's Heights Hotel" on a picturesque bluff near the present site of the Ausable Club. This was a large inn by Adirondack standards of the day, the largest in Keene Valley, three stories high and 105 feet long. It throve and soon expanded as the base for much Adirondack tramping. Besides the three mountains that Orlando's trails had opened up, there was Marcy itself, reached via the upper lake. During the 1870s there may also have been a trail up Gothics from the upper lake, one that did not last long, and there may have been another one, also of short life, cut (or at least blazed) by Ed Phelps to the Wolf Jaws. Not far away were the Phelpses' trail up Hopkins and a couple of new ones on scenic Baxter Mountain.

By the late 1880s another force entered the picture. A preservationist association of wealthy Philadelphians grew alarmed over plans to log the mountains overlooking Ausable Lakes. Having the wherewithal to back their convictions, they purchased outright substantial acreage, including both lakes, under the name of the Adirondack Mountain Reserve. Thus began, in 1887, the long stewardship of the AMR, which continues to this day, though most of the mountaintops have been conveyed (some quite recently) to state ownership. In 1890 the Beedes sold out to the AMR. When the original inn burned to the ground, a successor was promptly built and christened St. Hubert's Inn, known since 1906 as the Ausable Club. In the woods around the main building, a considerable colony of summer cottages gradually germinated. The pace of trail construction quickened. Even before the inn was purchased, AMR guides cut a trail up Gothics from just below the lower lake. In 1888 a new trail to Dix was cut through the pass between Noonmark and Bear Den.

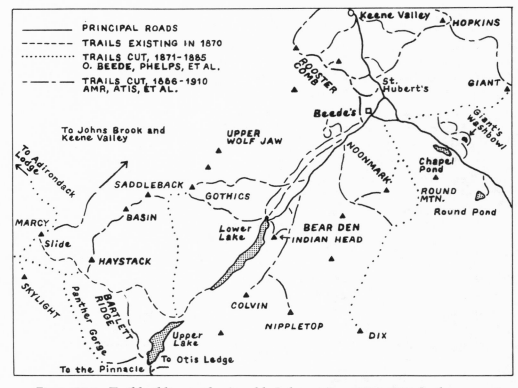

Figure 21.1. Trail building in the Ausable Lakes region, 1870–1910 In the 1870s Orlando Beede began cutting trails to the mountain heights surrounding his inn at the south end of Keene Valley. When the Adirondack Mountain Reserve took over the property in 1890, the pace of trail making quickened, especially with the formation of the Adirondack Trail Improvement Society (ATIS) in 1897. While this activity laid the foundations of the modern trail network in this end of the Adirondacks, alert modern hikers may note that several of these older trails have not survived—for example, the slide route up Marcy, the southern approach to Gothics, the western approach to Noonmark, and the trail through the pass east of Bear Den.

In the 1890s the importance of trail work was signaled by a singular event. According to the story, three AMR summer visitors were climbing Noonmark in 1897 when they met with a chaotic jumble of blowdown, over, under, and through which they expended considerable energy. Of the three climbers the best known to the outside world was Dr. Felix Adler, founder of the Ethical Culture movement. The others became well known in the narrower circle of Adirondack vacationers: William Augustus White and S. Burns Weston. As they struggled with crisscrossed timber, Dr. Adler paused astride an uppermost log to intone, "My friends, we should at once establish an Adirondack trail improvement society." Such at least is the legend.[b]

The Adirondack Trail Improvement Society (ATIS) was organized at St. Hubert's on September 14, 1897, with W. A. White as president, and Adler and Weston among the nine founding fathers. Although the group had no official connection with the AMR or the subsequent Ausable Club, its field of activity and base of operations were (and still are) the mountains around St. Hubert's and the Ausable Lakes. Besides trail construction and maintenance, ATIS has been concerned with conservation, forest fire control, and later with educational and recreational programs for children, including supervised mountain climbing. White remained president through its first thirty years, and Weston was also extremely active in its leadership during that time.

Thomas P. Wickes was one of the most active trail workers in the early days of ATIS. Even before the founding of that organization, Wickes had interested himself in constructing new trails up Gothics (the 1886 trail from the east) and Mount Colvin (see figure 21.1). Under ATIS, Wickes took the lead in inspecting trails and ensuring their upkeep. In 1905 he worked out a trail to Rocky Peak from Giant, via a small pond that he named for his daughter, Lake Mary Louise.

ATIS's first report, put together by Weston, listed an impressive number of trails built or improved by 1898, especially when one recalls the rudimentary state of Adirondack trails not long before.[c]

In 1905 one of the greatest mountain walks in the Northeast was opened by Ed Phelps, Ed Isham, and Charlie Beede: the Great Range trail, connecting Gothics with Saddleback, Basin, Haystack, and thence to Marcy. Sections of this peak-hopping aerial promenade are as rugged as any Northeastern trails.

At this time in the Johns Brook valley, on the other side of the Great Range, a few families built small private camps, and to these camps came a coterie of hikers, looking for worlds to conquer. The old Phelps trail, never clearly defined and now "almost impassable," was finally well established all the way from its origin in Keene Valley to the summit of Marcy,

---

[b]In some versions of this widely told anecdote, the frustrated blowdown-sitter is Carl Jung (letter from Nancy Lee to L&GW, Jan. 29, 1983), but usually it is Adler.

[c]Besides those already mentioned, Weston's report listed a new trail up the west side of Noonmark; Indian Head via Gill Brook, as well as directly from Lower Ausable Lake; a new trail to Pinnacle, with a side trail to a popular lookout, Otis Ledge; a new approach to the Giant's Washbowl and on to Roaring Brook; Hopkins from St. Hubert's; Baxter; trails connecting St. Hubert's with the lower lake on both sides of the river; and even a purported trail over the Great Range itself between Gothics and Haystack. The last claim is disputed by Adirondack trailsmen, however, who date this important route to 1905—Weston may have converted dreams to reality on paper a bit ahead of the actual work of ax and saw. No less an authority than William James, the philosopher, alluded to an 1898 scramble from Marcy to Bason (*sic*) following a trail of blazes, but there had been no clearing of the footway. Around 1900 a way was cut from the lower lake into the col between Gothics and its southern neighbor, Pyramid Peak, and hence to the summit; this trail had a brief history, reportedly being swept away by a slide shortly after it was cut, though Ausable Club hikers still used it enough to make the track discernible into the 1920s. Figure 21.1 shows the extent of Ausable Lakes trail construction during these years.

the work done by guides and volunteers from those camps in 1902. When Ed Isham finished the Great Range trail, he worked on feeder trails to the Range from Johns Brook, one up Orebed Brook to Gothics Col and one up to Wolf Jaws Notch. Permanent establishment of these trails, however, dates from later. These first steps began to open up the Johns Brook valley to more tramping, but the full development of that now popular locale awaited the 1920s and the building of Johns Brook Lodge.

A variety of smaller trails on the hills west of St. Hubert's, including a link connecting to trails on Rooster Comb, also date from this period.

Adirondack Lodge

A second center of Adirondack hiking and trail building opened during the last two decades of the century, this one associated with the colorful Adirondack innkeeper Henry Van Hoevenberg. In 1877 Van Hoevenberg, an inventive but eccentric twenty-eight-year-old electrician for the Baltimore and Ohio Railroad, developed insufferable hay fever, and doctors recommended a summer in the Adirondacks. So the young man betook himself to the Ausable Lakes. In the clear mountain air at Beede's, he found both health and true love, courting a young lady from Brooklyn named Josephine Schofield. One day they climbed Marcy together and in a moment of rapture, the sweeping panorama beneath them, vowed to marry, build a wilderness tourist lodge, and settle down after the fashion of Beede or Paul Smith. From the summit of Marcy they picked out a little-frequented body of water known locally as Clear Pond, nestled at the foot of a charming little mountain. After returning from the romantic heights, Josephine encountered strong family opposition to the marriage and was whisked home to Brooklyn for good. Heartbroken, as the story goes,[d] Henry Van Hoevenberg proceeded anyway, buying 640 acres around Clear Pond (which he sentimentally renamed Heart Lake) and its little mountain (forever Mount Jo). There in 1880, he built Adirondack Lodge. (This was before the innovative spelling reforms, which will be described later in this chapter.) The original lodge was a luxuriously appointed "camp" boasting an 85-foot frontage, built entirely of logs, some of them gargantuan in girth, with easy access to a wealth of mountains and other striking scenery: Indian Falls, Avalanche Pass, Indian Pass, the precipice of Wallface, and the panorama from Mount Jo. It was said to be the largest log building in the country at the time, as well as the first lodge to offer a real bathtub in the Adirondacks.

Even before the final logs were in place, Van Hoevenberg had scouted a trail to the summit of Marcy. The great Bill Nye was hired to cut what has

---

[d]But then, sometimes the story has it that Josephine died a dramatically tragic death within a year of the Marcy climb, which is not true.

become the most traveled major trail in the Adirondacks. The route went past Indian Falls, where a commanding view of the MacIntyre Range combined with the attractions of the foreground to create an irresistible camping spot for future generations. This well-tramped trail has undergone three major relocations in its lower portions during the course of its first century of existence (see figure 21.2).

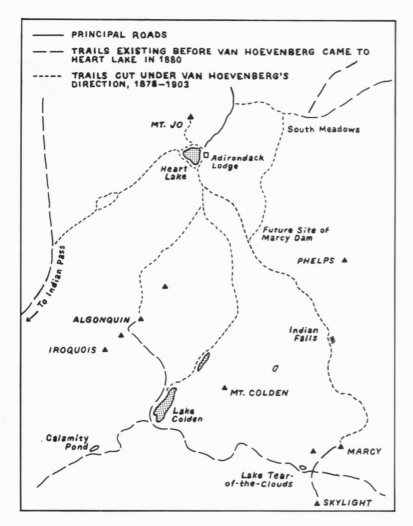

Figure 21.2. Trail building in the Heart Lake region, 1878–1903 When Henry Van Hoevenberg built Adirondack Lodge, he created a network of trails for his guests to enjoy. Some of the most heavily used trails in the Adirondacks were cut during this period, including the well-known Van Hoevenberg Trail to Marcy. Note the old spelling of Adirondack Lodge: the modern "Adirondak Loj" dates from its takeover by the Dewey family, with its campaign for spelling reform.

Another early project for Van Hoevenberg was the improvement of the track to Indian Pass. By bringing the northern terminus of this major tourist itinerary directly out to Heart Lake, the shrewd innkeeper not only provided his own guests with another major scenic trail, but placed Adirondack Lodge squarely on the itinerary of "The Round Trip" from St. Hubert's over Marcy and through Indian Pass.

Next came a trail into Avalanche Pass, to the precipitous shores of Avalanche Lake. Here the uncompromising terrain forced the trail out onto boulders in the shoreline waters before it could continue on to Lake Colden and link up with the established trails coming in from the southwest.

In 1881, under Van Hoevenberg's direction, guides Pete McCree and Will Trudeau cut a trail from the lodge to the summit of Algonquin. This gave Adirondack Lodge guests the only direct access to both of the highest summits in the Adirondacks.

Altogether, in the space of a very few years, Van Hoevenberg established 50 miles of hiking trails in the vicinity of Adirondack Lodge. Along with the trails, he constructed a few shelters for his guests, forerunners of the many shelters that now ring the shore of Heart Lake. From a little-visited pond in the wilderness, Heart Lake became almost overnight a major center for Adirondack mountain recreation. Van Hoevenberg must certainly be ranked as one of the major "improvers" in this classic period of Northeastern trails history.

"Mr. Van" cultivated a memorable image. Short of stature (5 ft., 4 inches), luxuriantly bearded and browed, stocky and muscular, he stood out in a crowd by wearing a suit all of leather. It was said he had a dozen leather suits, each a different color. He prided himself as a raconteur and even poet, grinding out long north woods epics that fell somewhere between Longfellow and Robert Service in style, if not in lasting contribution to American literature.

Though adept at laying out a trail system to satisfy a growing market for mountain recreation, Van Hoevenberg proved otherwise not suited to the inn business. During the 1890s he became increasingly harassed by financial strains and litigation until he was finally forced to sell his beloved lodge. Heartbroken once more, he was lucky to find work as postmaster and telegraph operator for the Lake Placid Club. Luck came in cycles for Van Hoevenberg during those years. In 1900 the Lake Placid Club purchased Adirondack Lodge and installed Mr. Van as resident manager. He was back at the old stand for three glorious years when the great fire of 1903 swept over the lodge and destroyed his dream. From then until his death in 1918 he continued to work in Lake Placid, mostly for the club. In those years his continued interest in mountain hiking took the form of presiding over the Adirondack Camp and Trail Club, of which more later.

The third major nucleus of Adirondack trails during the late 1800s was Whiteface Mountain and the shores of Lake Placid, which Whiteface overlooks (see figure 21.3). The early Whiteface trails have been cited already, but development of a trail *system* began in 1893 with the formation of a summer colonists' organization known as the Shore Owners' Association (SOA), its membership composed of those who owned lakefront or island property. Its objectives, as spelled out in its bylaws, included trail building:

> The preservation of Lake Placid; the preservation of the pollution of its waters; the maintenance of suitable surface levels; the supervision of

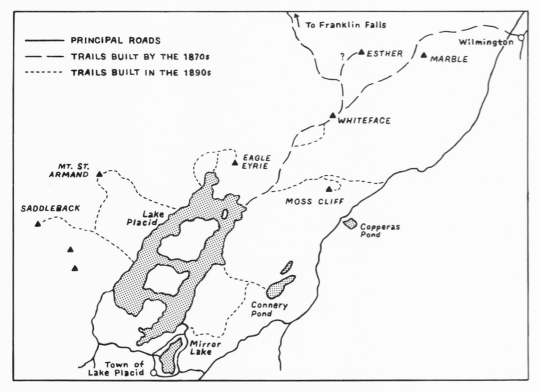

Figure 21.3. Trail building in the Lake Placid region, the 1890s The trail system for the mountains surrounding Lake Placid was largely built during the 1890s, after formation of the Shore Owners' Association. Whiteface had trails dating from earlier in the nineteenth century, including the earliest known hiking trail in the Adirondacks. Note the 1890s names, which differ from their modern counterparts: St. Armand has become Moose Mountain, and Saddleback is now Mount McKenzie.

traffic on the Lake; the maintenance of trails and landings; the promotion of aquatic sports; and the care and protection of the common interests of its members.

The association's trails opened up recreational opportunities on many of Whiteface's southwestern satellites. Among the lesser mountains to which routes were cut during the 1890s were Mount St. Armand (now Moose Mountain—with two separate approaches); Saddleback (now called McKenzie); the Eagle Eyrie; and Moss Cliff Mountain. Later (1915) the association also rebuilt the old Nye trail up Whiteface from Lake Placid which had been substantially obliterated by lumbering operations, bypassing the troublesome landslide area. These trails are noteworthy because of the role of the summer folk in directing the work of guides and assuming responsibility for trail maintenance. Along with the ATIS crowd at St. Hubert's, the association activists were bringing Adirondack trail work in the direction that Randolph and the AMC had taken in White Mountain trail work (see chapters 20 and 22).

Ultimately an even greater impact on Adirondack trail history was made by the arrival in town of Melville Louis Kossuth Dewey. Dewey is best known as the father of modern library science and the inventor of the decimal classification of books. He was also an ardent champion of spelling reform: he simplified his own first name to Melvil and revised the spelling of the inn at Heart Lake to its present Adirondak Loj. Like Van Hoevenberg, Dewey came to the north country as a victim of hay fever. In 1895 he purchased five acres on the shore of Mirror Lake, adjacent to the main lake, and organized a private association called the Lake Placid Club. Dewey's idea was "by cooperation of congenial people to provide at cost an ideal summer home in ideal surroundings." Whatever the vagaries of his spelling theories, Dewey ran a popular club, starting with 30 members the first year and boasting more than 1,000 by the 1910s. By the 1920s the club had 9,600 acres, 365 buildings, and close to 800 members.

From the beginning the Lake Placid Club capitalized on its association with Whiteface and its reasonable proximity to the northwest approaches to Marcy. Shortly after Van Hoevenberg became ensnared in his fateful lawsuits, the Lake Placid Club purchased Adirondack Lodge and, after changing its spelling, installed Mr. Van again as manager. The older "Loj" became a kind of southwest branch of the club and base station for members to climb peaks besides the Whiteface group. In the 1901 handbook, the club announced (translating into orthodox spelling):

> Adirondack Lodge with 50 miles of trails through the forest to the finest scenery in eastern America has been known for 20 years as the best point of the Adirondacks for camping parties and mountain climbing. This will be made one of the Club's great specialties hereafter. . . . A carriage will run regularly each way between Club and Lodge materially

reducing labor and expense of making these excursions and opening the way for more outdoor life in the heart of the Adirondacks.

From this time on, the fortunes of the Lake Placid Club and the Deweys (Melvil and his son, Godfrey) were intertwined with those of Van Hoevenberg and Heart Lake. The Lake Placid Club was the dominant partner in the alliance. Mountain recreation for the western side of the high peaks was, for a couple of decades, dominated by the LPC as it was on the eastern side by the Ausable Club. The enthusiasm of the Lake Placid Club climbers extended even to winter, beginning in 1904 (see chapters 33 and 34).

The great fires

Meanwhile one more event had a major impact on preautomobile Adirondacks trail history. In April and May of 1903, following a winter of little snow, a severe drought gripped the Adirondack forests, which normally at that time of year were still wet from spring runoff. Dead and down wood became tinder dry. Slash lay around in the wake of the logging companies. The consequences were not hard to predict.

Between late April and the coming of rains after June 8, a series of forest fires devastated large areas of the high peak region. New York State figures for annual acres burned during the period from 1890 to 1902 were never more than 16,071 acres and averaged fewer than 6,000 per year. But in 1903 a total of 464,189 acres went up in smoke, the "worst holocaust of its kind in the history of the State" (see figure 21.4).

The power of those large-scale fires and the terror they aroused are hard to imagine today. Given poor roads and few telephones, rumor replaced knowledge as to just where the fires were and where to expect them next. People were repeatedly called out with no notice and dispatched to fight a conflagration many miles away, never knowing whether their own homes might be next.

The fire that swept down on Adirondak Loj caught Van Hoevenberg away fighting another blaze. He and his men rushed back and took what measures they could, releasing horses, throwing silver into the shallow lake, setting prized tools in clearings. Then Mr. Van instructed his men to flee toward Indian Pass—now the only escape—while he himself, in total distress, entered the lodge, prepared to go up with it. Only the stubborn refusal of one loyal employee to leave without him induced him to go. That night, from their camp way up in Indian Pass, they heard a crash that told the end of "the largest log building in the country."

Forest fires leave the woods a tangled mess of charred and misshapen remains. For a hiking trail, a fire means not merely that blazed trees and bridges are burned, but that a jumble of other trees come crashing down

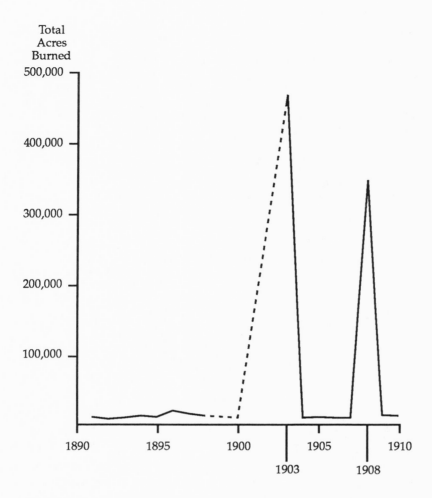

Total
Acres
Burned

Figure 21.4. The great fires of 1903 and 1908 In 1903, mostly during the month of May, a spectacular series of forest fires raged through the Adirondack high peaks region. Five years later still more fires rampaged through the woods. As this chart shows, the scale of destruction in those two years far exceeded the normal. One result, especially of the 1903 conflagrations, was that many hiking trails were wiped out, some of which were never restored.

across and along the footway, virtually erasing it from recognition. Among the immediate consequences of the 1903 blaze were the following:

The popular Van Hoevenberg Trail to Marcy was destroyed throughout its lower half. So chaotic were the remains of Bill Nye's great work that no immediate effort was made to restore it. In 1904 a new approach was put in from the Avalanche Pass Trail over to join the old route at Indian Falls. This was used until the original path could be recut in 1919.

The trail up Algonquin was likewise annihilated. For more than a decade the only trail up Algonquin was the one from Lake Colden.

Little Mount Jo, with all of its sentimental attachments for Mr. Van, lost its trail.

Trails up two popular lesser peaks, Cascade and Porter, were gone.

Fire burned savagely through Railroad Notch, but the old "road" itself was kept in service for salvage lumbering. Its end was in sight, however, as the whole blackened and charred area no longer had appeal for recreational hiking.

South of St. Hubert's Inn, soon to become the Ausable Club house, another 1903 fire destroyed the AMR trail to Dix via the Noonmark–Bear Den notch.

By destroying Adirondak Loj, the 1903 fire shifted the center of initiative in trail work even more to the Lake Placid Club. With no base close to the peaks, the decisions regarding trail construction and maintenance on the western end of the high peaks were made increasingly from the shores of Mirror Lake.

As a vehicle for this work, an activist group at the Lake Placid Club formed the Adirondack Camp and Trail Club in 1910. The popular Mr. Van was the first president, Godfrey Dewey was secretary, and Edward S. Woods was the third member of the organizing troika. The club's purposes and activities were comparable in the western end of the high peaks to those of the Adirondack Trail Improvement Society in the east. During its first twelve years, 1910–22, this club had a small membership, drawn largely from Lake Placid Club guests; in 1921 membership was just forty-two. Active in its leadership, besides Van Hoevenberg and Woods, were T. Morris Longstreth, the writer-conservationist, and Harry Wade Hicks, longtime Lake Placid Club executive. Though small the club devoted itself energetically to trail work, mainly at first in the Lake Placid Club area, through the woods to nearby places like Copperas and Connery Ponds and Sunset Notch. In 1915 it hired a small paid trail crew headed by Henry Ives Baldwin, a Saranac Lake resident who knew the woods and mountains well, and over the next five years this crew built or rebuilt many trails and shelters in the Heart Lake–Marcy–Algonquin region. Besides maintaining camps and trails, the club conducted a progressive program of what would today be called outdoor education, with special activities for boys aged twelve to seventeen and (separately) girls, to introduce them to the proper way to camp and hike—"to teach proper care of the great legacy of the public park existing for the use of all, and the reasons why it should be preserved." The club kept in touch with the state Conservation Commission and sought to cooperate in its recreational and conservation programs.

Thus the Lake Placid side of the mountains, with its Adirondack Camp and Trail Club and the Shore Owners' Association, and the Ausable Lakes, where ATIS was at work, both functioned well into the twentieth century as two separate trail and hiking centers. As in the White Mountains, it was not until the advent of improved transportation and a single unifying club—in this case the Adirondack Mountain Club, formed in 1922—that trampers and trailsmen perceived the entire high peaks region as a single unified system of trails.

Chapter 22

Randolph

MEANWHILE, in the White Mountains during the 1880s the first intensively creative burst of trail building exploded over the Northern Presidentials and the Randolph hills. In eight years, Randolph folk built more than 50 miles of hiking trails, with about 30 miles on the flanks of the Northern Presidentials and another 20 on the Randolph side of the valley. Figure 22.1 shows how the map of the Northern Presidentials filled up with a spiderweb of trails as the improvers opened up ways to every scenic point and vista they could find. Even today these slopes remain as thoroughly crisscrossed with trails as any area of comparably difficult terrain in the Northeast.

There was a special quality to this great age of Randolph trail making. While earlier trails and bridle paths in the Presidentials had been "designed to increase the monetary receipts of the builders," the new Randolph trails were "made by pedestrians for the use of pedestrians"—so observed naturalist Arthur Stanley Pease, a later Randolphian. To the Crawfords or Osgood, building a trail was just hard work, one may surmise. The new Randolph trail-builders raised calluses and sweat too, but also their voices in laughter and song.

A special buoyancy lit up Randolph in those years. A small group of lively summer residents fused with half a dozen local woodsmen-mountaineers to form a creative alliance for trail work, as well as an atmosphere crackling with physical vitality and uproarious good times. Randolph in the eighties was one of those rare and precious moments in any region's history when the bloom was fresh and new worlds of enterprise and adventure were there to be grasped, amid lots of hard work, camaraderie, and joy.

The center of this vibrant scene was the Ravine House. Opened as an inn in 1877 and gradually expanded until it sprawled in grand disarray over the open fields at the foot of King Ravine, the Ravine House was the summer residence of the principal figures among the trail-builders. Presiding as its proprietor and host was the "genial and kindly" Laban M. Watson, who was only thirty when he began to build trails in 1880 for his

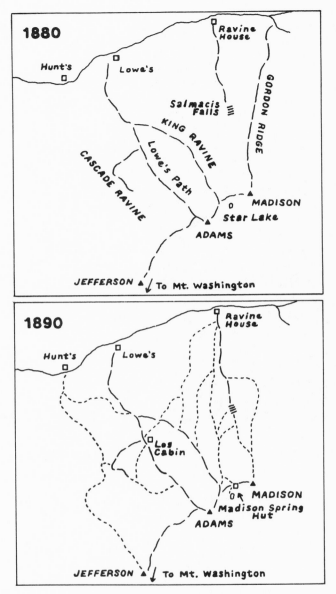

Figure 22.1. Trail building at Randolph, 1880s The difference between the sparse Northern Presidentials trail map of 1880 (above) and the crowded one of just ten years later (below) indicates that a great burst of creative trail building had taken place during the 1880s. Spurred mainly by the leadership of the energetic and imaginative guests at the Ravine House, "everybody . . . became path finders and path makers." White Mountain hikers may note differences between the 1890 paths and modern ones: the Castle Trail to Jefferson stayed in the valley longer before climbing to the ridge; trails not now existing connected the bottom of that trail with Lowe's Path and ascended the Cascade Ravine; and the Valley Way, probably today's most heavily used route, was not yet built.

guests. "Tall and broad-shouldered, with muscle, endurance, and wit strengthened and tempered in the school of the farm and the logging camp," Watson soon took his place beside Charles Lowe, plus another local woodsman named Hubbard Hunt, as one of the three most active trail workers of the year-round population.

While Watson held sway at the Ravine House, Lowe operated the Mount Crescent House, while a third center of summer hikers and trail-builders developed at Kelsey Cottage (later known as Mountain View House). Gradually some of the summer residents began to build their own summer cottages in Randolph, but at first they met at these three central resorts. It was in the Ravine House, Crescent House, and Kelsey's that the traditions of dancing, charades, Fourth of July picnics (at the Crescent House), hiking, and trail work began, traditions that Randolph hikers still carry on. Though the Ravine House closed its doors in 1960, and almost every family now stays in its own cottage, much of the spirit of life and humor that began during the 1880s has continued in Randolph summer life through each succeeding generation.

Beginning in 1882 the center of this busy stage was preempted by Eugene Beauharnais Cook of Hoboken, New Jersey. "A slender, wiry man with long black curly hair, heavy 'Burnsides' and large merry blue eyes laughing under heavy brows," Cook was an indefatigable hiker, ever curious explorer, industrious trail-builder, incorrigible punster, chess fan, and bon vivant who loved to dance, play his violin, or give vent to "a loud merry laugh." He first summered in the White Mountains at Philbrook Farm in Shelburne in 1872, later moved to Sugar Hill on the Franconia side, but settled on the Ravine House in Randolph in 1878. Unlike most early AMC figures, he was equally at home in both camps, improvements and explorations. No one built more miles of new trail than he during the nineteenth century, and he is credited with inventing the string method of laying out trails, long used by trail-builders since. Yet he was also a bold and inventive explorer, delving curiously into the less-traveled ranges.

Cook's perennial partner, both on trails and explorations, was a book publisher from Chicago who spent twenty-five summers at Randolph, William H. Peek. These two "indefatigable leaders of the march of improvement" showed superficially different personalities: Cook is recalled as "athletic, brilliant and erratic . . . hating all injustice and oppression," while the milder Peek was "learned, kindly, serene in high religious faith." But they shared a common fervor for trail work and rugged hikes . . . and bad puns. If the musician Cook is credited with naming a trail that they marked with a rusty can the "Intermezzo Rusticano," Peek takes responsibility for naming the railroad station near the apple orchard of the Ravine House (now the trail-head parking area); after noticing a group of unhappy little boys who had eaten too many green apples, Peek suggested immortalizing both their plight and the fledgling AMC with the name "Apple-achia."

Cook, Peek, and their circle, including Cook's vivacious sister, Lucia Pychowska, and her daughter Marian (see chapter 26), were filled with a love of the mountains and were "eager to share their worship with others," recalled Louis Cutter in a memoir written forty years later. Their trail work was "a labor of piety." It was also a spark to the entire Randolph summer population. Recalled one subluminary of that constellation:

> Everybody, under the inspiration and guidance of Mr. Peek or Mr. Cook or Madame Pychowska, became path finders and path makers. We counted that day lost whose low descending sun saw no new waterfall discovered, no new path pushed many rods through the scrub, no new view cleared of brush to wider prospects. In the evening, in the parlor circle, we reported and enlarged upon our works, discussed and named our discoveries.

Others later came to loom large in Randolph: J. Rayner Edmands, Louis Cutter, and a separate circle who stayed at Kelsey Cottage. But in that extraordinary burst of trail-building during the 1880s, most of the miles were blazed and cut by Cook, Peek, and Laban Watson. As trail mileage increased and maintaining existing trails became a major job, the AMC turned to Charles Lowe and his sons, Thaddeus and Vyron, as well as to Hubbard Hunt. But after 1880 Lowe cut few new trails.

Figure 22.1 shows the volume of new trails built in Randolph between 1882 and 1889. Included were some classics that remain favorites today, such as the Castellated Ridge on Jefferson, the Air Line on Adams, the Watson Path on Madison, Amphibrach (sometimes called Chicago Avenue in honor of Chicagoan Peek), and the Short Line.

The Randolph trail-builders ignited a burst of White Mountain trail building so that by the turn of the century clusters of trails could be found emanating from wherever there was a summer colony of hikers (see figure 22.2).

During the early 1880s, AMC trail-builders cut a splendid crest line from the town of Twin Mountain south over the two peaks of the Twins, and on over Guyot and Bond, directly down the middle of the vast Pemigewasset Wilderness. At this time the heart of that wilderness remained primeval forest, untouched by the logging that began to strip it bare during the next decade. It is a sign of how wild the Pemigewasset was that, despite this trail's scenic qualities, it received little use and had to be cut fresh many years later. The southern end of the trail remained confused for a long time, finally being brought down the southeast ridge off Bond, not over the southwest Bondcliff as at present.

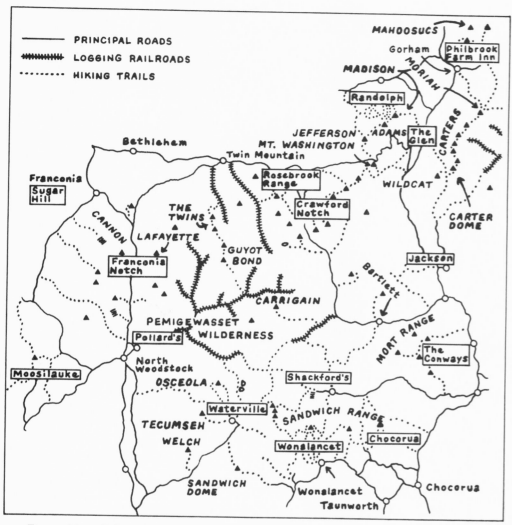

Figure 22.2. White Mountain trail clusters, ca. 1900 Around the year 1900, White Mountain trails were clustered around a few key vacation centers, like Randolph, the Glen in Pinkham Notch, Waterville Valley, and Wonalancet. Other minor centers can be noted on this map, some just a single inn or boardinghouse, such as Philbrook Farm Inn at the foot of the Mahoosucs or Pollard's at the southwest corner of the Pemigewasset Wilderness. Relatively few connecting links joined these separate trail systems. Note that this was a period of intensive logging, and logging railroads penetrated many areas that had been pristine wilderness until late in the nineteenth century.

During the mid-1880s Nowell masterminded another major ridgeline trail, this one across the entire Carter Range, previously virgin ground for almost 10 miles from Carter Dome to Moriah. This "magnificent mid-air promenade," as Sweetser called it, was made with Nowell as "engineer-in-chief, axe-man, packman, commissary, cook, and whatever else might be needed," a happy gang of teenagers, some of them also Nowells, plus Hubbard Hunt, Thaddeus Lowe, and some other locals, not to mention Nowell's eight-month-old Saint Bernard–Newfoundland, Osman Pasha. Extensions were added up the nearby summit of Wildcat at the southwest end of that range and over the lesser Moriahs at the northeast, thereby opening up substantial hiking country east of the Presidentials.

The Twin and Carter trails were single, lengthy, ridge-crest trails; more characteristic of the valley-based trail *system* was what took place on the Sandwich Range in the 1890s. The key figure here was a young woman in her twenties, "small, blond, with deep blue eyes, and a high-pitched voice," and "a veritable dynamo" in the life of the small community. Diminutive Katherine Sleeper ran a farm-inn at Wonalancet single-handed from 1890 until she married in 1902, saw to the upgrading of local roads, cleaned up the look of the town, established a post office, brought in the first telephone, transformed the farm hamlet into a minor tourist center, founded the Wonalancet Out Door Club, and secured the preservation of the heart of the Sandwich Range from the depredations of the loggers. "All her life," writes one admiring local historian, "she possessed the rare quality of inspiring others to want what she wanted." In 1890 she was looking for ways to make her new inn profitable and quickly figured that walking trails in the mountains above her backyard might prove an attraction. So she invited AMC trail-builder Charles E. Fay to a gathering of local residents at her house. A few days later Fay led "an enthusiastic body of men" in cutting the trail from Dicey's Mill to the summit of Passaconaway, an experience that incited the locals to further action: Nat Berry built the scenic Brook Path up Chocorua in 1892, Tom Wiggin the steep Wiggin Trail up Whiteface in 1895. Fay and Berry constructed the first shelter high on Passaconaway, maintained later as Camp Rich. In 1898 Kate Sleeper organized the Wonalancet Out Door Club (WODC) and much more began to happen: the Lawrence Trail on Paugus; a third route on Whiteface, the beautiful Blueberry Ledges Trail; the first trail up Chocorua from the north; and the elegant curving ridgeline trail between Passaconaway and Whiteface. Between 1891 and 1900 another 50 miles of prime hiking paths had been created and a new trail system to rival the one in Randolph (see figure 22.3).

Waterville, though blessed with Greeley's well-established trail network, added an occasional path and formed the Waterville Athletic and Improvement Association in 1888. The prime figures during this period were A. L.

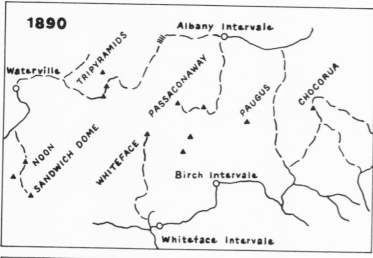

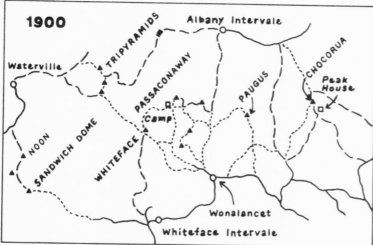

Figure 22.3. Trail building at Wonalancet, 1890s As Randolph had built trails during the 1880s, so the quiet community of Birch Intervale, changing its name to Wonalancet, went to work on mountain trails during the 1890s. Initially prodded to action by the forceful Katherine Sleeper, the Wonalancet trail-builders opened access to all of the peaks of the Sandwich Range, with an integrated network of connecting paths to make possible a rich variety of hikes. By 1900 two of the old shelters had been built—Camp Rich on Passaconaway and Camp Shehadi on Whiteface—while Chocorua boasted a full-service hotel, the Peak House, on a level spot just below the rocky summit cone.

Goodrich, a summer visitor, and Silas and Carrie Elliott, the innkeepers who had succeeded Nathaniel Greeley in 1883. While Goodrich thought up new trails, the Elliotts dispatched their hired hands throughout the nearby hills to keep the existing network maintained for their walking guests.[a]

Chocorua, initially an eastern province of the Wonalancet Out Door Club, declared independence in 1908 with the establishment of the Chocorua Mountain Club. The CMC maintained trails on its mountain, staged spectacular Fourth of July fireworks on Lake Chocorua, and pointedly excluded the WODC from operating within its jurisdiction.

Up at the north end of Crawford Notch, the upgrading of the Mount Pleasant House in 1895 from a small inn to a major hotel generated a plexus of trails on the Rosebrook Range, a chain of small but picturesque peaks running north from Mount Tom. At the height of their popularity during the early 1900s, the Rosebrook Range trails connected all the modest summits—Tom, Echo, Stickney, Rosebrook, Oscar—with feeder trails both from the notch on the east and the Zealand Valley on the west. Early AMC guidebooks devoted one of eleven chapters to the Rosebrook Range trails. This little empire of footpaths symbolizes the era of the independent cluster of trails around a specific mountain resort, just as the passing of that era eventually led to the abandonment of the entire network of Rosebrook trails. The 1938 hurricane, World War II, and the closing of the Mount Pleasant House combined to effect the complete obliteration of this once flourishing trail system.

The Crawford House also had its small network of local trails. Maj. Curtis B. Raymond, the man who had built the Raymond Path to Tuckerman Ravine when he summered at the Glen House during the 1870s, made the Crawford House his base of trail-building operations during the 1880s.

In Franconia Notch, until about 1890, the major instigator of trail work had been Isabella Stone, an independent-minded friend of the Pychowska women, who chose to summer on the western side of the hills instead of Randolph, and who prodded local woodsmen such as William Sargent to build trails on Moosilauke and its satellites, into Georgianna Falls, Bridal Veil Falls, and elsewhere. Beginning in the 1890s, however, a hiking and trail-building community began to evolve in summer cottages near North Woodstock. The initial leader of this effort was Frank O. Carpenter, schoolteacher from English High School in Boston. Carpenter explored all the existing trails in the area, produced a guidebook in 1898, and attempted to put various routes up the west flank of the Franconia Ridge. He had the ill luck to undertake his work precisely at the height of logging activity in that area. Some of his ideas were brilliant—a trail that he cut in 1897 directly up the aesthetic western arête to the summit of Lincoln, for example, as well as an attempt to reopen the long-defunct Old Bridle Path

---

[a]It was in Waterville around the turn of the century that a young trio of ardent mountaineers first tasted the attractions of trail work: Paul R. Jenks, Charles W. Blood, and Nathaniel Goodrich (A.L.'s son). Remember those names: in future years Jenks, Blood, and Goodrich became the most active and skilled triumvirate of trailsmen in the entire Northeast (see chap. 36).

—but each year's logging would smother his summer's work with slash. Thus few of his labors bore lasting fruit. Today Carpenter's ridge on Lincoln is trailless, and the Old Bridle Path remained lost for another generation. But Carpenter was soon joined by two Wesleyan college professors, Karl Pomeroy Harrington and Herbert W. Conn, together with Edmund K. Alden of Brooklyn and a Miss Cummings of the Wesleyan faculty, and others. Out of this group was formed, in 1897, the North Woodstock Improvement Association, "with the specific purpose of rendering more accessible the many points of interest in this part of the Pemigewasset Valley." Alden and Miss Cummings were the early leaders in the association, but Harrington proved to be the master trail-builder of the group, taking over Carpenter's mantle in the North Woodstock area after 1900.

These fractured clusters of mostly unconnected trail systems scattered around the White Mountains are characteristic of the years before 1910. The major accomplishment of trail work after 1910 was to connect these independent states—Randolph, Wonalancet, Waterville, Franconia— with through trails that ultimately created a single system of White Mountain trails (see chapter 36). But before 1910 the time had not arrived. The most important factor keeping the early trail systems separated was the difficulty of transportation prior to the spread of automobile ownership and paved highways. Hikers came to summer in one spot, and it was simply not feasible to climb Lafayette if they were living in Randolph, nor Adams if they were staying at the Elliots' or Kate Sleeper's. Another factor, probably related, was that the Appalachian Mountain Club was not yet the dominant force throughout the area. Unification of White Mountain trails into a single system awaited the more complete extension of the AMC's influence over the entire region, a development that local trail-builders and the smaller clubs were not necessarily ready to welcome. During the early 1880s AMC Councillor of Improvements A. E. Scott had an idea for a trail on Mount Field; he received a curt letter from Major Raymond, then the established trail-skeeper for the Crawford House, advising him:

> I think . . . that we there can make the path; and let the Appalachians put their money, which they would spend for this purpose, upon some other important development in some other district, which will be a clear gain. Later, perhaps, a path to Thoreau Falls, which I have often thought of, may be extended by people at the Crawford House in the same way, without the Appalachians taking any trouble or expense about it; which also will enable the latter to continue their excellent work of developments in other sections of the mountains.

In plain words, Major Raymond was telling the AMC to keep out of his private preserve, including not just Mount Field but Thoreau Falls. Clearly the time was not yet ripe for considering the White Mountains as a single unified trail system.

Chapter 23

Other trail systems

In the northern ranges, trails were long and taxing. For most hikers a full day's journey began when they started up Lowe's Path or the Van Hoevenberg Trail. But on some lesser ranges a different character of trail system sprang up, roughly simultaneously with those of the north country. Three examples of these systems were the paths of Monadnock, Mount Desert, and Greylock.

The Grand Monadnock

The classic pattern of late nineteenth-century trail building was exhibited on the Grand Monadnock. This popular mountain had routes of access from all sides, but until the early 1890s well-traveled trails were limited to three or four main arteries: the heavily tramped over White Arrow Trail on the south side, the old Dublin Trail on the north, a newer ridgeline trail built by Prof. Raphael Pumpelly in 1884, and (less used) the traces of an old trail from Marlboro. Besides the Dublin and Pumpelly trails, Dublin climbers of the late nineteenth century made regular use of a well-known bushwhack up Mountain Brook, through "fine forest growths and through ravines of ever-changing and subtle charm." But as late as 1890, no real effort seems to have gone into creating a Monadnock trail system.

A substantial "Half Way House" had been built on the south side of Monadnock during the late 1860s. Beginning around 1894, some of the guests became infected with the trail-cutting bug, just as the Randolph, Wonalancet, AMR, and Lake Placid trailblazers had been. From then until 1910 an orgy of trail cutting converted the small area south of the summit into a close-woven fabric of picturesque and varied little trails. Here a natural amphitheater is formed by ridges that extend southwest and southeast from the summit, the one culminating in a little rock spire known as Monte Rosa, the other on Bald Rock; in the high valley between lay the Half Way House. Within this amphitheater approximately thirty short paths were laid out between 1894 and 1910 (see figure 23.1).

The guiding genius of this movement was Scott A. Smith of Providence, Rhode Island; others who played major roles included George H. Noble and George A. Parker. An admiring Half Way House guest wrote of their trail work:

> Miles of these sun-flecked narrow paths thread through deep, quiet forests, broken constantly by the outcropping crags . . . ; lines of miniature cairns beckon along the calm and sunny cliffs; countless

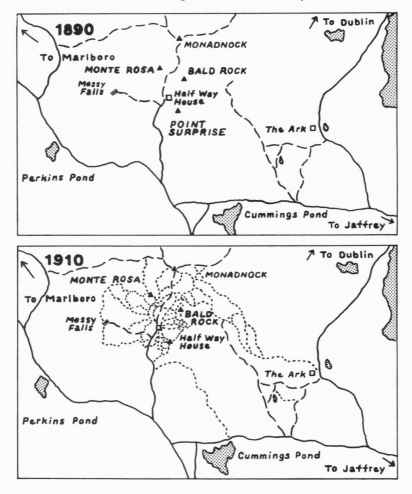

Figure 23.1. Trail building on the Grand Monadnock, 1890–1910 Until 1894 the Grand Monadnock had only a few basic trails. Then guests of the Half Way House began a sustained campaign of building short trails to every conceivable beauty spot or point of interest in the high country just south of the summit. Many of these "sun-flecked narrow paths" have disappeared, due to lack of use during the second half of the twentieth century. Others can be faintly traced by a careful observer. Still others, of course, remain as well-marked and cleared trails.

mossy nooks sheltered by overhanging rock and huge tree sentinels invite the loiterer to rest; up above in the sunshine, hundreds of stone-wrought couches upholstered with gray-green moss allure one. Up here one can gaze his fill at the grave, brooding Titan reigning supreme, outlined against the ultra-marine sky, giving his majestic salutation alike to distant sea and to encircling plain. . . . One may stay at the little hostelry for many weeks and not be able to explore every threadlike path with all the twisting links and visit every nook he loves; . . . something has always been left to next year.

A second center of Monadnock summer hikers grew up around another inn, the Ark, lower down on the east flank. Ark guests built three basic routes up the mountain from this side during the years when Smith and his Half Way House friends were at work. The original line was known as the Pasture Trail and was completed in 1897. Paralleling it to the south, the Ark Trail was begun in the same year but not fully completed until 1909. Meanwhile in 1900 a major revision of the Pasture Trail was laid out and called the White Spot Trail. Pioneers of these early efforts included Dr. and Mrs. William P. Wesselhoeft, Dr. and Mrs. George H. Parker (not to be confused with George A. Parker of the Half Way House), summer guests; Arthur E. Poole, of the family who ran the Ark; and "Big Will" Royce, a local woodsman employed by the Ark. Gradually during the twentieth century, most of the original Pasture Trail faded away or was absorbed by other trails, while the White Spot (now Dot) Trail and a relocated version of the Ark (later Red Cross and now White Cross) Trail survived to become extremely popular. Ark guests also built a modest network of lower-elevation paths, mostly during the 1910s, though not nearly as dense as the Half Way House mosaic.

Mount Desert

Mount Desert's picturesque crags sprouted a trail network at about the same time as Monadnock. Since Thomas Cole's visit in 1844 this island gem had attracted tourists, some of whom established walks and paths on the small but rugged mountains, especially those known as Green, Dry, and Newport (respectively, Cadillac, Dorr, and Champlain today). With the creation of the Bar Harbor Village Improvement Association in 1890, mountain trail building took a big step forward. The VIA's first president, Parke Godwin, defined one of the prime objectives of the society as:

> To open the grand forests that surround us, by means of paths which shall penetrate their almost inaccessible jungles, and connect their various points of magnificent outlook by unfatiguing travel.

A committee on roads and paths set about marking and regularly clearing up to 60 miles of hiking trails, under the vigorous leadership of successive chairmen Herbert Jacques (1894–99) and Waldron Bates (1900–1909). Other villages on Mount Desert created similar associations and also nurtured their own networks of walking trails.

A new phase of Mount Desert trail building began in 1912 and gave that region's "paths" an utterly unique character. In that year Rudolph E. Brunnow took over as chairman of roads and paths and began to conceive new trails that, for their steepness and bold exposure, made Cook and Peek's Presidential trails look like garden walks. In 1914 Brunnow persuaded the committee to authorize construction of the aptly named Precipice Path up the steep east flank of Mount Champlain. The route wound through and in some cases directly up a succession of steep ledges for almost 1,000 feet, with iron rungs and railings provided wherever stone steps were insufficient to overcome verticality. Hikers on the Precipice Path today can only shake their heads in disbelief at the contemplation of long-skirted ladies and full-suited gentlemen of the pre-1920 era who deftly surmounted its airy course. During the next three years, Brunnow created other trails almost as bold. One on the south side of the Beehive was perhaps even more "steep and dizzy," though for a shorter distance.[a] It is astonishing what a liberal use of iron rungs and railings could make feasible for the fashionable walkers of that age, as today's rock climbers must reflect when incongruously coming across old neglected ironwork in the middle of the seemingly vertical cliff of the South Bubble. Nor was the work unaesthetic, as the use of iron may imply: some of the rock steps built in those years had a picturesque charm that blended beautifully with the qualities peculiar to Mount Desert's landscape, an outstanding sample being visible today in the first few hundred feet of the 1916 path from Sieur de Monts Spring up Dorr Mountain.

Mount Greylock

On Greylock the timing of trail developments was roughly parallel to that of Monadnock and Mount Desert—but the auspices under which these developments were conducted and the character of the resulting trails were altogether different.

Greylock had enjoyed several well-established trails during the 1850s, but, as on so many other mountains, the trails of that era had deteriorated by the mid-1870s. The ancient Wilbur road had been substantially improved some time between 1850 and 1853. Around 1850 the route above Wilbur's clearing was reported to be a maze of fallen trees, but in 1854 a newspaper describes "a tolerably good road . . . from the village

---

[a]This terrain was not entirely unknown "to the lovers of a tough scramble" back in the 1870s (see Clara Barnes Martin, *Mount Desert on the Coast of Maine*, p. 77).

of North Adams," giving the date of its construction as "of late years." By the latter half of the nineteenth century this was known locally as the "Notch Road," but it had once again fallen into a state of disrepair (see figure 23.2).

Another approach from the northeast came through "a choice mountain passage" known as the Bellows Pipe. This route had become a definite trail at least by 1851. It may have existed in some form as far back as the 1830s or even before. Certainly the lower part was a well-used road, with farms along it, during the eighteenth century. From the end of the road to the top of the mountain, however, the dating of a definite trail is more tenuous before 1850. A 1914 newspaper referred to a "century old

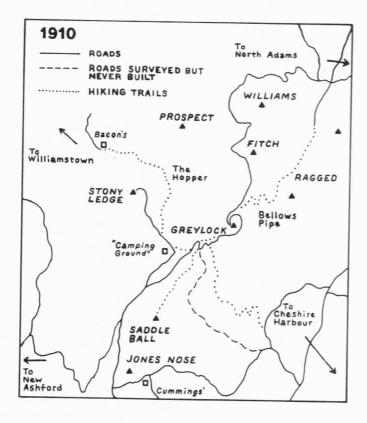

Figure 23.2. Trail building on Mount Greylock, 1897–1910 When the Greylock Commission took over the management of Massachusetts's highest mountain, none of Greylock's roads or trails were in good condition. The commission gave prompt attention to improvements. By 1904 the mountain could claim two good roads (from the northeast and southwest) and three trails to the top (the Hopper, Bellows Pipe, and Cheshire Harbor routes). In 1907 the Rockwell Road from the south, today's most popular route of access, was constructed. It was not until shortly after 1910 that other hiking trails were opened on the mountain.

path" and placed Thoreau's ascent as via this route "over 70 years ago." But at least one authority interpreted Thoreau's account as a bushwhack by compass, not on a trail. In any case the upper trail portion of the Bellows Pipe route had also lapsed into disuse and decrepitude by the later years of the century. For example, a descent by this route in 1893 was described thus: "At times it was nothing more than the bed of a brook but as we neared the bottom of the mountain it widened."

There may also have been some ascents from the south. Two routes went up from this side. One was an old stage road over the saddle near Jones Nose, but this route was no longer maintained and was becoming overgrown. At some point, an old right-of-way was established up the southeast side from Cheshire Harbor, but just when and how much it was used during the nineteenth century is not known; it is of interest because nearly a century later it became the route of the famed Appalachian Trail. Still other trails may have existed on the Greylock Range during these years. One can read, for example, in the *Williams Quarterly* in 1855: "The Hopper [was] passed, a doubtful choice having been made between several paths . . . " A Pittsfield newspaper in 1849 told of a "practicable route" from Williamstown over Mount Prospect. Trails or not, these were scarcely well groomed. A Williams College publication deplored the lack of any good path. Some of the ascents were exciting, as this 1853 party attests:

> After scrambling up the sides of precipitous cliffs, and through stony chasms, winding around the edges of projecting rocks, and crawling over the smooth surface of almost perpendicular ledges, the party . . . reached the top.

In 1885 the Greylock Park Association was formed to buy and preserve 400 acres on Greylock. Later the protected area was expanded to take in most of the mountain. This signaled the beginning of major improvements on Massachusetts's premier peak. One of the first acts of the association was to upgrade substantially the Notch Road up the north side to allow carriages once again to reach the top.

Sometime during the late 1890s Rollin H. Cooke worked out a route up the mountain from New Ashford on the west, possibly using the old stage road for the lower half of the way. He and others, including E. H. Robbins and George A. Bauer, blazed a definite foot trail up this route first, then set about raising money to widen it into a "road" (by which they meant passable for horses and small carriages, but not for motorcars). When they had sufficient funds, Bauer took on the job of building this road. It was done to within a mile of the top by 1899.

In 1898, the Greylock Park Association turned over its lands to the newly formed Greylock Commission. This commission initially focused on maintaining, completing, and extending the roads suitable for driving carriages up the mountain, making sure each of the surrounding towns was served with convenient access. By 1900 the commission had arranged with Bauer to complete Cooke's road, and for the first time Mount Greylock boasted road access from two sides.[b]

Meanwhile, until the establishment of the commission, the hiking trails do not seem to have had much use or care. In 1903 the commission opened its first endeavor at making a footpath, the Cheshire Harbor Trail from the southeast. Apparently some attention was given to the state of the Hopper and Bellows Pipe trails. Thus the commission was able to state by 1904, "There are now two roads to the summit, and three trails."

However, for another five years, the chief preoccupation of the commission continued to be with roads. In 1906 legislation authorized work on what became the Rockwell Road from due south, now the mountain's most-used motor route. Most of the work was done in 1907, the finishing touches in 1908, under the supervision of George Bauer, who was now superintendent of the Greylock Reservation.

By 1910 a side-road ran past a "camping ground" long used by Hopper Trail excursionists, running onto Stony Ledge, a scenic outlook. Original plans called for extending this road down through the Hopper to Williamstown, possibly following the route of the Hopper Trail. But this was never carried through.

In 1909 a connecting road between Cheshire and the new Rockwell Road was added, coming up via the old Cummings Farm. This was the original right-of-way up the southeast side. In 1910 still another road was added, connecting the one from Cheshire with the base of the Cheshire Harbor Trail, contouring roughly along the line of the old stage road.

With the major roads in place by 1910 and more and more visitors on the mountain, the attention of the Greylock Commission at length turned to constructing (or formalizing already worn) trails to points of scenic interest.[c] The commission began a second footpath (after the Cheshire Harbor Trail of 1903) in 1909 and completed it the following year; it ran along the south ridge of the mountain to the features called the Saddle Balls, paralleling the new Rockwell Road. Other trails followed. By 1913 the commission listed seventeen foot trails, including ones leading to such scenic spots as Jones Nose, the rim of the Hopper, the "Heart of Greylock" gorge, and the obligatory Sunset Rock. (The last

[b]In 1899 the commission surveyed the route for a road up from Cheshire Harbor, possibly using the bottom of the old stage road, then splitting off to follow what later became the Cheshire Harbor Trail for awhile, before branching southwest of that trail to go up to the Saddle Balls. This road was never built, however, and there is no evidence of its use as a hiking trail. In 1907 it was "marked anew" by the Greylock superintendent and continued to be spoken of hopefully both in commission reports (for example, 1908, p. 3), commission maps (for example, 1913 report, back of book) and even in local newspaper articles (for instance, "Routes by Which to Get to Greylock's Summit," *Berkshire Eagle*, Sept. 30, 1914, p. 13). However, the commission itself dropped this route from its 1914 map, and there is no evidence it was ever definitely established and used to climb the mountain.
[c]Commission records do not state clearly whether these were in every case newly built trails. It seems likely that some were already well-worn foot paths used by walkers who knew the mountain.

two were offshoots of a trunk trail from the west leading directly to the camping ground along Roaring Brook.) Within the next two years, additional paths were in use on most of the range's subsidiary summits—Williams and Fitch, Mount Prospect, and Ragged Mountain (then called Ravenscrag). Thus by the middle of the second decade of this century, Greylock, like Monadnock and so many mountain centers in northern New England and the Adirondacks, had a well-developed system of foot trails affording access to a wealth of scenic spots.

Other Massachusetts trails

Elsewhere in the Berkshires, the pace of trail building quickened. In 1887 appeared *The Book of Berkshire, Describing and Illustrating Its Hills and Homes for the Season of 1887.* Within its pages were descriptions of some dozen walks around Lenox and Stockbridge, most of them up modest eminences that gave fair prospects over the pastoral landscape. The chief attractions that approached the status of mountain were Monument Mountain in Stockbridge and Lenox's Yokun's Seat, which at 2,080 feet was hailed as the "highest mountain in town." During the remaining years of the century, the Berkshire Life Insurance Company regularly issued detailed booklets describing "Drives and Walks" in Stockbridge and other Berkshire towns. (This and most similar booklets are undated, but references such as one to "a convenient point where you can leave your team" suggest they precede the age of the automobile.) That these walks were not all garden-variety strolls is demonstrated in the comment on one: "At least 25 miles but starting after breakfast gives time enough to reach home before dark and take it very leisurely."

In the early years of the twentieth century, a circle of vigorous Stockbridge pedestrians organized the Pathfinders, or the "Leg-It" Club, led by such literary luminaries as an aging R. R. Bowker and a youthful Walter Prichard Eaton. Richard Rogers Bowker (1848–1933) founded and edited *Publishers Weekly* for fifty years, helped establish the influential *Library Journal* as well as the American Library Association, and was a feisty political reformer from the time of Grover Cleveland to the New Deal. Walter Prichard Eaton (1878–1957) was a prolific writer of nature and children's books, as well as essays and fiction on a wide range of subjects, and editor of *Stockbridge* magazine during the 1910s. The Leg-It Club also included sculptor Daniel Chester French, portrait painter John C. Johansen, Robert Underwood Johnson, and a number of other diplomats of prominence at that time. This group opened trails and placed signs on Monument Mountain, Burgoyne Pass, and other local destinations.

To the west the Bash Bish Inn in the Taconics had a number of hill paths laid out for its guests, in a miniature replica of what was going on at Monadnock's Half Way House, Kate Sleeper's in Wonalancet, and Adirondak Loj. Following an excursion to the area in 1888, the Appalachian Mountain Club arranged to open trails over Mount Alander to Bash Bish Falls, between the falls and Sage's Ravine, and elsewhere in the Taconics. The precise history of these early trail activities in this area, however, is not well documented.

Farther east, the Holyoke Range was the scene of yet another splurge of trail building, this one under the aegis of a newly formed Amherst Mountain Club. This group—more of a faculty club than a student outing club on the Dartmouth model—built on the base that Edward Hitchcock had laid half a century earlier (see chapter 13). Although the founding documents of this organization did not mention trail building as one of its main functions, other records of activities referred to trails built and maintained not only on the principal Holyoke Range but as far afield as Mount Toby. The club seems to have been active for possibly a decade following its founding in 1903. A college publication in 1928 laments that "for about fifteen years the Amherst Mountain Club has consisted of just enough members of the Faculty to furnish it with officers, and there has been no student organization of hikers." The old Amherst Mountain Club then gave way to the new Amherst Outing Club, a true student outing club.

During these years, walking trails also sprouted on the lesser hills nearer Boston—on Mount Wachusett, in the Middlesex Fells, and on the Blue Hills. From within sight of Massachusetts Bay to the Heart of Greylock, as on Monadnock and Mount Desert, it was an era for trail cutters to open walkways for the pedestrians of the new age of hill walking.

Chapter 24

Trails that failed

WHEREVER there were mountains to be climbed, trail building proceeded throughout the Northeast, though not everywhere at the same pace—nor with the same lasting success. Not every area was blessed with the cohesive summer communities of amateur trail makers and experienced guides, such as came together at Randolph and Keene Valley, Monadnock and Mount Desert. Sometimes ambitious trail systems were sown on barren soil and withered after only a few years. Often the forest relentlessly reclaimed the ground and the proud works of the trail makers were swallowed up and lost in the wide womb of nature's private world.

Maine

Katahdin provides several examples of trails that failed. Pamola was not easily appeased.

Throughout the mountain's history, the climber's approach to Katahdin has continually shifted with various radical changes in access to the base of the great mountain. We have seen how the first climbers (other than the hapless Monument Line surveyors) came from the southwest, up the Abol Slide. During the 1840s appeared the Reverend Marcus Keep with his long path from the east. These routes and the subsequent changes in access are shown in figure 24.1.

A sweeping change occurred in the 1880s, when the logging firm of Tracey and Love commenced major operations in the broad wilderness watershed of the Wassataquoik, due north of Katahdin. For this purpose, in 1882 they substantially upgraded the old Wassataquoik tote road and threw up bustling lumber camps that became known as Old City and New City. Tracey and Love wound up their operations in 1891, but in that year another company, Ayer and Rogers, began logging the South Branch of the Wassataquoik, between the north peaks and the Turner mountains. In 1892 a good lumber road was built to what was known as McLeod Camp, creeping even closer to the citadel of the woods.

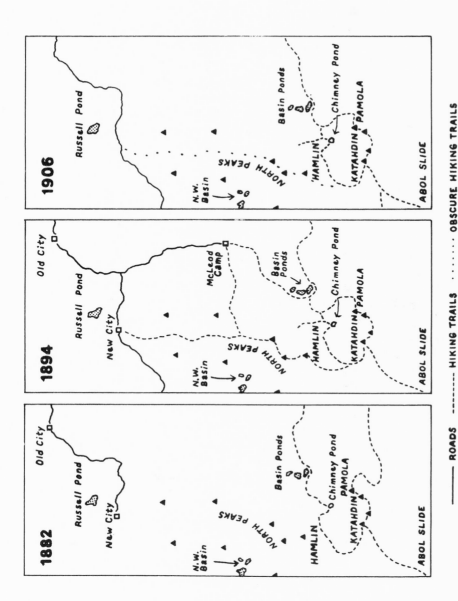

Figure 24.1. The rise and fall of Katahdin's northern trails, 1882–1906 During the period of intensive logging in the Wassataquoik region north of Katahdin, a well-built system of trails sprang up on the northern flanks of Maine's greatest mountain. Bustling logging camps throve at such now deserted sites as Old City, New City, and McLeod Camp. The spectacular forest fires of 1903 destroyed this system completely, and it was not until the 1930s and after World War II that trails on the north side were restored. Katahdin hikers may note that the trail up Pamola in those days lay farther east than the later Dudley Trail.

It is difficult to believe today, wandering the deep, seemingly primeval forests around Russell Pond, the scope of these operations and the population of lumbermen and associated people and horses that filled the entire area during the 1880s and 1890s. Much of their impact has been completely repaired by the inexorable return of the great north woods of Maine, except that the virgin timber is gone. Something of the scale of bustling activity and vitality can still be grasped—almost heard—by the imaginative visitor to the stillness and wilderness solitude of such sites as Old City and New City today, each but a short walk from Russell Pond Campground.

In one swoop, that arrival of the logging camps transformed the access problem for Katahdin climbers. Now instead of the long, slow water route to the Abol Slide or the wearying tramp through the woods from the east, a party could jounce by buckboard all the way through the Maine wilderness to an improved camp within 6 miles of the very summit of Katahdin. Trails sprang up over the north peaks (figure 24.1). In 1885 Tracey and Love, the first loggers in the area, constructed a trail up the gentle northern flanks of the massif, wending along the high plateau past the north peaks and Hamlin to the true summit, gaining gradually the heights that had to be so fiercely overcome by the old approaches. Indeed, when first constructed, the Tracey-Love Trail was so tame that riders could take horses to the top. Tracey himself waxed enthusiastic about the future of tourism in the area:

> The discovery of this bridle path to the top of the mountain is going to do much to attract people to this place. There will be a buckboard road to within six miles of the top of the mountain, and then the rest of the way will be traversed by horses.

The optimistic lumberman was even quoted in the newspapers as envisioning "a favorite resort" to be developed on the north slope.

For twenty years the north was the preferred route to the peak. When Ayer and Rogers began their logging operations in 1891, they cut a good road down along the South Branch to McLeod Camp. From this camp, they built the McLeod Trail westward to join the Tracey and Love Trail, shortening still more the distance from the camp to the top. In 1894 Edwin Rogers built a trail all the way through to Basin Ponds from the north, thereby making it possible to reach the scenic basins under the eastern ramparts as well as the peak itself, all from the new northern approaches. Indeed, from the 1880s on, with extensive lumbering on virtually all sides, numerous wood roads, horse tracks, and footpaths must have been roughed out throughout the area. Only the more permanent ones survive in historical records.

Thus during the heyday of trail building in Randolph and Wonalancet, at Beede's and Adirondak Loj, Katahdin too was enjoying its first boom in recreational trails, albeit with a rough lumberman's flavor rather than that of the polished Cook-Pychowska circle or that of Mr. Van with his varicolored leather suits. Still, the Maine woods aura suited the ambitious Katahdin trampers. The September 1894 issue of the *Maine Sportsman* praised the convenience of the lumbermen's facilities at New City and McLeod Camp. "whence the ascent of the northern slope of the mountain may be made without difficulty." In November 1900 this magazine proclaimed, "Never before has the trip up the big hill been as popular as now." By 1903 the magazine reported, "At one time last season there were as many as fifty different guests camped in the great basin."

The ink was scarcely dry on that issue before the great fires of 1903 erupted, bringing the sudden demise of the entire north peaks trail system. The twenty-year idyll of Katahdin-from-the-north went up in flames in one week, June 2–9, 1903. The tremendous fire raged over the Wassataquoik country, greedily feeding on twenty years of slash, devouring with one tongue of flame McLeod Camp, all the trails that emanated from it, and 132 square miles of timber as well. The McLeod and Rogers trails never were seen again. The Tracey and Love Trail over the north peaks became a faint, little-used track, not to be revived for another generation. Seldom has an entire network of trails disappeared so quickly and so decisively.

Meanwhile, over on the other side of the mountain, trails came and went with like capriciousness. In 1887 the AMC held its first "August Camp" at Chimney Pond, hiring Clarence Peavey to cut a new trail from the east and to construct a shelter at Chimney Pond. Since AMC members were known then as Appalachians, this trail was the first to be given the name Appalachian Trail. From Chimney Pond Peavey also marked other routes up (1) Katahdin's summit via an old slide leading to the "saddle" between the main peak and its northern subsidiaries, (2) Pamola, and (3) the North Basin. This was the start of the Chimney Pond complex of hiking trails.

The original Appalachian Trail enjoyed but a short life. By 1894 a visitor found the remains of the trail "very rough and hard," with one especially provoking patch of blowdown. Two AMC members found it overgrown and abandoned in 1896. However, when Ed Rogers put the trail through from McLeod Camp to join the Appalachian Trail at Basin Ponds, the Chimney Pond area continued to see use. In 1902 Rogers cut a new trail from the east to replace the abandoned Appalachian Trail. It would be more than thirty years before another trail of that name would be associated irrevocably with the destinies of Katahdin.

Meanwhile still another approach—from due west—opened up. During the 1890s Irving O. and Lyman A. Hunt, grandsons of old William Hunt, whose farm had been the original jumping-off point from the east in the midnineteenth century, turned up as operators of a sporting camp on Sourdnahunk Stream west of the mountain. Around 1900 they built a camp on Daicey Pond and cut the trail known ever since as the Hunt Trail. One legend had it that Irving Hunt, who called himself "the Old Eagle of Katahdin," blazed the entire trail from base to treeline in a single day, single-handed. The Hunt Trail gave Katahdin climbers their first approach from due west—the fourth access direction, still omitting the southeastern approaches that later became the most used.

During the last years of the nineteenth century, despite the opening up of so many new routes, the Abol Slide never lost its appeal. Numerous contemporary references documented its persistent use. The AMC guide to Katahdin, published in the club's 1925 guidebook, described the Abol Slide as "until 1921, the best-known route." For all the passing prominence of the Keep Path, the Appalachian Trail, and Tracey's schemes for the northern approaches, that judgment is not far off the mark.

Elsewhere in Maine trail building gradually spread to other mountains. In 1839 Josiah Swift had climbed Saddleback Mountain by "the route commonly taken by parties in ascending the mountain," implying that it was regularly climbed—but Swift goes on to say that he

> could however see no traces of the foot or hand of man, except in one instance, (where we saw two marked trees, probably lot line trees,) until we had nearly reached the summit.

If Saddleback had anything like a trail in those years, it must have been one of the more arduous ascents of the era. It is a high peak bristling with steep slopes and formidable forests; Swift called it "a steep and rugged ascent frequently up granite precipices, up which we had to draw ourselves by our hands."

Farrar's 1880 guide to the Rangeley region names a blazed path up Bald Pate, a fully cleared trail up Bald, and a good carriage road to within a mile of the top of White Cap. On these peaks, again, the impermanence of Maine mountain trails in the nineteenth century may be seen. Farrar's 1890 guide calls the Bald Pate path "very blind," adding, "If you have not considerable experience in woodcraft, the chances are ten to one that you will lose it before reaching the summit." *A Maine Sportsman* correspondent lost the trail up Bald well below the top, lamenting, "From there on it was 'a go as you please' over the rocks and through the scrub pine." And an AMC explorer described White Cap as more of a maze of blueberry pickers' paths than a maintained hiker's trail. Farrar's Androscoggin guide described a trail up Mount Aziscohos as "much improved in the last two years," and one on Mount Blue as "a good path through the woods." In 1892 one writer pronounced Mount Blue "a celebrated place of resort" with a sublime view for "the tourist who ascends its cliffs." Hubbard's guide described a path up Squaw Mountain as "bushed out and cut anew in 1880." Even the rugged Chairback Range had a "spotted trail over the mountain" around 1900 but not to the true summit. Little

Mount Agamenticus on the coast was a popular destination for residents of Kittery, Eliot, South Berwick, and Wells, and must have had a well-trodden trail. Kineo had two routes, one of gentle grade up the southwest side, the other next to the cliffs, "where by the aid of trees men can find foothold for a very steep climb." By 1899 this rugged route had been tamed with "a flight of stairs" and "chains" for support. Twentieth-century accounts, however, suggest that many of these trails had but brief careers.

Vermont

In Vermont, the period from 1870 to 1910 was a checkered time for trails. Mount Mansfield had participated in the bridle path boom of the 1850s, but pure footpaths had little lasting success until the twentieth century. The first path to Mansfield of which any definite record exists ascended from the west side in 1847. Apparently it was very obscure. An 1848 party described its course:

> Through tangled underbrush, over fallen trees, creeping and climbing, through the midst of roots laid bare, down one ravine and up another, crooking and crouching this way and that. . . . on down the rocky precipices, up their craggy sides, over boggy, mossy morasses that shook and trembled under us as we walked through muddy, winding paths, first tearing out a buttonhole on this side of our coat, and then on the other, walking, falling, rising, climbing, until we stood at last upon the top.

When the Halfway House was built in 1850, this trail received more traffic and, befitting the era of bridle paths, was made passable for horses by 1859 or 1860. In 1856 a second trail from the west was cut up the Maple Ridge, but it did not last long in its first incarnation, completely disappearing long before its replacement was built in the 1950s, almost one hundred years later. On the east side, Bingham's fine hotel and carriage road were in place by the mid-1850s. In 1862 another small and short-lived "hotel" was built at Big Spring, well up the road through Smugglers' Notch, and Bill Russin, while employed in this building project, cut a trail up the approximate line taken by the Hell Brook Trail today; the hotel was abandoned in 1869, and it is doubtful whether Russin's trail lasted much beyond that. In 1866 plans were laid for a road up from the northwest, through Pleasant Valley, past Lake of the Clouds, but were never realized. During the 1870s a 5-mile path from Cambridge via Pleasant Valley was cut to the top of Mansfield, using "a spur called Blue Ridge at the left side of the slide." This trail has had its ups and downs during the twentieth century, pretty much disappearing by 1910, being reestablished during the early 1920s, fading out again by the late 1930s, being reopened in the 1960s, only to fade once more during the 1970s. Thus of five or six routes up Mansfield, only one on the west and one on the east gained anything like a permanent footing until the era of the Green Mountain Club in 1910 (see figure 24.2).

The north-south orientation of the long rugged Mansfield ridgeline meant that for all these years its development was strictly an east-west side story. Simply forcing roads through the north and south notches—Smugglers' and Nebraska, respectively—was a struggle. A road through Smugglers' Notch was engineered in the late 1860s; it is presumed that a footpath existed long before and certainly would have been in use during the 1850s. A much older road went through Nebraska Notch, but it was falling into disuse by the 1850s; periodic proposals to reopen this road have been made as recently as the 1920s and 1930s but have never been followed through. Nebraska Notch is now probably a wilder place than it was 150 years ago.

Figure 24.2. The short-lived trails on Mount Mansfield, ca. 1875 Between 1856 and 1875, three trails were built on Mount Mansfield, none of which survived to the end of the century. All three were subsequently restored, though by the 1980s one of the three had once again faded into obscurity. The Maple Ridge Trail, built first in 1856, was soon allowed to fade away but was rebuilt exactly one hundred years later. A short-lived hotel at Big Spring resulted in a trail, built in 1862, which disappeared some years after the hotel was abandoned in 1869, but it probably used essentially the same route as the modern Hell Brook Trail cut in 1921. The trail from Pleasant Valley has faded in and out several times over the years.

As far back as the 1830s, the ascent of Camel's Hump (or the Camel's Rump, or the Couching Lion) was "yearly becoming one of increasing interest to the lovers of the sublime." One approach was from the town of Huntington on the west, at the home of a Mr. Snyder, from which visitors could ride horses for 2 miles, then following a steep footpath to the top. By about 1850 farmers on the northeast slope were occasionally guiding people up the mountain, though no good trail was available on that side until later in the decade. In 1859 Samuel Ridley opened his hotel in the clearing just north of the summit, as well as the bridle path—carriage road combination from North Duxbury on the northeast (see figure 24.3). The hotel was not destined for a long career, however; nor did other footpaths emerge until the next century.

During these years, lower and more accessible eminences around the Green Mountain State were probably climbed regularly by local residents. Ascutney was certainly a favorite in the Windsor area, Burke Mountain near Lyndonville, Anthony near Bennington, Killington near Rutland, Mount Hunger near Montpelier. Green Mountains chronicler W. Storrs Lee says,

> By the middle of the century, Sunday-afternoon paths had been worn to the summits of most of the higher mountains, through back yards, upland pastures, and into the rough.

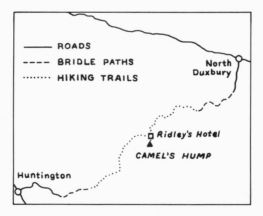

Figure 24.3. The Camel's Hump trails to Ridley's hotel, ca. 1860 In 1859 entrepreneur Samuel Ridley constructed a hotel just one quarter of a mile below the summit of Camel's Hump. The clearing on the Long Trail, at the trail junction above Gorham Lodge, is all that remains to remind twentieth-century hikers of that hostelry, which burned during the 1870s. The trail most used by Ridley's guests followed a route completely different from modern hiking trails. An alternate route from the Huntington side has survived as a hiking trail throughout the twentieth century.

There was supposed to be a path up Lincoln Peak (then bearing the less distinguished title of Potato Hill) by the 1850s, but one party failed to find it when they bushwhacked to the top in an exhausting overnight effort, scrambling through dense growth and along at least one precipitous ledge.[a]

During the late nineteenth century, a few Vermont peaks enjoyed a late-blooming and short-lived interest in summit houses and associated horse paths that elsewhere had passed away when Starr King moved west. Theron Bailey, proprietor of the Pavilion House in Montpelier, built a toll road up Mount Hunger in 1877–78; it seems to have had a short career as a functioning road but provided that mountain with a convenient path from then on. During the 1880s Snake Mountain boasted a road up to a hotel known as the Grand View House, with croquet grounds, a dance hall, roller skating rink, and a 65-foot observation tower, for which ten cents was charged—all now memories.

On Killington Peak an even more substantial "improvement" took place but, again, enjoyed only a brief day in the sun. A government signal station was erected in 1879, and a road led to this installation, ascending the west side of Killington. Alert entrepreneurs soon put up a hotel on the level patch just below the summit where the Long Trail cabin (Cooper Lodge) now stands. For the rest of the century Killington was an oft-climbed peak. At some point during the 1880s a second path came up from West Bridgewater on the east. By 1893 when the U.S. Geological Survey topographic map of the mountain was drawn, there was a second trail from the east and one that went out to the north over neighboring Pico Peak. But shortly after 1900 Killington lost popularity. The hotel was abandoned and began to fall apart, and the trails to the north and east became overgrown. By 1911 James Taylor described even the old carriage road as "like the stony bed of a mountain torrent," and was not even aware there ever had been a trail over to Pico. By 1913, when Woodstock money built what became known as the Juggernaut Trail from West Bridgewater, the trail-builders had to start from scratch, so little remained of the old trail from that side.

By 1910 Green Mountain Club founders claimed that Vermont mountains had virtually no trails. An overstatement, surely; figure 24.4 shows that almost forty peaks in Vermont had trails to their summits before 1910. But they were not well maintained and nowhere was a true trail system in evidence. The modern trail era in Vermont awaited the clarion call of James P. Taylor and the GMC (see chapter 35).

The Catskills

The Catskills had given the Northeast its first true mountain vacation center at Pine Orchard. Now, during the golden age of trail building

---

[a]The party included Philip Battell, father of the eccentric millionaire-conservationist Joseph Battell (see chap. 31).

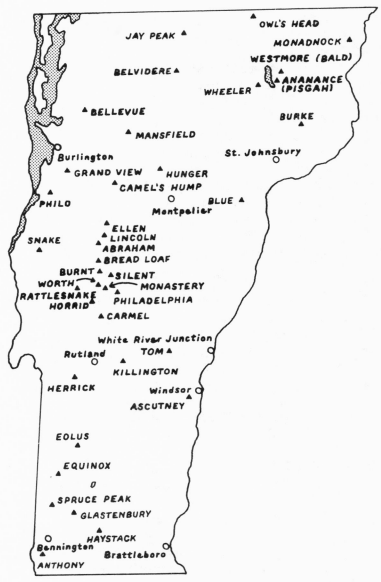

Figure 24.4. Vermont mountains with trails, ca. 1910 The founders of the Green Mountain Club encouraged the belief that Vermont's mountains lacked hiking trails and that therefore it was imperative that one Long Trail be built connecting summits throughout the state from Massachusetts to Canada. In fact trails led to the tops of almost forty Vermont mountains in every corner of the state, as this map shows.

throughout the region, Catskill trails grew but at a notably slower pace. Nothing like the youthful rush of Randolph or the Ausable Lakes could be found in the sleepy hills of Rip Van Winkle. As mountain walking rose in popularity elsewhere, the trend in Catskill recreation shifted toward valley-based amusements. No major trail systems developed on the plentiful summits and ridges that might have seemed fully as rich in hiking opportunities as their White Mountain and Adirondack counterparts. Pine Orchard still had its modest network of walking paths. When the Overlook Mountain House opened in 1871, a similar system of trails sprang up for its guests. After the railroad reached Haines Falls in 1883, a summer colony of cottages took root, the owners of which developed hiking trails connecting with those of Pine Orchard and thoroughly exploring Round Top and High Peak from the west; a local brochure from shortly after 1900 listed thirty-three mountain walks, most of them short. On beyond Haines Falls, on the area's second highest peak, three trails were developed on Mount Hunter, with a side trail to its graceful subsidiary, the Colonel's Chair. Farther north, around 1900, a winding road climbed Mount Pisgah to an observatory on top. Other observatories and associated paths arose on neighboring Nebo and Tower and, farther south and west, Belle Ayre. Down in the heart of the Catskills, in the land that Guyot's explorations and the Ulster & Delaware's railroad had made known, paths brought hikers up mountains like Tremper, Tobias, and Pleasant, though only Tremper retains an official trail today. The southern outpost of High Point was climbed. Shortly after the turn of the century, Mounts Balsam Lake and Utsayantha had definite paths. Somewhat later, construction of fire towers opened a few more trails that hikers could use.

Slide Mountain, the newly acknowledged monarch of the range, had lots of new mountain-hiking traffic and the most significant trail building of this period. Toward the end of the 1870s James W. Dutcher, who ran a boardinghouse in the valley west of Slide, built the first definite trail up the big peak and guided parties regularly. Dutcher built his trail with flair and an eye to both the tastes and comforts of his guests: the route wound through and around picturesque rock formations and, at the steeper places, provided not only rock steps but even rock or log benches for resting. Though it is still possible to trace the remains of this path, it is no longer a maintained trail. During the 1880s, however, it was the fashionable route of ascent.

Slide's eastern neighbors Wittenberg and Cornell also nurtured hiking traffic during this period. Summer residents of Woodland Valley were among the more energetic walkers in the Catskills during the late nineteenth century, and soon opened a trail that at first was clearly maintained only as far as the Wittenberg. When John Burroughs attempted to climb Slide from Woodland Valley in 1884, he went not much farther than the Wittenberg before being "forced to turn back." It is not improbable that hardier hikers kept on over the ridge to Cornell and Slide even during the nineteenth century, and gradually a trail was cleared. According to Raymond Torrey, members of the New York Fresh Air Club finally opened the trail through to Slide during the early years of the twentieth century.

Meanwhile other approaches from the west had developed. In 1893 and 1894, with the aid of state funds, a bridle path was put through not far to the south of Dutcher's trail. This popular route has ever since been well trampled and is a jeep road today. In the wake of the Curtis-Ormsbee tragedy on Mount Washington (see chapter 27), members of the Fresh Air Club memorialized their fallen compatriots by building a trail up Slide Mountain in their memory. It followed the ridge that runs west-southwest of the summit plateau, a trail maintained to this day.

Nevertheless, when compared with what was going on in the northern ranges or on Monadnock, Mount Desert, and Greylock, the Catskills failed to sustain trail making of "golden age" credentials. Numerous sectors of the range were ignored. No record exists, for example, of hiking trails south of Belle Ayre over Balsam, Haynes, Eagle and Big Indian; nor any over the great chain of peaks crossed by today's Devil's Path; nor even on the curving ring of peaks near Windham where once Thomas Cole had frolicked. The Catskills as a whole seemed to be entering a curious phase of being relatively passed by. Throughout the first half of the twentieth century, New Yorkers tended to tramp on the nearby Hudson Highlands or to go all the way to the Adirondacks. Recreation in the Catskills took other forms, with mountains merely as visual backdrops, not as a pedestrian playground.

Chapter 25

Backcountry camping in the eighties and nineties

Overnight camping trips—the word *backpacking* is a twentieth-century invention—made a tentative beginning in the late nineteenth century.

The old mountain guides had offered overnight trips long before the Civil War: Cheney and Phelps taking city folk up Marcy, Keep and others escorting adventurous celebrities to Katahdin, the Crawfords shepherding their clients through the southern peaks to Mount Washington. For such trips, the night out in an improvised pole-and-bark shelter was one of the thrilling elements in the experience.

Now, however, a somewhat broader-based impulse to get back to nature began to induce more excursionists to sample the pleasures and excitements of sleeping in the wilderness by an open fire. By 1877 this trend had produced what was probably the first manual on the subject: *How to Camp Out*, by Maj. John M. Gould of the Portland White Mountain Club. Guidebooks of this period usually included sections of advice on camping, as well as day hiking.

Sleeping out in the nineteenth century was either under the open sky, with hopes of a clear night, or in the hasty bark or bough shelters that the guides so proficiently threw together. But guides were on their way out, and the new generation of hikers found bark construction "difficult to make" and boughs "leaky in wet weather." One Katahdin party that deployed boughs in the roof found, during a nighttime downpour,

> The fir boughs would keep out about as much rain as a lawn tennis net, and even the best lawn tennis net will leak in a heavy rain. We estimated that roof of fir boughs would leak for four days after the rain had ceased.

Nevertheless, the rough-hewn, three-sided shelter continued to appeal to early campers. Long before either trails or loggers invaded the Pemigewasset Wilderness, the valley of the East Branch abounded in "bark shelters left by some of the fishing-parties which frequent the flatter regions." In the Adirondacks the legacy of Cheney and his contemporaries ultimately sired what became known generically as the Adirondack lean-to, a more solidly built three-sided log shelter upon which twentieth-century campers later came to rely. In the White Mountains a similar structure was carried to more elaborate and comfortable proportions in the "camps" erected principally on the northern slopes of the Presidentials, some of which survive today in such Randolph Mountain Club facilities as Crag Camp and Grey Knob.

While the improvised shelter was gradually maturing into the Adirondack lean-to and the Randolph camp, another outdoor facility made its first appearance in the Northeastern mountains: tents.

The first camping tents were either enormous portable palaces unsuitable for carrying any distance from the wagon, such as the 18-foot circular Sibley tent carried by the Pemigewasset Perambulators of 1866, or else the simple, A-shaped pup tents inherited from common soldier use, with no floor or fly—far more portable but not much of an improvement over the bark shelter either. Gould's 1877 treatise gave directions for how to make your own tent, designed in the A pattern or "wall." By 1880 an Adirondacks manual promoted "an 'A' tent of cotton cloth waterproofed," weighing about 10 pounds, sleeping three campers. On the other hand, the guidebook writer Sweetser and others favored the shed-tent, which was more directly derived from the familiar old bark shelter design. This model gradually became extremely popular, to judge from manuals of around 1900 vintage.

In time tents became a more common mode of backcountry shelter, but well into the twentieth century they remained heavier than most backpackers would now be willing to carry. These tents seldom had floors sewn in. While canvas was a common material, it was, put mildly, "burdensome to carry." Serious mountain campers indulged in cotton or silk to reduce weight.

Besides authentic backcountry camping in shelters or tents, two parallel traditions remained in some vogue in the late nineteenth century, though they were fading. One was the tour via roads with horse and wagon to carry the gear, which had enjoyed such popularity on the student pedestrian tours of the 1860s and 1870s. In 1877 Major Gould was still dispensing advice on this method of camping. A Burlington, Vermont, newspaper declared in 1880 that the first principle of camping was: "If possible, buy or borrow a horse, and we would recommend the first—it will cost very little for any old beast. No matter if he be blind of one eye, or foundered, he will do." However, this style of travel was passing from the serious mountain tramping scene.

The other modus operandi was the old-fashioned tour on which travelers stayed in farmhouses—the American equivalent of the British bed and breakfast accommodations. Though English trampers may have continued to employ this method widely down to the present, its use in the New World seems always to have been limited. New England and New York mountain vacationers tended to come to stay in one mountain center. Nomadic vagabonding between farmhouses and country inns failed to catch on as a basis for northeastern U.S. mountain walking, though isolated examples of its application can certainly be found throughout the region.

Let's return to that generation's true backcountry campers. Sleeping bags were virtually unknown to nineteenth-century overnighters. Campers depended on a blanket or two. First they spread a "rubber blanket" or raincoat on the ground, then fir boughs (the softest of mattresses), then their wool blankets. The bough bed, destined to become the target of environmentally concerned campers a century later, was not assembled with restraint: one 1880 adviser exhorts, "Hemlock or balsam boughs, and plenty of them"; Sweetser recommended one or two entire fir trees worth, per bed. By around 1900 a few campers began to use sleeping bags, but early models weighed as much as 18 pounds, and the tried-and-true blanket system remained in widespread use well into the twentieth century. From 1910 on, camping manuals promoted sleeping bags as the modern method but conceded that "most old campers . . . prefer a pair of blankets to a sleeping bag." In 1916 an AMC manual found the issue still undecided.

Blankets were also the first widely used backpacks. Long before "knapsacks" or pack-baskets came into general use, the standard procedure was to roll all of one's camping needs in a bedroll and carry the awkward bundle looped over the shoulders. A 1912 manual still prescribed this technique. In 1913 Boy Scouts in the Berkshires were "not afraid to shoulder a blanket, a frying pan, and a pound or two of bacon, and spend the night in the mountain," according to nature writer Walter Prichard Eaton. One Adirondack tramper recalled that knapsacks did not fully replace the bedrolls until around 1920.

Few references to packs of anything approaching modern design can be found in nineteenth-century camping narratives. Sweetser, ever in the forefront, advocated "knap-sacks" as "indispensable to the forest-traveller," but Gould remained skeptical, recommending the over-the-shoulder blanket roll: "It feels bulky at first, but you soon become used to it. On the whole, you will probably prefer the roll to the knap-sack." The Adirondacks' Seneca Ray Stoddard advised that campers could get by with

> a common grain-bag, with two straps attached about half way up, which, passing over the shoulders and back, under the arms, fasten to the lower corners, the load resting well down the back.

The other Adirondack authority, Edwin R. Wallace, favored a knapsack "when it can be procured"; otherwise he recommended "a common enameled double satchel." A popular day-trip substitute was the haver-sack, a pouch with strap, slung over the shoulder.

What went into the bedroll or pack? Gould enumerated the necessary items as rubber blanket or light rubber coat to double as ground cloth; spare shirt; tent (no poles, since they can be cut in the woods); hatchet; long-handled frying pan, coffee pot, and pail; personal items such as towel, soap, and comb; shotgun; and fishing tackle. He added that one might want to carry a tin cup handy on pack or belt—an early ancestor of the Sierra Club cup. It is not surprising that Gould cautioned against backpacking unless one were accustomed to strenuous exercise.

Other equipment lists of the period agreed with Gould's or added other items: change of socks; large silk handkerchief; pair of sneakers or slippers for around camp; whiskbroom (for brushing yourself to be pre-sentable on walks through towns—touted by one fastidious writer as a "necessity"); repair kit; ax, as a substitute for the hatchet, with a small whetstone; candles or a carbide lamp; umbrella; opera glasses; song-book (on many lists of essentials); "some good brandy (for medical use only)"; a muslin pillowcase, to fill with balsam cuttings for a pillow; and "a small bottle of bay-rum with which to cool the ankles at night."

Attire knew no high-technology fabrics, such as are used widely to-day. For men, clothes were a simple matter. Most just wore the old clothes they wore at home on Sunday afternoon, not bought in any spe-cialty store, and certainly not mail-ordered or imported. All were made of natural fibers. To put together clothing for a mountain trip in the late nineteenth century, campers rummaged through their closets, or maybe their father's, went to the woodshed for the ax, into the wife's (or mother's) sewing kit for repair items, then down to the pantry for grub. "Wear what you please if it be comfortable and durable," admonished Gould. "Coarse and trustworthy trousers" were the foundation of the outfit recommended by B. J. Lossing in 1866. Another expert advised in 1882: "A good stout suit of woolen clothing, such as we wear in winter, . . . a soft felt hat, . . . woolen stockings, a pair of stout boots, not coarse and clumsy." None of the manuals of the day recommended any-thing but comfortable old clothes, with emphasis on durable materials. Hiking boots as such were as yet unknown, though adding nails to the sole of "stout" (a much used adjective) walking shoes was a common practice. A necktie was optional, but old photos show that it was not uncommon to wear one in the backcountry.

Wool was king. "To start with," wrote an 1890 mentor, "let your maxim be, *all wool.*" "I am a member of the wool cult," wrote Allen Chamberlain in the early years of this century. Wool remained enthroned for a full century, grudgingly giving way to a variety of manmade "high-technol-ogy" materials only during the 1970s and 1980s.

What to eat in the woods? Nineteenth-century camp comestibles were surprisingly similar to today's backcountry fare. Freeze drying lay far in the future, of course, but dried foods were widely used. Milk and eggs in powder form and dried vegetables for the evening stew were staples. The rudiments of modern Gorp—"Good Old Raisins and Peanuts"—were often lunch, along with chocolate, cheese, and dried fruits. Oatmeal was a breakfast mainstay, then as now. Early accounts suggest that campers ate more breads and biscuits, baked at the fire, devoted more time and fuss over preparing coffee and tea, and relied more on fishing and hunting small game.

These differences from modern camp cuisine account for some of the heavier items of cookware lugged along. Cast-iron frying pans and kettles of assorted sizes and shapes were standard equipment, along with a variety of baking devices. On the other hand, nineteenth-century backpackers went unburdened by the camp stove and fuel carried by their modern counterparts. One guidebook's section on "Camp Stoves" turns out, on inspection, to describe different types of iron grilles to be laid over a good old fire. Wood fires were the universal means of cooking backcountry meals. Considerable comfort and cheer were associated with the blazing campfire, before which the tired trampers cooked, conversed, perhaps repaired some gear, perhaps sang a camp song or two, and then stretched their bedrolls for the cool night.[a]

From the beginning writers of hiking and camping manuals found it irresistible to instruct the mountain walker in minute particulars. Even how to walk was fit subject for instruction. Major Gould sounded a popular note in urging a moderate pace and frequent rests:

> Rest often whether you feel tired or not; and when resting, see that you do rest. . . . Avoid all nonsensical waste of strength, and gymnastic feats.

One of the early guidebooks, in an introductory list of "Maxims for Mountaineers," cautioned against haste: "Take it cooly at first." Edward Everett Hale, the Katahdin explorer, admonished: "Remember . . . that you are not running a race with the railway train." Another writer offered specific instructions on just how to rest:

> In resting on a mountain climb do not sit down, as the knees get stiff in that position. Lie flat on the ground or best of all lean against a tree.

The majority of experts in this period warned the hiker not to drink or eat too much while climbing:

---

[a]The signal fire on mountain summits was a diversion of the day, virtually unknown today. Campers from a summer resort would climb the local mountain and that night set a huge bonfire on the summit for the amusement of family and friends in the valley below. See, for example, Alice S. Nichols and Charles W. Bacon, *One Night in a Mountain Camp* (Boston: S. E. Cassino, 1886), which tells of a night time bonfire on the top of Osceola, answered by signal fires from friends below in Waterville Valley.

One should be careful to drink but little water while climbing, as the stomach overloaded with water often gives out under the great muscular strain.

Dissent was heard on this point, however. One of the AMC's more active climbers wrote some "Observations on the Physiology and Hygiene of Climbing" for *Appalachia* in 1903 which read remarkably like modern advice. He favored "frequent small drinks," as well as plenty of food during the day's climb.

Mountain walkers debated the use of walking sticks or alpenstocks. Pickering's Guide opined:

> Alpenstocks are seldom carried by the stronger pedestrians in the White Mountains, as they find them more of a hindrance than a help; but the novice is advised to take one at first.

Various insect repellents were advanced or dismissed, most of them abominable gooey mixtures of pine tar, camphor, and other substances of undoubted repellent qualities. One guide analyzed seven different recipes for insect repellent, the ingredients being various combinations of, in the order named, pennyroyal, melted mutton tallow, camphor, creosote, carbolic acid, sweet oil, tar, peppermint, common petroleum, glycerine, turpentine, and castor oil. One may gauge the effectiveness of the various recipes by the dosage recommended by one druggist to a White Mountain tramper: "One drop to each mosquito as often as necessary." Special remedies for other ills were touted—milk for sunburns, soap for blisters.

Attention to trailside etiquette and consideration for landowners got off to an early start in Northeastern hiking. "Do not be saucy to the farmers," lectured Gould. Early manuals counseled courtesy to fellow hikers and those who permitted hikers to cross their land. "Try to be civil and gentlemanly to everyone" was the guiding principle.

Much early camping may strike modern readers as uncomfortably primitive compared with today's backcountry conveniences. We can recognize, nevertheless, the aura of exploration and of companionship in the tales of early backpackers. Nineteenth-century accounts of camping breathe an excitement that each generation partially recaptures for itself but that seems to have been uniquely fresh in those truly pioneering days of the bedroll stretched on springy boughs under the bark shelter before the blazing campfire. Moreover the nineteenth-century camper developed some skills that his descendants are losing or have lost: how to start a fire under all conditions, how to lay a bough bed with a maximum of comfort and a minimum of prickliness ("very much as shingles are fastened on a roof," admonished Sweetser), how to assemble and carry a blanket roll. Each era had its own style and the skills requisite to carry off that style; and each its own attractions that other eras can never fully recapture.

Chapter 26

Pychowskas ascendant

LATE nineteenth-century mountain walking unfolded during a period of rapid change in the status of women in American society. The first Women's Rights Convention was held in 1848, and even by then the word *feminism* was not new to the vocabulary. Nevertheless it was right after the Civil War that women began a sustained push toward equal rights, carrying on with ups and downs until achieving suffrage in 1920. Before the end of the century names such as Margaret Fuller, the Grimké sisters, Susan B. Anthony, and Lucy Stone were well known to American women, especially those who had leisure to contemplate mountain trips. During the 1880s, women's clubs sprang up around the country, culminating in the formation of the General Federation of Women's Clubs in 1890.

Despite all this social change, skepticism and controversy persisted about women's place in the backcountry. Major Gould's *How to Camp Out* had this advice for women: "Where there is a road, or the way is open and not too steep, they may attempt it; but to climb over loose rocks and through scrub-spruce for miles, is too difficult for them." Hubbard's Moosehead Lake guide said in 1893, "Ladies have climbed Ktaadn, but only the strongest can do it." At about the same time Catskill rover John Burroughs heedlessly wrote,

> The regular way to the top of Slide Mountain is by Big Indian Valley, where the climb is comparatively easy. But from Woodland Valley up the slide itself only men may assay the ascent.

But others spoke up for women in climbing. In 1869 no less an authority than Adirondack Murray urged women as well as men to take to the woods. Mrs. Murray set an example that impressed the local guides: "She's a dashing, independent sort of woman, who don't let thoughts of what people may say interfere with her plans." By 1878 Keene Valley had come to expect the annual appearance of "city ladies" prepared to clamber about the mountain trails who came in their mountain costumes of daring ankle length skirts and tin cups on their belts, making tinkling sounds as they took their seats.

In the White Mountains, Moses Sweetser, the most forward looking of the day's guidebook writers in his coverage of true mountain trails, almost recognized equality for women:

> In these days of advocacy of female suffrage and woman's rights, it needs hardly to be stated that American ladies can accomplish nearly everything which is possible to their sturdier brethren.

As we have noted, the Appalachian Mountain Club encouraged women's participation in hiking, on and off trail, as well as trail clearing in the summer communities of Randolph and elsewhere. Women formed a majority on the first AMC excursion to Katahdin in 1887. In Field and Forest Club activities, women were almost as active as men, leading Saturday outings as well as putting on evening programs. The first recreational snowshoeing in the high mountains in winter was pursued by women as much as men (see chapter 32).

Though encouraged by male support from influential quarters like Murray, Sweetser, and the AMC, in the end it was women who could speak most eloquently to women. In early *Appalachias*, some AMC women wrote pioneering articles on topics such as "Camp Life for Ladies." Not much later, Mary Alden Hopkins wrote articles for *In the Maine Woods* proclaiming the equal ability of women to roam the wilderness and climb its mountains.

> In many a camp one will find a party of women, or a group of school-girls with their teacher, who tramp and climb and fish. . . . No woman need hesitate to take a woods trip for fear she lacks strength, for the strength will come to her there. . . . The Maine forest is a place where sick women grow well and well women accumulate muscle and happiness.

Dress was the key issue for most women hikers. A rigorously enforced modesty decreed that lower limbs be draped with yards of heavy material.[a] By the time mountain hiking came into popularity, at least the hoopskirts and tight-laced stays of an earlier era had been abandoned. "No lady should ever wear a corset into camp," cautions an 1890 manual. Only one generation earlier (1864), one handbook had felt compelled to admonish women hikers, "Abandon crinoline and hoop." But still, even into the twentieth century, long skirts bespangled with frills and

---

[a]In 1867 one young woman was overheard, while crawling over a down tree on the path to the Crystal Cascade: "Lizzie, when you get in such a place as this, you do have to show your extremities" (T. R. B., "Bummers Records at the White Hills," manuscript in the collections of the New Hampshire Historical Society, p. 89). Reprinted with permission.

furbelows must have posed almost insurmountable obstacles to scrambling up steep mountainsides. One young woman, Margaret Twitchell Steele, whose family belonged early to the Chocorua Mountain Club, worked out a technique for rapidly descending mountains without fear of the skirt snagging on bush or rock: her brother would run behind with a stick, releasing her skirts as "the two went pell mell down the trail." Troublesome enough on summertime hiking trails, skirts' effects on bushwhacks or snowshoeing trips were unimaginable. An "indispensible" item of equipment, according to one female explorer, was an ample supply of "pins, needles, thread (plenty of them), hair-pins." Wholly apart from the constant catching and tearing of clothing on branches, mountain undergrowth was often soaking wet. The weight of drenched flannel or wool skirts must have been considerably increased after the first few minutes in the bushes. Early female snowshoers dragged long hems through the snow, which became wet, then frozen and still heavier.

From the Austin sisters in 1821 until just before World War II, the story of women's climbing is one long gradual emancipation from Victorian dress codes that were peculiarly unsuited to mountaineering. In 1877, in the first *Appalachia* article on the subject of women's hiking dress, Mrs. W. G. Nowell, wife of the AMC trailsman, proclaimed,

> Our dress has done all the mischief. For years it has kept us away from the glory of the woods and the grandeur of the mountain heights. It is time we should reform.

In this opening salvo in the battle for rationality in women's climbing garb, Mrs. Nowell recommended "a plain, untrimmed skirt a few inches shorter than regular street dress." Even this radical shortening, however, spared not the wearer from "skirt entanglements," so Mrs. Nowell moved further and audaciously declared for wearing "a good flannel bathing suit" as no more improper on the mountain heights than on the beach. The modern reader should not envision a bikini; Mrs. Nowell's bathing suit was "made of stout gray flannel":

> The upper garment is a long sack, reaching to the knees. This is neatly buttoned and makes all the skirt that is needed. It is confined at the waist by a loose and adjustable belt. The sleeves are full and are gathered into bands at the wrist. The lower garments are loose, full, Turkish pants gathered into a band around the ankle.

It is unknown, however, whether Mrs. Nowell's bathing suit proposal ever gained acceptance. Sweetser tells of encounters with "beach-costumed maidens, ranging the woods from their camps half-way down Mount Washington," but this was a rare vision, to judge from other available evidence. Throughout the last two decades of the century, ankle-length skirts were still the principal feminine costume in the woods.

In 1879 another AMC hiker, Miss M. F. Whitman, advocated "a short skirt about to the tops of the boots, with another longer if it is desired for wear in public conveyance." The wear and tear (especially the latter) of off-trail travel for Whitman and others caused her to recommend that, on camping trips, two full suits be brought along, plus "a generous supply of thick stockings."

By 1887 the flamboyant Lucia Pychowska, a leading light in the luminous Randolph circle of the 1880s (see chapter 22), was still obliged to acknowledge her generation's scruples. She recommended an outfit of gray flannel trousers, knickerbocker length, covered by two skirts, the inner one reaching just below the knee, the outer to the top of the walking boot. As an ardent bushwhacker, Madame Pychowska undertook the revolutionary measure of "a temporary shortening of the dress" by pinning up the outer skirt for "a rapid transit through hobble bush," assuring her Victorian readers that "when the difficulty is surmounted, the pin may be loosened and affairs restored to their original condition." While conceding that this arrangement was "cut somewhat scanty," the redoubtable Pychowska insisted that her garb had

> ascended Mts. Tahawus, Whiteface, Hopkins, Hurricane, and other peaks of the Adirondacks, gone through Indian Pass, travelled in twelve hours over the peaks of the White Mountains from Washington, over Clay, Jefferson, Adams, and Madison; and through the thickets on Madison down to the Glen Road; . . . it last summer came down through Tuckerman's ravine when the streams were at their fullest; and yet it has appeared at the end of these walks sufficiently presentable to enter a hotel or a railroad car without attracting uncomfortable attention.

In the Adirondacks, the leading guidebook writer, Seneca Ray Stoddard, recommended a short walking dress over "Turkish trowsers, buttoned at the ankle." His rival Wallace concurred in almost identical words.

Women's hiking apparel, whatever its inconvenience, often afforded bright contrast with the drab male costume of the day. Accounts of women on excursions to rugged mountaintops could read like a description of the Easter parade. A Waterville Valley party set forth for Osceola with one woman attired in

> a navy-blue jersey, relieved by a sacque of cardinal red, falling over a skirt of the same bright hues. . . . [while] Lady Eleanor's gentle spirit found fit expression in a quiet suit of brown, splashed here and there with doubtful white, the whole surmounted with a jaunty cap of red.

After 1900 skirts began a gradual retreat. The provocative Mary Alden Hopkins, who advocated women's hiking in the Maine woods, recommended that the skirt clear the ground by 12 inches, but that was 1902;

and it *was* Hopkins; and of course such a skirt was to be worn over knickerbocker bloomers *and* union underwear.

It was not until after the turn of the century that even the most unconventional women climbers discarded the outer skirts and hiked in plain, knee-length bloomers or Turkish pants. Even then, wrote Marjorie Hurd in a historical review published in 1935: "However, a skirt was carried in the pack, or even more conveniently on the belt for quick donning on the approach of other parties." Hurd dates the first "public" wearing of just bloomers to 1914 and the acceptance of knickers for women to 1916. A manual called *Equipment for Mountain Climbing and Camping* gave its blessing to knickers for women in that year. Before that, it had been a slow process of letting go of the skirts. During that long period of transition, one guidebook reflected,

> Modesty is not so much a matter of dress as of demeanor. One woman can wear knicker-bockers without a skirt and appear perfectly natural and modest while another—simply can't.

As late as the 1920s, many women hikers felt they were flouting convention to entrain for Sunday excursions dressed in pants.

Burdened with these extraordinary accoutrements, as well as with the manners of the age, women seem not to have carried much else in the way of weight. On an 1882 White Mountain trip, each woman carried "her own satchel, attached to a leather belt, and a small canteen," but "all other luggage is delivered to the packman." An 1897 Katahdin party of eight included four women: "The ladies started bravely, with a small hand-bag and shoulder-strap. One of them volunteered to carry the camera." The four men had 50 pounds each to carry. No nineteenth-century accounts of women in the mountains mention their carrying loads of consequence. Amid the constraints of the Victorian vision of women's role in society, their self-sufficiency and full participation in the hiking and climbing world would have to await a later generation.

A handful of unconventional women defied the strictures of the age and the handicap of long dresses to throw themselves into mountain hiking, off trail and on, with as much gusto as the leading men of their times. That women were climbing in the Adirondacks and up at Katahdin in the post–Civil War years is known, but unfortunately few incidents or personalities of special note have come down to us. No such dearth dims the White Mountain scene, however. There we find several instances of women keeping pace with their male contemporaries.

These heroines certainly include M. F. Whitman, though historical records deny us even the privilege of knowing her full first name. One of Whitman's adventures may serve as an example of how women of her time could rise to an occasion, long skirts and Mount Washington's worst weather notwithstanding.

One mid-August Whitman joined a camping trip of fellow Appalachians in the White Mountains. From their base camp, they made daily journeys into the peaks. After lunch at the Crystal Cascade one sunny afternoon, a gentleman "who had often been our leader in exploration" suggested following the stream up to the snow arch in Tuckerman's. Whitman was the only taker, so giving their "heavy wraps" to the others, the pair set off. It was a little past 2:00 P.M. What had been a path to the ravine was "considerably overgrown, and in many places the blazes are obscure." The ramble turned into a wet slog, much of it in the stream itself, to bypass impenetrable alder thickets on either side. But eventually the pair reached their goal, since, as Whitman put it, "we were accustomed to accomplish whatever we attempted."

By now the benign weather of midday had changed. Clouds thickened, wind shrieked, and rain began to fall. The climbers became wet through, shivering with cold, and night was fast approaching. Having left warmer clothes with their companions, their possessions consisted of Whitman's knife, wet matches, two hard crackers, and "a very small pocket-flask, with not more than a spoonful of brandy." Whitman knew it was not time to be that high in the ravine with nothing but water-soaked thickets below, "but what was in the mind of my companion I knew not, for little had been said during the last hour and I would not by a question indicate to him that I had the slightest anxiety."

At this juncture, her companion suggested, "To return is impossible; our only hope is to reach the top. Are you equal to it?" Whitman responded, "I think I am."

So, with no clear knowledge of the vast mountainside above them, as clouds descended over it and rain continued to pelt down, in fading light, with no bivouac gear of any kind, the two turned uphill, selecting a route that "seemed to be the bed of a spring torrent or the track of a slide." When they at length dragged over the lip of the ravine,

> The storm struck us with its full force, compelling us to cling to each other for support. Night was hard upon us and the clouds so dense we could hardly see a dozen rods ahead.

Taking their bearing as best they could, they struck off across the storm-swept alpine zone, "bareheaded and with skirts close-reefed." After a long struggle, a break in the clouds gave them a momentary glimpse of a summit ridge that they knew to be Mount Monroe. Shortly thereafter they came across the Crawford Path, and with much relief were able to follow it upward, "sometimes on foot, often on hands and knees." When they finally reached the old corral used for horses (just off the summit), they paused and allowed themselves the last spoonful of brandy. Here, so close to the top, Whitman's companion remarked drily that "Lizzie Bourne perished even nearer the summit than we were" (see chapter 27).

Fortified, they carried on and "so thick was the night that we struck the platform which surrounds the house before we discerned a gleam of light." Their entrance into the summit hotel was a sensation: "Hatless, with remnants only of shoes, stockings, and skirts, before the wondering crowd which surrounded the blazing fire."

During the 1880s an even more outstanding pair of women on the mountaineering scene were the Pychowska family: Lucia the mother, and Marian the daughter. The sister of Eugene Cook, Randolph's leading hiker in the 1880s, Lucia yielded nothing to her well-known brother in vitality of personality. Married to a celebrated Polish musician-aristocrat (the tall, slender, aloof nonhiker, Chevalier Pychowski), Lucia Cook—or Madame Pychowska, as she became—was "a most restless, agile, lovable little lady whose flashing thought and rapier repartee found a match only in her daughter." Marian Pychowska grew into a dazzling personality on the Randolph scene in her own right, not overshadowed by mother, father, or uncle. Her map of the Northern Presidentials superseded that of Pickering himself and remained in use until Louis Cutter created his masterpiece fifteen years later. The two Pychowska women were full participants in both the trail building and the off-trail exploration of the vigorous Randolph summer circle. In 1879 both mother and daughter were delivering papers before the AMC on their investigations of the rugged Mahoosucs. In 1884 Marian Pychowska and another young woman, exploring around the top of Huntington Ravine, thought nothing of creeping out on the narrow crest of that gigantic arête known to later generations as the Pinnacle. Two years later the ebullient Marian astonished the AMC hierarchy by showing them where she and her friend had frolicked:

Mr. Edmands asked me to show them the projection of which I had previously spoken to him and Mr. Lowe. So in effect, I had the satisfaction of introducing our crag officially to the president of the AMC [Edmands]. He did not think it a safe place to invite the party to follow. Consequently Messrs. Lowe, Lawrence, Nowell, and one other were the only ones to venture down the slide. I was surprised to find that the spot was new to all of them, as well as flattered by the enthusiastic interest they showed in viewing the great crag from all sides. Mr. Lowe was so inspired as to spout verse,—and his enthusiasm . . . pleased me more than anything else. The crag is a jutting ridge of rock, extending down the ravine wall 500 ft or more, and showing a superb cleavage, with great smooth surfaces and bold angles. One can easily walk out to the point of the promontory and look down the abyss. From under the slide which leads down to the crag, flows an icy cold streamlet.[b]

[b]The icy cold streamlet, in winter, becomes the Pinnacle Gully, a premier ice-climbing route in the twentieth century. The "slide" referred to is evidently the scree slope above the Pinnacle. The delegation that ventured down on Marian Pychowska's airy perch was distinguished indeed: Charles Lowe was the chief guide and most respected mountain man in Randolph at the time; Rosewell Lawrence and W. G. Nowell were among the most robust of the early AMC mountaineers.

The Pychowskas' friend Isabella Stone did almost as much exploring in the western end of the Whites as the Pychowskas did in the east. When the club named Mount Waternomee on a list of "unexplored mountains," Stone undertook its ascent, only to find confusion as to which of several peaks (among a constellation of Moosilauke's northeastern neighbors) was in fact Waternomee, what was the order of elevations, and whether in fact most existing maps of the range were in error. Enlisting the aid of her North Woodstock landlord, George F. Russell, and armed with compass, faulty maps, and an earlier reconnaissance from the summit of Moosilauke, Stone embarked on a series of bushwhacks during which she straightened out the topography of that complex mountainside, in the process climbing and sorting out the names for Mounts Blue, Cushman, and Jim, as well as more than one summit of what she eventually determined to be Waternomee. This involved "rough work,—over rocks, prostrate logs, moss-covered pitfalls, and through thick underbrush."

It is a loss to history that we do not know the names of two of the three women who accompanied A. E. Scott on an arduous weeklong journey through the Pemigewasset Wilderness in 1882. It was an epic that Scott had done all he could to avoid, and affords a fitting conclusion to our chapter on this era of women's climbing.

At that time the central range of that wilderness—North and South Twin, Guyot, Bond, and its satellites—was as yet unexplored save by the Hitchcock surveyors (see chapter 17). Some AMC parties had attempted to reach the summits of the Twins but had been repulsed by the exceptionally thick undergrowth above 4,000 feet. Within the AMC, the Twins and Bonds had begun to be regarded as "an interesting field for exploration." As reports of the dense upper-elevation scrub filtered back, the AMC's new councillor of improvements, Scott, decided that what was needed was a trail up to and along the entire range.

But first it fell to Scott to undertake a reconnaissance. Anticipating a forced march of several days, he determined to make his survey accompanied only by a single woodsman. Much to his surprise and chagrin, word of his plan leaked out. He received in the mail an inquiry from a journalist named Charlotte E. Ricker, who claimed "much experience among the mountains" and requested to accompany him. Scott replied by painting a vivid picture of the difficulties anticipated: long-continued off-trail bushwhacking, clothes-tearing thickets, sleep without shelter or blanket, extremes of heat and cold, need to travel through storms, thirst, and hunger. He closed with a deft ploy in which he announced that if Charlotte Ricker still wished to come, then, to preserve the proprieties, he would invite another woman—"the only lady I know for whom the undertaking is feasible"—trusting to be quite sensibly turned down and thereby taken off the hook. Dismayed again, Scott found that the second woman—and a third! —eagerly wished to join the party and that his words of warning had not dampened but merely incited the ardor of the journalist.

I was fairly caught. I had painted the probable difficulties of the proposed expedition in glowing colors, and had rather disdainfully expressed a willingness to invite ladies to accompany me if they dared attempt it; and here were three ladies who not only dared, but were eager to go. I would not retract, although I had many misgivings, and some doubts of their reaching even the first summit.

Thus it was that Scott's original light two-man team ballooned into a party of six: himself, Charlotte Ricker, two other women whom the sources, alas, do not identify, and two local woodsmen, a youth known only as Odin and an older man named Allan Thompson. On the morning of August 3, 1882, they set off for the Twins and beyond, country seldom trod before and never yet by women (see figure 26.1).

The first day's travel was mostly along the approach valley. That night was spent well down from the top of North Twin. On the second day they came to grips with the problem. Wrote Scott:

We have reached the line of scrub spruces, and are soon floundering helplessly. We are familiar with scrub as it appears on Adams, Carrigain, and other summits, but the worst places on those summits seem

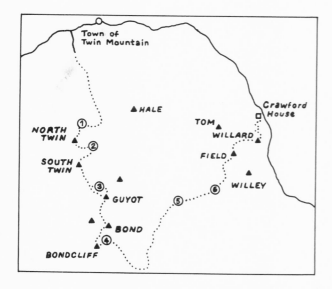

Figure 26.1. The Scott-Ricker adventure of 1882 In the early 1880s the Twin Range was completely trailless, a genuine virgin wilderness where the scrub above 4,000 feet was especially dense and tangled. AMC Councillor of Improvements A. E. Scott and two women whose names are lost to history made a remarkable seven-day journey through this formidable wilderness. The six numbers on this map refer to their bivouac campsites. Most of the way, they were reluctantly accompanied by a long-suffering journalist, Charlotte E. Ricker, and two disgruntled local woodsmen.

to us like pleasure-grounds compared to this. Twin Mountain scrub is unique; it is indescribable.

At this point it became clear that Ricker had used journalistic license in describing herself as "experienced." Nothing like Twin Mountain scrub had she ever attempted before. To her,

> There is no way that you can meet and defy this pitiless enemy—unless you pause to hew it from your path. Is it of average height, with a small interstice at the bottom? You must crawl under it. Is it short and tangled? You must make it your footstool. Is it knit tightly from top to bottom? You must fight your way through its unbending branches. It will scratch you mercilessly, it will aim for your face, your hands, your person; it will make voyages of discovery in your eyes, will entangle your feet, will push aside your hat, and relentlessly Absalomize you. You may force it down—it will fly back and strike you. You may tread it under your foot—it will assert itself just in time to give you a parting thrust. Vainly will you search for favoring inlets and outlets. One scrub differs from another only in its increasing fiendishness. It is an army of porcupines over and under and around you; it is a phalanx of broadswords by which you are surrounded. Once involved in its intricacies there can be no retreat, no quarter. Are you a great man or a graceful woman? The more dignified your carriage the greater the inconvenience it causes you, the more cringing the attitudes to which it subjects you. And your raiment! It is rent and tattered in a myriad places; shreds and remnants are the trophies of this inexorable scrub. If your garments are not iron-bound, you will become a travelling rag-bag, a deplorable shade of your former self. And you must be prepared to be mutilated; scratches, bruises, wrenches count for nothing. . . . Whoever reads this and pronounces it an exaggeration, let him traverse fifteen rods that are overgrown with spruce scrub, and he will say "the half was never told."

Finally around 1:00 P.M. they reached North Twin, battered and torn, their water improvidently consumed against the warnings of Scott and the two more experienced women. During the afternoon they found water—in the form of a steady rain that soaked not only themselves but the branches through which they must push all afternoon. The reader will recall that this was the age of long skirts, now shredded, drenched, and much heavier. Finding no drinkable water on the ridge, they descended to a landslide on the side of North Twin, well down which they found water, but no level ground. The night was spent "fitted in among the rocks," the journalist "showing slight symptoms of discouragement," but the others "wet and torn, but all jolly."

Starting earlier on the third day, they reached the summit of South Twin, the local men once again consuming the day's water supply before the morning was out. En route to Guyot they encountered "scrub worse than any we have yet seen." By this time the party separated both physically and psychologically into two groups: Scott and the two experienced women plunged happily on to Guyot only to discover that Ricker and the two local men, being both demoralized and parched with thirst, had headed downhill for water. When Scott and the others realized what had happened, they attempted to get back to Ricker's group, but each contingent ran out of daylight and was forced to bivouac in the dense woods, still separated. By this time the journalist and both woodsmen were thoroughly discouraged, but Scott and the other two still going strong.

On the fourth day they managed to reunite and, despite her state, Ricker expressed a wish to continue with the planned course. Somehow they struggled with the scrub and steep terrain all the way over Bond and down to the open ledges of the Bondcliff. There, in spite of the ordeal, they found the scenery captivating—or at least Scott and the two experienced women did:

> The old man declares he never will attempt another trip like this, the young man would give a thousand dollars (which he does not possess) to be at home, and the journalist begins to discuss the easiest way of emerging from the valley below.

From that night's camp below the Bondcliff, on the stream that today's trail follows, they soon descended to the floor of the Pemigewasset Wilderness and turned east, heading for Crawford Notch. They camped near Thoreau Falls, enjoyed fresh trout for dinner, but were rained on for a while during their fifth night out.

The next day the two woodsmen and the journalist started on the quickest way out, via Ethan Pond. In a weakened condition, however, the journalist collapsed and the party reunited for a sixth night out.

In the morning while the three demoralized members of the party made their way down, Scott and the remaining two women ("nearly as fresh and unwearied as at starting") struck off up an almost unexplored stream valley and bushwhacked up the steep west side of Mount Field—a tough trip any time and an almost incredible accomplishment on the seventh day of this epic:

> The climb is difficult; there is no soil,—nothing but immense fragments of rocks, covered with moss which treacherously conceals the pitfalls; and we are an hour and a half in reaching the ridge. We follow the ridge to the summit with little difficulty.

From the top of Mount Field the intrepid trio descended on a straight line to Mount Willard and the carriage road. ("It is very steep and ledgy, but we are expert after our seven days' climbing.") Breaking into the civilized clearing on the top of Willard, they encountered a crowd of genteel tourists, up by carriage to enjoy the vista. After seven days of bushwhacking through intermittent rain, and six nights spent out, under improvised shelter only on some of them, the women wearing long skirts the whole time, now thoroughly shredded and tattered, the threesome must have made a grand entrance.

What eludes posterity is who these two amazing women were who not merely accomplished the seven-day exploration, but seem to have taken the hardships effortlessly in stride, backtracking when necessary to help the journalist and the two hapless local woodsmen, and launching the final ascent up the back side of Field on the seventh day "nearly as fresh and unwearied as at starting"—symbols of what women could overcome in the Victorian era.[c]

---

[c]Ricker's account gives no clue to the identity of the other two. Scott tells us that they were AMC members, that one was a doctor and the other a medical student. The profession appears to rule out the redoubtable Pychowska women. The only female doctor listed in the 1881 AMC register of members is Dr. Mary J. Safford. That name, however, is not mentioned elsewhere in club annals as participating in vigorous trips. Whitman was a club member and could well have justified Scott's characterization as "the only lady I know for whom the undertaking is feasible," but there is no evidence that Whitman engaged in medical studies. The two heroines must remain anonymous— but not forgotten.

Chapter 27

Death in the mountains

WITH swarms of adventurous trampers afoot in Northeastern mountain storms, it was only a matter of time and fate before some unfortunate individual would prove imprudent or unlucky.

A curious thing about mountain accidents is the selectivity of public response to them. Every few years there occurs a particular incident that especially transfixes public attention, and the story becomes widely told and retold, with fascination far exceeding that of dozens of other accidents and fatalities, some of them in the same mountains or involving more people. Some particular ingredients of drama or pathos strike a peculiarly responsive chord of sympathy or fascination, perhaps morbidity, perhaps a feeling that some special blend of heroism or fatalism was involved.

This selectivity of public response extends far back in history. During colonial times it is not unlikely that occasionally a number of individuals would be lost in the woods around the lower flanks of the mountains; but one forlorn girl, who perished in pursuit of an unfaithful lover, achieved immortality in early White Mountain literature and even had a major mountain and a brook named after her: Nancy Barton. In 1885 a slide on Cherry Mountain devastated a farm, smashed the farmhouse, and killed one man, but that event has virtually vanished into obscurity while pages and pages of prose, poetry, and fiction have been inspired by a similar incident on Mount Willey in 1826. Some chemistry about Nancy and the Willey family touched emotional depths in people that the others did not.

Considering the notorious Mount Washington weather and the fact that people had been climbing the mountain for two hundred years, it is remarkable that up through 1850 no stories of climbing deaths have come down to us. The Crawfords had an almost spotless record. The only injury noted by the Crawfords was the sprained ankle of a sea captain on his descent in August 1822. The victim walked out, but he holds the distinction of being Mount Washington's first recorded accident victim. If other trampers occasionally went astray, Ethan Allen Crawford would call them in with a 6-foot horn.[a]

Frederick Strickland, a wealthy young Englishman, was the first to die in a genuine climbing accident in the mountains of the northeastern United States. He perished on Mount Washington in October 1851, a victim of his decision to persist upward alone when his guide and another client turned back. The route was the Crawford Path, the weather wintry, with snow and cold. His trackers ascertained that Strickland reached the summit but succumbed on the descent. His body was found in the valley of the Ammonoosuc, face down in a stream.

Four years later, on September 15, 1855, a young woman passed away after being benighted near the summit during a foul weather ascent. The following year, an elderly hiker named Benjamin Chandler was lost in a storm and perished. One might expect that Strickland, as the first victim of the Northeastern mountains, would be the best known of these three victims. Or perhaps that Chandler, for whom a major ridge and brook on Washington have been named, might have a memorable story, oft retold. In fact, most histories scarcely mention either gentleman's name. But the young woman who died in the storm, Lizzie Bourne, has been immortalized in reports, legends, poetry, painting, and a monument on the mountain itself; in 1916 Kilbourne called her death "more widely known than that of any other person who has perished on the Presidential Range," a judgment that remains true today.

Why has Lizzie Bourne attracted so much sympathy? She was young (twenty-three), the daughter of a Kennebunk, Maine, judge, and soon to be married. With her uncle and his daughter, she started up the bridle path late in the day. They failed to heed advice to stay the night in the Halfway House, were caught in high winds, wet clouds, and darkness, and finally sank exhausted and soaking wet not 200 yards from the top, where unknowing guests were enjoying a cozy and convivial dinner. Unable to rouse the fallen girl, her uncle improvised a stone windbreak and kept himself and his daughter alive through the night, but not, alas, poor Lizzie.

Later in the same year occurred another incident that, though not involving death, has been a favorite for retelling in mountain histories and anthologies. A Boston physician named B. L. Ball, experienced in the Alps and with other foreign travel, started up Mount Washington in late October, armed with no more mountain gear than an unbelievably stout umbrella, an equally stout determination to reach the top, and a thorough unwillingness to face facts. On the first day of ferocious weather above treeline, he came to within one-half mile of the top, reaching a 6,000-foot knob since known as Ball Crag. Lost and running

[a]This method of helping lost persons find their way out of the woods is used still today in the White Mountains: the city of Berlin, on the edge of the Mahoosucs, has a siren called Big Bertha, which is sounded to help lost hunters get their bearings.

out of daylight, he retreated to treeline and bivouacked under his umbrella amid the scrub growth, in what was now a full-scale snowstorm. Having survived one night, Dr. Ball had the misfortune next morning to glimpse through broken clouds a summit that he assumed to be Washington but that later analysts guess may have been Adams, far off across the Great Gulf. All that day, still aiming for the summit, he wandered around trying to decipher what had by now become completely baffling topography and unrelenting hostile weather, still with no visibility and no idea where he was. As darkness came on again, he was forced to endure once more—and somehow to survive once more—a second night under the umbrella. Wandering farther on the third day, he chanced upon a search party, which escorted him down to safety, incredibly unharmed by the ordeal. Dr. Ball published an interminable account of his three days in 1856. Sixty years later a fascinated Kilbourne devoted seventeen pages to the episode, not less than 4 percent of his entire *Chronicles of the White Mountains*. The anecdote continues to absorb the attentions of succeeding generations. More than one hundred years after the original incident, Dr. Ball's own write-up was reprinted in entirety (in several installments) and without explanation, in an obscure underground climbers' rag known as the *Vulgarian Digest*, given mainly to ribald humor and tall tales. Most of *Vulgarian Digest*'s readers assumed the farce was yet another outrageous inspiration of editor Joe Kelsey's mad imagination—yet every word was from Dr. Ball's original account. Such is the inexplicable staying power of certain incidents in mountain history.

Although several climbers died on Mount Washington as the years went by, it was not until 1900 that the next occurrence caught the public fancy with anything like the fervor that Lizzie Bourne had aroused. This was the first double fatality on Washington, one that shocked the climbing fraternity and had far-reaching effects on Northeastern mountain history. Unlike Strickland, Chandler, or Lizzie Bourne, obscure walkers of probably only ordinary ability, these victims were noted athletes of their generation, famed as outstanding mountain walkers, who showed themselves not immune to the same kinds of fatal mistakes as other victims before them.

Saturday, June 30, 1900, was the opening day of a field meeting of the Appalachian Mountain Club, to be held on the summit of Mount Washington. The cream of the crop of White Mountain climbers converged on the top, including club president John Ritchie, Jr., Louis Cutter, Herschel Parker (later famed for his work on Mount McKinley), and J. Rayner Edmands. The veteran Randolph guides Vyron and Thaddeus Lowe came up through Tuckerman Ravine that day. The Reverend Harry Nichols and his son completed a multiday climb of then trailless Montalban Ridge. Most of the dignitaries, however, came up by stage or cog railway, because the mountain that day was wracked by ferocious storm, with high winds, low visibility, and driving rain at lower elevations, rain, sleet, and snow above treeline.

Alone of those who walked up, William B. Curtis and Allan Ormsbee chose to ascend the long Crawford Path, exposed to the full force of the storm for almost five miles over such intermediate summits as Clinton, Pleasant (Eisenhower), and Monroe. The fury of the storm may have been accepted as a challenge by the self-confident pair. "Father Bill" Curtis, then sixty-two years old, was founder of the Fresh Air Club, hailed widely as "the father of athletics in America," and celebrated for the vitality of his hiking pace. The younger Ormsbee, twenty-eight, was in the prime of his prowess and also proud of his speed over the hills.

The pair made it over each of the southern peaks, signing in at the summit registers. On Pleasant they noted: "Rain clouds and wind sixty miles—Cold." Just above there two descending hikers passed them, noted the thinness of Curtis's clothing and urged them to turn back. Neither of the ascending pair replied; perhaps even then the storm had weakened their perceptions and responses. Not far beyond Monroe, Curtis succumbed. Ormsbee continued almost to the top before he too collapsed. AMC search parties were hampered by the continuing storm throughout Sunday, but the bodies were found on Monday.

The hiking and climbing community was stunned. For the first time since the popularity of mountain walking had blossomed after 1875, the full powers of Northeastern mountain storms stood revealed. Two stronger hikers could scarcely have been named—yet even they had been unable to survive a walk up one of the standard hiking trails, in summer. Nothing could have more forcefully called attention to the seriousness of bad weather on Mount Washington.

The chain of events that followed took an unexpected direction. Spurred by a desire to prevent the recurrence of such a tragedy, the AMC constructed a sturdy wood-frame refuge, 10 feet by 10 feet, not far from the spot where Curtis had died. This shelter, erected in 1901, was announced as intended "exclusively as a refuge"—that is, it was not meant to be a regular camping spot. The AMC distributed circulars to this effect to all mountain hotels and placed a large sign on the door of the refuge itself reading "Not for pleasure camping." Despite these precautions, campers soon adopted the new shelter as a regular station on the summit cone. By the following summer, the club found it abused and damaged, and as the years went by, maintenance of the little building became a troublesome nuisance. Finally in 1915, a little lower on the ridge, the Lakes-of-the-Clouds Hut was erected as a more substantial facility, intended for regular use by summer hikers, under dependable supervision, but at the same time fulfilling the emergency functions of the older building. Thus the most popular of the AMC's high-mountain huts today owes its origin and location in part to the circumstances of this influential accident in the summer of 1900.[b]

Mount Washington was not only the first Northeastern peak to claim victims, but it continues to be by far the cruellest mountain in the region, probably because of the combined effect of its vast above-treeline exposure and its popularity. In recent years, the Adirondacks, Katahdin, and other peaks have been the scene of fatalities, but Mount Washington continues its grisly record as the number one killer. It is a grim pattern that began with Frederick Strickland, Curtis and Ormsbee, and poor Lizzie Bourne.

---

[b]Response to the Curtis-Ormsbee accident set a pattern that has recurred in subsequent incidents during the twentieth century. In the immediate aftermath of tragedy, responsible officials feel an overwhelming need to respond with action designed to deal directly with the specific events of that accident. This reaction has produced "emergency" buildings on top of Marcy, at Edmands Col in the Northern Presidentials, and at half-mile intervals along Mount Washington's auto road. In each case —as in the pattern-setting Curtis-Ormsbee incident and its resulting "emergency shelter"—the hiking public has soon adopted the building as a regular place to camp, and it has become littered and damaged. In each case mentioned, officials have eventually torn down the shelter, apparently concluding that its possible value in an emergency did not justify the environmental degradation that resulted.

Chapter 28

Trail policy issues

As recreational trails pullulated through the Northeast in the late nineteenth century, the beginnings of some thorny issues of trails policy—many of which continue to this day—tentatively surfaced. None of them was resolved during the period under discussion. Indeed none of them has been finally resolved today. But they can be identified as having been raised and discussed almost a century ago.

How civilized should a trail be? During Randolph's golden years, a friendly debate arose in the Ravine House parlor of a summer evening or out on the trails during the day. The primary antagonists were the irrepressible Eugene Cook and the great trail-builder whom the reader will meet in the next chapter, J. Rayner Edmands. At issue were the steep, rocky, ax-blazed trails of the former and the graded, smooth, well-manicured paths of the latter. This gentlemanly difference was but one facet of the larger question of how much "improvement" was appropriate in the mountain setting. This is the gut issue, of course, between the improvements and explorations points of view, but within the improvers there were important divisions.

Over at Heart Lake, Van Hoevenberg ordered his trails cut wide and well cleared, reflecting his fundamental views:

> He believed, moreover, that a tramping expedition should be made as comfortable as possible for all concerned. He was among the first to realize that the charm of unavoidable hardships is not increased by unnecessary ones, and he was most successful in demonstrating the theory. His tramping and camping parties were always provided with dainty food and the best of bedding.

At the other extreme, the trails built on Katahdin during the 1880s and 1890s were but the roughest of cuts through the north woods. Katahdin pilgrims liked them that way. Rosewell Lawrence described the old Appalachian Trail of 1887 as crossing a "wet and difficult" bog but added, "Fortunately, for it affords a view which is remarkably fine"; encountering a "quite steep" section, where "the climbing is rewarded"; and crossing the

Knife Edge on which "some actual climbing is necessary; and a cloud or gale might render the trip unsafe, especially to a novice." To the Katahdin adventurer, roughness in the track was part of the experience.

In the White Mountains, early path makers were fired with a zeal to mark the way plainly. A Portland White Mountain Club member proposed that the route between Tuckerman Ravine and the top of Mount Washington should be lined with iron posts, "with perhaps a connecting wire between them." In his first report, Nowell recommended paths 6–8 feet wide, cleared of all underbrush and trip roots, with holes filled in, and well blazed and signed. After 1900, however, AMC councillors were expressing concern not to overbuild. In the 1901 report, Parker Field argued for gradations of improvement, a spectrum ranging from trunk routes "thoroughly cleared of all incumbrances," to "simple blazed paths through the forest . . . for those who enjoy a rough scramble beside an enchanted brook." James Sturgis Pray, councillor from 1902 to 1904 was described by a young admirer named Benton MacKaye as "a pioneer in keeping improvements *out* of the wilderness" (italics in original); Mac-Kaye called one of Pray's trails "an improvementless way which was opened by the Councillor of Improvements."[a] By the term of Warren Hart, from 1908 to 1910, the pendulum in the AMC (at least as long as Hart was in charge) had swung well back. A Boston newspaper described the Great Gulf trails built then in these terms:

> Unlike most of the paths in the White Mountains these trails have not been cut to avoid obstacles or to smooth them away as much as possible; they were not designed for the pastime of curious women, and they have not been made like to the highly superfluous "boulevards" of piled stone work that a perverted energy has built here and there upon the mountains [presumably a reference to Edmands] . . . They have been content to let the roughness of forest or ledge, or boulder remain the grateful roughness that it is.

The debate was not confined to the AMC. One of the points of divergence between the Wonalancet path makers and the rebel Chocorua Mountain Club concerned the former's elegant blue signposts and meticulous blazing. The Chocorua upstarts fought to keep such improvements out of their end of the Sandwich Range.[b]

---

[a]The same young MacKaye who admired Pray's "improvementless trail" in 1897 wrote in 1921 the landmark article advocating creation of the 2,100-mile Appalachian Trail (see chap. 45). As that trail neared completion during the 1930s—built as a plainly marked and broadly cleared trail under the leadership of others than himself—MacKaye once again cried out for a more wilderness-oriented path. These issues persist.

[b]The difference of opinion endured. In a letter dated Oct. 14, 1921, the secretary of the New England Trail Conference, Arthur C. Comey, suggested impishly one possible discussion topic for a forthcoming meeting: "1. A symposium for and against the general use of color or metal for blazes. The C. M. C., W. O. D. C. and others to fight it out." (Letter to Steering Committee of NETC in the James P. Taylor Papers, Vermont Historical Society, Montpelier, Vt. Reprinted with permission.)

Private corporations permitting public use: Maine's mountains on paper company lands, the Pemigewasset Wilderness and the Mahoosucs, the latter two still owned by logging companies far into the twentieth century, before coming into the White Mountain National Forest

Private individuals or families: the Shawangunks, New York's section of the Taconics, much of the Green Mountains, and the wooded hills of Connecticut[c]

It is interesting to recall that in the East, the conservation movement came long after the physical extent of wilderness had reached its low point and was actually coming back. During the midnineteenth century, remember, northern New England had based a short-lived economic prosperity on agriculture and sheep raising, at which time many of today's sweeping forest vistas were cleared for pasture. Starr King had observed with pleasure the field of rye planted high on Moriah in the 1850s. A description of now wooded Moosilauke in 1879 refers to the upper slopes as "up where the grass grows green, where sheep and cows graze." Much of the Catskills were stripped clean by the tanning industry, and John Burroughs complained in 1894,

> The most annoying animal to the camper-out in this region, and the one he needs to be most on the lookout for, is the cow. Backwoods cows.

When Boston planners first succeeded in setting aside the Blue Hills, that now completely wooded domain was largely cleared pasture.[d] So was

---

[c]The Northeast is not unique, but the proportion of wild land that has depended for its conservation on private, rather than public, ownership is far greater here than in other regions in the United States. This may partly explain why today's national prowilderness organizations sometimes are at odds with Northeastern conservation groups. This history of acceptance of private land ownership as consistent with the cause of conservation is largely unknown and poorly understood elsewhere. Yet in the Northeast, some conservationists have held that private land can be just as effectively preserved as public. History equips them with the numerous examples cited in this chapter.

[d]The 1895 annual report of the Metropolitan Park Commission points out that every part of the Blue Hills had been cut. One substantial area, now woods, was called "the Hancock pasture"; another was referred to as "the ancient pasture on the slopes of Chickatawbut," which had been thoroughly browsed by sheep. Indeed, says the report, "With the exception of the hill tops, pools, bogs, swamps and meadows and the open or recently converted pastures, the reservation is 'sprout land' covered with stumps. . . . In other words the ground is covered with a dense thicket of brush, a crop of scrubby sticks or a forest of poles" (p. 74). See also Bacon, *Walks and Rides*, in which the north slope of Great Blue Hill is described as "gently rolling pasture" (p. 343); a viewpoint to the southwest from the same hill is portrayed as "sweeping over the beautiful expanse of meadow and cultivated land" (p. 340); and "meadows" and "pastures" are noted elsewhere on the reservation (for example, pp. 335, 342, 349). Bacon observes, "The devastation long ago begun by the axe had been continued by frequent brush fires" (p. 336). It is also noteworthy that the MPC favored retaining some of the 1890s pastures as open land and deliberately *not* allowing the woods to return, mainly through the mechanism of allowing grazing to continue: "Open growth, fragments of forest and inferior groups alone are particularly interesting in landscape. An extensive and unbroken wilderness of wood affords but a dreary prospect and an unattractive journey." (Words of early conservationist Wilson Flagg, quoted on p. 80 of the 1895 annual report.)

Mount Greylock. For New England landscape as a whole, the scene has been aptly described thus:

> By 1840, much of the New England landscape was like a photographic negative of itself before settlement; not a thick forest punctuated by small openings, but a shorn landscape with scattered tufts of trees.

Paradox as it may seem, the illusion of wildness may be far more available to today's hikers than it was to our ancestors of 100 or 125 years ago.

It was not until after the collapse of the economic systems that had cleared so much of the land that the conservationist movement began. By then—during the 1880s in New York, but the 1890s in most of New England—wild forest was beginning to come back in many places. Only then did summer visitors from a rapidly industrializing and urbanizing society start to value forest. *Then*, when new threats arose from loggers and developers, the urban-based conservationists moved to protect and preserve woods that in many cases were scarcely as old as themselves.

Chapter 32

The first mountain snowshoers

Winter climbing afforded another form of "exploration." It will be recalled (from chapter 14) that Mount Washington was not climbed in winter conditions until the 1850s and not in calendar winter until the 1860s; and yet in the 1870s men stayed on top all winter long, even maintaining a government office there. But while Washington was thus tamed, very little additional winter climbing was done until the 1880s. Then, with the formation of the AMC Snow-Shoe Section, recreational winter climbing finally began in earnest.

Apparently even Washington's neighbors in the Northern Presidentials—Adams, Jefferson, Madison—saw no winter visitors until the 1880s. In late April 1871 Professor C. H. Hitchcock and another visiting gentleman traversed the range from the summit building of Mount Washington, going over Clay and Jefferson to Mount Adams and back. This feat was duplicated by S. A. Nelson and a Boston reporter named L. L. Holden on May 6. Because both parties met snow in patches, these journeys had some of the characteristics of winter climbing above treeline. Still they can hardly be claimed as true winter ascents. Similarly with an April stroll by Nelson over to the Lakes of the Clouds, during which he may have climbed Mount Monroe. Given J. H. Huntington's adventurous spirit, it is surprising—and to the mountaineering reader, disappointing—that he never seized some favorable midwinter day to traverse the other peaks of the range.[a]

Outside the Presidentials as well, there is little evidence of winter climbing until the 1880s. As related in chapter 14, Captain Partridge's intrepid school lads camped on Ascutney in 1840. On March 13, 1872, three men climbed Mansfield and spent a couple of nights in the summit house. Independently, just three days later, two professors and eight

---

[a]During the 1880s an early AMC winter climber wrote in a Boston newspaper, "The summit of Adams has also been reached in winter, selecting a perfect day, and by starting from the house on Mt. Washington; but even that is not the same thing as attacking the mountain from its very base." It is not known whether this statement alludes to the April jaunts of the Hitchcock and Nelson parties, or to subsequent calendar winter forays by Signal Service men or others. (W.H.P. [William H. Pickering], "A Winter Ascent of Mt. Adams," *Boston Transcript*, Feb. 21, 1884, p. 6.)

students from the University of Vermont—including yet another of the ubiquitous Torrey clan, Augustus Torrey, Jr.—climbed Camel's Hump with snowshoes in a high wind but moderate temperatures, "the difficulty of the undertaking only making it more exciting"; though they considered their ascent "grand sport," they did not claim it was unprecedented. In 1876 Samuel Drake enjoyed a winter ascent of Kearsarge. In that year Sweetser wrote in his guidebook,

> The ascent of the ridges and the exploration of the ravines can then be conducted on snowshoes, the traveller gliding thus over dwarf forests and ragged rocks on a carpet-like covering of snow.

This certainly implies that winter climbing was going on, but no specific ascents are mentioned.

The reason why the extensive wintertime activity on Mount Washington is such an isolated phenomenon lies not alone in the unique attractions of the region's highest peak. One of the most difficult obstacles in winter climbing is not the windswept summit ridge, where walking can be relatively easy in good conditions, but the long approach through the steep-slope dense forest with its tremendous load of winter snows. Mounts Washington and Moosilauke each had carriage roads to their tops; so did the other peaks mentioned—Ascutney, Mansfield, Camel's Hump (road partway, bridle path the rest), and Kearsarge. Climbers can't lose the way on a road below treeline, and the wind may blow much of the snow off its upper reaches or else pack it densely enough to support weight much more easily than on a sheltered narrow trail. Since the art of snowshoeing on steep terrain was undeveloped, and skiing but an exotic Scandinavian oddity, these open graded carriage roads made Washington and Moosilauke almost uniquely accessible.

During the 1880s this situation finally changed. By a curious coincidence three snowshoeing clubs originated in the same year, the winter of 1886–87: one in Concord, New Hampshire, for which records are meager, with no evidence of mountains having been climbed; one at Williams College called the Mohican Snowshoe Club; and an AMC "Snow-Shoe Section" under the leadership of Rosewell Lawrence and John Ritchie, with forty-six charter members, twenty of whom were women. This last-named group became a major force in the earliest recreational winter mountaineering.[b]

On February 1, 1882, a group of sixteen winter pioneers boarded a specially chartered car of the Eastern Railroad at Boston. Of the eight men and eight women, the former included Samuel Scudder, the veteran Williamstown alpinist, and J. Rayner Edmands, then a thirty-one-year-old

---

[b]That formal clubs were organized suggests that informal snowshoeing had been getting more popular during the years immediately preceding 1887. The AMC's snowshoeing is known to have started at least five years earlier.

merrymaker, not the stern trail-builder of later years. The group members were transported with all their warmest clothing and their snow-shoes to the railroad depot at Glen, New Hampshire. There they transferred to two sleighs, the larger of which was described as "affording room for twelve to fourteen, if peaceably inclined." By sleigh they sped up the snow-lined road to the "comfort and cosiness" of Arden Cottage in the little town of Jackson, on the southern flanks of the Presidentials. Their outing was all in the spirit of fun and good times, not determined exploration or challenge seeking. Much of what those merry vacationers did—speeding over the snow in open sleighs, enjoying the vistas of snow-clad peaks far above them, tobogganing down long slopes by moonlight "with shouts of merry laughter and screams of delight," enjoying the warm hearths of cheery inns—sounds very like the occasional winter trip of Starr King and his contemporaries. But there are two differences of historical importance: first, they *did* climb a mountain on their snowshoes, albeit a modest 2,287-footer named Thorn Mountain, involving a moderate grade of scarcely more than 1,000 feet; and second, this was the first in a continuing series of annual winter excursions that, over the next thirty-six years, took on more and more snowshoe climbs of increasing difficulty or remoteness. By the end of this period—that is, by World War I—it had become common enough for winter climbing enthusiasts to spend Christmas vacation climbing the Northern Presidentials in much the same style as many parties do today (if without the blessings of plastic boots, freeze-dried food, and Gore-tex) and with about as high a success rate in reaching summits. In these thirty-six years, winter mountaineering passed from the isolated foray of the visionary and the eccentric to a regular pastime of the hardy outdoors set.

The new AMC outings were an instant success. In 1883 twenty-three people returned to Jackson, this time in January. The next year they chose a different base, moving to the Ravine House in Randolph.

During the 1884 Ravine House week, two of AMC's strongest "explorers," Samuel Scudder and William Pickering, attempted to climb Adams from the valley along with two other men and with Laban Watson and Hubbard Hunt as guides. They spent their first evening "discussing how and when we should make our ascent, and adjusting snowshoes." (This phrase has a modern ring: thus is spent many an evening before the big climb even today.) The redoubtable Charles Lowe dropped in to dispense advice on both issues.

On the morning of January 26, which dawned clear and cold (2 degrees above zero at the Ravine House), they set forth at 7:30 A.M. The guides carried pack-baskets for the lunches, extra clothing, and "photographic apparatus," as well as a rope for the anticipated icy slopes. Each man carried "a compass and a spirit flask—necessary appendages of the cautious pioneer." They all took turns breaking trail up Lowe's Path, the lead man displacing 6–8 inches of soft snow. As the trail steepened, "many a fall did we have, and many an ignominious backward slide, to the amusement of those behind"—indications that winter climbing has not changed over much in a century. It was well after noon before they reached treeline. Clouds had moved in from the west, and the wind had picked up noticeably. In the shelter of the last clump of low timber, they put on their heavy clothes: "Wraps and ulsters, hoods and caps." Breath froze on mustaches, beards, and eyelashes. Shortly above this point, exposed to a buffeting wind, two of the men weakened and the party decided to divide; the two stronger men (Scudder and Pickering) and one guide (Watson) continued up, while the other guide (Hunt) returned to a lower sheltered spot with the two who had tired. Scudder, Pickering, and Watson here doffed their snowshoes and donned creepers ("an iron calk armed with four sharp spikes about an inch in length . . . just in front of the heel") that had been made especially for them by a Randolph blacksmith only a day or two before. They reached the subsidiary summit known as Adams 4, at about 5,340 feet, and continued along the open plateau above toward the final summit cone. However, time was getting away from them, visibility was reduced by the blowing icy fog, and the wind was gaining strength at the higher elevations. At quarter before three, probably somewhere near the open flatland now called Thunderstorm Junction (where at present stands an outsized cairn), they reluctantly abandoned their goal. (Until Thunderstorm Junction, Lowe's Path slabs the east side of another subsidiary summit known as Sam Adams, gaining some respite from the normal northwestern winds; it seems possible that the 1884 trio made their turnaround decision as they passed out of the lee of Sam Adams into the full force of the wind on the final summit cone of Adams itself.) Once turned around, their descent was rapid, including many voluntary and involuntary glissades, and they were back at the Ravine House at 6:15, in time for dinner with their friends.

The 1884 climb is in many ways the start of "serious" recreational winter climbing. Adams became a prestigious objective for winter climbers during the late 1880s. The first recorded ascent is attributed to Charles Lowe, on February 17, 1887. Lowe apparently climbed alone, carrying "a strong staff with a pick, which he could stab into the ice." It is sad that more is not known about this historic climb. On February 21, 1889, Rosewell Lawrence and Laban Watson made the second known ascent and spent the night in the new hut at Madison Springs. On February 22 they made the first recorded winter ascent of Madison before descending to the valley. They climbed on snowshoes to treeline, then changed to creepers, with Lawrence wielding a 6-foot alpenstock. They were "in high glee" for much of the time. On Adams:

> It was growing colder, the wind was blowing, and at times it was impossible to stand against it, much less make any progress. It was an exhilarating climb, and we enjoyed the sport.

Coming off Madison into the wind the next day:

> The descent of the peak to the hut in the teeth of the wind required some gymnastics. We climbed, slid, crawled, and when we were not careful we blew and flew up hill again.

Descending to the valley, once below treeline, was pure pleasure: "We had great fun coasting down on the steep slopes, only to be buried deep in the soft snow."

During the following winter an AMC party of three women and five men, including Lawrence and Watson, spent the night at Madison Hut. On March 4, 1890, two of these women and three of the men climbed Adams. The two women who deserve credit for this significant first female winter ascent of Adams are two of the following three: Mrs. A. F. Butler, Mrs. C. H. Frank, Miss F. A. Smith; it is frustrating to historians that the records for this climb fail not only to tell us their first names, but even to say *which* two made the ascent and which one remained in the hut.[c] During the Christmas week of either 1889 or 1890, a student party made the ascent, spending the night at the hut and making a difficult escape the next day from one of the Presidentials' ferocious weather displays. Another student group made a Christmas-week ascent in 1892.

Meanwhile the AMC's Snow-Shoe Section was moving up on other fronts. During its second winter in existence, 1888, one of its parties climbed Mount Willard (February 29) and attempted 4,843-foot Carter Dome (February 27). The following year, success was achieved on the Dome, on February 16, 1889.

During the 1890s, the Snow-Shoe Section traveled each February to the White Mountains, and occasionally to Vermont, to spend a week or two climbing mountains and having fun. The latter was important—snowshoe races on the snow-covered road in front of the Ravine House, tugs-of-war, races climbing ladders in snowshoes. One evening's entertainment featured

> "the Ascent of the Mantel Horn" when hardy alpinists with rope and ice axes skirted around the upper part of the office on window casings, lintels, and the high frame of the mantel-piece in true alpine style.

They stayed at inns such as the Elliott House in Waterville (1891–92, 1898), Eagle Mountain House in Jackson (1894), and Vermont's Woodstock Inn (1893 and 1897), fine old north country establishments where the host's conviviality and cuisine were invariably praised. But climbing

---

[c] The first recorded women's winter ascent of Mount Washington was made by two of Lucy and Ethan Crawford's daughters in 1874 (Lucy Crawford, *History*, p. xix). This was a less noteworthy achievement than the Adams ascent ten years later, because by 1874 people were streaming up and down Washington in good weather. Adams was still very much a rare adventure in 1890.

peaks became an increasingly important part of the agenda. AMC snow-shoers reached the following peaks during the 1890s:

Osceola (February 19, 1891)

Tecumseh (February 23, 1891)

Sandwich Dome (February 19, 1892)

North Tripyramid (February 21, 1892)

Chocorua (December 28, 1892)

Passaconaway (December 1892)

Ascutney (February 1893)

Carrigain (February 24, 1896)

Killington (February 1897)

Tom (Vermont; February 1897)

South Tripyramid (February 1898)

Giant Stairs (February 1899)

Some of these may have been first winter ascents, though there is surely no way to be certain. Of the peaks listed, earlier winter ascents are documented only for Ascutney (1840), Osceola (late 1880s), and probably Chocorua (1891?).

If the AMC party of February 24, 1896, was the first to climb the formidable Carrigain in winter—and no earlier winter ascent is known—Miss M. A. Furbish's presence in the seven-person party merits special observance. The reader should recall the obstacles confronting women winter climbers of that day, from the social restraints to the physical handicap of long skirts, which must have been frightfully heavy and awkward as the hems became coated with ice and snow. Considering these obstacles, Furbish's participation in such a difficult first winter ascent as Carrigain is extraordinary. Ample other historical evidence tells us that at least two of the men in the party, Rosewell Lawrence and Herschel Parker, were exceptionally strong winter climbers. Evidently Furbish was too. Women were also on the first winter ascent of North Tripyramid in 1892. Women climbed just about everything the men did during the early days of the AMC Snow-Shoe Section.

Some of these climbs were mass assaults—twenty-five climbers on Ascutney, thirty-six on Killington—though the more difficult pioneering climbs were usually made by parties of four or five, often with a local guide along.

North Tripyramid may have been the scene of the discovery of that notorious evil spirit that plagues winter climbers at roughly the 4,000-

foot level where so many dwarf evergreens are covered with snow—the spruce trap. When snow drifts over the branches of a small tree it does not consolidate nearly as much as it does on surrounding terrain. The unwary snowshoer who passes over such a hidden tree may plummet instantly to nearly the full depth of the tree, in extreme cases sinking over his or her head. The branches of the tree then interlock around the snowshoe in intricate patterns that so defy efforts at extrication that some unhappy victims have started rumors of malignant snow-dwarves who dwell at the bottom of spruce traps and wrap chains around snowshoes that fall their way. On February 21, 1892, atop North Tripyramid occurred history's first documented incident of a spruce trap:

> Stepping on the top of one tree that projected above the snow, one of the party went down almost out of sight, and it took considerable floundering to get out again.

By around 1900 winter climbing in the White Mountains had spread beyond the AMC's Snow-Shoe Section. Moriah's summit register showed ascents on November 20, 1898, and December 23, 1899, neither by AMC parties. Wonalancet publications of that period advertise the availability of camps for winter climbers on Whiteface, Passaconaway, and Sandwich Dome. Gordon H. Taylor blazed several trails in the Sandwich Range specifically for snowshoers, one of which became far more popular as a summer hiking trail, the Blueberry Ledges Trail. In Waterville the Elliotts opened special accommodations for winter climbers in 1901. Beginning in the winter of 1902–3, Philbrook Farm Inn guests began to do some winter climbing in the Mahoosucs, under the lead of F. G. Goodale and P. R. Parker. In 1904 the AMC's councillor of improvements cited demand for a closed cabin in Carter Notch as a base for winter climbing. By 1905 a Boston newspaper was calmly assuring its readers, "Winter mountain climbing in New England is extremely invigorating, seldom dangerous and always interesting."

Beginning in 1899 the Snow-Shoe Section settled down to stay at Jackson, where they had started seventeen years earlier, and made the Iron Mountain House their regular base every year from then until the group disbanded in 1919. However, they sometimes made a second trip to some other location. Noteworthy climbs in the years just after 1900 included:

Wildcat (February 23, 1903)—possibly the first time since old Bill Perkins more than fifty years before, by six men and two women

The west peak of Wildcat, known to today's 4,000-foot peakbaggers as Wildcat E (February 26, 1904)

A traverse of both Wildcats (February 22, 1905)

A traverse of Washington, up the Carriage Road and over the range (omitting other summits, however) and down to Randolph (January 26, 1905)

A traverse of Adams and Madison, up from Randolph and down the Osgood Ridge to the Glen House (January 22–23, 1906)

A traverse of Washington, up Huntington Ravine and down through the Gulf of Slides (1906)

Mount Pleasant (today's Eisenhower; February 1906)

Field (February 22, 1907)

Isolation (February 26, 1910)

The sociability of the group reached a high point during the early years of the century, with parties of 54 climbing Clinton together in 1902, 80 ascending Thorn on one day in 1904, and 84 people at least starting up Wildcat together in 1911 (though not all made it to the top). More than 100 people signed up for the Iron Mountain House stays of 1902 through 1904 and again in 1907 and 1909, with highs of 141 people in 1910 and 134 in 1911. Obviously these were not all gung-ho climbers, and the pure fun quotient remained high. "The exciting ride down the four miles of the Carriage Road (starting from treeline at the Halfway House) on a tandem toboggan" highlighted the 1911 sojourn at Mount Madison House in Gorham. Some of the noteworthy individuals who attending outings included Frank Mason and Willard Helburn, both of whom were instrumental in the start of rock climbing; and one who became a mainstay and superstar of the Snow-Shoe Section, Herschel C. Parker.

Parker, who later rose to mountaineering fame for his pioneering climbs in the Canadian Rockies and attempts on Mount McKinley, used the Presidential Range in winter as his principal training ground, as so many alpinists have since. Parker made eleven winter ascents of Washington, mostly during the last decade of the nineteenth century, by such various routes as the carriage road, the cog railway tracks, Tuckerman Ravine, the northern peaks, and the Crawford Path. He made five other unsuccessful attempts during this period, proving his words of warning: "The terrible storms that sometimes rage about the summit . . . constitute a menace that even the strongest climbers should never face."

Like many subsequent climbers who spent a lot of time in the Presidentials, Parker had his share of adventures, some in epic proportions. One ticklish moment occurred when he was alone, having undertaken, on December 31, 1890, to climb Mount Washington from Gorham via the carriage road. He broke trail through extremely soft snow, a very fatiguing effort, getting only as far as the Halfway House, where he passed a solitary night. On New Year's Day in threatening and heavy clouds, he continued on. "It may interest friends who have accompanied me on some of my later climbs," he wrote, "to know that I had no ice-creepers or alpenstock of any description, that I wore moccasins of the softest and lightest kind, and was further handicapped by wearing an overcoat." While crossing one of the huge drifts that covered the carriage road, Parker slipped, dropping one of the snowshoes that he had been carrying under his arm, and slid out of reach of it. "Here was a very unpleasant situation," he wrote.

> I could not keep my footing on the icy snow in order to climb up and reach the shoe, neither could I return through the deep soft snow on the lower portion of the carriage road without it. Luckily I remembered that I had a large pocket knife with me, and by means of this I was able to cut steps in the hardened snow, and so regain the shoe.

Despite low visibility and high winds, Parker succeeded on this solo ascent.

In 1894, he was rebuffed by ill weather on another attempt to ascend the carriage road, but two days later (February 22, 1894) he walked up the cog railway track with ease.

Parker saw Tuckerman Ravine in winter as a splendid gymnasium for practicing "real alpine work." After one unsuccessful attempt in December 1894, he returned that February and succeeded in scaling the headwall of Tuckerman's, reaching the summit at 4:50, and descending the railway in gathering darkness, followed by "a long dark walk" out to his inn at midnight. Three times in later winters (1895, 1896, 1899), Parker made ascents of the famous headwall.

At the end of December 1896, Parker and his frequent climbing companion Dr. Ralph C. Larrabee walked up to Madison Hut and spent the night. The next day, fine and clear, with mild temperatures, they grabbed the opportunity to cross all the northern summits, arriving at Washington at 1:00 P.M. Then they proceeded down the Crawford Path and out over the southern summits, not getting to Crawford Notch until 7:25, as they were delayed by ice on the summit cone of Washington. Parker noted, "This was, perhaps, the first time that a complete traverse of the Great Range [the Presidentials] had been made in winter." If that is the case, Parker and Larrabee deserve credit for accomplishing the very first winter Presidential traverse, a plum destined to become a status symbol for many succeeding generations of winter mountaineers.

In February 1899, Parker and a Mr. Holmes started up the Mount Washington carriage road in perfectly still and mild weather. At the Halfway House all was serene, but at the 6-mile post it began to snow, and the last 2 miles to the top were "a desperate struggle against the terrible wind and flying cloud and snow."

Almost blinded by the stinging frost and exhausted by the fierce wind, we had just strength to reach the summit and enter the stage office. Here a most uncomfortable night was spent. The wind blew with hurricane force, the chains pounded like sledge-hammers against the roof, and at times the building, quivering in every timber, seemed about to be blown to pieces.

In the morning they made good their escape, the wind having moderated somewhat, and descended to the valley that they found to be as still and warm as when they had left it, "with no indication of the terrible storm that was raging just above."

Parker made two more climbs of note in the Presidentials. One, on February 19, 1901, was to ascend Washington by way of the Crawford Path, which, he wrote, "had seemed to me the most dangerous way, not only on account of its great length, but also because there is no practical way by which a descent to the valley can be made along its entire extent." Parker's three companions on this venture were each strong individuals: Alec Newhall and Alfred Haskell were mainstays of winter climbing then, Newhall having been (with Parker) on the first winter ascent of Carrigain; and George N. Whipple participated in some difficult ascents, including one of the Great Gulf headwall.

Parker's last significant climb in the Presidentials almost turned into a one-day traverse. Since the party did not reach Washington's summit until 3:25 P.M., they judged it too late to continue, coming down by the railroad instead and continuing to Fabyan's that night—still a pretty big day. The coveted one-day winter traverse lay in the future. It was not to occur for more than a decade.

Chapter 33

Winter pioneering on Mount Marcy

FIRST winter ascents—like the summer ascents—came late to the Adirondacks. Not until 1893 is there any record of Mount Marcy's being climbed in winter. Even the remarkably tough and adventurous surveyor of the 1870s, Verplanck Colvin, and those hardy woodsmen-guides of his era—Bill Nye, Alvah Dunning, Old Mountain Phelps, and the rest—could not conceive of withstanding winter on Marcy. Colvin and his guides made many of their pioneering ascents in October and November, however, and coped with some winterlike conditions. When Colvin and Old Mountain Phelps climbed 4,736-foot Gothics on October 11, 1875, it was in a temperature of 22 degrees, with high winds and "glary slopes of ice" covering the steep summit ridge. Descent was the more terrifying in gathering darkness. In the winter of 1877 Colvin and his survey crew spent two weeks in February snowshoeing around the woods and lakes southwest of the high peaks. This was an adventurous winter camping trip, but they climbed only one peak, the broad, low, forested ridge of Seventh Lake Mountain. In late 1882 and even into January of 1883, Colvin's chief assistant Mills Blake was at work in the field, occupying stations on peaks such as Gore, Mount Snowy, and Balm of Gilead—not 4,000-footers to be sure, but substantial mountains nonetheless.

But to Colvin and his post–Civil War contemporaries, winter in the high peaks was a time of unimaginable cold, snow, and wind, a time of furious storms and arctic blasts that no one could possibly survive.[a]

The rise of winter climbing in the White Mountains—and not in the Adirondacks—can be explained by several forces. The White Mountains by this time had spawned a sizable hiking community during the summer months, well organized by the Appalachian Mountain Club. Washington and other high peaks were not as far in sheer mileage from well-traveled roads as Marcy, Haystack, and most Adirondack high peaks. The

---

[a]A curious point is that Colvin's most active period of explorations came right on the heels of Huntington's winterings-over on Moosilauke and Washington. Colvin must have known about those White Mountains winter exploits, yet there is no mention of them in his writings. In all his speculation about how fierce winter must be on Marcy, he does not draw on the obvious examples so readily provided by Huntington's experience.

White Mountains as a range were closer and more accessible to a big city (Boston) than the Adirondacks. There were better roads, more convenient train connections, and more comfortable winter inns. Carriage roads to the tops of Washington and Moosilauke, not to mention hospitable buildings on top, made these winter ascents more feasible. Not least among the causes must be listed the vision of J. H. Huntington and others who pulled off the winter occupations of Moosilauke and Washington: that bold stroke must have fired the imaginations of New England's potential winter adventure seekers in a way that was not paralleled west of Lake Champlain.

These are some of the reasons why it was not until 1893 that Mount Marcy or any other great Adirondack peak was climbed in winter. In that year John W. Otis was employed as forester and game warden for the Adirondack Mountain Reserve. He was stationed for the winter at a camp on the Upper Ausable Lake, 9 long miles over snow and frozen lake from the nearest road. Benjamin Pond also worked for the AMR that winter, stationed at a clubhouse on the road. The two men spent much of that winter snowshoeing around the woods as they performed their duties. In view of what they did on Marcy and the route they took, it is worth noting that this winter happened to have more snow than usual. "As I look back," Pond later wrote, "it seemed to me that I never before experienced such cold weather and deep snow as we had in that region that winter."

One evening in late winter the pair snowshoed into Otis's camp. That night, over their dinner, they joked about climbing Marcy on the next clear day. As though the mountain gods sought to call their bluff, the very next morning, March 18, dawned cold (-18 degrees) but crystal clear and without a breath of a breeze: perfect weather for the job. So, after an ample breakfast of flapjacks and syrup, sausage and coffee, the two woodsmen set out to make good their banter of the night before. They made no effort to stay on the trail over the Bartlett Ridge down into Panther Gorge (see figure 33.1) so confident had they become at making their way in the woods. Panther Gorge is notorious for being one of the snowiest places in the Adirondacks, as snow blowing off the bare summits of surrounding Marcy, Haystack, and Skylight seems to know no other place to go. Finding tougher going then, they snowshoed slowly up Marcy Brook, estimating the snow to be as much as 10–12 feet deep at the head of the gorge, until they reached the high col between the windswept summit cones of Marcy and Skylight.

At treeline they took off their snowshoes and proceeded carefully to pick their way up on a crust that was all "covered with a thick coating of glistening ice." Here, wrote Pond, finding the "climbing was exceedingly difficult and hazardous," they chopped steps in the ice with an "ax"— doubtless a woodsman's ax, *not* the climber's tool. But lack of crampons or a proper ice ax did not stop this pair, and at high noon they stood on Marcy's summit, windless and sunny on this rare climbing day.

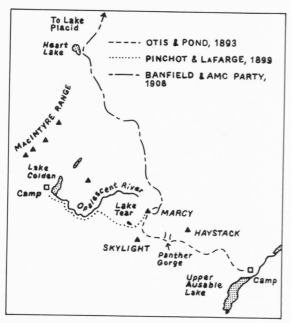

Figure 33.1. Pioneering winter ascents of Mount Marcy, 1893–1908 Mount Marcy was not climbed in winter until 1893, when two employees of the Adirondack Mountain Reserve (AMR) snowshoed up from the southeast. The second successful ascent was from the west, involving two figures destined for future fame, Gifford Pinchot and Grant LaFarge. The route most commonly used in winter today—the Van Hoevenberg Trail from the northwest—was not ascended until 1908, by a visiting party of climbers from the Appalachian Mountain Club, including the first woman to climb Marcy in winter.

Three years later Otis ran into two young men on their way toward the Marcy trail in late winter, intending to make the ascent and camp at the col between Marcy and Skylight. Otis went as far as the start of the trail up Shanty Brook and gave them what advice he could. Two days later, however, the men showed up in Keene Valley and reported they had not reached the top.

The second recorded winter ascent of Marcy was not to come for six years. The big mountain was climbed then from the west, and everything about this ascent provided contrast with the straightforward snowshoe of Pond and Otis.

To begin with, the cast of characters was composed not of modest local woodsmen with their ax, but of two distinguished personages of the day. C. Grant LaFarge was from a renowned Boston family of wealth and position, several members of which contributed significantly to American arts and letters over the course of a century. Gifford Pinchot served as chief of the U.S. Forest Service, later twice as governor of Pennsylvania, and his farsighted policies and concern for conservation won him the sobriquet Father of American Forestry.

In February 1899 these two plus an English friend named Lethbridge arranged to spend a week at a camp located on Lake Colden, which was inaccessible by road and thus guaranteed for privacy. As for climbing Marcy, LaFarge wrote, "We allowed that project to subside into a sort of mild joke; each of us, I think quite convinced that the other was not going to let him fail to have a try at it."

For most of the week, unfavorable weather gave little chance for any such venture, but the idea nevertheless gained hold on their minds. At length, despite a morning when the "gale was still raging and the cold bitter," LaFarge, Pinchot, and two local guides set out up the Opalescent River toward Lake Tear-of-the-Clouds (see figure 33.1). All morning they snowshoed up the steep grade, at noon reaching the tiny lake, frozen and so deep in snow it looked more like a clearing in the forest than the highest wellspring of the great Hudson River. While they were fortifying themselves with lunch, LaFarge "heard a brief exclamation from Pinchot, indicating that in his opinion it would be no great task to go on to the end, to which I instantly assented."

They had underestimated the difficulties that lay ahead. The cold and wind sharpened as they climbed through the final scrub growth. The roar of the gale meant they had to shout to be heard. Above Lake Tear they encountered a breakable crust, that worst of snowshoeing conditions in which the surface is hard and slippery at one step and breaks through at the next. The four men foundered in many a spruce trap. In turn, the guides found good and sufficient reason to bow out, one claiming his snowshoes were too long to maneuver in the thickets, the other testifying one leg had gone numb.

Now Pinchot and LaFarge were on their own in the ferocious wintry environment of New York's highest mountain in a begrudging mood. When the pair reached firmer ground they took off their snowshoes, tying them securely to the top of a fir just sticking through the snow.

Upward they pushed. "The wind was no more to be faced than a battery of charging razors; and to stand upright in it was more than we cared to attempt," wrote LaFarge. Reduced to crawling on "all fours," they groped slowly up the icy slopes "with only occasional patches of snow or little projecting tips of rock to afford hold for hands and knees." At the stronger blasts "we lay prone at full length and buried our faces in our folded arms, . . . and hoped not to be dislodged from that precarious holding. . . . The cold was such as I had not ever imagined."

It finally became too much for LaFarge. Only 200 feet below the swirling summit he knew his feet were freezing and "I simply could no longer stand the cold, which was benumbing my whole body." Leaving Pinchot to go on alone, LaFarge crawled down to the snowshoes, tramped a hole in the snow, "and proceeded by stamping my feet to restore circulation to them." He could just make out his friend on Marcy's high slopes, "creeping upward with many pauses."

Somehow Pinchot forced his way up to the signal pole marking the highest point and even took a photograph of it. "On the topmost rock of Tahawus he had felt the unbroken weight of the merciless gale, and everything from New Hampshire to North Carolina was beneath him. But of it he saw nothing, for the panorama was hidden by the stinging drift."

They hesitated little on the descent. All four were back together at Lake Tear by 2:30 P.M. and down to the warm and welcoming camp on Lake Colden before dark.

Nine years passed before the next new winter route on Marcy. The venerable Appalachian Mountain Club, whose members had been accumulating considerable winter climbing experience in the White Mountains during the 1880s and 1890s, made their first jaunts to the Adirondacks in the winters of 1908 and 1909, lodging at the Lake Placid Club. In 1908, this group succeeded in making what may have been only the fourth winter ascent of Marcy, and the first known climb from the northwest, by far the most common route today.

In anticipation of the AMC party's arrival, Lake Placid Club leaders expressed the belief that "nothing will do more for mountain lovers and for the members of this great mountain club." That the AMC's style of winter outings was new to the Adirondacks was indicated when "our oldest guide said he had never been on a winter picnic before, but that it was the most enjoyable he had ever shared in." The appreciative club concluded, "The Appalachians brought the spirit of real mountain lovers, and left an inspiration for our own 'mountain climbing section,' which will be organized this year."

The northwest approaches to Marcy were being logged heavily at the time, and the AMC snowshoers were able to turn this fact to advantage. After two men devoted a day to finding where the trail left the edge of the logging operation, they were able to arrange to ride horse-drawn sleighs into this point.

Accordingly, at 8:40 A.M. on January 14, 1908, two groups—one of six men, the other of about twenty, including several women—departed the Lake Placid Club, traveling 12 miles to the lumber camp at the foot of Marcy. The advance guard of six then set out swiftly on the trail, the others following behind. At treeline they met "a gale so strong that it was almost impossible to face it." These odds forced four of the men to turn back, leaving Lewis Wells and D. A. Harrington to tackle the job alone.

But as Harrington and Wells were moving up over the ice and packed snow on Marcy's north side, they were overtaken by Laura Banfield and Alec Newhall, the only two out of the second party of twenty who had persevered to attempt the summit. These two took a somewhat more southeasterly course to gain the peak, for although it was steeper it was more in the lee of the terrific wind that was sweeping relentlessly down on Wells and Harrington. With the advantage that this tactic provided, the second pair actually passed the first, and at 4:10 P.M. Laura Banfield stepped on the summit of New York's highest mountain. As Wells proudly wrote, she thereby became

> the first woman on record to ascend Mount Marcy in winter, the first member of our party to arrive, and the only lady in it who ventured above tree-line. Mr. Newhall arrived immediately after, and Mr. Harrington and myself, after a futile attempt to ascend by way of the ridge, followed their route up the steep incline and reached the top at 4:15.

As the Lake Placid Club had hoped, the AMC snowshoers' visit touched off a time of enthusiasm for winter sports at Lake Placid. In 1904 a wintertime social and outings group had been formed at the Lake Placid Club. Emboldened by the AMC group's example, these and others began climbing neighboring Whiteface as well as Marcy and other Adirondack peaks, usually on snowshoes.[b] Still, ascents of such magnitude remained rare at first. The early Lake Placid group confined itself mostly to skating, tobogganing, and modest snowshoeing and skiing around the club.

Scattered reports of Adirondack winter or near winter climbs may be found during the first decade of this century. An Easter 1901 ascent of Dix by J. B. Burnham, a December 1903 ascent of Marcy via the fresh-cut Johns Brook trail, a February 1910 ascent from the Ausable Lakes (repeating the first winter ascent route), a March 1910 (?) climb of Giant by Ed Isham and a New York Athletic Club wrestler trying to lose weight, not to mention some early ski ascents (which will be covered in the next chapter): these attest a gradual spread of the spirit of exploration into the winter season in the land of the Cauchsachrage, a spiritual heritage of the boldness of Charles Brodhead and of Redfield and Emmons.

---

[b]This was not the first winter ascent of Whiteface: two high school boys snowshoed up on February 22, 1905, and claimed a first winter ascent (letter from A. L. Goff to the *Post & Gazette* [city and page unidentified], Feb. 27, 1905, in Comstock Scrapbooks [item no. 151], archives, Keene Valley Library).

Chapter 34

The first mountain skiers

When the AMC's Snow-Shoe Section romped at the Eagle Mountain House in Jackson, New Hampshire, in February 1888 (see chapter 32), the members found that a previous guest of the house, from Norway, had left there "a pair of skees." The snowshoers were curious, amused, but baffled by these "foreign shoes." Early experiments on them foundered helplessly, affording

> ample opportunity to study the principles of mathematics and physics. When the skees mark out for themselves divergent tracks, and are permitted to follow their divided purposes, the resultant force is always in the vertical and downward. When this fact has been proven experimentally, the skees, freed from their limiting tendencies, skim like birds over the snow to the lowest possible level, each after its own fancy, forming in a twinkling an isosceles triangle with the late passenger at the apex. At Jackson there was usually the choice of wading in the deep snow, rolling on the light crust, going around by the road, or having some one on snowshoes assemble the separated elements.

Eventually one persistent "Skee-man" mastered, after several false tries, a run down the toboggan slide, compared with which the toboggan "seemed but a tame affair."

For the earliest winter climbers, snowshoes were the only way to cope with deep soft snow. The idea of floating over the top on long boards seemed preposterous.

Despite a long and honorable history in Scandinavia, skis were unknown in North America until 1881, when they were reported in Montreal. In 1885 a Pennsylvania Railroad engineer designed his own skis, 8 feet long, made of ash (the traditional snowshoe wood), with corrugated rubber attachments for ascents. In the famed blizzard of 1888, the brother of this fellow is said to have introduced skis to New York City, skiing over the snow-covered Brooklyn Bridge and up Broadway to Herald Square. Sometime around 1892 a Canadian visitor amazed the locals of the Saranac Lake region with his rapid glides through the Adirondack woods. About the same year, a Dartmouth medical student was using skis around Hanover but did not recall seeing anyone else with a pair in town.

By 1900 a Montreal Ski Club had been formed, and in 1904 two hundred pairs of skis were estimated to be in use in Montreal. By this time skis were surfacing more regularly south of the border as well. Skis were reasonably common in Hanover around the turn of the century, and boys who couldn't afford the real thing careened down the slopes of the golf course on barrel staves. Over in Vermont, during the years between 1902 and 1905, as one veteran of that period recalled,

> A few of us took two hardwood boards and bent up one end by soaking them in hot sawdust. We then nailed some toestraps about the center and thought we were ready to ski.

Commercial skis were available by then from sources in Minnesota, where Scandinavians had settled more thickly. The price seemed steep: two gentlemen from Schenectady, New York, ordered skis in 1898 for $3.75 per pair and demanded a lower price the following year.

At some date, which local historians have been unable to pin down, a group of young Scandinavians who had come to live in Berlin, New Hampshire, formed the Nansen Ski Club. Membership was limited at first only to Scandinavians, but later the rules were amended to allow "any young man of good character" able to pay the annual dues of fifty cents. Though Berlin is within sight of the Presidential Range, no evidence is found that the club or its members took much interest in mountain skiing. Their chief preoccupation was ski jumping, and they built several "slides" for jumps. Berlin remained a ski-jumping center for years.[a]

The man for whom the Berlin club was named, Fridtjof Nansen, is sometimes regarded as having given the greatest single boost to popular interest in skiing in those early days. Nansen's polar explorations and especially his crossing of the Greenland ice cap in 1888 made him a hero widely publicized in the United States, and his use of skis was much discussed. A Norwegian, Nansen himself made a visit to the United States in 1912 and gave some demonstrations of his skiing around Lake Placid, including an ascent of Whiteface mountain.

By the end of the first decade of the twentieth century, skiing was no longer a novelty in the Northeast. Climbing *mountains* on skis, nonetheless, was apparently still unheard of. However, several independent but

---

[a]The origin of the Nansen Ski Club is placed by some as early as 1872, by others as late as 1905, with 1883 also mentioned. The 1872 date seems early for the name at least, as young Fridtjof was but eleven years old then. Isolated references to notes left by Scandinavians on the top of 3,860-foot Goose Eye in the Mahoosucs hint that possibly one or more of the Nansen Ski Clubbers got out to the mountains at least by 1910 or 1912, but again no hard evidence exists. See J. K. Wright, "Northern Mahoosucs: 1910–1911," *Appalachia* (Dec. 1965), p. 640.

nearly simultaneous pioneers in Hanover, Schenectady, and Lake Placid were about to show what heights could be reached on the magic boards.

Fred Harris and the Dartmouth Outing Club

In New England the long, snowy winters at Dartmouth College provided a logical arena for the new sport. Indeed, Dartmouth pundits had been wondering aloud as early as 1896 why students didn't take better advantage of winter's challenges. "How strange it is," editorialized *The Dartmouth*," that more interest is not given to snow shoeing here." College officials worried about student inactivity when "winter has finally closed in upon us and deprived us of all our varied out door sports." There was much deploring of "stuffy rooms, hot stoves, card games, and general sluggishness resulting from a lack of exercise."

Into this stale setting came a freshman from Brattleboro, Vermont, in the fall of 1907 by the name of Fred Harris. Harris was a fine tennis player who won tournaments for the Big Green during his Dartmouth years (1907–11), but that's not why his name enters these pages. Besides his tennis racket, Harris brought with him to college a pair of 9-foot skis, with a single pole of equal length, having already mastered their use around the hills near Brattleboro.

During his first two years at college, Harris skied alone across the rolling slopes around the outskirts of Hanover and set up his own "homemade ski jump" in back of Davison's farm. But he was not by nature a loner. When the winter of 1909–10 came around, Harris wrote a letter to *The Dartmouth*, printed on December 7, 1909, in which he changed history. That letter proposed "a ski and snowshoe club" to stimulate college interest in "out-of-door winter sports" and outlined a program of weekly cross-country runs on skis, one long excursion ("say to Mooselac"), construction of a ski jump and contests thereon, and a winter carnival with ski and snowshoe races, as well as gala social festivities. "By taking the initiative," Harris exuded, "Dartmouth might well become the originator of a branch of college organized sport hitherto undeveloped by American colleges." Prophetic words.

In January 1910 sixty students responded to Harris's call for an organizing meeting. The Dartmouth Outing Club was created and Harris elected its first president. Several faculty members endorsed the idea, and the DOC soon had official college blessing, which it has enjoyed ever since. Outings began immediately, led by the spirited Harris, meets and races were held, and the first Dartmouth Winter Carnival was staged in 1911. Harris himself set the first Dartmouth ski jump record with a prodigious leap of 60 feet. In less than ten years the Outing Club was a Dartmouth institution, and one magazine painted this picture of the Big Green student:

When a Dartmouth freshman enters college, the first thing he buys are textbooks. Then, likely enough, he joins the DOC and 10 minutes later is in a sporting goods outfitter's store picking out a pair of skis. . . . Of course he has no immediate use for these but somehow a Dartmouth student doesn't feel exactly at home unless he owns a pair.

Harris was the man of the hour:

Not only the founder of the club but he was its foster-father, wet nurse, Treasury Department and about everything else you can think of, up to the time that the club was an assured success and intercollegiately known.

As an undergraduate Harris threw himself into making the DOC a success. Ceaselessly he preached the new gospel of ski: "If snowshoeing be the prose, then skiing is the poetry of winter sports," he pealed. Besides leading the outings and organizing the events, he supplied a steady barrage of press releases to both college and community press. He lined up interesting speakers, including one from the AMC Snow-Shoe Section (John Ritchie, Jr.). Wrote one admirer:

For two whole winters it was Fred who routed the lazy out into the drifts; kept *The Dartmouth* and the New England dailies supplied with Outing Club news; shouldered personally impeding financial difficulties; injected huge blocks of his enthusiasm into every wavering tyro, and of a weekend was always on hand in person to lead away from Dartmouth Hall. But now, from some near vantage point, he sees a *college* out on trails where two score months ago meagre and lonesome tracks were all that broke the surface of the hills.

In 1911 Harris led a seven-man DOC attempt on Mount Washington that was turned back by ferocious weather. Harris wore skis, the others snowshoes. They went up the carriage road as far as the Halfway House without difficulty. Above that Harris and another student drew away from the pack. The others soon turned back in the face of the terrible weather, but Harris and the other youth struggled on as far as Nelson Crag before giving up. On the descent Harris showed one advantage of skis, by whooshing down the 4 miles below the Halfway house in just fourteen minutes. ("Fourteen minutes is the record. Fourteen spills is *not* the record," commented an admiring DOC neophyte, Nat Goodrich.) An experienced snowshoer from the Ravine House, C. T. Jones, accompanied by another DOCer, went up to check on Harris's safety, and by taking a shortcut passed him without knowing it; these two reached the summit before descending, giving Jones the honor of being the first DOC member to climb Washington in winter on a college outing club trip.

In 1913, as a graduate, Harris was back to forge the way for a seven-teen-man DOC party to reach the top. Harris and two others went all the way on skis, claiming a first ski ascent of Mount Washington.[b]

Other firsts followed: Carl E. Shumway, another early DOC president, and G. S. Foster skied all the way from Hanover to the summit of Moosilauke in three days, and then skied back by a different itinerary. This was claimed as the first ski ascent of Moosilauke. Shumway also skied up Monadnock. Other mountains near Hanover, such as Cube, Smart, and Moose, were often climbed on early DOC trips.

Not every mountain objective was attained. In 1919 a DOC leader, Sherman Adams, and three buddies attempted a ski traverse of the new Monroe Skyline section of the Long Trail, from Middlebury Gap north toward Camel's Hump, a 43-mile trip to be completed in four days. Like many a collegiate dream, this proved far more than they could accomplish, especially when they encountered 20-below weather and deep-drifted snow. After a couple of cold nights and very little progress the trip was aborted—"obviously a foolhardy venture to begin with," recalled Adams sixty-two years later.

As a graduate, Harris continued to support and stimulate the growth of the DOC and raised a lot of alumni financial support, which guaranteed the permanence of the club. Other alumni soon joined, the most notable being a generous enthusiast named John E. Johnson, whose munificence enlarged the original DOC shack at the foot of Moose Mountain into a chain of cabins throughout the hills from south of Hanover to Moosilauke and beyond.

The Dartmouth Outing Club was the first place on record where people thought of climbing New England mountains on skis. Harris was the first up a peak on skis, and his fourteen-minute glide down the bottom of the carriage road presaged a future downhill ski movement that would one day change the economy and spirit of north country winters.

Langmuir, Apperson, and the General Electric skiers

Almost simultaneously with the start of skiing in New England mountains, two separate circles of Adirondack skiers took up the sport as well.

---

[b]For earlier claims to the first ski ascent of Mount Washington, documentation is slender. These include an 1899 ascent by a "Dr. Wiskott" of Germany, cited by Dudley in *60 Centuries* (p. 61), for which Dudley says merely: "This information was given by C. J. Luther, editor of *Der Winter*." F. A. Burt, in *The Story of Mount Washington* (Hanover, N.H.: Dartmouth Publications, 1960), credits a February 16, 1905, ascent by Norman Libby of Bridgton, Maine, but contemporary accounts in a Gorham, New Hampshire, weekly, *The Mountaineer* ("Skiing on Mount Washington," Feb. 22, 1905, p. 1, and "Up Mt. Washington on Skiis [sic]," March 8, 1905, p. 1), indicate that Libby wore skis, with a piece of water-soaked burlap frozen under each foot, only to ascend to treeline—on the tracks of the Cog Railway!—at which point he switched to creepers for the summit cone. Libby also skied to the Halfway House on the carriage road several times for the joys of skiing down the lower 4 miles, giving that popular pastime an early precedent.

One centered on the General Electric Company in Schenectady, New York, the other on the Lake Placid Club.

Irving Langmuir is best known to the world as the Nobel Prize winner for chemistry in 1932. He spent a long and creative scientific career at the research laboratory of the General Electric Company in Schenectady. Less well known is Langmuir's lifelong secondary interest in vigorous outdoor exercise, mountain climbing, and conservation.

Though raised primarily in Brooklyn, young Irving spent three years as a teenager in Paris, where vacations gave him a taste for the Alps. As a graduate student in Germany, his interest in climbing continued, and it was here that he first learned of "Norwegian snowshoes" (skis) and ordered a pair. Soon "every minute he could spare from lectures he practiced skiing" and introduced many fellow students to the subtle art of the long boards. In 1906, back in the United States, Langmuir began skiing up Northeastern mountains in the winter of 1906–7, making him the first American ski climber of whom any record can be found. On February 23, 1907, he skied up the Wittenberg in the Catskills. The following winter, he skied up Greylock. In 1909 Langmuir moved to Schenectady. At first he indulged his hobby of hiking in the nearby Helderberg hills, later in the Lake George area and the Adirondacks. Through an associate from General Electric, he met Dan Beard, who was then launching the scouting movement. Langmuir started a Boy Scout troop that camped and rambled all over the Helderbergs.

In the fall of 1910, Langmuir had the unaccustomed experience of encountering a fellow GE employee with whom he could not keep up on a hike. This was John S. Apperson. A most extraordinary character, Apperson had come from the South and studied unsuccessfully at the Virginia Military Institute, class of 1889, where he either quit or was expelled, whereupon he went to Schenectady because his brother had a job there. He soon fell in love with the woods and hills of New York State and became thoroughly at home on his own in the backcountry. For the rest of his long life, he roamed the Adirondacks and the hills around Lake George. Said one observer:

> "Appie" was a tall, rugged bachelor who possessed legendary stamina and an Indian's knowledge of woodlore. Throughout his long life he disdained to take any bride but the wilderness.

Later the strong-willed Apperson became a major conservation advocate, fighting for the maintenance of wilderness in upper New York State with vigor and controversy.

Back in 1910, however, Apperson and Langmuir became close friends through their shared love of hiking and the great hill country in which both were so much at home. Langmuir introduced Apperson to skiing and in turn Appie brought the scientist to the Adirondacks. The pair formed the nucleus of a Schenectady group of outdoorsmen who grew to be proficient in the use of the "Norwegian snowshoes."

Scattered sources over the years have claimed a ski ascent of Marcy in 1908; some of these rumors credit Apperson, some Langmuir. However, the sources for such an early date for either man have but slender claims to authenticity.

The date that is now accepted for the earliest ski ascent of Marcy is 1911. In that year Apperson teamed up with Jean Canivet and a third Schenectady man (Paskey?) to ascend essentially the same route as that of the 1908 AMC party. Glass slides now preserved at the Adirondack Research Center in the Schenectady Museum show the skiers at a lumber camp en route and, clad in capelike ponchos that served as windbreakers, on the Marcy summit cone.

Just what else they climbed in those early years was unfortunately not systematically documented. Apperson's papers indicate that he had been up Marcy in winter on at least two occasions before 1915; that he climbed Washington in winter in 1912 and again in 1914; that he skied up Greylock via the Cheshire Harbor Trail in 1914, descending "by a fine coast down to the Hopper and out to Williamstown"; and that he skied two other mountains near Greylock, Prospect and the one he knew as "Black." Later Apperson was on the Adirondacks' third highest, the magnificent Haystack, in March 1920, for its first ski ascent of record. Both men skied up Gothics in 1927, Apperson also doing Basin and Saddleback that year. How many other Adirondack peaks may have been climbed by one or both is not recorded, one of the difficulties being Apperson's pronounced aversion to publicizing his winter climbs.

Both Langmuir and Apperson remained devoted to the mountains throughout long and active lives. Of Langmuir, one of his colleagues said,

> Whether in the Lab or in the mountains, an intense curiosity about natural phenomenon constantly pervaded his thoughts. In fact, I have never met anyone else who was so well coupled to nature.

His close associate of many years, Vince Schaefer (who conceived the Long Path), recalled an overnight hiking trip with Langmuir:

> We lay awake in our bedrolls for hours watching the stars that night, while Langmuir tried to figure out the evolutionary pattern that accounted for those strange excrescenses.

Winter never deterred but only sharpened Langmuir's enthusiasm for the outdoors. All through the 1920s and 1930s he continued to ski. When Schaefer was frequently visiting the Mount Washington Observatory to do research during World War II, Langmuir came over to join him on some of his winter ascents. Recalled Schaefer:

> Although then over 60 years of age he climbed the mountain on skis several times with [me]. We would go the short steep route by way of Tuckerman's Ravine and Lion's Head. His climb was a steady slow pace interspersed with pauses during which all manner of natural phenomena would be discussed.

Apperson's style was altogether different, but his devotion all the more intense. He threw himself into conservation controversies with the same zest with which he attacked a steep snow slope. He founded the militant Forest Preserve Association and is generally given the lion's share of credit for preserving the shoreline of Lake George from development. But he seems to have been prickly and self-righteous, and as a result his reputation is recalled differently by different people. "He was beautiful," recalled one Schenectadian; "He loved a fight," reminisces another; "One of the most irritating men I ever knew," responded a fellow conservationist, who added, "He was 'right' on any subject he chose to talk about." Perhaps the most fitting assessment placed him in the realm of legend:

> His love of adventure is unbounded. If he had lived in the sixth century, there is no doubt in my mind that King Arthur might have added immensely to the brilliant history of the Round Table by enlisting this man, whose fame as a knight would surely have surpassed that of Sir Launcelot himself.

Jackrabbit Johannsen and the Lake Placid Club

In the winter of 1904–5, the Lake Placid Club staged a winter gathering, and ten hardy outdoors people went to the club for a week to cavort on snowshoes, skis, skates, and toboggan. Godfrey Dewey, son of owner Melvil, and Henry Van Hoevenberg acted as hosts. Five of the eight guests were women. The event was a smashing success and was repeated every year thereafter with more and more participants. By 1920 they formed a club, calling themselves the Sno-birds, and by 1922 had five hundred members. By then someone was calling Switzerland's famed St. Moritz "the Lake Placid of Europe."

The Lake Placid enthusiasts did not at first consider climbing the high peaks, but in 1915 a forty-year-old newcomer changed all that. Herman Smith-Johannsen was born in Norway in 1875. (He claimed his family name was really just Johannsen, but his father disliked having such a common name and so arbitrarily added the exotic moniker "Smith" to give it distinction.) Herman was educated in Germany in the 1890s and migrated to North America before the turn of the century. At first he led a roving life as a railroad engineer in western Canada—"I was after adventure, wanted to see the world"—but in 1907 settled down, married, and started his own engineering business. Since his profession still involved a lot of travel, he decided his family could live anywhere and chose the north country as the best place to raise children. From 1915 to 1928 the Johannsens lived at Lake Placid, then moving to the Montreal area.

Once settled in Lake Placid in 1915, the Norwegian expatriate took advantage of the snowy winters to resume his boyhood love of skiing. In that year he first skied up Marcy, via the old Opalescent River route. Later ascents were via the Van Hoevenberg Trail and from the Upper Ausable Lake. Whiteface became a frequent objective. He also skied up Giant and numerous smaller peaks.

Johannsen's energy and skiing skill opened eyes at Lake Placid. "I have never before or since seen such agility and strength," recalled one seasoned outdoorsman of the area. "All of us were in awe of the grace and speed that Jackrabbit displayed on his narrow birch skis," said another. "Jackrabbit?" That nickname was applied early and stayed forever. Johannsen explained its origins thus in a 1980 television interview: "We had hare and hound races and I was the hare, the jackrabbit. They tried to catch me. They haven't caught me yet." (At this date the Jackrabbit was 104 years old.) Under his inspiration the Lake Placid winter set became more adventurous, particularly after Johannsen and his family moved into residence at the club in 1920.

In 1920 Johannsen joined forces with Langmuir and Apperson and a Schenectady group to do some mountain skiing. On this occasion, they headed one day for remote Haystack, one of the tougher Adirondack peaks to reach in winter. After spending the night in Keene Valley, they skied up past the Ausable Lakes and started up the Bartlett Ridge. It was a long, hard, uphill pull, and at the top of the ridge Langmuir and all the others turned back, save Johannsen and Apperson. The summit pair continued on, bushwhacking without regard to the trail, which was obscured by deep snow. Just before sunset they reached treeline 300 feet below the summit. Here they switched to crampons and continued to the top. The first ski ascent of Haystack was a memorable moment, as the sun was setting over Marcy simultaneously with the moon rising over Giant. Johannsen and Apperson paused briefly to savor the unforgettable scene before heading briskly back through the frigid dusk and then the moonlight to rejoin their friends at the camp on the upper Lake. Nighttime descents or even overnight bivouacs rarely bothered the Jackrabbit. He often came off Marcy in the dark. He devised a light sled that his dog could haul that carried a sleeping bag and meal, with the aid of which he could do overnight circuits. Among the peaks that he climbed, besides the early conquests mentioned already, was Skylight, a remote and difficult objective by today's standards. In 1932, when the Winter Olympics brought the world's top skiers to Lake Placid, Jackrabbit escorted them on a long pleasure tour—in one day—from Adirondak Loj through Indian Pass, down to Tahawus, and back via Lake Colden. This was an itinerary for which many summer hikers might take three or four days. As they came up by Colden in the afternoon, the fifty-six-year-old leader puckishly inquired if they'd like to go back over the top of Marcy. When the group rose to the bait, Johannsen turned his skis uphill and led them up the 2,600-foot ascent, reaching the top at sunset. Down the Van Hoevenberg Trail by moonlight, they skied into the Loj, a tired but jubilant crew.

At the age of 72, Johannsen placed third in the Stowe Derby, a race in which his youngest competitors were one-fourth his age. That was thirty-five years before the authors interviewed him for this book. Then he was still living near Montreal at age 106—and still skiing! It appeared that he might never stop. Jackrabbit Johannsen, born in the administration of Ulysses S. Grant, was no longer bushwhacking up Marcy or Haystack at sunset, but he was still gliding over cross-country trails near Montreal, and the gleam of youth had not faded from his twinkling eye, nor the cutting edge from his sharp wit. This extraordinary life ended on January 5, 1987, in his 112th year.

On the nature of early skiing

These first mountain skiers—Harris, Langmuir, Apperson, Johannsen—saw skis as a way to move around all kinds of mountainous terrain in winter, including climbing to the summits. To them, sliding downhill was only part of the sport, albeit probably the most fun. Downhill was the frosting on a rich cake that they enjoyed in all its layers. Going across country was part of the sport too, but also only a part.

Today most skiers consider the sport to have at least two major and two minor subdivisions, neatly compartmentalized and segregated, even requiring different types of skis, different boots, specialized bindings, and wholly different techniques (plus different wardrobes, for those to whom fashion counts). The two major branches, both enormously popular and fashionable today, are downhill and cross-country. Two relatively esoteric or elite further subdivisions are ski mountaineering and jumping. The more sophisticated practitioners distinguish even more subdivisions, but for the purposes of our discussion consider just these four. The first Northeastern skiers saw all four subdivisions as elements of one sport, skiing. The complete skier did all four. In spirit their perception of skiing was probably closer to that of today's ski mountaineer than any of the others, but to them that included what we think of today as downhill and cross-country. Surprisingly, too, jumping was a big part of skiing for many of the early people.

Besides combining all four in one undifferentiated skill, the skiers of the early 1900s otherwise exhibited many obvious differences from their descendants at this end of the century. The reader has noticed repeated references to boards 8 and 9 feet long. They were wooden, of course. Steel edges were unknown till the 1920s. The weight, as against today's light materials, must have been atlasian. Nothing like present-day poles were in universal use. Many skiers used nothing at all in their hands but lots of body English, many had one long heavy pole, some used two more wieldy wands. As late as the 1920s, Adirondack enthusiast Fay Loope would climb Marcy on skis with no poles, cutting a slender birch log on the way up near treeline; for the fast descent of the Van Hoevenberg Trail, he would straddle the pole and control turns by leaning on it one way or another. Others did not control turns, but simply crashed—a technique perhaps not entirely extinct.

But if the techniques, equipment, and certainly the clothing were different, something of the spirit surely survives and flourishes today as it did for so much smaller a circle of hardy pioneers back then. Something of the inimitable thrill of swift gliding through snow-laden glades in the clear, cold, clean, mountain air was surely the same then as now. Skiing had entered the Northeastern mountain recreation scene for keeps.

Our history concerns mountain *climbing*, so it covers only *uphill* skiing. We shall make no effort to pursue the lively and colorful history of *downhill* skiing, which became the dominant branch of the sport sometime during the 1930s, and the almost exclusive department of it for almost a generation after World War II. That specialization, however, awaited developments of ski tows and lifts, specialized equipment, ski trains, and major investments in a ski industry that soon grew to have little in common with the climbing or hiking world.

But these developments still were dreams in the promoters' imaginations until well into the 1920s. In the skilled hands of Fred Harris and Langmuir and Apperson and the incredible Jackrabbit, and of a still small but growing cadre of other hardy pioneers of the 1920s, skiing remained an adventurous branch of winter climbing for yet a few years.

PART FOUR

Mountains as escape from urban society: 1910–1950

In July 1902 newlyweds Mr. and Mrs. Herbert J. Sackett of Buffalo, New York, took their honeymoon journey in an "automobile," driving to the Ampersand Hotel on Lower Saranac Lake. The horseless carriage, a novelty in those parts, was a sensation. When the Sacketts drove up the dusty unpaved roads to Paul Smith's camp, that "pioneer of the oxmobile" greeted them and the very first automobile to invade his sanctuary. "Their passage was long remembered," recalled Adirondack historian Donaldson:

> In Saranac Lake village and along the highway the puffing and pounding motor spread terror before it and left wreckage and anathema behind it. In spite of many runaways [terrified horses], however, there was no really serious accident.

No really serious accident . . . except, that is, the death of Paul Smith's way of life. The Sacketts' motorcar and those that followed it up those dusty roads had a revolutionary effect not only on the quiet Adirondacks, but everywhere in American life.

In August 1903 a party from Philbrook Farm Inn went by horse and carriage to a picnic at Crystal Cascade in Pinkham Notch. While in the notch, they were surprised by the arrival of not one but three automobiles. A chronicler of that summer's events noted that "Mr. Philbrook took the opportunity to lead his horses up and around these strange machines accustiming [sic] them to the novel sight." The story is of interest not only for revealing something of the novelty of automobile traffic in 1903, but for a certain poignancy: Mr. Philbrook could little realize that his own grandnephew, Douglas A. Philbrook, as president of the Mount

Washington Summit Road Company, would preside over the annual visit of several thousand automobiles to the top of the mountain. For all the mountains, things were never again the same.

Life speeded up. Roads were built and improved. The once inaccessible places became accessible to all. Come along with me, Lucille, in my merry Oldsmobile.

Vacation habits changed. Whereas people had once stayed for a month or more at great resort hotels, the two-week or one-week vacation now became possible, followed in time by The Weekend as an American institution. Soon not only the well-to-do few could come to the mountains but anyone well off enough to own a car. And just about anyone could, once Henry Ford began mass-producing his Model T at a low price. James P. Taylor, the supersalesman trailsman who conceived and promoted Vermont's Long Trail, loved to call the first inexpensive Fords "the chariot of Democracy." Proclaimed Taylor, "Like the Constitution of the United States, the Ford makes us all free to pursue happiness."[a] Whether happiness was thus attainable, everyone—or at least a broad cross section of society—was free to pursue a vacation in the hitherto exclusive mountain vacation centers.

The large, opulent hotels and private camps like Paul Smith's declined, particularly the fashionable ones. Fashion is often linked with a show of exclusivity, and the automobile left nothing exclusive. Further, though many *more* visitors now came to the mountains, the irony is that quicker and cheaper transportation enabled them to spend *less* time there. Many of these new visitors had neither means nor time nor inclination to spend an entire summer at one grand hotel. Instead they looked for tourist camps or cottages, and eventually motor courts and the modern motel. A longtime vacationer who had enjoyed the leisurely summers of gracious living at the Profile House in Franconia Notch is reported to have shaken his fist when the first automobile roared up to the hotel entrance. "This," he intoned, "is the end of the Profile House." He was, like many exaggerating prophets of doom, perfectly right.

Russell Carson wrote in 1927 of the automobile and the good roads that were built for it,

> Indirectly they have totally changed the character of those who are enjoying the high mountain region. An ascent of a high peak, instead of being limited largely to natives or summer-long visitors, is now possible of accomplishment by week-end visitors.

Donaldson had already observed in 1921, "They have changed a great wild spot with a few parks, into a great park with a few wild spots."

[a]As the reader will see again in chap. 35, Taylor's irrepressible enthusiasm was not to be derailed by little things like missing the distinction between the Constitution and the Declaration of Independence.

As usual, the wilder Adirondacks remained innocent longer than the rest of the Northeast. The Catskill Mountain House built its first "Automobile Garage" as early as 1909. Already back in 1899 a Stanley "locomobile" had ascended Mount Washington's carriage road; it was not many years before Mount Washington became a test run for many early American cars, and by 1911 the venerable "carriage road" had become the "auto road."[b] By 1913, down in the Berkshires, Walter Prichard Eaton mused,

> Nobody walks any more, except the Appalachian Club, Boy Scouts, and President John Finley, of the College of the City of New York—really walks, that is.

The automobile and the changing American vacation were in evidence in all New England mountain centers by the time of World War I.

Eaton's eulogy for walking proved premature, however. It was not long before many hikers noted the double-edged impact of the automobile. On the one hand, walking along country roads was no longer fun. As one summer camp found, "No longer could the road walking be done in a massed bunch over the whole road. One hugged the ditch and watched the cars." But the result was an increase in *off*-road walking. When the *New York Times* ran an editorial deploring the automobile's takeover of country roads, and concluding "the foot-path is not for Americans," walker-columnist Raymond H. Torrey, ombudsman of the thriving New York–area hiking community, fired back a letter to the editor pointing out,

> It is true that the old country dirt roads, which were once attractive and safe for walkers twenty or thirty years ago, are now . . . so frequented by automobiles that they are no longer desirable foot-ways. But this very change has driven the walker into the woods, made him discover the old wood roads, which exist everywhere. . . . It has also led many walking clubs to develop and mark new routes, over the sky-lines, and to discover forest solitudes which were formerly unknown to the walker.

In 1920 Percy Stiles deplored the inroads of the automobile, but conceded that "indirectly the pedestrian had gained something by the intolerable condition of the highways for it is this which is stimulating the trail-building."

---

[b] At first automobiles were not allowed regular use of the Mount Washington road because they frightened the horses. On Aug. 6, 1906, *Among the Clouds* reported that the carriage road would be open to automobiles on Sundays only ("Automobiles on the Carriage Road," p. 4). The gradual transition to autos-only use in 1911 is described by Douglas A. Philbrook in "The Mount Washington Auto Road," *Forest Notes* (Summer 1967), pp. 14–17.

Furthermore, as Stiles noted, the automobile enabled the hiker to get to trails more quickly. This point was soon picked up by others—for example, the AMC's John Ritchie in 1926:

> The auto gives to the mountain climber a new item of equipment wherewith, from what were impossible distances in the old days, he may speed to his point of attack on a mountain. His field of exploration [from a given base] is enormously increased.

Different patterns of leisure generated different patterns of hiking. In the preauto days of the grand hotels and summerlong leisure, hiking traffic was more diffused in the area immediately around the hotels, less concentrated on the one or two trade routes. A charming diversity of short paths led to a wider variety of scenic attractions than we have today: waterfalls, vistas, unusual natural features. On the other hand, for large stretches of the mountains, away from the vacation centers, very few trails yet existed. During the 1920s and 1930s that changed: trails and hikers sallied forth all over the mountains.

To illustrate this contrast, consider Franconia Notch. Today's hiking traffic concentrates on perhaps half a dozen trails, the summit of Lafayette being the principal attraction; the few well-used trails are worn and eroded from the volume of traffic and require constant maintenance work. One hundred years ago, with grand hotels such as the Profile House and Flume House in their glory, pedestrians strolled a much wider variety of shorter paths near the hotels. After all, they had all summer to walk and naturally looked for new paths every few days. But beyond easy reach of the hotels, the mountains remained truly wild. No path defiled the wooded sanctuaries of the Kinsman Ridge south of Cannon, while to the east of Lafayette, the entire watershed of the East Branch—the Pemigewasset Wilderness, with all its rich offering of mountains—was seldom visited.

Or in the Adirondacks, around the valley of the Ausable Lakes, a cornucopia of popular walking paths sprang up during the last quarter of the nineteenth century. Almost all of these were short and untaxing. Meanwhile, the Great Range, with its bristling phalanx of summits and ridges, remained trackless and untraveled save for the single trail up Gothics from the lakes.

With the advent of the automobile and its eager, mobile, independent hikers, trails and people assaulted and took possession irretrievably of the Kinsman Ridge, the Pemigewasset Wilderness, and the Great Range itself. Huts, shelters, and lodges were built in glades that had been but the haunt of bear and raven two generations before—or, in some cases, of logging camps during the immediately preceding generation. But with the new hikers venturing farther into the hills, and fewer grand hotel patrons, the wealth of close-by paths went neglected; many grew in quickly and disappeared forever.

Beginning in Vermont in 1910 a new conception of trail building spread throughout the Northeastern mountains. In place of a focus on independent clusters of short trails, regionwide consciousness grew. Everywhere path makers began to see local trails in relation to trails elsewhere, to link up one cluster with another, forming much greater systems of trails. For the first time, vacationers began to think of the White Mountains or the Adirondacks as one big place to hike, instead of as a variety of disconnected centers. Over the next two decades, a new generation of trail-builders began the work of linking up one trail cluster with another until they formed one cohesive White Mountain trail system, another unified Adirondacks system—both with offshoots leading into other mountains in the Northeast.

The full maturing of this new concept produced the "through-trail": linkups that opened the opportunity to hike clear across the region or substantial parts of it. The fruits of this movement were, first, Vermont's Long Trail, then a wave of other long-distance regional trails, and finally the 2,100-mile Appalachian Trail, running the length of the country from Georgia to Maine.

The Long Trail and the Appalachian Trail are major milestones in Northeastern trails history. They have qualities in common, yet striking differences as well. Both were conceived by brilliant visionaries who were unsuited to the task of eventually building them. That is not intended as criticism: James P. Taylor and Benton MacKaye richly deserve the plaudits of posterity as "fathers" of the LT and AT respectively. But in both cases other men did the actual building: Judge Cowles, Professor Monroe, storekeeper Laurence Griswold, and a score more in Vermont: Murray Stevens, Ned Anderson, Helon Taylor, and well more than a score more along the northeastern sectors of the AT. In the case of both trails, the builders did not originally intend that people would hike from one end to another. The *trail* went from Massachusetts to Canada, but it was assumed that an individual hiker would see only a part of it. The builders of the AT actually condemned as a "stunt" the notion of end-to-end hiking, or even of walking, say, the entire Maine part of the trail in one stint. Both trails took a long time to complete—twenty years for the LT, sixteen for the AT (even just its New England sector took that long). Both suffered from attempts to rush it to completion with ill-considered trail sections, which produced unsatisfactory results that had to be largely rebuilt later. For all these similarities, however, the two great trails evolved wholly different personalities, despite the fact that they coincide for almost one hundred miles (more than one-third of the LT's length). The LT was and is pure Vermont, homespun, relatively homogenous in character, heavily forested and richly green, rarely spectacular, always comfortable, and taciturn in respect to publicity, once Taylor's original whoopla died away. The AT was almost from the start a national celebrity, discussed among famous thinkers like MacKaye, Lewis

Mumford, and their high-powered circle, destined to become a National Scenic Trail, receiving the attentions of presidents, Congresses, and well-known writers. The AT was enormously varied in terrain and spirit, climbing far above treeline, striding down the main streets of numerous towns, traversing a variety of ecosystems, often in the newspapers, the theme of a score of books, brassy, splashy, "the flagship of American trails." In these two long footpaths—so like, so unlike—the history of trail making in the 1910–50 period appropriately begins and ends. Nothing so richly documents the double-edged impact of the automobile as the observation that these two splendid monuments to the quintessential walker were, in fact, products of the Automobile Age.

The automobile was but the single most obvious item in the catalogue of sweeping economic and social changes that transfigured Northeastern mountain recreation. The affluence of the 1920s, the Great Depression of the 1930s, the rise of the cities and the transition of America from a quiet rural to a bustling urban society, the increased social and geographical mobility of the American population, the economic prosperity of a large middle class, the growing social independence of newly enfranchised women—all these forces changed both the numbers of people interested in the mountains and the expectations of those people when they went there. The newly urbanized generation sought escape from the pressures of city life. A key factor that made such escape possible was the new leisure, in the form of the shorter work week, with many now getting Saturday afternoons off, as well as paid vacations.

The hiking and camping style of the 1920s and 1930s was a long step removed from that of the nineteenth century; but it was another long step from today's.

The nineteenth-century tramper kept nature respectfully at a distance, staying in valley hotels or hiring guides for the occasional night out in improvised lean-tos, with blazing bonfire all night. The development of long trails and backcountry shelters showed that the children of the Automobile Age were far more ready to stay in the woods longer, more self-sufficiently, more on nature's terms. On the other hand, the casual form-less approach to camping and the virtual vacuum in the retail outdoor equipment business contrasted sharply with the backpacking boom of recent years.

Freed from dependence on a guide or from the dusty, roadbound, horse-and-wagon camping of the old student excursions, the hikers of the 1920s and 1930s went off the roads and into the cool green woods on their own. No need now to come out of the woods and down to the valley at night. They could stay at an Adirondack shelter, a Long Trail lodge, or an AMC hut—or they could set up their tents anywhere: near a gushing stream, on the trail itself, or even above treeline in the lush alpine vegetation. Environmental impact was no concern, in part because of the still small number of hikers and, perhaps more important, because the beginnings of the impact problem were largely unperceived. Regulations telling hikers just how and where to camp were as yet undreamed of. Both the backwoods and backwoods accommodations were completely uncrowded. It was a golden, carefree age.

With access to the north country becoming greater, the four major ranges of northern New England and New York (counting Katahdin as a major range unto itself) developed distinct personalities as twentieth-century recreational centers in the 1920s and 1930s. The hiking environment as we know it today in each of those ranges was largely shaped during this period. The mountain backcountry was "developed"—not in the sense of residential housing or commercial buildings, but in the institutional fabric required to support the hiking and camping style peculiar to each region: the huts, lodges, or shelters, and the network of trails on the peaks. Not merely were the physical structures built, but the tone and style both of the recreation that took place there and of what was later called backcountry management were basically set on their present course during the 1920s and 1930s.

Institutions formed—the AMC's hut system and trail crew, the Adirondack Mountain Club and the Forty-Sixers, the GMC's Long Trail Patrol, Baxter State Park, the Civilian Conservation Corps, the Appalachian Trail. Legendary figures strode the hills. It was a time when larger-than-life individuals towered over various walks of American life—the age of Lindbergh and Amelia Earhart, Hemingway and Gertrude Stein, Babe Ruth, Al Capone, Paderewski and Heifetz and Bessie Smith, Valentino and Harlow, Charlie Chaplin, Dempsey and Tunney, Will Rogers, Huey Long, FDR, W. C. Fields, and Mae West. In the hiking and camping arena of northern New England and New York, this was the era of Roy Dudley and Percy Baxter, Sherman Adams and Joe Dodge, C. W. Blood and P. R. Jenks, Jim Taylor and Roy Buchanan, Robert Marshall and Raymond Torrey, Myron Avery—each an extraordinarily dominant personality, though their styles were as different as those of Capone and Chaplin.

If we would understand the shape of Northeastern hiking and camping today, we must look at these institutions, physical and personal, and at why and how they grew, for it is in the extended shadows of these giants that Northeasterners of the waning twentieth century still hike and camp.

But for all the flamboyance of the superstars of the era, perhaps the greatest change after World War I was simple numbers: the much larger flow of ordinary people coming to the hills. The stage on which our history of Northeastern climbing is enacted suddenly becomes much more crowded. It will be increasingly difficult to keep track of the cast. No longer can we easily discern a limited number of actors, each with reasonably prominent roles. From now on the arena of the Northeastern hills teems with hundreds and thousands of trampers, of all ages and from a much broader range of American society. As early as 1921 a Massachusetts newspaper observed:

> No longer is the hiker's pack a novelty; nor do tanned and rough looking trampers excite more than passing curiosity, except as mingled with envy.

Thus the paradox of hill walking in the Automobile Age: it would not be long before social critics and pundits would deplore the stultifying influence of motorized travel on American exercise and on the physical fitness of the average American; and perhaps they were generally right. But up in the hills of the Northeast, the Automobile Age brought more mountain walkers and climbers than had ever peopled the wildest dreams of Ethan Allen Crawford or the Reverend Marcus Keep, or even of Adirondack Murray himself.

Chapter 35

The Long Trail

AT the turn of the century Vermont's mountains were not as well trampled as New Hampshire's or New York's. The upsurge in hill walking, that struck the White Mountains and Adirondacks after 1875 largely bypassed the Green Mountain State. If anything Vermont mountains had grown even wilder than before. An 1862 brochure for the Manchester resort area identified numerous mountain walks, but its 1905 updated edition gave none at all. Wrote *Harper's* magazine:

> Of the Green Mountains one might probably say, . . . they are more generally admired than visited. Poets sing without seeing them. They have furnished ready and familiar figures to orators who could hardly point them out on the map. That they stimulate the virtues of the patriot, . . . is one of those axioms which one meets over and over again in the pages of writers who have never felt their rugged breezes.

The first stirrings of change took place not on the great 4,000-footers of the main range, but on graceful, isolated, little Ascutney, on the shores of the Connecticut River. Ascutney had a trail as early as the 1820s (chapter 7) and a stone hut on top in the 1850s (chapter 8). In 1903 renewed interest was shown by the formation of the Ascutney Mountain Association. That a club was formed invites the speculation that climbing had been on the rise for several years before. Led by George Duncan, Frank Clark, Houghton Hoisington, Luther White, and Dr. Dean Richmond, all of whom lived near the mountain's base, the association rebuilt the 1858 stone hut on the summit and improved the two old trails, even relocating sections of the original trail on the Windsor side. Dr. Richmond dramatized the caliber of this reconstruction by driving a horse and buggy to the top on October 20, 1903. By the following year, no fewer than 700 celebrants turned out for dedication ceremonies on the summit. An annual picnic on top attracted as many as 500 each year, evidence of considerable local interest in mountain excursions. A trailhead register maintained by the association showed 664 sign-ins in 1905, 635 in 1906, and 670 in 1907 (none of these totals counting the Labor Day crowd, nor children, nor winter traffic). The farmer at the base kept for hire, at a dollar per trip, a threesome of "burrows" named Wilson, Taft, and Roosevelt. That must have been around the autumn of 1912. "The custom was to unload at the top, turn him [Wilson et al.] around and he would trot along on home for the next customer." In 1906 a new trail was opened on the previously little-visited south side of the mountain.

The example of Ascutney was soon followed at Camel's Hump. On June 20, 1908, a group of local businessmen came together to form the Camel's Hump Club, with the purpose of developing Camel's Hump as a mountain resort that would appeal to mountain walkers. C. C. Graves was elected president. The first, and possibly the only major accomplishment of the Camel's Hump Club was the provision of camping facilities just below the summit of the Hump. At first, four large tents were furnished at the clearing, three of them big enough for 12 people each and one monstrosity that slept 20. Each tent was equipped with stove, lantern, dishes and utensils, a supply of foodstuffs, "fragrant boughs for bedding," and "clean, new blankets." In 1910 this tenting area attracted 700 visitors, the following year 1,100. In 1912 a 14-foot-by-20-foot hut was erected at the site. "It in no sense offers the ease and luxuries of the great houses of other mountain resorts," conceded the Camel's Hump Club, "but to those who 'love the call of the wilderness' and long to live close to nature in all her rare and changing beauties it comes a distinct boon." This building was roughly comparable to the contemporary AMC hut at Madison Springs. Though a caretaker was provided, nothing was designed to emulate the elegance of, say, the Catskill Mountain House. The little clearing below the summit, well known to hikers today, is the lasting legacy of its effort. Otherwise, the Camel's Hump Club accomplished little—it built no new trails, for example—but it was a significant organizational precursor of the Green Mountain Club.

Neither the AMC nor the CHC altered the statewide neglect of Vermont's mountain scenery, save on their home peaks. How Vermonters changed that neglect into one grand celebration of their statelong chain of mountains is the story of the building of the Long Trail. It is remarkable how, as this drama unfolded, a succession of key figures entered the stage at just the right time to keep the action going: first the educator-turned-chamber of commerce drumbeater, James P. Taylor; then the small group that Taylor organized as the Green Mountain Club; then Judge Clarence Cowles; then foresters Austin Hawes and Robert Ross; then Prof. Will Monroe; then the rest of the state of Vermont; and finally the little man who placed it all on a permanent footing, Roy Buchanan.

When the curtain opened on this drama, Vermont seemed in a state of apathy toward its beautiful hills. One of the early GMC enthusiasts, Louis Paris, with characteristic overstatement, defined the problem, as it existed in 1910:

The main range continues unopened territory known only to the lumberman and the hunter. . . . No one had interest enough to clear a single mile of trail until very recently. The beautiful mountains have become a distant scenic background.

Dr. Paris went on to observe that Washington Irving had glamorized the Catskills in public fancy, Adirondack Murray had similarly blessed the Adirondacks, Starr King the White Mountains, and half the leading romantic men of letters the Berkshires. But, lamented Paris, "the song of the Green Mountains remains unsung."

Enter James P. Taylor.

Taylor was not a man to leave a song unsung. Headmaster of the Vermont Academy for Boys at Saxtons River, Taylor was a spiritual descendant of Alden Partridge, who believed that education was incomplete without robust outdoor exercise. Taylor formed a Vermont Academy Mountain Club, gave special awards to students for climbing mountains in all seasons, and personally led the way on many trips, even spending a winter night on Mount Ascutney, just as Captain Partridge's cadets had done sixty years before.

But Taylor soon began to deplore the limited number of mountains on which good trails and overnight shelters could be found. On Killington, he frowned, "they could find for shelter only the ell of the wreck of an ancient mountain house." On nearby Pico he found no trail at all. One hot day on the top of Mansfield, Taylor grew inordinately thirsty and could see only the beautiful Lake of the Clouds, almost a mile distant, as a place to get a drink. Wrote he, in the florid oratory in which he recounted tales about himself in the third person:

> [He] swore no pilgrimage could be complete without anointing his brows in the waters of that lake. But Vermonters had made no trail connecting these two sacred spots.

The lack of trails on Vermont's hills became an obsession to the schoolmaster:

> Should the Green Mountain Range continue to be sacrosanct to the spirits of the first "Green Mountain Boys," and to hedgehogs, and untouchable to everybody else?

Eventually Taylor's frustrations gave birth to the idea of a series of trails up each of the many peaks that form the long, north-south spine of Vermont, with connecting trails between, so as to form one long trail from Massachusetts to Canada: *the* Long Trail. To build and maintain this footpath, Taylor envisioned a Green Mountain Club, which would take its place beside the venerable AMC as a center for New England outdoorspeople. Both the supertrail and the second great hiking club were bold and original conceptions; both succeeded astonishingly.

Destiny made the strange choice of James Paddock Taylor to father such precocious twins. Born in New York State on September 9, 1872, educated at Colgate, Harvard, and Columbia, a lifelong bachelor, he was a teacher and school administrator for the first twenty years of his career, and a chamber of commerce executive for the next thirty-seven. Although he had led a good many hikes at Vermont Academy, he was not thereafter much seen on the trails that he inspired. John Paulson of Bennington, an early follower, recalls Taylor as "a speechmaker and backslapper" who did little physical trail work. He was a promoter, a dreamer, a salesman, a compulsive after-dinner speaker. His career soon departed the quiet halls of academia in favor of the hucksters' haven, as secretary of the Vermont State Chamber of Commerce, where he used his fertile imagination to dream up an endless stream of publicity stunts to attract attention to his beloved adopted state. His zeal for publicity and the popular appeal of the Green Mountains led him to back wholeheartedly a 1930s plan for a skyline highway along the approximate route of his own Long Trail—a sacrilege to many others who had built the trail and jealously guarded its wildness and sylvan solitude.[a]

But all that came later. First Taylor needed the organization to convert his dreams to reality. He went to Boston to appeal to the Appalachian Mountain Club but found little interest in Vermont trail building among the AMC hierarchy. "Apparently, to the 'Apps,' the Green Mountain State was as flat as a pancake," recalled Taylor later. "If a mountain trail system were to be constructed in the Green Mountains, Vermonters would have to build it."

So Taylor launched a series of meetings up and down the state with anyone who would listen to his idea for a long trail. Armed with nothing more than "a line on a map and a spiel," he pursued movers and shakers wherever he could find them, always promoting his dream. At his first public address on the subject, he found only two backers: one was a New Yorker and the other moved to Michigan three days later. But the supersalesman kept selling and gradually won enough supporters to form the skeleton of a statewide organization, at least on paper.

---

[a]Besides being father of the Green Mountain Club and the Long Trail, James Taylor was perhaps the grandfather of the Dartmouth Outing Club's Winter Carnival. DOC's Fred Harris, as an undergraduate, ran into Taylor on a train and the sight of the student's 9-foot skis led Taylor to tell him about the Winter Carnival that Taylor had organized at the Vermont Academy. In after years, Harris liberally credited Taylor with planting the idea for the DOC's famed Winter Carnival in his mind. See Fred Harris, "Skiing and Winter Sports in Vermont," *The Vermonter* (Nov. 1912), pp. 680–81, and a letter from James P. Taylor to Congressman Frank L. Greene, Feb. 7, 1920, in the Taylor Papers, Vermont Historical Society, Montpelier, Vt.

On March 4, 1910, Taylor sent a "call" to eighteen prominent citizens to form a "Green Mountain Club." The stated purpose was to "make the Vermont mountains play a larger part in the life of the people. . . . to awaken an interest in the mountains of Vermont, to encourage mountain climbing, to make trails, build shelters, and aid in the preparation of maps and guide books." The founding meeting was held at the Van Ness House in Burlington on Friday, March 11, at 2:00 P.M. Among the twenty-three men present (no women), of particular importance were Taylor himself, who naturally was elected president; Judge Seneca Haselton of Burlington, vice president, who later arranged for cutting the popular trail on Mansfield that bears his name; Frank H. Clark of Windsor, then president of the Ascutney Mountain Association (AMA); M. E. Wheeler of Rutland, who offered one hundred dollars as seed money for the new club; and, in a then minor capacity, a young Burlington lawyer named Clarence P. Cowles, soon to become a vital, almost indispensable figure in the early fortunes of the Green Mountain Club.

The result of this historic meeting was the formal organization of the Green Mountain Club, with a constitution that pledged, "The object of the Club shall be to make the Vermont Mountains play a larger part in the life of the people." This is the organization that adopted the single objective of building the Long Trail—eventually to become a 262-mile footpath through the forests and over the crags for the entire length of the state from Massachusetts to Canada. The GMC was the first true *trail* club, as distinct from a hiking or all-purpose outdoor club, such as the AMC. Though its scope has broadened over the years, it has never lost sight of the primary mission of tending the one long trail. Provision of shelters and closed cabins, building of access trails, and the many outings and excursions scheduled by the club have all been subservient to the unifying theme of building and maintaining the Long Trail. Nonetheless, it became the second of the three great north country mountain clubs that dominate the region to this day.

Taylor treated the launching of the GMC like a political campaign. Both predecessor organizations were courted: the AMA's Clark was asked to speak at the first meeting on his club's founding and activities; C. C. Graves of the CHC, though not present, was elected to a spot on the governing council. The governor of the state was also elected a councillor, and Taylor gave it out to the press that the GMC enjoyed the "patronage of the Governor and many others. . . . Many of the most prominent men in Vermont are interested." Old Colonel Battell of Middlebury was persuaded to let the trail pass over his extensive landholdings around Camel's Hump and points south. College presidents, the state forester, and many well-known political figures were brought in, at least on paper, whether they were outdoorsmen by nature or not.[b] (Taylor referred to one early backer, whose financial support he was glad to accept, thus: "His age and weight would make a mountain trail for him pure theory, not applied practice.")

Taylor took to the banquet circuit, giving hundreds of speeches to any audience that would listen—garden clubs, historical societies, chambers of commerce. He fired off a continual stream of letters, appealing for public support, shaping up a county-by-county organization, raising funds, "inspiring and congratulating others who worked on the trail." The performance was a model of political action.

Soon after the club's founding, Taylor received important help from two other tireless publicists who picked up the Long Trail dream: Louis Paris, who produced a prolific flow of magazine articles and newspaper stories on the GMC, and Theron S. Dean, who became secretary of the club and carried on a prodigious correspondence with new members, trail workers, and public officials. Crucial early support also came from *The Vermonter*, a widely read statewide magazine that began to devote considerable coverage to the Green Mountains. Its May 1911 issue was wholly devoted to the Long Trail and the GMC, and stimulated a lengthy and favorable editorial in the *New York Sun*, which ended, "At last Vermont is waking up."

Thus James P. Taylor was the organizing genius of the Green Mountain Club, the creative imagination that conceived the Long Trail, and the supersalesman for everything in the Green Mountain State. One thing James P. Taylor was not, and that was a practical, persevering, patient trail-builder. After the first year or two, for all of Taylor's enthusiasm, the Long Trail remained just "a line on a map and a spiel" with which to spellbind after-dinner audiences. Through all the heady hoopla of organizing the GMC, lining up the governor, holding meetings, making speeches, fanning publicity, and otherwise beating the drums for the Long Trail, it gradually became clear that lasting credibility could only come from actually producing a real-live trail on some real-live mountains.

In fairness, it should be kept in mind that Taylor's dream was a completely new idea in trail making at the time. One long "through-trail" had never occurred to the great nineteenth-century trail-builders at Waterville or Randolph or Wonalancet, or around Ausable, Heart, or Placid lakes. This was 1910—more than ten years before Benton MacKaye was to conceive the Appalachian Trail, a dozen years before the 130-mile Northville–Placid Trail was thought of, and even a couple of years before anyone in the AMC tried to connect one continuous route from Moosilauke to the Mahoosucs across the White Mountains. Taylor's dream was

---

[b]Among the original eighteen invitees appeared the name of Warren R. Austin, then a thirty-three-year-old rising political star, later to become U.S. senator and ultimately the United States' first representative at the United Nations. Taylor could smell a comer years away.

truly pioneering, the first conception of a long-distance hiking trail as the ultimate expression of mountain walking. So it is not surprising that the trail did not spring to life full-blown during those first years.

To get the ball rolling, Taylor and the GMC founders decided to focus first on connecting a through-trail between the two best-known mountains of the state, to dramatize the scope of a statelong trail. Mansfield and Camel's Hump were almost 30 miles apart as the trail would have to go, much of it over difficult terrain (see figure 35.1).

During the first two summers, 1910 and 1911, Taylor spent some time in the woods with members of the club from Burlington. However, physical toil was not his forte. To Taylor, after one week's work, "the Club's commitment *in toto* from the Massachusetts line to the Canadian border began to seem a bit oppressive." He gloomily called the Long Trail a "long trial." This may have been the only time that Taylor's unbounded optimism was ever daunted. His reaction to the physical challenge showed that up to that time the Long Trail was proceeding along the lines of the Camel's Hump Club—organized and directed by promoters and businessmen, with tourist revenue in mind. It was not like the Randolph circle's trails, "made by pedestrians for the use of pedestrians." What was missing was at least one vigorous pedestrian to get out there in the woods and go to work.

Enter Judge Cowles.

The thirty-five-year-old Burlington attorney had occupied a back seat at the organizational meeting of the GMC in March 1910. Events now thrust him to the fore. The reason was that he differed from most of the other founding fathers in one important respect: he was a doer, a hiker, a physically robust man. At a later banquet meeting of GMC trustees, one writer reported:

> I asked a trustee with a thought of asperity: "How many of these people ever climbed a mountain?" "Very few," was his reply. "They joined the club to make it easier for those who do. In Middlebury we have 100 members and only 12 hike."

By contrast Cowles was interested in building trail with his own two hands. Taylor asked him in May how things were faring in Burlington, and Cowles replied that no one was building trail, being "too busy" or "attending Supreme Court in Montpelier." Taylor responded by prodding Cowles into taking the lead himself, and my mid-August the Burlington Section of the GMC held an organizational meeting, electing Cowles president. That fall things began to happen.

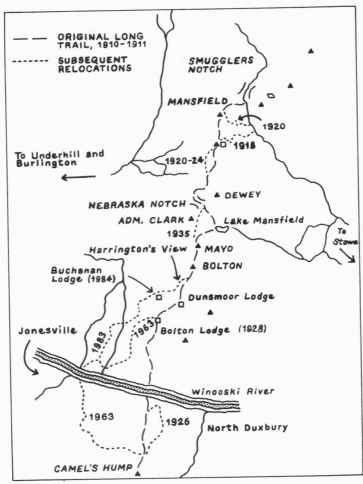

Figure 35.1. The Long Trail: First sections, 1910–1911 Linking Mansfield and Camel's Hump, Vermont's two most prominent mountains, was the opening move in construction of the state-long Long Trail. On October 1, 1910, Clarence P. Cowles and Craig O. Burt marked 3 miles of the new trail, from the south end of Mansfield's summit crest down to Nebraska Notch. The next year they carried their new trail on to the Winooski River, where for years a primitive ferry conveyed hikers to the southern shore and the original Long Trail straight south to Camel's Hump.

On a crisp October 1, 1910, Cowles and Craig O. Burt of Stowe started south from the top of Mansfield with the intention of scouting trail all the way to the road south of Bolton Mountain. At the time a side trail led from the Nose of Mansfield, above the Summit House, over the crest to the Forehead. Cowles and Burt soon decided that this side trail did them little good because dropping straight south off the Forehead would take them over a series of cliffs. So they worked out a new route, skirting the cliffs and passing to the west of Dewey Mountain. Toward the end of a rugged day, they scrambled down the steep north side of Nebraska Notch and found the remains of the old road, which they followed out to Lake Mansfield. From that point Burt descended the road home to Stowe, while Cowles made the first of many end-of-the-day trudges back over the old Nebraska Notch road to Underhill, where he caught the trolley back to his home in Burlington.

Although they had not reached as far as they had planned, the original stretch of the Long Trail had been launched. In two more scouting trips they had an acceptable route worked out on this first section, Mansfield to Nebraska Notch and out to the road at Lake Mansfield. Early in the summer of 1911, Cowles and Burt blazed and cleared the entire first section.

The importance of this first five miles of the Long Trail should be noted. Had Cowles not picked up an ax and clippers and gone to work, all of the publicity that Taylor and his allies were drumming up might have gone for naught. Had the Long Trail *not* succeeded, the idea of long-distance trails might have had a very different and less fruitful future. But once Cowles began to make it a physical reality, others were encouraged to take it further.

In June and July of 1911 Cowles and Burt returned to Nebraska Notch and resumed scouting trail over the shoulder of Mount Clark to the summits of Mayo and Bolton, and down over the forested ridges to the Winooski River. Passing an abandoned lumber camp en route, they took over one of its buildings as a shelter, calling it Dunsmoor Lodge—the first of what was to become a system of shelters along the entire length of the trail.[c] Also in 1911, Cowles went back to the top of Mansfield and worked out a way north along the summit ridge and down to Smugglers' Notch, via the steep Hell Brook.[d] The Burlington gang was working fast: in October 1911 Dr. Paris was writing to Taylor, "Cowles didn't even find out how much we had in our Treasury before he began operations. It put us in a bad hole." But he was getting action. The year 1911 ended with a complete trail from Smugglers' Notch over Mansfield, Nebraska Notch, and Bolton, to the Winooski River.

Linking the work of Cowles with that of Taylor in his one week on Camel's Hump in July 1911, plus existing trails of the Camel's Hump Club, the Long Trail had reached and even slightly exceeded its initial

[c]In 1928 Bolton Lodge was built, replacing Dunsmoor Lodge, which had fallen into ruin. Bolton Lodge was unique among Northeastern backcountry shelters in that it was built to resemble an English or Welsh cottage, topped by a four-sided roof with round corners and irregular shingles meant to look like a thatched roof. It served Long Trail hikers for fifty-five years, until a major relocation of the trail made it off-route.
[d]It is uncertain whether the Hell Brook Trail was thoroughly cleared in 1911. It is so indicated in some of the writings of Dr. Paris in the collections cited, but Judge Cowles's own 1946 reminiscence places its construction in 1921. Possibly it was blazed or rough-cut in 1911 but then thoroughly cleared ten years later.

goal during the first full year: 29 miles from Camel's Hump to Mansfield, and on to Smugglers' Notch.

Under Judge Cowles (somewhere along the line the young attorney of 1910 ascended to the bench), the Burlington Section became one of the most exuberant sections of the GMC. It has been ever since. Among the innovations that Cowles pushed was the admittance of women. As soon as he was installed as head of the Burlington Section in 1910 he wrote Taylor, "Please let us know whether we are right in taking ladies into our organization." Again Cowles was not waiting for an answer before taking the initiative. Within a few years the presidency of the Burlington Section passed to Laura Cowles, the judge's wife.

Cowles remained an active hiker and trail worker long after his 1910–11 work on the Long Trail, but for the most part he chose to concentrate on Mansfield, rather than extending the LT farther north or south. He built at least five other trails on the mountain as well as its most prominent hikers' shelter, Taft Lodge. Mansfield was "his playground." Over a lifetime of hiking, winter and summer, he inspired a whole family of devoted hikers, as well as a wide circle of friends from Burlington. Fittingly he died at age eighty-seven on the Long Trail, savoring the pleasures of a GMC excursion among friends. He lives on in memory as the second critically important figure in the saga of the Long Trail.

In 1912 work on the Long Trail bogged down again. Partly this was blamed on an unusually rainy summer, but partly it reflected the fact that outside of Burlington no one had yet been found to pick up the gauntlet from Judge Cowles. The only addition to the trail was a short section from Smugglers' Notch north to Sterling Pond (3.5 miles), cut by workmen under the direction of W. W. Adams, proprietor of the Mansfield Summit House. The following year an active nucleus of trail workers emerged north of Mansfield, formed the Sterling Section, and cut another 10 miles from Sterling Pond north to the town of Johnson.[e] Among these earliest Sterling Section trail workers the most notable was Fred W. Mould of Morrisville, who continued to maintain this part of the trail, and to build and take care of camps throughout a long life; like Judge Cowles, he died hiking on the Long Trail in 1950. But also like Cowles, Mould and other Sterling workers restricted their efforts to their own locale. The Long Trail still lacked people to extend it up and down the state.

---

[e]A Sterling Section was first organized in Morrisville in 1911, but it focused not on the Long Trail so much as on construction of a trail up Elmore Mountain at the north end of the Worcester Range. This early effort soon lapsed. Then on June 27, 1913, a new Sterling Section (originally "Mount Sterling Section") was formed in the town of Johnson. After the Long Trail work was accomplished by this group (1913–15), it too faded, though Fred Mould continued active. In 1915 a "Pathfinders Section" of the GMC was organized at Johnson High School but was also short-lived. (Sterling Section history is thoroughly documented in an unpublished paper by Robert L. Hagerman, a copy of which is in the GMC archives at the Vermont Historical Society, Montpelier, Vt.)

During the summer of 1912 Taylor approached the Vermont state forester, Austin F. Hawes, to see if his department might help. As usual, Taylor picked the right man. Through a long career in forestry, both in Connecticut and Vermont, Hawes showed a consistent interest in hiking trails. As a young forester in Maine he climbed Squaw Mountain and remained a vigorous mountain walker thereafter. Furthermore, as Vermont's first state forester, appointed in 1909, he had already begun contemplating the need for access routes along the forested ridges of the main range of mountains, for fire control. A budget-minded legislature had given him little money, however. Hawes agreed to have his men build more of the Long Trail, provided it could be located so as to serve fire control needs and provided the GMC raise funds to pay for the labor. Anxious to see trail built, Taylor quickly agreed.

Hawes designated an able young forester on his staff, Robert M. Ross, to work with the GMC on extending the trail south from Camel's Hump to Killington. In late 1912 Ross went into the woods and began scouting (see figure 35.2).

In three weeks in May 1913 Ross and a crew of six cut a well-cleared trail 35 miles north from Killington to Mount Horrid. In June he and his crew started from Camel's Hump and put through another 28 miles south to Lincoln Gap. At this point the GMC funds ran out, with a missing link of about 35 miles still uncompleted between Lincoln Gap and Mount Horrid. That was no small obstacle, as Ross had been through the area in 1912 and pronounced it

> the queerest jumble of peaks, valleys, cross ridges he had encountered in Vermont and he had no more idea of where the best route for a trail lay than before he had crossed.

But Taylor's publicity efforts had paid off. The once aloof AMC now organized a Labor Day excursion to walk the new trail from Killington to Camel's Hump and offered a sizable contribution toward completing the missing link. A Chicago man who summered near the south end of that link, Albert G. Farr, announced he would personally supply the rest of the money. With this financial backing, Ross again struck out across that "queerest jumble" and this time picked a way through. His crew went to work and got the new trail section done by August 26.

Now, at Labor Day of 1913, the Long Trail measured almost 150 miles from Killington to Johnson, north of Smugglers' Notch. Taylor was jubilant. In little over three years his dream of a statelong trail was more than half completed. In the first flush of success, Dr. Paris wrote rapturously of the felicitous harmony of interest between the GMC and the state foresters:

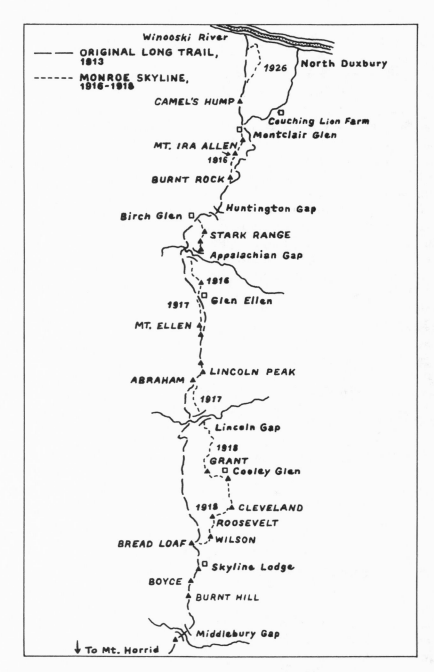

Figure 35.2. The Long Trail: The Monroe Skyline, 1916–1918 South of Camel's Hump, the original Long Trail, built by the state foresters with forest fire control as one objective, proved unpopular with Green Mountain hikers. So Prof. Will Monroe spearheaded a campaign to move the trail off the lower slopes and onto the ridge crests. The resulting "Monroe Skyline" elevated this part of the Long Trail from a routine walk along low-elevation woods into one of the most interesting and scenic hiking trails in the Northeast.

The Forestry Department located and blazed the trail, and furnished super-intendance in its construction, while the Green Mountain Club provided the funds. As a result the Green Mountain Club has its Long Trail, and Vermont has a fire-patrol trail for its Forestry Service, the gift of the Green Mountain Club, a happy result for all concerned.

Alas, the euphoria of 1913 was short-lived. It was soon clear that not all Green Mountain Club members were so happy. Hawes and Ross built the kind of trail they thought appropriate. It was primarily designed for fire control, and thus avoided ups and downs, moving no more than a 15 percent grade across lower flanks of the ridges, with very few summits included. Hawes defended this kind of trail as best suited to the average walker:

> I still feel very strongly that the trail should not be kept exclusively for strenuous hikers, but should be made possible for the great majority of people who do not care for strenuous trips.

But many GMC hikers had other ideas. Several parties expressed disappointment in the "weary and monotonous" trail they found. Built through lower-elevation hardwoods and in some cases burnt-over regions, the Forest Service sections were quickly overgrown with sprouts in a single season. Harry Canfield lost the trail five times in a single trip. The peppery Army officer Herbert Wheaton Congden reported, "There is no visible trail underfoot." Further, the low-level itinerary was plain dull. Congden was dismayed to find the trail "a mile below the summits and ridges." Within a year or two even the perennially optimistic Dr. Paris was critical of what they were stuck with. Influential outdoors writer Allen Chamberlain walked part of the trail in 1916 and summarized the problem thus:

> Unfortunately, however, the necessities of the forest patrol did not fully harmonize with the ideals of the tramper. A route across the ridges was too meandering and laborious to meet the foresters' needs, and the trail that they ran on easy grades along the slopes was far too tame and unspectacular for those whose quest was scenery.

Dissatisfaction with the Forest Service section, combined with a withdrawal of James Taylor's interest in the project (now that it was ostensibly well established), left the GMC in the doldrums, its members inactive and feeling discouraged. The years 1914 and 1915 were "years of disillusionment." At a meeting in October 1916 Dr. Paris actually "put the matter of continuing the existance [sic] of the club fairly before the meeting." Though unanimously voting to carry on, the Green Mountain Club was clearly at a crossroads.

Enter Will S. Monroe.

Born in Pennsylvania on March 22, 1863, Monroe was as different a figure from Taylor as one could imagine. Well educated at Stanford and at European universities, a renowned botanist, author of a dozen books, friend of Walt Whitman, characterized by Judge Cowles as "the most scholarly man I ever knew," appointed by President Woodrow Wilson to the U.S. Peace Inquiry Commission in 1918, Monroe was also the most eccentric of the early Long Trail architects. He was constantly surrounded by a regiment of large shaggy dogs (collies, Saint Bernards, Newfoundlands, Great Pyrenees), to which he was inordinately devoted, so much so that his grave below Camel's Hump is surrounded by half a dozen granite markers honoring the remains of his canine associates. He was almost equally fond of a flock of fifty pigeons, each named (Wotan, Siegfriede, Brunhilde, and so on), and of plantings of exotic flowers, ferns, and trees, on which he kept meticulous records. He was a gourmet cook, known for his Brunswick stew, "Wyanokie pudding," and rose-petal jam from a Turkish woman's recipe. In appearance he was outlandish: wool knickers year-round, blue smock, an ever present red bandana draped over his bespectacled head, wispy beard at loose ends. He earned devoted friendships and was always hospitable to passing hikers. He also earned a reputation for being self-centered, strong-willed, and quick to take offense. "The wiry Rommel of the Camel's Hump region," one later writer called him.

Professor Monroe was an avid climber in Europe each summer until World War I interfered. This made him seek closer hiking worlds, and he fell in love with two. One was the Wyanokie hills in New Jersey near his regular residence in Montclair, where he taught college. The other was Camel's Hump.

When Monroe first summered on the University of Vermont faculty in 1914 and 1915, he quickly decided that south of Camel's Hump the GMC "had on its hands the sort of a trail that it did not want and that it was not worth keeping clean." Monroe believed the Long Trail simply must move out of the lowlands and onto the high ridges and peaks. In 1915 he corresponded with GMC leaders and secured agreement that he and some of his New York–area friends might work on the trail the following summer. Whatever the GMC may have expected from this eccentric professor, it soon discovered that he came prepared to work long and hard hours at scouting, marking, and clearing trail.

On June 20, 1916, Professor Monroe and two associates, J. Ashton Allis and Kerson Nurian, met Dr. Paris's son, Olden, at Burlington, traveled by train to North Duxbury, by auto to a farm that the professor later bought, and by ox cart two miles farther into the woods high on the shoulder of Camel's Hump. Here they set up base camp in a quiet nook that Monroe dubbed Montclair Glen, in honor of his New Jersey home. During the next eighteen days of trail work, it rained on fourteen:

And no one but Allis, Nurian, Olden Paris and I will ever know what we suffered from the torments of the Canadian black-fly and the midgets—no-see-ums, as called by natives. But we pushed our trail south through the unbroken forest of balsam firs and spruces, over Ethan and Ira Allen and Burnt Rock Mt.

Monroe proved a genius at trail location. Hikers on that 1916-vintage skyline from Montclair Glen south over the Allens and Burnt Rock are rewarded with this first sample of his artistry as a trailsman. He painstakingly combed the ridges for spots of exceptional interest or beauty, then linked them together for his trail, so that the miles roll by in a dazzling succession of rock outcrops, mossy glades, secluded hollows, airy ledges, arching hogbacks, boulder heaps and caves with mysterious openings leading to unfathomed recesses, or exposed rock slabs commanding sweeping views of rugged mountainsides. Trail makers had found forest nooks before and climbed high ridges before, but Monroe may have been the first to combine such meticulous attention to detail with an overall skyline sweep. His work elevated the Long Trail from one that was merely long to one that was a classic for beauty and interest as well.

The work of 1916 was only the beginning. Later that summer, during weekends away from his teaching duties, Monroe rounded up Judge Cowles and Theron Dean and pushed the new ridgetop trail on to Birch Glen, south of Huntington Gap. At the end of that summer, before returning to New Jersey, Monroe had a last fling with Olden Paris, a New York friend named Frederic N. Brown, and two hired men, and cut the new trail over the bristling Stark range to Glen Ellen. By the end of 1916 they had 13.5 miles of new trail—a significant beginning, but Monroe recognized that much more work was needed to remake the trail into what he wanted.

That fall, back in Montclair (New Jersey, not the glen), he set about creating the organizational backing that his efforts would require. After a letter-writing campaign to friends throughout the New York area, he called the first meeting of the New York Section of the Green Mountain Club at the St. Agnes Branch of the New York Public Library on October 24, 1916. Fifty-one enthusiastic hikers attended, Monroe was elected president and chairman of the Trails and Shelter Committee (made up of himself, Allis, and H. N. Mussey), and by year's end membership was up to 146. At that first meeting, "animated discussion" and a formal resolution criticized the Forest Service trail and called for substantial rerouting. This first meeting of the New York Section set the tone for its continuing history—a stormy, independent fiefdom within the parent GMC, frequently at odds with the club as a whole, always vigorous, often the largest section in membership, never the quietest. The GMC was one of the most active groups in the swirl of New York City–area hiking, often giving more of its rambunctious energy to that scene than to Vermont, though a vital force in the latter area as well.

Back in the Green Mountains the following summer, Professor Monroe and his New York–area friends, often joined by Vermonters Judge Cowles, Theron Dean, and Olden Paris, pushed on across the summits and high ridges, obliterating the memory of the state Forest Service's overgrown, low-level trail. By the end of 1917 they had cut another 8 miles to Lincoln Gap. In 1918 another 19 miles brought them to Middlebury Gap. Into the 1920s work continued, not only south but north of Camel's Hump, with the relocation of the trail from the Winooski River out of the ravine onto a scenic route over Spruce Knob (today's Bamforth Ridge Trail). Through these years time was always taken for thoroughly blazing and clearing the earlier work and for building lodges at several points along the route, including the original structures at Montclair Glen, Birch Glen, Glen Ellen, and Cooley Glen, and later, to honor his GMC associates, Cowles Cove and Theron Dean Shelter.

By 1926 Monroe's work was complete. By this time this New Jersey professor with his international background had adopted northern Vermont as his home. After summering at "Couching Lion" (as he insisted on calling Camel's Hump) for several years, he purchased the farm by the same name high on its eastern slopes and retired there in 1925, to live with his trail, his dogs, and one sister until his death in 1939.

Meanwhile his new ridgetop route was hailed as the "Monroe Skyline" and is regarded by many GMC members today as the heart of the Long Trail. At the time it was not without controversy. Austin Hawes was understandably miffed:

> Mr. Munroe [sic] entirely disregarded grade and all principles of the proper location of trails, placing his trail directly over the main peaks of the range, so that it is full of steep pitches.

But few hikers shared this view. Allen Chamberlain was lavish in his praise:

> A hiker's joy. Not only does it find the high spots where broad views abound, . . . but it hunts out every interesting charming dell and glade and ravine, every picturesque cliff, every refreshing spring. . . .
> There is not a monotonous inch in the whole twenty-seven miles from the Lincoln-Warren Pass to the Duxbury Valley.

A Massachusetts newspaper called Monroe "a genius in selecting the most scenic courses for his trail and the spots with the grandest views for his lodges." *The Burlington Free Press* especially dwelt on the charms of the section over the Starks:

There were ledges one-half mile long and as the trail wound round these all sorts of fairy caverns came into view. It gave us a feeling that fairies, imps and gnomes scampered to cover just in time to hide from us.

Will Monroe, third of the great trinity of Long Trail founders, had elevated the trail of 1913 from an embarrassment to one of the crown jewels of Northeastern hiking trails.

Meanwhile, south of Killington, the Long Trail pressed on. In 1914, before dissatisfaction with the Forest Service trail set in, the call was to complete the trail from Killington to the Massachusetts line. Crowed Dr. Paris: "From now on the watchword is 'Killington to Graylock' [sic]."

Enter the rest of the state of Vermont.

In southern Vermont a Stratton Mountain Club existed already. Formed in 1912, and with a membership of fifty-three by 1914, it had built a trail up Stratton from the east and constructed a tower on top. However, the club was based in West Wardsboro, somewhat off the route of the Long Trail. Though relations with GMC were generally cordial, the Stratton Mountain Club did not become directly involved in the Long Trail effort.

An uncoordinated network of wood roads laced the southern ridges, and the state Forest Service had blazed and cleared some paths for fire control. GMC leaders saw these existing routes as simply needing to be hooked up to supply at least a preliminary Long Trail route. "A surprising amount of trail and wood road can be discovered when it is sought," urged Dr. Paris. By diligently counting every wood road and forest trail he could find, he estimated that there were 139 miles of "trail" already existing in the regions south of Killington to be traversed by the Long Trail, and that only about 28.5 miles of new trail were needed to link up the pieces into a continuous route all the way to Massachusetts.

Nevertheless, to put this together local leadership was essential. To get it, the original Taylor civic-booster approach was invoked. GMC leaders appealed to chambers of commerce along the route, pointing out the tourist dollars that might result from making their towns into resort centers, featuring access to the Long Trail. Dr. Paris painted a picture of a popular Long Trail aswarm with cheerful tourists, together with radiating loop trails leading down off the main ridge to each town, where tourists could descend each night to spend their money on food and lodging:

Sooner or later all of the towns near the Long Trail will get in contact with the Long Trail, and according to the charm and accessibility of their own region will become mountain centers, great and small.

The Rutland Railroad joined the crusade with a booklet issued that summer (1914) highlighting the Green Mountains' recreational opportunities, with two pages devoted to the new Long Trail. As a result of these efforts, new GMC sections were formed in Bennington and Manchester, and "expressions of interest" were detected in Dorset, Arlington, and Peru.

As usual most early club members' interest was casual. But in J. Laurence Griswold, owner of a Bennington sporting goods store, that section found a man of action and leadership. In 1914 he began scouting the route north toward Manchester, and in 1915 a route was laid out from the Bennington-Brattleboro highway north over Stratton Mountain to Prospect Rock, a distance of 30 miles (see figure 35.3). In the interests of getting the trail through, Griswold and his helpers used the low-level wood roads more than they or future GMC officials wanted, and virtually all of this original route was displaced to the west before World War II. But, unlike the work of the foresters to the north of Killington, this was deliberate strategy for getting temporary trail completed fast. Griswold's intentions from the beginning were made clear in an undated four-page memorandum addressed "to the Officers and Members of Bennington Section, Green Mountain Club, Inc.":

> When the Bennington Section was put through it took the most accessible route with two or three objective points in view. Desiring to be early recognized as a part of the Long Trail system all haste was given in marking our section and every available existing trail and wood road was utilized with the result that the location all through perhaps is not ideal.

The Bennington group soon went back and improved the route to take in more ridgetops and popular local mountains such as Glastenbury.

In 1916 the Bennington Section, now boasting ninety-nine members, pushed south to the Massachusetts line, hooking up with the Williams College network that led to Greylock. The following year, the missing link was filled in between Manchester and Killington.

In 1917, with the trail a reality from Massachusetts to the town of Johnson, the Green Mountain Club issued its first Long Trail guidebook, a Vermont institution that by the 1980s had run through more than twenty editions.

The south end of the trail required repeated refinements and revisions during the early years. Indeed, parts of the trail between Killington and Greylock were apparently still more in the realm of theory and hope than club leaders cared to admit. Especially dubious was the 45-mile distance between Killington and Manchester, allegedly completed in 1917. Reports throughout 1918 and 1919 kept alluding to "new" sections' being opened, and sections that had been pronounced open were much later

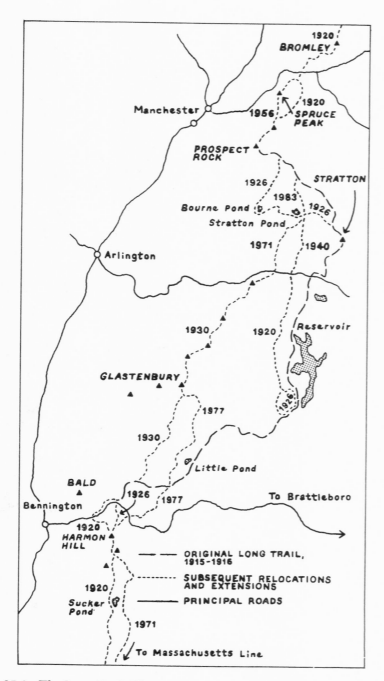

Figure 35.3. The Long Trail: The southern front, 1915–1931 The work of extending the Long Trail south to the Massachusetts line took years to accomplish. Even after it was first opened during the late 1910s, trail workers continued to find better routes, taking in more varied attractions, such as Glastenbury Mountain and the lovely Stratton Pond. Major relocations have been made during every decade since the original trail was built. The years shown on this map refer to the edition of the guidebook in which each relocation first appeared.

reported to be "in pretty good shape now." By 1920, however, most of the difficulties seemed ironed out, and a second edition of the guidebook, issued that year, was able to give a detailed route all the way to the Massachusetts line.

A trail as long as the Long Trail, traversing such varied landscape, inevitably went through many changes, large and small, over the years. Relocations proved a way of life. The first major reroute, indeed, can be dated to the second year of the trail's existence, when the Burlington Section decided that Judge Cowles's Hell Brook route off the north end of Mansfield was too steep for regular use, and switched the Long Trail designation to a new and less strenuous trail down from the Nose, cut under the direction of Judge Seneca Haselton, which was originally called the Running Water Trail and is known today as the Haselton Trail. In 1920 and during the next few years, several other changes were made in the Mansfield area of the Long Trail: When the Taft Lodge was built in 1920 Judge Cowles cut a new trail to it from the road, and gradually this supplanted Judge Haselton's as the designated Long Trail route. About the same time minor changes were made in the route just south of the Nose. Professor Monroe's extensive relocations during the period between 1916 and 1926 have already been described. During the 1920s the Bennington Section rerouted the trail north of Stratton Mountain to swing it west by lovely Stratton Pond and Bourne Pond. And the Sterling Section moved the north end of its part of the trail away from "downtown" Johnson. During the 1930s the Bennington Section made a major change to bring the trail up over Glastenbury Mountain; a cutoff removed Stratton Mountain entirely from the itinerary; in the middle, just north of Middlebury Gap, a minor relocation moved it east and onto a ridge; the Burlington Section eliminated the drop into the valley at Lake Mansfield; and finally, the Sterling Section relocated the climb out of Smugglers' Notch. More changes followed after World War II.

As they did with the trail, club workers built or remodeled lodges—GMC terminology (usually) for small enclosed cabins. On July 4, 1917, the Killington Section erected a new lodge on the site of the old hotel below the summit of Killington, a one-day blitz performed with the aid of Boy Scouts and Camp Fire Girls. In 1919 three Middlebury College professors built the lodge near Lake Pleiad, originally as a base from which Middlebury students could work on the trail south to Brandon Gap. Other lodges sprang up along the route. By 1923 the GMC's thirty-three shelters, together with nine other private and public establishments, made it possible to walk the Long Trail with no more than 8 miles between overnight stops, save for four sections of a bit more than 10 miles each.

With the south end complete by 1920, GMC ambitions swung again to the north end. In 1922 James Taylor was back on the warpath, crusading to complete the trail north at least as far as Jay Peak, the elegant pyramid "whose charms he regards as sadly neglected." In 1923 the first link north of Johnson was put through to Belvidere Mountain (see figure 35.4). In 1924 the trail pushed another 8 miles forward as far as Hazen's Notch. Despite the slogan "Jay Peak or Bust," it took another two to three years to get there. As fervor diminished, GMC planners lowered their sights apace, and Jay Peak was for several years touted as the logical end point for the great trail. During this time it was proudly described as extending "from the Massachusetts line to within a few miles of the Canadian border."

Enter Roy Buchanan.

In 1929 two brothers made up their minds: "We better get rid of the almost." Bruce and Roy Buchanan, with the latter's son Chester, struck off into the woods north of Jay Peak. On their first tries, they found the country baffling, especially toward the end of the first day when, after circling among curving ridges and bedeviled by "a particularly vicious race of mosquitoes," they beheld the sun setting in the east. Before pitch dark they "finally succeeded in returning the sun to its rightful place (and ourselves to camp and supper)." Subsequent trips brought them better results, and by June 1, 1931, they finally had worked out a route all the way from Jay Peak to Line Post 592, an iron marker on the international boundary. "We had removed the 'almost' from the Long Trail," they grinned.

The Buchanans' scouting trips were accompanied by some rumors not usual in trail-building annals. This was the height of Prohibition, and, as Raymond Torrey observed, interest in Canada ran high in some circles other than those of Long Trail completers:

> In view of the interest in Canada at this time, by some persons devoted to other than geographical considerations, some Vermonters have jocularly proposed a bootleggers' chapter of the Green Mountain Club to build and maintain this extension, on the theory that it would be useful to contraband smugglers. This brings up rather hilarious mind pictures of Federal officials chasing bootleggers' agents from crag to crag over the rocks of Jay Peak, which would be rather hazardous for the contraband.

When the Buchanan brothers' scouting trips first required them to park along the road farthest north in Vermont, they struck into the woods for a full day's work. On their return they deposited packs, boots, ax, and other heavy gear in the trunk, and drove off with the trunk sagging noticeably over the rear wheels. Concerned citizens were said to have branded their activities as something other than trail cutting.

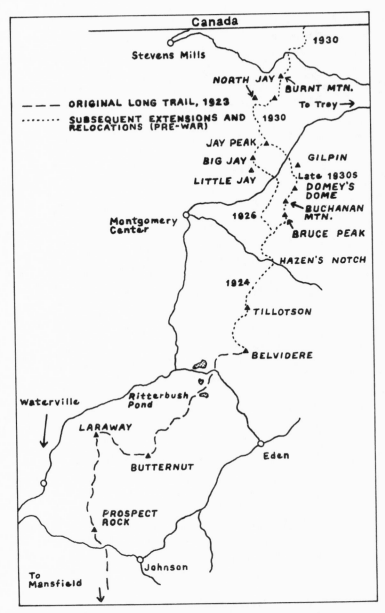

Figure 35.4. The Long Trail: On to Canada, 1923–1930 At first the Green Mountain Club regarded the Long Trail as complete when it stretched from the Massachusetts line to a point north of Mansfield. During the 1920s ambitions were raised again, and the trail pushed on—first to Belvidere Mountain in 1923 and to Hazen's Notch in 1924, then to Jay Peak by 1926, and finally on to the Canadian line in 1930.

In the summer of 1930 a party from the University of Vermont headed by geologist Charles G. Doll and English instructor Phillips D. Carleton were hired to cut the final sections that the Buchanans had blazed. They spent three months almost entirely camped in the woods, not only cutting the trail but also building Laura Woodward Shelter. Twenty years after James Taylor had called the first meeting of the Green Mountain Club, the Long Trail stretched at last from Massachusetts to the Canadian line.

Chapter 36

Unification of the White Mountain trails

IN the same two decades of the teens and twenties, when the Long Trail was knitting Vermont together, both White Mountain and Adirondack denizens began to perceive their entire high peaks regions as cohesive trail systems, instead of independent clusters. Both the White Mountains and the Adirondacks became, in effect, single, unified hiking centers.

Up through 1910, the White Mountains were balkanized into the separate summer colonies of Randolph, Wonalancet, Waterville, and other centers. This was before the unified ownership of the White Mountain National Forest, and before the AMC was established enough to command a regional following. But what mainly kept the early trails separated was the slowness of transportation around the mountains. Even after 1876 when the railroads had greatly speeded up the process of getting from Boston and New York to the mountains, it was still a long slow journey to get, say, from Gorham to North Woodstock, or from North Conway to Randolph or Twin Mountain (see figure 36.2). Therefore, hikers of those days wanted circle routes by which they could return to their summer base of operations. The idea of a through-trail system from Pinkham Notch clear to Franconia Notch—the standard milk run for today's mountain vacationers—had to await the Automobile Age. Not until hikers could drive their cars around the perimeter roads to any trailhead they chose did they first begin to think of the White Mountains as one big place to hike, instead of as clusters of smaller ones.

Although no significant *action* was taken to unify White Mountain trails before 1910, the *idea* of unification can be traced as far back as 1901. Louis F. Cutter, mapmaker nonpareil and doyen of the later Randolph trail-building set, became the AMC councillor of improvements that year. Cutter called for viewing the White Mountains as a single trail system:

> In general, Club money should not be spent for improvements of merely local interest, but for paths and camps that will be of use to the membership as a whole. This condition is fulfilled by paths joining two or more settlements, and by paths giving access to points of general

interest, such as the principal mountain summits and great ravines. Furthermore, paths that are connected together in systems can be maintained with less expense than can isolated bits of paths.

Cutter proposed as the first goal to connect Waterville trails with the rest of the White Mountains. In James Sturgis Pray he found an eager volunteer. Pray scouted possible routes over the next two years and in 1903 cut a trail up the Swift River valley, following roughly the present course of the Kancamagus Highway, and then down past Greeley Ponds to Waterville (see figure 36.1). Pray was assisted by a young Harvard hiker on whom the significance of linking up local trails to form long-distance hiking routes was not lost: Benton MacKaye later recalled this early experience with Sturgis Pray as planting the seed of the idea of the Appalachian Trail, which finally germinated in 1921.[a]

Cutter was councillor of improvements for only one year, but he was succeeded by Pray, who continued what he called "the Club's proposed system of trunk lines," and

> advocated the gradual development and subsequent maintenance of a system of interrelated main paths connecting local centers, —the maintenance of purely local paths to be left to local organizations interested.

Though Pray had progressive ideas, his three years in office (1902–4) were hampered by illness and travel. His successor, Harland A. Perkins (1905–7), finally pushed through the Carrigain Notch Trail in 1906, connecting Waterville to the Pemigewasset trails.

Under Perkins, the club's first printed guidebook appeared. The original plan for this 1907 guidebook was, as Perkins assured Waterville trailbuilder A. L. Goodrich, "to cover those regions not now covered by local guides." Hence Waterville, the Sandwich and Franconia ranges, and Moosilauke were all omitted from the 1907 edition. But the inclusion of all sides of the Presidential Range in one book showed that Perkins was at least pushing in the direction of perceiving the White Mountain trails as one system. In October 1907 the "Guidebook Committee" was made a standing committee of the club, evidence of the club's commitment to the White Mountains trail system as a whole. Still, before 1910, all this remained largely in the realm of theory.

---

[a]MacKaye was a little hazy on his White Mountain topography at this point, describing the area thus: "It connected the East and the West, the Swift River country with the Waterville country, separated by the quite real wilderness of Carrigain Notch" (Dorothy M. Martin, "Interview with Benton MacKaye," Potomac Appalachian Trail Club *Bulletin*, [Jan.–March 1953] p. 12). Since Carrigain Notch lies several miles north of both the Swift River and the Waterville country and runs unmistakably north-south, it seems likely that MacKaye's memory fused two separate projects, the Swift River–Waterville trail which was cut in 1903, and possible scouting trips into Carrigain Notch, where the trail was not actually cut until 1906 (figure 36.1). As we shall see in chap. 45, MacKaye was a grand strategist and global thinker of tremendous importance, who was never troubled by trivial errors in his supporting documentation.

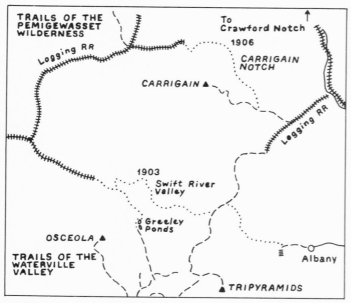

Figure 36.1. White Mountain trails: Strategic links, 1903–1906 In the late nineteenth century, White Mountain trails were built in isolated clusters around the leading vacation centers of the area. In the early 1900s, a few far sighted AMC leaders envisioned linking up all these clusters to form a single White Mountain trail system. The first moves toward this objective were small but strategic links that joined east to west over the future route of the Kancamagus Highway (1903), and that joined the trails of Waterville Valley in the south to those of the Pemigewasset Wilderness in the north, going through Carrigain Notch (1906).

Back around that time, three of the Waterville Valley summer residents most interested in trail work were Paul R. Jenks, Charles W. Blood, and Nathaniel L. Goodrich. In 1912 Jenks transferred his summer base to a farmer's house in the town of Whitefield. That season he enjoyed climbs of Webster and Jackson but lamented the lack of a trail between those two, making a pleasant one-day circuit (see figure 36.2). In the summer of 1912, Jenks cut a trail from Webster to Jackson, the first step in what grew into a relentless nineteen-year campaign to hook up all the trails of the White Mountains into one unified system.

It occurred to Jenks next that a trail from Jackson on through to Mount Clinton would connect with the Crawford Path, thereby opening up a variety of circular day-hikes and through-trips. In 1913 he persuaded fellow Watervillian Charles ("C.W.") Blood to join him in cutting the Jackson-to-Clinton hookup.

In 1914 Jenks and Blood observed that from the top of Webster they could cut a scenic route along the sweeping cliffs on its western flank (the eastern wall of Crawford Notch) and then carry the route down into the

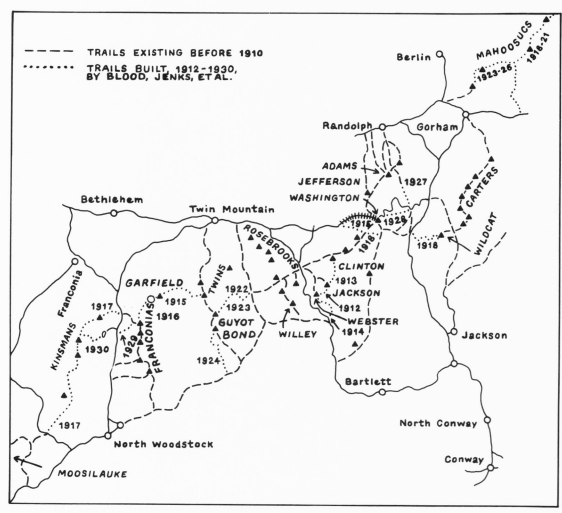

Figure 36.2. White Mountain trails: Unification, 1912–1930 Between 1912 and 1930 the systematic unification of White Mountain trails was planned and executed, a few miles each year. The architects of this achievement were four men: Paul R. Jenks, Charles W. Blood, Nathaniel L. Goodrich, and Karl Pomeroy Harrington. In this map, note how almost every new trail built after 1910 served to link together previously unrelated clusters of trails. For sustained and significant trail work over two full decades, Jenks and Blood especially were remarkable in their impact on the White Mountains hiking world.

notch to meet the trail up Willey and into the Pemigewasset region on the other side. For this task they roped in another old Waterville crony, Nat Goodrich, and went to work. Louis Cutter recalled going by to visit them early in the job and being amazed at the speed and efficiency with which the three made progress. Cutter and the older AMC trailsmen had assumed they would "spend the whole week locating the trail, leaving it to other groups to cut it later." Instead they completed the entire Webster Cliffs Trail, one of the handsomest hiking routes in the Northeast, in four days (August 3–6, as Europe stalked into World War I). The old guard was finding out what kind of trail work to expect from Messrs. Jenks, Blood, and Goodrich. "It was our first step," later wrote Blood, "in the development of a unified trail system across the White Mountains."

At the end of that summer Blood and Jenks, with three others from Waterville Valley (Ed Lorenz, Fred Crawford, and Nat Goodrich's brother, Hubert), went over to Mount Garfield, set up a base camp at Hawthorne Falls, on a trail now abandoned, and began to scout the possibility of a trail connecting the Twin Range to Garfield, and Garfield to Lafayette. They only laid out the approximate route in 1914. The Garfield Ridge is rugged up-and-down country, bristling with dense, coniferous growth, a trail-builder's nightmare. Back in 1876, Moses Sweetser had sampled the terrors of the Garfield Ridge and described it as "surpassingly difficult, leading through long unbroken thickets of dwarf spruce." Shortly thereafter, the redoubtable Eugene Cook had found tough going through "the serried ranks of spruces, which stood with open arms to receive us and to prove their strong attachment." Blood noted, "It was evident then that this new trail was going to be a big undertaking."

In 1915 Blood, Jenks, Goodrich, and a couple of others cleared the trail from South Twin to Garfield Pond. In 1916 they hit the worst of the spruce, trying to push the route from Garfield to Lafayette. Their first attempts were defeated:

> But further way found none, so thick entwined,
> As one continued brake, the undergrowth
> Of shrubs and tangling bushes had perplexed
> All path of man or beast that passed that way.

Goodrich wrote of the epic struggle:

> I recall in point the famous hump between Garfield and Lafayette. We just had to get through to Lafayette that week. And the hump was one solid blowdown. It slopes gradually on the north, breaks off in a small cliff to the south. The trail runs east and west along the ridge. We ran a line over the top—a horrible mess. We tried to contour on the north slope—just as bad. We tried between the two—no better. We knew that under the cliff to the south was too low down and bad footing. We had now crawled through that awful tangle six times and were desperate. Also there were bugs. Finally as a forlorn hope, I went through just at the very edge of the cliff and found a delightful narrow corridor of good going.

This Garfield Ridge Trail was completed in 1916, a major step to unifying the mountains, linking Franconia Notch to the Twin Range, from which by turning south over Bond and down, one could hike through to Crawford Notch via Ethan Pond, and there connect with the Webster Cliffs Trail and the entire Presidentials. Wrote Blood: "The idea of a series of connecting ridge trails maintained by the club across the mountains was beginning to take shape."

The AMC made Blood councillor of improvements in 1914. He served three years and was succeeded by Jenks, who was succeeded by Goodrich, who was succeeded by the fourth man in their dynasty, Karl Pomeroy Harrington, and, recalled Blood, "for more than twenty years . . . our group continued opening new trails, having what we liked to call 'trail sprees' almost every year." The roll call of their trail work accomplishments between 1915 and 1930 reads as follows (also see figure 36.2):

In 1915, aside from the South Twin–to–Garfield section, Blood reopened the completely obscured Ammonoosuc Ravine Trail, and the outlying Mahoosucs first drew their attention, with cutting of the Success Trail.

In 1916, besides the Garfield Ridge, the group cut the Notch Trail in the Mahoosucs.

In 1917 they began the long Kinsman Ridge Trail, to link the Franconia Ridge and Cannon with Moosilauke. The triumvirate laid it out, but the bulk of the actual cutting was done under the direction of Harrington, by what is sometimes regarded as the first paid AMC trail crew. As was noted in chapter 28, a single worker had been employed as early as 1911, but the 1917 crew was the first group of students hired for most of the summer, and the first in an uninterrupted chain of annual summer crews employed ever since. The leader of the first crew was a young Dartmouth woodsman with a future ahead of him, Sherman Adams. More on the growth of the AMC trail crew will unfold in chapter 43.

In 1918 they laid out the Wildcat Ridge Trail, linking Carter Notch directly to Pinkham Notch at the base of the Tuckerman Ravine Trail. (Anticipating the sentiments of many an exhausted hiker today, Blood noted, "Considering its length, the route is much harder than would be expected.") They also put the Camel Trail across the Presidentials, providing a direct route from Lakes of the Clouds to Boott Spur, the Davis Path, and Pinkham Notch.

Between 1918 and 1921 they pushed trail through the first major section of the anguine Mahoosuc Range, from Old Speck to Gentian Pond, where it connected with logging roads to the valley. With trails coming off the northeast end of the Carter-Moriah range, the hiker could now continue from the Presidentials across the Carters and on through the Mahoosucs. Earlier work had been done in the Mahoosucs by Arthur Stanley Pease, but mostly just scouting possible routes.

During 1922 and 1923 Blood and Gray Harris laid out a trail from Zealand Notch up the steep side of Zeacliff and on to Mount Guyot, where it connected with the Twin Range Trail. The actual cutting was done by an AMC trail crew.

In 1924 Harrington restored the route south off Bond to its present Bondcliff location, providing more useful access to the southwest.

From 1923 to 1926 attention returned to the Mahoosucs, where they completed the route from Gentian Pond southwest to Mount Hayes and Gorham. By the end of 1925 "the whole splendid trip of twenty-seven miles" was open. The following year they added access trails.

In 1927 the Madison Gulf Trail was extended from its bottom end in the Great Gulf to connect with the auto road on Washington near where the Old Jackson Road from Pinkham also joined. This made a new direct connection between Pinkham Notch and the hut at Madison.

In 1928 the Nelson Crag Trail was put in, providing a new option for connecting Mount Washington with the valley.

In 1929 Jenks, Blood, and the trail crew resurrected the oft-rebuilt-and-as-often-lost Old Bridle Path up Lafayette. This was its final reincarnation—it has been maintained continuously ever since.

In 1930 Blood and others opened the Fishin' Jimmy Trail to connect the Kinsmans directly with Lonesome Lake, and thereby with Franconia Notch and the various peaks of the Franconia Range.

The result of all this was that the White Mountain hiker who chose among a variety of different and largely unrelated trail clusters in 1910 was confronted, by 1930, with a single unified trail system extending across the state of New Hampshire, from Moosilauke to Maine. All the great peaks and passes of the Northeast's highest range were now linked together to form one great hiking center.

In addition, the pattern of White Mountain hiking was very much affected by two related institutions that evolved during the 1920s and 1930s. One was structural: the AMC hut system. Expanded to nearly their present scope by the early 1930s, the huts have been fundamentally unchanged (physically) for more than fifty years. The other institution was personal and thus mortal, though it seemed as if he would go on forever at times: Joe Dodge. We'll get to him in a few pages—no way to get around that compelling presence in White Mountain history.

But first the AMC huts. In the terminology of northern New England, the words used to denote backcountry buildings have taken on more or less precise meanings. Three-sided overhanging-roof constructions, with or without floors, are usually called *shelters*, or less often *lean-tos*, or generically *Adirondack lean-tos*. Four-sided closed buildings, with a door and window(s) are called *cabins*, *camps*, or (especially the larger ones in Vermont) *lodges*. All of these, however, presuppose self-sufficient hikers, carrying their own food and usually, though not invariably, their own cook-gear and bedding. In New England the term hut is normally reserved for that unique backcountry building where a resident crew provides the food and does the cooking. They are, in effect, primitive off-road inns. The principal examples are those of AMC in the White Mountains, described in this chapter. Johns Brook Lodge in the Adirondacks (chapter 37) is an essentially similar facility—in New England terminology, it is more a *hut* in the AMC sense than a *lodge* in the Vermont sense.

The first full-fledged hut was built during the 1880s in the high col between Mounts Adams and Madison. AMC members had often camped in this col, to such an extent that they were having a noticeable impact on the pristine alpine vegetation there. Litter was getting to be a problem. Laban Watson, manager of the nearby roadside inn, the Ravine House, had constructed "Camp Placid," a very substantial" shelter off the Air Line Trail in 1885. The idea gradually formed of establishing a more permanent structure for camping in the col.

The motivation for building Madison Spring Hut is hard to pin down from the distance of a century away. Later chroniclers of the AMC hut system have emphasized its function as a refuge in bad weather, but contemporary accounts do not mention this concern. The convenience of a high base for tramping excursions seems more likely to have been the primary motivation. The example of Swiss huts was probably in the minds of club members who had climbed in the Alps.

In the summer of 1888 work began on what was recognized at the time as "the most considerable single undertaking on which the Club has yet ventured." The original structure was built of flat stones, with walls 2 feet thick, pointed with cement, two windows, and a single door. The inside dimensions were 16.50 by 12.25 feet, constituting a single room, though one end could be curtained off for ladies' privacy. The work was performed by paid labor from Randolph and Gorham. All materials were carried by horses to treeline, under Laban Watson's direction, but were hand-carried from there. Ill luck provided the builders with an especially rainy summer in which to work, but the building was ready for occupancy nonetheless by the following summer (1889).

One century, one major fire, several reconstructions, and many changes in management techniques later, Madison Spring Hut continues to serve club members and the public. The modern, comfortable, full-service facility of today, however, is a far cry from the original, simple, one-room stone dungeon, dank and dark, equipped with stove, bunks, and cook-gear. Back in the 1890s, visitors did their own cooking and otherwise took care of the building. A caretaker and later a full crew were unknown in that first decade.

Following the Curtis-Ormsbee tragedy of 1900, a second refuge was built in the Presidentials, intended for emergency use, as described in chapter 27. As hikers made regular use of it anyway, the AMC built a more permanent and spacious stone building at the Lakes of the Clouds in 1915. By this time the AMC had already built a hut in Carter Notch, not for emergency refuge, but because that scenic location had been a favorite camping spot for club members and other hikers.

Thus by 1916 the AMC had three huts in the high mountains. Beginning at Madison in 1906, resident caretakers were provided seasonally, but most visitors still expected to bring their own meals.

Meanwhile, the club had also leased from a lumber company some land in the heart of Pinkham Notch, including two favorite attractions, Crystal Cascade and Glen Ellis Falls. Originally the area was secured to prevent logging from desecrating these picturesque spots. After the acquisition of the area by the White Mountain National Forest, the club put up two log cabins in 1920 in the notch below Crystal Cascade. By then it was evident that, as at the high huts, a resident caretaker was needed. In 1921 a Natick, Massachusetts, man named Bill Loker spent the summer as Pinkham Notch's first full-time hutmaster.

With a network of four huts now to supervise (see figure 36.3) and hiking traffic starting to grow fast, the AMC needed a manager for what was, for the first time, perceived as a "hut system." Into that job in 1921 stepped Milton "Red Mac" MacGregor, a wiry Scot from Rhode Island. He ran the system for seven years and continued to be a well-known figure around the Presidentials well into his nineties. Red Mac was a colorful personality, but the man he hired as Pinkham hutmaster in 1922 put him and everyone else in the north country in the shade. Soon after he arrived in the notch, Joe Dodge preempted the central role in the White Mountains.

Joseph Brooks Dodge was born on the Massachusetts seacoast on December 26, 1898. During World War I he saw submarine service as a wireless operator, acquiring a lifelong love of radio. On June 9, 1922, he started work as hutmaster at Pinkham Notch. That summer was a bountiful one for the porcupines that infested those primitive log cabins in the notch, and a truck driver working under Joe christened the establishment "Porky Gulch," which became the insider's name for Pinkham Notch from then on.

Joe Dodge was mayor of Porky Gulch, "poobah of the Presidentials," and "master table thumper of them all." A large and powerful man, with strong jaw, stentorian voice, and an infamous repertoire of blue language, Joe built an image for Porky Gulch and himself which made both the notch and its mayor the chief magnets for hikers in the 1920s and

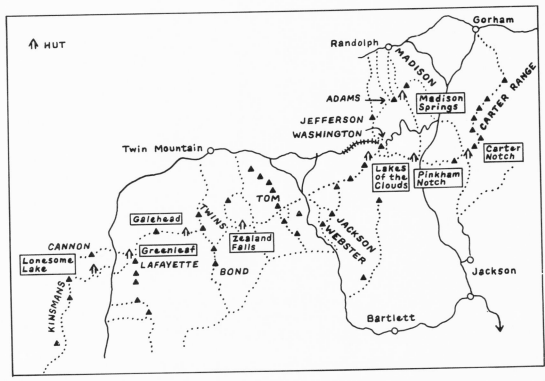

Figure 36.3. The AMC hut system, 1930s During the early 1930s construction of several new overnight facilities in the mountains west of Crawford Notch created the modern AMC hut system. This system reflected the fact that the trail system was already fully linked up (figure 36.2.). The chain of huts symbolized the unification of White Mountain trails which had been accomplished by Jenks, Blood, and the trail-builders of the two decades before 1930. During the 1960s another high hut was added at Mizpah Springs, between Mount Clinton and Mount Jackson.

1930s. Joe had personal contact with most of the hikers: "Though he knows only 2000 visitors by name or face, friends estimate that 250,000 Easterners are acquainted with him," reported the *Saturday Evening Post*. Legends grew of his capabilities as mountaineer, cook, builder, repairman and improvisational mechanic, skier, fisherman, weatherman, and master of the swearword:

> Joe ran a good show. He was a showman, there's no question about it.
> . . . He knew they liked to hear him swear so he would accommodate
> them.

One of his former employees observed, "I don't believe any one ever found it necessary to say to Joe, 'Sorry, I didn't quite catch that.' " This same former employee recalled, "For thirty-six years, he *was* Pinkham, and for those of us who worked with him and for him, he always will be."

For the first four years he was at Pinkham Notch only in the summer. Beginning with the winter of 1926–27, Pinkham remained open, with Joe battling the worst of the storms, talking to himself when no one else was around (which was most of the time), snowshoeing up to check on his three huts, Madison, Lakes, and Carter, and eventually concluding that his life would henceforth be inextricably bound to the White Mountains. From that winter of 1927, the AMC's Pinkham Notch Camp remained open year-round, and for the next third of a century the man in charge of this wintry outpost was Joe.

On January 1, 1928, Joe Dodge succeeded Red Mac as manager of the AMC hut system. Under his forceful leadership, common sense, and aggressive (sometimes abrasive) drive, the system grew from three small refuges to a chain of seven full-service inns and spread from the immediate area of Porky Gulch all the way across the White Mountains westward past Crawford Notch and Franconia Notch. In 1927, at Lakes of the Clouds, a separate crew room was built. In 1929, at Madison, major renovations and new construction resulted in five separate rooms: dining room, kitchen, men's and women's bunkrooms, and crew quarters. The same five rooms were provided in the new huts that began to spring up in 1929 (figure 36.4). This had more than architectural significance. It signaled that the new huts aimed to provide a different level of service and thereby an altogether different mountaineering experience from what had been envisioned by the builders of Madison Hut in 1888. In 1929 Greenleaf Hut was erected on a bluff high on a shoulder of Lafayette. Across Franconia Notch, in the same year, two long-standing fishing camps around Lonesome Lake, acquired by the state of New Hampshire, were added to the growing AMC system. In 1931 and 1932 respectively, the ridges between the Franconias and the Presidentials were provided with two more huts, Galehead and Zealand Falls, so situated as to fashion a chain convenient for nightly stops on a continuous hike across the unified trail system that Blood and Jenks had fashioned (see figure 36.3).

As implied by the size and floor plan of the newly built western huts and the greatly expanded Presidential pair, the AMC huts now provided much more than minimal protection from the weather. With a dependable flow of mountain walkers, augmented by large parties from summer camps, business now required staffing by more than a single caretaker. Teams of two to four "hut-men" were recruited from the colleges, with a strong Dartmouth bias. The young men welcomed the special life of hard work, clean air, and spectacular surroundings. The "croos" (or, more strictly rendered, "Da Croo") provided clean blankets and hot meals, the latter soon acquiring hearty renown among hikers. White Mountain travelers grew accustomed to a level of comfort, though scarcely of luxury, that was not available in the Green Mountains or Adirondacks. The

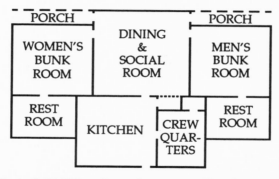

Figure 36.4. Typical AMC hut floor plan, 1930s The three western huts built during the 1930s—Greenleaf, Galehead, Zealand Falls—were designed in a similar way, as shown in this floor plan. There were minor variations in each hut. In postwar years the sex barrier was broken in the bunkrooms, so that men and women occupied either side. Another postwar trend in some other huts was toward separate buildings for bunkhouses.

accommodations had a special flavor and appeal to large numbers of AMC members and others but earned a measure of disdain from more primitive campers, some of whom resented these "hotels" in the mountains. Certainly they had come a long way from that simple stone refuge at Madison Spring in 1888.

For all his colorful self-promotion, Joe Dodge also proved a stunningly successful business manager of the expanding hut system. He understood his market, the hikers of the 1920s, 1930s, 1940s, and 1950s. He was a natural genius at devising workable solutions to the physical problems of maintaining facilities in such remote and difficult settings. On the people side, though his bombastic and domineering style might not have worked in the 1960s and 1970s, it was just right for his time. Many who worked under him attested his "amazing gift of getting the very best out of all those who worked for and with him." One of his employees recalled, "Joe had the art of taking boys and getting men's work out of them."

Though Joe Dodge stepped down in 1959 after thirty-one years, the system he built has lasted and remains a distinctive characteristic of White Mountain hiking. Changes have been introduced since World War II, such as the hiring of women on crews, the addition of an eighth high hut (at Mizpah Springs—to reduce the gap between Lakes and Zealand Falls), and the opening of two huts for winter use. The summertime volume of guests has greatly increased since the quiet days of the 1930s. But the basic system is surprisingly little altered from that which Joe Dodge put in place more than fifty years ago.

The transition from isolated trail clusters to a unified trail system in the White Mountains had an interesting side effect in the Pemigewasset Wilderness: the tilting of the trail axis from north-south to east-west.

In 1910 the orientation of the fledgling trails in the Pemigewasset was north-south. The major mountaintop trails were the Franconia Ridge on the western edge, a trail up Garfield (east of the present trail), the Twin Range Trail, the roadbed of the abandoned Zealand Valley logging railroad, the ridgeline trail along the Rosebrook Range (now abandoned), and the Willey Range Trail over Willey and Field (see figure 36.5). Note especially the decided north-south orientation of the Twin Range Trail, running from the town of Twin Mountain over North and South Twin, Guyot, Bond, and down to the logging railroad (by a more easterly ridge than that used today).

East-west trails were confined to the perimeter. No one wanted to go west from the Twins over the uninviting lanate humps of the Garfield Ridge, nor east from Guyot over the shapeless Zealand Ridge. Indeed, twenty years after it was first cut, even the Twin Range Trail was so little used that it was hard to follow and had to be cut afresh.

Today, what was built originally as one north-south trail goes by four different names for each of four segments: North Twin Trail, North Twin Spur, the Twinway, and the Bondcliff Trail. Why? Because today's hikers perceive that range as part of an east-west artery running from Franconia Notch to Crawford Notch, and connecting with other trails farther east and west (see figure 36.5). The Twinway is seen as a way to get between the Galehead and Zealand huts. The North Twin Spur and the upper Bondcliff Trail are perceived as spur trails to reach interesting side attractions, and the North Twin Trail and lower Bondcliff are viewed as access routes to get up onto the main ridge.

Thus by 1932, with the connecting trails built by Blood, Jenks, Goodrich and Harrington, plus the new western AMC huts (Greenleaf, Galehead, Zealand), the orientation of the entire district switched to east-west. The north-south trails took on an aura of side trails.

It is tempting to assume that the opening of the huts played the key role in the new perception of hikers. However, it may be noted that the western huts came only *after* the trail system was basically complete. Virtually all of the key trails were built during the 1920s, the western huts not completed until 1932.

Not all trail cutting in the Blood-Jenks era involved virgin forests like those of the Garfield Ridge. The Pemigewasset Wilderness had by this time seen the worst of the logging, and much of what is now rejuvenated forest was then a wasteland of charred stumps superfused with a growth of brambles, berries, and hobblebush. Elsewhere the woods had somewhat come back, but the old logging roads could still be found and often served as trailbeds. Robert Underhill, editing *Appalachia* during the late 1920s, reflected on the place of the trail makers in the overall scheme of White Mountain topographical history:

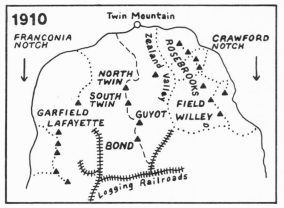
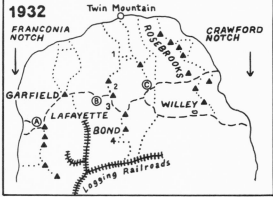

Key to symbols in 1932 map

A. Greenleaf Hut
B. Galehead Hut
C. Zealand Falls Hut

1. North Twin Trail
2. North Twin Spur
3. The Twinway
4. Bondcliff Trail

Figure 36.5. The tilting axis of the Pemigewasset trails, 1910–1932 As late as 1910 the Pemigewasset region—the diverse mountain country between Franconia and Crawford notches—had few trails, and they tended to run north-south. After the building of trails and huts, the orientation of hiking in this region shifted to east-west. One consequence was that the Twin Range Trail of 1910 became fragmented and known as four different trails, with the Twinway (no. 3 in the 1932 map) conceived as a link in the east-west route through the hut system. Today most hikers think of the usual route through this area as running east-west, as do the Appalachian Trail and the standard hut-to-hut itinerary.

> It reverses the order of nature. Or rather it is as if an older unknown civilization has come and gone, and we had overlaid our newly primitive paths upon its stately remains—like setting tents upon the sites of ancient Babylonian palaces.

The four leading trail makers of this age—Blood, Jenks, Goodrich, Harrington—were a distinctive quartet. If Joe Dodge preempted center stage, these four were certainly worthy, if less-noticed, side shows. Their prestige in New England trail circles during the 1920s and 1930s was awesome. "The definition of a standard trail by Nat Goodrich," it was once said, "did more than any other single influence to produce better amateur trails in New England." They styled themselves the "Old Masters."

They were all strong personalities. Blood was a Boston lawyer, with a steel-trap mind and an unfailing memory for detail. Jenks and Harrington were teachers of Latin, the former at a Flushing, New York, high school, the latter at Wesleyan University. Goodrich was librarian at Dartmouth College. All but Harrington—back to him in a moment—are remembered as hard-driving, purposeful men, with little patience for casual or sloppy work. Wrote Goodrich:

> There is an edge, a tenseness, about this work. The day is a long strain of keen concentration, of quick decisions, of driving through scrub and blow-downs.

Blood and Jenks were described by a contemporary as "two of the worst trail cranks of those mountains." Neither one brooked conflicting opinions; fortunately they saw eye to eye on most trail issues until near the end of their long careers, when they had a falling-out. Of Jenks, Blood said, in words that others might have equally applied to Blood,

> To him a thing was either right or it was wrong. Unless in his opinion it was right, he would not tolerate it, no matter what his friends thought or how utterly unimportant the matter might seem to some of us.

Goodrich was less assertive than Blood or Jenks, a tall, lean, proper, unsmiling ascetic. Though his writings reveal grace and a subtle sense of humor, his presence did not, according to Sherman Adams, who worked under him both at Dartmouth and on the trail.

Yet these tough-minded men had a warm spot in their hearts for the mountains which glowed with uncommon fervor. The humorless Jenks could reminisce about work on the Mahoosucs, writing,

> Of nigh a hundred miles of heavy packing; of nearly as much string paid out through the rough; of forty days' camping beside high waters; of much bacon and corncake, coffee and cocoa; of some two thousand biscuits baked before the blaze; of a trail varied, interesting, fascinating for every one of twenty-five miles; and withal the outcome of men's vacations, for the vacations of men to come.

Blood, nearing old age at the Ravine House, could admit:

> I am happy, however, just to go into the forest and put a new handrail on a bridge or putter over a few rods of trail, for, above everything, I am a trail man.

The austere Goodrich could reflect:

> The trails we have made together, three of us, latterly another, unroll before my eyes, and the thrill comes back. Always there has been the faint spice as of adventure, of exploration; always the keen, joyous concentration as of those enwrapped in a great task to which they were not inadequate—and yet all in a sort of play. So, summer after summer, hot, dirty, redolent of dope, we have struggled through blowdowns and scrub while the white string unrolled behind. Always

there was the odor of balsam, the song of thrushes, the drift of cloud shadows.

Of the lot Harrington alone is remembered with warmth and affection. A short man, soft-spoken, self-deprecating, he has been described as the archetypal absent-minded professor. He wore old suits when in the woods, complete with jacket and tie, finding that "the pockets of the coat were handy for sandwiches." His solitary rambles in the trailless parts of the mountains, including unplanned bivouacs, were legendary around North Woodstock, his summer home. Yet he too accomplished much trail work, and was a guiding light on outdoors matters for a generation of Wesleyan students. One of their number paid Harrington the kind of compliment that, in a measure, is richly deserved by all four of the great trailsmen who between 1912 and 1930 built the White Mountain trail clusters into a single unified system, essentially the trail system that White Mountain hikers know today:

> [Harrington] was indeed a patron saint of the Outing Club when I was an undergraduate, and his inspiration meant much to many Wesleyan people who went climbing in the White Mountains.

Chapter 37

The Adirondacks become one hiking center

As in the Green Mountains and the White Mountains, so in the Adirondacks—but a little bit later: hikers finally perceived them as a unified mountain center during the 1920s.

It will be recalled that during the nineteenth century the Catskills had been the premier mountain playground of New York State, thronged with mountain-loving enthusiasts (if only at the Pine Orchard corner of the range), while the Adirondacks were virtually unknown. During the first half of the twentieth century these positions were almost totally reversed.

In 1924 the one-thousand-room Hotel Kaaterskill went up in flames. The Catskill Mountain House was in its final days, a decaying shadow of former glory. The stock market crash of 1929 ruined whatever hopes it had for revival, and when World War II began it finally closed its doors to guests. The Catskills—the mountains, that is, as distinct from the thriving valley-based resorts—were largely bypassed and went into relative eclipse in climbing history. It was said:

> The Catskill summer tourist is not a climber. He is a two-week porch sitter or road walker who knows or cares little for the wild peaks and cloves a few miles from his inn.

To the hiking generation of the 1920s, the Catskills seemed "too far from New York for a day trip and . . . too close for a good weekend." By the end of the 1930s they were perceived but dimly, as "perhaps the one mountainous place within four or five hours of New York which is becoming wilder all the time." The hills that had rung with the merry laughter of Mountain House guests for so many decades now lay silent. Some hiking persisted, but well into the 1940s and 1950s it was so light that Ed West, a Conservation Department man who knew the range as well as anyone, could say, "First I heard anything about hiking here in the Catskills was about 1960."

Thus the Catskills replaced the Adirondacks as New York's unknown mountains. Rip Van Winkle slumbered in peace.

Meanwhile the Adirondacks enjoyed a burst of popularity, spear-headed by the emergence of the third and last of the great Northeastern mountain organizations. The Adirondack Mountain Club was born amid a succession of curious paradoxes.

The first man who took action on the idea of an Adirondackswide mountain organization was one whose long subsequent outdoors career is associated with New Hampshire, not New York: Henry Ives Baldwin, later woodlands manager for Brown Paper Company of Berlin, New Hampshire, still later forester at Fox State Forest, New Hampshire, and author of the guidebook to Monadnock. Baldwin was a rangy youth who grew up in Saranac Lake, New York, and so his first mountains were the Adirondacks. He headed the trail crew in the Marcy region each summer during the years 1915-19. On a sunny autumn day on Whiteface in 1916, he and some buddies organized and named their own "Adirondack Mountain Club." However, they erected no formal organization and for several years functioned without publicity or growth in membership.

A second paradox was that it was a New York real estate developer who later took to Florida Lands development, who built on Baldwin's gang of friends to create what became a major force in preserving the Adirondacks *from* development. Meade C. Dobson, then secretary of the New York State Association of Real Estate Boards, was a summer vacationer in upstate New York who knew of the AMC's role in the White Mountains and had pondered the need for a similar organization in his beloved Adirondacks. Dobson had some proven talent for this sort of thing, having been a prime mover in organizing both the Utica Tramp and Trail Club and the Palisades Interstate Park Trail Conference, predecessor to today's New York–New Jersey Trail Conference. Somehow he heard of Baldwin's little Adirondack Mountain Club and began to see it in larger terms.

Legend supplies a further irony: it was Dobson's violation of conservation laws, by catching a trout out of season, that led to his being hauled before State Conservation Commissioner George D. Pratt in February 1921, at which time Dobson took the opportunity to propose to Pratt that there ought to be a single Adirondackswide club, "to do for the Adirondacks what the Green Mountain and Appalachian Mountain Clubs were doing for those areas." Pratt liked the idea, decided to involve the Conservation Commission, and assigned forester William G. Howard to help Dobson get it going.

Dobson and Howard soon had talks with Baldwin, and the unlikely trio—youthful woodsman, well-connected real estate developer, and state bureaucrat—began to work together. That summer they got up a mimeographed sheet to sound out others. The first newspaper publicity appeared in the *Adirondack Enterprise* on August 10, 1921, describing the club and its objectives, and citing Baldwin, Dobson, and Howard as people for interested parties to contact. That fall Baldwin made a special trip to Boston to study the AMC's organization: "We got many hints on constitution and by-laws from that club," recalled Baldwin in 1955.

Meanwhile, within the state, Dobson and Howard worked with organizational skill and flair that even James Taylor must have admired. On December 5, 1921, they assembled a meeting of forty interested persons in New York City, in the "log cabin" inside the plush sporting goods emporium of Abercrombie and Fitch. Leroy Jeffers, secretary of the Associated Mountaineering Clubs of America, was persuaded to preside, though one of those present commented later that Dobson really ran the meeting. Howard gave the principal talk to inspire the august forty with their idea.

The December 1921 meeting appointed an Organizational Committee, with Dobson as chairman. This group laid the groundwork for a second meeting, April 10, 1922, and a certificate of incorporation, signed on April 25. George Pratt, just retired as conservation commissioner, was elected president; Dobson was one of three vice presidents; J. Ashton Allis, a New York banker-trailsman, was Treasurer; and the New York journalist-trailsman extraordinaire, Raymond H. Torrey, was recording secretary. The charter membership of 208 was skillfully selected to include all the right people calculated to ensure the success of an Adirondack club, including the Lake Placid Club's Melvil Dewey and Harry Wade Hicks; Henry L. DeForest, the aptly named Adirondack Mountain Reserve (Ausable Club) president; a vice president of the Adirondack League Club (still the largest property-holding club in the region), George H. Storm; Allis and Torrey, both of whom were extremely influential in the burgeoning New York City–area hiking circles; the founder and head of the New York Section of the Green Mountain Club, Will S. Monroe; Adirondack historians Alfred L. Donaldson and T. Morris Longstreth; *New York Times* editor and superwalker John H. Finley; prestigious former U.S. chief foresters Gifford Pinchot and Henry S. Graves, the latter now dean of the Yale Forestry School; and influential New York politicians such as Robert Moses, Louis Marshall, and the chairman of the Taconic State Park Commission, a rising political star by the name of Franklin Delano Roosevelt. Taylor must have been green with envy.

In his 1921 keynote address, State Forester Howard proposed three fundamental objectives:

1. An Adirondack Mountain Club can stimulate interest in the out-of-doors and encourage hiking and mountain climbing.

2. An Adirondack Mountain Club can, by the development of public trails and campsites, open up a wider field and increase the pleasure of those who have already heard and responded to the call of the wild.

3. An Adirondack Mountain Club can, as one man has put it, "improve the camping manners" of the public.

Howard's first two points placed the club squarely on the road paved by the AMC and the GMC in New England. They amounted, in plain language, to hiking and trail work. When the ADK drew up "objects of the club" for the certificate of incorporation, these two activities took center stage, number one being: "To open, develop, extend and maintain trails for walkers and mountain climbers in the Adirondack mountains." Other objects included shelter construction, maps and guidebooks, excursions, and support of like-minded local walking and trail-building clubs throughout New York State.

Two big projects occupied the club's earliest years, both designed to establish its identity as a trail-building and hiking presence in the Adirondacks. The first was laying out the 130-mile Northville-Placid Trail, to be described in chapter 44. The second was the construction of Johns Brook Lodge as a hiking base in the heart of the high peaks.

The latter had considerable symbolic importance. The ADK's acquisition of a site in the Johns Brook valley signaled the rise of modern hiking in the Adirondacks and explicitly displaced two older traditions. In the first place, the land was acquired from a lumber company, which had basically completed logging operations in the area. Thus wilderness exploitation yielded to wilderness recreation. Moreover, the specific site was the very one occupied by old Mel Hathaway's squatter's cabin, last vestige of the old mountain guide tradition. Hathaway was ousted. Thereby did the era of guided hikes give way to that of self-reliant hikers and campers.

Building Johns Brook Lodge, 3 miles from the nearest road, was tough work. Several tons of building materials were hauled by team from Keene Valley over the old logging road, much washed out by heavy rains that summer and fall. Some of the materials were delayed until winter, when snow cover made horse-drawn hauling possible again. Costs soared from the initial budget of eight thousand dollars to about fifteen thousand. By June 1925, however, the lodge was completed and opened with much fanfare.

Johns Brook Lodge became a center of Adirondack Mountain Club hiking from the beginning. Accommodations were available for people, who were encouraged to bring their own food and cooking gear. Caretakers were provided—initially Mr. and Mrs. Harvey Branch—and they had supplies on hand for sale and occasionally cooked for guests, Harvey's "succulent flapjacks" being especially memorable. Thus in general style, Johns Brook Lodge resembled the AMC White Mountain huts as they then functioned (Madison, Carter, Lakes of the Clouds). In 1929 the ADK acquired an additional seven acres adjoining its plot, with two much smaller cabins already on the land. These became known as Grace Camp and Winter Camp. Along with Johns Brook Lodge and a satellite cabin housing its crew, they continue to this day to serve as a four-building complex in the heart of the high peaks, for the use of ADK members and the public. It is noteworthy that this is where ADK drew the line. No system of full-service huts or even of closed camps took root in the Adirondacks. A road-based facility was acquired when the club took over Adirondak Loj in 1932. But, except for the JBL complex, the only overnight accommodation available to hikers in the high country remained the occasional old open-front lean-to. To this extent the spirit of Adirondacks camping remained wilder.[a]

The real significance of Johns Brook Lodge was its strategic location. It may be recalled that up until this time the two chief centers of Adirondack tramping had been the Ausable Club and the Lake Placid Club (with its subsidiary, Adirondak Loj). The Ausable Club had a wealth of paths, largely maintained by the Adirondack Trail Improvement Society. The Lake Placid Club-Adirondak Loj end of the mountains also had trails in abundance, and organizations like the Shore Owners' Association and the Camp and Trail Club performed a role somewhat analogous to that of ATIS. But in between, the only connections lay where both systems reached Marcy and its high neighbors, Haystack and Skylight, or along the low-elevation, now deteriorating Tight Nipping Road through Railroad Notch. A single trail climbed through Johns Brook valley, past old Mel Hathaway's cabin, not part of any "system."

Stirrings of interest in more Johns Brook trails can be detected prior to 1925. In 1919 the Range Trail to Haystack was linked to the Johns Brook trail up Marcy at the head of Panther Gorge. In 1921 State Forester Arthur S. Hopkins laid out a trail from Johns Brook at Bushnell Falls to the Van Hoevenberg Trail up Marcy. It is uncertain exactly when the way from Hathaway's cabin to Gothics Col was a definite trail, but it definitely preceded the coming of the lodge.

When the ADK moved into the valley, however, a small but strategically significant upswing in trail building took place. A New York newspaper reported in the summer of 1926,

> The various trail projects from the [Johns Brook] Lodge, up the mountains on either side of the valley of Johns Brook, are being pushed rapidly, with volunteer labor.

The formerly sparse look of the trail maps of the high peaks rapidly changed during the 1920s and 1930s (see figure 37.1). Most active among the trail-builders were, at first, the old Adirondack Camp and Trail Club, which functioned as an arm of the ADK club during the late 1920s; the rangers of the Conservation Department, sometimes working closely

---

[a]The ADK's governing body went on record in favor of constructing something similar to the AMC's hut system as late as 1934. At that time it was the Conservation Department that stopped the move, by declaring it impossible under the "forever wild" constraints of the constitution (see John J. Bennett, Jr., "Attorney General Rules Closed Shelters in Forest Preserve Inadvisable," *High Spots* [Apr. 1934], pp. 35–37).

with the ADK's Trails Committee; and ATIS workers from the Ausable side. New trails emanated north from Johns Brook Lodge to Big Slide, east to Wolf Jaws Notch on the Great Range, south to Gothics Col, and west through Klondike Notch to Adirondak Loj. The trail into the lodge, and both trails from there up toward Marcy, saw a considerable increase in traffic.

The direct effect of all this was to enhance the tramping options available to lodgers at Johns Brook. The underlying effect was to fill in the missing middle of the Adirondacks trails map. Combined with the advent of the automobile and good roads (so that all trail-heads were available from all summer places), these connecting links had the effect of unifying the Adirondacks as a hiking region, in much the same way that Vermont and New Hampshire mountains had been knit together during the preceding fifteen years. Yet not quite so systematically: the Adirondacks,

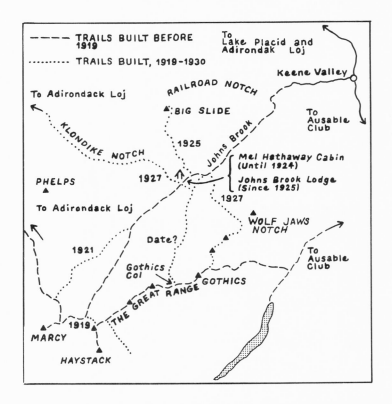

Figure 37.1. Adirondack trails near Johns Brook Lodge, 1919–1930 The Adirondack Mountain Club took over the site of an old guide's cabin in the Johns Brook valley, lying between the Ausable Club trail network on the east and Adirondak Loj and its trails on the west. In 1925 the ADK opened Johns Brook Lodge on this strategically centered site. The trails that grew up around Johns Brook Lodge had the effect of knitting together the trails of the high peaks into a single Adirondack-wide system.

with their trailless peaks, their outlying Sewards, their wild perimeter valleys, remained as they always had been, a trifle wilder than most of the Northeast, always just a bit more resistant to unification or systematization.

Thus, despite its youth, the Adirondack Mountain Club played a key role in transforming the Adirondacks into a single hiking center. By opening the Johns Brook valley to hikers, the ADK instantly and forever filled in the center of the Adirondacks hiking map, tying together the formerly separate trail systems of the Lake Placid–Adirondak Loj and Ausable Club circles. For mountain trampers from this point on, the Adirondacks meant the entire high peaks region, not two isolated subregions. By occupying that core ground, the ADK symbolically took over as the central club of the Adirondacks.

Hiking and trail building flourished in the Adirondacks during the later 1920s and 1930s. A register kept at once pristine Lake Colden recorded visits by more than one thousand people each summer in the years 1932–34, more than two thousand annually from 1935 to 1937. Another register at Marcy Dam, on the most popular route up Marcy, showed numbers soaring to more than three thousand in 1937.

The failure of more developed facilities to catch on in the land of the Cauchsachrage reflected the presence there of a burning policy issue that did not surface with such urgency in New England for another generation. This was the gut issue of preservation versus use. It will be recalled that in Howard's keynote address in 1921 the third objective for the new club was to "improve the camping manners" of the public. Here Howard challenged the ADK to adopt a modern concern for the outdoor environment. To Howard in 1921 this meant primarily correcting abuses such as littering, peeling bark, defacing signs and picnic tables, and being careless with campfires. But in urging that the new club "must stand for high ideals in conservation," Howard gave the club an initial push in directions not yet of central concern to the recreation-oriented New England clubs.

The ADK did not rush headlong into the conservation issue.[b] At its 1922 meeting a resolution to involve it more deeply was deferred, and conservation sank to eighth and last of the objectives in the certificate of incorporation. Not until the presidency of Pirie MacDonald in 1928 did the club adopt a strong policy. By 1930, when the club prepared a "call to action for much of the decade of the 1930s," it listed first and foremost:

> RECREATION. An expanding trail policy to keep pace with ever increasing yearly use of the State Forest Preserve by the people, but with a due regard to the preservation of large areas of wilderness.

---

[b]Throughout this chapter we use the older term *conservationist* to apply to those who sought to minimize the intrusion of people on the natural world. In modern debate, the term *preservationist* has arisen for one who most staunchly resists intrusion, and *conservationist* has been pushed back to mean one who accepts a low level of human use and impact. The conservationists, or at least the "strict conservationists," of the 1930s were akin to today's "preservationists."

In short, while recreation was still in first place, it was now modified by the caveat phrase "preservation of large areas of wilderness." Listed second was:

> CONSERVATION. Creation of a widespread understanding of correct trail manners and customs and of the need for unceasing caution against fire, and the development of public appreciation of the Forest Preserve.

As the decade of the 1930s progressed, these twin objectives proved not always as compatible as the club's early leaders had hoped. These were years that one appraiser of club trends labeled "Sturm und Drang." At issue was interpretation of the "forever wild" clause for the Forest Preserve. On one side were ranged the strict conservationists, such as the strong-willed John S. Apperson and guidebook writer Walter Collins O'Kane. On the other side were the ardent recreationists, led by peakbagging historian Russell Carson, skier Hal Burton, and others who wanted improved access, especially for the increasingly popular sport of skiing. Robert Marshall, a peakbagger *and* archadvocate of wilderness preservation, proposed a zoning system with some totally wild areas, others with limited trails, and some areas with intensive trail development. Whatever Marshall's stature today as a giant of the conservation movement, that proposal was loudly deplored by the ADK's conservationist wing in the 1930s.

It should be understood that this was not a badly polarized debate all the time. As a guidebook writer, O'Kane clearly accepted the idea that people should have access to mountains, while both Marshall and Carson were eloquent spokesmen for wilderness. "In all our thinking about recreational development," Carson warned his own side of the debate, "we ought constantly to remember that wilderness and natural beauty are the real charm of the Adirondacks, and that preservation is as much our objective as helping more people to share our joy in them."

Nevertheless differences were real and fundamental. Two issues caused special acrimony. One was the building of "truck trails" and other access roads, intended for fire control as well as to provide access for recreationists. These were proposed projects of the Civilian Conservation Corps (CCC). In 1933 the ADK supported a state Conservation Department plan to improve roads within the Forest Preserve but by 1936, after bitter debate, went on record as opposed to the CCC truck trails, "other than those already finished or on which work has been started." In 1936 the club urged too that, on CCC trail projects (which it had always supported), "the trail shall not be unduly manicured, graded or widened."

The other issue was the construction of ski trails in the high peaks region. As conservationists fought resolutely for the strictest interpretation of "forever wild," the club's enthusiastic skiers found themselves increasingly uncomfortable with that posture. When the Whiteface ski development came up for discussion during the late 1930s and early 1940s, the club opposed it, but when it came to building trails slightly wider to accommodate skiers, as on some CCC work or the club's own Wright Peak ski trail of 1939, the club's skiers were ready for some flexibility in the concept of wildness. Harry Wade Hicks of the Lake Placid Club and a group of skiers from Schenectady spearheaded a campaign to cut ski trails not only on Whiteface and Wright, but on the southwest shoulder of Giant. The latter proposal was rejected, but the first two prevailed.

In October 1935 the club sponsored a trails conference in Albany that "developed into an animated and somewhat turbulent discussion," ending in acrimony. A sizable bloc felt that conservation was being overstressed to the detriment of the basic mountain-climbing orientation of the club. "What this Club needs above anything else," cried Trails Chairman A. T. Shorey, "is to become trail conscious again—a mountain club that does not climb mountains has no excuse for being alive." The conservationist wing held firm, O'Kane solemnly warning,

> The more that's done for hikers in the forests and woods and mountains, in that far do they fail to get the most out of it. . . . We must retain the challenging character of the wilderness.

Sturm und Drang indeed. During the years when the AMC's Joe Dodge and the GMC leaders in Vermont were happily building huts and lodges, the ADK seethed with controversies over these conservation issues that little troubled their New England counterparts. Be it noted that what was peculiarly a New York issue in the 1930s was destined to become a central concern of conservationists and, in 1970s parlance, environmentalists throughout the Northeast—indeed, throughout the nation —but not until a full generation later. Thus in organizing after the AMC and the GMC, the Adirondack Mountain Club borrowed much from those clubs in deciding how to build and maintain trails and conduct excursions and other sociable events; but it added a distinctive touch of its own that foreshadowed concerns that touch the entire community of hikers and conservationists today.

Chapter 38

Baxter State Park

KATAHDIN'S interesting and checkered history took important new turns during the first half of the twentieth century. Earlier chapters have seen Maine's great mountain go from the wild northern outpost that tested the resources of the Monument Line surveyors of the 1820s and 1830s and the adventurous recreationists of the 1840s and 1850s; to the relatively easily climbed peak that the logging operations made accessible during the 1880s and 1890s; then back to remote isolation following the great fire of 1903. By the 1910s Katahdin was again a difficult peak. It was seldom climbed, usually by one of three routes: the old Abol Slide, which had never been entirely neglected; the newer Hunt Trail from the west; and an arduous 27-mile pilgrimage from the east across logged and burned forest by indifferently maintained trails, successors to the now lost Keep Path (see figure 38.1). In the years between 1910 and 1914 a brief flicker of resurgence was felt when renewed logging took place in the Wassataquoik; new tote roads were brought down from the north via the Pogy Pond region, offering a new though long and taxing approach; Tip Top Camp was built on the northwest spur of Katahdin. But this time the climbers did not respond, and by 1920 all the northern trails were but faint tracks in a returning wilderness.

In 1917 a veteran Maine guide named Leroy Dudley built a simple camp barely big enough for three people on the shore of Chimney Pond —"Dudley's Den"—and made it his summer headquarters. This was the first in a chain of events that once more shifted the hiking and camping scene at Katahdin and placed its center of gravity squarely over Chimney Pond. It has remained there ever since.

Mark Leroy Dudley became as much a part of Katahdin mythology as the storm god Pamola. Born on June 24, 1874, in Wesley, Maine, he moved as a child to Stacyville, the old logging town east of Katahdin. By age eighteen he was guiding parties up the great mountain and had established a regular campsite beneath a large shelving rock on the far side of Chimney Pond. He was in and out of that cirque for the next quarter century before he built Dudley's Den in 1917. After that, for a

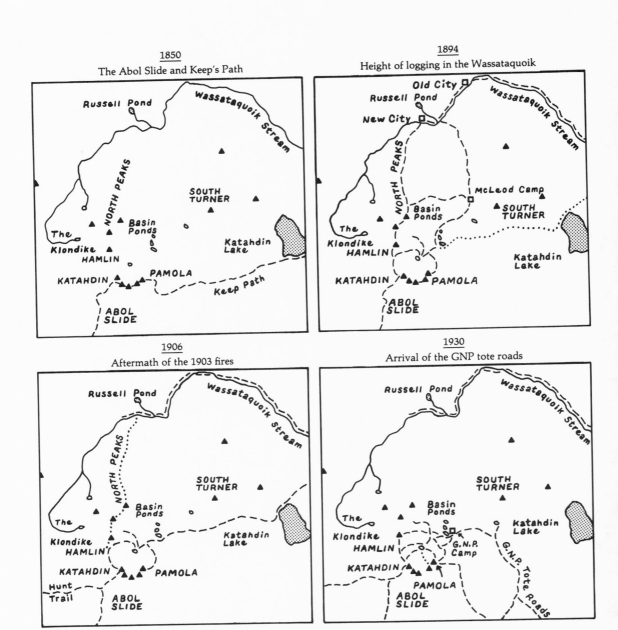

Figure 38.1. Changing approaches to Katahdin, 1850–1930 The preferred routes of access to Katahdin underwent radical changes over the years between 1850 and 1930. In 1850 the newly built Keep Path was the principal approach route. With the coming of major logging operations along the Wassataquoik, trails opened up from the north. When these trails were largely destroyed by the 1903 forest fires, approaches reverted to east and west, the latter via the newly opened Hunt Trail. The major change that ushered in the modern trails era at Katahdin came when the Great Northern Paper Company built tote roads from the southeast and a commodious camp at Basin Ponds. The one route that was always in use despite all these radical changes elsewhere was the Abol Slide.

second quarter century, he held court to the growing volume of Katahdin hikers coming through Chimney Pond. Lean and wiry, a pipe forever implanted in his mouth, with the creased smile of the authentic backwoodsman's leathery face, Dudley was renowned for his knowledge of the Katahdin country, as well as for his homey friendliness, understated repartee, and stories of Pamola. His base at Chimney Pond earned him an intimate acquaintance with the mountain and its neighbors, making him rightful heir to the tradition of Marcus Keep. Helon Taylor, a later Katahdin legend in his own right, recalled Dudley's story-telling virtuosity even more vividly than his mountaincraft or woodsmanship: "I don't know any entertainer who could keep a group entertained the way he did." A typical party's experience illustrates:

> In the evening, all who could crowded into the limited quarters of Roy Dudley, guide and character of the campgrounds. . . . For nearly an hour he entertained his guests with tales of the Indian Spirit, Pamola, and of some of his supposed adventures.

Dudley might ask a listener after one of his stories, "Did you like that story?" "Oh yes, Mr. Dudley." "Well, there's some truth in it too." Thus did Pamola's greatest servant carry on until Saint Valentine's Day in 1942, when a trivial misstep in front of a logging truck on an icy road suddenly snuffed out his vibrant life—but not his legend nor those of Pamola which he had spun.

The decisive event that thrust Dudley and Chimney Pond onto Katahdin's center stage came in 1921, when the Great Northern Paper Company began major lumbering operations on the eastern slopes, between Turner and Katahdin. This brought a usable road to within six miles of the Great Basin, and a good walkable route right up to Basin Ponds, just 1.3 miles from Chimney Pond. At Basin Ponds, the Great Northern built a spacious though primitive camp to house its lumbermen in winter months but made it available to hikers in the summers. This building and the tote road approaches to it suddenly made the southeast approach wonderfully accessible. Until its burning in 1936, the Basin Pond Camp with its five bunks was a frequent base for Katahdin climbers.

Leroy Dudley then went to work to make Chimney Pond a major hiking base. Between 1923 and 1925 he improved the trail between Basin and Chimney ponds and cut three new trails up the peaks: the Cathedral Trail up Katahdin in 1923, the Dudley Trail up Pamola in 1923, and the Hamlin Ridge Trail up Hamlin in 1925 (see figure 38.2). He also relocated and improved the Saddle Trail and kept open a track to the base of the Chimney. This latter spectacular ascent, regarded today as a technical climb, was called the "Chimney Trail" in those days and regarded as a "short sporting path to the summit" suitable for ladies, be they sufficiently enterprising.[a] In short, in three summers of work, Dudley put in place virtually the entire network of trails most commonly used on the Katahdin massif today. During the 1920s other trails left more directly from Basin Ponds for Hamlin and Pamola, but the growing popularity of Chimney Pond and Dudley's trails preempted the hiking traffic.

The pattern of Katahdin climbing swiftly shifted to this new locale. The AMC began running trips to the area and built and maintained several lean-tos at Chimney Pond. Many others flocked there. In 1925 the state replaced Dudley's Den with a larger and more comfortable cabin, in which Mr. and Mrs. Dudley spent their summers from then on. In 1925 also, Gov. Owen Brewster and his wife made a much publicized trip, filmed by Pathé News, to stay at Chimney Pond one night; to be guided up the Saddle Trail by Dudley to spend a second night atop the mountain; and (according to the plan) to do the Knife Edge the next day. A storm drove them and the Pathé News cameras back down in disarray. No matter: the following year Governor Brewster proudly reported a doubling of the tourist volume on the great mountain. By 1930 one hundred campers crowded the shores of Chimney Pond on Labor Day weekend alone.

While climbing activity expanded at Chimney Pond, it contracted elsewhere. The old trails over the North Peaks were labeled "OBSCURE" or "OVERGROWN" on the maps of the time. The old road from Stacyville to Hunt's Farm was no longer passable by auto. One explorer of the Katahdin backcountry, pointing to the near exclusive focus of visitors on Basin and Chimney ponds, said in 1929, "With the exception of the Hunt Trail, the other routes have fallen into practical disuse."

Beginning with its construction in 1923 by W. H. St. John and a friend, the St. John Trail enjoyed two decades of existence before fading into obscurity. It left the tote road near Windey Pitch and cut northwesterly to the base of the old avalanche track used by the ancient Keep Path, which it followed to the top of Pamola. Another trail was cut by Walter Leavitt, author of a popular book on Katahdin trails, running from Pamola almost due east to where it struck the tote road. This too is now gone.

In 1929 botanist Judson Ewer and Amherst College librarian E. Porter Dickinson poked around the back side, exploring the Klondike and, with

---

[a]The "Chimney Trail" was shown on the standard maps of Katahdin for many years (for instance, *In the Maine Woods'* map of 1927, the AMC's of 1931, Walter Leavitt's of 1941) and routinely described among the trail descriptions in Leavitt's *Katahdin Skylines*, pp. 59, 77–79. A Yale Outing Club party, with time to kill on rainy days, thoroughly cleared, blazed, and cairned the trail between Chimney Pond and the base of the Chimney itself on June 8–10, 1935 (R. S. G. Hall in a letter to "A.M.C.," June 23, 1935, Avery Papers, Maine State Library). Some people used the Chimney as a quick descent route (see Harry Brook, "Katahdin Weekend," *Appalachia* [Dec. 1932], pp. 238–39). A story that a dog had descended the Chimney with his master turned out to be an error: the dog went down the next gully to the west, still a remarkable feat (see Parker B. Field, "The Most Hazardous Crag Climbing Stunt in New England," *Boston Transcript*, Sept. 5, 1923, p. II-5).

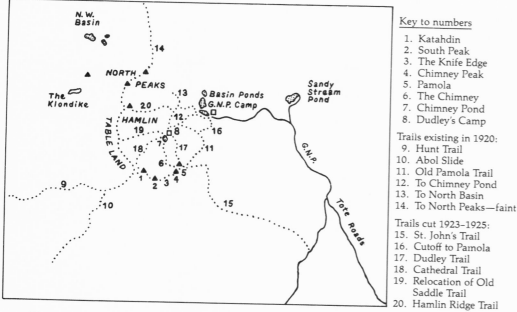

Key to numbers

1. Katahdin
2. South Peak
3. The Knife Edge
4. Chimney Peak
5. Pamola
6. The Chimney
7. Chimney Pond
8. Dudley's Camp

Trails existing in 1920:

9. Hunt Trail
10. Abol Slide
11. Old Pamola Trail
12. To Chimney Pond
13. To North Basin
14. To North Peaks—faint

Trails cut 1923–1925:

15. St. John's Trail
16. Cutoff to Pamola
17. Dudley Trail
18. Cathedral Trail
19. Relocation of Old Saddle Trail
20. Hamlin Ridge Trail

Figure 38.2. The Chimney Pond trail network, 1923–1925 Once the Great Northern Paper Company made Katahdin accessible from the southeast, a rich assortment of trails sprouted on that side of the mountain. Chimney Pond became the popular base camp for Katahdin hiking, and has remained so ever since. Many of the most celebrated hiking trails on the mountain were built during a three-year period, 1923–25. These splendid paths were largely the work of the great guide Leroy Dudley.

two couples whom they met at Chimney Pond, found a way into the Northwest Basin. Not even Dudley had been there at that point. Thereafter, the remote cirque saw a handful of visits each year. Otherwise the backcountry north and west of the Tableland became the exclusive preserve of a handful of adventuresome Katahdin specialists, among whom the foremost was Ron Gower, an AMC leader who led numerous forays during the 1930s. Most others stuck to the Chimney Pond area and Dudley's trails. They still do.

Meanwhile, management of the Katahdin area underwent a major change, from unstable patterns of private ownership to lasting status as a state park. The governments of each of the Northeastern states developed their own systems of state parks and forests during the 1910s, 1920s, and 1930s. These were of modest importance in both recreation and conservation history, but in only one place in New England did a state park become the main focus of backcountry hiking and camping. That was Maine's Baxter State Park.

As we have seen, the woods surrounding Katahdin were repeatedly and heavily logged from the midnineteenth century on. Fires devastated large swaths from time to time. Conservationist forces called for preservation of the mountain area beginning at least as early as 1895, when the Maine Hotel Proprietors Association (of all things) proposed the establishment of state parks around Katahdin, Moosehead Lake, and the Rangeley region. The next year the Maine Sportsmen's Fish and Game Association called for establishing a game preserve around the mountain, and in 1901 a Bangor newspaper editorial urged,

> It should be made the duty of the state to own Katahdin, to be forever kept for the use of the people as a great public reservation.

Two theories of how to preserve Katahdin evolved. One school favored making it a national park, and a Maine congressman, backed by the Maine Sportsmen's Fish and Game Association, so urged as early as 1916. Other Mainers, suspicious of Federal ownership, called for state purchase, and in 1919 a bill was introduced in the legislature to attain this goal. In 1921 the author of that bill became governor of the state of Maine: Percival Proctor Baxter.

Baxter was the archetypal eccentric millionaire. Born in Portland, Maine, on November 22, 1876, he was heir to a father who had made a fortune in the canning industry and risen to prominence as civic leader, philanthropist, and mayor of Portland. An avid fisherman, he introduced young Percival to the great outdoors at an early age and took him along to Kidney Pond near Katahdin as a young man. Percy inherited not only his father's wealth, but also his outdoors interests, philanthropic ideals, and taste for politics. As a Bowdoin student he was arrested at a political demonstration and jailed overnight ("student of the common long-haired variety," one newspaper reporter described him). Elected to the state legislature while still in his twenties, Baxter held political views that were an eclectic combination of orthodox Republicanism (he supported Taft against Teddy Roosevelt in 1912) with progressive crusades for public power and state parks. He was a passionate lover of animals, and as governor ordered the flags on state buildings to half-mast upon the death of his Irish setter. He was a lifelong bachelor. As a politician he quickly earned a reputation for quiet tenacity of purpose. A newspaper editor called him "the most patient and persistent person I ever knew," and observed that "he has certain arts of retreat from difficult positions but he always take his weapons with him when he retreats."

Governor Baxter's fight for Katahdin displayed these qualities of persistence and patience. In the summer of 1920 he climbed Pamola, escorted by Dudley, traversed the Knife Edge, and stood on the highest summit. There he discussed the preservation of the mountain with other political leaders along on the trip and resolved to fight for the state ownership, which led, eleven years later, to that peak's being officially renamed "Baxter Peak." As governor, during the years 1921–24, he repeatedly but fruitlessly urged the legislature to acquire the mountain as a state park. Thwarted on that front, he began to buy up the land himself. By early 1931, eleven years after that climb across the Knife Edge with Dudley, he initiated the process of turning over about five thousand acres around Katahdin to the state of Maine (see figure 38.3).

In 1933 the legislature created Baxter State Park. The original area was small, barely covering the main peak, but this patient and persistent man persevered and, over the next thirty years, expanded the park to include a total of 200,000 acres. Throughout these years he retained a strong personal interest in the administration of the park, constantly looking over the shoulder of Helon Taylor—the strong-limbed Bigelow guide and AT-builder (we shall meet him in chapter 45) whom Baxter persuaded to act as park supervisor from 1950 to 1967)—and the three-person Baxter State Park Authority. Both by the terms of his transfer to the state and by his personal attentions thereafter, Baxter guaranteed that the park "shall forever be left in the natural wild state." Only one perimeter road was allowed, motor vehicles were restricted to that road (a restriction somewhat relaxed later for snowmobiles), and hunting limited to certain areas only. Baxter repeatedly argued these principles:

> Everything in connection with the Park must be left simple and natural and must remain as nearly as possible as it was when only the Indians and the animals roamed at will through these areas. . . . I do not want it locked up and made inaccessible: I want it used to the fullest extent but in the right unspoiled way.

Baxter's gift of the state park, oddly enough, did not end agitation to make it a national park. During the 1930s, ex-governor Owen Brewster, now a congressman, led a major push to create a Katahdin National Park. Myron Avery, who by now had gained prominence as leader of the Appalachian Trail movement, became one of the most vociferous supporters of the idea, believing that the state's administration was being too laissez-faire, which was leading to squalid camping practices around Chimney Pond. In 1935 the National Park Service drew up an ambitious plan for the development of the area and the accommodation of many more visitors, through motor roads skirting the base of the mountain, many more trails, "a large lodge and cabin development" at Basin Ponds, increased accommodations at Chimney Pond (to include "several individual cabins for less hardy visitors"), and other buildings scattered around the park "along the lines of the Appalachian Mountain Club huts in the White Mountains." Through tenacity and political adroitness, Baxter held off this threat to his ideals, with important support from the AMC, the Wilderness Society, and the widely respected Robert Marshall. It is clear that the area around the great mountain would have a very different look today had it become a national park.

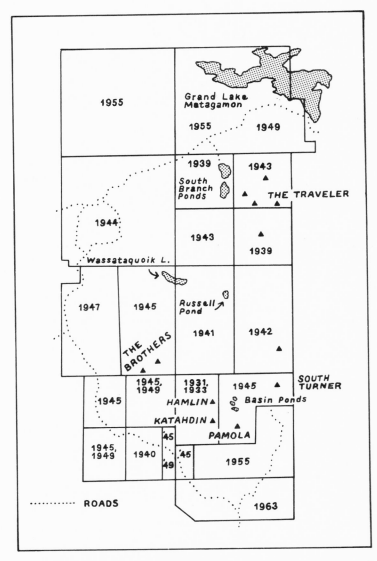

Figure 38.3. The formation of Baxter State Park, 1931–1963 The Katahdin area was reserved as primitive hiking country largely through the energies and personal wealth of one man, Percival P. Baxter. This map, showing the dates of additions to Baxter State Park, is based almost entirely on a similar map drawn for John W. Hakola's landmark history of Baxter State Park, *Legacy of a Lifetime: The Story of Baxter State Park* (see p. 75 of that book). The authors are grateful for permission to adapt this map to show the relation of the park's growth to the principal mountain areas discussed in the text.

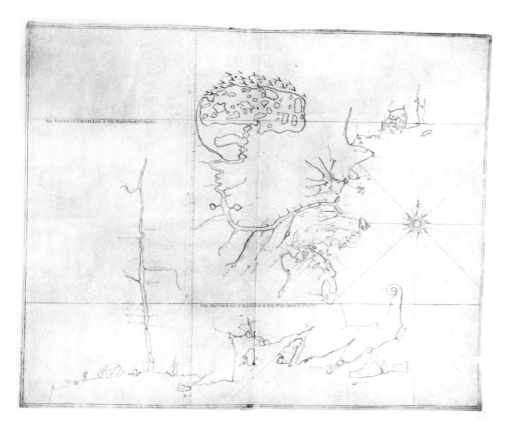

(top) How the Northeast mountains looked to the first colonists. This seventeenth-century map, from the so-called Blathwayt Atlas, shows coastal areas and major rivers in detail but only vague notions of the interior wilderness. The large lake with islands is presumably Lake Winnepesaukee, and to the north lies possibly the first cartographical representation of New Hampshire's White Mountains. (Courtesy of the John Carter Brown Library at Brown University.)

(bottom) Crawford Notch before highway and railroad. Nineteenth-century photographer Baldwin Coolidge caught this scene of an artist painting in the picturesque notch. The road as shown here was a major north-south artery through the White Mountains beginning in 1803, and was the approach used by many hikers bent on climbing Mount Washington via the early Crawford paths. (Courtesy of the Society for the Preservation of New England Antiquities; photograph by Baldwin Coolidge.)

The Southern Presidentials, as seen from Mount Washington. This terrain is rich in historical associations. The deep cut in the background of the picture is Crawford Notch, and the peaks between that and the foreground include, in ascending order, Mount Jackson, Mount Pierce (Clinton), Mount Eisenhower, Mount Franklin, and Mount Monroe. Darby Field may have reached some of these peaks on his first ascent of Mount Washington in 1642 (chapter 1). The oldest continuously used mountain trail, the Crawford Path, was built over these peaks to Mount Washington in 1819 (chapter 5). The tragic Curtis-Ormsbee double fatality occurred on this terrain (chapter 27) and led indirectly to the first major expansion of the Appalachian Mountain Club hut system (chapter 36). (Courtesy of the Mount Washington Observatory; photograph by Greg Gordon.)

The Katahdin massif, as seen from the Turner range. This formidable mountain country confronted the Monument Line surveyors in 1825 when they ran their survey across East Turner and the shoulder of South Turner. At that time the Katahdin country was little known, and the peak had previously been climbed only from the more accessible other side. The surveyors ran their line up the extreme right edge of this picture, then proceeded to make the probable first ascent of Hamlin (right) and fourth recorded ascent of Katahdin (left) before descending. Chimney Pond, center of much twentieth-century hiking activity, lies in the hidden cirque below the largest horizontal snowfield left of the center of the picture. (Photograph by Paul A. Knaut, Jr.)

(right) The first house built on a mountain summit in the northeastern United States was the 1821 structure shown in the middle of these three drawings. It was built atop Massachusetts's Mount Holyoke and was the first of many nineteenth-century summit houses (chapter 8). It gradually expanded to the more commodious size pictured above and below. By 1854 an inclined railway whisked thousands of guests up the mountainside each summer. (From Mount Holyoke and Vicinity [Northampton, Mass.: Gazette Printing Company, 1887].)

(left) "The Astor House of those altitu Vermont's Mount Mansfield boasted perhaps the most comfortably appoin the many nineteenth-century summit houses, complete with "cozy bedroom fifty, dining room and bar, plus a cro court outside on the tundra. In the background loom Mansfield's highest summit, the Chin (left), and the lower Adam's Apple (right). Over the latter Ira Allen ran his survey line in 1772, t first recorded ascent of Vermont's high peak (chapter 2). (Courtesy of the Ve Historical Society.)

Mount Washington's Carriage Road. For the convenience of guests of the many summit houses built atop Northeastern mountains during the middle of the nineteenth century, many bridle paths and carriage roads were built to the tops of mountains. The most famous was the road to the top of the Northeast's highest summit, Mount Washington. In the twentieth century, this road was adapted for automobile use and continues to serve tourists today. Most of the other carriage roads and bridle paths have fallen into disuse or have become hiking trails. This scene looks across the Great Gulf toward the Northern Presidentials. (Courtesy of the Appalachian Mountain Club.)

Changing styles of backcountry camping.

(left) This nineteenth-century party has set up its tent in an area that appears to have been logged recently. Note the gentlemen wearing jackets and ties, the woman in long skirts, the makeshift pole supports for the tents, and heavy kettle and pot. Card games are often mentioned in nineteenth-century accounts of camping (chapter 25). (Courtesy of the Vermont Historical Society.)

(below) The first half of the twentieth century saw widespread adoption of the three-sided lean-to, or "Adirondack" shelter. Before the backpacking boom of the 1960s–1970s, the backcountry shelter was still a quiet retreat from urban civilization, and many parties enjoyed reflective moments like this one before the evening campfire (chapter 42). (Courtesy of the Green Mountain Club.)

Contrasting approaches to trail building.
(above) The finely graded paths built by J. Rayner Edmands in the Presidential Range during the 1890s and 1900s represented one philosophy of trail building. This photo shows the Westside Trail on Mount Washington. (Courtesy of the Mount Washington Observatory; photograph by Greg Gordon.)

(below) The steep, rugged trails in the Presidentials' Great Gulf, in contrast, represented an entirely different philosophy. These trails were built by Warren W. Hart during the years 1908–10. These sketches record vivid impressions of the Six Husbands (left) and Adams Slide (right) trails, drawn within a year or two of their opening by the talented journalist and tireless hiker George A. Flagg. (From the Sketchbooks of summer life in Randolph, New Hampshire, drawn by George A. Flagg, 1909 and 1910; reprinted by permission and through the courtesy of Marion Flagg Foynes and Shirley Foynes Hargraves.)

The earliest winters spent above treeline.

In 1869–70, when winter climbing was still almost unheard of, two men spent the winter in this building on top of Moosilauke in the White Mountains. One was the photographer A. F. Clough. The other, possibly pictured here before the door, was the remarkable scientist-adventurer Joshua Henry Huntington. (Courtesy of the Society for the Preservation of New England Antiquities; photograph by A. F. Clough.)

During the following winter, 1870–71, Clough, Huntington, and others wintered over on Mount Washington. As this picture attests, they observed and recorded data on extraordinarily severe winter conditions. Weather observation continues to this day at the year-round Mount Washington Observatory. (Courtesy of the Society for the Preservation of New England Antiquities; photograph by Clough and Kimball.)

Thorn Mt. 1912.

Early mountain snowshoe trips.

(top) In 1882 snowshoers from the Appalachian Mountain Club made the first recorded recreational snowshoe ascent of a mountain: little (2,287 ft.) Thorn Mountain near Jackson, New Hampshire. The photo above was taken thirty years later on another AMC climb of Thorn. Note the large party, characteristic of many early winter climbs. (Courtesy of the Appalachian Mountain Club.)

(left) Snowshoers from the Green Mountain Club often climbed Mansfield and Camel's Hump during the 1910s. The 1915 party shown here is planning to camp overnight on top of Camel's Hump. Note the blanket rolls instead of sleeping bags: a cold night lay ahead. (Courtesy of Cathy Paris.)

(bottom) In these early days of winter climbing, women coped with the extraordinary handicap of long skirts, which must have become excruciatingly heavy and awkward when encrusted with snow and ice. (Courtesy of the Appalachian Mountain Club.)

(left) Among the early winter climbers, the youths from the Dartmouth Outing Club were especially active, following organization of the DOC in 1909 (chapter 34). Although the Dartmouth group was noted for its pioneering in the use of skis to climb mountains, this 1920 party used snowshoes below treeline and is seen crossing the exposed Franconia Ridge carrying its snowshoes. Note the length: they are much longer than modern snowshoes. (Courtesy of Doris Richardson.)

(below) The first ski ascent of Mount Marcy in the Adirondacks was led by John S. Apperson in 1911. Here Apperson's cloaked companions view Skylight from the top of Marcy. It may be observed that the remote Skylight was the last major Northeastern summit to remain unclimbed. Its first recorded ascent was not until 1873 (chapter 17). (Courtesy of the Adirondack Research Center, the Schenectady Museum, and William M. White.)

(left) Katahdin's stupendous chimney route. Ever a magnet for the adventurous climber, the Chimney is the prominent gully ascending all the way up to the skyline. The peak left of the gully is Pamola; the peak immediately right of the gully is Chimney Peak. (Courtesy of the Appalachian Mountain Club; photograph by Will Thompson.)

(upper right) An intrepid team of winter climbers completes the final moves to the top of Chimney Peak. This photo was taken during the 1926 expedition, which included many of the most talented and headstrong winter climbers of the day, among them Willard Helburn, leader of the original Bemis Crew (chapter 47); Robert Underhill and Miriam O'Brien, possibly the United States' leading male and female mountaineers, respectively; J. Ashton Allis of New York; and the redoubtable Arthur Comey, first man to ski up Katahdin (chapter 48). (Courtesy of the Appalachian Mountain Club; photograph by Arthur Comey.)

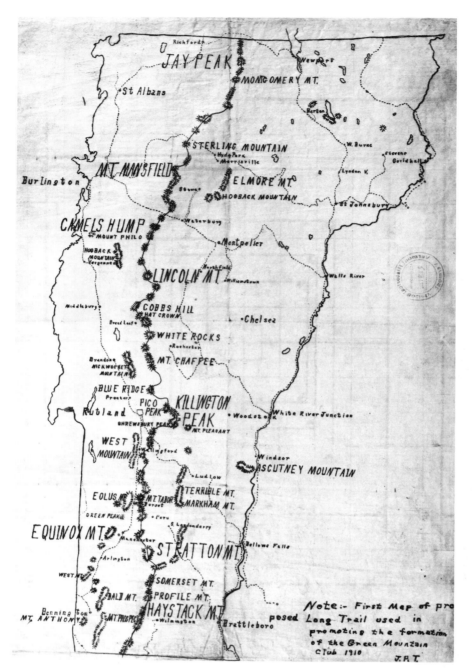

"A line on a map and a spiel" (chapter 35). As the handwritten caption (added years later) indicates, this map was the first conception of Vermont's Long Trail, as developed in 1910 in the fertile imagination of James P. Taylor ("J. P. T."). Taylor used this map in a series of talks all over the state to drum up support for the idea of forming a Green Mountain Club and building one long trail from Massachusetts to Canada, the first such long-distance hiking trail ever proposed. (Courtesy of the Vermont Historical Society.)

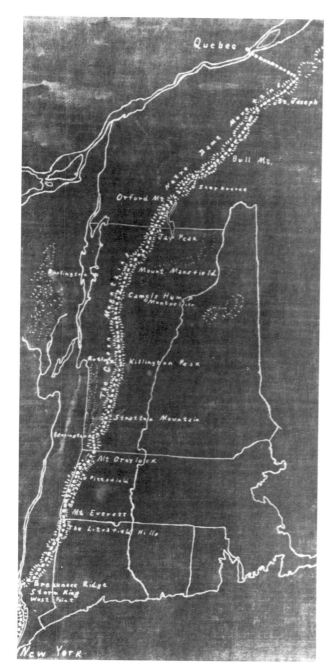

New York City to Quebec. Not long after the launching of the Long Trail, James Taylor's vision expanded again, and he proposed a hiking trail from New York City to Canada. In plans like these, Taylor and other visionaries within the Northeastern trails community foreshadowed the yet bolder scheme proposed by Benton MacKaye in 1921 for building a single trail extending the entire length of the Appalachian mountain chain: what became the 2,100-mile Appalachian Trail. (Courtesy of the Vermont Historical Society.)

The Monroe Skyline. Prof. Will Monroe, an eccentric teacher from Montclair, New Jersey, played a key role in the extension and enhancement of Vermont's Long Trail. Over a decade of hard-working summers, Professor Monroe relocated a major part of the Long Trail so as to improve its scenic quality and hiking interest. (Both photographs courtesy of the Green Mountain Club.)

(left) The colorful Monroe paints a blaze on his new trail.

(below) A work party at rest in front of Montclair Glen Lodge, built by Monroe, who is seated at the right.

The Appalachian Trail. Shown here is Judge Arthur Perkins, one of the indispensable leaders in the movement to transform Benton MacKaye's bold dream of a long-distance Appalachian Trail into the reality of a 2,100-mile blazed and cleared trail. (Both photographs courtesy of Helen D. Perkins.)

(right) Judge Perkins nails up a trail sign during a 1927 scouting expedition to Maine, during which he and his party plotted a tentative route from Katahdin to Moosehead Lake. Later the route was substantially relocated.

(below) Judge Perkins (left) and party on a work trip during the late 1920s. A bit of canoeing and fishing was evidently included along with the trail work. But note the trail measuring wheel in foreground.

Impact of the backpacking boom on hiking trails. During the late 1960s and early 1970s an unprecedented volume of hikers took to the trails. The stamp of so many more feet produced severe erosion and large patches of mud.

(right) A Green Mountain Club trail worker stares glumly at a washed-out section of the Bear Pond Trail. Note the original level of the terrain on either side of the eroded trail bed. (Courtesy of the Green Mountain Club.)

(bottom) Two Appalachian Mountain Club trail workers wade over their boot tops in mud while attempting to secure a log bridge for the benefit of future hikers crossing this section, and to protect the trail environment from further damage by hikers seeking to avoid the mud patch. (Courtesy of the Appalachian Mountain Club.)

Chapter 39

Metropolitan trails

THE NORTHERN ranges were for folks on vacation. You made a complete break from city life when you went up to the Adirondacks or the White Mountains. Even when the automobile brought them closer, they were still a day's journey away, so you went to stay a while, long enough to forget the city environment.

However, demand for a different category of recreation began to appear some time around 1910 or 1920. To a much greater degree than ever before, city dwellers began to think in terms of weekend excursions. This was a break from earlier patterns, where hiking took place mainly on extended trips. In light of later twentieth-century developments—when weekend hiking has become at least as important as longer jaunts, if not more so—this is a highly significant change. Its origins merit our attention.

Around Boston the roots of the new style went back further than elsewhere. From its birth in 1876, the AMC held excursions around the metropolitan region. Creation of the Metropolitan Park Commission in 1892 and its subsequent acquisitions of the Blue Hills and the Middlesex Fells gave Bostonians opportunities for a day's genuine hiking, as contrasted with mere Sunday strolls or walks around city sidewalks or parks. In 1915 a knowledgeable New Yorker could write that "walking had hardly been discovered" in the New York area; it was, however, a mature avocation in Boston. In the 1920s, networks of hiking trails sprouted on both the Blue Hills and the Fells, attesting the growth of interest in metropolitan area hiking. Connecticut's cities enjoyed a surge of interest in nearby hills too.

However, it was in the New York City area that hebdomadal hiking most dramatically blossomed during the 1920s and 1930s. Here emerged a weekend outing style and society wholly different from the north country tramps with which this history has so far been concerned. Instead of spectacular mountain crags, above-treeline biomes, spruce-fir forests, solitude, and grand hotels below, the big-city weekender turned to low rolling hills, second-growth and largely hardwood forests, a myriad of old wood roads, cellar holes and abandoned iron mines to poke around, large sociable groups of other weekend sojourners in the woods, and fond traditions of Sunday afternoon return trips aboard some favorite trolley line, ferryboat, or "the dear old Erie" Railroad.

Mountaineering? No. But a significant part of the history of northeastern U.S. hiking and climbing? Emphatically, yes.

The Hudson Highlands before 1920

The chief attractions for the New Yorkers were the Hudson Highlands and the hills to their west. One hiker of the times, Frank Solari, expressed the feelings that distinguished the hiking community from the rest of New York's millions when he said, "New York does several things very well, but to my mind its supreme achievement is being within forty miles or so of Bear Mountain."

These low (under 1,500 ft.) hills gave ever present views down upon the local towns and bustling commercial life of the Hudson River. The area had been well populated before the American Revolution. By the middle of the nineteenth century, however, the once populous heights were fast being abandoned and were returning to nature, restoring a wilderness playground for future recreationists. Already by the 1830s the ascent of Mount Beacon was praised as "worthwhile" and easily accomplished "by the help of some boy-guide, to be picked up at the 'Corners' " (see figure 39.1). Walkers could also obtain a guide at Cornwall Landing across the river for the ascent of Storm King via a steep trail said to have been established by "those who gathered hoop-poles upon the mountain." The travel writer N. P. Willis pronounced the Crow's Nest, Storm King's southern neighbor, "one of the most beautiful mountains of America for shape, verdure, and position." An early AMC member recalled exploring the secret recesses and ravines of the Crow's Nest as a child with his father before the Civil War, and could find at least one "old path" in 1879. Bear Mountain and the Dunderberg, Breakneck Ridge and Mount Taurus (or Bull Hill, for the less classically inclined) were all so close to towns then thriving that they were doubtless occasional locales for picnics or after-school romps. How much is not known, however; the area was not yet the hikers' haven it was to become much later.

"Father Bill" Curtis and the athletic pedestrians of the Fresh Air Club dominated these hills during the last quarter of the nineteenth century. By this time they were starting to be reforested and were laced with a fascinating tangle of old wood roads, faint cart tracks, dimly perceptible footpaths, and other ancient traces of a civilization now gone (see figure 39.2). One of Curtis's contemporaries, William T. Howell, became the poet laureate of the Hudson Highlands, writing rhapsodically of their charms:

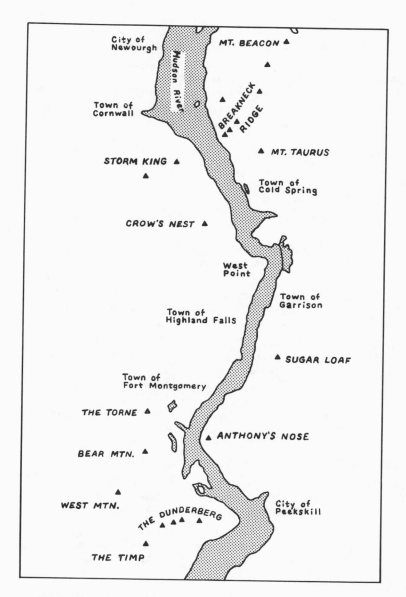

Figure 39.1. The Hudson Highlands Scarcely 50 miles from downtown New
York City, the Hudson Highlands afforded a hiking haven among rugged hills
of varied interest and exquisite beauty. This was the playground of the Fresh
Air Club and stalwart trampers such as "Father Bill" Curtis and W. T. Howell
around 1900. When New Yorkers' interest in hiking rose during the 1920s,
these hills became the focus of much imaginative trail building.

The wood roads are legion. For two centuries they have been coming into being, growing up and disappearing, until today they form a labyrinth more perplexing than helpful to the wood novice, but useful, interesting, and tempting in a high degree to the man who knows his mountains. They lead everywhere and—nowhere; . . . they always bring one to some surprise or point of interest hidden from the voyager on the travelled road.

Of the Crow's Nest, Howell wrote,

How famous it is, as a beautiful natural feature, . . . yet how wild and little trod. Emerson must have had some such mountain in mind when he said "The mountains are silent poets."

On the modest bluff known as the Dunderberg, scarcely 1,000 feet high and within sight of downtown Peekskill:

Its long sweeping lines and comparatively low elevation are deceiving. . . . Not only is its surface area large, but its woods are so wild and thick . . . and its long summit ridge is so broken into hills, valleys and faulted rock arrangements, that it is difficult to explore the mountain thoroughly at one time. I refer to the whole formation, from the river to the Timp Pass, three miles westward. . . .

The charm and mystery of Dunderberg for me rest largely on these conditions. After years of coming to this mountain I do not feel that I know it at all well, although I have cut across its forests in all directions and at all seasons of the year.

Howell and his friends explored all the creases and folds of those ancient hills. They discovered hidden delights, like Bat Cave on the Crow's Nest, mines abandoned for more than a century, tiny level camping sites on the ledges of steeply sloped mountainsides. They cut no paths and maintained none. Rather, they came to know all the intricate byways of the hills, every faint track of an overgrown wood road, so that they could embark on a 20- or 30-mile ramble with full confidence in their itinerary, though to any other eyes they seemed to be in trackless forest. They often camped out and for that purpose maintained caches of tents, cooking supplies, and food in secret spots throughout the hills. Years later puzzled New York–area bushwhackers occasionally stumbled on the remains of some of these abandoned stores.

Though they scrambled up steep rock faces, for which the next generation roped up, and though they tramped through winter's fiercest weather, a decidedly patrician air never left them. They were wilderness-loving explorers, but their mealtimes betrayed their cultured origins. A typical lunch was "Appetizer, Vegetable Soup, Broiled Chicken, Rolls, a bottle of Chianti, Demi-tasse, Cigars." On a 1911 trip to the Crow's Nest the dinner menu consisted of:

Three Star Haig and Haig; stuffed olives; soup; broiled Frenched Lamb chops; hot house tomatoes; celery; chocolate wafers; black coffee; and a smoke.

Howell devoted himself passionately to the cause of preserving this land from the return of civilization. His photographs illustrated several influential articles, which marshaled public opinion to the cause of conservation. He studied the history of the area diligently, absorbing much from the highlands' oldest inhabitants themselves—fringe farmers, woodsmen, hunters, honeybee tracers. Yet he grew aware that the wildness of the highlands as he knew them was a fragile moment in history, poised between the ancient farms and wood roads whose traces he explored and the coming generation of hikers who would demand, build, and maintain trails along these hills, eradicating the spirit of wildness that he and his small circle of friends were privileged to enjoy.

The creation of Bear Mountain and Harriman parks in 1910 was the event that opened the floodgates to a sea of change. This vast area, now sixty thousand acres, is not the only place where New Yorkers hike, but it is the lodestone. Howell argued strongly, even passionately, for keeping development of any kind to a minimum, though he sensed his ideas were not destined to prevail. In November of 1910 this man who had known and loved the wild highland hills as well as anyone ever would, wrote one last appeal for a disappearing paradise:

> There is but one perfect solution as to the preservation of the Highlands, though I know in my heart that it will never be realized. That is, to leave them alone. By that I mean, keep out all foreign influences. That means more than quarries and manufactures. It means hotels and parking projects, and even . . . roads and easy paths. There is something more at stake here than the preservation of the scenery. . . . There is a wild charm and isolation about the Highlands that will fly forever when the "improvements" begin to come in. Lake Mohonk is as beautiful as ever. So is the Delaware Water Gap. They have their place, with their great hotels, and their graveled paths and summer houses; . . . but there is a place, too, for those who love nature for herself, and especially for her wild self . . . and you can't keep it when the tourist enters the scene. . . .
>
> Part of my argument is meant to imply that such persons have Mohonk and the Water Gap, and a thousand other spots. But the stamping grounds of the lover of wild nature are yearly growing more restricted. Some day there will be none left. And then, a valuable species of citizen is going to grow extinct. . . . A plea for the Natty Bumpos [sic], before it is too late!

But it was too late. With New York's teeming millions now aware of the prize within a day's easy jaunt, "development" began.

First to come marching in were the Boy Scouts. George D. Pratt, the same who later became conservation commissioner and first president of the ADK, was at this time an oil company executive who served his home community of Brooklyn as chairman of its Boy Scout Council. In the fall of 1912, at Pratt's instigation, the park invited a Brooklyn Scout leader named Thomas Leeming to bring five or six senior Scouts up to the newly acquired woods. The Scouts picked an area for camping and in 1913 brought a contingent of Brooklyn Boy Scouts to enjoy this touch of nature so remote in spirit from the sidewalks of Flatbush but in miles so close. In 1914 the park put up a rough camp building for their use on what was called Carr Pond (enlarged and more elegantly named Lake Stahahe today). By 1916 Scouts from Manhattan and Queens joined the happy throng, and Camp Kanawauke was created as a large central area around which scouting activities were organized. Soon another corner of the park was set up for Girl Scouts—affectionately referred to by the boys as the "Adamless Eden." In 1917 a Camp Department was established in the park's administrative organization and city camps were provided with sites in the park, including the "fresh air camps" that did so much to give city-bred kids a taste of an outdoor world their parents little dreamed of.

Meanwhile adult hikers were starting to move in. Their presence looms first not in Harriman Park itself, but across the Ramapo River on New Jersey's Wyanokie Plateau. When the New York Chapter of the Appalachian Mountain Club was formed in 1912, it was most active in the Wyanokies. Beginning in 1917, the New York Section of the Green Mountain Club moved in as well. Close on their heels came a group of German-born outdoor enthusiasts calling themselves Nature Friends, who established a camp in the area in 1920. As the GMC gravitated toward Harriman Park after acquiring its own lodge there in 1922, Nature Friends became the dominant hiking club in the Wyanokies, their camp growing into a bustling social center, with more than one hundred cabins scattered through the woods, a three-hundred-bed dormitory, and a 400-foot swimming pool. The hills west of Wanaque rang with a merry German ascent.

Still the bulk of the Hudson Highlands backcountry remained untamed—"in a measure the most primitive section of the state (for the Adirondacks and Catskills are overrun and cheapened by tourists)," Howell had written just a few years before.

Major Welch and the Harriman Park trails

The man who changed this world was an Army officer named William A. Welch, who as the Palisades Interstate Park's general manager decided to stimulate a systematic expansion of hiking trails. Welch was the fount from which New York's metropolitan trail system flowed. This remarkable leader was no narrow-thinking military engineer. He had, in the eyes of one of the earliest volunteer park workers, "a very broad social philosophy . . . a genial and persuasive attitude . . . and a marvellous feeling for people." A big burly man with jet-black hair and a strong jaw, Welch had an easy and confident manner, along with a bottomless bag of old war stories with which to entertain meetings amidst the serious business of trail planning. These assets, one hiking leader recalled, "filled us with enthusiasm for his project of a network of trails throughout the Interstate Park." Welch was among the first to grasp the significance of the trends that were creating a demand for outdoor recreation available to urban populations, and he was as much as anyone the designer of that balance between true wilderness and development which has prevailed in the Hudson Highlands. If that balance came down too heavily on the side of development to suit men like Curtis and Howell, it doubtless seemed uncomfortably primitive for many others who would have paved over more of the park. In any event, Welch's design won and has been indelibly printed on the pattern of outdoor recreation for many thousands of New Yorkers.

During the summer and fall of 1920, Major Welch explored the prospects of Harriman Park trails with various hikers and trail club representatives. Among these were William W. (Billy) Bell of the New York AMC and J. Ashton Allis of New York's GMC. Finally, with the aid of that consistent catalyst in outdoors organizations, Meade Dobson, Welch convened a meeting on October 19, 1920. To this meeting came representatives of the AMC, the GMC, the Fresh Air Club, the Tramp and Trail Club, and the umbrella-group Associated Mountaineering Clubs of North America. In a shrewd move to guarantee press attention, Welch and Dobson included Albert Britt of *Outing* magazine and a *New York Evening Post* writer and hiker named Raymond H. Torrey.

This historic meeting organized a permanent federation of hiking clubs, known at first as the Palisades Interstate Park Trail Conference; with a broader focus after 1922, it was more widely known as the New York–New Jersey Trail Conference. Its first chairman was Britt of *Outing*, but he soon was succeeded by Torrey; of these two writers, the former faded into obscurity as far as this history is concerned, while the latter became unquestionably the most influential figure on the whole bustling New York hiking scene.

A second result of Major Welch's 1920 meeting was the launching of actual trail work. Welch had issued a trail map for the park earlier that year—the first of many hikers' maps to come—showing what then passed for the park's trail system: mostly old wood roads in various states of overgrownness and disrepair (see figure 39.2). These were not specifically built as scenic hiking trails but evolved over many years for a variety of utilitarian purposes; thus they tended to shun the rugged heights and interesting places where a true hiker's trail would want to go. Meade Dobson wrote an article for the *New York Evening Post* in the summer of 1920, telling of this map and promoting the idea of hiking in Harriman Park:

> Almost every mountain in the park has a fire patrol trail to its summit.
> . . . They usually lead out from an old road. Aboriginal trails and old
> lumber and mine roads in a veritable maze. . . . Trails shown on the
> park map generally trace an old road that finally dwindles down to a
> footpath. Many roads have blind ends reaching up to old timber cut-
> tings and mine dumps.

Now, however, began a deliberate program of new trail construction. The procedure was for Major Welch to outline a general destination for each trail and then to invite hikers familiar with the region to find the best route for getting there. In the summer of 1920, the Major proposed a single 20-mile trail to cross the park, linking scenic points from Jones Point on the Hudson to Tuxedo on the Ramapo River. The West Shore Railroad ran by the foot of Jones Point and Tuxedo was a station on the Erie, so both ends could be easily reached by New York's weekend hikers. In between, the projected trail would climb the Dunderberg, that long graceful curve overlooking the Hudson; cross the sharper summit of a rugged outcrop known as the Timp; drop into Timp Pass; then proceed over lower ridges past the park's new Lake Tiorati; cross over Fingerboard Mountain, with its picturesque features such as the Pot Hole and Ship Rock; and continue on over other wooded ridges toward the Ramapo on the western edge of the park. Thus was born the Ramapo-Dunderberg Trail—the "R-D" to subsequent generations of New York hikers—first of the great transpark trails in Harriman (see figure 39.3).[a]

Welch laid out the general route, promised to supply trail signs, twine, and tools, and turned the trail cutters loose. Almost instantly a coterie of avid and effective workers sprang forward to take up the challenge. Within three weeks of the initial meeting, though in November, Will Monroe assembled a group of volunteers to start work on the Ramapo-Dunderberg. When the professor fell ill before the appointed day, his trusted co-worker, J. Ashton Allis, picked up the banner and, on November 20–25, 1920, led out the first contingent of New York trail makers— the advance troops on whose tracks an army has followed. The Ramapo-Dunderberg was completed in 1921, under the overall supervision of Meade Dobson, with Allis, Monroe, and Cecil Earle the most active in the field.

Welch kept the trail cutters moving on to new assignments. Even before the R-D was finished, the Major suggested a side trail from Timp

---

[a]During the early years the western end of the R-D was better known as the Tuxedo–Tom Jones Trail, although it seems to have been viewed clearly by all as part of one long trail.

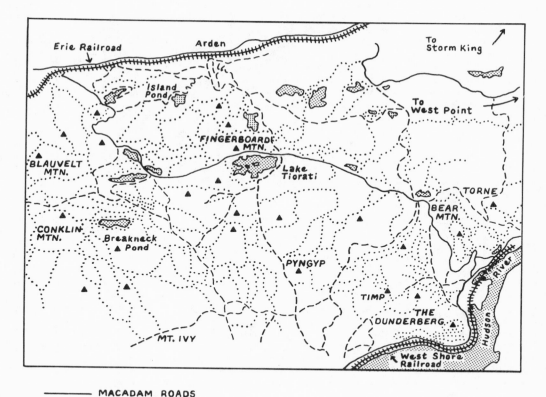

Figure 39.2. Harriman Park trails, ca. 1920 Trails shown here are the old wood roads and faintly defined paths known to the woods-wise experienced hikers of the W.T. Howell generation. Their heyday was before the building of modern hiking trails in Harriman Park. Note that there was as yet no Bear Mountain Bridge at this date. This map is based on one prepared by the Palisades Interstate Park Commission in 1920, a copy of which is on file in the commission's map records. The authors are grateful for the opportunity to reproduce this adaptation of that 1920 map.

Pass, to climb over the long ridge of West Mountain and descend to the north to that sharp little spike of a peak, the Popolopen Torne. This ridgeline trail connecting two of the most striking spots in the park, the Timp and the Torne, was cut mainly by Billy Bell and the New York AMC. It immediately earned a reputation as one of the finest hiking trails in the park, "the most concentratedly scenic of all," wrote Torrey.

By the next year, 1922, the Appalachian Trail idea was on the move, and the trail cutters' efforts turned in that direction. With Welch's blessing, Torrey scouted a route from the new Bear Mountain Bridge up over

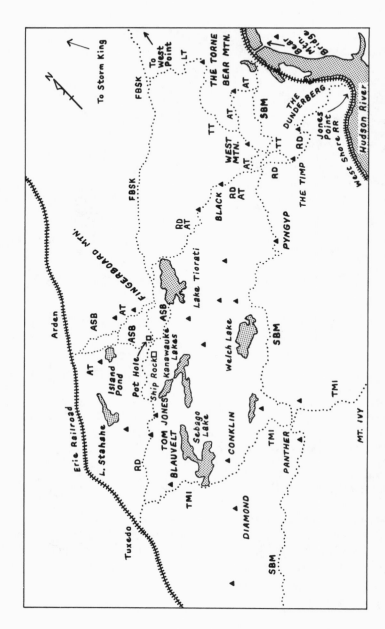

Figure 39.3. Harriman Park trails, 1921-1927 Under the guidance of Harriman Park's general manager, Maj. William A. Welch, New York hikers constructed a succession of modern hiking trails crisscrossing the park's prime hill country. This trail network became the leading attraction for the energetic and enthusiastic generation of metropolitan hiking clubs during the 1920s and 1930s. This map is based on those produced over the years largely by William Hoeferlin, a leader in the New York-area hiking scene for many years. The authors gratefully acknowledge permission granted by Walking News, Inc., New York, for producing this adaptation of those maps.

Bear Mountain; on to West Mountain to share some of the nicest parts of the Timp-Torne; west to pick up the Ramapo-Dunderberg over to Fingerboard Mountain; then striking northwest past the beautiful Island Pond to the town of Arden; whence the AT could continue its long journey to Georgia. Again it was AMC trail cutters who built most of this trail, in 1922 and 1923.

Also in 1922, Allis reopened his 1917 trail that ran north from Fingerboard Mountain out of the park, past West Point to Storm King, four miles up the Hudson. Though a splendid trail, its future was clouded by its crossing over the West Point military reservation, and it was later closed. During this year, Allis also cut a 1.5-mile connecting link between this trail and the Timp-Torne. Thus an integrated network of linked-up trails was taking shape, a true trail *system*, in which loops and circuits of various lengths could be worked out to suit any hiker's inclinations.

In 1923 Welch designated a route from Tuxedo down through the southern part of the park to the town of Mount Ivy. In the same year GMC trail cutters put in the Arden-Surebridge Trail.

During the years between 1920 and 1923, the Boy Scouts worked out what was known as the White Bar Trail but which was actually a system of trails radiating like spokes of a wheel from the Scouts' camping center at Lake Kanawauke.

By 1923 New York–area trails had proliferated to the extent that a guidebook was published. Until then, Frank Place of the Tramp and Trail Club had personally kept track in detail of all trails, not just in Harriman but throughout the New York area. Torrey persuaded him to make his data available and agreed to help edit detailed route descriptions and discursive essays on the glories of the New York hiking scene. A third author, Robert L. Dickinson, who had already published a booklet on the Palisades, was brought in, largely to do illustrations. The three men collaborated splendidly ("We have brought out a book and the authors are *still good friends,*" marveled Dickinson), to produce the first edition of the *New York Walk Book*. This classic among Northeastern guidebooks was in its fifth edition sixty years later.

In the years between 1925 and 1927, the last of the great Harriman Park trunk trails was built, running the width of the park from Suffern in the southwest to Bear Mountain in the northeast. Again, Major Welch was the instigator and architect; this time Place headed the "elephant squad" who cut it through.

The New York hiking scene of the 1920s–1930s

Such a magnificent burst of trail building reflected, of course, the emergence of a tremendously vigorous hiking population in the New York metropolitan area. These weekend walkers became a distinctive subculture within the huge metropolis, though their pre–World War II numbers were never great. Their style was entirely at odds with north country vacationers'. Two contemporary accounts convey something of the flavor:

> Another Sunday has arrived. Out they scatter from the big city, popping up out of the subway, down off the elevated, piling out of trolley cars, headed for Westchester or the open country across the Hudson, the weekend walkers with their knapsacks on their backs. They have stout shoes and stout hearts. They roam the hills, climb the cliffs and their voices come echoing up from the valley. Spring calls them; Summer lures them; Autumn entrances them; Winter does not deter them.

> On Sundays and holidays, from September to June, rucksack-laden stalwarts assemble at ferry-houses and railroad stations, bound for the Hudson Highlands, the Ramapos, or whatever other parts the Walks Committee, in its wisdom, may have seen fit to designate as the scene of the day's outing. No fair-weather strollers these, but seasoned hikers, knights of brush and brier, modern Bayards, without fear and above reproach. It would be superfluous to add that they are enthusiasts, and perhaps they are slightly tinged with madness.

A motley mix of men and women of all ages, sizes, and cultural backgrounds (including substantial numbers of foreign-born), the weekend walkers cultivated an exuberant informality, a good-humored vigor. They could not take themselves seriously, but they sometimes took trail work or long hikes or nature study very seriously indeed.

Attire showed complete unconcern for urban fashions of that day and none of our time's preoccupation with specially designed and marketed hiking wear. Comfortable old clothes were the only uniform, often topped with some eccentricity of personal value:

> Of course most everyone had a favorite old hat which they had cut down from an old felt or straw. Some were decorated with feathers, trout flies, or emblems that had been collected along their trips.

One professionally respected engineer, Bulgarian-born Kerson Nurian, regularly donned the same threadbare business suit and trusty fedora for every weekend's excursion; returning to Manhattan on the Sunday evening ferry after an exhausting weekend on the trails, slumped against the rail, battered old hat in hand, Dr. Nurian was startled to see a kindly stranger drop a coin into that hat. But such was the image of the New York hiker to the New York nonhiker.

Limitations of leisure time and transportation in prethruway years confined their outings to a few choice spots nearby. Harriman Park, with its splendid new trails, and the Ramapos got most of the traffic, with not much less on the hills east of the Hudson (Sugarloaf, Mount Taurus,

Breakneck Ridge, and Mount Beacon). Slightly farther afield were those two oddly dissimilar independent mountains, the graceful, beautifully proportioned Storm King, and the formless, sprawling Schunemunk. To go farther still—to Connecticut's blue-blazed trails or even the Catskills —you really needed a full two or three days.

Within this tight little world of backyard wildernesses, the weekenders grew to know and treasure each ridge and hollow. No Kangchenjungas or Matterhorns or even Katahdins for them—so Letterrock and Fingerboard and Pyngyp and the Timp and the Torne were endowed with the qualities of high adventure. Frank Place could refer quite seriously to Schunemunk's overgrown wooded hump, surrounded by roads and towns, as "another inspiring massif." Albert Stürcke sang of "beetle-browed Breakneck, rocky-ribbed Storm King, and the rest of the towering crags of the Highlands, . . . the sylvan glens and spooky gorges of the Ramapos," and concluded, "They couldn't be much more wild and picturesque if they were a thousand miles away from our much vaunted civilization."

Though the New Yorkers were the ruggedest and rankest of individualists, somehow there emerged a high degree of cohesion in their hiking community. Within the ranks of metropolitan walkers, unity derived from the common love of the land they hiked, the exciting work of cutting and maintaining the new trails and the magnetism of the leading figures. Everyone seemed to know everyone else. Travel limitations and Saturday morning work kept everyone in the same small geographical circle, and you were bound to run into other clubs on the train if not on the trail. Only a limited number of outfitters catered to the outdoors set, so if you missed meeting your fellow hikers on the Erie or the Timp-Torne Trail, you would probably bump into them at Camp and Trail Outfitters, or David T. Abercrombie's, or Charles Harris's Camping Equipment on Chambers Street. Albert Stürcke recalled one hike over Breakneck Ridge to Mount Beacon in 1924 where the party of five consisted of persons whose primary affiliations were, respectively, the Adirondack Mountain Club, Nature Friends, Paterson Ramblers, Tramp and Trail Club, and himself, a kind of maverick who was equally at home in the ADK or the GMC.

The hike itself was the main attraction, but getting to the trail-head and back became a rich part of the experience and certainly contributed to the unique flavor of New York hiking. Because of Saturday morning work for most people, Sunday was the big day. On a typical Sunday morning those who lived in the city would arise in the wee small hours, converge on the Chamber Street ferry via a variety of subways, elevateds, buses, or long walks, take the ferry across the broad Hudson in the misty stillness of dawn in time to catch the 5:55 A.M. milk train or perhaps just the 7:30 of the Erie Railroad, where they would be joined by another crowd of those who lived in the Jersey satellite towns.

These weekenders loved the Erie Railroad—"good old Erie!" They would congregate in one car and the conductors got to know them. The

"Will you walk a little faster!" said the Goldthwaite to his guest,
"I should count it a disaster if you failed to reach the crest.
See how eagerly the Ingraham and the Spadavecchia prance!
They'll be lunching on Black Mountain—will you come and join the dance?
Will you, won't you; will you, won't you; will you join the dance?
Will you, won't you; will you, won't you; won't you join the dance?

"You can really have no notion how delightful it will be
When I get you from Buchanan up the Beacons before three!"
But the guest replied, "Too far, too far!" and eyed the map askance;
He said he valued wind and limb too much to join the dance.
Would not, could not; would not, could not; would not join the dance.
Would not, could not; would not, could not; could not join the dance.

"What matters it how far we go?" replied his agile friend;
"There's another railroad train, you know, when we reach the other end.
The further off from Erie's line, the nearer the West Shore.
So do not rest, beloved guest, but haste a little more.
Will you, won't you; will you, won't you; will you join the dance?
Will you, won't you; will you, won't you, won't you join the dance?

Behind them lay the Hogencamp,
  And Fingerboard behind them lay;
And Pyngyp, West, and Letterrock
  Lay in their wake at close of day.
The sad guest said, "It's going to rain!
  And lo! the very trail is gone.
Brave leader, get us to the train!"
  He said, "Walk on! walk on! and on!"

They walked. They walked. Then spake the guest:
  "The woods are dangerous at night!
I think I need a little rest!
  How can I walk without a light?
What will you do, O leader dear,
  If we see naught but trees, at dawn?"
The leader answered with a sneer—
  He said, "Walk on! walk on! and on!"

They walked. They walked as snails might go.
  The guest unto another said,
"It is so dark, he wouldn't know
  If all of us should fall down dead!
What would you do, proud leader, say,
  If you found one of us had gone?"
He muttered, crashing on his way—
  "Walk on!" he said, "Walk on! and on!"

Reprinted from *Appalachia* by permission of the
Appalachian Mountain Club.

railroad offered special fares to hiking clubs on weekends. Round-trip to Arden was $1.01. Friendly conductors would stop the train at nonscheduled places convenient to trail-heads. Recalled one regular rider:

> For a while it almost became a ritual to board the popular 7:30A.M. Erie train on Sunday, and roam up and down the car aisles, greet trail acquaintances, exchange information and news of the latest trail clearing progress, and form small groups for that Sunday's work. And, of course, there was always Ray Torrey with his sage advice.

For the GMCers and ADKers bound for their clubs' camps in Harriman Park, the routine began earlier with a frantic dash from the office after Saturday's midday closing hour, so as to catch the crowded ferry and the 1:30 Erie train to Tuxedo (ADK) or Arden (GMC) and begin the walk in to camp. Office clothes might be exchanged for hiking garb in the Erie's restrooms. Some made simpler changes. A Brooklyn attorney, Ed Ingraham, had a regular routine in the railroad station of doffing his tie, loosening his collar, and punching his hat out, all operations performed on the move, thereby instantly transforming himself from a punctilious lawyer into an outdoorsman ready for brush or brier; the process would be reversed at the station on Sunday evening, as tie came out of the pack and back around the secured collar, while the hat was deftly and ceremoniously punched back into respectable format. If you missed the train or were a slow walker, you might arrive at camp after dark, but that only added spice to the walk in.

Even in these early days, some New York hikers traveled by car, but they did not enjoy the pleasant and sociable commute of those on the Erie. Ferries were even more crowded for motorists, and a forty-five-minute wait to drive the car on was not uncommon. Coming home, the road threading between Harriman and the Ramapos through Arden and Tuxedo could be one long traffic jam.

For those who returned by train, the atmosphere was more congenial. Hikers would converge on the Arden and Tuxedo stations of the Erie or the equivalent stops alone the West Shore line.

> Sometimes we were so wet from rain or snow that we'd have to strip, discreetly and completely, at the Arden Station, and bless the Station Master for the warm fire he kept.

The regulars brought their Sunday suppers (or leftovers from lunch) in their packs, and referred to their congenial gatherings as the "third class diner." Tales of the weekend trail were exchanged, plans for the next week hatched, and an occasional offbeat episode livened proceedings.

> One of our members taught biology in Brooklyn and used to collect specimens for class. One day she caught a small black snake, stunned

it and put it into the pack. When she got on the train, she rummaged into the pack for a snack and the snake was gone. She politely asked the people on the seat in front of her if they had seen the snake. Needless to say in two minutes most passengers were standing on the seats and screaming. The snake crawled down the aisle where the conductor managed to corner it and throw it off the train.

The train ride over, the weekend hikers dispersed, many to take the ferry back across the Hudson, weary and footsore, leaning against the rails to gaze at the evening lights of the big city, returning to the ants' nest of their urban weekday world from the joyful weekend on the Timp-Torne or Breakneck Ridge.

The entire weekend ritual was as much a part of the New York hiking scene of the 1920s and 1930s as the trails and summits the hikers escaped to. One hiker recalled the conclusion of a hiking weekend in softly glowing terms: " . . . and then along winding roads back to Monroe and the old reliable Erie, and so home and to bed." Another spoke for the generation: "We had a wonderful time; the depression of the 1930s was forgotten."

Raymond H. Torrey

While the shared experience may have been sufficient to knit the New York hiking scene together, there was also a proliferation of hiking clubs, described in chapter 41. More important than the formal club structure was the extraordinary energy and diplomacy of the dominant individuals who crossed over, between, and among a lot of the clubs. Leaders like J. A. Allis, Bill Burton, Bill Gorham, and Percy Olton were apt to hold membership and even offices in two or even all three of the big clubs' chapters (AMC, ADK, GMC), and perhaps an independent club affiliation or two as well. Joseph Bartha, a New York hotel head waiter, was active in the leadership, at various times, of the Paterson Ramblers, the Nature Friends, the ADK, the Interstate Hiking Club, and his own creation, the Geneva Hiking Club. Ernest Dench started with the Paterson Ramblers in 1923, broke away to form the Interstate Hiking Club in 1931, soon moved on to start the Hiking Trips Bureau, and from there founded the Woodland Trail Walkers in 1937.

The most potent unifying force of all was Raymond H. Torrey, supreme ombudsman in the boiling consortium of New York hiking clubs, universally known and liked, extending the help of his newspaper column to one and all, acting as midwife at the birth of several of the clubs, always in touch with everyone, smoothing ruffled feathers, prodding to action, admonishing the recalcitrant, inspiring waning spirits, sparking jovial laughter, setting an exuberant pace on the trail.

Born in Georgetown, Massachusetts, on July 15, 1880, Torrey began work as a newspaperman in western Massachusetts, but moved to New York City in 1903 to write for the *New York American*, then for the *Tribune*, and finally, and for twenty golden years, the *New York Evening Post*. His "Long Brown Path" column (the title is from a Walt Whitman poem) was the bible of New York hikers of all clubs from near the beginning of the 1920s to the end of the 1930s. It appeared weekly at first as the "Friday Outing Page" but soon became a daily feature.

There has probably never been a phenomenon like Torrey's "Long Brown Path" column. Throughout the 1920s and until Torrey's sudden death in 1938, it was almost literally universally read by New York hikers. Aside from news of the clubs and trails, especially new ones, answers to readers' questions, and assorted editorial comments, the most important feature was the weekly listing of hikes. As many as twenty or thirty trip notices, from almost as many different clubs, would appear in these listings.

Nor was Torrey bound to typewriter and desk. He was out on the trail as much as the most faithful of his hiking readers, cutting or flagging new trail, maintaining old, helping a new club get off to a good start, or scouting potential new routes. "Torrey was the dynamo, the power, the driving force behind all the trail scouting, locating, clearing, and maintaining that occurred in the early years." He scouted the very first section of the Appalachian Trail and participated in the Byzantine negotiations required for the AT's ultimate location all through New York State. His diplomatic abilities on right-of-way deals with recalcitrant landowners could have earned him an ambassadorship. The other giant of those times, his buddy Frank Place, recalled,

> Owners of large tracts, frowning on trespassers of any sort, had to be persuaded to permit markers to be put up. This meant long waits, letters, telephone calls, visits. This Torrey did for years. . . . The fact that the Appalachian Trail now runs the whole distance from the Ramapo to the Delaware is due principally to his long-continued efforts.

The correspondence of trail workers in the 1920s is laced with repeated references to Torrey as the fount of all knowledge of where next weekend's work was to be done. ("I can find out from Torrey when he crosses the wood to climb Pyngyp and then locate the spot from his description," "You know what Torrey had in mind and can take it up where he left off.") At a time when few got to the Catskills, Torrey knew their trails, existing and former, as well as details of their vegetation.

Besides new trail work, Torrey never failed to support the more pedestrian job of trail maintenance. "Scarcely a party went into the park for scouting of which he was not a member," Place wrote. "No 'elephant squad' was complete without Torrey and his clippers."

Somewhere in all this flurry of important trail work, the man found time to go on just plain hikes, study highland vegetation (he became expert on lichens), and explore interesting historical sites. A side interest in a pre-Revolutionary iron mine speculator was carried to such depths as to earn him the nickname of "Baron Hasenclever" among his close friends.

The volume and scope of Torrey's accomplishments strain belief. Besides all his local hiking affiliations, which were not confined to memberships but included several chairmanships, presidencies, and other offices, Torrey was secretary of the Association for the Preservation of the Adirondacks and secretary of the American Scenic and Historic Preservation Society, and in 1925 he was asked by the National Conference on State Parks to do a survey of state parks throughout the United States, publishing an exhaustive report in 1926. When Leroy Jeffers was killed in a plane crash, Torrey stepped in as head of the Associated Mountaineering Clubs of North America and soon made its magazine, *Mountain*, a widely read and quoted source.

> Is there a trail to Pamola? Ask Torrey. Who knows about the botany of the Blue Ridge? Ask Torrey. How do you account for Schunemunk Mountain? Where is the best skiing south of the Berkshires? Who is who in Massachusetts conservation circles? Torrey will know.

Physically Torrey was an unlikely, large, "roundish-looking" figure, not easily taken for a strenuous hiker, though he enjoyed a reputation for maintaining a moderate pace all day long "without let-up for hill, dale, swamp, rock, or brier."

On his fifty-eighth birthday, July 15, 1938, this incredible dynamo suddenly ceased to exist: Raymond H. Torrey was dead. The New York hiking scene was stunned. It was the end of that glorious era of the 1920s and 1930s for which Torrey was symbol and center. In a ceremony that must have been one of the more memorable moments in the Hudson Highlands, his friends gathered to place a memorial atop Long Mountain in Harriman Park, the inscription reading "A Great Disciple of the Long Brown Path." Frank Place scattered Raymond Torrey's ashes to the winds that blew them over the hills he had known and helped so many to know, while a solitary bugler played taps.

The noisy Trail War and the quiet Long Path

But it is a mistake to dwell long on leaders like Torrey, Place, and others. If ever there was an egalitarian, populist, leveling hiking scene, it was that of New York City in the 1920s and 1930s.

One event that richly characterized the era was the "Trail War" of around 1930. During the late 1920s the trail-building boom that Major Welch and his Trail Conference had set in motion took on a self-perpetuating vitality of its own. "Volunteers probably ran into the hundreds," recalled one trail worker of the time. Like the legions of the sorcerer's apprentice, these enthusiastic trail cutters knew not when or where to stop.

> A number of the old-timers became involved in a sort of cult of vanity and went out on their own and built bits and pieces of trails to which they attached their own names.

Eventually and inevitably swords crossed over conflicting routes in the same area. Like jealous highland chieftains, each trail cutter painted on his own colors. The great "Trail War" was on. One marauder showed up with black paint, which he smeared over competing trail blazes. Torrey's newspaper columns were used to air rival charges and countercharges. Although the identity of the combatants was not always disclosed, it was common knowledge that among the most active and uncontrolled trail cutters were Joseph Bartha, Emil Unger, Alexander Jessup, Kerson Nurian, and Howard Tiger. Bartha was known as "the Demon Trail Painter of the Ramapos." He, Jessup, and Nurian were often at cross-purposes, especially around the northwestern edge of Harriman Park and in the hills across the Ramapo River. Another area of friction was in the Wyanokies, where the GMC and Nature Friends were in jurisdictional dispute. Part of the problem during the Trail War was the lack of any overall leadership that all trail workers acknowledged. In the old days one roar from Major Welch would have swung everyone in line, but after 1927 the old lion took less direct personal interest in Harriman Park trails. Anyway some of the Trail War was being waged outside park boundaries. The New York–New Jersey Trail Conference, now that the main Harriman trails had been completed, had "quietly faded out."

Though many of the New York area's more interesting little trails were products of this stormy period, by 1931 the chaos was driving trail conservatives wild. To step into this leadership vacuum, Torrey, Frank Place, and William Burton, then president of the GMC's New York Section, determined to reactivate the Trail Conference as a means of restoring order. Burton issued a call for a meeting at the New York Telephone Company building on April 21, 1931. Here in the heart of Manhattan assembled most of the principal trail-builders and hiking leaders of the metropolitan area, including some of the extremists in the Trail War. It was especially fortunate that the latter were counted in on the meeting: Bartha and Jessup were there; both the GMC (Burton, Worth J. Smith) and Nature Friends (Emil Plarre) were represented. The New York–New Jersey Trail Conference was reinvented, and the universally respected Torrey installed as chairman. Angelique Rivollier of the women's hiking club, Inkowa, was elected secretary. Two key committees were named: Bill Burton headed one on trail marking and Frank Place chaired one that Torrey diplomatically labeled "allocation of trail work." These two committees submitted recommendations that were approved by the conference in June 1931 and incorporated in a "statement of principles" for coordinating both new trail construction and existing trail maintenance. Miraculously all the major factions agreed to the statement. To govern future trail work, an "advisory committee" was created under Torrey's chairmanship, with representation for the three major New York chapters and sections (AMC, GMC, ADK), as well as four of the leading independent clubs (Nature Friends, Tramp and Trail, Inkowa, and the New York Mountain Club). Included on this key committee with Torrey were the other two architects of the armistice, Burton (representing the GMC) and Place (for Tramp and Trail). The more cantankerous independents (Bartha, Unger, Jessup, Nurian, Tiger) were left off. But all of them signed the statement of principles.

In remarkably short order, this group established a rapprochement among the warring club chieftains. Guidelines for trail colors and the size and frequency of blazes were created and agreement reached that the conference would approve all new trails or major relocations. The more recalcitrant went through a couple of showdowns to test the conference's authority, but Torrey succeeded in cajoling, persuading, or browbeating them into agreement. One such incident, involving the fiery Bartha and his trail-making ally, Emil Unger, provoked the following parody of Pope's *Iliad* translation, written by friends of Bartha and Unger but cheerfully published by Torrey in his own column:

> Here on brave Torrey's speech Barthlides broke,
> And furious thus, and interrupting spoke:
> "Tyrant, I well deserve thy galling chain,
> To live thy slave and still to serve in vain,
> Should I submit to each unjust decree—
> Command thy vassals, but command not me!
> Seize on my markers, which some hikers deemed
> Perfect and fitting, as to me they seemed;
> And seize secure; no more Barthlides wields
> His painting brush in any hiking fields.
> I, like Achilles, will get out from under—
> I flee to Florida with Emil Unger.

As late as 1937 there was another outbreak of hostilities in the Trail War, but it was soon suppressed.

No doubt Torrey's extraordinary diplomatic skills were one factor in the conference's stunning success, but Torrey himself credited "a spirit of harmony and willingness to subordinate individual ideas to the general good." Whatever the cause, the New York–New Jersey Trail Conference hereby attained a position of leadership in the New York area hiking scene that it has never relinquished.[b]

Amid the crash and thrash of axes, clippers, and personal egos in metropolitan New York's trail-cutting boom of the 1920s and 1930s, one quiet idea stands in marked contrast. In 1929 General Electric scientist Vincent J. Schaefer and some of his friends in the Schenectady, New York, area organized the Mohawk Valley Hiking Club. During the next few years the idea began to take shape in Schaefer's fertile imagination of a "hiker's route" from New York City to the Adirondacks. Unlike the usual concept of a cleared path, Schaefer envisioned resourceful hikers making use of what they found along the way—whether hikers' trails, back roads, abandoned wood roads, tow paths, creek beds, game trails, plus occasional bushwhacks where that appeared to offer the most interesting route:

> . . . a route that a person having good "woods" sense could use to move across a region using compass and "topo" map, and that in a meandering way would lead such persons to most of the interesting scenic vistas, rock formations, choice or unique vegetation, historical sites, and similar items that a certain type of outdoors person enjoys.

Taking the name from the same Whitman source that had inspired Raymond Torrey's column, Schaefer said, "It rather was conceived as 'a long brown path leading wherever I choose.'" He explicitly sought to avoid the marked-trail syndrome: "The Long Path was never planned as a trail that would be marked by paint, blazes or trail markers." That it *not* be marked seemed a crucial point to Schaefer. He wrote to a Harriman Park official,

> There would be no cutting or blazing, for this trail would be a truly wild walk that wouldn't erode the land or scar the solitude . . . and each found site would be an adventure in orienteering.

In 1933 the Long Path attracted powerful support from Torrey and from W. W. Cady, a transplanted Colorado mountain walker. The latter

---

[b]Resurrection of the defunct Trail Conference in 1931 gives that organization three dates that could almost equally claim acceptance as its birthdate. The conference itself claims the year 1920, referring to the establishment of its predecessor, the Palisades Interstate Park Trail Conference, on October 19, 1920; since the New York–New Jersey trail Conference directly superseded this organization, there is nothing wrong with the claim. However, those who formally dissolved the PIPTC and created the NY–NJTC in 1922 clearly felt that something more than a mere name change was taking place (see William A. Welch letter to Frank Place, Jan. 20, 1940, in Frank Place, "Trail Clippings"; Torrey, "Publicly Owned Footways a Need," *New York Evening Post*, Jan. 28, 1921, p. 9; "N. Y.–N. J.–Trail Conference Formed," *New York Evening Post*, Aug. 28, 1922; and Benton MacKaye, "Some Early A. T. History," PATC *Bulletin*, [Oct.–Dec. 1957], pp. 92–93); so the year 1922 could as accurately be regarded as the birth of the present organization. Then, since there is ample evidence that the conference had "faded out" after 1927, a case could be made for taking April 21, 1931, as the date of the present organization's actual inception.

took on the job of scouting the general plan for the itinerary from the Harriman Park region north to the Catskills. From there on, Schaefer and his brother Paul worked out the route toward Marcy. Torrey supplied publicity in a series of columns written in early 1934.

The concept of an unblazed, nonspecific route, to be called a "path," proved a tough one for more orthodox trailspeople to swallow. In the standard thinking of the day, the Long Path was regarded as not yet built, because no one had been through with ax and clippers to clear the way, whereas to Schaefer the path "existed as soon as the route had been field explored and then marked on a 'topo' map, and so become available to the person who appreciates such things."

We shall find a similar divergence of thinking between the original concept of the Appalachian Trail in the mind of Benton MacKaye and the trail as it physically came to be cut, cleared, blazed, and signed by others who followed. Schaefer's ideal, like MacKaye's, was too subtle or perhaps too impractical for general acceptance.

Then World War II came along, Schaefer and Cady drifted away from the hiking scene, and the idea of the Long Path was held in abeyance. It was resurrected during the postwar period but transmogrified from Schaefer's original delicate concept into the firmer, more understandable one of a definite, marked-and-cleared trail, with its own blazes, logo, and route descriptions, and finally even a guidebook. A new and magnificent long-distance trail was born: an idea was lost.

Chapter 40

Connecticut's blue-blazed trail system

A METROPOLITAN trail system with an entirely different character and personality took shape not far away in the increasingly urbanized state of Connecticut, whose city residents were also discovering the pleasures of weekend hiking.

Connecticut's urban growth was different from that of most states, in that it developed no one giant metropolis, but rather half a dozen middle-sized and many small, independent cities scattered over almost the entire state. This demographic pattern created its own pattern of recreation. In each of the scattered urban areas—New Haven, Waterbury, Meriden, Hartford, Bridgeport, and elsewhere—recreationists made weekend and early evening use of nearby wooded or elevated land wherever the owners permitted. Philanthropists donated large chunks of undeveloped land for public parks: a good example was Walter Hubbard's gift to the city of Meriden of an extensive area that included the Hanging Hills, with their rugged cliffs and wooded heights. In 1895 the Connecticut Forestry Association (Forest and Park Association after 1924) formed to preserve woodlands wherever they could be had.

In 1913 the state established a park commission and hired forty-six-year-old Albert Milford Turner as field secretary. Turner, it was said, "combined the best features of a spark plug, a compass, and a crystal ball." Short of stature, he had, said one trailsman, "the longest stride for a little man of anyone I know." More important, he had a long view of Connecticut's recreational needs. In 1917 he sent the commission a memorandum powerfully stating the case for woodlands in an increasingly civilized state:

> We all recognize the value of education but have much yet to learn about the importance of recreation. I am inclined to think when we do realize it, the state will find recreation a close second to education in importance state wide, and that the state has a deep and permanent interest in it.

Turner passed over the idea of a few big wilderness parks in favor of adapting to the peculiar requirements of a state that was sprouting numerous small cities, rather than one giant metropolis. To Turner, this signaled the need for maintaining little patches of woodland throughout Connecticut:

> There should be many minor open spaces under the State Park Commission scattered all over the State, maybe one in every country town, for every town has some spot peculiarly its own, like the water-falls, the deep ravine, mountain or hill-top, lake or sea shore, meadow, fields, or groves that are well adapted for the outdoor use of the people of the town . . . where they can go and let the spirit of the woods, of the hills, valleys, brooks and ponds soak into them, refreshing and feeding their spirits, strengthening their courage and renewing their youth. They need not be very large, an acre or so in extent, surely not over five acres.

Turner argued that relatively small acquisitions could open large worlds of recreation. "When you are in a park, all that you see is in the park"—meaning that if a hiker could walk through a small strip of wildness in the foreground, his spirit could do the rest and claim the farthest horizon as part of his recreational experience. Echoing Emerson's doctrine of landscape, Turner pointed out, "The blue distance is always pleasing; he who looks on it owns it as much as anyone can."

Turner was a strong champion of pedestrianism: "Only the man on foot can reap the full reward from the State Parks." During the 1910s it was a relatively new realization that "only the man on wheels has any longer any right worth defending in our public highways. Let the walker beware." So much more reason to reserve the parks for pedestrians. Having lost the country roads, the walker badly needed the backcountry beyond the roads. Therefore, beginning in the years from 1917 to 1919, Turner began to devote his efforts to encouraging the development of trails on parklands.

The system of Connecticut forests and parks that developed from Turner's philosophy was admirably shaped to suit the demographics of the Nutmeg State. More than eighty parks and thirty state forests are distributed through every corner of the state—none large, a score of them fewer than one hundred acres, but providing green space for the numerous cities' walkers.

Yet Turner's vision was only partially realized in that Connecticut's formally state-owned parks and forests by no means constitute the total land available for public recreation. Neither Turner nor other pioneer advocates of Connecticut parks foresaw the phenomenon of so much public recreation on private lands. This is the genius of Connecticut's trail system. But Turner was right on target in painting a picture of recreation land coexisting side by side with increasing urban development. Both in general theory and in practical support of specific trail projects, Turner was the original inspiration of the system of pedestrian recreation for which Connecticut's blue-blazed trails were built.

At first Connecticut trail makers groped but slowly toward the kind of trail system suited to this urbanized state. In Meriden's Hubbard Park, short footpaths were cleared around such attractions as West Peak and East Peak soon after the park was donated by Hubbard. Beginning around 1916 a small group of men began extending these paths northward from West Peak and eastward toward Mount Higby (see figure 40.1). The leader of this effort was Meriden resident Frederick W. Kilbourne, librarian, associate editor of Webster's International Dictionary, chronicler of the White Mountains, a competent amateur botanist, and ardent pedestrian, with means enough to enjoy leisure time. With help from local friends (Alfred P. Wheeler, Robert W. Carter, Robert A. Squires) and local Boy Scouts under John D. Roberts, Kilbourne gradually expanded his trails until in 1918 he conceived the idea of a single trans-Connecticut trail from Long Island Sound to Massachusetts. In 1919 this "Trap Rock Trail," as Kilbourne dubbed it, received important support from Turner and Allen Chamberlain: Turner made it Exhibit A in a December 1, 1919, memorandum "Concerning Trails" to the Connecticut State Park Commission, while Chamberlain published long articles on the proposed trail in the *Boston Evening Transcript*.

Others who pioneered Connecticut's foot trails included Herbert C. Warner, operating on city-owned lands west and north of Hartford; J. Walter Bassett, a Yale professor who roamed the Sleeping Giant, north of New Haven; Dr. A. A. Crane, a surgeon from Waterbury who used roller bandages for trail markers; Arthur Perkins, a Hartford judge who became interested in hiking during the 1920s and soon was engrossed with plans to build the Appalachian Trail through the northwest corner of the state; members of the newly formed (1921) Connecticut Chapter of the AMC; and doubtless many other more or less casual walkers who picked out routes through the woods on the outskirts of other cities.

The man who lifted these disconnected and haphazard trail projects into a statewide system of major importance to Connecticut's pedestrian life was a tall, lean, intense, bespectacled, and bushy-browed retired minister, Edgar Laing Heermance. A scarecrowlike figure, as long as Turner was short—a fellow trailsman recalled Heermance's bicycle: "I had never seen a bicycle seat raised as far above the frame, except in the circus"—Heermance was no less a powerful influence on the direction of Connecticut recreation.

Born in 1876, graduated from Yale Divinity School in 1899, Edgar Heermance had summered in the Catskills as a boy and in Waterville Valley and Wonalancet as a young man, where the Heermance Shelter on

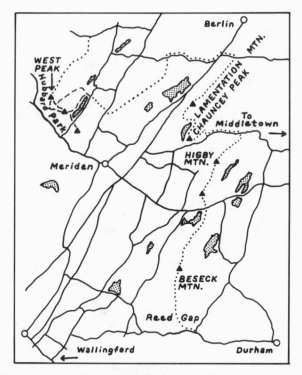

Figure 40.1. Connecticut's Trap Rock Trail, 1919 The first concept of a
through-trail in the populous state of Connecticut sprang from the
imagination of Frederick W. Kilbourne. Designated the Trap Rock Trail, it was
put together by Kilbourne and his friends between 1916 and 1919. It afforded
a pleasant walk linking woodlands and crags in the center of the state,
weaving around such densely populated urban centers as Meriden,
Middletown, and Berlin. This was a precursor of Connecticut's statewide
blue-blazed trail system of more than a decade later.

Whiteface was evidence of his involvement in trail and shelter construction back then. In 1912 he went west to preach in Minnesota but returned
to his beloved Connecticut in 1920 to retire to a life of study and writing,
with trail work as a hobby—an active hobby. He purchased a hilltop
property, which he called "Rocky Top," a few miles north of New Haven,
and there he rebuilt some dilapidated old cabins for his family's use. During the mid-1920s, he and his children started work on a trail from Rocky
Top along the crest of a ridge toward another outlook that they called
"Lone Tree Hill" (York Hill today). He then carried the trail westward to a
road at Bethany Gap. The eastern end was easily linked to nearby Sleeping Giant and its network of paths (see figure 40.2). Though but 4 miles
in length, Heermance's trail was in some respects the actual starting point
for Connecticut's blue-blazed system. That ever present adjective "blue-
blazed" dates directly from the Reverend Mr. Heermance's initial trail.

Borrowing the color used (and still used) by the Wonalancet Out Door Club, and perfecting the tint by mixing paints until he had one that could best be seen in twilight, Heermance not only blazed his own trail blue but succeeded in having that color adopted by trail makers all over the Nutmeg State.

In 1929 the Connecticut Forest and Park Association sensed the emerging importance of foot trails and created its first Trails Committee. The initial membership included Herbert Warner and Judge Arthur Perkins of

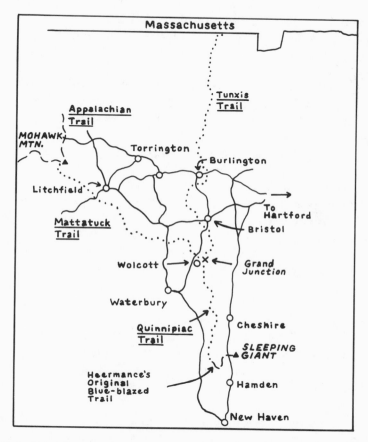

Figure 40.2. The three trails that met at Grand Junction Connecticut's blue-blazed trail system began with a short path built by Edgar Laing Heermance in the hills west of the Sleeping Giant. Under Heermance's leadership, other trail-builders soon were at work all over the state. By the mid-1930s, three long-distance hiking trails crossed the area north of New Haven and west of Hartford: the Quinnipiac, which was a northward extension of Heermance's original blue-blazed trail; the Tunxis Trail, reaching to Massachusetts; and the Mattatuck Trail, which ran northwest to link up with the Appalachian Trail. These three met at a single axis, known to Connecticut hikers as "Grand Junction."

Hartford, Robert E. Platt of Waterbury, and two Yale professors from New Haven, J. Walter Bassett and Everett O. Waters, with Heermance as chairman. Though in many ways a loner, the sage of Rocky Top was, in the words of a New Haven associate, "cursed with a certain executive ability which annoys his philosophical nature." Under his leadership, the Connecticut blue-blazed trail system sprang to life over the next two or three years, and the Trails Committee of the CFPA assumed general direction and coordination of the system, a role that it has maintained ever since.

The committee initially focused on Heermance's own 4-mile trail and its connection with the Sleeping Giant. Early in 1930 Professor Waters rounded up some Yale Outing Club lads and extended that trail northward from Bethany Gap another 17 miles over little hills, through picturesque hemlock groves, past a cemetery, crossing several roads (with a trolley line affording convenient access from nearby towns) to a spot near Spindle Hill just northeast of the town of Wolcott (see figure 40.2). By April 19, 1930, the 21-mile trail was declared open and christened the Quinnipiac Trail, inaugurating a policy of naming virtually all Connecticut trails after Indian tribes.

That same year, 4 miles north of Wolcott in the town of Bristol, the chamber of commerce called a meeting for the purpose of organizing the building of hiking trails on nearby hills. Attending that meeting was a General Motors patent attorney named Romeyn (pronounced "Romine") A. Spare, who had joined the AMC in 1925 to do a bit of walking but who was bitten by the trail-making bug at that 1930 meeting, gave up golf and yachting and the other dignified pastimes of a General Motors attorney, and dedicated his extraordinary vitality for the next thirty years to trail work. A follower of his observed: "He had a one-track mind. He thought always of trails. He ate, slept, and dreamed trails."

During the summer of 1930 Spare commenced work on what was called the Tunxis Trail, running north from Wolcott through the high land south of Bristol, swinging west of that city and beginning its circuitous way toward Massachusetts (see figure 40.2). With a few friends, notably Newton Manross, Spare

> went out nearly every other night scouting through woodlands and meadows, over old cart paths and wood roads, beside brooks and along ledges, toiling and clearing as they went.

By the end of the following year the Tunxis Trail reached 44 miles from its junction with the Quinnipiac at Wolcott to a road crossing (now Route 4) north of Burlington. By the end of the decade, Spare had not only carried the route to within a couple of miles of the Massachusetts line, but had also created a series of loops and circular side trails along the main trunk line, so that the Tunxis was not just one trail but its own minisystem of trails. In the process, Spare wore out some of his old business friendships: "Golfers and yachtsmen have little taste for brambles, mosquitoes, and mud—to say nothing of Connecticut's merciless humidity," recalled a later associate. But others pitched in, including his family—wife Bessie, daughters Ardella and Betty, brother-in-law Perry Deming and his wife Alice, with the steadfast support of Manross.

With Heermance and Ned Anderson, the Connecticut AT-builder whom we shall meet in chapter 45, Romeyn Spare was among the first of the giants of Connecticut trails, that handful of men who truly dominated some section of the blue-blazed trail system and became walking legends. Most of these men were primarily post–World War II figures— Seymour Smith, Harold Pierpont, Kornel Bailey, Ned Greist, George Libby, and a few others—so their story belongs to a later time. But in prewar titans such as Heermance, Anderson, and Spare all the elements of the genre are there: the single-minded devotion to good trail work, the fierce dedication, the volcanic energy, the unabashed pride, often tinged with disdain for those less dedicated, the marvelous decades-long record of achievement. Spare was known as Baron von Tunxis, a title expressive of the feudal sway over their trails that these men exercised.

With the Quinnipiac in place and the Tunxis forging northward, a third trail sprouted from that corner on Spindle Hill northeast of Wolcott. The Mattatuck Trail was laid out to head westward, north of Waterbury, south of Litchfield, cutting over the graceful Litchfield hills to join the newly constructed Appalachian Trail at the western edge of the state (see figure 40.2). Conceived and in large measure marked out in 1930, though not cleared thoroughly until 1932, this trail was the fruit of the labors of Dr. Crane, the Waterbury surgeon, and two executives of the Scovill Manufacturing Company in Waterbury, Bennet Bronson and Roger Sperry. From 1932 on, Sperry involved a friend named Ronald Malia, who devoted many years to the maintenance of the Mattatuck.

The confluence of three major trails on Spindle Hill gave that unassuming road-crossing the exalted name of "Grand Junction." It was a landmark on Connecticut trail maps of the 1930s.

Meanwhile two other major blue-blazed trails grew out of Kilbourne's old ax-blazed Trap Rock Trail of vintage 1919 (figure 40.3). The southern part of that trail was given the name of Mattabesett. The combined efforts of the Yale and Wesleyan outing clubs were instrumental in its construction. Having pioneered the upper Quinnipiac with his brawny Yale lads in 1930, Professor Waters now brought his crew to Reed's Gap, southeast of Meriden, and in 1931 extended Kilbourne's trail south to the site of Coe's Mill, a distance of a little more than 5 miles. Enthusiastically cooperating with the new system, Kilbourne and his friends went over the southern end of his old trail to paint his blazes blue in late 1931. In early 1932 Karl Pomeroy Harrington, the Wesleyan professor who had been one of the leaders in White Mountain trail work for many years, turned out the Wesleyan Outing Club and extended the Mattabesett another 3 miles to the southeast. Later that year Kilbourne completed and remarked the northern end of his original trail. During the rest of the decade of the 1930s, Harrington and the Wesleyan youths pushed the Mattabesett east and eventually circled back north until they reached the Connecticut River at White Rocks. Thus was made a continuous hiking trail of almost 50 miles right up against the most densely populated heart of Connecticut, threading between and around the cities of Meriden, Berlin, Wallingford, Durham, and Middletown.

The northern half of Kilbourne's old trail became the Metacomet. During the 1930s it was pushed northward from Meriden's West Peak, at first over Ragged and Rattlesnake mountains by the efforts of William Burling, and later in discontinuous sections north toward the Massachusetts line through the work of Mark Goedecke.

Elsewhere during the 1930s blue-blazed trails sprang up (see figure 40.4). The Appalachian Trail was pushed through the northwest corner of the state between 1929 and 1932. The AT, with the three big trails that converged on Grand Junction (Quinnipiac, Tunxis, Mattatuck), and the two that grew from Kilbourne's old Trap Rock Trail (Mattabesett, Metacomet) were the major original trails. But smaller ones grew up in the eastern part of the state, and were also given Indian names: the Narragansett, Pequot, Mohegan, and Nipmuck. In the southwest corner there was a short-lived Mianus Trail through the northern sections of the city of Stamford. Near New Haven were the Naugatuck Trail, the Salmon River Trail, and the George Washington Trail (which was supposed to follow an old route traveled by the first president). When the Civilian Conservation Corps camps moved into some of the state parks and forests, they built hiking trails, as well as roads, picnic areas, and observation towers.

By 1933 Connecticut counted 250 miles in the blue-blazed system and claimed more trail mileage than any other New England state except New Hampshire.

Of greater significance than the sheer mileage was the uncommon accomplishment of building reasonably lengthy trails through the most consistently populated, paved, and built-up sector of New England. Living in the heart of civilization, Connecticut's blue-blazed trails acquired certain characteristics totally foreign to those of the White Mountains or the Adirondacks. Built in large measure on private land, they existed at the whim of the landowner. One of the Mattatuck's architects, Bennet Bronson, enunciated a cardinal precept of Connecticut trail making when he said, "It is always understood that permission is informal and revocable if the trail gets to be a nuisance." One of the early Mattabesett workers, Norman Wickstrand, recalled,

> The amazing thing about the old trails is that it was all done on a voluntary basis, and with such very nice friendly courteous landowner permission.

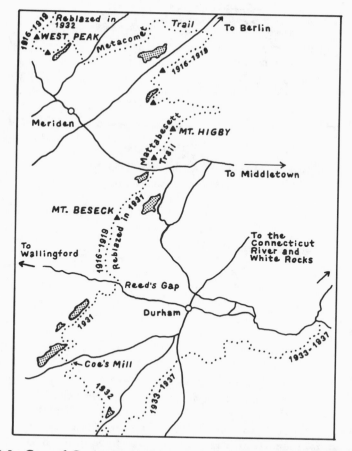

Figure 40.3. Central Connecticut's blue-blazed trails The original Trap Rock Trail of 1919 provided the starting point for a much longer trail known as the Mattabesett, which was extended southward first by Yale Outing Club students under Prof. Everett O. Waters in 1931; and then eastward by Wesleyan students under Prof. Karl Pomeroy Harrington between 1932 and 1940. The north end of the old Trap Rock Trail was designated the Metacomet Trail. This too was extended, largely through the efforts of William Burling during the early 1930s and of Mark Goedecke during the late 1930s.

Wrote the Baron von Tunxis, Romeyn Spare:

> It has been said that the best trail maker is one third Indian to scout out the most interesting route, one third diplomat to secure permits, and the remaining third a combination of other qualities such as enthusiasm, imagination, and executive ability.

This close association with a diversity of private landowners created continuous challenges in trail maintenance, as we shall see in chapter 43.

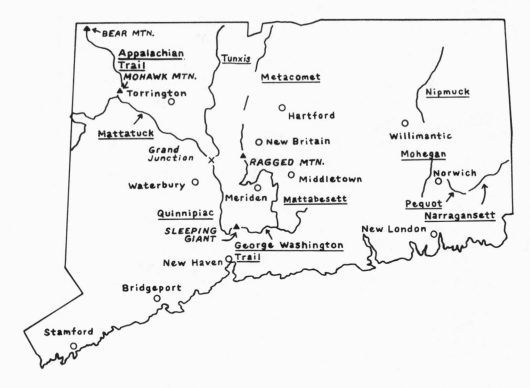

Figure 40.4. Connecticut's through-trails, ca. 1940 By the end of the 1930s, Connecticut claimed to offer more miles of hiking trails than any other New England state save New Hampshire. The blue-blazed trails could be found in virtually every corner of the state. This and the foregoing maps of Connecticut trails are based largely on the maps in various editions of the *Connecticut Walk Book.* The authors gratefully acknowledge permission from the Connecticut Forest and Park Association to make these adaptations of their maps.

Most remarkable was the fact that Connecticut trail makers maintained their precarious relationships with private landowners largely without benefit of organized hiking clubs. To be sure, among the trail makers themselves, the CFPA played an important coordinating and leadership role. Nevertheless, the trail makers were a bunch of creative individuals, headstrong, self-reliant, geographically dispersed, not easily led. Among the broader constituency of ordinary trail hikers, organized clubs were not dominant as in New York. True, the Connecticut Chapter of the AMC was a thriving social group by the mid-1920s and has continued so ever since. The New Haven Hiking Club enjoyed prosperous years during the 1930s. At the same time, in the northwest corner, the Housatonic Trail Club was a small but spirited group under the leadership of AT-builder Ned Anderson. Waterbury had its Half-a-League Club. But for trail work, these independent Connecticut Yankees did not band together so consistently as the weekend walkers of New York City. Yet in both areas the phenomenon of metropolitan trails was brought to maturity during the decades of the 1920s and 1930s.

Chapter 41

The proliferation of hiking clubs

THE THREE big clubs—the AMC, the GMC, the ADK—dominated the hiking scene on the northern ranges, but a scattering of smaller clubs surfaced from time to time during the 1920s and 1930s, lending diversity and individuality to the hiker's world.

Maine

The *Eastern States Mountain Club* was an all-male group founded by YMCA hikers from Portland, Maine, on a climb of Pleasant Mountain in 1931. Their guiding spirit was the popular and versatile bachelor, Arthur M. Fogg (generally called "Foggie"), an orchestra leader, artist, civic leader, expert roller skater, and strenuous outdoorsman, beloved by young and old. The group scheduled hikes regularly during the 1930s, climbing many of the lesser-visited mountains of western Maine, as well as Katahdin and the White Mountains. Its members, headed by George P. LaBorde, built the steep Chimney Trail up Tumbledown, and for a while it maintained a section of Maine's Appalachian Trail. Despite internal debates over the issues, the club never officially opened its doors to women, but during the late 1930s some of the members formed a skiing auxiliary called the *Penguins*, in which women were active. Finding that experience felicitous, the ESMC voted to merge with the Penguins, thereby indirectly breaking down the sex barrier. The group disbanded when World War II came along.

The *Maine Alpine Club* was the brainchild of Stanley B. Attwood, city editor for Lewiston, Maine, newspapers. Founded in 1936, the club concentrated exclusively on climbing the mountains of the Pine Tree State. It also built a trail up Goose Eye in the Mahoosucs and maintained a section of the AT for awhile. The club survived World War II but faded out during the 1950s.

The *Maine Appalachian Trail Club* was organized in 1935 explicitly to maintain the Appalachian Trail throughout Maine, directly or by delegating responsibility to other individuals or organizations. This group was an important force in the history of the Appalachian Trail and is described more fully in chapter 45.

New Hampshire

Hiking and trail clubs formed around specific portions of the White Mountains, spurred by summer folk concerned with either maintaining local trails or arranging a schedule of sociable hikes. *The Randolph Mountain Club, Wonalancet Out Door Club, Chocorua Mountain Club, Waterville Athletic and Improvement Association, North Woodstock Improvement Association,* and *Squam Lake Association* were the most important groups in pre–World War II days. Most of these clubs were involved with trail maintenance, so they are described more fully in chapters 22 and 43.

Vermont

The *Stratton Mountain Club* was organized by ten friends on July 27, 1912, and grew to a membership of more then fifty within two years. In 1912 the group built a trail to the top of Stratton Mountain and a 65-foot observation tower. No record of its activities is found during the 1920s and 1930s, so the club was presumably short-lived.

The *Brattleboro Outing Club* is similarly little celebrated in historical annals. Organized in 1922, it seems to have been the outlet for the boundless organizing talents of Fred Harris, the effervescent founder of the Dartmouth Outing Club, after his graduation took him away from the hills around Hanover. It reportedly blazed a 40-mile trail (partly on roads) from Brattleboro to the top of Stratton Mountain during the early 1920s and was active enough in 1926 to be discussing affiliation with the GMC. How much longer it enjoyed independent existence is not known.

The *American Fun Society* was the cheerful name of a group of Lake Willoughby vacationers, organized at Pisgah Lodge during the late 1920s. Though it claimed a membership of 350, only 25 persons attended its "annual field meeting" in 1930, and how long it lasted is not known. One noteworthy member was Judge Clarence P. Cowles, charter member of the GMC and builder of the original section of the Long Trail.

Upstate New York

The *Adirondack Camp and Trail Club,* formed in 1910 under the leadership of Henry Van Hoevenberg and the Lake Placid Club hikers, puttered around at trail building mainly near Lake Placid during the 1910s. Reorganized in 1923, the club constituted itself a major trail-building arm of the newly formed ADK and entered on a more aggressive period of trail work in the Marcy-Colden-Algonquin mountains during the middle and late 1920s. As soon as the ADK's own Trails Committee was in full operation, the Camp and Trail Club withered away.

Haskell's Raskels was the informal name of a circle within the Camp and Trail Club, led by Edward Haskell and specializing in very strenuous hiking.

The *Elizabethtown Trails Club* was a small and informal club organized by Judge A. N. Hand of Philadelphia, businessman W. Houston Hubbard of New York, and other summer residents of Elizabethtown in 1926. The group was responsible for getting the Conservation Department rangers to cut a trail connecting Elizabethtown to the top of Giant Mountain and other local eminences. Never elaborately organized, the club faded out during the 1930s.

The *Catskill Mountain Club* was created in 1926 by a New York City trailsman named Alexander Jessup, as an attempt to stir interest in Catskill hiking and trail building. Extolling the virtues of the Catskills' highest peak, Jessup coined the club slogan "Slide, Kelly, Slide!" after a popular song about a turn-of-the-century baseball star. Jessup's scheme never took off—a reflection of the curious absence of general interest in Catskills hiking during the 1920s. "He had the dream," recalls one of Jessup's early recruits, "but somewhere there was no drive; it simply ran into the sands."

The *Mohawk Valley Hiking Club* was organized in 1929 by a General Electric scientist, Vincent Schaefer, whose interesting career and innovative ideas for trails were described in chapter 39 and whose winter adventures will be encountered in chapter 49. The club was active in hills around Albany, with occasional trips to the Adirondacks during the 1930s.

The *Taconic Hiking Club* filled the need for a hiking and trail club in the Taconic Range, along the New York–Massachusetts border. Though discussions were underway as early as 1929, the formal organization of the club occurred in November 1932. The original nucleus of membership was from the Troy, New York, YMCA, which had an active hiking contingent during the 1920s, but others swelled the ranks to more than one hundred during the late 1930s. A regular schedule of trips took them to the Taconics for day-trips and to the Green Mountains, Berkshires, and Catskills on weekends. This club survived a drop in membership during World War II and flourishes today, having assumed major responsibility for trail maintenance in the Taconic Range.

The *Adirondack Forty-Sixers* are a group of major importance, described in chapter 46. They were formed with the single purpose of climbing all Adirondack peaks over 4,000 feet in height, which at the time were thought to number forty-six.

It was in the New York City–area hiking scene where hiking clubs found their most fertile soil. To begin with, each of the "big three" Northeastern clubs had New York chapters (or sections)—but that was just the beginning.

The AMC's New York Chapter. The New York Appies tended to have broader interests than the other two big clubs. Canoeing, cycling, and seashore rambling at the club's camp on Fire Island (off Long Island) competed for members' leisure hours, along with hiking and trail work. Lacking a central hikers' camp in Harriman Park, the Appies never developed the close-knit social weekend life of the GMC and ADK chapters. This tended to make the other two more of a presence for the New York hiking community.[a] On the other hand, the Appies had a reputation for more strenuous hiking.

The GMC's New York Section. Prof. Will S. Monroe founded this GMC section and dominated its activities until at least 1922. In that year, Raymond Torrey negotiated with Major Welch for the use of the spacious off-road house on the shore of the newly built Lake Tiorati in Harriman Park. On Christmas Eve of 1922 the section took over this camp. "Thendara" became the local headquarters and spiritual weekend home for GMC members. Every weekend a designated member was in charge; those who loved to hike used Thendara as a centrally located base, while many came simply to socialize at the lodge.

The ADK's New York Chapter. When the ADK was formed in 1922, it did not hesitate a moment before setting up a New York chapter. Raymond Torrey had been among the founding members of the parent organization and was authorized immediately to organize a New York chapter. By the spring of 1923 the first schedule of walks was published. Like the GMC, the New York ADK soon acquired a base in Harriman Park: a commodious camp on the shores of Lake Sebago, 5 miles west of Thendara, built in 1926. This was Nawakwa, and its function for the ADK was analogous to that of Thendara for the GMC. One had to walk to the camp until after World War II, when park authorities required road access for fire control, much to the disgust of old-time members.

Together, these three groups shared many qualities, including a rambunctious independence from their parent clubs. New York members thought of themselves first as New York hikers; formal affiliation with Boston or Vermont or the Adirondacks took a distant backseat. Laura Woodward (later Abbott) was a charter member of the GMC's New York Section, its secretary from 1921 to 1927, and president in 1928 and 1929 —yet never set foot in the Green Mountains until 1927.

---

[a]One indication of the Appies' lower profile is an article by Ernest A. Dench, "Hiking—the Sport of Four Seasons," *Charm Magazine* (Oct. 1927), pp. 20–21, 83, in which ten prominent clubs are named, including the ADK and the GMC, but not the AMC.

Whatever the dominance of males in mountain walking elsewhere, the New York hiking scene showed no such inclination. Quite the contrary: both the ADK and the GMC continually wrestled with a tendency to grow overbalanced with too many women. The ADK once ran a mock classified ad in its newsletter: "Men wanted: Must be of good character, have hiking and camping ability. . . . Needed to help balance the ADK membership woman surplus!" The GMC even adopted a formal rule requiring "sex balance," a "smile-provoking by-word" that resulted in its 1924 membership of 298 being composed of precisely 149 men and 149 women.

Though women were not discriminated against, other people certainly were. One reason for the many independent clubs among minority groups and foreign-born was a persistent hint of exclusivity about the three major clubs. These comments from women active in the New York City clubs in the 1930s are relevant:

> Back in the early days, it was quite a status symbol to belong to a hiking club such as the big 3. They had rigid membership requirements, physical, educational. There were religious and color lines.

> I did not like their [GMC's] admission policy. You had to come to Thendara to get in and having a guest card didn't help unless you had a friend who could bring you to Thendara. Also they excluded Jews and of course blacks.

In fairness it should be made quite clear that these policies prevailed during the 1920s and 1930s, not today. That was a different era, the heyday of Jim Crow and isolationism. The point is mentioned only because the phenomenon *did* exist: historical completeness requires recording this unsightly blot on the otherwise attractive New York hiking scene.

These big three were a strong presence, but by no means did they intimidate the host of independent clubs of all shapes and sizes. It was an era of "joining." The more prominent of the independents included, roughly in order of age:

The Torrey Botanical Club. Organized during the 1860s (see Chapter 18), it remained very active during the 1920s.

The Fresh Air Club. During the last quarter of the nineteenth century, "Father Bill" Curtis's band of hardies had a structure and schedule, but by the 1920s they had abandoned all formal organization. Yet they remained a formidable presence on the scene. The club was at once the most exclusive group and the least structured. It had no meetings, notices, or dues, but certain individuals were known to be "members," and it was listed in a 1930s bulletin as among the clubs coordinating volunteer trail work. Its principal pursuit, however, was certainly not trail work but strenuous hiking. No group surpassed the ambitious itineraries or jet-speed pace of the Fresh Air Club boys of summer (no women were permitted).

The Paterson Ramblers. Next in point of age were the Paterson (New Jersey) Ramblers, organized in 1904 by Philmer Eves. All trips started at city hall in Paterson and went from there largely to New Jersey hills, though sometimes to Harriman Park and Storm King.

The Walkers' Club of America. Organized in 1911 and based in New York City, the Walkers' Club had both a women's affiliate, the *Ladies Walking Club* (1913) and a rival, the *American Walkers' Association* (1915). These groups were still scheduling hikes during the early 1920s.

The Tramp and Trail Club. Of major importance was this group organized by Edgar D. and Jessie Stone in 1914. This was the first unaffiliated New York hiking club that (*a*) welcomed both sexes, with balanced participation, (*b*) engaged in trail work regularly, and (*c*) occupied as significant a niche as the big three in the New York hiking scene, thanks to its leading figure, Frank Place. An industrious trail-builder and maintainer and a tireless hiker (known to some as Mr. Miles), Place was active in many groups, but his chief allegiance was always the Tramp and Trail Club, which he served as president all through the 1920s and 1930s. The "Tramps" scheduled 8–12-mile hikes every Sunday, mostly in the Hudson Highlands, rain or shine. Club schedules bore the legend "No trips postponed on account of weather." Besides walks and trail maintenance, this club pursued what would be called today an environmental education program, urging good woodsmanship and practical concern for the hiking environment.

Inkowa[b] In 1918 three well-heeled ladies with outdoor interests—Mrs. E. H. Harriman, Mrs. Daniel Guggenheim, and Anne Morgan—formed this all-women hiking club, as an adjunct of the national Inkowa, founded in 1915. Its hikes were listed regularly in the "Long Brown Path" columns, and it maintained a city house on Spuyten Duyvil and a country house on Greenwood Lake, New Jersey. Men were sometimes asked to lead more strenuous trips; one recalls "finding myself surrounded by a flock of girls on an overnight camp trip; one man and a congregation of females; very disturbing!"

Nature Friends. Mention has already been made of this interesting group. The transplanted counterpart of a society organized in Germany in the early twentieth century, Nature Friends combined the philosophical ideals of a mild form of socialism with love of the natural world and exuberant physical exercise. Though their political beliefs exposed them to harassment from the right both in prewar Germany and in the postwar United States, they were among the most vigorous hiking and trail-maintaining clubs of the 1920s and 1930s, with a major base in the Wyanokies and a lesser one in the Kaaterskill Clove of the Catskills.

---

[b]One source explains the name as a word, perhaps of Indian origin, meaning "trust" or "trustworthiness" (Torrey, "Long Brown Path," March 2, 1928).

Wanderlust (later *Wandervögel*, still later *Wanderbirds*). This second important German group went through two distinct phases. During the 1920s it was a close-knit group of friends who

> kept to themselves, did little publicity work (except in the German newspapers), and simply practiced German Gemütlichkeit in the out-of-doors and on the trail instead of a beerstube.

In 1929, when some of the original leaders left the scene, one of its newest members, Bill Hoeferlin, was just beginning to come into his own as a leading New York trailsman. Hoeferlin anglicized the name and transformed the club into a vehicle for his personal activities as hiking leader, trail cutter, and, most important, designer of the maps used in the New York area for fifty years.

The New York Hiking Club. Founded in 1922 with an emphasis on the health benefits of exercise, the NYHC proclaimed the slogan "Health is wealth! Let's hike!" Dr. Royal Copeland, then health commissioner (later U.S. senator) was its founder.

The City College Hiking Club (later *College Alumni Hiking Club*). Originally (1922) an adjunct of the Geology Department of City College, this flourishing group combined collegiate affability with extraordinary energy and humor. "Leave compasses and maps at home," admonished one trip notice. "Nothing can keep us from getting lost." Fast-moving, long-distance hikes for the ambitious were balanced with shorter, sociable rambles to the accompaniment of their own hiking songs. After the original group graduated, the club expanded to take in other colleges in the city and changed its name. Whatever the racial or national restrictions of other clubs, the CAHC was open to all, an uproarious melting pot that reflected the polyglot city from which it drew its following. Concern for good hiking and camping practices was expressed in the "Club Hikers' Code," a catechism found among several clubs of that era.

The New York Ramblers. In 1923 another club notorious for fast-paced hikes was organized on the summit of New Jersey's High Mountain. The Ramblers, like almost all the leading clubs of the time, devoted its energies to trail maintenance as well.

The Yosians. This group was J. Otis Swift's personal creation, the name being a corruption of his own first name, Joshua. The Yosians (1925) were one of the more conspicuous clubs of the late 1920s and 1930s, turning out in groups of from one hundred to two hundred, the men wearing suits and ties, the women sometimes long dresses. Swift would coordinate the outing with the aid of a bullhorn. More than a walking organization, the Yosians sought "to promote the spirit of friendliness and kindness and harmony," held a religious view of nature, and invested Swift with quasi-priestly powers. The organization ceased to prosper after Swift's death in 1948.

The Westchester Trails Association. Although members hiked all the traditional highlands areas, this group was formed (1923) specifically to foster trails development in Westchester County (east and south of most of New York's hiking locales).

The Union County Hiking Club. On the opposite side of the metropolis from Westchester, the Union County (New Jersey) group stemmed originally (1938) from nature walks sponsored by the Union County Park Commission.

The Interstate Hiking Club. In 1931 a group led by Ernest A. Dench split off from the Paterson Ramblers to form this club, which became one of the most active of the 1930s. Dench was the guiding spirit until his attentions were transferred to the . . .

Hiking Trips Bureau. During the mid-1930s this enterprise was not so much a club as it was a subscription hiking service, offering a variety of one- and two-day guided trips, led mostly by Dench—who, however, soon devoted his attentions strongly to the . . .

Woodland Trail Walkers. Dench founded the "Woodies" in 1937 and was their leader until 1949, by which time the club had become one of the more consistently active in the New York area.

Others. These were the prime, roughly in order of founding and in the might of their presence on the hiking scene of the 1920s and 1930s. The rest were long to tell, though far less renowned save to their own enthusiastic members. Something like seventy-five clubs were putting people on the trails of Harriman Park and the Ramapos during those two decades. Hike notices in "Long Brown Path" columns and other contemporary sources tell about the *New York Mountain Club,* the *Cygian Society,* the "*Warwick Group,*" the *Boot and Pack Club,* the *Steppers,* the *Jolly Hikers,* the *Native Walkers,* the *Lingernots* (see chapter 18), the *Reptile Study Society,* the *Amateur Insects Group,* the *Metropolitan Council of Geography Teachers* (one of the most active walking groups for a while), the *Bohemians,* the *Pagans,* the *North Star Altar,* the *Sunshiners* (for people aged sixteen to twenty-three), the *Summit Club,* the *Hygiologists,* the *Mycological Society,* the *Snow Month Group* (a January-only hiking club), the *Vagabonds,* the *Pathfinders,* the *Arrowhead Club,* the *Trail Campers of America,* the *Staten Island Bird Club,* the *Hudson Hikers,* the *Local History Group,* the *Manhattan Hiking Club,* the *James King Hand Association,* the *Oasis Hiking Group,* the *Ramapo Mountain Club,* the *Geneva Hiking Club,* the *Union City Ramblers,* the *Timeology Society,* the *Tomorrow Hiking Club,* the *Microscopical Society,* the *Thoreau Walking Club,* the *Dickinson Hiking Club,* the *Young Circle League of American Hiking Club,* the *Shore and Mountain Club,* the *Outdoor Group* of the *Cosmopolitan Club of Montclair,* the *New York University Outdoor Club,* the *Linnaean Society,* the *Elizabeth* (New Jersey) *Nature League,* the *Fellowship of Nature,* the *Brooklyn Botanical Garden,* the *American Nature Association,* the *New York Botanical Club,* the *Roselle*

Park Nature Club, the *Tour and Trail Club of Westchester*, and the *Hill-side Nature Club*.

Southern New England

In southern New England other walking clubs surfaced. In Connecticut the early 1930s saw the birth of the *New Haven Hiking Club*, Waterbury's *Half-a-League Club*, and the *Housatonic Trail Club* in the northwest corner of the state. In Massachusetts the old *Field and Forest Club* was active into the 1920s. Even earlier the Berkshires had a group of intellectual hill walkers known as the *Pathfinders* or *Leg-It Club*. Cambridge, Massachusetts, was home base to an early group known as the *Cambridge Walking Club*. Two separate circles formed hiking clubs in Andover and Lynn, Massachusetts, but by pure coincidence chose nearly identical names: the *Pequawket Mountain Club* in Andover and the *Pequaket* (no w) *Club* in Lynn. The Andover group was especially active on hikes in northern New England from its founding in 1928 and for half a century thereafter. During the 1930s two important trail-maintenance clubs were the *Mount Greylock Ski Club* of Pittsfield and the Massachusetts State College's faculty outing club, called by the name of *Metawampe*. A major force in southern New England, both for excursions and trail work, were the AMC chapters born during these years in Connecticut, the Berkshires (drawing membership largely from the Springfield-Northampton area), and Narragansett (Rhode Island).

College outing clubs

The phenomenon of the college outing club burst upon the Northeastern camping/hiking scene full bloom during the 1920s and 1930s. The first of the modern college outing clubs had been born at Dartmouth in 1909. The Dartmouth Outing Club was so thoroughly oriented to winter sports that it was described in chapter 34. This winter focus characterized other early college outing clubs at Colby, Maine (1914), Middlebury, Vermont (1916), and Williams, Massachusetts (1916). The state colleges of Massachusetts, New Hampshire, and Vermont all had outing clubs before 1920. In the period of 1920–23 came a flurry of new groups. The Bates Outing Club was formed in the fall of 1920. By the following spring another was framed at the University of Maine. Also in 1921 came Smith College and Mount Holyoke. In 1922 Norwich University's outing club was marching. In 1923 MIT's Outing Club (MITOC) hit the trails, destined to become one of the most influential on the Northeastern college scene. Others followed year by year: Yale, 1927; Amherst, 1928 (replacing a defunct Amherst Mountain Club); University of Connecticut,

1929; Massachusetts State (reincarnating a defunct group at what is now called the University of Massachusetts), 1930; and Middlebury, 1931 (the 1916 club having lapsed). During the middle 1930s came another flurry: Union, 1933; Colby, 1934 (another reincarnation of an earlier lapsed club); and in 1935, Brown, Radcliffe, Rensselaer Polytechnic Institute, Syracuse, and Wesleyan. Oddly enough—or perhaps understandably—the prestigious and aloof Harvards were among the last club to form a college outing club (1941).[c]

The college outing clubs went off to the mountains, though they also went canoeing, skiing, and skating, just plain picnicking and off-campus partying, and occasionally rock climbing and caving. Mount Washington was a popular goal for a serious outing, and Maine groups climbed Katahdin. Middlebury was often in the Green Mountains of the Breadloaf region, Williams on Greylock, and New York State colleges aswarm the Adirondacks. Trail maintenance and the construction of cabins for use on student hiking trips (and parties!) were major functions at many schools. As winter climbing spread during the 1930s, many clubs focused on attempting winter ascents of the bigger peaks. As important as the climbing accomplishments was the spirit of the excursions. One statement drawn up in 1939 expressed it thus in defining the purpose of a college outing club: "To recreate the individual after a week of study, . . . to get together in a natural, free social manner . . . to get fresh air, sunshine, FUN!!"

Within the college outing club movement, the importance of the Dartmouth model merits notice. Many of the other early clubs consciously patterned themselves after the Hanoverian precedent. Maine students aspired to create "a real organization similar to the well-known Dartmouth Outing Club," and Colby's was described as "a club similar to the Dartmouth Outing Club." Faculty members recently graduated from Dartmouth were credited with suggesting the outing club idea at Bates and at Williams. Middlebury's 1916 club hoped to build a series of cabins across Vermont to connect with Dartmouth's, as did Norwich's in 1922. Thus Dartmouth can be taken as the starting point of the college outing club movement in more than just chronological terms. Even today the DOC is probably perceived by more hikers as the most visible and effective of college outing clubs.

All-male Dartmouth's example was *not* followed in one respect. Most clubs stressed the nearly equal participation of both sexes in almost all activities, with the exceptions of winter climbing and trail work, where women were largely left out. The Colby Outing Club was heralded by the college's historian as "one of the earliest organizations [at Colby] to have members of both sexes from its inception." Women's colleges early joined

---

[c]A junior version of the college outing club emerged at a few New England prep schools. Among the most prominent were Exeter and Berkshire.

the movement, starting with Smith and Mount Holyoke in 1921. The Mount Holyoke group was especially vibrant—"almost every girl in college is a member," boasted the *Alumnae Quarterly*—outings went on year round, and the club maintained a cabin in a nearby state park. The social side of outing club activity was expressed in joint outings—in one year, for example, the Amherst men climbed Lafayette with the women of Radcliffe, Greylock with Skidmore, and many nearby Connecticut River valley hills with Mount Holyoke—and in winter carnivals, in which skiing and other competitive events were mingled with dances and dates. By providing opportunities for women to participate in hikes and climbs on an equal (or nearly equal) footing, the early college outing clubs not only reflected the growing interest of women in hiking, but also got many young women started on a lifelong interest in the mountains of the region.

A characteristic of the college outing clubs is the volatile swings in the level of activity, as different waves of students pass through, with differing degrees of interest in outdoor activity. Perhaps only at Dartmouth and possibly Bates—where all students are automatically assumed to be members—has a reasonably consistent level of interest been sustained from the earliest years.[d]

An event of considerable importance in the history of college outing clubs was the formation in May 1932 of the Intercollegiate Outing Clubs of America (IOCA; pronounced "eye-*oh*-kuh"). Again Dartmouth's leadership may be seen, as the initial meeting was held on Moosilauke, the idea coming from the DOC's Ellis B. Jump. The original purpose was stated with unusual clarity for organizational pronouncements: "to keep the different outing clubs in touch with each other." Fourteen Eastern colleges were in on the founding: Bates and the University of Maine, Dartmouth and the University of New Hampshire, Williams, Massachusetts State, Jackson, Smith, Mount Holyoke, Yale, and the University of Connecticut, and only three outside of New England—Vassar, Skidmore, and Swarthmore. By 1938 the membership was up to thirty-five clubs. An annual conference and bulletin were established, but most important was the inauguration in 1932 of "College Week," a grand gathering of all the colleges for one week of hiking and camping in a mountain setting in the fall, just before most college openings. The first College Week was held in the Great Gulf in the White Mountains. In 1933 the collegians descended on the Marcy region, and, ever since, Lake Colden's lean-tos have often rung with September's laughter and song of college outing clubs.

---

[d]This feast-or-famine student participation has one consequence for history: the founding dates of many clubs are elusive. A club would be formed with appropriate hoopla one year, run along with enthusiasm for a couple of years, and then disappear completely from campus life, to be organized anew three, seven, or maybe fifteen years later. Thus the Middlebury Outing Club was formed in 1916, was inactive by 1918, reorganized with fanfare in 1919, faded into extinction by the mid-1920s, and organized again in 1931. The Colby Outing Club was launched in February 1914 but dropped from sight so completely that it was "founded" again in 1934. At the University of Maine the club held its first trips in 1920, was officially organized in 1921, but lapsed and was organized anew by a fresh group of students in 1925.

Scouting groups

Membership in the Boy Scouts and Girl Scouts grew phenomenally after World War I. As Roderick Nash has pointed out, few statistics reveal so much about developing American attitudes toward mountain wilderness as the fact that during its first twenty years the Scouts' *Handbook* outsold every other book in the United States except the *Bible*—an estimated 7 million copies. The Scouts not only tramped over the hiking trails of the Northeast, they also helped to build and maintain them. By as early as 1921, New England's Regional Scout Executive could boast before the New England Trail Conference that Scouts had contributed extensively to the construction of hiking trails and shelters throughout New England —from Gilead, Maine, and Burlington, Vermont, to New London, Connecticut, and even Providence, Rhode Island—and urged NETC member clubs to put Scouts to work more often. Scout groups built cabins for campers at Boston's Blue Hills reservation, cut the White Bar trail system in New York's Harriman Park, and were especially active in putting the Appalachian Trail through western Massachusetts.

Summer camps

One feature of many scouting programs was the summer camp, but this phenomenon was by no means limited to scouting. During the 1920s more summer camps were launched than in any other decade: eighteen in Massachusetts alone during those ten years, and another fifteen in Maine and fifteen in New Hampshire (see figure 41.1). White Mountain trails were thronged with eager campers, particularly active parties emanating from the Mowglis camps on Newfound Lake (boys), Camp Kehonka on Lake Winnipesauke (girls), Camp Pasquaney (with its tradition of "long walks" to the mountains), Camp Pemigewasset from its base near Mount Cube, and, from just across the Connecticut River, the complex of camps started by the Gulick family at Lake Fairlee, Vermont (the Aloha Camp for girls, Aloha Hive for younger girls, and Lanakila for boys). In Vermont some seven thousand people populated summer camps in 1926; had they all been in one place, they would have ranked among the top ten largest cities in the state. The oldest and most active in the Green Mountains were the Keewaydin camps on Lake Dunmore. Maine had more summer camps than any other state, according to a 1926 study, with more than eighty camps around the shores of Sebago and Long lakes. In the Adirondacks, the White Mountain scene was duplicated on a later and more modest scale, the roads and facilities being more limited. Here, however, almost because the climbing was more difficult to get to, several camps adopted strenuous "tripping" programs, among which those of Camp Pok-o-moonshine (founded in 1906, but taking to major climbing trips in 1918) and Camp Lincoln (1920) soon became outstanding. Down in New York City's nearby Palisades Interstate Park System, summer camps programs exploded; by 1936 no fewer than sixty thousand campers were provided space. Like the college outing clubs and the Scouts, summer camps contributed to trail construction and maintenance, on a limited scale; outstanding pre–World War II examples were the work of the Mowglis on Mount Cardigan and Camp Pemigewasset on Mount Cube.

These mechanisms for getting young people into the mountains had far-reaching consequences. Outdoor writer Harvey Manning has

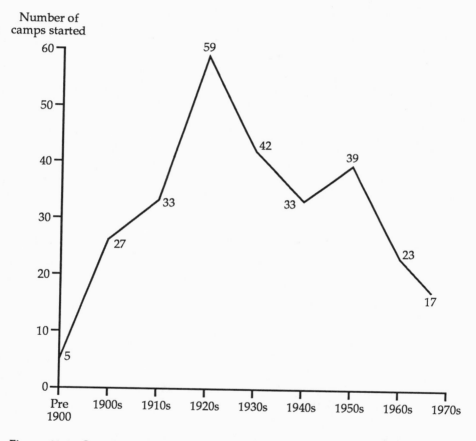

Figure 41.1. Summer camps started in northeastern states during the 1920s and 1930s One indication of growing interest in the outdoors during the 1920s and 1930s was the boom in children's summer camps. This chart shows the number of summer camps that were started during each decade since 1900, and that had survived through 1980. Note that more camps were launched during the 1920s and 1930s than in any other decade. Data for this chart are taken from the 1982 edition of the American Camping Association's *Parent's Guide to Accredited Camps.*

propounded a theory that each generation of an outdoors-oriented family tends to progress one step further into the wilderness. If your parents took you car-camping as a child, you may take trips to the AMC huts as an adult. If you were taken to huts, you may become a backpacker as an adult. The children of backpackers become mountaineers. If there is substance to Manning's theory, the effects of the 1920s boom in summer camps, Scouts, and college outing clubs produced large numbers of adults in the next generation with a predilection for hiking and camping. The taste of outdoor living and acquaintance with the mountain world available in the Northeast produced a postwar generation ready for the backpacking boom to come.

Chapter 42

Backcountry camping in the twenties and thirties

BACKCOUNTRY camping entered a new phase after World War I. Many more people took to the woods for weekends or multiday trips, toting their own gear aback, and enjoying the quiet nights under the stars, in tents, or at the AMC huts, Adirondack lean-tos, and Long Trail lodges. Though their numbers were small compared with the boom of fifty years later, there definitely was a backwoods camping set.

By the 1920s, long skirts and Victorian scruples having faded, women were full participants in the hiking world. Having won suffrage after a long political battle, the newly unfettered American woman turned away temporarily from serious political effort to enjoy her newfound freedoms. Nowhere was this more in evidence than on Vermont's Long Trail.

In 1927 three women traversed the entire Long Trail from Massachusetts to the Canadian line, and became the toast of the Green Mountain Club. The three were Kathleen Norris and her gym teacher, Hilda Kurth, both of Schenectady, New York, and Catherine Robbins, a Brandon, Vermont, schoolteacher. Working out techniques later perfected by LT and AT "through-hikers," they cached some food along the trail and mailed other food packages ahead to farms along the route, so that they could keep pack weights to 20–25 pounds each. Hilda toted a pack-basket, the others knapsacks. Sleeping in blankets at shelters, they were "always wet," especially their footgear, but their spirits never dampened. The northern part of the trail was not yet cut, merely blazed, and they once went six days without seeing other hikers. The thirty-two day trip had a quality of pioneering adventure unobtainable today.

This journey became a public relations coup for the Long Trail and the GMC. The three women were hailed as the "Three Musketeers," and their story hit the newspapers from coast to coast, with photos in the "Roto" section of the New York *Herald Tribune* and in the San Francisco *Sunday Examiner*, while Vermont papers played up the event with gusto. The press consistently marveled at their lack of protection: "They Carried No

Firearms, and Had No Male Escort," headlined the San Francisco paper. The Green Mountain Club honored them at the 1928 annual meeting:

> At this point the three musketeers entered and were joyfully received. They were informally introduced and each gave a running account of their hike and experiences over the entire trail the past summer.

Fifty years later the club paid an anniversary tribute to these heroines of early LT hiking.

In 1929 another all-women party of four duplicated the feat, in 1930 a group of four women walked a substantial segment, and in 1933 two more did the entire trail. In the latter year, Thelma Bonney and Erna Clayton began a series of trips on the Long Trail and elsewhere in New England in which they'd be off for a week or two in the woods, enjoying an informal (though entirely "proper") camaraderie with Roy Buchanan's Long Trail Patrol, having a wonderful time, and taking in stride whatever the mountain weather threw at them. Bonney's journal for their first Long Trail hike records one all-day rain:

> All the way down Killington, it poured. Rain was in our eyes, in our faces, in our hair, in our necks. In our shoes. . . . Erna would be walking ahead and when I looked at her back—the bulgy pack and flopping poncho—I'd have to laugh. Then we'd both stop and laugh. We had not a care in the whole wide world. It was raining. We were soaked in spots, but still dry in the vital spots and we knew we'd have a dry bed and warm food for the night. It was raining and we were in the woods. It was glorious, so we laughed. We looked ridiculous, so we laughed. We were happy, so we laughed.

These Long Trail escapades hint of a hiker's world quite different from that of Major Gould and the 18-pound sleeping bags described in chapter 25 but equally distant from modern backpacking. Women and men alike were discovering the lilting freedom of the backcountry, not just in Vermont but also in the forests and crags of the Adirondacks, the quiet majesty of Chimney Pond, and previously little-visited corners of the White Mountains as well. Consider this remembrance of a Boston Appie, Marjorie Hurd, an attorney who walked and climbed all over New England woods and hills for half a century beginning in the early 1920s:

> Do you remember your first balsam bed? You were visiting school mates in Chocorua when an overnight trip to Passaconaway was suggested. What fun! Blankets were rolled and fastened to packs bulging with goodies and you trudged off down the road and up through the woods to the shelter. After a glance at the twigs and dried needles on the floor, the grown-up in charge sent you scurrying for balsam. Spicy armfuls were brought in, the prickly spruce cast aside (you had not

made that mistake) and under skillful tutelage you started thatching the bed. Then for the first time you heard the never ending arguments as to the proper way to lay a balsam bed—what size twigs should be used, should the bow of the branch be up or the needles, should the butt be toward the head or the foot.

The bough bed symbolizes that generation's sleeping arrangements; a later and more numerous generation condemned it as environmentally wasteful and destructive. But who could foresee then what damage later multitudes would bring? Against the smaller numbers of 1920s and 1930s campers, the mountain environment simply sloughed off their inconsequential impact and grew new forest, effortlessly. So in its day the bough bed was perfectly valid—indeed, a fragrant luxury and, as Marjorie Hurd's account indicates, an art not easily mastered.[a]

What went on top of the balsam bough bed might be a sleeping bag, but to many sleepers of those times it was an army blanket, with or without safety pins to hold it in place during the long night's squirm. Sleeping bags "were for the rich, or the clever who could make them" in the eyes of many. The AMC designed and sold a 3.5-pound sleeping bag of wool bat, with waterproof cover—$10.00 for the bag, $4.50 for the cover. Enterprising members of the Mohawk Valley Hiking Club and others designed homemade down bags in a mummy style during the 1930s. By 1940 the Phillips Polar Cub Sleeping Bag made a good and inexpensive down bag commercially available.

Meanwhile, for large numbers of hikers, the blanket was not only the sole sleeping accommodation, it was also the backpack. Belongings were rolled in the old traditional blanket roll and slung over the shoulders. For a Long Trail hike during the 1930s one woman recalled carrying all her gear in "a poncho with shoulder straps."

But by now the serious hiker used a backpack. Often these early packs were plain, roomy, rectangular canvas bags, the weight borne fully on the shoulders. A popular, slightly more sophisticated model was the Norwegian-designed Bergen. Others inherited Army rucksacks from World War I. In the Adirondacks the wicker pack-basket enjoyed a popularity that it never established elsewhere. Some campers adopted the Trapper Nelson packboard, a wooden frame with cloth sack attached, a heavy precursor of the aluminum pack-frame that became widely used during the 1960s and 1970s.

Most of this generation of campers traveled heavy-laden. One Adirondack hiker's "grub and duffle" list included heavy canvas tent, blankets, rubber blanket to serve both as groundcloth and poncho, extra woolens, ax or hatchet, two nesting aluminum pails, frying pan, plates, and food in cotton cloth bags. Advice in an ADK publication as late as 1940 recommended "at least 5 pounds of blanket," waterproof ground

---

[a]More discussion of environmental concerns of a later generation will be found in chap. 52.

cloth, two extra wool shirts, three pairs of wool slacks, "suit of flannel pajamas," light ax plus sheath, three nested cake tins, aluminum kettle, coffee pot, canvas bucket, and fry pan or reflector oven, and extensive repair kit. A 1947 *Long Trail News* writer reminisced about backpacks of the 1930s: "One expected to enjoy the trip in spite of the pack and the garb."

While most hikers of the interwar years grunted under atlaslike loads, the go-light school had its early advocates. A. T. Shorey snorted, "Most Adirondack Hikers carry too much. Some of them seem to think that a heavy pack makes a he-man." In 1924 Arthur C. Comey of the AMC, NETC, and Chocorua Mountain Club wrote a short pamphlet called *Going Light*, which became a fast-seller. Comey promoted the virtues of the "ten-pound pack," with which he claimed to be comfortable for a week at a time in the wilds. He once boasted that when scouting the future Appalachian Trail in Maine, the 10-pound pack "worked perfectly" for a nine-night trip. "Camping and particularly camping on the hike," wrote Comey, "is an art." A 10-pound pack for overnight camping is almost unheard-of today, for all our modern lightweight gear and freeze-dried food, and yet Comey's 10 pounds found room for an ax and sheath, whetstone, moccasins, bathing trunks, soap, washcloth, razor, and shaving soap.

The Mohawk Valley Hiking Club drew up recommendations during the 1930s that recognized three different levels of comfort, convenience and weight:

1. The "Mohawk" pack for a single day in the open—8–10 pounds, with options of 10–12 extra pounds
2. The "Helderberg" for a two-day trip, sleeping out—21–23 pounds, with 5–7 pounds in extra options to consider
3. The "Adirondack" pack for a week's sojourn in the wilderness, sleeping out of doors and independent of civilization—29–31 pounds, with 4–5 extra for options.

In one respect pre–World War II campers went lighter than their children of half a century later: few carried tents. Wherever one wandered in the Northeast, one was likely to find a backwoods structure empty, be it AMC hut, GMC lodge, or Adirondack lean-to. Tents were more available than they had been during the nineteenth century, but few had need of them. Most tents were still heavy, despite having no floor, but the beginnings of more modern design could be had for a price. Abercrombie and Fitch sold a light, two-person model, of breathable fabric, with sewn-in ground cloth and bugproof zippers, for the stiff price of thirty dollars. But the typical tramper of those days simply headed for one of the numerous backcountry shelters and rarely had to share it.

The hiker's uniform of the 1920s and 1930s was whatever was comfortable in the way of old clothes. No "backpacker chique" or specialized materials filled the pages of outfitting catalogues. Wool was still the basic medium, especially for colder weather.

A faint reminder of old-time formality clung to backwoods attire throughout the interwar years. For men the tie was not completely discarded. Widely read guidebook writer Walter Collins O'Kane counseled the male hiker to wear a flannel shirt of dark gray or brown, adding, "With this he usually wears a tie until he has covered ten minutes of climbing." One great rock climber, Ken Henderson of the Boston AMC, rarely appeared on the cliffs without a necktie and jacket.

Women had once and for all shed the hampering absurdity of long skirts in the woods but still wore "voluminous bloomers" or knickers. Adirondack packbagger Grace Hudowalski recalled preparations for her first trip up Marcy in 1922:

> My voluminous bloomers were carefully pressed, my middy blouse, complete with the large red square of a tie (twice the size of today's kerchief), hung in readiness on a hanger.

For members of the older generation, bloomers were radical enough. A White Mountain peakbagger recalled roundabout early morning starts because of female dress scruples: "We walked to Atkinson Depot to catch the train as mother refused to be seen in downtown Haverhill [sic] in bloomers!"

In *The Gentle Art of Tramping* (1926), Stephen Graham recommended, for men, "workmen's trousers, suspended by workmen's braces" plus jacket; and for women, "khaki blouse and knickers, green putties or stockings, and a stout pair of shoes."

Shorts—almost universally worn by summertime hikers today—made a most hesitant entrance on the stage of 1920s–1930s hiking. Overwhelmingly even men still wore long trousers, but as the years went by more and more unconventional individuals braved the disgrace of showing their knees on the hiking trail. By 1936 the general manager of the Palisades Interstate Park made a public announcement that it was henceforth permissible to wear shorts on Hudson Highlands trails. "I see no use in interfering with hiking costumes," mused the manager, "because the hikers are going to wear what they please in any event." He reassured the public, however, that bathing suits would be limited to beaches and pools and not allowed in the woods. Still, the hiking world of 1936 had come a long way from the heavy skirts of Miss Whitman and Madame Pychowska.

Few hikers wore specialized hiking boots. Those who had been on European mountain holidays might come back with hobnailed boots or Tricounis, but the enormously respected Nathaniel Goodrich advised,

"Sneakers are deservedly popular. . . . They are light and stick where hobnails will not." George Goldthwaite, reputedly the speediest hiker in the New York area of the 1920s and 1930s, wore sneakers and acquired many imitators. O'Kane recommended to his legions of readers "a pair of good quality canvas shoes with crepe-rubber soles." Moccasins with leather bottoms were often worn. "Army last" boots from World War I were put to peacetime use on hiking trails. Veteran trailsman Jim Goodwin in the Adirondacks recalled children in sneakers, their elders wearing workboots.

Each hiker had his or her own approach to coping with rain. Wearing a heavy rubber poncho meant that "the victim will stew in his own juice for his sweat cannot get out." GMC veteran Louis Puffer advised, "When the hiker gets into camp, he should take off his wet clothes, put on his flannel pajamas. He can probably get his clothes dry by morning, if not, let him set out wet. If the weather is dry, the clothes will soon be dry, too; if it is still rainy, they would be wet anyway."

Freeze-dried food was unheard of and few lightweight foods were available. During the early 1930s the Northwestern climber Ome Daiber was credited with being the first to distribute dehydrated foods nationwide. Will Monroe, the Long Trail professor, carried dried bean meal and evaporated egg powder. Even so, dried fare was not consistently palatable. "You knock a lot of weight off most foods if you draw off the water," pointed out one Vermonter, who added pointedly, "and in my opinion you knock even more off your appetite." The foods still needed cooking—just adding water and waiting for the miracle of rehydration was well in the future. Hence, the culinary department required all those tins, pails, and fry pans mentioned earlier among the gear.

Bread, biscuits, or cornmeal muffins were often baked on the trail. Ingenious ways of carrying bulk and perishables were devised. Adirondack tramper Orra Phelps described rolling up potatoes, carrots, and even a can of soup in her bedroll. She transported fresh eggs in a cooking pail padded with loose shredded wheat, carried carefully by hand. Breakfast included oatmeal, dried fruits (stewed and heated up), or bacon. Dinners often included meat, soup, and vegetables, most of it canned and heavy. Lunches were usually based on breads of various kinds, including pilot biscuits (a staple for many hikers of that day), but peanuts and chocolate and raisins were beginning to come together as the standard fare familiar in the post–World War II world.

Needless to say, the campfire was the traditional way of cooking. References to portable camp-stoves are virtually nonexistent in accounts of Northeastern camping during the 1920s and 1930s, though such devices were not unknown, as we saw even earlier in chapter 25. The campfire was a symbol of outdoor life, evoking deep responses, almost primeval instincts, in a long generation of backcountry trampers seeking escape from urban society. The arts of building a fire in a rainstorm, of selecting good wood for maximum cooking power, of using only what was needed, of always leaving enough dry wood for the next party, became the marks of an experienced camper.

If we look beyond the glowing light of the wood fire on the happy circle of campers, we may note another shape moving in the shadows. The North American porcupine was known long before the 1920s–1930s generation and shall be ever with us, but in that era his presence loomed so large as to merit due recognition in the history of the times. If Pinkham Notch justly earned its nickname as Porky Gulch, it by no means held a monopoly on the population. Up in the Mahoosucs, it was said that "every lean-to has a caretaker (with quills)." Down in the Catskills, there was more than one around some spots:

> The top of Wittenberg is an enlarged anthill, a porous rind, actually moving under your feet with ambitious porcupines, practicing and rehearsing their parts for the evening's performance on the Wittenberg stage. At sunset the sergeant-at-arms ushers in the first coterie of damsels who cavort and whine to the elation of their more pod-like consorts. Spiny tails thump the ground, and teeth are ground on axe-handles or tin boxes as the case may be. The rising moon beholds the four hundred approaching from the catacombs just over the edge of the cliff, and the orgy is on!

Many who know the region well award first place in the porcupine department to the Green Mountains. Scarcely an account of the Long Trail during the 1920s and 1930s does not bristle with barbed references to the quilled varmints:

> No telling where porkies may lurk. . . . I nearly stepped on one. They mowed and mumbled around the camp at night. The record at Laura Woodward Camp was seven killed two nights before we came, four the night before.

By 1942 the roundup story on the menace to shelters along the Appalachian Trail reported that "the damage and nuisances caused by porcupines are particularly bad in Vermont." In 1951, with annual bounties costing the state nearly twenty thousand dollars per year, State Forester Perry Merrill convinced the legislature to give its august attentions to *Erethizon dorsatum* and to appropriate two thousand dollars for research on ways to check the depredations of the beast. Whatever the researchers came up with, it didn't work; when last heard from, the shelters and camps of the Long Trail were still aswarm with porcupines.

Chapter 43

Trail maintenance comes of age

WHEN the Blood-Jenks-Goodrich-Harrington dynasty began its long hegemony over White Mountain trails, it inherited an unresolved problem: how to ensure yearly maintenance of hundreds of miles of footpaths. Pondering the problem while in charge of the lunchroom at Flushing High School during the winter of 1919, schoolteacher Paul Jenks found himself staring at two of his favorite students, "Bus" Fyles ("pitcher of the nine") and "Stilly" Stillwell . . .

> both of them brainy and brawny. As I stared at them, thinking hard and fast, the light dawned. The solution of my problem was right there: such boys could clear our trails!

Jenks's tale surely oversimplifies. Blood had been harping on the need for maintenance for several years. The same solution had occurred to Nat Goodrich in Hanover almost two years earlier, when he hired several Dartmouth youths to cut the Kinsman Ridge Trail in 1917. Nevertheless, during the summer of 1919, the first full-time summerlong staff was expressly hired to clear existing trails—the first AMC trail crew.

Flushing's Bus Fyles and Stilly Stillwell were on that first seven-man crew in 1919, but its chief was the Dartmouth student who had proved his worth on the Kinsman Ridge in 1917. Sherman Adams was only 5 feet 4 inches, but he strode tall in White Mountains woods lore. Born in East Dover, Vermont, on January 9, 1899, Adams went to Dartmouth College in 1916 and fell in love with the north woods. "Slender, wiry, and with muscles of steel," he proved an extraordinary walker on mountainous terrain, and turned in feats of long-distance hiking that have scarce been equaled since. With the trail crew he relished the daily exercise of going to work by climbing more than 2,000 vertical feet up Cannon Mountain after breakfast at the crew's base in the servant's quarters of the Profile House, or later of climbing Mount Willey every day from Ethan Pond when the crew was fixing up the Willey Range Trail. After two years of running the trail crew and after graduating from Dartmouth, he went to work in the woods for the lumber companies. What he lacked in size he made up for in shrewdness, toughness, skill, and drive. He rose to become woodlands manager for Parker-Young, the huge company that owned and logged the Pemigewasset Wilderness until 1936. By that time Adams was such a prominent figure in the north country that he turned in his double-bit ax and his peavey and embarked on a meteoric political career, becoming successively state legislator, Speaker of the New Hampshire House, congressman, governor, and special assistant to the president under Dwight Eisenhower. During those years he was a nationally known politician, but had he never won public office, he would already have established a place in history as first paid head of AMC's pioneering trail crew. He "has been the hero figure to all trail men," recalled Harland Sisk, of the AMC trail crew of the 1920s.

The seven-man crew over which Adams presided in 1919 and 1920 was composed of roughly equal parts Dartmouth and Flushing High School. During the 1920s college youths predominated, always with a strong Dartmouth accent. Their primary job was, first, to do "ax-patrol" on all trails every year, which consisted of clearing the blowdowns with a double-bit ax, kept razor-sharp and guarded with fierce possessiveness; and, second, to "standardize" existing trails as needed, if possible every three years, which involved widening and thoroughly clearing the footway. In those days very little was done on erosion control, the job that preoccupies trail crews today, because hiking traffic was so light that erosion was hardly a problem. They also seldom worked on new trails; that privilege was reserved to the "old masters" (Blood, Jenks, Goodrich, Harrington, and an occasional crony).

Trail crew work was a unique job for a young man of the 1920s. Pay was low: $1.00 a day for the first-year men, $1.50 or $2.00 for second- or third-year men, and a whopping $4.00 per day for trail master as the senior man came to be known during the 1930s. But if the pay was low, at least the hours were long and the work bone-wearying tough: in 1926, for example, the trail crew counted 413 cross-logs cleared from the Davis Path in two and a half days. The food was good and plenty, and the exercise built the young men into superb physical condition.

Most important were the intangibles of trail crew traditions. As years went by, this elite band came to know more about the specialized task of trail maintenance than all but a handful of senior individuals in the Northeast. A fierce pride and spirit evolved—pride in their woodcraft, in their toughness, in their knowledge of the interstices and mysteries of the White Mountains, in their hiking speed and strength. They worked hard, played hard, bathed seldom, ate enormously, developed close friendships, and looked down on the rest of the world which knew not how to go through a blowdown, keep an ax sharp, or find the way out of the Mahoosucs in the dark after all-day work on the trail. Harland Sisk, sixty years later, after a successful business career, called his four years on the trail crew "a high spot in my lifetime of work. It gave me a balanced perspective of the work of man and his environment." A later trail crew member captured the spirit of the experience more quaintly when he described his firstborn child:

> the kid's first shoes were L. L. Bean ground grabbers, . . . his first toys were a pot-kit, an A. M. C. guidebook and a three-foot machete (he refuses to use clippers), and his first two words were "Pemigewasset Wilderness."

The 1929 crew was once observed as it headed for the woods and described as follows:

> . . . a varied assortment of lawyers, professors, school-teachers, and other of the intelligentsia, followed by a husky gang of young roughnecks that made me think of a varsity football field. They bore double-bitted axes, cross-cut saws, machetes, packs of various sorts, and a prodigious quantity of grub. . . . at least one officer to each and every private.

The last observation is telling: throughout the 1920s, the trail crew worked very much under the supervision and control of the club's volunteer trail leaders. In this partnership, the "old masters" were the senior partners, knew more about the work, and were looked up to by the young paid hands. That point is emphasized because of the change that soon evolved: during the 1930s, the Blood-Jenks generation of trail men was never succeeded by a comparably experienced and dedicated group from the club membership. Into this vacuum of leadership the young trail crew moved. Those youths who had been on the crew for two or three summers began to find that they knew as much or more about trail maintenance as their older adult supervisors. These supervisors spent less time in the field, did not have the enormous prestige formerly accorded the old masters, and came to rely more and more on the two- and three-year "veterans" of the college-age crew. The term *trail master*, once applied with a great show of exclusivity to the Blood-Jenks-Goodrich-Harrington quadrumvirate, was adopted as the job title for the eldest of the paid crew. The role of supervisor of the trail crew remained in the hands of a volunteer part-time club leader until 1937, but the practical authority lay largely in the hands of the young trail master and the senior crew members. Beginning in 1938 a Syracuse University forester named John Hutton became supervisor. Hutton had risen through the trail crew ranks between 1933 and 1936. Thus his background ensured that trail crew traditions and autonomy would be maintained. By this time the trail crew had attained a high degree of independence—and, in the eyes of some concerned elders, of arrogance. Though nominally taking orders from the Forest Service on the one hand and the club's volunteers on the other, the trail crew in practical reality governed itself and the vast network of the AMC's White Mountain trails. During the post–World

War II period this independence led to several crises in relationships with the Forest Service, with AMC hut crews, and with the volunteer leadership of the club. But through it all, the on-the-ground supremacy of the trail crew remained unchallenged.[a]

Trail maintenance on Vermont's Long Trail was a problem immediately after its construction. Many sections of the trail pass through lower and generally more fertile country than high-elevation spruce-fir forest and the even harsher alpine zone. Not for nothing are they called the "Green" Mountains! At lower elevations, vegetation springs to life much more quickly. It will be recalled that one of the criticisms of the original Killington to Camel's Hump route was how quickly it became obscured by fast-growing greenery. By the early 1920s GMC officials were aware that the LT was not being kept open as well as it should be.

Never at a loss for ideas, James Taylor proposed a spectacular (of course) one-day trail-clearing blitz, in which every mile of the Long Trail would be patrolled, blowdown and bushes cleared, and major repairs noted for future scheduling. This one-day walk-through would be held early in the hiking season, with suitable publicity (of course). Taylor even came up with a catchy name (of course), which proved prophetic: Long Trail Patrol Day. Charles C. Cooper, then GMC president, scheduled the first Long Trail Patrol Day for May 20, 1922, with the intention that it be an annual event. While the first was reasonably successful, the tradition did not catch on.[b]

During the 1920s the club relied on its various geographically organized sections to maintain specific parts of the trail. The system worked very unevenly. Probably the most consistently effective trail maintainer during the 1920s was Fred W. Mould of Morrisville, "Guardian Angel of the Sterling Range." From 1915 until 1950 Mould devoted his spare hours to taking good care of the Long Trail and its tributaries, mainly on the heights just east and north of Smugglers' Notch. A little man (5 feet 2 inches), but agile and athletic (a former semipro baseball player), he was one of several dedicated trailsmen who achieved that enviable goal: to die while working happily on the trail. Mould was eighty-one years old, and busy reblazing the Long Trail on Sterling Mountain when the end came on June 10, 1950. But few men were cut from this mold. Elsewhere up and down the state, maintenance was an unresolved problem. The New

---

[a]One individual occupied a unique position in the trail crew of the late 1930s: Vern Sampson. He was an aging professional woodsman who worked with the crew, exercising no supervisory role but enormously respected for his woodsmanship. Though small of stature and walking with a limp due to some old logging injury, "he could and did outwork all of us," recalled one old trail crew member of that time. "He literally would not sit down except to eat. . . . There are few people who have impressed me more, as regards his high personal standards for the amount of work he required of himself and the quality of what he turned out." (Letter from Kent Eanes to L&GW, May 2, 1985. Reprinted with permission.)

[b]Oddly enough, the technique of a single-day blitz of a long trail, though largely unsuccessful before World War II, has found acceptance in several areas during the 1980s. As usual, Taylor's ideas were ahead of his time.

York Section eventually began contracting to pay for getting its trail sections cleared. This got the job done but at a cost that other sections were not prepared to match. Others relied on club members, some of whom put in the time, while others couldn't or didn't.

In 1929 the GMC determined to formalize arrangements and voted to fund the annual hiring of a small summer crew of paid workers—college kids much like the AMC's—to work under the supervision of volunteer club leaders. For the first three years, Wallace M. Fay was the adult in charge of the Long Trail Patrol. Other club members pitched in to help supervise. Among them was a college professor named Roy Buchanan, who began to devote much of his summer vacation to Long Trail work in 1931, driving the crew and tools to and from trail-heads in "Patrol Truck No. One," a new 1931 Chevrolet pickup. After three years Fay stepped down, and Roy Buchanan took over the Long Trail Patrol. It was thirty-five years before Buchanan laid down his ax and twenty-three before "Patrol Truck No. One" retired from the fray. By that time both man and truck had earned GMC immortality.

Roy O. Buchanan was born in West Glover, Vermont, on December 13, 1881. He was a Phi Beta Kappa graduate of the University of Vermont in engineering and taught there until his "retirement" in 1949, at which point he continued his professional work with the Central Vermont Power Company and other employers until well into his eighties. He lived to be ninety-six years old, always in Vermont.

Buchanan was forty before his brother introduced him to hiking. During the 1920s he became more and more interested in mountain walking, not only in Vermont but, beginning in 1927, in the Adirondacks as well. By the end of the decade, he had walked the entire Long Trail (the first of three times) and become active in the push to extend its northern terminus to the Canadian border. In 1931 he started work on the Long Trail Patrol and in the following year succeeded Fay as supervisor—and continued in the job each summer until 1967. Under Buchanan the LTP not only maintained whatever trail the section volunteers couldn't handle, but did most of the major construction work as well. The crowning achievement of the early years of the LTP was the filling in of the chain of shelters and lodges, so that from Massachusetts to Canada hikers were guaranteed a roof over their heads for the night at intervals of never more than 8 miles (see figure 43.1). The characteristic Buchanan "camp" was a small enclosed cabin with bunks, shuttered windows, a single table with benches, and a wood stove. Though the Long Trail Patrol worked on all parts of the trail, most of its early camp construction was north of Mansfield, where the gaps were greatest when Buchanan came on the scene: French and Barrows were built in 1931, Parker in 1932, Journey's End and Ritterbush in 1933, Shooting Star in 1934, and numerous replacements and reconstructions over the subsequent years. Butler Lodge, on the southwest slope of Mansfield, was the largest of the early Buchanan works and the one of which he was most proud. When he retired in 1967 it was estimated that under his direction and personal involvement, the Long Trail Patrol had built thirty-seven of the camps then in use.[c]

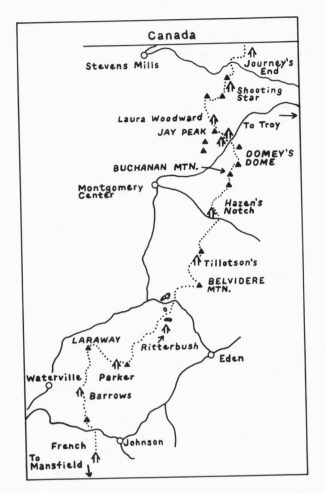

Figure 43.1. The Long Trail "camps" of Roy Buchanan Prof. Roy O. Buchanan headed the Long Trail Patrol for thirty-six years. During that period one of his enduring legacies was the chain of small cabins (known in Vermont as either "camps" or "lodges") built under his direction at the northern end of the trail. These were largely products of the early 1930s. Built to such exacting specifications as "to within a foot-and-a-half" and large enough for "six hikers or six porcupines, but not six hikers and six porcupines," most of the original structures in this chain survive to this day.

---

[c]LT shelters *not* built by Buchanan's LTP included the old Taft Lodge on Mansfield and several others built by the Burlington Section, many along the Monroe Skyline by the New York Section, several in the Breadloaf region by Middlebury College professors and students, a brace in the southern section by the Worcester Section when Ralph Van Meter and John Vondell were in their glory years, and others by a variety of individuals or clubs.

Buchanan was not imposing physically, at 5 feet, 2 inches in height, "his legs worn short by much hiking" (as longtime close friend Louis Puffer explained), balding and bespectacled, soft-spoken and amiable. Where many other great trail masters of his era and earlier—Edmands, Blood and Jenks, Avery, for example—tended to be self-important and brusque with novices, Buchanan was mild, warm, friendly, and self-effacing. One of his young patrol workers remembered him as "always ready with repairs, help, advice, moral support in general, entertaining stories, mystic directions." His methods were relaxed. In place of the careful string method of trail layout perfected in the White Mountains, Buchanan used what he called the "yell method." When constructing camps, he would instruct co-workers to get the measurements exact "to within a foot-and-a-half." He identified one trail-head thus: "The trail starts where the pile of lumber used to be." He described his camps as accommodating "six hikers or six porcupines, but not six hikers and six porcupines." As he held the leadership of the Long Trail Patrol until age eighty-five and remained active in the GMC until well into his nineties, he became one of the best-loved figures who ever came through the north country hiking scene. "That man never had an enemy in the world," recalled one GMC president. "I never saw that man upset."

As for Patrol Truck No. One?

That was some truck. It would go just about anywhere. However, getting there could be interesting. It had mechanical brakes that required much foot pressure and praying to bring it to a stop. Luckily it did not go over 35 downhill with a tail wind. Neither side window existed and the windshield, which was on hinges to be opened, would not clamp shut. It had tires that were removed from the rim to change and by the end of the season we had no more casing.

It may be obvious by now that the Long Trail Patrol had neither the fierce independent pride nor perhaps the rugged competence of the AMC trail crew. But the picture of casual amiability painted by so many of the endless Buchanan stories should in no way obscure the accomplishments of this little professor. He and his patrol built a complete chain of camps over the better part of a 262-mile trail and helped to maintain the footway in reasonably good condition over a period of thirty-five years. It was as if he gave the Long Trail a solid endowment, in the form of a dependable maintenance crew. That all this was accomplished while everyone involved had a lovely time and no one was ever angry with the boss for long tells more about effective leadership style than most volumes on the subject.

In the Adirondacks, as in New Hampshire, trail maintenance fell largely to paid crews, rather than to volunteers. ATIS in the east, the Adirondack Camp and Trail Club in the west, and the Shore Owners'

Association around Lake Placid all employed guides or other local labor to open the trails each summer. By the 1920s rangers from the Conservation Commission (later the Conservation Department, still later the Department of Environmental Conservation) began maintaining some of the trails, including the 130-mile Northville-Placid Trail. Since hiking traffic was decidedly lighter in New York than in the White Mountains, maintenance was less of a problem, and none of the Adirondack crews accumulated the rich traditions and glowing pride of either the AMC's crew or Buchanan's LTP.

A minor tradition of volunteer trail maintenance persisted through the years in the Adirondacks. Most of the trails that emanated from Johns Brook Lodge after 1925 were maintained by ADK volunteers, much of the work being blitzed in June work weekends. Some longtime summer vacationers maintained specific trails: one example was the 1907 trail from Hopkins to Giant, built and then maintained for many years by Will Glover and Fritz Comstock.

During the 1930s a significant change occurred in ATIS's trail maintenance methods. By this time the Adirondacks guide tradition was a pale shadow, and the local labor had become expensive by the standards of the Great Depression, as well as having little incentive now that unemployment compensation was available. Beginning in 1934, ATIS adopted the AMC and GMC practice of hiring summertime crews of college-age youths to get the maintenance done. The guide tradition died out around Lake Placid as well, and almost all trail maintenance in the Whiteface region fell to Conservation Department rangers. The Camp and Trail Club disbanded. The Adirondack Mountain Club did not hire a trail crew until well into the postwar period, however.

In the Adirondacks as elsewhere throughout the region, prewar trail maintenance meant clearing blowdown and clipping brush. The age of erosion control and tread-hardening was still many years in the future, save for a few farsighted individuals who did a little work on controlling drainage.

Down in the metropolitan areas in the southern part of the region, a stronger tradition of club and individual volunteer maintenance became the rule. Around New York City, the same clubs and eccentric personalities who had built the trails also did the maintenance. The terms negotiated by Torrey, Place, Burton, and the others at the peace conference of 1931 governed maintenance as well as new trail construction. Thus the New York–New Jersey Trail Conference adopted a loose overseer role, while the same colorful cast—Bartha, Nurian, Jessup, Hoeferlin, and the major hiking clubs—continued to do the actual work.

In Connecticut, the maintenance problem had a special flavor all its own because of the amount of privately owned land traversed by the blue-blazed trails. For Connecticut trail maintainers, as one early worker noted, "diplomacy is more useful than huskiness": a recurring need to revise, relocate, sometimes close, sometimes reopen, patiently negotiate and renegotiate, sometimes move fast, sometimes wait, always stand ready to improvise in a never ending effort to keep a continuous route open in the face of industrial, commercial, residential, and highway growth and change. One state trail maintainer described his trail as "the epitome of instability." Connecticut trailspeople became masters of diplomacy, resourcefulness, and flexibility, on a scale never needed elsewhere.

Beyond the negotiating skill and tact of the trail makers, the Connecticut system required a genuine respect for and tolerance of the landowner which had important implications. A "courtesy" sign was widely posted to encourage good trail manners on the part of Connecticut hikers: "This trail is on private land and used only by courtesy of the owner, whose rights must be respected." An early map of the state's trails carries this admonishment: "This [trail system] has been made possible by the cooperation of private land owners and of the State Commission." The executive director of the Connecticut Forest and Park Association, John Hibbard, summarized this important aspect of Connecticut's trail system thus:

> Any history of the trails program would be incomplete without recognizing the role of the private landowner who has in reality been the backbone of the system throughout its history.

As Hibbard has pointed out elsewhere, the land managers for corporate owners merit special credit for their tolerance of hikers and trails: "They really stick their necks out within their corporations." One Connecticut trailsman, after negotiating as recently as 1983 the lease to the state of 1,100 acres owned by the Stanley Iron Works, made this statement:

> Anyone who sees this property will fall in love with it, as I have. DON'T BLOW IT! Our lease is on a yearly basis. If the Stanley Works finds there are too many infractions or problems they may well revoke the lease.

In its never ending efforts to ensure hiker courtesy and good behavior, the Connecticut trail-making community was led into a program of hiker education that foreshadowed by almost a full generation what other areas would be forced to do during the backpacking boom of the postwar years. The earliest CFPA maps, for example, always included a page of warnings about neat camping practices, careful control of campfires, and respect for the land:

> Except on State land, which is open to the public for proper use, our trails exist merely by courtesy of the owner. Trampers have the privilege of following the route indicated, but are not expected to roam

through the property at will. Destroy no vegetation, respect rare flowers, and leave no litter. Trampers should constitute themselves a voluntary patrol to see that these necessary rules are enforced.

Thus did tiny Connecticut, with the shortest formal history of recreational hiking trails, show the way to the older areas in what a later generation would call environmental education or backwoods ethics.

Chapter 44

Regionwide consciousness

WITH one Long Trail creeping along the Green Mountains toward Canada, and unified trail systems knitting together in the Whites and the Adirondacks, regionwide consciousness was the dominant theme in the 1910s. Out of this frame of reference grew two interrelated movements. One was to formalize New England's growing sense of unity into a single organization or confederation of trail groups. The other was to seek opportunities to build more long-distance trails patterned on the GMC's success.

In 1914, always thinking big, James P. Taylor spoke at a meeting of New England chambers of commerce. Here he expounded on the possibilities of long trails not just in Vermont but connecting all New England, ideas "elaborately illustrated and reinforced by sets of six blueprints of proposed mountain trail routes throughout the New England states." In the audience that day was Philip W. Ayres, forester of the Society for the Protection of New Hampshire Forests. Fresh from victory in creating the first Eastern national forest, this practical forester was thinking ahead of how to build a constituency of forest defenders. Taylor's vision triggered ideas about how to unite a broad interest group among hikers and trailbuilders. Ayres invited Taylor to come before a joint meeting of the Society and the AMC, "to rehearse dreams and to distribute blueprints." The AMC's joint sponsorship proved hard to pin down, so the meeting did not come off until late 1916.

By then other centripetal forces were building in the region. In May 1916 the Associated Mountaineering Clubs of North America was formed, with headquarters in New York, and nine clubs as founding members. Within two years this umbrella group had twenty-two constituent societies, including the AMC and the GMC, and its magazine, *Mountain*, was widely read and quoted during the late 1920s. By the early 1930s this organization had faded, but its founding in 1916 was a further indication of the regionwide thinking then spreading.

That fall Frank H. Burt wrote a paper for publication in the December 1916 *Appalachia*, in which he offered the proposition that an annual conference of mountain clubs would be helpful, embracing the local clubs of Randolph, Wonalancet, Waterville and other places, as well as the Green Mountain Club and any other kindred organizations within easy reach.

By this time the cause had attracted the formidable talents of Allen Chamberlain, the prestigious outdoors writer for the *Boston Transcript*, activist in forestry circles, and former president of the AMC. Chamberlain perceived hiking trails as a means to an end: a way of attracting a broad constituency to the forests, forming a political base for support of wise, long-range forestry practices.

In the fall of 1916, at Chamberlain's urging, Ayres finally called his meeting, inviting a cross section of regional trail clubs and interested individuals, under the joint sponsorship of the AMC and the Society for the Protection of New Hampshire Forests. On December 15, 1916, the meeting was held at the AMC offices in Boston, presided over by the Society's president, U.S. Sen. Allen Hollis. Featured addresses were by Chamberlain and William L. Hall of the U.S. Forest Service. Messrs. Blood, Jenks, and Goodrich were all there, taking an active part, as were Taylor and C. P. Cooper from Vermont. Taylor unfurled his "blueprints" of regionwide trails, as their author modestly put it, "nailed to the mast like a flag."

Regionwide consciousness took a giant step forward that day. Before the afternoon was over, a committee of five was appointed to "make arrangements for a permanent New England Trail Conference, with the aim of furthering coordinate enterprise in building and maintaining trails." The five were Ayres, Taylor, and three leading AMC figures: Chamberlain, former improvements councillor Harland Perkins, and active trail-builder Nat Goodrich (who officially represented the Dartmouth Outing Club). Working quickly, this committee called the first full meeting of the New England Trail Conference for March 16, 1917. Its purpose was officially defined thus: "To promote cooperation in the creation and maintenance of a system of connecting trails in New England." The original membership of the New England Trail Conference, as established in 1917, included all the major hiking and trail clubs.

For New Hampshire:

Appalachian Mountain Club

Chocorua Mountain Club

Dublin Trail Association (from the Monadnock area)

Gorham Improvement Association

Intervale Improvement Association

Lake Tarleton Club (located near Mount Moosilauke)

New Hampshire Hotel Association

North Woodstock Improvement Association

Randolph Mountain Club

Society for the Protection of New Hampshire Forests

Waterville Athletic and Improvement Association

Wonalancet Out Door Club

U.S. Forest Service

For Vermont:

Green Mountain Club "and its branches"

Vermont Forestry Association

For Massachusetts:

Boy Scouts, Central Council of Boston

Field and Forest Club

Massachusetts Forestry Association

New England Federation of City Planning Boards

New England Hotel Association

For Connecticut: Connecticut State Park Commission.

College outing clubs:

Amherst Mountain Club

Dartmouth Outing Club

Metawampe (The University of Massachusetts faculty outing club)

Pack and Paddle (MIT)

Williams Outing Club

In 1920 the conference published the first in a series of census reports on trails, showing that 23 constituent societies were maintaining 302 trails for a total of 1,072 miles. Trail construction plus membership growth in the NETC combined to push those totals up in biennial censuses that followed:

In 1922, 43 clubs maintained 535 trails, with a mileage of 2,008

In 1924, 49 clubs maintained 758 trails, with a mileage of 2,441

In 1929, 49 clubs maintained 876 trails, with a mileage of 3,194

The creation of the NETC was hailed at the time as an event of immense significance. Jenks touted the original conference of 1916 as

> perhaps the most noteworthy of its kind ever held in that section as regards attendance, the importance of the societies represented, the personnel of the representatives, and the interest shown.

Chamberlain invoked the vernacular of the Roosevelt-Wilson era to label the fledgling NETC "the New England Trail Trust":

> Except that it does not seek to establish a monopoly but invites all individuals and organizations that may be interested to join in on equal terms and to share in the enterprise and the profits.

The founders' pride seemed for a while to be justified. During the 1920s the NETC was a vigorous presence on the New England trail scene. Its meetings were well attended and widely reported. Its publications program generated not only the annual trail census, but also manuals on trail construction and maintenance, and pamphlets such as the immensely popular *Going Light* designed to show how the hiker could thrive with minimum baggage for days in the woods. For a while there was talk of expanding onto New York to form a "Northeastern Trail Conference," a step never accomplished.

The vigor and prestige of the NETC have passed through cyclical fluctuations since the organization's glory years of the 1920s. After a period of relative inactivity during the early 1930s, the NETC obtained a new lease on life by fusing its identity with a series of "Recreational Conferences" sponsored by the Massachusetts State Agricultural College (now the University of Massachusetts) at Amherst. Under the able leadership of John Vondell of the Massachusetts State faculty, the "Mountaineering Section" of these conferences drew a wide attendance from hiking clubs all over New England beginning in 1934. Recognizing a common interest, then NETC chairman Edgar L. Heermance suggested holding the NETC's annual meeting at the Massachusetts Recreational Conference in 1937. The outcome was so successful, with a wide representation of trail-maintaining clubs present and reporting on the state of their trails, that the NETC continued to use this forum for its annual meetings thereafter. Vondell became chairman of the trail organization in 1939. Another low point occurred during World War II, when men were in the military. Few could attend to trail work, and travel was restricted. Shortly after the war, however, at the prodding of Vondell and C. W. Blood, among others, the meetings were resumed. In 1955 the Massachusetts Recreational Conferences were officially discontinued, but the NETC continued to hold its annual meeting at the University of Massachusetts. This meeting, at which each trail club reported on the status of its trails, became the principal function of the NETC.

The NETC provided a formal organizational rallying point for the regionwide consciousness that had been growing among New England trail-builders during the 1920s. The single idea that appealed to many as best expressing this regionwide unity was what came to be called "through-trails"—routes that a hiker could follow for days and weeks on end, traversing the region as a whole or some substantial part of it.

Between 1914 and the culmination of this concept in the Appalachian Trail (1921), an articulate diversity of spokesmen raised the banner for through-trails.

Vermont's Long Trail was the archetype of a through-trail, of course. Its founder was never known to be content with the easily attainable goal. Well before the Long Trail had reached Massachusetts, much less Canada, Jim Taylor's fertile imagination had jumped miles beyond. At that meeting in 1914, where his oratory had inspired Ayres, Taylor showed a map on which he had drawn a trail reaching from New York City to Quebec. Taylor intermittently but rather ineffectually promoted this dream for the next decade or so, treating it as usual like a chamber of commerce promotion:

> I have another hobby [he wrote to a friend] which is being pushed by the New England Trail Conference, which aims to unify and systematize the mountain and lowland both throughout New England. . . . Some day I hope to see New England as a senic [sic] unit, playing this up more effective in its competition with the national parks of the west. The only way to do this is to play the territory as a unit.

Taylor deserves credit as the first to start thinking about a truly long-distance Atlantic states trail. It takes nothing away from the singular brilliance of Benton MacKaye's Appalachian Trail of 1921, nor from the far-sightedness of the others who anticipated him, to acknowledge that this slightly shabby, slightly disreputable chamber of commerce huckster, this amiable schemer, this compulsive promoter, this mercurial and most un-Vermonterish grand champion of Vermont was on the field first, waving his baton and ready to lead the parade. If the practical trail-builders had picked up his idea when he first anticipated it and actually cut that New York-to-Quebec trail, you can bet Taylor would have been talking about Georgia next. When they got to Springer Mountain, he'd have been looking for a way to walk dry-shod to Cuba.

Taylor got others thinking. Allen Chamberlain, employing his facile pen to help Ayres get the NETC started, wrote an article for the *Proceedings of the Society of American Foresters* in July 1916, in which he pointed out how the trail systems of the AMC, the GMC, and the Dartmouth Outing Club could be linked up to realize an "ambitious plan to lay a foot-way that might eventually connect New York City with the province of Quebec, along the Highlands of the Hudson and over the mountainous ridges of western New England."

When the NETC held its initial meeting on December 15, 1916, the air was alive with through-trail thinking. Both Taylor and Chamberlain spoke on the subject. While Taylor's "blueprint" envisioned the use of the entire Long Trail to Canada, the idea of branching east over the White Mountains to Katahdin was first broached at this 1916 meeting by Sumner R. Hooper of the summer resort at Kineo on Maine's Moosehead Lake. Here indeed lay the very route of the future Appalachian Trail. Even more prophetic was the vision of U.S. Forester William L. Hall, who went so far as to speak

> of the desirability of completing a system of trails to traverse all the New England mountain ranges, and be linked ultimately with the southern Appalachians.

This is the earliest known instance of someone's envisioning a foot trail extending up and down the entire Eastern seaboard—almost five years before the publication of Benton MacKaye's celebrated article on the Appalachian Trail.[a]

Others who played around with long-distance trail ideas during the years before 1920 include Ayres, Warren Hart, Connecticut's Albert Turner, and Prof. Will Monroe. But the most concrete through-trail plan came from Monroe's friend and co-worker J. Ashton Allis, the New York City banker. Allis came forth with a plan to extend the Long Trail south across the Berkshires and Taconics down to the Hudson River at Mount Beacon and Breakneck Ridge; thence across the Hudson by the Beacon-Newburgh ferry to Storm King; and then down among the Hudson Highlands to pick up the Ramapo-Dunderberg Trail across into New Jersey; and on, via Professor Monroe's trail system, to the Delaware Water Gap. Allis's plan sparked serious discussion within the NETC, and he was asked to make a written report, with maps, at the 1922 meeting. One speaker suggested extending the trail northeast by a cross-path from Killington to the White Mountains. Allis and others actually scouted route

---

[a]The remarkably farsighted Hall deserves more attention than he has hitherto received in New England environmental history. He was district forester for district 7 of the U.S. Forest Service in 1916, a post roughly equivalent to that of regional forester today. This gave him general supervision of most Eastern national forests, including the White Mountains and those of the south. His office was in Washington, D.C. Apparently he played an important role in acquiring lands for the White Mountain National Forest. Ayres, a recognized giant, had towering respect for Hall, whose unrecognized work in putting together the WMNF awed him. He once called Hall "a red-headed man from Kansas who came up our way and beat the Yankees out of their boots in the matter of careful buying" (undated typescript, ca. 1920, entitled "National Forests in the Eastern Mountains," in the archives of the Society for the Protection of New Hampshire Forests. Reprinted with permission.)

possibilities through Connecticut and New York. It is not unlikely that Allis's plan might have reached fruition had it not been for the almost simultaneous publication and more inspirational vision of MacKaye's proposal for a 2,100-mile Appalachian Trail.

The AT idea channeled efforts for the "big one" into that dream after 1921, but the idea of through-trails embraced a diversity of middle-range proposals as well (see figure 44.1). Berkshires nature writer Walter Prichard Eaton conceived the idea of a trail running the width of Massachusetts, north-south through the Berkshires, but he did little to promote it. In 1919 Frederick W. Kilbourne began pushing the idea of a cross-Connecticut through-trail from Long Island Sound to Mount Tom in Massachusetts, but it was ten years before Connecticut was ready for serious work on through-trails. In 1922 and 1923 W. F. Robbins, a trail-builder from the town of Rindge, New Hampshire, laid out a through-trail from Mount Watatic in Massachusetts to Pack Monadnock in southern New Hampshire; though but 20 miles long, the "Wapack" trail was a landmark in that it represented one of the earliest completed through-trails outside of Vermont and was a genuine interstate trail. By 1928 a southern extension to Mount Wachusett was added by the Field and Forest Club of Boston, under the leadership of Frank Sprague. Also in the early 1920s the New Hampshire Forest Society took advantage of its status as key landowner on Mount Monadnock to create a through-trail running north along abandoned town roads and cart paths to Mount Sunapee, 40 miles north; the original Monadnock-Sunapee Trail was more of a road-walk than its modern reincarnation, but it was said to provide "rural charm as it led trampers through small, historic villages where innkeepers offered simple room and board."

The largest through-trail yet, save the Long Trail, was the initial project of the newborn Adirondack Mountain Club in the years 1922 and 1923: the 130-mile Northville-Placid Trail. Northville was selected as the southern terminus because the main line of the New York Central Railroad reached that far and no farther. Lake Placid was an obvious destination as a major hiking and recreation center. In between, the Northville-Placid Trail was quintessentially a tramper's trail, spurning big-name peaks, threading undulating waves of hills, valleys, and saddles, "a valley route with occasional sections of skyline." Its highest point was the 3,008-foot pass near Tirrell Pond. It is interesting to note the diversity of tastes: the Adirondacks' long trail was well-received on the grounds that it *was* a valley trail, avoiding peaks, whereas only a few years before, Vermonters (and New Yorkers, led by Will Monroe) had revolted against the first version of the Long Trail *because* it avoided summits and ridge crests.[b]

_____

[b]When newborn, the Northville-Placid Trail was christened the "Long Trail," but confusion with the teenage Vermont sibling caused that name to be dropped in favor of the prosaic but descriptive name it has kept ever since.

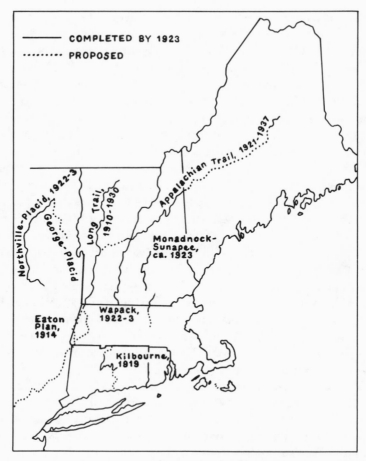

Figure 44.1. Long-distance hiking trails, 1910–1930 Regionwide consciousness spread throughout Northeastern hiking and trail-building circles during the 1910-30 period. What had been fragmented and separated systems of trails began to be perceived as parts of a regionwide whole. One manifestation of this new thinking was the growth of several long-distance hiking trails. The first was Vermont's Long Trail, begun in 1910. The culmination was the 2,100-mile Appalachian Trail, stretching from Maine to Georgia. But others sprang up around the region, especially during the early 1920s, as this map shows.

During 1923 an abortive start was made on a Lake George–Placid Trail as a companion piece, to go from Bolton Landing on Lake George up through the high peaks of the Adirondacks, over Marcy itself, and down to Lake Placid.

Back in New England through-trail mania was kept alive largely by the peripatetic Arthur Comey. A brilliant but erratic individual, Comey was a city planner from Boston, a summer trailsman at Chocorua, New Hampshire, an early NETC leader, an active AT scout in Maine, not to mention a daring and resourceful skier and winter climber. Probably the most active promoter of long-distance walking outside the AT orbit, Comey prepared a comprehensive map showing a still largely theoretical Appalachian Trail; the Long Trail in Vermont; a projected northern New Hampshire path running north from the White Mountains to Dixville Notch; the Monadnock-Sunapee; the nearby Wapack; and two alternative routes in western Massachusetts, where the route of the AT had not yet been selected.

The first flush of through-trail enthusiasm, which produced the Long Trail, the NETC, and eventually the Appalachian Trail itself, was perceived by Comey as the wave of future mountain recreation. In fact, once the great AT had been built, the crusading spirit for long-distance trails quieted down until its revival in more recent years, under the impetus of national legislation and new ideas for long-distance trails throughout the nation. Nevertheless, the regionwide consciousness that the through-trail ideas of those early pioneers in the Northeast embodied has become a permanent attribute of the Eastern hiking scene.

Chapter 45

The Appalachian Trail

T HE ONE big supertrail was inevitable. By around 1920 promoter James Taylor was hawking "blueprints" of a Quebec–New York City trail. Prof. Will Monroe was extending that to the Delaware Water Gap. Forester William Hall was musing at public meetings about linking up with the southern Appalachians. Trail-cutter J. A. Allis was mapping connections between Vermont and Harriman Park. Philip Ayres, Allen Chamberlain, and Albert Turner were all mulling over the idea. The Appalachian Trail from Maine to Georgia awaited only the right person to give the word in the right place. The surprise was that the person and place were both completely outside the Northeastern trail community as we have been watching it develop.

Benton MacKaye

Benton MacKaye was born in the urban confines of Stamford, Connecticut, on March 6, 1879. When he was nine, the family moved to Shirley, Massachusetts, 30 miles west of Boston, where he found wooded hills to roam. He and his childhood buddies formed a secret society called the Rambling Boys' Club. It is tempting to suggest that MacKaye's original concept of the purpose of the Appalachian Trail could scarcely be better summarized than by the stated purpose of the Rambling Boys' Club of around 1890:

> To give to the members an education of the lay of the land in which they live, also of other lands, taking in the Geography, Geology, Zoology, and Botany of them.

Monadnock was the first mountain that MacKaye climbed. As a Harvard freshman, he made his first trip to the White Mountains in 1897. The summer after graduation (1900) he and classmate Horace Hildreth embarked on an extended hike through the Green Mountains, starting at Haystack on the southern end and working their way by trails, wood roads, cart paths, bushwhacks, and back roads across low land and high, over Stratton to Killington, and on northward as far as Mansfield— virtually the Long Trail-to-be ten years before Taylor had his vision. Thus a yen for long-distance hiking was part of MacKaye from his college days. Three summers later the concept of linking existing trail systems together was added to his fermenting ideas when he worked under James Sturgis Pray, scouting how to link the AMC's Mount Carrigain Trail to Waterville Valley. (The reader will recall that Pray and Louis Cutter were struggling with the unification of the White Mountain's clusters of trails.) Further study at Harvard gave MacKaye a degree in forestry in 1905, the year that Gifford Pinchot organized the U.S. Forest Service. MacKaye went to Washington, D.C., to work for Pinchot, who immediately sent him back up to the White Mountains to survey the forests— part of the groundwork for the White Mountain National Forest. During the 1910s MacKaye worked in Washington for the Forest Service and the Department of Labor, and his ideas on conservation, land use, and regional planning continued to evolve.

In Washington MacKaye grew into a "dignified, affable philosopher with the ever-present pipe clamped firmly between his teeth." He became one of those large-scale, imaginative thinkers whose vague idealism and facile way with words and ideas may change the world but are the nemesis of more precise thinkers or practical doers. At one agency he was provided with "an upstairs cubbyhole where he welcomed anyone in for a 'pow-wow.'" Here he would sit, smoke his pipe, and think, except that

> once a week, he'd come downstairs to the staff meeting and pep up the others with new ideas and diagrams and imagination, and then disappear upstairs again.

One perceptive MacKaye-watcher called him a "walking anachronism," in that he was

> a nineteenth century New England reformer strayed into the Jazz Age. His political radicalism partook of pre-Marxist utopian socialisms, bucolic and spiritual, rather than the urban, gritty proletarianism of this century.

The modern reader looking at his articles, speeches, and reminiscences, is struck with the continental sweep, the glittering generalities, the quasi-mystical epigrams, the frequent minor errors of fact, arranged against an overall vision that stirs the imagination even now and changed forever the walker's world of 1921.

In late June 1921 MacKaye began noting down ideas for what he alternately called an "Appalachian Trail" or an "Appalachian Skyline." On July 10 he visited a friend, Charles Harris Whitaker, editor of the *Journal of the American Institute of Architects*, who introduced him to a community planner named Clarence S. Stein. The three men spent the day spinning philosophical notions, and Whitaker suggested that MacKaye put down in an article his idealistic ideas about the use of the Appalachian skyline. The piece appeared in the October 1921 issue.

MacKaye's original vision was much more than just an Appalachian Trail. It was a utopian plan "to develop the opportunities—for recreation, recuperation, and employment—in the region of the Appalachian skyline." With the trail and shelters along it, MacKaye imagined a series of "community camps" of one hundred acres or more, where families could live simply and cheaply, engaging in various pursuits of self-improvement; and ultimately the development of "food and farm camps" providing "permanent, steady, healthy employment in the open." All this was to provide "a sanctuary from the scramble of every-day worldly commercial life." In later rhetoric, he portrayed the trail as designed "to preserve the primeval environment" and called on hikers to "organize a Barbarian invasion," first assaulting and capturing (through the AT) the ridgeline, to protect it from civilization, and then working downward: "Cabins and trails are but a line of forts." Thus, and much more, ran the grand vision.

With a product worth pushing, MacKaye began to introduce himself and his idea to the Northeastern hiking community. Heretofore Mac-Kaye had been on the fringe of that community: as an occasional hiker and an interesting ideas-man, he had formed friendships with Allen Chamberlain and a few other prominent outdoors leaders in the region. These contacts were a good start. But he had not been active in any of the regional clubs or trail-building projects. Now he sought out influential leaders to sell them on the Appalachian Trail. He attended his first NETC meeting in 1921, where he talked with Albert Turner and Arthur Comey, both fellow global thinkers and long-trail proponents. Over the winter, in Cambridge, he conferred with Allen Chamberlain and with his old mentor, Sturgis Pray. In March, Stein introduced MacKaye to a newspaperman in New York whom Stein thought might be helpful: Ray Torrey. Four days later, in Flushing, he reviewed his dreams and schemes with Boy Scouts impresario Dan Beard.

In Torrey, of course, MacKaye won an invaluable ally. A "Long Brown Path" column soon appeared, providing "the first big broadside newspaper account" of the AT idea. On April 6, 1922, at the City Club in New York, Torrey brought Stein and MacKaye to the same dinner table with Major William Welch and J. A. Allis. MacKaye's vision perfectly suited the action plans of those two eminently practical doers: Welch was looking for trails to lay out through Harriman Park, and Allis had already been working on connecting that park with the Long Trail. From this meeting was launched the first concrete plan for the initial section of trail explicitly built as part of the Appalachian Trail. That summer Torrey and Allis scouted the route and stimulated the New York Appies (including a young trail worker named Murray Stevens) to begin cutting it.

MacKaye—like James Taylor, a celestial dreamer who left the dirty work to other hands—was off to Washington and more conferences. He also hit the banquet circuit in 1923, with talks to the NETC and a Bear Mountain Conference of New York trail workers. Finally, on March 1–3, 1925, he spoke at a specially convened meeting in Washington, held under a name that was to stick around from then on: the Appalachian Trail Conference.

The first Appalachian Trail Conference was an important step. It established a vehicle for getting the Appalachian Trail out of the hands of the global thinkers and into the hands of the doers. Except for what Torrey and Allis had achieved in New York, the trail was not making physical progress. The Community Planning Committee of the American Institute of Architects, chaired by Stein, had made some vague plans for building the trail, but it lacked the necessary contacts with real-life trail-builders. Allis was bogged down with his plans for eastern New York. MacKaye and Torrey attempted to enlist the support of the chairman of the Taconic State Park Commission, Franklin D. Roosevelt, without substantive success. MacKaye continued to spin his ideas at meetings, but the trail was not moving across the hills.[a]

At the first meeting of the ATC, Major Welch was elected chairman but did not throw his proven talents for action into the AT. For another year or two, the trail plan drifted along without action. By 1926 it was "practically moribund."

Arthur Perkins

The turning point came with the entry of two new men. The first was Judge Arthur Perkins of Hartford, Connecticut. Perkins had climbed the Matterhorn as a youth but otherwise had devoted himself to a law career until he was well along in his fifties. By then a distinguished barrister, Perkins began to give some time to latent outdoor interests. In 1923 or 1924 he spent the summer in Chocorua, New Hampshire, climbed that

---

[a]The negotiations of MacKaye and Torrey with Franklin D. Roosevelt constitute an obscure but interesting chapter, discernible in various papers, mainly in the MacKaye Family Collections at the Dartmouth College Library, the ATC Archives, and the Franklin D. Roosevelt Library at Hyde Park, New York. MacKaye went to see Roosevelt in the spring of 1925, and Torrey followed up with long letters to him, advocating a trail route northward along the east side of the Hudson River, through the Taconic State Park into Massachusetts—bypassing Connecticut completely. On May 16, 1926, Torrey even ran a map of the proposed all–New York route in the *New York Times* ("Hiking Footpath to Dixie Urged" p. VIII-16), perhaps an effort to put pressure on the commission. Roosevelt expressed personal support but pleaded opposition within the commission as reason not to push that route. Commissioner Francis R. Masters was indeed strongly opposed (see Masters to Roosevelt letter, Jan. 19, 1926, in the Hyde Park Library). Later as governor of New York, FDR lobbied for the AT at the 1930 Governors' Conference (see Roosevelt to Robert U. Johnson, June 25, 1930); as president, he wrote notes to AT enthusiasts about establishing a continuous reservation from Maine to Georgia along the highlands, thereby seeming to anticipate federal protection legislation of a generation later (for example, Roosevelt to Johnson, Aug. 24, 1934). But during the 1920s the rising politician's support was only verbal, at a time when more verbiage was not the critical need.

peak several times, and became a devoted hiker. By 1925 he was involved in trail work and was named to fill a New England vacancy in the ATC. In 1926 he was scouting possible routes both in his own state's northwest corner and, during a vacation at York's Twin Pine Camps, in the state of Maine. In 1927 he became trails chairman of the AMC's Connecticut Chapter. By the end of that year he was in very active touch with Welch and Torrey, pushing suggestions at them about the future course of the AT all up and down the East. Largely at his instigation, a second Appalachian Trail Conference was called in Washington on May 19–20, 1928. By this time Major Welch was ready to step down as chairman. Perkins was appointed, first, chairman of a committee on reorganization, and then, in late 1928, chairman of the ATC, succeeding Welch. During the late 1920s, Judge Perkins roamed up and down the trail corridor, enlisting workers, forming Appalachian Trail clubs, and plotting specific routes. Practical leaders began to emerge in specific localities. These were the true heroes of the Appalachian Trail, which in the end was built from the bottom up by those men who took on a section of perhaps fifty miles in length and got the job done. But the leader who, more than any other, originally found and motivated them was Judge Perkins.

Myron Avery

Among the trail groups that Judge Perkins encouraged to organize was the Washington-based Potomac Appalachian Trail Club, formed in 1927. The key figure in this outfit was a young maritime lawyer named Myron Avery. Though but twenty-seven years old, Avery seemed interested in the trail and a capable and effective organizer. Perkins asked him to serve as assistant chairman. With the work finally moving forward, and as the date for the Appalachian Trail Conference of 1930 approached, Perkins was stricken with an illness from which he never recovered; he died in 1932. Avery was made acting chairman for 1930, then chairman in 1931, and occupied that post in name and deed for the next twenty-two years.

If Benton MacKaye was indispensable to the creation of the Appalachian Trail, so was Myron Halliburton Avery. Two less compatible characters could scarcely be conjured. It is not surprising that they did not get along. Against MacKaye's rambling, pipe-smoking, airy visions, Avery displayed a pragmatic, no-nonsense dedication to results.

Avery was once described thus: "Mr. Avery is a blonde [sic] son of the forest, medium statured, husky, weatherbeaten, with all the appearance of a football halfback." He was born in North Lubec, Maine, so far down east it's almost in Canada, on November 3, 1899. After distinguishing himself as an honors student at Bowdoin College and Harvard Law School, he entered the practice of admiralty law first in Hartford, where he came to the attention of Judge Perkins, and then for the U.S. Maritime

Commission in Washington, D.C. He was a charter member of the Potomac Appalachian Trail Club (PATC) and its president from 1927 to 1941. He was also instrumental in founding the Maine Appalachian Trail Club and was its dominant figure from 1935 to 1952. He was chairman of the Appalachian Trail Conference from 1931 to 1952. It seemed simply not possible for Myron Avery to be associated with an enterprise without running it. He was possessed of singular intelligence, energy, discipline, organizing skill, aggressive drive, and personal egotism. That so remarkable a man died of a heart attack at age fifty-two is a cruel irony.

From the time of his becoming ATC chairman in 1931 until World War II, Avery devoted every spare moment to the trail. He made it his personal business to go over every foot of the route, and to know the status of each local group that had responsibility for a piece of it, not just in its construction but in its subsequent maintenance. He devised trail standards and specifications for trail signs with meticulous attention to details and insisted on their being observed. Although he appointed numerous committees, he generally knew more about their activities than the chairmen he appointed, and often dictated letters for their signatures, not always discussing the contents with them in advance. Though his principal affiliations were with the Potomac and Maine clubs, he seemed in perpetual motion up and down 2,100 miles of trail, spurring local trail workers to action, personally reviewing new sections and measuring their precise mileage, insisting on high standards of trail work, demanding to know what work was next on the local agenda, ceaselessly troubleshooting, problem solving, questioning, prodding. His febrile energy level constantly astounded local workers.

Almost before the Appalachian Trail was completed, Avery was the first person to walk every mile of it, though he never did it as one continuous walk.

Under Avery the Appalachian Trail Conference became more than a biennial meeting. It became a highly structured organization with authority to set standards for 2,100 miles of trail, a federation of clubs from Maine to Georgia. Memoranda and instructions on trail marking, signing, and maintenance standards flowed from the Washington headquarters. Theoretically local clubs retained autonomy in their trail sections, but it quickly became clear where Avery saw the real authority. In discussing trail standards with Perkins in 1931, he wrote,

> I first planned to have a draft adopted at the Conference. Then it seemed to me that it would be hard to keep people from airing their pet ideas and that the most effective thing would be to have the Standards adopted by the Board of Governors after being prepared by the people who really know about such things.

In 1934, while engaged in a test of power with a Pennsylvania trail worker, Dr. H. F. Rentschler, Avery wrote to an associate,

Rentschler has written you that he will not accept any supervision of "outside agencies." This, of course, is utter nonsense, for any work in Pennsylvania—as in Virginia or New York—is bound to be subject to Trail Conference standards and supervision.

Though the local clubs and a growing army of dedicated individuals did the actual work, the ATC exercised strong leadership from above—this in sharp contrast to the NETC, which exercised no authority over its constituent clubs.

No misty-eyed disciple of Thoreau or Starr King, Avery devoted little time to dreams. He was there to get action and had little patience for talk and less for procrastination. If he felt that a local trail worker was ineffective, he would not hesitate to replace him with someone who would get the job done. "Myron was easy to work with if you were willing to work hard and do things his way," recalled one early PATC associate. Another conceded that he might be "a 'dictator' who strongly objected to anyone who opposed his Trail ideas," but that he was "a very capable man when working with details." Said a third: "Myron left two trails from Maine to Georgia. One was of hurt feelings and bruised egos. The other was the A. T."

Avery's single-minded concern for results left him no time for vague principles. Wilderness, for example, was not a concept he troubled himself much about. "Mere woods travel" had "a sort of monotony" for him. Although associates resisted the building of the Skyline Drive near Virginia's wild Blue Ridge AT section, Avery was all for the parkway: it would give more people access to the trail. He deplored the inaccessibility of New Hampshire's Mahoosucs and their "amateur trail with a very rough footway."[b] Although he was the most dedicated of amateurs himself and recognized the chief reliance of the AT on volunteers ("The Appalachian Trail is in every sense an enormous amateur recreational project," he wrote), he eagerly accepted governmental aid when he could get it. When the CCC came into the Maine picture, he was not one to raise the banner of pure volunteerism, though his successors in Maine have become the chief opponents of professionalism.

Under Avery the concept of the Appalachian Trail changed from a broad, vague social program, as originally envisioned by MacKaye, to a simple, single, tangible, well-cleared footpath. This change caused MacKaye himself some pain at first. The old visionary had argued,

> High and dry above the stupendous detail of our job we should hold the reason for it all. This is *not* to cut a path and then say—"Ain't it beautiful!" Our job is to open a realm. This is something more than a geographical location—it is an environment.

---

[b]The "amateurs" who built the Mahoosucs trails were, of course, C. W. Blood and P. R. Jenks, who had been building trails in the White Mountains every summer since the thirty-seven-year-old Avery had been in kindergarten. See chap. 36.

In 1925 he insisted, "The path of the trailway should be as 'pathless' as possible; it should be the minimum path consistent with practical accessibility." Ten years later, as the Appalachian Trail neared completion, MacKaye cautioned Avery not to be preoccupied with a "connected trail": "Wilderness, not continuity, is the vital point."

To Avery this was nonsense. A trail was a trail and should be continuous, plainly marked, broadly cleared, and unmistakable to follow: "Trails should be marked and maintained in a manner to eliminate the necessity of labor and uncertainty in finding one's route." Even Perkins criticized Avery's tendency to overblaze. MacKaye was anguished and wrote to Avery that he was losing sight of the goal, that the original concept of a wilderness way was being destroyed by overcivilizing the trailway. To this Avery responded with a six-page outburst in which he heatedly disagreed and charged that "no thanks are due to you for our long-delayed eventual success," and that the father of the AT "had consciously placed himself at the disposal of the elements which have attempted to wreck the project and prevent its completion."

A prickly antagonist, Avery had his battles with MacKaye, with Torrey, with Heermance, with Robert Underhill (*Appalachia* editor and the prestigious dean of American mountaineers), with Percy Baxter, with the AMC, with various publications. Never a generous spirit, he questioned the veracity of the first man who claimed to have walked the AT continuously, perhaps because the feat upstaged his own of having walked it all piecemeal. Inordinately sensitive to criticism, he seethed with contempt for anyone who tried to comment on trail policy who had not actually been out on the trail working.

His critics deplored his rebarbative egotism and desire to control results. "Myronides I," he was called. "Not a pleasant man," recalled Underhill, "but he got things done." Baxter State Park historian John Hakola described him as "convinced he was God," but went on to praise his "enormous contribution to Katahdin." One local trail worker addressed a letter in 1929 thus: "To Myronides, Emperor of Hither (and Thither) Appalachia: Hail!"

Yet he was liked, indeed almost worshipped, by his liege followers in the Potomac and Maine circles. "A hell of a fine fellow," said PATC coworker Frank Schairer. "And he was fun to be with," added another, Shailer Philbrick, "one of the greatest men I ever knew." His successor in the Maine organization, Roy Fairfield, recalled, "He was a whiz."

Avery's controversial personal qualities should not eclipse his stature in the history of the Appalachian Trail. Without him—and Judge Perkins —the vague dreams and meetings and philosophical concepts of MacKaye and the others might never have been welded into a cohesive 2,100-mile AT, with its clearly defined character and unity. Outside of New York and New England, Avery is justly rated as an enormously effective leader, perhaps because there he had relatively few established leaders to challenge his authority, and he worked best when he was completely in charge. In the Northeast his record of effectiveness is more uneven, because here he had to contend with existing organizations and other strong leaders, neither of which was he temperamentally well-suited for dealing with. Between New York and New Hampshire, Avery contributed little to the building of the AT: in New York and Connecticut, the key local leaders were found by others (Stevens by Torrey and Allis, Anderson by Perkins); in Massachusetts Avery's influence may have been counterproductive; in Vermont and New Hampshire, trails already existed. But in Maine, where new work was needed, in a vacuum of local leadership, Avery's skills came to the fore. Indeed, pushing the trail through Maine might well have been abandoned as too difficult and complicated had it not been for Avery.

The Appalachian Trail is too monumental an accomplishment to lay at the feet of one man or even two, and its essence is that it was built from the ground up by the local workers all along the route; but if single names must be mentioned, that of Myron Avery deserves, though it rarely gets, equal billing with that of Benton MacKaye.

AT building: New York

Meanwhile, to return to the story of the Appalachian Trail itself, by 1932 Avery was able to report the Northeastern sections complete from New Jersey to the Maine border. That meant a lot of work had been done in five years.

For purposes of this history, we will take the Ramapo River as the southwestern limit of our focus. From the Ramapo to the Hudson, Torrey and the New York AMC had already built one section. The route from the Hudson east to Connecticut exhibited all the worst problems that the original AT-builders had to overcome: almost entirely private land ownership, a civilized area crisscrossed with public roads and villages of various sizes, and no previous history of hiking trails.

The man principally responsible for steering through these troubled waters was Murray H. Stevens of the New York AMC. Born in 1895, Stevens was an engineer who lived in New York City most of his life, but had tasted hiking trails at summer camp in New Hampshire, spent his honeymoon hiking in the White Mountains in 1925, and joined the New York Chapter of the AMC. He worked on the original AT crew west of the Bear Mountain Bridge; in 1927 or 1928 he took on the challenge of finding the way onward east from the Hudson River.

As the problem was archetypal, so Murray Stevens's solution was a model of how the great AT-builders worked. First, Stevens laid out his ideal route on the maps, trying to piece together as much scenic, wooded, and hilly country as he could identify. Next, he went out and walked the prospective route, modifying it by what he found on the land. Then came the tough part: approaching and negotiating with all the landowners to secure their permission or at least their tolerance of having the Appalachian Trail cross their private land. Not all agreed, but many were surprisingly cooperative:

> One man told me I could run right through his house if I wanted to; his explanation was that he had met his wife on the Trail.

Worried landowners were given a written release, in which the ATC disclaimed any permanent rights and acknowledged the owner's right to remove markers at any time.

Stevens worked his way east-northeast from the Bear Mountain Bridge, passing steeply over Anthony's Nose (a magnificent hill since closed to hikers by a military reservation) and alongside some abandoned iron mines of Baron Hasenclever (the eighteenth-century original, not Torrey), and crossing several roads before reaching the shores of Lake Celeste. After crossing more roads, Stevens brought the trail up over Candlewood Hill and gained the boundaries of Fahnestock Memorial State Park. After enjoying several miles of undeveloped woodlands here, the route proceeded over almost 20 miles of wood roads and narrow dirt lanes past Pawling. The trail then picked up more wooded country through the valley of Ten Mile River, until it reached the Connecticut line on the broad wooded summit of Schaghticoke Mountain, overlooking the Housatonic River near Kent (see figure 45.1).

Following his diplomacy with the landlords, Stevens went to work in 1929 cutting the trail through the woods and blazing it along the roads. He usually worked with only one or two others but sometimes organized work trips of eight or ten fellow Appies. Over two years, 1929 and 1930, the AT through to Connecticut was basically complete . . . in a way:

> But then it materialized that this was only the beginning; in the next 20 years I had to relocate 40 out of the original 55 miles. An interstate highway used five miles. A state insane asylum had the Trail running right through the main entrance. Most of the remaining changes were the result of change in ownership or usage of the property.

This is the story of all the AT workers who built and maintained the trail through the built-up areas of New York, Connecticut, and Massachusetts, and some of the northern states as well. The work was never "done." Landowner relations were continually in jeopardy because of occasional offensive actions by thoughtless hikers, or simply because of a change in ownership, or even a change of heart by the original owner. Like the Connecticut blue-blazed trail makers, the AT maintainer had to be one-third trail worker, one third organizer of other trail workers, but three-fourths diplomat among the landowners.

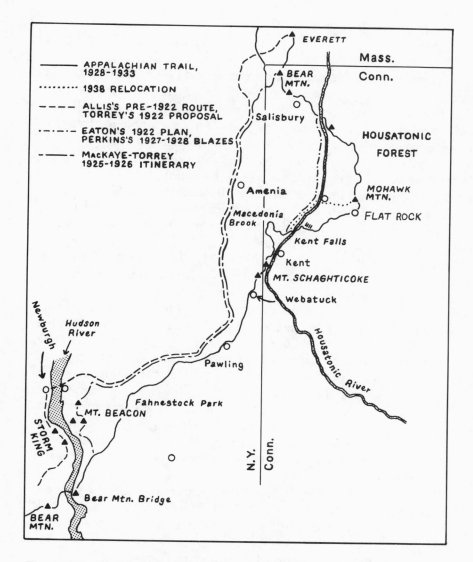

Figure 45.1. Building the Appalachian Trail in New York and Connecticut The route that the Appalachian Trail should take from the Hudson River to Massachusetts was a subject for prolonged debate and numerous alternative and conflicting proposals. Several of the early plans would have by-passed Connecticut altogether, or would have included only the northwestern tip of the state. The route that was finally selected was the result of the initiative of Ned Anderson. Like Murray Stevens in New York, Anderson was a practical trail-builder who got the job done, thereby resolving the debate.

In Connecticut many alternatives were explored before the original Appalachian Trail route was selected (see figure 45.1). Even before MacKaye's 1921 article appeared, New York trail-builder J. A. Allis was working on a through-trail route that would have completely bypassed Connecticut. Allis's route would have gone north from Harriman Park over Storm King Mountain; crossed the Hudson River on the Beacon-Newburgh ferry (the Bear Mountain Bridge was not yet built); then journeyed northeast through New York State before reaching Mount Everett in Massachusetts. When MacKaye's AT proposal was first discussed by New York–area trail-builders, this all–New York route was the original plan, according to Raymond Torrey.

However, Connecticut trailsman Albert M. Turner entered the picture early in 1922 with a proposal that the trail should run through Connecticut. He described a route through Macedonia Brook and Kent Falls state parks and Mohawk and Cornwall state forests. This implied an "elbow" swinging to the east side of the Housatonic River, very much along the lines that the trail actually took ten years later. At some point in 1922, Allis and Torrey walked a proposed route south from Mount Everett over Bear Mountain and down through Connecticut, but sticking to the west side of the Housatonic. Later that year, Massachusetts trailsman Walter Prichard Eaton proposed a Connecticut route, also sticking to the west side of the Housatonic. By 1924 at least, Torrey was persuaded that this approximate route was the best. By 1926 an influential Connecticut political figure and ardent walker, Roger S. Baldwin, also supported essentially this route.

In 1925 and 1926, however, the New York route regained support. MacKaye and Torrey dickered with Taconic State Park Chairman Franklin D. Roosevelt over a possible route running west of such towns as Amenia, New York, and entering Connecticut only briefly to climb Bear Mountain, just before entering Massachusetts. Eaton still argued for Connecticut, however.

In 1926 and 1927 Arthur Perkins took a strong interest in a Connecticut AT route, favoring the west side of the Housatonic River. By February 1927 Torrey had been converted back to the Connecticut route. During the summer of 1927 Perkins "scouted and temporarily marked" a 35-mile route entirely west of the Housatonic. At this point Perkins was unable to obtain landowner permissions to take the AT over Bear Mountain, so he worked out a "tentative route" bypassing Bear to the west.

Thus by 1927, three routes were still very much under consideration: a virtually all–New York route; a western Connecticut route; and Turner's "elbow" route east of the Housatonic. In reviewing these three possibilities, MacKaye wrote to Torrey,

My own idea about this is to encourage the first individual or group who will take up any of these routes and push it through in real earnest.

That is where matters stood when the first on-the-ground trail-builder finally came along: Ned Anderson. It was Anderson's practical initiative which broke the logjam in favor of Turner's "elbow" route and got the trail built.

Born on October 2, 1885, Nestell Kipp Anderson was a farmer in the town of Sherman who enjoyed a lifelong love of the woods, combined with a Puritan zeal for hard work and straight living. "If there is a truly good man, it is Uncle Ned," wrote one youthful admirer.

> He seems the happiest when he has a group of young people around him eager to learn and listen. He is never too busy to take us on some new trail or to a new cave.

He neither drank nor smoked and claimed that "ginger ale would put him under the table." He started a Boy Scout troop in Sherman and soon had the boys at work building the AT; later, during the 1930s, he organized the Housatonic Trail Club, consisting largely of friends who visited his farm, and put club members to work maintaining the trail that he and his Scouts had cut.

Anderson came into the AT picture suddenly when discovered by Perkins in the woods in the summer of 1929. Heermance and the other active Connecticut trail makers of 1930 had never heard of him. "How you ever discovered him is a mystery to me, as he lives on the top of the world," Heermance wrote Perkins. But Perkins sparked Anderson's interest in trail work and turned over the maps on which he had sketched the AT route possibilities. Anderson started right in:

> After farm chores were done, his Scouts labored with him, cutting and clearing, hacking and blazing, from the entrance of the Trail into Connecticut at Dog Tail Corners in Webatuck at the Kent line all the way up to Bear Mountain at the Massachusetts border.

By the end of the summer of 1930, Anderson had marked and cleared the AT through Macedonia Brook State Park and as far as Flanders Bridge north of Kent. Crossing the river, he took the trail eastward through scenic Kent Falls, past Flat Rock (where the Mattatuck Trail would soon take off on its easterly course for Grand Junction), and north to Mohawk Mountain. Just before Kent Falls, with a railroad to cross, the resourceful Yankee farmer directed the AT through a culvert under the railroad tracks, which Avery called "the only instance, to my knowledge, where the Trail does such a thing." With the mileage now quite distant from the Anderson farm in Sherman, Perkins, Avery, and

Heermance were looking for someone else to finish the north end of the state. They underestimated Anderson's zeal and physical energy. In 1932 Anderson all but completed the route north through the Housatonic State Forest, to beautiful Dean's Ravine and Barrack's Mountain, then back across the Housatonic River and north to Bear Mountain (Connecticut's, not New York's) via its craggy subsidiary, Lion's Head. In that year, to provide access to the trail at Bear Mountain, he also cut the Under Mountain Trail. In 1933 he put the finishing touches on his work, connecting his trail with Murray Stevens's on the south end and the Massachusetts AT to the north (see figure 45.1).

As in New York, maintenance and relocations proved a continuing challenge. Cantankerous landowners were not so much a problem here, but the elements enforced one major change when a 1936 flood swept away Flanders Bridge across the Housatonic River. Anderson moved the trail north to Cornwall Bridge, where he joined it to an existing trail through Dark Entry Ravine and thence on to rejoin the old route at Mohawk Mountain.[c] Although the AT suffered by missing the spectacular Kent Falls, it more than made up the loss by adding the enchanted hemlock grove and silvery stream of Dark Entry. This relocation involved building 15 miles of new trail—no small job. Elsewhere, Anderson and his Housatonic Trail Club not only maintained the rest of the trail but attempted some minor improvement each year, eliminating a road walk here, adding a mountaintop there.

AT building: Massachusetts

MacKaye's home state of Massachusetts was the first to take the AT idea seriously enough to start planning a specific route—yet (except for Maine) the last to complete a continuously cleared footway and provide for its regular maintenance.

The first plan for an AT route across Massachusetts goes back to 1922. With the ink scarcely dry on MacKaye's original article, nature writer Walter Prichard Eaton outlined a route that started from existing trails on Mount Everett in the south, traversed in a northeasterly direction much as the present trail does, until reaching October Mountain Forest, less than halfway up the state. Here, however, Eaton's proposal diverged sharply from the present trail: his plan was to have the trail swing hard west, south of Pittsfield, and proceed north along the crest of the Taconic highlands, all the way to Mount Greylock. Going north off Greylock, he proposed following the Bellows Pipe Trail, not the ridge to its west as it does now (see figure 45.2).

---

[c]When the AT abandoned Flat Rock for Mohawk Mountain, the Mattatuck Trail adopted that change, moving its western terminus from the former to the latter.

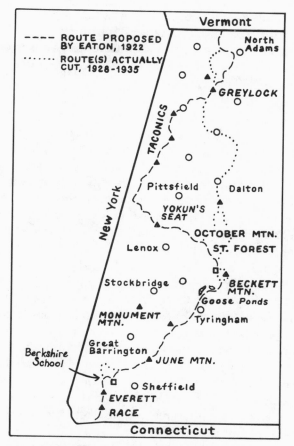

Figure 45.2. Building the Appalachian Trail in Massachusetts When the Appalachian Trail was first proposed in 1921, Massachusetts writer-outdoorsman Walter Prichard Eaton mapped out a route, the northern half of which swung to the western edge of the state where it traversed the heights of the Taconic Range. After years of inaction, however, several groups of activists—not always working in harmony—built the trail farther east in the Berkshire hills. The Massachusetts AT history was a stormy one, leaving a residue of bitterness still felt today.

Eaton, however, as events repeatedly proved, was more a writer than a doer, more a local-level MacKaye than an Avery or Anderson. Several false starts sputtered in the Berkshires during the mid-1920s, with the most actual trail work being accomplished by Berkshire school boys under Eaton's wing. During these years of inaction, 1923–27, optimistic statements emanated from outside sources (MacKaye, Torrey, and others) as to the progress being made in western Massachusetts. Their optimism is not supported by tangible evidence in other sources that any trail had actually been built, however. Eaton himself made no such claims and indeed wrote MacKaye in 1926 that "I doubt if it can ever be completed, anyway, without state aid." As late as February 10, 1928, Torrey described the AT route through Massachusetts as going over Monument Mountain and otherwise a different course from that over which it was constructed in the years 1928–31.

The first sustained Connecticut-to-Vermont effort was launched in 1928 under a countywide promotional organization called the Berkshire Hills Conference. This group established a three-man Trails Committee on June 4, 1928, consisting of Eaton, representing the south end; Archie K. Sloper, secretary of the Mount Greylock Commission; and Franklin L. Couch, a Dalton civic leader who drew the responsibility for the all-important connections between Greylock and the south end.

Within this group, Couch emerged as leader and chairman. Born in 1895, Couch had served in World War I and remained a State Guard commander in Berkshire County, edited the *Village Press* in Dalton, worked as personnel director for a local manufacturer, and presided over a phenomenally active Boy Scout movement in the towns east of Pittsfield, reportedly the largest single Boy Scout troop in the world between 1922 and 1936. Known as "the conscience of the town" and familiarly as "Cap," Couch was an immensely popular figure locally, with a warm human touch to complement his talent for organizing large numbers of community volunteers.

Over the next four years, 1928–31, Couch and his Berkshire Hills Conference group built a nearly complete AT across Massachusetts. How thoroughly this was done varied along the way, but except for one stretch in the south end, between Mount Everett and June Mountain (Eaton's country), and some ambiguity around the October Mountain Forest, a continuous trail was established. The route sharply differed from Eaton's 1922 plan by staying east of Pittsfield all the way to Greylock— that is, a truly Berkshires, as opposed to a Taconic, route. The most effective trail-builders were the Williams Outing Club and a Williamstown school principal, John B. Clarke, in the north; Archie Sloper and the Boy Scouts whom he turned out to cut the southern flanks of Greylock; Couch and his Boy Scouts around Dalton; and a remarkable naturalist from the Pittsfield area named S. Waldo Bailey, who probably cut more miles of actual trail than all the rest.

In 1931 the Berkshire Chapter of the AMC began to send work parties over to the Berkshires to work on the AT, functioning completely independently of the Berkshire Hills Conference locals. Despite its name, the "Berkshire Chapter" trail workers came almost exclusively from outside Berkshire County. Its leaders were J. E. Partenheimer of Springfield, chapter chairman in 1931; John B. Dickson of Northampton, who succeeded him in 1932; and Payson T. Newton of Holyoke, who followed Dickson in 1933.

A schism developed between the locals and the Berkshire Chapter "outsiders" (as they were perceived by Cap Couch's trail workers).

Communication was never established between the two. Confusion resulted. The locals, with the blessing of Perkins, had marked a route over Beckett Mountain, for example; ignorant of this plan, the Berkshire Chapter blazed a route straight to Finerty Pond, bypassing Beckett. At one point Couch's crew found Berkshire Chapter AT signs up where they didn't expect them and actually took them down.

In an effort to resolve the problem, Arthur Comey used his position as chairman of the NETC to appoint an overall AT coordinator, to supervise the work of both groups. Comey's choice was a splendid trailsman: a young General Electric engineer named Harland P. Sisk, who had served several summers on the AMC's White Mountain trail crew and was C. W. Blood's stepson. But, though probably the most knowledgeable nuts-and-bolts trail-builder in western Massachusetts at the time, Sisk also was something of an outsider to the locals.

From the distance of more than half a century later, relying on fragmentary reports, newspaper stories, correspondence, and memorabilia and recollections of one or two of the original participants and a number of their descendants, it is difficult to establish how much of the real work of building the trail was done by which group. It seems fair to say that the Berkshire Hills Conference group (Couch, Bailey, Sloper, and others working with them) had constructed virtually the entire AT throughout Massachusetts but that they never quite finished all the sections. Newspaper articles of the period repeatedly report sections as "practically completed," "nearly completed," "all finished except . . . ," and similar phrases. A longtime hiker who moved to the Pittsfield area in 1928 recalls that the trail was mostly completed then. However, it was neither well marked nor consistently maintained. By the summer of 1931 outside observers felt that the Massachusetts AT picture was "pretty stagnant."

In November and December 1931, at Comey's request, Myron Avery made two trips to "whirl through the Berkshires." Far from bringing the factions together, Avery snapped to the opinion that the AT's best interests lay with the Berkshire Chapter, so he set about undermining the authority of Couch, and eventually even of Comey and Sisk. During one of his "whirls" through the Massachusetts AT, accompanied by John Dickson of the Berkshire Chapter, Dickson proposed visiting Couch for the purpose of coordinating plans—but Avery opposed the idea of even visiting him. While at first backing Sisk over Couch, Avery soon lost patience with Sisk, described Comey's arrangements as "an absolute failure," and strove to have the Berkshire Chapter assume full authority for the state. Perkins and Comey defended Sisk's role but to no avail. Comey warned Avery that he was antagonizing many local trail workers. In January 1933 Couch wrote a one-page letter to Avery, asserting the continuing authority of the Berkshire Hills Conference. He got back a stinging three-page reply in which Avery denounced Couch's group for inaction and use of unauthorized trail signs, praised the Berkshire Chapter, and made clear that the

ATC would not recognize any statewide role for Couch's committee. As a mild and peace-loving Scout leader, Couch apparently was not one to keep up a controversy with so formidable an antagonist; his role and that of most of the previously active locals seems to have ceased altogether after 1932.

Under the skillful leadership of Dickson and Newton, the Berkshire Chapter volunteers completed the entire Massachusetts AT during the years 1932–35, but the alienation of the locals had its price. Once the original work was done, a period ensued (1936–37) during which little interest could be generated among Berkshire Chapter people in traveling west to work on the AT. ("The Berkshire Chapter of the A. M. C. were on the other side of the Connecticut River and had other interests," one local hiker told Torrey in 1938.) Trail maintenance virtually ceased, and the Massachusetts AT was well on its way to disappearing.

Between 1937 and 1940 two new groups saved the situation. The Mount Greylock Ski Club, formed in 1932, was made up primarily of skiers who devoted summertime weekends to trail maintenance. They agreed to take over the northern half. From this local group emerged a man who became increasingly interested in taking responsibility for the Massachusetts AT. Max Sauter began work in 1938. For the next four decades, he was a one-man trail crew, and Massachusetts finally was blessed with what had been missing during the 1920s and 1930s: a single dedicated, energetic, capable trail worker—the role played by Stevens and Anderson in their respective states during the formative years.

The second group was Metawampe, the faculty outing club of Massachusetts State College (now the University of Massachusetts) at Amherst. This club adopted the central section between Tyringham and Washington, leaving the Berkshire Chapter just the south end. Though an "outsider" group, Metawampe was going through a period of dynamic leadership under such men as John Vondell and Ralph Van Meter. From 1940 on they became reliable maintainers.

The stormy Massachusetts story illustrated several aspects of early AT history: the value of one strong, dedicated leader, such as Stevens and Anderson; the potentially counterproductive effects of strong national (ATC) leadership when not sensibly managed; and above all the importance of a strong local base of trail workers. Though a combination of outsiders and belated local efforts eventually completed the AT through the Berkshires, a legacy of bad feelings has haunted AT activity in that area ever since.

AT building: Vermont and New Hampshire

Putting the trail through Vermont and New Hampshire was greatly simplified by the prior existence of the Long Trail in the former; the long-standing AMC trails in the White Mountains, then in the process of being linked together by the work of Blood, Jenks, Goodrich, and Harrington; and the trails near the Connecticut River built and maintained by the Dartmouth Outing Club. All that was required was to designate which of these trails were to be used for the AT's odyssey. The only new work was an 18-mile link between the Long Trail at Sherburne Pass near Killington and the westernmost DOC trails across the river from Hanover. In 1927 DOC trail workers marked at least part of the way. In 1928 the Norwich Outing Club, heirs to the Alden Partridge mantle, worked on more of it. Apparently the college lads did not clear this route consistently, however, as in 1930 it was recut by GMC trailsman Willis M. Ross. Even the GMC was lax about keeping it cleared for a couple of years, but from 1934 on it seems to have been well maintained until the neglect occasioned by World War II, when it became virtually impassable.

MacKaye had originally conceived Mount Washington as the northern terminus of the supertrail. When Blood and Jenks opened the Mahoosucs into Maine by 1926, there seemed no good reason not to extend the trail over that magnificent country. Once it was in Maine, Katahdin beckoned. But even after the rest of the Northeastern AT was substantially complete, the Maine woods presented a 280-mile problem.

AT building: Maine

In 1925 Arthur Comey made the first foray beyond the Mahoosucs, scouting route possibilities from Grafton Notch over Baldpate and Moody Mountain as far as Old Blue and Elephant Mountains (see figure 45.3),

> following fishermen's and hunters' trails and even deer runs, along old lumber roads, along streams and across divides—unsigned, uncleared, yet often with excellent or at least unmistakable footways.

In autumn of that year a man named Henry Poor actually cut an isolated fragment of the Maine AT from Black Brook Notch to the summit of Old Blue. In 1927 Judge Perkins and the Connecticut AMC started from the other end, scouting and marking a route "on existing trails and wood roads" from Katahdin's Hunt Trail to Ripogenus Dam. They walked on along auto roads to Big Squaw Mountain near Moosehead Lake. And somewhat more hastily they took wood roads and rangers' trails westward to the edge of the Bigelow Range. In 1929 Comey returned to cross the remaining gap between Old Blue and Bigelow, traversing some wild country and such stunning summits as Elephant, Saddleback, Abraham, Sugarloaf, and the Bigelows. As of 1929 Comey and Perkins thought they had roughed out a good route all across Maine,

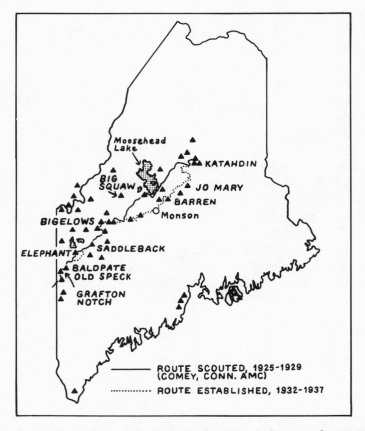

Figure 45.3. Building the Appalachian Trail in Maine In 1925 the versatile and eccentric Arthur Comey was the first to scout a proposed route for the Appalachian Trail through the state of Maine. In 1927 a group from the AMC's Connecticut Chapter marked out a route from Katahdin to Moosehead Lake, following a totally different path from today's AT. In 1929 Comey did more scouting for this northern route. All these efforts came to naught, and new trail-builders during the mid-1930s located the AT in an entirely new place.

considerably north of where the present AT lies. However, neither they nor anyone else followed up on the ground, and all that work went down the drain.

So in 1932 began a fresh start, with the appearance of two key figures. The first was Walter D. Greene, a Broadway actor who summered regularly at Sebec Lake in central Maine and knew intimately the bristling ridges of the Barren-Chairback Range, one of the knottiest stretches of Maine woods but also one of the most interesting. In 1932 he began to scout the new route. The second was Shailer S. Philbrick, a geologist who undertook in 1931 and 1932 a detailed topographic and geologic map of the Barren-Chairback Range and its environs. Avery heard about

Philbrick's project and sought him out to obtain a copy of his map. Sensing a good worker, Avery suggested that Philbrick might wish to help mark and clear Greene's new route. Philbrick agreed:

> I was receptive to Avery's suggestion about Barren because it would be necessary to camp on Barren or Fourth to study the geology of those two mountains. Why not mark the Trail on Barren and do the geology from the same camps and at the same time?

In the summer of 1932, with the help of two unemployed woodsmen, Lyman Davis and Elwood Lord, Philbrick marked much of the route through the thickest of the wilderness.

By 1933 Avery felt that most of the rest of the AT was completed and the stage was set for going to work in earnest on Maine. Though a Washington lawyer, Avery was delighted at the prospect of returning to his native state. On August 19, 1933, Avery, Philbrick, and two of Avery's PATC friends assembled on the summit of Katahdin with paintbrushes and buckets, paint both blue and white, signs and galvanized iron AT markers, a post, axes, hammers and nails, and half a bicycle, a device for measuring trail mileage. They planted their post in the summit cairn of Katahdin, nailed up a board sign, declared it the northern terminus of the AT, and began marking with paint and cairns across the Tableland and down the Hunt Trail, heading for Georgia. For two weeks they cleared and blazed along the tote roads, old trails, and, with Greene joining them, over the newly marked route on the tough spruce-fir ridge of the Barren-Chairback and on to Monson. To reach their goal, the group worked literally from dawn until past dusk on the last four days, blowdowns giving them fits. But they *did* get through by Labor Day. In that pioneering fortnight's work, Avery's wheel recorded 118.7 miles from the summit of Katahdin. During the next month Philbrick came back and, with the help of Elwood Lord and local fire wardens, pushed the route another 54.8 miles to the Bigelows. A gap of just 100 more miles remained to Grafton Notch and the Mahoosucs.

In 1934 two more vital pieces of the puzzle fitted into place. One was a great tree of a man, Helon Taylor, a north country original, born and raised in the shadow of Bigelow Mountain. Taylor became a Maine guide at age eighteen and entered the Maine Warden Service in 1929. Taylor sparked legends of his strength and prowess on snowshoes or afoot through the wilderness. In 1932 Avery sent him a letter asking him to explore an AT route across the Bigelows. Taylor flew into the job with the force of a hurricane. In 1933 and 1934 he scouted and cut a spectacular stretch of trail across the horned summits of the Bigelows and south over Sugarloaf, Maine's highest peak outside the Katahdin group. In 1935, with the help of two other wardens, he pushed the trail through dense conifer forests to the rocky ridge of Saddleback. Taylor also cut side trails on the Bigelow Range, opening up that striking country to hikers for the first time.

The last major piece to be filled in fell to the Bates College Outing Club. In 1934 Avery contacted a Bates faculty member, William H. Sawyer, Jr., faculty adviser to the Outing Club, and suggested scouting the AT as a club project. Sawyer picked up the challenge. That summer Sawyer and three high-spirited Bates students (Sammy Fuller, '35, Ed Aldrich, '35, and Harold ["Ace"] Bailey, '36) spent a week scouting a route for the missing section between the Mahoosucs and Helon Taylor's trail on the east. The following year Professor Sawyer, Ace Bailey, and some new Outing Club recruits were back to clear part of the route.[d]

By 1935 the Maine AT was largely scouted and marked, but a thorough clearing of the western sections had not been completed. At this point James W. Sewall, forester for CCC camps in Maine, offered to put his legions to work clearing the AT. Avery eagerly accepted. By the following summer six crews of fifteen CCC workers each were clearing a wide swath through that once daunting "utter wilderness." On August 14, 1937, on the south slope of Sugarloaf, the last leg of the entire Maine-Georgia trail was cleared by a CCC crew and Avery pronounced the Appalachian Trail complete (see figure 45.3).

The Maine AT was and remains a distinctive part of the great trail. As originally laid out it was largely a patchwork of old logging roads and its shelters largely sportsmen's camps, then a popular feature of the Maine woods. (In an odd juxtaposition, the earliest route descriptions, which mention repeatedly the "utter wilderness" character of the Maine AT, incorporated names and locations of sporting camps where indoor accommodations could be enjoyed, with prepared meals, telephone hookups, and other civilized conveniences.) But over the years relocations took the trail out of the valley wood roads and away from the sporting camps, many of which were passing from the scene. Gradually more primitive, open-front shelters were built along the entire route, at first by the CCC crews. Trail relocations and the later shelters alike were built by the Northeast's sole major club organized exclusively for work on the AT: the Maine Appalachian Trail Club. During prewar years Avery and his Washington, D.C., friends constituted the active membership of MATC, making annual work trips from there to Maine for trail maintenance. Not until postwar years did membership and ultimately leadership as well pass to Maine locals. Under the watchful eye of MATC trail workers, the Maine AT evolved a hiking flavor all its own, regarded by generations of through-hikers as one of the most memorable stretches of the 2,100-mile trail.

---

[d]Besides Bates, other groups became involved briefly in scouting this part of the trail. The section just west of Saddleback was initially scouted in the spring of 1934 by that small Portland-based club with the imposing name, Eastern States Mountain Club (Torrey, "Long Brown Path," June 26, 1934). That fall (after the Bates boys had been through) some Bowdoin students laid string on Baldpate (letter from John S. Holden to L&GW, June 7, 1984).

Characteristics of the Appalachian Trail in its early days

The Appalachian Trail is such an established institution today that we tend to take many of its attributes for granted. From its genesis in the fertile imagination of Benton MacKaye, however, it might have embarked on roads quite different from the one it has taken (see figure 45.4). For example, it became strictly a trail; the food and farm camps and associated socialist utopian schemes never materialized. Furthermore, it is strictly a foot trail, with as little road walking as possible, and decidedly a backpacker's trail, rather than a casual inn-to-inn stroller's. These are qualities that were not inevitable: the AT might have become more like the "Mohawk Trail" and other highway routes, slightly reoriented to pedestrian purposes. That it did not was through the accident of which people came to dominate its directions—in the Northeast this was the hiking community of which MacKaye was not originally a part, but from which came Torrey, Stevens, Anderson, and the clubs that valued wilderness attributes ahead of creature comforts.

The extensive use of private land for the trail route and the extraordinary decentralization of responsibility were two other distinctive qualities established during the formative years. Early correspondence among the trail's initial planners—MacKaye, Stein, Torrey, Turner—conveys the impression that they were convinced that it would have to be entirely on public lands, that it would be hopelessly unmanageable to have a 2,100-mile trail that greatly depended on the goodwill of private owners. In fact one reason the project bogged down during the first five years was the planners' disappointment at being unable to string together publicly owned land, for example, in eastern New York and Connecticut. These early AT planners may have envisioned the entire trail as something that just a few of them would have to put together—hence the utter impossibility of dealing with a myriad of local landowners. They did not foresee the incredible diversity and dispersion of authority that came to characterize the AT community. The key to building and maintaining a 2,100-mile trail, so much of which marched across private land, turned out to lie in a chaotic and virtually uncontrolled decentralization of responsibility down to the Murray Stevenses and Ned Andersons and their successors on the trail-maintenance front, like Max Sauter and the MATC-PATC maintainers. Through the diplomacy of the early trail-builders and the cooperation of a long list of private owners, not least the paper companies that owned the Maine woods, a tradition of responsible recreational use of privately owned land was nurtured. The trail corridor became a mosaic of many kinds of land ownership.

For the job of trail maintenance, less enterprising pioneers might have believed that only some governmental agency, state or federal, could supply the paid manpower to keep the long trail cleared. Indeed, for a

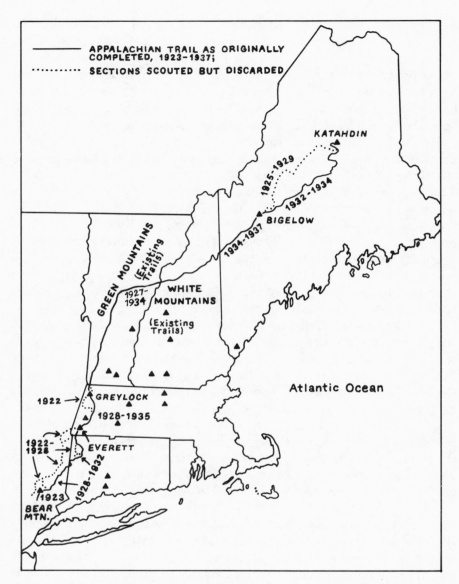

Figure 45.4. The Appalachian Trail: Dreams versus reality This map shows the general route that the Appalachian Trail took through the Northeast when it was finally completed in 1937. Also shown are the various major alternative locations that were considered during the planning stages, largely during the 1920s.

while in Maine, under Avery's arrangements with the CCC, it almost went this direction. Instead, the more difficult but ultimately more successful system of individuals and hiking clubs doing the work themselves took firm root.

Today most people associate the AT with long-distance "through-hiking." That was *not* the case at its origins, not until well after World War II. It was designed and used for relatively short trips. Avery and others actually frowned on the "stunt" of hiking long distances. Walter Prichard Eaton had predicted, "Nobody, or practically nobody, would ever tramp more than a fraction of its length." Even a segment like the Maine AT was not intended for through-hiking, as Avery made clear:

> We do not regard the existence of the Trail in Maine as presenting an opportunity for a stunt; that is, to travel the entire 266-mile section in the state in one summer.

Several individuals announced plans to do the whole route continuously, some with great fanfare, but they were viewed as a nut fringe. A bearded and long-haired Dane, Eiler U. Larson, precursor of a generation that lay forty years ahead, started out in 1930 to do a through-hike, but dropped out and wound up a much photographed fixture at Dupont Circle in Washington, D.C., greeting office workers with a flashing smile, hoping "to pull at least one depression-bowed mortal out of the doldrums each day."[e]

During the prewar years the AT occupied a relatively modest niche in Northeastern hiking. The region's trail makers perceived their local trail systems as providing the primary benefits for hikers, and the AT was a kind of novelty side attraction. "The A. T. is of minor importance in New England," Connecticut's Heermance told NETC colleagues. Those who stayed in AMC huts and tramped around the White Mountain trails rarely gave a thought to when they were or weren't on the AT. Its prewar importance loomed larger in the South, which had no long tradition of preexisting networks of local recreational trails.

Sometimes in fact the importance that ATC "outsiders" attempted to attach to what they sometimes called "the Trail" irritated New England locals. After one galling exchange with Avery, Heermance complained that the AT "has been a continual headache." For a while GMC trailsmen refused to allow AT markers on the Long Trail. In 1928 the Dartmouth Outing Club balked at permitting the AT on DOC trails and cabins.

The big trail's more prominent and positive profile of recent years is an outgrowth of postwar developments: the growth of long-distance through-hiking, the steady flow of end-to-enders encountered on the various segments of the trail during the latter part of the summer, publicity that some of them have sought and obtained in books and high-circulation magazines, federal legislation providing for the trail's protection,

---

[e]Other early through-hiking aspirants, none of whom succeeded in completing a continuous end-to-end hike included R. R. Ozmer of Tennessee in 1929 (Torrey, "Long Brown Path," Apr. 25, 1929, and "Walking the Entire Appalachian Trail," *Mountain Magazine* [July 1929], p. 88); and Edward Damp of New Hampshire in 1939 (Damp, "Of Mules, Mice, and Madison," *Appalachia* [Dec. 1980], p. 55).

and the association of the federal protection program with the conservationist cause. Before the war the AT enjoyed a quieter, more modest, more innocent youth. But the seeds of its greatness were planted back there on the dusty roads of eastern New York State by Murray Stevens, through the rambling hills on northwestern Connecticut by Ned Anderson, among the Berkshire ridges by Cap Couch's Boy Scouts, and across the coniferous forests of Maine by Helon Taylor, Shailer Philbrick, and a dozen others. Here and throughout its 2,100-mile length, an army of unpaid mercenaries transformed MacKaye's dream into a hiker's terrestial paradise.

Chapter 46

Superhiking

FROM time to time in every age and mountain range, individuals of exceptional strength or determination set out to show what they can do in that most rugged of physical testing grounds, the mountains. We shall call this fine form of fanaticism "superhiking."

Alden Partridge was the spiritual father of American superhikers, of course. After him, the earliest records of deliberately competitive mountain walking in the Northeast included a flurry of fast walks up Mount Washington during the 1850s.

In the next generation, Randolph hikers Eugene Cook and George Sargent conceived the one-day traverse of all the peaks in the Presidential Range, a feat that has remained a test piece ever since. On September 27, 1882, Cook and Sargent walked from Randolph across the entire range—24 miles and about 10,000 feet of uphill—in time to enjoy supper at the White Mountain House in Crawford Notch. After supper they set out by road over Jefferson Notch, walking 18.5 miles back to Randolph by 1:24 A.M. On July 12, 1904, another strong pair, Herschel Parker and Warren Symonds, duplicated this feat, adding a bushwhack over then trailless Jackson and Webster, completing the task in just over twenty-two hours. Symonds later did a double Presidential traverse: Crawford Notch to Randolph by lunchtime, then back over (not around) all the peaks, reaching Crawford House at precisely midnight. To this day superhikers relish the Presidential traverse as proof of prowess, though they generally miss the spice of bushwhacking part of the way or walking 18.5 miles after dinner (see figure 46.1).

In the Adirondacks superhikers focused on the Great Range. In July 1892 the Reverend Walter Lowrie and a friend, Malcolm MacLaren, hiked from Keene Valley up the Johns Brook valley to Marcy and over to Haystack by noon, then embarked on a long bushwhack over Basin and Saddleback to Gothics, then down via trail. On August 5, 1894, Newell Martin pulled off what a later superhiker called "probably the most remarkable one day's climbing ever done in the Adirondacks" by doing the Lowrie route in reverse but adding Skylight. The Great Range traverse

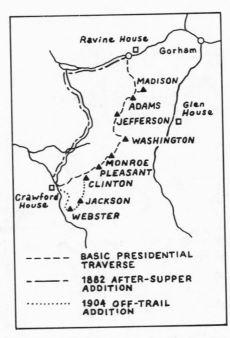

Figure 46.1. The Presidential traverse, then and now A major test piece for ambitious hikers from the late nineteenth century to the present day is the one-day traverse of all the major peaks of the Presidential Range in the White Mountains. The basic itinerary is shown on this map, along with some of the variations thrown in by the hearty. Note that when the 1904 party included Webster and Jackson in the traverse, they had no marked trails to help them but bushwhacked that entire portion of the trip.

continued to be popular during the early 1900s, especially for the spirited youth of the Putnam Camp, but by their day a definite trail had softened the bushwhack ordeal that Lowrie and Martin had known. Like the Presidential traverse, the Great Range continues to attract the attentions of superhikers today (see figure 46.2).

In the Catskills, during the first decade of this century, the Lingernot Society sponsored a competition for walking the most miles in a summer.

Dartmouth's long walks

Soon after the Dartmouth Outing Club was launched (1909), it began to award prizes for those undergraduates who covered the most miles during the school year on foot, skis, and snowshoes. This led to a series of walks that merit high rank in the annals of superhiking.

In 1919 a husky junior named William P. Fowler compiled a record 681 miles on foot on club outings. On April 29, 1919, Fowler and a friend

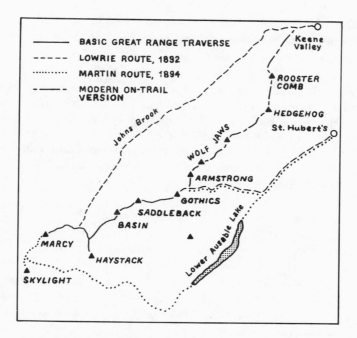

Figure 46.2. The Great Range traverse, then and now In the Adirondacks, a test piece comparable to the Presidential traverse is the one-day crossing of the major peaks of the Great Range, culminating with Mount Marcy. This feat was first attempted during the 1890s when much of the route was trailless. A modern version of the Great Range traverse includes even more summits than those originally climbed—as many as eleven distinct summits to be climbed in one day—but the existence of a good hiking trail eases the rigors of the trip.

walked 52 miles from Hanover to the town of Pike, New Hampshire, in a single day. Rising to the challenge, a senior by the name of Sherman Adams took off from Hanover less than a week later (May 4), forcing himself 62 miles to the town of Putney. "The only reason that I stopped at Putney," scoffed the future trail crew boss and governor of New Hampshire, "was because I could neither see, walk, nor eat." One week after that, Fowler and classmate John Herbert set off to break that record, doing 66 miles in one day from Littleton to Lyme Center. At the first break between classes the next day, Fowler met Adams in the hall to tell him they'd beaten his record. Adams had news for him. On the same day, still another Big Green superwalker, Warren F. Daniell III, had covered 69 miles from Hanover to Woodsville and partway back. Daniell's record held for all of one year.

In the summer of 1919, Adams worked on AMC's trail crew, climbing Willey before work each day. That winter, as president of the Outing Club, he led a succession of formidable winter trips. "By spring," he recalled, "I was as tough as a boiled owl forgotten by the chef and grossly overcooked." During April and May he climbed Happy Hill and back, a 10-mile round trip, before morning classes each day. Fowler recalled the 130-pound Adams in those days as

> slender, wiry, and with muscles of steel—a living refutation of the theory that long legs are essential to fast walking. . . . Of him alone will I admit that I have seen times when he could walk me ragged. He was a driver, sparing neither himself nor companions. . . . Neither Dan [Warren Daniell] nor I ever had quite the speed and dash that Sherm could display as he snapped along for mile after mile, his whole frame shaking from his machine-like muscle-action.

That spring saw Fowler in top condition too. Taller and more heavily built than Adams, Fowler was noted for endurance more than speed. "He possessed more sheer guts than most anybody I ever knew," said Adams in 1971, having known a few people in the intervening years. Both were dedicated to physical fitness—"didn't drink, smoke, and was not addicted to hell-raising," said Adams of Fowler approvingly, in reference to qualities that not all Dartmouth undergraduates then or now might have perceived as positive.

At midnight on the thirty-first of May, 1920, Adams and Fowler left Skyline Cabin, north of Franconia Notch, at a blistering pace. Over Franconia Notch, Kinsman Notch, and the shoulder of Moosilauke, on through the Dartmouth chain of mountain cabins, 83 miles to Hanover, with a vertical rise of 5,600 feet and descent of 6,500 feet, "over a course that was crammed with natural obstacles," combining 23 miles of hiking trails with another 60 of roads, the two established the premier one-day hiking feat in DOC annals, ever since recalled but never repeated by generations of DOC trampers. That fall Warren Daniell outdid their mileage by pacing off 86 miles from Hanover to Hinsdale, New Hampshire, in one day, an incredible feat in its own right but never saluted as much by posterity, perhaps because it did not involve the rugged mountainous terrain. College outing clubs being subject to cyclical turns of fancy, the mania for long walks suddenly died after 1920, leaving the Adams-Fowler tour de force of that year as its lasting monument.

The Adirondack forty-six

The next outstanding superhiking achievement had an entirely different objective and style. Louis Marshall, a great lawyer and New York civic leader, had a summer home on Lower Saranac Lake and was a charter member of the Adirondack Mountain Club. His teenage sons, Robert and George, began to climb mountains, starting with Ampersand in 1916. In 1918 a Saranac guide who had rarely climbed a mountain before in his life, named Herbert Clark, a regular employee of the Marshall family during previous summers, set about to take the boys on various hikes up Whiteface, Marcy, Algonquin, and Iroquois. As they surveyed the panorama of peaks from those summits, ambitions formed of climbing them all. In 1918 Robert was eighteen and George fifteen, while Clark was forty-eight; but the number with which the names of all three became indelibly linked was "forty-six"—the number of peaks that they figured were over 4,000 feet in height.

When the Marshall brothers and Herb Clark set out to climb the Adirondack forty-six, it was the start of one of the golden adventures of twentieth-century hiking. Whatever "stunt" quality may be associated with later peakbagging, this first voyage into that realm had the aura of a quest. No account of their climbs fails to convey a magic mixture of high spirits, awe and admiration of the rugged beauties of the peaks, sheer physical delight in strenuous exercise, and close companionship. The relationship between the two boisterous youths and the quiet, middle-aged woodsman was close. Another Adirondack hiker who met them on a remote mountainside during their original quest recalled,

> Clark was obviously more mature, but their relationship seemed to be that of three pals, not that of leader and followers. I *think* I remember noting that the two boys were not handsome but that they seemed like nice guys to be camping with. . . . Nothing was mentioned about the fact that they were in the process of climbing all the 4000-foot mountains in the Adirondacks.

Bob Marshall crackled with joyous energy and humor, a rugged six-footer brimming with "great gusto and infectious enthusiasms," under all of which lay a profound love and respect for the primitive qualities of wilderness, along with an unquenchable zest for robust physical exertions. Another trait, for which history can thank him, was an accountant's passion for keeping elaborate statistics on all his climbs. He could recount with precision that, as of October 1937, he had been on two hundred 30-mile one-day walks, fifty-one 40-milers, and others up to 70 miles in one day. In later life he became "one of the most significant and vigorous conservationists in American history," holding high government posts from which he tirelessly promoted the cause of wilderness, until suddenly struck dead at age thirty-nine.

George Marshall spent a long lifetime in the shadows, first of Bob's larger-than-life presence and later of his brother's memory as a kind of martyr to the wilderness cause. Yet George was almost his brother's equal afoot in the hills and in the promotion of conservation causes throughout a long life.

Of Herbert Clark, Bob Marshall said,

> Herb has been not only the greatest teacher that I ever had, but also the most kindly and considerate friend. . . . a constantly refreshing and stimulating companion. . . . the happy possessor of the keenest sense of humor I have known.

Throughout their explorations of the then little-known 4,000-footers, Clark kept up a constant banter and needling of the youths, invented yarns and doggerel for every occasion, conveyed to them his quiet reverence for the loveliness of the woods or the magnificence of a mountain vista, while keeping up their spirits with nonstop humor during the low moments of rainy bushwhacks through the cripplebrush. (He solemnly assured them that the battle of the *Monitor* and the *Merrimac* had been fought on the Ausable River just east of Lake Placid, pointing out for proof holes where shells had landed.) His personal qualities aside, he discovered a natural talent for the Adirondack wilderness—"the fastest man I have ever known in the pathless woods," according to Bob Marshall, and possessed of an uncanny sense of direction and of sensing the path of least resistance through blowdown and scrub.

The realm of the Adirondack high peaks that these three first climbed during the early 1920s was a different world from what it is today. Lumbering operations rendered some areas at once more accessible of approach and more difficult to navigate in once one left the logging roads (due to slash and the inscrutability of the course of abandoned roads). Only about half of the forty-six peaks had trails. Perhaps as many as eight had never been climbed before—three in the Dix Range, Street and Nye west of Algonquin, Couchsachraga in the Cold River country, remote Allen, and the little peak with three names, two of which attempt to honor the three first ascensionists (Marshall or Herbert—or Clinton). Over many a blowdown, through many a rainstorm, into many a twilight stagger through the woods and long walk back along dusty roads, to popular lodestones like Marcy and featureless plateaus of thickets like Table Top, finally ending together on Mount Emmons on June 10, 1925, the three close friends took their solitary way, etching an unforgettable chapter in the records of northeastern mountain history.

Climbing the Adirondack "forty-six" was at first an isolated feat by those three. Within the growing community of Adirondack hiking, it was not long before others took note of the accomplishment. In Ausable Club circles, Henry Goddard Leach, Joseph Boyce, and Adelaide Marble started a club to promote climbing them all, more or less under the tent of the Adirondack Trail Improvement Society. The twin brothers Jerry and Peter Hunsaker were the first in this group to complete all forty-six peaks. Independently, Fay Loope of the Schenectady YMCA reached that goal in 1933, followed two years later by that Florida tiger, Herbert Malcolm, a speedy tramper of whom more will be heard presently.

Still another circle of interest was in Troy, New York, during the mid-1930s. Among many outdoor-lovers in that town was a group of sturdy hikers who attended the Grace Methodist Church, where the minister himself, the Reverend Ernest R. Ryder, was a vigorous devotee of Adirondack high country, not above holding the Sunday service on a peak if that was the weekend's agenda. The Reverend Mr. Ryder and some of the parishioners, notably Edward C. Hudowalski, gradually raised their sights from casual mountain climbing to systematic peakbagging, completing the Marshalls' forty-six on Dix in a dense fog on September 13, 1936. Soon after, others of the parish took out after the goal and in the process formed a club destined to evolve into a major force in the Adirondacks, second in importance only to the Adirondack Mountain Club itself. The original club was known as the Forty-Sixers of Troy, New York. It was the antecedent of today's Adirondack Forty-Sixers, organized on May 30, 1948, with Troy's Grace Hudowalski (Ed's wife) as first president. During postwar years the numbers of Forty-Sixers swelled annually, passing the one thousand mark in 1974 and two thousand in 1984. Though new topographical measurements have played havoc with the original list of forty-six peaks, several of which proved to be well under 4,000 feet, loyal forty-sixer followers clung to the original list as constituting the peaks to be climbed by all those who aspired to the roster. The first three numbers on that roster proudly record the names of Herbert Clark, Bob Marshall, and George Marshall.

"Big days"

An offshoot of Bob Marshall's peakbagging was his zest for the pleasures of a big day in the mountains. Once in 1920, from a camp in Panther Gorge, the threesome climbed Haystack, Basin, Saddleback, and Gothics, and then went back over the same route to their camp. Other big days followed, until in 1930 they broke Newell Martin's record of six peaks in a day by surmounting nine, though with more help from trails than Martin had. Now this new challenge was thrown out, and other joined in. On August 20, 1931, a professor from Syracuse University, Ernest S. Griffith, climbed ten peaks in a day. The following July Bob Marshall upped that to fourteen peaks in a day. That summer a new contestant entered the lists and soon established records that none could surpass. Australian-born Herbert L. Malcolm, a "demon of energy," had been a schoolmaster in Lake Placid in the 1910s and early 1920s, before moving to Florida to become a successful hotel manager. Still summering in Lake Placid, Malcolm took up the gauntlet in October 1932 by climbing sixteen peaks in a single 30-mile day, topping that with eighteen peaks and 40 miles a year later. Malcolm also set records for vertical ascent, breaking Griffith's 1932 record of 16,930 vertical feet with 20,067 uphill feet in 1933, and eventually, on July 29, 1936, at age fifty-two, a single twelve-hour day in which he climbed 25,551 vertical feet, though by this time the itinerary was getting a bit contrived, including four separate ascents of Noonmark, three of them in succession at the end of the day.[a]

Meanwhile, over in New Hampshire, similar movements were underway. During the 1930s various lists of White Mountain 4,000-footers were compiled, so that by the AMC's traditional August Camp in 1935, people were conscious of "the determined assault of the 4000-foot mountain collectors." Peakbagging had spread from New York to New Hampshire. The original White Mountains list numbered forty-six too, providing perfect symmetry with the Adirondacks' forty-six. Subsequent topographical measurements raised the number of qualifying peaks in the White Mountains to forty-seven and later forty-eight. It is interesting to note the contrast in reaction to the news of new elevation figures. The Adirondack Forty-Sixers clung to tradition, rather than change their original list of peaks, inherited from the Marshall brothers and Herb Clark. The AMC committee in charge, lacking the sentimental loyalty to the Marshall tradition, added new peaks to its list when new measurements were announced. The explanation may lie in the preponderance of humanists (ministers, schoolteachers) in the ADK group, versus a preponderance of technical people (to whom either a peak is 4,000 feet or it isn't!) on the AMC committee. Whatever the cause, the two ranges now have not only different numbers (forty-six versus forty-eight) but different criteria (historical tradition versus strict measurement).

Besides peakbagging, the New Hampshire climbers also adopted the zeal of the Adirondacks for big achievements in a single day. The mortar in the last of the AMC huts was scarcely dry in 1932 before the crews of hutmen, waxing robust from much heavy packing of food and supplies, first conceived the idea of a nonstop traverse of the entire system of huts —a course of somewhat more than 50 miles and approximately 15,000 vertical feet. (The exact figures depend upon several minor options in the route.) On August 9, 1932, Stilly Williams, Hub Sise, and Dick Dodge, paced most of the way by Ray Falconer, walked from the hut at Lonesome Lake all the way across Mount Lafayette and the peaks of the Pemigewasset Wilderness, down into Crawford Notch, then up and over almost the entire Presidential Range to Madison Hut in just under twenty-four hours. That same summer, two other hutmen named Ev Loomis and Ralph Batchelder walked the entire hut system, Lonesome to

---

[a]Care must be taken with some old accounts of superhikes. Trail mileages had not been measured with precision and were often overestimated. For example, the Marshalls recorded their Panther Gorge–Gothics trip as a 20-mile day with nearly 10,000 feet of elevation, and their Dix traverse as a 30-mile day, 20 of it off-trail, with 7,800 feet of elevation gained. An attempt to trace these itineraries on modern maps suggests that the former was more like 12 miles with 7,000 feet of elevation, and the latter not quite 25 miles (depending on what road walking was involved getting to and from trails), with fewer than 7 miles off-trail and an elevation gain of less than 7,000 feet.

Madison and then down to Pinkham and over the rugged Wildcat ridge to Carter Notch, over a period of two days. The following year, Loomis and Batchelder took the obvious next step: on August 30–31, 1933, starting from Carter at 6:00P.M., they walked the entire chain of high huts (skipping the Wildcat Range but still including Pinkham) in just under twenty-four hours—over 50 miles and an ascent of 13,000 feet. This record lasted for three years, at which time the redoubtable Herbert Malcolm moved his place of summer vacation from Lake Placid to Randolph, New Hampshire. To Malcolm, a mountain hiking record was too clarion a challenge. On July 7, 1936, he cruised the huts course in a new record of twenty-two hours, after which he sat around Lonesome Hut with the crew, "the boys joshing me about going right on to Moosilauke." Two weeks later, July 22, 1936, he bettered that time over the same course in twenty-one hours, forty-three minutes. The remarkable aspect of Malcolm's huts traverse was that he started at Carter Notch and went over the Wildcats to Pinkham, before proceeding with the rest of the trip. Furthermore, when crossing the Presidentials he went over each summit. Thus his itinerary took in almost 3 miles and 3,500 feet of elevation more than the normal modern one-day huts traverse.

Various other kinds of "big days" developed in the White Mountains during these years. The spiny, twisty Mahoosuc Range was covered in a single day for the first time in 1940. Skier Sel Hannah walked all the known hiking trails of the White Mountains in a single summer. Batchelder carried 1,000 pounds of cement from the summit of Washington to Lakes-of-the-Clouds Hut in a single day, taking ten carries, each over 100 pounds (counting packboard), for a total distance of 30 miles and 13,000 feet up and another 13,000 fully-laden, knee-buckling feet down. In 1936 the first competitive road race up the 8-mile Mount Washington auto road was held, twelve runners participating; it has been held every year since, the time gradually being lowered to one hour from Francis Darrah's surprisingly good time of one hour, fifteen minutes, forty-eight seconds in 1936.

Speed hiking found a welcome home in the New York City hiking scene of the 1930s. Some of the new trans–Harriman Park trails were between 20 and 30 miles long, with railroad stations at each end. This was too obvious a challenge for one rugged day's walk by a strong hiker. The paint blazes on those classic trails may have been dried in part by the breezes created by passing speedsters trying to see how fast they could go from one end to the other. The star of these escapades was George Goldthwaite, the black-sneakered speed champion of the Fresh Air Club. He soon set records of five and a half hours for the 20.8-mile Ramapo-Dunderberg Trail and six hours, forty-four minutes for the somewhat longer Suffern–Bear Mountain route. During the late 1930s a kind of intercollegiate rivalry developed along the Suffern–Bear Mountain Trail. The City College Hiking Club and the New York University Outing Club entered representatives in what was billed then as a 29-mile race (compare with the present guidebook distance of 24.3 miles). In 1936 the CCHC's Fred Wandel broke Goldthwaite's record with a winning dash of six hours, thirty-five minutes. The following year his teammate Jack Friedman won honors with a new record of six hours, twenty-two minutes. With the passing of Torrey and his column in 1938, these events ceased to be so well reported, but metropolitan students and other New York hikers continued to use the Harriman Park transcontinentals for tests of hiking prowess.

A most rare species of the genus superhike was attained over a July weekend in 1932. When the Great Northern Paper Company's Basin Pond Camp opened up the east side of Katahdin in 1923, Allen Chamberlain had observed, "For exceptionally sturdy trampers the traverse of the mountain is now almost within the realm of a weekend trip." Nine years later, Katahdin's most enthusiastic tramper, Ron Gower, persuaded friends to help make that prophecy literally come true. The goal: to climb Katahdin from Boston in a weekend. This feat is not so difficult today, with all-day Saturday off, a good road all the way to within 3.5 miles of Chimney Pond, superhighways almost to Millinocket, and speedy, comfortable cars. In 1923 conditions were different: Saturday morning working hours, earlier vintage cars, and poor roads, especially near Katahdin. The four friends crammed into a Ford in front of Gower's house in Newton, Massachusetts at 1:00P.M. on Saturday and sped north. They traveled the 360 miles from Newton to Windey Pitch on the Millinocket Tote Road (then the last drivable stretch) in thirteen hours, averaging a heart-stopping 27 mph over the narrow, twisty, high-crowned, low-shouldered highways, including the final "twenty-three miles of bumps" from Millinocket. As refreshed as one might expect to be from thirteen hours in an old Ford over such roads, they started up the trail by flashlight at 2:30 A.M. on Sunday morning. For purposes of this feat, they declared that to climb Pamola was to climb Katahdin. They were on top at daybreak. Their choice of descent route is interesting: the Chimney. Today the Chimney is regarded as a technical climb, and park authorities require registration and special permission, plus approved technical equipment, including hard hat. But Gower and his friends, having driven and climbed all night, now plunged happily *down* the Chimney—as it began to rain and blow hard. "A sixty mile gale was blowing up it," recalled one of the party, "and the rocky walls were dripping water." When Gower's hat blew off, it sailed 100 feet *up* the Chimney. With a single 120-foot rope, they executed three rappels, on one of which they swung free under a waterfall, which ran down the neck and out the trouser-leg of each rappeler. On the bottom chockstone, the rope snagged—by this time it "was about as flexible as a wire cable"—and was therewith abandoned. They reached Dudley's cabin at 1:00 P.M. on Sunday, where they rested for an hour and enjoyed tea. Then they raced down the trail to the waiting Chariot of Democracy at Windey Pitch. The drive home began at 6:00 P.M., and took another thirteen and a half hours. Right on schedule, the old Ford pulled up in front of Gower's house at 7:30 A.M., and he was back in the office by 8:00 A.M. Monday—Katahdin in a weekend.

End-to-enders

People walking the entire 2,100-mile Appalachian Trail from Georgia to Maine have become such a frequent presence on today's Northeastern hiking scene that it is surprising to discover how recent is the phenomenon of long-distance hiking for recreation. The "end-to-end" movement indeed did not exist on the Appalachian Trail until after World War II. End-to-end hiking started on the Long Trail during the 1920s. For many years the Green Mountain Club officially ignored the achievement, uncertain whether to approve. In 1942 the club established an "emblematic award" and began keeping records of those who had walked the entire 262-mile trail. By the 1980s the total was well over one thousand.

One of the earliest to set his sights on the whole trail—even before the Jay-to-Canada section was complete—was also one of the most controversial. On June 30, 1926, Irving D. Appleby of Roxbury, Massachusetts, started from Jay Peak, then the northern terminus, and headed south. Appleby's register entries exhibited increasing swagger as he sped south: "They say Mansfield is a tough old climb but watch me hit it! . . . I feel the strength and speed of a panther! . . . If any son-of-a-gun ever does it faster I hope he chokes." On July 15 he was at the Massachusetts border. Having taken off a couple of days en route, he announced his record time as thirteen days and four and a half hours.

In 1927 Appleby was back, whirling south to north this time, and announced a new record of ten days and nineteen hours. By this time he was basking in the limelight of celebrity. On Mansfield he arrived at the Summit House at noon to find a "big crowd there. Splendid welcome." Writing from Boston to fellow publicity-lover James P. Taylor, he reported,

> During the coming two weeks the boots that I wore will be on exhibition in the main show window of a big shoe store on one of our busiest corners. They will have my whole outfit in the window, including several pictures. I estimate that over a million people will see the exhibit and a big show card will tell the story.

Taylor was delighted of course. He made sure that the Vermont State Chamber of Commerce gave full publicity to Appleby's performances and put out a special brochure of clippings about the feats, with an introductory reminder of the value of such publicity.

Officials of the Green Mountain Club were less impressed and considerably less pleased. In 1927 *The Long Trail News* wrote up the first trip, raising doubts on grounds that Appleby's reported itinerary was vague and, of course, that no one was with him to verify his claims. After the second trip the LTN again pointed out his lack of a specific record of dates and distances and went on to observe what it considered to be errors in his route description. Concluded the GMC fathers:

> In view of the seemingly incredible performance which he claims to have accomplished, and in the absence of more definite data, it is not surprising that there are some doubting Thomases among those who know the Trail well.

Angry exchanges of letters followed, until Appleby withdrew in a huff, canceling plans to do it again in 1928. By 1930 Appleby was regarded as a bad joke in GMC circles.

Later observers, even within the GMC hierarchy, are less certain that Appleby was in fact a fraud. Others have shown that 20-mile days are not out of the question. The doubts raised at the time have a nitpicking, mean-spirited ring. Whether his boasts were true or not cannot be determined today. The entire episode reflected no credit on anyone, least of all on the spirit of superhiking.

Superhiking never gained acceptance in the Green Mountains comparable to its prestige in the Adirondacks and the White Mountains. The Green Mountain Club has rather pointedly adopted a posture of discouraging speed records on the Long Trail. Though a club executive was quoted in 1978 as saying, "We don't encourage or discourage records," postwar Long Trail publications have carried admonitions against record setting and warned that the GMC wished to discourage "a competitive climate around the End-to-End accomplishment."

Critics of Superhiking

The GMC's skepticism reflects the fact that superhiking is not to everyone's taste. That some should find it "a rather tiresome pursuit" is not surprising. That others should react with emotional fury or attack the practice as a "distortion of values" or "sin," and that such criticism may be found from the very beginning, may surprise some readers—and appear quite logical to others. The strong feelings on either side of this issue are heated and have their roots deep in Northeastern hiking history.

During the 1880s, when the Randolph trails were just being built, an AMC party signed the new register on Mount Adams with scornful sarcasm:

We do not care what time we started nor how long it took to get here. What we know is we are here and are perfectly happy and are going but when we get ready.

Sweetser's pioneering guidebook castigated "foot-cavalry exploits," heaping ridicule on "the absurd rate of speed" of some students of that day. A 1905 critic voiced the complaint still heard today:

The desire to make record trips and travelling at speeds inconsistent with proper appreciation of the view and the peculiar charms of these lofty trails are apparently common faults.

When Sherman Adams and his DOC buddies set their records for long walks, their Dartmouth elders gently chided them in the *Alumni Magazine*:

One hesitates to bestow too much réclame upon performances like this, however interesting the records may be, because they evidently miss the real point in a walking tour and do not at all represent the usual intent and purpose of the Outing Club.

Robert Marshall himself took a genial, self-deprecatory view of his own exploits, comparing them to flagpole sitting and marathon dancing, two other popular pursuits of the 1920s. It was "like eating goldfish or anything else," recalled DOC superwalker Warren Daniell. "Records are really insignificant," Marshall added, "compared with the beautiful woods and mountain views seen on the way." The *New York Times'* well-known pundit John Kieran wrote disapprovingly of the "deliberate attempt to cover ground on foot, mile after mile." Lectured Kieran:

While this can be recommended as good for the body, it is not particularly good for the soul. It induces a certain superior attitude, an air of condescension toward those who cover lesser distances or no distance at all. It becomes a game, like golf, and the distance walker, boasting of the miles he has put behind him, may be quite as boring as the golfer going over his strokes before an audience that wishes him in Gehenna.

An early Appalachian Trail walker found her own goal acceptable, but only if taken at a relaxed pace. Of speedier superhikers, she disdained: "What folly to race through paradise!"

The superhikers' response

Superhikers themselves rarely came up with written defense of their activity, but some did. British alpinist Geoffrey Winthrop Young spoke eloquently in *Mountaincraft* both of the value of a good "pace" for safety reasons (the importance of getting off snow slopes before the warm afternoon sun made them avalanche-prone) and for the inherent pleasure in moving fast. Harry Wade Hicks of the Lake Placid Club argued that hikers gained a comparable pleasure, that superhiking could be undertaken in "the spirit of the true mountaineer." Herbert Malcolm, the most impressive (or most guilty, depending on the viewpoint) of prewar superhikers, spoke up for his ilk in a 1936 essay:

> My answer is that it is thoroughly enjoyable. . . . Dogs, birds, etc. seem to take a lot of exercise just for the joy there is in graceful motion. Why should not men and women get a thrill from using their strength just for the fun of it? There is an ecstacy in sustained motion among beautiful surroundings, in breezing over a mountain range seeing the whole gamut of views and lights and shadows in a single day, and coming in hungry and full of life at the end. . . . There is an elemental joy in this struggle with mountain, darkness and storm, spiced perhaps with a dash of fear which weakens your pride in your strength just enough to make the battle interesting, a joy that lingers delightfully in your memory.

A soothing commentary on this debate came, oddly enough, from one more accustomed to inflaming controversy than resolving it: Myron Avery. Himself both an extraordinary hiker proud of his prowess and also a critic of early long-distance AT hiking, Avery urged tolerance of many different ways of enjoying the mountains:

> Perhaps charity is lacking. Let him who seeks the hills do so for what reasons he may have or seem sufficient to himself. He may be there for sustained physical exertion, oblivious to all else, the desire to conquer a peak because it has beaten off all other aspirants, or "the zeal to learn visual geography," or the desire to know trees, study geology, insects, birds or revel in the sensuous delights of far-spread panoramic views. Granted that a minimum combination of all these rewards would represent the maximum to be derived from mountain or woods travel. But, if in lieu of the ideal, the recreationist concentrates upon any one of these factors, does it not require extreme confidence in the correctness of one's viewpoint dogmatically to condemn the impelling motive? Is it not enough that he is there for whatever motive seems sufficient to himself?

Chapter 47

The Bemis Crew

SUPERHIKING was one outlet for the ambitious. Another was winter climbing. Let us return to the snowshoers and skiers and see what kinds of adventures they were up to during the 1920s and 1930s

By the 1910s the venerable AMC Snow-Shoe Section had lost much of the zest it had displayed during the 1890s. Large numbers of happy Appies still turned out for Snow-Shoe Section outings, but the thirst for true adventure was gone. Its sojourns at the Ravine House and elsewhere were gradually becoming more and more social, clubby mass gatherings, with little new exploration or surprise. Some of the younger AMC winter climbers grew restless. The more impatient soon struck out on independent paths.

Willard Helburn was a big bluff man, a competent mountaineer with an enterprising turn of mind. He was one of New England's earliest pioneers in rock climbing, and winter climbing in New England appealed to him as another way to practice mountaineering arts needed for summertime climbing in the Alps. Helburn also saw winter escapades as a chance to have a lot of fun in the bargain. He joined the AMC Snow-Shoe Section on a couple of outings but soon decided that he could do better on his own.

In 1915, during an AMC winter excursion at the Ravine House, Helburn resurrected Herschel Parker's old dream of traversing all the major peaks of the Presidential Range in one day during the winter. As a veteran of big days in the Alps, he considered himself a fit candidate to try to achieve what had eluded the redoubtable Parker. Nevertheless, his first tries (in 1916 and 1917), starting from Randolph, were stopped short of Mount Washington by strong winds, ever the crucial factor in the success or failure of winter Presidential traverses.

On February 20, 1918, Helburn and his bride of less than a year (the former Margaret Mason), together with Henry Chamberlain and his wife, crossed over Mount Madison from the Ravine House to the Glen, descending the long Osgood Ridge on a smooth, hard crust that led to many an involuntary glissade and sitzmark. After a layover day in the Glen House, the two men set forth before dawn on Washington's

Birthday. For a couple of hours they snowshoed by candlelight, following the "dents" of their descent's mishaps. At treeline they switched from snowshoes to creepers and were up and over Madison in time to see "a beautiful sunrise glow" on Washington. The glow turned out to be prelude to a stormy day. Hurrying along the Gulfside Trail, looping over each summit as they went, they were engulfed by a snowstorm, which raged about them for most of the day. Despite this formidable distraction, they were over Adams, Jefferson, Clay, and Washington, and down to the Lakes of the Clouds by lunchtime. In the continuing storm, they lost track of the Crawford Path as they descended Monroe and plunged partway down into Oakes Gulf before realizing their mistake, necessitating a tedious backtrack. Indeed Chamberlain insisted that they reclimb Monroe to be sure they had really been on that summit in the clouds. On over Franklin and Pleasant (today's Eisenhower) they whirled through the storm, switching back to snowshoes in the trees south of Pleasant. From Clinton down they were delighted to find that other snowshoers (their AMC friends) had broken out the trail up from Crawford Notch. Twenty-two miles, nine summits, and fourteen hours after their morning's start, they arrived in Crawford Notch just too late for the afternoon train to Jackson but in time for a hearty supper and a night's lodging under lots of horse blankets. The next day they walked down the train tracks to Bartlett to join their fellow AMCers' special train back to Boston.

The importance of this event owes not so much to its intrinsic accomplishment, though 22 miles and nine summits (Monroe twice) is unusual in winter, especially under adverse conditions above treeline. But the day merits the attentions of posterity because of the symbolic importance that posterity has seen fit to bestow on the winter Presidential traverse. It has been ever the single biggest status symbol for the winter mountaineer, the Grand Prix or Stanley Cup or Heisman Trophy of winter climbing, the one big trip to which most aspiring practitioners of this mad art dedicate their ambitions. The success rate remains low and probably always will because of the caprices of Presidentials weather. Especially admired, and seldom attempted, is the feat of pulling it off in one day—or one moonlit night, as later (and much madder) climbers would attempt. Such lasting symbolic importance demands that history honor that long walk of Helburn and Chamberlain on February 22, 1918.

Other adventurous winter trips followed for Helburn. He and Chamberlain, along with Richard Mayer, traversed Mount Jefferson, descending the awesomely steep Six Husbands Trail, drenched in snow, some of which was "taken in a series of exciting jumps." Helburn later told Robert Underhill that this was his toughest winter trip ever, more of a trial than the traverse of the entire range. In March 1923 he and Margaret, with Chamberlain and four other AMCers made a trip to Katahdin, during which Helburn led the group up the Chimney and across the Knife Edge; and on another day, up the slide on South Turner.

Finding the typical AMC winter excursion too tame for his active tastes, Helburn and others of his fiber decided to organize a group of hardy winter climbers who could take on tough winter trips to interesting places. An official club trip had to take anyone who signed up, so the pace and ambitions might be limited. Furthermore, the group was not always congenial. The AMC had reached such a size that a smaller, more harmonious subculture might hold more attractions. Helburn and his friends wanted adventure.

Sic transit the Bemis Crew.

In February 1923 a select group of about twenty climbers gathered to spend a week at the Inn Unique in Crawford Notch, otherwise known as the old Bemis Place, where Dr. Samuel Bemis had once summered. Helburn put the group together as a like-minded, high-spirited, able-bodied collection of enthusiastic and competent climbers, without strict regard to club affiliation. Some were from New York, most from Boston. None were faint of heart.

Each day they snowshoed or skied, climbed mountains, and flagged freight trains up and down Crawford Notch. Each evening they gathered at the inn to feast, talk, sing, play cards, repair gear, and plot the next day's escapades. In that first year they climbed mainly around Crawford Notch—mountains such as Carrigain and Bemis, the steep slides on Webster Cliffs, trailless nooks in Oakes Gulf. Foul weather all week limited their mountaineering accomplishments during this first year but not their uproarious spirit. It was "a very congenial and fast travelling bunch," recalled one of the original members fifty-eight years later.

The first winter's outing was such an unqualified success that they decided to make it an annual event, and a tradition was born. The following winter, again in mid-February, the group reconvened at the Glen House but retained the name of its original location, ever after calling itself the "Bemis Crew."

The 1924 crowd was enlarged to thirty-six strong. They traveled by train from Boston and New York to Gorham, where they loaded trunks, ice axes, a few skis and ski poles, and a mountain of miscellaneous gear aboard a two-horse sled. Then, donning their snowshoes and rucksacks, they struck out up the unplowed road, leaving the horses, driver, sled, and gear to take their own time up the 9 miles to the hotel. Some of the snowshoers walked the road all the way, the others climbed up and over 2,404-foot Pine Mountain en route.

On the next day they all stormed up the carriage road, 8 miles and 4,600 vertical feet, to the summit of Mount Washington. For most parties that would be the day's adventure, to be followed by an easy descent back down the road. Not so for the Bemis Crew. Leaving the summit at

1:30, they struck over to the edge of the formidable Great Gulf, dropped off the headwall and plunged down into the gulf, picked up the trail and snowshoed out to the Glen House just at twilight—a 15-mile-plus day.

The morrow was no rest day. The group went up to Carter Notch, scrambled up Carter Dome, crossed over to Mount Height and back down, reveling in the long snowshoe glissades en route. Each day held new exploits: the Tuckerman headwall, descent over Boott Spur, Adams and Madison via Parapet Brook, Wildcat Mountain, the headwall of Huntington Ravine, ski runs down the bottom half of the Carriage Road, another ascent of Washington, in which they cavorted on the roofs of the summit buildings.

Bemis Crew trips continued every year: the Ravine House in 1925, Glen House in 1926, the Adirondacks in 1927, back to the Glen House in 1928, Lincoln in 1929.[a]

Snowshoes were the dominant Bemis mode of travel all through the 1920s, though some brought skis as well and used them for moderate ascents and on such downhill runs as the carriage road and the 19-Mile-Brook Trail out of Carter Notch. Helburn dispensed advice on equipment, recommending "stout," short, flat-toed snowshoes with coarse mesh. Snowshoe creepers or "Swiss crampons" were indispensable. He also insisted on ice axes for all:

> An ice axe is a pretty toy. It looks professional in the snapshots, serves to hook around the next tree on a steep woods-path, and is no heavier or more trouble on the trail than a loaded shotgun. However, I should as soon be in mid-ocean without a boat as on the headwall of Tuckerman's without an ice axe. Some of the notorious Bemis picks will be along for those who can't beg, borrow or steal ice axes, but the axe is the lesser evil.

Within the first year or two the group began to apply incongruous nautical terminology to their strictly landlocked voyages. They called themselves the Bemis "crew," referred to each winter's escapades as "the cruise of the good ship Bemis," and their mountaineering objectives as "ports of call." For tough trailbreaking in deep snow they employed the universal stratagem of switching the lead frequently, so that no one would be worn out from breaking trail. When it was time to switch trailbreakers, the call would go up, "Breakers ahead!"—adding further to the nautical irrelevance.

On some trips the crew historians kept careful track of mileage and elevation climbed by each crew member. An indication of the energy level of the crew is glimpsed from the fact that eight of the 1924 crew registered 20,000 feet of elevation climbed during the week. Three of those eight were women.

---

[a]The 1927 Adirondacks trip is described in chap. 49.

The Bemis Crew was such a volcanically democratic bunch of strong-minded individuals that it seems an affront to single out specific names as outstanding, other than Helburn, the originator. Besides Willard and Margaret Helburn and their perennial climbing crony Henry Chamberlain, some of the leading lights were:

Engineer Joe Wolcott, from the Helburn leather factory, who earned renown for his gargantuan repair truck full of tools and spare parts, by means of which he kept snowshoes, crampons, and other gear operative despite the formidable punishment inflicted upon it during each day.

Attorney Marjorie Hurd, that spirited, diminutive spitfire who was a pioneer in New England rock climbing, and her brother Jack, who functioned as the crew's "historians" on the early trips.

Various interesting individuals whom the reader has met before in wholly different contexts, such as the New York trail-builder J. Ashton Allis, Hanover's Nat Goodrich, and guidebook writer Walter Collins O'Kane.

On the later trips, such strong personalities as the rock climbers Robert Underhill and Miriam O'Brien, and the superb skier Arthur Comey.

A contingent of New York mountaineers with Western high-mountain experience, including Daniel Underhill (Robert's distant cousin), Ruth Langmuir (Irving's niece), John Van de Water (a "powerhouse," recalled Jack Hurd), alpinist Frank Waterman, and the flamboyant Nicholas Spadavecchia[b]

A formidable array of female climbers, who gave little ground to the males: Jessie Doe, who had climbed Katahdin's Chimney in winter with the Helburns in 1923; Wilhelmina Wright, a rock leader as well as winter climber; Florence Luscomb, alias "Haircomb," perennial champion of feminist causes and all other causes; the Pennock sisters, Grace and Helen; plus the aforementioned Margaret Helburn, Marjorie Hurd, Miriam O'Brien, and Ruth Langmuir.

In that 1924 Glen House gathering, Jack Van de Water had set the pace for the week with 26,800 feet of ascent, including two 4,600-foot days. Right behind him was Ruth Langmuir at 26,000 feet. In third place—ahead of all the men but Van de Water—was Helen Pennock at 24,900 feet, and not far behind was the effervescent Marjorie Hurd at 19,800 feet.

---

[b]This Frank Waterman, an active AMC winter climber from the New York City area during the 1920s, with a reputation for much mountaineering experience in the Alps, was no relation to the authors, as far as anyone knows.

It was a close-knit crew. Van de Water, finding himself relentlessly pursued around the peaks by the indefatigable Langmuir, soon married her. Beyond this match and that of Robert Underhill and Miriam O'Brien, the crew members felt themselves to be a close social unit, an elite. Their solidarity was most severely tested by the occasional presence of that most explosive of temperaments: Arthur Comey. To learn more of this intriguing personality requires us to move from the popular haunts of the Glen House and Mount Washington to that most remote of all winter testing grounds in the Northeast, Comey's special domain: Katahdin in winter.

Chapter 48

Katahdin in winter

R<small>EMOTE</small> and wild in the great north woods, Katahdin must seem an even more difficult objective in winter than the relatively accessible summits of Washington, Adams, and Marcy, all of whose early winter ascents were such stirring sagas. During the 1950s and 1960s, when the latter three had become reasonably routine winter objectives, climbing Katahdin in the snowy season was regarded as a major expedition, not often undertaken. Surely its early winter ascents must have been adventures on a grand scale?

Surprisingly, early in the history of Northeastern winter climbing, from the mid-1880s until the early 1900s, Katahdin was a relatively common and not terribly difficult winter ascent. This was because access was so easy. With the logging camps operating at full blast all through the season, the peak was quickly reached by logging roads, and the old northern approaches were not very steep.

There is not even a good record of when the first winter ascent was made. Lore Rogers climbed the peak on February 28, 1892, and wrote it up for *Forest and Stream* that year. Thus that ascent gained a certain credence as the first winter ascent and has traditionally been so cited. In fact, however, Rogers's own account merely claimed that the climb from the Wassataquoik camp in winter "is not very often undertaken." That was the ninth year of logging operations in that area: at least as far back as 1887, other parties had been up. One earlier tale tells of an 1887 ascent with no particular fanfare and certainly not claiming a "first ascent":

> A tramp of eight miles along the "Eureka road," discovered and blazed
> by Mr. Tracey and conceded to be the most direct and best route,
> brought us to the top of Katahdin.[a]

No exact date is given for this excursion, so it is conceivable that by "winter" the author actually alluded to a late November or early April jaunt.

---

[a]A round-trip of 16 miles in winter could actually be formidable if it meant breaking trail on snowshoes on steep terrain. The "Eureka road" may have been partially broken out by working loggers, and the route was "very gradual," as noted by the 1911 party (discussed later).

Still, no reading of this account could leave one feeling that winter ascents had not occurred at other times during this period of peak activity in the Wassataquoik.

Other published accounts of Katahdin winter ascents trickled in after the Rogers story. In November 1897, in what seem to have been "full winter conditions," a party of four men and four women spent several days tramping around the region, making one unsuccessful attempt from McLeod Camp, then moving on to camp somewhere between Basin Ponds and Chimney Pond, from which point three of the men made the ascent via the Saddle. In 1905 three Harvard alumni of the class of '97 also ascended the Saddle route, one of them apparently sleeping out on the Tableland on the night of February 25. In 1909 an AMC climber found an entry in the summit cylinder that told of a group of climbers from Philadelphia that had made no fewer than three attempts to climb Katahdin in winter via "a little-known trail landing them about half way along the big ridge."[b] In 1911 two climbers made a straightforward winter ascent from the north, during that last period when logging was resumed on that side.

In the annals of the pioneering Northeastern winter climbs, the Katahdin ascents are a distinct anticlimax. No Huntingtonian struggles against wind and cold, no Pinchot crawling to the top of Marcy, just "a tramp of eight miles." Lore Rogers commented, "We had come prepared for an Arctic coldness but were much surprised to find it quite warm." The 1911 party called the grade "very gradual." Indeed, one wonders if the November crossing of the Tableland by the Norris party in 1825 may not have been a more impressive "winterly" climb than these true winter ascents from the north. Or perhaps wintertime timber cruising of mountain country elsewhere in Maine, virtually undocumented, may have actually produced tougher winter climbing. One forester named Austin Cary conducted a thorough investigation of Maine forests for the state Forest Commission during the 1890s, and although no specific winter ascents of Maine mountains can be identified in his lengthy report, he did climb Washington on February 27, 1894, just for fun—"a delightful trip, just a pleasing variety for an active and cool-headed man." Such men may well have been on Maine mountaintops in winter in the course of their work. Their epics remain unsung.

Meanwhile, when the Wassataquoik lumber camps closed up, Katahdin became a more problematic winter objective. This greater difficulty and the advent of ski mountaineering converged in the 1920s to present a challenge that the redoubtable Arthur Comey could not resist.

Arthur Comey was not only the nemesis of Bemis Crew solidarity, but president of the Chocorua Mountain Club, a leading advocate of

---

[b]The context implies that the big ridge was the Knife Edge, but the "little-known trail" is a mystery, unless this party was trying to come in, in winter, via the old Keep Path! It is too bad that the Philadelphians' epic defeats on the Knife Edge have not come down to posterity. They might have been among the more exciting winter attempts of the day, unsuccessful or no.

through-trails, a prolific mapmaker, secretary and later chairman of the New England Trail Conference, and the man who first scouted the Appalachian Trail route through the Maine north woods. In private life Comey was a leading city and regional planner, influential in developing the concept of zoning in the United States. But, if those impressive emoluments have conjured up the picture of a dignified and respectable civic leader, it is time to introduce new evidence.

Comey was one of the most tireless and innovative Northeastern climbers of the 1920s, winter and summer, on trail and off—but he also had one of its most explosive and unpredictable temperaments. Equipped with a skyrocketing temper and given to extravagant candor, he went through four marriages (two to the same woman) and spent part of each friendship in high dudgeon. Trailsman Arthur Perkins said,

> The trouble with Arthur Comey is that I can never tell which way he will jump, except that it is generally the way I don't want him to.

Among the climbers and skiers, Comey's presence was even more of a gamble. "A raw product," said Robert Underhill, one of his closest friends. When he lost his temper, it was quite a show; recalled John Holden, "He would almost literally bare his teeth." Helen Pennock marveled, "Arthur could be very charming and intelligent in the woods, but you get him at a party—he might throw the watermelon." The Bemis Crew included Comey on a couple of trips, at first enchanted with his zest for adventure and high jinks. But after some vintage Comey tirades, the crew "blacklisted" him from future outings. "The trouble with Arthur," explained one tactful crew member, "is that he is not a gentleman." This was true, conceded another: "Comey would say things which no gentleman would say to another without smiling." If the wild and woolly individualistic gang of the good ship Bemis found Comey too much to take, his personality must have been strong medicine indeed.

Nevertheless, whether in or out of favor with the Bemis Crew, Arthur Comey rarely missed a weekend in the mountains, especially in winter. For a while he kept a careful record of his winter outings and over three winters totaled 1,115 miles on skis. Other top skiers of the era recall his form as less than polished but his grit incredible. "A very utilitarian skier," was Holden's characterization: "He could hold a stem better than anyone I ever knew." He also skied through krummholz, over rocky ridges, and even up fire tower ladders. From a cabin at the base of Chocorua, he often climbed that mountain and even constructed a ski trail on it. He was also instrumental in widening the Wapack Trail for skiers' use. He skied many a mountain in the Northeast, but his first love was always for Katahdin.

In March 1926 Willard Helburn led another winter expedition to Katahdin, this time assembling in one party of nine some of the most headstrong personalities on the Northeastern winter climbing scene: himself and Margaret, Henry Chamberlain, Robert Underhill, Miriam O'Brien, J. Ashton Allis, Avis Newhall, J. W. MacKenzie, and Arthur Comey, with Leroy Dudley along as host and supplier. This star-studded array of leaders-in-search-of-a-follower, as Allis recalled, "behaved themselves remarkably well—considering the extraordinary proportion of generals to privates!" Hearing of the planned trip, John Holden mused, "Who is King Beetle?" Helburn led them up the Chimney again—child's play to this cast—across the Knife Edge and, with snowshoes, down from the Saddle "at lightning speed in a cloud of snow." On a later day Helburn also led an ascent of the Elbow Gully in the North Basin. Meanwhile, however, Comey and Underhill set out to climb the peak on skis, via the Saddle; as the angle steepened near the top, Underhill relented and switched to crampons for the last 200 feet, but not Comey, who gritted out the steepening slope on his skis, completing the first pure ski ascent of Katahdin. Later that week he also skied up Hamlin (with Allis), over to the Northwest Basin, and on the last day skied 27 miles out to Grindstone (then the nearest town), "seeming none the worse for it," as Allis recalled. Comey returned on several occasions to ski up Katahdin and explore various descents and traverses on the rugged contours of that massif.

One result of Katahdin's relative inaccessibility after 1920 was that, aside from Helburn and Comey and their companions, few out-of-staters coped successfully with the necessary logistics. In 1922 a pair of snowshoers from Providence, Rhode Island, took three days to trudge over 20 miles from Millinocket to a lumber camp on the Abol Slide side, hauling 200 pounds of supplies on a sled. From there they were unsuccessful in getting up the slide. After several days they hauled their gear around to the Basin Ponds Camp, then operated by a paper company, and managed a successful climb of the Saddle route. In 1929 a pair of strong college skiers made what they believed was the first ski ascent via the Hunt Trail. These were Lewis Thorne, Yale man and rock-climbing protégé of John Case in the Adirondacks, and Terris Moore of Williams (later Harvard), who later climbed to fame on Alaskan peaks and the 24,900-foot Chinese giant, Minya Konka. In 1934 an all-Yale party, which included another future world-class climber, Bill House, made a successful ascent of the Abol Slide. Otherwise prewar parties of out-of-staters were rare.

Winter ascents by locals were more common. During the early 1920s forestry students at the University of Maine at Orono made something of an annual tradition of a winter ascent of the great mountain. These were usually on snowshoes rather than skis, though occasionally the snow was light enough or crusty enough for them to get up without either. By the 1930s UMO's Outing Club had developed a hardy group that made the ascent almost every year, led by such strong winter outdoorsmen as Win Robbins. Another source of winter climbers in the 1930s was the nearby town of Millinocket, where the locals formed a Katahdin Outing Club for a while.

Both skis and snowshoes were used on Katahdin during the 1930s. One veteran of three such ascents recalled these twin patterns of local dominance and use of both types of footgear:

1933: ascent by three from Millinocket, one on skis, two on snow-shoes;

1934: ascent by four locals and one "from outside," two on skis, three on snowshoes;

1938: ascent by five locals and one outsider, all on skis.

Other than Katahdin, Maine's mountains were rarely the focus of winter climbing. The big guide, warden, and AT-builder Helon Taylor was often in the winter woods on both skis and snowshoes but climbed peaks rarely; he did get up Sugarloaf, Bigelow, and others during the 1930s, but summits were not his occupational interest. The Eastern States Mountain Club of Portland (see chapter 41) had some interest in winter climbing but went to the White Mountains principally. A single ascent of note was the 1941 climb of far-off Traveler, north of Katahdin, by Harold J. Dyer, then Baxter Park supervisor, when he was on a winter check of moose winter habitat; though equipped with snowshoes, he and his part-ner, Henry Souci of Millinocket, benefited from a thaw followed by a hard freeze and walked right up on a hard crust.

As these accounts attest, skis and snowshoes were both in use on Maine mountains during the 1930s. This reflects a regionwide discussion and debate over the merits of the two modes of travel—the subject of our next chapter.

Chapter 49

Snowshoes versus skis: The great debate

THE ISSUE of whether snowshoes or skis were best suited for North-eastern winter climbing had an interesting test in a historic gathering in February 1927. This brought together the leaders of the Bemis Crew—primarily snowshoers—with the Schenectady contingent which had pioneered ski mountaineering in the Adirondacks. Representing the Bemis Crew were the Helburns, Robert Underhill, Allis, Spadavecchia, Wilhelmina Wright, Joe Wolcott, Frank Waterman, Ted Dreier, and others—"a hand-picked, hard-boiled crew of old sailors," according to their pretrip mailing. For the Schenectady group, Irving Langmuir and John Apperson headed the list, not the young tigers they had been fifteen years earlier but still going strong and ably supported by young David Langmuir (a nephew) and other Schenectady friends. The ground chosen was the Adirondacks, with a base at a camp on the Upper Ausable Lake. The mountains climbed were the cream of the Adirondack high peaks: Marcy, Haystack, Skylight, the Gothics, Basin, and Saddleback.

On both sides, curiosity as to the other's mode of travel was rampant, and it soon became clear that a test of sorts was underway. "Apperson and Langmuir had hoped to show that skis were better than snow-shoes," recalled Dreier, and doubtless Helburn and his crew were anxious to have at the famed Adirondack high peaks with their web-shoes.

On the first big day the group took on the formidable Haystack—or rather two groups headed out by separate paths. A sizable party of Bemis Crew snowshoers took off in one direction, apparently (records are spotty) led by Helburn and Underhill. Apperson and the Langmuirs, with a smattering of AMC skiers (including at least Dreier and Margaret Helburn) took another route. The result was an eye-opener. The snowshoers "had a glorious time, reaching the summit at some obscenely early hour such as 10 A.M.," as recalled by one of the envious skiers, glissaded uproariously down, and were back in camp by midafternoon (2:15, according to one participant's recollection, 4:00, according to another). The skiers worked their way more slowly up, expecting to overtake the snowshoers on the descent. Struggles with the dense conifers and steeper patches, however, slowed them down, and they finally limped into camp at 9:30 P.M., four hours after dark.

Snowshoers and skiers climbed Marcy together that week, but this time the skiers strapped snowshoes to their packs. A mile before the high col between Marcy and Skylight, where the going steepened, the skiers switched to snowshoes. "What a revelation it was!" recalled David Langmuir. On the descent the difference seemed even more in favor of the snowshoe.[a] Some of the Bemis tigers, led by Spadavecchia and Allis, took in a side trip to Skylight. During this eventful week, they also climbed Basin, Saddleback, and Gothics—all possible first winter ascents.

At the time the 1927 trip seemed a clear victory for snowshoes over skis. In 1929 another Adirondacks trip sparked "rivalry between the minority on skis and the majority on snowshoes"; again, after three days, "the advantage was conceded to the snowshoers, who reached the tops sooner and made the total returns faster."

But how transitory are such victories! The very next year a party of skiers and snowshoers ascended Marcy by going up the long Johns Brook valley; the skiers reached the top first by a mile, and took an hour less time and considerably less effort in the descent. Two years after that one of the "victorious" 1927 snowshoers, Robert Underhill, penned an essay in *Appalachia* entitled "What of the Snowshoe?" in which he argued that "the snowshoe is fighting a retreating battle," and asked,

> Will it eventually disappear from the mountains, at least so far as sport is concerned, withdrawing again to the lumber camps and hunting quarters from which, a generation ago, it sallied forth into general usage and acclaim?[b]

All through the 1930s skiers continued to enjoy immense success in climbing Northeastern mountains, on and off trail. But—so did snowshoers.

The difference between the two was the subject of an essay written a decade later (1949) but applicable even more to the 1930s scene than it was to the postwar world for which it was written. "A social barrier" was noted by the essayist Richard L. Neuberger: "The folk on opposite sides barely communicate." A difference in fundamental personality type produced two distinct images of winter sport:

> The fellow on snowshoes is the backwoods dweller of long standing.
> . . . He acts as if he had been in the frosty fastnesses since the year

---

[a]To the layman skis may seem to have distinct advantages on descent. The problem is on steep and narrow trails, where skiers have difficulty keeping their speed down sufficiently to maintain control.
[b]Underhill's illuminating essay, while extolling the many virtues of the ski, ended with a concession that the snowshoe remained the better tool for certain ground: " . . . of the sort where one walks up a 40-degree slope of hard snow, trusting desperately to one's snowshoe-creepers; or mounts by stemming widely between tree-bases, after the manner of chimney technique; or hauls oneself up bodily, by the arms, from trunk to trunk." A familiar scenario to snowshoers—and no place for the ski!

one. He can light a campfire in a blizzard and survive a night outdoors at 70 below. . . .

The skier is the "dude," the part-time inhabitant of the ranges. He is in the woods for fun. . . .

The snowshoer is a strong silent man. . . . He wants to be alone and the skiers intrude on his private domain. . . .

The skiers, on the other hand, regard the snowshoers with condescension. Snowshoeing seems such hard work, skiing such exhilarating sport. . . . They insist they would rather whiz across the tundra at 40 miles an hour than plod across it at four.

The question of which is the more appropriate winter climbing tool will continue to be answered differently by different generations and by different individuals within each generation. An entire generation during the 1950s and 1960s believed that snowshoes were *the* only feasible winter climbing footwear. In the 1970s and 1980s skillful backcountry skiers rose again to prove them wrong. Which is more appropriate depends on the details of the terrain. On the steeper trails and denser bushwhacks the snowshoe's advantages are unquestioned. On moderate downhills through open woods or along broad trails, the speed and pleasure of the skier is tenfold that of the snowshoer. Underhill praised the skill required and the grace of motion in skiing. But there is a skill in rugged snowshoeing not to be underestimated (though little grace!). Perhaps the real answer lies with the individual wearing either of them. A good snowshoer can get places unthinkable by any other means. But a good skier can do wonders too. When David Langmuir descended the steep Marcy cone in 1927 wearing snowshoes for the first time, he marveled at the ease of gliding down; but one comment of his is worth noting: "Only a very expert skier could have gone down that narrow trail on skis faster than we did it on snowshoes." The key phrase may be "only a very expert skier." Doubtless Jackrabbit Johannsen would like to have been along to show them how!

Snowshoes had their day on the 1927 trip and have had many since. But the issue was not settled. For the rest of the prewar period, both snowshoes and skis carried a still small but growing number of winter climbers to the tops of Northeastern mountains. A lengthy litany would be required to record them all; it would be fruitless to attempt, tedious to read. What should be noted is some indication of the scope and style of various circles active in those years.

The White Mountains

The key events for winter climbers in New Hampshire mountains during the 1920s and 1930s were the year-round opening of the AMC's Pinkham

Notch Camp; the installation there of Joe Dodge; the plowing of the road partway in the winter of 1926–27 and all the way in 1929–30; and the reopening of the Mount Washington Observatory year-round in 1932–33, with expert skier Bob Monahan in residence.

In January 1931 a new chapter in the continuing saga of the winter Presidentials traverse was written. Amid ferocious weather, and with the aid of open refuges at the Mount Washington summit and Madison col, two skiers made the first all-ski traverse of the Northern Presidentials: up from Pinkham to the top of Washington (the route unspecified); one day cooped up in shelter there; across over Clay, Jefferson, and Adams to the Madison Hut; a desperate ascent of Madison in high winds; then down the Osgood Ridge. The participants were Milana Jank, an experienced German alpinist, and Fritz Wiessner, a well-known rock climber and world-class mountaineer. According to her account at the time, Jank made a side trip by herself to take in the Southern Presidentials during the bad-weather layover on Washington, but Wiessner's recollection emphatically denied the claim.

Snowshoers and skiers alike were active in the White Mountains. Perusal of the *AMC White Mountain Guides* of the 1920s and 1930s shows increasing tidbits of advice on the use of trails in winter, until finally in the 1934 edition a special section on "Mount Washington in Winter" first appeared; it has been in every edition of the guidebook since. The guidebook counseled that "snowshoes are still the only practical means of travel where trails are steep and narrow," and it seems likely that most mountain *climbing* was done on showshoes all through the 1920s and 1930s in New Hampshire.

Skiing—undifferentiated at first but increasingly focused on downhill —swept the White Mountains by storm during the late 1920s and 1930s. Many events contributed. The great Otto Schniebs arrived and became ski instructor to hundreds, first through the AMC and from 1930 on at Dartmouth. A pack of wildly enthusiastic ski clubs sprang up, such as the Ski Club Hochgebirge of Boston, Harvard's Stem-Like-Hell Club, Dartmouth's Hell Divers Ski Club, a Lowell-Lawrence (Massachusetts) contingent calling themselves the Black and Blue Trail Smashers, and something called the Silver Ski Geschnozzle-Bashers. Numerous ski trails were designed exclusively for downhill runs, in which the Civilian Conservation Corps (CCC) played a major role, though private enterprise was soon active as well. Highly publicized races were staged, first on Moosilauke's carriage road in 1927, and culminating in Tuckerman Ravine's infamous Inferno, in which nineteen-year-old Toni Matt set the skiing world on its ear by schussing the Tuckerman headwall in 1939 ("like jumping into a 600-foot deep hole from a speeding car"). Enterprising clubs arranged for "snow trains" to bring the multitudes up from Boston beginning in 1931. *Ski Bulletin* appeared, at first as a series of mimeographed postcard notices of ski conditions and scheduled events, developing into an avidly read printed magazine during the 1930s. At Cannon Mountain the region's first tramway was born, and soon a variety of tows and lifts all but eliminated uphill from the art and lexicon of skiing. By 1937 the AMC had an estimated one thousand club members regularly turning out as skiers. More to the point was that the AMC accounted for but a small sector of a proliferating clientele of the popular sport. The bustling world of downhill skiing—not just in the White Mountains, but also on Mansfield and Killington and Greylock and Whiteface and elsewhere throughout the region—became a vivid, hectic, colorful world of its own, but it is not part of a history of mountain climbing. The downhill skiers congregated in large centers, with road access, busy social activities, and a life quite separate from those who plodded uphill to lonely summits. Increasingly, during the 1930s uphill work was left to the snowshoers, at least in the White Mountains. Wrote one denizen of the world of the web feet in 1932: "Concrete roads have made the mountains more accessible, but the top is still an arctic waste, remote and apart from the valleys below."

The Green Mountains

Judge Clarence Cowles and the original Green Mountain Club folk of Burlington were avid snowshoers. Their prime years were the 1910s, when jovial outing groups plodded up and careened down peaks such as Killington and Lincoln, Camel's Hump and Bolton, and Mansfield by such ambitious routes as Hell Brook Trail and the Maple Ridge. Judge Cowles counted sixteen winter ascents of Mansfield alone. Laura Cowles, the judge's wife, was scarcely less active. A tradition of enormous parties enjoying Washington's Birthday on a snowshoe outing reached such popularity that seventy-one snowshoers were counted in Smugglers' Notch on February 22, 1920. James P. Taylor himself was an occasional participant, Professor Monroe more rarely. University of Vermont students also climbed Mansfield before 1920. In the south of the state, GMC Bennington Section snowshoers cavorted on Glastenbury, Bald Mountain, and Greylock as early as 1917.

On February 1, 1914, Nat Goodrich, a protégé of Harris's DOC, made the first ski ascent of Mansfield, via the toll road, accompanied by AMC trailsman C. W. Blood on snowshoes. "I had a lot of fun," recalled the then novice Goodrich, "but my stops, voluntary and otherwise, were very frequent." Blood *descended* almost as fast on snowshoes. J. R. Norton and a friend named Aldrich skied to within 100 feet of the top of Camel's Hump in February 1912.

During the 1920s skis were more commonly seen on the Green Mountains. GMC outings of that decade included both skiers and snowshoers, but for a while the latter did not do as much climbing as the earlier

Cowles generation had. On February 5, 1927, Edwin H. Steele and Robert Cate of Montpelier claimed the first ski ascent of Mansfield by a route other than the toll road, going up the Long Trail from the northeast.

In 1933 the CCC began cutting ski trails on Mansfield, in 1934 the Mount Mansfield Ski Club was formed (succeeding the 1931 Stowe Ski Club), and in 1935 the first ski tow went in on the mountain. Mansfield soon became one of the chief downhill skiing attractions in the Northeast. But elsewhere throughout the 1930s both snowshoers and "uphill" skiers continued to enjoy Green Mountain climbs. A 1942 GMC report indicated that right up until World War II the friendly rivalry was in the winter air over Vermont:

> The long-standing feud between skis and snowshoes throve merrily. . . . Roy Buchanan on skis claims to have led Louis Puffer on snowshoes around the new ten mile cross-country loop cleared by the Long Trail Patrol last summer. But when a group of skiers rode exaltedly to the top of the lift, they found Miss Erne Camradt of Bennington beaming down at them from the top of Little Pico, which she had scaled on snowshoes.

The Adirondacks

Adirondack snowshoers had reached Haystack on February 12, 1915, five years before Johannsen and Apperson skied up. Snowshoers also reached Giant that same winter, and other peaks as the years went by: Algonquin in 1923; Basin, Saddleback, and Gothics in 1927 (the Bemis Crew); Allen in 1928.[c]

But the Adirondacks seem to have been much more of a ski climbers' center than was any other part of the Northeast, a tendency greatly accentuated after the 1932 Winter Olympics were held at Lake Placid, but already an established pattern before then. Beginning in 1927 Fay Loope, later executive of the Adirondack Mountain Club, was the ringleader in a YMCA group, which included women, that regularly skied up Marcy, sometimes starting in the middle of the night so as to view the winter sunrise from the top. (By 1948 Loope had more than thirty winter ascents of Marcy.) The Reverend Andrew B. Jones made a solo ski ascent of Big

---

[c]The difficulty of determining first winter ascents is illustrated by the case of Gothics. In the Jan. 1985 issue of *Adirondac*, Bill Toporcer wrote a brief piece recalling his ascent of Gothics on Feb. 2, 1931, and noting that Russell Carson had credited his party with the first winter ascent of that magnificent peak ("A Winter Ascent of Gothics," pp. 12–13, 33). In the June issue, Peggy O'Brien sent in a letter written by her brother, Jim Goodwin, on Feb. 2, 1928, describing his ascent in January of that year, clearly preceding Toporcer (pp. 25, 38). Both ascents, of course, came after the 1927 Bemis Crew trip on which Gothics, Saddleback, and Basin were all climbed. It would be reckless to claim with any air of certainty a "first winter ascent" for the Bemis Crew. It may be noted that T. Morris Longstreth wrote in 1920 that "the St. Hubert mountains" had been climbed in winter; whether this term included Gothics is not known (Longstreth, "Climbing Up Whiteface in Winter," *Outing* [Dec. 1920], p. 115).

Slide in 1930. Jim Goodwin and various companions made many ski ascents of Marcy, Algonquin and Wright, Big Slide, Whiteface, Giant, and Hurricane. The Lake Placid Club continued a winter sports center, dispensing both skiers and snowshoers on ascents of Whiteface, Marcy, and Algonquin all during the 1920s and 1930s. A club newsletter offered "guided daily trips during early March" up Marcy on skis.

In 1928 a stone shelter was erected on the top of Marcy, and the following New Year's Day three students inaugurated what became a minor tradition of skiers camping overnight right on the very top of New York's highest peak—an airy perch, well above treeline and exposed to winter's worst, without the amenities of the larger buildings atop Mount Washington. The three pioneers were Dwight Little, then captain of the Williams College ski team, classmate Terris Moore, and Lewis Thorne of Yale. The mountain provided appropriate weather to welcome its first overnight winter guests, and the three climbers

> had lots of time to hear the black night winds seize the chill little hut and drum on the door with icy fingers during the long night.

Subsequently (1933) yet another General Electric Research Lab group —Guy Suits, Klaus Sixtus, Larry Shaw—spent five nights in this exposed perch, skiing the leeward summit snowfields and fulfilling Verplanck Colvin's dream of sixty years earlier by taking weather observations on the summit in winter. The weather cooperated by turning on a display that the careful scientist Suits recalled as "awesome": a measured -40 degrees (Fahrenheit) on more than one night, the summit cone in dense cloud and blowing snow most of the time, with a steady wind strong enough so that

> when the wind was high, it was very interesting to put your hand near the frost covered, 4" thick, poured concrete wall. The wind seepage thru the wall could be felt easily.

Another GE Research Lab winter climber during the 1930s was Vincent Schaefer, author of the Long Path. Schaefer and his Mohawk Valley skiing friends established a Schenectady Winter Sports Club and were instrumental in arranging for the first snow train to the Adirondacks.

Winter camping

The earliest winter climbers did day-trips. They wanted to be back in the warmth of the Ravine House or Adirondack Lodge by nightfall, or at least in some loggers' camp with a stove. A very few hardy souls might bivouac infrequently—Jackrabbit Johannsen with his dog, Judge Cowles and his friends on occasion.

The first printed treatment of winter camping as "the new sport" goes back to 1913, but at this point camping does not seem to have been much associated with climbing. For one thing the weight of the gear was prohibitive. The 1913 manual prescribes "a sixteen-pound [sleeping] bag, or the same weight of blankets," for starters.

By 1920 winter camping among AMC members was common enough to generate the first "how-to" article on the subject in *Appalachia*. The recommended camping method was to sleep out in the open in a triple-layer sleeping bag—wool inner, feather outer, and waterproof silk shell, the total package weighing just over 10 pounds—on bough beds thrown on the snow. Everyone wore all his or her clothes into the sleeping bag, including heavy wool underwear, three heavy sweaters, with a wool skullcap topped by a hunter's cap with earflaps. One capacious tent was lugged along to serve for storage during the daytime and as a "center for assembly before the evening campfire." The program envisioned campers taking the Saturday afternoon train to some place such as Monadnock (remember the Saturday morning working hours), snowshoeing for a couple of hours to the campsite, and enjoying a highly convivial campfire circle, before turning in around midnight; on Sunday the summit would be reached, followed by a quick descent and return to Boston. The parties seemed to stay warm at least: for the climbing, this 1920 instructor sounded modern with his advice that "one of the secrets of comfortable outdoor travel in the winter is keeping cool enough!" (He noted that novices tended to overdress, work up a sweat, then chill rapidly later in their damp clothing.)

By 1925 winter camping was part of the programs of the AMC in the White Mountains, the Sno-birds at Lake Placid, and to a lesser extent the GMC in the Green Mountains. A *Book of Winter Sports* issued in that year included extensive discussion of camping techniques. By this time a lean-to style or Baker's tent was standard equipment, though still without sewn-in floor, and fur sleeping bags had improved ("some of these bags will weigh under ten pounds.")

In 1927 the Boy Scouts of America issued a handbook on winter camping, described as "a comparatively new phase of Scouting. . . . so new that only meager information could be found in print on the subject." Much of this handbook dealt with closed-cabin camping, but some discussion of tent camping was included. The recommended sleeping outfit was a kind of packsack sleeping bag with wool lining weighing roughly 8 pounds, though elsewhere in the manual wool blankets weighing 14 pounds were touted.

In 1928 *Appalachia* updated advice to the club's winter campers, with a tent now prescribed (but still no floor) and sleeping bags now down to a two-layer combination weighing 8 pounds. During the early 1930s the Schenectady winter sports set did a fair amount of sleeping out. GE Research Lab scientists—some of the top scientific minds in the country at the time—sneaked in a lot of research, perhaps not always strictly off company time, on sleeping bag materials and design. This practice had started at GE long before the 1930s, with Langmuir and Apperson. Down bags of remarkably sophisticated design were worked out, along with ingenious methods and materials for insulation, far advanced over the old bough bed. Schaefer invented a sleeping bag with slots on the edges; the sleeper cut slender poles and ran them through the slots; supported at each end by logs, this device kept the sleeper suspended off the snow or frozen ground, thereby eliminating the need for an air mattress or foam pad; the slots were designed to admit skis in place of cut poles.

Throughout the 1930s winter camping remained a relatively esoteric branch of winter climbing, with few participants relative to the number of active snowshoers and, of course, dwarfed to insignificance by the boom in downhill skiing. Adirondack Mountain Club write-ups of the subject around 1940 expressed the prevalent feeling toward those who did not have sense enough to come in out of the cold at night, by describing the practice as "a whole new field" and a "hazardous stunt."

Chapter 50

Depression, hurricanes, and war

T HREE external phenomena exerted a powerful effect on the closing years of the period we've been observing in these chapters. These were the Great Depression of the 1930s, two hurricanes—one hitting New England in 1938, the other the Adirondacks in 1950—and World War II. Coming in the space of twenty years, these events left a radically altered hiking scene in their wake.

The Great Depression

The economic collapse that was signaled by the stock market crash of 1929 took the United States into the deepest depression of its history. At its nadir in 1932, one-fourth of the country's job seekers were unemployed. Incomes and prices dipped to low levels.

The effects on the hiking scene were mixed. On the one hand, people had less income and a feeling of far less security, and therefore they indulged less in long drives and carefree vacations in the mountains. Membership in all three of the Northeast's major hiking clubs fell off markedly (see figure 50.1).

On the other hand, working hours were cut in an effort to share the work, so that a great many people had longer weekends available, and the boon of escape to the natural world was relief eagerly grasped. It seems likely that metropolitan area excursions like those described in chapter 39 were more popular than ever. One of the few solid statistical indicators of outdoor recreation from that period, the series on public campsite use in the Adirondacks, shows steady increases every year but one during the 1930s. While predominantly roadside tourism rather than true backcountry activity, it is at least evidence that people went to the Adirondacks more than before, rather than less.

Thus a paradox: as previously noted, increasing affluence was a long-range factor in stimulating interest in hiking. But during the 1930s, in the short run, *decreasing* affluence, brought about by the Great Depression, also stimulated hiking.

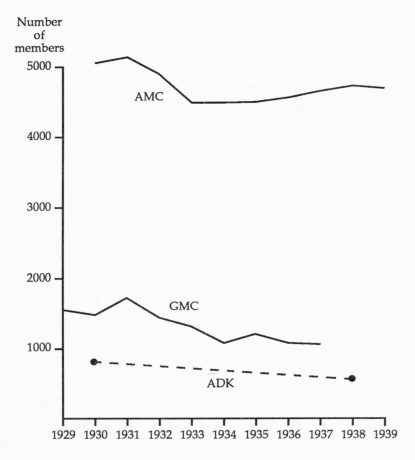

Figure 50.1. Club membership trends, 1929–1939 The Great Depression of the 1930s had mixed effects on the Northeastern hiking scene. Membership in all three of the major hiking clubs declined but not drastically. Indeed, after a 13 percent drop in membership during the early 1930s, the Appalachian Mountain Club's membership figures held even and slightly rose thereafter. Green Mountain Club membership declined more, proportionately: a drop of 35 percent between 1931 and 1937. Data for the Adirondack Mountain Club is not consistently available, but it is known that between 1930 and 1938 ADK membership fell 37 percent. (Data from the clubs.)

One direct outgrowth of the Depression years was the creation by the federal government of the Civilian Conservation Corps, known to that generation as the "CCC," or more familiarly as the "Cs." This was a program for providing employment for thousands of unemployed young men (ages seventeen to twenty-five), put to work mainly in national and state parks and other natural areas, building fire roads, picnic areas, campgrounds, nature trails, ski trails, bridges, cabins and shelters, observation towers, and a variety of related projects. The program only lasted nine years, being phased out when World War II began and the nation had other needs for young men aged seventeen to twenty-five.

At their height, though, the CCC camps were a major presence in the New England states and their work can be seen today all over the region. It has been argued that "the CCC program sent the state park movement forward a good fifty years." In Massachusetts, perhaps the most active CCC state, as many as fifty-one camps employed more than ten thousand men working in state forests. Among projects that affected the hiking environment were the widening of the Appalachian Trail through most of western Maine and the building of several open-front shelters along it; extensive trail improvements on Mount Greylock in Massachusetts; the development of campgrounds and hiking trails (usually short ones) in state forests in almost every state, most notably in Vermont, Massachusetts, and the Catskills; some of the side roads that provided greater access to the White Mountains, including the Bear Notch, Evans Notch, Tripoli, and Zealand roads, and the widening and partial relocation of the old carriage road up Mount Willard; and many shelters and cabins throughout the region.

Because the CCC camps were so prominent in so many areas, there is some tendency to exaggerate the impact of their work on the hiking and camping environment, but the fact is that most of this work was done on roadside facilities or on trails extending but a short distance up minor mountains. No major trail system or network of truly backcountry facilities in the Northeast can be credited to the CCCs.

Nevertheless, their work was of peripheral significance throughout almost every district within the region covered by this history. There is scarcely a hiker today who has not at some time walked up a trail, slept in a lean-to, or crossed a bridge that was constructed by the men and boys of the CCC.

A second child of the Depression, also conceived as a job-creating program, was the movement for scenic skyline highways in the fashion of Virginia's Blue Ridge Parkway. Had two such plans prevailed, the look of Northeastern high country and the experience available to hikers would have been radically altered.

During the early 1930s White Mountain hotel magnate W. A. Barron proposed a 25-mile motor highway winding up from Crawford Notch and along the alpine zone of the Presidentials past all the great peaks and down to the north. Some survey work for this trans-Presidentials highway was actually ordered by the state. The outcry from White Mountain loyalists was so anguished, however, that the project mercifully died.[a]

---

[a]A serious but even more bizarre proposal twenty years earlier would have placed an electric trolley line up the slopes of Jefferson, over Clay, spiraling around the summit cone to a giant resort hotel complex on the top of Washington—a scheme also luckily abandoned. See F. A. Burt, *Story of Mount Washington*, p. 102, and C. Francis Belcher, "Trolley on the Presidentials," *Appalachia* (June 1957), pp. 320–28.

During the mid-1930s Vermont was wracked by a heated debate over a plan to authorize a national park along the crest of the Green Mountains, with a 220-mile skyline parkway running from Jay Peak to Woodford (near Bennington). Defeated in the Vermont House of Representatives in 1935, by the narrow margin of 126 to 111, it was repeatedly revived by a friendly governor, until finally submitted to a referendum, where the state's voters resoundingly turned it down, 42,318 to 30,897. The pages of GMC publications at the time were crowded with discussion of the issue. Surprisingly, the club was not solidly against it. One straw vote of the membership came out 196 for, 272 against. Although votes taken among the club leadership were strongly opposed (for example, a 14 to 2 rejection by the trustees in 1934), some influential figures, such as James Taylor and Judge Cowles, supported the plan. At the national level, influential opponents were, publicly, Robert Sterling Yard of the Wilderness Society and, behind the scenes in government, Robert Marshall.

Hurricanes

September 1938 was a rainy month in New England. By the twentieth of the month, streams and rivers were unusually high and the forest soil was saturated, so that the root systems of even large trees had poor anchorage and were in a vulnerable state.

With that as backdrop, at 2:50 P.M. on September 21, 1938, the most devastating hurricane in New England's recorded history arrived on the southern shore of Long Island, swept across Long Island and the sound, and up the valley of the Connecticut River at exceptional speeds, passing New Haven at 3:50 P.M., Springfield about 5:00, then veered off over Burlington at 8:00 P.M. and on into Canada that evening (see figure 50.2). The storm center's forward motion averaged about 60 mph for much of the time. This meant that winds on the eastern edge of the whirling maelstrom were in excess of 100 mph. The greatest damage occurred from the center of the storm's path well out to the east, because of the effects of this circular rotation. The accompanying downpours combined with the month's earlier rains to produce record precipitation figures (for instance, more than 14 inches in Hartford in ten days, September 12–21), disastrous floods, and in the mountains great swaths of blowdown. It was estimated that 35 percent of the land area of New England had down timber. The forests of Massachusetts and New Hampshire were hardest hit. The White Mountain National Forest lost an estimated 200 million board feet of timber. Large-scale salvage operations that fall and for the next several years attempted to reduce the economic loss. The piles of slash were a stupendous fire hazard.

The impact on hiking trails was unprecedented. It took twenty-five trail-clearing sessions to reopen Massachusetts's Wapack Trail. On parts

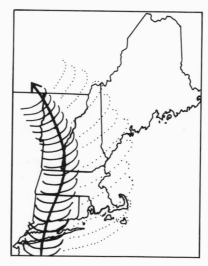

Figure 50.2. Path of the 1938 hurricane The 1938 hurricane has been called the most devastating storm ever to hit New England. Because of the circular movement of the wind and the high speed at which the eye of the storm moved northward, the destruction extended far to the east of the storm center. While the eye passed through New Haven, Connecticut, and Springfield, Massachusetts, the White Mountains and even the forests of western Maine were severely affected.

of the Long Trail near Belvidere Mountain, "there were miles where it was almost impossible even to find the blazes." The Madison Springs hutmaster, Bob Ohler, started down from the hut on the morning of September 22 with a load of blankets, taking along an ax in case of blowdowns; "nightfall found him three quarters of a mile down the trail, an entire day spent chopping through the blowdowns." On Monadnock the Pumpelly and Red Cross trails, two of the mountain's most popular, were still closed the following spring. On the Maine AT, the Elephant Mountain section (though a long way from the eye of the storm) was still in chaos ten years later. Many trails throughout New England, including the entire network of Rosebrook Range trails, once so well trodden, were irretrievably buried and never reopened. For the 1940 edition of the *AMC White Mountain Guide*, eleven of twelve trail maps had to be thrown out and drawn from scratch, so great were the changes. Thus this one weather event had an impact on the hiking environment of New England far greater than more elaborate plans of mankind.[b]

The Adirondacks were spared in 1938—only to be devastated in their turn in 1950. The damage from this blow was said to be "beyond

---

[b]While much was written lamenting the destructive impact of the 1938 storm in New England's mountain areas, a refreshing perspective was provided by Robert L. M. Underhill, "In Praise of Hurricanes," *Appalachia* (Dec. 1939), pp. 564–65.

anything ever experienced in this State and possibly anywhere in the country." The western high peaks were hardest hit, leaving "oceans of fallen, tangled trees" athwart the Seward and Santanoni ranges, as well as such trailless peaks as Marshall, Street, and Nye. The tangle was so great that much down wood was suspended well above the ground in intricate lacework, so that it did not rot quickly but simply dried out in place and left vast acreage of tinder-dry wood, a fearful fire risk. For safety, the state simply closed off a substantial bloc of what had been prime hiking country.

The first impact of the 1950 storm on Adirondack hiking was therefore starkly explicit: would-be peakbaggers found that the Sewards and Santanonis, with all seven of their 4,000-footers, were legally closed. An official statement from the Adirondack Forty-Sixers warned:

> Recognizing the danger of climbing these peaks from any approach is hazardous as well as unethical and illegal, . . . The Adirondack 46ers are declaring these seven peaks off-bounds and cannot, therefore, recognize ascents of these mountains from any approach. . . . until the ban was lifted.

It is the 1950 storm that accounts for the strange pattern of the annual number of new Forty-Sixers during the decade, as shown in figure 50.3.

When the woods reopened, the first hikers who ventured into the devastated areas received a shock. Heading for trailless summits in the Santanonis, one hiker reported, "the first hour out from the lean-to was through the worst blowdown I have ever seen in the Adirondacks." His pace was so slowed that he was forced to bivouac that night in the mess. Another entering the Seward Range described the shorn trunks on the ridge between Donaldson and Emmons as "a broken-toothed comb," adding,

> The real shock occurs when you reach the south end of the Donaldson summit ridge and gaze out over that scene of desolation: a vast tangled mass of intertwined limbs and trunks.

By this time, of course, a thick new growth of spruce was coming up through the tangled old trunks.

Ever since that storm the Adirondacks have richly deserved their reputation as having the worst blowdowns in the Northeast. A bushwhack through such an area became "an art in itself" and "a truly unique Adirondack experience," anathema to some, but a cherished challenge and source of pride to many Adirondack partisans, helping to preserve that range's status as the most genuinely wild and difficult in the Northeast.

Figure 50.3. Number of new Forty-Sixers, 1947–1957 Trends in new members added to the ranks of the Forty-Sixers—that is, people completing the ascents of all the Adirondack 4,000-footers—would appear incomprehensible to an observer who did not know about the impact of the 1950 hurricane. That storm caused extensive blowdowns throughout the high peaks region, with especially severe damage in the Seward Range. Resulting fire risk was so high that large portions of the Adirondacks were legally closed to hiking for several years. Even when the woods were reopened, the bushwhacking on trailless peaks remained a major obstacle and has given Adirondack bushwhacking its special reputation ever since. (Data from Hudowalski, ed., *Adirondack High Peaks*, pp. 306–312.)

World War II

On the heels of the Great Depression and the New England hurricane came World War II. Few events so drastically altered the Northeasterners' hiking and climbing world.

The immediate effect, of course, was to reduce greatly the number of people in the woods. Multitudes of the nation's young men marched off to military duty. Others, both men and women, were pressed into jobs in defense industries. Those not directly involved were kept busy with the myriad disruptions of the war and volunteer duties (air raid wardens, plane spotters, USO and other troop-support services), and with coping with housing shortages, transportation difficulties, and wartorn family life. Long working hours reduced available hiking time precipitously, especially with unpredictable emergency overtime for many in war-related occupations. Noted one New York–area hiker: "During the war some, like my father, worked seven days a week with one Sunday off a month." Restrictions on travel alone were enough to depopulate north country hiking regions—gas rationing, rubber tires hard to get, trains and buses very crowded. Beyond the physical constraints, the attention of the country was fully absorbed in the serious business of winning the war.

Nevertheless, a few people managed to get to the northern ranges. The AMC continued to staff the White Mountain huts and the trail crew. "We had the roads and the woods pretty much to ourselves," recalled one trail crew worker. "Sometimes there would be an entire week when we saw no other people in the woods." With the shortage of young men, crews had to be improvised by hiring high school boys or older family men. Some of the latter were accompanied by their wives, resulting in the first female "hutmen" and the only ones until the 1970s. One of these—Calista Harris, who joined her husband Stuart, seven-year-old daughter, and four-year-old son in running Zealand Hut—became one of the best-known "Old Hutmen" (OH) in the system and was still tramping up to visit huts in the 1980s, though herself "fiercely in her eighties," as one admiring fellow OH noted.

Trail maintenance was naturally at a minimum. Few trail crews could operate, so even well-known trails became overgrown. If Long Trail hikers were inconvenienced by blowdowns or a leaky shelter roof, counseled the GMC, "blame Hitler or Hirohito instead of the Green Mountain Club." The Appalachian Trail was hard hit, with many stretches becoming overgrown and Appalachian Trail Conference meetings simply suspended for the duration.

Katahdin was most affected, as befit its remoteness. By coincidence it was the first winter of the war when Leroy Dudley was killed by a logging truck, and Baxter State Park did not immediately replace him. Chimney Pond became "an abandoned camp," with the forests and crags around it "a deserted land."

One perverse effect was to increase demand for trails located near enough to metropolitan areas to be reached on Sunday excursions. Thus Harriman Park remained vital to New Yorkers and Boston's parks to its hikers, while in Connecticut

> the Connecticut Forest and Park Association noted that the crowding of new defense workers into industrial centers was stimulating the market for trails, making it more important than ever to keep open these opportunities for recreation, in time of strain.

College outing clubs carried on during wartime. The Intercollegiate Outing Clubs of America declared gamely: "War or no war, we had college week!" In 1943 the collegians gathered at Lake Colden in greatly reduced numbers but undimmed enthusiasm. Patriotic consciences were soothed with best wishes from IOCA boys in service:

> They all want the rest of us to keep the gang together and even more to keep the outing club spirit that we stand for alive until they get back and times are normal again so that we can all get back to our mountains, clean air, skis, and snow. We'll do our best, boys.

Despite such bravado, everyone felt the war years were an interruption. Outdoorspeople awaited the return to peacetime before mountain weekends and vacations would be what they once were. When the war ended, they were ready. An AMC hill worker recalled the pent-up urge to get back to the White Mountains and how it exploded:

> We were in the woods when V-J Day occurred, and it was several days before we knew the war was over. A few weeks later, Harry Truman ended gas rationing. Again we were in the woods and didn't know it. I remember we were working some place off the lower end of Crawford Notch, and came out Thursday afternoon to find a steady stream of traffic headed north. Our first reaction was that the war had started again, that we had been invaded, and that all citizens were fleeing to Canada. We'd never seen so many cars on the road. Everybody was looking happy however, so we figured it must be O.K.

World War II's impact did not end with V-J Day, however. Many trails that had grown in were never reopened. In the White Mountains' Rosebrook Range, for example, where a complex of trails had taken prewar hikers to such pleasant summits as Echo, Stickney, Rosebrook, and Oscar, the triple-barreled impact of the 1938 hurricane, the war, and the war-related closing of the trail head hotel resulted in all of those trails' fading out of existence, so completely that few White Mountain hikers today could even identify where the range is and fewer have ever trod its four summits.

On the other hand, wartime equipment developments had a positive impact on the hiking scene. Military research produced new sleeping bags, tents, winter clothing, freeze-dried and dehydrated foods, and climbing rope, all of which became dominant in the hikers' and climbers' postwar world. The most significant impacts here were on winter climbing.

When the considerable dust settled that had been raised by these three events—the Great Depression, the two hurricanes of 1938 and 1950, and World War II—the scene that opened on the postwar generation was irretrievably changed from that of the 1920s and 1930s. Another era had passed, like that of Starr King and the preautomobile grand hotels. Once more a new dawn brought in a new hikers' world, leading in time to the backpacking boom of the 1960s and 1970s, and all its related developments so familiar to today's generation of trampers, spiritual heirs to that long-gone world of Joe Dodge, Leroy Dudley, and the dear old Erie Railroad.

PART FIVE

Mountains as places for recreation: Since 1950

THE PROVERBIAL Martian observer, set down once at Lake Colden or Chimney Pond or Tuckerman Ravine in 1950 and then again a quarter-century later, might have guessed he had visited two different planets but for the constancy of the beautiful mountain walls above him. During the years between 1965 and 1975 profound changes had altered the hiking and climbing scene. In 1950 our Martian would have seen something very similar to what his father had seen during the 1930s: old, well-worn clothes, a heavy canvas tent, bough beds, canned food cooked in an iron skillet over a campfire, and (unless he hit College Week at Colden, August Camp at Chimney, or spring skiing at Tucks) only one or two parties enjoying the quiet solitude of their intimate campfire circle. In 1975 our extraplanetary visitor would have blinked to find brightly colored, lightweight nylon clothing, tents, and sleeping bags, freeze-dried food cooked on portable white-gas stoves, not an ax in sight, and enormous numbers of voluble campers spread about in every conceivable sleeping site. It *was* a different world, Martian!

The obvious changes were greater numbers of people in the backcountry and high-technology innovations in clothing and equipment—new materials, fabrics, designs, fashions, gadgets. Less obvious but perhaps more important from a historical perspective were changes in the purposes and expectations of hikers and climbers, and the resulting spirit of backcountry life.

We have seen how Americans' attitudes toward their mountains evolved from hostility and fear of wilderness (before about 1830); to veneration of the sublime scenery (the midnineteenth century); to vigorous pursuit of pedestrian exercise (after 1870); and finally (in the twentieth century) to the perception of mountains as a place to escape the pressures of an urban society. During the late twentieth century, attitudes evolved one step further. For the new generations, mountains were highly accessible recreation grounds, an alternative setting for relaxation, exercise, release, self-development, and renewal in an increasingly complex and impersonal post-industrial age.

Wilderness had changed in subtle ways, often unnoticed. For Robert Marshall and his contemporaries, wilderness was genuinely wild, vast, at odds with civilization, a realm of nature wherein a resourceful individual might forge a highly personal kind of experience. By the late 1960s, or at least the 1970s, the mountain world had been brought within the deliberate purview of humankind, a sort of garden set aside for recreation, over which people (or at least "wilderness users," in the popular phrase) held stewardship. With these new attitudes came a strong sense of responsibility for the mountain environment, but also a diminution of the spirit of wildness and wonder that had infused the adventures of Verplanck Colvin, Charles Fay, and George Witherle.

These changes occurred in a slow evolution over almost half a century, but there are moments and circumstances in which the changes seemed more sudden, more of a revolution.

Our vantage point is too close in time to give us good perspective on the country's social history since World War II, but one might speculate that future histories will discern three distinct phases in postwar American life, at least as it affected backcountry recreation. These three phases reached their high watermarks at roughly fifteen-year intervals: 1955, 1970, and 1985.

During the first postwar years, the tone of America was set largely by veterans fresh from military service in the most destructive war in world history. Their attitudes and values, strongly conditioned by vivid war experience, permeated American society during the 1950s. These were men who had seen enough excitement and adventure for one lifetime and were not keen on pursuing the voluntary adventure of life in the backcountry. Many went camping, but with little change in style from the way their parents had camped before the war. When they indulged in higher-risk outdoor pastimes, such as rock climbing or winter climbing, they tended to be conservative and safety conscious. They were a sober and serious generation on the whole, who remembered the prewar Depression as vividly as the war and who therefore placed high priority on jobs, income, and economic security. So they came back from war to go to work, not to escape to the backcountry. These people had already "gotten away from it all"—and were anxious now to get back to it all. They watched Ed Sullivan, listened to Perry Como, and voted for Dwight Eisenhower.

The only major change was the injection of military equipment into the camping scene in wholesale lots. War-surplus sleeping bags, packs, tents, fatigues, snowshoes, and ice axes put in their appearance at shelters and along the trails of the postwar decade. Most campers, whether veterans or not, bought much of their gear at Army-Navy stores. Winter climbers were almost completely outfitted with Tenth Mountain Division clothing and equipment.

Otherwise the backcountry was little changed. For the last time in the history that this book has related, the Northeastern backcountry was still an uncrowded, unhurried, unspoiled Eden.

Sometime during the 1960s, in association with all that social ferment that was such a striking characteristic of a decade of youth, long hair, drugs, rock music, and political turmoil, a lot of young people took to the woods in the country's second big back-to-nature movement (for the first, see chapter 31). A "backpacking boom," by no means confined to youth, then swept the country. Between 1965 and 1975 an unprecedented increase in hiking filled the once quiet mountains with nature seekers. Organized outdoor programs flourished, from Outward Bound and a host of imitators, to new summer camp programs, college credit courses in wilderness skills, technical climbing schools. All over the Northeast, as throughout the country, it seemed as if an entire generation wanted to "find itself" in the backcountry. The impact on the mountain environment was formidable and seen at the time as potentially disastrous: soil compaction, trail erosion, campsite devastation, litter, noise, sanitation problems, and loss of solitude.

By the late 1970s, as the back-to-nature generation grew up, different values surfaced—or resurfaced. Young people went back to school, especially to law school and business school. Hair was shorn, suits and ties put on again, dress hems lowered. Making money was once again socially desirable. Youths who had dropped out of the affluent society and played the guitar were replaced by those who cashed in on that affluence and played the stock market. A new image of the young urban professional displaced that of the flower children.

Where the young people of 1965–75 had swarmed into the backcountry to get away from the world, their 1980s successors perceived a vigorous program of outdoor exercise as part of the sharper image of the bright young man or woman. Thus, whatever future historians may conclude about differences between the two generations, the perceptions of both generations of their place in the backcountry had strong elements in common—and in contrast with the approach of prewar generations. With affluence, leisure, and interstate highways, the Northeastern mountains were so easily accessible as to become an alternative habitat. The 1965–75 generation might aspire to live all the time in touch with nature; the 1980s group was more at home in boardrooms and at conference tables, but a sizable number of them also wanted the mountains regularly in their lives. To them the backcountry was a readily available natural gymnasium in which to find vigorous physical tests, a cleansing of the spirit, and the deliberate pursuit of challenge under controlled conditions, in which to develop the body and refresh the mind.

And so the impact of large numbers of "backcountry users," as the "backcountry managers" called them, continued even after the personal style of those users changed.

With the heightened awareness of the outdoors, a new kind of conservation movement emerged, with different implications for the term *conservation*. Until the late twentieth century, conservation had meant safeguarding wild land from the incursions of somebody else, not us: loggers, mining interests, commercial developers, home builders. Now, all of a sudden, in Pogo's oft-quoted words, "We have met the enemy, and he is us." That is, the largest single threat to the integrity of Northeastern backcountry had become the impact of the hikers and climbers and backpackers themselves.

So the new conservation involved efforts to pick up litter, to educate campers to reduce their impact on campsites, to develop management plans for shelters and trails, and otherwise to awaken the environmental conscience of an entire generation of hikers and campers. It was a new ethic—and sometimes a controversial one, as we shall see.

The old meaning of conservation was not obsolete either. Good old-fashioned conservation crusades continued to snatch victory from defeat in specific campaigns to preserve some choice parcel of wild land from the threat of a developed ski resort or an electric power company or a large-scale second-home developer. Some of the glorious battles fought and, for the most part, won by conservationists in the postwar Northeast include:

Defeating a proposed giant recreation and second-home complex that had been designed for Maine's magnificent Bigelow Range

Obtaining designation of "wilderness areas" under the national Wilderness Act for several large chunks of forest and mountain terrain in both New Hampshire and Vermont

Negotiating patiently and repeatedly for workable compromises with Vermont's ski industry, so that the Long Trail could continue to run along the crest of several mountains on which ski resorts were blooming

Creating the Adirondack Park Agency and strengthening New York State's commitment to the "forever wild" character of both the Adirondacks and the Catskills

Repulsing a proposed resort development at Minnewaska on the Shawangunk ridge

Saving the Hudson Highlands' graceful little mountain Storm King from a proposed pumped storage hydroelectric plant

Painstakingly arranging for public authority to take over that rock climber's playground, the Quincy quarries south of Boston, which had been slated for condominiums

Securing classification of the Appalachian Trail as a National Scenic
Trail, with the objective of permanently protecting an off-road trail
corridor for its entire 2,100 miles

These victories were won at the cost of exhausting efforts by organizations and individuals, some of which have been well chronicled but
many of which have gone unsung. Their story will not be told in these
pages—not because it is unimportant but because it is too important to
be folded into the prime focus of this history, which is the hiking and
camping that took place on the land the conservationists saved.

The chapters that remain will sketch some of the new ways in which
the successive postwar generations—the veterans, the nature children,
the young urban professionals, along with all their less stereotyped contemporaries—have enjoyed the Northeastern backcountry since 1950,
and some of the issues that their large numbers have raised.

Such recent history must be more tentatively recorded than what came
before World War II. Both these writers and our readers are too close to
what has happened—in many cases, have been too personally involved
—to have adequate objectivity. Time is needed for perspective. In James
Hilton's *Lost Horizon*, one of the characters chides an old Chinese sage
for having no interest in current world news.

"Quite a lot of things have happened in the world since last year
[1930], you know," says the English visitor.

"Nothing of importance, my dear sir," responds the sage, "that could
not have been foreseen in 1920, or that will not be better understood in
1940."

Historians go further. Not ten years, but more like half a century's perspective is needed. We cannot properly interpret the history of the last
fifty years, for the simple reason that we do not know what will happen
in the next fifty. We cannot distinguish between an accelerating trend
and a distracting aberration. Historian Barbara Tuchman cautions,

> The contemporary has no perspective; everything is in the foreground
> and appears the same size. . . . The historian fifty or a hundred years
> hence will put them in a chapter under a general heading we have not
> yet thought of.

Therefore the remaining chapters will not attempt to provide the detail
or the generalizations given heretofore. This may frustrate readers who
believe, like Hilton's Englishman, that quite a lot of things have happened
in the hiker's and camper's world since 1950. We agree that a great many
changes indeed have taken place, but we also agree with Hilton's sage
that we shall understand them better ten or fifty years from now. So we
shall record salient events that future historians will have to deal with.
We envy their opportunity: the years since 1950—especially since about

1965—are filled with vitality, change, controversy, and every bit as many colorful and provocative personalities as the previous periods we've recorded. In the pantheon of the Northeastern backcountry, Alden Partridge, Ethan Crawford, Marcus Keep, and Old Mountain Phelps will have worthy company from the twentieth-century gods, not only Robert Marshall and Sherman Adams and Jackrabbit Johannsen, but many men and women of the backcountry of our own time.

Chapter 51

The backpacking boom

FOR almost twenty years after World War II, surprisingly little changed in the Northeastern outdoors scene. It was the lull before the hurricane. What happened in the late 1960s and early 1970s was a major break from the past, both in quantitative terms and in spirit. The backpacking boom was born.

As large as the backpacking boom was, few statistics provide us with a good picture of it. A few dramatic numbers can be cited—see figure 51.1 —but most data were not collected early enough or carefully enough to be useful. Nevertheless, there is no mistaking that, as everyone realized at the time, use of the outdoors was booming as never before.

Membership in hiking clubs surged, especially in the AMC. In the seven years between 1969 and 1976, AMC hut use increased 97 percent. (The oft-repeated myth that a 1961 *National Geographic* article on the huts by Justice William O. Douglas produced the big crowds in the huts does not stand up under scrutiny: the numbers went up for a year or two after that article was published, then leveled off; the real growth came later.) Data for Long Trail shelters was not systematically collected until 1972, but during the next three years those numbers shot up too—42 percent in Mount Mansfield's four lodges, for example. Some peripherally relevant series are helpful. In almost every series of numbers the trend shows (*a*) little or no growth between 1960 and 1965, (*b*) an acceleration between 1965 and 1970, and (*c*) a takeoff between 1970 and 1975. Camping along the Allagash River in Maine rose from roughly 4,000 people per year in the period 1966–68 to 9,477 in 1975. Massachusetts forests and parks had between 500,000 and 600,000 campers annually in the years 1964–68; by 1974 that annual figure was over 1 million. Before 1967 only 53 people had ever hiked the full length of the Appalachian Trail during the thirty years of its existence. In 1968, 10 more hardy souls completed the AT; in the single year 1972, 68. By 1973 that annual figure had soared to 166. Where 26 completed the Long Trail in 1968, 118 completed it in 1975. Peakbagging in the Adirondacks showed only slightly less of a spurt: from 15 people finishing the round of all 4,000-footers in

Figure 51.1. Portrait of the backpacking boom The data shown here are among the few reliable statistical indicators of the extent and timing of the boom in backcountry hiking and camping during the 1960s and 1970s. Where data is missing, a dotted line is shown. Note the general tendency for the numbers to grow slowly from 1960 to 1965, more rapidly for the next five years, and very rapidly indeed between 1970 and 1975.

Sources for data: Appalachian Mountain Club, Adirondack Mountain Club, Green Mountain Club, Maine Bureau of Parks and Recreation, Massachusetts Division of Forests and Parks, Appalachian Trail Conference, Adirondack Forty-Sixers, and Mohonk Preserve, Inc.

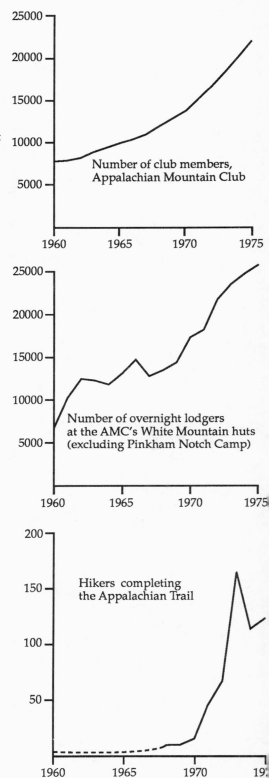

Number of club members, Appalachian Mountain Club

Number of overnight lodgers at the AMC's White Mountain huts (excluding Pinkham Notch Camp)

Hikers completing the Appalachian Trail

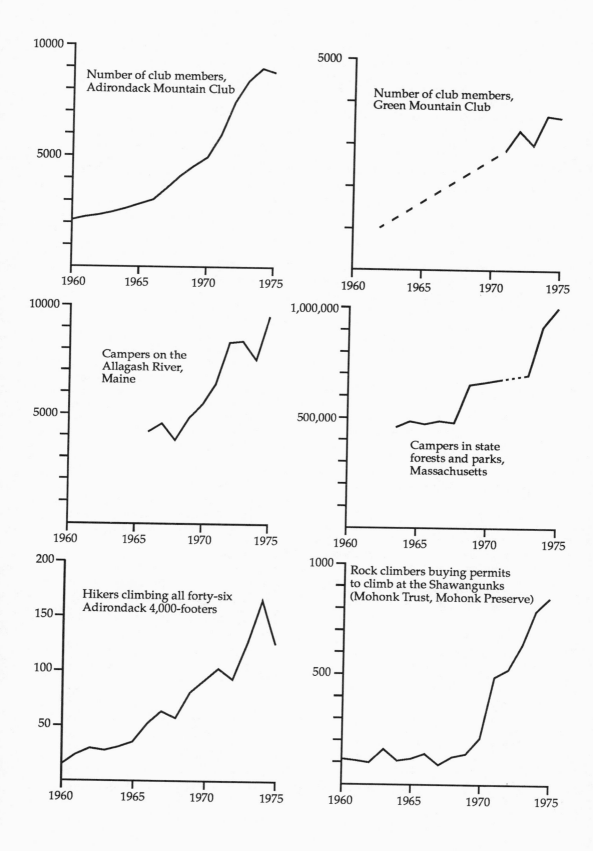

1960, to 36 in 1965, 70 in 1970, and 126 in 1975. Rock climbers annually bought about one hundred permits to climb on Shawangunk cliffs between 1960 and 1967; by 1975 that number exploded to more than eight hundred in a single year.

Why? What created the backpacking boom?

Some of it was inevitable in the demographics of population changes: the babies brought into the world by that family-oriented, conservative postwar generation began to reach an age where they could go camping on their own. Population dynamics were aided and abetted by social and economic forces, among which major contributions were:

Postwar affluence: continually rising family incomes.

An even faster rate of increase in discretionary income—that is, as basic needs were more easily met, people had extra cash to devote to leisure-time activity and recreation.

Increased leisure, and especially the trend to receive the increased leisure not in the form of a shorter workweek but as paid vacations and holidays instead.

Improved transportation and especially the interstate highway system. The importance of I-93 and I-91 to the White Mountains, I-95 to Katahdin, and New York State's Thruway and Northway to the Adirondacks can scarcely be exaggerated.

Demographics, economics, leisure, and transportation were basic influences, but something more happened that set the boom on fire. That was the new patterns of thought and behavior associated with the late 1960s and best conjured up by a host of catchphrases descriptive of that era: the back-to-nature movement, the hippies, the flower children, the now generation, the counterculture, the environmental movement, the greening of America. One phase of that multifaceted cultural turmoil was a torrid love affair with nature on the part of virtually the entire generation. This was the age when so many took to the woods or went back to the land, where lug-soled boots and backpacks seemed to be on two of every three college freshmen—and on a far higher proportion of the many who dropped out of higher education in those years. Armed with their parents' affluence and their own leisure and with the interstates to travel, this generation swarmed to the mountains in unprecedented numbers.

Factors that began as *effects* of this movement soon became contributing *causes* as well. The hikers and climbers became a significant market for the first time in business history, and a newborn outdoor equipment industry catered to their needs. The exterior-frame backpack, most prominently associated with the trade name of Kelty at first, became a widespread symbol of the backpacking boom. Down parkas spread so pervasively that near the end of the period (around 1975) it became almost a status symbol of the true outdoorsperson *not* to wear a down jacket, so thoroughly had the garment been adopted by everyone else. Down sleeping bags and various synthetic imitators crowded the pages of equipment catalogues. New kinds of tents appeared: free-standing exoskeleton models during the late 1960s, not requiring stakes or external poles to stand up, and dome designs beginning in the early 1970s. Portable stoves, once available in only a few heavy models, were subjected to steady technological innovations, which resulted in lighter, more dependable stoves and many more brands from which to choose. The freeze-dried and dehydrated food companies expanded and multiplied, while many more orthodox packaged foods appeared on supermarket shelves that backpackers found serviceable in a camping setting. The growing availability of all this convenient, lightweight gear acted as a further stimulus to the backpacking boom.

Outfitting stores were transformed from small specialty shops to lucrative chains eyed appreciatively (and eventually bought up, in many cases) by big business. At first such shops remained scarce, and many Northeastern backpackers haunted Army-Navy surplus stores or ordered through the mail from Recreational Equipment, Inc., familiarly known as "the Seattle Co-op." But gradually retail outlets expanded. Some of the small, old shops, such as Maine's L. L. Bean, flourished and grew enormously. Others, such as Camp and Trail, New York City's beloved, musty, second-floor walk-up, were overwhelmed by more modern competitors and went under at the first sign of slack in the boom. Among the new stores of this period which enjoyed golden years, when they were home to hundreds of backpackers and/or technical climbers, were Skyline Outfitters in Keene, New York (opening in 1965), Leon Greenman's of New York City (1967), Climbers' Corner in Boston (1968), Rock and Snow in New Paltz, near the Shawangunks (1970), and International Mountain Equipment in North Conway, New Hampshire (1975). Some of these were short-lived, others continued to prosper for many years. The biggest commercial success story in the Northeast was Eastern Mountain Sports, which began with a single store in the Boston area in 1967 and grew to be a multimillion-dollar enterprise, with thirty retail stores from the Baltimore-Washington area to Maine, plus Minnesota and Colorado outlets.

As backpackers emerged as an identifiable market, advertising and special publications rose to address their wants and needs. Cigarettes and beer, ironically, were sold by ads displaying their use in sparkling sylvan settings where they tasted good like they should. *Wilderness Camping* magazine was first issued in 1971, *Backpacker* in 1973. Books on how to go camping and on the experiences of longtime hikers filled the shelves of outfitting stores and the specialty sections of general bookstores and catalogues. Of twelve how-to guides reviewed in the first issue of *Backpacker*, the dates of publication say much about the rate of increase in the boom: one title in 1968; none in 1969; one in 1970; two in 1971; eight in 1972.

What about the mountains themselves during the height of the backpacking boom? What was the result of all this growth and change up in the quiet realm, that Starr King had romanticized, Marcus Keep had admired, and Verplanck Colvin had explored?

It was devastating. As the lean-tos and camps filled up, the land around them showed the brutal effects of overuse and misuse. Hundreds of fire builders pushed back the tree cover, and many novices hacked indiscriminately and ineffectually at green trees nearby, leaving a widening circle of dead stumps, often bludgeoned off well above ground level. As the shelters filled up every weekend, sleeping bags were laid out on the ground around, or tent sites leveled and ditched. The battered earth around the shelters became compacted, further inhibiting recovery of vegetation. At upper elevations, approaching and above treeline, where greenery had an uphill battle to begin with, the impact at shelter sites was particularly harsh. If the site had not been selected with heavy use in mind, the area immediately in front of the shelter often turned into a muddy quagmire on rainy days. Outhouses filled up—or were chopped down for firewood. Almost exactly one hundred years after the surveys of Charles Hitchcock and Verplanck Colvin had opened up the backcountry of the White Mountains and the Adirondacks, that backcountry had finally had enough.

Over and above the physical damage, the wilderness experience suffered grievously. Robert Marshall had warned, "There are certain things that cannot be enjoyed by everyone. If everybody tries to enjoy them, nobody gets any pleasure out of them." Applied to the backpacking boom of 1965–75, that principle was ceaselessly exhibited. Shelters that had been such a quiet and peaceful haven for the solitary hiker or intimate group were transmogrified when the crowds began to fill them to overflowing. Between the physical degradation of the surroundings and the social disintegration caused by noise, crowding, and lack of privacy, the experience was not the same. For those who took to the woods envisioning an idyll of spruce-scented solitude, many a weekend fell far short of the dream, being spent huddled in a crowded, dark, 8-foot-by-12-foot hovel with not always compatible company, as rain beat relentlessly on the mud outside and sleeping bags and clothing grew dank in the humid air. Lamented a couple who had known Vermont's Little Rock Pond in quieter days, "What was paradise for two or three or five people might become hell for twenty or thirty or how many."

The trails suffered as badly as the popular campsites. The merciless march of so many lug-soled boots churned up the ground, leaving it vulnerable to severe erosion during every rainstorm and especially during spring thaws. Upper elevation soils were especially susceptible to damage.

As trail corridors filled with water or bottomless muddy ooze, hikers understandably skirted to the sides, progressively widening the path of destruction. Deep trenches opened. It was not uncommon to observe that the ground level on either side was three or four feet above the eroded trailbed. Exposed trip-roots and loose rocks made for uncertain footing as well as a pathetic visual blot.

Our account thus far describes the worst-case scenes. It would be easy to exaggerate the extent of both the crowding and the impact. A point to underscore is that the crowds and the impact were sharply focused on the well-known, already popular, highly scenic areas: the Presidentials and Franconias, the Pemigewasset "Wilderness" (AMC guidebooks began using the ironic quotation marks in 1969), Mount Marcy and its approach trails, Lake Colden, Mansfield and Camel's Hump; especially picturesque backcountry ponds like Maine's Chimney and Horns, New Hampshire's Garfield and Greeley, Vermont's Stratton and Little Rock, and Massachusetts's Upper Goose; Monadnock, Slide Mountain; Sage's Ravine (on the Massachusetts-Connecticut border) and Harriman Park. Throughout the 1970s and since, large stretches of Northeastern backcountry remained lightly used. Even during the height of the boom, informed sources widely believed that "90% of the hikers use 10% of the trails." Avid peakbagger Fred Hunt found in the Adirondacks during the height of the boom that "on well over half of all ascents, I was totally alone on that particular mountain." Even the time of day was crucial: before 8:00 A.M. even during the most popular summer weekends, the trails were virtually empty. Opportunities for solitude in the Northeastern mountains always remained obtainable but were seldom experienced by the overwhelming proportion of new hikers. Relatively few knew how or where to avoid the crowds.

By 1975 the boom had gone on long enough to invite some terrifying projections. Concerned backcountry managers saw no reason to assume that the trend would level off. The general supposition in 1975 was that if the situation was this bad now, wait till you see it in the year 2000! One report on "Backcountry Management Problems" in the early 1970s predicted, "Hiking and camping occasions will at the very least triple between now and 2000," and warned, "Control on the numbers of people entering the woods inevitably will come." Desperate scenarios were painted of new regulations needed to cope with ever geometrically increasing use levels, with the backcountry trapped in an Orwellian nightmare of crowds, devastated campsites, strict regulations, paved-over trails, hopelessly polluted streams, and complex permit systems.

What happened to thwart these projections? Several things.

First, the boom suddenly turned itself off. Immediately after 1975 the alarming upward trends virtually all leveled out, and many actually turned downward. The picture varied in different areas, but a few examples in figure 51.2 illustrate how quickly and unexpectedly the pattern changed.

Some of the reasons for this remarkable turn-around are simply the obverse of the factors that had generated the boom ten years earlier. The baby boom generation had worked through the years of youth, and no longer were such large numbers entering the ranks of potential first-time hikers. More important, attitudes and values were swinging away from those of the rebellious, back-to-nature counterculture. The image of the backcountry was not quite so compelling. As one AMC spokesman commented during the late 1970s,

> Hiking and backpacking went through a period of very rapid growth in the late 1960s and early 1970s. . . . Media coverage made them trendy. People with avant garde leanings were drawn in even though they might have been happier in other pursuits. Now the growth has tailed off as trendiness has gone to racketball and jogging.

Figure 51.2. The end of the backpacking boom The backpacking boom accelerated so rapidly between 1970 and 1975 that alarmed observers at the time made terrified predictions of numbers to come and the expected impact on the backcountry environment. But after 1975 the boom unexpectedly leveled off and even declined in many areas.

Pictured below are the annual numbers of campers in Massachusetts forests and parks between 1964 and 1975, together with a range of projections that any reasonable observer might have made from the viewpoint of, say, 1976 (see dashed lines). The only question seemed to be whether the rate of increase would moderate or continue to accelerate.

But what really happened after 1975 was this:

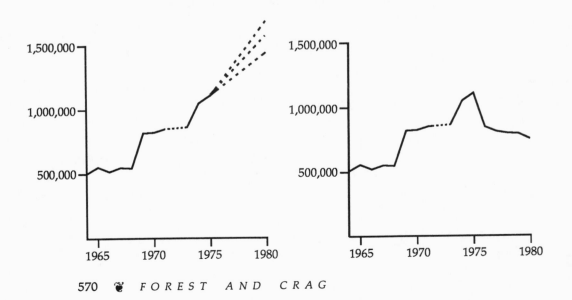

The number of "through-hikers" completing
the Appalachian Trail went from fewer than
10 per year in the mid-1960s, to 166 in the
single year 1973. Anyone might have
projected continued increases during the late
1970s.

But in fact here's what really happened:

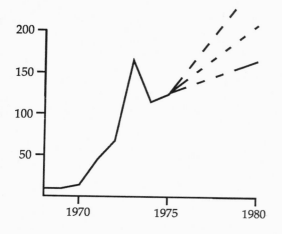
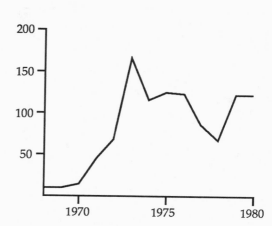

In the Adirondacks, the number of hikers
completing the ascent of all forty-six 4,000-
footers showed a similar accelerating trend.

But in later years this trend also moderated:

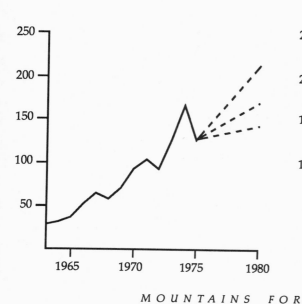
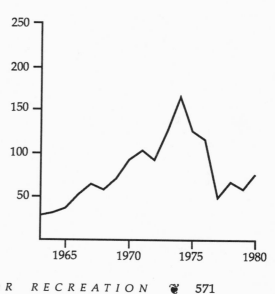

In the AMC hut system, from an early 1960s spurt associated with a *National Geographic* article to the takeoff that began in 1967, all signs pointed skyward. Plans were laid for expanding hut capacity to meet the expected demand.

In this case, as a result of growth-oriented policies, no downturn took place. But the rate of increase slowed. Part of the post-1975 increase shown here was due to the huts' being open for longer periods in the spring and fall seasons.

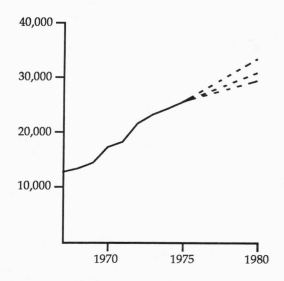

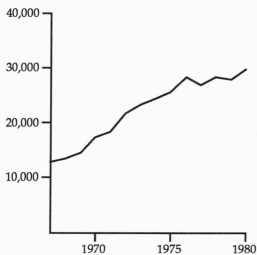

On the other hand, in the Green Mountain Club lodges on Mount Mansfield (where data was not systematically available until 1972), here was the trend through 1975:

And here's what happened after 1975. The GMC did not actively promote more business in its lodges and, in fact, discouraged overuse of the Long Trail.

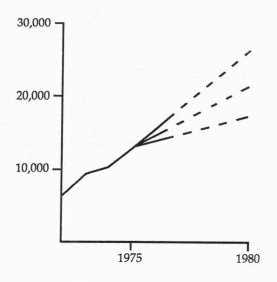

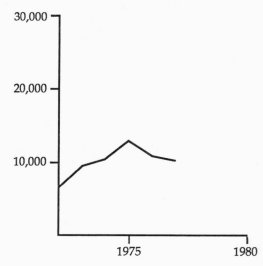

Unquestionably a major shock that checked the momentum of the boom was the oil crisis of 1974–75. The sudden price rise and sporadic shortages of gas made leisure trips to the mountains more difficult and expensive. The long-range impact of this factor was probably overemphasized in early assessments, however; the boom continued to taper long after gas prices stopped rising and even declined. Short-term economic setbacks also received more credit than they deserved. The most important basic explanation, besides the underlying population curves, was a distinct shift in attitudes and values, especially among young people—from the era of the 1965–75 back-to-nature generation to that of the young urban professionals of the 1980s.

One reason why the trend could reverse direction so quickly was the relatively short period of time that most of the new generation of hikers devoted to their interest in the outdoors. Many of the backpackers, peakbaggers, rock climbers, and other recreationists entered the sport with gusto for about two or three years, then almost as quickly withdrew in favor of some other hobby or career. So when the rate of entry slackened, it was not long before total numbers dropped back.

Along with the end of the upturn in numbers, two other major factors saved the Northeastern backcountry from the dire predictions of the early 1970s. One was the institution of backcountry management through the cooperative efforts of public agencies and concerned private groups, especially the major hiking clubs (the AMC, GMC, and ADK). The second was the pervasive spread of an environmental ethic. Neither was altogether new. There had been supervision of the backcountry before, by state agencies and National Forest personnel. Responsible campers had always followed courteous camping practices. But the scale and impact of both took giant strides in response to the unprecedented numbers of the backpacking boom. The influence of backcountry management and environmental ethics is not just the subject of the next chapter; it pervades everything that has happened in the hikers' world since 1970.

Chapter 52

Environmental ethics and backcountry management

I<small>N</small> 1950 Catskills campers were advised to burn green wood, "if you want a fire for all-night service," cut bough beds for comfort, and "always trench for drainage around your campsite." These holdovers from prewar tenets guided Northeastern campers when the backpacking boom began. Such practices could not survive when the numbers began to escalate.

The antilitter drive

The first major expression of environmental concern addressed the subject of litter. Thoughtful hikers had always avoided casually discarding waste papers, but such care was by no means universal. Furthermore, even the most progressive of prewar campers either buried such trash as tin cans—the more conscientious would remove the labels and flatten them first—or made use of generally accepted garbage pits located more or less discreetly in back of shelters or popular tenting areas. These pits were called "the goat" or other local nicknames. As the backpacking boom caught hold, these pits rapidly began to fill up and overflow until they became all too conspicuous "islands of blight in the woods."

The first organized and well-publicized antilitter campaign to marshall broad support and achieve dramatic results took place in the spring of 1965. That year Elizabeth Levers became chair of the Conservation Committee of the New York Chapter of the Appalachian Mountain Club. Levers had been active in New York hiking circles since before World War II, but in 1965, with her leadership on the litter issue, she began to emerge as one of the Northeast's prime movers and shakers on environmental concerns, a role she played with increasing effectiveness for many years thereafter.

That spring, under Levers's leadership, the AMC chapter turned out sixty people, working in crews of ten or fifteen over a string of eight weekends. They marched into each of twelve shelters in Harriman Park and began picking up every piece of paper, every can, every bottle, every bit of plastic, foil, glass, and miscellany, stuffing it all in enormous trash bags. Some thirty to forty bulging bags of litter were carried out, either by individuals toting packboards or by two people carrying a long pole from which the monstrous bags were suspended like primitive hunters' quarry. Finding Boy Scouts camped at a couple of the shelters, Levers pressed them into service, the boys picking up trash, their leaders helping to carry it out.

Recognizing that litter would be an annual crop and that "the job will never be finished," Levers broadened the program during the following year to involve several other clubs in the New York area, as well as Boy Scout troops. Before long, the annual litter pick-up became one of the most visible programs of the New York–New Jersey Trail Conference. Twenty years later it was still going strong, though the amount of litter picked up each year was down by at least one-third, thanks to public education (and a New York State bottle bill).

The message spread rapidly during the late 1960s. In the White Mountains, the AMC's trail crew systematically closed up the "goats," carefully burying every trace. The GMC took corresponding action in the Green Mountains. In the Adirondacks, the ADK and the Mohawk Valley Hiking Club, under the lead of Almy Coggeshall, organized a shelter cleanup in the Marcy area in 1966 and annually thereafter. The Forty-Sixers' organization joined in a few years later with a massive program for distributing litter bags at trail-heads, a practice later followed by Baxter State Park authorities at Katahdin. At besieged Monadnock, cleaning up the trails was a major focus of a coordinated program that culminated in the establishment of an ecocenter there in 1970.

The antilitter forces early recognized that an ounce of prevention would be worth the many pounds of cure that they were picking up and carrying out. Campaigns developed to spread the message to the incoming swarms of campers and hikers. Various slogans were tried. "You *can* take it with you" was a theme of the AMC's first spring cleanup in Harriman Park. Levers had noticed a poster in a Michigan state park that read "Leave nothing but footprints." This was later expanded to include the gospel of not destroying vegetation, as "Take nothing but pictures, leave nothing but footprints." Connecticut trailsman Ned Greist spread the idea of and term *hiker's pocket*, as he encouraged everyone he hiked with to pick up every shred of litter all day, then derive satisfaction from emptying a bulging pocketful into a trash container at end of day. He and other Northeastern hiking leaders did a lot by setting a personal example. But the most widely used slogan ultimately was a simple one: "Carry In—Carry Out."

Of all the environmental programs spawned in response to the backpacking boom, none was more fully accepted and widely successful than the antilitter campaign. Indeed the message was so thoroughly put over that many take it for granted today. A generation of hikers has grown up with an almost instinctive aversion to simply dropping a candy wrapper. There remained offenders, and litter carry-out programs continued to be big events at Harriman Park and throughout the region, but Northeastern trails and shelters remained remarkably litter free even during the most hectic years of the boom. As the early zeal for environmental protection slackened during the 1980s, some creeping increase in litter was noted in places, illustrating the need for continuing emphasis as new generations of hikers take to the woods. But the basic message was solidly established by the programs that began with Elizabeth Levers's 1965 litter pickups.

Next in chronological order was a resolve to stop casually picking or cutting vegetation. The "take nothing but pictures" portion of the slogan just cited was directed at such malpractices as peeling bark from white birches and picking pretty wildflowers. This message too spread quickly and effectively. As with the antilitter campaign, success was not 100 percent, but nothing like the indiscriminate vegetative destruction of the 1960s seemed likely to recur.

But litter pickup and respect for flowers, though essential and badly needed, were the easy, noncontroversial, and relatively superficial elements in the awakening environmental consciousness. By the end of the 1960s, with the new army of backpackers invading Northeastern mountains, much more basic questions had to be confronted. For these, answers would be neither easy nor popular.

1969: Year of awakening

The year 1969 was a landmark for acknowledging the problem almost simultaneously in every major mountain sector of the Northeast, and along a wide variety of fronts.

At *Katahdin*, in August 1969, Baxter State Park authorities decided that Chimney Pond had taken such a beating that its beleaguered shores needed and deserved a thorough rest. So they announced plans to close the area to camping and to transfer all overnight traffic down to Basin Ponds. "We have to move," said a Chimney Pond ranger. "We find we are destroying what we are trying to preserve." The announcement sent shock waves through the ranks of hikers who knew Chimney Pond. That Baxter State Park would close down such a beautiful and historic campsite, the magnificent amphitheater of Marcus Keep, the home of Leroy Dudley, the haunt of most Katahdinophiles for over a century! It must indeed be a crisis!

In the *Green Mountains*, 1969 was a year of great change, in which several distinct events signaled a rising environmental consciousness. One was the start-up of a coordinated program for managing Mount Mansfield's summit area. Cooperating groups included Vermont's Forest and Parks Department, the Mount Mansfield Company (which operated Mansfield's ski and other tourist facilities), the Green Mountain Club, and the University of Vermont. A progressive and imaginative director of Forests and Parks, Rodney Barber, played a key role in bringing action. Besides coordinating the joint efforts of everyone involved, Barber hired the first full-time ranger to patrol the summit area during the summer of 1969, the first step toward a strong environmental education campaign. Also that summer, the GMC's Burlington Section reinstituted a caretaker system at Taft Lodge, Mansfield's most crowded shelter; although originally viewed as protecting the club's property from vandalism, shelter caretakers soon joined forces with Barber's summit rangers on the front line, contacting hikers and educating them on more sensitive use of the outdoors.[a] In October 1969 a Green Mountain Profile Committee was organized under the leadership of another key environmentalist figure of the time, University of Vermont botanist Hubert Vogelmann; building on Vogelmann's in-depth research on upper-elevation environments, this committee sought to develop an ecological approach to the preservation of the Green Mountain profile. And it was in 1969 that Shirley Strong became president of the GMC. Perhaps the most dynamic of all Vermont's environmental leaders at that time, Strong was active everywhere: she was "the driving force, the real organizer" of the Green Mountain Profile Committee, according to Vogelmann; she constantly prodded Barber and his staff to action; she was the GMC's first female president and also the first GMC president to move that club decisively toward bold responses to the impact of the backpacking boom. In an early message to GMC members, Strong focused club attention on

> the increasing number of hikers and increasing use of shelters. This interest in hiking and the outdoors is certainly wonderful; the trail is there to be used and enjoyed. But greater use brings greater responsibility and more problems of maintenance.

In the *White Mountains*, most of the change came later, during the early 1970s, but here too 1969 saw one landmark event; the release of a report by an AMC trail crew study team (Edward Spencer and Mark Dannenhauer) on the sorry state of White Mountain shelters and their environs, which were reeling under the impact of the backpacking boom. Spencer and Dannenhauer recommended bold action to deal with an unacceptable situation. Within a year the AMC and the White Mountain National Forest were moving along radical lines to remedy the abuses that the Spencer-Dannenhauer report identified, as we'll see presently.

In the *Adirondacks*, 1969 marked the first full year of the Temporary Study Commission on the Future of the Adirondacks, created by Gov. Nelson Rockefeller on September 19, 1968. This was recognized by conservationists as "the state's first response to the question of use and preservation of the character of the Adirondacks." Its recommendations, issued

---

[a]Employing shelter caretakers resurrected an old system. Back in the 1930s, with jobs scarce elsewhere, several GMC Long Trail lodges had hired caretakers.

in 1970, were the basis for official action to preserve the high peaks environment. In 1969 both the Adirondack Mountain Club and the Adirondack Forty-Sixers were beginning to produce educational materials urging more responsible use of the backcountry. And it was in 1969 that a member of the Forty-Sixers, Mason Ingram, stirred up a hornet's nest within that peakbagging society by proposing what he called "wilderness paths" on what had been regarded up until that time as trailless peaks. Ingram's point was that these peaks were becoming so riddled with "herd paths" that they were no longer genuine bushwhacks. The damage created by all the different paths, he argued, could be reduced by recognizing just one path and blocking off others. The plan was greeted with a chorus of protest from other Forty-Sixers and resoundingly rejected. But within two years the Forty-Sixers began to move decisively into programs of environmental protection of their beloved mountains.

No Northeastern peak was more overrun with visitors than New Hampshire's solitary but highly accessible southern sentinel, the *Grand Monadnock*. In 1968 a Monadnock Advisory Committee formed, representing the state's Department of Resources and Economic Development, the Society for the Protection of New Hampshire Forests, and interested individuals. In 1969 this committee drew up plans to "orient the climbing public to take better care of the mountain" and to "make the public more aware of the importance of the natural environment for good recreation and maintaining a quality environment for the future." To implement these goals, an "ecocenter" was opened in 1970 at the state park's most used trail-head and parking area.

From these beginnings in 1969, new ways of thinking and new action programs evolved throughout the Northeast, directed toward preserving the hiking and camping environment. Land managers, hiking and trail clubs, schools, summer camps, and an entire generation of individual hikers and backpackers changed their ways so as to mitigate the impact of the backpacking boom.

It was an exciting time of change and idealism. All over the Northeast —indeed, all over the United States—the outdoor community felt a sense of mission, a new dedication to safeguarding the precious islands of wildness left in an urban society. Not many generations really get to "save the world," but the hikers and climbers and backpackers and land managers of the early 1970s genuinely believed that they *were* saving *their* world, the mountains and woods and waters in which they enjoyed their outdoor adventures.

Different approaches to backcountry management

In the brief outline of that time that follows, note the variety of response within the major mountain areas of the Northeast: Katahdin, the Green

Mountains, the White Mountains, the Adirondacks, and the lesser ranges farther south. Special note should also be made of the unique problems of the alpine zone, found in varying degrees in each of the four major northerly ranges. These divergent approaches were based on very different philosophies of backcountry management, yet they shared a profound concern for preserving the mountain environment.

KATAHDIN. Chimney Pond in the 1960s illustrated vividly many of the maladies of the backpacking boom: butchered vegetation, trampled soils, quagmires in front of the shelters, overflowing outhouses, pollution of water sources. Hence came Baxter Park's 1969 announcement that the area would be closed. After thoroughly investigating the alternative site at Basin Ponds, park officials opted for retaining the original campground at Chimney after all. But along with that decision came fresh moves by park management toward closer supervision of all visitors.

Since 1950 Baxter Park had differed from other Northeastern areas in exercising greater control over hiking and camping practices. Over two decades these rules had been gradually tightened. In 1971 park officials issued a new and still more comprehensive set of regulations. These included complete control of access to the park; required advance registration; allowed absolutely no camping except at a dozen or so official campgrounds (each of them ranger-patrolled); required knowledge on the part of the rangers of exactly where each visitor was camped each night and what his or her planned itinerary was each day; required ranger approval of each hiker's clothing, footgear, and camping equipment; and even included decisions as to whether to permit or prohibit climbing of Katahdin at all, according to weather conditions, and (on days when climbing was permitted) designating hours beyond which no one was permitted to start up a hiking trail.

Here was one extreme school of backcountry management. Through these rules, Baxter State Park probably secured a prompter and more thorough control of unsound camping practices and of campfires than any other Northeastern hiking center. Of course this protection of the physical resource was achieved at a considerable cost in reduced freedom for Katahdin campers.

THE GREEN MOUNTAINS. Vermont's response was at the opposite end of the scale: primary reliance was placed on educating hikers to behave more responsibly, on obtaining voluntary cooperation rather than using stringent rules, and on awakening an environmental conscience.

The rangers installed on the summit of Mount Mansfield beginning in 1969 were a new breed. During the early 1970s, both on Mansfield and Camel's Hump, the job description broadened and deepened into what was called a "ranger-naturalist." Instead of the old enforcement or fire control duties, these new-style ranger-naturalists focused on "low-key on-site educational encounters with the hiking public." They spent hours simply sitting on top of the mountain. When a hiking party showed up, the ranger-naturalist casually joined the group and initiated conversation on the unique qualities of the alpine zone, leading to the "message" of everyone's helping to save the vegetation by staying on trail or on rocks. No orders were given, no summonses issued, no regulations quoted. Duties included some work on trails and availability for search and rescue, but the chief focus was always educational. "We keep watch over tundra like a lifeguard over a beach," said one ranger-naturalist.

> There, I have just seen someone walking upon the sedge meadow. I wander over and strike up a conversation. Sooner or later I bring up the subject of the alpine vegetation. My message in its essence is this: let's walk on the rocks so our children's children may experience this alpine summit undisturbed: otherwise the rare plants will be trampled to death.
>
> Getting this message across takes initiative, tact, and sensitivity. Above all, a ranger-naturalist should not carry an attitude of overbearing authority or superiority. I am an educator, not a policeman; my tools are common sense and the power of persuasion, not regulations and a strident voice.

Down below treeline a new educational emphasis infected the shelter-caretaker jobs that the GMC's Burlington Section had launched at Taft Lodge in 1969. During the early 1970s GMC caretakers sprang up at more shelters along the Long Trail until by 1975 the GMC (the parent club now) had twenty-one seasonal caretakers, chiefly around Mansfield, Camel's Hump, and popular ponds such as Stratton and Little Rock. This growth was directed largely by Kenn Boyd, one of the early Mansfield ranger-naturalists and a thoroughly education-oriented leader. Boyd and others guided the original watchdog function into a broader "multi-purpose" job description. As summarized by Boyd, they were "public relations people, historians, environmentalists, guides, and a friend to all hikers." Like the ranger-naturalists above treeline, the shelter caretakers were the frontline missionaries for the new ethic. "We're not here just to enforce rules," a Little Rock Pond caretaker told *Vermont Life*, "but to show people how they can help protect a beautiful but fragile area." On Mansfield and Camel's Hump, ranger-naturalists and shelter caretakers worked closely together to put across the message of the new environmental ethic.

For budgetary reasons, the GMC could never afford to staff its entire chain of Long Trail facilities with paid help. The gaps in coverage were partially filled with the launching of an "Adopt-a-Shelter" program in 1970, under which any GMC member might sign up to look out for one particular shelter. The "adopters" would visit their shelters anywhere from two or three times a year to nearly every weekend, depending on how much time they had and how much their interest was engaged. At its peak, the GMC's Adopt-a-Shelter program covered forty shelters.

Katahdin's locale was limited enough, the Green Mountains' crowds small enough, so that the one's dependence on a set of rules and the other's on education seemed sufficient to handle the job. In the White Mountains and the Adirondacks, use levels were far higher, the area broader and more diffused. More innovative and in some ways more radical approaches seemed to be demanded. Backcountry managers reacted accordingly.

THE WHITE MOUNTAINS. On July 26, 1970, the time-hallowed Liberty Springs Shelter in the woods below the Franconia Ridge was torn down by the AMC trail crew. In its place, wooden platforms on which backpackers could put up their own tents were constructed at scattered sites throughout the nearby woods. A new outhouse was installed. The "goat" was closed up. Fires were not completely outlawed, but were restricted to two sites, and portable gas stoves were highly recommended. Most important was the installation of a full-time caretaker throughout the peak camping season. Like that of Vermont's ranger-naturalists and shelter caretakers, his role was partly educational. Wandering among the campers, he counseled against cutting live firewood or fir boughs, pointed out the advantages of stoves, reminded everyone to carry out trash, answered questions about why the shelter was gone, and generally preached the gospel of saving the backcountry environment. However, the AMC's shelter caretakers were also out-and-out "managers" of their areas as well, assigning platforms as campers arrived, ensuring good behavior, safeguarding against illegal camping. "The kingpin of the whole program," said AMC Trails Supervisor Robert D. Proudman, "was caretaking—having knowledgeable personnel always at the site."

In 1971 the Liberty Springs experiment was followed up by tearing down the old shelter at Garfield Pond and closing that lovely, fragile, much abused area to camping. A new site was chosen, on the other side of Mount Garfield, and once again emphasis was on tent platforms and the educational-managerial presence of a caretaker. In succeeding years the trail crew moved through the chain of most used shelters—Guyot, Ethan Pond, Mizpah, the Imp, Speck Pond—forcing White Mountain trampers to convert from shelters and campfires to tents and stoves at designated sites.

These strong measures reflected changes in management thinking, both in the White Mountain National Forest offices and at the AMC. For the WMNF, the unprecedented crowds assaulting the White Mountains elicited the most innovative response in the history of backcountry management in the White Mountains. In 1971 WMNF officials banned all camping in Tuckerman and Huntington ravines except at designated sites and prohibited all campfires there. The next year, the WMNF broadened the attack, designating seventeen "Concentrated Use Areas" (later "Restricted Use Areas" or "RUAs") throughout the White Mountains, including many of the sites where the AMC had built tent platforms and installed caretakers. In these areas, camping was restricted to designated sites or 200 feet away from streams, trails, or roads. In 1975 the WMNF placed even tighter controls on use of federally designated Wilderness Areas—just two at that time in the White Mountains. Here, instead of concentrating use at designated sites, the WMNF experimented with dispersed camping, removing the old shelters and promoting a more diffused pattern with more opportunities for solitude, a pattern deemed more appropriate to a wilderness experience. Under a succession of able forest supervisors beginning with Paul Weingart in 1973, WMNF officials encouraged new and experimental responses both within WMNF personnel and among cooperating private groups, notably the AMC. WMNF officials also carried their case to the hiking public, setting up twenty-one "working groups" to advise them, soliciting hiker comment on proposed policies (1,300 responses counted officially in the three-year period 1973–75), and otherwise sought both to evoke and to respond to the aroused environmental conscience of the hiking community.

In 1971 the AMC reorganized staff operations, greatly expanding its north country office at Pinkham Notch and creating the post of educational director. Dynamic young leadership was provided by Thomas S. Deans as associate executive director in charge of the north country and by John B. Nutter as educational director. Before the year was out, the club was trying to reach every hiker in the White Mountains with the environmental message. Handouts, posters, presentations, and the pages of club publications hammered the theme. Ultimately the AMC's Education Department developed a wide range of evening programs, weekend and week long seminars, and exhibits at the Pinkham Notch facility; posters and informal talks by AMC crews and visiting "hut naturalists" at the off-road huts; and a variety of other imaginative measures for getting the point across to New England hikers through outfitter stores, magazines, and direct contacts with schools and summer camps.

THE ADIRONDACKS. The 1970 demolition of Liberty Springs Shelter seemed to be the beginning of the end of a way of life in the Northeastern backcountry. Shelter camping—the twentieth-century legacy of the old mountain guides' bark lean-tos—was winding down in the White Mountains and was soon in retreat in the Adirondacks as well.

The Adirondacks' Temporary Study Commission warned in 1971 that shelters were serving as attractions for excessive camping in fragile areas, and urged the closing of all shelters above 3,500 feet. The issue was debated warmly for several years, but by the end of 1976 New York's Department of Environmental Conservation (DEC) removed seven Adirondack lean-tos, all above 3,500 feet, each a magnet for crowds of campers. Whereas White

Mountain shelters had come down with relatively little controversy, the Adirondack lean-to was deeply rooted in ancestral memories, going back to the old bark contrivances of John Cheney and his generation. The older camping generation in 1976 had been nurtured on enchanted nights ensconced in open-front shelters at Lake Arnold and Indian Falls or high up at Four Corners, back in earlier and quieter years. The DEC's shelter removal therefore engendered a heartfelt anguish not met elsewhere. Still, the program proceeded, readily accepted by most of the new wave of hikers. Besides removing shelters, the DEC later instituted camping restrictions, requiring tents to be 150 feet from roads, trails, or bodies of water, or at designated sites; and prohibiting camping or fires above 4,000 feet in the Adirondacks or 3,500 feet in the Catskills.

After the mid-1970s official zeal for shelter removal relented. Neither in the White Mountains nor in the Adirondacks were backcountry shelters totally abolished. At critical points—grossly overused sites or environmentally sensitive ones such as those above 4,000 feet, or sites too close to roads (and thus prey to the incursion of nonhiker parties, often well lubricated with beer or more potent influences)—the shelters were removed. Elsewhere they remained as welcome havens to more limited traffic. The downturn in the backpacking boom after 1975 made it possible for backcountry managers to withhold the ax from many less-affected shelter sites.

As in New Hampshire and Vermont, Adirondack officials, both public (the DEC) and private (the ADK, the Forty-Sixers) launched an aggressive educational program during the early 1970s. In 1974 the ADK set up a ridge-runner staff, with functions similar to those of Vermont's ranger-naturalists. Three young people were hired that first summer, primarily to talk with campers and hikers about prudent treatment of the mountain environment. The ADK's ridge-runners had wider responsibilities than their Vermont counterparts, as they covered both below-treeline camping centers and alpine zones, and were involved with safety and equipment counseling, searches and rescues, and litter pickup. Still, a large part of the job was educational. Commented one of the early ADK ridge-runners:

> My job is to make people behave a bit better than they have been, and chief goal was to educate the public and, having failed to educate, then pick up after them. Since I prefer to educate rather than pick up, I emphasized education.

In 1975 the DEC reassigned one of its young Catskill rangers to the Marcy area, then a seething cauldron of too many hikers and campers, with the ADK's educational efforts barely started. Ranger C. Peter Fish made himself, over the next decade, possibly the best-known single figure in the Adirondack backcountry since Old Mountain Phelps. He combined an outgoing personality, easygoing, self-deprecating sense of humor, inner toughness, long hours on the job, and a fast hiking pace that enabled him to be seemingly everywhere at once. Tirelessly roaming the trails, loitering around trail-head parking areas, or basking among the crowds atop sunny summits, he always seemed to be where the problem was. He spoke at countless gatherings of hiking clubs and summer camps, was always available to the media, yet seemed to pop up at some distant backcountry nook whenever someone was about to set up an illegal campsite, cut a live tree, or wash a pot in a brook.

Fish was by no means a one-man gang. Both the ADK and the Forty-Sixers were tuning up educational efforts around the time he arrived on the scene. In fact, Fish quickly recognized the efficacy of the fledgling ADK ridge-runner program and urged DEC higher-ups to copy it. The result was the hiring in 1978 of ten young adults as seasonal "park rangers" (as distinct from "forest rangers"), with educational rather than primarily enforcement duties similar to those of the ADK's ridge-runners, but with the added clout of official DEC status and uniform. This program was expanded to include more than twenty rangers per year during the 1980s before budget cuts pared it down.

ELSEWHERE. The ridge-runner concept spread during the late 1970s to areas far from the alpine zones where the concept had been born. In Connecticut's low, forested, but nonetheless overused hills, the AMC's Connecticut Chapter volunteers began roving the 55-mile section of the Appalachian Trail to counsel hikers on proper camping practices. In 1979 paid seasonal ridge-runners were hired to carry on this work. Later the program was picked up in western Massachusetts as well. In the mountains of western Maine, the Maine Appalachian Trail Club initiated programs similar to those of the AMC, the GMC, and others, tailored to the specific problems of heavily used areas such as the Bigelow Range.

THE ALPINE ZONE. A place where backcountry management was vital during the backpacking boom was the land above treeline.

The Northeastern alpine zone is a place of paradox. The winter weather is notoriously vicious, often touted as the worst anywhere outside the polar regions. Surely here is one of the most hostile environments imaginable for plant life. The rich variety of alpine flowers, sedges and grasses, mosses and lichens have to be among the toughest, most determined, most resilient specimens of vegetation in the world. They endure winds that people can't stand up in. Their regular residence is a realm that, for many months of the year, people can't even visit without elaborate protective clothing. Yet this same plant community, so tough in some respects, is also painfully fragile. The tiny flowers are easily uprooted. Thin clumps of soil may be kicked away by a single passing hiker. In one weekend the work of decades of plant colonization can be trampled back to ground zero—an apt application of that term.

The backpacking boom was particularly hard on this region. The appeal of camping out above the trees under the wide mountaintop sky was irresistible to the back-to-nature generation. Tents and sleeping bags were often slapped down on what started as luxuriant beds of alpine flowers. Boot traffic cut broad swaths through the tundra. The scene was the same wherever summits were truly above treeline: the Presidentials and Franconia Ridge, Katahdin and the Bigelows, Mansfield and Camel's Hump, Marcy and half a dozen other Adirondack peaks. Below treeline the backpacking boom created an environmental problem; above the trees it created an environmental crisis.

From Katahdin to Marcy all public authorities ultimately declared the alpine zones off limits to camping—at Katahdin and Mansfield in 1971, in the White Mountains' extensive zones in 1973, in the Adirondacks in 1977. But the next step—how to keep day-hikers from continuing to trample the plant communities—varied widely from place to place in both form and timing.

During the mid-1960s—note how early in relation to the awakening of environmental consciousness described heretofore—two Syracuse University foresters began to study the destruction of alpine plant communities in the Adirondacks. One was Raymond E. Leonard, who later moved to New Hampshire, where he played a lead role in backcountry research and development of environmental programs. The other was Edwin H. Ketchledge, who remained in New York to become a driving force in promoting environmental consciousness among Adirondack hikers. They worked at first on Mount Dix, later broadening out to all the alpine summits and especially those of the MacIntyre Range (Algonquin, Wright). Ketchledge's and Leonard's studies contributed useful understanding of the basic mechanisms of alpine ecology. More important historically, Ketchledge and Leonard undertook direct action to reverse the degradation they were observing. After completing carefully watched experiments, they evolved strategies for reseeding summits with precisely tailored combinations of commercial grass seeds and fertilizers. The commercial grasses acted as temporary catalysts, enabling original native alpine species to move back into the "artificial lawns." Ketchledge, Leonard (until his move to New Hampshire), and a large number of interested graduate students and volunteers devoted long hours to summit reseeding work. By 1988 Ketchledge had climbed the MacIntyre Range more than two hundred times.

But Ketchledge recognized that neither plant science nor dedicated volunteer work could solve the problem. If the trampling hordes of lug soles continued to crisscross the alpine zones, no vegetation could catch hold permanently. Either the traffic had to stop or it had to be channeled into a single path, leaving the rest of the alpine zone to grow in peace. There was little prospect of stemming the tide of hikers. What could be done to get everyone to stay on one trail?

This was the beginning of Ketchledge's involvement with the Forty-Sixers, the organization that he reasoned could best reach the hikers frequenting the alpine summits of the Adirondacks. The story of the Forty-Sixers' response to this challenge is told in chapter 58.

Meanwhile, however, others were taking action to preserve and protect the alpine zones of New England. In Vermont, as before noted, the ranger-naturalist program was centered on the state's two significant alpine zones, Mansfield and Camel's Hump. The emphasis here was almost purely educational: direct, low-key contacts with hikers, plus articles in GMC publications, plus educational signs erected at treeline. White Mountain crowds were so much larger, the alpine zone so much bigger and potentially more dangerous in bad weather, that educational efforts here took a backseat to the ever present need for enforcement and safety concerns. The difference between the two areas is illuminated in the signs greeting hikers at treeline in the two ranges. In the White Mountains the big, bright yellow sign stressed safety:

STOP

THE AREA AHEAD HAS THE WORST WEATHER IN AMERICA. MANY HAVE DIED THERE FROM EXPOSURE, EVEN IN THE SUMMER. TURN BACK NOW IF THE WEATHER IS BAD.

In the Green Mountains the equivalently located sign, in subdued brown, dwelt on environmental concerns:

The Area Ahead Is One of the Two Arctic Alpine Zones in Vermont. The plants—grasses and sedges are rare and very fragile. Footsteps kill them! Please walk only on the rock trail.

In the Adirondacks also the message was environmental:

Please stay on the marked trail to prevent trampling of the fragile summit vegetation.

With damage to the tundra still proceeding in the White Mountains, despite educational and enforcement efforts, the AMC's trail crew launched strong measures to define one trail and block off alternatives, so as to confine hiker traffic (see chapter 56).

A major focus of White Mountain alpine zone management was a small patch of ground northeast of Mount Monroe. There, on an unlikely patch of gravelly rubble, grew the world's only known colony of a dwarf cinquefoil originally spotted by William Oakes in the nineteenth century and named to honor his fellow botanist J. W. Robbins. The *Potentilla robbinsiana* was an endangered species if there ever was one: the heavily traveled Crawford Path plus a side trail to Oakes Gulf ran right through the tiny plant's sole known habitat. Not only was it pulverized by casual passersby, but botanists from all over made pilgrimages to the "Monroe Flats" to see it —and so obscure was its tiny form that many curious viewers trampled the few, surviving plants in the very process of trying to find them. During the 1970s research teams from the Forest Service, the AMC, and the University of New Hampshire agonized over how to save the threatened plant. By the early 1980s a multipronged strategy had evolved. The side trail was relocated away from the area. The officially approved treadway of the Crawford Path was demarcated by low walls of scree rock on either side, and warning signs gave prominent mention to the fine for stepping outside. An earlier proposal to reroute the historic path to the other side of Monroe was strongly considered but ultimately rejected on practical, safety, and sentimental grounds.

BACKCOUNTRY PLANNING. The measures described so far were aimed at specific targets: shelter sites, alpine zones, rare plants. As backcountry management matured during the late 1970s, the concept broadened. Comprehensive integrated planning for entire mountain areas or trail systems evolved. A new wave of backcountry managers perceived planning as an essential tool for preserving the values sought by hikers and campers. The theory was that never again would uncontrolled abuses be allowed to take their own course, if backcountry management could be effectively implemented at an early stage. As the computer offered its useful services, backcountry management enlarged its scope voraciously. From the broadest theaters of operation—for example, the White Mountain National Forest, the Adirondacks high peaks region, the Appalachian Trail—down to the lowliest parcel of suburban woods, municipal watershed, or tiny cluster of nature trails, every sorcerer's apprentice developed a "management plan." Sometimes backcountry management seemed awash in a sea of paperwork. One 1979 "presidential unit plan" prepared by the White Mountain National Forest ran 269 pages. A 1981 "comprehensive plan" for the Appalachian Trail ran to 163 pages, with nine appendixes. The very next year a "case study" for the AT consumed 143 pages on its own. But despite voluminous inputs of individuals' time and attention, endless meetings, a most extraordinary output of paperwork, plus a new and bewildering jargon, land managers believed that the new methods ensured more prudent advance planning and a broader perspective on alternative solutions.

From the problems of the much fussed-over dwarf cinquefoil, to those of hundreds of campers in Tuckerman Ravine on a single weekend, to those of restructuring the land management of 2,100 miles of Appalachian Trail, the impact of the backpacking boom inexorably summoned a new level of response. Backcountry management became a presence throughout Northeastern recreation areas, an inescapable consequence of the backpacking boom, an influence on camping and hiking ethics from the Hudson Highlands to Katahdin.

Chapter 53

Backcountry camping in the seventies and eighties

W HAT of the hikers and campers who were the object of all this backcountry management? Earlier we described backcountry camping in the 1880s and 1890s, the age of bedrolls and bark shelters, and in the 1920s and 1930s, with Bergens, campfires, and Comey's 10-pound pack. What changes came with the postwar years?

When we last left the backcountry overnighter (chapter 42), he (or, only occasionally then, she) was clad in red-and-black-checkered lumber shirt, rough wool trousers, and work boots, carrying a sagging ruck-sack, and heading for an Adirondack lean-to, one of Buchanan's Long Trail camps, or a White Mountain shelter. In the 1950s and even the early 1960s, this uniform still prevailed, augmented only by a smattering of Army-Navy surplus clothing and equipment. However, by the late 1960s to early 1970s, the image suddenly changed. The aluminum frame pack, at first almost synonymous with the brand name of Kelty, swept the field at that time, almost completely replacing the old rucksack and other 1950s pack styles. Long pants were discarded in favor of shorts, so completely that the sight of full-length trousers on a summer hiking trail became nearly as rare as a blanket roll. Brightly colored nylon rushed into the backpacker's world and took over—in tents, sleeping bags, and parkas.

A special niche was carved out in Northeastern hiking by an Austrian bootmaker who emigrated to Intervale, New Hampshire, within sight of Mount Washington, where he set up a family business producing limited numbers of custom-made hiking boots. Three generations of Peter Limmer & Sons churned out an unchanging, fashionless, colorless (black) product, winning a degree of loyalty among Northeastern hikers that is perhaps without parallel in the annals of the outfitting business. Limmer boots were the uniform of White Mountain hikers from the 1950s on, even when demand outpaced the family's ability to produce them so that the waiting period for a new pair ran as high as three-and-a-half years.

Throughout the Northeast, leather hiking boots with "waffle-stomper" lug soles were standard footgear.

During the 1950s and early 1960s the Adirondack lean-to and its equivalents reached ascendancy. Shelters were constructed all along Maine's Appalachian Trail, largely under the direction of the MATC's master lean-to-builder, Louis Chorzempa. Chorzempa and his helpers built an average of two shelters per year from 1953 through 1959, forging a complete chain throughout the AT in Maine. Shelters were then available almost anywhere one might wish to stay in the Northeastern backcountry—and one usually had it all to oneself (and the local porcupine, especially in Vermont).

The full force of the backpacking boom brought more sweeping changes in the overnight camper's world. Backcountry camping in the 1970s and 1980s was characterized less by a new set of hallmarks than by a constantly changing kaleidoscope. Modern technology leaped to the fore. Whatever revolt against the machine age had been identified with the 1960s was replaced by the 1980s generation's eager acceptance of all that science could bring. Into the world of wool and leather and war surplus marched plastic and rip-stop nylon in flashing colors and an abundance of other manmade fabrics and design innovations. The changes— not merely compared with 1950 or the 1960s, but even within the 1970s and 1980s—are suggested by a comparison of leading outfitters' catalogues of the early 1970s with those of the late 1980s.

> Tents of the 1970s were mostly A-frame designs, and the Gerry Himalaya was almost unique in offering wands to bow out the sides; in the catalogues of the 1980s, many pages of tents exhibited a wide variety of designs, with emphasis on domes and variants on the dome principle, most of them employing flexible poles to bow out the sides.

> Sleeping bags of the early 1970s were primarily down, and the top of the line model cost $130; after a period of popularity for synthetic fibers, down had returned to fashion by the late 1980s, but the warmest models cost more than $500.

> Packs of the early 1970s were virtually all draped on aluminum frames; by the late 1980s, external frames had dwindled in popularity in favor of back-hugging internal-frame models.

> Stoves of the early 1970s tended to be heavy, and ranged from less than $10 to just over $20 for the 4-pound Optimus 111B, the favorite among Northeastern winter campers; by the late 1980s emphasis was on light, technologically refined models, many hooked directly to fuel bottles (eliminating the weight of a separate tank), with prices ranging from $25 to $85.

Underwear of the early 1970s was fishnet of either cotton (summer) or wool (winter); late 1980s underwear was quick-drying, less-absorbent polypropylene and other new fabrics.

During the early 1970s the latest rage with hikers and climbers was the "60/40" wind parka, a fabric of 60 percent cotton and 40 percent nylon, originally marketed by Sierra Designs and selling for about $35; during the late 1980s wind and rain protection was often combined in a single Gore-tex-coated parka that could cost as much as $275.

The once universal all-leather hiking boot of the early 1970s was still dominant in summer hiking circles, but it now had competition from a variety of heavy-duty running shoes, a few Gore-tex-covered models, and lightweight, superwarm plastic double boots for winter hiking.

The remarkable advance in the price of outdoor gear—far outstripping the 170 percent increase in the general Consumer Price Index between 1971 and 1986, for example—was even more noteworthy when one considers that an apparently larger proportion of outdoor recreationists were dabblers for a few years at most, unlike the lifelong campers of preboom years. A 1983 *Business Week* article showed the directions in which backpacking had moved. Affluent readers were advised that a complete outfit for camping required an initial outlay of $750–$1,250; but that this investment was prudent because it "is sturdy and normally used only three or four times each year." In other words, many campers of the 1980s were (*a*) well heeled; (*b*) equipped with a costly array of state-of-the-art gear, and (*c*) expected to dabble in the activity for only a few days per year.

But more significant than the technology of equipment or its price was a change in the style of camping. The image that the hiker emulated had shifted from that of the old woodsman of the 1950s and 1960s to that of the young mountaineer of the 1970s and 1980s. By the 1980s the transition was complete: advertisements in one issue of *Backpacker* magazine featured seven testimonials from leading American technical climbers (Lou Whitaker twice, John Roskelly twice, Galen Rowell and Jim Wickwire once each, and one from an entire American Everest team); not a single red-and-black-checkered lumber shirt was to be found.

The new breed of campers widely embraced the new environmental ethic. Virtually no one cut bough beds or trenched tents. Portable gas stoves largely displaced the traditional campfire, and most backpackers stopped carrying an ax or hatchet—indeed would not have known how to use one. Sanitation received more attention: people stopped washing dishes or themselves in streams and were more careful about latrine location. Litter was rare, in areas away from the roads, and birch bark was no longer peeled. Aside from physical conservation, efforts were made to preserve the psychological "experience" as well. Club, summer camp, and Scout groups tried (for the most part) to reduce group size, so as not to invade the quiet ridges with noisy gangs of twenty or thirty. Parties made efforts to keep noise down, especially in the evening. Some sought to reduce the visual impact on others by choosing less gaudy colors for tents and packs.

Shelters remained the prime place to spend the night in Maine and Vermont. However, with the removal of so many shelters in New York and New Hampshire, many backpackers carried their own tents. Whether in shelters or tents, campers of the 1980s were less likely to be by themselves overnight. Backcountry camping was more often a social experience than one of solitude. The arts of sharing a lean-to or of the complex community relations of tenting areas required social skills that postboom backpackers had far more practice with than had their 1950s or prewar predecessors.

In the White Mountains the AMC hut system remained but underwent some drastic changes. One of the most conspicuous was the end of the male exclusivity on crews: women joined AMC hut crews during the early 1970s. With much greater numbers of guests each night, the experience of a night in the huts acquired an altogether different flavor from preboom days. Then a hut had been a quiet, backwoods haven shared with perhaps three or four like-minded outdoorspeople. During the 1970s and 1980s it was an animated sociable scene, with thirty or forty guests mingling and sharing the experiences of the day. The management style of the crews changed accordingly. Where the old crews had enjoyed the privileges of being extremely informal with guests—sometimes to the point of being surly, with impunity—the crews that ministered to the demands of the crowds of the 1970s and 1980s were selected for their ability to be efficient and friendly and to provide a climate of "mountain hospitality for all." The price of this service climbed understandably, so that many backpackers of those years found themselves priced out of the AMC huts. A gap grew between the hut-user and other backpackers, with consequences touched on in chapter 57.

In many areas, much of the tone of backcountry life and its prevailing environmental ethic were set by summer camps. During the late 1960s and 1970s the popularity of hiking or "tripping" programs at summer camps blossomed. At first most camps' leadership was poorly prepared to take their groups through the backcountry without leaving environmental havoc in their wake. All the prominent Northeastern clubs—the AMC, the GMC, the ADK, the Forty-Sixers, the Maine Appalachian Trail Club—directed special efforts to reach camp leaders with the new ethic, beginning in the early 1970s. Before long many summer camps and the newer "challenge" programs like Outward Bound, heartily if sometimes belatedly picked up the theme of environmental concerns. For some the new ethic evolved a step further to a doctrine of "clean" or "no-trace" or "low-impact" camping, under which the objective was to leave "no trace" of the group's having camped. These truly "clean" campers dispersed quietly to hidden campsites off trail, slept off the ground in hammocks, changed to sneakers once in camp, never went to and from water sources by the same route, meticulously picked up litter, and never camped more than once in the same spot. No-trace camping was enthusiastically adopted by some summer camps and other educational groups, thus indoctrinating legions of young campers in the new ethic.

Nationally the environmental cause was warmly championed by the Sierra Club, Wilderness Society, National Audubon, and other groups. Some new how-to books on backpacking were eloquent on environmental concerns, notably Harvey Manning's *Backpacking: One Step at a Time* and Albert Saijo's *The Backpacker*. Two leading magazines, *Backpacker* and *Wilderness Camping*, were major influences in spreading the new ethic. *Backpacker*, for example, filled its early issues with readable but stern exhortations: "Outing Impact," by Jack Hope in the first issue (spring 1973), no fewer than three pieces with the message in the second issue, Saijo's quietly eloquent "Go Light Backpacking" in the third, publisher William Kemsley's repeated editorials, and culminating in Manning's vigorous "Where Did All These Damn Hikers Come From?" which appeared at the very apex of the boom (summer 1975). *Wilderness Camping*'s Harry Roberts promoted these themes too and in 1975 contributed a full-length book, *Movin' Out*, which was not only the foremost Northeastern-oriented how-to backpacking manual of its day, but was suffused with the new ethic. Both Kemsley and Roberts were Northeasterners and thus viewed the issues in the light of this region's acute problems. Their efforts were joined in 1975 by a regional magazine, *New England Outdoors*, which regularly ran columns on hiking and camping ethics. During the late 1970s, books devoted entirely to environmental concerns for hikers and campers began to appear.

Outfitters pitched in with pamphlets devoted to the new ethic, notably Gerry's *How to Camp and Leave No Trace* (1972) and Quabaug Rubber's (the chief supplier of Vibram soles) *Stepping into Wilderness* (1978). The influential Recreational Equipment, Inc. (REI), ran editorials in catalogues. The willingness of commercial businesses to divert resources from selling products to getting across the public-interest message should not go unnoticed: REI, Gerry, Quabaug, Kemsley, Roberts, and like-minded entrepreneurs deserved a warm salute from the backpacking community for putting their money where their hearts lay.

There was another side of the coin. Backcountry campers during the 1970s and 1980s found themselves under unprecedented pressure from their own numbers, the impact they generated, and the desire to preserve the backcountry environment. It was harder to have that old feeling of complete freedom in the wilds and control over one's own actions there that the solitary, preboom campers had enjoyed. On every hand, it sometimes seemed, authorities or even one's own fellow hikers admonished against cutting trees, washing in the brook, tenting at the water's edge or up on the mountaintop. The generation that grew up with the new ethic could accept these restraints and take pride in their stewardship of the outdoors that restraint implied. Some of their elders, who had grown up free to stoke up the campfire and cut the bough bed, found it a strange and sometimes alien world. Some quickly adjusted, some resentfully defied, some fled to the less-frequented byways where the old ethic might yet prevail, for a time. The backcountry was always a lot roomier than those who followed only the well-trodden trails to the popular peaks realized. During the 1970s and 1980s, for those who looked hard enough, solitude could still be found amid the multitude.

During the decade of the 1980s, as the more frantic days of the backpacking boom receded in memory, and as the spirit of backcountry crowds moved from the back-to-nature innocence of the 1960s to the exercise-and-challenge sophistication of the 1980s, the zeal for environmental education diminished. Many caretakers and ridge-runners reverted to more of the administrative-enforcement role, rather than the strongly educational one of the 1970s. Club educational efforts were beamed more at teaching skills or at entertainment or old-fashioned nature walks. The media changed its messages. Kemsley and Roberts having moved on from their influential editorships, the magazines (both commercial press and club publications) switched from environmental themes to pushing innovations in clothing, equipment, and "backpacker chique," so appealing to the 1980s readers. As a result, the backcountry scene reflected some slippage in ethics—a bit more litter, a few more illegal campsites and campfires, fewer no-trace camping groups among summer camps.

But the environmentalist crusade of the 1970s, along with the new backcountry management policies, had left its mark. An indelible stamp would remain on the habits of Northeastern campers and hikers, reflecting attitudes of respect for and stewardship over the mountain environment.

Chapter 54

The clubs cope with change

T HERE is evidence that postwar hiking was more of an individual or family activity, less dominated by hiking clubs. It was easier to learn about the outdoors and acquire experience without dependence on a hiking club, as the outdoor press and equipment suppliers reached the hiking public directly. Improved highways and broader automobile ownership made trail-heads more accessible. Social clubs were generally in decline in American culture.

Yet the evidence is ambiguous: some clubs grew spectacularly, while others did not, considering the increase in outdoor use.

The AMC, eldest and always most extroverted of the three major hiking clubs, gathered members at a phenomenal rate for a while (see table 54.1).

More meaningful is what happened in individual chapters. Before the boom, the AMC's decentralized chapter form of organization helped preserve a small-club atmosphere for many members. The Connecticut Chapter, a "family" of fewer than 500 before the boom, numbered almost 2,000 by 1970 and shot over 3,000 during the early 1980s. Meetings

Table 54.1
GROWTH IN AMC MEMBERSHIP, 1955–1980

Year	Total Number of Members	Increase from Five Years Before	
		Number	Percent
1955	6,000	500	9
1960	7,500	1,500	25
1965	10,000	2,500	33
1970	13,900	3,900	39
1975	22,700	8,800	63
1980	25,300	2,600	11

Source: Appalachian Mountain Club.

shifted from members' homes to large public halls. The Maine Chapter, with just 124 members in 1965, doubled to 251 by 1970, then more than doubled again to 643 members by 1975. The New York Chapter, commented one member, "reached some kind of critical mass and has almost exploded." New York Appie outings in the Hudson Highlands grew into crowds of 50, 75, or more than 100 participants.

The change was more than quantitative, but the qualitative change was viewed differently by different members. Many younger and newer members welcomed the bustling spirit of expansion, vitality, and potential political power that growth implied. The diversity of interests of the membership spawned enthusiastic subcultures within the club, many of which lie outside the scope of a hiking and climbing history: white-water canoeing, bicycling, windsurfing, overseas touring. Evening programs with big-name speakers attracted turnouts of hundreds. On the other hand, some of the older and longtime loyal members felt a weakening of the sense of community and camaraderie. Leaders no longer knew all the members of a chapter and vice versa. Of the Berkshire Chapter, one of its stalwarts and early leaders, Carl O. Chauncey, commented ruefully, "It was a club; now it isn't a club, it's an organization."

In the ADK, growth was more erratic. From fewer than 2,000 in 1955, ADK membership hit 3,000 in 1966, then grew with the peak years of the backpacking boom to 5,000 by 1978. There followed a quiet period during which ADK membership settled at about the 5,000 level. A shift to a more growth-oriented club policy in the mid-1980s brought renewed growth, with the 8,000th member welcomed aboard in 1986 and the 9,000th less than two years later. Again, some ADK chapters grew even more sharply, some hardly at all.

GMC membership doubled from before the boom to after—from about 2,000 to about 4,000. In view of the hectic behavior of other numbers associated with those years, that was not a fast pace. The Burlington Section, however, grew at a bustling pace.

Along with these trends came the emergence of professional staff. Until long after World War II none of the Northeastern hiking clubs had true professional headquarters staffs, though the larger ones had paid office secretaries who became well-known pillars of the organization, such as the GMC's beloved Lula Tye, who served for twenty-nine years. The first paid executive directors—the AMC's C. Francis Belcher and the ADK's Fay Loope, both hired in 1956—were longtime prominent club members. Though they were highly respected and vital to club operations thereafter, their duties were confined to the mechanics of club administration and to carrying out the policies and programs determined and initiated by the more active club members.

In 1971 the AMC shook up its Pinkham Notch facilities, appointing an associate executive director, Thomas S. Deans, who in turn created a management staff to place the north country operations on a fully professional footing, with managers of huts, trails, research, education, and the Pinkham facility. In 1975, the dynamic young Deans, then just thirty-four, replaced Belcher as executive director in Boston and began to build up the staff there, until by the 1980s the AMC had more than fifty full-time staff employees, with fully staffed departments of publications, education, conservation, volunteer coordination, and (the inevitable concomitants of staff growth) a large business office and full-time fund-raisers.

During the 1980s the ADK moved in a similar direction, if not as decisively. The GMC was more cautious, its professional staff never exceeding four during these years. Nevertheless, in all three clubs, the role of professional staff altered significantly the previous role of volunteer leadership. Increasingly policy tended to be both initiated and implemented by the paid staff. With large staff came much of the paraphernalia of modern large organizations, including periodic fund-raising drives, growing dependence on corporate donors and foundation grants, and spasmodic budget crises.

In short, the three big hiking clubs of the Northeast were greatly changed from their simpler, quieter, more informal identities. Now they dealt with big issues of land management and recreation policy, took on tough controversies, negotiated with high-level government officials and representatives of other large-scale private interests. For those who yearned for the simple, quiet, informal spirit of the 1950s and before, the new realities of the 1980s were hard to take. For those who welcomed change and lived apace with the modern world, the 1980s were exciting times.

While the major clubs expanded into fully professional organizations, the postwar years saw relatively few new hiking clubs in the Northeast.

Sub Sig was perhaps the most unusual. The Submarine Signal Company was an industrial firm in the Boston area producing underwater equipment. The employees organized an outing club in 1947. The following year the company went out of business, but the outing club endured and prospered. What transformed this venture from the obscurity that presumably befell dozens of similar clubs was the charismatic leadership of Jabe Whelpton during the club's early years. "Jabe was a very dynamic guy," recalled one former member. "If you didn't agree with some of the things he did, it was best to just go somewhere else. He was utterly unstoppable." Whelpton dreamed up and led a variety of interesting hikes to the White and Green mountains, with a smattering of winter climbing, downhill skiing, canoeing, and square dancing. The membership was a young crowd of technical people, many fresh from MIT and its outing club, full of spirit and humor. In 1949 a discarded school bus chassis was adorned with an elaborate superstructure that housed a full kitchen, complete with eight-burner gas stove and ample cabinets and counter space, sixteen sleeping bunks suspended from the ceiling, and other comforts, and it became the central object in the successful functioning of Sub Sig. Where Sub Sig went hiking, there to the trail-head went the monster bus, becoming possibly (as Sub Sig claimed) "the best known motor vehicle in New England."

The Wilton Outing Club and the Maine Trail Trotters were small Maine clubs that formed around leading figures in the Maine Appalachian Trail Club: the WOC around Louis Chorzempa and Lawson Reeves in the early 1950s, the MTT around Carl Newhall during the early 1960s. The parent MATC was an all-business trail-maintaining club that scheduled no purely recreational excursions, so these smaller clubs filled a niche in providing sociable outings and just plain hiking to go along with the serious work of trail maintaining.

The Berkshire Knapsackers started during the 1970s around Pittsfield, Massachusetts, under the leadership of Jack Murphy, soon ably supported by stalwarts from other clubs like the AMC's Kay Wood and the ADK's Werner Bachli. With the AMC's Berkshire Chapter heavily involved in trail work, the Knapsackers too constituted a club devoted strictly to hikes, without involvement in the distractions of trail maintenance.

Elsewhere in Massachusetts, organizations developed for the purpose of supporting some particular hiking locale. Examples were Friends of the Holyoke Range, Friends of the Blue Hills, and the Mount Tom Advisory Committee. Such groups sponsored educational and recreational programs, opened and maintained trails, and provided a focus for nearby residents who wanted to know more about and support actively the local hiking opportunities.

Doubtless other small New England groups formed during the post-war years, more or less permanent or transitory, according to whether leadership emerged to survive the eventual passing of the founders.

As usual New York City was different. The New York–area hiking scene remained the same swirling, bubbling melting pot of diverse hiking clubs that it had been before World War II. Here there was no shortage of new clubs to leap into the churning waters. As mentioned earlier, the AMC's New York Chapter grew solidly (see table 54.2). The schedule of Appie excursions each weekend became a complex program of varied events, and the traditional fare of Hudson Highland hikes now attracted enormous crowds. The AMC's expansion dwarfed that of the ADK's chapter and the GMC's section and most of the independent clubs as well. Comparing fall 1982 bulletins for the AMC and GMC (their New York affiliates) shows the GMC's twenty-two pages long, with eight pages of hike notices, while the AMC's runs sixty-eight pages, with thirty-seven pages of hikes.

In addition to the local chapters of the big three, the same potpourri of independents from before the war crowded the stage. Among the proliferation of hiking clubs of the 1920s and 1930s (see chapter 41) some had

Table 54.2
GROWTH IN THE AMC'S NEW YORK CHAPTER, 1955–1980

Year	Total Number of Members	Increase from Five Years Before	Percent of Total AMC Membership
1955	804	156	13
1960	1,028	224	14
1965	1,534	506	15
1971	2,493	959 (6 years)	16
1976	3,528	1,035	16
1980	4,836	1,308 (4 years)	19

Source: Appalachian Mountain Club.

faded into oblivion, like the Fresh Air Club, the all-women Inkowa, and the once vibrant Nature Friends. Some still existed but were not very active, like the Tramp and Trail Club. But others, like the Woodland Trail Walkers, still flourished, sending squads of enthusiastic hikers on the trails of Schunemunk, Storm King, and Slide Mountain every weekend. Several new groups forged to the fore, most of them owing their origins to the height of the backpacking boom. Several examples illustrate the diversity.

The *Essex County Trailwalkers* was a characteristic product of those years. A group of women in Essex County, New Jersey, wished to enjoy the local woods but feared hiking alone. With support from the Essex County Park Commission, they organized a group initially called the Wednesday Walkers, and turned out forty-four women and one lucky man for their first hike on April 12, 1967. As the years went by, male participation rose and the club changed its name, reflecting a busier schedule of hikes. The club took on trail work too, opening up 20 miles of new trails in the Pequannock Watershed.

The *Co-op City Hiking Club* was a vintage New York City group. Drawing members exclusively from an enormous cluster of thirty-five high-rise (twenty-six to forty-three story) apartments in the northeast Bronx, the club prospered for ten years at the height of the backpacking boom, under the leadership of Nat Lester, but failed to survive a falloff in interest during the 1980s.

The *Long Island Greenbelt Trail Conference* gave as much emphasis to trail work as to scheduled hikes. This brave band worked against the tide of megalopolis to build hiking trails on every scrap of green space they could salvage from the preserves of urban sprawl.

The *College Alumni Hiking Club* was not really a new club but an expansion of the former City College Hiking Club, with many members well past college age. This club became one of the area's most vigorous hiking groups, under such popular leaders as Harry Weitz. True to the egalitarian traditions of its origins (see chapter 41), this club probably turned out more black and Hispanic hikers than any major New York City outdoors club. Besides the usual hiking outings, the CAHC conducted canoe, bike, and ski trips.

The *Sundance Outdoor Adventure Society* organized with 15 members in 1980 to provide a gay hiking group for homosexuals of both sexes. Within a few years it reached 150 members, with outings to the usual New York–area hiking havens, occasional longer trips, canoeing and biking, and maintaining one trail in Bear Mountain Park. Sundance sought to provide a healthy alternative for gay people to meet each other and enjoy the outdoors outside of the usual context of bars or political groups.[a]

Ralph's Peak Hikers, also of recent origin, grew out of an adult education class in backpacking taught by one Ralph Ferrusi during the late 1970s in Dutchess County, on the east side of the Hudson north of New York City. One of his "courses" was a nine-day hike on the Appalachian Trail. The initial group kept getting back together for more hikes, adding members, formally adopting their unusual name, and finally taking on trail maintenance as well. With the latter tangible job to do, Ralph's Peak Hikers tore into their assigned trail section with energy, enthusiasm, and creativity. They soon maintained more than 20 miles of AT (fully 1 percent of the total!) and built several shelters, one of which they claimed was

> the only shelter on the AT with a mail box with the zip code listed in the guidebook, a garage, a mowed lawn, lawnchairs, a bird bath, a kitchen and dining area, plus . . .

Somewhat embarrassed by the name, Ferrusi "once suggested we change it to something like Dutchess County Hiking Association and almost caused a riot. The gang likes 'Ralph's Peak Hikers.' "

A world of its own was the college outing club movement.

That sturdy original, the Dartmouth Outing Club, continued to hold its place as the most prominent and emulated of the genre. Its role at Dartmouth was by now central to the life of the college in a way found elsewhere only at Bates. One Dartmouth president dismayed the academic faculty and football-oriented alumni alike when he expressed his opinion that "The Dartmouth Outing Club perhaps more than any other undergraduate activity gives this College its distinctive personality." Indeed the college administration gave strong institutional backing to the DOC, with a home of its own (Robinson Hall) and a succession of top-flight professional advisers, from the mountaineer-forester Robert

---

[a] In Boston a gay hiking club was also formed during these years, the Chiltern Club.

Monahan and Mountain Troops veteran John Rand during the first postwar generation, to Al Merrill and Earl Jette during the 1970s and 1980s. From "Freshman Week," when initiates who had yet to attend their first lecture were led into the White Mountains for a week of camping and hiking under DOC upperclass role models, through four Winter Carnivals, innumerable parties at DOC cabins, and strenuous hikes along DOC-maintained trails, the sons of Dartmouth—and, when women were admitted, the daughters as well—supported the DOC with intensity and pride.

Less well known but almost more dominant still in college life was the Bates Outing Club. Every student at Bates was automatically a member. Roaming the mountains of western Maine, with longer trips northeast to Katahdin or southwest to Washington, Bates students not only hiked but maintained more trail mileage than any other collegians. At one time the BOC maintained 50 miles of the Appalachian Trail and though that assignment was reduced by the 1980s, the students remained active participants in the MATC and in other Maine trail work.

Other New England college outing clubs that were especially prominent in postwar years were those of the University of Maine, the University of New Hampshire, Alden Partridge's spiritual descendants at Norwich University in Vermont, and the Massachusetts Institute of Technology (MITOC). In New York State, several college outing clubs were especially active in winter climbing, notably those of Rensselaer, Syracuse, and Cornell. A handful of secondary schools fostered extremely successful outing clubs, including Berkshire, Exeter, and Holderness.

In the first postwar generation, the umbrella organization of the Intercollegiate Outing Clubs of America (IOCA) was a major force in spreading and elevating the college outing club movement. IOCA provided a mechanism for getting the different clubs together, a channel through which active clubs might help reactivate moribund ones, an alumni organization (IOCAlums) whereby graduate members remained involved, and a sense of unity to all outing clubs. Ostensibly nationwide, IOCA was always centered in the Northeast, with Lake Colden and Katahdin its favorite haunts for clubwide gatherings.

During the 1960s IOCA enjoyed its highest pitch of activity and prestige under the leadership of MITOC's Gardner Perry III. "G-P-3," as he was universally known to collegiate hikers and climbers, understood precisely what the outdoors students of the 1960s were looking for and tailored IOCA activities to those demands. He vigorously promoted hikes and parties, rock climbing and winter climbing, and offbeat adventures such as moonlight Presidential traverses. The latter was first suggested impetuously by Perry to restore sagging spirits at the end of a work weekend in 1960; it became an IOCA tradition. After graduating from MIT, Perry remained in the Northeast in various occupations but with his chief focus still on IOCA affairs. He personally directed the Winter

Mountaineering School for many years (see chapter 59) and managed an outfitting store in between bouts of employment in the computer field. He seemed scarcely the correct image of a collegiate outing clubber—soft-spoken, laconic, often inclined to be a bit overweight—yet he fit every need: surprisingly hardy in winter, surprisingly light on his feet on a rock climb, surprisingly creative and durable at the wildest of parties. Perry was always available to assist any college's leaders yet seemed personally accessible to the lowliest freshman. Not the least valuable of his attributes was the uncanny ability to drive car, van, truck, or hearse (the preferred mode of conveyance for large MITOC parties), fully loaded with spirited IOCAns, all night to reach a trail-head or climbing area, hike or climb all weekend, then drive through the night back to college.

IOCA declined as a force in the college outing club movement during the 1970s and 1980s. Perry and his inseparable Mary went west in 1973. It would be tempting to connect IOCA's decline to this event, but far more probable that deeper causes were at work. Indeed the decline was well underway by 1970. One major contributing factor was the admission of women at most formerly all-male Northeastern colleges, eliminating the boy-meets-girl function of IOCA. Another factor was the rise of numerous activist social causes during the late 1960s, draining off much of the organizational spirit of that generation to subjects more serious than climbing a cliff or crossing the Presidentials by moonlight. Where outing interest remained high, as at Dartmouth, Bates, MIT, and elsewhere, the individual clubs grew stronger, reducing the need for support from IOCA.

Thus did the mountain-oriented clubs of the Northeast carry on through the era of the backpacking boom, the tradition that had begun in Williamstown, Massachusetts, with the formation of the Alpine Club there in 1863. The major clubs might grow, such as the AMC, to such size as to lose their intimacy; others, such as IOCA or Tramp and Trail, might dwindle in influence; some, such as the Forty-Sixers, might radically alter the original purpose for which they were formed and become reinvigorated (see chapter 58); others, such as MATC, might rigidly adhere to that original purpose, yet continue to prosper (see chapter 56); some, such as the AMC, might proudly claim a century-plus heritage or, like the DOC, celebrate a seventy-fifth anniversary by dispatching members to all the summits of the New Hampshire 4,000-footers simultaneously; others, such as Ralph's Peak Hikers, might spring up overnight with verve and spunk. Whatever the variety of their personalities, the Northeastern hiking clubs played, and in all likelihood will continue to play, a colorful and distinctive role in the mountain recreation of the region.

Chapter 55

Northeastern trail systems mature

NORTHEASTERN trail building—with all its rich heritage from the old gods who strode the earth to bring trails to hikers, from Marcus Keep to Leroy Dudley, Eugene Cook and J. Rayner Edmands, Professor Monroe and Professor Buchanan, Bill Nye and Jim Goodwin, Frank Place and Ray Torrey, Edgar Heermance and Romeyn Spare, Murray Stevens and Ned Anderson—entered a distinctly new period following World War II. The time for creating something new was over; the time for preserving and enhancing the legacy of the past had arrived.

The trail systems of northern New England and the Adirondacks were all basically built before World War II. In the Adirondacks, Vermont, and Maine, total trail mileage remained roughly stable during postwar years. That doesn't mean that no new trails were built. But additions were balanced by the abandonment of many trails. As a result of an excess of zeal on the part of 1920s trail-builders, together with the make-work psychology of much of the 1930s Depression-inspired trail work, there was more trail mileage in the northern ranges than most hikers would ever use and much more than trail-maintainers could ever keep open. The conversion from fire towers to aerial surveillance for fire control put an end to many old wardens' trails. The hurricanes of 1938 and 1950, and years of neglect during World War II accentuated the trend. The veterans-dominated era of the 1950s brought no great waves of hikers to the backcountry to demand new trails, so overworked forest rangers sought ways to cut back their load. Later, excessive use and resulting erosion contributed to declining trail mileage, which led to decisions in some cases simply to abandon a trail rather than try to rebuild and maintain it.

In Baxter State Park, a number of new trails were cut to peaks west and north of Katahdin: the Brothers, Coe, O-J-I, the Owl. But these additions were offset by the abandonment of many trails to the east of Katahdin. Near the great mountain itself, the few new trails built were more than offset by the numbers of those that were surrendered back to the Maine north woods, as shown in figure 55.1.

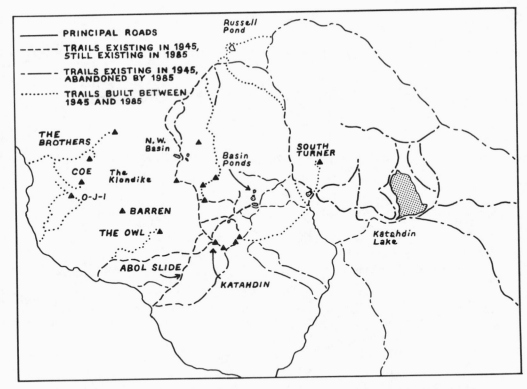

Figure 55.1. Trails built—and abandoned—Katahdin, 1945–1985 During the years following World War II, new trails were built in Baxter State Park to such previously trailless peaks as the Brothers, Coe, O-J-I, and the Owl. But during the same years many older trails were abandoned and reverted to nature. It is hard to tell whether there was a net increase or decrease in hiking trails for the Katahdin area as a whole.

In the Adirondacks, a few new trails were added—on Colden, Gothics, through Algonquin Pass, and in the St. Hubert's area (not to mention the unofficial "herd paths" that grew up on the "trailless" 4,000-footers as peakbagging rose in popularity). But these gains were partially offset by the disappearance of trails on Wright, Colden (again), and the hills east of Keene Valley.

On Monadnock, with the closing of the road to the site of the long-closed Half Way House, many of those "sun-flecked narrow paths" were abandoned.

In the White Mountains, trail mileage actually shrank markedly. From Waterville Valley to the Carters and Mahoosucs, numerous old trails, some of them logging roads and railroad beds or fire-control "man-ways," reverted to nature. In the Twin Mountain area, the shrinkage was most noteworthy. The original common routes of ascent for Garfield and North Twin were yielded back, never to be reclaimed. Mount Hale had four routes of ascent at V-J Day—but only two by 1960. The Rosebrook Range's fine network of pleasant paths were all gone and virtually undiscernible a generation later (see figure 55.2).

Only in the previously less developed hills farther south was substantial new mileage created. Most notable were the trail systems that grew up in the shadow of the big cities, sanctuaries of wild land tenaciously grasped and held in defiance of the megalopolis.

On Long Island, for example, urban trail-builders carved out a network of green paths between, around, and amongst the ribbons of concrete highways and urban sprawl, organizing themselves into the Long Island Greenbelt Trail Conference. It was an achievement of vision and boldness. One of the architects of the Nassau-Suffolk Trail, George Fisher, recalled how he started in 1982:

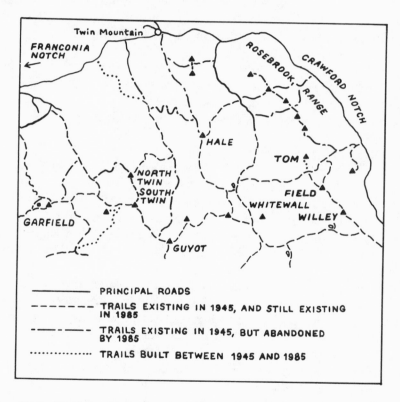

Figure 55.2. Trails built—and abandoned—White Mountains, 1945–1985
During the postwar era, total trail mileage in the White Mountains was substantially reduced. This phenomenon is noteworthy, for example, in the northern section of the Pemigewasset Wilderness and on the northern slopes of the peaks in that area, near the town of Twin Mountain. Traditional early routes up Garfield, the Twin Range, and Hale were abandoned and an entire network of trails on the Rosebrook Range disappeared. Very few new trails were built.

In an effort to find hiking room in Nassau County, I began looking through my Hagstrom's atlas for large areas of green or white—open space for walking. Obviously, there wasn't a lot, and what there was could hardly be called wilderness. But there was *some*, even in 1982, and all of it was just a short drive away.

So Fisher, Bob Kess, and Bill Sommerville plunged in "on a cold and rainy January day in 1983" and began the delicate work of weaving a genuine hiking trail through the midst of humanity. Other Long Island trail-builders followed, until they grew into one of the more spirited and unquenchable trail clubs in the New York area. No wilderness lay here: instead of traversing mountains, Long Island trails might run "from Northern State Parkway at Sunnyside Boulevard to Jericho Turnpike"; instead of vistas of vast wilderness tracts, hikers might still be rewarded with views of a different character (on a high point of the Nassau Greenbelt Trail, quoth the trail description of the Conference, "The World Trade Center and Empire State Building, some thirty miles distant, loom on the horizon"); trail workers caught in a downpour might seek shelter for lunch under the nearby Long Island Expressway. But such trails were a boon to citybound outdoorspeople. Other trail systems, only slightly less hemmed in by megalopolis, sprouted in New Jersey and Rhode Island.

Just north of New Haven, the charming contours of the Sleeping Giant provided a setting for an elaborate network of imaginatively conceived trails laid out during the years from 1958 to 1962 by two men—Richard Eliot, and a man who as a youth had worked with Edgar Heermance himself, the founding father of Connecticut's blue-blazed trail system, on some of the original Quinnipiac Trail: Norman A. ("Ned") Greist. An extensive system of trails was built in eastern Connecticut, largely through the efforts of Larry Tringe.

In the Catskills, DEC rangers built a number of new trails during the 1960s, especially in the Windham High Peak–Blackhead–Black Dome area (see figure 55.3). This activity reflected the dawning of interest in hiking in the land of Rip Van Winkle, between the Hudson Highlands and the Adirondacks, which had so long been bypassed.

The state that showed the most significant new trail activity in the postwar years was Massachusetts. Here a number of longer trails, crossing the state north-south, were created in somewhat the way Connecticut's blue-blazed trails had been built during the prewar Heermance-Spare-Anderson years. During the late 1940s, largely under the leadership of veteran Katahdin tramper and rock climber Ron Gower, the AMC built the 35-mile Warner Trail in the southeast sector of the state. At about the same time, Massachusetts State College trail-builders conceived a 70-mile trail connecting New Hampshire's Monadnock with Connecticut's Metacomet Trail, and over the course of fifteen years,

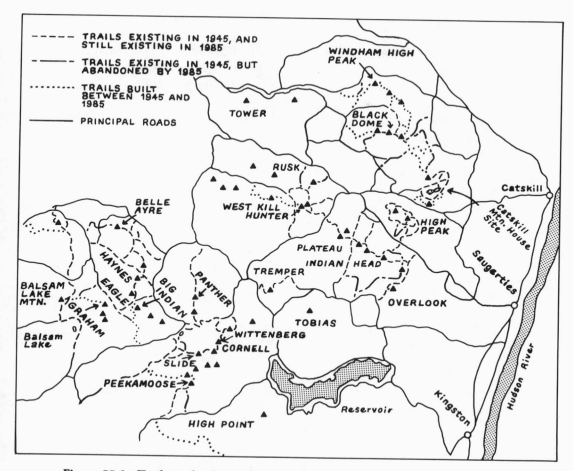

Figure 55.3. Trails in the Catskills, 1945–1985 As in other areas, so in the Catskills: some new trails were built and some old ones abandoned during the years following World War II. However, the relatively greater popularity of the Catskills in recent years, as compared with their comparative neglect by hikers before 1950, meant that new trail mileage was more significant in these hills. The splendid network of new trails in the Windham High Peak–Blackhead–Black Dome area, and additions to the routes over the Devil's Path and the Haynes–Eagle–Big Indian range are particularly noteworthy. Relatively few hiking trails of importance have been abandoned in the Catskills.

under the constant prodding and promotion of Walter Banfield, and with help from the AMC's Berkshire Chapter and the GMC's Worcester Section, this Metacomet-Monadnock Trail was built. A trio of long-distance trails was put together in the extreme western end of the state (nipping into the neighboring states from time to time), and named the Taconic Crest, Taconic Skyline, and South Taconic trails. The guiding light in this effort was retired American diplomat Robert Redington. During the 1980s the old Mid-State Trail north of Worcester was reopened, rebuilt, and extended west of the city and south to Connecticut so as to form yet another north-south transstate trail (see figure 55.4).

The two most ambitious additions to the Northeastern trails directory were also renovated prewar conceptions. The Society for the Protection of New Hampshire Forests dusted off the old plan for a Monadnock to Mount Sunapee trail, except that in this reincarnation it was moved from the country lanes of old up onto the wooded ridges and given a name appropriate to its new setting: the Greenway.

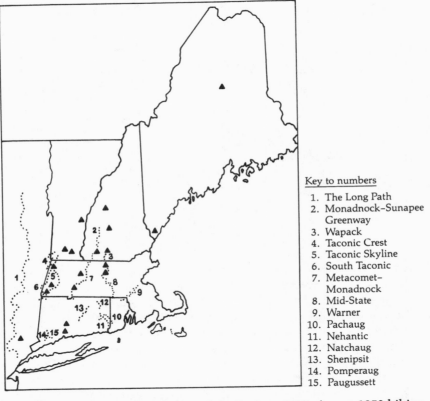

Key to numbers
1. The Long Path
2. Monadnock–Sunapee Greenway
3. Wapack
4. Taconic Crest
5. Taconic Skyline
6. South Taconic
7. Metacomet–Monadnock
8. Mid-State
9. Warner
10. Pachaug
11. Nehantic
12. Natchaug
13. Shenipsit
14. Pomperaug
15. Paugussett

Figure 55.4. Long-distance hiking trails built since 1950 A post-1950 hiking phenomenon has been the popularity of long-distance hiking, reflected in a substantial upsurge in the numbers of hikers completing the end-to-end walk of the 263-mile Long Trail and the 2,100-mile Appalachian Trail. Throughout the country, many other long-distance hiking trails have sprouted since 1950. In the Northeast—although a region already well supplied with hiking trails by 1950—this phenomenon was reflected in the development of New York's Long Path, New Hampshire's Greenway, and several long trails in Massachusetts and Connecticut. Some of the trails shown on this map (for example, the Wapack) were started before 1950 but extended thereafter.

In New York State, Vincent Schaefer's old dream for a Long Path meandering from the George Washington Bridge to the top of Mount Marcy was brought to life, marked out, and cleared. By the mid-1980s, the Long Path ran continuously 215 miles from Manhattan Island to the northern edge of the Catskills, with plans to carry it through to the Adirondacks before the end of the century. When completed, the 400-plus-mile trek will become the second-longest trail in the Northeast, displacing Vermont's Long Trail from the number two spot behind the Appalachian Trail.

But these new trails were exceptions. For most of the Northeast in the years after World War II, trail systems were mature, and the assignment for the postwar generations was to maintain them. Not to the builders, then, but to the maintainers belongs the story of postwar Northeastern trails history.

Chapter 56

New paths for trail maintenance

WITH few new worlds to conquer, Northeastern trail workers of the postwar years made a virtue of necessity: they exalted trail maintenance to an honored vocation. Indeed, in the hands of some of the masters of the trade, it was elevated to the status of a fine art.

The history of postwar trail maintenance divides into two distinct periods. The watershed between them is the point at which the crisis in trail conditions created by the backpacking boom was recognized—sometime around 1969 or 1970. Postboom trail work in turn further divides into two phases.

Paint brush and swizzle stick

Before 1970 trail maintenance primarily involved clearing blowdowns and clipping back branches and brush, plus freshening up the paint blazes and keeping trail signs in good order. The tools of the trade were preeminently the paint brush and can, along with a variety of weapons for controlling the growth of underbrush. One of the superstars of this era of trail work was Seymour Smith, who operated a small manufacturing operation in Watertown, Connecticut, where (along with other items) he designed and produced heavy-duty clippers especially for woods work. Smith developed another vital tool for the arsenal, the swizzle stick, which proved invaluable in clearing the track of lighter growth like ferns, brambles, and long grass. A razor-sharp blade suspended between the forks of a Y-shaped handle, it was swung with enthusiasm and effect. Sometimes with heady enthusiasm: novice Massachusetts trail workers were cautioned not to approach within a quarter-mile of Walter Banfield with a functioning swizzle stick in motion. The clippers and swizzle stick were the emblems of the age, the universal accoutrements of trail-clearing parties from the 1950s through 1970—and, for lighter maintenance work, still thereafter. Some more exotic devices surfaced: Massachusetts trail maintainer and guidebook editor Mead Bradner imported a Japanese tool called the *Nata*, which was a conversation piece among his trail-work parties. For clearing blowdowns the double-bit ax and small bow saw were standard. Chain saws were little used before 1970: early models were considered prohibitively heavy for the backcountry; the noise was regarded as offensive to the serenity of the woods and hills; and the need was simply not that great except where hurricanes and ice storms played exceptional havoc with trails.

The trail maintainers who wielded these tools consisted of a small oligarchy of organized groups in the northern ranges and a heterogeneous mobocracy of individualists in the southern part of the region.

Tops in prestige was AMC's tradition-rich trail crew. Priding themselves in their rugged independence, woodsmanship, mastery of the arts of trail maintenance, and colorful high jinks, "the" trail crew (in those days, it was unnecessary to qualify them as the AMC trail crew, since no other outfit fully merited the title) patrolled the region's most extensive and difficult trails, those of the White Mountains. Some sub-cultures within the White Mountains region sustained their own small trail crews, either of volunteers or, later, of hired college-age youths—Randolph Mountain Club, Chatham Trails Association, Wonalancet Out Door Association, for examples—but the dominant force in the White Mountains always was the parent AMC's trail crew. Hard-working and high-living, the eight to ten young men selected for the crew each summer enjoyed a remarkable lack of adult supervision until 1960, and they exploited that freedom to the fullest. They worked long dirty, sweaty, muddy hours, avoided soap, ate gargantuan meals, swore with illuminating intensity, played as hard as they worked, and reveled in the "laughter and joy in being part of the best group they knew." Besides tending to the trails, they cultivated an image of boisterous unruliness—one 1958 crew member was said to be "the only man in the world to flip a jeep end over end"—occasionally warred on the more civilized hut crews, and finally were subjugated, first to a full-time seasonal supervisor after 1960, and then to full integration into the AMC's staff headquarters at Pinkham Notch under a full-time year-round trails supervisor in 1971. It was a golden era and many old trailsmen viewed its close with bitter regret, little realizing that yet more honors lay ahead for the AMC trail crew in the new role that it assumed after 1971.

Less well known to the outside world and entirely different in structure and spirit, but scarcely less important in pre-1970 northern New England trail maintenance, was the Maine Appalachian Trail Club. Originally created by Myron Avery to preserve the freshly cut 270-plus miles of Appalachian Trail in Maine, the MATC was at first dominated by a handful of Avery's old friends from Washington, D.C. During the postwar years, local leadership emerged and gradually replaced the out-of-staters until by the 1960s a fiercely for-Mainers-only spirit infused the group. Not an outings club at all, the sole function of the MATC was to maintain the trail. Membership was limited to active workers, all of them volunteers and most of them enormously dedicated to their work as a lifetime commitment. As trail workers they developed a high level of skill, yielding nothing to their professional neighbors from New Hampshire, with whom relations were not always cordial.

In Vermont, Roy Buchanan's Long Trail Patrol, which had built the GMC's lodge and camps along the Long Trail before the war, now turned largely to trail maintenance. Professor Buchanan, a beloved legend in the state, stepped down in 1967 after thirty-five years at the helm, to be succeeded by another veteran Vermont trailsman and woodsman, Jack Harrington. The LTP crew was smaller than the AMC's—typically half a dozen members each summer—but other Long Trail maintenance was carried on by volunteers from the various GMC sections, with some individuals like Harrington, Gene Bamforth, Rod Rice, and Donald Wallace devoting most of the waking hours of their private lives to the maintenance of the trail and its cabins. Unlike the amateur purity of the MATC and the completely professional operation of the AMC in New Hampshire, Vermont worked out a satisfactory mix of paid crew and volunteers to get the job done.

In the Adirondacks, a similar mixed system prevailed. State rangers did much of what trail maintenance was done on state land, while the Adirondack Trail Improvement Society's seasonal trail crew worked on many of the trails on land controlled by the Ausable Club. In addition, a scattering of individuals, most of them leaders in the Adirondack Mountain Club, contributed long hours to trail work.

One other organized crew played a major role in trail maintenance during the era of brush and clippers. This was the Connecticut roving trail crew. Starting as a trip to the AMC's Lonesome Lake Hut by Seymour Smith and three friends in 1956, this group became an important force in Connecticut trail-clearing efforts year-round for the next twenty years, with time out each summer for a stay at one of the AMC huts to work on White Mountain trails as well.

But the more common pattern in Connecticut and elsewhere in the southern part of the region was one of rugged individualism. This was the era when trail maintainers came out of the woodwork to take on a section of trail, be it short or long, and to devote a lifetime of leisure hours to ensuring its navigable condition. In Connecticut this produced some of the modern-day giants of trail work. For the most part denied the creative process of cutting new trails by the historical accident of being born too late, they nonetheless pitched in with unflagging energy for many years of dedicated trail work in the humbler arts of maintenance. Among the Connecticut trail workers of stature were the following:

Seymour Smith, who not only designed the tools of the trade and launched the Connecticut roving trail crew, but who almost singlehandedly maintained Connecticut's Appalachian Trail for thirty years after inheriting the mantle from Ned Anderson. Such a pivotal figure was he during the quarter-century following World War II that one could do worse than to call those years, for Northeastern trails history, the Age of Seymour Smith.

Kornel Bailey, the big, burly, gentle man who began hiking with the Boy Scouts in 1914, became active in the New Haven Hiking Club in 1931, started maintaining trails on the Quinnipiac the next year, and stepped down from official trail responsibilities just fifty years later, having served as chairman of the Connecticut Forest and Park Association's Trails Committee for the preceding fifteen years.

Harold Pierpont, a one-man army. At one time it was alleged that Pierpont singlehandedly maintained 100 [*sic*] miles of Connecticut trails.

George K. Libby, who inherited the complex Tunxis Trail system from Romeyn Spare in 1956 and kept it up for thirty years. Libby developed a unique crew of helpers by recruiting the very young: boys and girls mostly aged ten to fourteen. Wholly apart from the trail work accomplished, the values instilled in hundreds of youngsters over the years of responsibility for wild lands and of satisfaction derived from careful work, constituted a beautiful thing for Libby to have done with his spare time for a quarter-century. "I know for a fact that my kids can do a better job than any paid trail crew," said Libby, "because the kids, especially the little girls, are so fussy."

Norman A. ("Ned") Greist, who was physically handicapped to a degree that would have confined most people to a sedentary indoors life, but who chose instead to become a hiker extraordinaire (AT end-to-ender and holder of most peakbagging honors to be acquired in the region). In between his hiking exploits, he gave countless hours to trail work. He built much of the Sleeping Giant trail network, devoting all weekends to the work and sneaking in additional hours before going to work on weekdays.

Mary Toth, who almost singlehandedly maintained three trails in the southwest corner of the state, in the face of vexing relocation problems brought on by suburban development, highway construction, and even a hurricane. When she married, she talked her husband into joining in the work. When his health made that no longer possible, she carried on alone until others could be found to help.

Larry Tringe, who built more than 50 miles of new trail on state forests in eastern Connecticut, then helped form the Pequot Outing Club and recruited Boy Scout troops to provide a reliable corps of maintainers for the new paths. Tringe began work in 1954 and regularly put in eight hours each Saturday and Sunday, plus a two-week vacation, on trail maintenance for the next twenty years.

Robert Redington, a maverick on the Connecticut scene, who took up trail maintenance after a career in the U.S. diplomatic corps and put in a decade of intensely creative trail building and maintenance in both northwestern Connecticut and southwestern Massachusetts, where he built the South Taconic Trail shown in figure 55.4. Suddenly afflicted with blindness in 1982, Redington had a restless energy that refused to let him give in and give up outdoors pursuits. He explored all the possibilities for what the blind can do in outdoor recreation, even returning to trail maintenance on a modest scale in 1986. Redington became with Greist an inspiration to all by showing how much can be overcome with moral strength.

Connecticut seemed to be an unaccountably fertile breeding ground for trail colossi, but the postwar years produced others of corresponding stature on their home preserves, including:

Walter Banfield, the willful and eccentric czar of the Metacomet-Monadnock and other Massachusetts trails, whose fiery leadership and lethal swing of swizzle stick and brush hook continued with undiminished force into his upper eighties.

Robert Humes, the inverse of Banfield in personality—quiet, unobtrusive, patient—but a steady force in Northeastern trail work for almost as many years, on the Mid-State Trail and on networks on Massachusetts's Wachusett and Vermont's Wheeler Mountain area.

A battery of New York–New Jersey area personalities, among whom William Hoeferlin, Elizabeth Levers, and Frank Oliver are only the first of many nearly equally dedicated and distinctive trail maintainers.

Adirondacks trail-maintaining titans like the veteran James Goodwin and his son Tony, L. Morgan Porter, Rudolph Strobel, and other ADK leaders.

Another elite, those who maintained the Appalachian Trail. This came in two waves: the first postwar generation—New York's Harry Nees, Connecticut's Seymour Smith, Massachusetts's Max Sauter and his successor, Arthur Koerber, Maine's Steven Clark; and those who took over under the federal protection program—New York's Levers, Connecticut's Norm Sills, Massachusetts's Kay Wood, Maine's David Field, and others.

These and other leading trail maintainers of the postwar years were as distinctive and individualistic a bunch of headstrong personalities as can be imagined. Some, like Redington, were upper crust and Ivy League; others, like Bailey, were self-made men. Some, like Greist and Levers and Field and Sauter, crackled with electric energy and swept all before them; others, like Smith and Libby and Wood and the elder Goodwin, sat back with an amused detachment and twinkle in the eye, achieving results with patience and philosophy. Some, like Banfield, were cantankerous and opinionated; others, like Humes, were mild and boundlessly tolerant.

But there were also character traits in common. These trail maintainers were all possessed of firm convictions; were unafraid to make decisions and assume full responsibility for getting the job done; were terribly hard workers themselves and not always effective delegators of work to others; were sometimes inclined to be contemptuous of those less dedicated than they; and were apt to believe that there was one right way to fix a trail (theirs). One co-worker of Max Sauter recalled, "There were two ways to do things: the wrong way and Max's way." Above all, these giants of modern trail maintenance were committed for life to the hard work, the joys, the vexations, and the extraordinary sense of accomplishment in trail maintenance. The contribution these people made to the pleasure of hikers who walked their trails is beyond measure.

Under these and other leaders served a less celebrated polyphony of anonymous club members who turned out for trail-work parties and knew something of those rewards, those frustrations, and that feeling of achievement. Stretched above them all was the umbrella organization, the New England Trail Conference, which served as a vital meeting ground for the exchange of information, ideas, and inspiration. The NETC was really little more than a once-a-year one-day meeting, but under a highly respected dynasty of chairmen during the postwar years —John Vondell, Carl O. Chauncey, John Hitchcock, Walter Banfield, and Forrest E. House—it provided a kind of town meeting and convention combined, where trail workers could report, to an audience whose interest was guaranteed (!), what they had done for the past year, talk shop, and come away rejuvenated for another year with the swizzle stick and paint brush. In New York a somewhat analogous role was played by the New York–New Jersey Trail Conference.

Thus was the work of Cook and Monroe and Heermance and Torrey preserved in quieter years and handed on intact—until the backpacking boom burst in on Eden.

Postboom trail work

WATER BAR AND SCREE WALL. A fundamental shift in both the organization and content of trail work occurred in response to the backpacking boom. The invasion of the Vibram-soled army brought new stresses to Northeastern trails for which the old methods of brush clipping and paint blazing were simply inadequate. An AMC trail crew leader in 1971 summarized the change simply:

> Ten years ago . . . the job of the Trail Crew was to make passage through the mountains easier for the people who hiked. Now the main concern of the Trail Crew is to lessen the impact on the environment that great numbers of people make.

The first manifestation of the new conditions was mud. Lots of mud. Very deep mud. Soft, squishy mud. As boots churned up the mountain soils in the narrow track of the trail, and as those long days of rain and/or spring melting set in, corridors of ten, twenty, or one hundred feet of trail would settle into bottomless seas of mud. Hikers would avoid the central depths, thereby progressively widening the track and, ultimately, broadening the sea of mud. Most troublesome and tragic were the high-altitude bogs through which many trails passed—delicate, lovely, quiet ecosystems where the muddy track appeared as a starkly inappropriate intrusion.

The old way of dealing with mud was "corduroy." This tactic involved cutting logs of roughly equal diameter to a length equivalent to the width of the muddy track, and laying them side by side for the length of the muddy section. When first laid on a not-too-muddy stretch, corduroy provided a reasonable solution to the problem. However, the logs tended to be slippery in a rain, and, worse, as the muddy spots grew wider and deeper, the logs simply sank out of sight. As the problem grew (or sank) during the late 1960s, corduroy proved inadequate.

In 1966, AMC trail crew leader Alan Thorndike was assigned to deal with some whale-sized mud traps on the Mizpah Cut-off, a short path near the Crawford Path. Thorndike came up with the idea of deliberately importing mineral soils and rebuilding the track. He and his crew also began placing large rocks across the muddy patches. This was the beginning of new tactics. Ultimately the solution to the worst of the mud was log bridging. During the early 1970s, "across every delicate, easily-destroyed bog in the Mahoosuc Range," the trail crew placed, by actual count, 442 split-log bridges.[a]

A tenfold worse trail problem was erosion. When mud formed on any kind of slope, rainfall would wash loose earth downgrade. In spring run-off or a sustained rain, the trail became nothing less than a stream, and the top layers of earth loosened by the Vibram army poured down the mountainside. When Ketchledge and Leonard began their studies of trail damage in the Adirondacks during the 1960s (before they zeroed in on the alpine zone), their research concluded that on steeper slopes, erosion was proceeding at a rate of 1 inch per year both downward and laterally —that is, the trail was getting both deeper and wider. In places, popular trails were already 3, 4, or 5 feet below the surface of the surrounding woods.

The imperative solution to trail erosion was to get either the hikers or the running water off the trail. Except in some places, the former was unlikely to happen. The latter meant major drainage work. In some cases, drainage was achieved by grubbing out a long ditch beside the

[a]During the later 1970s the technique of splitting logs for bridges gave way to top-log bridging, in which a flat surface would be roughed out along the upper edge of the log, rather than splitting it down the middle. Top-log bridges were found to last longer than split-log ones.

trail, sometimes in association with complicated devices for raising the level of the trail itself—log cribs filled with rock or mineral soil, or just plain rock and lots of it. But the key tool for combating trail erosion was the water bar. As the backpacking boom and consequent erosion progressed in the 1970s, the water bar became the single most important tactic in the response of trail workers—ultimately, the symbol of the new era in trail maintenance.

Water bars were hardly an invention of modern times. Country road builders of the premacadam age, especially in hilly New England, knew well the necessity of getting water out of the wheel ruts and had provided earth, log, or stone across-the-road ditches (sometimes called "thank-you-ma'ams") at intervals on hills. The more careful trail-builders of the early years, such as Edmands and Blood, had provided for drainage. During the postwar years, some voices had spoken up for more attention to erosion control in trail maintenance: a remarkably prophetic article by Robert S. Monahan in *Appalachia* in 1954 warned that drainage ditches were not being kept open (they tend to silt in unless regularly grubbed out). Seymour Smith's crews regularly built and maintained water bars. When he was almost eighty years old, C. W. Blood roused himself to write a set of instructions in 1957 for the construction and maintenance of water bars which was almost forgotten when the art was rediscovered in the 1970s: the old master's words on the subject compare favorably to most manuals written during the 1970s and 1980s.

But with the new levels of hiking traffic after 1965, the problem of trail erosion escalated to heights—depths, rather—for which earlier methods and tools had never been designed. The AMC trail crew began to install dozens of water bars on popular trails and to spread the word on their value and on how to build them correctly to other trail maintainers. Knowing how to put in an effective and long-lasting water bar became the mark of a good trail worker. Constant attention to keeping water bars free of silt and leaves became the mark of a careful trail maintainer. The mattock and hazel hoe, varieties of short stubby hoes designed for scraping earth and prying small stones, rose to number one status in the arsenal of modern trail tools. Monahan's forward-looking 1954 article had recognized the need: "The versatile mattock should not be relegated to a position below the ax and saw."

Even drainage control and bridging proved unequal to some of the new trail problems, however, as erosion widened and deepened all over the Northeastern backcountry. The next step up in the escalating battle to save the trails was tread hardening. Where soils were irretrievably degraded and/or erosion out of control, serious trail workers turned to rebuilding the trailbed itself with large rock. Log steps were used at first but of course were by no means permanent. Small rock could not be stable. Very large rocks—upwards of 100 pounds—were essential for a stable and lasting treadway. For this purpose, the long, straight crowbar assumed its place beside the mattock as a valued tool for modern trail work.

The first large-scale effort toward tread hardening was the reconstruction in 1972 of the short trail between busy Lakes-of-the-Clouds Hut and the picturesque summit of Mount Monroe. This "Staircase to the Stars" was shortly followed by the steep 0.9-mile trail between Galehead Hut and the top of South Twin. As with water bars, the AMC trail crew exported the techniques it learned in the White Mountains. Rock work for hardening the tread spread to all areas of the Northeast within about ten years.

Still more extreme measures followed but were not so universally embraced. In 1975 the White Mountain National Forest created its own trail crew, its first full-time forestwide crew. Among the innovations in trail stabilization techniques that the WMNF crew tried out were come-alongs (or winches) to move yet larger rocks; pin-steps, a method for attaching blocks of treated lumber into the rock surface so as to form a step or long series of steps up steep, rocky slopes; jackhammers to blast steps into rock ledges; and flown-in treated-lumber planks instead of on-site-hewn split-logs or top-logs for bridging. Some of these new techniques were adopted elsewhere, some discarded. The AMC trail crew, arbiter of taste for most of the trail community during those years, accepted the use of come-alongs, but balked at the more extreme tactics, such as pin-steps or jackhammered steps. Treated-lumber bridging was adopted widely in the Adirondacks and elsewhere. Chapter 57 discusses some points of disagreement on what were acceptable techniques and tools.

Above-treeline trails presented a special problem. The delicate ecosystem of the alpine zone was exceptionally vulnerable to trampling by boot traffic. All that could be hoped for was that the crowds of visitors could be encouraged to walk on one trail and let the rest of the tundra grow in peace. But at the height of the backpacking boom such a hope seemed forlorn, and many alpine summits exhibited an advanced degree of devastation.

In the Green Mountains and Adirondacks (the latter in connection with Ketchledge's summit reseeding program described in chapter 52) broad-based educational efforts urged people to stay on the trails, including on-site ranger-naturalists and ridge-runners, positively worded educational signs at treeline and posters at trail-heads, and rock cairns to mark the trail. In the White Mountains, little was done until by the late 1970s the situation had grown desperate. Then, in 1977, the AMC trail crew took bold action: along the Franconia Ridge, a crew outlined a single 3-foot-wide track with "scree walls," piled-up loose rock on either side of the trail, for a stretch of two miles. Though controversial at first, this action sent a clear message to above-treeline hikers that they should stay off the alpine flowers. Scree walls were widely adopted in the White Mountains during the next few years, on Katahdin during the mid-1980s, and in much modified form in the Adirondacks.

As many of these examples illustrated, new trail techniques—erosion control, tread hardening, extreme above-treeline tactics—typically started in the White Mountains and spread. The AMC's trail crew played an influential role in developing new methods and propagating their use. It was one of the most creative periods in that interesting institution's long history, stretching back to Sherman Adams in 1917 and down through Blood and Jenks and the hell-raising days of independence in the 1930s and 1950s. The leaders during this modern period were Robert D. Proudman, a tough, young, bearded, Camel-smoking, monosyllabic backwoodsman-mountaineer whose antiestablishment image was just right for providing leadership in the rebellious years of the early 1970s; and his successor, the taciturn and unflappable Reuben Rajala. Under Proudman and Rajala, the trail crew both developed new strategies for coping with White Mountain problems and reached out to spread the message of modern trail maintenance to the rest of the region. They conducted workshops for volunteer trail maintainers and crews from other areas. At the slightest hint of an invitation, they would dispatch a team to spend a weekend or two weeks working with local trail workers at any trouble spot. Proudman also authored a pioneering and widely read manual, the *AMC Field Guide to Trail Building and Maintenance.*

As the new methods spread, trail work enjoyed its greatest upswing in popularity since trail building began during the 1880s and 1890s. Existing outfits such as the MATC and the Long Trail Patrol enjoyed boom years, both in numbers and in the spirit of the workers. Organizations that had merely dabbled in trail work before now hired full-time seasonal crews for the first time. The ADK started its own crew in 1979 and brought major trail reconstruction on the AMC model to the Adirondacks' steep and sadly worn trails. Within its sphere, ATIS modernized and expanded its maintenance operations, even hiring a year-round part-time executive director; with symbolic appropriateness, the job went to Tony Goodwin, son of longtime Adirondack trailsman Jim Goodwin. Governmental units started up trail crews and undertook serious tread hardening to a degree never considered before—for example, crews of New York's Department of Environmental Conservation (DEC) in the Catskills. Even more a sign of the times was the explosion in volunteer trail crews, many of which achieved a high level of competence in heavy-duty trail work: a crew started by the Forty-Sixers in 1977, which the reigning dean of Northeastern trail building, Jim Goodwin, agreed to lead for a few years before turning over the reins to younger hands in 1982; a New York–New Jersey Trail Conference trail crew, launched in 1981 under the leadership of John Schoen, which undertook the heavy rock work on Hudson Highland trails; an AMC New Hampshire Chapter trail crew initially led by Hal Graham, which became an additional force in the well-traveled White Mountains; and many others among smaller clubs, from the veterans of the Woodland Trail Walkers to the brand-new and irrepressible Ralph's Peak Hikers. New trails organizations appeared: among the first were two in eastern Vermont, the Ascutney Trails Association and the Trails Committee of the Westmore Association (for the area around Lake Willoughby), both of which started in 1967. In Connecticut the Central Connecticut Women Outdoors organized an all-female trail crew and took over maintenance of 10 miles of the Mattabesett Trail. Older associations started Adopt-a-Trail (and Adopt-a-Shelter) programs, under which individual club members or small groups of friends might agree to take over a short section of some favorite trail and jealously protect it from blowdowns and erosion alike. Government agencies, federal and state, funded programs for putting disadvantaged youth and young adults to work in the woods, and many club and state agencies eagerly assigned them to trail work. Workshops in trail maintenance became a popular item on the agendas of many club meetings and conferences.

New Yorker Schoen spoke for the new breed of trail maintainer when he called for full recognition of trail work, which he felt was not adequately appreciated as compared with such hiking feats as walking the Appalachian Trail:

> We have to get away from looking at maintenance as a "duty" and as "work," and start selling it as a fun sport separate from hiking with its own types of equipment, styles, methods, approaches, rewards, etc.
>
> Why is the maintainer looking up to the hiker? Why is the greater dream to walk 2000 miles and not to maintain the perfect 5-mile section?

CORRIDOR AND "RELO." During the 1980s a major program of new trail construction came disguised under the label of trail relocations, or "relos." The program was touched off by the Appalachian Trail's federal protection program. This was one of the most important developments in postwar Northeastern trails history, not only for the total mileage of new trail built, but for the revolutionary character of the program, the new concepts that it germinated, and the issues that it raised.

Ever since the original conception of the Appalachian Trail in the fertile imagination of Benton MacKaye, and long before its physical completion in the 1930s, influential voices had called for public ownership of the entire trail corridor. As early as 1922 Walter Prichard Eaton had exhorted those who visualized the yet unbuilt trail: "Let us not stop with a mere dream of an Appalachian Trail. Let us dream of an Appalachian Reservation, from Georgia to the Presidentials." In 1924 the farsighted Connecticut trailsman Albert Turner had favored public rights-of-way for long distance trails. Myron Avery had come around to this view and made it a major theme of his farewell report when stepping down as ATC chairman in 1952. His successor, New York AT-builder Murray Stevens, had considered public ownership "the only solution for the permanence of the Appalachian Trail."

In 1968 this concept was written into federal law with passage of the National Scenic Trails Act, empowering the National Park Service to "protect" the whole length of the AT and other designated National Scenic Trails. The plan was to purchase a "corridor" of land over which the trail passed, or to work out protective agreements with private landowners. The ultimate power of seizure by eminent domain was authorized, but the intent was to exercise that force only as a last resort. It was hoped that voluntary sales or satisfactory covenants could be reached with almost all landowners.

For another ten years, lack of appropriations and, even more, lack of a coherent plan of action entailed few results. By the mid-1970s, some members of the AT community warned that time was running out: that land development pressures were going to preclude the survival of a continuous trail corridor unless federal protection could be arranged soon. Others were expanding the vision. In 1974 Ann Satterthwaite, a Washington, D.C., planning consultant, wrote a far-reaching report urging that much more than a narrow trail corridor be preserved, that a broad belt of wilderness, an "Appalachian Greenway" was essential to the integrity of the AT. This widely noticed report was written at a point when the federal program seemed at a standstill, while the backpacking boom was at fever pitch, with no sign of slackening off.

Finally in 1978 new legislation provided the basis for a more aggressive approach. The National Park Service began to work out protective arrangements all up and down the AT, with strong support from the Appalachian Trail Conference, the trail clubs that maintained the great through-trail, and large numbers of individual trail workers from Georgia to Maine.

It was a gargantuan task. Over a period of years a host of trailspeople labored hard to identify a route that could be protected permanently, to negotiate with landowners, to scout and build new trail where needed, to provide proper monitoring of the final corridor, and to meet all the paperwork requirements inherent in a large government program. The number of trail workers involved at this phase doubtless exceeded the army that Myron Avery had marshaled to build the original trail, and the complexity of the job they did fully matched that of Avery's forces as well.

Overseeing the whole, and wielding ultimate authority where the going got sticky, was the able and politically astute David A. Richie, who headed the National Park Service's AT unit until his retirement in 1987. Richie not only presided over and guided the enormous diversity of work, but made himself personally familiar with the whole trail, was accessible to local workers wherever obstacles seemed insurmountable, showed up to handle delicate issues, solve problems, bolster morale, and provide leadership along a 2,100-mile front. Though many contributed Herculean labors,

Richie personified this new phase of the Appalachian Trail's saga, as Mac-Kaye and Avery had at earlier stages. As one observer assessed the scene:

> The truth of the matter is, since the National Park Service became fully involved in the A. T. project in the mid-1970s, David A. Richie has been running the show.

The full story of the federal protection program for the AT deserves its own book. Some of the issues and controversies that the program raised are mentioned in chapter 57.

The point to focus on here is that, under this program, major sections of the AT were substantially relocated in an effort to provide the most scenic and interesting trail on land where it could be permanently protected. Through-hikers grew accustomed to expect a relocation—*relo* soon became the accepted jargon—as a regular part of the trail experience every few days. The trail workers who had been developing their skills in the age of the water bar now won a chance to turn loose their trail-building puissance in this age of the relo. Throughout every state in the Northeast, Rhode Island alone excepted, AT relocations were so extensive that the period in fact may be characterized as a significant era of new trail building.

Over the years, for the better part of a century, trail maintainers had relocated badly worn or poorly placed sections of trails. Connecticut's master trailsfolk were richly experienced in relocations to accommodate the whims of landowners. However, such relocations were usually short. Furthermore, the ruling theory was that relocations should be a last resort. Proudman's 1977 guide to trail work had counseled against relocation except in extreme cases, pointing out that fresh locations often turned up problems as vexing as those of the existing trail.

When the AT program was launched, the original idea was to protect the existing Appalachian Trail. However, as federal authorities and local trail workers dug into their work, several forces pushed them away from the original trail location and toward relocations. The National Park Service believed that its mandate was to get the trail off roads wherever possible; this goal alone led to extensive new-route scouting in Northeastern states such as New York and Massachusetts, where the old trail followed country roads for many miles. In some areas landowners who had accepted the trail in its prefederal informal status balked at granting permanent protective arrangements; these situations also generated relocations. Elsewhere, notably in Maine, the realization that the federal program would produce a permanent trail location spurred trail workers to find the most scenic and interesting terrain and to relocate the trail there, whether the old location had problems or not. Meanwhile external pressures were felt. Second-home developments pushed the trail off some places. Ski resorts expanded on some mountains, notably in Vermont and western Maine, coming into conflict with the trail. All these forces generated more and more relocations.

By the mid-1980s AT planners no longer considered themselves bound to the old location but turned loose their imaginations—and the exuberant energies of the new generation of enthusiastic and competent trail workers—to finding and opening up relos.

In New York, the Harriman Park section already enjoyed the protection of public ownership, but across the Hudson River, Murray Stevens's handiwork of the 1920s had depended mostly on the shifting patterns of private land ownership, and more and more sections had been forced out on to public roads. When the National Park Service began purchasing and otherwise protecting the land for a largely off-road permanent route, volunteer trail workers followed along to scout and cut the final trail. Under the leadership of Elizabeth Levers, the New York–New Jersey Trail Conference coordinated work by numerous hiking clubs and individuals on this effort. Where heavy-duty tread hardening was deemed necessary—rock work and extensive water bars—the conference's special volunteer trail crew was called in. Elsewhere Levers recruited scout groups to make Eagle Scout projects out of specific trail problems. During the decade following 1978, more than 40 miles of New York's AT were relocated. The result, reported Levers, was "a whole new world of woodlands and views which will be a revelation to the hiker in New York accustomed to trudging along roads."

In Connecticut a historic change in Ned Anderson's original route took place. It will be recalled (chapter 45) that a great debate occurred during the 1920s over the Connecticut route, with the verdict ultimately awarded to Albert Turner's "elbow" route, swinging east of the Housatonic River for more than 20 miles. More than half a century later, Judge Perkins's route west of the Housatonic finally prevailed over Turner's elbow: the AT was relocated so as to eliminate completely the swing east of the Housatonic.

In Massachusetts, bitter controversies with landowners attended the relocation program. Much of the old route traversed dirt roads through pastoral countryside, and the National Park Service made the decision to move the trail entirely off such roads. While the Park Service wrestled with the public hearings, lawsuits, newspaper headlines, and other accoutrements of altercation, the volunteer trail workers, led by Katherine Wood and other Berkshire Chapter figures, followed quietly along behind to scout, mark, and cut the new trail sections.

In Vermont, controversy also swirled for a time, but GMC leaders patiently negotiated a series of compromises to eliminate several road walks and conflicts with incompatible uses.

In New Hampshire, the existing White Mountain trail network meant that relatively little relocation was required. One large exception was found where the AT crossed the Connecticut River at Hanover. Here the Dartmouth Outing Club undertook to relocate substantial mileage.

In Maine, virtually an entire new AT was built. The Maine Appalachian Trail Club decided to use the powers that the federal legislation provided to select and create the best possible permanent route through the vast north woods of Maine, much of it originally over paper company land. The MATC's president during the critical years of the 1980s was David Field, a University of Maine forester, an aggressive and incisive leader in negotiations with both landowners and government, and a tireless trail worker himself. It was a case, as another MATC leader observed, of "the right man in the right job at the right time." Under Field's incessant prodding, a new route was established over much of Maine's long AT mileage.

The pressures on the AT and the passion for building relos spread outward to other trails during the 1980s.

The northern two-thirds of the Long Trail (the part that did not coincide with the AT) reached a critical point with the pressures from land development. During the 1970s both the GMC and Vermont's political leaders had rejected National Scenic Trail status for the Long Trail, distrusting the net effect of federal government involvement. National publicity would add to the overuse problem, GMC officials reasoned, and the federal presence would jeopardize long-standing cordial but informal relationships with landowners along the Long Trail. (For New England Yankees, the role of the federal government even in such a seemingly desirable program as trail protection was sometimes viewed as a mixed blessing.) But as second homes and ski resorts crowded against the northern Long Trail, some form of protection now loomed as imperative. So in the second half of the decade of the 1980s, the GMC undertook a campaign for public protection of the entire LT corridor. Meanwhile, Long Trail workers also cut loose with many relocations, some by necessity, some in anticipation of problems, and some simply to improve the physical trail. In the ten years between 1975 and 1985, more than 60 miles of the Long Trail were rebuilt, over 20 percent of the trail.

In the White Mountains and Adirondacks, in Connecticut and the Hudson Highlands, the 1980s were the age of the relo. As the volunteer trail crews of the 1980s mastered the arts of building a solid, sustainable footway, they itched to showcase their skills on brand new trail sections. Lacking any credible rationale for extensive new trail construction, they latched onto relocation as an outlet for demonstrating their prowess. The result was a new chapter in the long and honorable history of Northeastern trail building and maintenance.

Nothing symbolizes better the fully awakened environmental consciousness of the Northeastern hiking community than this renaissance of concern and caring for its most important asset, the network of trails on which hiking depended. This outpouring of interest and attention to the needs of Northeastern trails in this era of the backpacking boom was a fitting climax to the long history of trails that began with Colonel Gibbs's rough cut through the scrub of Tuckerman Ravine in 1809.

Chapter 57

Points of controversy

NORTHEASTERN hikers had a strong community of interest on most issues raised by the impact of the backpacking boom. But all was not unanimity and sweetness and light. To present a balanced picture of hiking and trail work since World War II requires turning the spotlight on some dark and stormy nights of controversy.

Some areas of disagreement have been touched upon in the foregoing chapters.

Reference has been made to the pain that removal of Adirondack shelters caused in some quarters. The DEC and many environmentalists believed strongly that high-elevation shelters were a magnet drawing too many campers to places that could not stand the impact. But many old-time campers considered the Adirondack lean-to a unique and precious heritage, the destruction of which was unthinkable. They believed that the experience of camping at such remote and picturesque havens was too rich to be denied to future generations.

Similarly, the move away from campfires aroused deep-seated attachments to what for many was a symbol of the backcountry experience. In 1975, when two GMC trustees proposed that the Vermont club institute a complete ban on fires throughout the Long Trail, bitter debate ensued, ending with a compromise policy to "discourage" fires only.

Another issue that aroused criticism was the charging of fees for camping at backcountry sites, a practice begun by the AMC in the White Mountains in 1972 and soon followed by other clubs. Many backcountry managers believed that the preservation and management of wild land cost a lot of money and that the direct beneficiaries, those who camped at backcountry facilities, should pay that cost. But to others, the idea of paying for the age-old privilege of sleeping in the great outdoors went down hard. Others argued that the existence of wild land was a benefit to the public at large and should not be charged to the few who camped out.

In the Presidential Range, the extensive restrictions on camping, especially above treeline, seemed to create a lengthy zone where virtually no one could stay overnight except at AMC huts. This resulted in two kinds of resentment. One was a generalized hostility toward the AMC on the part of some White Mountain campers who saw the huts as a privileged sanctuary exempt from the restrictions imposed on everyone else, a feeling exacerbated as the price of hut lodging soared to motel-like rates and caretaker fees were imposed (and then repeatedly raised), at designated camping sites.

The second was a resentment on the part of through-hikers along the Appalachian Trail, directed against the White Mountains in general, which seemed to them to be uniquely (with Baxter State Park) full of camping regulations and harassments and expense not encountered elsewhere along the trail. Backcountry managers believed the higher use-levels in the Whites were at the root of the problem.

Baxter State Park regulations, especially after 1971, produced heated opposition from outdoorspeople who regarded them as undue interference with the freedom and initiative long cherished as part of the backcountry experience. Such policies as "closing" Katahdin in bad weather, constant surveillance by park rangers, and the detailed control of winter climbing and rock climbing, evoked much criticism. Some Northeastern hikers and climbers simply refused to go there and be subjected to such rules. Baxter Park authorities believed that these policies were essential to the mission imposed by Governor Baxter of preserving the park.

These half-dozen issues largely involved restraints on formerly uninhibited use of the backcountry. The controversies stemmed from outrage on the part of those groups that were restricted by management actions. The issues were ones of self-interest. Were the sacrifices demanded of campers and the limitations on individual freedoms really necessary to the public interest or not?

Preservation versus use

More deeply rooted philosophical divisions centered on the long-standing and never fully resolved debate over preservation versus use. Here were heard twentieth-century echoes of the fundamental divergence in the early days of the AMC between the forces of improvements and exploration. Were the mountains a boundless public asset to be made more accessible so that they could be shared? Or was the "wilderness experience" inherently debased for all by throwing open the floodgates to large numbers? The split involved basic philosophy. In the heat of debate, the modern-day "improvements" wing often accused the "explorations" advocates of selfishly seeking to keep the mountains for their own private enjoyment, but such arguments did a disservice to the real issues.

During the 1970s this long-standing conflict surfaced over the question of whether to attempt to curb the numbers of new backpackers or to welcome them and encourage more. Two cardinal principles came into direct conflict: minimizing overuse of the mountains on the one hand, and the tradition of friendly mountain hospitality and a renewed enthusiasm for sharing the wilderness experience on the other. Was the problem really *overuse*? Or was it *misuse*, which could be corrected through education?

This was an issue that tended to find the GMC on one side and the AMC on the other. The division mirrored the personalities of the two New England states: Vermont (and the GMC) introverted, taciturn, uncomfortable with crowds, deeply attached to and protective of its land; New Hampshire (and the AMC) extroverted, ambitious for recognition by the outside world, hospitable to crowds. Meanwhile, over in New York, within both the ADK and the Forty-Sixers the Adirondack community was divided, as it had been before World War II, between the conservation wing and the recreation wing.

In the eyes of many, the backpacking boom unmistakably gave evidence that excessive numbers were incompatible with the preservation of either the physical resource or the quality of the experience. By 1977 the National Wilderness Society concluded,

> The question has become not how people can be drawn into wilderness in order to appreciate and enjoy it, but how the wilderness can survive, without being overwhelmed by sheer numbers.

On that basis the Wilderness Society decided that year to discontinue its eighteen-year program of organized trips for members and the public. That program had aimed to encourage wilderness use, thereby "to spread awareness of the ecological significance of wild places and the importance of their preservation." By 1977 the society felt that wilderness preservation had become a widely supported goal and that the backcountry was becoming overcrowded to the point where access had to be restricted.

Such considerations had already prompted the White Mountain National Forest, during the early 1970s, to limit camping in the Great Gulf, Baxter State Park to control access to Katahdin, and the Allagash Wilderness Waterway management to restrict entry to the Allagash river corridor. The Massachusetts Trustees of Reservations expressed a prevalent theme:

> Where enjoyment and preservation of a property may come in conflict, the Trustees of Reservations thinks first of its duty to preserve scenic and ecological values.

During the height of the boom, the Green Mountain Club quietly worked to turn away the flow of new hikers. The Vermonters discouraged publicity about the Long Trail and resisted having it designated a National Scenic Trail under federal legislation, fearing that the attendant publicity would attract yet more hikers. The GMC also actively urged members and the public to refrain entirely from hiking on the LT or other trails on Mansfield and Camel's Hump during mud season (roughly the month of April and, for higher elevations, May). In both the Green Mountains and the Adirondacks, all organized groups were urged to limit group size to ten or fewer. The focus was on dampening the boom and reducing the rate of increase in numbers.

The Forty-Sixers actually held meetings during the early 1970s at which they debated terminating their organization, because of concerns that their very existence spurred more people to climb the forty-six peaks. Ultimately, however, as shown in the next chapter, the Forty-Sixers decided instead to reorient the club's program toward environmental stewardship as an even more useful response.

Over in New Hampshire, some voices warned of overuse. Philip D. Levin argued, in a widely noticed essay, for the abolition of the Four Thousand Footer Club:

> I believe that the artificial inducements of these organizations create similar artificial use patterns in the mountains at a time when use and overuse is already subjecting these "wilderness areas" to fast-growing and unprecedented problems of land management.

But within the AMC, a far stronger impulse, based on long-standing club tradition, was to continue to encourage people to come to the mountains. The feeling was expressed by an outside observer of the AMC's programs:

> So much has been written—and legislated—about wilderness as a place for solitude, and I suppose that solitude has its rightful place. But there is also a lot to be said for the back country as a place for sharing, and that is the cause that the Appalachian Mountain Club serves.

The AMC's far-flung programs of education and recreation were dedicated to giving more people a chance to experience the outdoor life. While some voices within the club (such as Levin's) might counsel restraint, others whooped it up for larger turnouts at the friendly huts, efforts to reach new groups such as innercity youth, new workshops on every facet of outdoor life and ever larger and more frequent club-sponsored hikes. The philosophical rationale for such activities was that more backcountry users would strengthen the political base for the support of conservation. "Wilderness needs friends," argued the Sierra Club. AMC Education Director John Nutter took this view in a rebuttal to Levin's essay in *Appalachia*. Philosophy aside, a more urgent motive was added in the 1980s: as the AMC eagerly expanded its activities, club expenses began to outrun income, and a severe budget squeeze produced strong financial pressures to seek more income-generating use of club facilities at Pinkham Notch, the huts, and elsewhere.

Thus at a time when the GMC was urging people to stay out of the mountains in May, the AMC opened up the huts during that month for the first time and solicited guests.[a] At a time when the ADK and New York's DEC were limiting group size to ten or fewer, the AMC was expanding its programs of "range walks," under which twenty-five or more merry, sociable hikers would spend a week parading across the popular trails of the Whites. At a time when the Forty-Sixers were contemplating their own deliberate demise, the AMC was thinking up new workshops and other programs to turn out more people. These contrasts should not be read as simply a callous disregard for environmental concerns on the part of the AMC. The club's heavy involvement in education showed that it shared such concerns. In many areas, the AMC took strong steps to protect the environment at the expense of hikers' short-run preferences, as in tearing down shelters, charging fees, and building scree walls above treeline, all of which showed genuine commitment to protecting the physical resource. Rather, the contrasts reflected a fundamental divergence in analysis of the problem and response to it. The GMC and others saw the issue as clearly involving over use as well as misuse, and sought to reduce the growth in numbers. The AMC and like-minded observers insisted that *over*use was unproved, that *mis*use was the problem, and that through education and adroit backcountry management the crowds could be accommodated and a broader political base in support of conservation obtained.

Membership growth in the clubs

A related but separate issue on which opinion differed within as well as between the clubs concerned the question of deliberately courted membership growth. Strong factions within each club believed deeply in both

---

[a]A large-type notice in an AMC publication in April 1986 reminded readers that three huts opened on May 7, while two others "never close!" and went on to urge: "Discover the quiet times. . . . Call now for reservations. . . . MC and VISA accepted" ("Galehead, Greenleaf . . . " *Appalachia Bulletin* [Apr. 1986], p. 25).

The split over mud-season hiking was clearly posed in publications of the GMC and the AMC's new Vermont Chapter in May 1983. The GMC's *The Long Trail News* for that month ran a story headlined "Spring Hiking Discouraged" (p. 7) that reiterated the club policy against use of the LT in spring. At almost exactly the same time (spring 1983) the AMC's Vermont Chapter announced a scheduled hike on the Long Trail for Saturday, May 21, in its newsletter, *Vermont Adventures*, p. 4.

The AMC's approach did not stem from deliberate policy. In fact, a Backcountry Recreation Task Force established by the club in 1975 declared flatly, "The AMC opposes the unlimited marketing of backcountry to the general public, with the exception of specific outreach programs" (Backcountry Recreation Task Force, "Goals and Policies for Managing Backcountry Recreation," full report printed in *Appalachia* [June 1978], pp. 117–44. The quoted passage is on p. 140.) But in practice, this official policy was largely negated during the 1980s by budget pressures, an expansionist philosophy on the part of club officers and staff, and the enthusiasms of specific groups within the club.

the inevitability and desirability of growth. These factions grew dominant in the AMC during the late 1970s and in the ADK during the mid-1980s. Throughout the period, however, other factions questioned the wisdom of a policy that promoted more growth than would naturally flow from interest in the outdoors. This belief was held by some long-standing members of the clubs who felt that important values were lost when an organization became too big; others feared the financial consequences of overextending club resources; while others felt concerns about the environmental and experiential effects of promoting yet higher use levels in the backcountry. The debate over growth was of course by no means confined to hiking clubs: it was a cultural phenomenon of the late twentieth century.

Wilderness areas

During the early 1980s a gradually building division between regional conservation and national preservationist spokesmen finally produced a definite break over New England land management issues. Early in that decade the White Mountain National Forest established a program for expanding the number of "wilderness areas" designated by Congress under the Wilderness Act. A coalition of New Hampshire interests negotiated long and hard to reach a compromise consensus on adding new areas to that status, including a large tract in the Pemigewasset, so that this "wilderness" no longer needed to be placed in quotation marks. National organizations, with the Wilderness Society leading the charge, insisted that the extent of new "wilderness" was too limited and pushed for adding more—without success. In Vermont, at about the same time, the GMC and several ski resorts whose trails crossed the Long Trail hammered out agreements whereby the ski interests could expand operations but with limitations on the interference with hikers on the LT. Again, national organizations severely criticized the GMC for yielding ground to the resorts. During the mid-1980s the White Mountain National Forest completed a Forest-wide management plan for the next ten years. After criticizing early drafts of this plan as insufficiently sensitive to recreational interests, the AMC and other regional organizations secured concessions in the final version, whereupon they supported the plan with few reservations. On this issue national organizations waxed irate, charging that timber-harvesting interests had been heeded more than recreation and conservation. On all these issues, the New England organizations that had such long-standing reputations as champions of conservation in the region—the AMC, the Society for the Protection of New Hampshire Forests, the GMC—found themselves in the unwonted role of differing with old allies such as the Wilderness Society.

Trail work also drew its share of controversy during the years when trail maintainers struggled to devise strategies for coping with the backpacking boom.

When the AMC's trail crew first began probing for solutions to the problem, idealism ran high and careful thought went into preserving the spirit of wilderness, or at least of wildness. Steve Page, the first caretaker at Liberty Springs in that pioneering year of 1970, with manifest concern for wilderness values, reflected on early efforts to restrict hiker traffic from trampling vegetation adjacent to trails:

> A large decaying log placed next to the trail parallel to it is an excellent barrier—both physically and visually. . . . Another, less subtle barrier is the rock wall. . . . Split rail fences are a possibility for drastic no-access areas but somehow we must keep our backcountry from turning into a suburbia. . . . It means sensitivity to the surroundings in planning and building the trails, then a lot of work in repairing the continual erosion created by feet.

Trails Supervisor Robert Proudman, though spearheading the radical adoption of trail-hardening measures, worked hard to get his crews to take the time and effort to have rock work look natural. The 1973 work on South Twin remains a brilliant example of artfully placed rocks that simultaneously control hiker traffic, divert runoff, yet look remarkably as if placed there by nature.

As the years went by, however, the early idealism faded and, both in the White Mountains and elsewhere throughout the region, rock work and other measures became less subtle. Often the size of the job and the urgency of preserving the physical environment moved spirit-of-wildness considerations into the background. By the late 1970s, jackhammered steps blasted into the rock and knee-high scree walls trumpeted the message to hikers with all the quiet charm of seventy-six trombones.

When the WMNF trail crew introduced the jackhammer and pin-steps, many Northeastern trail workers blew the whistle. That strong measures were needed to stabilize trails was agreed, but many insisted that beyond a certain point the overcivilizing of trail work and the look and spirit of the completed trail were matters for legitimate concern. When the AMC refused to install pin-steps on the Wildcat Ridge Trail out of Pinkham Notch, the WMNF crew put them in. The public protest was so clamorous that the technique was not widely used thereafter. Blasting steps into the rock also met with disfavor and was not widely adopted. The AMC's above-treeline scree walls in turn met with protest among some trail workers and hikers, and subsequent efforts were directed toward softening their visual impact and making use of a broader range of tools to control tundra traffic, including greater emphasis on educational messages. As trail-hardening methods were more widely employed in the Adirondacks, the ADK's Trails Committee urged the DEC not to overbuild all trails just because the popular ones up Marcy obviously required strong measures:

> There are some intrusions almost universally agreed to "tear a big hole" in the wilderness, such as A-10 jet aircraft and the sound of a chainsaw. In an area where the use does not justify it, a highly engineered trail can cause the same effect. In fact, wilderness can be enhanced by leaving some trails a little rough in appearance. . . . Hikers deserve a chance for a wild wilderness experience.

A question on which opinions divided was the use of the chain saw. Some of the most important trail crews—the Maine Appalachian Trail Club, for example—enthusiastically accepted this new tool and believed that effective trail work was impossible without it. In the Adirondacks, DEC policy frowned on this noisy intrusion and instructed trail workers to confine its use to off-season. The AMC trail crew waxed hot and cold on this issue, depending on the personal values of each year's trailmaster. In the Hudson Highlands, the leading trail worker of the day, John Schoen, was personally opposed to chain saws but conceded that others loved them: he proposed a separate trail crew to be armed with chain saws and called the "Chain Gang" or the "Power Brokers."

A different kind of controversy on trail work surrounded the issue of amateurism versus professionalism. Oddly enough, this appeared to be an important issue in Maine and New Hampshire but a nonissue in Vermont and New York. In Maine, MATC leaders felt strongly that volunteer efforts could remain viable only if paid trail crews were not available to fall back on. So a rigorous principle of amateurism was enforced. At one point the AMC trail crew was granted a 9.5-mile section of the Maine AT to maintain, and AMC leaders sought to increase the club's role in Maine trail work. MATC leaders found themselves increasingly uncomfortable with having a professional crew within their jurisdiction, however, fearing that professionals tend to drive out volunteers. After several years of feuding, the grant of the trail crew's section was summarily revoked in the late 1970s, with the MATC's president warning the AMC,

> We cannot allow our long-term attempts to better organize ourselves to be undermined by the temptation to resort to hiring professionals to do our job.

On the other side of this issue, in the White Mountains, the AMC's professional trail crew carefully preserved its hegemony over AMC trails against the incursions of amateurs. An Adopt-a-Trail program, under which AMC volunteers were to take over maintenance of White Mountain trails, enjoyed limited success at first; adopters sensed trail crew reluctance to relinquish control of any trails. But in the Green Mountains and Adirondacks, this issue was moot. Paid trail crews (the Long Trail Patrol, ADK's seasonal crew) worked harmoniously on trails adjacent to those maintained by volunteers from the GMC, the ADK, ATIS, and the Forty-Sixers.

Appalachian Trail protection program

The Appalachian Trail protection program, while commanding very wide support in the Northeastern trails community, sparked some points of controversy. To many leaders in the Appalachian Trail Conference, the "melding" of private with public agencies—the trail clubs with the National Park Service—was an unprecedented and wholly positive step. Without this radical move, they contended, the AT could not have survived as a continuous footpath and would have been increasingly forced off the wooded ridges and onto the roads. They heralded the willingness of the Park Service to delegate management authority to the ATC as an innovative step in public land management.

But enlisting the federal government had its price. Landowners and town leaders in some communities, notably in western Massachusetts, were embittered by a feeling that the National Park Service was riding roughshod over local concerns, all for the promotion of a footpath for the amusement of an insignificant number of hikers. Landowner resentments might have been anticipated as inevitable in any program of land acquisition, but controversial opinions also grew among trail workers and hikers.

Some longtime trail workers had labored long and hard to promote a philosophy that landowner rights were absolute, and that hikers had an unshirkable obligation to respect private property over which a trail was allowed to pass. This tradition was especially strong in Connecticut, where trail maintainers had lived for fifty years with the necessity of respecting landowner rights. When federal legislation changed the basic relationships between trail workers and land owners, some of these longtime trail workers balked. Now, instead of being responsible for preserving good terms with landowners, the government could order landowners to accept the trail over their land, with seizure by eminent domain the ultimate threat. Veteran Connecticut trailsman Kornel Bailey recalled conversations with Seymour Smith, who had maintained Connecticut's AT section for almost fifty years.

> Seymour Smith and I felt that if it got to the point of taking land away from land owners, then we didn't want any part of it.

Another Connecticut trailsman spoke for this viewpoint when he commented,

The clubs are copping out on a moral issue when they have been using a person's land for 30–40 years and then promote condemnation of their land. . . . We could not get into a situation of not abiding by what we have said since 1929, that is, being able to get the Trail off the land if the landowner wants.

Some of these trail workers felt that the AT's widely publicized squabbles with landowners, especially in Connecticut and Massachusetts, jeopardized landowner relations on innumerable *other* trails where the threat of eminent domain was *not* available.

AT through-hikers were not always the strongest supporters of the federal protection program either. During the 1980s the letters column of *Appalachian Trailway News* was peppered with dissenting views. Park Service policy of eliminating road walks was regretted by through-hikers who recalled idyllic rambles on country roads and pleasant encounters with townsfolk. "The diversity of the Trail is one of its special charms," wrote one through-hiker. "Keep a few road-walks." "Why is it a sin for a hiker to see a house?" demanded another. "Why are we working so hard to make the Trail as monotonous as possible?" Some feared deterioration in the good relations between hikers and landowners: "Do we really want our organization to be known for its seizure of ancestral farms and homes?"

The issue was exacerbated by a feeling among some in the trail community that this community had lost control of basic trail decisions when the National Park Service acquired responsibility for the AT. In the view of one who talked to a wide representation of people connected with the AT,

Since the passage of the Trails Act many things have changed in the administration of the Trail. No longer a volunteer recreation project under the loose and casual leadership of a private organization, the Trail is now a government project. . . . The Park Service now has final responsibility for the Trail and exercises it with the full panoply of red tape.

This feeling seemed confirmed when disputes with landowners were portrayed in the media as involving landowners on one side and the federal government on the other. For all the pious declarations that the AT remained the work of volunteers and their clubs, when the chips were down, the NPS called the shots. This caused concern among some supporters of the trail:

The question remains concerning whether or not the small-is-beautiful concepts and working arrangements, which were employed in the first few decades of the Trail's existence, will be irreparably damaged by the participation of "big government."

It should be emphasized, however, that this sentiment was the view of, apparently, a small minority within the trail community. Overwhelmingly, the opinion of hikers and trail workers was united in support of the AT protection program. Against the minority's concern about landowner relations and the federal government's role, the majority felt that federal protection was the only way to preserve the continuity of the great trail in the face of growing land development pressure.

Indeed, nothing in this chapter should be construed as implying that the Northeastern hiking or trails scene was rife with controversy or seriously divided for very long. The points cited in this chapter were more like irritations than major issues. They were like pesky bites from the Northeast's backwoods black fly, not a life-threatening cancer. A broad consensus supported the new backcountry management and the environmental ethic that arose in response to the backpacking boom. Whatever the minor disagreements mentioned here, the general view was staunchly in support of preserving an environmentally healthy but still relatively unfettered Northeastern mountain world.

Chapter 58

Peakbaggers and end-to-enders

THE MARSHALL brothers started something when they climbed the "Adirondack forty-six" during the 1920s. Climbing the Northeast's 4,000-footers became an irresistible lure to those who derived joy from physical challenge and reaching goals.

The backpacking boom was a boon to peakbagging. The Adirondack Forty-Sixers welcomed many more new members (that is, people who qualified by climbing all forty-six 4,000-foot peaks). During the entire decade of the 1950s an average of fewer than 10 new Forty-Sixers per year were recorded. During the 1960s the numbers rose until by the early 1970s more than 120 new members per year was the average. In 1984 the Forty-Sixers' roster passed the 2,000 mark and kept rolling. In New Hampshire, the AMC formally established a Four Thousand Footer Committee in 1957 and handed out scrolls to similar numbers each year. At intervals of seven years thereafter, the peakbagging horizons expanded. In 1964 a full New England list of 4,000-footers—originally numbering sixty-three (forty-six in New Hampshire, twelve in Maine, five in Vermont)—was compiled, climbed, and made the basis for a new "club." After that it was but a short and logical step to the "111 Club of the Northeast" in 1971: the New England sixty-three plus the Adirondack forty-six plus Slide and Hunter in the Catskills. With new estimates of elevation, especially in New Hampshire where two "new" 4,000-footers were identified, this total crept upwards. Another direction the peakbagging mania took was toward the "Hundred Highest," a New England list being drawn up in 1964, and lists for individual states soon thereafter.

In the Catskills there were only two 4,000-footers, so the targeted list of peaks became the 3,500-footers. The origin of this list was unusual. In 1949 two couples who loved hiking—C. William and Kathleen Spangenberger and William and Elinore Leavitt—first came up with the idea of climbing the Catskill 3,500-footers. The idea did not catch on with others, but the Spangenbergers completed their climbs in 1952. Ten years later another hiking couple, Brad and Dorothy Whiting came up with the idea independently, only to discover that the Spangenbergers had beaten them to it. This time, however, a slightly broader interest among other Catskill hikers was discovered, so an organizing committee met on October 20, 1962, at the Mohonk Mountain House. There the aid of still another couple was enlisted, Daniel and Virginia Smiley. Dan Smiley had conducted a study, with Fred Hough, another local naturalist, of the Bicknell's Thrush, a bird that they noted was often found in balsam fir stands, which in turn they believed would most often be found above 3,500 feet. For this study, therefore, Smiley had compiled a list of 3,500-foot peaks, refining an earlier list that had appeared in a 1931 book, and publishing the list in a 1961 magazine article.[a] At the organizing meeting in 1962, attended by Brad Whiting, Bill Spangenberger, Dan Smiley, and Nancy Locke, Smiley was appointed to draw up the official list of peaks, and his wife Virginia agreed to design the club's patch.

Armed with this new list, the Catskill 3500 Club was born. Since the list differed slightly from that used by the Spangenbergers ten years earlier, the Leavitts stole the honor of completing the list first, becoming charter members numbers one and two on April 13, 1963, followed six weeks later by the Spangenbergers, with the Whitings and another couple, Betty and Jerome Hurd, in close succession. Charter membership was held open through 1965, at which point twenty-seven members were enrolled.[b]

Like the Adirondack Forty-Sixers and the New Hampshire peakbaggers, the Catskill 3500 Club attracted much interest during the next few years because of the backpacking boom. By the end of 1975 it had added more then two hundred new members in ten years. A newsletter, *The Catskill Cannister*, designed to keep members informed, was skillfully edited by Franklin Clark, himself a devoted Catskill hiker. One member, Sam Steen, had been around to all the peaks at least twenty times. He and Dick Davis climbed each of the peaks in each of the calendar months. Such feats were atypical, however, of an organization described by one of its members as

> permeated by a wholesome sense of humor and an ability to laugh at ourselves. After all, when you are grabbing peaks that are only 3500 feet high, you have to have a sense of humor and a love for the woods.

---

[a] By coincidence, Smiley's influential article in the New York *Conservationist* bears the same date (Aug. 1961) as William O. Douglas's famous article on the AMC huts in the *National Geographic* —see chap. 51—doing almost as much to open up hikers' interest in the Catskills as Douglas's may have for the White Mountains. Actually Smiley's list originally appeared in a less widely read publication, *The Chirp*, newsletter of the John Burroughs Natural History Society.

[b] Naturalists Smiley and Hough had, of course, climbed all the peaks on the trail of the elusive Bicknell's Thrush during the late 1950s. However, the Catskill 3500 Club introduced some additional criteria for membership—notably that four named peaks (Slide, Blackhead, Panther, and Balsam) had to be climbed in winter conditions. Not being peakbaggers by nature, Smiley and Hough never fulfilled that additional requirement.

The longer trails of the Northeast—Vermont's Long Trail, the North-ville-Placid Trail, and, of course, the 2,100-mile Appalachian Trail coming up from Georgia—gave impetus to an impulse that was somewhat like and somewhat unlike peakbagging: walking a long trail from end to end. Earlier chapters mentioned such accomplishments on the LT and Northville-Placid before the war. But although Myron Avery had been on every foot of the AT, no one had walked the trail in one continuous trip. Indeed, the idea of end-to-end walking was not in vogue before World War II, and very few even gave it a thought.

On August 5, 1948, Earl V. Shaffer reached that famous cairn on Ka-tahdin's summit to finish walking the entire Appalachian Trail, Georgia to Maine, in one continuous trip. That accomplishment had an impact on the thinking of a lot of hikers, almost comparable in psychological effect to the first 4-minute mile six year later. Soon others set out on the 2,100-mile walk, usually taking about six months to complete it. Along with those few who walked it in one continuous trip, many more under-took to walk all 2,100 miles in smaller discontinuous chunks, using sum-mer vacations and long weekends to bite off 25-mile or 125-mile segments until they filled in their maps. The total numbers of people completing the big undertaking remained small until the backpacking boom, but during the 1970s the rolls of AT end-to-enders swelled to roughly 100 per year, with a peak of 166 in 1973.

By then the phenomenon of the end-to-ender was no longer a curiosity but a regular feature of the Northeastern hiking scene, particularly in late summer, as the troops that began in Georgia in March and April began to file through the northernmost sections, heading lemminglike for Katah-din. The experience of a continuous AT walk was altogether different from ordinary weekend hiking, as it involved several months during which it was an all-absorbing occupation and became a way of life. Said one through-hiker,

> It's like being on two different planets. Time stretches out on the trail—
> I have more experiences in a single day than in two weeks back home.

End-to-enders were often solitaries, given to colorful habits, garb, and nicknames,[c] but those who were walking the trail in any given year grew to know each other, sometimes walking together for a few days or stop-ping at the same shelters, and otherwise keeping in touch through entries in registers provided at the shelters. Gradually each year's batch of end-to-enders would become knit into a cohesive community, albeit a mov-ing community not tied to a physical spot but very closely tied together by the common experience of the long walk. Some individuals went back

---

[c]Sample nicknames: Kaptain Wilderness, the Boston Strollers, Rambling Rat, Redbeard and the Gypsy, the Trail Tots, the Hobbit, the Cheshire Cat, the Irish Wonder, the Hog, A Pilgrim in Prog-ress, Minnesota Two-Sticks, the Connecticut Connection, Rockhopper, Droopalong, Flatfoot, Bumbles, and the Bag Lady.

for a second or third trip. During the early 1980s Stephen ("Yo-Yo") Nuckolls walked from Georgia to Maine, touched the cairn on Katahdin and turned around to walk back, turned around again at Georgia and returned to Katahdin, surely one of the first uninterrupted walks of more than 6,000 miles and a remarkable demonstration of the magnetic power of that way of life.

Along with the extended feats of the peakbaggers and end-to-enders, the postwar Northeastern hiking scene witnessed an extravaganza of other unusual pedestrian accomplishments.

One was multiple peakbagging. Many hikers had been known to sigh, with reference to a Couchsachraga (Adirondacks), or an Owl's Head (Whites), or a Rocky (Catskills), that having done *that* miserable little mountain once, they were glad they'd never have to do it again. Nevertheless, as completion of each of the lists became less rare, a few intrepid and incurable peakbaggers set out, like Yo-Yo Steve of the AT, to repeat the rounds. The hiking grandmother Trudy Healy completed six rounds of the Adirondack forty-six before moving west to Utah to carry on her passion for mountains in the Wasatch Range. That veteran climber Jim Goodwin never moved away and gradually worked his way up toward twenty rounds of the forty-six, with almost 200 individual ascents of Marcy. In the White Mountains, some have passed 15 rounds of the 4,000-footers, and 200 ascents of individual favorites, such as Washington or Lafayette. The professionals who work on the summits of Mount Washington or Mansfield year-round, or who regularly patrol Marcy, amass totals that probably exceed any unpaid recreationist's by far. One unusual feat was John Winkler's ascent of each of the Adirondack forty-six by bushwhack routes, an accomplishment duplicated in the White Mountains where one devotee also did them all from all four points of the compass.

One of the most astonishing hiking careers was that of one Fred Hunt, who hiked in the Adirondacks from 1969 to 1978. Hunt was brought up near New Hampshire's Monadnock, which he climbed many times from the age of nine on. He developed a strong love for being in the woods on foot. He entered the profession of forestry in which he could indulge his passion for tramping over hill and dale all day long. But in the fall of 1968 he took a job teaching forestry at Paul Smith's College in the Adirondacks and suddenly found himself saddled with long hours in the classroom and college office. For one who had always walked in the wilds, claustrophobia threatened. He decided to try hiking the mountain trails. On September 4, 1969, as he climbed Marcy, Hunt met a Forty-Sixer named Alder Tanton, who told him about the list of peaks and the club. Shortly thereafter, Hunt read in a log book about another Forty-Sixer who was contemplating the possibility of climbing each of the forty-six in each of the four seasons. These events triggered possibly the greatest binge of peakbagging the Adirondacks has ever seen. In a ten-year period, before he moved away to Vermont, Fred Hunt climbed each of the forty-six in each of four *consecutive* seasons, from December 21, 1969, to December 13, 1970; climbed each of the forty-six in each *month* of the year, finishing on Allen on March 4, 1973; climbed all forty-six at night; in one three-and-a-half year period, averaged three peaks per week year-round; climbed Marcy each month for 110 consecutive months. Hunt generally hiked alone, signing summit registers as "The Lone Ranger." An interesting conclusion to the story was how quickly Hunt's interest in peakbagging disappeared (as quickly as it had surfaced). After ten years of whirlwind climbing, a job change resulted in a move to Vermont and a chance to work in the woods again—whereupon Hunt apparently ceased recreational hiking altogether.

Inevitably some fast walkers conceived plans for covering the 4,000-footers in a sudden burst over as few days as possible. In 1966 a man, two boys, and a dog climbed all the New Hampshire 4,000-footers in one continuous trip of fourteen days. In 1969 the indefatigable Catskill peakbagging priest, Fr. Ray Donahue, and his friend Norman Greig climbed the Adirondack forty-six in nine days. The gauntlet having been thrown down, others began systematically assaulting these records, reducing the required time to four days, eighteen hours, eighteen minutes for the Adirondack Forty-Six (Sharpe Swan and Ed Palen, 1977), and four days, ten hours, twenty-four minutes for the Catskill 3,500-footers (Damon Douglas and Marshall Child, 1980).

One-day superwalks attracted those who loved the vigorous outing. In the White Mountains the big test pieces were the traverse of the Mahoosucs Range (slightly more than 30 miles and slightly less than 10,000 feet of uphill) and the traverse of the hut system (slightly less than 50 miles as usually done, and well over 10,000 feet of uphill, probably closer to 15,000). A Harvard student and AMC hutman named Chris Goetze broke Herbert Malcolm's old prewar records during the late 1950s. These feats picked up in popularity during the late 1970s. Hutmen Jonathan Waterman and Samuel Osborne broke Goetze's record for the huts traverse with a time of sixteen hours, two minutes in 1977, only to see that record smashed the next year by Michael Young's solo time of fourteen hours, fifteen minutes—a record which lasted until the Trail Crew's Robert Biddle's fourteen hours, five minutes in 1981.

Another White Mountains test piece was the Dartmouth Outing Club's "Trail Walk": Kinsman Notch north of Moosilauke to Hanover, comparable in distance to the huts traverse but involving less uphill. A DOC hiker summarized the mixed attractions of such a grueling one-day effort in a marvelously diverse comparison: "It's the DOC equivalent of beer chugging, earning a Varsity letter or becoming a grandmaster in chess."

Similar one-day tests, probably none quite as demanding as the White Mountains' hut traverse, became popular in all the ranges, from the Adirondacks Great Range to the old Harriman Park "Transcontinentals" (see chapter 46), from the quiet and remote 28.5-mile Taconic Crest Trail to the suburban, wooded, 30-mile network of the Sleeping Giant near New Haven, and even to the 34-mile Greenbelt Trail in the heart of Long Island.

An extension of the one-day long walk was the multiday speed hiking of long trails. Marathon runners attempted to set records on the 2,100-mile AT. In 1969 a U.S. cross-country Olympic ski squad walked the 263-mile Long Trail in nine days, four hours, only to have their mark bettered by an individual speedster, Warren Doyle, in 1978 (Doyle's time: eight days, thirteen hours, twenty-five minutes).

In an altogether different spirit was the new twist put on the old goal of a Presidential traverse. Several college groups, most often from Harvard or MIT, accomplished this feat by moonlight. One way to do it was to start from Randolph in late afternoon and arrive at Madison Col about dark. Then, if predicted good weather held, the happy party would walk leisurely the dozen or so miles of open alpine zone by glorious moonlight, and drop into Crawford Notch at daybreak.

One last superhiking feat deserves mention. Readers may recall the tour de force of the 1930s in which Ron Gower and his friends climbed Katahdin from Boston in a single weekend (chapter 46). In those days a weekend meant from Saturday noon to Monday morning, with access over narrow, twisty highways. During the late 1960s a group of three college outing club climbers elected to see whether they could climb Katahdin from New Jersey in a single weekend. Of course, conditions were radically changed: a weekend began late Friday afternoon and almost all the driving was on interstate highways. The trio left New Jersey at 6:00P.M. Friday, rotated drivers and sleepers to knock off the 600 miles of driving at an average clip of just over 50 mph (compare with the 1930s group's 27 mph), arriving at Roaring Brook Campground at 6:00 A.M. Saturday morning. From then on it was easy. They were up the Dudley Trail to Pamola, across the Knife Edge to the top, and down the Saddle Trail in perfect weather by 3:00 P.M. Saturday (compare the 1930s descent of the Chimney in a driving rain on Sunday). A bit groggy from the all-night drive plus hike, they drove to the first rest area on the interstate and threw sleeping bags unceremoniously on the ground, sleeping til dawn. On Sunday they had time to stop off in Boston to visit the outing clubbers' guru, Gardner Perry III—the opening conversation can be imagined ("What brings you boys up from New Jersey this weekend?" "Oh, happened to be climbing Katahdin and thought we'd drop in.")—before returning home at a quite reasonable hour. Katahdin in a weekend from New Jersey during the 1960s had proved much easier than Katahdin in a weekend from Boston during the 1930s.

Some other unusual feats of peakbagging involved winter ascents, but since there is a special quality to winter climbing, their tale is best reserved for chapter 60.

It may be clear that the goals set by peakbaggers and end-to-enders were diverse. Some emphasized speed and strength, but others frowned on such values and touted peakbagging or long-distance walking as delightfully accessible to the nonathletic duffer who simply enjoyed mountain walking at whatever pace suited, no matter how slow. Some end-to-enders regarded peakbagging as perfectly ridiculous, while some peakbaggers confessed they'd be bored to distraction by walking continuously on one trail for weeks. De gustibus. . . .

Meanwhile, in the rest of the hiking community—the *non*peakbaggers —a groundswell of criticism arose. Opposition centered on a conviction that superhiking took place at the expense of real appreciation of the mountain environment. Critics felt that to race through the hills was at best a waste of time spent in such surroundings, at worst a sacrilege. One critic lumped peakbagging with competitive climbing and pursuit of a "life list" by birders as "sins in thought in the wilderness." Philip Levin's critique, cited in chapter 57, was aimed at both the adverse impact on otherwise pristine summits and the degraded spirit of the enterprise. A director of a summer camp that encouraged hiking said,

> Above all, one must prevent hiking from turning into a competition for speed records. Campers should be ashamed of bragging that they "made the Diamond Trail over the Ridge in twenty minutes." Or rather their leaders should be ashamed of this distortion of values.

In a trail-head parking lot, an anonymous critic who saw the license plate of inveterate peakbagger Eugene Daniell III ("PKBGR"), traced "You're Sick" in the dust next to the plate. The Green Mountain Club continued to adorn literature on the Long Trail with such exhortations as "The L. T. is no place to break speed records." An Adirondack Park Agency official once warned a meeting of the Forty-Sixers, "You may now be taking in your last Forty-Sixers. You have got to get off these mountains. They can't take it anymore." In a gentler spirit, some ADK critics had long ago mocked the Forty-Sixers. One group in the 1950s started a countergroup called the "Non-46ers," whose objective was to abstain from reaching summits: "The goal to be attained by the faithful is a state of pristine purity unblemished by any taint of ascent whatever." A former ADK president, J. Kenneth W. Macalpine, promoted "the fun of stretching a two-hour hike into an all-day outing":

> Why not try it? On your first attempt you may find yourself back at three o'clock with nothing to do until dinner, but if you persevere you will find you can spend longer and longer days on shorter and shorter hikes.

Perhaps the ultimate criticism was pronounced by the fates: in June 1972 two robust climbers attempting to break the speed record for the

Adirondack forty-six were struck with unseasonably ferocious weather on the summit cone of Marcy on the fourth day of grueling effort—and one of the climbers died.

The most characteristic response of the peakbaggers and end-to-enders was to ignore the critics and carry on to the next mountain. Some tried to articulate a conviction that superhiking had its own unique rewards and was a thoroughly valid expression of love of the peaks. Herbert Malcolm's prewar evocation of dogs and birds who revel in the joy of the strenuous exercise of their powers was one defense (see chapter 46). Among those who responded in letters to *Appalachia* following Levin's critique, some insisted that peakbaggers savored the qualities of the mountains fully and that the added element of overcoming challenge was a legitimate aspiration:

> If Mr. Levin doesn't like such things [the physical challenge] he doesn't have to do them but don't take them away from those who do enjoy it so much.

Quoth an ADK peakbagger:

> I become slightly weary of others trying to tell me why I am not enjoying my climbs—simply because I do not climb for the reasons they feel I should.

The region's most accomplished peakbaggers, the leading 3,000-footer climbers, defended their activity mostly on grounds that they derived immense satisfaction from setting a very difficult goal and persevering until it was accomplished—and that such activity in no way intruded on others' enjoyment of the hills. Said one:

> I regard peakbagging lists more as an itinerary than a goal, tend to be sad rather than exultant when I complete a list (as if I'd lost a friend), and I always try to find a new list—if not several—as soon as possible.

One AT hiker responded to a critic of certain end-to-enders' practices with a plea for tolerance reminiscent of a similar viewpoint expressed by the AT-builder Myron Avery fifty years before:

> More disheartening to me is the phenomenon of people who take it upon themselves to closely monitor how others hike and to criticize them if they do not hike in a prescribed manner. . . . What is important is that a hiker be true to his or her own goals, not to what [critics] or I believe his or her goals should be. . . . Please, I beg of you, be true to your own ideals and allow other hikers to be true to theirs.

At one level, the peakbaggers' reply was simpler: from the days when people first began climbing mountains, the appeal has always been to see if one can get to the top. In that sense, peakbagging needed neither defense nor apology—it was what mountaineering had always been about. But the most convincing reply to the critics was probably to be found in a good look at some of the most incorrigible peakbaggers of the Northeast: no one who knew them could for one moment dream of leveling the accusation of failing to appreciate Northeastern mountains at such individuals as Robert and George Marshall, or Robert and Miriam Underhill; or at Grace Hudowalski and Jim Goodwin and Trudy Healy and Ed Ketchledge of the Adirondacks; or at White Mountain irreclaimables like Eugene Daniell and Thomas Sawyer; or at the Catskills' Fr. Ray Donahue.

Nevertheless, in the face of the environmental consciousness of the 1960s, many peakbaggers found that both their critics' barbs and their own consciences hurt. The response of the Adirondack Forty-Sixers formed an interesting tale, with an outcome that might not have been easily predicted at the start.

The first phase of the Forty-Sixers' reaction was the Great Herd Path War of the summer of 1966. Reacting to the charge that Adirondack wildness was being compromised by the proliferation of well-marked "herd paths" to the summits of ostensibly trailless peaks, some individual Forty-Sixers, led by James ("Beetle") Bailey and a Camp Pok-o-moonshine group under his direction, began a campaign to knock down cairns and to brush in the start of the herd paths to trailless summits. The intent was idealistic but the consequences chaotic. Others angrily restored the cairns and cleared the brush off the paths. Bailey and his allies returned a few days later to erase them, and even to build misleading cairns in the wrong place. Wrathful restoration forces were on the scene within days to correct the artifice. The pages of the fall 1966 issue of *Adirondack Peeks*, the Forty-Sixers' newsletter, resounded with charges and countercharges. Prestigious members of the club could be found on both sides of the issue. *Peeks* editor Trudy Healy backed the wreckers:

> The 46ers are trying to recover the trailless state of some of the official "trailless" mountains by removing cairns marking the beginning of trailless routes. Since they were put up by 46ers to speed their future ascents when taking other hikers, it seems not only their right, but their duty to remove the signs of their weakness. . . . Trailless mountains are for those who appreciate wilderness conditions and can handle them.

But Jim Goodwin lent his prestige to the opposite viewpoint, questioning whether these peaks would ever be truly trailless again—"You couldn't get the toothpaste back in the tube"—and fearing that bad judgment by the wreckers had turned loose unhealthy forces:

> The kids who were allowed to wreck the paths for the most part were not inspired by idealism to preserve the wilderness. They just enjoyed wrecking.

During the late 1960s mounting criticism was directed at the Forty-Sixers for the impact of herd paths and the promotion of peakbagging on the once pristine wilderness of the high peaks. David Newhouse, a perennial leader of the conservationist wing of the Adirondack Mountain Club, warned,

> The 46ers are really faced with what seems to me to be an evident fact that the existence of the club, its requirements for membership, and its maintenance of Summit registers are probably a prime cause of the problem. Without these incentives, without promotion by the 46ers, . . . the "trailless" peaks would doubtless be much closer to being trailless and their characteristics might have been such that their qualities might have been sustained, for the enjoyment of those motivated to climbing them without the incentives provided by summit registers and membership qualifications in a climbing club such as the 46ers.

In 1970 two men new to the leadership of the club came to the fore. Glenn W. Fish, a big, hearty, affable sportsman-turned-peakbagger, assumed the presidency of the club. That summer he received a long thoughtful letter from Dr. Edwin Ketchledge, the Syracuse University forester-turned-peakbagger, who had, with Ray Leonard, been wrestling with the problems of reseeding alpine summits. Ketchledge challenged Fish to convert the Forty-Sixers from being a cause of the problem to becoming its solution, to becoming "stewards of the High Peaks." At the club's next meeting Fish read Ketchledge's letter, and in the next few months held a series of huddles with small groups of concerned members. Fish started by boldly opening up the question of whether the club should vote itself into extinction, but his meetings slowly turned the club resolutely in the other direction: to direct its energies into saving the environment of the high peaks. Through a combination of the strong environmental conscience and intellectual discipline of Ketchledge, the artless amiability and organizing skill of Fish, and the creative ideas and practical hard work of dozens of other Forty-Sixers, a transformation was effected during the 1970s.

The first big step was—as it had been for the environmental movement itself (see chapter 52)—an antilitter campaign. Plastic litter bags bearing the logo and exhortatory message of the Forty-Sixers were systematically distributed at trail-heads, so that thousands of hikers were encouraged to carry out their own and others' trash. This program lent itself to Fish's salesmanship, and he himself frequently handed the bags out personally to passing hikers, taking the opportunity to regale them with the environmental ethic.

The summit reseeding effort became a formal part of the Forty-Sixers' program, under Ketchledge's direction. Along with this work went an effort to define a single path above treeline and to minimize aimless wandering on the alpine vegetation.

The herd path issue was resolved in favor of defining and unobtrusively marking a single herd path on trailless peaks but carefully refraining from widening or "improving" that path.

The Wilderness Leadership Workshop sponsored by the Forty-Sixers was used as a means for reaching camp groups with the environmental message.

In 1977 a program of trail maintenance was launched, at first under the leadership of Walter Herrod and Michael ("Big Axe") Shaw. The next year Jim Goodwin agreed to direct the Forty-Sixers' trail crew and over the next few years built it into a significant factor in Adirondack trail maintenance.

Also in 1977 a "46ers Conservation Service Award" was instituted to promote and honor volunteer work on these various projects.

When water pollution brought the threat of giardia to the Adirondacks high peaks during the 1980s, the Forty-Sixers launched a program of distributing trowels at trail-heads, with instructions on how to dispose of human wastes in the most constructive manner.

The net impact of all these efforts on the Adirondack backcountry was significant. Ketchledge, the original spark that lit the fire in the program, summarized the results seven years after his 1970 letter:

> We've turned the orientation around from just climbing the peaks to one of stewardship for the peaks. We are to a degree the conscience of the recreational user of the High Peaks.

Commented DEC ranger C. Peter Fish (no relation to Glenn W.): "For a small group, these people [the Forty-Sixers] probably put more of their time and backs into the area than anyone else."

Other superhiking organizations followed suit. The Catskill 3500 Club took up trail maintenance and litter pickup. The Appalachian Trail Long Distance Hikers Association promoted trail work among its members. Somewhat later than the rest, the AMC's Four Thousand Footer Club began cosponsoring trail work sessions with the New Hampshire Chapter's volunteer trail crew.

But pure unadulterated peakbagging did not die. While the critics sniped and the Forty-Sixers salved their consciences with constructive projects, the hard core of true peakbaggers forged on to new lists and ever more obscure summits.

Somewhere around the mid-1970s, a major escalation in the vision of peakbagging took place. At this time, the quest for the New Hampshire Hundred Highest (the NHHH, to insiders) attracted new faces, among whom were Eugene Daniell III, Thomas Sawyer, Bruce O. Brown, Deane Morrison, Ray Chaput, Sam Hagner, Beverly Nolan, and Frank Pilar. Encouraged and inspired by their "mentor," the indefatigable White Mountain summer and winter peakbagger Richard Stevens, most of this group completed the NHHH in 1975 and 1976 and looked around for more peaks to conquer. In 1975 Daniell circulated a list of 3,000-footers for New Hampshire, a total of 180 peaks (later raised to 185). Off they charged. By 1977, Sawyer, Chaput, and Nolan (the premier woman in peakbagging circles) had "done" that list and were looking around for more. Hagner and Pilar finished in October 1978, Daniell and Morrison two and a half years later. Morrison meanwhile had been first over the Vermont 3,000-footers, finishing in 1979, closely followed the next year by Daniell and Sawyer. On June 23, 1980, Sawyer left them all in the dust, completing all 445 (!) New England 3,000-footers on an ascent of Maine's lonely sentinel of the north, the Traveler.

Contemplation of the extraordinary activities of this group might conjure up a picture of youthful, muscular, macho men in constant training and humorless pursuit of their goals at all costs. The reality was different. Most were garden-variety Appie hikers, many active on the White Mountain guidebook committee. Several were over fifty years old. Few were technical climbers or true mountaineers—indeed few were remarkably fast-paced walkers. The prevailing attitude toward their unusual pastime was one of self-deprecating humor, acknowledgment of the notoriously unspectacular nature of many of the summits to be bagged, and garrulous enjoyment of the company on each climb. Some, like Sawyer and Pilar, did a lot of solo hiking, but most peakbagging was done in loquacious, slow-moving groups. "We are not an elite of super-macho-hero-climbers (no Henry Barbers we!)," confessed Daniell, pointing out, "This is an activity which becomes silly if one takes one's accomplishments too seriously; most hikers could do it if they wanted to enough." The spirit in which these ultimate peakbaggers approached their goals was well expressed by one of their number, Bruce Brown, in words that might describe the values of hiking in general for many a Northeastern backcountry tramper down through the years that the preceding 57 chapters of this history have traced:

> Climbing the NHHH had great rewards for me, partly with the woodsmanship and outdoor experience and confidence I learned and gained. But the greatest feature of those 2 years was the almost symbiotic and permanent bond formed between the people who gathered for the AMC and private trips. How wonderful it is for a group of mostly scrubby and trailless peaks to unite people of such diverse ages and backgrounds. The cares of the world just faded behind us when we planned and executed an assault on those seemingly insignificant peaks. . . . The immutable bond we formed will always remain and those inanimate hunks of scrub-laden rocks will live in us always.

Chapter 59

The "school" of winter mountaineering

W<small>ORLD</small> W<small>AR</small> II had a more immediate and direct effect on winter climbing than on any other branch of Northeastern mountaineering. The elite of American alpinism from the 1930s went to Washington to work on developing cold weather equipment for the military, and to Alaska or the Yukon or sometimes New Hampshire's Presidentials to conduct field tests. Out of this concentrated research and development came the Army bearpaw snowshoe, improved crampons, down mummy sleeping bags, lightweight tent fabrics, "monster mitts" (huge ungainly layered mittens, with gauntlets almost to the elbow and a fur patch on the back), wind-protective clothing, and better dehydrated foods. Progress was made in boots, but the key development in footgear awaited the Korean War and the big, insulated rubber "Mickey Mouse" boot.

For the winter climbers of the 1950s and 1960s, all of these developments meant "hiking comforts heretofore undreamed of." Reported the *New York Times* in 1947:

> GI material originally designed for the Aleutians and points north is now getting a good work-out in the public parks of the metropolitan area.

Lacking any other winter climbing supply industry in the United States, an entire generation outfitted themselves almost entirely with war surplus from Army-Navy stores. The baggy, olive-drab wind pants became almost the uniform for the 1960s winter climber—"We wore them all the time, wind or no," recalled one active during those years. Mouse boots became standard footgear. The price was right too: as late as 1959 REI offered Army ice axes for $5.95, snowshoes (with harness) for $7.95, down sleeping bags from $24.95 to $59.95. The Cornell Outing Club offered crampons to college climbers in April 1950 for $1.50 per pair.

Apart from the R & D contribution to equipment, a significant wartime phenomenon was the Tenth Mountain Division. Into this outfit poured many of the prewar climbers, and out of it, at the war's end, came many of the postwar climbers. Though actual mountain warfare was limited to a brief campaign in Italy, the Tenth Mountain's training exposed a lot of young men to winter climbing conditions and created a fraternal bond, mystique, and memories that stayed with them for life.

One direct outgrowth was the formation of a Mountain and Cold Weather Training Program at Vermont's Norwich University, under the leadership of ex–Tenth Mountain man Les Hurley, closely followed by a similar program across the Connecticut River with the Dartmouth Outing Club under another Tenth Mountain sergeant, John Rand. These programs were the first to develop experience-based search and rescue techniques in the Northeastern mountains. One graduate of the Norwich program, Roger Damon, became one of the region's top winter climbers and a leading authority on avalanches in the Northeast.

Under the influence of wartime equipment and the Tenth Mountain Division legacy, Northeastern postwar winter climbing departed from prewar practice in major ways.

First, skiing and mountaineering traveled divergent paths for a period of about a quarter-century. The occasional rope tows and specially built ski trails of 1940 ballooned after the war into a thriving industry of ski resorts, groomed trails for all grades from novice to expert, and multifarious contrivances for airlifting the crowds to the top of the slopes. Downhill skiing was in, cross-country out. In the Adirondacks, cross-country ski trails built before World War II went unused after the war until they were abandoned during the 1950s, at the same time that downhill skiing boomed. New York voters, who had approved a Whiteface ski area by the narrowest of margins before the war, gave a whopping two-to-one approval for Belleayre and Gore ski areas after. With downhill skiing in ascendancy, fewer and fewer climbers still used skis to go *up*hill.

Snowshoes became the near-universal vehicle for climbing Northeastern hills and held the field almost exclusively until the 1970s. As snowshoers more aggressively pursued more remote summits, the prewar diversity of odd shapes and sizes gradually shook down. For climbing Northeastern peaks, the longer varieties proved unsuitable. So did those with sharply turned-up toes. By the mid-1950s Northeastern snowshoers settled on a strong preference for one of two models: the army bearpaws or a modified beavertail type, of which the preferred make was the Westover. For the next twenty years virtually all Northeastern winter climbing was done on bearpaws or Westovers—so much so that by the end of the 1960s many winter climbers never knew that skis had been regularly used for climbing during the 1930s and firmly believed that snowshoes were the only medium possible. A later generation revived ski mountaineering, but for the 1950s and 1960s it was the Age of the Snowshoe.

Overnight camping in winter, virtually unheard-of before the war, slowly became a regular pastime of a few hardy postwar climbers. Despite some exciting climbing by the Adirondack pioneers such as Johannsen and Apperson, the Bemis Crew, Arthur Comey, and others of the prewar vintage, nightfall usually found them back in the valley in a heated lodge, or at best huddled around a stove in some closed cabin. Postwar climbers took to staying up there on the mountainsides, using tents with floors, air mattresses or pads, and warm sleeping bags. At first almost all this gear was war surplus. The trend to backcountry camping in winter reinforced the preference for snowshoes over skis. Backpacking overnight loads proved considerably more awkward and arduous on skis.

Winter climbing during the 1950s and 1960s had an unmistakable tone and style of its own—what we may call the Adirondack school. This was both a "school" in the general sense of a common set of beliefs and values about how to climb in winter, as well as in the more specific meaning of a formal, weeklong "school" held each year beginning in 1954. Though there was plenty of winter climbing in the northern New England states, it was the Adirondacks that embodied and defined the style of early postwar winter climbing.

The Adirondack school began when a small group of hardy winter climbers emerged in the Adirondack Mountain Club right after World War II and started to take on not just Marcy, Algonquin, and Whiteface, but some of the less-visited peaks as well. In 1949 one of the leaders of this group, Kim Hart, became chairman of the Winter Activities Committee of the ADK. Under his creative leadership, the committee drew up a highly formalized program for encouraging the college outing clubs to do more winter climbing and camping. An array of badges and trophies was set up for college climbers to aspire to: an Adirondak Loj Trophy, "for that college outing club which has contributed most to the cause of winter mountaineering," another trophy for the outstanding single day's winter climb, and a badge for climbing one 5,000-footer and four 4,000-footers in winter. Annual Winter Mountaineering Conferences were held at which the coveted awards were handed out and appropriate speeches intoned.

These moves by the ADK touched off a flurry of winter climbing by the colleges. Enthusiasm ran high, fired in part by a feeling of pioneering in pursuit of "first winter ascents." The collegians combined climbing with a much bigger commitment to winter camping than their prewar predecessors ever had. One common plan was to pack in tent and provisions several miles on one day and set up camp: climb a peak (or peaks!) on the second day and return to camp; perhaps do another on the third day; and finally pack out and drive home on the fourth. Thus the college climbers explored not just terrain but new methods of winter camping, cooking, and sleeping, as well as climbing. Using these new techniques and inspired by the ADK's trophy system, the eager collegians took after peaks that, as far as anyone then knew, had never before been visited by human feet in winter.[a]

---

[a]Probably they were right in most cases, but prewar ascents by Johannsen, Apperson, Goodwin, the Bemis Crew, and others were often overlooked by the postwar generation.

In December 1948 four members of the Rensselaer (RPI) Outing Club set up base camp at Lake Colden on the nineteenth; climbed Cliff on the twentieth; climbed Herbert on the twenty-first in a snowstorm, reaching the top at 3:15; and packed out on the twenty-second. In a similar four-day push, several Cornell climbers climbed Dial and Dix later that month, while a Yale throng did most of the peaks of the Great Range.

On February 16, 1949, Kim Hart and Art Heidrick of Cornell enjoyed a big day climbing Marcy on trail, bushwhacking over to Gray Peak, previously unclimbed in winter, regaining the trail at remote Four Corners with but an hour of daylight left, and speeding down to Lake Colden for a night in the ranger's cabin there. The next morning they walked out.

In December 1949, Paul Van Dyke, Gil Barker, and Bob Collin—all destined for leading parts in Northeastern winter climbing—spent two days working into a base camp at the foot of the Macomb Slide in the Dix Range. A storm set in, so they sat out a day in their tent. The next day, Christmas Eve, they packed up the slide, reaching Macomb's summit in a renewal of the snowstorm, and slogged over to South Dix where they set up camp after dark; on Christmas Day, still going strong, they made a side jaunt to East Dix and back, climbed Hough and again reached camp after dark; on the twenty-sixth, they finally packed out.

After just two days for drying out and regrouping, Van Dyke, Barker, and Collin snowshoed up to Uphill lean-to high on the ridge between Marcy and Colden, to watch the temperature sink to -20; the next day the strong party climbed remote and trailless Redfield, bushwhacked from there to Skylight, and threw in Marcy as well before descending to camp by moonlight.

Later that winter a Syracuse group reached Esther; an RPI party bagged the lonely and distant Allen; and a mixed team from RPI and Vassar climbed Sawteeth.

During the winter of 1950–51, Barker and Van Dyke elaborated the new methods by stocking food caches in July, to reduce weight hauling. With these caches tactically deployed, they went after such remote bastions as Santanoni and Seward.

During 1951–52 the Princeton Outing Club entered the competition when Nick Colby, Marty Harris, and John Rupley did a four-day stint in the Great Range, climbing both Wolf Jaws, Armstrong, and Gothics.

During 1952–53 a Cornell party completed the Santanoni Range by bagging not only the main peak but the previously unclimbed Panther and far-off trailless Couchsachraga as well.

During 1953–54 the last of the reportedly unclimbed forty-six fell, a Syracuse party making Donaldson in December and a Cornell group going in to Emmons later. These two of the four peaks in the Seward Range are widely regarded as the toughest of the winter "forty-six".

The competitive spirit of these college climbing trips was remarkable in a sport not usually thought of as a form of competitive athletics. Describing his 1949 ascent of Gray, Heidrick wrote,

> Until this day Gray Peak, 4902 feet high, was the highest mountain in the state that had not been climbed in winter. [I] was anxious to . . . claim Gray Peak for Cornell.

A write-up of the 1949 traverse of the Dixes begins: "On December 21, 1949, the opening date of the winter competitions, . . . "

Having fostered this spirit of competition, the ADK and some of the leading college climbers began to have second thoughts about the prudence of encouraging untrained college kids to go plunging out into the harsh winter environment to win a prized trophy for dear old State U. Safety consciousness began to take hold of the leaders of this activity.

These safety concerns were the basis for several new moves by the ADK: still another award, this one for winter leadership; publication of a how-to manual; and the establishment of the Winter Mountaineering School. The first item had a modest impact for a few years. The second was later expanded into a full-length book by John A. Danielson which was regarded as authoritative for many years. But the Winter Mountaineering School (WMS—or "Winmouse," in the jargon of 1960s insiders) was undoubtedly the most important influence in defining the style of Northeastern winter climbing for a generation.

The original Winter Mountaineering School was conducted at Adirondak Loj for four days between Christmas and New Year's, 1954, under the direction of Paul Van Dyke. The format gradually lengthened to one week, from December 26 to 31. Van Dyke, the ablest college climber of the first postwar wave, was director for eight years, then turned over the reins to IOCA's Gardner Perry for the next eight. Curriculum centered on snowshoeing from the beginning, with some cramponing above treeline thrown in. During the early years students also learned ice climbing at Cascade Pond. Winter camping, not included in the first year's program, was gradually introduced and, under Perry, became a major emphasis. A square dance was held on the last night in 1955 and became a tradition that continued for more than thirty years. Enrollment was twenty-three students in 1954, rising to forty-four the following year, and to upwards of one hundred students at its peak during the 1960s and 1970s.

College outing clubs were a major source of students at the WMS, but other aspiring winter climbers signed up from all over the Northeast. One year the U.S. Army sent four men who took copious notes on equipment—an irony, since the WMS still used mostly surplus gear from World War II and the Korean War, apparently a novelty to those soldiers of the late 1950s. As a font of knowledge, the WMS had no competitors until the late 1970s, when colleges, "challenge" programs such as Outward Bound, and others entered the field. As a result, throughout the 1960s a significant proportion of Northeastern winter climbers learned their methods from the WMS or indirectly therefrom through the burgeoning numbers of its alumni.

The conventional wisdom of postwar winter climbing all came from the WMS: how to plan a trip, where to climb, what clothing to wear, how to stay warm in camp, how to cook a meal, what equipment to take on a climb, and proper safety precautions. The program's emphasis on safety seemed appropriately conservative, considering the newness of the sport, the intimidating weather of the Northeastern hills, and the conservative tradition then prevailing in rock climbing and most other phases of hiking and camping during those years dominated by the veterans. The WMS stressed a healthy respect for the dangers in the Northeastern mountains in winter. An ascent of Haystack, declared Kim Hart in 1957,

> must always be considered hazardous in winter; and under no circumstances to be attempted except by a four-man party prepared to camp out for several days, and thoroughly grounded in all safety rules of the Winter Mountaineering Manual.

A sign was posted at Adirondack trailheads reading:

W A R N I N G !

> Winter mountain climbing is dangerous. The mountains are beyond range of ski patrol rescue. Travel at your own risk. Turn back if storms threaten. Don't fail to read ADK Winter Handbook.

The ADK felt a "duty" to inform the public of "the dangers of the mountains in winter, and the necessity for adherence to rules universally approved by the experienced." These "rules" were accepted as essential, and "the first rule" in winter climbing was "to take no chances."

Out of this era came the hallowed principles of winter mountaineering: never go out with fewer than four in a party, always carry plenty of spare clothing, plus a sleeping bag, tent, stove, pot, extra food, and extensive first aid kit in case of emergency. The characteristic WMS-trained winter party of the 1960s was clad almost exclusively in war surplus gear, of which the baggy, olive-drab wind pants and the Mickey Mouse boots were the most prominent, and carried full frame packs with ponderous reserves for emergency even on day-trips.

This description is not intended as criticism of what was unquestionably a safe tradition and perhaps one appropriate to its day. It should be remembered that when Van Dyke and his friends were back up beyond Marcy, they were often literally the only people for miles around, with no conceivable prospect of rescue, and conservative tactics may well have seemed prudent. This description is meant merely to contrast the style of this era with the lighter, more mobile, less nervous styles of both prewar and post-1970 winter climbers. Some of the prewar climbers ridiculed the Adirondack school's "rules" in letters to *Adirondac* or recalled more flexible axioms of wilderness explorers. To the later generation, the conservative style of the 1950s and 1960s made winter climbing appear as a joyless ordeal rather than a delightful experience.

But to the climbers of the 1950s and 1960s those years were rich in rewards. Because there were so few climbers up there in the hills, these climbers felt a tremendous pride and camaraderie as a tiny elite in a tough, unforgiving, and enormously satisfying discipline. A rough, macho banter enlivened their conversation, but a genuine and profound appreciation enriched their encounters with the fathomless aesthetics of the mountains in winter. Paul Van Dyke recorded his feelings on a late descent after climbing Redfield, Skylight, and Marcy in one day:

> Our dreams shall ever be haunted by memories of a moonlit trail thru sparkling powdered snow and a blue sky filled with stars as big as apples.

Atop Algonquin the following winter, Van Dyke recalled, "For that hour we would have exchanged places with no one."

Over in New England winter climbers of the 1950s and 1960s approached their snowclad hills in much the same spirit as did those in the Adirondacks. During the 1950s a number of more or less separate circles took a strong interest in the snowy season. Among the earliest were Charlie and Pat Osgood, who lived near the mountains and spent a lot of time in the Northern Presidentials, camping at Crag Camp during the early 1950s. Ex–Bemis Crew stalwarts Robert and Miriam Underhill and a small circle of their friends were avid snowshoers. Roger Damon and Dan Brodien of Vermont came over to New Hampshire to "bang around the mountains a lot." The Boston AMC rock climbers of the 1950s, led by Bob Kruszyna and Charlie Fay, regarded winter climbing as their chief diversion when the rock was too icy and cold, as well as a splendid training ground for the big mountains. A few college outing clubs sprouted strong winter climbing contingents: Dartmouth around Moosilauke, Harvard and MIT in the Presidentials, the University of Maine up at Katahdin. During the 1960s these groups were joined by others, and the hills became a trifle less lonely in winter. The New York Chapter of the AMC stepped up winter mountaineering under the leadership of Alaskan expedition leader Boyd Everett, as well as Arthur Fitch and Edward Nester. An AMC leader from the Boston area, Clarence LeBell, led several parties to Katahdin during the early 1960s; during the later 1960s another AMC leader, George Smith of Augusta, Maine, headed several Katahdin trips. MITOC and the DOC also sent out Katahdin expeditions almost annually. Clyde

Smith, the top-rank mountain photographer who lived in the Lake Champlain valley, could be found on Adirondack peaks, Mount Mansfield, and the Presidentials in winter. The AMC trail crew, in the early days of Bob Proudman's leadership, had a strong interest in winter climbing. Over in Vermont, a smattering of GMC hikers kept alive the snowshoeing tradition started by Judge Cowles fifty years before.

Around 1960, two AMC climbers gradually emerged among the most prominent winter climbers in New England: Chris Goetze and Robert Collin.

Goetze was an accomplished mountaineer with Alaskan first ascents to his credit. He was also the Northeast's top superhiker of the day, holding the record times for summer traverses of the Mahoosucs and of the hut system. In winter he was not only a gritty climber but a ceaseless innovator, experimenting with different styles of tents and emergency bivouac methods in the foulest of weather above treeline. He organized formidable undertakings such as traversing the wild Mahoosucs in winter. His wife, Lydia, was often with him, even on one night bivouacked at 6,000 feet on Mount Washington at zero degrees and appalling winds,

> the most miserable night either of us had ever spent—just to see what it would be like if we ever had to do it.

Goetze was a loner, disliking crowds and commonplace objectives. Increasingly he and Lydia traveled their own way, probably doing as challenging winter trips as anyone in the Northeast during the 1960s, but with diminishing influence on others.

Collin was an altogether different type of climber—more pedestrian, less mountaineer, and far more interested in providing leadership to others. After attending the Adirondacks' Winter Mountaineering School in 1957, he became the single most active winter trip leader in New England. Within the next two winters, he was the acknowledged authority on New England winter climbing, with a twenty-two-page mimeographed manual on "Equipment for Winter Climbing and Camping" and a state-of-the-art piece in Appalachia. The AMC organized an annual Winter Leadership Clinic at Pinkham Notch during the early 1960s, under Collin's direction. In 1965 a job change took Collin to Rochester, New York, whereupon he founded the Rochester Winter Mountaineering Society, providing the base on which a strong winter climbing community developed in that city. Like Goetze's, Collin's wife was equal to her assignment: Nancy Collin was a strong winter climber as well as an able rock climber.[b]

---

[b]Husband-wife combinations in winter climbing are a strong tradition in the Northeast: the Helburns and Van de Waters from the prewar Bemis Crew (see chap. 47), the Underhills, the Osgoods, Goetzes, Collins, and later the Adirondacks' Chrenkos, the Sawyers on the Long Trail, and several couples in the Bemis II group (see chap. 60).

The spirit of New England winter climbing throughout the 1950s and 1960s bore a close family resemblance to the Adirondack school, partly because of the pervasive grip of the conservative tradition and partly through direct osmosis, so many climbers having attended the Winter Mountaineering School (for example, Collin). As in the Adirondacks, climbers in New England emphasized the discomforts and hardships of winter. As the lead sentence in his definitive *Appalachia* piece, Collin quoted Antarctic explorer Apsley Cherry-Garrard about polar exploration being "the cleanest and most isolated way of having a bad time" and went on to counsel his readers, "If you insist on being comfortable at all times you had better stay at home; you will be unhappy on an overnight winter trip." Safety was always the prime consideration, and packs were heavily laden with reserves of emergency gear. As the Adirondack school had stressed from the beginning, "Safety must prevail over speed."

For all this, New England winter climbers accomplished some feats that are impressive when one recalls that they almost always broke out every trail they used; that many New England peaks with trails after 1970 were trailless before then; that the Kancamagus Highway was not plowed, making the peaks of the Pemigewasset far more remote; and that they climbed with such enormous packs. Winter peakbagging was launched by the Underhills: Miriam and Robert finished climbing all the 4,000-footers of the White Mountains in December 1961. Right behind them were Boston AMC climbers from the Collin group (though oddly enough not Collin himself, nor Goetze), plus Damon and Brodien from Vermont. Collin led an attempt to traverse the AMC hut system in winter in 1962, a formidable commission in those days of unbroken trails. Though unsuccessful, they gritted it out for nine grueling days and might have made it had weather in the Presidentials favored them. That difficult feat was not accomplished until 1980, under altogether different and easier circumstances. As mentioned, Chris and Lydia Goetze led a traverse of the Mahoosucs. Over in Vermont during the early 1960s, George Pearlstein became the first to walk the entire Long Trail in winter, not (needless to say!) in one continuous trip.

One of the more remarkable trips engineered by Collin was the south-to-north traverse of the long, low, densely thicketed hump of Owl's Head in the Pemigewasset Wilderness. Collin thought he had climbed it before, but the Underhills later found what seemed a higher point on the ridge—and twitted him about having missed a true summit. After an inglorious epic struggle all day with full packs through the thickets, as they stood on the final downhill in gathering dusk, Collin turned to his teammate Bob Leach and said with a wry grin, "Well, Miriam Underhill, sometime, somewhere today—I don't know just when, I don't know just where—we stood on the summit of Owl's Head."

The winter Presidential traverse acquired unique status during these years as a test piece for winter mountaineering. The typical itinerary was to ascend the Valley Way to the col between Madison and Adams; go up Madison and back; then slog across the entire Presidential Range over Adams, Jefferson, Clay, Washington, Monroe, Eisenhower (then called Pleasant), and Clinton, with Jackson and Webster sometimes included, sometimes not. For New England winter climbers this was the pinnacle of achievement, as it involved prolonged above-treeline exposure. Most parties took three or four days for the job, though some crawled along more slowly or were pinned down by bad weather, while others whisked over in less time, even in just one day (or moonlit night!). The success rate was low: the notorious Mount Washington weather frustrated the majority of attempts. Harvard climbers, for example, tried for three winters without success before completing a traverse in 1961, led by Goetze; then they were unsuccessful the next two years before repeating in 1964. Although victorious parties felt like tigers, success or failure on a Presidential traverse was not really a measure of a party's strength. Far more crucial was the weather. In good conditions, the trip could be almost easier than in summer; in bad conditions no one could think of it. Nevertheless, the feeling of that time was that even to attempt it was the mark of an accomplished winter mountaineer.

By common consent of winter peakbaggers, the Adirondacks' 4,000-footers as a group were a more difficult winter objective than were their White Mountains counterparts. Neither the early collegians nor WMS leaders of the 1960s aspired to attempt all of the "forty-six" in winter.[c] Nevertheless a group of Schenectady-based climbers, most of them General Electric engineers and scientists, and thus heirs to the tradition of Langmuir and Apperson, Suits and Schaefer, began to work on that goal. By 1962 Edgar B. Bean became the first "Winter 46er." The next year James W. F. Collins followed in his footsteps. Then Collins had the luck to be transferred to a Massachusetts job, positioning him for a shot at the White Mountains' 4,000-footers as well. On February 22, 1970, Collins became the first to do all 4,000-footers of both the Adirondacks and the White Mountains in winter. He followed that by pursuing the rest of New England's 4,000-footers, becoming the first to do the "Winter 111" on January 2, 1971. He held that distinction alone for more than seven years.

---

[c] A noteworthy exception was an ambitious plot hatched by Richard Andrews and Evan Bergan of the Rensselaer Outing Club in 1966 to do all the peaks in one continuous trip. The scheme was carefully planned, but foundered after only twelve of the forty-six had been reached. One of the four-man party was injured, and the others, after evacuating him safely, felt that "continuing the trip with only three wasn't safe." (Letter from Richard Andrews to L&GW, March 18, 1981. Reprinted with permission.)

Chapter 60

The winter recreation boom

As Jim Collins plodded up the last of his peaks during the early 1970s, change was in the winds of the winter climbing scene. The snowshoe world of the Adirondack school was about to be engulfed by new faces, new forces.

As with hiking, camping, rock climbing, and other outdoor pursuits, the boom years of 1970–75 brought a sharp increase in the numbers of winter climbers. A 1976 *New York Times* article called cold weather camping "the hot new sport." Unlike most of the summertime activities, however, interest in winter climbing did not level off after 1975 but kept rising through the 1980s. The AMC and the ADK expanded their programs of weekend trips and workshops on wintertime activities in the mountains. The AMC opened two of its high huts (Zealand and Carter) for winter use and made available a single basement room at Lakes-of-the-Clouds Hut as a refuge for parties attempting Presidential traverses. When Ranger Peter Fish of the DEC came to the Adirondacks during the mid-1970s he began regular winter patrols of the popular Adirondack trails. Colleges and special "challenge" programs such as Outward Bound sponsored winter climbing and camping sessions.

The White Mountains and the Adirondacks, and to a much lesser extent the mountains of Maine and Vermont, were now regularly climbed all winter long. Popular trails to the well-known peaks saw traffic every weekend. Climbers visited the less-known mountains much more commonly than during the 1960s. A sign of the times was the change in the title and scope of the chapter on winter climbing in the *AMC White Mountain Guide.* Until the 1966 edition that chapter went by the name of "Mount Washington in Winter"; beginning in 1966, the name was changed to "Mt. Washington Range in Winter," reflecting the growing interest in the Presidential traverse and the lesser peaks of that range; then in 1976 it was changed again to "White Mountains in Winter"—now the crowds were fanning out all over the hills.

With the eager newcomers came a very different image and spirit from that of the Van Dyke-Perry-Collin-Goetze era. As the sport attracted multitudes, previously dominant elements such as the Winter Mountaineering School, the Boston AMC leaders, and the college outing clubs declined in influence. People entered winter climbing from a wider variety of sources. They learned their winter skills not from the WMS, but from the media or from outfitting stores or from workshops staged by diverse sponsors. The Army surplus look, the macho toughness, the preoccupation with the dangers and all the safety precautions faded out in place of a jaunty, bright stylishness and an equally jaunty frame of mind.

A revolution in the winter climber's outfit began during the early 1970s, accelerated rapidly during the late 1970s, and was complete by the early 1980s. Baggy, olive-drab wind pants sank from sight. Bright colored fabrics shone brilliant in the winter sun and snow. Snappy pile and bunting shirts and jackets in modish colors replaced the old heavy wool. The once preferred 60/40 parka yielded to vivid Gore-tex models. Underwear moved from wool fishnet to polypropylene. Plastic boots caught hold widely, although many winter climbers still preferred either leather boots or the old reliable Mickey Mouse or Sorrel standards. Small, rectangular aluminum snowshoes almost completely displaced the wooden bearpaws and Westovers. Metal ice axes took over from wooden.

The new image reflected new attitudes as well. The drift of thinking swung away from a preoccupation with safety. Partly this reflected simply the decline of the conservative tradition everywhere. Partly it was an acknowledgment that winter climbing really was less risky with so many people out there, so many trails broken out, so many facilities to head for in emergencies. Partly it was just a swing of the pendulum independent of objective reality: winter *was* still a potentially dangerous season on the mountains, and accidents periodically reminded climbers and rescuers of that fact—but nonetheless the new generation was sometimes hard to convince.

But the fact was that the conditions of winter climbing *had* radically altered. No longer was it the lonely, committing adventure of the 1960s. Having other people on the mountains every weekend made it a very different experience. The fact that trails were commonly broken out to every major summit was a condition that made summits significantly easier to attain. Having the shelter of AMC huts in Zealand and Carter notches and, during the 1980s, a hostel in the formerly deserted Crawford Notch and a warming hut in the Johns Brook valley also reduced the sense of isolation and commitment. The boom in cross-country skiing generated a large volume of traffic on lower-level trails in the backcountry, providing better access and less sense of remoteness to peaks once considered quite isolated. For example, skiers regularly traversed the low-level trails and wood roads of the Pemigewasset Wilderness, providing packed highways in to the base of peaks (for example, the Bonds, Hancocks, Zealand) that had previously seemed lonely and difficult snowshoe trips. By the late 1970s wintertime peakbagging, once the eccentric pursuit of perhaps a dozen individuals in New Hampshire and another dozen in New York, became a popular pastime, with the result that trails to the top of every 4,000-footer were regularly broken out.

In winter the significance of other people's presence in the mountains is far greater than in summer. One must understand this point to appreciate the profound change between winter climbing as experienced by the Van Dyke-Perry-Collin-Goetze generation and as enjoyed by the growing multitudes who cavorted in the hills after 1970. In summer anyone can still find a solitude experience simply by staying primarily on the less-traveled trails, by bushwhacking, and by camping anywhere other than the popular magnets. But in winter the indelible mark of a packed trail inescapably alters the experience. Before 1970 any party that ventured well up into the Adirondack high peaks, say, up in the high country south and southwest of Marcy, or in the mountains west of Crawford Notch, had to rely on its own resources. Throughout the winter climbers could expect to break trail wherever they went. Not only break trail, but find it: in deep snow, staying on trail was a very taxing art, requiring much experience to master. These conditions meant that if an emergency arose, members of the isolated party knew they might have to break trail a long way, slowed further by the difficulties of finding the trail along the way, before safety could be reached. When the much greater numbers penetrated the hills, with access made easier by open huts and hostels and backcountry patrol and nearby cross-country ski trails, then no party could experience that complete sense of isolation that the Van Dyke-Perry-Collin-Goetze generation had known. Emergencies could still be real, but the proximity of packed trails everywhere greatly reduced the objective and subjective hardships of getting out to safety. Emergencies aside, the spirit of solitude that suffused the earlier experience was irretrievably altered. The awareness that a packed trail was never far away was totally different from knowing that unbroken soft snow lay around for miles and miles of forbidding terrain.

From a historical standpoint, one of the most interesting changes of the 1970s and 1980s was the second coming of the ski. The exclusive grip of the snowshoe on Northeastern winter climbing lasted roughly a quarter-century. When cross-country skiing first competed for popularity with downhill during the early 1970s, it remained largely a valley-oriented pastime, aimed more at pleasure than challenge. The Van Dyke-Perry-Collin-Goetze generation had firmly believed that the upper elevation realm was exclusively attainable by snowshoes, and even the first cross-country skiers agreed with them. But gradually individuals and small circles of more ambitious and able skiers turned their long boards uphill and headed for the peaks. Ascents proved surprisingly easy. Coming *down* the steep hiking trails called for a high level of skill indeed, or of judgment—and patience for long stretches of side-stepping.

But presently a new breed of backcountry skier developed more skill at handling rough and unpredictable terrain. By the 1980s their éclat was extraordinary. Among their playgrounds, for example, were the steep slides of Colden, Marcy, and Macomb in the Adirondacks, and virtually every major gully in the many cirques on Mount Washington, including some that had long been regarded as technical ice climbs. Who were the advance guard of these new forces? In the Adirondacks, many of the same technical climbers who brought difficult rock climbing to the Adirondacks, led by Plattsburg's Geoff Smith, led the headlong pursuit of high-peak ski mountaineering. Calling themselves the Ski-to-Die Club, they lived by such slogans as "Skiing is a controlled fall." In the White Mountains, the pioneers included a few new-breed technical climbers such as Michael Hartrich, Andy Tuthill, and John Imbrie, plus a handful of the AMC's wintertime employees such as Carl Krag, Dave Moskowitz, and Mark Dindorf, who took advantage of their year-round residence in the mountains to become highly proficient ski mountaineers.

Aside from these extreme performers, many other winter climbers of more earthly ambition used skis for ascents or at least for long approaches to remote peaks, carrying snowshoes for use on the final steep uphill.

While skis rose, the snowshoe went into decline. Three factors were involved. One was the competing use of skis and their obvious advantages on certain kinds of terrain, notably the long gradual descent on the way out. A second factor was the greater number of winter climbers and consequent packing out of at least one trail to every major summit all winter long. These packed trails tended to consolidate firmly, making snowshoes superfluous. Often it was perfectly easy to walk up the packed snow in boots alone. The term *bare-booting* came into vogue. As packed trails and bare-booting became more prevalent, many climbers came to view snowshoes as a specialized tool only occasionally required, instead of the essential sine qua non of the Van Dyke-Perry-Collin-Goetze era. Indeed, many climbers went through entire winters of avid peakbagging without wearing snowshoes more than a couple of times. Then came the third factor: the winter of 1979–80 when virtually no snow fell until February, and not much even then. That winter and the following (also light on snow) further weaned the new climbers away from the assumption that snowshoes were useful.

The Age of the Snowshoe was over, but snowshoes by no means disappeared. There were still snow conditions and trails—not to mention bushwhacks—where the snowshoe still seemed the essential tool. Furthermore, snowshoeing continued to be the focus of teaching at the Winter Mountaineering School. This venerable institution endured as a force in Northeastern winter climbing, albeit a relatively diminished one. In 1970 Gardner Perry relinquished direction of the school. The ADK and the AMC joined forces to expand the WMS into three sections: a beginners section based indoors and focused on day-trips, held in the White Mountains; an intermediate section much like Perry's had been, in the Adirondacks; and an advanced section at Katahdin. This format continued through the 1970s and 1980s with few changes. The advanced section was discontinued after 1974, because of difficulties posed by Katahdin's terrain and Baxter Park's regulations and paperwork. In its place, beginning in 1978, a small program for training leaders of winter climbing parties was instituted and conducted thereafter in the White Mountains. The Winter Mountaineering School continued to be an influence on the sport but never again had as decisive an impact as the Adirondack School had in the smaller snowshoe world of the 1950s and 1960s.

Although most winter climbers of the 1970s and 1980s took a relaxed and casual approach to the sport, challenge still summoned some to adventure. Adirondack snowshoers still found blowdowns and bushwhacks in terrain where skis were unthinkable. One White Mountain group specializing in remote, off-trail adventure, emulated the spirit of the old Bemis Crew even to the point of adopting the name Bemis II.

Winter peakbagging, still mostly on snowshoes, enjoyed a burst of popularity in the 1970s and 1980s. Before that it had been the exclusive preserve of a handful of odd fellows. By the mid-1980s close to fifty people were Winter Forty-Sixers in the Adirondacks, and more like one hundred had scaled the New Hampshire 4,000-footers. Elsie Chrenko, who became in 1973 the first woman to bag the Adirondack forty-six in winter, went back to do them all twice again, while her husband, Dick, completed four rounds. In the White Mountains, by 1987, one winter climber-incurable had done all the New Hampshire 4,000-footers six times each in winter, including each one from all four points of the compass. In 1985 Dot Myers of the GMC's Burlington Section became the first woman to duplicate Jim Collins's once unique feat of doing all the Northeastern 4,000-footers in winter. All-women parties achieved such prestigious plums as the Presidential traverse (first in 1980) and the winter ascent of Katahdin (1981). The superpeakbaggers described in chapter 58 extended their quests to the snowy months. When Tom Sawyer and Gene Daniell first began talking about the New England Hundred Highest in winter, one of the experienced 4,000-footer climbers of the 1970s, Joe Creager, told them they were crazy and it was impossible. "He was right on the first point," recalled Daniell, "and wrong on the second." Sawyer was again the pacesetter, being first to climb both the New England Hundred Highest and the New Hampshire Hundred Highest. Sawyer and his wife, Diane, also traversed the full length of the Long Trail on a continuous series of weekend trips over two winters.

Incidents involving lost or stranded climbers, sometimes resulting in fatalities, increased with the popularity of climbing. While precise data is unavailable, it seems probable that, although the absolute number of winter accidents and rescues rose, the proportion relative to the tremendously increased volume of winter climbing did not rise.

Of course accidents were by no means exclusively a winter occurrence, but they were often more serious in that season. The examples that follow are drawn from all four seasons. As in the nineteenth century (see chapter 27), the level of public attention attracted by any one accident seemed unrelated to objective factors, capricious. Every few years, some accident seemed to attract the kind of morbid curiosity and relentless follow-up analysis that Lizzie Bourne's death had attracted in 1855. Meanwhile other fatalities were duly recorded but little heeded. As with poor Lizzie Bourne, some combination of drama or human interest engaged public and media attention in the former, not in the latter. The more publicized incidents were often accompanied by clamorous but often short-lived outcries for restrictions on winter climbing.

On Thanksgiving weekend, 1956, with Mount Marcy mantled in deep snow, two young men climbed from Lake Colden to Marcy via Lake Tear-of-the-Clouds. The day was cold, the effort exhausting in the new-fallen snow. In the raw exposure above treeline, one of the tired men, Norman Nissen, collapsed. His companion, Tim Bond, half dragged, half carried him down to the shelter of the trees, and placed him in his sleeping bag, using their four snowshoes for insulation. Already the hypothermic Nissen was semidelirious and sporadically resisted Bond's efforts to warm him. Frantically Bond raced down the trail for help, soon overtaken by darkness. At 9:30 P.M. he stumbled into camp at Lake Colden, and three friends set off in the dark to reach the victim. At 1:30 A.M. they found Nissen dead.

This fatality received a lot of attention, and analysis sought lessons from the grim experience. The principle that winter climbing required no fewer than four people in the party received a strong boost: with just two, Bond had been forced to choose between going for help or staying with his friend. During the years of the conservative tradition in the Winter Mountaineering School, this accident was repeatedly cited as a dreadful example of the consequences of casual disregard for safety procedures.

In August 1959 two young men from Connecticut, having little serious experience in rock climbing and nothing more than two 40-foot ropes, a carpenter's hammer, and some homemade pitons of no value, attempted a long rock route on the cliff of Cannon Mountain in New Hampshire's Franconia Notch. Partway up the cliff they became stranded, unable to climb up or down. Sightseers spotted them and reported their predicament to state park authorities as darkness approached. Overnight a team of AMC rock climbers from the Boston area was assembled and drove northward. The next day the weather turned foul, wind and rain sweeping the rock face all day long. Heroic efforts, in the face of such adverse conditions, enabled the climbers to reach the boys, but again hypothermia claimed their lives.

The double fatality also attracted much notice. AMC leaders pointed to the lack of experience of the young men, and the example helped marshall support for a broad program of mountain leadership training and qualifications certification. Much of this program was short-lived, and a later generation of climbers rejected its formal trappings. However, one lasting institution created during those years was an annual five-day Mountain Leadership School for training group leaders in leading mountain trips of a nontechnical nature.

In late October 1963 two women were hiking on Katahdin's Knife Edge when one of them elected to leave the trail and descend via a steep gully. She found herself stranded and bivouacked for the night. The ranger at Chimney Pond, Ralph Heath, noted forecasts of bad weather and set out in the dark, with food and rescue equipment, to attempt to bring her down. That was the last seen of Ranger Heath. Other rescuers arrived the next day and searched all day amid frightful weather, including a foot of new snow. Rescue personnel from all over the Northeast poured in during the next few days in fruitless efforts to find the popular ranger. His body was never found.

This accident rang loud and clear to all Northeastern mountaineers the dangers inherent in rescue operations. Ranger Heath became a hero who symbolized all the risks faced by those who go out in bad weather and darkness to attempt to rescue others who foolishly blunder into difficulties.

Two incidents eleven years apart involved the notorious weather of the Presidential Range and an emergency shelter that existed in Edmands Col.

In February 1964 a group of four Syracuse University students attempting a winter Presidential traverse were pinned down by bad weather at Edmands Col. They waited for three days in that emergency shelter, managing remarkably well, so well that they continued across the range on the next clear day. In the meantime, however, concerned authorities had set the wheels of a massive search and rescue program in motion. Personnel from federal and state agencies were joined by volunteer technical climbing specialists and supported by aircraft. With all that effort mobilized, rescuers insisted on landing a helicopter dramatically on the high slopes of Mount Jefferson to evacuate the four students— who were equally insistent that they were in good shape and needed no help, though they eventually agreed to get in the helicopter on the insistence of the rescue leader.

In April 1975 two young hikers were stranded at the Edmands Col shelter by a heavy snowstorm. The pair had no snowshoes and indeed wore only summer hiking boots. Again, the wheels of a massive rescue effort were set in motion, as rescuers combed the range, helicopters buzzed around (ineffectually because of the weather), and the media eagerly reported the whole affair. At length rescuers reached the pair at Edmands

Col and escorted them safely down to the road, where press and television cameras engulfed the tired party.

These two incidents at Edmands Col displayed the enormous amount of effort and attention that a rescue effort could marshall. The cost to public agencies and private groups that became involved, such as the AMC, was extraordinary. Direct costs of the 1964 incident were estimated at more than five thousand dollars, those of 1975 closer to ten thousand. AMC people devoted more than six hundred person-hours to the 1975 search. Furthermore, the hue and cry produced an alarmed public reaction. Editorials and letters to the editor in various newspapers demanded restrictions on winter climbing and various proposals for making hikers pay for rescue costs. The two cases are linked not only by the size of the rescue operations and the extensive media coverage, but also because both involved the Edmands Col shelter. (One eventual result was the the Edmands Col shelter was removed, partly on grounds that its presence invited a false sense of security to parties attempting winter Presidential traverses.) The two cases differ, however, in that the 1964 party was competent and well equipped, and indeed needed no help; the 1975 party was clearly in over its head. But public outcry little heeded this important distinction.

In June 1972 a strong hiker died of a heart attack during foul weather on the summit slopes of Marcy while attempting to climb all the 4,000-footers in five days. This incident was mentioned in chapter 58, but is repeated here because of the widespread attention it provoked, putting it in a class with the other accidents described. The lessons that it appeared to convey, of the consequences of persevering in the face of bad weather, above-treeline exposure, and physical resources reduced by fatigue and immense effort, were too obvious to require belaboring.

On January 31, 1974, six winter technical climbers, in two parties, began difficult routes on the steep, ice-clad cliffs of Pamola in Baxter State Park. They did not complete their climbs in one day but rendezvoused on one ledge for a bivouac. That night the temperature dropped well below zero and a storm of incredible ferocity pounded the mountain. On February 1, the battered climbers did their best to evacuate, but one died and another suffered major frostbite and subsequent loss of limb. The remote location of Baxter Park made the mounting of rescue efforts necessarily slow, and weather conditions made those efforts arduous and hazardous. Even removing the one dead climber's body proved a major difficulty.

This incident received widespread attention and analysis. The decisions made by the climbers were subject to minute scrutiny. The case seemed to spotlight the peculiar difficulties of climbing at such a remote setting as Katahdin and the exceptional difficulty of rescue operations there. Baxter Park authorities interpreted the incident as requiring closer controls over winter climbing.

In November 1974 two backpackers clad in cotton clothing were surprised by a major snowstorm while hiking in the MacIntyre Range near Lake Colden. One, Steven Collier, finally collapsed and died before his partner could obtain help.

This accident illustrates how, though many people have died in the mountains, occasionally one fatality can attract an uncommon share of attention. The Collier death vividly portrayed the risks of hypothermia and the folly of poorly prepared hiking in late autumn. As a result, the incident was told and retold in newspapers, magazines, reprints posted at Adirondack hiking centers and stores, handouts at workshops, and countless lectures on the dangers of hypothermia in the mountains at any season.

In January 1982 two expert technical climbers completed an ice climb in Huntington Ravine, emerging high on Mount Washington in poor visibility. With little experience on that mountain and no map, compass, or snowshoes, the pair blundered off the wrong side of the mountain and eventually mired to a halt in deep snow in the Great Gulf. As two days of foul weather ensued, another massive rescue operation began. This time an avalanche swept away two highly skilled and respected technical rescuers, killing one of them, Albert Dow. Eventually others located and evacuated the lost climbers, both of whom suffered loss of limb due to frostbite.

This incident echoed the two Edmands Col cases cited earlier in the size of rescue operations, the costs incurred, and the media publicity. Added this time was the tragedy of a rescuer's death. Like Ranger Heath's death nineteen years before, Albert Dow's became a symbol of the risks that rescuers run as a result of the mistakes made by others. Again, this incident provoked widespread demands for legislation, especially to meet the costs of rescues. An odd sequel to this case was that one of the lost climbers, who had both feet amputated because of frostbite, went on to resume technical climbing with such total commitment that he became, even with artificial limbs, one of the region's half-dozen best climbers within three years of the accident.

As the publicity and fanfare surrounding these postwar accidents indicates, Northeastern hiking took place under conditions greatly altered from those of the nineteenth century when Lizzie Bourne quietly succumbed or Dr. Ball crouched under his umbrella in solitude and storm. Search and rescue had assumed a major place in the sun. During the 1970s, more formal and professionally competent search and rescue capabilities were established. Until then, rescues were improvised by contacting known competent climbers and assembling a team from whoever was available. Following the evolution of a guiding profession among technical climbers in North Conway, New Hampshire, during the 1970s, the Mountain Rescue Service was formed, under the direction of Rick Wilcox, a leading local technical climber, and consisting largely of the active winter technical climbers and guides. The system worked extremely well, since it marshaled the services of some of the very best and most consistently active winter climbers in the Northeast. For rescue from nontechnical situations in the White Mountains, reliance remained chiefly on the New Hampshire Fish and Game Department, which had statutory responsibility for search and rescue in the state, on state park and U.S. Forest Service personnel, and most of all on the AMC employees who worked in the mountains and were thereby quickest to be summoned. In the Adirondacks, where rescues were more often nontechnical in nature, albeit sometimes arduous and hazardous by being remote, rangers under Peter Fish were the prime resource. Winter climbers at Baxter State Park were long required to have a backup team lined up for rescue purposes before entering the park; during the 1980s the park developed rescue capability on its own ranger staff. Throughout the region, however, many rescues continued to be handled on an improvised basis, where such an option seemed adequate.

Epilogue

THE MOUNTAINS of the Northeast will have more history to record as the twenty-first century unfolds. But what direction that history will take—how our successors will view the mountains—is as unpredictable as New England weather. We have seen these mountains move from "daunting terrible" to sublime, from places where the strenuous find exercise to a sanctuary from the pressures of urban society, and finally to a readily accessible recreational playground.

In the process the metaphor of climbing has seen much metamorphosis. The same forests and crags that were a challenge for Alden Partridge and Herschel Parker and Herbert Malcolm were healing balm for Adirondack Murray's generation, a vehicle for uproarious fun for the Bemis Crew, a workshop for creative craftsmanship for C. W. Blood, the key to social change for Benton MacKaye, and a call to environmental stewardship for Edwin Ketchledge. Trail-builders conceived their creations as differently as the proverbial blind men perceived the elephant, J. Rayner Edmands paving the way for transplanted tea parties at the very same time that Warren Hart pointed straight up the steepest arêtes on Jefferson and Adams.

Whatever else, these hills of the Northeast have been and will be unfailingly *interesting*. Certainly they are small—absurdly small to be called mountains in comparison with the world's great ranges. But that smallness gives them their intimate connection to people. Robert Marshall, who knew the vast wilderness of Alaska and the West, wrote of the Adirondacks,

> All day we passed through luxuriant virgin forest and had time to enjoy three different mountain views. Had we done our 5,300 feet of climbing all on one mountain, we undoubtedly should have found much less beauty, and probably no more excitement.

The great guidebook writer, Walter Collins O'Kane wrote respectfully of "the infinite diversity" of Northeastern mountains and concluded, "Their interest is as many-sided as that of the great company of persons who visit them." The very scale and difficulty of the world's big ranges limit the possibilities of human activity in them. Only the few well-trained mountaineers can make them their playground or experience their varied moods. But the hills of the Northeast—capable of savage ferocity on occasions but of friendly welcoming on others—are available to all who respond to the natural world at any level.

The history that has been recorded in these pages reflects these two facets in which Northeastern mountains are as rich as any mountains anywhere: diversity, and a long and close association with people. As the chronicles have unfolded, we have seen the mountains in many moods—from the "terrible freesing weather" encountered by Darby Field in 1642; to the resplendent sublimities of the sunsets that Starr King and his romantic generation basked in from their summit houses of the 1850s; to the blasting furies of a winter storm shrieking down on Gifford Pinchot on Marcy in 1899 or the summertime tempest that brutally killed the strong athlete "Father Bill" Curtis on Washington in 1900; to the warm, companionable "sun-flecked narrow paths" of Monadnock and the Sleeping Giant and the Wyanokies, or the pink granite oceanside vistas of Maine's Mount Desert. Considering the scope, diversity, and depth of their human relationships, these little hills may well be the most interesting mountains on the face of this earth.

Appendix

Mountains over 4,000 feet in the Northeastern United States, their elevations, and first known ascents

THE LIST of mountains set forth below is based on elevations given for Adirondacks peaks in the Adirondack Mountain Club's *Guide to Adirondack Trails: High Peaks Region* (1987 edition); for Green Mountain peaks in the Green Mountain Club's *Guide Book of the Long Trail* (1985 edition); for White Mountain peaks in the Appalachian Mountain Club's *AMC White Mountain Guide* (1987 edition); for Maine peaks in the AMC's *AMC Maine Mountain Guide* (1985 edition); and for Catskill peaks in the "Catskill Trails" maps (numbers 41 and 43), prepared jointly by the AMC and the New York–New Jersey Trail Conference.

The basis on which mountains are identified as separate peaks varies: for example, for the New England peaks, the AMC requires a rise of 200 feet above the col between that peak and any neighboring peaks; for the Adirondacks, the criterion is 300 feet or simply three-fourths of a mile distance to the next highest peak.

For the Adirondacks, this list includes four peaks that are currently found to be less than 4,000 feet. The reason is that these were among the peaks thought to be 4,000 feet high when the first "peakbaggers" drew up their original list, based on surveys then available. Since the Adirondack Forty-Sixers still recognize that original list of forty-six peaks, these four peaks are included here. By the same token, Mount MacNaughton was not on the original list, though it is now considered to be 4,000 feet high. In the White Mountains, a list identical in length to that of the Adirondacks —forty-six peaks—constituted the official list for many years; the present list includes two (Bondcliff and Galehead) that have more recently been determined as qualifying.

Elevations are those given in the sources cited above.

The first known ascents for the Adirondacks reflect the research of Russell M. L. Carson, as modified by later scholars, notably Philip G. Terrie, Jr., in his introduction to later editions of Carson's 1927 classic, *Peaks and People of the Adirondacks*. First known ascents for New England peaks, where available, have been assembled by the authors from a variety of sources cited in the notes for the chapters in which these ascents are mentioned. Because Northeastern mountains are not "technically" difficult to climb, reasonable doubt may be entertained as to whether almost any of these "first known ascents" are the very first ascents ever. An asterisk (*) indicates an especially high possibility that other unrecorded ascents preceded the "first known ascent," or other grounds for significant doubt concerning the date or party.

Peak	Range	Elevation (ft.)	First Known Ascent
1. Washington	White	6,288	1642— Darby Field and Indian(s)
2. Adams	White	5,774	*1820— Lancastrians
3. Jefferson	White	5,712	*1820— Lancastrians
4. Monroe	White	5,384	1642— Field and Indian(s)
5. Madison	White	5,367	*1820— Lancastrians
6. Marcy	Adks.	5,344	1837— Ebenezer Emmons and party
7. Katahdin	Maine	5,267	1804— Charles Turner and party
8. Lafayette	White	5,260	*1826— Franconia party
9. Algonquin	Adks.	5,114	1837— Emmons and party
10. Lincoln	White	5,089	— unknown
11. Haystack	Adks.	4,960	1849— Old Mountain Phelps and party
12. Skylight	Adks.	4,926	1873— Verplanck Colvin, Phelps, and party
13. South Twin	White	4,902	1871— C. H. Hitchcock and a Dartmouth student
14. Whiteface	Adks.	4,867	1814— John Richards and party
15. Dix	Adks.	4,857	1807— surveyor Rykert and party
16. Gray	Adks.	4,840	1872— Colvin and Bill Nye
17. Iroquois	Adks.	4,840	*1883— William H. Brown
18. Carter Dome	White	4,832	— unknown
19. Basin	Adks.	4,827	ca. 1870— James J. Storrow and Orlando Beede
20. Moosilauke	White	4,802	*ca. 1770— Chase Whitcher
21. Eisenhower	White	4,761	1642— Field and Indian(s)
22. North Twin	White	4,761	*1871— Hitchcock and Dartmouth student

Peak	Range	Elevation (ft.)	First Known Ascent
23. Hamlin	Maine	4,751	1825— Joseph Norris and party
24. Gothics	Adks.	4,736	ca. 1870— Storrow and Beede
25. Colden	Adks.	4,714	1849— Robert Clark and Alexander Ralph
26. Bond	White	4,698	1871— Warren Upham and a Dartmouth student
27. Carrigain	White	4,680	1857— Arnold Guyot and party
28. Giant	Adks.	4,627	1797— Charles Brodhead and party
29. Nippletop	Adks.	4,620	1837— Emmons and party
30. Middle Carter	White	4,610	— unknown
31. Santanoni	Adks.	4,607	1866— Theodore R. Davis and David Hunter
32. Redfield	Adks.	4,606	1894— Ed Phelps and party
33. Wright	Adks.	4,580	*1893— Charles H. Peck and Charles Wood
34. West Bond	White	4,540	1871— Upham and Dartmouth student
35. Saddleback	Adks.	4,515	ca. 1870— Storrow and Beede
36. Garfield	White	4,500	*1871— three Dartmouth students
37. Liberty	White	4,459	— unknown
38. Panther	Adks.	4,442	1904— Daniel Lynch
39. South Carter	White	4,430	— unknown
40. Table Top	Adks.	4,427	1911— Jim Suitor
41. Wildcat	White	4,422	— unknown
42. Rocky Peak Ridge	Adks.	4,420	1878— Fred J. Patterson and Samuel Dunning
43. Macomb	Adks.	4,405	1872— Arthur H. Wyant and Melville J. Turnbull
44. Hancock	White	4,403	— unknown
45. Armstrong	Adks.	4,400	1875— Ed Phelps and Thomas P. Wickes
46. Hough	Adks.	4,400	1921— Marshall brothers (Robert & George) and Herb Clark
47. Mansfield	Green	4,393	1772— Ira Allen
48. Seward	Adks.	4,361	1870— Colvin and Alvah Dunning
49. Marshall (Clinton, Herbert)	Adks.	4,360	1921— Marshall brothers and Herb Clark
50. South Kinsman	White	4,358	— unknown

Peak	Range	Elevation (ft.)	First Known Ascent
51. Allen	Adks.	4,340	1921— Marshall brothers and Clark
52. Osceola	White	4,340	*1725— Samuel Willard and party
53. Flume	White	4,328	— unknown
54. Field	White	4,326	— unknown
55. Pierce (Clinton)	White	4,310	— unknown
56. Willey	White	4,320	— unknown
57. North Kinsman	White	4,293	*1871— A. A. Abbott and A. M. Bacheler
58. South Hancock	White	4,274	— unknown
59. Bondcliff	White	4,265	*1871— Upham and Dartmouth student
60. Zealand	White	4,260	— unknown
61. Killington	Green	4,241	— unknown
62. Big Slide	Adks.	4,240	1812— John Richards and party
63. Esther	Adks.	4,240	1839— Esther McComb
64. Sugarloaf	Maine	4,237	— unknown
65. Upper Wolf Jaw	Adks.	4,185	1875— Colvin, Ed Phelps, and party
66. Slide	Catskills	4,180	— unknown
67. Old Speck	Maine	4,180	— unknown
68. Lower Wolf Jaw	Adks.	4,175	1875— Ed Phelps
69. Cabot	White	4,170	— unknown
70. Crocker	Maine	4,168	ca. 1794— surveyor Ballard and party
71. Street	Adks.	4,166	1921— Marshall brothers and Clark
72. Phelps	Adks.	4,161	1904— Charles Wood
73. East Osceola	White	4,156	— unknown
74. West Bigelow	Maine	4,150	— unknown
75. North Brother	Maine	4,143	*1884— George Witherle and Clarence Peavey
76. Donaldson	Adks.	4,140	1870— Colvin and Dunning
77. North Tripyramid	White	4,140	*1874— Charles E. Fay and friend
78. Seymour	Adks.	4,120	ca. 1870— Guyot and Ernest Sandoz
79. Saddleback	Maine	4,116	ca. 1794— Ballard and party
80. Middle Tripyramid	White	4,110	— unknown
81. Sawteeth	Adks.	4,100	*1875— Newell Martin

Peak	Range	Elevation (ft.)	First Known Ascent
82. Cascade	Adks.	4,098	*1872— Lon Pierce
83. Bigelow: Avery Peak	Maine	4,088	— unknown
84. Camel's Hump	Green	4,083	— unknown
85. Ellen	Green	4,083	— unknown
86. Cannon	White	4,080	— unknown
87. Passaconaway	White	4,060	— unknown
88. South Dix	Adks.	4,060	1921— Marshall brothers and Clark
89. Porter	Adks.	4,059	1875— Ed Phelps and Noah Porter
90. Colvin	Adks.	4,057	1873— Colvin, Old Mountain Phelps, and party
91. Hale	White	4,054	— unknown
92. Jackson	White	4,052	— unknown
93. Abraham	Maine	4,049	— unknown
94. Moriah	White	4,049	— unknown
95. Tom	White	4,047	— unknown
96. Wildcat E	White	4,041	— unknown
97. Hunter	Catskills	4,040	— unknown
98. Emmons	Adks.	4,040	*1870— Colvin and Dunning
99. Owl's Head	White	4,025	— unknown
100. Galehead	White	4,024	— unknown
101. The Horn	Maine	4,023	ca. 1794— Ballard and party
102. Dial	Adks.	4,020	1884— Ed Phelps and Ed Beede
103. East Dix	Adks.	4,012	1921— Marshall brothers and Clark
104. Whiteface	White	4,010	— unknown
105. Abraham	Green	4,006	— unknown
106. Waumbek	White	4,006	— unknown
107. Isolation	White	4,005	— unknown
108. Tecumseh	White	4,003	— unknown
109. MacNaughton	Adks.	4,000	— unknown
110. South Crocker	Maine	4,000	ca. 1794— Ballard and party
111. Blake	Adks.	3,960	1874— Ed Phelps and client Miller
112. Cliff	Adks.	3,960	1917— Arthur S. Hopkins
113. Nye	Adks.	3,895	1921— Marshall brothers and Clark
114. Couchsachraga	Adks.	3,820	1924— Marshall brothers and Clark

Glossary

SOME terms from the vocabulary of hikers and campers may not be found in the dictionary. Others may be used with unusual meanings. The definitions below focus on applications to hiking and camping and reflect northeastern usage—and inevitably some personal preferences of the authors. For example, a BIVOUAC does not have to be in the mountains, but in the context of this book that is its usual application. A CHAIN obviously has several definitions more commonly encountered than that given here, but the surveyor's CHAIN is the one that readers may wish to know about when reading this book.

Words defined in this glossary appear in CAPITAL LETTERS throughout this section.

ABOVE-TREELINE: That part of a mountain above the point where trees will grow. The term is not precisely defined. It is sometimes used to mean the area above *all* trees, and sometimes to mean the area where trees cannot grow higher than the height of an adult person (approximately). There is a substantial zone on many mountains where patches of stunted or dwarfed trees (see KRUMMHOLZ, PUCKERBRUSH, and SCRUB) may be found in sheltered pockets of the mountainside, and many people include this zone in their concept of ABOVE-TREELINE. Some mountains have EXPOSED summits, on which bare rock dominates and no trees grow, but this condition does not necessarily mean they are technically ABOVE-TREELINE; the lack of trees may simply reflect lack of soil in which to take root. The altitude at which true TREELINE is reached varies widely in the northeastern United States and elsewhere: see TREELINE.

ABYSS: A deep chasm or drop-off.

ALPINE ZONE: That part of a mountain above the point where trees grow; often used interchangeably with ABOVE-TREELINE. The ALPINE ZONE is a useful term for ecologists because it refers to an environment altogether different from forested mountain terrain, with unique characteristics of climate, vegetation, and geology. Some students of alpine ecology believe that conditions ABOVE TREELINE in northeastern mountains are so extreme that a more appropriate term is ARCTIC ZONE.

ARCTIC ZONE: See ALPINE ZONE.

ARÊTE: A RIDGE, usually applied to an especially sharp or well-defined RIDGE, and most often applied to one that is ABOVE TREELINE, or at least EXPOSED.

AX BLAZE: See BLAZE.

BEARPAW: A short, flat, oval-shaped, tailless wooden snowshoe, made in large quantities for the military during World War II and therefore widely used in Northeastern winter climbing during the 1950s and 1960s.

BIOME: An environmental community whose characteristics are shaped by soil and climate.

BIVOUAC: As a noun, an arrangement for overnight camping in the mountains where developed facilities are unavailable. It usually implies an unscheduled, hasty arrangement, although planned BIVOUACS may be made. As a verb, to BIVOUAC is to spend the night out under such arrangements.

BLAZE: As a noun, a mark showing where the trail is, usually on a tree. The mark may be a small chip cut in a tree, often by an ax or hatchet (an AX BLAZE); or a dab of paint on tree or rock (a PAINT BLAZE); or both (an AX BLAZE on which paint has been applied).

BLOWDOWN: A place where wind has blown an unusually large number of trees down. The term is sometimes applied to the downed trees, rather than to the general area. A BLOWDOWN is most often referred to among hikers as an area through which hiking is extremely arduous, as the tree trunks and branches often lie in chaotic disarray, making travel most difficult.

BUSHWHACK: As a noun, an off-trail hike. Originally the term probably applied to off-trail hiking where the going was difficult—that is, where many BUSHES had to be WHACKED. Now it is often used to mean off-trail travel regardless of whether the going is difficult or not. As a verb, to BUSHWHACK is to travel off-trail.

CAIRN: A pile of rocks used to mark the trail, especially where trees are not available for BLAZES. CAIRNS are the traditional method for marking trails ABOVE-TREELINE in the Northeast.

CHAIN: As a noun, a surveyor's tool, in the days before tape measures, for measuring distance along a survey line. The term is also applied to the length of the surveyor's CHAIN: 100 links, or 66 feet. As a verb, to CHAIN is to run a survey line, measuring its length.

CHOCKSTONE: A rock wedged in a more-or-less vertical crack.

CIRQUE: A natural amphitheater, high on a mountain, with steep sides, caused by glacial erosion.

CLIMBING: See TECHNICAL CLIMBING.

CLOVE: A stream valley. The term is almost exclusively used in the Catskills and Shawangunks.

COL: The low-point or saddle on a ridge between mountains. A pass.

COME-ALONG: A strong cable fitted with a ratchet to gain mechanical advantage for moving heavy objects over the ground with comparative ease. It is often used in modern trail work to move large rocks. Also known as a cable-jack.

CONE: See SUMMIT CONE.

CORNICE: A projecting lip of snow along a RIDGE or at the edge of a cliff, created by high winds. A significant point for climbers is that a CORNICE is unstable, yet the extent of its projection may not be apparent from above. Climbers must use caution in walking along a corniced ridge, lest they step out on the CORNICE and break through.

CORRIDOR: See TRAIL CORRIDOR.

CRAG: A rocky summit or outcrop.

CRAMPONS: Metallic framework which may be attached to and removed from boots, with sharp points projecting downward about an inch or more. CRAMPONS give traction for crossing or climbing ice or hard snow. They are usually held on by straps or (modern versions) spring-loaded cables or cams, and may be donned or removed in the field, as terrain conditions require. Modern CRAMPONS often have ten points projecting down and may, for TECHNICAL CLIMBING, have two additional points projecting forward at the toe end. These are called ten-point and twelve-point CRAMPONS respectively. But early CRAMPONS exhibited a wide variety in the number of points, and some modern technical CRAMPONS do as well.

CREEPERS: A type of CRAMPON, usually with fewer than ten points. Not as serious a mountaineering tool. In older usages CREEPERS may be almost synonymous with CRAMPONS, but in modern usage CREEPERS usually have but four or two points and are attached with just a single strap to the boot instep.

CRIPPLEBRUSH: See KRUMMHOLZ, PUCKERBRUSH, and SCRUB.

CRUISER: See TIMBER CRUISER, TIMBER CRUISING.

ESCARPMENT: A cliff, especially one that is miles long and relatively uniform. An ESCARPMENT usually separates two relatively level areas of differing elevations, as opposed to cliffs on mountains that may occur in more varied terrain. ESCARPMENTS are often formed by erosion or faulting. Prominent examples of cliffs in the pattern of ESCARPMENTS are found at the Shawangunks.

EXPOSED: This term has two distinct meanings in a mountain setting. The first is the quality of being open to the elements—that is, not protected from the wind by trees or other features. An EXPOSED summit is one on which no protection from the wind is readily available. The term applies to most ABOVE-TREELINE areas, of course, except where wind direction and projecting rock surfaces afford possibilities for protection. A different use of the term is by ROCK CLIMBERS and others to refer to a steep and high rock face, where the climbers are or should be aware of the risk of falling.

FROST FEATHERS, FROST WINGS: A build-up of RIME that resembles feathers or wings. The patterns formed by wind and precipitation ABOVE TREELINE are often astonishingly delicate and beautiful when examined closely. The comparison with feathers on a bird is sometimes remarkably apt.

GLACIAL CIRQUE: See CIRQUE.

GLISSADE: As a noun, a controlled but reasonably rapid descent of a steep snow slope without skis, by sliding either in a standing or sitting position. As a verb, to descend a steep slope in this manner.

HEADWALL: The steep upper portion of a GLACIAL CIRQUE, usually its center section.

HERD PATH: An unofficial, unmaintained trail. The term is most commonly used in the Adirondacks, applying to the clearly discernible tracks that develop on officially "trailless" peaks, created by the "herds" of aspiring 4,000-footer climbers.

HOGBACK: A sharp ridge with steep drops on both sides. This term is normally applied to relatively small ridges or sections of ridges.

ICE AX: A climber's tool consisting of a shaft of wood, metal, or other strong material, with a straight metal spike at one end and a metal cross-piece at the other. The cross-piece has one pointed end (the pick) and one scalloped or otherwise functional end (the adze). The shaft is typically two to three feet in length, although older ICE AXES were longer and some with much shorter shafts are used in modern TECHNICAL CLIMBING of ice.

KNIFE-EDGE: An exceptionally narrow ridge or ARÊTE, EXPOSED, and often ABOVE TREELINE. In the relatively rounded mountains of the northeastern United States, a KNIFE-EDGE is not as narrow or exposed as a KNIFE-EDGE in larger, more spectacular mountains; most KNIFE-EDGES in the Northeast are wide enough to be hiked along without ropes if appropriate care is observed. The most celebrated northeastern KNIFE-EDGE is the one connecting Katahdin's Baxter Peak with Pamola, and that ridge is known as the Knife Edge.

KRUMMHOLZ: A patch of stunted, often twisted trees at the edge of the TREELINE. Literally, KRUMMHOLZ is German for "crooked wood." Sometimes the trunks may be more horizontal than vertical.

LEDGE: Commonly used in two different ways. LEDGE may refer to an entire rock cliff, as in New Hampshire's Cathedral Ledge. Or it may refer to small horizontal portions of an otherwise vertical cliff, as when ROCK CLIMBERS speak of climbing up to reach a LEDGE or placing one foot on a small LEDGE.

MASSIF: A mountain mass, possibly comprising more than one summit, as opposed to a single mountain. Thus, one may refer to the Katahdin MASSIF, meaning the entire raised area around Katahdin, including Baxter Peak (the principal summit) and subsidiary peaks along the same uplifted area, such as Pamola, Hamlin, and others.

NOTCH: A deep pass between mountains. This term differs from COL in that COL usually refers to a small saddle high on a ridge, at precisely the high point of the pass, whereas NOTCH may refer to a larger section of the pass. While the term NOTCH may be found in most sections of the Northeast, it is especially used in the White Mountains. In the Green Mountains, NOTCHES are more often called gaps; in the Adirondacks, they may be passes.

OFF-SET: A surveyor's term (among other meanings) describing an intentional temporary departure from a straight surveyed line, usually at right angles and to a new line parallel to the original, necessitated by encountering terrain where the line cannot be measured directly.

PAINT BLAZE: See BLAZE.

PEAKBAGGER, PEAKBAGGING: PEAKBAGGERS are people who aim to climb a large number of peaks, usually a list of specific peaks, such as the 4,000-footers of a particular range, state, or region (the Adirondacks, New Hampshire, New England). PEAKBAGGING is the pursuit of this activity. The term is used by some with connotations of disdain for the activity, but by others as simply descriptive, with no value judgments implied. In this book it is used in the latter way: no approval or disapproval of the activity is implied simply by calling it PEAKBAGGING.

PENEPLAIN: A large (possibly hundreds of square miles) and nearly flat land surface that represents an advanced state of erosion. If, in the course of geologic history, a peneplain is later uplifted and dissected by streams and/or glaciers, it may become a mountainous area distinguished by peaks with flat summits and rather uniform elevations. A frequently cited example of such an uplifted and eroded peneplain is the Catskills.

PIN-STEP: A trail maintenance device, in which a block of treated lumber is secured to a levelled piece of rock so as to form a step, or (more commonly) a series of steps, for surmounting a steep section of rock on a trail.

PITON: A metal wedge that ROCK CLIMBERS hammer into cracks in the rock face, for the purpose of securing protection on TECHNICAL CLIMBS.

PRECIPICE: Cliff.

PUCKERBRUSH: Short, densely thicketed trees or shrubs, difficult to travel through. Often used interchangeably with KRUMMHOLZ, SCRUB, or CRIPPLEBRUSH, although local usages may sometimes ascribe more specific meanings to each of these terms.

RAPPEL: As a noun, the descent of a cliff by means of a rope temporarily secured to the top of the cliff. As a verb, to descend a cliff in that manner.

RIDGE: An elongated crest between two valleys. Often used to mean the raised part of a mountainside, forming a logical line of ascent to the summit.

RIME: An accumulation of ice or snow on EXPOSED rock or other objects, usually ABOVE TREELINE. The buildup is *into* the wind, and can be impressive—see FROST FEATHERS.

ROCK CLIMBER, ROCK CLIMBING: While these terms may apply to people scrambling on steep, rocky terrain, they are usually distinctly applied to exceptionally steep terrain where a rope and TECHNICAL CLIMBING techniques are employed to overcome difficulty and maintain safety.

SCHUSS: To ski straight down a slope without checking speed by turns.

SCREE: Loose rocks on a mountain slope, from gravel size to somewhat larger (but smaller than the boulders which form TALUS).

SCREE WALLS: Short (roughly 3–18 inches in height) walls, built with rock or SCREE, intended to define a hiking trail ABOVE TREELINE, with the objective of encouraging hikers to stick to one trail through the alpine vegetation, thereby minimizing environmental impact on the ALPINE ZONE.

SCRUB: Short, tangled trees at or near TREELINE. Sometimes used interchangeably with KRUMMHOLZ, but sometimes applied to a wider variety of forest conditions, all characterized by short, densely thicketed trees, difficult to travel through without a cut trail. Some prefer to use SCRUB to apply primarily to hardwood thickets.

SITZMARK: A fall on snow, normally by a skier, possibly landing in a sitting position at first.

SLAB: As a noun, a relatively smooth expanse of horizontal or sloping (but not truly vertical) rock. As a verb, to SLAB is to contour or TRAVERSE across a mountain slope, as opposed to ascending straight up it.

SLASH: The tops and branches of trees left in the forest by loggers after they remove the trunks.

SLIDE: In addition to many other meanings, a SLIDE on a mountain refers to an open swath directly down a mountainside where sliding earth, rocks, and vegetation have left a bare scar. The surface of a SLIDE may be a rock SLAB, earth, SCREE, or any combination of this or other underlying material.

SPRUCE TRAP: A natural phenomenon that victimizes unsuspecting snowshoers or others travelling through deep snow. When heavy snow drifts over the branches of a low-growing conifer, it does not consolidate nearly as firmly as it does on surrounding terrain. A snowshoer travelling in deep snow may become accustomed to sinking a small amount with each step (say, 1–18 inches). But when that snowshoer steps over a small conifer, which may be mostly or even completely hidden from view by the snow, he or she will suddenly, and often unexpectedly, sink in far more—as much as 6 or 8 feet in extreme cases. This effect is referred to by snowshoers as a SPRUCE TRAP. Extrication from a deep SPRUCE TRAP, when surrounding snow is unconsolidated, may be difficult, time-consuming, and (for outside observers, if not the victim) amusing. The conifers that create SPRUCE TRAPS are usually at higher elevations (where snow is deeper) and are therefore usually spruce or balsam fir. While some northeasterners may occasionally refer to a fir trap, most use the general term SPRUCE TRAP regardless of what kind of tree created the effect. During the period when a snowshoer is attempting to get out of the SPRUCE TRAP, a variety of other terms may be applied, most of them inappropriate for inclusion in a book intended for general audiences.

SUMMIT CONE: The upper part of a mountain, including the summit; especially that part of a mountain that projects above a generally uplifted region and surrounding ridges, and that may be roughly conical in appearance.

TALUS: Loose boulders on a mountain slope, often found below a vertical rock face.

TARN: A small lake or pond set in mountainous terrain. Geologists employ more precise meanings related to the glacial origins of the lake.

TECHNICAL CLIMBERS, TECHNICAL CLIMBING: Applied to climbing, the term TECHNICAL implies the use of rope and other climbing equipment to ensure the safety of the climbers. For some people, the term CLIMBING alone means TECHNICAL CLIMBING, as distinguished from hiking; however, other people use the term CLIMBING to mean going up mountains whether by TECHNICAL CLIMBING or hiking. It is usually thought to take two distinct forms: rock climbing and ice climbing. Snow climbing is sometimes distinguished from ice climbing, and the term *mixed climbing* is used where both rock and ice or snow must be dealt with by technical means.

THROUGH-HIKER, THRU-HIKER (or -HIKING):   A hiker who is traveling from one end of a long-distance hiking trail to the other, usually over a period of weeks or months, usually (though not necessarily) in one continuous trip. For northeasterners, the term is most often used for Appalachian Trail hikers.

TIMBER-CRUISER, TIMBER CRUISING: One who goes through a section of forest to determine the potential yield of lumber to be cut therefrom.

TIMBERLINE: Usually synonymous with TREELINE. However, some people prefer to use these terms with a precise distinction, TREELINE referring to the point beyond which trees of any significant size will not grow, while TIMBERLINE refers to the point beyond which trees of marketable value as lumber will not grow. See ABOVE-TREELINE, TREELINE.

TOPO MAP, TOPOGRAPHICAL MAP: A map that indicates information about the surface features of the region, especially including elevations (by means of contour lines). Such maps are normally more accurate and detailed than other maps. Often northeastern hikers use these terms to refer specifically to the maps published by the United States Geological Survey, as contrasted with maps prepared by hiking organizations like AMC, ADK and GMC—even though the latter may also include considerable topographical detail.

TOTE ROAD: A road through the woods intended for use by wagons or other hauling equipment to remove logs from the woods or transport other material into or out of the woods. Nineteenth-century tote roads were built for horse-drawn wagons and skidders, and the term often implies roads originally built for such conveyances. However, it may apply to modern wood roads as well.

TRAIL CORRIDOR: A trail plus the zone on either side of it. This term has become common in discussion of measures to protect the Appalachian Trail by securing control of not just the trail itself but a relatively wide buffer zone on both sides of the trail.

TRAPROCK: Dark-colored igneous rock, typically appearing in prominent step-like formations. It is noteworthy in Connecticut, where outcrops of TRAPROCK are often the most prominent hills.

TRAVERSE: To cross a mountain slope or cliff either horizontally or (more often) on a moderate incline, rather than to ascend directly up.

TREAD-HARDENING: Any of several techniques used to prevent erosion of a trail surface. Most often it refers to rocks placed as stepping-stones where hikers are expected to walk.

TREELINE: The elevation on a mountainside beyond which trees cannot grow. In the Northeast, TREELINE varies greatly according to EXPOSURE to the wind and other weather influences and various other factors, but will generally be found between 4,000 and 5,000 feet, possibly a bit lower on parts of the Katahdin MASSIF. TREELINE sometimes means the point beyond which virtually no trees can grow and sometimes means the point beyond which trees of substantial size (over five or six feet tall) cannot grow. See above-treeline.

WINCH: See COME-ALONG. However, the term WINCH is more general, applicable to a broad array of devices for using a drum driven by a handle and gears, around which a cable is wound, so as to provide mechanical advantage for moving heavy objects.

Reference notes

THE NUMBERS on the left refer to the page in the text. The words in boldface type are normally the first words in the quotation on that page for which the source is given, or otherwise indicate the subject matter for which references are provided.

During the course of nine years of research for this history, the authors accumulated a variety of specialized sources—pamphlets, hiking club bulletins and schedules, special reports, unpublished papers, and the like. Many of these sources were generously supplied to us by people who thought they might be useful. Along with most of our research notes, these have been donated to the Dartmouth College Library, Hanover, New Hampshire. Therefore, when a source is cited as from the authors' collections, it can in most cases be found at Dartmouth.

Much of the authors' research took the form of interviews or conversations with knowledgeable individuals. Information gleaned from these talks is cited in the notes as "conversation with John Doe." Our notes on these conversations will also be found in the material donated to Dartmouth.

Another important source was correspondence. Where items are referred to as "letter from Jane Doe to L&GW," the last term refers to the authors. All of this correspondence has been given to Dartmouth.

INTRODUCTION: THE MOUNTAINS

xxviii **The fastest observed:** Comprehensive coverage of the measuring of the famous gust was provided on the occasion of the fiftieth anniversary, in the "World's Record Wind Edition" of the *Mount Washington Observatory News Bulletin* (Spring 1984), pp. 1-10.

xxix **"From horizon to":** Charles Dudley Warner, *In the Wilderness* (Boston: Houghton, Osgood, 1878), p. 107.

xxx **"They are friendly, gentle":** Tom Slayton, "Northeast Mountains: Cold, Hard, Exhilarating," *Sunday Rutland* [Vt.] *Herald and Sunday Times Argus*, June 6, 1982, sec. 5, p. 8. Reprinted with permission.

xxxvii **"Long horizontals":** Walter Prichard Eaton, intro., Federal Writers Project, *The Berkshire Hills* (New York: Funk & Wagnalls, 1939), p. xiii.

xxxviii **' . . . the woods":** William Thompson Howell, *The Hudson Highlands* (New York: Lenz and Riecker, vol. 1, 1933, vol. 2, 1934; reprinted in one volume, New York: Walking News, 1982), vol. 2, p. iii. Reprinted with permission.

1   **The nearly complete:** For how mountains were perceived in western civilization prior to the eighteenth century, the landmark source is Marjorie Hope Nicolson, *Mountain Gloom and Mountain Glory: The Development of the Aesthetics of the Infinite* (Ithaca, N.Y.: Cornell University Press, 1959).

2   **Seventeenth century geographers:** Yi-Fu Tuan, "Fragile Majesties," *The Sciences* (Apr. 1982), p. 25.

"Hillocks, Mole Hills": Quoted by Nicolson, *Mountain Gloom*, p. 67.

This European attitude: Roderick Nash, *Wilderness and the American Mind* (New Haven: Yale University Press, 1967; rev. ed. 1973, 1982, especially the first two chapters. See also Peter N. Carroll, *Puritanism and the Wilderness: The Intellectual Significance of the New England Frontier, 1629-1700* (New York: Columbia University Press, 1969); Hans Huth, *Nature and the American: Three Centuries of Changing Attitudes* (Berkeley: University of California Press, 1959); Howard Mumford Jones, *O Strange New World: American Culture, the Formative Years* (New York: Viking, 1952); Henry Nash Smith, *Virgin Land: The American West as Symbol and Myth* (Cambridge: Harvard University Press, 1950); John R. Stilgoe, *Common Landscape of America, 1580-1845* (New Haven: Yale University Press, 1982); and any of the standard histories of the period (for example, Oscar Handlin, *The Americans: A New History of the People of the United States* (Boston: Little, Brown, 1963).

When they first came: A useful summary of early sightings of the White Mountains may be found in Frederick W. Kilbourne, *Chronicles of the White Mountains* (Boston: Houghton Mifflin, 1916), pp. 17-19. Verrazano's report was made in a letter to the king of France, July 8, 1524; the quoted words are from a translation by Edward Hagaman Hall, quoted in Kilbourne, *Chronicles*, p. 17. Champlain's 1604 trip is described by Charles Pomroy Otis, trans., "The Voyage of Samuel de Champlain on the Coast of Maine, from the Saint Croix to the Penobscot in the Month of September 1604," *Bangor Historical Magazine*, vol. 2 (June 1887), pp. 229-34. Early sightings of Mount Agamenticus are related in Charles B. Fobes, "Mount Agamenticus, Maine," *Appalachia* (Dec. 1953), pp. 488-96. Camden Hills sightings are mentioned in William D. Williamson, *The History of the State of Maine* (Hollowell, Maine: Glazier, Masters, 1832), p. 95. The Blue Hills' early mention is cited by Edwin M. Bacon in *Walks and Rides in the Country about Boston* (Boston: Houghton Mifflin, 1897), p. 334. Jacques Cartier's view of the Adirondacks is mentioned by Samuel Eliot Morison, *The European Discovery of America: The Northern Voyages, A.D. 500–1600*, (New York: Oxford University Press, 1971), p. 414, and described in more depth by Neal Burdick, "Jacques Cartier's 'Hilles on the Southe,' " *Adirondac* (Oct.-Nov. 1985), pp. 13-14. Champlain's mountain sightings, the Adirondacks as well as the Green Mountains, are noted in his journal entries in Charles Pomroy Otis, trans., *Voyages of Samuel de Champlain* (Boston: Prince Society, 1878), vol. 2, pp. 217-18. Hudson's trip upriver is chronicled in the journal of his officer, Juet, an edition of which is printed in Roland Van Zandt, *Chronicles of the Hudson: Three Centuries of Travelers' Accounts* (New Brunswick, N.J.: Rutgers University Press, 1971), pp. 11-14.

2   **"At the start":** Handlin, *The Americans*, p. 28.

     "A waste and howling": Written by Michael Wigglesworth in 1662; quoted by Henry Nash Smith, *Virgin Land*, p. 4.

     "Horrid hills": Henry Andrews Wright, *The Story of Western Massachusetts* (New York: Lewis Historical Publishing Co., 1949), vol. 2, p. 902.

3   **"Even higher mountains":** Kenneth Roberts, *Northwest Passage* (Garden City, N.Y.: Doubleday, 1937), p. 225.

     In the lower: Evidence of Indian activity in the lesser ranges of the region may be found in H. A. Haring, *Our Catskill Mountains* (New York: G. P. Putnam's Sons, 1931), pp. 49-57; Michael Kudish, "Vegetational History of the Catskill High Peaks" (Ph.D. diss., State University College of Forestry at Syracuse University, 1971), p. 58; Alf Evers, *The Catskills: From Wilderness to Woodstock* (Garden City, N.Y.: Doubleday, 1972), pp. 7-11; Elizabeth D. Levers, "The Hills of the Shattemuc," in the Appalachian Mountain Club, *In the Hudson Highlands* (Lancaster, Pa.: Lancaster Press, 1945; second edition published by New York: Walking News, n.d.), p. 108; W. T. Howell, *The Hudson Highlands*, vol. 1, p. 25; Charles Taylor, *History of Great Barrington (Berkshire) Massachusetts, 1676–1822* (published by the town of Great Barrington, 1928), pp. 39-42; letter from George R. Horner to L&GW, Feb. 3, 1984; Edgar L. Heermance, *The Connecticut Guide: What to See and Where to Find It* (Hartford, Conn.: Emergency Relief Commission, 1935), p.255; Connecticut Forest and Park Association, *Connecticut Walk Book*, 13th ed. (East Hartford, Conn.: Connecticut Forest and Park Association, 1981), p. 14; and Long Island Greenbelt Trail Conference, Inc., "Map Guide to the Long Island Greenbelt Trail," n.d. (ca. Jan. 1983).

     On these more: CFPA, *Connecticut Walk Book*, p. 15.

     But the Indians: See, for examples, J. H. Spaulding, *Historical Relics of the White Mountains* (Boston: Nathaniel Noyes, 1855), p. 7, and Benjamin G. Willey, *Incidents in White Mountain History* (Boston: Nathaniel Noyes, 1856), p. 43.

     Katahdin, for example: Pamola legends are recounted in a two-page pamphlet prepared for Baxter State Park by a local historian, Marion Whitney Smith, *Pamola—The God of Katahdin*. In John W. Hakola, *Legacy of a Lifetime: The Story of Baxter State Park* (Woolwich, Maine: TBW Books, 1981), Pamola is well covered, with over a page of text and no fewer than nine illustrations: see pp. 2-6.

     The sole report: John Giles, *Memoirs of Odd Adventures, Strange Deliverances, &C in the Captivity of John Giles, Esq.* (Boston: William Dodge, 1736; reprinted Cincinnati: Spiller and Gates, 1869), pp. 45-47. Rumors of other unsuccessful aboriginal attempts on Katahdin may be found in Fannie Hardy Eckstorm, "History of the Chadwick Survey," *Sprague's Journal of Maine History* (Apr.-June 1926), pp. 62-89, and Williamson, *History of Maine*, p. 92.

4   **Capt. Samuel Willard:** Captain Samuel Willard, "A Journal of My March," read in the Massachusetts House of Representatives, Nov. 10, 1725, *Massachusetts Archives*, 38A, pp. 109-10; the quoted passage is on p. 109. An even earlier Indian scouting party went up Monadnock in 1706 but not necessarily all the way to the top; see Albert Annett and Alice E. Lehtinen, *History of Jaffrey, New Hampshire* (Peterborough, N.H.: Transcript Printing Company, 1937), pp. 16, 505.

Chase Whitcher: William Little, *The History of Warren, a Mountain Hamlet Located among the White Hills of New Hampshire* (Manchester, N.H.: William E. Moore, 1870), p. 229.

Besides, the northern: The obstacles to settlement of northern New England are vividly portrayed in Lois Kimball Mathews, *The Expansion of New England* (Boston: Houghton Mifflin, 1909). See also Francis Parkman's series of histories, collected and reprinted in *France and England in North America* (New York: Viking, 1983).

If New England's: For early Adirondack history, see Alfred L. Donaldson, *A History of the Adirondacks* (New York: Century, 1921).

"Stanley had found": *Ibid.*, vol. 1, p. 11.

"Cauchsachrage an Indian": Russell M. L. Carson, *Peaks and People of the Adirondacks* (first published by New York: Doubleday, Page, 1927; reprinted Glens Falls, N.Y.: Adirondack Mountain Club, 1973, 1986), p. 3. Reprinted with permission.

Capt. Joseph Chadwick: Chadwick's explorations and a reproduction of his map may be found in Eckstorm, "Chadwick Survey," pp. 62-89.

5   **"Being a remarkable":** Quoted in Eckstorm, "Chadwick Survey," p. 83.

"Daunting terrible": John Josselyn, *New England Rarities Discovered* (1672; Boston: William Venzie, 1845), p. 36.

CHAPTER 1. DARBY FIELD ON MOUNT WASHINGTON

7   **The earliest maps:** The two earliest maps printed in New England are those of John Foster (1677) and a "Blathwayt Atlas" map estimated at about the same vintage; both are analyzed by Bradford F. Swan, "The Earliest Map of the White Mountains," *Appalachia* (Dec. 1946), pp. 386-88.

Darby Field was: The most authoritative studies of Darby Field and his background are by Warren W. Hart, "Darby Field," *Appalachia* (June 1908), pp. 360-66, reprinted by permission of the Appalachian Mountain Club, and "The First Ascent of the White Hills," *Appalachia* (June 1942), pp. 9-15.

"Could not write": Jay Mack Holbrook, *New Hampshire Residents: 1633–1699* (Oxford, Mass.: Holbrook Research Institute, 1979), p. 151.

In that year: The primary sources concerning Field's ascent of Mount Washington are (1) a letter from Thomas Gorges, deputy governor of the province of Maine, to Ferdinando Gorges, June 29, 1642, reprinted in Robert E. Moody, ed., *The Letters of Thomas Gorges* (Portland, Maine: Maine Historical Society, 1978), pp. 112-19; and (2) the journal kept by Massachusetts governor John Winthrop between 1630 and 1649, published as John Winthrop, *The History of New England from 1630 to 1649* (Boston: Little, Brown, 1853), pp. 80-82. The quoted material from *The Letters of Thomas Gorges* is reprinted with permission.

8   **"Terrible freesing weather"**: Gorges, *Letters*, p. 115.

    "Found them drying": Winthrop, *History of New England*, p. 82.

    "His relation at": *Ibid.*, p. 81.

9   **In Lucy Crawford's**: Lucy Crawford, *History of the White Mountains*, p. 4. This, and all subsequent quotations, are reprinted by permission of the Appalachian Mountain Club, from Stearns Morse, ed., *Lucy Crawford's History of the White Mountains* (Boston: Appalachian Mountain Club, 1978).

    The first careful: Edward Tuckerman, in Thomas Starr King, *The White Hills: Their Legends, Landscape, and Poetry* (Boston: Crosby, Nichols, 1859 [1860]), pp. 34-46.

10   **The next writer**: Frederick Tuckerman, "Early Visits to the White Mountains and Ascents of the Great Range," *Appalachia* (August 1921), pp. 111-27.

    In 1930 John: J. Anderson and Stearns Morse, *The Book of the White Mountains* (New York: Minton Balch, 1930), p. 237.

    In 1942 Warren: Hart, "The First Ascent of the White Hills," p. 13.

11   **Frederick W. Kilbourne**: Kilbourne, *Chronicles*, p. 22.

    Through the centuries: A description of the dramatic surfacing of the Gorges letter in 1984 is in Barbara Tetreault, "New Info Surfaces on Darby Field's Mt. Washington Climb," *Sunday News* (Manchester, N.H.), Nov. 18, 1984, p. 12B.

    "In a sorry state": Moody, ed., in his introduction to Gorges, *Letters*, p. xii.

12   **"This much I certify"**: Gorges, *Letters*, p. 115.

13   **"We know too much"**: Lytton Strachey, *Eminent Victorians* (Garden City, N. Y.: Garden City Publishing, n.d.), p. v.

    One theory is: Examples of the three theories cited here may be found, respectively, in Hart, "Darby Field," p. 366; "Various Notes: White Mountains," *American Alpine Journal* (1943), pp. 153-54; and "The White Hills: Their Early History and an Account of the First Ascent of Mount Washington," *White Mountain Echo* (Bethlehem, N.H.), Aug. 20, 1898, p. 2.

    "Muscovy glass" (mica): Winthrop, *History of New England*, p. 82.

14   **"The exploit of"**: "The White Hills," *White Mountain Echo*, Aug. 20, 1898, p. 2.

    Neal was an agent: Jeremy Belknap, *The History of New Hampshire* (Philadelphia: Robert Aitken, 1784). This misinformation appeared in Belknap's first edition of his *History* (p. 23), published in 1784 and was deleted from the 1792 edition.

14   **In other accounts:** See, for examples, Eliphalet and Phinehas Merrill, *Gazetteer of the State of New Hampshire* (Exeter, N.H.: C. Norris, 1817), p. 206; George Barstow, *The History of New Hampshire from Its Discovery, in 1614, to the Passage of the Toleration Act, in 1819* (Concord, N.H.: I. S. Boyd, 1842), p. 58; and as late as Georgia Drew Merrill, *History of Carroll County* (Boston: W. A. Ferguson, 1889), pp. 49-50.

      After the first ascent: Winthrop, *History of New England*, pp. 82, 107; see also Gorges, *Letters*, pp. 120, 126.

CHAPTER 2. IRA ALLEN ON MOUNT MANSFIELD

16   **"It was an obstruction":** W. Storrs Lee, *The Green Mountains of Vermont* (New York: Henry Holt, 1955), p. 9.

      As every Vermont: Background on the activities of the Allen family as a whole is contained in Charles A. Jellison, *Ethan Allen: Frontier Rebel* (Syracuse, N.Y.: Syracuse University Press, 1969).

      "The family seems": James Truslow Adams, *New England in the Republic, 1776–1850* (Boston: Little, Brown, 1926), p. 101.

17   **Ira Allen was:** A two-volume biography is James Benjamin Wilbur, *Ira Allen: Founder of Vermont, 1751–1814* (Boston: Houghton Mifflin, 1928). The first fifty-nine pages of this work consist of Ira's own lively autobiography of his early years as surveyor and speculator. His adventures on the mountains are found chiefly on pp. 20-27, 32-34, and 37; except where otherwise noted, quoted passages are from these pages.

      "A short, well-built": Wilbur, *Ira Allen*, pp. 61-62.

      "Founder of Vermont": *Ibid.*, title.

      "Ira, the brilliant": Jellison, *Ethan Allen*, p. 3.

18   **Ira Allen's climbing exploits:** Allen's itinerary on this march has been traced by Llew Evans, in "Mount Mansfield: Capstone of Vermont," *Appalachia* (June 1944), p. 42.

CHAPTER 3. THE BELKNAP-CUTLER EXPEDITION TO MOUNT WASHINGTON

21   **The Belknap-Cutler:** This ascent of Mount Washington is described by Jeremy Belknap in *Journal of a Tour to the White Mountains in July 1784* (Boston: Historical Society, 1876). Among additional accounts by Belknap, notable are a paper entitled "Description of the White Mountains in New Hampshire," published in *Transactions of the American Philosophical Society* (1786), pp. 109-14; a second version of this paper, apparently identical, published in the *American Museum or Repository of Ancient and Modern Fugitive Pieces* (Feb. 1788), pp. 128-32; vol. 3 of Belknap's *History of New Hampshire*, pp. 48-50; a letter to Ebenezer Hazard, in *Collections of the Massachusetts Historical Society*, vol. 3, 5th ser., pp. 170-78; and a letter to his

son, Sammy, Sept. 2, 1784, in the manuscript collections of the New Hampshire Historical Society. Cutler kept a journal, which was printed in William Parker Cutler and Julia Perkins Cutler, *Life, Journals and Correspondence of Rev. Manasseh Cutler, L.L.D.* (Cincinnati: Robert Clarke, 1888), pp. 96-113. A third member of the expedition, Daniel Little, also kept a journal, a typescript of which is in The Brick Store Museum in Kennebunk, Maine. Quoted phrases from Little's Journal are reprinted with permission of The Brick Store Museum. A well-annotated edition of Belknap's *History*, shedding useful light on this climb, is that of Gary Thomas Lord, published in 1973.

22   **Of the dozen:** The backgrounds of the principal members of the party are described by C. Deane, editor of Belknap's published *Journal*, in a "prefatory note" to the 1876 edition, p. 4, and by Jeanette E. Graustein in "Early Scientists in the White Mountains," *Appalachia* (June 1964), pp. 44-45.

"Being the heaviest": Belknap, letter to Hazard, pp. 173-74.

"Left family, friends": Chester B. Jordan, "Col. Joseph B. Whipple," *Proceedings* of the New Hampshire Historical Society, vol. 2 (June 1888-June 1895), p. 289.

23   **"Built a hut":** This and remaining quoted passages in this and the next two paragraphs are from Belknap, *Journal*, pp. 9-10.

24   **"Exceedingly steep":** Belknap, letter to Sammy. Reprinted with permission.

"Like steep stairs": Little, "Journal."

For years most students: Examples of these three theories may be found in Moses F. Sweetser, *The White Mountains: A Handbook for Travellers* (Boston: James R. Osgood, 1876), p.9; Frederick Tuckerman, "Early Visits to the White Mountains," p. 125; and Anderson and Morse, *Book of the White Mountains*, p. 239.

A party of eight: For an account of this bicentennial expedition and its conclusions, see Peter Crane, "The Belknap 200th," *Mount Washington Observatory News Bulletin* (Fall 1984), pp. 52-53.

"First summit": This and other quoted passages attributed to Cutler are from his *Journal*, pp. 102-5.

25   **"By regular steppings":** Little, "Journal."

"Had the mortification": Cutler, *Journal*, p. 105.

Exact times: Cutler, *Journal*, pp. 102-5, and Belknap, *Journal*, p. 11.

Altitude comparisons: Cutler, letter to Belknap, Aug. 9, 1784, in *Life of Cutler*, p. 221, and Belknap, *History*, p.49.

"As cold as November": Little, "Journal."

"Nearly deprived": Belknap, *History*, p. 50.

Carving "N. H.": *Ibid.*

25   **"Partridges and neats tongue"**: Cutler, *Journal*, pp. 106-7.

       At 3:57 P.M.: Belknap, *Journal*, p. 11.

26   **"Slipped, and was gone"**: Belknap, *History*, p. 50.

       "Was either killed": Cutler, *Journal*, p. 108.

       At length the enterprising: *Ibid.*, p. 109.

       "Happily, without any": Belknap, *History*, p. 50.

       5:50 P.M.: Belknap, *Journal*, p. 11.

       "Wider, more steep": Cutler, *Journal*, p. 108.

       A winding gully": Belknap, *History*, pp. 50-51.

       "Par-boiled and smoke-dried": Belknap, letter to Hazard, p.177.

       Paine Wingate: Belknap, letter to Cutler, Jan. 25, 1785, in *Life of Cutler*, p. 224.

       When queried: Cutler, letter to Belknap, Feb. 28, 1785, in *Life of Cutler*, p. 227.

27   **"Two hundred-weight"**: Belknap, letter to Cutler, Jan. 25, 1785, in *Life of Cutler*, p. 225. Cutler's plans for trips that never materialized are described in letters to Belknap, dated Feb. 28, 1785, June 29, 1785, and July 25, 1786. See *Life of Cutler*, pp. 227-28, 232, 247.

       The 1784 expedition: For specific citations of the various accounts, see the first note in this chapter.

       Twenty years later: *Life of Cutler*, pp. 110-13.

CHAPTER 4. ALDEN PARTRIDGE: THE FIRST REGIONWIDE HIKER

29   **Alden Partridge was**: The facts of Alden Partridge's life may be found chiefly in William Arba Ellis, ed., *Norwich University, 1819-1911: Her History, Her Graduates, Her Role of Honor* (Montpelier, Vt.: Capital City Press, 1911), vol. 1, "General History"; N. L. Sheldon, "Captain Alden Partridge, A. M.," *New England Magazine* (Oct. 1904), *pp. 228-36*; Col. Lester A. Webb, *Captain Alden Partridge and the United States Military Academy, 1806-1823* (Northport, Ala.: American Southern, 1965); and N. L. Sheldon, "Norwich University Illustrated," a brochure reprinted from *New England Magazine*, March 1899. The authors also profited from the invaluable assistance of Prof. Gary Thomas Lord, chairman of the History and Government Department, Norwich University, and from access to the special collections of the Norwich University Library, Northfield, Vermont.

       West Point: Besides Colonel Webb's book cited above, see Edgar Denton III, "The Formative Years of the United States Military Academy" (Ph.D. diss., Syracuse University, 1964), especially pp. 172-76, and James William Kershner, "Sylvanus Thayer: A Biography" (Ph.D. diss., West Virginia University, 1976), especially pp. 134-38. Thayer succeeded Partridge as superintendent.

29 **When he insisted:** Jacqueline S. Painter, ed., *The Trial of Captain Alden Partridge, Corps of Engineers* (Northfield, Vermont: Friends of the Norwich University Library, 1987).

 He has been called: Lester A. Webb, "The Origin of Military Schools in the United States Founded in the Nineteenth Century" (Ph.D. diss., University of North Carolina, 1958), P. 32.

30 **He later referred:** Letter from Partridge to the *National Intelligencer*, Sept. 10, 1816, p. 2.

 Among the summits: Samuel Akerly, *The Geology of the Hudson River and the Adjacent Region* (New York: A. T. Goodrich, 1820), pp. 9-10. Bear Mountain is here rendered "the Bare mountain."

 In the summer of 1811: Letter from Partridge to the *American Monthly Magazine and Critical Review* (Dec. 1818), pp.124-29. The quoted passage is on p. 127. See also letter from Partridge to William Paddock, Sept. 12, 1820, in the Alden Partridge Papers, Norwich University Library, Northfield, Vermont.

 Later that year: Letter to the *American Monthly Magazine and Critical Review* (Dec. 1818), p. 124.

 In 1817: *Ibid.* (Sept. 1817), pp. 51-52.

 In 1818: *Ibid.* (Nov. 1818), pp. 51-54.

31 **Maine border climbs:** Partridge, journal of a northeastern boundary survey, part 1 (June 22-Sept. 4, 1819), and part2 (Sept. 4-12, 1819) pedestrian excursion to Lake Champlain, in Alden Partridge Papers, Norwich University Library, Northfield, Vermont.

 The scope of: Letters from Partridge to the *National Intelligencer*, Sept. 10, 1816, and Aug. 5, 1820.

 Professor Ritchie: Quoted in "Conference of New England Trail Makers," *New Hampshire Forestry*, vol. 2, no. 2 (1917), p.4.

 In a "Lecture on Education": Quoted by Roxanne Marie Albertson, "Physical Education in New England from 1789 to 1860: Concepts and Practices" (Ph.D. diss., University of Oregon, 1974), pp. 37-38. Reprinted with permission.

32 **"It was seen":** *Catalog of the Corporation, Officers and Cadets of Norwich University, 1848-1849*, p. 57. Italics in original.

 "The physical power": *Ibid.*, 1847-1848, p. 48.

 To Partridge, physical: An editorial in a Middletown, Connecticut, newspaper contrasted Partridge's emphasis on excursions with the indoor exercise at Yale University's new gymnasium ("Gymnastics," *Sentinel and Witness*, Nov. 8, 1862, p. 3).

 "On these excursions": Quoted by Ellis, *Norwich University*, p. 48.

32   **"We continued our course"**: *Ibid.*, p. 43.

One of the first: Alden Partridge, "Excursion to the White Mountains, August 1821," Alden Partridge Papers, Norwich University Library, Northfield, Vermont. (Typescript.) Reprinted with permission.

Other 1821–22 excursions: Ellis, *Norwich University*, pp. 21-23.

33   **"A youth of"**: Partridge, "Prospectus and Internal Regulations of the American Literary, Scientifick and Military Academy to be Opened at Middletown," quoted in *Catalogues of Norwich University, 1820–1828*, p. 29.

"Very steep indeed": William G. Brooks, "Journal of an Excursion to Manchester, Vermont, by a Party of the Norwich Cadets, 1823" Manuscript in the collections of the Vermont Historical Society. Reprinted with permission.

"The view alone": *Ibid.*

The year 1824: Ellis, *Norwich University*, pp. 27-35.

"We scaled their": W. J. Bennett, I. E. Morse, and H. L. Barnum, *Journal of an Excursion Performed by a Detachment of Cadets Belonging to the A.L.S.&M. Academy, Under the Command of Captain Alden Partridge*, Nov. 1st, 1826 (Middletown, Conn., 1826), p. 10. Reprinted with permissions. For the variety of excursions from Middletown, see Ellis, *Norwich University*, pp. 44-48.

"These young men": Untitled news item, Middletown, Conn., *Sentinel and Witness*, Apr. 27, 1825, p. 3.

Lafayette (1837): Ellis, *Norwich University*, pp. 79-80.

"Seemed to progress": Cadet Riley Adams, "Journal," *Vineland* [N.J.] *Historical Magazine*, vol. 4, no. 3 (Apr. 1919), p.10.

"All (except the Captain)": *Ibid.*, p. 7.

"Captain Partridge": François Peyre-Ferry, *The Art of Epistolary Composition. . . .* (Middletown, Conn.: E. & H. Clark, 1826), p. 255. Wesleyan University Archives copy consulted.

34   **At the age of forty-five**: Letter from Partridge, entitled "A Card," to the *Eastern Argus* (Portland, Maine), Dec. 7, 1830, p. 1.

There is a tale: Anecdote related by H. P. Davidson, (Norwich, class of 1867), letter to the editor, *Norwich University Record*, Aug. 8, 1912, p. 2. Reprinted with permission. Davidson concludes the anecdote thus: "I give the account as I heard it about three score years ago. How literally true the above account is I do not know."

"Not having had": Letter from Partridge, "Exercise Walking," to *Newark* [N.J.] *Daily Advertiser*, Aug. 20, 1849.

CHAPTER 5. THE CRAWFORDS OF CRAWFORD NOTCH

37   **"Was taxed heavily"**: King, *The White Hills*, p. 187.

37   **"Had noted the existence":** Frederic J. Wood, *The Turnpikes of New England* (Boston: Marshall Jones, 1919), p. 223.

This path was used: Unidentified clipping from a Lancaster, N.H., newspaper, ca. 1886, in the scrapbooks of John W. Weeks, John W. Weeks Papers, collections of the New Hampshire Historical Society.

In fact, Timothy Nash: Warren W. Hart, "Timothy Nash," *Appalachia* (June 1919), pp.383–90; see especially pp. 386–87.

38   **Nathaniel Hawthorne:** Nathaniel Hawthorne, "Sketches from Memory by a Pedestrian," *New England Magazine* (Nov. 1835), p. 324.

"On account of": Wood, *Turnpikes*, p. 223.

"Not much better": Undated news clipping cited earlier in notes to this chapter. Reprinted with permission.

39   **The first path:** Gibbs's Path is mentioned in Jacob Bigelow, "Some Account of the White Mountains of New Hampshire," *New England Journal of Medicine and Surgery*, vol. 5 (October 1816), p. 327. Cutler mentions that Col. George Gibbs called on him en route to his first trip to Mount Washington; see Cutler's journal, *Life of Cutler*, p. 341. It is important to distinguish this Gibbs's Path from others that may have been known by the same name later. For example, Franklin Leavitt's "Map of the White Mountains, N.H." (1852) labels the original Crawford Path as "Gibb's Path," reflecting the arrival on the Crawford Notch scene of hotel proprietor J. L. Gibb. This is a case where the placement of the apostrophe relative to the letter s is crucial.

Around 1791: The starting point for reading about the Crawfords is Lucy Crawford, *History of the White Mountains*, originally published in 1845. A useful edition is edited by Stearns Morse and published by the Appalachian Mountain Club. The Crawfords have been written about extensively by historians of the White Mountains. See, for example, Kilbourne, *Chronicles*, numerous references.

40   **"The largest house":** Letter from Ethan Allen Crawford to Philip Carrigain, June 20, 1832, in New Hampshire Historical Society. Reprinted with permission.

Winter brought: "White Mountains in 1825: How They Were Reached and What Was Seen in Them Sixty-Nine Years Ago," *White Mountain Echo*, July 7, 1894, pp. 1-2.

41   **The Crawford Path:** Paul T. Doherty, "Pathway of the Giant," *Appalachia* (Dec. 1969), pp. 595-610.

43   **One of the first:** The Rev. Samuel Joseph May, *Memoir of Samuel Joseph May* (Boston: Roberts Brothers, 1873), p. 50.

"The logs and underbrush": Letter from Alden Partridge to William Paddock, Sept. 12, 1820, Alden Partridge Papers, Norwich University Library, Northfield, Vermont. Reprinted with permission.

"A narrow footpath": Ellis, *Norwich University*, vol 1, p. 34.

43   **"Deep mud holes"**: G. W. Nichols, "Popular Notices of Mount Washington and the Vicinity," *American Journal of Science and Arts* (July 1838), p. 77.

Mount Washington was: An account of the Lancastrians' expeditions was written by one of its leaders, Adino Nye Brackett, "Sketches of the White Mountains," in J. Farmer and J. B. Moore, eds., *Collections, Historical and Miscellaneous* (Concord, N.H.: Hill and Moore, 1822), pp. 97–107. Ethan Crawford's version of the same events is in Lucy Crawford, *History*, p. 6.

44   **"Loaded equal to"**: Crawford, *History*, p. 6.

"Could only express": *Ibid.*

"Known by its sharp": Brackett, "Sketches," p. 98.

"To correspond with": Conversation between Brackett and John Bellows, related in a letter from Thaddeus William Harris to Edward Tuckerman, Aug. 17, 1853, quoted in Frederick Tuckerman, "A Naturalist's Visit to the White Mountains in 1853," *Appalachia* (June 1918), p. 257.

Furthermore, the field notes: "Survey Establishing Heights of Major Peaks in the White Mountains," in manuscript collections of the New Hampshire Historical Society. Reprinted with permission.

45   **"Second to Washington"**: Gideon Welles, "Journal of an Excursion from Norwich, Vermont, to the White Hills in New Hampshire," unpublished manuscript quoted in Ellis, *Norwich University*, Vol. 1, p.33. Reprinted with permission.

An 1839 gazetteer: John Hayward, *The New England Gazetteer* (Concord, N.H.: Israel S. Boyd and William White, 1839), unpaged; listing is alphabetical, under "White Mountains."

G. P. Bond: G. P. Bond, "A Map, with Views, of the White Mountains," 1853, in the collections of Douglas A. Philbrook.

Eastman guidebook: Samuel C. Eastman, *The White Mountain Guide* (Concord, N.H.: E. C. Eastman, 1858), p. 60.

"Most of this summer": Crawford, *History*, p. 106.

46   **Man named Garland**: Unidentified letter dated 1834, in the manuscript collections of the New Hampshire Historical Society.

Daniel Webster: Crawford, *History*, pp. 130–31.

47   **The botanists**: Sources for the botanists' explorations include Arthur Stanley Pease, "Notes on the Botanical Exploration of the White Mountains," *Appalachia* (June 1917), pp. 157–77, and Jeanette E. Graustein, "Early Scientists in the White Mountains," *Appalachia* (June 1964), pp. 44–63.

Two of the best-known: Jacob Bigelow, "Some Account of the White Mountains of New Hampshire," *New England Journal of Medicine and Surgery* (Oct. 1816), pp. 321–38.

47   **William Oakes:** For more information on this leader among the botanists, see Robert L. Goodale, "William Oakes, Pioneer Botanist in the White Mountains," *Appalachia* (Dec. 1969), pp. 579–85. See also William Oakes, *Scenery of the White Mountains* (Boston: Little, Brown, 1848; reprinted Somersworth, N.H.: New Hampshire Publishing, 1970).

"**There is now no corner**": Quoted by Pease, "Notes," p. 168.

"**Dark ravine**": *Ibid.*

Tuckerman is credited: Sweetser, *White Mountains*, p. 153.

"**Erect and vigorous**": Samuel Adams Drake, recalling the impressions of Dr. Samuel A. Bemis, in an interview reported in *White Mountain Echo*, Sept. 4, 1897, p. 2.

48   "**Honest, simple minded**": Capt. Oscar Coles, "The White Mountains in 1823: Recollections of an Observing Octogenarian Who Visited Them in Boyhood," *White Mountain Echo*, Sept. 19, 1896, p. 8.

"**Very deaf**": All quoted phrases in this sentence are found in the previously cited unidentified letter of 1834, in the manuscript collections of the New Hampshire Historical Society. Reprinted with permission.

The lack of pretty girls: *Ibid.*

Another visitor: Joseph Barrett, letter to "Dr. Torrey," Apr. 1, 1834, quoted by Pease, "Notes," p. 166.

"**He is a large man**": N. P. Willis, *American Scenery* (New York: Virtue & Yorston, n.d. [1840?]), vol. 1, p. 133.

CHAPTER 6. THE MONUMENT LINE SURVEYORS ON KATAHDIN

49   "**Prince of eastern mountains**": William Clark Larrabee, "The Backwoods Expedition," in *Rosabower: A Collection of Essays and Miscellaneous*, quoted by Edward S. C. Smith, "Larrabee and 'The Backwoods Expedition,' " *Appalachia*, (Feb. 1926), p. 287.

"**It stood alone**": *Ibid.*

"**Unbroken, silent**": *Ibid.*, p. 288.

50   "**A mountain which**": Letter from Belknap to Cutler, Nov. 18, 1785, in *Life of Cutler*, p. 235. Belknap here passes along to Cutler an account of a journey in Maine by another member of the 1784 Washington party, Daniel Little.

Maine was part: Turner's account of the first recorded ascent of Katahdin was published in the form of a letter written in the summer of 1804, in Masssachusetts Historical Society, *Collections*, vol. 8 (2nd series), pp. 112–16. All quoted phrases and other information in this and the subsequent two paragraphs are from his letter.

51   **In October 1819:** Excerpts from the 1819 journals of Colin Campbell are in the Barclay Papers of the Maine Historical Society, box 6. However, the entries for Oct. 13–19 are missing. A manuscript for part of this period is in the collections of John W. Hakola.

52   **In August 1820:** An account of this ascent, apparently written by Daniel Rose, was found and published with notes by L. Felix Ranlett, in "Third Recorded Ascent of Katahdin, Aug. 10, 1820," *Appalachia* (June 1968), pp. 43–52.

       In 1825 Joseph C. Norris: The field notes kept by Joseph Norris, as well as a large number of other early surveyors' records are preserved in a remarkable collection of archives at the James W. Sewall Company in Old Town, Maine. Our quotations are reprinted with permission. Extracts from the accounts of Norris in 1825, as well as Edwin Rose in 1833, were published by Myron Avery in "The Monument Line Surveyors on Katahdin," *Appalachia* (June 1928), pp. 33–43; reprinted with permission of the Appalachian Mountain Club. This article also provides valuable perspective on the surveyors' trips. (Curiously, Avery omits mention of the Webber-Bradley survey of 1832.)

54   **"Steep and broken":** These and other quoted words are from Norris's field notes.

55   **Five years after:** The 1832 journey is described in the field notes of John Webber, in the collections of the James W. Sewall Company.

56   **"Which is extremely dangerous":** These and other quoted words are from Rose's account, as reprinted in Avery, "Monument Line Surveyors," pp. 41–42.

CHAPTER 7. JANUS ON THE HEIGHTS DURING THE 1820S

57   **Timothy Dwight:** Timothy Dwight, *Travels in New England and New-York.* (A useful edition is edited by Barbara Miller Solomon (Cambridge, Mass.: The Harvard University Press, Belknap Press, 1969); the original was published in four volumes in 1821 and 1822).

       The Blue Hills: Bacon, *Walks and Rides*, p. 339; Mark L. Primack, *Greater Boston: Park and Recreation Guide* (Chester, Conn.: The Globe Pequot Press, 1983), p. 76; and *The Historic Blue Hills*, a pamphlet prepared by the Friends of the Blue Hills, p. 5.

       "Blew down": *The Historic Blue Hills*, p. 5.

       "Three stories high": Bacon, *Walks and Rides*, p. 339.

58   **Meanwhile, however, the prototype:** A complete description of the building of the Prospect House is in Henry M. Burt, Burt's *Illustrated Guide of the Connecticut Valley* (Springfield, Mass.: New England Publishing Co., 1866), pp. 84–85, 221–35. A description of it at a later stage is in John Eden, *The Mt. Holyoke Hand-Book and Tourists' Guide; for Northampton and Its Vicinity* (Northampton, Mass.: Hopkins, Bridgman, 1851), p. 17.

       "A most beautiful prospect": Jedidiah Morse, *Geography Made Easy* (Boston: Thomas & Andrews, 1813), p. 127.

       "A place of": Alden Partridge, letter to *American Monthly Magazine and Critical Review* (Dec. 1818), p. 126.

58   **"A little water"**: Burt, *Illustrated Guide*, p. 222.

In 1825 it rated: G. M. Davison, *The Fashionable Tour in 1825* (Saratoga Springs, N.Y.: published by the author, 1825), p. 150.

Travel accounts: Dwight, *Travels*, pp. 317, 352–57, 380–82; Philip M. Perry, "Banfield's Harvest," *New England Galaxy* (Fall 1975), pp. 19–24.

59   **The state's highest:** Myron Avery, "The Appalachian Trail: Massachusetts," *Appalachia* (Dec. 1932), p. 317. Some errors in that article may be corrected by reference to Susan Denault, "The Jeremiah Wilbur Homestead," unpublished manuscript in the files of the Berkshire County Regional Planning Commission. For discussion of the evidence concerning the precise location of Wilbur's road (see figure 7.1), the authors are grateful to Susan Denault (letter to L&GW, July 11, 1986) and Lauren R. Stevens (letter to L&GW, May 8, 1986). These two authorities on Greylock history provided interesting analyses of this historical puzzle.

On May 12, 1830: "Saddle Mountain" (a common name for Greylock then), *American Advocate*, May 19, 1830, p. 27.

"A visionary scheme": *Ibid*.

The prime mountaintop: The definitive study of the Catskill Mountain House is Roland Van Zandt, *The Catskill Mountain House* (New Brunswick, N.J.: Rutgers University Press, 1966). For other aspects of its early history, see also Evers, *Catskills*, pp. 308–9, 313, 351–54.

"Rural Ball": Evers, *Catskills*, pp. 352–53.

61   **"An early symbol":** Van Zandt, *Catskill Mountain House*, p. ix.

62   **Meanwhile in southern:** For Monadnock, the prime source is Allen Chamberlain, *Annals of the Grand Monadnock* (Concord, N.H.: Society for the Protection of New Hampshire Forests, 1936; reprinted 1975). for dates of early trails on Monadnock, see also Henry Ives Baldwin, *Monadnock Guide*, 3rd ed. (Concord, N.H.: Society for the Protection of New Hampshire Forests, 1980), pp. 87–100.

"A fashionable place": "Hermit" (author), "The Grand Monadnock," *New Hampshire* [Keene] *Sentinel*, Sept. 30, 1825, p. 1.

"Erected a convenient building": Josiah Amadon, "Grand Monadnock Hotel," *New Hampshire Sentinel*, Aug. 15, 1823, p. 3.

In 1824 John Fife: John Fife, "Monadnock Entertainment," *New Hampshire Sentinel*, Aug. 6, 1824, p. 3: and Fife, "Monadnock Entertainment, 4th of July," *New Hampshire Sentinel*, June 17, 1825, p. 3. See also Chamberlain, *Annals*, pp. 41–44.

Even more substantial: Thomas Dinsmore, "Monadnock Mountain," *New Hampshire Sentinel*, July 21, 1826, p. 3; Chamberlain, *Annals*, pp. 45–47. The authors are indebted to Richard A. Scaramelli for showing them the foundations of Dinsmore's "shantee" and the inscribed rock, Apr. 25, 1984.

63 **Definite evidence:** The authors enjoyed the assistance of Dan H. Allen, Natalie Davis, Nancy L. Rich, and the warden atop Kearsarge South in attempting to locate the oldest initials on the summit rock, Apr. 28, 1984.

64 **"During the last":** William G. Brooks, "Journal of an Excursion to Manchester, Vermont, by a Party of the Norwich Cadets, 1823." Manuscript in the collections of the Vermont Historical Society. Reprinted with permission.

"The rich and diversified": Davison, *Fashionable Tour*, p. 165.

A corresponding tribute: Lafayette's visit to Windsor may be glimpsed in A. LeVasseur, *Lafayette in America in 1824 and 1825* (Philadelphia: Carey & Lea, 1829), vol. 2, p. 212; Mary Grace Canfield, *Lafayette in Vermont* (Woodstock, Vt.: privately printed, 1934), p. 12; and Jane Bacon MacIntire, *Lafayette, the Guest of the Nation: The Tracing of the Route of Lafayette's Tour of the United States in 1824–25* (Newton, Mass.: Anthony J. Simone Press, 1967), p. 224.

"So that the Kingdoms": Canfield, *Lafayette in Vermont*, p. 12.

65 **One Charles Brodhead:** Field notes for Brodhead's Adirondack survey are in a *Book of Old Records*, no. 11, p. 111, on file at the New York State Archives, Cultural Education Center, Room 11D40, Empire State Plaza, Albany, N.Y. A transcript of these notes is in the archives of the Keene Valley Public Library. For a step-by-step analysis of Brodhead's line, the authors are indebted to a letter from Tony Goodwin, Apr. 2, 1981. Mr. Goodwin also treated this survey in more condensed form in "Exploring Giant," *Adirondack Life* (July–Aug. 1982), p. 30.

"Even today": Letter from Tony Goodwin to L&GW, Apr. 2, 1981. Reprinted with permission.

The southeast corner: Quoted phrases throughout this paragraph are from Brodhead's field notes, p. 111.

66 **Adirondack historians:** See Carson, *Peaks and People*, p. 126.

67 **Besides Brodhead:** For other surveyors' activities on high peaks, see Carson, *Peaks and People*, pp. 88, 109, 17–18.

PART TWO. MOUNTAINS AS SUBLIME: 1830–1870

69 **European perceptions:** For the European background, see Edmund Burke, *A Philosophical Inquiry into the Origin of Our Ideas of the Sublime and Beautiful*, ed. by Charles W. Eliot (New York: P. F. Collie & Son, 1909), and Nicolson, *Mountain Gloom*.

"During the first": Nicolson, *Mountain Gloom*, p. 3.

The new attitudes: For changing American perceptions of wilderness during the 1830–70 period, see *Nash, Wilderness and the American Mind: Huth, Nature and the American;* Raymond J. O'Brien, *American Sublime: Landscape and Scenery of the Lower Hudson Valley* (New York: Columbia University Press, 1981); and Leo Marx, *The Machine in the Garden: Technology and the*

Pastoral Ideal in America (New York: Oxford University Press, 1964). A vivid discussion of how pre-Civil War visitors saw the Northeastern wilderness as both terrifying and compelling is found in Philip Terrie, *Forever Wild: Environmental Aesthetics and the Adirondack Forest Preserve* (Philadelphia: Temple University Press, 1985), pp. 44–67.

70   **"Enthusiasm for wilderness"**: Nash, *Wilderness and the American Mind,* p. 51.

Nine attributes: Burke, *A Philosophical Inquiry;* the nine attributes of the sublime are discussed on pp. 36–74; the quoted passage appears on p.36.

"All that expands": Lord Byron, "Childe Harold's Pilgrimage," canto 3, stanza 62, lines 596–98.

71   **"Almost everything":** Belknap, *History,* p. 51.

Timothy Dwight: Dwight, *Travels.*

Dwight specifically uses: *Ibid.,* p. 377.

"Grand and sublime": Partridge, letter to *American Monthly Magazine and Critical Review* (Nov. 1818), pp. 51–52.

By 1825: Davison, *Fashionable Tour,* p. 28; and ("truly majestic"), p. 41.

"The sublime and awful": Joseph T. Buckingham, *Personal Memoirs and Recollections of Editorial Life* (Boston: Ticknor, Reed, & Fields, 1852), p. 172.

A visiting minister: B. K. Z. (Fred Hall), *A Trip from Boston to Littleton through the Notch of the White Mountains* (Washington, D.C.: Jacob Gideon, Jr., 1836), p. 11, and ("sublime in the highest"), p. 28. The Reverend Hall's trip was taken in 1833.

72   **"More absolutely isolated":** Thomas Wentworth Higginson, "Going to Katahdin," *Putnam's Monthly Magazine* (Sept. 1856): p. 244.

In art: Treatments of the Hudson River school and its attention to mountain scenery may be found in James Thomas Flexner, *That Wilder Image: The Painting of America's Native School from Thomas Cole to Winslow Homer* (New York: Dover Publications, 1962); Barbara Novak, *American Painting of the Nineteenth Century: Realism, Idealism, and the American Experience* (New York: Praeger, Publishers, 1969); and John W. McCoubrey, *American Art, 1700–1960: Sources and Documents* (Englewood Cliffs, N.J.: Prentice-Hall, Inc., 1965). The White Mountain artists are described in Catherine H. Campbell, *New Hampshire Scenery: A Dictionary of Nineteenth Century Artists of New Hampshire Mountain Landscapes* (Canaan, N.H.: Phoenix Publishing, 1985). Adirondack artists are similarly covered in a series of many articles appearing in *Adirondac* magazine during the years 1984–87 under the authorship of Peggy O'Brien.

Some critics: See, for example, *The White Mountains: Places and Perceptions,* a brochure to accompany a 1980–81 exhibition; Catherine H. Campbell, "Artists in the White Mountains," in *Edward Hill: A Man of His Time*

(1843–1923), a brochure to accompany a 1985 exhibition at Plymouth State College, Plymouth, N.H., pp. 7–12 (especially p. 10); and C. Francis Belcher, "Early White Mountain Scientists, Artists, and Writers," in Frank R. Kenison and Sherman Adams, *The Enterprise of the North Country* (New York: Newcomen Society in North America, 1980), p. 20.

73   **"[September 3, 1844]":** Richard W. Hale, *The Story of Bar Harbor* (New York: Ives Washburn, 1949), p. 126.

One astute innkeeper: This was S. W. Thompson, who opened his tavern in North Conway in 1840. See "A Live Resort: The Beginning of North Conway and How It Has Risen into Fame," *White Mountain Echo*, Sept. 3, 1892, p. 1.

As the Hudson: The writers of the period are best read in their original works. See Ralph Waldo Emerson's essay on "Nature," William Cullen Bryant's poem, "Thanatopsis," Nathaniel Hawthorne's short stories cited in our text, and Henry David Thoreau's mountain writings, which have been conviently assembled in William Howarth, ed., *Thoreau in the Mountains: Writings by Henry David Thoreau* (New York: Farrar Strauss Giroux, 1982).

"I think 'tis": Emerson, "Country Life," quoted in Aaron Sussman and Ruth Goode, *The Magic of Walking* (New York: Simon and Schuster, 1967), p. 357.

"Go forth": Bryant, "Thanatopsis," lines 14–15.

Henry David Thoreau: Thoreau's celebrated anthem to wilderness values is *Walden: or Life in the Woods* (originally published in 1854; see the accessible Riverside edition, Boston: Houghton Mifflin, 1893). He recounted his first trip to the White Mountains in *A Week on the Concord and Merrimack Rivers* (originally published in 1849; see the edition edited by C. Horde, Princeton: Princeton University Press, 1980). His second trip there was related in his *Journals*, vol. 17, pp. 21–36, covering May 2–12, 1858 (Bradford Torrey, ed.; Boston: Houghton Mifflin, 1906). The Katahdin climb was originally described in a series of five articles, "Ktaadn and the Maine Woods," *Union Magazine*, 1848, but the series is best known now for its inclusion in a book called *The Maine Woods* (originally published in 1864; a modern edition is Dudley C. Lunt, ed., New York: Bramwell House, 1950). A convenient compilation is Howarth's *Thoreau in the Mountains*, cited earlier. Useful analyses of Thoreau's trips to Katahdin are Robert C. Cosbey, "Thoreau on Katahdin," *Appalachia* (June 1961), pp. 409–11; and Howarth's commentary in *Thoreau in the Mountains*, pp. 141–52. For discussion of his second trip to the White Mountains, see Frederick W. Kilbourne, "Thoreau and the White Mountains," *Appalachia* (June 1919), pp. 356–67; Richard B. Erickson, "Transcendentalists among the Hills," *New England Galaxy* (Summer, 1975), pp. 43–50; Howarth, *Thoreau in the Mountains*, pp. 252–66; and Chris Stewart, "Savaged in the Wilds: Thoreau's Mount Washington Misadventures," *Appalachia* (Summer 1984), pp. 32–39.

74   **Fannie Hardy Eckstorm:** Quoted by Hakola, *Legacy of a Lifetime*, p. 16.

74   **"Puns flying off"**: Cornelius Mathews, "Several Days in the Berkshires," *Literary World* (August 24, 1850), p. 145.

"We scattered": Evert Duyckinck, then editor of the *Literary World*. Quoted in Richard D. Birdsall, *Berkshire County: A Cultural History* (New Haven: Yale University Press, 1959), p. 360.

The White Hills: The most complete biography of King is Charles W. Wendte, *Thomas Starr King: Patriot and Preacher* (Boston: Beacon Press, 1921). See also Lawrence Shaw Mayo, *Three Essays: An Appreciation with a Biography* (Boston: privately printed, 1948). Briefer but more accessible profiles are those of Kilbourne, *Chronicles*, pp. 128–131; and L. S. Mayo, "The White Mountains in Three Centuries," *Appalachia* (Dec. 1950), pp. 202–3.

75   **A rumor that**: Kilbourne, *Chronicles*, p. 128.

"There is no such": King, *The White Hills*, pp. 324–26. Remaining quoted passages are from pp. 103, 383, 156, 46 (not directly quoted), 266–67, 308, 288, 5, 9–10, 7, and 203–4, in that order.

77   **The grand style**: See, for example, a wry passage in A. E. P. Searing, *The Land of Rip Van Winkle: A Tour through the Romantic Parts of the Catskills, its Legends and Traditions* (New York: G. P. Putnam's Sons, 1884), p. 2.

"Will never be equaled": Kilbourne, *Chronicles*, p. 130.

CHAPTER 8. THE FIRST MOUNTAIN TOURISTS

79   **The artists, writers**: The economic changes in the hill country of northern New England during the period 1830–70 form an important backdrop for the growth of mountain tourism and can be studied in Harold Fisher Wilson, *Hill Country of Northern New England: Its Social and Economic History, 1790–1930* (New York: Columbia University Press, 1936), and Charles E. Clark, *The Eastern Frontier: The Settlement of Northern New England* (New York: Alfred A. Knopf, 1970). For economic developments in the Catskills, see Evers, *Catskills*, chap. 46–48, 53–59.

A detailed study: Peter B. Bulkley, "Identifying the White Mountain Tourist, 1853–1854: Origin, Occupation, and Wealth as a Definition of the Early Hotel Trade," *Historical New Hampshire* (Summer 1980), pp. 106–62; the quoted passage appears on p. 124.

A traveler coming: "A Moosehead Jornal," *Putnam's Monthly* (Nov. 1853), p. 457.

A man who had: Elon Jessup, "Up Vermont Way," *Outing*, March 3, 1919, p. 298.

Another, whose farm: Samuel Adams Drake, *The Heart of the White Mountains* (New York: Harper and Brothers, 1882), p. 175.

Starr King asked: King, *The White Hills*, p. 273.

80   **Another farmer**: *Ibid.*, pp. 254–55.

80   **Early chroniclers:** Sweetser, *White Mountains*, p. 193; and Tuckerman's chapter in King, *The White Hills*, p. 43.

The first respectable map: G. P. Bond, "A Map, with Views, of the White Mountains."

Travel to and fro: No one source covers comprehensively the nature of transportation between population centers and mountain resorts during the antebellum years. Information in this section is drawn from a wide variety of railroad brochures, hotel advertising, town histories, and contemporary accounts. For the Catskills, also see Evers, *Catskills*; Van Zandt, *Catskill Mountain House*; and Van Zandt, *Chronicles*. For the White Mountains, see also Kilbourne, *Chronicles*; and Peter B. Bulkley, "A History of the White Mountain Tourist Industry, 1818–1899" (master's thesis, University of New Hampshire, 1975). For prerail river travel, see Elizabeth D. Levers, "The Hudson Was Their Highway," in AMC, *In the Hudson Highlands*, especially pp. 158–60.

82   **These were the years:** See Van Zandt, *Catskill Mountain House*, and Evers, *Catskills*.

Harriet Martineau: Harriet Martineau, selection from "Retrospect of Western Travel," in Van Zandt, *Chronicles*, p. 335.

In the White Mountains: A useful compendium of White Mountain hotel activity is Donald A. Lapham, *Former White Mountain Hotels* (New York: Carlton Press, 1975). See also much information in Kilbourne, *Chronicles*, and Bulkley, "White Mountain Tourist Industry."

Horace Fabyan: An interesting study of this important figure is Peter B. Bulkley, "Horace Fabyan, Founder of the White Mountain Grand Hotel," *Historical New Hampshire* (Summer 1975), pp. 53–77.

In Vermont: See Robert L. Hagerman, *Mansfield: The Story of Vermont's Loftiest Mountain* (Canaan, N.H.: Phoenix Publishing, 1975), pp. 57–62; Edwin L. Bigelow and Nancy H. Otis, *Manchester, Vermont: A Pleasant Land among the Mountains, 1761–1961* (published by the town of Manchester, 1961); Harriet Myers Fish, *The Westmore Story: A Bicentennial Project* (pamphlet dated 1976); and for a contemporary view, Zadock Thompson, *Northern Guide: Lake George, Lake Champlain, Montreal and Quebec, Green and White Mountains and Willoughby Lake* (Burlington, Vt.: S. B. Nichols, 1854). The quote about Lake Willoughby's accessiblity appears on p. 37 of the last named.

The Berkshires: See R. Dewitt Mallary, *Lenox and Berkshire Highlands* (New York: G. P. Putnam's Sons, 1902), especially pp. 28–45; Electa F. Jones, *Stockbridge, Past and Present; or, Records of an Old Mission Station* (Springfield, Mass.: Samuel Bowles, 1854); Allen T. Treadway, *Souvenir of the Red Lion Inn*, a brochure in the collections of the Berkshire Athenaeum, Pittsfield, Mass.; and Clark W. Bryan, *The Book of Berkshire: Describing and Illustrating Its Hills and Homes for the Season of 1887* (Great Barrington, Mass. and Springfield, Mass.: Clark W. Bryan, 1887), pp. 35, 60.

84   **The first hotel:** The story of Mount Washington's summit buildings is recounted in most of the major books about the mountain. See, for example, Kilbourne, *Chronicles*, chap. 11.

87   **South of the White:** Chamberlain, *Annals*, pp. 48–52, 34–37.

88   **Mount Mansfield:** Mansfield's summit developments are well covered in Hagerman, *Mansfield*, chap. 8–11. Except as otherwise noted, our information is from this source.

    "An occasional trip": "Trip to Mansfield Mountain," *Burlington Free Press*, Sept. 6, 1859, p. 2.

    "A far more complete": S. C. Eastman, *White Mountain Guide* (1864 ed.), p. 227.

    "The Astor House": "Adventures on a Mountain Top," *The Knickerbocker* (Apr. 1860), p. 363.

89   **Camel's Hump:** J. H. R., "How to Reach Camel's Hump, Green Mountain House, Messrs. Ridley & Sons, North Duxbury, Vermont," *Burlington Free Press*, July 31, 1860, p. 2. See also Lyle S. Woodward and Stanley Chase, *The Camel's Hump Story*, a typed brochure of the Waterbury Historical Society, p. 4. The local experts on the history of Camel's Hump, John Willey and William Gove, were most helpful to the authors.

    Ascutney: Frank H. Clark, *Glimpses of Ascutney* (Bradford, Vt.: The Opinion Press, 1905), p. 11.

90   **Burke Mountain:** Bradford F. Swan, "Joseph Seavey Hall: White Mountain Guide," *Appalachia*, (June 1960), p. 58.

    Lake Willoughby: Fish, *The Westmore Story*, and letter from Norman R. Atwood to L&GW, Oct. 4, 1982.

    Maine: Richard Rollins Wescott, "Economic, Social and Governmental Aspects of the Development of Maine's Vacation Industry, 1850–1920" (master's thesis, University of Maine, Orono, 1961); Cleveland Amory, *The Last Resorts* (New York: Harper and Brothers, 1952); Charles B. Fobes, "Pleasant Mountain, Maine," *Appalachia* (June 1952), pp. 60–67; and George B. Dorr, "Our Seacoast National Park," *Appalachia* (Aug. 1921), pp. 174–82.

    One of the more bizarre: The authors are indebted to Theodore C. Tryon of the James W. Sewall Company, Old Town, Maine, for pointing out the map and field notes for this project both of which are in the archives of the Sewall Company. Quoted passages are from the handwritten field notes of David Haynes, surveyor. Reprinted with permission.

91   **There is no record:** Charles B. Fobes, "Mt. Kineo, Maine," *Appalachia* (June 1976), pp. 521–27.

    The horses bagged: B. K. Z. (Fred Hall), *A Trip from Boston*, p. 23.

    "Though it is": James G. Carter, "A Geography of New Hampshire," quoted in Chamberlain, *Annals*, p. 1.

93   **Katahdin filled this:** The best summary of Katahdin ascents, as well as the backdrop of its increasing accessibility during the period 1830–70 is given in Hakola, *Legacy of a Lifetime*, pp. 11–29.

    "Lodestone of great power": This apt phrase was applied by Percival Sayward in "A Winter Ascent of Mt. Ktaadn," *Appalachia* (June 1915), p. 227.

94   **First serious botanical investigations:** Jacob W. Bailey, "Account of an Excursion to Mount Katahdin in Maine," *American Journal of Science & Arts* (July 1837), pp. 20–34. The same article also ran in *The Maine Monthly Magazine*, vol. 1 (1837), p. 54ff. Quoted passages in this paragraph are from pp. 22, 24, and 31–32 of the former version.

95   **Another 1836 party:** The Rev. Joseph Blake, "An Excursion to Mount Katahdin," *Maine Naturalist*, vol. 6, no. 2 (June 1926), pp. 71–73.

    Charles Thomas Jackson: Jackson's life is described in Allen Johnson, ed., *Dictionary of American Biography* (New York: Charles Scribner's Sons, 1927); and in Dirk J. Struik, *Yankee Science in the Making* (Boston: Little, Brown, 1948), pp. 247–49. He published the results of his Maine survey work as *Reports on the Geology of the State of Maine* (Augusta, Maine: Smith & Robinson, three annual reports, 1837–1839).

    Saddleback and Bigelow: Jackson, *Third Annual Report* (1839), pp. 109–11.

96   **In the Presidentials:** Frank H. Burt, "The Nomenclature of the White Mountains," *Appalachia* (Dec. 1915), p. 376.

    "His was a wonderful": Struik, *Yankee Science*, p. 249.

    After some lesser climbs: Jackson, *First Annual Report* (1837), pp. 45–47, 55–57; *Second Annual Report* (1838), p. 149.

    Party to Katahdin: Jackson, *Second Annual Report* (1838), pp. 10–20. However, the trip is best described in Larrabee, "The Backwoods Expedition." William Larrabee was a thirty-four-year-old schoolteacher, and his account is the most vivid and interesting of Katahdin before Thoreau's. It is retold with useful commentary by Edward S. C. Smith, "Larrabee and 'the Backwoods Expedition,'" *Appalachia* (Feb. 1926), pp. 284–90.

    Hale and Channing: Edward Everett Hale. "An Early Ascent of Katahdin," *Appalachia* (Apr. 1901), pp. 277–89. This article includes a narrative originally appearing in the *Boston Daily Advertiser*, Aug. 15, 1845.

97   **"Steep and hard":** This and other quoted phrases in this paragraph are from Hale, "An Early Ascent," pp. 285–88.

98   **The Rev. Marcus Keep:** Keep awaits a biographer, who will do his remarkable personality justice. The only profile of consequence is in Hakola, *Legacy of a Lifetime*, pp. 16–19. Otherwise the fragments of the portrait remain disassembled, chiefly in three sources: (1) a letter signed "S. C.," dated July 18, 1906, from Presque Isle in *Bangor* [Maine] *Daily Commercial*, July 21, 1906, p. 4; S. C. is identified as Sidney Cook in the same newspaper one week later

(July 28, 1906, p. 16); (2) the Rev. Joseph Blake, "A Second Excursion to Katahdin," *Maine Naturalist* (June 1926), p. 74; and (3) Frederick Sumner Davenport, "Some Pioneers of Moosehead, Chesuncook, & Millinocket," *The Northern* (Nov. 1922), p. 6. The characterizations of Keep that we quote are drawn from these three sources.

98   **In 1847 Keep led:** Keep wrote up this journey in "Mount Katahdin," *The Democrat* (Bangor, Maine), Dec. 7, 1847, p. 1. See also Fannie Hardy Eckstorm, *The Penobscot Man* (Somersworth, N.H.: New Hampshire Publishing Company, 1972; a facsimile of the original 1924 ed.), pp. 108–12.

99   **Within a month:** Keep, "Mount Katahdin," *The Democrat*, Dec. 7, 1847, p. 1.

     The next summer: Hakola, *Legacy of a Lifetime*, pp. 18–19. See also Myron H. Avery, "The Keep Path and Its Successors," *Appalachia* (Dec. 1928), especially pp. 135–41.

     Hannah Taylor ascent: Marcus R. Keep, letters to *The Democrat:* "Mount Katahdin—Again," Oct. 9, 1849, p. 2; "Mount Katahdin—Again (Continued), a Sermon Preached upon Mount Katahdin, on Sunday, Aug. 19, 1849," Oct. 16, 1849, p. 2; and "Mount Katahdin—Again (Concluded)," Oct. 23, 1849, p. 2. The ill-fated naming of the peaks may be found in the Oct. 23 issue.

     State geological team: Keep, "Maine's Scientific Survey," *Aroostook* [Maine] *Times*, Aug. 23, 1861, p. 2; and subsequent accounts under the same title in the issues of Aug. 30, p. 2; Sept. 6, p. 2; Sept 13, p. 2; and Sept. 20, p. 2, all in 1861. See also *Sixth Annual Report of the Secretary of the Maine Board of Agriculture* (1861), pp. 394–99.

     Not until 1881: Charles E. Hamlin, "Routes to Ktaadn," *Appalachia* (Dec. 1881), p. 323.

100   **In 1847 a small squad:** George Thurber, "Notes of an Excursion to Mount Katahdin," *Providence Journal*, Sept. 26, 1847. In the same month an account also appeared in the *Bangor* [Maine] *Whig and Courier*, signed "By One of the Party," and entitled "Dr. Young's Botanical Expedition to Mount Katahdin," in the issues of Sept. 7, 8, 9, 10, and 11, 1847. These two were reprinted in *Maine Naturalist*, under the following titles: George Thurber, "Notes of an Excursion to Mount Katahdin" (Dec. 1926), pp. 134–51; and J. K. Laski, "Dr. Young's Botanical Expedition to Mount Katahdin" (June 1927), pp. 38–62.

     Another minister: John Todd, *Summer Gleanings or Sketches and Incidents of a Pastor's Vacation* (Northampton, Mass.: Hopkins, Bridgman, 1852), pp. 121–32.

     William L. Jones: Letter from William L. Jones to his brother, Apr. 19, 1853, published in *Lewiston* [Maine] *Journal*, Nov. 5, 1927, p. A-1. In Hakola, *Legacy of a Lifetime*, p. 21, this trip is erroneously dated Apr., 1853 (the date of the letter); the trip itself was in August, apparently the summer before. This point is of passing importance, since an April ascent, as Hakola points out, might have involved a formidable amount of snow and in many respects deserved much more attention as exceptionally early and quasi-winter climbing. No such luck: it was just another summer climb.

100 **A large party:** Unsigned (but attributed to Thomas Wentworth Higginson), "Going to Mount Katahdin," *Putnam's Monthly Magazine* (Sept. 1856), pp. 242–56. Higginson's authorship is cited in Allen Chamberlain, "When Colonel T. W. Higginson Was a Guide to Katahdin in 1855 and Now," *Boston Evening Transcript*, July 14, 1923, p. v-1. An odd aspect of the Higginson trip was how it came to be written up. The story came out in *Putnam's Monthly Magazine* for September 1856, apparently written by one of the women members of the party, who, however, did not disclose her name. Years later, shortly before his death, Colonel Higginson confessed his authorship.

The Rev. Joseph Blake: The Rev. Joseph Blake, "A Second Excursion to Mount Katahdin," pp. 74–79.

A Bowditch party: Henry I. Bowditch, "Life in the Woods for a Fortnight on a Trip to Katahdin, Moosehead Lake, in the Summer of 1856," an unpublished manuscript, later printed as "A Trip to Katahdin in 1856," in *Appalachia* (Dec. 1958), pp. 145–62, and (June 1959), pp. 331–48.

Col. Luther B. Rogers: Myron H. Avery, "The Keep Path and Its Successors (Conclusion)," *Appalachia* (June 1929), p. 226.

In 1856 Frederic Church: Theodore Winthrop, *Life in the Open Air* (New York: United States Book Company, 1863), pp. 3–119.

CHAPTER 10. THE ADIRONDACKS AT LAST

101 **In 1835 Eaton:** Events leading up to the survey of 1836–42 are described in Mary C. Rabbitt, *Minerals, Lands and Geology for the Common Defence and General Welfare*, vol. 1; Before 1879 (Washington, D.C.: Government Printing Office, 1979).

102 **Emmons and Hall:** Emmons's career is described in profiles in Jules Marcou, "Biographical Notice of Ebenezer Emmons," *American Geologist* (Jan. 1891), pp. 1–23; "Sketch of Dr. Emmons," *Williams Quarterly* (June 1864), pp. 260–69; and Charles Coulston Gillispie, ed., *Dictionary of Scientific Biography* (New York: Charles Scribner's Sons, 1970–1976). Hall's life and character are outlined in John M. Clarke, *James Hall of Albany: Geologist and Palaeontologist, 1811–1898* (Albany, N.Y.: printer not indicated, 1921); and in Gillispie, *Dictionary of Scientific Biography*.

A letter from Emmons: In papers of James Hall, manuscript collections of the New York State Library. See also, in these papers, a letter from Ebenezer Emmons, Jr., to Hall, unfortunately undated, asking Hall to lend *him* fifty dollars. It should be noted that sums like four hundred dollars or even fifty dollars were substantial in the 1830s.

102   **William C. Redfield:** Redfield's career is described in Gillispie, *Dictionary of Scientific Biography.*

He demonstrated his: Terrie in his introduction to the 1973 edition of Carson, *Peaks and People*, pp. lxii–lxiii. An account of his trip to Ohio was written up by Redfield, "Journal of a Pedestrian Tour from Connecticut to Ohio in 1810," manuscript in the possession of a descendent, Alfred G. Redfield of Lexington, Mass.

103   **"I got the party":** Redfield, "Field Notes" (see next note), p. 2.

In August 1836: The 1836 explorations are described in two documents by Redfield: his own field notes, as loaned by Charles B. Redfield to Verplanck Colvin, copied by Mills Blake in 1875, whose copy in turn was copied by Russell M. L. Carson on Apr. 4, 1926, a typed version of which is in the collections of the Adirondack Museum at Blue Mountain Lake, N.Y., MS 63-273, p. 2, reprinted with permission; and an article, "Some Account of Two Visits to the Mountains in Essex County, New York, in the Years 1836 and 1837," *American Journal of Science and Arts*, 33 (Jan. 1838), pp. 301–23. See also Ebenezer Emmons, *First Annual Report of the Second Geological District of the State of New York*, Assembly Documents, 60th sess. (1837), vol. 2, pp. 97–105. All direct quotes describing the 1836 trip are from Redfield, "Field Notes," pp. 4–8.

105   **"Probably the greatest":** Emmons, *First Annual Report*, p. 103.

The summer of 1837: The 1837 explorations are described in Redfield's two accounts cited above, plus his letter to the *New York Journal of Commerce*, Aug. 24, 1837, p. 2; Ebenezer Emmons, *Second Annual Report of the Second Geological District of the State of New York*, Assembly Documents, 61st Sess. (1838), vol. 4, pp. 240–50; James Hall, letter to *Albany Daily Advertiser*, Aug. 15, 1837, p. 2; and a letter from John Torrey to Benjamin Silliman, Aug. 23, 1837, quoted in Andrew Denny Rodgers III, *John Torrey: A Story of North American Botany* (Princeton: Princeton University Press, 1942), p. 131. An analysis of the historical evidence relating to the ascents may be found in Philip G. Terrie's introduction to the 1973 edition of Carson, *Peaks and People*, pp. xliii–lii. A convenient survey of the 1837 Marcy climb is Terrie's "The High Peak of Essex," *Adirondac*, the magazine of the Adirondack Mountain Club (Aug. 1987), pp. 20–22.

106   **Marcy summit party:** Terrie meticulously examined (Carson, *Peaks and People*, pp. xliii–xlix) the question of who went to Marcy's summit in 1837. Terrie's scholarship necessarily refuted lists of the summit party made by Carson (pp. 53–54), Donaldson (in *History*, vol. 1, p. 152), and the plaque on the summit of Marcy itself, all of which seem to be in error.

"Extraordinary elevation": Redfield, "Some Account," p. 312.

Ice on the vegetation: This is consistently reported in the Marcy accounts: *Ibid.*, p. 315; Redfield, "Field Notes," p. 12; Hall, letter to *Albany Daily Advertiser*; and Torrey, letter to Silliman (Aug. 23, 1837) in Rodgers, *John Torrey.*

106   **"We immediately found"**: Redfield, "Some Account," p. 314. The time of arrival on top is variously reported. While this account gives 10:00 A.M., Redfield's field notes say 12:00 noon (p. 12), and Hall's letter to the *Albany Daily Advertiser* implies they were at least still on top at 2:00 P.M.

107   **"There are probably"**: Emmons, *Natural History of New York, Geology* (final report), 1842, vol. 4, part 2 (Albany, N.Y.: W. & A. White & J. Visscher, 1842), p. 210. Terrie discusses the attitudes toward wilderness on the part of the original Marcy party in his *Forever Wild*, chap. 2.

"Sublime grandeur": Redfield, "Some Account," p. 316.

"Steep and difficult": Emmons, *Geology*, p. 216.

1:00 or 1:20 P.M.: Again, accounts differ on the summit arrival time. Redfield's "Some Account" says 1:00 P.M. (p. 317); the field notes say 1:20 P.M. (p. 13).

Nippletop: Emmons, *Geology*, pp. 219–20.

Cascade: *Ibid.,* p. 229.

108   **Seward**: Carson, *Peaks and People*, p. 92.

The artist, Ingham: Warder Cadbury, "The Improbable Charles C. Ingham," *Adirondac* (Aug. 1987), pp. 23–25.

The same year: Mr. Hogan is quoted in Carson, *Peaks and People*, p. 5; reprinted with permission. Henry J. Raymond is quoted in "The Adirondacks in 1854," *Adirondac* (Sept.–Oct. 1952), p. 81.

109   **"Quite a tourist infestation"**: We are indebted to a letter from Mary MacKenzie, May 5, 1984, for pointing out evidence that Whiteface was being regularly climbed well before the Civil War. The quote is from that letter, reprinted with permission.

Charles Fenno Hoffman: Charles Fenno Hoffman, *Wild Scenes in the Forest* (London: Richard Bentley, 1839).

Farrand Northrop Benedict: Letter from Benedict to Emmons, published in Emmons, *Geology*, p. 195.

Joel T. Headley: Joel T. Headley, *The Adirondack: Or, Life in the Woods* (New York: Baker and Scribner, 1849). A pirated and partial edition appeared in 1850 as *Letters from the Backwoods and the Adirondac* (New York: John S. Taylor, 1850). For a discussion of Headley's various versions, see Philip Terrie's introduction to the 1982 reprint by Harbor Hill Books, pp. 10–14.

Charles Lanman: Charles Lanman, *Adventures in the Wilds of the United States* (Philadelphia: John W. Moore, 1856).

John Cheney: Biographical sketches of Cheney include Ruth V. Riley, "Historical Adirondack Character Series. No. 1. John Cheney, 'The Mighty Hunter,'" *High Spots* (June 1930), pp. 12–13; and Donaldson, History, vol. 1, pp. 168–71. *High Spots* was the regular magazine of the Adirondack

Mountain Club before the start up of *Adirondac*. Colorful contemporary accounts of his guiding include Hoffman, *Wild Scenes in the Forest*, pp. 35–39, 81–90; and Lanman, *Adventures in the Wilds*, pp. 225–36.

110 **"I expected":** Lanman, *Adventures in the Wilds*, p. 229.

"An amicable, kind-hearted": These three tributes are, respectively, from an item labeled "from an unsourced scrapbook," in the biographical vertical file on Cheney, in the collections of the Adirondack Museum, Blue Mountain Lake, N.Y., reprinted with permission; Riley, "John Cheney," p. 12; and Henry Dornburgh, in a pamphlet on the McIntyre Iron Works, quoted in Maitland C. DeSormo, *The Heydays of the Adirondacks* (Saranac Lake, N.Y.: Adirondack Yesteryears, 1974), p. 121.

"This formidable Nimrod": Hoffman, *Wild Scenes in the Forest*, p. 37.

Ascent of Seward: Cheney told this tale to the guidebook writer Edwin R. Wallace, who put it into his *Descriptive Guide to the Adirondacks and Handbook of Travel* (New York: American News Company, 1875), p. 216. The question is analyzed with skepticism by Terrie in his introduction to Carson's *Peaks and People* (1973), p. liii, and by George Marshall in his "Adirondack Guides" chapter in Grace L. Hudowalski, ed., *The Adirondack High Peaks and the Forty-Sixers* (Albany, N.Y.: The Peters Print, 1970), pp. 122–23.

The other guide: Biographical sketches of Holt include Marshall, "Adirondack Guides," pp. 115–19; Carson, "Great Adirondack Guides No. 5: Harvey Holt," *High Spots*, (Jan. 1934), pp. 18–22. Hoffman includes a brief but vivid picture in *Wild Scenes in the Forest*, p. 33.

One rumor: This report is in Nettie Holt Whitney, "Reminiscences of Keene Valley and Personal Experiences," manuscript in the archives of the Keene Valley Library, pp. 30–31. No other substantiation of what seems an unlikely event has been found, and historians are disinclined to believe that any trail to Marcy's summit existed that early: see, for example, Terrie, introduction to Carson, *Peaks and People*, pp. xlix–li. Nevertheless, the possibility cannot be entirely discounted.

John Brown's daughter: Letter from Annie Brown to John Brown, Jr., July 18, 1857, printed in *The Placid Pioneer*, vol. 1, no. 1 (Spring 1968), p. 8.

According to the chronicler: Carson, *Peaks and People*, p. 261.

CHAPTER 11. THE MOUNTAIN GUIDES

111 **First true trail:** Wallace, *Descriptive Guide to the Adirondacks*, p. 144. A charming tale of a trip over Phelps's original trail, some of it long abandoned, is Ed Hale, "Climbers Follow Ghost up Mt. Marcy," *Adirondac* (Dec. 1985), pp. 9–11.

Speaking of guides: Good general descriptions of the nineteenth-century guiding profession's requirements can be found in George Marshall, "Adirondack Guides of the High Peak Area," in Hudowalski, *Adirondack*

High Peaks (1970), pp. 105–31; in a passage in Paul F. Jamieson, ed., *The Adirondack Reader* (Glens Falls, N.Y.: The Adirondack Mountain Club, 1982), pp. 123–30; and in poetic form in T. Morris Longstreth, "The Guide," in *The Sky through Branches* (New York: Century, 1930), pp. 55–59.

113 **"Adirondack" Murray:** William Henry Harrison Murray, *Adventures in the Wilderness, or Camp-Life in the Adirondacks* (Boston: Field & Osgood, 1869), pp. 36, 35, and ("Bronzed and hardy") p. 38. Adirondack Murray will be met in chap. 16.

"If he is": Henry Van Dyke,"Ampersand," in Stuart D. Ludlum, *Exploring the Adirondack Mountains 100 Years Ago* (Utica, N.Y.: Brodock & Ludlum, 1972), p. 59.

114 **"The Maine guide":** "Maine's Guides," *In the Maine Woods* (an annual publication of the Bangor & Aroostook Railroad) (1900), p. 41.

"It is the guide": Palmer H. Langdon, "Down the Penobscot, up Katahdin," *In the Maine Woods* (1912), p. 37.

"Should resemble a general": "A Glimpse into the Wilderness," *The Tech* (publication of the Massachusetts Institute of Technology), Feb. 16, 1888, p. 132.

"Respectful, which": Letter from P. F. Schofield to H. S. Harper, Nov. 29, 1918, recalling a trip taken in or about 1878, in the papers of Alfred L. Donaldson, Adirondack collection of the Saranac Lake Free Library, Saranac Lake, N.Y. Reprinted with permission.

"Who for years": Joseph P. Ranney, "Reminiscences of Keene Valley 1866 to 1881," archives, Keene Valley Library. Reprinted with permission.

"The guides of the north woods": "Maine's Guides," *In the Maine Woods* (1910), p. 41.

115 **"Leatherstocking was losing":** Jamieson, *Adirondack Reader*, p. 128.

White Mountain guides: An example of Crawford employees acting as guides is the reference to "Garland, mountain guide," in the 1834 letter cited in chap. 5. Starr King's description of James Gordon is in *The White Hills*, p. 352. Osgood will be met twice later in this book: as pioneer winter climber (chap. 14) and as builder of the first Great Gulf Trail and the one up Madison by way of the ridge that today bears his name (chap. 20). Randolph's Lowes will be met again in chap. 20. A vivid picture of Jim Clement emerges from a long, handwritten journal kept by his brother in the year 1879; see D. Q. Clement, "Journal: Moosilauke, 1879," in the manuscript collections of the New Hampshire Historical Society.

"There are but few": Sweetser, *White Mountains*, p. 41.

"Being in charge": "Maine's Guides," *In the Maine Woods (1910)*, p. 41.

"For at Kineo": Langdon, "Down the Penobscot," p. 37. Italics added.

116 **Mitchell Sabattis:** Biographical sketches include Ruth V. Riley, "Famous Adirondack Guides No. 8: Mitchell Sabattis," *High Spots* (Oct. 1934), pp. 11–12; Headley, *Letters from the Backwoods*, p. 84; DeSormo, *Heydays*, pp. 122–24; and Donaldson, *History*, vol. 2, pp. 81–87. His conversion from a dissolute early life is described in L. E. Chittenden, *Personal Reminiscences: 1840–1890* (New York: Richmond, Croscup, 1893).

Lyman Eppes, Sr.: Biographical sketches are not as detailed as for the other guides mentioned. Some information may be found in Marshall, "Adirondack Guides," p. 126, and in P. F. Schofield, "A Trip through Indian Pass," *Adirondac* (Nov.–Dec. 1955), pp. 114–17.

Alvah Dunning: Biographical sketches include an obituary in the *Syracuse Sunday Herald*, March 16, 1902; DeSormo, *Heydays*, pp. 126–27; Donaldson, *History*, vol. 2, pp. 105–17; and Marshall, "Adirondack Guides," pp. 120–22.

Bill Nye: Biographical sketches include an unsigned profile, "Billy Nye—His Adventures on Land and Sea!" *Essex County Republican* (Keeseville, N.Y.), Aug. 7, 1890, reprinted with the same title in *The Placid Pioneer* (Summer 1970), pp. 7–12; Mary MacKenzie, "Discoverer of the Hudson's Source," *New York State Conservationist* (Feb.–March 1969), pp. 28–31; Ray Bearse, "The Adventuresome Life of an Unsung Mountain Hero," *Adirondack Life* (Spring 1974), pp. 10–11, 46–48; Marshall, "Adirondack Guides," pp. 124–26; and Terrie's introduction to Carson's *Peaks and People*, pp. lxiv–lxv.

"First ascents": The climbs of Dunning and Nye with Colvin are related in chap. 17.

Orson Schofield Phelps: More attention has been paid to Phelps in Adirondack literature than to any other guide. The writeup that launched his fame was Charles Dudley Warner's 1878 essay, "A Character Study," in *In the Wilderness.* This essay also appeared in *The Atlantic* magazine during the same year. An even earlier description had appeared in Seneca Ray Stoddard's guidebook, *The Adirondacks Illustrated* (Albany, N.Y.: Weed, Parson, 1874), pp. 137–43. Twentieth-century biographical sketches include Herbert McAneny, "Old Mountain Phelps," *High Spots*, vol. 9, no.2 (Apr. 1933), pp. 13–15; DeSormo, *Heydays*, pp. 125–26; and Donaldson, *History*, vol. 2, pp. 53–62.

"Settled down to": McAneny, "Old Mountain Phelps," p. 14. Reprinted with permission.

Several leading clergymen: A pleasing picture of some of these "climbing clerics" is in Peggy O'Brien, "Frederick Baylies Allen (1840–1925)," *Adirondac* (Sept.–Oct. 1985), pp. 19–20.

"He was not": Donaldson, *History*, vol. 2, p. 53.

117 **"Lazy, shiftless":** McAneny, "Old Mountain Phelps," p. 13. Reprinted with permission.

117   "The vulgar estimate": Warner, *In the Wilderness*, p. 89.

"He was a great": Carson, *Peaks and People*, p. 209. Reprinted with permission.

"A little man": Quoted in DeSormo, *Heydays*, p. 125.

"A Character Study": Warner, *In the Wilderness*. these two phrases appear on pp. 86 and 84, respectively. further quoted material from this source maybe found on pp. 87–89, 92, 105, and 120.

118   "Devoted himself": Donaldson, *History*, vol. 2, p. 54.

"Took to posturing": Jamieson, *Adirondack Reader*, p. 126.

"Phelps was a man": Quoted in Carson, *Peaks and People*, pp. 154–55. Reprinted with permission.

"That wily scamp": The phrase is Mary MacKenzie's. See her comments in papers of Russell M. L. Carson, manuscript collections of the Adirondack Museum, Blue Mountain Lake, N.Y., box MS-73-4. Reprinted with permission.

CHAPTER 12. THE AUSTIN SISTERS AND THEIR LEGACY

119   **Austin sisters:** Lucy Crawford, *History*, pp. 50–51. All other information and quotations concerning Mount Washington climbing in this chapter is from this source, pp. 75–81.

121   **Mrs. Daniel Patch:** Little, *History of Warren*, p. 493.

Esther McComb: The first ascent of Mount Esther is an oft-told tale in Adirondack lore; see, for example, Carson, *Peaks and People*, pp. 96–97.

122   **Mary Cook and Fannie Newton:** Carson, *Peaks and People*, pp. 67–68. Reprinted with permission.

Mr. and Mrs. B. J. Lossing: Benson J. Lossing, *The Hudson: From the Wilderness to the Sea* (Troy, N.Y.: H. B. Nims, 1866), pp. 4–40.

Keene Valley woman: Typescript entitled "Material about Keene Valley in the Diaries of Elizabeth Baldwin Camp Russ 1854–1939," in the manuscript collections of the archives, Keene Valley Library.

123   **Mrs. E. Oakes Smith and Hannah Taylor Keep:** Marcus R. Keep, letters to *The Democrat:* "Mount Katahdin—Again," Oct. 9, 1849, p. 2; "Mount Katahdin—Again (Continued), a Sermon Preached upon Mount Katahdin, on Sunday, Aug. 19, 1849," Oct. 16, 1849, p. 2; and "Mount Katahdin—Again (Concluded)," Oct. 23, 1849, p. 2.

Higginson Party: Unsigned (attributed to T. W. Higginson), "Going to Mount Katahdin," pp. 242–56. See chap. 9 for additional description and full source information.

112 **Edward Hitchcock:** Our principal source for information on the elder Hitchcock's career is a biographical sketch by Frederick Tuckerman, "President Edward Hitchcock," *Amherst Graduates' Quarterly* (Nov. 1920), pp. 3–13. Hitchcock wrote prolifically for newspapers and periodicals, and many of these pieces are cited in references that follow.

By 1817, at age twenty-four: Letters to Professor Silliman can be found in the archives of Amherst College; see especially ones dated Sept. 1, 1817, and Sept. 28, 1818.

"The neglect of": A copy of this address, delivered before the Mechanical Association at Andover Theological Seminary on Sept. 21, 1830, is in the Amherst College Archives.

"Mechanical or agricultural": *Ibid.*

"Among the mountains": Sketch "by the editor," "How a Poor Boy Became One of the Greatest of Men," *The Christian Advocate*, Apr. 14, 1892, p. 256.

Hitchcock himself explored: Our list of mountains climbed by Hitchock is compiled from a multiplicity of sources, the most useful of which are four: (1) *Reminiscences of Amherst College, Historical, Scientific, Biographical and Autobiographical* (Northampton, Mass.: Bridgman & Childs, 1863); (2) his *Final Report on the Geology of Massachusetts* (Amherst, Mass.: J. S. & C. Adams, 1841), especially vol. 1: pp. 234–50; (3) a series of articles he wrote, all called "History of Western Masssachusetts," all in the *Springfield Daily Republican*, May 8, 15, 22, 1854, all on p. 1; and (4) a chapter on geology, that he contributed to Josiah Gilbert Holland, *History of Western Massachusetts* (Springfield, Mass.: Samuel Bowles, 1855).

126 **"The gem of Massachusetts mountains":** Hitchcock chap. in Holland, *History of Western Massachusetts*, p. 384.

"Down to the last": A tribute quoted by Frederick Tuckerman in his biographical sketch in *Amherst Graduates' Quarterly*, p. 12.

Arnold Henri Guyot: Guyot's life and character are unfolded in an unsigned obituary, "Professor Arnold Henry Guyot," *New York Daily Tribune*, Feb. 9, 1884, p. 5; another obituary, unsigned and untitled, in *Transactions* of the New York Academy of Science, vol. 3 (1883–84), pp. 66–68; William Libbey, Jr., "The Life and Scientific Work of Arnold Guyot," *American Geographical and Social Journal*, vol. 16 (1884), pp. 194–221; and Philomena Muinzer, "'Instructive Panorama': Arnold Guyot's Barometrical Explorations, 1848–1884" (senior thesis, Princeton University, Apr. 29, 1977).

"Remarkable not only": Obituary in *New York Daily Tribune*.

"Singularly pure and sweet": *Transactions, p. 67.*

"One of the loveliest": S. Hastings Grant, "With Professor Guyot on Mounts Washington and Carrigain in 1857," *Appalachia* (June 1907), p. 235. Reprinted with permission of the Appalachian Mountain Club.

127   **"Indeed, he seems":** Letter from David M.Sherman to L&GW, Feb. 15, 1982. Reprinted with permission.

128   **Mount Carrigain:** Grant, "With Professor Guyot," pp. 229–37. See also letter from Guyot to A. D. Bache, Oct. 8, 1857, in the microfilm publication M642, "Correspondence of A. D. Bache, Superintendent of the Coast and Geodetic Survey, 1843–1865," National Archives, Washington, D.C. Quoted material is from Grant's account except for the characterizations of Carrigain by Huntington, from C. H. Hitchcock, *Mount Washington in Winter, or The Experiences of a Scientific Expedition upon the Highest Mountain in New England, 1870–71* (Boston: Chick and Andrews, 1871), p. 130; and by "a later writer," who is Nathaniel L. Goodrich, in *Trail Location*, a pamphlet (no. 14) published by the New England Trail Conference (1926), p. 11. Professor Fay's error is in his article on "Mount Carrigain," in *Appalachia* (July 1880), p. 111.

       Seward Range: George Marshall, unpublished manuscript on Guyot in collections of the Adirondack Museum, Blue Mountain Lake, N.Y.

129   **"Impossible to tell":** Carson, *Peaks and People*, p. 217. Reprinted with permission.

       Catskill 3,500-foot peaks: Guyot, "On the Physical Structure and Hypsometry of the Catskill Mountain Region," *American Journal of Science*, vol. 19, no. 114, 3d ser. (June 1880), pp. 430–51; and "On a New Map of the Catskill Mountains," *Appalachia* (July 1880), pp. 97–108. Guyot read the latter paper in presenting his landmark map at a meeting of the Appalachian Mountain Club on Dec. 10, 1879.

       Before he was through: For a peak-by-peak review of the thirty-four peaks and the evidence as to whether Guyot climbed them, as summarized in the footnote to the next paragraph, the authors are deeply indebted to the knowledgeable assistance of Edward G. West and Fr. Raymond Donahue.

       "The wilderness of": Guyot, "On the Physical Structure," p. 430.

130   **In the White Mountains:** Guyot, "On the Appalachian Mountain System," *American Journal of Science and Arts*, vol. 31, 2d ser. (May 1861), pp. 181–83, and Guyot, "Karte der White Mountains (Weissen Berge) zur Übersicht der Höhenmessungen," no. 89 in collections of the Boston Public Library. A close student of Guyot's career, David M. Sherman, has pointed out that this list of known White Mountain ascents probably understates the case, because Guyot was in the White Mountains for extended periods and was certainly not a man to sit idly on hotel verandas (letter to L&GW, Dec. 1984). The authors completely agree. However, no documented records have been found for summits other than those listed.

       In the Adirondacks: Guyot, "Hypsometrie," in box no. 3, collections of Clark University Library, pp. 140–41.

       In Vermont: Guyot, "On the Appalachian Mountain System," p. 183.

130 **Farther south:** *Ibid.*, p. 173. For Guyot's activities in the Shawangunks, see especially Daniel Smiley, "Arnold Henry Guyot, 1807–1884, Geology and Meteorology," Historical/Cultural Note no. 1, of the Mohonk Preserve, Inc., New Paltz, N.Y., Feb. 1984.

Beyond question: Paul M. Fink and Myron H. Avery, "Arnold Guyot's Explorations in the Great Smoky Mountains," *Appalachia* (Dec. 1936), p. 253; reprinted with permission of Appalachian Mountain Club. A useful overview of Guyot's mountain activities is Muinzer's " 'Instructive Panorama' " paper.

CHAPTER 14. WINTERING OVER ON MOOSILAUKE AND WASHINGTON

131 **Starr King made:** King, *White Hills*, p. 376.

Thomas Cole and others: Charles Rockwell, *The Catskill Mountains and the Region Around* (1867; Cornwallville, N.Y.: Hope Farm Press, 1973), p. 291.

"For two-thirds": Spaulding, *Relics*, pp. 50–51.

"Frost clouds," "To be caught," and "The first known": The two quoted phrases are from a contemporary writeup in the *Coos Republican* of the December 1858 ascent. This account is quoted at length in an excellent description of the climb in Hitchcock, *Mount Washington in Winter*, pp. 50–52. Another newspaper account is in an unidentified clipping preserved in the back of the Tip Top House register for 1853–55, in the collections of the New Hampshire Historical Society. A third version was written by Osgood, appeared in *Among the Clouds*, Sept. 6, 1907, p. 1, and was reprinted as J. Lloyd Spaulding and Irving A. Spaulding, "An Osgood Account of the First Winter Ascent of Mt. Washington," *Mount Washington Observatory News Bulletin* (Fall 1986), p. 59. See also, by the same authors, "The First Winter Ascent of Mt. Washington Revisited," *Mount Washington Observatory News Bulletin* (Spring 1986), pp. 2–8.

132 **The second winter ascent:** Hitchcock, *Mount Washington in Winter*, pp. 52–58. The 1862 climb was also described by "J. H. S." (Spaulding), "First Winter Visit to the Summit of Mount Washington," *Among the Clouds*, Sept. 4, 1878, pp. 1–2. Quoted passages in our paragraph are from the former.

133 **Early fears:** Discussion of winter conditions in Northeastern mountains may be found in numerous sources, of which reliable samples include Dan H. Allen, *Don't Die on the Mountain:* (published by the New Hampshire Chapter, Appalachian Mountain Club, 1972); John A. Danielson, *Winter Hiking and Camping*, 3d ed. (Glens Falls, N.Y.: Adirondack Mountain Club, 1982).

231 mph, on April 12, 1934: Interesting accounts of the record wind may be found in the fiftieth anniversary commemorative edition (beginning with Alexander A. McKenzie. " 'Through a Glass Darkly . . . ,' ") of the *Mount Washington Observatory News Bulletin* (Spring 1984). For a particularly brutal combination of wind and cold, see Greg Gordon, "Worst Ever?" *Mount Washington Observatory News Bulletin* (March 1968), pp. 6–9.

133 **Men with such diverse:** Peary's opinion is cited by Willard Helburn, in a note quoted in Marguerite D. Barnes, "A Snowshoe Trip in 1924," *Appalachia* (June 1961), p. 349; Odell's view was recalled by Robert L. M. Underhill in several conversations with the authors; and Washburn was quoted in John Noble Wilford, "Atop Brutal Mt. Washington, Scientists Measure the Nation's Worst Weather," *New York Times*, Jan. 13, 1981, p. C-1.

"Mount Washington is the coldest" and **"Patagonian winds":** Conversation with John Bragg, Apr. 8, 1983.

"When I went": Letter from Michael Young to L&GW, Feb. 9, 1985. Reprinted with permission.

134 **"One of the great":** Letter from Jonathan Waterman to L&GW, March 15, 1984. Reprinted with permission.

135 **"[Western climbers] don't":** Gene Prater, *Snowshoeing*, 2d ed. (Seattle, Wash.: The Mountaineers, 1980), pp. 98–99, 118.

"If you've camped": Pam Kerr, quoted in an interview by Sharon Hainsfurther, "One Thing at a Time," *New Hampshire Spirit* (Winter 1987), p. 26.

136 **"There is beauty":** Thomas Cole, "The Falls of Kaaterskill in Winter," *New York Evening Post*, March 29, 1843, p. 2.

"It must be": The Rev. F. W. Sanborn, "How Frank and I Spent Two Weeks in the White Mountains of New Hampshire, 1874," in manuscript collections of the New Hampshire Historical Society. Reprinted with permission.

The early settlers: Evidence is the fact that during the 1784 ascent of Mount Washington, Cutler noted that some of the locals employed as guides, encountering the thick scrub at treeline, "wished for their snowshoes" (Cutler, *Life*, p. 102).

Some of the Indian-hunting: Frederick Tuckerman, "Early Visits to the White Mountains and Ascents of the Great Range," *Appalachia* (Aug. 1921), p. 115.

Ethan Crawford and Charles Stuart: Lucy Crawford, *History*, pp. 45–46.

But in general: In May 1858 a party headed for Mount Mansfield and was told by locals that the mountain simply would be unclimbable until the snow was gone ("Ascent of Mansfield Mountain, May 10th," *Burlington Free Press*, May 19, 1858, p. 2).

137 **The earliest known record:** Letter from Edward Crowell to his parents, Jan. 20, 1840, Nineteenth Century Student Papers, Norwich University Library, Northfield, Vermont. (Typescript.) Quoted passages in this paragraph are from this letter. Reprinted with permission.

137   **"Over the brow":** "A Day in the Carter Notch," *Putnam's Monthly* (Dec. 1853), p. 676.

    One unsuccessful attempt: Hitchcock, *Mount Washington in Winter*; p. 50.

    It is a measure: The story of wintering over on Moosilauke and Washington is told in detail in Hitchcock, *Mount Washington in Winter*. Except where otherwise indicated, all quoted material in the remainder of this chapter comes from this book.

138   **Moosilauke:** The winter on Moosilauke is the subject of chap. 5 of Hitchcock's book, pp. 87–100.

139   **"If it blows":** Clough's diary, quoted in D. Q. Clement, "Moosilauke—1879," handwritten journal in the manuscript collections of the New Hampshire Historical Society, p. 12. Reprinted with permission.

140   **Ten years after:** This unusual episode in winter mountaineering history is recounted in the handwritten journal of D. Q. Clement, "Moosilauke—1879." All quoted material in this paragraph is from that journal. Reprinted with permission of the New Hampshire Historical Society.

141   **Washington:** Chaps. 6–15, pp. 101–280, of Hitchcock's *Mount Washington in Winter*.

144   **Polar exploration:** Two readable summaries of the history of early polar activity are by Farley Mowat, *The Polar Passion: The Quest for the North Pole*, rev. ed. (1967; Toronto: McClelland and Stewart, 1973), and *Tundra: Selections from the Great Accounts of Arctic Land Voyages* (Toronto: McClelland and Stewart, 1973).

PART THREE. MOUNTAINS AS PLACES TO WALK: 1870–1910

145   **Mount Adams summit register:** R. M. D. Adams, "The Register Cylinders of the Club," *Appalachia* (June 1905), pp. 40–47.

146   **"We failed to observe":** C. R. Miller, "A Trip to the Mountains, No. II," *The Dartmouth* (Oct. 1871), p. 355.

147   **The Grand Hotels:** The era of the grand hotels is grandly recalled in many sources. Van Zandt's *Catskill Mountain House* covers not only that institution but many of its lavish rivals as well. Much of the spirit of the times in the Catskills may be gleaned from the large-size illustrated guides prepared by Richard Lionel DeLisser, *Picturesque Catskills: Greene County* (Northampton, Mass.: Picturesque Publishing Company, 1894: reprinted, Cornwallville, N.Y.: Hope Farm Press, 1967), and *Picturesque Ulster* (Kingston, N.Y.: originally published in eight numbered parts, 1896–1905; reprinted, Cornwallville, N.Y.: Hope Farm Press, 1968). The Shawangunks resorts are described in Larry E. Burgess, *Mohonk: Its People and Spirit* (New Paltz, N.Y.: Smiley Brothers, 1980). For New England, invaluable background on the period is in Wilson's landmark *Hill Country of Northern New England*. White Mountain hotels are listed in Lapham, *Former White Mountain Hotels*, and more colorfully described in Randall E. Spaulding,

"The Grand Hotels, the Glory and the Conflagration," in *The Enterprise of the North Country of New Hampshire*. Much White Mountain period flavor is available in Kilbourne, *Chronicles*. For the period in Vermont, see Lee, *Green Mountains*, Hagerman, *Mansfield*, pp. 58–62, and Madeline C. Fleming, *An Informal History of the Town of Sherburne, Vermont* (no publication data given; a copy may be found in the collections of the Vermont Historical Society). Sherburne is located near Killington Peak. The evolution of Bar Harbor's hotels and cottages can be read in G. W. Helfrich and Gladys O'Neil, *Lost Bar Harbor* (Camden, Maine: Down East Books, 1982). The Kineo resort business is described in contemporary articles in *Maine Sportsman*: see "The Development of Kineo: How the Grand Moosehead Lake Resort Has Been Evolved from Nature's Fastness" (Nov. 1893), pp. 1, 8, and James S. Rowe, "Moosehead Lake and Kineo" (July 1899), pp. 7–13. Berkshires developments are richly recounted in Clark W. Bryan, *The Book of Berkshire*, and William H. Tague, Robert B. Kimball, and Richard V. Happel, *Berkshire: Two Hundred Years in Pictures, 1761–1961* (Pittsfield, Mass.: Eagle Publishing, 1961).

148   **"Summer-boarding centers":** Evers, *Catskills*, p. 466.

The guidebooks of the time: Among thirty–eight establishments listed in Van Loan's first Catskill guidebook in 1876, few are very large; see Walton Van Loan, *Catskill Mountain Guide, with Maps; Showing Where to Walk and Where to Ride* (Van Loan & Van Gorden, 1876).

"Can Accommodate 20": *Ibid.*, p. 51.

"Nearly every Catskill": DeLisser, *Picturesque Catskills: Greene County*, p. 5.

Resort prices: Perusal of advertisements throughout Ernest Ingersoll, *Illustrated Guide to the Hudson River and Catskill Mountains* (Chicago: Rand McNally, 1893).

149   **Monadnock always:** The Half Way House, Shattuck Inn, and The Ark are described in Chamberlain, *Annals*, pp. 26–37. The successive developments of farm boardinghouses and summer cottages near Monadnock are discussed in George Willis Cooke, "Old Times and New in Dublin, New Hampshire," *New England Magazine* (Aug. 1899), pp. 745–62, and Levi W. Leonard and Josiah L. Seward, *The History of Dublin, N.H.* (Dublin, N.H.: published by the town, 1920), pp. 605–12.

On one hike: George C. Mann, "The Excursions of Our First Decade." *Appalachia* (Dec. 1886), p. 358.

A note on: George C. Mann, "Excursions of the Season of 1886," *Appalachia* (June 1888), p. 159.

For the AMC field meetings: After 1886 detailed records of AMC excursions and field meetings may be found in each issue of *Appalachia*, in the reports of the Excursion Committee, the recording secretary, or under other headings.

CHAPTER 15. THE PLEASURES OF PEDESTRIANISM

151 John Huston Finley: Obituary in *The Trail Marker*, a publication of the Adirondack Mountain Club (March 1940), p. 3. See also "John Huston Finley: As He Was Seen by Members of the New York Times Staff," *New York Times*, March 10, 1940, p. E–9.

Edward Payson Weston: The extent of press coverage of Weston's longer walks as they took place is amazing, as demonstrated in twenty–eight pages of clippings reproduced in George D. Trent, ed., *The Gentle Art of Walking: A Compilation from the New York Times* (New York: Random House, Arno Press, 1971), pp. 52–79.

"It is a common": "Walking the Fashion," *New York Times*, Jan. 15, 1887, p. 3.

152 "Perhaps their ruby": *Ibid.*

"Linger among": "Walking as a Fine Art," *New York Times*, May 31, 1885, p. 4.

Modest beginnings: One of the earliest examples of the kind of walking tour that later became so popular was by Henry James Tudor and a friend from July 21 through August 7, 1831, the record of which was published over a century later, as Henry James Tudor, "A Journey on Foot to the White Hills," *Appalachia* (June 1946), pp. 23–28.

Portland student group: Elizabeth M. Gould, "How We Did It," from contemporary Portland newspaper accounts reprinted in *Appalachia* (Dec. 1968), pp. 223–37. This trip was well reported in the press. A scrapbook assembled by Maj. John M. Gould, who was apparently the adult chaperone on the trip, includes accounts appearing in the *Boston Globe* (July 30, Aug. ?, Aug. 22, Sept. 2, 1873), *Buffalo Express* (July 28, 1873, and others undated), *Boston Daily News* (Aug. 18 and Sept. 2, 1873), and *Portland Transcript* (Sept. 27, Oct. 11 and 25, Nov. 8, 1873, and one undated). This scrapbook is in the collections of the Dartmouth College Library.

Lightweight equipment: Both tent and stove are described in John B. Bachelder, *Popular Resorts, and How To Reach Them* (Boston: John B. Bachelder, 1875), pp. 17–18.

"We seldom walked": J. H. Wickes, "The Pedestrians," *Williams Quarterly*, vol. 8 (Nov. 1860), p. 112.

153 Anthony Trollope: Anthony Trollope, *North America* (London: Chapman & Hall, 1862), vol. 1, p. 58, 56, respectively.

"Avoid all nonsensical": John M. Gould, *How to Camp Out* (New York: Scribner, Armstrong, 1877), p. 55.

From most of the leading colleges: The closest look so far at the phenomenon of walking tours by students in the nineteenth century is William A. Koelsch, "Antebellum Harvard Students and the Recreational Exploration of the New England Landscape," *Journal of Historical Geography*, vol 9, no. 1

(1983), pp. 362–72. Dr. Koelsch develops the thesis that long walks were an outlet for exercise prior to formal athletic programs at colleges and that the subsequent rise of organized athletics was associated with a decline in pedestrian exercise.

153   **"It is pleasing"**: Moses F. Sweetser, *White Mountains*, (1876 ed.), p. 34.

"There is a certain age": Bachelder, *Popular Resorts*, p. 13.

154   **"The young ladies"**: Quoted in Mildred S. Howard, "A Century of Physical Education," *Mount Holyoke Alumnae Quarterly* (Feb. 1936), p. 213.

"Mountain Day": Mildred S. Howard, "History of Physical Education at Mount Holyoke College, 1837–1955," typescript in the physical education records, Mount Holyoke College Library/Archives, p. 2. See also Irene Snider, "Mount Holyoke's Secret Day," *Yankee*, (Oct. 1964), pp. 74–75, 118, 120.

"All young ladies": Howard, "History of Physical Education," p. 2.

Harvard: Koelsch, "Antebellum Harvard Students." Examples of Harvard mountain walks in the 1850s may be found in *Harvard Magazine*: "Varieties in College Life" (Oct. 1855), pp. 415–16; "A Vacation Ramble" (Jan. 1857), pp. 14–20; "Retrospect" (March 1857), pp. 61–68; Spaulding '60, "Among the Mountains" (Oct. 1858), pp. 336–41; "A Walk"" (Jan. 1859), pp. 22–30; and "The Adirondacs" (June 1860), pp. 289–96. Continuing interest in such activity in the 1860s and 1870s is attested in "Walking," *Harvard Magazine* (Nov. 1862), pp. 81–89; in *The Advocate*: Loquax, "Cambridge Pedestrianism," May 11, 1866, pp. 8–9; Tahn, "The Environs of Cambridge," Nov. 25, 1870, pp. 56–57; and "Up Mount Kearsarge by Moonlight," Nov. 10, 1871, pp. 37–38; and *The Magenta*: B. H. C., "Walking," Apr. 18, 1873, pp. 79–80; and E. F. F., "Black Mountain," Jan. 9, 1874, pp. 90–91. Indeed Harvard's eminent historian Samuel Eliot Morison traces student rambles back into the eighteenth century; see Morison, *Three Centuries of Harvard* (Cambridge: Harvard University Press, Belknap Press, 1936), pp. 111, 207. For the Georgianna Falls and Pemigewasset Wilderness examples see Koelsch, "Antebellum Harvard Students," pp. 364–68, and Appalachian Mountain Club, *Guide to the White Mountains* (1925 ed.), p. 329.

Erastus Everett: Frank Burt, "White Mountain Album: Excerpts from the Registers of Ethan Allen Crawford," *Appalachia* (June 1941), p. 315.

"Established custom": "A Trip to the Mountains," *The Dartmouth* (Sept. 1871), p. 311. This publication is the source for our other information and quotations on Dartmouth pedestrian activity. See J. R. Willard, "The Dartmouth Mountaineers: A Pedestrian Excursion to the White Mountains by the Class of '67 during the Summer of 1866, No. 1" (June 1867), pp. 217–23; "A Trip to the Mountains and Northern Vermont, No. 2" (Oct. 1870), pp. 341–44; C. R. Miller, "A Trip to the Mountains, No. II" (Oct. 1871), pp. 351–56; "A Trip to the Mountains, No. III" (Nov. 1871), pp. 393–98; and "A Trip to the White Mountains, II" (Oct. 1874), pp. 302–4. For this and other colleges, where numerous illustrations could be cited, we shall confine the list of references to six especially vivid examples.

155 **Indeed everyone else:** In addition to the New England colleges cited in the text, nearby New York State colleges were not immune to the passion for pedestrianism; see the vigorous excursions of geology and botany students from Rensselaer Polytechnic Institute (Troy, N.Y.), in the 1860s and 1870s: "Editorial," *The Transit* (March 1867), p. 4, and "Transit," *The Transit* (March 1870), pp. 7, 40; "The Mining Expedition," *The Polytechnic* , Oct. 9, 1869, pp. 21–22; the summer vacation tramps to the White Mountains by two RPI students (scrapbook of E. Ray Thompson, 1876, in RPI manuscript collections, p. 85); and a ramble to Howe's Cave by students from Union College (Schenectady, N.Y.) in 1861 (Porter Farley, "Howe's Cave," *Union College Magazine* [Feb. 1861], pp. 231–35).

Brown University: Ralph Tingley, "White Mountain Pedestrians," *New Hampshire Profiles* (July 1973), pp. 22–24, 66, 68–75; and J. R. Willard, "The Dartmouth Mountaineers, No. 2," *The Dartmouth* (July 1867), p. 270.

156 **Yale:** For examples, see *Yale Literary Magazine:* H. K., "A Summer Experience" (Nov. 1861), pp. 62–71; W. B., "Bash–Bish" (Feb. 1867), pp. 115–20; M. E., "Mountain Thoughts" (Nov. 1879), pp. 56– 59; and William L. Phelps, "An Adirondack Memory" (Nov. 1885), pp. 51–56. See also Senior '73, "A Geological Trip into the Azoic Regions of New York," *The College Courant*, June 28, 1873, pp. 1–2, and "Vacation Reminiscences," *The Yale Record*, Apr. 1, 1874, pp.335–37.

Wesleyan: For examples, see *The College* (Wesleyan) *Argus:* "To Holyoke," Nov. 5, 1868, p. 22; D. H. H., "A Vacation Ramble on the Catskill Mountains," Sept. 29, 1869, pp. 4–5; "A Trip to the White Mountains," Dec. 4, 1872, pp. 82–83; H., "M. S. A. Excursion" [Middletown Scientific Association], Oct. 8, 1873, p. 16; A. G. K., "Physical Exercise in College," March 20, 1877, p. 113; and Naper, "A Trip to Wachusett Mountain," May 14, 1878, pp. 133–35.

Williams College: Williams's White Mountain tours are described in J. H. Wickes, "The Pedestrian," p. 112, and in "Editorials," *Williams Athenaeum*, Nov. 14, 1874, p. 15. Mountain Day in the 1850s is described in "College Holidays," *Williams Quarterly* (June 1856), p. 379. Post–World War I changes in attitude are compiled in "Nevermore Shall Be," *Williams Alumni Review* (Nov. 1935), pp. 64–65.

Middlebury College: J. H. Barrett, "Reminiscences of the Class of 1845," *The Undergraduate* (June 1894), p. 115, "Editorial," *The Undergraduate* (Apr. 1879), p. 102. See also David Stameshkin, "The Town's College: Middlebury College, 1800–1915" (Ph.D. diss., University of Michigan, 1978), pp. 395–96.

Colby College: "A Ramble with Our Friends," *The Colby Echo* (July 1877), pp. 58–59, and similar columns in subsequent issues.

156   **Pemigewasset Perambulators:** *A Record of the Perambulations of the Pemi-gewasset Perambulators,* by their scribe. A copy is in the collections of Dartmouth College Library.

157   **Oatmeal Crusaders:** Henry Carpenter, *The Oatmeal Crusaders, or a Nine Day's Wander round, up and down Mount Washington* (Portland, Maine: Stephen Berry, 1875), pp. 3, 38.

The Bummers: "T. R. B.," "Bummers Record at the White Hills," 1867, and the Rev. Leander Thompson, "The Journey of the Mu Sigma Pedestrians to the White Mountains," July 11–Aug. 10, 1865. Both manuscripts are in the collections of the New Hampshire Historical Society.

Williams's Mountain Days: All four quoted passages are cited in "Nevermore Shall Be," *Williams Alumni Review* (Nov. 1935), pp. 64–65.

158   **"Old-time pedestrians":** "The Bootless Trail," *The Colby Echo* (Feb. 1883), pp. 52–54.

"The alarming development": Sweetser, *White Mountains,* p.35.

Another reason: The influence of price changes is suggested by Thomas D. S. Bassett, a close student of the history of New England recreation, in a letter to L&GW, July 16, 1985.

"In our college days": Barrett, "Reminiscences," p. 115.

Football match: "Athletic Sports," *The Dartmouth,* May 16, 1878, p. 473.

Baseball: *The Dartmouth,* issues of the 1860s, 1870s, 1880s, and 1890s.

In other colleges: As mentioned above, this relationship between the decline of pedestrian tours and the rise in organized athletic programs has been most thoroughly examined by Koelsch in his 1983 article in the *Journal of Historical Geography.* Most students of recreation history agree that organized athletics emerged "in the last three decades of the nineteenth century" (Peter Berg, in a book review, *Baseball History* [Winter 1986], p. 63). After extensive reading in nineteenth–century college publications, the authors agree with this assessment. However, a convincing reminder that organized athletics were well advanced by the middle of the nineteenth century is well documented in Melvin L. Adelman, *A Sporting Time: New York City and the Rise of Modern Athletics, 1820–1870* (Urbana: University of Illinois Press, 1986).

"If our 'far away' ": "The Bootless Trail," p. 52. For other examples, see this transition noted at Wesleyan in the gradual change in emphasis spread over three sample articles in its *College Argus,* from "Boating," June 11, 1868, p. 5, where walking is perceived as one of "the chief methods employed among us to develop muscle"; to "Physical Exercise in College," March 20, 1877, p. 113; to an editorial, Nov. 29, 1881, pp. 38–40, where walking is not even mentioned, exercise having become virtually synonymous with organized athletics. See also the same trend at Williams in Frederick Rudolph, *Mark Hopkins and the Log: Williams College, 1836–1872* (New Haven: Yale University Press, 1956), pp. 136, 162, and at Middlebury in Stameshkin, "The

Town's College," pp. 395–96. Intercollegiate football began in the 1870s and grew in popularity in the 1880s. At the secondary school level, the Interscholastic Football Association was formed in Boston in 1888; see Stephen Hardy, *How Boston Played: Sport, Recreation, and Community, 1865–1915* (Boston: Northeastern University Press, 1982), p. 112. Hardy has traced the development during these years of sporting clubs in Boston for every kind of contest––yachting and rowing, cricket and baseball, track and field, driving and trotting, golf and tennis, lacross and curling: "Name a sport—it had its share of representative clubs" (Ibid., p. 135).

159 **At least one writer:** Albert Handy, "Walking Clubs of New York," *New York Evening Post* (Saturday magazine), May 6, 1916, pp. 8–10.

CHAPTER 16. ADIRONDACK MURRAY'S FOOLS

161 **The man who:** The most complete biography and profile of Murray is Harry V. Radford, *Adirondack Murray: A Biographical Appreciation* (New York: Broadway Publishing, 1905). Many books on the Adirondacks include colorful accounts of this intriguing personality —for example, Donaldson, *History,* vol. 1, pp. 190–201. Useful appraisals are those of Warder Cadbury in an introduction to a 1970 reprint of Murray's most famous book, *Adventures in the Wilderness,* and of Philip Terrie in *Forever Wild,* pp. 68–76. Murray's own writings are invaluable primary sources for understanding Murray.

"A big, husky": Donaldson, *History,* vol. 1, p. 190.

"Handsome and good-natured": Radford, *Murray,* p. 43.

"Fairly took Boston": *Ibid.,* p. 55.

"There has perhaps": *Ibid.,* pp. 13–14.

162 **"Now, tramping":** William Henry Harrison Murray, *Adirondack Tales* (Boston: Golden Rule Publishing, 1877), p. 452.

"Some say": Donaldson, *History,* vol. 1, p. 193.

"Kindled a thousand": Wendell Phillips, quoted in Frank Graham, Jr., *The Adirondack Park: A Political History* (New York: Alfred A. Knopf, 1978), p. 26. The analogy with Marlowe's Helen seems irresistible to Murray-watchers. Another writer refers to him as "the voice that launched a thousand guide-boats" (Jamieson, *Adirondack Reader,* p. 88.)

"A literal construction": Donaldson, *History,* vol. 1, p. 198. The skeptical view was not unknown in Murray's day. A Yale student signing himself "J. H. P." advised, "Get Murray's book and read it. The first part is true and the last interesting" ("A Trip to the Adirondacks," *Yale Literary Magazine* [Dec. 1869], p. 156). A Harvard student referred to the successful author as "that gay deceiver, Murray" ("A Ball in the Adirondacks," *Harvard Advocate,* June 21, 1872, p. 154).

163 **"It displaced":** Donaldson, *History,* vol. 1, p. 193.

163 **"Either the timing"**: William Chapman White, *Adirondack Country* (New York: Duell, Sloan & Pearce; Boston: Little, Brown, 1954), p. 112.

"Up and down": Unsigned (by Charles Hallock, according to Donaldson, *History*, vol. 1, p. 195), "The Racquette Club," *Harper's Magazine* (Aug. 1870), p. 324. The article's title may be a rare example of a triple pun.

"A moving phantasm": *Ibid.*, p. 325.

"The stampede into": White, *Adirondack Country*, p. 115.

164 **By some estimates:** Borden H. Mills, Sr., "Adirondack Hostelries of the 19th Century," *Adirondac* (Jan.–Feb. 1951), p. 4. Except where otherwise indicated, information in this paragraph is from this article. Donaldson's *History* is also full of anecdotal material on Adirondack hotels and boardinghouses. See also George Crossette and Paul H. Oehser, "The Adirondacks," *American Forests* (Oct. 1973), pp. 29–30.

Prospect House: Crossette and Oehser, "The Adirondacks," p. 29.

Enterprising men acquired: For the Adirondack "camps," see Harvey H. Kaiser, *Great Camps of the Adirondacks* (Boston: David R. Godine, 1982).

"Riches and rusticity": Philip Langdon, "Compromise with Nature," *Historic Preservation* (Sept.–Oct. 1979), pp. 14, 16. See also Kaiser, *Great Camps of the Adirondacks*. Another perceptive discussion of the balance between elegance and backwoodsiness in Adirondack accommodations is Philip G. Terrie, "Urban Man Confronts the Wilderness: The Nineteenth Century Sportsman in the Adirondacks," *Journal of Sport History*, vol. 5, no. 3 (Winter 1978), pp. 7–20.

The archetype: Donaldson devotes a chapter to Paul Smith in *History*, vol. 1, pp. 320–29. See also Neil Suprenant, "Paul Smith," *Adirondack Life* (July–Aug. 1979), pp. 19–21, 38–40.

"Paul Smith's is": *By-Ways*, brochure of the Central Vermont Railroad (1887), pp. 48–49. In the collections of the Vermont Historical Society, Montpelier, Vt. Reprinted with permission.

The backwoods host: Suprenant, "Paul Smith," p. 19. Reprinted with permission.

"Morgans, Whitneys, Vanderbilts": John G. Mitchell, "Gentlemen Afield," *American Heritage* (Oct.–Nov. 1978), p. 99.

165 **Pine Knot:** Langdon, "Compromise with Nature," p. 17.

Theodore Roosevelt: White, *Adirondack Country*, p. 31.

Robert Louis Stevenson: Darwin Benedict, "Robert Louis Stevenson at Saranac," *Cloud Splitter* (Sept.–Oct. 1947), p. 8.

Philosopher William James: Henry James, ed., *The Letters of William James*, Vol. 2 (Boston: Atlantic Monthly Press, 1920), pp. 76–77. The quoted words are on p. 77.

168   **Charles Henry Hitchcock:** Charles H. Hitchcock's life is summarized in Johnson's *Dictionary of American Biography* and in the *Amherst College Biographical Record* (1963); his character and personality are hinted at there and in his own writings cited below. The New Hampshire survey was written up in C. H. Hitchcock, *The Geology of New Hampshire* (Concord, N.H.: Edward A. Jenks, 1874).

Verplanck Colvin: Our information on Colvin's life is drawn from a heterogeneous collection of old newspaper clippings and excerpts from publications assembled in a folder on Colvin in the biographical file of the Adirondack Museum at Blue Mountain Lake, N.Y. His own reports and other writings, cited below, richly augment the assessments of his character and personality that virtually every major writer on the Adirondacks has provided. One of the more balanced and informed recent appraisals is in Philip G. Terrie, "Conservation, Preservation, and the Origins of the Forest Preserve," *Adirondac* (Aug. 1983), pp. 21–23. A detailed study of his life and the relationship of his work to Adirondack development is in progress by Joseph M. Jillisky. The Adirondacks surveys were reported in Verplanck Colvin, *Report on a Topographical Survey of the Adirondack Wilderness of New York*, Albany, N.Y.: The Argus Company, for early reports, and Weeds, Parsons & Company for later ones, the first appearing in 1873 (covering activities of 1872), and others from time to time thereafter, with inconsequential changes in the title. Besides the first (1873) report, the most important from the standpoint of mountaineering accomplishments are the second (1874) and third, which did not appear until 1879 and contained the third through seventh annual reports in one volume.

Avalanche Pass in 1869: Letter from Verplanck Colvin, *Albany Evening Journal*, Sept. 20, 1869.

Shot a bear: "Narrative of a Bear Hunt in the Adirondacks," read before the Albany Institute, Jan. 18, 1870, published in leaflet form (Albany, N.Y.: Joel Munsell, 1970).

Mount Dix: Letter from Colvin, *Albany Evening Journal*, Aug. 26, 1871.

169   **Nursing vengeance:** Colvin's railroad schemes are described in "A Raid on the Adirondacks," *Elizabethtown* [N.Y.] *Post & Gazette*, March 9, 1891, p. 3, and "Railroad Rivalry in the Adirondacks," *New York Times*, Sept. 14, 1902, p. 3.

170   **If these contrasting:** The authors are grateful to Nina H. Webb for presenting a strong case for Colvin's more positive qualities; see letter to L&GW, Apr. 21, 1986.

171   **"As yet":** Spaulding, *Relics*, p. 11.

Class of 1871: Dartmouth College records list the names of eighty-three members of the class of 1871; of these eighty-three, nineteen (23 percent) show up in Hitchcock's various reports as participating in the survey work.

171   **"To furnish":** Hitchcock, *Geology*, p. 16.

Vose knew his subject: For information on George Vose and his previous visits to the White Mountains, see Charles B. Fobes, "The White Mountain Club of Portland, Maine, 1873–1884," *Appalachia* (June 1955), pp. 390–91; Dumas Malone, ed., *Dictionary of American Biography* (New York: Charles Scribners' Sons, 1936), and a scrapbook of Portland newspaper obituaries, in the collections of the Maine Historical Society, vol. 9, p. 11.

"Almost exactly": Hitchcock, *Geology*, p. 628. Vose's account of this trip to Carrigain originally appeared in the *Oxford* (Maine) *Democrat*, Oct. 8, 1869, p. 2. Other quoted passages here are from this source. In the late twentieth century, the friendly branches along Cobb's Stairs were spruce and fir, not pine.

173   **Webster cliffs:** Hitchcock, *Geology*, pp. 174–75.

174   **"Our houses were":** *Ibid.*, p. 32.

175   **Verplanck Colvin had already:** Verplanck Colvin, "Ascent and Barometrical Measurement of Mount Seward," in the twenty-fourth *Annual Report* of the New York State Museum of Natural History, for the year 1870 (Albany, N.Y.: Argus, 1872), pp. 3–9.

177   **Snowy Mountain:** Colvin, *Report* for 1872 (published 1873), p. 11.

Bald Mountain: *Ibid.*, p. 14.

178   **Giant:** Colvin, *Report* for 1873 (published 1874), p. 27.

Dix: *Ibid.*, pp. 29–30.

Algonquin: *Ibid.*, p. 42.

"Not a particle": *Report* for 1872 (published 1873), p. 43. One of Colvin's clearest discussions of the requirements imposed on his guides was in the *Report* published in 1879, pp. 447–48.

"On the whole": Carson, *Peaks and People*, p. 177. Reprinted with permission.

179   **"Almost all of them":** Colvin, *Report* for 1873 (published 1874), p. 14.

A peak in the Ausable Lakes region: *Ibid.*, p. 31. He cannot have been unhappy that the guides (he says) chose to name this particular gem Mount Colvin, the name it bears today.

"Seventh Lake Mountain": Colvin, *Report* for 1877 (published 1879), pp. 158–60.

Trying days on Marcy: Colvin, *Report* for 1883 (published 1884), pp. 160–61.

U.S. Geological Survey: Carson, *Peaks and People*, p. 220.

179   **"Filled with a mass"**: Letter from Irving J. Morris, secretary of New York Commission of Highways, to Alfred L. Donaldson, Feb. 15, 1919, in the Adirondack collection of the Saranac Lake Free Library. Reprinted with permission.

180   **Not just a few trees:** For one of many vivid examples, see Colvin, *Report* for 1873 (published 1874), p. 46.

    While burning brush: Colvin, *Report* for 1876 (published 1879), p. 95.

    "If it had not been": Peter Preston, "Colvin of the Adirondacks," *Adirondack Life* (July–Aug. 1982), p. 22.

    "The Colvin reports": Philip G. Terrie, "Conservation, Preservation, and the Origins of the Forest Preserve," *Adirondac* (Aug. 1983), pp. 21–23, reprinted with permission. See also Terrie, *Forever Wild*, pp. 77–91.

CHAPTER 18. THE FIRST HIKING CLUBS

183   **During the 1920s:** See the comment of Myron Avery, in *The Appalachian Trail*, publication no. 5 of the Appalachian Trail Conference (Jan. 1934), p. 5: "As late as 1926, with the exception of the two-year old Smoky Mountain Hiking Club at Knoxville and smaller local groups in a few cities, all the mountaineering organizations in the eastern United States were confined to New England and the region adjacent to New York City." Outside of the eastern seaboard, two hiking-climbing clubs with nineteenth-century origins are California's Sierra Club (1892) and Oregon's Mazamas (1894).

    The Alpine Club: Samuel H. Scudder, "The Alpine Club of Williamstown, Mass.," *Appalachia* (Dec. 1884), pp. 45–54, and Arthur Latham Perry, *Williamstown and Williams College* (New York: Charles Scribner's Sons, 1899), pp. 579–81.

    President James Garfield: James A. Garfield, quoted in Burke A. Hinsdale, *President Garfield and Education* (Boston: Houghton Mifflin, 1895), p. 43. In the retelling of the celebrated epigram, Garfield's original "bench" became a "log," so much so that a previously mentioned history of Williams College by Frederick Rudolph took the title *Mark Hopkins and the Log: Williams College, 1836–1872.*

    As a youth in 1836: Albert C. Sewell, *Life of Prof. Albert Hopkins* (New York: Anson D. T. Randolph, 1870), p. 154.

    "Not a glen": *Ibid.*, p. 214.

184   **"To explore"**: Scudder, "Alpine Club," p. 46. Quoted passages in the remainder of this section are from this source, pp. 47–54.

185   **Professor Hopkins was losing:** Perry, *Williamstown*, p. 581.

    Scudder moved: Harvard University, *Quinquennial Catalogue of the Officers and Graduates: 1636–1930*, and Malone, *Dictionary of American Biography.*

    "Rather in the pleasant": Scudder, "Alpine Club," p. 54.

185   **Another energetic college:** The Torrey Botanical Club is described in correspondence of John Torrey, in Andrew Denny Rodgers III, *John Torrey: A Story of North American Botany*, p. 290; Raymond H. Torrey, "Art of Walking Saved by the Hiking Clubs," *New York Times*, Apr. 25, 1926, sec. 9, p. 10; Ruth Gillette Hardy, "John Torrey," *Appalachia* (June 1965), p. 563, and an informative letter from a 1980s club official, Richard T. F. Forman, to L&GW, July 14, 1981. The authors very much appreciate the assistance of the last named.

       The exact year: References in Torrey correspondence put it as early as 1865, an early club publication mentions 1866, earliest records in the club date from 1867, its bulletin began publication in 1870, and it was finally officially incorporated in 1871. The first two items are mentioned by Rodgers, *John Torrey*, p. 290. The last three items are cited in the letter from Forman to L&GW, July 14, 1981.

186   **New York's oldest:** For the Fresh Air Club, see many references, especially Torrey, "Art of Walking"; Will S. Monroe, "A Brief Survey of Outing Clubs," *Mountain Magazine* (July 1928), p. 8, and Albert Handy, "Walking Clubs of New York," *New York Evening Post* (Saturday magazine), May 6, 1916, pp. 8–9. All quotations from this article reprinted with permission. The authors are also indebted to numerous veteran hikers of the New York City area for their recollections of the Fresh Air Club; see several of the specific citations below.

       Hoary club legend: Handy, "Walking Clubs of New York," p. 9.

       "What the Appalachian": *Ibid.*

       Afternoon tea break: Letter from Robert Schulz to L&GW, June 1981. Reprinted with permission.

       "One of the first women": Handy, "Walking Clubs of New York," p. 8.

       "The story was": Letter from Grace J. Averill to L&GW, Oct. 2, 1981. Reprinted with permission.

       "Women friends": Handy, "Walking Clubs of New York," p. 9.

187   **Westchester Hare and Hounds:** *Ibid.*, p. 9.

       White Mountain Club: On the Portland White Mountain Club, see White Mountain Club of Portland, Maine, *Records and Memoranda*, a hand written journal in the collections of Charles B. Fobes; quotations reprinted with permission. See also Charles B. Fobes, "The White Mountain Club of Portland, Maine, 1873–1884," *Appalachia* (June 1955), pp. 381–95, and obituaries of leading members in scrapbooks of "Portland Obituaries" in the collections of the Maine Historical Society. On all matters relating to this club, the reigning expert is Mr. Fobes, whose gracious and generous assistance to the authors was invaluable.

       "It is," wrote: "Ascent of Mt. Carrigain," *Portland Transcript*, Sept. 13, 1873, p. 190.

187   **The club was organized:** Besides those already mentioned, another source of information on the 1873 Carrigain climb is a delightful long sing-song narrative poem, privately printed and unsigned, entitled "A Song of Mt. Carrigain, Dedicated to those members of the White Mountain Club who survived the memorable expedition to its summit, 1873," in the collections of the Maine Historical Society.

In August of 1874: This trip was memorialized in a second long narrative poem, also privately printed, "Another Song of Mt. Carrigain," in the collections of Charles B. Fobes.

189   **"The weather prevented":** *Records and Memoranda,* entry for Feb. 20, 1884.

Appalachian Mountain Club: The origins of the AMC are described, among many sources, in a letter from J. B. Henck, Jr., *Appalachia* (May 1902), p. 102; an address by E. C. Pickering, *Appalachia* (March 1877), pp. 63–70; C. Francis Belcher, "A Century of the Appalachian Mountain Club," *Appalachia* (June 1976), pp. 5–44, and early club records as preserved primarily in the pages of early issues of *Appalachia.*

190   **"Amusement rather than":** Pickering, 1877 address, p. 64.

The idea germinated: There are two versions of the specific occasion on which the idea of the Appalachian Mountain Club was conceived: one places the historic moment on Mount Attitash with Professor Henck, the other on Mount Adams with Mr. Edmands. Henck on Attitash is given in Henck's 1902 letter, Edmands on Adams in Lois P. Williams and Henry E. Childs, " 'Path No. 1' Site of August Camp, 1935," *Appalachia* (Nov. 1935), pp. 452–54.

191   **"It seems to me":** Obituary for Thomas Wentworth Higginson, *Appalachia* (July 1911), pp. 276–81. Reprinted with permission of Appalachian Mountain Club.

The 1887 "August Camp": George C. Mann, "Excursions for the Season of 1887–1888," *Appalachia* (Dec. 1888), p. 255.

192   **The Catskill Club:** "Fun in the Catskills: A Tea Party without any Tea," *The Examiner* (Catskill, N.Y.), Aug. 28, 1875, p.3

The Agassiz Association: Rollin Hillyer Cooke, ed., *Historic Homes and Institutions and Genealogical and Personal Memoirs of Berkshire County, Massachusetts* (New York: Lewis Publishing, 1906), pp. 71–73.

The Wlwascackbwgmsaesfssjhe Pedestrian Association: Summit register, Carter Dome, July 17, 1881, in the collections of the Appalachian Mountain Club.

193   **The Waterville Athletic:** See below, chap. 20.

A climbing club: Carolyn Dickerman, "Prosperous Colony Growing about Pretty Mt. Carmel," *New Haven Saturday Chronicle,* Sept. 21, 1907, p. 6, and Nancy D. Sachse, *Born among the Hills: The Sleeping Giant Story* (Hamden, Conn.: Sleeping Giant Park Assoc., 1982), pp. 9–11.

193 **The Intermediates and the Lingernots:** The Twilight Club, Fiftieth Anniver-
sary of Twilight Park, 1888–1938, booklet dated Aug. 27, 1938, in the collections of the Haines Falls Public Library, Haines Falls, N.Y.; "Walking Club
Gives 'Doctor of Pedestry' Degree," *New York Times*, July 10, 1910, p. 78;
"Degrees Given by Lingernots," clipping identified as from the *New York
Times* and dated 1939, in the collections of the Haines Falls Public Library
(although the authors have been unable to find the original in the *New York
Times* for that year). See also brief references in Haring, *Our Catskill Moun-
tains*, p. 221, and in a letter from John A. MacGahan to the Catskill Canister
(Summer 1985), pp. 2–3.

"Doctor of Pedestry": "Degrees Given by Lingernots," unidentified clipping
cited in the previous note.

The Sierra Club: Stephen Fox, *John Muir and His Legacy: The American
Conservation Movement* (Boston: Little, Brown, 1981), p. 107. Fox attributes the original form of organization of the Sierra Club to the AMC model.

The Field and Forest Club: Henry P. Nickerson, *Selective Studies in Nature
for the Ramblers' Group* (Boston: Field and Forest Club, 1924), p. 2; see also
early records of the Field and Forest Club in the collections of the Boston
Public Library.

CHAPTER 19. THE FIRST MOUNTAIN GUIDEBOOKS

195 **General travel guides:** G. M. Davison, *The Fashionable Tour in 1825* (Sara-
toga Springs, N.Y.: published by the author, 1825); Theodore Dwight, *The
Northern Traveler, and Northern Tour* (New York: J. & J. Harper, 1830), and
Nathaniel P. Willis, *American Scenery* (New York: Virtue & Yorsten, 1840).
A partial list of John Disturnell's guides and gazetteers, all published by him,
would include *A Gazetteer of the State of New York* (1842), *The Northern
Traveller, with Hudson River Guide* (1844), *New York Traveller* (1845),
Guide through the Middle, Northern, and Eastern States (1847), *Summer
Arrangements* (1848), *Railroad, Steamboat, and Telegraph Book* (1849),
Hudson River Guide (1850), *Springs, Waterfalls, Sea-Bathing Resorts, and
Mountain Scenery of the United States* (1855), *Railway and Steamship
Guide* (1856), and *The Picturesque Tourist* (1858).

By the 1850s: Samuel C. Eastman, *The White Mountain Guide* (Concord,
N.H.: E. C. Eastman, 1858 and subsequent years); Henry M. Burt, *Burt's Illus-
trated Guide of the Connecticut Valley* (Springfield, Mass.: New England Pub-
lishing, 1866); D. Appleton, *Appleton's Handbook of American Travel* (New
York: D. Appleton, 1871); James R. Osgood, *New England: A Handbook for
Travellers* (Boston: James R. Osgood, 1873), and Charles Newhall Taintor, *New
York to the White Mountains* (1867), *The Northern Route* (1869), *The Hudson
River Route* (1869), *The Connecticut River Route* (1875).

196 **In 1876:** Moses Foster Sweetser, *The White Mountains: A Handbook for
Travellers* (Boston: James R. Osgood, 1876).

He told Frederick Tuckerman: Tuckerman also recalled, privately to E. Porter Dickinson, that he once encountered Sweetser in the Presidential Range

in dense fog, totally lost and in need of directions (conversation with E. Porter Dickinson, Nov. 8, 1984).

196   **"Could make a routine":** Dan Brenan, ed., *The Adirondack Letters of George Washington Sears* (Blue Mountain Lake, N.Y.: Adirondack Museum, 1962), p. 22.

"Imparts to the ascent": Jamieson, *The Adirondack Reader*, p. 389.

Soon guidebook writers: H. Perry Smith, *The Modern Babes in the Woods: or Summering in the Wilderness* (Hartford, Conn.: Columbia Book Company, 1872), on which the title page includes this notation: "To Which is Added a Reliable and Descriptive Guide to the Adirondacks" by E. R. Wallace; Seneca Ray Stoddard, *The Adirondacks Illustrated* (Albany, N.Y.: Weed, Parson, 1874); Edwin R. Wallace, *Descriptive Guide to the Adirondacks and Handbook of Travel* (New York: American News Company, 1875).

197   **In Maine:** John M. Way, *Guide to Moosehead Lake and Northern Maine* (Boston: Bradford & Anthony, 1874); Charles A. J. Farrar, *Illustrated Guidebook for Rangeley, Richardson, Kennebago, etc.* (Boston: Farrar & Johnson, 1876); and other guides to other areas in Maine, mostly first appearing during the 1880s: Lucius L. Hubbard, *Summer Vacations at Moosehead Lake and Vicinity: A Practical Guide-book for Tourists* (Boston: A. Williams, 1879); Thomas Sedgwick Steele, *Canoe and Camera: A Two Hundred Mile Tour through the Maine Forests* (New York: Orange Judd, 1882); George Henry Haynes, *Seaside, Mountain and Lake Summer Resorts* (Lewiston, Maine: Journal Press, 1886), and Leroy Thomas Carleton, *Carleton's Pathfinder and Gazetteer of the Hunting and Fishing Resorts of the State of Maine* (Dover, Maine: Observer Publishing, 1899).

In the Catskills: Walton Van Loan, *Catskill Mountain Guide, with Maps; Showing Where to Walk and Where to Ride* (Catskill, N.Y.: Van Loan & Van Gorden, 1876); Samuel E. Rusk, *An Illustrated Guide to the Catskill Mountains, with Maps and Plans* (Catskill, N.Y.: no publisher given, 1879); Ulster & Delaware Railroad, *A Catskill Souvenir: Scenes on the Line of the Ulster and Delaware Railroad*, a brochure (New York: Aldine, 1879), and Edward Coykendall and N. A. Sims, *The Catskills Mountains*, a booklet (Rondout, N.Y.: Kingston Freeman Press, 1902).

Toward the end: Clark W. Bryan, *The Book of Berkshire* (Great Barrington, Mass., and Springfield, Mass.: Clark W. Bryan, 1887); Rollin Hillyer Cooke, *Drives and Walks in the Berkshire Hills* (Pittsfield, Mass.: Berkshire Life Insurance Company, 1895), and James H. Dana, *The Four Rocks of the New Haven Region, with Walks and Drives about New Haven* (New Haven, Conn.: Tuttle, Morehouse, & Taylor, 1891).

CHAPTER 20. THE FIRST TRAIL SYSTEMS

199   **While growing numbers:** The distinction between the vision of the backcountry as seen by the improvements and explorations advocates is implicit in much twentieth-century discussion of conservation issues. See, for

example, Roderick Nash, *Wilderness and the American Mind.* An unusually clear discussion focused on this distinction is in Joseph L. Sax, *Mountains without Handrails: Reflections on the National Parks* (Ann Arbor: University of Michigan Press, 1980).

201 **The single exception:** The early history of Waterville Valley is well told in two volumes by residents devoted to its memories: Nathaniel L. Goodrich, *The Waterville Valley: A Story of a Resort in the New Hampshire Mountains* (Lunenberg, Vt.: North Country Press, 1952), and Grace Hughes Bean, *The Town at the End of the Road: A History of Waterville Valley* (Canaan, N.H.: Phoenix Publishing, 1983).

"Town at the end": Bean, *Town at the End of the Road,* title.

"Proprietor of the Valley," and **"His spare form":** N. L. Goodrich, *Waterville Valley,* p. 4.

202 **Waterville trails:** Early maps from N. L. Goodrich, *Waterville Valley,* and A. L. Goodrich, *The Waterville Valley: A History, Description, and Guide* (Auburndale, Mass.: no publisher identified, first edition, 1892; second edition, 1904; third edition, 1916); it is useful to study the changes among the various editions).

203 **In the White Mountains:** The keys to early trail-building history in the White Mountains are three: Appalachian Mountain Club councillor of improvements reports; guidebooks published between 1876 and 1908; and maps, many of which were associated with guidebooks. Councillor of improvements reports may be found in many issues of *Appalachia,* beginning in 1876. Among guidebooks, the basic series at this time was Moses F. Sweetser, *The White Mountains: A Handbook for Travellers,* which also begins in 1876. See also W. H. Pickering, *Guide to the Mount Washington Range* (Boston: A. Williams, 1882), A. L. Goodrich, *The Waterville Valley: A History, Description, and Guide* (1892, 1904, 1916); F. O. Carpenter, *Guide Book to the Franconia Notch and the Pemigewasset Valley* (Boston: Alexander Moore, 1898); Wonalancet Out Door Club, *Guide to Wonalancet and the Sandwich Range of New Hampshire* (Cambridge, Mass.: Press of Powell, 1900), and *Guide to the Paths and Trails of the Sandwich Range* (revised and published by WODC, 1908), and the AMC's first *White Mountain Guide* (Boston: AMC, 1907). Maps generally appeared in conjunction with these guidebooks and in *Appalachia.* One drawn by J. B. Henck, Jr., which appeared in the first issue of *Appalachia,* is a valuable record of pre-AMC trails, but it should be studied with caution, as Henck included not only existing trails, but "proposed" new ones as well. See also H. F. Walling's "Atlas of the State of New Hampshire," 1877. For a later date, Louis Cutter's 1898 masterpiece ("Map of Northern Slopes of Madison, Adams and Jefferson") is especially important for the Northern Presidentials. This map is in the collections of the Appalachian Mountain Club.

William G. Nowell: George N. Cross, *Randolph Old and New: Its Ways and Its By-Ways* (published by the town of Randolph, N.H. 1924), pp. 256–57.

203   **"Great physical strength"**: *Ibid.*, p. 257.

205   **"When the setting sun"**: Nowell, "Report of the Councillor of Improvements," Appalachia (March 1877), pp. 110–11.

Charles E. Lowe: *American Series of Popular Biographies*, New Hampshire ed.; a brief obituary by Charles Fay et al. in *Appalachia* (June 1907), p. 321; and Cross, *Randolph Old and New*, pp. 259–60. The authors have also benefited from conversations with his grandson, Gordon Lowe, on Aug. 15, 1981, and on numerous later occasions. As of the late 1980s, the family still operated a business on the road at the base of Lowe's Path.

A "companionable" nature: The word companionable is used in Sweetser, *White Mountains*, p. 228, and in the June 1907 *Appalachia* obituary, p. 321.

"Paths to be Made": Nowell, "Report of the Councillor of Improvements," *Appalachia* (June 1876), pp. 51–57.

"We remember with what": A. E. Scott, "Report of the Councillor of Improvements," *Appalachia* (July 1880), p. 184.

Chapter 21. Three Adirondack Trail Centers

209   **Adirondack trails**: Adirondack trails history is not as richly documented as that of the White Mountains. Early guidebooks and maps are not as useful as their New Hampshire counterparts, but some information may be gleaned therefrom, especially from Stoddard, *The Adirondacks Illustrated*. Russell Carson assembled much trails information in *Peaks and People*, and Alfred L. Donaldson included a little in his *History of the Adirondacks*. In his editor's introductions to the 1973 and 1986 editions of *Peaks and People*, Philip G. Terrie, Jr., richly augmented Carson's data. Various other Adirondack writings contain scattered references to the contemporary state of trails. The single most valuable source of information to these authors, however, was the personal memory and notes of longtime Adirondacks trailsman James A. Goodwin. Mr. Goodwin drew up maps depicting the status of Adirondack trails at ten-year intervals, accompanied by copious notes under the heading "Notes on Adirondack Trail History Maps." These were made available to the authors, who in turn have deposited them in the archives of the Keene Valley Library for the use of other students of trails history.

Early Whiteface trails: Mary MacKenzie, town historian for Lake Placid, has studied the early history of Whiteface climbing and its trails, and discovered the earliest known reference to an Adirondack mountain trail, in G. T. S., "Visit to Whiteface," *Elizabethtown* (N.Y.) *Post & Gazette*, Aug. 13, 1859, p. 1. Other trails are described by Carson and Terrie in *Peaks and People* and the 1973 editor's introduction to that 1927 book, pp. 19 and xxxviii–xxxix, respectively. See also various articles in *Lake Placid News* by El Hayes: "Mount Whiteface—1860," May 4, 1928, p. 7, "The Second Trail to Whiteface and the First from Lake Placid," May 25, 1928, p. 7, and "The Pony Trail to Whiteface," June 22, 1928, p. 10.

209 **By this time:** For example, see G. H., "A Trip to Mount Marcy," *Burlington Free Press*, Sept. 29, 1870, p.2.

Marcy's first trail: Carson, *Peaks and People*, pp. 69–70 (among many sources).

210 **Second Marcy trail:** The status of whatever the Phelpses put through Johns Brook valley is difficult to document. It was described in the 1870s as "blind and full of wind slashes," with blazes far apart (Martin Bahler, "Personal Reminiscences of Keene Valley," typescript in the archives, Keene Valley Library, p. 3); in the 1890s as "almost impassable in places" ("For a Trail up Mount Marcy: Proposition to Build a Bridle Path to Near the Top of the Peak," *New York Times*, Aug. 6, 1895, p. 3); and around 1900 as "in what the politicians call a state of 'innocuous desuetude' " (unidentified newspaper clipping dated Dec. 1903, in the Comstock Scrapbooks, item no. 125–6, archives, Keene Valley Library). Walter Lowrie said that Old Mountain Phelps told him he "made" such a trail before 1860 but that it was soon abandoned in favor of the Upper Lake route (Lowrie, "Mountain Climbing in Keene Valley in the Latter Part of the Eighties and Later," typescript in Princeton University Library, with a copy also in the archives, Keene Valley Library, p. 5). Carson indicates that the trail was cut as far as the head of Panther Gorge by Ed Phelps and Seth Dibble in 1871 (Carson, *Peaks and People*, p. 76). The 1895 *New York Times* story also tells of a plan "to open a bridle path and trail to the summit of Mount Marcy" via the route. This project seems never to have proceeded very far toward realization.

Hopkins trail: Carson, *Peaks and People*, p. 127.

When Colvin's surveyors: Colvin, *Report* for 1873 (published 1874), p.26.

"No regular trail": Letter from George Notman to his mother, Mrs. Peter Notman, Aug. 21, 1874, archives, Keene Valley Library. Reprinted with permission.

Colvin trail work: The Colvin-built trails are mentioned in his reports for 1873 (published 1874), pp. 35–40, and for 1875 (published 1879), p. 97; and in the case of the earlier work on Dix, in Carson, *Peaks and People*, p. 88.

211 **Beede family:** The Beedes have not been nearly as well publicized or documented as the Crawfords. Episodic allusions are scattered through Donaldson's *History*, Carson's *Peaks and People*, and most other Adirondack volumes. See, for example, Carson (p. 122): "Yet it is quite likely that Storrow and Orlando Beede had climbed all the peaks over which the Range Trail now passes [long before the trail was cut]." The manuscript collections in the archives of the Keene Valley Library contain some helpful information, including two typed sheets of Beede family genealogy and family data, and Joseph P. Ranney, "Reminiscences of Keene Valley, 1866 to 1881" (1933). An unidentified news story in the Comstock Scrapbooks, vol. 1, p. 32, gives biographical background for Smith Beede. Later members of the family were profiled in *High Spots*—for example, Verde Beede in a reminiscence by William A. E. Cummings, Apr. 1932, pp. 14–15, and Charlie Beede in one by

Newell Martin, July 1933, pp. 9–10. This interesting family deserves a good biographer someday.

211 **Beede trail work:** Carson, *Peaks and People*, pp. 89, 127. See also James A. Goodwin, "Notes on Adirondack Trail History Maps," p. 2.

"Beede's Heights Hotel": Donaldson, *History*, vol. 2, pp. 48–50.

Gothics and Wolf Jaws trails: Carson, *Peaks and People*, pp. 122, 149.

Adirondack Mountain Reserve: The development of the Adirondack Mountain Reserve, while touched on by Donaldson (*History*, vol. 2, pp. 48–50), is more extensively treated by Edith Pilcher, in *Up the Lake Road: The First Hundred Years of the Adirondack Mountain Reserve* (Keene Valley, N.Y.: Centennial Committee for the Trustees of the Adirondack Mountain Reserve, 1987), and by Harold Weston, in *Freedom of the Wilds: A Saga of the Adirondacks* (St. Hubert's, N.Y.: Adirondack Trail Improvement Society, 1971), especially pp. 61–62.

New Gothics trail: Carson, *Peaks and People*, p. 122.

New Dix trail: *Ibid.*, p. 89.

213 **ATIS:** The anecdote has been widely told; for example, see the *75th Anniversary, 1897–1972* booklet by the Adirondack Trail Improvement Society, p. 9, in the archives of the Keene Valley Library. The formation and development of the Adirondack Trail Improvement Society (ATIS) is recounted in this booklet; in James A. Goodwin, "The Adirondack Trail Improvement Society," *Adirondac* (June 1974), pp. 55–56, 67; and more briefly in Weston, *Freedom of the Wilds*, pp. 70–71.

Wickes's trails: Carson, *Peaks and People*, pp. 122, 180, 203.

ATIS's first report: Document in possession of James A. Goodwin. For an analysis of the trails listed, see Goodwin, "Notes," pp. 3–4.

Great Range trail: William B. Glover, ed., "Reminiscences of Ed Isham of Keene Valley," *Adirondac* (Jan.–Feb. 1957), p. 9.

214 **Side trails:** *Ibid.*; see also letter from Glover to *Adirondac* (Nov.–Dec. 1969), p. 126, and Goodwin, "Notes," p. 4.

Smaller St. Hubert's trails: Goodwin, "Notes" and accompanying maps.

Henry Van Hoevenberg: Van Hoevenberg has been a popular subject among Adirondack historians and writers. See especially the obituary by Godfrey Dewey in the *Lake Placid News*, March 1, 1918, pp. 1–4; Donaldson, *History*, vol. 2, pp. 23–28; Harry Wade Hicks, "Henry Van Hoevenberg," *High Spots* (Jan. 1940), pp. 75–81; Hicks, "Early Days of Adirondak Loj," *Adirondac* (Jan.–Feb. 1959), pp. 5–7; Godfrey Dewey, "The Adirondak Loj of Long Ago," *Adirondac* (July–Aug. 1963), pp. 52–56; and William G. Distin, "Heart Lake before the Big Fire," *Adirondac* (March–Apr. 1964), p. 25.

217   "The preservation of": *The Shore Owners' Association of Lake Placid*, booklet published by that organization in 1928 (Lake Placid, N.Y.), in the collections of Mary MacKenzie.

218   **SOA trails:** Goodwin, "Notes," p. 3, and accompanying maps. See also T. Morris Longstreth, *The Lake Placid Country: A Guide to 60 Walks and Climbs from Lake Placid* (Lake Placid, N.Y.: Adirondack Camp & Trail Club, 1922).

   Old Nye trail: El Hayes, "The Second Trail to Whiteface."

   Melville Dewey: Dewey's career and his creation of the Lake Placid Club are recounted in Grosvenor Dawe, *Melvil Dewey—Seer: Inspirer-Doer— 1851–1931* (Essex Co., N.Y.: Melvil Dewey Biografy [*sic*], 1932), and in T. Morris Longstreth, *The Adirondacks* (New York: Century, 1917), pp. 240–57. See also Harry Wade Hicks, "History of Lake Placid Club: An Experiment in Intelligence," manuscript dated Sept. 7, 1938, in the archives of the Keene Valley Library.

   "By cooperation of": The phrase is noted by Stoddard, *Guide* (1903 ed.), p. 113.

   "Adirondack Lodge with": *Lake Placid Club Handbook* (for 1901), p. 167.

219   **1903 fires:** Norman J. Van Valkenburgh, *The Adirondack Forest Preserve (Blue Mountain Lake, N.Y.: Adirondack Museum, 1979), pp. 333–34. The big fires of 1903 have been described in Harry Wade Hicks,* "Great Fires of 1903," *The Conservationist* (Aug.–Sept. 1947), pp. 10–11; Donaldson, *History*, vol. 2, pp. 214–16; Hicks, "Henry Van Hoevenberg," pp. 75–77; USDA Bureau of Forestry, circular no. 26, "Forest Fires in the Adirondacks in 1903"; and elsewhere in Adirondacks literature. Contemporary news clippings concerning the fires abound in the Comstock Scrapbooks in the archives of the Keene Valley Library.

   "Worst holocaust": Hicks, "Great Fires of 1903," p. 10.

   Trail effects of 1903 fire: These have been meticulously traced in Goodwin, "Notes," p. 4, and accompanying maps.

221   **Adirondack Camp and Trail Club:** A brief sketch is in Carson, *Peaks and People*, pp. 252–53. Numerous accounts of the formation and activities of this group appeared in *Lake Placid Club Notes*, of which the following are representative: "Camp and Trail Club" (Apr. 1913), pp. 430–31; "Great Tramping Year" (Sept. 1923), pp. 1114–15; "Tramping in 1924" (Oct. 15, 1924), p. 1216; "'Facilis Ascensus'" (Oct. 1925), pp. 1348–49; "Camp and Trail Club" (Apr. 1926), pp. 1448–50; "Mountain Climbing" (July 1926), p. 1495; "Adirondak Loj" (Apr. 1928), pp. 1823–24; "All-Year Sports Leadership" (Apr. 1928), p. 1825; "For the Hiker" (Apr. 1928) pp. 1822–23; "Leaders" (Apr. 1929), p. 1979. A complete set of the *Notes* is in the collections of Mary MacKenzie of Lake Placid, N.Y. *The Lake Placid News* also carried articles on the Camp and Trail Club; for example, "What Camp and Trail Club is Doing" (Oct. 7, 1921, p. 1); "Camp and Trail Club Plan Great Improvements" (Sept. 11, 1925, p. 12); and

Harry Wade Hicks, "Annual Meeting of Camp and Trail Club August 24," (Aug. 19, 1927, p. 8).

CHAPTER 22. RANDOLPH

223   **Meanwhile, in the White Mountains:** For Randolph history, an invaluable source is George N. Cross, *Randolph Old and New: Its Ways and By-ways.* See also numerous articles in *Appalachia*—for example, Arthur Stanley Pease, "Early Trailmakers at Randolph and the Founding of the R. M. C." (Dec. 1960), pp. 187–93—and the correspondence and journals of the Pychowska women and Isabella Stone, in a collection jointly owned by George A. Kent and Douglas A. Philbrook.

"Designed to increase": Pease, "Early Trailmakers at Randolph," p. 188.

"Genial and kindly": Richard E. Dodge, "A Winter Trip to the Top of Mts. Washington and Adams in 1892," *Appalachia* (March 1898), p. 367.

225   **"Tall and broad-shouldered":** Louis F. Cutter, obituary for Laban M. Watson, *Appalachia* (June 1937), p. 417. Reprinted with permission of the Appalachian Mountain Club.

"A slender wiry": Cross, *Randolph Old and New*, p. 55.

"A loud and merry laugh": *Ibid.*

"Indefatigable leaders": Letter from Marian Pychowska to Isabella Stone, Sept. 18, 1885, in collections of Kent and Philbrook. Reprinted with permission.

"Athletic, brilliant": Louis F. Cutter, "The Edmands Paths and Their Builder," *Appalachia* (Aug. 1921), p. 139.

"Learned, kindly": *Ibid.*

And bad puns: George N. Cross, "Randolph Yesteryears," *Appalachia* (Dec. 1916), pp. 57–58.

226   **"Eager to share":** Cutter, "Edmands Paths," p. 140.

"A labor of piety": *Ibid.*

"Everybody, under the inspiration": Cross, "Randolph Yesteryears," p. 57. Reprinted with permission of the Appalachian Mountain Club.

228   **"Magnificent mid-air promenade":** Sweetser, *White Mountains* (1887 ed.), p. 109b.

"Engineer-in-chief": Nowell, "Report of the Councillor of Improvements," *Appalachia* (March 1886), p. 270.

"Small, blond": Mabel Hidden and Jean Ulitz, eds., *Tamworth Recollections* (North Conway, N.H.: Reporter Press, North Conway Publishing, 1976), p. 102. Katherine Sleeper and the changes in Wonalancet during the 1890s are described in this source, and in Marjory Gane Harkness, *The*

Tamworth Narrative (Freeport, Maine: Bond Wheelwright, 1958), especially pp. 232–56.

228   **"A veritable dynamo":** Hidden and Ulitz, *Tamworth Recollections*, p. 102.

"All her life": *Ibid.*

"An enthusiastic body": Charles E. Fay, "Mount Passaconaway," *Appalachia* (Jan. 1892), p. 315.

Tom Wiggin: WODC, 1900 *Guide*, p. 35.

230   **Chocorua:** Besides the usual sources for trails history cited earlier, see Samuel I. Bowditch, "Recollections of a Summer Complaint," typescript in Chocorua Public Library; notebook labeled "Chocorua Reminiscences" in Chocorua Public Library; Marion L. Nickerson and John A. Downs, *Chocorua Peak House* (Center Conway, N.H.: Walker's Pond Press, 1977); John E. Pember, "Axes Fly when 'C. M. C.' Boys 'Clean Up' Mt. Chocorua," *Boston Sunday Herald*, July 1, 1923, p. D-11; and Frederick W. Kilbourne, "Chocorua: The Complete Mountain," *Appalachia* (Dec. 1942), pp. 155–66. The authors also profited from conversations with Samuel I. Bowditch and Hutcheson Page, Sept. 15, 1981, and with Mr. and Mrs. Robert Lloyd, Apr. 13, 1982; and from correspondence with Robert Ward, Dec. 1981.

Rosebrook Range: The history of the Rosebrook Range trails has never been well documented. The Mount Pleasant House's transformation is cited by Kilbourne in *Chronicles*, pp. 337–38, and isolated references may be found to the trails in *Appalachia* (for example, June 1907, pp. 280, 311). Otherwise their history can be inferred from comparing various editions of White Mountain guidebooks and maps over the years. The single most useful source on this area for the authors was the personal recollection of Raymond W. Evans, and walks with him over the range where once the trails were.

Crawford House: Major Raymond's guiding hand in trails around Crawford Notch is evident in councillor of improvements reports during the 1880s. See, for example, *Appalachia* (Apr. 1883), pp. 188–89.

Franconia Notch: Isabella Stone's activities can be traced in the councillor of improvements report, *Appalachia* (Dec. 1884), pp. 84–86, and in correspondence from the Pychowskas, in collection of Kent and Philbrook. Carpenter's efforts are set forth in Frank O. Carpenter, *Guide Book to the Franconia Notch and the Pemigewasset Valley*, and in councillor of improvements reports, *Appalachia*, especially from May 1902 (pp. 98–100) and thereafter. The North Woodstock Improvement Association's classic statement of the "Improvements" philosophy, as quoted (**with the specific purpose**), appears in *A Little Pathfinder to Places of Interest in or Near North Woodstock, New Hampshire*, a booklet of the North Woodstock Improvement Association, 4th ed. (1921). The turn of the century trail work in the North Woodstock region is described in Mabel Potter, ed., *Karl Pomeroy Harrington: The Autobiography of a Versatile and Vigorous Professor* (Boston: Thomas Todd, 1975); see especially pp. 210–21.

231   **"I think . . . that we there":** A. E. Scott, "Report of the Councillor of Improvements," *Appalachia* (Apr. 1883), pp. 188–89.

CHAPTER 23. OTHER TRAIL SYSTEMS

233   **Monadnock trails:** See Chamberlain, *Annals of the Grand Monadnock*, pp. 64–67; Henry Ives Baldwin, *Monadnock Guide*, 3d ed. (Concord, N.H.: Society for the Protection of New Hampshire Forests, 1980), pp. 83–103; and compare the following maps: "Topographical Map of Monadnock Mountain, New Hampshire," Jan. 1891, *Appalachia*, placed between the issues of July 1891 and Jan. 1892; Scott A. Smith, "Monadnock Trails, laid out and developed by Scott A. Smith, 1894 to 1907," and E. J. Harling, "Trails Up Mt. Monadnock, Jaffrey, N.H., 1916," both in the collections of the Monadnock State Park headquarters, Jaffrey, N.H.; and Riding and Walking Club of Dublin, N.H., "Map of the Town of Dublin, New Hampshire," 1921. The authors were greatly assisted, both in research and on-the-ground investigations, by Richard A. Scaramelli, a local authority on Monadnock history.

    Prof. Raphael Pumpelly: This engaging individual is described in Henry Darracott Allison, *Dublin Days: Old and New* (New York: Exposition Press, 1952), p. 123.

    "Fine forest growths": H. H. Piper, "A Sketch of Dublin," *Granite Monthly* (Aug. 1896), p. 82. See also George Willis Cooke, "Old Times and New in Dublin, New Hampshire," *New England Magazine* (Aug. 1899), pp. 745–62.

234   **"Miles of these":** Elizabeth Weston Timlow, *The Heart of Monadnock* (Boston: B. J. Brimmer, 1962), pp. 6–10.

235   **Mount Desert:** Early guidebooks of the area refer to walks and paths but are not very explicit. See E. H. Dodge, *Guide Book and Map to and over Mount Desert* (Portland, Maine: Loring, Short, and Harmon, 1872—the cover says 1874, but the title page and map give the earlier date); Clara Barnes Martin, *Mount Desert on the Coast of Maine* (Portland, Maine: Loring, Short, and Harmon, 1874); *Handbook of Mount Desert* (Boston: A. Williams; New York: T. Whittaker; Bar Harbor, Maine: A. W. Bee, 1880); *Bar Harbor Blue Book and Mount Desert Guide* (Boston: Albert W. Bee, 1881); and W. B. Lapham, *Bar Harbor and Mount Desert* (Augusta, Maine: Maine Farmer Job Print, 1888). Early records of the Village Improvement Association are preserved in a bound volume of *Bar Harbor Village Improvement Association Reports, etc., 1890–1905* and subsequent separately bound annual reports in the collections of the Bar Harbor Historical Society. The VIA's trail-building efforts eventually generated a new and much more comprehensive and detailed guidebook, Waldron Bates, Edward L. Rand, and Herbert Jacques, *A Path Guide of Mount Desert Island Maine* (Bar Harbor, Maine: W. H. Sherman, 1915). See also Richard Walden Hale, Jr., *The Story of Bar Harbor* (New York: Ives Washburn, 1849), especially pp. 192–94, and Gladys O'Neil, "Acadia's Memorial Paths," *Maine Life* (June 1981): pp. 24–26. For an account of trail building elsewhere on the island, see William W. Vaughan, *Northeast Harbor Reminiscences by an Old Summer Resident* (No city given: White and Horne, 1930), especially pp. 68–71.

235 **"To open the grand"**: Address by Parke Godwin, printed in the fifth annual report of the Bar Harbor Village Improvement Association, Sept. 1894, p. 11.

236 **"Steep and dizzy"**: Bates, Rand, and Jacques, *Path Guide*, p. 13.

Greylock: The key source is the *Annual Reports* of the Greylock Commission, from its beginnings in 1899. The Berkshire Athenaeum in Pittsfield, Mass., is one of the few places where a full set of this valuable series may be found. The authors also benefited from the advice of Robert Hatton, who knows the mountain and its history as well as anyone.

A maze of fallen trees: "Greylock Mountain," *The Berkshire Hills*, Jan. 1, 1902, pp. 2–6.

"A tolerably good road": Edward Hitchcock, "History of Western Massachusetts," *Springfield* (Mass.) *Daily Republican*, May 22, 1854, p. 1. An almost identical account of the building of this road is given by Edward Hitchcock in his chapter on geology in Josiah Gilbert Holland's *History of Western Massachusetts* in 1855.

237 **"A choice mountain passage"**: Evert A. Duyckinck, "Notes of Excursions: An Ascent of Mount Saddleback," *Literary World*, Aug. 30, 1851, p. 161.

Certainly the lower part: Denault, "The Jeremiah Wilbur Homestead."

"Century old path": "Routes by Which to Get to Greylock's Summit," *Berkshire Eagle*, Sept. 30, 1914, p. 13.

238 **One authority**: J. Parker Huber, *The Wildest Country: A Guide to Thoreau's Maine* (Boston: AMC, 1981), p. 145.

"At times it was": "Roughing It on Greylock," *Pittsfield Sun*, July 20, 1893, p. 6.

There may also: "Greylock Mountain," *Berkshire Hills*, Jan. 1, 1902, p. 2.

An old right-of-way: Referred to as "discontinued as a public right of way some years since" in the Greylock Commission *Annual Report* of 1906, p. 5.

"The Hopper": H. A. Edson, "Mountains and Tramps," *Williams Quarterly* (June 1855), p. 359.

A Pittsfield newspaper: L. A., "Excursion to Greylock," *Pittsfield Sun*, June 7, 1849, p. 2. Further evidence for an established trail over Prospect to Greylock is found in a 1916 guide that refers to such a trail as "apparently that used by Williams men of sixty years ago to ascend Greylock" (Francis William Rockwell, Jr., *Greylock Guide*, copyrighted by the author, 1816, ed. of 1817, p. 19). An 1860 account describes a route over Prospect "which to some extent has been cleared," though apparently not all the way to the top (Calvin Durfee, *A History of Williams College* [Boston: A. Williams, 1860], p. 392.)

A Williams College: "Editorials," *Williams Athenaeum* (Nov. 1874), p. 15.

238   **"After scrambling up"**: C. A. Stoddard, "Greylock," *Williams Quarterly* (July 1853), p. 10.

One of the first: "Greylock Mountain," *Berkshire Hills*, Jan. 1, 1902, p. 2. See also John Bascom, "Greylock Reservation," in *Collections of the Berkshire Historical and Scientific Society*, p. 260; and Greylock Commission, *Annual Report* (1913), p. 4.

Sometime during the late 1890s: Bascom, "Greylock Reservation," p. 262, and "What the State Reservation Has Done," *Berkshire Eagle*, Sept. 11, 1905, p. 8.

239   **"There are now two"**: Greylock Commission, *Annual Report* (1904), p. 3. Except as otherwise noted, the remainder of this discussion of Greylock's trails history is based on the commission's reports. See also Williams College records in "Good Government Club Scrapbook' (1915), pp. 5, 17, 23.

240   **"Highest mountain in town"**: Bryan, *The Book of Berkshire*, p. 48.

"A convenient point": Berkshire Life Insurance Company, "Drives and Walks: Pittsfield and Vicinity," p. 9.

"At least 25 miles": *Ibid.*, p. 54.

Pathfinders: Names of members are listed on a loving cup dated Sept. 4, 1923, in the collections of the Stockbridge Library, Stockbridge, Mass. Their trail work is described in early issues of *Stockbridge* magazine—see, for example, "Monument Mt. Trail" (July 1914), p. 4; "The Reservation" (May 1915), pp. 54–55; "Stockbridge Trails and By-Ways" (June 1915), pp. 73–76; and "Editorial" (July 1915), p. 83.

Bash Bish Inn: Hiram C. Todd, "Bash Bish Falls: Moquin's Famous Inn Brought Elite to Copake Falls," *Chatham* (N.Y.) *Courier*, Aug. 20, 1964, unpaged.

241   **AMC excursion:** "Report of the Councillor of Improvements," *Appalachia* (Dec. 1888), p. 252.

Amherst Mountain Club trails: Amherst Mountain Club Papers, in the collections of the Amherst College Archives. Some of these trails were recalled for the authors by old-time hikers in the area (conversation with Carl O. Chauncey, Oct. 25, 1982).

"For about fifteen years": Paul D. Bartlett, "Mountain Trails and the Amherst Outing Club," *Amherst Graduates' Quarterly* (Aug. 1928), p. 231.

CHAPTER 24. TRAILS THAT FAILED

243   **Katahdin trails:** As usual, Hakola's *Legacy of a Lifetime* is an excellent starting point for Katahdin trails history. For the 1870–1910 period a second key source is the two-part analysis by Myron H. Avery, "The Keep Path and Its Successors," *Appalachia* (Dec. 1928, June 1929). See also H. Walter Leavitt, *Katahdin Skylines* (Orono, Maine: University of Maine Press, 1942).

243   **A sweeping change:** For the lumbering era of the 1880s and 1890s, besides Hakola, see Augustus A. Hamlin, "Routes to Mt. Ktaadn," *Maine Sportsman* (Sept. 1894), p. 6, and "Up Katahdin on Horseback," *Maine Sportsman* (May 1903), pp. 171–72.

245   **Tracey and Love trail:** Avery, "Keep Path" (June 1929), p. 225.

"The discovery of": Unidentified clipping in a scrapbook dated 1885, book 6, file 7, in the collections of the James W. Sewall Company, Old Town, Maine. Reprinted with permission.

"A favorite resort": *Ibid.*

McLeod Trail: Avery, "Keep Path" (June 1929), p. 226.

Rogers 1894 trail: *Ibid.*, pp. 226–27. See also "Up Katahdin on Horseback," pp. 171–72.

246   **"Whence the ascent":** Hamlin, "Routes to Mt. Ktaadn," p. 6.

"Never before has": Frank Hazelwood Rowe, "Up Maine's Big Hill," *Maine Sportsman* (Nov. 1900), p. 57.

"At one time": "Up Katahdin on Horseback," p. 172.

The ink was: The "great burn" of 1903 is richly described in Avery's "Forest Fires at Mount Katahdin," *The Northern* (June 1928), pp. 3–4.

Appalachian Trail: R. B. Lawrence, "Improvements at Mount Ktaadn, Me.," an appendix to the "Councillor of Improvements Report," *Appalachia* (June 1888), pp. 156–58.

"Very rough and hard": Letter from Samuel Merrill to Myron H. Avery, Dec. 22, 1931, Avery Papers, Maine State Library. Reprinted with permission.

Two AMC members: Fullerton L. Waldo, "Notes on a Recent Visit to Ktaadn," *Appalachia* (Nov. 1896), p. 190.

Rogers 1902 trail: Avery, "Keep Path" (June 1929), pp. 228–30.

247   **Irving Hunt trail:** The legend is cited in "Field Notes: The Katahdin August Camp—1925," *Appalachia* (Feb. 1926), p. 372. The "old Eagle" moniker is given by H. Walter Leavitt, *Katahdin Skylines*, p. 37. The Hunt Trail is described by Hakola, *Legacy of a Lifetime*, p. 42. There is confusion as to the date of its construction. We accept the circa. 1900 date given by Hakola and an article in *In the Maine Woods*, 1927 (Frederic Bulkeley Hyde, "The Taming of Mt. Katahdin"), pp. 52–53. On the other hand, Leavitt gives the date as 1890 (*Katahdin Skylines*, p. 31) and so does a later *In the Maine Woods* article (1939, Myron Avery, "Katahdin: Its History," p. 21). The 1900 date seems more consistent with what is known about the movements of the Hunt brothers. A 1908 article cites the Hunt Trail as "recently cut" (Frederic Bulkeley Hyde, "Under Katahdin's Shadow," *In the Maine Woods* [1908], p. 94).

247 **Abol Slide trail:** See, for examples, Newman Smith, "The Lake Country of New England," *Scribner's Magazine* (July 1890), pp. 493–506; Hubbard's Moosehead *Guide* (1893), pp. 74–75; "Down the West Branch," *Maine Sportsman* (Jan. 1898), p. 13; Frank Hazelton Rowe, "Up Maine's Big Hill," *Maine Sportsman* (Nov. 1900), p. 57; A. Radclyffe Dugmore, "Alone up Mt. Katahdin," *Everybody's Magazine* (June 1901), pp. 547–59; "Up Mount Katahdin," *Maine Sportsman* (July 1902), p. 229, and "The Fish and Game Region," *In the Maine Woods* (1905), p. 47.

"Until 1921, the best-known route": Appalachian Mountain Club, *Guide to Paths in the White Mountains and Adjacent Regions* (1925 ed.), p. 459.

"The route commonly taken," "Could however see no traces," and "A steep and rugged": Josiah S. Swift, "Saddleback in 1839: The Account of an Ascent," with some remarks added by Benton L. Hatch, *Appalachia* (Dec. 1945), pp. 491–92. Reprinted with permission of the Appalachian Mountain Club.

Farrar's 1880 Guide: Charles A. J. Farrar, *Guide* (Rangeley; 1880 ed.), pp. 213, 175, 203.

"Very blind," and "If you have": Farrar, *Guide* (Androscoggin; 1890 ed.), p. 285.

"From there on": G. S. O., "A Morning on Bald Mountain," *Maine Sportsman* (Feb. 1897), p. 6.

AMC explorer on White Cap: Gaetano Lanza, "A Sojourn in Andover, Maine" *Appalachia* (May 1881), p. 247.

"Much improved in": Farrar, *Guide* (Androscoggin; 1888 ed.) p. 63.

"A good path": *Ibid.* (1890 ed.), p. 196.

"A celebrated place," and "The tourist who": John S. C. Abbott, *The History of Maine*, 2d ed. (Portland, Maine: Brown, Thurston, 1892), p. 500.

"Bushed out and cut": Lucius L. Hubbard, *Guide to Moosehead Lake* (1882 ed.), p. 44. A Bates College student climbed this trail in October of that year and contributed an account to the student paper (H. Woodbury, letter to *The Student* [Feb. 1881], pp. 23–24).

"Spotted trail": "Rustling Leaves," *Maine Sportsman* (Nov. 1901), p. 41. See also Hubbard, *Guide* (Moosehead; 1893 ed.), pp. 149–50, and Herbert W. Rowe, "Across the Chairback Range," *Maine Sportsman* (June 1901), pp. 229–32.

248 **Little Mount Agamenticus:** See, for example, Justin Henry Shaw, " 'Agamenticus Majestic': York County's Mountain and the Legend of 'Saint Aspenquid,' " *Sprague's Journal of Maine History* (Apr.–June 1923), pp. 72–73.

"Where by the aid": Hubbard, *Guide* (Moosehead; 1882 ed.), p. 52.

"A flight of stairs": James S. Rowe, "Moosehead Lake and Kineo," *Maine Sportsman* (July 1899), pp. 11–12.

248 **Mount Mansfield trails:** Hagerman's *Mansfield* is the prime source for any trails information on this mountain.

"Through tangled underbrush": Quoted by Lee, *Green Mountains*, pp. 206–7.

Maple Ridge trail: Green Mountain Club, *Guide Book of the Long Trail*, 19th ed. (1968), p. 111.

1862 Big Spring trail: Clarence P. Cowles, "Trails up Mount Mansfield," p. 2, typescript dated Jan. 27 1946, in Cowles Papers, manuscript collections of the Bailey-Howe Library, University of Vermont. Dates for the hotel are given in Hagerman, *Mansfield*, p. 52.

1866–67 road plans: Frederic J. Wood, *The Turnpikes of New England*, p. 282, and "The Mount Mansfield Turnpike Co.," *Burlington Free Press*, Apr. 18, 1867, p. 4.

"A spur called Blue Ridge": R. D. E., "A Trip to Mount Mansfield," *Burlington Free Press*, July 9, 1878, p. 3.

Pleasant Valley trail: An Appalachian Mountain Club party in 1885 descended over the north end to Smugglers' Notch and implies that there was no trail on that side ("Excursions of the Season of 1885," *Appalachia* [March 1886], p. 282. On the other hand, an account of an ascent in 1892 refers to coming up from Cambridge that year, apparently by trail ("The Force of the Floods: A Graphic Description of the Last Slide on Mount Mansfield," *Burlington Free Press*, Sept. 2, 1892, p. 4). By 1909, when he was on the mountain James Taylor found no trail that led over to Lake of the Clouds (for one of the more colorful of many versions of Taylor's experience, see his address at the Long Trail Lodge, Sept. 12, 1931, pp. 2–3, in collections of the Vermont Historical Society). But Judge Cowles recalls that when he first worked on the Long Trail in 1910 there was a "trail up from Pleasant Valley" (Cowles, "Trails up Mount Mansfield"). By the time the Green Mountain Club published the first Long Trail *Guides*, in the late 1910s and early 1920s, whatever had been there was at first ignored. In the 1930 *Guide*, however, the Pleasant Valley Trail appears, though marked "Obscure and little used." By 1932 it is called "No longer maintained." Beginning in 1935 it was dropped from GMC maps, presumably indicating its virtual disappearance. During the 1960s the Clyde Smiths (father and son) reopened this old trail, and for a while it was informally maintained by the younger Smith, Jack Harrington, and others, but by the 1970s these efforts had again faded, and the route lapsed back to wilderness. (Conversations and correspondence with Clyde Smith, Jack Harrington, Pieter Crow, and others.)

249 **Smugglers' and Nebraska notches:** Hagerman, *Mansfield*, pp. 48–56, 78–80.

250 **"Yearly becoming one":** William Slade, "Excursion to Camel's Hump," *Family Magazine* (1838; no month given), p. 252.

Trail from Huntington side: *Ibid.*

250   **Guiding by farmers:** An account of an ascent circa 1850 tells of farmers apparently negotiating with visitors to get a fee for guiding them up. See John H. Rheyn, "The Couching Lion," *Sartain's Union Magazine* (June 1851), p. 381.

        Ridley's road: J. H. R., "How to Reach Camel's Hump," *Burlington Free Press*, July 31, 1860, p. 2.

        "By the middle": Lee, *Green Mountains*, p. 204.

251   **Lincoln Peak path:** Philip Battell, "Potato Hill," manuscript in collections of the Sheldon Art Museum, Middlebury, Vermont, date uncertain but estimated to be between 1849 and 1858. The authors are indebted to Polly C. Darnell, librarian of the Sheldon Art Museum, for alerting us to this manuscript.

        Mount Hunger road: Perry H. Merrill, *Vermont under Four Flags: A History of the Green Mountain State, 1635–1975* (Montpelier, Vermont: published by the author, 1975), p. 248; see also Walter Collins O'Kane, *Trails and Summits of the Green Mountains* (Boston: Houghton Mifflin, 1926), p. 275.

        Snake Mountain road: Lee, *Green Mountains*, pp. 216–17.

        Killington developments: The development of Killington's hotel and associated trails may be pieced together from Julia C. R. Dorr, "Going up Mount Killington," *The Vermonter* (July 1905), pp. 389–94; Mortimer R. Proctor, "Killington Peak," *The Vermonter* (Feb. 1911), pp. 39–43; O'Kane, *Green Mountains*, p. 104; and Fleming, *History of Sherburne*, p. 55. See also USGS topographical map for Rutland, 1893.

        "Like the stony bed": James P. Taylor, typescript of an address to a University of Vermont audience in Boston, dated 1911, in Taylor Papers, collections of the Vermont Historical Society.

        Figure 24.4: Mansfield, Camel's Hump, Killington, and Ascutney had long-established trails, which were referred to in earlier chapters. Owl's Head near Lake Memphremagog had a trail frequently alluded to in nineteenth-century tourist guides. It is mentioned as late as 1906 in J. C. Hubbard, "A Message from Memphremagog," *The Vermonter* (June 1906), p. 175. Jay Peak's trail is also refered to in tourist guides and is described in "Mountain Directory," *The Vermonter* (May 1908), p. 142, and in an article by Lilian Wright, "Jay Peak," *The Vermonter* (July 1910), p. 210. Belvidere had a path in a listing of Vermont trails dated 1911–14 in the James Taylor Papers in the Vermont Historical Society's collections; it is shown on the USGS topographical map for 1925 (a trail independent of the Long Trail, which was cut over Belvidere about that date). Pisgah (then Ananance), Westmore (now Bald), and Wheeler are all mentioned as having had trails around 1910 by Harriet Fish, a local resident with personal memory of them (conversaton with Harriet Fish, July 30, 1982). This area was a prominent resort in the late nineteenth century. Burke Mountain had a trail cut around 1910 or 1911, as cited by Perry Merrill in *Vermont under Four Flags*, p. 249, as well as in Bradford F.

Swan, "Joseph Seavey Hall: White Mountain Guide," *Appalachia* (June 1960), p. 58, and in John B. Chase, "Burke Mountain," *The Vermonter* (June 1910), pp. 185–86. A Hunger Mountain trail is also referred to by Merrill, p. 249, by O'Kane, *Green Mountains*, p. 36, and by E. R. Plaisted, "Mount Hunger," *The Vermonter* (Sept. 1910), p. 269. Mount Philo, south of Burlington, is written up by Samuel E. Bassett, "Mount Philo," *The Vermonter* (June 1910), pp. 169–73, with a trail to the top specifically mentioned. Several mountains in the vast land holdings of Joseph Battell had trails built in the last years of the last century, and these trails were actively used by people staying at the Breadloaf Inn in the years around 1910. These paths are described in the promotional literature of the inn during those years, and include the following mountains: Ellen, Lincoln, Abraham, Bread Loaf, Burnt Hill, Silent Cliff, Worth Mountain, Monastery Mountain, and Philadelphia Peak. This literature is available in the special collections of the Middlebury College Library. Rattlesnake Mountain, east of Lake Dunmore, is shown on the USGS map for 1902 as having a trail to the top. Snake Mountain in the town of Addison is mentioned as climbed via a path in Lee, *Green Mountains*, pp. 216–17. Mounts Horrid and Carmel are both mentioned in a brochure written by Louis J. Paris for the Brandon Inn in 1914. At that time, Horrid had two paths up it, Carmel three. Mount Tom near Woodstock had a path up it as early as the latter part of the nineteenth century (letter from Mrs. John H. McDill to L&GW, Sept. 17, 1982). Mount Equinox had a trail on the USGS map of 1894, and it is described in Sarah W. Orvis, "Mount Equinox," *The Vermonter* (July 1910), pp. 212–14, as well as in "Mountain Directory" (May 1908), p. 143. Glastenbury has a long history as a popular peak for blueberry pickers from the city of Bennington, as attested by such longtime residents as John Paulson (conversation with Paulson, Oct. 16, 1981, and Oct. 5, 1982). Haystack, lying between Bennington and Brattleboro, was climbed from both towns. An Appalachian Mountain Club excursion went up its path, as mentioned in "Excursions," *Appalachia* (March 1900), p. 209, and this trail is described in "Old Home Week," *The Vermonter* (Sept. 1900), p. 22. For other peaks indicated in figure 24.4, see contemporary USGS maps; the authors are indebted to the indefatigable researcher-hiker George A. Pearlstein for pointing out these trails on USGS maps.

252   **Catskill trails:** Consult Evers, *Catskills*, and the invaluable Ph.D. dissertation by Michael Kudish, "Vegetational History of the Catskill High Peaks."

253   **Overlook Mountain House:** Evers, *Catskills*, pp. 470–80.

Haines Falls trails: Charles T. Wingate, *Round about Twilight Park*, undated brochure estimated about 1910; Linger Not Society, *Handbook of Walks in the Vicinity of Twilight Park*, brochure dated 1912. Both these documents are in the collections of the Haines Falls (N.Y.) Library.

Mount Hunter trails: Ulster & Delaware Railroad, *The Catskill Mountains*, promotional brochure dated 1902, p. 101.

Mount Pisgah road: J. B. Beers, *History of Greene County* (New York: George MacNamara, 1884), pp. 75–76.

253   **Nebo, Tower, Belle Ayre:** USGS topographical map for Durham, 1892 ed. (for Mount Nebo); DeLisser, *Picturesque Ulster*, p. 193 (for Belle Ayre).

Tremper, Tobias, Pleasant: Ulster & Delaware Railroad, *The Catskill Mountains*, pp. 53–55.

High Point trail: "The ascent is no longer difficult, there being a well marked road over half the way" (*ibid*, p. 51).

Balsam Lake and Utsayantha: *Ibid.*, pp. 80–81.

Fire tower trails: Section on "Observation Stations" in New York Forest, Fish, and Game Commission, Sixteenth annual report, (1910), pp. 25–26; see also Michael Kudish, "Towers, Trails, and Campsites," unpublished typescript in Dr. Kudish's files.

James Dutcher trail: Evers, *Catskills*, pp. 555, 576–80; DeLisser, *Picturesque Ulster*, p. 221; letter from Michael Kudish to L&GW, June 18, 1985.

Wittenberg and Cornell: Ulster & Delaware Railroad brochure, *A Catskill Souvenir: Scenes on the Line of the Ulster & Delaware Railroad*, dated 1879, text to accompany sketches no. 4 and no. 6. See also Raymond Torrey, "Trails in the Catskills," *Appalachia* (June 1928), p. 47.

"Forced to turn back": Haring, *Our Catskill Mountains*, p. 15.

Fresh Air Club: Torrey, "Trails in the Catskills," p. 47.

254   **Curtis-Ormsbee trail:** DeLisser, *Picturesque Ulster*, p. 221; Torrey, "Trails in the Catskills," p. 47. The legislation explicitly providing funds "for completing the public path leading to the summit of Slide Mountain" was in chap. 356 of the laws of 1892, state of New York.

No record exists: For example, USGS maps for Durham, 1892, show no trails on the Windham High Peak–Black Head–Thomas Cole chain; and for Phoenicia, 1900, show none on the Belle Ayre–Big Indian ridge. These maps are *not* an infallible guide to the status of trails, but no literature of the period alludes to trails in these areas until the 1920s and 1930s.

CHAPTER 25. BACKCOUNTRY CAMPING IN THE EIGHTIES AND NINETIES

255   **Overnight camping trips:** The best way to study nineteenth-century camping practices is to read the first generation of how-to manuals. These include special sections in the leading guidebooks of the day, notably Sweetser's *White Mountains Guide* (1876) and Stoddard's (1874) and Wallace's (1875) Adirondacks counterparts. A very early independent book is John M. Gould, *How to Camp Out* (1877). Two later manuals with important influence were Horace Kephart's *Book of Camping and Woodcraft* (New York: Macmillan, 1906) and the AMC's publication prepared by Allen Bent, Ralph Lawson, and Perceval Sayward, *Equipment for Mountain Climbing and Camping* (Boston: AMC, 1916). For a dozen others that appeared between Gould and Bent-Lawson-Sayward, especially after 1910, see other specific citations in the notes for this chapter. Others not specifically cited include D. C. Beard, *The Field and Forest Handy Book* (New York: Charles Scribner's

Sons, 1906); George S. Bryan, ed., *The Camper's Own Book* (New York: Log Cabin Press, 1912); Charles Stedman Hanks, *Camp Kits and Camp Life* (New York: Charles Scribner's Sons, 1915); Howard Henderson, *Practical Hints on Camping* (Chicago: Jansen, McClung, 1882); Oliver Kemp, *Wilderness Homes* (New York: Outing Publishing, 1908); Warren H. Miller, *Campcraft* (New York: Charles Scribner's Sons, 1915); Ernest Thompson Seton, *The Book of Woodcraft* (Garden City, N.Y.: Doubleday, Page, 1912); Frederic Shelford, *Pioneering* (New York: Spen & Chamberlain, 1909), and C. A. Stephens, ed., *Camping Out* (Boston: James R. Osgood, 1872). Another source of information on camping habits is, of course, the many narratives of camping trips during these years.

255 **"Difficult to make":** Sweetser, *White Mountains*, p. 39.

"The fir boughs": Frank E. Wolfe, "Pamola: An Ascent of Mt. Katahdin, Maine," *Forest and Stream*, Jan. 1, 1898, p. 5.

256 **"Bark shelters left":** J. Rayner Edmands, "A Day on Flume Mountain and a Night in the Wilderness," *Appalachia* (March 1886), p. 198.

Tents: Gould, *How to Camp Out*, pp. 75–79; A. Judd Northrup, *Camps and Tramps in the Adirondacks* (Syracuse, N.Y.: Davis Bardeen, 1880), p. 273; Sweetser, *White Mountains*, p. 39. Another proponent of the shed design was John B. Bachelder, in *Popular Resorts, and How to Reach Them*, p. 15.

"Burdensome to carry": Sweetser, *White Mountains*, p. 39.

In 1877 Major Gould: Gould, *How to Camp Out*, pp. 25–34.

"If possible, buy": "Camping Out," *Burlington Free Press*, Aug. 3, 1880, p. 4.

257 **"Hemlock or balsam":** Northrup, *Camps and Tramps*, p. 275.

Sweetser recommended: Sweetser, *White Mountains*, p. 37.

By around 1900: The eighteen-pound model is lauded in G. O. Shields, *Camping and Camp Outfits* (Chicago: McNally, 1890), p. 32.

"Most old campers": Edward Breck, *The Way of the Woods* (New York: G. P. Putnam's Sons, 1910), p. 49.

An AMC manual: Bent, Lawson, and Sayward, *Equipment*, p. 5.

A 1912 manual: Dillon Wallace, *Packing and Portaging* (New York: Outing Publishing, 1912), p. 107.

Boy Scouts in the Berkshires: Walter Prichard Eaton, "Joys of the True Walker," *American Magazine* (June 1913), p. 13.

One Adirondack tramper: Letter from Herbert McAneny to L&GW, May 30, 1982. Marion Foynes of Randolph, N.H., recalled carrying bedrolls in White Mountain hikes of the 1910s (conversation with Foynes, July 13, 1983).

257   **"Indispensible to the"**: Sweetser, *White Mountains*, p. 39.

"It feels bulky": Gould, *How to Camp Out*, p. 18.

"A common grain-bag": Stoddard, *Adirondacks*, p. 4.

"When it can be": Wallace, *Adirondacks*, 8th ed., p. 240.

258   **A popular day-trip**: The haversack seems to be recommended by Sweetser for less ambitious excursions than those for which a knapsack is needed (*White Mountains*, p. 39). Bachelder advocates the haversack for day-trips (*Popular Resorts*, p. 15). A photograph of a 1906 outing shows them in use (collection of Marion Foynes).

What went into: Gould, *How to Camp Out*, pp. 11, 14.

Whiskbroom: Allen Chamberlain, *Vacation Tramps in New England Highlands* (Boston: Houghton Mifflin, 1919), p. 26.

"Some good brandy": J. R., Jr., "Outfit for the Adirondacks," *Forest and Stream*, Aug. 3, 1882, p. 5.

"A small bottle": Sweetser, *White Mountains*, p. 39.

"Wear what you": Gould, *How to Camp Out*, p. 12.

"Coarse and trustworthy": Lossing, *The Hudson*, p. 27.

"A good stout suit": J. R., Jr., "Outfit," p. 4.

"To start with": Shields, *Camping*, p. 11.

"I am a member": Chamberlain, *Vacation Tramps*, p. 24.

What to eat: Most of the how-to guides cited in the preceding notes dispense extensive advice on camping food of the day.

259   **One guidebook's section**: H. H. Windsor, ed., *The Boy Mechanic: 1000 Things for Boys to Do* (Chicago: Popular Mechanics, 1915), vol. 2, p. 97.

"Rest often whether": Gould, *How to Camp Out*, pp. 50, 55.

"Maxims for Mountaineers": John Ross Dix, *A Handbook for Lake Memphremagog* (Boston: Evans, 1864), p. 36.

"Remember . . . that you": In a passage contributed by Edward Everett Hale to Gould's *How to Camp Out*, p. 114.

"In resting on": Frank O. Carpenter, *Guide Book to the Franconia Notch*, p. 129.

260   **"One should be careful"**: *Ibid.* This advice was concurred in by Gould (*How to Camp Out*, p. 58), and William H. Pickering, *Guide to the Mount Washington Range*, p. 12, though the latter urged drinking copiously before the day's hiking.

"Frequent small drinks": Ralph C. Larrabee, "Observations on the Physiology and Hygiene of Climbing," *Appalachia* (May 1903), pp. 170–72.

260   **"Alpenstocks are seldom":** Pickering, *Guide*, p. 9.

One guide analyzed: Wallace, *Adirondacks* (1875 ed.), pp. 245–46.

"One drop to each": Charlotte E. Ricker, "The Wilderness," *White Mountain Echo*, Aug. 26, 1882, p. 5.

Special remedies for: Pickering, *Guide*, p. 10.

"Do not be saucy": Gould, *How to Camp Out*, p. 56.

"Try to be civil": *Ibid.*

"Very much as shingles": Sweetser, *White Mountains*, p. 37.

CHAPTER 26. PYCHOWSKAS ASCENDANT

261   **Late nineteenth-century:** Of many treatments of this subject, see, for examples, Eleanor Flexner, *Century of Struggle: The Woman's Rights Movement in the United States* (Cambridge, Mass.: Harvard University Press, Belknap Press, 1959), and Betty Friedan, *The Feminine Mystique* (New York: Norton, 1963), pp. 73–94.

Despite all this: Although books have been compiled about women climbing in the Alps or other great ranges —see, for example, Cicely Williams, *Women on the Rope: The Feminine Share in Mountain Adventure* (London: George Allen & Unwin, 1973), and Luree Miller, *On Top of the World: Five Women Explorers in Tibet* (No city given: Paddington Press, 1976)—no single work describes women hikers and climbers of the northeastern United States in the nineteenth century. For specific issues, incidents, and people, many of the sources given as specific citations may be of interest.

"Where there is a road": Gould, *How to Camp Out*, p. 59.

Hubbard's Moosehead Lake: Hubbard, *Guide* (Moosehead; 4th ed. [1893]), p. 75.

"The regular way": Quoted in Haring, *Our Catskill Mountains*, p. 253.

In 1869 no less: Murray, *Adventures in the Wilderness*, pp. 58–62.

"She's a dashing": A guide identified only as "Baldwin" is credited with these words in Stoddard, *Adirondacks*, p. 59.

262   **"Who came in":** Blanche Isham, "The History of the Keene Valley Congregational Church," mimeographed paper dated 1879, in the archives of the Keene Valley Library. Reprinted with permission.

"In these days": Sweetser, *White Mountains*, p. 35.

Women formed a majority: George C. Mann, "Excursions for the Season of 1887 and 1888," *Appalachia* (Dec. 1888), p. 255.

In Field and Forest: See Field and Forest Club records in the collections of the Boston Public Library.

262 **The first recreational snowshoeing:** Appalachian Mountain Club, Snow-Shoe Section, *List of Excursions, Parties, Mountain Climbs, 1882–1911,* a privately printed compilation, a copy of which is in the AMC Library.

In early *Appalachias*: See Mrs. W. G. Nowell, "A Mountain Suit for Women," *Appalachia* (June 1877), pp. 181–83; M. F. Whitman, "Camp Life for Ladies," *Appalachia* (June 1879), pp. 44–48; and Lucia D. Pychowska, "Walking-Dress for Ladies," *Appalachia* (Dec. 1887), pp. 28–30.

"In many a camp": Mary Alden Hopkins, "Women in the Woods," *In the Maine Woods* (1902), pp. 123–25. Hopkins contributed a similar piece to the 1904 issue.

"No lady should": Shields, *Camping and Camp Outfits,* p. 24.

"Abandon crinoline": Dix, *Lake Memphremagog,* p. 36.

263 **One young woman:** Hidden and Ulitz, *Tamworth Recollections,* p. 39.

An "indispensible" item: Charlotte E. Ricker, "The Wilderness: Wild Places and Rugged Peaks First Visited by Woman," *White Mountain Echo,* Sept. 9, 1882, pp. 8–9.

"Our dress has": Nowell, "Mountain Suit," p. 183. Other quoted passages from this article are from pp. 182–83.

Sweetser tells: Sweetser, *White Mountains,* p. 35.

264 **"A short skirt":** Whitman, "Camp Life," p. 47.

"A generous supply": *Ibid.*

By 1887: Pychowska, "Walking-Dress." Quoted passages are from pp. 29–30.

In the Adirondacks: Stoddard, *Adirondacks,* p. 4.

His rival: Wallace, *Descriptive Guide,* p. 245.

"A navy-blue jersey": *A Night on Osceola* (unsigned; privately printed, 1887), p. 10.

The provocative: Mary Alden Hopkins, "Women in the Woods," p. 124.

265 **"However, a skirt":** Marjorie Hurd, "Fashion on the Peaks: 1876–1935," *Appalachia* (Nov. 1935), p. 378. Back in 1882, this trip-end dress was known as a "civilization garment," carried by women throughout the hike solely as something "in which to make their appearance at the end of the journey" (Ricker, "The Wilderness," Sept. 9, 1882, p. 8)

A manual called: Bent, Lawson, and Sayward, *Equipment,* p. 8.

"Modesty is not": Breck, *Way of the Woods,* p. 61.

"Her own satchel": Ricker, "The Wilderness," Sept. 9, 1882, p. 9.

"The ladies started": Wolfe, "Pamola," p. 2.

265   **M. F. Whitman:** This account is taken entirely from M. F. Whitman, "A Climb through Tuckerman Ravine," *Appalachia* (June 1877), pp. 131–37.

267   **"A most restless":** Cross, *Randolph Old and New*, p. 151.

      In 1879: For example, Lucia D. and Marian Pychowska, "Baldcap Mountain," *Appalachia* (July 1880), pp. 121–27.

      "Mr Edmands asked": Letter from Marian Pychowska to Isabella Stone, July 30, 1886, in Kent-Philbrook collection. Reprinted with permission.

268   **The Pychowskas' friend:** Isabella Stone, "Mt. Waternomee and the Blue Ridge," in councillor of explorations report, *Appalachia* (Dec. 1884), pp. 75–78, and a letter from William Little to Isabella Stone, Aug. 2, 1884, in the Kent-Philbrook collection. The description of the difficulties appears in the former, p. 78.

      It is a loss: Two accounts of this odyssey may be consulted: A. E. Scott, "The Twin Mountain Range," *Appalachia* (Apr. 1883), pp. 107–21, and Charlotte E. Ricker, "The Wilderness: Wild Places and Rugged Peaks First Visited by Woman," *White Mountain Echo*, in three installments, Aug. 26, 1882, pp. 5–7, Sept. 2, 1882, pp. 5–6, and Sept. 9, 1882, pp. 8–9. All quoted passages are from one or the other of these two versions.

CHAPTER 27. DEATH IN THE MOUNTAINS

273   **Nancy Barton:** This tragic tale has been oft told; for example, by Starr King, *The White Hills*, pp. 184–85, and Kilbourne, *Chronicles*, pp. 55–56. Ambiguity concerning her last name is discussed in a footnote by the latter, p. 55.

      Willey family: The Willey slide is even more widely recounted than Nancy's saga. Again Starr King (*The White Hills*, pp. 187–202) and Kilbourne (*Chronicles*, pp. 85–87) give ample versions.

      Considering the notorious: A systematic record and chronological numbering of fatalities on Mount Washington are kept by Charles B. Fobes of Portland, Maine. See, for example, a representative entry concerning death number 86, in Fobes, "Accidents—No. 86," *Mount Washington Observatory News Bulletin* (Summer 1983), p. 28.

      The only injury: Lucy Crawford, *History*, p. 53.

274   **If other trampers:** *Ibid.*, pp. 100–101.

      Frederick Strickland: *Ibid.*, pp. 187–88.

      Benjamin Chandler: *Ibid.*, pp. 191–94.

      Lizzie Bourne: Lizzie Bourne's celebrated tragedy can be read in Lucy Crawford, *History*, pp. 188–91, or Kilbourne, *Chronicles*, pp. 269–71. See also Peg Hendrick, "120 Years Ago Lizzie Bourne Died on Mount Washington," *Mount Washington Observatory New Bulletin* (Sept. 1975), pp. 50–54, and a reprinting of a contemporary account, dated Sept. 14, 1855, and attributed to J. H. Spaulding, under the title, "The Way It Was," *Mount Washington Observatory News Bulletin* (Sept. 1976), pp. 54–55.

274　　**"More widely known":** Kilbourne, *Chronicles*, p. 270.

B. L. Ball: Dr. Ball's story is related at length in his own small book on the subject, *Three Days on the White Mountains; being the perilous adventures of Dr. B. L. Ball on Mount Washington, during October 25, 26, and 27, 1855* (Boston: N. Noyes, 1856), and is somewhat more accessible in Kilbourne, *Chronicles*, pp. 285–301. Further light on his itinerary is shed by Paul R. Jenks, Charles W. Blood, and Ralph C. Larrabee, "The Famous Case of Dr. Ball," *Appalachia* (Dec. 1931), pp. 448–53.

275　　**More than one hundred years after:** Dr. B. L. Ball, "Three Days on Mount Washington," *Vulgarian Digest*, no. 1 (Spring 1970), pp. 12–14, no. 2 (Fall 1970), pp. 13–21, and no. 3 (Spring 1972), pp. 13–20.

276　　**Curtis and Ormsbee deaths:** The Curtis-Ormsbee incident was described in a contemporary analysis by an Appalachian Mountain Club "Committee of Investigation." See "The Recent Fatalities on Mt. Washington," *Appalachia* (Apr. 1901), pp. 323–35.

"Exclusively as a refuge": Appalachian Mountain Club, report of the Building Committe, "The New Refuge on Mount Washington," *Appalachia* (May 1902), pp. 52–57.

"Not for pleasure camping": *Ibid.*, pp. 56–57.

By the following summer: *Ibid.*, p. 57; see also Dean Peabody, Jr., "The Evolution of the A. M. C. Hut," *Appalachia* (Dec. 1931), pp. 432–47, especially pp. 438–40.

CHAPTER 28. TRAIL POLICY ISSUES

279　　**"He believed, moreover":** Donaldson, *History*, vol. 2, p. 26.

Rosewell Lawrence's trail description: "Councillor of Improvements Report," *Appalachia* (June 1888), p. 157.

280　　**"With perhaps a connecting wire":** White Mountain Club of Portland, Maine, *Records and Memoranda*, p. 37. Reprinted with permission of Charles Fobes.

In his first report: "Councillor of Improvements Report," *Appalachia* (June 1876), p. 55.

"Thoroughly cleared of": *Ibid.* (Apr. 1901), p. 380.

"A pioneer in keeping," and **"An improvementless way":** Dorothy M. Martin, "Interview with Benton MacKaye," Potomac Appalachian Trail Club *Bulletin* (Jan.–March 1953), p. 12.

"Unlike most of the paths": "The Great Gulf Opened," *Boston Evening Transcript*, Aug. 25, 1909, p. 14.

The Chocorua upstarts: Recollections of Samuel I. Bowditch and Hutchinson Page, conversations on Sept. 15, 1981.

281　　**"Rocks along its course":** "Councillor of Improvements Report," *Appalachia* (June 1876), p. 55.

281   **One faction within:** *Ibid.* (Feb. 1893), p. 86.

"Let us no longer": *Ibid.* p. 87.

"A desecration": *Ibid.* (Apr. 1901), p. 389.

"Should be tabooed": *Ibid.*

"Visitors should remember": Sweetser, *White Mountains* (1886 ed.), p. 1 of section marked "Notes for 1886."

Witness Carpenter's frustrations: See chap. 22.

Witness the ruination: See chap. 21.

282   **In 1904, over on Mount Desert:** Bar Harbor Village Improvement Association *Annual Report* for 1904, p. 7.

Hunt kept up: "Councillor of Improvements Report," *Appalachia* (Feb. 1893), p. 85.

"The club should": "Councillor of Improvements Report," *Appalachia* (July 1880), p. 185.

"Nature is at work": *Ibid.* (July 1885), p. 166.

283   **"The department is":** *Ibid.* (Apr. 1883), p. 183.

On the other hand: *Ibid.;* see also the complaints of Chubbock (1885–87), Frederic D. Allen (1888–90), and other councillors of improvements.

Sturgis Pray's systematic: *Ibid.* (May 1903), pp. 221–22.

Warren Hart's enthusiastic, and "With the cooperation": *Ibid.* (July 1910), p. 197. Reprinted with permission of the Appalachian Mountain Club.

W. J. Winninghoff: *Ibid.* (Apr. 1912), p. 400.

284   **"Found it so littered":** Letter from Marian Pychowska to Isabella Stone, July 30, 1885, in the Kent-Philbrook collection. Reprinted with permission.

"We all fear": Letter from Marian Pychowska to Isabella Stone, Aug. 16, 1885, in the Kent-Philbrook collection. Reprinted with permission.

"It is hoped": "Councillor of Improvements Report," *Appalachia* (Feb. 1893), p. 86.

WAIA rules: Bean, *Town at the End of the Road*, p. 146.

285   **"The landowner":** Bar Harbor Village Improvement Association *Annual Report* for 1906, pp. 18–20.

CHAPTER 29. J. RAYNER EDMANDS AND WARREN HART: A STUDY IN CONTRAST

287   **Edmands:** J. Rayner Edmands's life and personality have been frequently outlined. See the obituary in *Appalachia* (July 1910), pp. 158–62, and recollections by Louis Cutter ("The Edmands Paths and Their Builder," *Appalachia* [Aug. 1921], pp. 134–40), George N. Cross ("Randolph Yesterdays," *Appalachia* [Dec. 1916], p. 56), Hazel de Berard ("Memories of Randolph,"

Appalachia [Dec. 1956], pp. 190–97), and Arthur Stanley Pease ("Early Trailmakers at Randolph," *Appalachia* [Dec. 1960], pp. 188–90).

287   **"A special form,"** and **"A convenient pack-saddle":** Edmands's obituary, *Appalachia* (July 1910), p. 159.

        "Always rising but": Cutter, "The Edmands Paths," p. 136.

289   **"A high-strung organism,"** and **"Painstaking and conscientious":** Obituary, p. 161.

        "Kind and helpful": Cutter, "The Edmands Paths," p. 140.

        One old Randolph hiker: De Berard, "Memories," p. 192.

        "Left as far," and **"In no case":** "Councillor of Improvements Report," *Appalachia* (Apr. 1901), p. 380.

291   **Hart:** In contrast to the admiring attention paid to Edmands in print, Warren W. Hart is without a biographer. For the trail work and its underlying philosophy on which this chapter focuses, see the councillor of improvements reports in *Appalachia* for the period from 1908 to 1910 (July 1909, pp. 85–89; July 1910, pp. 196–202; and July 1911, pp. 309–15).

        "Thus, until the present": "The Great Gulf Opened," *Boston Evening Transcript*, Aug. 25, 1909, p. 14.

        Flagg expeditions: The ascents of 1902 and 1906 are described in George A. Flagg, "From the Sketchbooks of George A. Flagg," *Appalachia* (June 1959), pp. 352–60; that of 1907 is shown pictorially in the sketchbook for 1907, in the possession of Shirley Hargraves, Mr. Flagg's granddaughter.

292   **"We were so impressed":** "Councillor of Improvements Report," *Appalachia* (July 1910), p. 199. Reprinted with permission of the Appalachian Mountain Club.

294   **"Every member familiar":** "Councillor of Improvements Report," *Appalachia* (July 1909), p. 85. Reprinted with permission of the Appalachian Mountain Club.

        "Quite rough and difficult": "Councillor of Improvements Report," *Appalachia* (July 1910), p. 200.

        "In a talk": Charles W. Blood, obituary for Warren W. Hart, *Appalachia* (Dec. 1943), p. 526. Reprinted with permission of the Appalachian Mountain Club.

CHAPTER 30. THE LAST EXPLORERS

297   **"The exhilaration of that":** Robert Marshall, *Arctic Wilderness* (Berkeley: University of California Press, 1956), p. 4.

        Explorers in the White Mountains: Early pages of *Appalachia* abound in stories of White Mountain explorations, many of which are identified in specific citations below. See the reports of the councillor of explorations in almost any nineteenth-century issue of the journal.

298   **Sweetser-Huntington climbs:** Sweetser, *White Mountains.* Items mentioned and/or quoted in this paragraph may be found on pp. 36–40 and 199.

William H. Pickering: Vivid examples of Pickering's exploits may be read in the councillor of explorations reports in *Appalachia* for March 1877, p. 121, and June 1882, pp. 71–72; "A Three Day's Tramp on the Mt. Washington Range," *Appalachia* (July 1880), pp.117–21; and "Carter Dome, Huntington's Ravine, and the Montalban Ridge," *Appalachia* (Dec. 1881), pp. 345–51.

Eugene B. Cook: For examples, see E. B. Cook, "An Ascent of Mt. Haystack (Garfield)," *Appalachia* (Dec. 1883), pp. 275 -78, and other material in "Councillor of Explorations Report," *Appalachia* (Dec. 1883), pp. 255–82; and a series of three *Appalachia* articles, all by W. H. Peek and all entitled "An Exploration of the Pilot Range": (March 1886), pp. 219–25; (Dec. 1887), pp. 30–38; and (Dec. 1888), pp. 215–22.

Pychowska women and Isabella Stone: See, for examples, Mrs. L. D. and Miss Marian M. Pychowska, "Baldcap Mountain," *Appalachia* (July 1880), pp. 121–27; M. M. Pychowska, "Evans Notch, Royce, and Baldface," *Appalachia* (Dec. 1883), pp. 264–71; and Isabella Stone, "Mt. Waternomee and the Blue Ridge," *Appalachia* (Dec. 1884), pp. 75–78; see also numerous letters in the Pychowska correspondence in the Kent-Philbrook collection.

Charles Ernest Fay: John Ritchie, "Obituary for Charles Ernest Fay," *Appalachia* (June 1931), p. 303; Howard W. Vernon, obituary for Fay in *American Alpine Journal* (1931), pp. 373–76.

In September of 1880: C. E. Fay, "Exploration of a Gorge on Mt. Lincoln," *Appalachia* (May 1881), pp. 286–87. Quoted phrases in this paragraph are from this account.

299   **"May no season":** Charles E. Fay, "Mount Passaconaway," *Appalachia* (Jan. 1892), p. 316.

"Was it justifiable": *Ibid.,* p.304.

"To prolong the luxury": *Ibid.,* p. 318.

Some were recreationists: For examples, see Rosewell B. Lawrence, "From the Sources of the Connecticut to the Rangeley Lakes," *Appalachia* (July 1885), pp. 105–23; Frederick Tuckerman, handwritten notes retained in his copy of Sweetser's guidebook, in the collections of the AMC; Warren W. Hart, "Councillor of Improvements Report," *Appalachia* (July 1910), pp. 201–2; and "From the Sketchbooks of George A. Flagg," *Appalachia* (June 1959), pp. 352–60.

Others were out there: Louis F. Cutter, "Some Maps of the Northern Peaks," *Appalachia* (Oct. 1914), p. 168, and inferences from dates on old USGS maps—see David A. Cobb, *New Hampshire Maps to 1900: An Annotated Checklist* (published by New Hampshire Historical Society and distributed by University Press of New England, Hanover, N.H., 1981). Morris recounted some of his early adventures in *Reminiscences of a Yankee Jurist: An Autobiography* (Littleton, N.H.: Courier Printing, 1953), pp. 56–97.

299   **"Localities, of which":** L. F. De Pourtales, "Reports of the Councillors for the Spring of 1876: Explorations," *Appalachia* (June 1876), p. 49. Other councillor of explorations reports quoted in this paragraph are Charles E. Fay (June 1879), p. 73; W. H. Pickering (July 1880), p. 181; W. H. Pickering (May 1881), pp. 281–82; E. B. Cook (Dec. 1883), p. 256; and A. L. Goodrich (March 1894), p. 262.

300   **Leading Yale intellectuals:** For exploits of Porter, see Carson, *Peaks and People*, pp. 184–86; on Gibbs and Whitney, see letter from Newell Martin to *High Spots* (Jan. 1936), pp. 29–30; and for Bushnell, see Mary Bushnell Cheney, *Life and Letters of Horace Bushnell* (New York: Harper & Brothers, 1880), pp. 497–98.

Newell Martin: A key source is his letter to *High Spots* (Jan. 1936), pp. 29–30. See also Carson, *Peaks and People*, pp. 131–32.

"From that time": Letter to *High Spots* (Jan. 1936), p. 29. Reprinted with permission.

301   **"Were perfectly indifferent":** Letter from Walter Lowrie to Russell Carson, Jan. 9, 1928, published under the title "Walter Lowrie: Theologian in the Adirondacks," *Adirondac* (Sept.–Oct. 1969), p. 90. Reprinted with permission.

"Perhaps no one": Walter Lowrie, "Mountain Climbing in Keene Valley in the Latter Part of the Eighties and Later," p. 6, transcript prepared for the archives of the Keene Valley Historical Society, copies of which are in the archives of the Keene Valley Library and in Princeton University Library. Reprinted with permission.

302   **Walter Lowrie:** Lowrie's career and especially his Adirondack hiking can be traced in Donald Hardie Fox, *The Complete Bibliography of Walter Lowrie: Illustrated with Selections from His Wit and Wisdom* (Princeton, N.J.: Fox Head Press, 1979). See also Lowrie's letter to Carson cited earlier, *Adirondac* (Sept.–Oct. 1969), pp. 89–97; Lowrie's manuscript on "Mountain Climbing in Keene Valley" cited earlier; Lowrie's handwritten notes and maps, which he kept concerning his hikes, in the collections of Princeton University Library; and William D. Glover, "Climbs with Walter Lowrie," *Adirondac* (Nov.–Dec. 1956), pp. 110–12, 119.

"He wanted to climb": Letter from Cuthbert R. Train, *Adirondac* (Jan.–Feb. 1957), pp. 22–23. Reprinted with permission.

Putnam Camp: See Elizabeth Putnam McIver, "Early Days at Putnam Camp," manuscript in the archives, Keene Valley Library; Nancy Lee, "Putnam Camp," *Adirondack Life* (Nov.–Dec. 1980), pp. 43–46; more briefly, Harold Weston, *Freedom in the Wilds*, p. 57; and for profuse detail, the logs of the hikes dating back to the earliest days, kept at the camp, with microfilm copies at the Adirondack Museum at Blue Mountain Lake, N.Y., and the

Essex County Historical Society in Elizabethtown, N.Y. The authors are grateful to have been given the opportunity to review the originals of these logs at the camp.

303 **"Their policy was"**: Lowrie, "Walter Lowrie," p. 93. Reprinted with permission.

"An extremely difficult," "As nearly as possible," and **"In a drenching shower"**: These quotations and other information are from the logs of the Putnam Camp. Reprinted with permission.

"A kind of family": Weston, *Freedom in the Wilds*, p. 57.

"A Spartan regime": Helen Adler, "Felix Adler, One of the Early Pioneers in Keene Valley and at Beede's," manuscript in the archives of the Keene Valley Library, pp. 8–9. Reprinted with permission.

Witherle in Maine: George Witherle kept a remarkably full narrative record of his explorations. Portions of these appeared in *Appalachia* at the time: see George H. Witherle, "Excursions North of Katahdin" (Dec. 1883), pp. 222–31; Witherle, "An Autumn Visit to the Sourdnahunk Mountains and Katahdin," (Dec. 1884), pp. 20–34; and Witherle, "Explorations in the Vicinity of Mount Ktaadn," condensed from letters written to Charles Hamlin and Rosewell Lawrence and published with the councillor of explorations report (June 1888), pp. 147–51. (The different spellings of Katahdin [Ktaadn] reflect a disagreement at the time between Witherle and the editor of *Appalachia*.) The complete journals were later assembled and made available by his daughter, Amy C. Witherle, and mimeographed, together with an introduction by Henry R. Buck and Myron H. Avery, by the AMC in 1928. In 1950 the Maine Appalachian Trail Club reran these mimeographs, under the title "Explorations West and Northwest of Katahdin in the Late Nineteenth Century."

304 **"A monument of rough stones"**: Witherle, "Explorations," p. 227.

"There the landlady": *Ibid.*, p. 231.

306 **"Far too precipitous to be scaled"**: "Voyaging in the Maine Woods; On East Branch Waters," *In the Maine Woods* (1905), p. 111.

Clarence Peavey apparently: Peavey was reported operating a series of hunting camps "in the Aroostook region" by 1896. See Fullerton L. Waldo, "Notes on a Recent Visit to Ktaadn," *Appalachia* (Nov. 1896), p. 192.

Witherle was on Bigelow: His presence in the Bigelow Range in 1891 is documented in an entry he made in the summit register, now in the collections of the AMC.

"Practically virgin territory": Henry R. Buck, "Traveler Mountain and North of Katahdin, August 13–27, 1927 (Myron H. Avery, Henry R. Buck)," *Appalachia* (June 1928), p. 73.

One small body: Ronald L. Gower, "The Missing Northwest Basin Pond," *Appalachia* (Dec. 1933), p. 613.

306   **Hakola called Witherle:** Hakola, *Legacy of a Lifetime*, pp. 37–38.

"He was probably": Myron H. Avery, "Explorations West and Northwest of Katahdin Late in the Nineteenth Century," *Maine Naturalist* (Sept. 1928), p. 107.

CHAPTER 31. THE CONSERVATION MOVEMENT

307   **"More than five-sixths":** George C. Mann, "The Excursions of Our First Decade," *Appalachia* (Dec. 1886), p. 356. This point is also stressed by David Tatham in "Winslow Homer in the Mountains," *Appalachia* (June 1966), pp. 83–85, and R. Stuart Wallace, in Donald Keyes et al., *The White Mountains: Place and Perceptions* (Durham, N.H., Hanover, N. H., and London: published for the University Art Galleries, University of New Hampshire, by the University Press of New England, 1980).

"It was not": Stephen Hardy, *How Boston Played*, p. 67.

"An insulating barrier": Terrie, "Urban Man Confronts the Wilderness," p. 15. This quality of gentlemanly camping is also discussed in Terrie, *Forever Wild*, pp. 50–51; Langdon, "Compromise with Nature"; and Mitchell, "Gentlemen Afield."

308   **"Coffee, cigars, whiskey":** Quoted in Terrie, "Urban Man Confronts the Wilderness," p. 16.

Stuffed olives: Howell, *Hudson Highlands*, vol. 1, p. 92.

Nash, Schmitt, Fox: Nash, *Wilderness and the American Mind*; Peter J. Schmitt, *Back to Nature: The Arcadian Myth in Urban America* (New York: Oxford University Press, 1969); and Fox, *John Muir and His Legacy*. Except as otherwise noted, our brief summaries of the points that follow are drawn from these three excellent sources.

Magazines such as: For examples, *American Angler* (1881), *Outing* (1882), *Sports and Pastimes* (1883).

Summer camps: Data from the American Camping Association, *Parents' Guide to Accredited Camps*, 1982 ed. A prime source for the early history of the summer camp movement is Porter Sargent, *A Handbook of Summer Camps: An Annual Survey* (Boston: privately printed, annually beginning in 1924, throughout the rest of the 1920s and 1930s).

310   **On May 15, 1885:** Two comprehensive histories of the establishment and subsequent development of the Adirondack Preserve are Norman J. Van Valkenburgh, *The Adirondack Forest Preserve*, and Eleanor Brown, *The Forest Preserve of New York State: A Handbook for Conservationists* (Glens Falls, N.Y.: Adirondack Mountain Club, 1985). See also Neal Burdick, ed., *A Century Wild: Essays Commemorating the Centennial of the Adirondack Forest Preserve* (Saranac Lake, N.Y.: The Chauncey Press, 1985). For the background of Adirondack logging, see James A. Goodwin, "Lumbering High on the High Peaks," *Adirondac* (September 1982), pp. 3–5. See also Philip G. Terrie, "The Adirondack Forest Preserve: The Irony of Forever

Wild," *New York History*, (July 1981), pp. 261–88. In anticipation of the centennial in 1985, *Adirondac* magazine ran numerous articles that provide useful background: see most issues in 1983–85. These included a separate treatment of the Catskills forest preserve by Van Valkenburgh, "The Catskill Park: A Mystery," *Adirondac* (Apr. 1984), pp. 14–15, 33.

310   **In May 1891,** and **In June 1892:** The struggle for the birth of Massachusetts parks may be gleaned from several useful sources, including early annual reports of the Metropolitan Park Commission (forerunner of the later Metropolitan District Commission); Mark L. Primack, *Greater Boston: Park and Recreation Guide;* and Friends of the Blue Hills, *The Historic Blue Hills*, a 1980 publication, a copy of which is in the files of the Friends of the Blue Hills, Milton, Massachusetts. Also useful are studies focused on the key individual involved in the Massachusetts effort, Charles Eliot: a biography by his father, Charles W. Eliot, *Charles Eliot: Landscape Architect* (Boston: Houghton, Mifflin, 1902); and Mark Primack, "Charles Eliot: Genius of the Massachusetts Landscape," *Appalachia* (June 1982), pp. 80–88.

"An epidemic of parks": Quoted in Robert Walcott, "City Parks," *The Harvard Advocate*, June 26, 1895, p. 157.

In 1900: For the historical background leading to the creation of the Palisades Interstate Park, see Arthur C. Mack, *The Palisades of the Hudson* (Edgewater, N.J.: The Palisade Press, 1909); Report of the Commissioner of the Palisades Interstate Park for 1900; Palisades Interstate Park Commission, *Sixty Years of Park Cooperation, N.Y., N.J.: A History, 1900–1960* (Bear Mountain, N. Y.: Bear Mountain State Park, 1960?); and Nancy Newhall, *A Contribution to the Heritage of Every American: The Conservation Activities of John D. Rockefeller, Jr* (New York: Alfred A. Knopf, 1957).

In 1901: The swashbuckling saga of the White Mountain logging railroads is recounted with flair and scholarship in C. Francis Belcher, *Logging Railroads of the White Mountains* (Boston: Appalachian Mountain Club, 1980). A concise summary of the early New Hampshire conservation movement and legislative successes is in Theodore Natti, "Stirrings of Organized Forestry in New Hampshire," in Kenison and Adams, *The Enterprise of the North Country of New Hampshire*, pp. 13–15. The Society for the Protection of New Hampshire Forests is chronicled in Paul E. Bruns, *A New Hampshire Everlasting and Unfallen* (Concord, N. H.: Society for the Protection of New Hampshire Forests, 1969). The long struggle for the establishment of the White Mountain National Forest is recounted there and in many other sources, notably Charles D. Smith, "Origins of the Movement for a White Mountain National Forest, 1880–1903," *New England Quarterly*, (March 1960), pp. 37–56; Stephen R. Pendery and R. Stuart Wallace, "A Cultural Resource Evaluation of the White Mountain National Forest, New Hampshire–Maine" (Contract no.01-3210, in the files of the WMNF, Laconia, New Hampshire); and James R. Jordan, "White Mountain Trilogy: Decimation—Fire—Forest Rebirth," in Kenison and Adams, *The Enterprise of the North Country of New Hampshire*, pp. 16–18.

311   **In the Adirondacks:** Sources for the Adirondack Mountain Reserve include Harold Weston, *Freedom in the Wilds: A Saga of the Adirondacks*, and Edith Pilcher, *Up the Lake Road: The First Hundred Years of the Adirondack Mountain Reserve*.

      Down in the Shawangunks: See Bradley J. Snyder, *The Shawangunk Mountains: A History of Nature and Man* (New Paltz, N. Y.: Mohonk Preserve, Inc., 1981), and Burgess, *Mohonk: Its People and Spirit*.

      In the Taconic Range: See New York Department of Conservation, Division of Parks, and State Council of Parks, *New York State Parks: Twenty-Fifth Anniversary Report, 1924–1949* (brochure). The authors are also indebted to the recollections and researches shared with us by Francis Masters, in conversation, Oct. 7, 1983.

      In Massachusetts: See reports of the Greylock Commission from the first decade of this century; full sets of these documents are scarce, but one may be found in the Berkshire Athenaeum, Pittsfield's public library (Massachusetts).

      In Connecticut: The growth of Connecticut's blue-blazed trails, almost entirely on private land, is described in chap. 40.

      In Vermont: For Joseph Battell's conservation activities, see Lee, *Green Mountains*, pp. 193–202; the following articles in the *Middlebury Campus*: "Alumni Notes," Feb. 24, 1915, p. 4; "Joseph Battell Dead," March 10, 1915, pp. 1, 3; "Mr. Battell's Will," Apr. 7, 1915, pp. 1, 3; and Thomas E. Boyce, "Notes on Bread Loaf Inn and Its Founder," Feb. 1930, manuscript in collections of Middlebury College Library.

312   **"[People] go to Europe":** Quoted in a letter from Thomas E. Boyce to "Miss Scott," July 20, 1924, in special collections of the Middlebury College Library. Reprinted with permission.

      In New Hampshire: For Monadnock's preservation, see Bruns, *A New Hampshire Everlasting and Unfallen*.

      In Maine: The story of Katahdin's absorption into Baxter State Park in 1931 belongs to chap. 38.

      On Mount Desert: Sargent F. Collier, *Acadia National Park: George B. Dorr's Triumph* (Farmington, Maine: Knowlton & McLeary, 1965); see also J. Malcolm Barter, "George Buchanan Dorr: Father of Acadia National Park," *Down East*, (Aug. 1965), pp. 42–45, and Helfrich and O'Neil, *Lost Bar Harbor*.

313   **Starr King had observed:** Starr King, *The White Hills*, p. 156.

      "Up where the grass": D. Q. Clement, "Moosilauke—1879," p. 3. Reprinted with permission.

      "The most annoying": John Burroughs, *Riverby* (Boston: Houghton, Mifflin, 1894), p. 64.

313 **So was Mount Greylock:** See reports of Greylock Commission from the first decade.

314 **"By 1840, much":** Mollie Beattie, Charles Thompson, and Lynn Levine, "A New England Forest History," *Appalachia* (Winter, 1983–1984), pp. 114–31. Reprinted with permissin of the Appalachian Mountain Club.

CHAPTER 32. THE FIRST MOUNTAIN SNOWSHOERS

315 **In late April 1871:** Hitchcock, *Mount Washington in Winter*, p. 220.

This feat was duplicated: *Ibid.*, pp. 229–36.

Similarly with an April: *Ibid.*, p. 220.

Mansfield in 1872: L. L. A., "A Trip to Mt. Mansfield in Winter," *Lamoille* [Vt.] *News Dealer*, March 13, 1872, p. 2.

316 **Camel's Hump:** P., "Ascent of Camels Hump," *Burlington Free Press*, March 20, 1872, p. 3.

Kearsarge: Drake, *Heart of the White Mountains*, pp. 47–54.

"The ascent of the ridges": Sweetser, *White Mountains*, p. 33.

One in Concord: Edward French, "The First Snowshoe Club in New Hampshire," *Granite Monthly* (March 1896), pp. 170–75.

One at Williams College: "History of the Outing Club," *Williams Alumni Review*, Feb. 1935, p. 161.

An AMC "Snow-Shoe Section": The basic source regarding the AMC Snow-shoe Section is a printed booklet, a copy of which is in the AMC library, entitled *A. M. C. Snow-Shoe Section; List of Excursions, Parties, Mountain Climbs, 1882–1911*. Articles on Snow-Shoe Section activities appeared in *Appalachia*, both current articles during the period when the group was active and reminiscences in later years. Several of these are cited in specific notes below. The information as to its founders is given in an obituary for Ephraim Harrington, one of its ardent members, by J. W. Worthington in *Appalachia* (Dec. 1939), p. 526.

On February 1, 1882: John Ritchie, Jr., "The Winter Excursion to the White Mountains," *Appalachia* (June 1882), p. 42. The participants are not named in the article, but are listed in the booklet, *A. M. C. Snow-Shoe Section; List of Excursions*. Quoted passages in this paragraph are from the 1882 *Appalachia* article by Ritchie.

317 **During the 1884:** Samuel H. Scudder, "A Climb on Mt. Adams in Winter," *Appalachia* (Apr. 1884), pp. 314–23. Except where otherwise indicated, quoted passages that follow are from this source. Again, participants are not named in the article, and a variety of sources must be examined to establish who they were. In another write-up of the climb (by "W" [William H. Pickering? Laban M. Watson?], "Randolph," *The Mountaineer* [Gorham, N.H.], Feb. 1, 1884, p. 3), the five men and six women who were at the Ravine House are listed, and Watson is identified as the guide who went higher,

Hunt as the other guide. A minor accident temporarily incapacitated Charles Lowe, who was to have gone (Scudder, "A Climb on Mt. Adams in Winter," p. 315). In still another account (W. H. P., "A Winter Ascent of Mt. Adams," *Boston Transcript*, Feb. 21, 1884, p. 6), the initials identify Pickering (from among those listed in *The Mountaineer*) as one of the two men who went high with Watson. Scudder's authorship of the *Appalachia* piece suggests that he was the other. In a later article ("A Winter Excursion to Tuckerman's Ravine," *Appalachia*, July 1885, p. 127), Scudder refers to "What our Mt. Adams party saw last winter," the context tending to confirm that he was the third of the three who went high. The four nonguides in the party are identified in the booklet, *A. M. C. Snow-Shoe Section*, p. 9, and ths tells us that the two who did not continue up with Watson were Rufus A. Bullock and William B. Clarke.

318 **"An iron calk":** W. H. P., "A Winter Ascent of Mt. Adams," p. 6.

The first recorded ascent: Georgia Drew Merrill, *History of Coos County*, footnote on p. 935.

On February 21, 1889: Rosewell B. Lawrence, "A Dedicatory Visit to the Madison-Spring Hut," *Appalachia* (May 1889), pp. 312–19. Quoted passages that follow are from this account. The dates and personnel for these two ascents are confirmed in a retroactive entry in the register for Madison Spring Hut, Aug. 8, 1889, in the collections of the AMC.

319 **During the following winter:** Minutes of an AMC meeting on Apr. 9, 1890, at which Lawrence spoke on this trip, *Appalachia* (May 1890), p. 105. The eight who went up to the hut are listed in a March 4, 1890, entry in the register for Madison Spring Hut (in collections of the AMC).

During the Christmas week: John Corbin, "A Christmas Ascent of Mount Adams," *Outing* (Jan. 1892), pp. 261–68. The guide to this party told the students that the ascent "had been attempted three times and had been done twice." If the unsuccessful attempt was that of 1884, and the successful ones those of 1887 and February 1889, as described above, this would place this ascent in December (Christmas week) 1889. By the following year, the guide presumably would have known of three successful ascents.

Another student group: Richard E. Dodge, "A Winter Trip to the Top of Mts. Washington and Adams in 1892," *Appalachia* (March 1898), pp. 367–69.

Meanwhile AMC's Snow-Shoe Section: Except where otherwise indicated, ascents are listed in the booklet *A. M. C. Snow-Shoe Section*. In many cases these ascents are also written up in contemporary Appalachia articles.

"The Ascent of the Mantel Horn": Charlotte Endicott Wilde, "Reminiscences of the Snow-Shoe Section," *Appalachia* (June 1952), p. 57. Reprinted with the permission of the Appalachian Mountain Club.

320 **Osceola (late 1880s):** Julius H. Ward, *The White Mountains: A Guide to Their Interpretation* (New York: D. Appleton, 1890) pp. 268–69.

320 **Chocorua (1891?):** Frank Bolles, *At the North of Bearcamp Water* (Boston: Houghton Mifflin, first edition 1893, second edition 1917); in reference to the south side of Chocorua: "In winter this face is quite readily climbed upon the packed snow" (2d ed., p. 64); Bolles definitely climbed nearby Bear Mountain on December 21, 1891 (*Bearcamp Water*, 2d ed., pp. 243–51), so he may well have been up Chocorua and other peaks at about this time as well.

Carrigain in winter: Personnel on this party are shown in a summit register entry dated Feb. 24, 1896, in the collections of the AMC.

First winter ascent of North Tripyramid: Isaac Y. Chubbock, "Up Tripyramid on Snow-Shoes," *Appalachia* (Feb. 1893), pp. 14–18.

321 **"Stepping on the top":** *Ibid.*, p. 17.

Moriah's summit register: Summit register for 1898 and 1899 in the collections of the AMC.

Wonalancet publications: WODC, *Guide* (1900), p. 17.

Gordon H. Taylor: "Councillor of Improvements Reports," *Appalachia* (May 1899), p. 100.

In Waterville the Elliotts: N. L. Goodrich, *Waterville Valley*, p. 47.

Beginning in the winter of 1902–3: Unidentified manuscript notebook in the collections of Philbrook Farm Inn, Shelburne, N.H.

In 1904 the AMC's: "Councillor of Improvements Report," *Appalachia* (Apr. 1904), p. 337.

"Winter mountain climbing": "Appalachian Club's Winter Excursion to White Mountains," *Boston Sunday Globe*, Feb. 19, 1905, p. 4.

322 **"The exciting ride":** *A. M. C. Snow-Shoe Section*, p. 85.

"The terrible storms": Herschel C. Parker, "Winter Climbing on Mt. Washington and the Presidential Range," *Appalachia* (May 1902), p. 20. All remaining quoted passages in this chapter are from this article.

Mount McKinley: Parker's later activities on Mount McKinley are recounted and given perspective in American climbing history in Jones, *Climbing in North America*, pp. 54–64.

CHAPTER 33. WINTER PIONEERING ON MOUNT MARCY

325 **Colvin on Gothics:** Colvin, *Report* for 1875 (published 1879), p. 89.

Colvin on Seventh Lake Mountain: Colvin, *Report* for 1877 (published 1879), pp. 157–69.

Mills Blake in wintry conditions: Colvin, *Report* for 1883 (published 1884), pp. 160–61.

326 **1893 ascent:** Benjamin S. Pond, "The First Winter Ascent of Marcy," *High Spots* (Jan. 1932), pp. 2–3, and W. H. Pond, "First Winter Ascent of Mt.

Marcy," *Adirondac* (March–Apr. 1950), pp. 28–29. Quoted passages are from Benjamin Pond's account, pp. 2–3. Reprinted with permission.

327   **Three years later:** Journal of the Adirondack Mountain Reserve, entries for March 28 and 30, 1896, in collections of the Essex County Historical Society, Elizabethtown, N.Y.

328   **1899 ascent:** The 1899 ascent was described by the two principals in C. Grant LaFarge, "A Winter Ascent of Tahawus," *Outing* (Apr. 1900), pp. 69–75; and Gifford Pinchot, *Breaking New Ground* (New York: Harcourt Brace, 1947), pp. 145–46. Quoted passages are from LaFarge's version, pp. 69–75.

329   **"Nothing will do more":** "Appalachian Mountain Club" *Lake Placid Club Notes* (Dec. 26, 1907), p. 23.

   "Our oldest guide": "Appalachian Mountain Club" *Lake Placid Club Notes* (March 2, 1908), p. 39.

   "The Appalachians brought": *Ibid.*

   1908 ascent: The 1908 climb was written up by Lewis A. Wells, "A January Ascent of Mount Marcy," *Appalachia* (June 1908), pp. 340–43. Quoted passages are from Wells's article, reprinted with the permission of the Appalachian Mountain Club.

330   **Winter sports at Lake Placid:** Mary MacKenzie, "Home of the Hickories," *Adirondack Life* (Winter 1972), pp. 8–11.

   Dix in 1901: J. B. Burnham, "An Outing in the Snow," *Forest and Stream* (Apr. 5, 1902), pp. 262–63.

   Marcy in 1903: Unidentified newspaper clipping dated December 1903, in Comstock Scrapbooks (item no. 125–6), in the archives, Keene Valley Library.

   Marcy in 1910: Alexander F. Ormsbee, "Another Winter Ascent of Mount Marcy," *Appalachia* (July 1910), pp. 135–38.

   Giant in 1910 (?): William B. Glover, ed., "Reminiscences of Ed Isham of Keene Valley," *Adirondac* (Jan.–Feb. 1957), p. 11.

CHAPTER 34. THE FIRST MOUNTAIN SKIERS

331   **When the AMC's Snow-Shoe Section:** John Ritchie, Jr., "On Snow-shoes at Jackson," *Appalachia* (Dec. 1888), pp. 212–13. Quoted passages in this paragraph are from this article.

   Despite a long: Among many histories of skiing, especially useful are Charles M. Dudley, *60 Centuries of Skiing* (Brattleboro, Vt.: Stephen Daye Press, 1925), Elon Jessup, *Skis and Skiing* (New York: C. P. Dutton, 1929), and *America's Ski Book*, prepared by the editors of *Ski Magazine* (New York: Charles Scribner's Sons, 1958). A good regional study is E. John B. Allen, "The Development of New Hampshire Skiing: 1870's–1940," *Historical New Hampshire* (Spring 1981), pp. 1–37.

331 **A Pennsylvania Railroad engineer:** The 1885 and 1888 incidents are re-counted in Sig Steinwall, "Ski Pioneer," an unidentified magazine clipping sent to the authors.

Sometime around 1892: Mentioned by Henry Ives Baldwin, both in "The Relative Antiquity of Skiing in the Adirondacks," *American Ski Annual*, 1937–1938, p. 58, and in conversation with the authors, Aug. 29, 1982.

332 **About the same year:** William B. Rotch, "Growth and Development of the Dartmouth Outing Club, 1909–1937," unpublished typescript dated May 12, 1937, p. 3, kindly provided to the authors by Mr. Rotch. A copy is also in the Dartmouth College Library.

Montreal Ski Club: Thomas Drummond, "The Canadian Snowshoe," *Transactions of the Royal Society of Canada*, (Dec. 1916), p. 320.

Two hundred pairs of skis: Fred H. Harris, ed., *Dartmouth Out o' Doors: A Book Descriptive of the Outdoor Life in and about Hanover, N.H.* (Boston: George E. Crosby, 1913), p. 105.

Skis were reasonably common: Turn of the century barrel–stave schusses were recalled in a conversation with an old Hanoverian, Larry Moore, June 26, 1981.

"A few of us": Craig O. Burt, "We Lived in Stowe," unpublished and undated manuscript in the collections of Bailey-Howe Library, University of Vermont. Reprinted with permission.

The price seemed steep: Letters from Ernest J. Berg to Kennedy brothers, Minneapolis, Minn., dated Dec. 10 and 14, 1898, and Jan. 3, 1899, in the Berg Brothers Papers, Library of Union College.

Nansen Ski Club: Pamphlet issued by the city of Berlin, N.H., on the occasion of its sesquicentennial, 1979, a copy of which is in the Berlin Public Library.

333 **The Dartmouth Outing Club:** Origins of the Dartmouth Outing Club are amply recorded in DOC files in the archives of Dartmouth College. See especially the unpublished paper by William B. Rotch, "Growth and Development of the Dartmouth Outing Club, 1909–1937"; Nathaniel L. Goodrich, "The Dartmouth Outing Club," *Appalachia* (Dec. 1915), pp. 357–59; and copious writings of Fred Harris, including *Dartmouth Out o' Doors*.

"How strange it is": Untitled item in *The Dartmouth*, March 27, 1896, p. 381.

"Winter has finally closed in": *Ibid.*, Dec. 11, 1885, p. 149.

"Stuffy rooms, hot stoves": Rotch, "Dartmouth Outing Club," p. 1. Reprinted with permission.

"Home-made ski jump": W. Lee White, "A Salute of the Trail," in Harris, ed., *Dartmouth Out o' Doors*, p. 8.

333   **Letter to** *The Dartmouth:* Fred Harris, letter to *The Dartmouth,* Dec. 7. 1909, p. 279.

334   **"When a Dartmouth freshman":** Elon Jessup, "Winter Week Ends," *Country Life* (Dec. 1919), p. 48.

       "Not only the founder": Letter from W. Lee White to Dan P. Hatch, Jr., Dec. 13, 1934, Dartmouth Outing Club Papers, Dartmouth College Library. Reprinted with permission.

       "If snowshoeing be": Harris, "The Finer Points of Skiing: in Seven Lessons," *Country Life* (Dec. 1921), pp. 48–50.

       "For two whole winters": W. Lee White, "A Salute of the Trail," in Harris, ed., *Dartmouth Out o' Doors,* p. 8.

       "Fourteen minutes is the record": N. L. Goodrich, "Dartmouth Outing Club," p. 358.

335   **"Obviously a foolhardy venture":** Conversation with Sherman Adams, Sept. 17, 1981.

336   **Irving Langmuir:** C. Guy Suits, ed., *The Collected Works of Irving Langmuir,* vol. 12, *Langmuir, the Man and the Scientist,* including a biography by Albert Rosenfeld (New York: Pergamon Press, 1962), and a biography by Virginia Veeder Westervelt, *Incredible Man of Science: Irving Langmuir* (New York: Julian Messner, 1968). The authors also thank Vincent J. Schaefer, Langmuir's protégé and colleague of many years, for his recollections in several conversations and in correspondence.

       "Every minute he could spare": Westervelt, *Langmuir,* p. 43.

       Back in the United States: Dating of Langmuir's earliest ski ascents is largely based on notations on snapshots in family photograph albums, reported to the authors by Ruth Langmuir Van de Water, Irving's niece.

       John S. Apperson: An enormous volume of John Apperson's letters and other papers have been preserved; the authors originally looked at these in the basement of Apperson's longtime associate Philip Ham, but they now reside at the Adirondack Research Center of the Schenectady Museum, Schenectady, N.Y.

       " 'Appie' was a tall": Suits, ed., *Collected Works,* p. 94.

337   **Marcy in 1908:** The earliest references to a possible 1908 ski ascent are apparently in a Schenectady, N.Y., newspaper in 1936, as an editor's note preceding an article by Apperson ("Trails in Forest Provide Network of Trips for Skiers," *Schenectady Union-Star,* Dec. 17, 1936, p. 26). Soon after, a footnote appeared in Henry Ives Baldwin, "The Relative Antiquity of Skiing in the Adirondacks," *American Ski Annual,* 1937–1938, p. 61, which refers to it as "reported in print" but does not give the source. A Schenectady newspaper cited it again in the 1960s (Arthur E. Newkirk and Philip W. Ham, "Forest Preserve, Lake George and 'Conservation' Owe Great Debt to John S.

Apperson," *Schenectady Union-Star*, Feb. 5, 1963, p. 12), but a knowledgeable friend of both Apperson and Langmuir, Philip Ham, has since called that "hearsay from Apperson" (letter from Arthur Newkirk to L&GW, Apr. 19, 1983). There is no evidence of any 1908 ascent in the Apperson papers beyond these doubtful wisps.

337　　**Marcy in 1911**: John Apperson's glass slides are in the collections of the Adirondack Research Center of the Schenectady Museum, Schenectady, N.Y., as is correspondence that mentions the 1911 ski ascent of Marcy. The only evidence concerning the identity of the three-person party is an envelope containing photos of the trip, on the outside of which is written "Apperson, Canivet and Paskey (?)"; according to William M. White, who knew Apperson well, the note on the envelope is in Apperson's handwriting. See also William M. White, "Mount Marcy—Winter 1911," *Adirondac* (Jan. 1984), pp. 3–5; note, however, that this article erroneously gives Langmuir as a member of the 1911 party, as the note on the envelope had not been noticed when that article was written.

Other early climbs: All this information and the quoted phrases are from correspondence in the Apperson Papers, Adirondack Research Center, Schenectady, N.Y. Reprinted with permission.

"Whether in the Lab": Suits, in his introduction to the *Collected Works*, p. viii.

"We lay awake": Schaefer, quoted in Suits, ed., *Collected Works*, p. 8.

338　　**"Although then over 60"**: *Ibid.*, p. 188.

"He was beautiful": Conversation with Hilda K. Martin, Nov. 2, 1981.

"He loved a fight": Conversation with Philip Ham, Oct. 27, 1980.

"One of the most irritating": Conversation with Daniel Smiley, Oct. 24, 1980.

"His love of adventure": R. E. Doherty, "An Essay on Apperson," unpublished typescript, Aug. 28, 1918, Apperson Papers, Adirondack Research Center, Schenectady, N.Y. Reprinted with permission.

Jackrabbit Johannsen: A biography is *Jackrabbit: His First Hundred Years*, edited by Brian Powell (Ontario, Canada: Collier MacMillan Canada, 1975). The transcript of an interview by Doug Wilson on "ABC Sports," Feb. 2, 1980, was graciously provided to the authors by Mr. Wilson. A fair volume of correspondence between Apperson and Johannsen is preserved in the former's papers. A priceless experience for many writers, including the authors, was to meet and talk with the man himself when he was over one hundred years old and still skiing, still holding court in his home outside Montreal though well into his second century. Most of our information on his early climbs comes from a conversation with him on February 26, 1981.

Lake Placid Club: The best single description of the early Lake Placid winter scene is in Mary MacKenzie, "Home of the Hickories," *Adirondack Life* (Winter 1972), pp. 8–11.

338   **"The Lake Placid of Europe":** *Ibid.*, p. 8.

339   **"I was after adventure":** Conversation with Jackrabbit Johannsen, Feb. 26, 1981.

      "I have never before": John Herbert Price, in Powell, ed., *Jackrabbit*, p. 164.

      "All of us": Thomas D. Cabot, in Powell, ed., *Jackrabbit*, p. 48.

      "We had hare": Interview by Doug Wilson, "ABC Sports," Feb. 2, 1980. Reprinted with permission.

341   **As late as the 1920s:** Conversation with Fay Loope, Aug. 15, 1980.

PART FOUR. MOUNTAINS AS ESCAPE FROM URBAN SOCIETY: 1910–1950

343   **"In Saranac Lake":** Donaldson, *History*, vol. 2, p. 296. The phrase "pioneer of the oxmobile" is Donaldson's too (*ibid.*).

      "Mr. Philbrook took": Mrs. White, "1st Mount Washington Trip on Saturday," *The Philbrook Sunday News*, a typed "newspaper" prepared for sojourners at the inn that summer, Aug. 30, 1903, p. 1, in the archives of the Philbrook Farm Inn, Shelburne, N.H. Reprinted with permission.

344   **Life speeded up:** The automobile's impact on mountain recreation has been frequently discussed. Some who have described the effects with special insight are Peter B. Bulkley, "A History of the White Mountain Tourist Industry," see especially p. 121; R. Stuart Wallace, "White Mountain History: A Question of Access," *Forest Notes* (Summer 1984), pp. 2–6; and Van Zandt, *Catskill Mountain House*, especially pp. 295–300. Kilbourne also commented on the automobile's impact just as it was beginning to occur: see *Chronicles*, especially p. 405.

      "Like the Constitution": James P. Taylor, "The Chariot of Democracy: An Appreciation," *Burlington Daily News*, Aug. 14, 1920, p. 4.

      "This is the end": Shirley Barker, "The Heyday of the Grand Hotel," *New Hampshire Profiles*, (Sept. 1956), p. 28.

      "Indirectly they have": Carson, *Peaks and People*, pp. 247–48. Reprinted with permission.

      "They have changed": Donaldson, *History*, vol. 1, p. viii.

345   **"Automobile Garage":** Van Zandt, *Catskill Mountain House*, p. 300.

      Stanley "locomobile": Frank H. Burt, "Among the Clouds," *Appalachia* (Dec. 1938), p. 176.

      "Nobody walks": Walter Prichard Eaton, "Joys of the True Walker," *The American Magazine* (June 1913), p. 11.

      "No longer could": Charles Platt, *Pasquaney: The Long Walk (1895–1977)*, a booklet sent to the authors by Camp Pasquaney, p. 25.

345   **"It is true":** Torrey, "Many Still Use Their Legs" (letter to the editor), *New York Times*, Aug. 16, 1931, sec. 3, p. 2. Copyright ©1931 by The New York Times Company. Reprinted by permission. The editorial to which Torrey responded appeared on Aug. 8, 1931.

"Indirectly the pedestrian": Percy G. Stiles, *Wayfaring in New England*, p. 10.

346   **"The auto gives":** John Ritchie, Jr., "Fifty Years of Progress," *Appalachia* (Feb. 1926), p. 333. Reprinted with the permission of the Appalachian Mountain Club.

348   **"The flagship of American trails":** Ray Hunt, "A. T. the Flagship of U. S. Trails," *Appalachian Trailway News* (Sept.–Oct. 1985), p. 3.

A key factor: Sar A. Levitan and Richard S. Belous, *Shorter Hours, Shorter Weeks: Spreading the Work to Reduce Unemployment* (Baltimore, Md.: Johns Hopkins University Press, 1977), see especially pp. 6–7.

350   **"No longer is":** "Hiking Along the Sky-Line Trail in the Green Mountains," *Springfield* [Mass.] *Republican*, magazine and auto sec., Aug. 7, 1921, p. 1.

CHAPTER 35. THE LONG TRAIL

351   **An 1862 brochure:** W. H. Tyler and John Ross Dix, *Manchester and Its Vicinity: A Guide for the Use of Guests of the Equinox House, Manchester, Vermont* (Boston: Press of George C. Rand & Avery, 1862), pp. 6–9; and Manchester Development Association, *Manchester-in-the-Mountains* (Buffalo and New York: Mathews-Northrup Works, 1905).

"Of the Green Mountains": Herbert Tuttle, "A Vacation in Vermont," *Harper's Magazine* (Nov. 1883), p. 813.

Ascutney: See Frank H. Clark, *Glimpses of Ascutney*, and the current guide book of the Ascutney Trails Association, *Guide to the Trails of Ascutney Mountain* (Windsor, Vt.: Ascutney Trails Association, 3d ed., 1975). The authors also benefited from the privilege of looking at scrapbooks maintained by the Ascutney Trails Association, which contain additional historical information.

352   **"The custom was":** Ascutney Trails Association, *Guide*, p. 6.

Camel's Hump: Camel's Hump Club, *Camel's Hump: Vermont's Famous Mountain* (Waterbury, Vt., 1910), a sixteen-page pamphlet published by the club at the time of its formation, in the collections of the Vermont Historical Society, Montpelier, Vt. See also articles in *The Vermonter* for July 1909 (Charles A. Robie, "On Foot to the Summit of Camel's Hump," pp. 205–7); Apr. 1910 (Edwin Franklin Palmer, Jr., "The Trails up Camel's Hump," pp. 134–35); and a seven-page typed paper by Lyle S. Woodward and Stanley Chase, "The Camel's Hump Story," prepared for the Waterbury Historical Society. The authors are indebted to conversations with two reigning authorities on the history of Camel's Hump, John Willey (June 26, 1981) and William G. Gove (July 11, 19, 1983, and subsequent correspondence).

352   **Details on CHC shelters:** Camel's Hump Club pamphlet, pp. 3–5. Quoted phrases reprinted with permission of the Vermont Historical Society.

353   **"The main range":** Louis J. Paris, "The Green Mountain Club: Its Purposes and Projects," *The Vermonter* (May 1911), p. 155.

"The song of": *Ibid.*

James P. Taylor: Voluminous information on Taylor and his early efforts to promote the Long Trail and the Green Mountain Club are in the James P. Taylor Papers in the collections of the Vermont Historical Society. Except where otherwise noted, our information and quoted material in this section of the text are from various papers in this collection, reprinted with permission. See especially Taylor's address delivered at the Twenty-first Birthday celebration of the Green Mountain Club, at the Long Trail Lodge, Sept. 12, 1931. See also obituaries on Taylor: by Louis Puffer in the *The Long Trail News* (Aug. 1949), pp. 1–2, and "I Am at Home," *Vermont Sunday News* (Burlington, Vt.), Sept. 11, 1949, p. 14.

354   **"A speechmaker and backslapper":** Conversation with John Paulson, Oct. 16, 1981.

355   **Green Mountain Club:** The official history of the Green Mountain Club is Jane Curtis, Will Curtis, and Frank Lieberman, *Green Mountain Adventure, Vermont's Long Trail* (Montpelier, Vt.: The Green Mountain Club, 1985). An excellent shorter history is Reidun D. Nuquist, "The Founding of the Green Mountain Club, 1910," *Vermont History News* (May–June 1985), pp. 60–65.

"Make the Vermont mountains": A copy of the minutes of the founding meeting of the Green Mountain Club, March 11, 1910, is in the Taylor Papers. This document includes the text of the March 4 "call," a list of persons attending, and various related papers.

357   **Judge Cowles:** See the Clarence P. Cowles Papers in the Bailey-Howe Library of the University of Vermont. Among these papers, an especially valuable document is his unpublished paper, dated January 27, 1946, entitled "Trails up Mount Mansfield." The authors are also deeply indebted to John Cowles, son of the judge, who was most generous in supplying personal recollections and family papers otherwise unavailable.

"I asked a trustee": Charles R. Cummings, "The Long Trail Lodge," *The Vermonter* (July 1930), p. 160.

"Too busy": Throughout the remainder of this chapter, quoted phrases of Cowles, Taylor, and Louis J. Paris are drawn from the variety of diverse papers in the collections cited above, except as otherwise indicated.

361   **State Forest Service:** The Forest Service's activity on the Long Trail is described in three useful documents: an unpublished "History of Forestry in Vermont," by Austin F. Hawes, generously supplied to the authors by one of Mr. Hawes's successors as state forester, Arthur F. Heitmann; Robert M. Ross, "Green Mountain Trail," *The Vermonter* (Jan. 1914), especially p. 23;

and Louis J. Paris, "The Making of the Long Trail," an unidentified article in the GMC archives in the Vermont Historical Society. See also related information in the Austin Foster Hawes Papers, in the Manuscript Room of the Yale University Library.

361   **"The queerest jumble"**: Ross's description as recounted by Paris, "The Making of the Long Trail." Reprinted wtih permission.

363   **"The Forestry Department"**: Dr. Paris provided this summation in a brochure he prepared entitled *Brandon: A Mountain Center on the Long Trail*, dated 1914, in the collections of the Vermont Historical Society, Montpelier, Vt. Reprinted with permission.

"I still feel": Letter from Hawes to Taylor, Oct. 9, 1916, in the Theron S. Dean Papers, Bailey-Howe Library, University of Vermont. Reprinted with permission.

"Weary and monotonous": "New Green Mountain Club," *Burlington Free Press*, Oct. 30, 1916, p. 5.

Harry Canfield: Letter from Harry L. Canfield to Theron Dean, Sept. 27, 1916, referring to a trip of "two years ago" (Theron S. Dean Papers).

Herbert Wheaton Congdon: H. W. Congdon, "Report of March of Officer's Patrol, 23d Inf. N. G. N. Y., September 5th to 20th, 1914, on the Long Trail, Green Mountain Club," a copy of which is in the Congdon Papers, Bailey-Howe Library of the University of Vermont. Reprinted with permission.

"Unfortunately, however, the necessities": Chamberlain, *Vacation Tramps*, pp. 83–84.

"Years of disillusionment": Will S. Monroe, "A Brief Survey of Outing Clubs," *Mountain Magazine* (Oct. 1928), p. 46.

"Put the matter": Green Mountain Club files on microfilm, Bailey-Howe Library, University of Vermont. Reprinted with permission.

364   **Will S. Monroe**: Professor Monroe and his work on the Long Trail have been described in numerous articles and reminiscences, of which some of the more interesting include: Will S. Monroe, "The Short and Simple Story of the Poor," *The Long Trail News* (Nov. 1950), pp. 1–2; a posthumous collection of personal reminiscences, apparently given to Judge Cowles and supplied by him eleven years after Monroe's death to *The Long Trail News* (Louis B. Puffer, ed., "The Will S. Monroe Number," Feb. 1950, pp. 1–5); Cowles, "The Monroe Sky-line Trail," unpublished typescript in the Cowles Papers, Bailey-Howe Library of the University of Vermont; the New York Section's "History of Our First Fifty Years"; "Tramping Along the Sky-Line Trail in the Green Mountains," *Springfield* (Mass.) *Republican*, Aug. 7, 1921, magazine and auto sec., p. 1; and a series of remembrances by various authors in *The Long Trail News*, Feb. 1950.

"The wiry Rommel": Tom Slayton, "Vermont's Green Mountain Club," *Rutland* [Vt.] *Times-Argus*, Nov. 4, 1979, p. III-2.

364　　**"Had on its hands"**: Monroe, unpublished typescript history of the GMC, in club archives, Vermont Historical Society, Montpelier, Vt. Reprinted with permission.

365　　**"And no one"**: *Ibid.*, pp. 17–18. Reprinted with permission.

　　　The New York Section: The authoritative source for this interesting club within a club is its own typescript, "History of Our First Fifty Years." Copy in the authors' collections.

　　　"Animated discussion": "New Green Mountain Club," *Burlington Free Press*, Oct. 30, 1916, p. 5.

366　　**"Monroe Skyline"**: The term *Monroe Skyline*, was in use from the first years of this work: see "'Monroe Skyline Trail' Name of Mountain Pass," *Burlington Free Press*, Oct. 16, 1916, p. 8. The term was also used in the Green Mountain Club's first edition of *The Long Trail Guidebook* in 1917 (pp. 11, 13).

　　　"Mr. Munroe [*sic*]": Hawes, "History of Forestry in Vermont," p. 22. Reprinted with permission of Vermont Historical Society.

　　　"A hiker's joy": Allen Chamberlain, "Kicking the Leaves of Vermont," *Boston Transcript*, Oct. 3, 1917, p. II–4. Chamberlain was mildly critical of what he felt was Monroe's tendency to overblaze.

　　　"A genius in selecting": *Springfield Republican*, Aug. 7, 1921.

367　　**"There were ledges"**: Unsigned letter to Theron S. Dean, *Burlington Free Press*, May 9, 1919, p. 5. Reprinted with permission.

　　　"From now on": Louis J. Paris, "The Loops of the Long Trail: With the Trail Possibilities of the Woodstock Quadrangle," reprinted from the *Elm Tree Monthly*, Dec. 1913, for the Woodstock Inn, Woodstock, Vt., 1914, p. 4.

　　　In southern Vermont: See general references previously listed.

　　　Stratton Mountain Club: The Stratton Mountain Club is described by Louis J. Paris in "The Long Trail and the Trails of Bennington County," *Bennington County Review*, April 1, 1914, pp. 3–4. John Paulson of Bennington, a veteran of these earlier years, recalls at least one joint outing of the GMC and the SMC (conversation with John Paulson, Oct. 16, 1981).

　　　"A surprising amount": Louis J. Paris, "Killington to Greylock: The Long Trail of 1914," typescript in GMC archives of Vermont Historical Society, Montpelier, Vt., p. 4. Reprinted with permission.

　　　By diligently counting: Paris, "The Long Trail and the Trails of Bennington County," April 1, 1914, p. 7.

　　　"Sooner or later": Paris, "Killington to Greylock," p. 5. Reprinted with permission.

368　　**The Rutland Railroad:** *Ibid.*

368   **New GMC sections:** Paris, "The Long Trail and the Trails of Bennington County," p. 3.

     Bennington Section: See Louis J. Paris, "Green Mountain Trail Coming This Way," *Bennington* [Vt.] *Banner*, Jan. 15, 1914, pp. 1, 5. The early history of the Bennington Section has been well documented in "A Short History of the Bennington Section of the Green Mountain Club," an unpublished typescript, as well as in other papers in scrapbooks kept by John Paulson, an early member of the section. The authors are deeply indebted to Mr. Paulson for access to these papers.

     "When the Bennington Section": Undated four-page memorandum from J. L. Griswold addressed "To the Officers and Members of Bennington Section, Green Mountain Club, Inc." The authors saw this memorandum when it was in the possession of John Paulson. Paulson's Green Mountain Club material is now in the files of the Green Mountain Club. Reprinted with permission.

     Long Trail guidebook: Green Mountain Club, *Guide Book of the Long Trail*, 1917 and subsequent years.

     The south end: For examples of the ambivalence of reports of completed trail sections, see a November 1918 newspaper report that announces completion of an LT section south of Killington, though that was supposedly done in 1917 (unidentified clipping in Taylor Papers, Vermont Historical Society). At the 1919 Annual Meeting of the GMC, another trail section was described as "in pretty good shape now" (GMC Archives, Vermont Historical Society, Montpelier, Vt. Reprinted with permission). Even above Killington, the trail seemed to fade in and out. Though allegedly completed in 1913, the section between Middlebury Gap and Brandon was reported in 1919 to be under construction by Middlebury College students ("Midd Men to Work on Long Trail," *The Middlebury Campus* [Oct. 1, 1919], p. 1).

370   **A trail as long:** Beginning in 1920, the best source of information on trail changes is a comparison of edition-to-edition changes in the *Guide Book of the Long Trail*, and, after 1922, write-ups in the *Green Mountain News*, the name of which was changed in December 1925 to *The Long Trail News*.

     Killington Section's lodge: Louis J. Paris, "A 'Rising Bee' on Killington," *Burlington Free Press*, July 9, 1917, p. 7.

     Lake Pleiad Lodge: "Midd Men to Work on Long Trail, p. 1.

     By 1923: "Camps and Shelters on the Trail," *Green Mountain News* (Apr. 1923), p. 2.

371   **"Whose charms he regards":** Raymond H. Torrey, "Plans to Extend Long Trail over Quebec Border," *New York Evening Post*, June 16, 1922, p. 12. Reprinted with permission.

     Belvidere Mountain: Torrey, "Long Trail Extended," *New York Evening Post*, Nov. 9, 1923, p. 7.

     Hazen's Notch: "Work on The Trail," *Green Mountain News* (Dec. 1924), p. 2.

371 **"Jay Peak or Bust":** "Jay Peak or Bust Expressive Slogan," *Burlington Free Press*, Sept. 8, 1924, p. 6.

"From the Massachusetts line": Edith M. Esterbrook, "The Long Trail Safe for Women Hikers," *The Vermonter* (May 1929), p. 77.

Roy Buchanan: For more details on this interesting individual, see chap. 43.

"We better get rid": Quoted in *Guide Book of the Long Trail,* 20th ed. (1971), p. 7. The Buchanans' scouting expedition is described in Bruce Buchanan, "Taking the 'Almost' Out of the Long Trail," *The Long Trail News*, (Nov. 1953), pp. 1–3. Quoted passages in the rest of this paragraph are from this account.

"In view of": Torrey, "Plans to Extend Long Trail over Quebec Border."

Concerned citizens were said: Conversation with Larry Dean, long active in the GMC, Nov. 6, 1980.

373 **In the summer of 1930:** Besides contemporary write-ups in *The Long Trail News*, this last Long Trail work was written up in "Brown Men Complete Long Trail," *Providence* [R.I.] *Sunday Journal Magazine*, Oct. 11, 1931, pp. 3, 9, 16 (Carleton and Doll were both graduates of Brown University), and, as a fiftieth anniversary remembrance, by Robert L. Hagerman, "Axes, Machetes, Bugs, and Pumpernickel Mark Last Ten Miles of L. T.," *The Long Trail News*, (Aug. 1981), pp. 8–9. By an odd quirk, GMC records for many years reported this year of completion as 1931, even though the club's own publications in 1930 unequivocally reported the final work. In 1985 *The Long Trail News* ran a brief article pointing out the long-standing error and speculating on some of the possible reasons why it persisted ("When Was the Long Trail Really Completed?," *The Long Trail News* [Nov. 1985], p. 5). The date of 1931 *is* correct for the first newspaper article given here.

CHAPTER 36. UNIFICATION OF THE WHITE MOUNTAIN TRAILS

375 **In the same:** White Mountain trail work in the years 1912–30 is well documented in two landmark articles: C. W. Blood, "The Evolution of a Trailman," *Appalachia* (June 1965), pp. 427–46, and P. R. Jenks, "Twenty-Five Years of the A. M. C. Trail Crew," *Appalachia* (Dec. 1943), pp. 441–52. Of course annual write-ups in *Appalachia* during the years when the work was being done are an invaluable source. The series of White Mountain guidebooks published by AMC, beginning in 1907, is an essential reference for this history.

"In general, Club money": "Councillor of Improvements Report," *Appalachia* (May 1902), p. 95.

376 **Swift River trails:** Louis Cutter's proposals for these trails were contained in his "Councillor of Improvements Report," *Appalachia* (May 1902), p. 95. His original idea was "to pass through the depression immediately north of the north summit of Tripyramid," but inability to obtain landowner permission led to the more circuitous route shown in figure 36.1. Pray's work on the

Swift River trail is described in his "Councillor of Improvements Report," *Appalachia* (Apr. 1904), pp. 340–41.

376   **Benton MacKaye later recalled:** MacKaye described the importance of his participation in this work in an interview by Dorothy M. Martin fifty years later in the Potomac Appalachian Trail Club's *Bulletin* (Jan.–March 1953), p. 12.

"The Club's proposed system" and "Advocated the gradual": "Councillor of Improvements Report," *Appalachia* (Apr. 1904), p. 336.

Carrigain Notch Trail: "Councillor of Improvements Report," *Appalachia* (June 1907), p. 292.

First printed guidebook: Appalachian Mountain Club, *Guide to Paths and Camps in the White Mountains* (Boston: Appalachian Mountain Club, 1907). The publication of this guide is described in Perkins's report just cited, p. 293.

379   **"Spend the whole week":** C. W. Blood, "Evolution of a Trailman," *Appalachia* (June 1965), p. 432. Reprinted with the permission of the Appalachian Mountain Club.

"It was our first step": *Ibid.*

"Surpassingly difficult": Sweetser, *The White Mountains*, p. 270.

"The serried ranks": E. B. Cook, "An Ascent of Mt. Haystack [Garfield]," *Appalachia* (Dec. 1883), p. 276.

"It was evident": Blood, "Evolution of a Trailman," p. 433.

"But further way": John Milton, *Paradise Lost*, book 4, ll. 174–77.

"I recall in point": Nathaniel L. Goodrich, "Trail Location," paper delivered before the New England Trail Conference, Jan. 23, 1925 (pamphlet no. 14, pp. 5–6). Reprinted with permission.

380   **"The idea of a series":** Blood, "A Twentieth Anniversary: The Garfield Ridge Trail, 1914–1916," *Appalachia* (Dec. 1936), p. 280.

"For more than twenty years": Blood, "Evolution of a Trailman," p. 435.

"Considering its length": *Ibid.*, p. 436.

381   **Earlier work . . . in the Mahoosucs:** Arthur Stanley Pease, "The Mountaineer," *Boston Transcript*, Nov. 23, 1912, part 2, p. 6; Arthur Stanley Pease, "Mahoosuc Notch," *Appalachia* (June 1918), pp. 238–39; and obituary by C. W. Blood for Pease, *Appalachia* (June 1964), p. 154, in which Blood notes his astonishment, when working in the Mahoosucs, to see Pease emerge from the densest of thickets, "having run a string line across from Goose Eye for an extension of the Mahoosuc Trail to the south."

382   **The AMC huts:** The best published source on the early history of the AMC hut system is Dean Peabody, Jr., "The Evolution of the A. M. C. Hut," *Appalachia* (Dec. 1931), pp. 432–47. For a more up-to-date and complete picture

of the entire hut system, see William E. Reifsnyder, *High Huts of the White Mountains* (Boston: Appalachian Mountain Club, 1979). See also annual reports for the huts in *Appalachia* from 1933 on.

382 **Litter was getting:** See letter from Marian Pychowska to Isabella Stone, July 30, 1885, in Kent-Philbrook collection.

"Camp Placid": The only known references to this 1885 precursor of the Madison Spring Hut are in the correspondence between Marian Pychowska and Isabella Stone, in the Kent-Philbrook collection. One letter dated Sept. 18, 1885, gives it the name "Camp Placid." Reprinted with permission.

Madison Spring Hut: The building of Madison Spring Hut is described in Frederic D. Allen's "Councillor of Improvements Report for 1888," *Appalachia* (Dec. 1888), pp. 243–47, and Cross, *Randolph Old and New*, pp. 110–13.

"The most considerable": Allen, "Councillor of Improvements Report," p. 243.

383 **Joseph Brooks Dodge:** The colorful personality of Joe Dodge is partially captured in William Lowell Putnam, *Joe Dodge: "One New Hampshire Institution"* (Canaan, N.H.: Phoenix Publishing, 1986). See also an extended tribute compiled by Frederic A. Stott, "Joe Dodge," in *Appalachia* (June 1974), pp. 7–30. The authors have also drawn on countless reminiscences by hikers and AMC members who recalled the Dodge era.

Mayor of Porky Gulch: The origin of this title is unknown, but it became a cliche.

"Poohbah of the Presidentials": Reg Abbott, "Joe Dodge, Mountain Maestro, Ready for Year's AMC Hut Session," *Manchester* [N.H.] *Union Leader*, June 6, 1950, p. 18.

"Master table thumper": Sherman Adams, "Remarks Made at the Dedication Ceremonies for the New Summit Building on Mount Washington," *Mount Washington Observatory News Bulletin* (Dec. 1980), p. 73.

384 **"Though he knows":** Hal Burton, "The Mayor of Porky Gulch," *Saturday Evening Post*, Mar. 19, 1949, p. 144.

"Joe ran a good show": Edward Damp, "Of Mules, Mice, and Madison," *Appalachia* (Dec. 1980), p. 60.

"I don't believe": Jane Atwood Black, "Hutman F.: Pinkham Notch Camp in the Forties," *Appalachia* (Dec. 1987), p. 46. Reprinted with the permission of the Appalachian Mountain Club.

385 **"For thirty-six years":** *Ibid.*, p. 47.

On January 1, 1928: A perceptive analysis of change in the physical architecture of the huts and its relationship to changing social patterns is contained in an unpublished typescript dated spring 1981 by Peter Crane, "Carter Notch Hut: An Introductory Essay." A copy is in the authors' collections, kindly supplied by Mr. Crane.

386   **"Amazing gift of getting":** Putnam, *Joe Dodge*, p. xi.

         "Joe had the art": Conversation with Ted Brown, Oct. 27, 1985.

387   **It is tempting:** Enterprising hikers perceived the new east-west possibilities well before there were western huts: see the charming narrative, Leon Keach, *Glencliff to Gorham: A Cross-Country Adventure with the League for Leaner Loins* (Sheffield, Mass.: The Deacon's Seat Press, 1983).

388   **"It reverses the order":** Robert L. M. Underhill, "Untraveled Paths: II. Through North Fork Junction," *Appalachia* (Dec. 1929), p. 357. Reprinted with the permission of the Appalachian Mountain Club.

         "The definition of": P. R. Jenks, "Twenty-five years of the A. M. C. Trail Crew," *Appalachia* (Dec. 1943), p. 444.

389   **"There is an edge":** Nathaniel L. Goodrich, "The Attractions and Rewards of Trail Making," *Appalachia* (June 1918), p. 248. Reprinted with the permission of the Appalachian Mountain Club.

         "Two of the worst": Gray Harris, quoted in P. R. Jenks, "The Story of the Mahoosucs," *Appalachia* (Dec. 1933), p. 563.

         "To him a thing": C. W. Blood, obituary for P. R. Jenks, *Appalachia* (June 1953), p. 399. Reprinted with the permission of the Appalachian Mountain Club.

         According to Sherman Adams: Conversation with Sherman Adams, Sept. 18, 1981. Governor Adams told the authors, when recalling Goodrich: "If he had any sense of humor, I never detected it."

         "Of nigh a hundred": Paul R. Jenks, "The Story of the Mahoosucs," *Appalachia* (Dec. 1933), p. 564. Reprinted with the permission of the Appalachian Mountain Club.

         "I am happy": Blood, "Evolution of a Trailman," p. 446.

         "The trails we have made": Goodrich, *Trail Location*, p. 12. Reprinted with permission.

390   **A short man:** Among others, Sherman Adams reported the most pleasant recollections of Professor Harrington (Sept. 17, 1981, conversation).

         "The pockets of the coat": Hubert Goodrich, obituary for Karl Pomeroy Harrington, *Appalachia* (June 1954), p. 89.

         "[Harrington] was indeed": Letter (photocopy of carbon) from Waldo Beach to Charles B. Stone, Sept. 6, 1965, Harrington Lodge folder, Wesleyan University Archives. Reprinted with permission.

CHAPTER 37. THE ADIRONDACKS BECOME ONE HIKING CENTER

391   **It will be recalled:** The decline of Catskill hiking in the interwar years can be observed in the "Long Brown Path" columns by Raymond H. Torrey in the *New York Evening Post* of those years; T. Morris Longstreth, *The Catskills*

(New York: Century, 1921); W. Gray Harris, "Afoot in the Catskills," *Appalachia* (Dec. 1922), pp. 313–17; William J. Neisel, "The Fortress of Manitou," *Appalachia* (Dec. 1939), pp. 456–65; and Henry L. Young, "Catskill Adventures," *Adirondac* (July–Aug. 1950), pp. 88–89. Roland Van Zandt's description of the Catskill Mountain House's stalking drearily toward its final closing and eventual immolation is the best part of his excellent book (*The Catskill Mountain House*). The authors are also indebted to Edward G. West and Victor Schrader for illuminating recollections.

391   **"The Catskill summer tourist"**: Neisel, "Fortress of Manitou," p. 456. Reprinted with the permission of the Appalachian Mountain Club.

"Too far from New York": *Ibid.*, p. 457.

"Perhaps the one mountainous": *Ibid.*

"First I heard": Conversation with Edward G. West, Oct. 10, 1982.

392   **The first man:** The origins of the original Adirondack Mountain Club are revealed in Henry Ives Baldwin, "Early Days of the ADK," *Adirondac* (Nov.–Dec. 1955), p. 103. For the history of ADK, the most useful single source is the fiftieth anniversary issue of the club's publication, *Adirondac* (Nov.–Dec. 1972). In some fifty pages of this issue were marshaled an array of articles on various phases of the club's history, all of which are highly informative. Authors included Frank J. Oliver, Herbert McAneny, Clinton Miller, Robert J. Ringlee, and the then president of the club, Rudolph W. Strobel. A more recent summary of the formative years is Frank J. Oliver, "ADK's Birth—1921–1922," *Adirondac* (Nov. 1982), pp. 4–5, 28. The authors benefited greatly from conversations with both Mr. Baldwin and Mr. Oliver.

Utica Tramp and Trail Club: *History of the Tramp and Trail Club of Utica, 1921–1946*, a booklet prepared by the club and dated Feb. 15, 1946.

Palisades Interstate Park Trail Conference: See chap. 39.

Legend supplies: Meade C. Dobson, "Recollections of the Formation of the Adirondack Mountain Club," *Adirondac* (Nov.–Dec. 1947), p. 3. This anecdote is retold in several ADK accounts of the club's origin. See, for example, Frank J. Oliver, "The Founding Fathers of ADK," *Adirondac* (Nov.–Dec. 1972), p. 101, Russell Carson, "A Charter Member Looks at 25 Years," *Cloud Splitter* (Nov.–Dec. 1947), p. 2. Many versions of the origin of the club begin with the events of 1921 and omit the earlier Baldwin phase. The poached-trout story has the ring of legend since it seems unlikely that fishing-law violaters were routinely hauled before the state conservation commissioner himself.

The first newspaper: "Proposed Adirondack Mountain Club Would Open Region to People of State," *Adirondack Enterprise* (Saranac Lake, N.Y.), Aug. 10, 1921.

393   **"We got many hints"**: Baldwin, "Early Days of the ADK," p. 103.

393   **December 5, 1921, meeting:** Besides sources already cited, see a letter from George Marshall to his brother Robert, quoted by Oliver in "The Founding Fathers of ADK," p. 101.

         Howard gave the principal talk: Howard's address, "The Proposed Adirondack Mountain Club," was reprinted in *Adirondac* (Nov.–Dec. 1947), pp. 4–5.

         Three fundamental objectives: *Ibid.* Reprinted with permission.

394   **"To open, develop":** Rudolph W. Strobel, "Trail Activities of the Adirondack Mountain Club, 1922–1972," *Adirondac* (Nov.–Dec. 1972), p. 122. Reprinted with permission.

         Johns Brook Lodge: The history of Johns Brook Lodge is told by Frank Oliver in "The Beginning of Johns Brook Lodge," *Adirondac* (March–Apr. 1967), pp. 20–22, and "The 'Famous Trek' to JBL—1925," (May–June 1967), pp. 41–44. Contemporary accounts of the project appeared in *High Spots*, in just about every issue in early 1924.

         Mel Hathaway: The eviction of Mel Hathaway is affectingly related in Peggy Byrne, "Mel Hathaway and the 'Conservationers,' " *Adirondac* (May–June 1966), pp. 50–52.

         Grace Camp and Winter Camp: "Proposed Purchase at Johns Brook," *High Spots* (Apr. 1929), pp. 1–2.

395   **Stirrings of interest:** See Goodwin, Adirondack trail maps and accompanying notes; see also letter to L&GW, Feb. 1, 1986.

         "The various trail projects": Torrey, "Long Brown Path," *New York Evening Post* (Aug. 6, 1926). Reprinted with permission.

397   **Hiking and trail-building flourished:** Data from annual reports of the New York Conservation Department.

         The conservation issue: The early evolution of ADK conservation policy is described in Frank J. Oliver and Robert J. Ringlee, "ADK Conservation Policy: Its Evolution," *Adirondac* (Nov.–Dec. 1972), pp. 126–49; Frank J. Oliver, "Birth of Conservation Policy, 1928," *Adirondac* (Nov. 1982), pp. 6–7; and Arthur E. Newkirk, "Early ADK Conservationists," *Adirondac* (Jan. 1985), pp. 34–36.

         At its 1922 meeting: This proposal took the form of a resolution by Warwick S. Carpenter, former secretary of the state Conservation Commission, entitled "Mountain Slope Protection and Recreational Development in the Adirondacks: Memorial and Motion Received and Referred to the Conservation Committee of the ADK at its Second Organization Meeting, New York City, April 3, 1922," a copy of which was generously loaned to the authors by Frank J. Oliver.

         "Call to action": "Adirondack Mountain Club Projects," *High Spots* (June 1930), pp. 16–17. This statement of club objectives and its subsequent follow-through are analyzed by Herbert McAneny, "The Lean Years: 1930–1945," *Adirondac*, (Nov.–Dec. 1972), pp. 107–13.

398   **"Sturm und Drang"**: William A. Andrews, president of the club during the years 1932–35, in a reminiscence written for *Adirondac* (Nov.–Dec. 1947), p. 9.

Robert Marshall's proposal: Oliver and Ringlee, "ADK Conservation Policy: Its Evolution," pp. 133–34.

"In all our thinking": Carson, *Peaks and People*, p. xxi. Reprinted with permission.

CCC truck trails: Oliver and Ringlee, "ADK Conservation Policy: Its Evolution," p. 132.

Ski trails: *Ibid.* pp. 132–35. See also Weston, *Freedom in the Wilds*, pp. 169–70.

399   **"What this club needs"**: Quoted in Rudolph W. Strobel, "Trail Activities of the Adirondack Mountain Club, 1922–1972," p. 123. Reprinted with permission of the Adirondack Mountain Club, Inc.

"The more that's done": Walter Collins O'Kane, "The Mission of the Wilderness," *High Spots* (Oct. 1935), p. 14. Reprinted with permission.

CHAPTER 38. BAXTER STATE PARK

401   **Leroy Dudley**: Dudley's legend is preserved mainly by word of mouth among Katahdin old-timers. He is described at various points in Hakola's *Legacy of a Lifetime*, in numerous *In the Maine Woods* articles of the 1920s and 1930s, and in a brief obituary by Ronald L. Gower appearing in *Appalachia* (June 1942), p. 100. The authors are indebted chiefly to conversations with Helon Taylor, supervisor of Baxter State Park in post-Dudley years, and others.

403   **"I don't know"**: Conversation with Helon Taylor, July 16, 1982.

"In the evening": R. M. Hayes, "Barnstorming Mt. Katahdin," *In the Maine Woods*, 1936, p. 47.

"Did you like that story?": Conversation with Taylor, July 16, 1982.

Katahdin trails: While a variety of other sources are helpful, the best guide to the changing trail scene during the 1920s is the trail map published annually in *In the Maine Woods* during these years. Also helpful are Hakola, *Legacy of a Lifetime*, Leavitt, *Katahdin Skylines*, and numerous *In the Maine Woods* articles of the 1920s.

404   **"Short sporting path"**: Margaret Helburn, "The Chimney of Ktaadn," *Appalachia* (Nov. 1920), p. 56.

During the 1920s other trails: Many of these are mentioned in "How Two Men from Orono Climbed Katahdin in June," *Bangor Daily Commercial*, June 16, 1920, p. 10. Placing dates on the construction of Katahdin trails is complicated by the fact that many were well traveled informally for years before Dudley and others actually began clearing them. We have relied principally on the maps appearing annually in *In the Maine Woods* beginning in 1921 and on Leavitts' descriptions in *Katahdin Skylines*.

404 **In 1925 also:** Philip Ricker Shorey, "Maine Celebrities Climb to Katahdin's Peak: A Story of the Ascent Made by Governor Brewster and His Party in the Summer of 1925," *In the Maine Woods*, 1926, pp. 94–99.

No matter: Frederic Bulkeley Hyde, "The Taming of Mt. Katahdin," *In the Maine Woods*, 1927, p. 50.

"With the exception": Myron H. Avery, "The Keep Path and Its Successors," *Appalachia* (June 1929), p. 235.

In 1929 botanist: Grace E. Butcher, "The Opening Up of the Northwest Basin, Katahdin," *Appalachia* (Nov. 1935), p. 427, and conversations (Oct. 26, 1982, and other occasions) and correspondence with E. Porter Dickinson.

405 **Thereafter, the remote cirque:** Other tales of exploration behind Katahdin during these years include Ludwig K. Moorehead, "Atop Mt. Katadin [*sic*] and How It Was Reached: A Vivid Story of the Scramble through Craggy Passes and o'er Dizzy Paths," *In the Maine Woods*, 1922, pp. 9–17; Henry R. Buck, "Traveler Mountain and North of Katahdin," *Appalachia* (June 1928), pp. 72–74; Myron H. Avery, "A New Route to Mt. Katahdin," *In the Maine Woods*, 1929, pp. 12–26, and "The Katahdinaughauh," *In the Maine Woods*, 1929, pp. 12–27 (also written up for *Appalachia* [Dec. 1928], pp. 174–79, and [June 1930], pp. 90–96); and Ronald L. Gower, "Round about Katahdin, *Appalachia* (June 1932), pp. 74–85, and "Katahdin Circumambulated," *Appalachia* (June 1933), pp. 381–97.

Meanwhile, management: The authoritative source for the development of Baxter State Park is, of course, Hakola. See especially chap. 2, "The Drive to Create a Park at Katahdin," and 3, "Baxter State Park is Acquired."

406 **"It should be":** "Katahdin," *Bangor Daily Commercial*, July 13, 1901, p. 4.

"Student of the common": Quoted by Hakola, *Legacy of a Lifetime*, p. 284. Hakola devotes his chap. 16 to a biographical essay of Baxter.

"The most patient": Arthur Staples, editor of the *Lewiston* [Maine] *Journal*, quoted in Hakola, *Legacy of a Lifetime*, p. 288.

407 **"Shall forever be left":** *Ibid.*, p. 104. Hakola's chap. 4 covers "Percival P. Baxter and the Wilderness Concept."

"Everything in connection": *Ibid.*, p. 111.

National Park Service: A copy of the National Park Service's detailed plan (Arthur C. Sylvester, "A Report on the Recreational Development, Mount Katahdin Region, Millinocket, Maine," May 16, 1935) is in the Myron H. Avery Papers at the Maine State Library in Augusta, as is a large volume of Avery and Baxter correspondence and related papers. See also Hakola's chap. 6, "The National Park Controversy."

409   **"Walking had hardly"**: Frank Place, "Raymond H. Torrey," *High Spots* (Jan. 1939), p. 65.

410   **"New York does"**: Frank Solari, "Impressions," in AMC New York Chapter, *In the Hudson Highlands*, p. 184.

"Worthwhile," and **"By the help"**: Letters to Joseph C. Hart from "his friend," published as *Letters about the Hudson River and Its Vicinity, written in 1835 and 1836, by a citizen of New York* (New York: Freeman Hunt, 1836), p. 95.

"Those who gathered": Lossing, "The Hudson, p. 213. As to what hoop-poles or their function were, the authors are unable to assist the reader.

"One of the most beautiful": N. P. Willis, *American Scenery*, p. 24.

An early AMC member: W. Whitman Bailey, "Crow's Nest Mountain," *Appalachia* (Apr. 1884), pp. 345–48.

William T. Howell: William T. Howell kept diaries, and these were assembled and published after his death by his friend Frederick Delano Weekes in two volumes entitled *The Hudson Highlands: William Thompson Howell Memorial* (New York: Lenz and Riecker, Inc., vol. 1, 1933; vol. 2, 1934), This once scarce item was reprinted in a single volume by Walking News, Inc. (New York, 1982). All quotations in this chapter reprinted with permission of Walking News, Inc.

412   **"The wood roads"**: Howell, *The Hudson Highlands*, vol. 2, p. 163.

"How famous it is": *Ibid.*, vol. 2, p. 5.

"Its long sweeping": *Ibid.*, vol. 2, p. 78.

"The charm and mystery": *Ibid.*

"Appetizer, Vegetable Soup": *Ibid.*, vol. 1, p. 34.

413   **"Three Star Haig"**: *Ibid.*, vol. 1, p. 92.

His photographs: Examples include Edward L. Partridge, "A Forest Preserve for the Metropolis," *Country Life in America* (Sept. 1908), pp. 456–59, and Van Wyck Brooks, "The Highlands of the Hudson as a Playground for the People," *The World's Work* (Sept. 1909), pp. 12,001–12,009.

Fringe farmers: See, for example, one boyhood hero and hiking companion, the venerable woodsman named "Old Hager": *The Hudson Highlands*, vol. 1, pp. 29–31, 109, vol. 2, p. 26–31, 98.

"There is but one": *Ibid.*, vol. 2, pp. 89–90.

414   **First to come:** Invaluable recollections of the pre-1920 era for Scouting in Harriman Park were provided to the authors by Julian H. Salomon in conversations on Oct. 29, 1981, and Oct. 22, 1982. Mr. Salomon was one of those Scouts brought to the park in 1912.

414   **New Jersey's Wyanokie Plateau:** Sources for the early history of activity in the Wyanokies include Minnie May Monks, *Winbeam* (New York: Knickerbocker Press, 1930); William Hoeferlin, *Wyanokie Trail Guide* (Brooklyn, N.Y.: *Walking News*, 1943); Edgar F. Wright, "Wyanokie: 'The Place of the Sassafras,'" *Appalachia* (June 1971), pp. 106–15; Green Mountain Club, New York Section, "History of Our First Fifty Years: 1916–1966," p. 45; and Frank J. Oliver, "Trails in the Metropolitan Area Near New York City," a typescript generously prepared for the authors, July 6, 1981, p. 3. We also learned much from conversations with Mr. Oliver and with Xandi and Henry Roebig, both on Oct. 21, 1982. The modern spelling used in the area is *Wanaque*.

"In a measure": Howell, *The Hudson Highlands*, vol. 2, p. 41.

415   **"A very broad social philosophy":** Conversation with Julian H. Salomon, Oct. 29, 1981.

"Filled us with enthusiasm": Place, "Trails in the Metropolitan Region," *In the Hudson Highlands*, p. 217.

During the summer: The story of the start-up of trails in Harriman Park has been often recounted. Of central importance are the various editions of the *New York Walk Book*. This first appeared in 1923 under the joint authorship of Raymond H. Torrey, Frank Place, Jr., and Robert L. Dickinson. Subsequent editions have appeared in 1934, 1951, 1971, and 1984. A separate and smaller guide by Dickinson, *Palisades Interstate Park*, had been published by the American Geographical Society in 1921; it was incorporated into the *Walk Book* in 1934. Other useful sources are Place, "Trails in the Metropolitan Region," in the AMC's *In the Hudson Highlands*; Raymond H. Torrey, "New Mountain Trails Made for City Hikers," *New York Times*, May 2, 1926, sec. 9, p. 12; Torrey, "Volunteer Trail Making," *Mountain Magazine* (Oct. 1927), pp. 39–43; and contemporary "Long Brown Path" columns by Torrey in the *New York Evening Post*. A key source is a letter from Major Welch to Frank Place, written on Jan. 20, 1940, as the Major was about to retire, in response to a query from Place about the origins of New York area trail work. This is one of many vital documents set aside in the seventeen scrapbooks kept by Frank Place, referred to in more detail in a later note in this chapter. The authors have also been greatly aided by extensive correspondence with various old-time New York trail workers, among whom, for the earliest history, Herbert C. Hauptmann and Frank J. Oliver have been especially enlightening.

Among these were: Within the hiking community, who were the key people whom Major Welch called on to get the Harriman trails movement going? The sources do not agree, but a few names come up prominently. Welch's letter to Place, in which he says he consults his diaries, reports that he held "a preliminary talk with Allis, Bell, Torrey and Carl Buckingham (whom I can't quite identify) at luncheon somewhere down on Wall Street." Place himself says the October 1920 meeting was called by Welch "through Meade C. Dobson" (Place, "Trails in the Metropolitan Region," p. 217). The GMC's "History of Our First Fifty Years" assigns the major role for organizing the first trail workers to Professor Monroe (p. 45), but a Torrey article says that Bell and Allis "were named joint chairmen of a reconnaisance and trail-making committee which will organize volunteer workers," ("To Lay Out Trails in Interstate Park," *New York Evening Post*, Oct. 20, 1920, p. 13.)

415   **Figure 39.2:** The map shown as figure 39.2 is based entirely on a 1920 map prepared under Maj. William A. Welch, "Palisade Interstate Park: Harriman and Bear Mountain Section," a copy of which is in the maps collection of the Palisades Interstate Park Conference headquarters at Bear Mountain, N.Y.

416   **"Almost every mountain":** Meade C. Dobson, "Continuous Paths Would Add to Hiker's Delight in Hudson and Ramapo Highlands," *New York Evening Post*, Aug. 27, 1920, p. 7. Reprinted with permission.

417   **"The most concentratedly":** Torrey, "New Mountain Trails," sec. 9, p. 12.

419   **"We have brought out":** Place, "Raymond H. Torrey," *High Spots*, Jan. 1939, p. 68.

Such a magnificent: In compiling this picture of the New York hiking scene of the 1920s and 1930s, the authors have relied less on printed sources than on the immeasurably valuable personal recollections of many who generously took time to talk with us, write to us, and send us memorabilia of the era. At risk of omitting names, we must especially mention Eleanor and Percy Olton, Xandi and Henry Roebig, Herbert C. Hauptmann, Walter W. Shannon, Heinrich E. Kromayer, Julianna S. Irelan, Elizabeth Burton, Grace J. Averill, Alice Thorpe, Elizabeth Cook, Frank J. Oliver, Meyer Kukle, George Zoebelin, Lee Erde, and Elizabeth D. Levers. Not of the older generation, but most helpful catalysts in putting us in touch with it, were Esther Weitz, Barbara and Richard Tourin, and most especially Robert Schulz. The next best source is a remarkable set of seventeen scrapbooks entitled "Trail Clippings," containing a wealth of newspaper clippings, club publications, and other memorabilia, kept by Frank Place throughout the 1920s and 1930s. While the scrapbooks themselves are in the collections of the American Geographical Society, their deteriorated condition is such that they are best studied via microfilm, sets of which are available at the New York–New Jersey Trail Conference and at one or two other places. Our knowledge of this period owes a great debt to Mr. Place for putting these scrapbooks together; the American Geographical Society for preserving them; Howard Deller of that society and David M. Sherman of the National Park Service for arranging for the authors to obtain the microfilm of these invaluable records. Among the few printed sources that do justice to the special flavor of those times, the most important is the AMC New York Chapter's *In the Hudson Highlands* (Lancaster, Penna.: Lancaster Press, 1945; reprinted by Walking News, no date indicated). A less accessible gem is Albert Stürcke, *Hikes* (New York: privately printed, 1926). Torrey's "Long Brown Path" columns constitute an invaluable record of the times. Extensive collections of this column can be conveniently perused in three places: the collections of the Trailside Museum, Palisades Interstate Park Commission, at Bear Mountain, N.Y.; the library of the New York-New Jersey Trail Conference, New York,

N.Y.; and the microfilms of Frank Place's scrapbooks; as well as (less conveniently) in the newspapers in which they appeared, principally the *New York Evening Post*. The first edition of Torrey et al., *New York Walk Book*, is also of value. For the later part of the period, William Hoeferlin's publication *Walking News* picks up where Torrey left off.

420 **"Another Sunday has arrived"**: John Kieran,"Out of the City, Into the Open," *New York Times*, magazine sec., Dec. 6, 1931, pp. 12–13, 21. Copyright © 1931 by The New York Times Company. Reprinted by permission.

"On Sundays and holidays": Robert Livingston Schuyler, preface to *In the Hudson Highlands*, p. iii.

"Of course most everyone": Letter from Julianna S. Irelan to L&GW, Nov. 13, 1981. Reprinted with permission.

Kerson Nurian incident: *Ibid.*

421 **"Another inspiring massif"**: Frank Place, "Trails in the Metropolitan Region," *In the Hudson Highlands*, p. 224.

"Beetle-browed Breakneck": Stürcke, *Hikes*, p. 136.

"They couldn't be": *Paterson* [N.J.] *Morning Call*, Jan. 20, 1939.

Albert Stürcke recalled: Stürcke, *Hikes*, p. 29.

"Good old Erie!": Letter from Alice Thorpe to L&GW, Jan. 21, 1982. Reprinted with permission.

423 **"For a while it almost"**: Letter from Herbert C. Hauptmann to L&GW, Nov. 3, 1981. Reprinted with permission.

Ed Ingraham's routine: Conversation with Eleanor and Percy Olton, Apr. 13, 1982.

"Sometimes we were": Letter from Alice Thorpe to L&GW, Jan. 21, 1982. Reprinted with permission.

"Third class diner": Letter from Julianna S. Irelan to L&GW, Nov. 13, 1981. Reprinted with permission.

"One of our members": *Ibid.*

424 **"And then along"**: Raymond R. Goodlatte, "Maginnisville and Sugar Loaf Mountain," *In the Hudson Highlands*, p. 102.

"We had a wonderful": Unsigned obituary for Russell Lodge, "Obituaries," GMC *Bulletin* (July–Oct. 1979), p. 7.

Raymond H. Torrey: Torrey's personality and accomplishments are in part revealed in obituaries, notably Frank Place's in ADK's *High Spots* (Jan. 1939), pp. 64–71; Bill Gorham's in GMC's *Bulletin* (Aug.–Oct. 1938); J. Ashton Allis's in AMC's *Appalachia* (Dec. 1938), pp. 244–45; Benton MacKaye's in *The Living Wilderness*, March 1939), p. 8. Oddly enough, one of the best was written by one of the very few antagonists Torrey ever had, Myron H. Avery, in the Potomac Appalachian Trail Club's *Bulletin* (Oct. 1938), p. 95.

425　　　**"Torrey was the dynamo":** Letter from Herbert C. Hauptmann to L&GW, Jan. 11, 1982. Reprinted with permission.

"Owners of large": Place, Torrey obituary in *High Spots*, p. 68. Reprinted with permission.

"I can find," and **"You know what":** Letters from A. T. Shorey to H. C. Hauptmann, Jan. 20, 1925(?), and from Frank Place to H. C. Hauptmann, Jan. 19, 1925. Both of these letters were sent to Herbert C. Hauptmann, who saved them and sent them to the authors more than fifty-six years later.

"Scarcely a party": Place, Torrey obituary in *High Spots*, p. 65. Reprinted with permission.

426　　　**A side interest:** When needing a pseudonym for a question-and-answer column in *Mountain Magazine* (see, for example, the issue of July 1927, p. 2), he signed it "Baron Hassenclever." He also signed some of his personal correspondence with close friends by this name; and they refer to Mrs. Torrey as the Baroness (samples supplied by Herbert C. Hauptmann). His favorite hiking costume of knickers, coat, calf-high boots, and cap were known as his baronial costume (Place, Torrey obituary in *High Spots*, pp. 70–71).

"Is there a trail": Place, Torrey obituary, *High Spots*, p. 64. Reprinted with permission.

"Roundish-looking": Conversation with Eleanor and Percy Olton, Apr. 13, 1982, clearly confirmed by photographs.

"Without let-up": Place, Torrey obituary in *High Spots*, p. 71. Reprinted with permission.

427　　　**"Volunteers probably ran":** Letter from Herbert C. Hauptmann to L&GW, Nov. 3, 1981. Reprinted with permission.

"A number of": *Ibid.*

One marauder showed up: Torrey, "Long Brown Path," Nov. 22, 1937.

"The Demon Trail Painter": *Ibid.*, Apr. 1928, day not indicated, in Place's "Trail Clippings."

"Quietly faded out": *Ibid.*, Dec. 30, 1937.

Revival of the New York–New Jersey Trail Conference: The most authoritative account is William Burton, "The New York–New Jersey Trail Conference," in the AMC's *In the Hudson Highlands.* See also Torrey's contemporary "Long Brown Path" columns. A copy of the conference's landmark statement of principles was issued as an eight-page booklet under the title *Program for the Co-ordination of Volunteer Trail Work* by the conference; a copy of this document may be found in the Frank Place "Trail Clippings," vol. 8, pp. 100A–100G, and another is in the MacKaye Family Papers in the Dartmouth College Library.

428   **"Here on brave Torrey's":** "Long Brown Path," Feb. 26, 1932. Torrey attributed this epic fragment to Edward P. B. Laurence, then president of the Interstate Hiking Club. Reprinted with permission.

    Another outbreak of hostilities: See Torrey, "Long Brown Path" columns of Nov. 22, 1937, Jan. 20, 1938, and others.

    "A spirit of harmony": Torrey, "Long Brown Path," Apr. 24, 1931.

429   **"A route that a person":** Vincent J. Schaefer, "Memorandum relative to the Long Path of New York," Dec. 18, 1974, copy supplied to the authors by Dr. Schaefer. Except where otherwise indicated, quoted words are from this memorandum. Dr. Schaefer has also kindly explained much of the history and philosophy of the Long Path in conversations (Aug. 15, 1980) and in correspondence with the authors. Quotations from the "Memorandum" are reprinted with permission.

    "There would be": Letter from Dr. Schaefer to William Carr, quoted in Jean Craighead George, *The American Walk Book*, (New York: E. P. Dutton, 1979), p. 76. Reprinted with permission. Chap. 4 of this book gives a full description of the Long Path (pp. 75–85).

430   **Torrey supplied publicity:** Torrey, "Long Brown Path," beginning on Dec. 23, 1932, but mainly between April and June 1934.

    We shall find: See chap. 45.

CHAPTER 40. CONNECTICUT'S BLUE-BLAZED TRAIL SYSTEM

431   **A metropolitan trail system:** The start-up of the Connecticut Forest and Park Association's trails activities is told by John E. Hibbard, "A 50th Anniversary of the Blue-Blazed Trail System," *Connecticut Woodlands*, (Fall 1979), pp. 5–7. Various historical articles have appeared in *Connecticut Woodlands* during the 1980s, some of them cited in specific references below. Of great help to the authors were several conversations with Kornel Bailey, whose more than fifty years of leadership in CFPA trail work go back almost to the beginning. Talks and correspondence with Mr. Hibbard and several other Connecticut trailsmen also shed light on these earliest days: see specific citations below. A useful general article is Romeyn A. Spare, "Connecticut Trails," *Appalachia* (June 1946), pp. 131–33.

    "Combined the best features": "Albert M. Turner: The 'Temporary' Employee Who Stayed for 28 Years," Connecticut Department of Environmental Protection, *Citizens' Bulletin* (June 1978), p. 7.

    "The longest stride": Conversation with Seymour Smith, Oct. 22, 1981.

    "We all recognize": Memorandum from A. M. Turner to the State Park Commission, July 24, 1917, in the Herman Haupt Chapman Papers, Yale University Library. Reprinted with permission.

432   **"There should be":** *Ibid.*

432 **"When you are in a park":** A quotation attributed to George A. Parker ("of Hartford") by Turner in an address, "State Trails—A Corollary of State Parks," to the Fourth Annual Meeting, National Conference on State Parks, 1924; the text was published in Herbert Evison, ed., *A State Park Anthology* (Washington, D.C.: National Conference of State Parks, 1930), pp. 190–92.

"The blue distance": *Ibid.*, p. 192.

"Only the man on foot": Memorandum from A. M. Turner to the Connecticut State Park Commission, "Concerning Trails," Dec. 1, 1919, in the Herman Haupt Chapman Papers, Yale University Library. Reprinted with permission.

"Only the man on wheels": *Ibid.*

More than eighty parks: Connecticut Forest and Park Association, *Connecticut Outdoor Recreation Guide*, bicentennial ed. (East Hartford, Conn.: published by the Association, 1976).

433 **Meriden-area trails:** Trail building around Meriden between 1916 and 1929 is recounted in Norman M. Wickstrand, "Early Hiking Trails around Meriden," *Connecticut Woodlands* (Winter 1981–1982), pp. 19–20; a few of Kilbourne's own recollections were set down in Frederick W. Kilbourne, "Early Days of the Connecticut Trail System," *Appalachia* (Dec. 1946), pp. 271–74; Allen Chamberlain covered contemporary developments in two *Boston Evening Transcript* articles, "Making A Happy Dream Come True," Feb. 21, 1919, p. III-6, and "A Cure for Springtime Restlessness," May 10, 1919, p. III-5. The authors are greatly indebted to Norman M. Wickstrand for conversations about early days on May 26, 1983, and subsequent occasions.

Trap Rock Trail: Kilbourne himself recalled this date as "in or about 1919" ("Early Days," p. 273), but Turner's 1919 memorandum says Kilbourne had discussed the idea at a December 1918 meeting.

Edgar Laing Heermance: Kornel Bailey, "Edgar L. Heermance, Father of the Connecticut Trail System," *Connecticut Woodlands* (Summer 1983), pp. 17–18, is the best single source for Heermance's role in early Connecticut trails. Other good sketches are by Louise H. Tallman (Heermance's daughter), "Building of Camp Heermance," *Appalachia* (Dec. 1957), pp. 538-40, and Willis Birchman, "Faces and Facts: Edgar Laing Heermance," *New Haven* [Conn.] *Register*, Feb. 22, 1942, p. IV-4. An illuminating document is Heermance's own recollections, "The Heermance Book," in the possession of Mrs. Tallman. The authors are grateful to Mrs. Tallman for access to this family relic and for her own recollections of her father's trail work in correspondence and in conversation (March 26, 1984).

"I had never seen": Bailey, "Edgar L. Heermance," p. 17.

436 **"Cursed with a certain":** Birchman, "Faces and Facts: Edgar Laing Heermance."

Quinnipiac Trail: The original route description for the Quinnipiac Trail appeared in leaflets prepared by the Connecticut Forest and Park Association,

"Quinnipiac Trail," the first dated April 1930 and a revision dated September 1931. Its history was summarized by Kornel Bailey, "History of the Quinnipiac Trail," *Connecticut Woodlands* (Summer 1983), pp. 16, 18. The occasion of this trail's opening was used as the basis for a write-up, "Connecticut Trail System," in *Mountain Magazine* (May 1930), p. 15.

436   **"He had a one-track mind"**: Letter from George K. Libby to L&GW, Feb. 4, 1983. Reprinted with permission.

Tunxis Trail: Tunxis Trail route description appeared first in a CFPA leaflet dated October 1931, "Tunxis Trail." A vivid and complete picture of Romeyn Spare and his work on the Tunxis is contained in Dorothy Manchester, "Bristol Woodsman Ardent Lover of Nature's Amazing Handiwork," *Bristol* [Conn.] *Press*, June 14, 1965, p. 15. Two magnificent accounts by Spare's successor, George K. Libby, are "Twenty Years on the Southern Tunxis," *Connecticut Woodlands* (Summer 1982), pp. 19–22, and his obituary for Spare in the *Bristol Press*, Dec. 18, 1968. The authors profited immensely from conversation (Apr. 4, 1984) and correspondence with Mr. Libby.

"Went out nearly": Manchester, "Bristol Woodsman." Reprinted with permission.

"Golfers and yachtsmen": Letter from George K. Libby to L&GW, Feb. 4, 1983. Reprinted with permission.

437   **Mattatuck Trail:** The original route description for the Mattatuck was published by the CFPA in May 1932, "Mattatuck Trail." That its planning was well underway in 1930 is evident from a letter from Arthur Perkins to Myron Avery, May 27, 1930, in which Perkins says that "a good deal of progress has been made in building and marking this trail, and I think it will be completed to Mohawk this season" (Avery Papers, archives, Potomac Appalachian Trail Club, Washington, D.C. Reprinted with permission). Additional light was shed on this trail's history by a letter from Ronald Malia to L&GW, Feb. 7, 1983. No good recent account is known.

Mattabesett Trail: The CFPA route description for the Mattabesett appeared May 1932, "Mattabesett Trail." A good general source is Kornel Bailey's "History of the Mattabessett [*sic*] Trail," *Connecticut Woodlands*, (Spring 1983), pp. 8–9. Of great assistance also were conversations with Norman M. Wickstrand, correspondence from Albert E. Van Dusen (Dec. 29, 1982), and records of the Wesleyan Outing Club in Special Collections of the Wesleyan University Library.

438   **Metacomet Trail:** The CFPA route description for the Metacomet is dated October 1935, "Metacomet Trail." Kornel Bailey was very helpful to the authors on filling in its history. No good recent account of the early history exists.

Miscellaneous trails: An excellent published source for the general state of lesser Connecticut trails in the 1930s is Connecticut State Planning Board, *The Connecticut Guide: What to See and Where to Find It* (Hartford, Conn.: Emergency Relief Commission, 1935). It is understood that Heermance was the primary author of this study. Kornel Bailey's personal memory was another invaluable source for us.

438   **250 miles:** The Connecticut Telephone Company's newsletter, *Telephone News* (July 1933), made these claims in a write-up, "Connecticut Trail System Lures Many Hikers," pp. 1, 4.

    "It is always understood": Bennet Bronson, "The Connecticut Trail System," *Appalachia* (Dec. 1933), p. 620.

    "The amazing thing": Conversation with Norman A. Wickstrand, May 26, 1983.

439   **"It has been said":** Romeyn A. Spare, "Connecticut Trails," *Appalachia* (June 1946), p. 131.

440   **Connecticut Chapter of the AMC:** The Connecticut Chapter of the AMC published in 1984 a comprehensive history of itself, "History of Connecticut Chapter, 1921–1981," incorporating other histories prepared at various stages of its organizational existence.

    New Haven Hiking Club: Kornel Bailey, "History of the New Haven Hiking Club: 1931–1942," Jan. 23, 1983 (revised March 10, 1986); copies of these typescripts were generously supplied to L&GW by the author and are in their collections.

    Housatonic Trail Club: Records of the Housatonic Trail Club are contained in a scrapbook in the possession of Richard P. Donohoe of Sherman, Conn. Thanks are also due to letters to L&GW, concerning its early days, from Edna Anderson (May 6 and June 5, 1984), and from Joseph Ruddley (June 1, 1984).

    Waterbury Half-a-League Club: Mentioned in "Tales of the Trails," *The Trail Marker*, newsletter of the New York Chapter of the Adirondack Mountain Club (April 1940), p. 2.

CHAPTER 41. THE PROLIFERATION OF HIKING CLUBS

443   **Eastern States Mountain Club:** This club has left little trace of its passing. Our information comes almost entirely from recollections and papers (meeting announcements, trip schedules, and so forth) generously supplied to the authors by two former members of the club, Leroy D. Cross and George P. LaBorde.

    Maine Alpine Club: Stanley B. Attwood, "When the Maine Alpine Club Takes the Trail," *Lewiston* [Maine] *Journal*, Apr. 24, 1937, magazine section, p. A–8; "Maine Alpine Club's New Trail up Goose-Eye," *Lewiston Journal*, Jan. 21, 1939, magazine section, p. A–8; Attwood, "Maine Alpine Club Building the Robertson Trail to Goose-Eye," *Lewiston Journal*, Nov. 22, 1941, magazine section, pp. A–6–7; and P. G. Canham, "The Maine Alpine Club," *The Pine Cone* (Summer 1951), pp. 17–18. Leroy Cross again supplied information from his personal memories and papers.

    Maine Appalachian Trail Club: See notes for Chap. 45.

444 **Stratton Mountain Club:** See Louis J. Paris, "The Long Trail and the Trails of Bennington County," *Bennington* [Vt.] *County Review*, Apr. 1, 1914, pp. 3–4. The club is listed as a member of the New England Trail Conference, with maintenance for one 3-mile trail up the southeast side of Stratton, in the "1924 Census of New England Trails" of the NETC.

Brattleboro Outing Club: Harold A. Barry, Richard M. Mitchell, Richard H. Wellman, and Richard E. Michelman, *Before Our Time* (Brattleboro, Vt.: Stephen Greene Press, 1974), p. 134. A letterhead in correspondence in the MacKaye Family Papers, Dartmouth College Library, shows the Brattleboro Outing Club, Inc., with Fred H. Harris listed as president. Its 40-mile trail is mentioned in the NETC "1924 Census of New England Trails." In the GMC Archives at the Vermont Historical Society, there is a record of a "Trustees' Special Meeting" on July 16, 1926, at which the possibility of the Brattleboro Outing Club's affiliation with the GMC is discussed.

American Fun Society: A single document describes its 1930 field meeting, in the GMC Archives at the Vermont Historical Society.

Adirondack Camp and Trail Club: Both phases of this club are described in scattered issues of the *Lake Placid Club Notes*. See especially "Camp and Trail Club" (Apr. 1913), pp. 430–31; "Great Tramping Year" (Sept. 1923), pp. 1114–15; "Tramping in 1924" (Oct. 15, 1924), p. 1216; " 'Facilis Ascensus' " (Oct. 1925), pp. 1348–49; "Camp and Trail Club" (Apr. 1926), pp. 1448–50; "Mountain Climbing" (July 1926), p. 1495; "Adirondak Loj," (Apr. 1928), pp. 1823–24; "Leaders" (Apr. 1929), p. 1979. A complete set of these *Notes* is in the collections of Mary MacKenzie, Lake Placid, N.Y. The Camp and Trail Club is also described in the *Lake Placid News* as follows: "Camp and Trail Club Working on New Markers" (Aug. 19, 1927), p. 7; Harry Wade Hicks, "Annual Meeting of Camp and Trail Club August 24" (Aug. 19, 1927), p. 8; "What Camp and Trail Club is Doing" (Oct. 7, 1921), p. 1; "Camp and Trail Club Plan Great Improvements" (Sept. 11, 1925), p. 12. It is briefly described in a note in Carson, *Peaks and People*, p. 52.

445 **Elizabethtown Trails Club:** The authors are indebted to correspondence from Geoffrey Carleton, a longtime hiker in the Elizabethtown, N.Y., area. The club was mentioned briefly by Torrey in "Long Brown Path" (July 29, 1927), and in "New Trail to Giant Mountain," *Mountain Magazine* (Oct. 1927), p. 44.

Catskill Mountain Club: This club was described as "recently formed" in Torrey, "Long Brown Path" (Oct. 7, 1926), and as maintaining trails on Peekamoose, Schunemunk, and the Terrace Pond area in a November 1928 (date obscured) column.

"Slide, Kelly, Slide": The slogan appears on a letterhead in a letter from Jessup to Arthur Perkins, Apr. 21, 1931, in the archives of the Appalachian Trail Conference.

"He had the dream": Letter from Herbert C. Hauptmann, to L&GW, Jan. 11, 1982. Reprinted with permission.

445 **Mohawk Valley Hiking Club:** Descriptions and papers were supplied by Vincent J. Schaefer, in correspondence and conversations.

Taconic Hiking Club: A two-page history prepared by its first president, Edmour Germain, was published with the club's constitution and other articles in 1941. Early discussion of the need for the organization is in Edward T. Heald, *Taconic Trails: Being a Partial Guide of Rensselaer County Rambles by Auto and Foot* (Albany, N.Y.: J. B. Lyon, 1929), p. 201.

Adirondack Forty-Sixers: See notes for chap. 46.

446 **AMC's New York Chapter:** There is no good single published source of information on the AMC New York Chapter's early history, but the chapter maintains archives. The authors are also indebted to many old-time members of the chapter for their personal reminiscences.

GMC's New York Section: A superb typescript history, "History of Our First Fifty Years," was kindly supplied to the authors by Jan B. Hudgens. The authors also profited from a collection of early GMC *Bulletins* generously supplied by Lillian P. Lodge, as well as conversation and correspondence with Helen B. M. Kreig, Eleanor and Percy Olton, Elmer C. Perrine, and John Paulson, all early members of the New York Section.

ADK's New York Chapter: See the chapter's newsletter, *The Trail Marker*, an extensive collection of which was made available to the authors by Francis W. Penny. We also learned from conversations and correspondence with Herbert C. Hauptmann, Frank J. Oliver, and Walter W. Shannon, all very active in the chapter's early days.

447 **"Men wanted":** "Classified Ad—Men Wanted," *The Trail Marker* (Nov. 1950), p. 8. Reprinted with permission of Adirondack Mountain Club, Inc.

The GMC even adopted: GMC New York Section, "History of Our First Fifty Years," p. 14.

"Back in the early days": Letter from Julianna S. Irelan to L&GW, Nov. 22, 1982. Reprinted with permission.

"I did not like": Letter from Elizabeth Burton to L&GW, Oct. 11, 1982. Reprinted with permission.

Torrey Botanical Club: See the notes for chap. 18.

Fresh Air Club: See the notes for chap. 18. Many old-time New York–area hikers, affiliated with various other clubs, have vivid memories of the Fresh Air Club speedsters.

A 1930s bulletin: New York–New Jersey Trail Conference, "Program for the Co-ordination of Volunteer Trail Work," publication no. 1, 2d ed., 1940.

448 **Paterson Ramblers:** A club "Schedule of Outdoor Events, 1931–1932," contains a brief history and description (copy in authors' files).

448 **Walker's Club:** This club and its offshoots are described in Albert Handy, "Walking Clubs of New York," *New York Evening Post*, Saturday magazine, May 6, 1916, pp. 8–9.

Tramp and Trail Club: See *Tramps*, a booklet containing general information, schedule of events, and directory of membership, issued on the occasion of its twenty-fifth season, 1938–39. See also letter from Gray H. Twombley, a member for fifty years, to L&GW, March 2, 1982.

"No trips postponed": *Tramps: Issued by the Tramp and Trail Club of New York, Twenty-Fifth Season, 1938–39*, p. 6.

Inkowa: No club records have been found. See Torrey, "Art of Walking Saved by the Hiking Clubs," *New York Times*, Apr. 25, 1926, sec. 9, p. 10.

"Finding myself surrounded": Letter from Herbert C. Hauptmann to L&GW, Nov. 3, 1981. Reprinted with permission.

Nature Friends: While many old-timers have memories of the Nature Friends, the authors are particularly indebted to conversations and correspondence with Xandi and Henry Roebig and Naomi Sutter.

449 **Wanderlust:** This club was described in a letter from Herbert C. Hauptmann to L&GW, Jan. 11, 1928. Reprinted with permission.

"Kept to themselves": *Ibid.*

Bill Hoeferlin: Leon R. Greenman kindly arranged for access to a wealth of information on William Hoeferlin's long career, including his era of leadership of the Wanderbirds.

New York Hiking Club: An excellent little history appeared on the occasion of its sixtieth anniversary in 1982. A copy was sent to the authors by then president Leo Tamari. See also Oton Ambroz, "N. Y. Hiking Club Celebrates 60th," *Trail Walker*, Aug.–Sept. 1982, p. 4.

"Health is wealth!": Ambroz, "N. Y. Hiking Club Celebrates 60th."

City College Hiking Club: A wealth of printed material and personal recollections was most generously supplied by Lee Erde, Richard H. and Barbara Tourin, and Esther Weitz.

"Leave compasses and maps": City College Hiking Club, "Schedule of Hikes, Feb. 1939 to Aug. 1939," copy in the possession of Esther Weitz.

"Club Hiker's Code": *Ibid.*, and other club schedules of those years.

New York Ramblers: See "New York Ramblers—Fifty Hikeful Years," *Trail Walker*, Nov.–Dec. 1973, p. 1; also early club bulletins.

Yosians: Note a wide variety of incidental references in "Long Brown Path" columns and other contemporary sources, plus the Hoeferlin material cited above. A one-page circular describing the organization may be found in the Frank Place "Trail Clippings," vol. 6, p. 125.

"To promote the spirit": Club circular just cited.

450   **Westchester Trails Association:** See Jim Lober, "60-Year-Old Assn. Maintains 65 Miles of Trail," *Trail Walker,* June–July 1983, p. 3. See also a write-up on the dinner program for the fiftieth anniversary dinner in 1973, kindly supplied to the authors by Catherine Allen.

Union County Hiking Club: Fred Dlouhy supplied the authors with invaluable information on the history of this club.

Interstate Hiking Club: See Gerhardt Zauzig, "IHC Celebrates 50th Year," *Trail Walker,* June–July 1981, p. 7.

Hiking Trips Bureau: See sources for Dench's subsequent and related creation, the Woodland Trail Walkers.

Woodland Trail Walkers: Jennie Wander Valk, club historian, provided valuable information on their history. See also Oton Ambroz, "Off the Beaten Path: 40 Years with the Woodland Trail Walkers," *Trail Walker,* March–Apr. 1977, p. 3.

451   **Southern New England:** Information on the two Pequawket clubs was generously supplied to the authors by Robert B. Hatton of Andover, Mass. Sources of information for most of the other clubs in southern New England are cited elsewhere.

College outing clubs: The evolution of this interesting movement may be traced in student publications and sometimes special archives of college libraries. The authors are grateful for the assistance of special collections libraries in more than two dozen colleges in tracing outing club histories and other information.

452   **"To recreate the individual":** "Outing Club Organization," Bulletin of the Intercollegiate Outing Club of America, (Fall 1939), p. 1.

A real organization: "University Outing Club to be Organized," *Maine Campus* (Nov. 3, 1920), p. 1.

"A club similar": " 'Wind' and Brains Start Outing Club," *Colby Echo,* Feb. 11, 1914, p. 1.

Faculty members recently graduated: "Outing Club Activity Continues 25 Years," *The Bates Student,* Jan. 26, 1945, pp. 1, 4; Williams Outing Club Trail Commission, *The Mountains of Eph* (Williamstown, Mass.: W. O. C. Trail Commission, 1927), pp. 4–5; "The Outing Club Program" *Middlebury Campus* (Jan. 10, 1917), p. 2; "Outing Club Busy," *Norwich University Record* (Oct. 27, 1923), p. 50, and "Outing Club Organizes" (Sept. 27, 1924), pp. 40–41; and "The Outing Club," Norwich University *War Whoop* (1925), pp. 275–76.

"One of the earliest": Ernest Cummings Marriner, *The History of Colby College* (Waterville, Me.: Colby College Press, 1963), p. 446.

453   **"Almost every girl":** Charlotte Peterson, "The Outing Club," *Mount Holyoke Alumnae Quarterly* (Apr. 1922), p. 18, in the Outing Club records of the Mount Holyoke College Library/Archives.

453　　**IOCA:** Formation and early history of IOCA may be traced in the annals of the IOCA *Bulletin* and the IOCAlum *Newsletter,* the latter a publication of a very active IOCA alumni group. Early accounts of the formation of IOCA include "I. O. C. A.," Dartmouth Outing Club *Bulletin* (May 11, 1932), p. 1, and Bruce M. Gelser (Yale), executive secretary, a note under the heading of "Clubs," in *Appalachia* (Dec. 1933), pp. 625–26.

　　"To keep the different": Gelser, "Clubs," *Appalachia* (Dec. 1933), p. 625.

454　　**As Roderick Nash:** Nash, *Wilderness and the American Mind*, p. 143.

　　By as early as 1921: Remarks by R. N. Berry, regional Scout executive, prepared for the New England Trail Conference, Boston, Mass., Dec. 9–10, 1921, reprinted in "Boy Scouts and Trails," *Appalachia*, (Dec. 1922), pp. 317–23.

　　Summer camps: Data compiled by the authors from dates listed for each camp in the American Camping Association, *Parents' Guide to Accredited Camps*, 1982 ed. For the camping history of this period, see Sargent, *Handbook of Summer Camps*. The directors of numerous summer camps were most generous in taking time from busy schedules to provide information on their camp's histories and hiking programs.

455　　**Outdoor writer Harvey Manning:** Harvey Manning, "Where Did All These Damn Hikers Come From?" *Backpacker* (Summer 1975), pp. 36–41, 83, 85.

CHAPTER 42. BACKCOUNTRY CAMPING IN THE TWENTIES AND THIRTIES

457　　**In 1927 three women:** Among numerous write-ups of the Three Musketeers, see especially "A Feminine Record," *The Long Trail News* (Dec. 1927), pp. 2–3. These accounts were richly supplemented for the authors in conversations with Hilda Kurth Martin, Oct. 10 and Nov. 2, 1981, and with Catherine Robbins Clifford, Oct. 10, 1981.

　　"Always wet": Conversation with Hilda Kurth Martin, Nov. 2, 1981.

　　Newspaper coverage: Clippings in the scrapbooks of Hilda Kurth Martin.

458　　**"At this point":** Minutes of Jan. 14, 1928, annual meeting, Green Mountain Club Archives, in collections of the Vermont Historical Society, Montpelier, Vt. Reprinted with permission.

　　In 1929 another: The 1929 and 1933 treks were covered in *The Long Trail News;* see Agnes Watkins, "Females Do the Entire Trail" (June 1930), pp. 2–4, and "Notes," (Nov. 1933), p. 3, the latter also in Marion U. Urie, "Down the Long Trail," *The Vermonter* (Aug.–Sept. 1934), pp. 201–9. The 1930 hike was described to the authors by three of the four participants: conversation with Eldora Stevens, Apr. 17, 1984, and letters from Mildred W. Cull and Prudence F. Monroe, both dated Apr. 30, 1984.

　　"All the way": Journals of Thelma Bonney Towle, 1933. Reprinted with permission. The authors benefited from conversations with Thelma Towle and perusal of her hiking journals on July 10 and Dec. 7, 1980.

458 **"Do you remember"**: Handwritten notes in the possession of Marjorie Hurd's brother. The authors are grateful to John Hurd for the opportunity to review these notes and other memorabilia of Marjorie Hurd. Reprinted with permission.

459 **"Were for the rich"**: Frances Green, "War Surplus and the Hiker," *The Long Trail News* (Nov. 1947), p. 2. Reprinted with permission.

The AMC designed and sold: Advertisement in *Appalachia*, June 1929.

Enterprising members of: Conversation with Vincent J. Schaefer, Aug. 15, 1980.

Phillips Polar Cub: Albert H. Jackman, "Twenty Years of Hiking and Camping Equipment," *Bulletin* of the Potomac Appalachian Trail Club (Jan. 1948), p. 9.

"A poncho with shoulder straps": Letter from Prudence F. Monroe to L&GW, Apr. 30, 1984. Reprinted with permission.

"Grub and Duffle": Robert S. Wickham, *Friendly Adirondack Peaks* (privately printed, 1924), p. 19.

"At least 5 pounds": A. T. Shorey, "Camping Out," *Cloud Splitter* (May 1940), p. 7.

460 **"One expected to enjoy"**: Frances Green, "War Surplus and the Hiker," p. 2. Reprinted with permission.

"Most Adirondack hikers": A. T. Shorey, "What the Well Dressed Hiker Will Wear," *Bulletin of the Adirondack Mountain Club* (May 1937), p. 6.

Going Light: Arthur C. Comey, *Going Light*, New England Trail Conference, 1924, and subsequent editions.

"Worked perfectly": Letter from Arthur C. Comey to Benton MacKaye, Sept. 24, 1925, in MacKaye Family Papers, Dartmouth College Library. Reprinted with permission.

"Camping and particularly camping": Comey, *Going Light*, unpaged [p. 3].

MVHC's three packs: Mohawk Valley Hiking Club, "Duffle Lists," Hiking Committee bulletin no. 4 (Nov. 1935).

461 **"With this he usually"**: O'Kane, *Trails and Summits of the White Mountains* (Cambridge, Mass., Boston: Houghton Mifflin, 1925), p. 30.

"My voluminous bloomers": Grace L. Hudowalski, "Marcy Kaleidoscope," *Adirondac* (Mar.–Apr. 1953), p. 31. Reprinted with permission. In 1919 a female Long Trail hiker commented, "I can't picture anyone hiking the Trail in a skirt" (Theron S. Dean, "Skyline Trail Affords Opportunity for Pleasant Week-end Outing," *Burlington Free Press*, May 9, 1919, p. 5).

"We walked to": Excerpt from a letter from an applicant for membership in the New Hampshire Four Thousand Footer Club to Chairman A. S. Robertson, describing a 1924 hiking trip; printed in "Four Thousand Footer Clubs,"

Appalachia (June 1966), p. 170. Reprinted with the permission of the Appalachian Mountain Club.

461   **In *The Gentle Art:*** Stephen Graham, *The Gentle Art of Tramping* (New York: D. Appleton, 1926), pp. 24–25.

"I see no use": "Hikers in Shorts Safe in the Palisades Park," *New York Times*, July 28, 1936, p. I–6.

462   **"Sneakers are deservedly":** Nathaniel L. Goodrich, "The D. O. C. Equipment Manual" (1917), p. 7. Sneakers were also recommended in the Bates Outing Club Handbook for 1926–27, p. 27.

George Goldthwaite: Conversation with Percy Olton, Apr. 13, 1982, and other occasions.

"A pair of": O'Kane, *Trails and Summits of the White Mountains*, p. 27.

Jim Goodwin: Letter from James A. Goodwin to L&GW, Sept. 10, 1980.

"When the hiker": Quoted in W. Storrs Lee, ed., *Footpath in the Wilderness*, p. 25.

Ome Daiber: Yvonne Prater and Ruth Dyer Mendenhall, *Gorp, Glop & Glue Stew: Favorite Foods from 165 Outdoor Experts* (Seattle, Wash.: Mountaineers, 1982), p. 52.

Will Monroe, and "You knock a lot": Lee, *Footpath in the Wilderness*, p. 29.

Orra Phelps: Orra Phelps, in Prater and Mendenhall, *Gorp, Glop & Glue Stew*, p. 169.

463   **"Every lean-to":** Stanley B. Attwood, "Maine Alpine Club Members in Three-Day Trip over the Mahoosuc Range," *Lewiston Journal*, Jan. 25, 1941, magazine section, p. A–6.

"The top of Wittenberg": W. Gray Harris, "Afoot in the Catskills," *Appalachia* (Dec. 1922), p. 315. Reprinted with the permission of the Appalachian Mountain Club.

"No telling where": Ruth Gillette Hardy, "A Skyline for Valley Hounds," *Appalachia* (Dec. 1937), p. 495. Reprinted with the permission of the Appalachian Mountain Club.

"The damage and nuisances": "Porcupines—Lean-tos," *Appalachian Trailway News* (Sept. 1942), p. 49.

Perry Merrill: Perry Merrill, *History of Forestry in Vermont* (Montpelier, Vt.: Vermont State Board of Forests and Parks, 1959), p. 61.

Chapter 43. Trail Maintenance Comes of Age

465   **"Both of them":** Jenks, "Twenty-five Years of the A. M. C. Trail Crew," *Appalachia* (Dec. 1943), p. 442. Reprinted with the permission of the Appalachian Mountain Club.

465 **Blood had been harping"**: Blood, "The Evolution of a Trailman," *Appalachia* (June 1965), p. 430; and minutes of NETC meeting, Dec. 15, 1916, in archives of the Society for the Protection of New Hampshire Forests.

The same solution: See chap. 36.

The first AMC Trail Crew: Basic sources for early AMC trail crew history include Paul R. Jenks, "Twenty-five Years of the A. M. C. Trail Crew," *Appalachia* (Dec. 1943), pp. 441–52; C. W. Blood, "With the Trail Gang," *Appalachia* (June 1929), pp. 246–51; Karl P. Harrington, "Fifty Years of Progress: Appalachian Mountain Club Trail System," *Appalachia* (Feb. 1926), pp. 327–46; and the files of the AMC Trails Department. The authors are deeply indebted to AMC Trails Supervisor Reuben Rajala for making available material from these files, notably a memorandum written by Blood, "A. M. C. Trail Crew: Historical Background," dated Sept. 25, 1962, and for suggesting key members of early trail crews for consultation. Among these, particularly helpful were Gov. Sherman Adams, Harland P. Sisk, and William J. Henrich ("Hix," for those who might not recognize the little-used full name of this giant of the early crews). Among the second generation, we are particularly grateful to E. K. Eanes and Theodore Brown. The 1919 trail crew is covered in most of the general sources cited above, as well as in a variety of Sherman Adams's own published reminiscences. However, the authors have relied mainly on two conversations with Governor Adams, July 29, 1980, and Sept. 17, 1981, and correspondence.

"Slender, wiry, and with muscles": William P. Fowler, "From Midnight to Midnight: The D. O. C. 24-Hour Walks of 1919–20," *Appalachia* (Dec. 1932), p. 261.

466 **"Has been the hero figure"**: Letter from Harland P. Sisk to L&GW, May 15, 1984. Reprinted with permission.

"A high spot": *Ibid.*

467 **"The kid's first shoes"**: Warren Lightfoot, quoted in William "Hix" Henrich, "What Ho," in *Chips and Clippings* (a newsletter of the Trail Crew), Nov. 1970, p. 5. Reprinted with the permission of the Appalachian Mountain Club.

"A varied assortment": Ralph C. Larrabee, "The Trail Spree of 1929," *Appalachia* (Dec. 1929), p. 366. Reprinted with the permission of the Appalachian Mountain Club.

Into this vacuum of leadership: See especially Blood's Sept. 26, 1962, memorandum: "As I look back to conditions thirty years ago [that is, the 1930s], the Crew pretty much ran itself. Mr. Jenks had organized the Trail Crew and had made it a smoothly running institution. After the early thirties, however, except to put up signs, I think he rarely went into the woods to *work* with the Crew." (Reprinted with the permission of the Appalachian Mountain Club.)

468 **Vermont's Long Trail**: The origin and development of the Long Trail Patrol may be studied in the pages of *The Long Trail News* for the period October

1929 to June 1932. The authors are greatly indebted to several longtime GMC members for their knowledge of the patrol's history, notably Larry Dean, Jack Harrington, Harry T. Peet, Rod Rice, George Pearlstein, and Donald M. Wallace. Buchanan's career was always well covered in *The Long Trail News.* A profile, "Faculty Woodsman is Guardian Spirit of Long Trail," appeared in *The Vermont Alumnus,* a University of Vermont publication (Dec. 1938), p. 51. Most helpful to the authors were the wealth of Buchanan papers graciously made available by the family; special thanks are due Roy's son, Andrew Buchanan. These papers are now in the archives of the Green Mountain Club. Of particular value therein are a table giving a complete list of GMC lodges and a wealth of pertinent information on each; and Buchanan's letter to Ralph Bryant, Jan. 9, 1974, giving a personal recollection of the history of each shelter.

468   **One-day Long Trail Patrol project:** Accounts of the first Long Trail Patrol Day and how it came into being may be found in "To Establish Patrol Day on Long Trail," *Burlington Free Press,* May 20, 1922, p. 7, and numerous documents in the James P. Taylor Papers, Vermont Historical Society.

During the 1920s, the club: These early GMC trail maintenance efforts are described in the early issues of the *Green Mountain News.*

Fred W. Mould: This trail worker's career has been covered at various times in *The Long Trail News;* see especially "View vs. Water" (Aug. 1947), p. 6; "Age, No Deterrent on Long Trail" (Aug. 1948), p. 3; "Birthday!" (Nov. 1944), p. 4; and "Fred W. Mould" (Aug. 1950), p. 3.

469   **By the end of the decade:** Buchanan's participation in putting the final section of the Long Trail through to Canada is covered in chap. 35.

Long Trail lodges: In Buchanan's Jan. 9, 1974, letter to Ralph Bryant, the origins of the names of each shelter, along with the dates and builders of most, are given.

471   **"His legs worn short":** Louis Puffer, "Lee Vangeline: A Tale of Adventure," *The Long Trail News* (Feb. 1945), pp. 1–3.

"Always ready with repairs": Bill Allard, "A Look Into the Diary of a Green Mountain Patrol Leader," *The Long Trail News* (Feb. 1955), p. 4.

"Yell method," "To within a foot-and-a-half," and **"The trail starts":** Conversation with Andrew Buchanan, June 23, 1981.

"Six hikers or": Letter from Buchanan to Bryant, Jan. 9, 1974. Reprinted with permission.

"That man never": Conversation with Larry Dean, Nov. 6, 1980.

"That was some truck": Ted Goddard, LTP worker from 1955 to 1960, quoted in Robert L. Hagerman, "New LTP Truck Succeeds Two Long-Term Veterans," *The Long Trail News* (Aug. 1981), p. 4. Reprinted with permission.

471   **In the Adirondacks:** For Adirondack trail maintenance history, the basic source is a letter from James A. Goodwin to L&GW, Feb. 12, 1984; this is among the papers associated with Mr. Goodwin's trails history maps, now in the archives, Keene Valley Library.

"Diplomacy is more useful": Bennet Bronson, "The Connecticut Trail System," *Appalachia* (Dec. 1933), p. 619.

473   **"The epitome of instability":** Letter from George K. Libby to L&GW, May 17, 1984. Reprinted with permission.

"This trail is on": Quoted in "Connecticut Trail System," *Mountain Magazine* (May 1930), p. 15.

"This [trail system]": "Connecticut Trail System Lures Many Hikers," *Telephone News* (July 1933), p. 1.

"Any history of the trails": Hibbard, "A 50th Anniversary of the Blue Blazed Trail System," *Connecticut Woodlands* (Fall 1979), p. 6. Reprinted with permission.

"They really stick": Conversation with John Hibbard, Oct. 22, 1981.

"Anyone who sees": Joe Marks, quoted by Carolyn Nuzzi in "New Public Housatonic Land," *Connecticut Woodlands* (Winter 1982–1983), p. 19. Reprinted with permission.

"Except on State land": CFPA, "Quinnipiac Trail" (Sept. 1931). Reprinted with permission.

CHAPTER 44. REGIONWIDE CONSCIOUSNESS

475   **"Elaborately illustrated and reinforced":** This phrase appears in an unidentified set of page proofs in the Taylor Papers at the Vermont Historical Society, Montpelier, Vt., reprinted with permission. The tone and language of these papers invites the speculation that Taylor was the author.

"To rehearse dreams": *Ibid.*

Associated Mountaineering Clubs: Note on "The Associated Mountaineering Clubs of North America" in *Appalachia* (June 1918), pp. 294–95; and *Bulletin* of the Associated Mountaineering Clubs of North America, issues published in 1920 and 1921 (and possibly other years). Raymond H. Torrey devoted one of his "Long Brown Path" columns to a brief history of this group (*New York Evening Post*, May 9, 1935). In a letter to Benton MacKaye in July 1935, Torrey described the group's decline in the early 1930s; MacKaye Family Papers, Dartmouth College Library.

476   **"An annual conference":** Frank H. Burt, "The White Mountains Forty Years Ago," *Appalachia* (Dec. 1916), p. 49. Reprinted with the permission of the Appalachian Mountain Club.

By this time: Ayres credited Chamberlain with a crucial role: see letter from Ayres to Robert M. Ross, June 1, 1935 (in NETC Archives).

476 **Chamberlain perceived hiking:** See letter from Chamberlain to Theron S. Dean, Dec. 15, 1916. Theron Dean Papers, Bailey-Howe Library, University of Vermont. Reprinted with permission. "I see from your letter that you have the impression that the A. M. C. was responsible for today's meeting. They were not so much as consulted, not even informally, until those of us who yearned for it had decided to make the suggestion to you and to all the others. It is a fact that the three officers of the N. H. Forestry Society who started the ball are all members of the A. M. C. but the whole thing was conceived in the interest of stimulating a wider interest in forestry. We forestry cranks see an active supporter of national and state forests in every trail hitter. . . . The trails will draw the public. Make the forests accessible and attractive and the public will go to them, and once they get to know them we shall have an army of forestry boosters. Now you see the selfish motive that inspired this game."

"Nailed to the mast": Unidentified page proof in Taylor Papers, Vermont Historical Society.

"Make arrangements for": "To Encourage Trail Building in New England," *Boston Herald*, Dec. 16, 1916, p. 18. Reprinted with permission.

New England Trail Conference: The New England Trail Conference's archives are a valuable source, and the authors are indebted to Forrest House for access to this material. Much documentation of the first meeting and events surrounding it are in the archives of the Society for the Protection of New Hampshire Forests in Concord, N.H. The James P. Taylor Papers in the Vemont Historical Society also include numerous references. A useful printed source is Paul R. Jenks, "New England Trail Conference," *Appalachia* (June 1918), pp. 280–83. The later evolution of NETC may be traced in an unpublished paper, "The First Fifty Years of the New England Trail Conference," by John H. Vondell, and a scrapbook of papers kindly supplied to the authors by Carl O. Chauncey, who succeeded Vondell as chairman in 1952. The authors also profited from conversations with former NETC chairmen, including Mr. Chauncey (Oct. 25, 1982), John H. Hitchcock (Sept. 2, 1982), and Forrest E. House (Oct. 25, 1982).

"To promote cooperation": From the "Rules of Organization" adopted at the March 16, 1917, meeting, as quoted in Jenks, "New England Trail Conference," p. 281. Reprinted with the permission of the Appalachian Mountain Club.

Original membership of the NETC: Jenks, "New England Trail Conference," *Appalachia* (June 1918), pp. 280–83.

477 **Census reports on trails:** NETC, *1920 Trail Census*, publication no. 4, 1920. Subsequent censuses issued periodically during the 1920s.

478 **"Perhaps the most noteworthy":** Jenks, "New England Trail Conference," p. 281.

"Except that it does": Chamberlain, "Making a Happy Dream Come True," *Boston Transcript*, Feb. 21, 1919, p. III-6.

478 **Going Light:** Arthur C. Comey, *Going Light*, NETC publication no. 11, 1924. Trails manuals included Nathaniel L. Goodrich, *Trail Location* (1926), Paul R. Jenks, *Trail Clearing Expeditions* (1924), and William G. Howard, *Open Camps* (1922).

For a while there was talk: In a letter to Clarence Stein, Oct. 11, 1921, Benton MacKaye reports that Chamberlain "says they [NETC] expect to combine with the New York state groups and form a 'Northeastern Trail Conference' " (MacKaye Family Papers, Dartmouth College Library, reprinted with permission). Perhaps relying on this assurance, Stein repeats the rumor in his published introduction to MacKaye's celebrated Appalachian Trail article in the *Journal of the American Institute of Architects* (Oct. 1921), p. 2. In December of that year, Chamberlain brought up this idea, and was counseled by J. Ashton Allis that a plan was afoot that very month for an Adirondack Mountain Club (see chap. 37) and that "there might be lost motion if some alliance between the New England and New York trail makers is not fostered" (Raymond Torrey, "Long Brown Path," Dec. 16, 1921). Possibly the birth of ADK at just that moment served to divert the proposal to expand the NETC into New York.

479 **Through-trails:** The origins of the idea of through-trails, prior to the landmark article by Benton MacKaye (see chap. 45), have been little studied. See Laura Waterman and Guy Waterman, "Early Founders of the Appalachian Trail," *Appalachian Trailway News* (Sept.–Oct. 1985), pp. 7–11.

Taylor's map: This remarkable map is in the Taylor Papers, Vermont Historical Society, attached to a two-paragraph typescript urging the creation of this "international mountain and forest trail." It is otherwise unidentified as to source or purpose, but the language is unmistakably Taylorian.

"I have another hobby": Letter from Taylor to George E. Rix, secretary of the Lawrence, Mass., Chamber of Commerce, Apr. 14, 1920, in the Taylor Papers, Vermont Historical Society, Montpelier, Vt., reprinted with permission. Chamberlain wrote to Theron Dean on Dec. 13, 1916, giving Taylor "full credit for the big idea" of a trans–New England trail. (Letter in Theron S. Dean Papers, Bailey-Howe Library, University of Vermont. Reprinted with permission.)

Allen Chamberlain, employing: Allen Chamberlain, "Recreational Use of Public Forests in New England," *Proceedings of the Society of American Foresters* (July 1916), pp. 276–80. The quoted passage appears on p. 276.

480 **Sumner R. Hooper:** NETC, "Minutes of a Trail Conference, Friday, Dec. 15, 1916," in the archives of the Society for the Protection of New Hampshire Forests, p. 2.

"Of the desirablility": "To Encourage Trail Building," *Boston Herald*, Dec. 16, 1916, p. 18. Reprinted with permission.

Others who played: For Ayres's ideas see "Conference of New England Trail Makers," *New Hampshire Forestry* (a publication of the Society), vol. II, no. 2 (undated but probably 1916 or 1917), p. 4; and also his "Mountain Trails in

New England," *The American Review of Reviews* (July 1917), pp. 79–82. For Warren Hart's, see "War Training in Mountains," *Boston Herald*, Dec. 15, 1917, p. 11. For Turner's, see Raymond Torrey, "Long Brown Path," Dec. 16, 1921. For Monroe's plan, see *New York Walk Book* (1923 ed.), p. 172.

480 **Allis's plan:** Torrey, "Long Brown Path," Dec. 16, 1921. See also a report on the 1922 NETC meeting in GMC Archives, Vermont Historical Society.

481 **Berkshires nature writer:** W. P. Eaton, "Editorial," *Stockbridge* (July 1914), p. 3.

Frederick W. Kilbourne: Chamberlain, "Making a Happy Dream Come True," *Boston Evening Transcript*, Feb. 21, 1919, p. III–6, and "A Cure for Springtime Restlessness," May 10, 1919, p. III–5. Kilbourne himself describes his conception of the through-trail across Connecticut in "Early Days of the Connecticut Trail System," *Appalachia* (Dec. 1946), pp. 271–74. See chap. 40.

W. F. Robbins: The Wapack Trail and its construction are first described in Appalachian Mountain Club, *Guide to Paths in the White Mountains and Adjacent Regions* (1925 ed.), p. 437. See also subsequent editions of this guide, under the title *The AMC White Mountain Guide*, 7th ed. (1928), p. 464, and 8th ed. (1931), p. 465.

Monadnock-Sunapee Trail: Several printed pamphlets in the archives of the society tell of preparations for and eventual completion of this trail, but surprisingly few of these documents are dated. Allen Chamberlain wrote a feature on the trail project, "A Tangled Trail for Tried Trampers," *Boston Transcript*, Aug. 31, 1921, p. 2:5, but he was apparently anticipating the actual clearing of some parts of the trail. According to the society's newsletter, the trail was definitely cleared in the summer of 1922; see "What Are We Doing This Summer," *New Hampshire Forestry* (Aug. 1922), p. 4. However, the minutes of a meeting held on Nov. 10, 1924, indicate that the trail was still being worked on (archives of the Society for the Protection of New Hampshire Forests). The AMC first includes it in its White Mountains *Guide* for 1925 (pp. 450–53). By the 1931 edition of this guide it is described as "not recently . . . cleared and marked," though still discernible (p. 455). It continued to be carried in the AMC Guidebook throughout the 1930s.

"Rural charm as it led": Society for the Protection of New Hampshire Forests, *The Monadnock-Sunapee Greenway Trail Guide* (1980 ed.), p. 5.

Northville-Placid Trail: The history of the Northville-Placid Trail is touched on lightly in the ADK's *Guide to the Northville-Placid Trail* (1980 ed.), and is recounted in more detail in Edwin M. Noyes, "Building the Northville-Placid Trail," *Adirondac* (Oct. 1973), pp. 97–99. A contemporary account was "Long Trail Big Project Accomplished First Year," *High Spots* (Nov. 1922), p. 3. See also an account by the first person to walk the entire trail, Robert S. Wickham, *Friendly Adirondack Peaks*; and a letter to the editor by Henry L. Young on Frank J. Oliver's early hike, *Trail Walker*, (Feb.–March 1982), p. 2.

"A valley route": "Long Trail Big Project Accomplished First Year," p. 3.

482　　**Lake George-Placid Trail:** "New Trail Project to Link Lakes George and Placid," *High Spots* (May 1923), p. 3.

Arthur Comey's ideas: Arthur C. Comey, *Projected System of Through Trails in New England,* New England Trail Conference publication no. 13, 1925.

CHAPTER 45. THE APPALACHIAN TRAIL

485　　**The one big:** The archives of the Appalachian Trail Conference at Harpers Ferry, W.Va., are a rich source for information on the origins of the Appalachian Trail. A condensed history is contained in a chapter of the ATC's 1934 publication no. 5, *The Appalachian Trail.* A revised version is in the *Appalachian Trail Conference's Member Handbook,* 13th ed. (Harpers Ferry, W. Va.: Appalachian Trail Conference, 1988). The ATC's magazine, *Appalachian Trailway News,* publishes many reminiscences and historical studies.

Benton MacKaye: MacKaye has been the subject of numerous magazine articles and, because he lived to the age of ninety-six, left his reminiscences about the Appalachian Trail scattered through a score of personal interviews in later years. Particularly valuable are Dorothy M. Martin, "Interview with Benton MacKaye," *Bulletin* of the Potomac Appalachian Trail Club, (Jan.–March 1953), pp. 10–14, 34–35; an eighteen-page personal reminiscence prepared for his seventy-fifth birthday celebration by MacKaye himself at the home of Harvey and Anne Broome in Knoxville, Tenn., March 6, 1954 (MacKaye Family Papers, Dartmouth College Library); MacKaye, "Some Early A. T. History," PATC *Bulletin* (Oct.–Dec. 1957), pp. 91–96; E. John Long, "Benton MacKaye: The Verdant Prophet," *American Forests,* (July 1964), pp. 16–19; Constance L. Stallings, "The Last Interview with Benton MacKaye," *Backpacker,* No. 14, (Apr. 1976), pp. 54–57, 81–85; Gerald Broughton Lowrey, Jr., "Benton MacKaye's Appalachian Trail as a Cultural Symbol," (Ph.D. diss., Emory University, 1981); and a superb portrait by Anne Bennett, "Making the World More Habitable—Benton MacKaye: A Man and His Vision," *Appalachian Trailway News* (Nov.–Dec. 1985), pp. 11–15. A source of considerable importance is the collection of MacKaye Family Papers at the Dartmouth College Library. A thoroughly researched biography by Larry Anderson is in progress, and Anderson has published smaller articles that illustrate the depth of understanding he has for his subject. See, for example, "Benton MacKaye and the Art of Roving: An 1897 Excursion to the White Mountains," *Appalachia* (Dec. 1987), pp. 85–102, and "A Classic of the Green Mountains: The 1900 Hike of Benton MacKaye and Horace Hildreth," *The Harvard* [Mass.] *Post,* Dec. 19, 1986, pp. 22–25.

"To give to": Handwritten constitution of the Rambling Boys' Club, in MacKaye Family Papers, Dartmouth College Library. reprinted with permission.

White Mountains trip: See Anderson, "Benton MacKaye and the Art of Roving," as well as numerous letters in the MacKaye Family Papers, Dartmouth College Library. The MacKaye family was large and apparently richly endowed with aunts: Dartmouth's collections include letters written during MacKaye's first White Mountains trip to Maud, Aug. 21, 1897; to Aunt Emmie, Aug. 25, 1897; to Aunt Sadie, Aug. 28, 1897; and to his mother, Aug. 9 and 22, 1897.

486   **Green Mountains trip:** Letter to his mother, July 20, 1900. MacKaye was fond of recalling these trips in his various interviews, so they are often cited there. See also Anderson, "A Classic of the Green Mountains."

Work with Sturgis Pray: Martin, "Interview with Benton MacKaye," p. 12, and MacKaye, "Some Early A. T. History," p. 91. As pointed out in chap. 36, MacKaye's memories of just where he worked with Pray are confusing and conflicting.

"Dignified, affable philosopher": Lowrey, "Benton MacKaye's Appalachian Trail," p. 89. Reprinted with permission.

"An upstairs cubbyhole": Bennett, "Making the World More Habitable," p. 14. Archives, Appalachian Trail Conference, Harpers Ferry, W.Va. Reprinted with permission.

"Once a week": *Ibid.*

"Walking anachronism": Stephen Fox, "We Want No Straddlers," *Wilderness* (Winter 1984), p. 7. Reprinted with permission.

"A nineteenth century": *Ibid.*

487   **Original AT article:** Benton MacKaye, "A Project for an Appalachian Trail," *Journal of the American Institute of Architects* (Oct. 1921) pp. 2–8. Except as otherwise noted, quoted passages in the following paragraph are from MacKaye's original article.

MacKaye's original vision: For perspective on MacKaye's ideas in relation to the evolution of American thinking on wilderness, two useful analyses are Schmitt, *Back to Nature*, pp. xix–xx, and Nash, *Wilderness and the American Mind*, p. 243.

In later rhetoric: The last three phrases in this paragraph are from MacKaye, "Vision and Reality," an address to the Appalachian Trail Conference, May 20, 1930, and MacKaye, "Outdoor Culture, the Philosophy of Through Trails," an address to the New England Trail Conference, Jan. 21, 1927. Both of these addresses are in the MacKaye Family Papers, Dartmouth College Library; reprinted with permission.

With a product: MacKaye's early moves to promote the AT may be followed in numerous documents in the MacKaye collections of the Dartmouth College Library, especially diary entries for 1921–25, and correspondence during this period. See also Martin, "Interview with Benton MacKaye," p. 13, and MacKaye, "Some Early A. T. History," pp. 91–94.

A "Long Brown Path" column: Torrey, "2000-Mile Trail on Appalachian Ridges Planned," *New York Evening Post*, Apr. 7, 1922, p. 9.

"The first big broadside": Martin, "Interview with Benton MacKaye," p. 13.

488 **"Practically moribund":** ATC, "The Appalachian Trail," publication no. 5, p. 12.

Arthur Perkins: Judge Arthur Perkins's life is briefly traced in H. C. Anderson, "A Tribute to Judge Arthur Perkins," PATC *Bulletin* (July 1932), p. 53, and other obituaries. Much of his correspondence, especially with Myron Avery, is preserved in the archives of the ATC in Harpers Ferry and of the Potomac Appalachian Trail Club in Washington, D.C.

489 **Myron Avery:** An extremely perceptive and well-balanced description of Myron Avery is David Bates, "Profile: Myron Halliburton Avery," *Potomac Appalachian* (Dec. 1982), pp. 5–9. See also Bates, *Breaking Trail in the Central Appalachians: A Narrative* (Washington, D.C.: Potomac Appalachian Trail Club, 1987). Among many obituaries, the most informative were in ATC's *Appalachian Trailway News* (Sept. 1952), p. 1, and Ken Boardman et al., in PATC's *Bulletin* (Oct.–Dec. 1952), pp. 100–3. A seemingly bottomless fund of information about and insights into Avery is provided by the three archives of his correspondence preserved at the ATC in Harpers Ferry, the PATC in Washington, D.C., and the Maine State Library in Augusta. The authors are also very grateful to many co-workers of Avery who communicated to us their recollections about and evaluations of his contributions to early work on the AT; especially helpful were letters from James W. Denton, Aug. 17, 1985; Florence Nichol, Sept. 15, 1985; Arch Nichols, Aug. 24, 1985; Shailer S. Philbrick, Apr. 8, 1985; and Egbert H. Walker, Aug. 18, 1985.

"Mr. Avery is a blonde": "Bowdoin Graduate Helping to Blaze the Appalachian Trail," *Portland* [Me.] *Sunday Telegram*, Oct. 4, 1931, sec. D, p. 2.

490 **Although he appointed:** Bates, "Profile," p. 5.

"I first planned": Letter from Avery to Perkins, Apr. 23, 1931, archives, Potomac Appalachian Trail Club, Washington, D.C. Reprinted with permission.

491 **"Rentschler has written":** Letter from Avery to William A. Welch, Nov. 16, 1935, archives, Appalachian Trail Conference, Harpers Ferry, W.Va. Reprinted with permission.

"Myron was easy": Letter from Florence Nichol to L&GW, Sept. 15, 1985. Reprinted with permission.

"A 'dictator' who": Marene Snow, quoted in Lowrey, "Benton MacKaye's Appalachian Trail," p. 89. Reprinted with permission.

"Myron left two": Bill Mersch, quoted in Bates, "Profile," p. 8, archives, Potomac Appalachian Trail Club, Washington, D. C. Reprinted with permission.

"Mere woods travel": Letter from Avery to Arthur M. Fogg, Aug. 18, 1932, archives, Appalachian Trail Conference, Harpers Ferry, W.Va. Reprinted with permission.

491   **Although associates resisted:** Extensive correspondence on the Skyline Drive controversy litters the various Avery archives, most heavily in those at the PATC in Washington.

"Amateur trail with": Avery, "Mountains of Western Maine—Little-Known Peaks Accessible by Appalachian Long Trail," *Lewiston* [Me.] *Journal*, Apr. 10, 1937, p. A–6.

"The Appalachian Trail is": Avery, "Maine and the Appalachian Trail," *In the Maine Woods* (1933), p. 98.

When the CCC: See ATC, *Guide to the Appalachian Trail in Maine*, 7th ed., especially pp. 23–25; Avery, "Developments along the Appalachian Trail in Maine during 1935," *In the Maine Woods*, 1936, pp. 95–103; and Harvey Paul McGuire, "The Civilian Conservation Corps in Maine: 1933–1942," especially pp. 72–76.

"High and dry": Address by MacKaye (to the NETC?), undated, copy in MacKaye Family Papers, Dartmouth College Library. Reprinted with permission.

492   **"The path of the trailway":** MacKaye, remarks to first Appalachian Trail Conference, March 1–3, 1925, as recorded in a "Brief of Proceedings," a copy of which is in the archives, Appalachian Trail Conference, Harpers Ferry, W. Va. Reprinted with permission.

"Connected trail," and "Wilderness, not continuity": Letter from MacKaye to Avery, Nov. 20, 1935, archives, Appalachian Trail Conference, Harpers Ferry, W. Va. Reprinted with permission.

"Trails should be marked": Avery, "Report of the Chairman," *Appalachian Trailway News* (Sept. 1952), p. 42.

Even Perkins criticized: Letter from Perkins to Avery, Oct. 22, 1928, PATC Archives.

"No thanks are due," and "Had consciously placed": Copies of this fiery exchange of letters are in the archives, Potomac Appalachian Trail Club, Washington, D.C., reprinted with permission, and elsewhere. The culmination is Avery's six-page single-spaced letter of Dec. 19, 1935 (softened very slightly from a Dec. 5 draft, also in the PATC's archives), and a one-page reply from MacKaye, on Feb. 4, 1936, in the PATC's archives, regretting especially the "calumnious accusations" quoted here, and ending, "For sometime past I have noticed in you a growing, self-righteous, overbearing attitude and a bullying manner of expression. Your statements to me now—of assumption, distortion, and accusation—constitute a piece of insolence which confirms my former observations, as well as various reports of your conduct which have come to me from individual club members both in the North and South. In your present frame of mind, therefore, I feel that further words are futile."

Never a generous spirit: Earl V. Shaffer, *Walking with Spring: The First Thru-Hike of the Appalachian Trail* (Harpers Ferry, W. Va.: Appalachian

Trail Conference, 1983), p. 1. When Shaffer's completed journey was reported in the newspapers, Avery commented to his associate, Jean Stephenson, "I wonder if he did." When next encountering Stephenson, who had a law degree, Shaffer found himself subjected to "a charming but thorough cross-examination" (*Ibid.*).

492   **"Myronides I":** Recalled in Boardman's obituary, PATC Bulletin, p. 102.

      "Not a pleasant man": Conversation with Robert L. M. Underhill, July 21, 1980.

      "Convinced he was God": Conversation with John Hakola, Sept. 25, 1980.

      "To Myronides, Emperor": Letter from Harold (Allen?) to Avery, March 15, 1929, archives, Potomac Appalachian Trail Club, Washington, D.C. Reprinted with permission.

      "A hell of a fine fellow": J. Frank Schairer, article called "Early Days of the Appalachian Trail" (unidentified as to source), reprinting a talk given at a PATC meeting, March 19, 1969, p. 56, in archives, Potomac Appalachian Trail Club, Washington, D.C. Reprinted with permission.

      "And he was fun": Shailer S. Philbrick, letter to the editor, *Appalachian Trailway News* (March–Apr. 1984), p. 24, archives, Appalachian Trail Conference, Harpers Ferry, W. Va. Reprinted with permission.

      "He was a whiz": Conversation with Roy Fairfield, Sept. 26, 1983.

493   **New York:** The history of building the Appalachian Trail's New York section (east of the Hudson River) has never been well documented. The authors are chiefly indebted to Murray Stevens for his personal recollections in correspondence during 1982 and 1984. Raymond Torrey occasionally covered events as they unfolded on this front: see especially "Long Brown Path" columns of Jan. 18, 1929, and May 8, 1931, plus "The A-T over Private Lands," *Mountain Magazine* (July 1929), p. 86. On this and all other sections, various ATC historical summations are useful, notably the history chapter in publication no. 5, *The Appalachian Trail.*

      Murray H. Stevens: For personal background, see his obituary in *Appalachian Trailway News* (March–Apr. 1985), p. 8.

494   **"One man told me":** Letter from Murray H. Stevens to L&GW, late April 1984.

      Worried landowners: The language of this release was published in *Mountain Magazine* (July 1929), p. 86.

      "But then it materialized": Letter from Murray H. Stevens to L&GW, late April 1984.

496   **Connecticut:** Ned Anderson's work on the Connecticut AT is described in "Ned Anderson: Appalachian Trail Pioneer," which appeared both in *Connecticut Woodlands* (Fall 1983), pp. 15–17, and, with the same title, in the *Sherman* [Conn.] *Sentinel*, Oct. 26, 1983, pp. 1–3. This article was also done up as a special four-page brochure for the occasion of the dedication of a

bridge across the Housatonic River in Anderson's name. The authors are also greatly indebted to Mrs. Edna Anderson for recollections provided in correspondence; to conversations and correspondence with Seymour Smith, who succeeded Anderson as maintainer of the Connecticut AT; and to Richard P. Donohoe of Sherman, Conn., for access to his files relating to Ned Anderson and his trail work. A thorough written report ("Report on the Appalachian Trail in Connecticut") from Anderson addressed to Perkins, Heermance, and Avery, dated Feb. 7, 1931, a copy of which is in the ATC archives, provides good information. The building of the Connecticut AT may also be traced in a Connecticut Forest and Park Association trail guide, "Appalachian Trail," publication no. 19N (May 1934); Torrey, "Long Brown Path," Jan. 29, 1932; correspondence in the various major AT archives at Harpers Ferry, Washington, D.C., and Dartmouth College (the MacKaye Family Papers); and Myron H. Avery, "Connecticut" (a note containing AT route description and capsule history), *Appalachia* (June 1932), pp. 165–68. The *Appalachia* article should be read with caution as regards the state of the trail in 1932. While it describes the trail as if it were completely finished, Torrey's column claims less, and various ATC reports and correspondence in ATC archives indicated continuing work in Connecticut well into 1933. In "Connecticut Trail System Lures Many Hikers," *Telephone News* (July 1933), it is called "complete with a few gaps."

496 **Allis's route:** Torrey, "The Long Brown Path," *New York Evening Post*, Dec. 16, 1926.

When MacKaye's AT: Torrey, "2000-Mile Trail on Appalachian," p. 9.

Turner's route: Torrey, "Connecticut Helps Appalachian Trail," *New York Evening Post*, Apr. 21, 1922, p. 7.

At some point: Letter from Torrey to MacKaye, Nov. 10, 1924, in MacKaye Family Papers, Dartmouth College Library. Unless otherwise indicated, correspondence from this era, cited below, is from this source.

Later that year: Eaton, *Skyline Camps* (Boston: W. A. Wilde, 1922), p. 91.

By 1924 at least: Letter from Torrey to MacKaye, Nov. 10, 1924.

By 1926 an influential: Letter from Eaton to MacKaye, Aug. 30, 1926.

In 1925 and 1926: Extensive correspondence between MacKaye, Torrey, and Roosevelt, in MacKaye Family Papers, Dartmouth College Library, and various other AT archives. See also Torrey, "Hiking Footpath to Dixie Urged," *New York Times*, May 16, 1926, p. VIII–16.

Eaton still argued: Letter from Eaton to MacKaye, Aug. 20, 1926.

In 1926 and 1927: Letters from Torrey to MacKaye, Jan. 7, 1927, and from Perkins to MacKaye, May 3, 1927.

By February 1927: Letter from Torrey to MacKaye, Feb. 12, 1927.

"Scouted and temporarily marked": Torrey, "Long Brown Path" columns of Oct. 7, 1927, and May 11, 1928; and two articles in *Mountain Magazine*

(July 1927), pp. 23–25, and (Oct. 1928), pp. 40–41, which shows a map of the upper sections of Perkins's route.

497   **"My own idea":** Letter from MacKaye to Torrey, Jan. 14, 1927.

"If there is," and **"He seems the happiest":** Janet Morren Judd, essay on Ned Anderson written in March 1942, a transcript of which is in the files of Richard P. Donohoe, Sherman, Conn. Reprinted with permission.

"Ginger ale would put": Edna Anderson, quoted in "Ned Anderson: Appalachian Trail Pioneer." Reprinted with permission.

"How you ever": Letter from Heermance to Perkins, Oct. 23, 1930. ATC archives, Harpers Ferry, W. Va. Reprinted with permission.

"After farm chores": "Ned Anderson: Appalachian Trail Pioneer." Reprinted with permission.

"The only instance": Myron H. Avery, "Connecticut," *Appalachia* (June 1932), p. 166.

With the mileage now: Heermance, as overall trail chairman for the Connecticut Forest and Park Association, alludes to "Anderson's work and that of the man working north of him" in a letter to Perkins on Oct. 23, 1930. Perkins wrote to Avery on Dec. 17, 1930, that "Mr. Heermance suggested that the trail be divided into two or three parts in charge of different chairmen." Avery agreed: "I think that some help must be found for him [Anderson] when he gets across the Housatonic for the second time" (letter to Perkins, May 12, 1931—all three of these letters are in ATC archives, Harpers Ferry, W. Va. Reprinted with permission.)

498   **Under Mountain Trail:** Mentioned in Avery's write-up of the Massachusetts AT, *Appalachia* (Dec. 1932), p. 313.

Flanders Bridge–Dark Entry relocation: "Connecticut," *Appalachian Trailway News* (Jan. 1939), p. 3, and letter from Seymour Smith to L&GW, Nov. 28, 1982.

MacKaye's home state: The history of the original construction of the Appalachian Trail in Massachusetts is exceedingly obscure. The only printed sources are a note (Myron H. Avery, "The Appalachian Trail: Massachusetts") in *Appalachia* (Dec. 1932), pp. 312–18, and references to Massachusetts in general in ATC historical publications, such as the "History" chapter in *The Appalchian Trail*, publication no. 5. These accounts suffer severely from the limited perspective that ATC officials had of the local scene, probably based on Myron Avery's "whirl through the Berkshires" in 1931. In these histories, the Berkshire Chapter is given credit for doing most of the work and for completing it by 1932 or 1933. The Berkshire Hills Conference group is mentioned once and erroneously, while one or two local figures (William Hunter, a Scout leader in Pittsfield, and Francis Kelly of Great Barrington) are given credit for more work than any other evidence suggests they did. In order to reconstruct the history that preceded the Berkshire Chapter's involvement, it is necessary to refer to relatively obscure sources, such as old *Berkshire Eagle* (Pittsfield,

Mass.) clippings, club records, surviving correspondence, and the papers and memories of descendents of the original participants. The authors wish to acknowledge a tremendous amount of help given to us by a large number of individuals in the Pittsfield area in trying to find our way back to these sources. Eaton's plan is described in *Skyline Camps*, pp. 91–98. For the Berkshire School's involvement, the authors are indebted to Arthur Chase, longtime Berkshire School teacher and Outing Club adviser; to Jane Carver of the School Library; and to several Berkshire alumni of that period who corresponded concerning their recollections of Outing Club activity during those years. Correspondence among MacKaye, Eaton, Chamberlain, and Comey, most of it in the MacKaye Family Papers at Dartmouth, and various "Long Brown Path" columns of Torrey are important sources for the situation as it evolved throughout the 1920s. Activity by the AMC's Connecticut Chapter in Massachusetts in the late 1920s is reported in a note by Herbert O. Warner, "Connecticut: The Appalachian Trail on Mt. Greylock," *Appalachia* (Dec. 1929), pp. 412-13, and in a report, "Trails on the Taconic Plateau," *Mountain Magazine* (Oct. 1928), pp. 46–47. The Berkshire Hills Conference archives for the years 1925–35 are preserved in a notebook, a copy of which was located and duplicated for the authors by George S. Wislocki of the Berkshire County Natural Resources Council; the activities of its Trails Committee are noted therein in general terms. More detailed accounts of trail work of that period appeared in the *Berkshire Eagle*: "Appalachian Trail in Berkshire Near Reality; Definite Action Taken," June 5, 1928, pp. 9, 13; "Completion of Long Trail through Berkshire County Hoped for This Year," Apr. 6, 1929, p. 3; "Half of 73 Miles of Trail in Berkshire Completed as Part of Appalachian Route," July 8, 1929, p. 9; "New Map Shows Berkshire Hikers New Trail Route," Jan. 25, 1930, p. 3; "Current Comment," Feb. 15, 1930, p. 10; "Only Few Stretches Remain Unfinished on Hiking Trail," Apr. 18, 1931, p. 7; "Long Footpath in County Will Be Ready for 1932," Aug. 13, 1931, p. 2; and, retrospectively, Joe Ski (pseud.), "Chunk Stove Chatter," Jan. 21, 1937, p. 10. The work is described by Torrey in "Long Brown Path" columns of Feb. 15 and May 15, 1929. Franklin Couch's career was covered as it developed in the *Eagle*; an especially noteworthy article is Jack Cook, "Franklin Couch to be Ordained at Service Sunday," Nov. 6, 1952, p. 24. The authors also benefited from a conversation with Mrs. Couch, Apr. 9, 1984. Of particular value to the authors were journals and records kept by two of the principal trail workers, S. Waldo Bailey and Archie K. Sloper, and made available by their sons, Richard Bailey and Roger Sloper. Richard Bailey recalled working with his father on the trail as a youngster. The Berkshire Chapter's involvement in the Massachusetts AT was highlighted in Avery's note in *Appalachia* (Dec. 1932), pp. 312–18, but the timing of the work done seems more accurately documented in scheduled work trips by the chapter as listed in *AMC Bulletins* for the years 1931–35; the authors are indebted to E. Porter Dickinson, retired reference librarian of Amherst College, who most generously did the compilation of the latter for the authors' use. (Mr. Dickinson had participated in some of these work parties as a young man.) The evidence of conflicts between locals and Berkshire Chapter and other "outsiders" has been pieced together from correspondence, mostly from ATC archives—see especially Comey to Perkins, May 15, 1931; Perkins to Comey, July 16, 1931; Comey to Perkins, June 26, 1931; Perkins to Avery, undated but apparently July 1931; Avery to Perkins, Dec. 4, 1931; Partenheimer to Perkins, Dec. 8, 1931; Partenheimer to Avery, Dec. 10, 1931; Dickson to Sisk, Dec. 18, 1931; Avery to Comey, May 25, 1932; Perkins to Avery, sometime between May 26 and June 7, 1932; Avery to Comey, June 8, 1932; Couch to Avery, Jan. 10, 1933; Avery to Couch, Jan. 17, 1933; and Avery to Comey, Feb. 13, 1933. Of special importance to the authors was a conversation with one of the original participants, Harland Sisk, July 12, 1984; and correspondence with one who was on the scene as early as 1928, Orin P. McCarty, letter to L&GW, Jan. 23, 1983. Appraisals of the situation in the late 1930s include Torrey's "Long Brown Path" column for Jan. 13, 1938; a trail report, "Massachusetts," in *Appalachian Trailway News* (Jan. 1939), p. 3; and Joe Ski (pseud.), "Chunk Stove Chatter," *Berkshire Eagle*, Jan. 21, 1937, p. 10. For recent perspectives, see Laura Waterman and Guy Waterman, "Trail Builders," *Berkshires Week*, a summer supplement to the *Berkshire Eagle*, August 1–7, 1986, pp. 14–18; and AT Committee of the AMC Berkshire Chapter, "Management Plan for the Appalachian Trail in Massachusetts" [n.d., 1987], chap. 1, pp. 6–7.

499 **Optimistic statements:** Raymond Torrey reported in a Nov. 10, 1924, "Long Brown Path" column that "Eaton has blazed a trail from Everett to Race." Comey wrote MacKaye in 1925 to the effect that Eaton had 32 miles finished from the Connecticut line well out across the valley northeast of Everett (Sept. 24, 1925). MacKaye wrote Chamberlain congratulating him on what he and Eaton had accomplished (Sept. 21, 1925).

500 **"I doubt if":** Letter from Eaton to MacKaye, Aug. 30, 1926.

As late as: Torrey, "Long Brown Path," Feb. 10, 1928.

"Conscience of the town": *Berkshire Eagle*, Aug. 22, 1964.

501 **A longtime hiker:** Letter from Orin P. McCarty to L&GW, Jan. 23, 1983.

"Pretty stagnant": Letter from Arthur Perkins to Myron Avery, July 1931, in the archives of the Appalachian Trail Conference, Harpers Ferry, W. Va. Reprinted with permission. Further correspondence on this period in Massachusetts is from the ATC archives, and the authors are grateful for permission to quote as we have.

"Whirl through the Berkshires": Letter from Arthur Comey to Perkins, June 26, 1931.

During one of his: Letter from Avery to Comey, Feb. 13, 1933.

"An absolute failure": Letter from Avery to Comey, Apr. 17, 1931.

Perkins and Comey, and Comey warned Avery: See Avery's reply to these points, in a letter to Comey, June 8, 1932.

In January 1933: Letter from Couch to Avery, Jan. 10, 1933, and letter from Avery to Couch, Jan. 17, 1933.

502 **"The Berkshire Chapter of the A. M. C.":** Torrey, "Long Brown Path," Jan. 13, 1938.

Mount Greylock Ski Club: The Mount Greylock Ski Club's assumption of AT reponsibility was reported in "Skiers Will Keep Appalachian Trail Cleared for Hiking," *Berkshire Eagle*, Jan. 21, 1937, p. 10, and may be followed in detail in the club records preserved with scrupulous care by Max Sauter and now in the possession of the Charles Goodrich family of Pittsfield, Mass. The authors are grateful to the late Mr. Goodrich for giving us access to these papers.

Metawampe: Metawampe's involvement in AT maintenance was announced in "Metawampe Club Takes Trail Assignment," *Appalachian Trailway News*, Sept. 1940, p. 52.

503 **In 1927 DOC trail workers:** *Annual Report* of the Dartmouth Outing Club for 1927, p. 12.

In 1928 the Norwich Outing Club: Unidentified news clipping, dated 1928, in scrapbooks dated 1928–29, ATC archives.

Apparently the college lads: Letter from Perkins to Avery, May 27, 1930, PATC archives.

Even the GMC was lax: "History" chapter in ATC publication no. 5, p. 16.

"Following fishermen's and hunters' ": Arthur C. Comey, "Field Notes: Exploration in Maine—1925," *Appalachia* (Feb. 1926), p. 377. As a precautionary note, a report by Alice Frost Lord, "Sunlit Trails," *Lewiston Journal*, Oct. 8, 1932, p. 4, is apparently in error in giving 1926 as the date of this trip.

Henry Poor's trail section: Comey, "Field Notes" (Feb. 1926), p. 378n.

"On existing trails": Torrey, "Long Brown Path," Oct. 7, 1929. Perkins described the work in letters to MacKaye, Sept. 23, 1927, and Sept. 28, 1927. As another precautionary note, an article by Perkins, "The Appalachian Trail," in the *American Civic Annual* for 1929, pp. 100–103 is apparently in error (a typo?) in giving 1928 as the year of the Connecticut AMC trip.

504 **Walter D. Greene:** Avery, "Marking the Appalachian Trail in Maine," *In the Maine Woods*, 1934, p. 30. Greene's involvement with the trail was richly reported in the magazine section of the *Lewiston Journal*; see issues of Dec. 3, 1932, p. A–1, and Dec. 10, 1932, p. A–1, for articles by Greene both titled, "Lure of Foot Cruising in the Maine Wilderness," and Feb. 25, 1933, p. A–1, for "Actor and Adopted Son of Maine to Start Work on Maine Portion Long Trail." Avery constantly credited Greene with an important role in reopening the Maine AT work, starting with an article "Outstanding Progress Reported," in the PATC *Bulletin* (Oct. 1932), pp. 66–67. See also, for example, Avery, "Maine and the Appalachian Trail," *In the Maine Woods*, 1933, pp. 99–100.

Shailer S. Philbrick: Shailer S. Philbrick, "Fifty Years After the Marking of the Appalachian Trail," typescript dated Jan. 21, 1983, provided by Mr. Philbrick to the authors, pp. 5–6. See also Shailer S. Philbrick, "Before and After the Avery Expedition," *Appalachian Trailway News* (Nov.–Dec. 1983, pp. 12–13.

505 **"I was receptive":** Philbrick, "Fifty Years After," pp. 5–6. Reprinted with permission.

On August 19, 1933: See "Fifty Years Ago on the 'Greatest Mountain,' " *Appalachian Trailway News* (Nov.–Dec. 1983), pp. 6–13. Earlier versions include Avery, "Marking the Appalachian Trail in Maine," pp. 18–32, and Emmie B. Whitney, "The Beginning of the Long Trail," magazine section, *Lewiston Journal*, Oct. 7, 1933, pp. A–1, A–8 ff.

During the next month: Avery, "Marking the Appalachian Trail in Maine," p. 32.

Helon Taylor: An excellent profile is Rima Farmer, "The 'Four-mile-an-hour Man' Is Right Where He Wants to Be!" *Appalachian Trailway News* (July–Aug. 1984), pp. 18–20. His work on the original AT is described there; in a short article in the Maine Appalachian Trail Club newsletter, "Percival Baxter—Some Eccentricities," *MAINEtainer* (June 1981), p. 3; and in the general AT histories previously cited. The authors profited greatly from conversation and correspondence with Mr. Taylor. A map of his early trails on Bigelow ran in the *Lewiston Journal*, Apr. 3, 1937, pp. A–6, A–7, along with an article by Avery, "Mountains of Western Maine—Little Known Peaks Accessible by Long Trail."

506 **Bates College Outing Club:** A log of the 1934 trip is in the archives of the Bates Outing Club, Bates College Library. See also "Bates Outing Club Completes Blazing of Appalachian Trail," *Lewiston Daily Sun*, Oct. 5, 1934, p. 3. The 1935 trip is described in the club's yearbook for 1936.

CCC work in Maine: Avery, "Developments Along the Appalachian Trail in Maine during 1935," *In the Maine Woods*, 1936, pp. 95–103; W. Clark Dean, "With the Trail Club in Maine," PATC *Bulletin* (Jan. 1936), pp. 11–12; and a mimeographed letter to MATC members over Walter Greene's signature, Apr. 8, 1937, ATC archives. For recent recollections, see Judy Jenner, "Early Trail-Builder Recalls CCC Effort," *Appalachian Trailway News*, (Nov.–Dec. 1987), pp. 9–10; and "The 'Splendid Work' of the Civilian Conservation Corps," *Appalachian Trailway News* (July–Aug. 1987), p. 11.

"Utter wilderness": This much favored phrase appears in virtually every write-up of the early Maine AT (for instance, ATC publication no. 5, p. 17).

On August 14, 1937: Avery, "White Blazes across Maine," *In the Maine Woods*, 1938, pp. 19–24. For a recent perspective, see Judy Jenner, "August 14, 1937: The Golden Anniversary of a 'Never-Ending Project,' " *Appalachian Trailway News* (July–Aug. 1987), pp. 7–13.

In an odd juxtaposition: ATC, *Guide to the Appalachian Trail in Maine* (1938), pp. 5–9.

Gradually more primitive: Greene's report to MATC for Dec. 15, 1937, MATC archives.

506   **Maine Appalachian Trail Club:** "Maine Club Organized," PATC *Bulletin*
(Oct. 1935), p. 78, and Avery, "Developments along the Appalachian Trail
in Maine during 1935," *In the Maine Woods*, 1936, pp. 100–101. A copy of
the original press release on the club's founding is in the archives of MATC.
The authors are deeply indepted to David Field, and to Barbara Clark and
Stephen Clark, all officials of the MATC, for generously making these archives available to us and for providing much background from their own
long experience with the club. Another rich source of information on the
MATC is the archive of Avery Papers at the Maine State Library in Augusta.
The original Washington, D.C., domination of the club is strikingly evident
from such facts as these: the original press release gives the club's address as
"1850 Park Road, Washington, D.C."; club officers included Greene as president (apparently a titular honor), with three others all from the Washington
area; five out of ten members of the board of directors were also Wash-
ingtonians.

509   **"Nobody, or practically":** Eaton, *Skyline Camps*, p. 89.

"We do not regard": Avery, report to MATC members, Dec. 15, 1941, p. 4,
in the archives of MATC.

Eiler U. Larson: "Hiker Covers Half of 2056-mile Trail." *Christian Science
Monitor*, Dec. 18, 1931.

"To pull at least": "Larson, Dispenser of Happiness, Tires of Streets, Takes
Open Road," *Washington Herald*, Apr. 17, 1933, p. 1.

"The A. T. is of minor importance": Letter from Heermance to Steering
Committee of NETC, March 18, 1938, ATC archives.

"Has been a continual headache": *Ibid.*

For a while GMC trailsmen: Letters to Avery from Wallace M. Fay, Sept. 26,
1933, and Willis M. Ross, Sept. 9, 1933; in ATC archives. The point was
recalled by longtime GMC member, Robert Humes, in conversation on June
6, 1981.

In 1928 the Dartmouth: Annual Report of the Dartmouth Outing Club for
1928, p. 12, and 1929, p. 13.

CHAPTER 46. SUPERHIKING

511   **In the next:** Eugene B. Cook, "The Record of a Day's Walk," *Appalachia*
(Dec. 1884), pp. 54–57; Herschel C. Parker, "A Day's Trip over the Presidential Range," *Appalachia* (June 1905), pp. 13–17; and two unsigned pieces in
Among the Clouds: "Mount Washington," July 29, 1904, p. 1, and "Another
Record Tramp," Aug. 1, 1904, p. 4. A precautionary note: Sweetser alludes to
the Cook-Sargent walk in *White Mountains*, 1886 and subsequent editions,
p. 193b, and apparently is in error in assigning it to the year 1884; all other
sources say 1882.

In the Adirondacks: Letter from Walter Lowrie to William D. Glover, published as "Marcy Reminiscences," *Adirondac*, (March–Apr. 1956), pp.

30–33; Newell Martin, *Six Summits*, a little pamphlet printed in 1927, in the archives of the Keene Valley Library; and logs of the Putnam Camp.

511 **"Probably the most remarkable"**: Carson, *Peaks and People*, p. 132. Reprinted with permission.

512 **In the Catskills**: "Walking Club Gives 'Doctor of Pedestry' Degree," *New York Times*, July 10, 1910, p. 78.

Dartmouth's long walks: William P. Fowler, "From Midnight to Midnight: The D.O.C. 24-Hour Walks of 1919–1920," *Appalachia* (Dec. 1932), pp. 261–78; and Sherman Adams, "Mission Impossible," *Appalachia* (Dec. 1971), pp. 53–64. The authors also had the advantage of talks with three principal participants: Sherman Adams (July 29, 1980 and Sept. 17, 1981), Warren F. Daniell III (May 8, 1981), and William Plummer Fowler (Oct. 4, 1981).

513 **"The only reason"**: Quoted in Fowler, "From Midnight to Midnight," p. 264. Reprinted with the permission of the Appalachian Mountain Club.

"By spring I was as tough": Adams, "Mission Impossible," p. 58.

514 **"Slender, wiry, and with muscles"**: Fowler, "From Midnight to Midnight," pp. 261–62.

"He possessed more": Adams, "Mission Impossible," p. 58.

"Didn't drink, smoke": Conversation with Sherman Adams, July 29, 1980.

"Over a course": Neal R. O'Hara, "Train for Great Endurance Test: Dartmouth Hikers Seek to Break the World's Walking Record over Blazed Mountain Trails," *Boston Post*, Feb. 14, 1921, pp. 1, 9.

The next outstanding: The original climbing of the Adirondack "forty-six" was described even while it was in process by Robert Marshall in a little booklet called *The High Peaks of the Adirondacks* (Albany, N.Y.: The Adirondack Mountain Club, 1922). See also Jim Glover, "The First Forty-Sixers," *Adirondack Life* (Feb. 1985), pp. 17–23. For descriptions of the principals, see especially James M. Glover, *A Wilderness Original: The Life of Bob Marshall* (Seattle, Wash.: The Mountaineers, 1986), George Marshall, "Adirondacks to Alaska: A Biographical Sketch of Robert Marshall," *Adirondac* (May–June 1951), pp. 44–45, 59; and Robert Marshall, "Herbert Clark," *High Spots* (Oct. 1933), pp. 8–11. A useful overview of the Marshalls and the start-up of the Forty-Sixers is Grace L. Hudowalski and Orville C. Gowie, "The Story of the Adirondack Forty-Sixers," in Hudowalski, ed., *The Adirondack High Peaks and the Forty-Sixers*, pp. 1–24. A complete roster of the first 518 Forty-Sixers appeared in this book, pp. 303–37, and subsequent names have been announced regularly in the club's newsletter, *Adirondack Peeks*. The authors were also helped by conversations with Grace Hudowalski (Nov. 3, 1981) and Fay Loope (Aug. 15, 1980).

515 **"Clark was obviously"**: Letter from Herbert McAneny to L&GW, March 25, 1982.

515   **"Great gusto and":** George Marshall, "Adirondacks to Alaska," p. 59.

He could recount: Robert Marshall's statistics are mentioned in *ibid.*, p. 45.

"One of the most": Stephen Fox, "We Want No Straddlers," *Wilderness* (Winter 1984), p. 7.

516   **"Herb has been":** Robert Marshall, "Herbert Clark," p. 9. Reprinted with permission.

He solemnly assured: Clark's *Monitor-Merrimac* yarn is mentioned by George Marshall in "Approach to the Mountains," *Adirondac* (March–Apr. 1955), p. 24.

"The fastest man": Robert Marshall, "Herbert Clark," p. 10. Reprinted with permission.

In Ausable Club: Information on early Ausable-circle peakbagging comes from several conversations with James A. Goodwin.

517   **"Big days":** Adirondack one-day mileage and elevation feats were reported in *High Spots*. See the following: Newell Martin, "Expunging Old Marcy Records" (Sept. 1930), pp. 17–18; "11 Peak-One Day Climbing Record Hung up by Professor H. L. Malcolm" (Oct. 1931), p. 21; Ralph H. Knight, "Free Wheeling over the Mountains" (Jan. 1932), pp. 30, 39; "Summary of Trip of Ernest S. Griffith" (Oct. 1932), p. 19; Samuel G. Carson, "A New Marathoner" (July 1933), p. 26; "Malcolm Breaks His Former Record" (July 1933), p. 24; "H. L. Malcolm Breaks Previous Altitude Records in Marathon Hike, Making 20,067 Feet in Ascent," (Oct. 1933), pp. 24–25; and Herbert L. Malcolm, "Mountain Marathon in the Adirondacks" (July 1936), p. 26. A summary was noted in "Record Walks in the Adirondacks," *Appalachia* (June 1934), pp. 138–39.

"Demon of energy": Klaus Goetze, obituary for Herbert L. Malcolm, *Appalachia* (June 1959), pp. 431–32.

518   **Meanwhile, over in:** New Hampshire peakbagging may be traced through articles in the following issues of *Appalachia*: Nathaniel L. Goodrich, "The Four Thousanders" (Dec. 1931), pp.479–80; Francis B. Parsons, "The Four-Thousand-Foot Peaks of New England" (Dec. 1949), pp. 461–67; and Roderick Gould, "More on the Four-Thousand Footers" (Dec. 1956), pp. 247–48.

"The determined assault": Lois P. Williams and Henry E. Childs, "'Path No. 1' Site of August Camp, 1935," *Appalachia* (Nov. 1935), p. 454.

Besides peakbagging: Big days in the hut system were reported in the following issues of *Appalachia*: Stillman P. Williams, "Lonesome to Madison: Twenty-four Hours" (Dec. 1932), pp. 304–305; "The Chain of Huts in Two Days" (June 1933), p. 477–78, Ralph F. Batchelder, "The Chain of Huts in Twenty-four Hours" (Dec. 1933), pp. 603–5; and Herbert L. Malcolm, "Breaking One's Own Record" (Dec. 1936), pp. 189–94. Information also came from correspondence with Ralph Batchelder (Aug. 17, 1980), Stillman Williams (Aug. 13, 1980, and Sept. 1, 1980), Evarts G. Loomis (Sept. 24, 1980), and from Raymond Falconer (Oct. 4, 1982) in conversation.

518 **On August 9, 1932:** In addition to cited published sources on 1930s hut traverses, the authors are indebted to Stillman Williams for correcting an error in the names given in the original account of the Aug. 9, 1932, jaunt (letter to L&GW, Sept. 1, 1980).

519 **"The boys joshing me":** H. L. Malcolm, "Breaking One's Own Record," p. 192.

The spiny, twisty: Stanley B. Attwood, "Maine Alpine Club Members in Three-Day Trip over the Mahoosuc Range," *Lewiston Journal,* Jan. 25, 1941, magazine sec. p. A–6.

Skier Sel Hannah: Conversation with Sel Hannah, Nov. 16, 1982.

Batchelder carried 1,000 pounds: Letter from Ralph Batchelder to L&GW, Aug. 17, 1980.

Speed hiking found: For Harriman Park superhiking, the chief source is the "Long Brown Path" column of Raymond H. Torrey in the *New York Evening Post;* see especially Nov. 30, 1923, May 4, 1928, Nov. 2, 1934, Oct. 30, 1936, and Nov. 8, 1937.

520 **In 1936 the CCHC's :** "Race Against Time to Mt. Washington's Peaks," *Boston Herald,* July 11, 1937, p. B–1.

A most rare: "Harry Brook Describes Week-End Trip to Mount Katahdin, Maine," *Pawtucket* [R.I.] *Times,* July 13, 1932, p. 2; and Harry Brook, "Katahdin Weekend," *Appalachia* (Dec. 1932), pp. 235–40.

"For exceptionally sturdy trampers": Allen Chamberlain, "When Col. T. W. Higginson Was a Guide to Mt. Ktaadn in 1855 and Now," *Boston Evening Transcript,* July 14, 1923, magazine sec., p. V–1.

"Twenty-three miles of bumps": Brook, "Katahdin Weekend," p. 236.

"A sixty mile gale": Brook, "Harry Brook Describes Week-End Trip," p. 2.

"Was about as flexible": Brook, "Katahdin Weekend," p. 238.

521 **End-to-end hiking:** The origins of the GMC End-to-End award are described in "End-to-Enders," *The Long Trail News* (May 1942), p. 15. Early numbers of qualifying hikers are given in "Green Mountain Club 'End-to-Enders' Award," *The Long Trail News* (May 1955), p. 6.

One of the earliest: Appleby's Long Trail exploits were reported and discussed in *The Long Trail News:* "A Long Trail Marathon" (July 1927), pp. 3–4; "Appleby" (Dec. 1927), pp. 1–2; "Appleby Writes a Letter" (Apr. 1928), pp. 2–3; "Communication" (Aug. 1930), p. 3; and "The Appleby Story" (May 1952), p. 5.

"They say Mansfield": Appleby's typewritten record of the 1926 trip, in GMC archives, Vermont Historical Society, Montpelier, Vt. Reprinted with permission.

"Big crowd there": Appleby's typewritten record of the 1927 trip, in GMC archives, Vermont Historical Society. Reprinted with permission.

521 **"During the coming"**: Quoted in *Novelty—Surprise—Suspense*, a brochure issued by the Vermont State Chamber of Commerce, n.d. (1927), James P. Taylor Papers, Vermont Historical Society, Montpelier, Vt. Reprinted with permission.

522 **"In view of"**: "Appleby," *The Long Trail News* (Dec. 1927), p. 2. Reprinted with permission.

"We don't encourage": Executive Director Steve Rice, quoted in "New End-to-End Record Set," *The Long Trail News* (Nov. 1978), p. 14.

"A competitive climate": GMC, *Guide Book of the Long Trail*, (1985 ed.), p. 14.

"A rather tiresome pursuit": Letter from Hope Cobb, *Appalchia* (Dec. 1973), p. 174. Reprinted with the permission of the Appalachian Mountain Club.

"Distortion of values": Kenneth Webb, *As Sparks Fly Upward* (Canaan, N.H.: Phoenix Publishing, 1973), p. 13.

"Sin": Justin Askins, "Magazine Pollution," *Appalachia* (June 1983), p. 151.

523 **"We do not care"**: Entry in the summit register on Mount Adams, Aug. 1, 1884, in the collections of the Appalachian Mountain Club.

"Foot-cavalry exploits" and **"The absurd rate"**: Sweetser, *White Mountains* (1884 ed.), pp. 34–35.

"The desire to make": Raymond W. Dow Adams, "The Register Cylinders of the Club," *Appalachia* (June 1905), p. 43.

"One hesitates to bestow": Quoted in William B. Rotch, "Dartmouth Outing Club," p. 28. Reprinted with permission.

Robert Marshall himself: Robert Marshall, "Adrirondack Peaks," *High Spots* (Oct. 1932), p. 14.

"Like eating goldfish": Conversation with Warren Daniell III, May 8, 1981.

"Records are really": Letter from Bob and George Marshall to Newell Martin, quoted in Newell Martin, "Expunging Old Marcy Records," *High Spots* (Sept. 1930), p. 18. Reprinted wtih permission.

"Deliberate attempt to cover," and **"While this can be"**: John Kieran, "Out of the City, into the Open," *New York Times* (Dec. 6, 1931), magazine sec., pp. 12–13, 21. Copyright © 1931 by The New York Times Company. Reprinted with permission.

"What folly to race": Dorothy Laker, quoted in "Who Has Walked the Whole Trail?" *Appalachian Trailway News* (Sept. 1969), p. 44.

Geoffrey Winthrop Young: Geoffrey Winthrop Young, *Mountaincraft*, 3d ed. (London: Methuen, 1934), pp. 74–76.

524 **"The spirit of"**: Harry Wade Hicks, "Climbs 16 Peaks of Adirondacks in One Day," *High Spots* (Jan. 1933), p. 10.

524   **"My answer is":** Herbert L. Malcolm, "Breaking One's Own Record," p. 194.

       "Perhaps charity is lacking": Myron H. Avery, "Records and Record-Breaking," Potomac Appalachian Trail Club *Bulletin* (July 1937), p. 69.

CHAPTER 47. THE BEMIS CREW

525   **Willard Helburn:** Helburn's importance in early (pre-1925) winter climbing was repeatedly emphasized to the authors by Robert Underhill and others of that era.

526   **Presidential traverse:** "In the Heroic Age," *Appalachia* (June 1932), pp. 136–37.

       Six Husbands descent: *Ibid.*

       Helburn later told: Conversation with Robert Underhill, July 21, 1980.

       Katahdin in 1923: Willard Helburn, "On Ktaadn in March," Appalachian (Apr. 1924), pp. 426–30.

527   **The Bemis Crew:** The best printed description of the Bemis Crew is T. P. Chandler, 2d, "Cruises of the Ship Bemis," *Appalachia* (Dec. 1930), pp. 145–51. Each year's trip was normally written up in *Appalachia*. A notable reminiscence is Marguerite D. Barnes, "A Snowshoe Trip in 1924," *Appalachia* (June 1961), pp. 340–49. More important than any printed sources were the papers of Marjorie Hurd, to which John C. Hurd generously gave us access, and conversations and correspondence with numerous Bemis Crew participants, notably Margaret Helburn, Robert Underhill, Jack Hurd, John Van de Water, Ruth Langmuir Van de Water, Helen Pennock Wiley, and Carleton Fuller.

       "A very congenial": Letter from Ruth and John W. Van de Water to L&GW, undated (early July 1981). Reprinted with permission.

528   **"An ice axe":** Memorandum from Willard Helburn addressed to "Ladies, Gentlemen and Crew of the Late [*sic*] Ship Bemis," in Marjorie Hurd Papers, in the possession of the Hurd family. Reprinted with permission.

       Nautical terms: From other Marjorie Hurd papers.

529   **"A powerhouse":** Conversation with John C. Hurd, July 11, 1980.

CHAPTER 48. KATAHDIN IN WINTER

531   **Lore Rogers climbed:** Lore Rogers (signed "L"), "Katahdin in Winter," *Forest and Stream* (Apr. 28, 1892), p. 395. For a citation of this climb as the first winter ascent, see for example Edward S. C. Smith, "An Early Winter Trip to Katahdin," *Appalachia* (Dec. 1926), p. 493. Hakola is more cautious in *Legacy of a Lifetime*, merely citing Rogers's 1892 ascent as "a winter ascent" (p. 39).

       "Is not very often": Rogers, "Katahdin in Winter," p. 395.

531   **"A tramp of eight miles":** G. M. Campbell, "Katahdin and Around There," *St. Croix Courier*, March 10, 1887, p. 2.

532   **November 1897 party:** Frank E. Wolfe, "An Ascent of Mt. Katahdin, Maine," *Forest and Stream* (Jan. 1, 1898), pp. 2–5.

1905 Harvard party: Smith, "An Early Winter Trip to Katahdin," pp. 493–96.

"A little-known trail": Perceval Sayward, "A Winter Ascent of Mt. Ktaadn," *Appalachia* (June 1915), p. 236.

1911 ascent from the north: *Ibid.*, pp. 227–38.

"A tramp of eight miles": Campbell, "Katahdin and Around There," p. 2.

"We had come prepared": Rogers, "Katahdin in Winter," p. 395.

"Very gradual": Sayward, "A Winter Ascent of Mt. Ktaadn," p. 232.

Austin Cary climbs: Cary's report was printed in the Forest Commissioner of the State of Maine, *Third Annual Report* (1896), pp. 15–203. The quoted passage is on p. 136.

Arthur Comey: Just about every New England climber or skier of the 1920s interviewed by the authors regaled them with stories of Arthur Comey. Most valuable was a conversation with his widow, Janet Comey (Feb. 2, 1981). Among printed sources see the obituary by William P. Fowler in *Appalachia* (June 1954), pp. 85–87. The first ski ascent of Katahdin is related in J. Ashton Allis, "March Days on Katahdin," *Appalachia* (Dec. 1926), pp. 509–12. For subsequent ascents, see Comey, "Skiing at Katahdin," *Appalachia* (June 1928), pp. 24–26, and a separate note, "Katahdin, by Saddle Slide, on Skis," on p. 72 of that issue; and Jessie M. Whitehead, "Skiing at Katahdin, 1931," *Appalachia* (June 1931), pp. 250–56. The authors are indebted to Thomas D. Cabot (Apr. 29, 1981) and Philip H. Lewis (Feb. 12, 1981) for letters vividly describing Katahdin skiing with Comey.

533   **"The trouble with":** Letter from Arthur S. Perkins to Myron Avery, June 1, 1928, in archives, Appalachian Trail Conference, Harpers Ferry, W. Va. Reprinted with permission.

"A raw product": Conversation with Robert Underhill, July 21, 1980.

"He would almost": Conversation with A. John Holden, Nov. 3, 1980.

"Arthur could be": Conversation with Helen Pennock Wiley, Oct. 10, 1981.

"The trouble with Arthur": Recalled in conversation with Robert Underhill, Feb. 18, 1982.

"Comey would say": *Ibid.*

"A very utilitarian skier": Conversation with A. John Holden, Nov. 3, 1980.

Up fire tower ladders: Conversation with William P. Fowler, Oct. 4, 1981.

533   **1926 Katahdin trip:** J. Ashton Allis, "March Days on Katahdin," *Appalachia* (Dec. 1926), p. 512. The authors also profited from a conversation with Margaret Helburn about this trip, Jan. 28, 1980.

534   **"Behaved themselves remarkably well":** Allis, "March Days," p. 512.

        "Who is King Beetle": Holden's question was recalled by Robert Underhill in conversation, July 21, 1980.

        "At lightning speed": Allis, "March Days," p. 510.

        "Seeming none the worse": *Ibid.*, p. 512.

        1922 Providence snowshoers: J. Earle Bacon, "A Winter Climb," *Atop Katahdin*, a promotional brochure by the Bangor & Aroostook Railroad, 1922, in the collections of the Portland, Maine, Public Library.

        1929 college skiers: Terris Moore, "Katahdin by the Hunt Trail," *Appalachia* (June 1929), p. 283.

        1934 Yale party: Conversations with William P. House on various occasions, but particularly on July 15, 1980.

        1920s forestry students: Conversation with A. D. Nutting, Sept. 23, 1980, and letter from Gregory Baker to L&GW, June 14, 1981.

        1930s UMO trips: J. Howard Lawson, "Climbing Katahdin on Skis," *In the Maine Woods*, 1937, pp. 66–72; letter from Robert G. MacKay to L&GW, undated, ca. May 1981; George Bell, "Climbing Mt. Katahdin in the Winter as the University Men Did," *Bangor News*, Apr. 8, 1939, p. 3.

535   **Katahdin Outing Club:** Dorothy Bowler Laverty, *Millinocket: Magic City of Maine's Wilderness* (Freeport, Me.: Bond Wheelwright, 1973), p. 74.

        One veteran of three: Letter from Robert G. MacKay to L&GW, undated, ca. May 1981.

        The big guide: Conversation with Helon Taylor, July 16, 1982.

        Eastern States Mountain Club: Letter from Leroy D. Cross to L&GW, Aug. 17, 1981.

        Traveler in 1941: Myron Avery in two articles for the *Lewiston Journal*, magazine sec.: "The Katahdinaugauh and Its Reigning Monarch, The Traveler," Apr. 2, 1949, pp. A–6–7, and "Magnificent Scenery Greets 'The Traveler' Region Explorer," Apr. 9, 1949, pp. A–6–7.

CHAPTER 49. SNOWSHOES VERSUS SKIS: THE GREAT DEBATE

537   **1927 Bemis-Langmuir trip:** The 1927 Adirondacks snowshoe versus skis trip was regrettably never written up for publication. Typed records of what was done were kept in some quantity apparently, because the authors found them in several places, the most generally accessible being the Apperson Papers at the Adirondack Research Center, in the Schenectady Museum, Schenectady, N.Y. Extremely helpful were detailed letters to the authors from

two of the participants, David Langmuir (July 22, 1981) and Theodore Dreier (June 7, 1981).

537   **"A hand-picked, hard-boiled crew"**: Trip-planning memorandum entitled "Fourth Voyage of the Good Ship Bemis A. M. C.," in Apperson Papers, Adirondack Research Center, Schenectady, N.Y. Reprinted with permission.

"Apperson and Langmuir had hoped": Letter from Theodore Dreier to L&GW, June 7, 1981. Reprinted with permission.

"Had a glorious time": Letter from David B. Langmuir to L&GW, July 22, 1981. Reprinted with permission.

538   **"What a revelation"**: *Ibid.*

"Rivalry between," and **"The advantage was conceded"**: Ruth G. Hardy, "Trip to the Adirondacks," *Appalachia* (Dec. 1929), p. 412.

But how transitory: For explicit discussion of the 1930s debate over snowshoes versus skis, see Robert L. M. Underhill, "What of the Snowshoe?" *Appalachia* (June 1932), pp. 131–134, and Richard L. Neuberger, "Ski versus the Snowshoe," *New York Times*, Jan. 9, 1949, p. X–15.

The very next year: "Seven Ascend Mount Marcy by New Route," *Glens Falls* [N.Y.] *Times*, date obscured [Feb. 26, 1930], Comstock Scrapbook, vol. 3, archives, Keene Valley Library.

"What of the Snowshoe?": Underhill, "What of the Snowshoe?" pp. 131–34. Reprinted with the permission of the Appalachian Mountain Club.

"Will it eventually disappear": *Ibid.*, pp. 133–34.

"A social barrier" and **"The fellow on snowshoes"**: Neuberger, "Ski versus the Snowshoe," p. X–15. Copyright © 1949 by The New York Times Company. Reprinted by permission.

539   **"Only a very expert"**: Letter from Langmuir, July 22, 1981.

White Mountains: Among innumerable written sources on 1920s–1930s skiing and snowshoeing, some samples of particular value include, for the White Mountains, Dyson Duncan, "Arctic Adventure in New England," *Appalachia* (June 1931), pp. 257–62; two notes by Robert Underhill in *Appalachia* (June 1932), "Mt. Washington in Winter," pp. 137–40, and "Tuckerman Headwall," pp. 140–42; Robert S. Monahan, *Mount Washington Reoccupied* (Brattleboro, Vt.: Stephen Daye Press, 1933), as well as an article, "The Genus Winter Climber," *Appalachia* (June 1933), pp. 465–67; P. Starr Cressy, "Out of Doors in Winter," *Appalachia* (May 1951), pp. 362–64; a chapter on "Skiing" in F. Allen Burt, *The Story of Mount Washington*, pp. 134–44; Francis Head, "Early Skiing in the A. M. C.," *Appalachia* (Dec. 1964), pp. 213–21; John Jay et al., *Ski Down the Years* (New York: Award House, 1966); Hal Burton, *The Ski Troops* (New York: Simon & Schuster, 1971); Henry Ives Baldwin, "Early Skiing on Mount Washington," *Mount Washington Observatory News Bulletin* (March 1977), pp. 2–4; William P.

Fowler, reprint of a January 3 or 4, 1934, radio talk, "New Hampshire Becomes Ski Conscious," *Appalachia* (Dec. 1978), pp. 122–24; Winston Pote, "Winter Experiences on Mount Washington Fifty Years Ago," *Mount Washington Observatory News Bulletin* (June 1979), p. 48, and (Dec. 1979), pp. 74–78; and E. John B. Allen, *New Hampshire Skiing,* a brochure prepared for the New Hampshire Council for the Humanities, ca. 1983. The authors also benefited from conversation and correspondence with William P. Fowler, Henry Ives Baldwin, Kenneth A. Henderson, Robert S. Monahan, Robert Livermore, Jr., Bradford Washburn, H. Adams Carter, Sel Hannah, Dorothy Gardner Burak, Leroy D. Cross, Raymond W. Evans, Charles M. Dudley, John Rand, William B. Rotch, George C. Sawyer, and Donald Hight.

540   **Presidentials ski traverse:** Milana Jank, "Mt. Washington–Mt. Madison, First Ski Traverse," *Appalachia* (June 1931), pp. 312–14; and conversations and correspondence with Fritz Wiessner.

"Snowshoes are still": *AMC White Mountain Guide* (1934 ed.), p. 469.

"Like jumping into": Quoted by John Jay in "Tuckerman Ravine," *Mount Washington Observatory News Bulletin,* (March 1968), p. 5.

541   **"Concrete roads have":** Francis Adams Truslow, "Mt. Washington for the Weekend," *Appalachia* (June 1932), p. 72.

Green Mountains: See Craig O. Burt, "We Lived in Stowe," an unpublished manuscript in the Bailey-Howe Library, University of Vermont. The GMC's *The Long Trail News* contains frequent stories of winter excursions throughout the 1930s.

Judge Clarence Cowles: The activities of the Burlington set are richly recorded in a variety of papers and clippings in the Clarence P. Cowles Papers and Theron S. Dean Papers, Bailey-Howe Library, University of Vermont; and the James P. Taylor Papers in the Vermont Historical Society. Further records and invaluable reminiscences were provided by John Cowles, the judge's son, and Larry Dean, long active in the GMC. Other representative early snowshoe trips up Mansfield are recounted in A. A. Twiss, "A Snow-shoe Hike over Mt. Mansfield," *The Vermonter,* vol. 23, no. 1 (no month), 1918, pp. 9–11; John K. Wright, "Stowe in Early Spring," in T. D. S. Bassett, ed., *Outsiders inside Vermont: Three Centuries of Visitors' Viewpoints on the Green Mountain State, an Anthology* (Canaan, N.H.: Phoenix Publishing, 1967), pp. 107–10; and Leroy L. Little, "Mount Mansfield on Snowshoes," *Outing* (Dec. 1920), pp. 128–31, 148.

Mansfield on skis: Letter from N. L. Goodrich to A. W. Coleman, Dec. 4, 1942, in the Charles D. Lord Papers, Bailey-Howe Library, University of Vermont. Reprinted with permission. See also in Llew Evans, "Mount Mansfield: Capstone of Vermont," *Appalachia* (June 1944), p. 52.

Camel's Hump on skis: The 1912 Camel's Hump trip is in J. R. Norton, "A Trip up Camel's Hump on Skis," *The Vermonter* (Jan. 1913), p. 23.

542   **Mansfield on skis via trail:** Robert Cate, "Operation Frostbite," *Mt. Mansfield Skiing*, (a publication of the Mt. Mansfield Ski Club), Apr. 1, 1948, pp. 1, 4.

"The long-standing feud": "Looking Back," *The Long Trail News* (May 1942), p. 14. Reprinted with permission.

Adirondacks: See especially William B. Glover, "Winter Climbs in the Adirondacks," *Adirondac* (July–Aug. 1957), pp. 64–66, 72; and *Lake Placid Club Notes* for the years 1925–29. For the authors, conversations and correspondence with Jackrabbit Johannsen, Fay Loope, Jim Goodwin, John Case, Hilda Kurth Martin, William Glover, Andrew B. Jones, and George W. Martin (sports director at the Lake Placid Club, 1927–33) were also important sources.

Haystack in 1915: Carson, *Peaks and People*, p. 106.

Giant in 1915: Glover, "Winter Climbs," pp. 64–66, 72.

Algonquin in 1923: Carson, *Peaks and People*, p. 234. T. Morris Longstreth asserts that Algonquin "and the St. Hubert mountains" were all climbed in winter before 1920; see Longstreth, "Climbing up Whiteface in Winter," *Outing* (Dec. 1920), p. 115.

Allen in 1928: Conversation with James A. Goodwin, Aug. 17, 1983.

The Reverend Andrew B. Jones: Letter from the Reverend Andrew B. Jones to L&GW, Oct. 16, 1982.

543   **"Guided daily trips":** "March Skiing," *Lake Placid Club Notes* (Nov. 1929), p. 2,112.

First Marcy overnight: The authors are grateful to two of the three participants for sharing their memories of this climb—in correspondence, Dwight Little (Dec. 27, 1980), and in conversation, Terris Moore (Dec. 9, 1980). See also Moore, "Winter Night on Marcy," *Mountain Magazine* (Oct.–Nov. 1929), pp. 18–20.

"Had lots of time": Moore, "Winter Night on Marcy," p. 20.

Suits-Sixtus-Shaw trip: Letters to L&GW from two of the participants: Chauncey Guy Suits, Feb. 9, 1981, and Lawrence H. Shaw, Dec. 12, 1980.

"Awesome" and "When the wind": Letter from Suits. Reprinted with permission.

Schaefer 1930s climbs: Newspaper accounts, mainly from the *Schenectady Gazette*, covering Schaefer's climbs were supplied to the authors from Dr. Schaefer's scrapbooks, in his possession.

Winter camping: See Warwick S. Carpenter, *Winter Camping* (New York: Outing Publishing, 1913); Perceval Sayward, "Under the Greenwood Tree in Winter and Rough Weather," *Appalachia* (Nov. 1920), pp. 45–54; W. Dustin White, *Book of Winter Sports* (New York: Houghton Mifflin, 1925); Boy Scouts of America, *Winter Camping* (New York: Boy Scouts of America,

1927); Clark S. Robinson, "Winter Camping," *Appalachia* (Dec. 1928), pp. 156–63; W. W. Cady, "Pointers on Winter Camping," *Walking News* (Feb. 1941), p. 7; A. T. Shorey, "Winter Camping," a three-part article in *Cloud Splitter* (Nov. 1941), pp. 8–9, (Dec. 1941), pp. 5–6, and (Jan. 1942), pp. 2–3; Elizabeth D. Levers and Frank Solari, "Winter Camping," *Appalachia* (Dec. 1945), pp. 529–30.

544   **"The new sport,"** and **"A sixteen-pound [sleeping] bag":** Carpenter, *Winter Camping*, pp. 14, 30.

First "how to" article: Sayward, "Under the Greenwood Tree." Quoted phrases in the remainder of this paragraph are from this article, pp. 47, 49.

"Some of these bags": White, *Book of Winter Sports*, p. 142.

Boy Scouts: B. S. A., *Winter Camping*. Quotations are from this manual, p. 5.

GE Sleeping bags: The authors had the privilege of seeing two of the original bags in the possession of Vincent Schaefer, Aug. 15, 1980.

545   **"A whole new field,"** and **"Hazardous stunt":** Shorey, "Winter Camping," part 3, p. 2, and part 1, p. 8.

CHAPTER 50. DEPRESSION, HURRICANES, AND WAR

547   **Membership in all three:** Of the three large clubs, only the AMC has good statistics on its own membership historically— at least until recent years, when club officials have been guarded about releasing data. For the other two, club publications (*The Long Trail News, Adirondac*) must be consulted, almost year by year.

One of the few: Norman J. Van Valkenburgh, *The Adirondack Forest Preserve*, appendix 8: "Recreational Use—Adirondack Forest Preserve."

548   **Civilian Conservation Corps:** John C. Paige, *The Civilian Conversation Corps and the National Park Service, 1933–1942: An Administrative History* (Washington, D.C.: National Park Service, 1985). See also chap. 38, "State Parks and the Civilian Conservation Corps," in Norman T. Newton, *Design on the Land: The Development of Landscape Architecture* (Cambridge, Mass.: The Belknap Press of Harvard University Press, 1971), pp. 576–95; Stan Cohen, *The Tree Army: A Pictorial History of the Civilian Conservation Corps, 1933–1942* (Missoula, Montana: Pictorial Histories Publishing, 1980); Conrad L. Wirth, *Parks, Politics, and People* (Norman, Okla.: University of Oklahoma Press, 1980), pp. 143–52; and Conrad Wirth and James F. Kieley, "It's 50 Years Since CCC Went into Action," *Courier* (the National Park Service Newsletter), Apr. 1983, pp. 1–3.

549   **"The CCC program":** Newton, *Design on the Land*, p. 576.

In Massachusetts: An impressive file of material on Massachuesetts CCC activity has been assembled in Region 5 headquarters of the Department of Environmental Management under the direction of Bernice O'Brien, who generously provided the authors access to this valuable collection of information. See also the annual reports of the state's commissioner of conservation during the 1930s. For other states, see a wide variety of sources, of which the following are illustrative: Harvey Paul McGuire, "The Civilian Conservation Corps in Maine: 1933–1942" (Master's thesis, University of Maine, 1966); White Mountain National Forest, "CCC 50th Anniversary, 1933–1983," an undated four-page newsprint article, ca. 1983; and Perry Merrill, *The Making of a Forester: An Autobiographical History* (Montpelier, Vt.: Published by Perry H. Merrill, 1984), pp. 118–25 (Vermont).

549   **During the early 1930s:** Few contemporary accounts can be found about the proposed Presidentials highway. A systematic argument against it by R. Ammi Cutter ("Some Objections to the Skyline Highway") appeared in the *Plymouth* [N.H.] *Record*, Oct. 27, 1934, pp. 1, 7. Raymond W. Evans of Crawford Notch recalls work on the survey for this road, (conversation with Raymond Evans, July 26, 1983). See "Skyline Drive," *Mount Washington Observatory News Bulletin* (Fall 1986), pp. 63–70.

550   **During the mid-1930s:** The Long Trail News between 1934 and 1936 contains many reports on the status of the Vermont skyline drive. A convenient summary has been written by John A. Douglass, "History of the Green Mountain National Forest, Vermont," an unpublished typescript in the files of the GMNF, see especially pp. 83–84. See Nancy Price Graff, "A Long, Winding Road Not Taken: The History and Legacy of the Green Mountain Parkway," *Vermont Life* (Spring 1986), pp. 14–19. The activities of Yard are alluded to in various letters to Perceval Baxter (July 16, 1937, and October 12, 1937), in the Baxter Papers, folder 73, Maine State Library; and of Marshall in Memoranda in the MacKaye Family Papers, Dartmouth College Library—for example, an undated memorandum "to the Secretary" on "The Proposed Green Mountain Parkway" (box 214, folder 4).

September 1938: A contemporary overview of the 1938 hurricane was compiled by the Federal Writers' Project, *New England Hurricane: A Factual, Pictorial Record* (Boston: Hale, Cushman & Flint, 1938).

It took twenty-five: Conversation with John Hitchcock, Sept. 2, 1982.

551   **"There were miles":** "The Trail," *The Long Trail News* (Oct. 1939), p. 2.

"Nightfall found him": John Hutton, "Windthrow," *Appalachia* (June 1939), p. 324. Hutton's article is an excellent summary of the impact on the White Mountain trail system.

On Monadnock: Letter from William P. House to Howard M. Goff, *AMC White Mountain Guide* editor, May 20, 1929, AMC trail crew files, Pinkham Notch Camp.

On the Maine AT: Conversation with Roy Fairfield, Sept. 26, 1983.

For the 1940 edition: "Report of the Councilor of Topography and Exploration," *Annual Report of the Appalachian Mountain Club*, 1940, p. 17.

551   The Adirondacks were: A description of the 1950 hurricane from the hikers' viewpoint is P. Schuyler Miller, "The Blow-Down," *Adirondac* (March–Apr. 1951), pp. 26–27, 40.

"Beyond anything ever": Letter from Peter B. Duryea, commissioner of the Conservation Department, to Nathaniel L. Goldstein, attorney general, Dec. 12, 1950, reprinted in *The Conservationist* (Feb.–March 1951), p. 2.

552   "Oceans of fallen": Editor's Introduction by Philip G. Terrie, Jr., in Carson, *Peaks and People*, 1973 edition, p. lxxxi; reprinted with permission. Terrie provides an excellent summary of the impact of the storm on Adirondacks hiking, pp. lxxxi–lxxxii.

"Recognizing the danger": Open letter from Grace Hudowalski et al. to fifty people classified as "Aspiring 46ers," June 28, 1954, published in *Adirondac* (July–Aug. 1954), p. 64. Reprinted with permission.

"The first hour": Rudolph Strobel, "After the Blowdown," *Adirondac* (May–June 1956), pp. 48–49, 56. See also Paul Van Dyke, "After the Storm," *Adirondac* (March–Apr. 1951), p. 33.

"Broken-toothed comb": Duane H. Nash, "The Sewards—1955," *Adirondac* (Nov.–Dec. 1955), p. 105. Reprinted with permission.

"The real shock": *Ibid.*

"An art in itself," and "A truly unique": Terrie, editor's Introduction to *Peaks and People*, 1973 edition, p. lxxxii. Reprinted with permission.

554   "During the war": Letter from Robert Schulz to L&GW, Oct. 6, 1982. Reprinted with permission.

"We had the roads": Letter from Theodore Brown to Reuben Rajala, Nov. 20, 1980, in trail crew history files, Appalachian Mountain Club, Pinkham Notch Camp. Reprinted with permission.

First female "hutmen": See Jane Atwood Black, "Hutmen F: Pinkham Notch Camp in the Forties," *Appalachia* (Dec. 1987), pp. 36–51.

"Fiercely in her eighties": Alex MacPhail, "Las Machas," *Appalachian Bulletin* (Oct. 1984), p. 12. The authors are grateful to Calista Harris for sharing her recollections of wartime Zealand Hut on several occasions.

"Blame Hitler": Louis B. Puffer, "Green Mountain Club in Wartime," *Cloud Splitter* (June–Sept. 1943), p. 2.

"An abandoned camp": Arthur W. Lord, "Pamola Pilgrimage," *Appalachia* (June 1943), p. 305.

"A deserted land": "1944 Work Trip to Maine," Potomac Appalachian Trail Club *Bulletin* (Apr. 1944), p. 25.

"The Connecticut Forest": W. R. Hamlin, "Annual Meeting of the New England Trail Conference," *Appalachia* (June 1942), p. 133. Reprinted with the permission of the Appalachian Mountain Club.

555 **"War or no war":** Letter from Margaret Fayerweather to *IOCAlum Newsletter* (Oct. 1943), p. 1. Reprinted with permission. A complete set of this newsletter is on file at the University of Wyoming.

"They all want": *Ibid.*

"We were in the woods": Letter from Theodore Brown to Reuben Rajala, Nov. 20, 1980. Reprinted with permission.

Rosebrook Range: The authors are indebted to Raymond W. Evans for showing us the location of the old Rosebrook Range trails, now almost completely undiscernible in the regrown forest.

PART FIVE. MOUNTAINS AS PLACES FOR RECREATION: SINCE 1950.

561 **"Quite a lot," and "Nothing of importance":** James Hilton, *Lost Horizon* (New York: William Morrow, 1934), pp. 133–34.

"The contemporary has": Barbara Tuchman, *Practicing History* (New York: Alfred A. Knopf, 1981), p. 28. In this book Tuchman gives her opinion that "a historian needs, I think, a perspective of at least twenty-five years, and preferably fifty, to form an opinion of any value" (p. 273).

CHAPTER 51. THE BACKPACKING BOOM

563 **The backpacking boom:** Of many articles describing the boom while it was in progress, a representative example is Susan Sands, "Backpacking: 'I Go to the Wilderness to Kick the Man-World Out of Me' " *New York Times*, May 9, 1971, sec. X, p. 1. One of the more lucid analyses of the forces behind the boom, also written at its height, was Harvey Manning, "Where Did All These Damn Hikers Come From?" *Backpacker*, (Summer 1975), pp. 36–41 ff. For many other sources, see specific citations in this and later chapters.

Figures 51.1 and 51.2: AMC membership and hut use: Appalachian Mountain Club. GMC membership and Mansfield shelter use: *The Long Trail News*. ADK membership: *Adirondac* and Adirondack Mountain Club. Allagash campers: Maine Bureau of Parks and Recreation. Massachusetts campers: Massachusetts Division of Forests and Parks. AT hikers: Appalachian Trail Conference. Forty-Sixers: Adirondack Forty-Sixers. Rock climbers: Mohonk Preserve. New York park campers: New York Department of Environmental Conservation.

1961 National Geographic: William O. Douglas, "The Friendly Huts of the White Mountains," *National Geographic* (August 1961), pp. 205–39.

568 **Of twelve how-to guides:** Denise Van Lear, "Books," *Backpacker* (Spring 1973), pp. 8–10.

"There are certain": Robert Marshall, quoted in Fox, *John Muir and His Legacy*, p. 208.

"What was paradise": Letter from Mildred and Armand Siegel, in *The Long Trail News* (Feb. 1973), p. 5. Reprinted with permission.

569 **"90 % of the hikers":** George S. James, "National Forest Backcountry in New England—Problems and Opportunities," *Appalachia* (Dec. 1970), p. 24.

"On well over half": Letter from Fred M. Hunt to L&GW, Apr. 27, 1982. Reprinted with permission.

One report on: Benjamin Read, "Backcountry Management Problems," unpublished AMC report, undated (ca. 1973), Research Department files, Pinkham Notch Camp. Reprinted with the permission of the Appalachian Mountain Club.

Desperate scenarios: See. for example, Edward L. Spencer and Mark Dannenhauer, "The A. M. C. Shelters: What Future?" unpublished AMC report, undated (ca. 1969), trail crew files, Pinkham Notch Camp; Philip D. Levin, "For Future Generations," *Appalachia* (Dec. 1970), pp. 5–19; and Read, "Backcountry Management Problems."

570 **"Hiking and backpacking":** Nelson Obus, quoted in Arlyn Powell, "The Future of Backpacking," *New England Outdoors* (Winter 1980), p. 28.

CHAPTER 52. ENVIRONMENTAL ETHICS AND BACKCOUNTRY MANAGEMENT

575 **"If you want":** Arthur C. Mack, *Enjoying the Catskills* (New York: Funk & Wagnalls, 1950), p. 74.

"Always trench for drainage": *Ibid.*, p. 75.

"Islands of blight": Elizabeth D. Levers, "Litterbugs and Hikers," *Appalachia* (Dec. 1965), p. 777.

The first organized: The pioneering litter cleanup was originally described in Levers, "Litterbugs and Hikers," pp. 776–77, and (a somewhat more extended description) in a note by Levers under the heading of "Conservation" in *Appalachia* (Dec. 1967), pp. 767–70. Among annual write-ups of litter cleanup efforts since, in *Trail Walker*, the journal of the New York-New Jersey Trail Conference, see especially Barbara Methvin, "Litter Day in Its 20th Year" (Oct.–Nov. 1984), p. 6.

576 **"The job will":** Levers, "Litterbugs and Hikers," p. 777.

In the Adirondacks: "Operation Cleanup," *Adirondac* (Sept.-Oct. 1966), pp. 86–87.

Levers had noticed: Levers, "Conservation" note, p. 769.

Hiker's pocket: Conversation with Norman A. Greist, Oct. 21, 1981.

577 **In August 1969:** "Erosion, Pollution Close Katahdin Camping Area—Baxter State Park," *Appalachia* (Dec. 1970), pp. 132–34. For background on this decision and its subsequent reversal, the authors also profited from a conversation with Baxter Park Supervisor Irvin C. Caverly, July 13, 1977.

"We have to move": "Erosion, Pollution Close Katahdin," p. 132.

577   **Mansfield's summit area:** "Mt. Mansfield Project," *The Long Trail News* (May 1971), p. 8. Many Vermonters involved in the first environmental protection efforts on Mansfield kindly shared their recollections of these early years, among whom we are particularly grateful to Kenn Boyd, Coralie Magoon, and Harry T. Peet, Jr., of the Green Mountain Club; Rodney Barber and Charles Johnson of the Vermont Department of Forests, Parks, and Recreation; and Hubert W. Vogelmann of the University of Vermont.

578   **First full-time ranger:** Vermont Department of Forests and Parks, *Biennial Report: 1969–1970*, p. 72.

       Also that summer: The start-up of the Burlington Section's caretaker program is not systematically documented in the parent GMC's *The Long Trail News*. The first mention is buried in the Burlington Section's report in the Nov. 1969 issue, p. 6. A more complete story was Kenn Boyd, "Why Caretakers?" (Aug. 1970), p. 4.

       In October 1969: The most useful source for information on the launching of the Green Mountain Profile Committee is a notebook labeled "Promotion of the State of Vermont" in the files of Hubert W. Vogelmann. Other relevant documents from these files, which Professor Vogelmann generously allowed us to peruse, include an unsigned brochure, *The Green Mountains*, dated 1970; Francis A. Young, "Profile for Posterity: Saving the Skylines of Vermont," *National Parks & Conservation Magazine* (Feb. 1971), pp. 20–24; and Green Mountain Profile Committee, Mountain Ecology, a brochure dated May 1971. A short but more accessible account is Hubert Vogelmann, "Committee Organized to Protect Green Mountain Profile," *The Long Trail News* (Nov. 1969), p. 1.

       An ecological approach: Unsigned typescript, "An Ecological Approach to the Preservation of the Green Mountain Profile," June 1969, in the files of Hubert W. Vogelmann.

       Shirley Strong: Virtually every Vermonter we asked about the beginning of environmental concerns in the Green Mountains went out of his or her way to express respect for the constructive and dynamic role played by Shirley Strong.

       "The driving force": Conversation with Hubert W. Vogelmann, May 6, 1987.

       "The increasing number": Shirley Strong, "President's Message," *The Long Trail News* (Feb. 1970), p. 1. Reprinted with permission.

       In the White: Edward L. Spencer and Mark Dannenhauer, "The A. M. C. Shelters: What Future," unpublished document in the files of the trail crew at AMC's Pinkham Notch Camp.

       In the Adirondacks: Reports of the Temporary Study Commission, *The Future of the Adirondacks*. The most useful edition is a two-volume publication by the Adirondack Museum, Blue Mountain Lake, N.Y., issued in 1971. The authors also learned much about the start-up of environmental safeguards in the Adirondacks from numerous individuals in both state agencies and conservation organizations, among whom special thanks are due to David Newhouse.

578   **"The state's first":** Conversation with David Newhouse, Aug. 18, 1986.

579   **In 1969 both:** Examples include *This Is the Adirondack Mountain Club,* informational brochure of the Adirondack Mountain Club, 1969; and *Mountain Manners—Don'ts, Why Nots, and Dos,* educational brochure of the Adirondack Forty-Sixers, 1969. Copies of both are in the authors' files.

And it was in 1969: See various articles and letters, *Adirondack Peeks* (Spring 1970), pp. 8–12, including a letter from David Newhouse to William Weissinger, p. 10.

No Northeastern peak: A full description of the Monadnock Ecocenter and its original purposes and programs is contained in an unpublished, unsigned and undated typescript entitled "Ecocenter" in the archives of the Society for the Protection of New Hampshire Forests. The ecocenter is also described in Baldwin, *Monadnock Guide,* pp. 12–13. See also Ann L. Royce, "Monadnock Past and Present," *Forest Notes* (Summer 1970), pp. 3–6.

"Orient the climbing": "Ecocenter," typescript, p. 1. Reprinted with permission.

"Make the public": *Ibid.*

580   **Since 1950 Baxter Park:** Baxter State Park's 1971 regulations were printed in their entirety in Baxter State Park Authority, "Notification of Changes in Rules and Regulations, Baxter State Park, Revision 1971," *Appalachia* (Dec. 1971), pp. 194–98. A complete history of earlier Baxter Park regulations is in Hakola, *Legacy of a Lifetime,* chap. 12, "Administration, 1950–1969: Rules & Regulations," pp. 229–42.

The rangers installed: The evolution of ranger-naturalist and shelter caretaker programs may be followed in the Green Mountain Club's *The Long Trail News,* beginning in 1969. See especially Gardiner Lane, Sally S. Spear, and Larry Van Meter, "Happenings on the Hump: A Comprehensive Ranger Program" *The Long Trail News* (Feb. 1975), pp. 1–3, and Van Meter, "Camel's Hump Ranger Program May Expand to Mt. Mansfield" *The Long Trail News* (May 1975), p. 2. The authors are also indebted to several GMC leaders for many conversations in which this evolution was described, notably Harry T. Peet, Jr. (Nov. 3, 1980), Kenn Boyd (Nov. 5, 1980), John P. Harrington (numerous occasions), Gardiner B. Lane (May 15, 1983), Roderick Rice (June 25, 1981), and Donald M. Wallace (Oct. 16, 1986).

"Low-key on-site": Van Meter, "Camel's Hump Ranger Program," p. 2.

581   **"We keep watch":** Pieter Crow, "A Day in the Life of a GMC Ranger-Naturalist," *Ridge Lines* (Burlington Section GMC, newsletter), June 1981, p. 2. Reprinted with permission.

"There, I have just": *Ibid.*

581   **Down below treeline:** Kenn Boyd, "Why Caretakers?" *The Long Trail News* (Aug. 1970), p. 4, and Boyd, "Caretaker Program," *The Long Trail News* (Nov. 1971), p. 4.

"**Multi-purpose,**" and "**Public relations people**": Boyd, "Why Caretakers?" p. 4.

"**We're not here**": John Vara, "Vermont's National Forest Is More Than Trees," *Vermont Life* (Summer 1982), p. 21.

Adopt-a-Shelter: This GMC program was announced in "GMC 'Adopt A Shelter' Program," *The Long Trail News* (Nov. 1970), p. 3. For additional information on its progress, the authors are indebted to conversations with GMC leaders mentioned above, especially Donald M. Wallace.

582   **On July 26, 1970:** The background for the AMC trail crew's shelter removal was a 1969 report by Edward L. Spencer and Mark A. Dannenhauer, "The A. M. C. Shelters: What Future," an unpublished document, a copy of which is in the trail crew files at AMC's Pinkham Notch headquarters. The early shelter removals are described in Stephen Page, "Liberty Springs Tentsite Area—Pilot Project," *Appalachia* (Dec. 1970), pp. 116–20, and Robert D. Proudman, "Caretaking on Mt. Garfield," *Appalachia* (Dec. 1971), pp. 199–201.

"**The kingpin of the whole program**": Proudman, "Caretaking on Mt. Garfield," p. 199.

In 1971 the Liberty: The authoritative history of White Mountain shelters, including the period when their numbers were substantially reduced, is Ned Therrien, "Hiking Trail Shelters and Their Management on the White Mountain National Forest," June 1987, a paper on file with the White Mountain National Forest, Laconia, N.H.

In 1971 WMNF officials: Robert B. MacHaffie, "Campsite Betterment," *Appalachia Bulletin* (May 1976), pp. 22–24. White Mountain National Forest regulations may be found in the files at WMNF headquarters in Laconia, N.H. The authors wish to thank Ned Therrien, public information officer of WMNF, for assistance in identifying key stages in their development.

583   **WMNF officials also carried:** Ned Therrien, "Search for the Silent Majority," *Appalachia Bulletin* (Aug.–Sept. 1975), pp. 11, 21.

In 1971 the AMC: Information on AMC programs may be found in issues of *Appalachia* and *Appalachia Bulletin* during the 1970s and 1980s. Two useful overviews on the early stages are George S. James, "National Forest Backcountry in New England," *Appalachia* (Dec. 1970), pp. 20–30, and a series of short articles by W. Kent Olsen et al., in a section entitled "White Mountain National Forest," *Appalachia* (June 1972), pp. 145–56.

The issue was debated: Some of the more eloquent pleas on both sides appeared in the pages of *Adirondack Peeks*. See, for example, Jim Dittmar, "In Memoriam" (Winter 1976), pp. 9–11; C. Peter Fish, "A Ranger's Outlook from the High Peaks" (Winter 1977), pp. 25–28; E. H. Ketchledge, "President's Message" (Summer 1978), pp. 28–33; and the moving letter to the editor from Carolyn Schaefer (Winter 1978), p. 6.

584 **Aggressive educational program:** See, for example, *For the Beginner Hiker: Some Trail Tips to Help You Enjoy Your Hike, For the Summer Backpacker,* and other informational brochures produced by the Adirondack Mountain Club during the mid-1970s; and Marion Fresn, "46er Wilderness Leadership Workshop," *Adirondack Peeks* (Spring 1972), p. 9, and write-ups of subsequent workshops in later issues of Peeks.

ADK ridge-runners: The original ADK ridge-runner program was described in Doris H. Herwig, "What Is a Ridge Runner?" a four-part series in *Adirondac* (Dec. 1974), pp. 130–33, (Feb. 1975), pp. 9–11 ff, (Apr. 1975), pp. 32–33 ff, (June 1975), pp. 52–53. See also Herwig, "Ridge Runners 1975," *Adirondac* (Feb. 1976), pp. 8–10. The authors are grateful for the opportunity to review memoranda on this program in the files of the Adirondack Mountain Club, Glens Falls, N.Y.

"My job is": "Tony Goodwin," typescript in files of the Adirondack Mountain Club, undated, ca. 1974. Reprinted with permission of the Adirondack Mountain Club, Inc. and Tony Goodwin.

C. Peter Fish: The authors' information on Ranger Fish comes principally from personal contact and correspondence with Fish, as well as conversations with numerous other Adirondack hikers. One published exposition of Fish's views appears in C. Peter Fish, "A Ranger's Outlook from the High Peaks," *Adirondack Peeks* (Winter 1977), pp. 25–28.

585 **The ridge-runner concept:** Connecticut's original ridge-runner program does not seem to have been well documented in any printed source. It is alluded to in the "History of the Connecticut Chapter, Appalachian Mountain Club, 1921–1981," pp. 109, 114, 119, but not fully described. The authors are indebted to conversations with Connecticut trail leaders, including especially Robert Redington (Apr. 13, 1984) and Norman Sills (Oct. 23, 1981), for an understanding of the background of this program. For its extension into Massachusetts, we profited from conversations with Robert Hatton (Apr. 16, 1986), Katherine Wood (Apr. 14, 1986), Rudy Yondorf (Apr. 14, 1986), and others. A perspective on the program in both states is Sue Van Der Zee, "Ridgerunners: Roving Caretakers Assist Trail Users in New England," *Appalachian Trailway News* (Nov.–Dec. 1984), pp. 14–15.

586 **During the mid-1960s:** The Adirondack summit reseeding program was described in its early stages in E. H. Ketchledge and R. E. Leonard, "The Impact of Man on the Adirondack High Country," *The Conservationist* (Oct.–Nov. 1970), pp. 14–18, and E. H. Ketchledge, "Progress Report: High Peak Erosion Studies, 1973," *Adirondack Peeks*, (Spring 1973), pp. 8–9. For later perspectives and a more complete analysis of the program, see E. H. Ketchledge and R. E. Leonard, "A 24-Year Comparison of the Vegetation of an Adirondack Mountain Summit," *Rhodora* (Oct. 1984), pp. 439–44, and E. H. Ketchledge, R. E. Leonard et al., "Rehabilitation of Alpine Vegetation in

the Adirondack Mountains of New York State," U.S. Forest Service, Northeastern Forest Experiment Station, Research Paper NE-553, 1985.

587 **At-treeline signs:** The messages were copied by the authors directly from signs at treeline in the three ranges.

A major focus: The best summary of the dwarf cinquefoil problem and the evolution of programs to deal with it is Kenneth Kimball, "Mountain Rescue for a Flower: AMC Research Focuses on a Rare Alpine Plant," *Appalachia Bulletin* (Sept. 1987), pp. 8–10. For more details, see Kenneth D. Kimball, "Potentilla Robbinsiana Recovery Program Progress," U.S. Department of Endangered Species Technical Bulletin X (5): 6, 11 (1985); E. A. Norse et al., "Conserving Biological Diversity in Our National Forest," The Wilderness Society, 1986, pp. 88–89; and K. D. Kimball and R. Paul, "Potentilla Robbinsiana —Autoecological, Reproductive Biology and Management Study (1985 Progress Report)," an Appalachian Mountain Club Research Technical Report.

588 **Management plans:** The three management plans cited as examples are White Mountain National Forest, draft, "Presidential Unit Plan," Dec. 20, 1978; Appalachian Trail Project Office, "Comprehensive Plan for the Protection, Management, Development and Use of the Appalachian National Scenic Trail," Sept. 1981; and Appalachian Trail Project Office, "Appalachian National Scenic Trail Case Study: Final Report," March 1, 1982.

CHAPTER 53. BACKCOUNTRY CAMPING IN THE SEVENTIES AND EIGHTIES

589 **A special niche:** Among profiles of the Limmer boot operation, see Laird Hart, "The Limmers Make Boots to Last—If You Can Affort to Wait," *Wall Street Journal* Nov. 11, 1974, pp. 1, 23; Allan Pospisil, "Waiting for Limmers," *Country Journal* (March 1980), pp. 88–96; and D. W. Roberts, "Limmers Boots Hike the World," *New Hampshire Profiles* (March 1987), pp. 47–55.

590 **During the 1950s:** The Maine shelter-building program is documented in the files of the Maine Appalachian Trail Club.

Comparison of leading outfitters': Two companies whose catalogues are of special value, because both were important suppliers to Northeastern backpackers throughout the period under discussion, are Eastern Mountain Sports of Peterborough, N.H., and Recreational Equipment, Inc., of Seattle, Wash.

591 **A 1983 Business Week:** "Backpacking Is Easier than Ever," *Business Week* (Aug. 1, 1983), p. 100.

Advertisements in one issue: *Backpacker* (March 1983), pp. 2, 6, 7, 17, 32, 35, 47.

The new breed: Among many discussions of the new approach to backcountry camping, one that was written during the backpacking boom is illustrative: John B. Nutter, "The New Outdoorsman," *Appalachia* (June 1972), pp. 75–81.

592   **AMC hut system:** Representative pieces include Peter Crane, "Carter Notch Hut: An Introductory Essay" (Spring 1981), a typescript in the authors' files; Alex MacPhail's three-part series on women in the hut system in *Appalachia Bulletin*, "Las Machas" (Oct. 1984), pp. 12–14, (Nov. 1984), pp. 12–21, and (Dec. 1984), pp. 16–19; William Reifsnyder, *High Huts of the White Mountains* (Boston: Appalachian Mountain Club, 1979); and Daniel Ford, *The Country Northward* (Somersworth, N.H.: New Hampshire Publishing, 1976).

593   **"No-trace" or "low-impact" camping:** One such program, that of Vermont's Killington Adventure camps, is described in David Langlois, "Clean Camping," *Appalachia* (Dec. 1975), pp. 83–89.

     Publication data for the books cited in the text are: *Manning:* Seattle, Wash.: REI Press, 1972. *Saijo:* San Francisco: 101 Productions, 1972. *Roberts:* Boston: Stone Wall Press, 1975.

     Books devoted entirely: Two examples are Laura Waterman and Guy Waterman, *Backwoods Ethics: Environmental Concerns for Hikers and Campers* (Boston: Stone Wall Press, 1979), and John Hart, *Walking Softly in the Wilderness: Sierra Club Guide to Backpacking* (San Francisco, Calif.: Sierra Club Books, 1984).

CHAPTER 54. THE CLUBS COPE WITH CHANGE

595   **The AMC, eldest:** Data on AMC membership is from club headquarters in Boston. Membership data has not been regularly reported during the 1980s. Reliable data is not available.

     The Connecticut Chapter: A superb historical document is the "History of Connecticut Chapter, Appalachian Mountain Club: 1921–1981," assembled under Gardner Moulton, chairman of the chapter's History Committee, 1981.

     "Family": The "family" analogy recurred in conversation with members of the AMC's Connecticut Chapter and in its literature. See, for example, "History of Connecticut Chapter," pp. ii–iii.

596   **The Maine Chapter:** Data from Leroy D. Cross, "A History of the Maine Chapter of the AMC: 1956–1975," *Appalachia* (Dec. 1976), p. 47.

     "Reached some kind": Letter from Harry Smith to L&GW, June 4, 1981. Reprinted with permission.

     "It was a club": Conversation with Carl O. Chauncey, Oct. 25, 1982.

     In the ADK: Data on voting membership from the Adirondack Mountain Club.

     The GMC's growth: Data compiled by authors from *The Long Trail News*.

597   **Sub Sig:** Conversation with George Ehrenfried, Aug. 29, 1982, and an address by Ehrenfried before the New England Trail Conference in 1954, a typescript copy of which was graciously loaned to the authors by Mr. Ehrenfried.

597   **"Jabe was a very":** Letter from Stewart Coffin to L&GW, Apr. 29, 1987. Reprinted with permission.

598   **"The best known":** Ehrenfried, 1954 address, p. 13.

       Wilton Outing Club: Letter from Mrs. Lawson Reeves to L&GW, June 9, 1982, and files of MATC.

       Maine Trail Trotters: Letter from Carl Newhall to L&GW, Dec. 26, 1981, and obituary by David Field for Newhall, *Appalachian Trailway News* (July–Aug. 1985), p. 22.

       Berkshire Knapsackers: Conversation with Werner Bachli, Apr. 7, 1984, and with Katherine Wood, Apr. 14, 1986.

       The AMC's New York Chapter: Data on chapter membership was kindly provided to the authors by Adele Lerner, Doris Davis, and Robert Bliss.

       Comparing fall 1982 bulletins: Copies of these bulletins are in the authors' files.

599   **Essex County Trail Walkers:** Letters to L&GW, with club material enclosed, from Al Kent, Aug. 17, 1981, and from Mary Cerulli, Aug. 22, 1981.

       Co-op City Hiking Club: Letter from Nat Lester to L&GW, Jan. 21, 1982.

       Long Island Greenbelt Trail Conference: Data from the conference's newsletter, *Greenbelting Long Island*, 1982–86.

       College Alumni Hiking Club: Conversation with Esther Weitz and Barbara and Richard H. Tourin, Jan. 31, 1982.

600   **Sundance Outdoor Adventure Society:** Letter from Leonard Magnus to L&GW, May 15, 1982.

       Ralph's Peak Hikers: Letter from Ralph Ferrusi to L&GW, with accompanying club material, Jan. 12, 1984.

       "The only shelter" and **"Once suggested we change":** *Ibid.* Reprinted with permission.

       The Dartmouth Outing Club: The quoted passage is from John S. Dickey, "A Word of Appreciation," *Dartmouth Out o'Doors* (Fall 1954), inside front cover. For background on the DOC, see its records in the archives, Dartmouth College Library, and a monumental history of the club by David Hooke, *Reaching That Peak: 75 Years of the Dartmouth Outing Club* (Canaan, N.H.: Phoenix Publishing, 1987). The authors also benefited from conversations with Robert Monahan, June 13, 1980, and July 8, 1980, and with John Rand, July 19, 1981.

601   **Bates Outing Club:** See club records in the archives at Bates College Library. The authors profited from conversations with Roy O. Fairfield, Sept. 26, 1983, Richard Sampson, Sept. 27, 1983, and Judy Marden, numerous occasions.

601 **IOCA:** The *IOCAlum Newsletter* is an invaluable source for IOCA history. The authors are grateful to Ann Knudsen for lending us voluminous files of this newsletter and related IOCA documents. Among many talks with ex-college outing club hikers, an outstandingly valuable conversation was with Gardner Perry III, June 8, 1981.

CHAPTER 55. NORTHEASTERN TRAIL SYSTEMS MATURE

603 **In Baxter State Park:** An excellent source for postwar trails history on Katahdin through 1970 is Hakola, *Legacy of a Lifetime*, chap. 15: "Administration, 1950–1969: Trails," pp. 269–80.

604 **In the Adirondacks:** The authors again gratefully acknowledge the guidance of James A. Goodwin in tracing Adirondacks trails history.

On Monadnock: See Henry I. Baldwin, *Monadnock Guide.*

In the White Mountains: In addition to comparisons of *AMC White Mountain Guides*, the authors were aided immensely by the personal knowledge of the area on the part of Raymond W. Evans.

605 **On Long Island:** The Long Island Greenbelt Trail Conference issues a quarterly newsletter, *Greenbelting L. I.*, with news of its trails and scheduled hikes.

606 **"In an effort":** George Fisher, "Planting the Seed," *Greenbelting L. I.*, (Spring 1987), p. 3. Reprinted with permission.

"On a cold": *Ibid.*

"From Northern State Parkway": Dick Schultz, "Blazes," *Greenbelting L. I.*, (Winter 1985–1986), p. 6.

"The World Trade Center": "Nassau Notes," *Greenbelting L. I.*, (Spring 1985), p. 4.

Trail workers caught in a downpour: George Fisher, "Nassau Notes," *Greenbelting L. I.*, (Winter 1984–1985), p. 3.

Sleeping Giant trails: The sleeping Giant Park Association distributes a brochure showing trails. Their history is touched on in Harrison Eldredge, "Sleeping Giant Marks 60th Anniversary," *Connecticut Woodlands* (Winter 1983–1984), pp. 4–5, and Nancy Davis Sachse, *Born Among the Hills: The Sleeping Giant Story* (Hamden, Conn.: The Sleeping Giant Park Association, 1982). The authors also learned much directly from Norman A. Greist (Oct. 21, 1981).

Eastern Connecticut trails: These trails have been reported on periodically in the *Norwich* [Conn.] *Bulletin;* see, for examples, Ralph W. Mills, "Volunteers Blaze Pachaug Trail, Newest in Eastern Conn. System," Aug. 20, 1960, p. 7; "Two New Trails in Area," Oct. 4, 1962, p. 16; Erwin Goldstein, "Weekend Trail Blazer Preserves Forest for State's Hikers," Aug. 14, 1974, p. 28. The authors are indebted to Lawrence Tringe for much information on these trails received in correspondence of March 7, 1983, March 17, 1983, and March 25, 1983.

606   **Catskills trails:** These trails are described in periodically updated booklets distributed by the DEC under the title "Catskill Trails." The authors were greatly assisted in dating the construction of Catskill trails by several active and retired DEC officials, including Edward Jacoby, Victor Schrader, Daniel Showers, Stanley Engel (these four on Oct. 18, 1982), C. Peter Fish (Sept. 27, 1982), and Edward G. West (Oct. 10, 1982).

During the Late 1940s: Among other sources, the authors are indebted to a conversation with Mead Bradner (Dec. 4, 1982).

At about the same: Philip M. Perry, "Banfield's Harvest," *New England Galaxy* (Fall 1975), pp. 19–24. The authors are also indebted to conversations wtih Walter Banfield (Oct. 15, 1982), Carl O. Chauncey (Oct. 25, 1982), E. Porter Dickinson (Oct. 26, 1986, and other occasions), Forrest E. House (Oct. 25, 1982), and correspondence with Alden Holt (Apr. 17, 1983, Apr. 19, 1983, and May 9, 1983).

607   **A trio of:** For the postwar history of these trails, the authors are most thankful for the personal recollections and invaluable record of Robert J. Redington (Apr. 13, 1984). For the Taconic Crest Trail, see also the guidebook by that name published and distributed by the Taconic Hiking Club of Troy, N.Y.

608   **Mid-State Trail:** Conversations and correspondence with Robert Humes and John Hitchcock.

The Society for: See the periodically updated trail guide, *The Monadnock-Sunapee Greenway*, a joint production of the Society for the Protection of New Hampshire Forests and the Appalachian Mountain Club.

609   **In New York State:** The progress of the Long Path has been reported frequently in *Trail Walker*, journal of the New York–New Jersey Trail Conference. For example, see "Long Path Celebration," and "A Happy Day in the Catskills," *Trail Walker* (Dec.–Jan. 1988), p. 1.

CHAPTER 56. NEW PATHS FOR TRAIL MAINTENANCE

611   **Novice Massachusetts trail workers:** Banfield's spectacular abilities with the swizzle stick were recounted by virtually every Massachusetts trail worker contacted by the authors.

Some more exotic: Conversation with Mead Bradner, Dec. 9, 1982.

612   **Tops in prestige:** No written word has ever adequately captured the history and spirit of the AMC trail crew. Illuminating glimmerings may be obtained from the AMC Trail Crew Associaton's newsletter *Chips and Clippings*, issued since March 1958. One effort to capture something of the flavor is Alan S. Thorndike, "Trail Crew Thoughts," *Appalachia* (Dec. 1966), pp. 357–69. The authors were greatly aided by talks with Robert D. Proudman (Sept. 7,

1982) and Reuben Rajala (Aug. 18, 1982), trails supervisors since 1971, and various postwar trail crew members.

612 **"Laughter and joy"**: Robert D. Proudman, "Keeping in Step: AMC Trail Crew," *Appalachia Bulletin* (Nov. 1977), p. 12.

"The only man": Cited in a note in *Chips and Clippings* (Nov. 1, 1959), p. 1.

Less well known: The authors are grateful to David Field and Barbara Clark for the opportunity to study the archives of the Maine Appalachian Trail Club. Those two and Stephen Clark also gave us the benefit of their long personal association with the MATC. Conversations as follows: Barbara Clark (July 18, 1981), Sephen Clark (July 15, 1982), David Field (July 13, 1981).

613 **In Vermont**: Postwar Long Trail maintenance can best be studied by perusal of the GMC's *The Long Trail News*. Helpful to the authors were conversations with many GMC leaders, including Andrew Buchanan, Lawrence Dean, John P. Harrington, Harry T. Peet, Jr., Roderick Rice, and Donald M. Wallace.

In the Adirondacks: Adirondack trail maintenance is not well reported in any single source, although the ADK's *Adirondac* contains articles on the subject from time to time, and *Adirondack Peeks* covers work by the Forty-Sixers. Two examples are Robert D. Hofer, "Sixty Years of Trail Activities," *Adirondac* (Nov. 1982), pp. 24–25, and John S. Wood, "Algonquin Rockwork," *Adirondac* (July 1983), pp. 8–9. The authors were generously advised on the subject by Terry Healy (Sept. 29, 1982), Herbert Lamb (Oct. 1, 1982), and C. Peter Fish of the DEC, James A. Goodwin and others.

One other organized: Seymour Smith (?), "Chapter Trail Committee 1957–1977," typescript on the Connecticut roving trail crew, supplied to the authors by Mr. Smith; AMC, History of *Connecticut Chapter*, p. 112; and conversation with John Hibbard and Seymour Smith, Oct. 22, 1981. In the "Notes" sections of *Appalachia* during the 1950s and early 1960s, activities of this crew were occasionally reported.

But the more common pattern: Our descriptions of individual trail maintainers and generalizations concerning the species are the product of several years of conversations with Northeastern trail maintainers and participation in many work parties.

614 **"I know for a fact"**: Conversation with George K. Libby, Apr. 4, 1984.

616 **"There were two"**: Conversation with Werner Bachli, Apr. 7, 1984.

NETC: Access to NETC archives was kindly provided by Forrest E. House. The authors also appreciated the opportunity to talk with past chairmen Chauncey, Hitchcock, and Banfield.

A fundamental shift: Robert D. Proudman, *AMC Field Guide to Trail Building and Maintenance* (Boston: Appalachian Mountain Club, 1977) is the basic document on modern trail maintenance. *Backpacker* magazine produced a three-part series on modern trail maintenance: Jim Chase, "Overuse: The Long Trail Back" (Nov. 1986), pp. 25–30; Perri Knize and Jim Chase, "The New Intruders" (Jan 1987), pp. 32–37; and Jim Chase, "Look, but Don't Touch" (March 1987), pp. 64–72. A prolific source of descriptions of trail maintenance techniques and specific work done, with primary emphasis on the Appalachian Trail, is the monthly newsletter on the subject prepared and distributed by the Appalachian Trail Conference, *The Register*. Other club publications frequently feature stories on trail maintenance. The authors are grateful to many leaders in modern trail methods for their recollections of the evolution of new tools and techniques, especially Robert D. Proudman, Reuben Rajala, Ned Therrien, Tony Goodwin, David Field, and others.

616   **"Ten years ago"**: Steve Page, "Trail Crew: 1971," *Appalachia* (June 1972), p. 147. Reprinted with the permission of the Appalachian Mountain Club.

617   **In 1966, AMC:** Alan Thorndike's early initiatives were stressed to the authors by both Proudman (Sept. 7, 1982) and his successor as AMC trails supervisor, Reuben Rajala (Aug. 18, 1982).

       "Across every delicate": Untitled note in *Chips and Clippings* (Nov. 1974), p. 4.

       When Ketchledge and Leonard: Ketchledge and Leonard, "The Impact of Man on the Adirondack High Country," *The Conservationist* (Oct.–Nov. 1970), pp. 15–16.

618   **The more careful trail-builders:** See Hazel de Berard, "Memories of Randolph: J. Rayner Edmands," *Appalachia* (Dec. 1956), p. 192; and Charles W. Blood, "Trail Erosion," *Appalachia* (June 1957), p. 354.

       A remarkably prophetic article: Robert S. Monahan, "Après Nous, le Déluge? A Plea for Better Trail Maintenance," *Appalachia* (Dec. 1954), pp. 249–51.

       Seymour Smith's crews: See Seymour R. Smith, "Interchapter Trail Clearing," *Appalachia* (Dec. 1962), p. 357.

       When he was: Blood, "Trail Erosion," pp. 353–56.

       "The versatile mattock": Monahan, "Après Nous, le Déluge?" p. 250.

619   **Franconia Ridge:** "Franconia Ridge: First Aid for a Mountain," *Appalachia Bulletin* (Nov. 1977), pp. 7–9.

621   **"We have to get away"**: John Schoen, "Take Trail Maintenance out of the Closet," *The Register* (March 1985), p. 2. Appalachian Trail Conference, Harpers Ferry, W.Va. Reprinted with permission. See also Schoen, "Trail Crew Leadership: The NY–NJ Experience," *The Register* (Sept. 1986), pp. 5–7.

       "Let us not stop": Walter Prichard Eaton. *Skyline Camps*, p. 104.

       In 1924 the farsighted: Turner's views are spelled out in an address to the Fourth Annual Meeting, National Conference on State Parks, 1924, published in *A State Park Anthology*.

621   **Myron Avery:** Myron H. Avery, "Report of the Chairman" (his farewell report), to the Twelfth Appalachian Trail Conference, May 30, 1952, reprinted in *Appalachian Trailway News* (Sept. 1952), pp. 41–42.

622   **"The only solution":** Quoted in an obituary, "Murray Stevens," *Appalachian Trailway News* (March–Apr. 1985), p. 8. Mr. Stevens recalled holding this view for many years in a letter to L&GW, late April 1982.

      "Appalachian Greenway": Ann Satterthwaite, "An Appalachian Greenway: Purposes, Prospects and Programs," report prepared for the Appalachian Trail Conference, Nov. 1974, copy loaned to the authors by George S. Wislocki.

623   **"The truth of the matter":** Judy Jenner, "Dave Richie," *Appalachian Trailway News* (March–Apr. 1984), p. 9.

      The full story: The AT protection program is the subject of a voluminous literature of governmental reports and articles in outdoor publications, but the definitive history of the program has not been written and probably will not be until its basic mission has been completed. Among dozens of people who provided background for the authors, one who continuously and faithfully kept us informed was David M. Sherman of the National Park Service. One full-length book is Charles H. W. Foster, *The Appalachian National Scenic Trail: A Time To Be Bold* (publication data not given, 1987), but this focuses on the political and administrative history and tells little of the trail itself. The *Appalachian Trailway News* is a key source for many stories on the federal program as it developed over the years. On-the-ground work on relocations is extensively reported in another ATC publication, *The Register,* with formal mile-by-mile information given in the annual *Appalachian Trail Data Book.* One positive overview, representative of numerous magazine pieces during the 1980s, is Charles Sloan, "Trail Blazers," *National Parks,* (Nov.–Dec. 1986), pp. 24–30. A more critical view is Paul Dunphy, "Unhappy Trails," *New England Monthly* (Aug. 1987), pp. 30–33. One difficulty in most 1980s writings on the subject is that the program is controversial, attracting enthusiastic loyalty from those involved and bitter opposition from a few landowners and their supporters. The result is that a thoroughly objective description of the program's history and discussion of the issues has not been written. There is risk that it may not be written until the facts are submerged in an incoming tide of partisan accounts on both sides.

      Proudman's 1977 guide: Proudman, *Trail-Building and Maintenance,* pp. 67–68.

624   **Eagle scout project:** Letter from Elizabeth Levers, *The Register* (Apr. 1987), p. 2.

      "A whole new world": Unpublished memorandum from Elizabeth Levers on the Appalachian Trail Project. The authors are grateful to Ms. Levers for lending us a copy of this memorandum and for permission to quote from it.

625   **"The right man":** Conversation with Stephen Clark, July 14, 1982.

625   **The northern two-thirds:** The Long Trail's situation was written up in national news stories: see John Donnelly, "Development Intrudes, Threatens Long Trail," *The* [Barre–Montpelier, Vt.] *Times-Argus,* July 29, 1986, pp. 1, 8 (an AP story widely carried in other newspapers), and "Club Moves to Protect Vermont Trail," *New York Times,* Aug. 24, 1986, p. 46. For measures taken by the GMC, see "Long Trail Protection Resolution Approved by Board of Directors," *The Long Trail News* (Nov. 1985), pp. 1, 4; "Long Trail Protection Task Force," *The Long Trail News* (Feb. 1986), pp. 1, 8; Preston Bristow, "The Long Trail Protection Fund of the Green Mountain Club," *The Long Trail News* (Aug. 1986), p. 7; and lead stories in nearly every issue of *The Long Trail News* throughout 1987 and 1988.

CHAPTER 57. POINTS OF CONTROVERSY

627   **Some areas of disagreement:** Among published analyses of late twentieth century backcountry points of controversy, one of the most important is Joseph L. Sax, *Mountains without Handrails: Reflections on the National Parks.* See also Garrett Hardin, "The Economics of Wilderness," *Natural History* (June–July 1969), pp. 20–27. A useful list of sources is Arlyn S. Powell, Jr., "The Backcountry Management Debate: A Selected Bibliography," *Appalachia* (Dec. 1980), pp. 85–93. As general background, see the most recent edition of Roderick Nash, *Wilderness and the American Mind.* However, much of the most useful discussion of these points of controversy took the form of casual conversations among hikers, backpackers, trail workers, and backcountry managers during the 1970s and 1980s. The authors heard much of such discussions during these two decades. Though unrecorded, and therefore of no use to future scholars, this source constituted a rich background for our own understanding of these issues.

Shelter removal: See especially the running debate over these issues in *Adirondack Peeks,* during the late 1970s: for example, Jim Dittmar, "In Memoriam" (Winter 1976), pp. 9–11; C. Peter Fish, "A Ranger's Outlook from the High Peaks" (Winter 1977), pp. 25–28; E. H. Ketchledge, "President's Message" (Summer 1978), pp. 28–33; and letter from Carolyn Schaefer (Winter 1978), p. 6.

Campfires: The GMC deliberations are reported in Donald M. Wallace, "Are Wood Fires a Luxury?" *The Long Trail News* (Feb. 1971), p. 3; "Fires on the Long Trail May 'Go Up in Smoke,' " *The Long Trail News* (Nov. 1975), pp. 2–3; and Robert L. Hagerman, "Fires Discouraged but Can Keep Burning on LT," *The Long Trail News* (May 1976), p. 3. Among discussions of the issue, an interesting contrast was afforded by companion pieces in *Backpacker* (no. 8, Winter 1974): Dick Anderson, "How to Build a Campfire in Deep Snow," p. 33; and Laura Waterman and Guy Waterman, "How to Keep Warm in Winter without a Campfire," pp. 32–33.

Fees at backcountry sites: The criticism and defense of this policy was carried on during the 1970s largely in verbal form among the backpackers and backcountry managers of the time; published comments do not fully reflect the issue.

628   **Hostility toward AMC huts:** One published critique of the huts was in Daniel Ford, *The Country Northward.* However, as with the foregoing issue, most of the criticism during the 1970s and 1980s went unrecorded. Anyone talking with backpackers in the White Mountains during the 1970s and 1980s heard plenty of this viewpoint, however. AMC publications of that era periodically defended the huts. See, for example, a series of articles in *Appalachia Bulletin* (May 1977), pp. 12–35, especially William Reifsnyder, "The AMC Hut System: Scourge or Savior of the Backcountry?" pp. 24–28.

Appalachian Trail hikers' views on the White Mountains: One published expression of these views can be found in Steve Sherman and Julia Older, *Appalachian Odyssey: Walking the Trail from Georgia to Maine* (Brattleboro, Vt.: Stephen Greene Press, 1977), p. 195. See also Jeffrey Worst, *Hiking through the Whites without Losing Your Shorts,* a small brochure distributed to AT hikers by the Appalachian Trail Conference, 1982. The authors learned much from informal conversations with numerous through-hikers along the AT, among whom special thanks are due to Jean Cooley.

Baxter State Park regulations: Again most of the criticism went unrecorded. For one example, see the authors' two-part article in *New England Outdoors,* "Anthem for Katahdin" (Oct. 1977), pp. 22–25, and "Requiem for Katahdin" (Nov. 1977), pp. 20–24.

629   **To curb numbers or welcome them:** A running debate on this issue appeared in *Appalachia* during the 1970s. See especially Philip D. Levin, "Toward a Recreated Wilderness: Notes on Abolishing the Four Thousand Footer Club," June 1973, pp. 132–40; John B. Nutter, "Towards a Future Wilderness: Notes on Education in the Mountains," Dec. 1973, pp. 86–91; William R. Burch, Jr., "In Democracy is the Preservation of Wilderness," Dec. 1974, pp. 90–100; and Levin, "Inward to Wilderness," a four-part analysis in the issues of Dec. 1975, pp. 49–62; Dec. 1976, pp. 18–35; June 1978, pp. 25–44; and Dec. 1978, pp. 57–86. See also Randel F. Washburne, "Wilderness Recreational Carrying Capacity: Are Numbers Necessary?" *Journal of Forestry* (Nov. 1982), pp. 726–28, and Theodore M. Edison, "Wilderness Values," *The Chirp* (bulletin of the John Burroughs Natural History Society), Nov. 1973, pp. 1–4.

"The question has become": "Wilderness Trips: A Valedictory," *The Living Wilderness* (Oct.–Nov. 1977), p. 47. Reprinted with permission.

"To spread awareness": *Ibid.*

"Where enjoyment and preservation": *The Trustees of Reservations: A Museum of the Massachusetts Landscape,* undated brochure distributed by the Trustees of Reservations.

GMC policies: On Federal involvement, see "National Trails Designation Not for LT, Say GMC and State," *The Long Trail News* (Aug. 1975), pp. 2–3, and "Trustees Approve LT Relocations, Oppose North Country Trail in Vermont," *The Long Trail News* (Feb. 1975), p. 4. On mud season policy, see "Mud Season Reminder: Camel's Hump 'Closed,' " *The Long Trail News* (May 1976), p. 7, and "Spring Hiking Now Discouraged on All of Long Trail

System," *The Long Trail News* (May 1977), p. 10; and reaffirmation of this policy throughout the 1980s: for example, "Spring Hiking Discouraged," Feb. 1988, p. 11. On group size limits, see "Guidelines for Use of the Long Trail," a leaflet prepared and distributed by GMC in the 1970s and early 1980s, copies of representative samples in the authors' files.

630   **"I believe that":** Levin, "Toward a Recreated Wilderness," p. 134. Reprinted with the permission of the Appalachian Mountain Club.

"So much has been written": David Abrahamson, "Taking the Mountain Airs," *Backpacker* (July 1982), p. 66. Reprinted with permission.

"Wilderness needs friends": John G. Mitchell, "Editorial," *Sierra Club Bulletin* (Sept. 1972), p. 28.

Nutter article: John B. Nutter, "Toward a Future Wilderness."

631   **The growth issue:** This subject was discussed in club councils during the 1980s, but the issues were never adequately aired in print.

632   **Wilderness areas:** A useful report on this debate is Fred Powledge, "The War of the White Hats," *New England Monthly* (June 1987), pp. 69–72.

633   **"A large decaying log":** Steve Page, "Speck Pond: Analysis of a Backcountry Shelter," *Appalachia Bulletin* (Dec. 1972), pp. 14–15. Reprinted with the permission of the Appalachian Mountain Club.

634   **"There are some intrusions":** Jim Cooper, "Policy Position on Trail Classification," *Adirondac* (Aug. 1984), p. 21. Reprinted with permission.

In the Hudson Highlands: John Schoen and Dick Warner, "Trail Crew News," *Trail Walker* (Apr.–May 1985), p. 4.

"We cannot allow": MATC Official Records and Minutes, Nov. 28, 1976.

635   **"Seymour Smith and I":** Conversation with Kornel Bailey, Oct. 27, 1982.

636   **"The clubs are copping out":** John Hibbard, quoted in Sally Kirk Fairfax, "Federal-State Cooperation in Outdoor Recreation Policy Formation: The Case of the Appalachian Trail," (Ph.D. diss., Duke University, 1973), p. 110. Reprinted with permission. Similar views were expressed to the authors by several longtime Connecticut trail workers.

Squabbles with landowners: See, for example, Brad Pokorny, "Battles on Appalachian Trail," *Boston Globe*, June 2, 1986, pp. 17ff., and frequent coverage of Massachusetts squabbles in Pittsfield's daily newspaper, *The Berkshire Eagle:* see especially the years 1984–1987. A good summary is James Niedbalski, "Trail Controversy," *Berkshires Week* (the Eagle's summer supplement), July 24, 1987, p. 7.

"The diversity of": Letter to the editor from Dan Orlinski, *Appalachian Trailway News* (March–Apr. 1987), p. 3. Reprinted with the permission of the Appalachian Trail Conference.

636   **"Why is it,"** and **"Why are we"**: Letter to the editor from Raymond H. Fadner, *Appalachian Trailway News* (May–June 1986), pp. 4–5. Reprinted with the permission of the Appalachian Trail Conference.

"Do we really": Letter to the editor from Roger Brichner, *Appalachian Trailway News* (July–Aug. 1984), pp. 4–5. Reprinted with the permission of the Appalachian Trail Conference. For a representative sampling of other letters in *ATN*, see those by Tom Watson (March–Apr. 1984), p. 24; John Hodgins (March–Apr. 1985), p. 29; and Frederick J. Gerty, Jr. (May–June 1986), pp 3–4. Similar viewpoints were noted among through-hikers in conversations with the authors—for example conversations with Jean Cooley, Oct. 1986.

"Since the passage": Fairfax, "Federal-State Cooperation," pp. 34–35. Reprinted with permission.

For all the pious: The authors are grateful to many trail workers, landowners, and town leaders in western Massachusetts who took the time to explain all shades of opinion on the controversy surrounding the AT in that state during the 1980s. Thanks are especially due to Dick and Tommy Bailey, Dana Bartholomew, Arthur Chase, Player Crosby, Arthur Delmolino, David Hapgood, Robert Hatton, Peter Jensen, George Osgood, Douglas Poland, Abby Pratt, George Wislocki, Kay Wood, and Rudy and Margot Yondorf.

"The question remains": Gerald Broughton Lowrey, "Benton MacKaye's Appalachian Trail as a Cultural Symbol" (Ph.D. diss., Emory University, 1981), pp. 103–4. Reprinted with permission.

CHAPTER 58. PEAKBAGGERS AND END-TO-ENDERS

639   **Adirondack Forty-Sixers**: The prime sources for information are Grace L. Hudowalski, ed., *The Adirondack High Peaks and the Forty-Sixers* (Albany, N.Y.: The Peters Print, 1970); the newsletter *Adirondack Peeks*; and the "Nell M. Plum Memorial Roster," issued in May 1986. The patient willingness of many officers of the club to answer queries over the years has been of invaluable assistance to these authors, with special thanks due to Grace Hudowalski, Adolph G. (Ditt) Dittmar, Philip B. Corell, Glenn W. Fish, and Edwin H. Ketchledge.

Four Thousand Footer Committee: The New Hampshire counterpart of the Forty-Sixers is not nearly as well documented or heralded in song and story. The original organization was described in Walter C. Merrill, "The Four-Thousand-Footer Club," *Appalachia* (Dec. 1957), p. 526, and Albert S. Robertson, "Four-Thousand-Footer Club of the White Mountains" (June 1958), pp. 105–9. Lists of those attaining this and related peakbagging accomplishments have been maintained by Eugene Daniell III.

New England 4000-footers: Albert S. Robertson, "New England 4000-Footer Club," *Appalachia* (June 1965), pp. 550–51.

639   **Catskill 3500 Club:** The original list appeared in Daniel Smiley, "Mountains of the Catskills: A Guide and Record," *The Conservationist* (Aug.–Sept. 1961), pp. 28–29. (An earlier list was published in 1931 in H. A. Haring, Our *Catskill Mountains*, pp. 256–57, but was not the source used by those who organized the club.) Invaluable records of the Catskill 3500 Club, including minutes of the first meeting, are in the collections of Fr. Ray Donahue, who generously allowed the authors to borrow them. The newsletter *Catskill Canister* is a fine source for historical as well as current information on the club. The authors are grateful for the recollections of early members C. W. and Kay Spangenberger, Father Donahue, Franklin Clark, Cy Whitney, and Edward G. West.

640   **"Permeated by a wholesome":** Henry L. Young, "Peak Bagging," *Catskill Canister* (Spring 1977), p. 2. Reprinted with permission.

641   **On August 5, 1948:** Earl V. Shaffer, *Walking with Spring: The First Thru-Hike of the Appalachian Trail* (Harpers Ferry, W.Va.: Appalachian Trail Conference, 1983).

       "It's like being": Jean Cooley, quoted in Beth Schwinn, "That Long, Long Trail A-Windin'," *Washington Post*, May 30, 1986, "Weekend" sec., p. 48.

642   **One unusual feat:** John E. Winkler, "How I Bushwhacked the '46,' " typescript sent to L&GW by Mr. Winkler.

       Fred Hunt: The authors are grateful to Fred Hunt for information supplied in correspondence (Apr. 27, 1982) and conversation (June 2, 1982).

643   **Speed records:** "The 46 in Nine Days," *Adirondack Peeks* (Spring 1970), p. 15; for more recent Adirondack records the authors relied on correspondence with participants and observers; for the Catskills, see "Mountain Feet, Mountain Mind," *Woodstock* [N.Y.] *Times* (Aug. 28, 1980), pp. 8–9.

       One-day superwalks: For White Mountains one-day extravaganzas, the authors are indebted to conversations with many of the participants, as well as correspondence with Lydia Goetze (Aug. 25, 1981), David Wolff (Apr. 5, 1982), David Warren (Sept. 9, 1982), and Jack Tracy (undated—1982).

       "It's the DOC equivalent": Letter from David Wolff to L&GW, Apr. 5, 1982.

644   **Katahdin in a weekend:** Conversation with Dick Andrews, one of the participants, Apr. 2, 1982.

645   **"Sins in thought":** Justin Askins, "Magazine Pollution," *Appalachia* (June 1983), p. 151.

       Philip Levin's critique: Philip D. Levin, "Toward a Recreated Wilderness: Notes on Abolishing the Four Thousand Footer Club," *Appalachia* (June 1973), pp. 132–40.

       "Above all, one must": Kenneth Webb, *As Sparks Fly Upward*, p. 13.

       In a trail-head: Letter from Eugene Daniell III to L&GW, Aug. 8, 1981.

645   **The Green Mountain Club:** Numerous GMC publications—for example, *Guidelines for Long Trail . . . by Backpacking Groups*, a 1981 brochure.

"You may now": Richard Lawrence, quoted in William Kemsley, "46ers: Is Peak-Bagging Dead?" *Backpacker* (Summer 1973), p. 59.

"The goal to be": Unsigned correspondence in letters columns, *Adirondac* (May–June 1956), p. 55.

"The fun," and "Why not try": J. Kenneth W. Macalpine, untitled article, *Adirondac* (Nov.–Dec. 1947), p. 7. Reprinted with permission.

Perhaps the ultimate: Winthrop A. Rockwell, "The Challenging Mountains: Two Men Attempt 46 Peaks in 5 Days," *New York Times*, Feb. 18, 1973, p. x-1.

646   **"If Mr. Levin":** Letter to the editor from Winifred L. Finbar, *Appalachia* (Dec. 1973), p. 178. Reprinted with the permission of the Appalachian Mountain Club.

"I become slightly": Letter from Glenn W. Fish to L&GW, Sept. 27, 1978. Reprinted with permission.

"I regard peakbagging": Letter from Eugene Daniell III to L&GW, Aug. 8, 1981. Reprinted with permission.

"More disheartening to me": Letter to the editor from Frank Krajcovic, *Appalachian Trailway News* (March–Apr. 1986), p. 4. Reprinted with the permission of the Appalachian Trail Conference.

647   **Great Herd Path War:** The pages of *Adirondack Peeks* throughout the mid-1960s reverberated to communiqués from the front of this conflict. See especially the letters columns in the issue of Fall 1966. Except where otherwise indicated, quotations that follow are from that issue. Reprinted with permission. The authors are also indebted to James A. and Tony Goodwin for recollections of this period.

"You couldn't get": Conversation with James A. Goodwin, Aug. 17, 1983.

648   **"The 46ers are really":** Letter to the editor from David Newhouse, *Adirondack Peeks* (Spring 1970), p. 10. Reprinted with permission.

"Stewards the High Peaks": Ketchledge's letter was printed under the title "46ing—An Ecological Disaster?" in *Adirondack Peeks* (Fall 1970), pp. 8–10.

649   **"We've turned the orientation":** Conversation with Edwin H. Ketchledge, Aug. 20, 1986.

"For a small group": Conversation with C. Peter Fish, Sept. 27, 1982.

650   **"We are not," and "This is an activity":** Letter from Eugene Daniell III to L&GW, Aug. 8, 1981. Reprinted with permission.

"Climbing the NHHH": Letter from Bruce O. Brown to L&GW, Apr. 5, 1980. Reprinted with permission.

651   **World War II:** The authors received invaluable guidance about the development of winter equipment during World War II from those directly involved,
notably Robert Bates, H. Adams Carter, John Case, William P. House,
Charles Houston, William L. Putnam III, and Bradford Washburn. An interesting series of articles appeared during World War II in the *Appalachian
Trailway News*, written by the staff of the Appalachian Trail Conference,
describing equipment developments as they affected winter climbing even
while the war was on. See, for examples, articles entitled "Post-war Hiking
and Camping Equipment" in the issues of Sept. 1943, pp. 34–36, Jan. 1944,
pp. 11–12, and Sept. 1944, pp. 35–36.

"Hiking comforts heretofore": Frances Green, "War Surplus and the Hiker,"
The Long Trail News (Nov. 1947), p. 3. Reprinted with permission.

"GI material originally": John B. Ehrhardt, "Winter Camping: Surplus
Army Equipment at Low Cost Is Adding Comfort to This Sport," *New York
Times*, Dec. 21, 1947, sec. 2, p. 21.

"We wore them": Letter from Dick Andrews to L&GW, March 18, 1981. Reprinted with permission.

The price was right: Equipment catalogue of Recreational Equipment, Inc.,
for 1959, and *IOCAlum Newsletter* (Apr. 1950).

Tenth Mountain Division: The authors appreciate the reminiscences shared
with them by numerous Tenth Mountain veterans, including James A.
Goodwin, Leslie Hurley, Thomas J. Johnston, William L. Putnam III, and
John Rand. A printed history is Hal Burton, *The Ski Troops* (New York: Simon & Schuster, 1971).

652   **One direct outgrowth:** Conversations with Roger Damon (May 9, 1983);
Leslie Hurley (June 30, 1981), Donald Jennings (June 29, 1981), and Gary
Thomas Lord (Nov. 7, 1980) of Norwich University; and John Rand of Dart-
mouth College (July 19, 1981). The archives of Norwich University and of
Dartmouth College provide source material on these programs.

653   **The Adirondack school:** The first publication by the Adirondack Mountain
Club describing the formal system developed during these years was *The
Advanced Winter Badge*, an undated brochure (ca. 1952), in the files of the
Adirondack Mountain Club. Contemporary articles in *Adirondac* provide
useful background too: see especially a note on the Winter Activities Com-
mittee's evolving program under the heading "Adirondak Loj Chapter"
(May–June 1949), p. 66; and Kay Flickinger and Kim Hart, "Skis, Snow-
shoes and Crampons" (Nov.–Dec. 1949), pp. 128–29.

"For that college": Flickinger and Hart, "Skis, Snowshoes and Crampons,"
p. 128.

Winter Mountaineering Conferences: "Winter Mountaineering Conference
Held," *Adirondac* (May–June 1949), p. 51. For subsequent conferences, see
reports annually thereafter during the early 1950s.

654   **RPI on Cliff and Herbert:** Dick Bailey, "First Winter Ascents of Two Adirondack Peaks," *Adirondac* (Jan.–Feb. 1949), p. 10.

Cornell on Gray Peak: Arthur G. Heidrick, "When Thaw-Time Plagues the Skier," *Adirondac* (May–June 1949), pp. 60–61.

Van Dyke, Barker, and Collin: David C. Hart, "Cornell on Dix," *Adirondac* (March–Apr. 1950), pp. 30–32; E. Gilbert Barker, "Winter Travel in the Big Blowdown," *Adirondac* (Nov.–Dec. 1951), pp. 106–9; Paul A. Van Dyke, "High Peak Camping in Winter," *Adirondac* (Jan.–Feb. 1952), pp. 4–5. See also "Winter Ascent," *Cloud Splitter* (March–Apr. 1950), pp. 6–7. Under Van Dyke's leadership, the Cornell Outing Club prepared detailed typewritten accounts of winter climbs, copies of which were retained by Van Dyke. The authors greatly appreciated the opportunity to read these reports during a visit to Van Dyke's home, Nov. 2, 1981. Among the important reports are David C. Hart on the Dix Range, Dec. 21–26, 1949; Paul Van Dyke on Redfield, Dec. 29–30, 1949; Bob Collin on the Great Range, Jan. 31–Feb. 3, 1950; Paul Van Dyke on the MacIntyre Range, March 20, 1950; E. Gilbert Barker on Santanoni and Seward, Christmas vacation, 1950 (subsequently printed in the *Syracuse* [N.Y.] *Post Standard*, Feb. 25, 1951, p. 21); and Peter Brackett Dirlam on Panther and Couchsachaga, Feb. 1953.

Syracuse on Esther: An attempt to summarize pioneering winter ascents in the Adirondacks is Katherine T. Flickinger, "Climbing the Forty-Six on Snow and Ice," in the first (1958) edition of Hudowalski, ed., *The Adirondack Forty-Sixers*, pp. 88–97. The Esther ascent is described on p. 95.

RPI on Allen: Flickinger "Climbing the Forty-Six on Snow and Ice," p. 96.

RPI and Vassar on Sawteeth: *Ibid.*

Princeton on the Great Range: Marty Harris, "Princeton Outing Club's Winter Range Trip," *Adirondac* (Jan.–Feb. 1953), pp. 4–5.

Cornell on Panther and Couchsachraga: Peter B. Dirlam, "C. C. C. Winter Ascents of Panther, Couchsachraga," *Adirondac* (Jan.–Feb. 1954), pp. 8–11.

Syracuse on Donaldson: Flickinger, "Climbing the Forty-Six on Snow and Ice," p. 96.

Cornell on Emmons: *Ibid.*

655   **"Until this day":** Heidrick, "When Thaw-Time Plagues the Skier," p. 60. Reprinted with permission.

"On December 21, 1949": Hart, "Cornell on Dix," p. 30.

Still another award: E. Gilbert Barker and Paul A. Van Dyke, "The Advanced Winter Badge," *Adirondac* (Jan.–Feb. 1953), pp. 7, 15.

How-to manual: *The Adirondack Winter Mountaineering Manual* (Gabriels, N.Y.: Adirondack Mountain Club, 1957). This manual was succeeded by the book-length John A. Danielson, *Winter Hiking and Camping* (Glens Falls, N.Y.: Adirondack Mountain Club, first edition, 1972; subsequent editions in 1977 and 1982). An updated manual on winter climbing, prepared by John Dunn, is to be published by the Adirondack Mountain Club in 1989.

655   **Winter Mountaineering School:** Kim Hart, "First Winter Mountaineering School Held at Adirondak Loj," *Adirondac* (Jan.–Feb. 1955), p. 17. For subsequent early years, see annual writeups in *Adirondac*. The authors are greatly indebted to early WMS leaders for sharing recollections of the start-up and early years of this important institution. Especially helpful were Paul A. Van Dyke, Gardner Perry III, Dick Andrews, Craig Fournier, and Kate Rezelman. A historical perspective is Stephen C. Frauenthal, "The Winter Mountaineering School: Middle-Aged and Going Strong," *Adirondac* (March–Apr. 1986), pp. 22–23.

One year the U.S. Army: Letter from Paul A. Van Dyke to L&GW, Nov. 5, 1981.

656   **The conventional wisdom:** The conservative tradition in Adirondack winter climbing can be seen in many of the write-ups of the time.

"Must always be": Kim Hart, "Tragedy on Marcy," *Adirondac* (March–Apr. 1957), p. 40. Reprinted with permission.

Warning signs: A copy of this sign was shown to the authors by Paul Van Dyke, who had a copy in his files. It was reported to have been drafted by Hart, Van Dyke, Flickinger, and A. T. Shorey.

"Duty": ADK, *The Advanced Winter Badge*, undated brochure (ca. 1952), in the files of the Adirondack Mountain Club. Reprinted with permission.

"The dangers of": *Ibid.*

"The first rule": Kim Hart, "Iroquois Conquered on Skis!" *Adirondac* (March–Apr. 1948), p. 8. Emphasis on the dangers of climbing, the importance of the rules, and the need to read the manual before entering the mountains in winter are all constant themes stressed in ADK literature of the 1950s and 1960s.

657   **Some of the prewar climbers:** See, for example, a letter to the editor from "Henry," *Adirondac* (Nov.–Dec. 1957), pp. 111–12.

More flexible axioms: For example, Geoffrey Winthrop Young, patron saint of the conservative tradition in mountaineering, had warned, "To carry unnecessarily heavy loads as precaution against cold or hunger in case of benightment—a very common custom—is to increase the actual probability of the event, by further checking the rate of progress" (*Mountaincraft*, p. 75). Antarctic explorer Ernest Shackleton had counseled that "those who burdened themselves with equipment to meet every contingency had fared much worse than those that had sacrificed total preparedness for speed" (Alfred Lansing, *Endurance: Shackleton's Incredible Voyage* [New York, London: McGraw Hill 1959], p. 65.)

"Our dreams shall": Typescript report by Paul A. Van Dyke, in his files. Reprinted with permission of his widow, Marilyn J. Van Dyke. The passage appeared only slightly revised in Van Dyke, "High Peak Camping in Winter," p. 5.

657   **"For that hour":** Notes on early Adirondack winter climbing in the collections of Paul A. Van Dyke. Reprinted with permission of his widow, Marilyn J. Van Dyke.

"Bang around the mountains": Conversation with Roger Damon, May 9, 1983.

658   **Goetze was an accomplished:** Chirs Goetze left few written records of his winter climbs. One sample is his "The Mahoosucs in February of '69," *Appalachia* (June 1969), pp. 484–86. Our description is based on the recollections of other winter climbers of the years around 1960 (Robert Underhill, Robert Collin, et al.) and a letter from Lydia Goetze to L&GW, Aug. 25, 1981.

"The most miserable": Letter from Lydia Goetze to L&GW, Aug. 25, 1981. Reprinted with permission.

Robert Collin: The authors talked with numerous White Mountain winter climbers of the 1960s, and most of them stressed the leadership role played by Collin. We also had the benefit of an evening's conversation with Collin and review of papers that he supplied. See especially Collin's typescript memorandum, "Equipment for Winter Climbing and Camping," dated Nov. 1959, copy in the authors' files, and Robert L. Collin, "Winter Climbing and Camping," *Appalachia* (Dec. 1959), pp. 480–87.

659   **"The cleanest and most isolated":** Collin, "Winter Climbing," p. 480. Reprinted with the permission of the Appalachian Mountain Club.

"If you insist": *Ibid.*, p. 481.

"Safety must prevail": Hart, "Iroquois Conquered," p. 8.

"Well, Mirian Underhill": Conversation with Robert Leach, Nov 2, 1983.

660   **Harvard climbers, for example:** The records of HMC attempts to accomplish a Presidentials traverse may be noted in the annual HMC Journals, 1958–64.

By common consent: A list of the known winter Forty-Sixers was compiled by Grace L. Hudowalski and printed with annotations in "Winter Forty-Sixers," *Adirondack Peeks* (Fall–Winter 1983–84), p. 26. The authors also were assisted by conversations over the past twenty years with several of the early winter Forty-Sixers.

CHAPTER 60. THE WINTER RECREATION BOOM

661   **As Jim Collins plodded:** For trends in Northeastern winter mountaineering since the 1970s, the authors have relied less on specific written sources and more on their own involvement during these years.

"The hot new sport": Philip Singerman, "The New Hot Sport of Cold Weather Camping," *New York Times* (Feb. 22, 1976), Travel and Resorts sec., pp. 10–11.

661   **A sign of the times:** See *AMC White Mountain Guides* for the years indicated.

664   **Ski-to-Die Club:** Tony Goodwin, "Challenge Skiing: High Peaks Adventures," *Adirondack Life* (Jan.–Feb. 1985), pp. 24–31.

       "Skiing is a controlled fall": *Ibid.*, p. 31.

665   **"He was right":** Letter from Eugene Daniell III to L&GW, Aug. 8, 1981. Reprinted with permission.

666   **On Thanksgiving weekend, 1956:** A complete report in typescript form is in the papers of Paul A. Van Dyke. For published accounts, see Kimball Hart, "Tragedy on Marcy," *Adirondac* (March–Apr. 1957), pp. 26, 40, and William Lange, "A Death on Marcy," *Adirondack Life* (Nov.–Dec. 1981), pp. 14–17.

       In August 1959: George T. Hamilton, John C. Perry, John E. Taylor, and David Sanderson, "The Cannon Mountain Tragedy," *Appalachia* (Dec. 1959), pp. 441–61.

667   **In late October 1963:** William Lowell Putnam, "A Tragedy of Errors on Katahdin," *Appalachia* (June 1964), pp. 178–81.

       In February 1964: N. K. Sheldon, "The Search for the Syracuse University Students," *Appalachia* (June 1964), pp. 175–78.

       In April 1975: Robert Proudman, "Search and Rescue of David Cornue and Jane Gilotti," *Appalachia* (Dec. 1975), pp. 115–17.

668   **In June 1972:** Winthrop A. Rockwell, "The Challenging Mountains: Two Men Attempt 46 Peaks in 5 Days," *New York Times*, Feb. 18, 1973, sec. x, p. 1.

       On January 31, 1974: George T. Hamilton et al., "The Katahdin Tragedy, January 31–February 1, 1974," *Appalachia* (Dec. 1974), pp. 121–37.

669   **In November 1974:** "Thanksgiving Weekend Death in High Peaks," an article originally from the *Lake Placid News*, reprinted in *Adirondack Peeks* (Fall 1974), pp. 9–11.

       In January 1982: Charles B. Fobes, "Albert Dow—Avalanche Victim No. 89," *Mount Washington Observatory News Bulletin* (Spring 1982), pp. 22–26.

EPILOGUE

671   **"All day we passed":** Robert Marshall, quoted by George Marshall in his preface to Carson, *Peaks and People*, 1973 edition, p. xiv. Reprinted with permission.

       "The infinite diversity": O'Kane, *White Mountains*, Foreword (unpaged).

       "Their interest is": *Ibid.*

Selected Bibliography

Because of the diversity of subject matter and geographical focus in this history, a complete alphabetical bibliography would be less useful to readers and researchers than one organized by subject. Therefore, our sources and suggestions for further reading or research are listed with the reference notes for each chapter.

Certain basic sources, however, merit special attention because of their pervasive importance to the history of mountain recreation in the Northeast. Therefore, these are listed here, with annotation.

Adirondac. Journal of the Adirondack Mountain Club. An invaluable source of contemporary accounts of Adirondack hiking and trail work since World War II. Also contains numerous historical articles about earlier times in the Adirondacks. Its predecessor, *High Spots*, is of special value in tracing the early years of the Adirondack Mountain Club.

Adirondack Peeks. Journal of the Adirondack Forty-Sixers. Another good source for Adirondack developments, especially since the mid-1960s. Its focus is on climbing the forty-six peaks originally thought to exceed 4,000 feet in elevation.

Appalachia. Journal of the Appalachian Mountain Club. The single most useful—indeed indispensable—source on White Mountains hiking and trail lore. Published since 1876, usually twice a year.

Appalachian Mountain Club, Publication Committee of the New York Chapter. *In the Hudson Highlands.* Lancaster, Pa.: Lancaster Press, 1945; reprinted, New York: Walking News, n.d. A compilation of essays on the hiking country just north of New York City. Includes valuable information on the early days of metropolitan area hiking and trail building.

Appalachian Trailway News. Journal of the Appalachian Trail Conference. The primary source for both historical and current information on the Appalachian Trail.

Ascutney Trails Association. *Guide to the Trails of Ascutney Mountain.* 3d ed. Windsor, Vt.: Ascutney Trails Association, 1975. Although primarily a guidebook, this little document is packed with historical information on Ascutney.

Carson, Russell M. L. *Peaks and People of the Adirondacks.* New York: Doubleday, Page, 1927; reprinted Glens Falls, N.Y.: Adirondack Mountain Club, 1973, 1986. The best source on the first ascents and trails history of the high peaks of the Adirondacks. Carson's original book (1927) was excellent, but the editor's introductions, added in 1973 and 1986 by Philip G. Terrie, Jr., add greatly to the accuracy and completeness of the data.

Chamberlain, Allen. *Annals of the Grand Monadnock.* 1936; reprinted, Concord, N.H.: Society for the Protection of New Hampshire Forests, 1975. The authoritative source for Monadnock hiking and trails history.

Connecticut Woodlands. Journal of the Connecticut Forest and Park Association. Although CFPA is primarily focused on other concerns, this is the organization that coordinates trail work on the far-flung blue-blazed trails of Connecticut. During the 1980s a steady flow of superb historical articles on Connecticut's major trails appeared.

Curtis, Jane, Will Curtis, and Frank Lieberman. *Green Mountain Adventure, Vermont's Long Trail.* Montpelier, Vt.: Green Mountain Club, 1985. An authorized history of the Green Mountain Club and the building of its Long Trail.

Donaldson, Alfred L. *A History of the Adirondacks.* 2 vols. New York: Century, 1921; reprinted, Harrison, N.Y.: Harbor Hill Books, 1977. The most comprehensive general history of the Adirondack region, with much information on its mountains.

Evers, Alf. *The Catskills: From Wilderness to Woodstock.* Garden City, N.Y.: Doubleday, 1972; rev. ed., Woodstock, N.Y.: Overlook Press, 1982. Does for the Catskills what Donaldson did for the Adirondacks, with the advantage of having been written half a century later and therefore covering much more of twentieth-century developments.

Greylock Commission. *Annual Reports,* beginning in 1899. There is no single good source for the mountain history of Greylock, the Berkshires, or the Taconic Range. However, the trails history during the area's crucial period was well covered in these annual reports.

Hagerman, Robert L. *Mansfield: The Story of Vermont's Loftiest Mountain.* Canaan, N.H.: Phoenix Publishing, 1971; rev. ed., 1975. Written in highly readable style, this book covers developments on Mount Mansfield in excellent detail.

Hakola, John W. *Legacy of a Lifetime: The Story of Baxter State Park.* Woolwich, Maine: TBW Books, 1981. A professional historian, Hakola did a more substantial job of covering Katahdin than most authors cited here did for other mountains. Special emphasis is given to the evolution of Baxter State Park and its administration. Unquestionably the most important source for information on Maine's greatest mountain.

Helfrich, G. W., and Gladys O'Neill. *Lost Bar Harbor.* Camden, Maine: Down East Books, 1982. Though its emphasis is on the social and cultural history of the area, this book is the best starting point for information on the hiking and trails history of Mount Desert.

Howell, William Thompson. *The Hudson Highlands.* New York: Lenz and Riecker, vol. 1, 1933, vol. 2, 1934; reprinted in one volume, New York: Walking News, 1982. Howell was a New York walker during the years around 1900 who kept a diary of his rambles in the Hudson Highlands. When he died young, his friends printed these recollections as a memorial to him. What raises them above ordinary interest is, first, that Howell was an observer and writer of uncommon sensitivity and, second, that he writes about a critical period in Hudson Highlands history, just before the transition to the modern era of developed hiking trails. Taken with the AMC's *In the Hudson Highlands*, these two books cover that region superbly.

Hudowalski, Grace L., ed. *The Adirondack High Peaks and the Forty-Sixers.* Albany, N.Y.: The Peters Print, 1958; rev. ed., 1970. A splendid compilation of diverse essays on the high peaks of the Adirondacks. For the student of Adirondack history, both editions contain useful information.

In the Maine Woods. An annual publication of the Bangor and Aroostook Railroad, this is a rich source of hiking and trails history in Maine, especially concerning Katahdin, during the 1910s and 1920s.

Jamieson, Paul, ed. *The Adirondack Reader.* 2d ed. Glens Falls, N.Y.: Adirondack Mountain Club, 1982. A rich anthology of writings on Adirondack mountain lore. The diversity of selections fills in much vivid detail that Carson and Donaldson do not cover fully.

Kilbourne, Frederick W. *Chronicles of the White Mountains.* Boston: Houghton Mifflin, 1916. Although written back in 1916, Kilbourne's work was so splendidly done that this book remains the generally accepted basic history of the White Mountains.

Lee, W. Storrs. *The Green Mountains of Vermont.* New York: Henry Holt, 1955. Highly readable, but light on detailed mountain history.

The Long Trail News. Journal of the Green Mountain Club. An indispensable source for information on hiking and trails history in Vermont since the 1920s.

Mount Washington Observatory News Bulletin. Journal of the Mount Washington Observatory. A most interesting diversity of articles. Regular contributors include some of the best White Mountain historians, so it is not uncommon for articles with new historical information or insights to appear in this little quarterly.

Nash, Roderick. *Wilderness and the American Mind.* New Haven: Yale University Press, 1967; rev. eds., 1973, 1982. One important influence on hiking and trails history is the evolution of underlying public attitudes toward mountains and wilderness. Many illuminating books have examined aspects of this subject, but the basic text remains this seminal study by Nash.

Snyder, Bradley, J. *The Shawangunk Mountains: A History of Nature and Man.* New Paltz, N.Y.: Mohonk Preserve, 1981. The Shawangunks are less important in hiking and trails history—in rock climbing, they are of central importance. Nevertheless, the range is of interest to New York City hikers, and this is the authoritative source on their history.

Trail Walker. Journal of the New York–New Jersey Trail Conference, published in tabloid newspaper form. The best source for current (and occasional historical) information on the New York metropolitan hiking scene.

Index

Abercrombie and Fitch, 393, 460
Abercrombie's, David T., 421
Abol Slide: early ascents, 50–55; mid-nineteenth century ascents, 94–100; trails on, 65, 247, 401–402; winter on, 534; Witherle on, 304
Abraham (Maine), xxxiv, 91; elevation of, 677; first known ascent of, 677; Jackson on, 96; trails on, 503
Abraham (Vermont), 677
Acadia. *See* Desert, Mount
Accidents, 273–277, 645–646, 665–670
Adams, James Truslow, 16
Adams, Sherman, 335, 380, 389, 465–466, 513–514, 523
Adams, W. W., 360
Adams, Mount, xxxii, 145, 287, 522–523; Alpine Club on, 184; Ball on, 275; elevation of, 674; first known ascent of, 44, 674; Hitchcock on, 173; King on, 75–76; Lancastrians on, 44–45; trails on, 205–206, 226, 281, 291–294; winter on, 315, 317–319, 526, 528, 540, 660; women on, 319
Adams Slide Trail, 292, 294
Adirondac, 657
Adirondack Camp and Trail Club: formation, 221; trail work, 221–222, 282, 395, 444–445, 471–472; Van Hoevenberg in, 216
Adirondack Forty-Sixers, 445; criticism and defense of, 645–648; environmental issues and, 576, 579, 584–585, 587, 620, 629–631, 645–649; formation, 517; growth of, 552–553, 639; Marshalls and, 514–516; trail work, 620, 649; unusual feats, 642–643; winter climbing, 660, 662–666
Adirondack League Club, 165, 393
Adirondack Lodge. *See* Adirondak Loj
Adirondack Mountain Club, 222, 392–399; environmental issues and, 393–394, 397–399, 445, 576, 579, 584–585, 629, 648; formation, 392–393; growth of, 548, 565, 596, 598, 631–632; New York Chapter, 421–424, 428, 446–447, 598; ridge-runner program, 584–585, 619; staff, 596–597; trail work, 395–396, 472, 481, 613, 620, 634; winter climbing, 545, 653–657, 661–665
Adirondack Mountain Reserve, 211–213, 311, 326, 393
Adirondack; Or, Life in the Woods (Headley), 109
Adirondack Park Agency, 560, 645
Adirondack Peeks, 647
Adirondack Trail Improvement Society (ATIS), 516; formation, 212–213; staff, 620; trail work, 213, 221, 282, 395–396, 471–472, 613, 620, 635

Adirondacks, the, xxvii–xxx, 57, 80; back-country management in, 397–399, 578–579, 583–585; Brodhead in, 65–67; Colvin in, 175–181; conservation of, 310–311; early sightings of, 2; environmental issues and, 560, 576, 578–579, 583–587, 627–630; exploration of, 3–4, 101–110, 150; fires in, 219–222; guidebooks to, 196–197; hurricanes in, 551–553; trails in, 65, 111, 209–222, 391–399, 471–472, 604, 613, 619–620, 634; winter in, 325–330, 335–340, 537–539, 542–543, 653–658, 661–665
Adirondak Loj, 149, 165–166, 214–221, 340, 395–396, 655
Adler, Felix, 165, 212–213, 303
Adopt-A-Shelter programs, 581–582, 621
Adopt-A-Trail programs, 621, 634–635
Adventures in the Wilderness, or Camp-Life in the Adirondacks (Murray), 162–163
Adventures in the Wilds of the United States (Lanman), 109
Agamenticus, Mount, xxxvi, 2, 248
Agassiz Association, 192
Air Line, 226
Alander, Mount, 241
Alden, Edmund K., 231
Aldrich, Ed, 506
Aldrich, Mr., 541
Algonquin, Mount, xxx, 302, 586; Colvin on, 178; elevation of, 674; first known ascent of, 67, 104–107, 674; Guyot on, 130; Marshalls on, 515; trails on, 210, 216, 221; winter on, 542–543, 657
Allen, Ethan, 16–17
Allen, Frederick Baylies, 118
Allen, Herbert, 206n
Allen, Ira, 4, 16–20, 49
Allen, 643; elevation of, 676; first known ascent of, 516; winter on, 542, 654
Allis, J. Ashton, 364–365, 393, 415–416, 419, 424, 480–481, 487–488, 496, 529, 534, 537–538
Aloha Camp, 454
Aloha Hive, 454
Alpine Club of Williamstown, Mass., 183–185, 189
Alpine zones, xxviii; environmental issues and, 281, 585–588, 627–628, 648; trail maintenance in, 619, 633–634
Alumni Magazine (Dartmouth), 523
Alumnae Quarterly (Mount Holyoke), 453
Amadon, Josiah, 62
AMC Field Guide to Trail Building and Maintenance, 620
AMC White Mountain Guide, 193. 198, 540, 551, 661
American Fun Society, 444

American Institute of Architects, 486–488
American Literary, Scientific and Military Academy. *See* Norwich University
American Museum or Repository, 27
American Philosophical Society of Philadelphia, 27
American Scenery (Willis), 195
American Scenic and Historic Preservation Society, 426
American Walkers' Association, 448
Amherst Mountain Club, 241, 477
Amherst Outing Club, 241, 451–453
Ammonoosuc Ravine Trail, 380
Ampersand Mountain, xxx, 165
Amphibrach, 226
Ananance. *See* Pisgah, Mount
Anderson, John, 10
Anderson, John F., 187
Anderson, Nestell (Ned) Kipp, 347, 437, 440, 495, 497–498
Anderson, Mount, 187n
Andrews, Richard, 660n
Anthony, Mount, 184, 250
Anthony's Nose, 30, 34, 186, 494
Appalachia, 190, 192, 262, 263, 387
Appalachian Greenway, 622
Appalachian Mountain Club (AMC), 149, 169, 174, 184, 275–276, 409, 492; in the Adirondacks, 329–330; Berkshire Chapter, 451, 500–502, 596, 598, 607, 624; Connecticut Chapter, 433, 440, 451, 489, 503–504, 585, 595–596; Education Department, 583, 630–631; environmental issues and, 199–200, 279–284, 582–583, 587–588, 592, 617–620, 629–632; formation, 189–192; in the Green Mountains, 354, 361; growth of, 191–192, 548, 563–564, 595–599, 631–632; hut system, 23, 200, 276–277, 285n, 381–388, 554, 563–564, 572, 583, 592, 628, 631; on Katahdin, 191, 246–247, 404, 407; Maine Chapter, 596; Narragansett Chapter, 451; New England Trail Conference and, 475–476; New Hampshire Chapter, 620; New York Chapter, 414–419, 424, 428, 446–447, 493–494, 575–577, 596–599, 657; Pinkham Notch Camp, 9, 23, 383, 385, 539–540, 583, 596–597, 612, 631; search and rescue and, 668–670; shelter caretakers, 582; Snow-Shoe Section, 315–322, 331, 525; trail building, 199–200, 205–208, 226–231, 241, 375–381, 386–388; Trail Crew, 283, 380–381, 465–468, 554, 576, 578, 582, 587, 612, 633–634, 658; trail maintenance, 281–283, 465–468, 554, 612, 616–620, 633–634; trail policy, 279–284, 616, 633–634; Vermont Chapter, 631n; women and, 191, 262–268
Appalachian Trail, 127, 183, 347–348, 481–483, 507–510, 588, 600; Avery and, 489–493, 501–502, 505, 508–509; in Connecticut, 437–438, 495–498, 613–615, 624; Long Distance Hikers Association, 649; MacKaye and, 280n, 376, 430, 485–488, 491–492, 496–497; in Maine, 443, 503–506, 549, 590, 601, 612–613, 615, 623–625; in Massachusetts, 238, 454, 498–502, 615, 623–624; National

Scenic Trail status, 561, 622–623; in New York, 417–419, 425, 493–495, 615, 623–624; Perkins and, 488–489, 492, 496–497; protection program, 621–625, 635–637; Richie and, 622–623; through-hiking on, 563–564, 571, 641–644; in Vermont and New Hampshire, 502–503, 623–624
Appalachian Trail (Katahdin), 246, 279–280
Appalachian Trail Conference, 488–494, 501–502, 509, 554, 622, 635
Appalachian Trailway News, 636
Apperson, John S., 336–341, 398, 537, 545, 652
Appleby, Irving D., 521–522
Appleton's General Guide to the United States and Canada, 197
Appleton's Handbook of American Travel, 195
Arbutus, Mount, 184
Arden-Surebridge Trail, 418–419
Ark, the, 149, 235
Armstrong, Mount, 654, 675
Ascutney, Mount, xxxii, 80; mountaintop structures on, 57–58, 64, 89; Partridge on, 30; student walking tours, 153–154; Taylor on, 353; trails on 63–65, 89, 201, 250, 351–352, 621; winter on, 137, 315–316, 320
Ascutney Mountain Association, 351–352, 355
Ascutney Trails Association, 621
Associated Mountaineering Clubs of North America, 393, 415, 426, 475
Association for the Preservation of the Adirondacks, 426
Atkinson, Purviance, 301–302
Atlantic, 117–118
Attwood, Stanley B., 443
Atwood, William, 189
Audubon, Mount, 184
Audubon Society, 308, 593
Ausable Club, 165–166, 211, 213, 221–222, 395, 613
Austin, Abigail, 119–120
Austin, Daniel, 119
Austin, Eliza, 119–120
Austin, Harriet, 119–120
Austin, Warren R., 356n
Automobiles, impact of, 343–350, 375, 396, 432, 566
Avalanche Pass, xxviii, xxx, 67, 103–107, 168, 214–216, 220–221, 302
Avery, Myron H., 130, 306, 407, 489–493, 497, 501–502, 505, 508–509, 524, 612, 621, 641, 646
Avery Peak. *See* Bigelow, Mount
Ayres, Philip W., 310, 475–476, 479–480
Aziscohos, Mount, 247

Bachli, Werner, 598
Backcountry management, 573, 577–585, 621–627, 632, 635–637; in the Adirondacks, 397–399, 578–579, 583–586, 627; in the alpine zone, 585–588, 627–628; on the Appalachian Trail, 621–625, 635–637; in the Green Mountains, 577–578, 580–582, 587, 627–629, 632; on Katahdin, 407, 577, 580, 628; in the White Mountains, 578, 582–583, 587–588, 627–629, 632

Clubs. *See names of individual clubs*
Cobb, John C., 171
Coe, Mount, 304, 603–604
Cog Railway, 43, 70, 84–85, 323, 335n
Coggeshall, Almy, 576
Colby, Nick, 654
Colby College: outing club, 451–452, 453n;
  student walking tours, 156, 158–159
Colden, David C., 103
Colden Dike, 107–108, 301
Colden, Lake, xxviii, 397, 557, 569; accidents
  at, 666, 669; college outing clubs at, 453, 555,
  601, 654; exploration of, 105–107; trails near,
  210, 216, 221; winter at, 328–329, 340, 654
Colden, Mount, xxx, 104–105, 302; elevation of,
  675; first known ascent of, 675; Guyot on,
  130; trails on 604; winter on, 654, 664
Cole, Thomas, 72–73, 131, 136
College Alumni Hiking Club, 449, 519–520,
  599–600
College outing clubs, 451–453, 555, 600–602,
  653–655, 657, 662. *See also individual colleges*
Collier, Steven, 669
Collin, Nancy, 658
Collin, Robert, 654, 658–659, 663
Collins, James (Jim) W. F., 660–661
Colonel's Chair, 253
Colvin, Verplanck, 116, 128, 167–170, 175–181,
  196, 210, 325
Colvin, Mount, 170, 300, 303; conservation of,
  311; elevation of, 677; first known ascent of,
  116, 175–176, 677; trails on, 213
Comey, Arthur C., 280n, 460, 482–483, 487,
  501, 503–504, 529–530, 532–534, 652
Comstock, Fritz, 472
Conant, C. H., 174
Concentrated Use Areas. *See* Restricted Use Areas
Congden, Herbert Wheaton, 363
Conn, Herbert W., 231
Connecticut: conservation in, 311; Forest and
  Park Association, 431, 435, 440, 473, 554,
  614; geological survey, 167n; State Park
  Commission, 431–433, 477; trail maintenance
  in, 472–474, 613–615, 635–636; trails in,
  431–441, 606
Connecticut Roving Trail Crew, 613
Connecticut, University of: outing club, 451–453
Connecticut Walk Book, 3, 440
Conservation Department. *See* New York
  Conservation Department
Conservation movement, 150, 307–314, 560–561
Cook, Eugene Beauharnais, 225–226, 279, 284,
  289, 298, 300, 379, 511
Cook, Mary, 122
Cooke, Rollin H., 197, 238–239
Cooley Glen, 366
Co-op City Hiking Club, 599
Cooper, Charles C., 468, 476
Cooper, James Fenimore, 73, 113
Copeland, Royal, 449
Copp, Benjamin, 23
Corduroy, 617
Cornell, Mount, 129n, 253
Cornell Outing Club, 601, 651, 654
Corway Peak. *See* Chocorua

Couch, Franklin L., 500–502
Couching Lion. *See* Camel's Hump
Couchsachraga, 642, elevation of, 677; first
  known ascent of, 516, 677; winter on, 654
Country Life in America, 309
Cowles, Clarence P., 347, 355, 357–360,
  365–366, 370, 444, 541, 543, 550
Cowles, Laura, 120, 360, 541
Cowles Cove, 366
Crane, A. A., 433, 437
Crawford, Abel, 39–43, 47–48, 82, 121, 148
Crawford, Ethan Allen, 32, 40–48, 82, 115–116,
  119–121, 136, 146, 273–274
Crawford, Fred, 379
Crawford, Hannah, 39–40
Crawford, Lucy, 9, 40, 119–121, 146
Crawford, Thomas J., 40–41, 46, 48, 82, 121
Crawford House, 40–41, 86, 128, 131n, 230–231
Crawford Notch, xxxii, 37–48, 72–73, 82, 148,
  271; Belknap-Cutler expedition in, 21, 26;
  exploration of, 37; Hitchcock in, 173–174;
  Partridge in, 30, 32; road through, 38–41, 43,
  46; student walking tours, 155; trails near, 87,
  202, 230, 377–379; winter in, 131, 662
Crawford paths, 12, 30, 32, 41–46, 59, 82, 83,
  136, 156, 201, 266, 274, 276, 322–324, 526,
  587, 617
Crawford State Park, 311
Creager, Joe, 665
Crocker, Mount, xxxiv, 91, 676
Crowell, Edward, 137
Crow's Nest, 30, 410–412
Crystal Cascade, 343, 383
Cube, Mount, 335, 454–455
Cudworth, Moses, 87
Cummings, Miss, 231
Curtis, William B., 186, 276–277, 410–411, 447
Curtis House, 83
Curtis-Ormsbee tragedy, 276–277, 383
Curtis-Ormsbee Trail, 254
Cushman, Mount, 268
Cutler, Manasseh, 47; Belknap-Cutler expedition
  to Mount Washington, 21–27, 38–39, 46, 49
Cutter, Louis F., 191, 200, 226, 267, 275,
  375–376, 378

Daiber, Ome, 462
Damon, Roger, 652, 657, 659
Damp, Edward, 509n
Dana, James D., 197
Daniel Webster (Scout) Trail, 185
Daniell, Eugene, III, 645, 647, 649–650
Daniell, Warren F., III, 513–514, 523, 649–650,
  665
Danielson, John A., 655
Dannenhauer, Mark, 578
Dark Entry Ravine, 498
Darrah, Francis, 519
Dartmouth, The, 333–334
Dartmouth College, 168; Hitchcock survey and,
  168, 171–173; outing club, 158, 333–335,
  354n, 451–453, 477, 503, 509, 512–514,
  600–602, 624, 652, 657; student walking
  tours, 146, 154–158
Davis, Dick, 640

Hale, Mount, 298, 604–605, 677
Half-a-League Club, 440, 451
Half Way House (Monadnock), 87, 149, 233–235, 604
Halfway House (Mount Mansfield), 88–89, 248
Halfway House (Mount Washington), 132, 322–323, 334
Hall, James, 101–108
Hall, Joseph Seavey, 89–90
Hall, William L., 476, 480
Hamlin, Charles E., 98, 99
Hamlin: elevation of, 674; first known ascent of, 53, 55, 675; Hale and Channing on, 97; trails on, 245, 403–405; Witherle on, 304
Hancock, Mount, 662, 675
Hand, A. N., 445
Hanging Hills of Meriden, xxxvii, 80, 130, 149, 431
Hannah, Sel, 519
Harding, George, 192
Harriman, Mary, 310, 448
Harriman Park, xxxviii; Appalachian Trail in, 417–419, 487; boy scouts in, 414, 419, 454; college outing clubs in, 519–520; conservation of, 310; environmental issues and, 569, 575–577; New York hikers and, 413–428, 446–450, 519–520, 554, 643; summer camps in, 414, 455; trails in, 415–419, 426–428
Harrington, D. A., 329–330
Harrington, Jack, 613
Harrington, Karl Pomeroy, 231, 378–381, 387–390, 437–439, 465–467
Harris, Calista and family, 554
Harris, Charles, 421
Harris, Fred, 333–335, 340–341, 354n, 444
Harris, Gray, 381
Harris, Marty, 654
Harrison, Benjamin, 165
Hart, Kim, 653, 656
Hart, Warren, W., 10, 13, 280, 283, 287, 291–295, 299, 480
Hartrich, Michael, 664
Hartshorne, Lucius, 132
Harvard University, 58; mountaineering club, 135n; outing club, 452, 657, 660; student walking tours, 154
Haselton, Seneca, 355, 370
Haskell, Alfred, 324
Haskell, Edward, 445
Haskell's Raskels, 445
Hatch, Bill, 128
Hathaway, Mel, 394
Hawes, Austin F., 361, 363, 366
Hawthorne, Nathaniel, 38, 73–74
Hayes, Mount, 82, 381
Haynes, David, 90–91
Haynes, George Henry, 197
Haynes, Thomas H., 90
Haynes, Mount, 254
Haystack (New York), xxix, 165, 302–303, 517; conservation of, 311, elevation of, 674; first known ascent of, 674; trials on, 210, 213, 395; winter on, 337, 339, 537, 542, 656; women on, 122
Haystack, Mount (Vermont), 485

Headley, Joel T., 109, 162
Healy, Trudy, 642, 647
Heath, Ralph, 667
Heath, Captain, 26
Hedgehog, Mount, 67
Heermance, Edgar Laing, 433–437, 478, 492, 497–498, 509, 606
Heidrick, Art, 654–655
Helburn, Margaret Mason, 525–526, 529, 534, 537, 658n
Helburn, Willard, 322, 525–529, 533–534, 537, 658n
Helderbergh Hills, 169n, 336
Hell Brook Trail, 248–249, 370, 541
Hell Divers Ski Club, 540
Henck, John B., Jr., 189–190
Henderson, David, 103–108
Henderson, Ken, 461
Henry, J. E., 299
Herbert, John, 513
Herbert, Victor, 165
Herbert. See Marshall
Herd paths, 579, 647, 649
Herrick, Mount, 130
Herrod, Walter, 649
Hibbard, John, 473
Hickok, Andrew, 209
Hicks, Harry Wade, 221, 393, 399, 524
Higby, Mount, 433–434
Higginson, Thomas Wentworth, 72, 100, 123, 137, 191
High Mountain, 449
High Peak, 30, 64, 129, 193, 253
High Point, 253
Hight, Mount, 528
Hiker's pocket, 576
Hiking clubs. See names of individual clubs
Hiking Trips Bureau, 424, 450
Hildreth, Horace, 485
Hincks, Mr., 208
History of New Hampshire (Belknap), 27
History of the White Mountains (Crawford), 9, 119
Hitchcock, Charles H., 99, 126, 137, 139, 141, 167–175, 191, 196, 315
Hitchcock, Edward, 125–126, 167n, 168, 241
Hitchcock, Edward, Jr., 173
Hitchcock, John, 616
Hodge, Hugh, 301–302
Hoeferlin, William, 418, 449, 472, 615–616
Hoffman, Charles Fenno, 109, 162
Hogan, William, 108
Hoisington, Houghton, 351
Hoitt, C. W., 174
Holden, John, 533–534
Holden, L. L., 315
Holderness School, 601
Hollis, Allen, 476
Holmes, Oliver Wendell, 74
Holmes, Mr., 323
Holt, Harvey, 103, 106, 110, 116, 122
Holyoke Range, xxxvii, 57–58, 80, 149, 598; Hitchcock on, 125–126; mountaintop structures on, 58; Partridge on, 34; student walking tours, 153, 156; trails on, 241

Jones Nose, 59, 238–239
Josselyn, Henry, 14
Journal of the American Institute of Architects, 486–487
Juggernaut Trail, 251
Jump, Ellis B., 453
June Mountain, 500
Jung, Carl, 213n, 303

Kaaterskill High Peak. *See* High Peak
Katahdin, xxviii, xxxii, 72, 115, 443; accidents on, 667–668, 670; Appalachian Trail on, 505; backcountry management of, 405–408, 567–577, 580, 586, 628–629; college outing clubs on, 452; conservation of, 312, 405–408; Dudley and, 401–407; elevation of, 674; environmental issues and, 279–280, 569, 576–577, 580, 586, 620, 628–629; exploration of 49–56; fires on, 246; first known ascent of, 50–51, 674; guidebooks to, 197; Jackson on, 96; Monument Line surveyors on, 52–56; Thoreau on, 73, 145; trails on, 90–100, 243–247, 279–282, 402–405, 601–604, 619; Turner on, 50–51; weekend climbs of, 520–521, 644; winter on, 526–527, 531–535, 657, 665; Witherle on, 303–306; women on, 99, 123–124, 262, 265, 665
Katahdin Outing Club, 535
Kearsarge, Mount, 86, 153, 156, 316
Kearsarge South, 63
Keely, George Washington, 94–95
Keep, Marcus, 90, 94, 98–99, 116, 123–124
Keep Path, 99–100, 304, 532n
Keewaydin Camps, 454
Kelsey, Joe, 275
Kelsey Cottage, 225–226
Kemsley, William, 593–594
Kess, Bob, 606
Ketchledge, Edwin H., 586–587, 617, 647–649
Kieran, John, 523
Kilbourne, Frederick W., 11, 77, 274–275, 433–434, 438, 481
Killington, Peak, xxxii; elevation of, 676; first known ascent of, 676; Guyot on, 130; MacKaye on, 486; mountaintop structures on, 90, 148, 251, 353; Partridge on, 30, 33; trails on, 250–253, 353, 361, 367–370, 480; winter on, 320, 541
Kimball, Henry, 129
Kimball, Howard A., 141–143
Kineo, Mount, xxxvi, 73, 91, 115, 123, 148, 197, 248, 480
King, Thomas Starr, 9, 74–77, 79–80, 131, 146, 313
King Ravine, xxxii, 76, 206, 298
Kinsmans, 130, 174, 346, 380. *See also* North Kinsman *and* South Kinsman
Kirby Peak, 18
Klondike, 54, 56, 305–306, 404–405
Knife Edge (Katahdin), 98–100, 123, 280, 304, 406, 644; accidents on, 667; winter on, 527, 532n, 534
Koerber, Arthur, 615–616
Krag, Carl, 664
Kruszyna, Bob, 657

Kurth, Hilda, 457–458

LaBorde, George P., 443
Ladies Walking Club, 448
LaFarge, C. Grant, 327–329
Lafayette, Mount, xxix, 44, 79, 298; elevation of, 674; first known ascent of, 674; Guyot on, 130; mountaintop structures on, 84; Partridge on, 30, 33; student walking tours, 153–157; Thoreau on, 145; trails on, 84, 201, 346, 379
Lake George-Placid Trail, 482
Lake Placid Club, 165–166, 216–219, 221, 282, 329–330, 336, 338–340, 395, 444, 543
Lake Tarleton Club, 476
Lake Tear-of-the-Clouds, 175–177, 210, 328–329, 666
Lakes of the Clouds, 11–12, 30, 41, 276, 315, 380, 519
Lakes-of-the-Clouds Hut, 383–385, 619, 661
Lamb, George, 116
Lamb, Levi, 116
Lanakila, 454
Lancastrians, 43–46
Langmuir, David, 537, 539
Langmuir, Irving, 336–341, 537, 545
Langmuir, Ruth (Van de Water), 529–530, 658n
Lanman, Charles, 109–110
Larrabee, Ralph C., 191, 323
Larrabee, William, 49
Larson, Eiler U., 509
Laura Woodward Shelter, 373
Laurel House, 82
Lawrence, Rosewell, 191, 267, 279–280, 299, 316, 318–320
Lawrence Trail, 228
Leach, Henry Goddard, 516
Leach, Robert, 659
Leavitt, Walter, 404
Leavitt, William and Elinore, 639–640
LeBell, Clarence, 657
Leeming, Thomas, 414
Leg-It Club, 240, 451
Leon Greenman's (store), 567
Leonard, Raymond E., 586, 617
Lester, Nat, 599
Lethbridge, Mr., 328
Letters from the Backwoods and the Adirondac (Headley), 109
Letters of Thomas Gorges, The, (Maine Historical Society), 11
Levers, Elizabeth, 575–576, 615–616, 624
Levin, Philip D., 630, 645
Libby, George K., 437, 614–616
Libby, Norman, 335n
Liberty, Mount, 174, 675
Liberty Springs Shelter, 582
Life in the Open Air (Winthrop), 100
Limmer, Peter & Sons, 589
Lincoln Peak (Vermont), 312, 674; trails on, 90, 251; winter on, 541
Lincoln, Mount (New Hampshire), 130, 230, 298, 674
Lingernot Society, 193, 450, 512
Linsley, D. C., 89
Lion Head, 24–27

Nancy, Mount, 174, 298
Nansen, Fridtjof, 144, 332
Nansen Ski Club, 332
Naromiyochknowhusunkotankshunk Brook, 3, 193n
Narragansett Trail, 438, 440
Nash, Roderick, 70, 308, 454
Nash, Timothy, 37–38
Nassau Greenbelt Trail, 606
Nassau-Suffolk Trail, 605–606
National Audubon. *See* Audubon Society
National Geographic, 563, 572
National Intelligencer, 31
National Park Service, 407, 622–624, 635–636
National Scenic Trails, 347, 561, 622, 625
Native Americans, 3, 7–9, 37, 50, 96
Natural History of New York, Geology (Emmons), 108n
Nature Friends, 414, 421, 424, 427–429, 448, 599
Naugatuck Trail, 438
Nawakwa, 446
Neal, Walter, 14
Nebo, Mount, 253
Nebraska Notch, 249, 359
Nees, Harry, 615–616
Nelson, S. A., 141–144, 315
Nelson Crag, 24–27, 381
Nester, Edward, 657
Neuberger, Richard L., 538–539
New England: A Handbook for Travellers (Osgood), 195
New England Federation of City Planning Boards, 477
New England Hotel Association, 477
New England Outdoors, 593
New England Trail Conference, 454, 476–483, 487–488, 616
New Hampshire: conservation in, 310–312; Fish and Game Department, 670; geological survey of, 96, 167n, 171–175; Historical Society, 131n, 154n; Hotel Association, 477; Hundred Highest (NHHH), 649–650
New Hampshire, University of: outing club, 451–453, 588, 601
New Haven Hiking Club, 440, 451, 614
New York American, 425
New York Evening Post, 415–416, 425
New York Hiking Club, 449
New York Mountain Club, 428, 450
New York-New Jersey Trail Conference, 392, 415–416, 427–429, 472, 576, 616, 620, 624
New York Ramblers, 449
New York State: Conservation Department, 395, 398, 445, 472; Department of Environmental Conservation (DEC), 583–585, 620, 627, 631, 634; geological surveys of, 101–108, 125, 167n; topographical survey of, 175–181
New York Sun, 356
New York Times, 109, 151, 345
New York Tribune, 309, 425, 457
New York University: outing club, 519–520
New York Walk Book, 419
Newhall, Alec, 324, 329–330
Newhall, Avis, 534
Newhall, Carl, 598

Newhouse, David, 648
Newport Mountain. *See* Champlain Mountain
Newton, Fannie, 122
Newton, Payson T., 500–502
Nichols, Harry, 275
Nicholson, Marjorie Hope, 69
Nipmuck Trail, 438, 440
Nippletop: Colvin on, 175; conservation of, 311; elevation of, 675; first known ascent of, 107, 675; Guyot on, 130; Phelps on, 116; Putnam Camp on, 303
Nissen, Norman, 666
Noble, George H., 234
Nolan, Beverly, 649–650
Non-46ers, 645
Noon Peak, 208
Noonmark, xxx, 211–212, 213n, 221, 518
Norris, Joseph C., Sr., 52–56, 65
Norris, Kathleen, 457–458
North Brother, 306, 676
North Dome, 129n
North Kinsman, 676
North Mountain (Catskills), 61, 129, 201
North Peaks (Katahdin), 54, 243–246, 404–405
North Tripyramid, 299n, 320–321, 676
North Twin, 604, 674
North Woodstock Improvement Association, 231, 444, 477
Northern Presidentials. *See* Presidential Range *and names of individual peaks*
Northern Traveller, The, (Theodore Dwight), 195
Northville-Placid Trail, 394, 472, 481, 641
Norton, J. R., 541
Norwich University, 29–33, 64, 137, 652; outing club, 451–452, 503, 601; Partridge and, 29–33
Notch of the Mountains. *See* Crawford Notch
Notch Road (Greylock), 236–238
Nowell, Mrs. William G., 191, 263
Nowell, William G., 190, 196, 203–206, 227–228, 267, 280–282
Nuckolls, Stephen, 642
Nurian, Kerson, 364–365, 420, 427–428, 472
Nutter, John B., 583, 630
Nye, Bill, 116, 175, 179, 209, 214–215
Nye, Mount, 516, 552, 677

Oakes, William, 47, 587
Oakes Gulf, 47, 526–527
Oatmeal Crusaders, 157, 159
O'Brien, Miriam (Underhill), 529, 530, 534, 647, 657, 659
O'Brien, Peggy, 542n
October Mountain, 500
Odell, Noel, 133
Odin, 269
Ohler, Bob, 551
O-J-I, Mount, 306, 603–604
O'Kane, Walter Collins, 398–399, 461, 462, 529, 671
Old Blue Mountain, 503
Old Bridle Path, 84, 230–231, 381
Old Speck, xxxiv, 380, 676
Oliver, Frank, 615–616
Olton, Percy, 424

Whiteface (New Hampshire), 433–434; elevation of, 677; first known ascent of, 677; Guyot on, 130; Hitchcock on, 171; trails on, 228–229; winter on, 321

Whiteface (New York), xxx, 64, 108–110, 127, 165, 515; elevation of, 674; Emmons on, 105; environmental issues and, 398–399; first known ascent of, 67, 674; Guyot on, 130; Murray on, 162n; trails on, 65, 209, 217–219; winter on, 330, 332, 541, 543, 652

Whiting, Brad and Dorothy, 639–640

Whitman, Fanny, 184–185

Whitman, M. F., 120, 124, 264, 265–267, 272n

Whitney, William Dwight, 300

Whittier, John Greenleaf, 73, 75

Wickes, Thomas P., 213

Wickstrand, Norman, 438

Weissner, Fritz, 540

Wiggin, Tom, 228

Wilbur, Jeremiah, 59–60

Wild Scenes in the Forest (Hoffman), 109

Wildcat, 298; elevation of, 675; first known ascent of, 675; Guyot on, 130; trails on, 87, 228, 380, 633; winter on, 137, 321–322, 528

Wildcat E, 321, 677

Wildcat Ridge Trail, 380, 633

Wilderness Act, 632

Wilderness areas, 560, 583, 632

Wilderness Camping, 567, 593

Wilderness Leadership Workshop, 649

Wilderness Society, 407, 550, 593, 629, 632

Willard, Samuel, 4

Willard, Mount, 271–272; Alpine Club on, 184; guidebook to, 195; Guyot on, 128; Hitchcock on, 174; King on, 77; student walking tours, 153–157; trails on, 86, 549; winter on, 319

Willey family, 73, 273

Willey, Mount, 47, 273; elevation of, 676; first known ascent of, 676; Guyot on, 130; Hitchcock on, 174; trails on, 208, 387–388

Williams, Stilly, 518

Williams College, 59, 101–102, 238; outing club, 451–453, 477, 500; student walking tours, 152–153, 156–157; trail work, 368

Williams, Mount, 240

Williams Quarterly, 238

Williamstown Alpine Club. *See* Alpine Club of Williamstown, Massachusetts

Willis, Nathaniel P., 47, 195, 410

Willoughby, Lake, xxxii, 82, 90, 148, 444, 621

Willoughby Lake House, 82, 90

Wilton Outing Club, 598

Windham High Peak, 606

Wingate, Paine, 26

Winkler, John, 642

Winninghoff, W. J., 283

Winter Camp, 394

Winter camping, 543–545, 652–654, 661–663

Winter climbing, 131, 144, 315–341; 525–545; 651–670. *See also names of individual mountains*

Winter Mountaineering School, 601–602, 655–658, 662, 664–665, 666–667

Winter Olympics of 1932, 542

Winthrop, John, 8–12

Winthrop, Theodore, 100

Wiscott, Dr., 335n

Wister, Owen, 308

Witherle, George H., 98, 303–306

Witherle, Mrs., 303–306

Witherle Ravine, 305–306

Wittenberg, Mount, 253, 463; winter on, 336

Wlwascackbwgmsaesfasjhe Pedestrian Association, 192–193

Wolcott, Joe, 529, 537

Wolf Jaws, 67, 303; trails on, 211, 214, 396. *See also* Lower Wolf Jaw *and* Upper Wolf Jaw

Women: Alpine Club, in, 184; Appalachian Mountain Club, in, 191; AMC Huts, in, 554, 592; Bemis Crew, in, 528–530; college outing clubs, in, 452–453; Eastern States Mountain Club, in, 443; first climbs by, 119–124; Fresh Air Club, in, 186; Green Mountain Club, in, 360, 457–458; hiking and, 119–124, 151–152, 261–272, 274, 457–461; Inkowa, in, 448; Katahdin, on, 99, 122–124, 534, 665; New York hiking clubs, in, 446–448; student walking tours, 154; winter climbing and, 319–320, 329–330, 525–530, 534, 658–659, 665

Wonalancet Out Door Club, 193, 228–230, 280, 434, 444, 477, 612

Wood, Kay, 598, 615–616, 624

Woodcraft Indians, 309

Woodland Trail Walkers, 424, 450, 599, 620

Woods, Edward S., 221

Woodstock Inn, 319

Woodward, Laura, 373, 446

Worchester, William L., 192

Wordsworth, William, 70

World War II, impact of, 553–555, 558–559, 603, 651–652

Worth Peak, 18, 312

Wright, Wilhelmina, 529, 537

Wright: elevation of, 675; environmental issues and, 586; first known ascent of, 675; trails on, 399, 604; winter on, 543

Wright Peak Ski Trail, 399

Wyanokies, xxxviii, 364, 414, 427, 448

Wyant, Alexander, 72

Yale University, 31; outing club, 404n, 436–437, 451–453, 654; student walking tours, 156

Yard, Robert Sterling, 550

Yokun's Seat, 240

Yosians, 449

Young, Aaron, 100

Young, Geoffrey Winthrop, 523

Young, Michael, 135n, 643

Zealand, 662, 676

Zealand Falls Hut, 385, 554, 661–662

About the Authors

Laura and Guy Waterman are Vermont homesteaders, avid hikers and trail workers, and outdoor writers. Authors of a 1979 book, *Backwoods Ethics: Environmental Concerns for Hikers and Campers*, they are contributors to *Backpacker* and *New England Outdoors* magazines, as well as publications of several Northeastern hiking clubs. They have hiked and climbed intensively throughout New England and New York. Special interests include trail maintenance—they have tended the White Mountains' Franconia Ridge Trail since 1980—and winter hiking and rock and ice climbing.

Before their move to Vermont, Laura was an editor for several New York publishing companies. When *Backpacker* magazine was founded, she was its first full-time employee and became associate editor. Guy has a varied background—working first as a jazz pianist in Washington, D.C., nightclubs, then as an aide and speechwriter for Washington political figures (he wrote speeches for three U.S. presidents, among others), and later as speechwriter for the president of General Electric Company.

In 1973 they moved to twenty-seven wooded acres in northern Vermont, where they have constructed their own buildings, raise much of their own food, and live without modern amenities— no electricity, plumbing, telephone, road access, or motors. (They cut seven cords of firewood a year with bow saw, ax, and peavey.)

Despite their backwoods life-style, they manage to pursue a variety of interests. Laura is both an accomplished cook and a pioneer in women's technical climbing; she was the first woman to climb Cannon Mountain's classic and difficult Black Dike ice route. Guy keeps up such diverse memberships as the Society for American Baseball Research (he contributes to *Baseball Digest* magazine) and the Milton Society (he can recite five hours' worth of *Paradise Lost* from memory). Laura is a devoted lover of grand opera, Guy a published authority on ragtime.